Give your students choices.

Pearson's History titles are available in numerous formats to give you and your students more choices.

CourseSmart eTextbooks

offer the same content as the printed text in a convenient online format—with highlighting, online search, and printing capabilities. *60% off the list price of the traditional book.* www.coursesmart.com

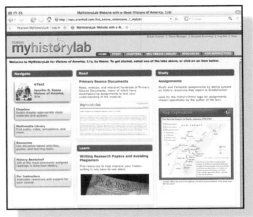

MyHistoryLab

is a dynamic website that provides a wealth of resources geared to meet the specific teaching and learning needs of every instructor and student. **MyHistoryLab** includes an interactive eText—identical in content and design to the printed text—so students have access to their text wherever and whenever they need it. It also features unabridged audio files of the entire text, which enable students to learn and review in a new way. **MyHistoryLab** may be packaged with a printed text for no additional charge or purchased as a standalone eText. *35% off the net price of the traditional book.* www.myhistorylab.com

Books à la Carte editions

feature the exact same text in a convenient, three-hole-punched, loose-leaf version at a discounted price—allowing students to take only what they need to class. **Books à la Carte editions** are available both with and without access to **MyHistoryLab**. *35% off the net price of the traditional book.*

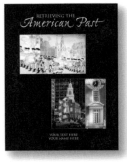

The Pearson Custom Library

lets you create a textbook that meets the specific needs of your course. Combine chapters from several best-selling Pearson textbooks and/or topical reading units in the sequence you want.

www.pearsonlearningsolutions.com

20TH CENTURY U.S. HISTORY (1945–PRESENT)

Brands America Since 1945 *
©2011, 9780205568482 / 0205568483
(Penguin Academic Series)

Moss The 1970s *
©2012, 9780205777655 / 0205777651

Opdycke Jane Addams and Her Vision of America *
©2012, 9780205598403 / 0205598404
(Part of the Library of American Biography Series) 20th Century U.S. History (1945–present)

THE COLD WAR

Judge & Langdon The Cold War: A Global History with Documents, 2/e
©2011, 9780205729111 / 0205729118

COLONIAL AMERICAN HISTORY (1492–1776)

Gallay Colonial and Revolutionary America: Texts and Documents
©2011, 9780205809691 / 0205809693

Kicza & Horn Resilient Cultures, 2/e *
©2012, 9780205693580 / 020569358X

Reich Colonial America, 6/e
©2011, 9780205743162 / 0205743161

HISTORIOGRAPHY

Hoefferle The Essential Historiography Reader
©2011, 9780321437624 / 0321437624

Sayegh & Altice History and Theory *
©2012, 9780136157250 / 0136157254

HISTORY OF AFRICAN AMERICANS

Carson, Lapsansky-Werner & Nash The Struggle for Freedom: A History of African Americans, Concise Edition, 2/e, Combined Volume
©2011, 9780205832408 / 0205832407
Also available in Volumes I & II
(Penguin Academic Series)

Hine, Hine & Harrold The African-American Odyssey, 5/e, Combined Volume
©2011, 9780205728817 / 0205728812
Also available in Volumes I & II

Hine, Hine & Harrold African Americans, 4/e, Combined Volume *
©2012, 9780205806270 / 0205806279
Also available in Volumes I & II

HISTORY OF NATIVE AMERICANS

Nicholas Sources in the Native American Past, Combined Volume *
©2012, 9780205742516 / 0205742513
Also available in Volumes I & II

Townsend & Nicholas First Americans: A History of Native Peoples, Combined Volume *
©2012, 9780132069489 / 0132069482
Also available in Volumes I & II

HISTORY OF SCIENCE AND TECHNOLOGY

Burns Knowledge and Power: Science in World History
©2011, 9780136155614 / 0136155618

HISTORY OF WOMEN IN AMERICA

Skinner Women and the National Experience: Sources in American History, 3/e, Combined Volume
©2011, 9780205743155 / 0205743153
Also available in Volumes I & II

THE SIXTIES (1960-1969)

Anderson The Sixties, 4/e *
©2012, 9780205744282 / 0205744281

U.S. HISTORY SURVEY

Comprehensive Texts

Keene, Cornell & O'Donnell Visions of America: A History of the United States, Combined Volume
©2010, 9780321066879 / 0321066871
Also available in Volumes I & II

Primary Source Readers

Gorn, Roberts & Bilhartz Constructing the American Past: A Source Book of a People's History, 7/e
©2011, Vol. I: 9780205773640 / 0205773648
Vol. II: 9780205773633 / 020577363X

Merrell & Podair American Conversations *
©2012, Vol. I: 9780132446839 / 0132446839
Vol. II: 9780131582613 / 0131582615

Unger & Tomes American Issues: A Primary Source Reader in United States History, 5/e
©2011, Vol. I: 9780205803453 / 0205803458
Vol. II: 9780205803446 / 020580344X

Secondary Source Readers

Youngs American Realities, 8/e
©2011, Vol. I: 9780205764129 / 0205764126
Vol. II: 9780205764136 / 0205764134

THE VIETNAM WAR

Hearden The Tragedy of Vietnam, 4/e *
©2012, 9780205744275 / 0205744273

For more information, please visit
www.pearsonhighered.com/gomakehistory

GO MAKE HISTORY
www.pearsonhighered.com/gomakehistory

Why Do You Need This New Edition?

6 good reasons why you should buy this new edition of *OUT OF MANY*, Brief Edition!

1. New and expanded coverage on topics such as native religious practices, the position of women in New England, class and ethnicity in the Revolution, the Spanish and the American Revolution, Southern Republicans in the reconstruction era, and the role of moderate white Southerners in the civil rights struggle.

2. New coverage of the election of 2008 and Barack Obama's first year as president as well as extensive treatment of the Great Recession.

3. New references to primary sources, videos, audio clips, and other resources on MyHistoryLab are included throughout the chapters and identified by icons in the margins.

4. A new *MyHistoryLab Connections* section at the end of the text lists documents, audio, video, maps, and images identified in the chapter and available on the MyHistoryLab website.

5. New topics in the special feature *Seeing History* include P.T. Barnum's "curiosities," and visualizing civil rights.

6. Extensive updating of numerous topics within the text make the sixth edition up-to-date with the most recent scholarship in the discipline.

Out of Many

Out of Many

Sixth Edition

A History of the American People

BRIEF EDITION

COMBINED VOLUME

John Mack Faragher
YALE UNIVERSITY

Mari Jo Buhle
EMERITA, BROWN UNIVERSITY

Daniel Czitrom
MOUNT HOLYOKE COLLEGE

Susan H. Armitage
EMERITA, WASHINGTON STATE UNIVERSITY

Prentice Hall

Boston   Columbus   Indianapolis   New York   San Francisco   Upper Saddle River
Amsterdam   Cape Town   Dubai   London   Madrid   Milan   Munich   Paris   Montréal   Toronto
Delhi   Mexico City   São Paulo   Sydney   Hong Kong   Seoul   Singapore   Taipei   Tokyo

Editorial Director: Craig Campanella
Publisher: Charlyce Jones Owen
Editorial Assistant: Maureen Diana
Associate Editor: Emsal Hasan
Senior Manufacturing and Operations Manager for Arts &
  Sciences: Nick Sklitsis
Operations Specialist: Christina Amato
Director of Marketing: Brandy Dawson
Senior Marketing Manager: Maureen E. Prado Roberts
Marketing Assistant: Samantha Bennett
Senior Managing Editor: Ann Marie McCarthy
Senior Project Manager: Cheryl Keenan
Manager, Visual Research: Beth Brenzel
Senior Art Director: Maria Lange

Cover Design: Red Kite Projects
Cover Art: "City Life." Detail of a mural, c. 1934, by Victor
  Arnautoff at Coit Tower, San Francisco, California.
  Photo credit: Erik Falkensteen/The Granger
  Collection, NYC.
AV Project Manager: Mirella Signoretto
Cartographer: International Mapping Associates
Director of Digital Media: Brian Hyland
Media Editor: Andrea Messineo
Full-Service Compositon and Project Management:
  GEX Publishing Services
Printer/Binder: Courier/Kendallville
Cover Printer: Lehigh-Phoenix Color
Text Font: 10/13 New Baskerville

Credits and acknowledgments borrowed from other sources and reproduced, with permission, in this textbook appear on appropriate page within text or on page C-1.

Library of Congress Cataloging-in-Publication Data
Out of many : a history of the American people / John Mack Faragher ... [et al.]. -- 6th ed., brief TLC ed.
  p. cm.
  ISBN 978-0-205-01064-6 (combined book) -- ISBN 978-0-205-01063-9 (volume 1 split) -- ISBN 978-0-205-01062-2 (volume 2 split) 1. United States--History--Textbooks. I. Faragher, John Mack, 1945-
  E178.1.O935 2012b
  973–dc22

                    2010044966

10 9 8 7 6 5 4 3 2 1

Combined Volume
ISBN-10: 0-205-01064-4
ISBN-13: 978-0-205-01064-6

Examination Copy
ISBN-10: 0-205-05411-0
ISBN-13: 978-0-205-05411-4

Volume 1:
ISBN-10: 0-205-01063-6
ISBN-13: 978-0-205-01063-9

Volume 1 à la Carte:
ISBN-10: 0-205-03462-4
ISBN-13: 978-0-205-03462-8

Volume 2
ISBN-10: 0-205-01062-8
ISBN-13: 978-0-205-01062-2

Volume 2 à la Carte:
ISBN-10: 0-205-03463-2
ISBN-13: 978-0-205-03463-5

Prentice Hall
is an imprint of

www.pearsonhighered.com

1

A CONTINENT OF VILLAGES, TO 1500 2

Seeing History

2

WHEN WORLDS COLLIDE, 1492–1590 24

Seeing History

3

PLANTING COLONIES IN NORTH AMERICA, 1588–1701 46

Seeing History

6

FROM EMPIRE TO INDEPENDENCE, 1750–1776 120

Seeing History

7

THE AMERICAN REVOLUTION, 1776–1786 148

Seeing History

8

THE NEW NATION, 1786–1800 174

9

AN EMPIRE FOR LIBERTY, 1790–1824   198

10

THE SOUTH AND SLAVERY, 1790S–1850S   228

Seeing History

11

THE GROWTH OF DEMOCRACY, 1824–1840   254

Seeing History

Interpreting the Past

12

INDUSTRY AND THE NORTH, 1790s–1840s   280

Seeing History

Interpreting the Past

13

MEETING THE CHALLENGES OF THE NEW AGE: IMMIGRATION, URBANIZATION, SOCIAL REFORM, 1820s–1850s   306

Seeing History

14

THE TERRITORIAL EXPANSION OF THE UNITED STATES, 1830s–1850s   332

15

THE COMING CRISIS, THE 1850s   358

Seeing History

16

THE CIVIL WAR, 1861–1865   384

Seeing History

17

RECONSTRUCTION, 1863–1877   410

Seeing History

Interpreting the Past

18

CONQUEST AND SURVIVAL: THE TRANS-MISSISSIPPI WEST, 1860–1900   442

Seeing History

19

PRODUCTION AND CONSUMPTION IN THE GILDED AGE, 1865–1900 474

20

DEMOCRACY AND EMPIRE, 1870–1900 502

23

THE TWENTIES, 1920–1929   592

Seeing History

Interpreting the Past

24

THE GREAT DEPRESSION AND THE NEW DEAL, 1929–1940   624

Seeing History

25

WORLD WAR II, 1941–1945   652

26

THE COLD WAR BEGINS, 1945–1952   682

Seeing History

29

30

31

THE UNITED STATES IN A GLOBAL AGE, 1992–2010   832

MAPS

CHARTS, GRAPHS & TABLES

OVERVIEW TABLES

Out of Many: A History of the American People, Brief, sixth edition, offers a distinctive and timely approach to American history, highlighting the experiences of diverse communities of Americans in the unfolding story of our country. The stories of these communities offer a way of examining the complex historical forces shaping people's lives at various moments in our past. The debates and conflicts surrounding the most momentous issues in our national life—independence, emerging democracy, slavery, westward settlement, imperial expansion, economic depression, war, technological change—were largely worked out in the context of local communities. Through communities we focus on the persistent tensions between everyday life and those larger decisions and events that continually reshape the circumstances of local life. Each chapter opens with a description of a representative community. Some of these portraits feature American communities struggling with one another: African slaves and English masters on the rice plantations of colonial Georgia, or *Tejanos* and Americans during the Texas war of independence. Other chapters feature portraits of communities facing social change: the feminists of Seneca Falls, New York, in 1848, or the African Americans of Montgomery, Alabama, in 1955. As the story unfolds we find communities growing to include ever larger groups of Americans: the soldiers from every colony who forged the Continental Army into a patriotic national force at Valley Forge during the American Revolution, or the moviegoers who aspired to a collective dream of material prosperity and upward mobility during the 1920s.

Out of Many is also the only American history text with a truly continental perspective. With community vignettes from New England to the South, the Midwest to the far West, we encourage students to appreciate the great expanse of our nation. For example, a vignette of seventeenth century Santa Fé, New Mexico, illustrates the founding of the first European settlements in the New World. We present territorial expansion into the American West from the viewpoint of the Mandan villagers of the upper Missouri River of North Dakota. We introduce the policies of the Reconstruction era through the experience of African Americans in Hale County, Alabama. A continental perspective drives home to students that American history has never been the preserve of any particular region.

Out of Many includes extensive coverage of our diverse heritage. Our country is appropriately known as "a nation of immigrants," and the history of immigration to America, from the seventeenth to the twenty-first centuries, is fully integrated into the text. There is sustained and close attention to our place in the world, with special emphasis on our relations with the nations of the Western Hemisphere, especially our near neighbors, Canada and Mexico. The statistical data in the final chapter has been completely updated with the results of the 2000 census.

In these ways *Out of Many* breaks new ground, but without compromising its coverage of the traditional turning points that we believe are critically important to an understanding of the American past. Among these watershed events are the Revolution and the struggle over the Constitution, the Civil War and Reconstruction, and the Great Depression and World War II. In *Out of Many*, however, we seek to integrate the narrative of national history with the story of the nation's many diverse communities. The Revolutionary and Constitutional period tested the ability of local communities to forge a new unity, and success depended on their ability to build a nation without compromising local identity. The Civil War and Reconstruction formed a second great test of the balance between the national ideas of the Revolution and the power of local and sectional communities. The depression and the New Deal demonstrated the importance of local communities and the growing power of national institutions during the greatest economic challenge in our history. *Out of Many* also looks back in a new and comprehensive way—from the vantage point of the beginning of a new century and the end of the Cold War—at the salient events of the last fifty years and their impact on American communities. The community focus of *Out of Many* weaves the stories of the people and the nation into a single compelling narrative.

Out of Many is completely updated with the most recent scholarship on the history of America and the United States. All the chapters have been extensively reviewed, revised, and rewritten. The final chapter details the tumultuous events of the new century, including a completely new section on the "war on terror," and concluding with the national election of 2008. The sixth edition offers two features designed to bring history vividly alive for students: *Interpreting the Past*, featuring primary sources and images on an historical issue and *Seeing History*, carefully chosen images that show how visual sources can illuminate their understanding of American history.

WHAT'S NEW TO THIS EDITION

With each edition of *Out of Many* we have sought to strengthen its unique integration of the best of traditional American history with its innovative community-based focus and strong continental perspective. This new version is no exception.

- New and expanded coverage on topics such as native religious practices, the position of women in New England, class and ethnicity in the Revolution, the Spanish and the American Revolution, Southern Republicans in the reconstruction era, and the role of moderate white Southerners in the civil rights struggle.
- New coverage of the election of 2008 and Barack Obama's first year as president as well as extensive treatment of the Great Recession.

- New topics in the special feature *Seeing History* include P.T. Barnum's "curiosities," civility and democracy, visualizing civil rights, and a comparison of the Carter and Reagan inaugurations.
- Extensive updating of numerous topics within the text make the sixth edition up-to-date with the most recent scholarship in the discipline.
- New references identified by icons cite specific documents, audio, video, maps, and images available on the MyHistoryLab website that enhance topics discussed in the chapters. A description of MyHistorylab appears on page xxxix.

Chapter-by-Chapter Changes

Chapter 1 There is more discussion of native religious practices. The chapter now incorporates new theories of migration from Asia.

Chapter 2 Expanded discussions are included on the "Merchant Class and the Renaissance" and the "Columbian Exchange," and the newest material on the demographic consequences of the conquest.

Chapter 3 There is new coverage of the position of women in New England, the Salem Witch Trials, and Bacon's Rebellion.

Chapter 4 The sections on slavery in the Spanish and French colonies have been thoroughly revised.

Chapter 5 Sections within the chapter have been revised for better narrative flow, and there is increased emphasis on the importance of religion.

Chapter 6 New emphasis on the importance of the Seven Years' War has been included as well as more explicit coverage of class and ethnicity in the Revolution and of soldiers in the early fighting.

Chapter 7 There are two new sections in this chapter on "The Toll of War" and "Women and the War" and new material on the Spanish and the Revolution.

Chapter 8 The discussions of American culture and on the writing and ratification of the Constitution have been extensively revised, and a new discussion of republicanism has been added.

Chapter 9 Two new historical views of the capitol building underline the point that the nation's new capital city had small and undistinguished beginnings. The updated bibliography describes the Missouri Compromise to make the point that differing views on slavery were a political danger as early as 1820.

Chapter 10 This chapter incorporates the newest scholarship to deepen student appreciation of the human costs of the slave system.

Chapter 12 A new set of maps emphasize the importance of transportation in the rapid development of the Yankee West and commercial agriculture and new detail has been added in readings on early factory conditions.

Chapter 13 A new **Seeing History** analyzes the popular appeal of PT Barnum's "curiosities."

Chapter 15 A revised **Seeing History** feature includes a new picture and poses a question about civility and democracy.

Chapter 16 There is a use of new scholarship to increase understanding of the impact of the Civil War on soldiers and civilians.

Chapter 17 The expanded discussion of Southern Republicans in the Reconstruction era emphasizes regional differences within the South.

Chapter 18 The section on "Producing for the Global Market" has been dropped, with the material integrated into "New Production Technologies," to streamline the outline.

Chapter 21 A new section discusses immigration from the Carriibean basin in the early twentieth century and includes a revised map of Immigration to the U.S., 1900–1920.

Chapter 22 The coverage of women's experiences during WWI has been revised.

Chapter 23 The coverage of the relationship between global commerce and U.S. foreign policy has been strengthened. The extensively revised bibliographies reflect a large amount of new scholarship on the 1920s.

Chapter 24 There are revised and updated statistics and analysis of "Underlying Weaknesses of the 1920s Economy."

Chapter 25 Much of the Isolationism section has been streamlined and merged into the section "Roosevelt Readies for War" to streamline the chapter outline.

Chapter 26 The section "Zeal for Democracy" is replaced by "The American Way," which is a phrase that comes up in the most recent scholarship on Cold War culture.

Chapter 27 Clarified are the major goals—and tensions within—Eisenhower's foreign policy.

Chapter 28 A new **Seeing History** explores visualizing civil rights. There is new material on the role of moderate white Southerners in the civil rights struggle.

Chapter 29 The chapter outline has been streamlined by grouping the sections "Playing the China Card" and "Foreign Policy as Conspiracy" under a new section, "Nixon's Foreign Policy." The section on Johnson and the Vietnam War has been revised to reflect recent historiographical tendency to characterize Johnson as more hesitant about escalating the war than earlier scholars contended and to assign more responsibility to his advisors.

A discussion of the founding of *Ms. Magazine* has been added.

Chapter 30 The **Seeing History** feature has been revised to compare the Reagan and Carter inaugurations.

Chapter 31 A new section, "Barack Obama and the Audacity of Hope," covers the election of 2008 and Obama's first year as president. Extensive treatment of the Great Recession examines its causes and its impact on American life. The chapter has been reorganized to more fully integrate political and economic developments in the Clinton/Bush/Obama years.

Out of Many offers a wealth of special features and pedagogical aids that reinforce our narrative and helps students grasp key topics and concepts.

One of the most characteristic features of our country is its astounding variety. The American people include the descendants of native Indians; colonial Europeans of British, French, and Spanish background; Africans; and migrants from virtually every country and continent. Indeed, at the beginning of the new century the United States is absorbing a flood of immigrants from Latin America and Asia that rivals the great tide of people from eastern and southern Europe one hundred years before. What's more, our country is one of the world's most spacious, sprawling across than 3.6 million square miles of territory. The struggle to meld a single nation out of our many far-flung communities is what much of American history is all about. That is the story told in this book.

Every human society is made up of communities. A community is a set of relationships linking men, women, and their families to a coherent social whole that is more than the sum of its parts. In a community people develop the capacity for unified action. In a community people learn, often through trial and error, how to transform and adapt to their environment.

The sentiment that binds the members of a community together is the mother of group consciousness and ethnic identity. In the making of history, communities are far more important than even the greatest of leaders, for the community is the institution most capable of passing a distinctive historical tradition to future generations.

COMMUNITY & DIVERSITY

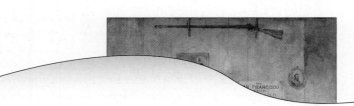

- **Community and Diversity.** This special introductory essay begins students' journey into the narrative history that unfolds in *Out of Many*. The essay acquaints students with the major themes of the book and provides them with a framework for understanding American History. (pp. xliii–xlvi)

AMERICAN COMMUNITIES
Cahokia: Thirteenth-Century Life on the Mississippi

AS THE SUN ROSE OVER THE RICH FLOODPLAIN, THE PEOPLE OF THE riverbank city set about their daily tasks. Some went to shops where they manufactured tools, pots, and luxury items—goods destined to be exchanged in the far corners of the continent. Others left their densely populated neighborhoods for the outlying countryside, where they worked the fields that fed the city. From almost any point people could see the great temple that rose from the city center.

The Indian residents of this thirteenth-century city lived and worked on the east banks of the Mississippi River, across from present-day St. Louis, a place known today as **Cahokia**. In the thirteenth century, Cahokia was an urban cluster of 20,000 or 30,000 people.  corn, beans, fif-

from the Atlantic coast. Cahokia's specialized artisans were renowned for the manufacture of high-quality flint hoes, which were exported throughout the Mississippi Valley.

Evidence suggests that Cahokia was a city-state supported by tribute and taxation. Like the awe-inspiring public works of other early urban societies in other parts of the world, most notably the pyramids of ancient Egypt and the acropolis of Athens, the great temple mound of Cahokia was intended to showcase the city's wealth and power. The mounds and other colossal public works at Cahokia were the monuments of a society ruled by a class of elite leaders. From their residences atop the mound, priests and chiefs looked down on their subjects both literally and figuratively.

The long history of North America before European colonization reveals that the native inhabitants developed a great variety of societies. Beginning as migrant hunting and gathering ... they found ways to fine-tune their subsistence st... environmental possibilities and ...

- **American Communities**. Each chapter opens with a story that highlights the experiences of diverse communities of Americans as a way of examining the complex historical forces shaping people's lives at various moments in our past.

Selling War

The Committee on Public Information (CPI), chaired by the progressive Denver journalist George Creel, oversaw the crucial task of mobilizing public opinion for war. Creel employed the most sophisticated sales and public relations techniques of the day to get Americans behind the war effort. The CPI created a flood of pamphlets, billboards, and news articles; sent volunteer "Four Minute Men" to make hundreds of thousands of patriotic speeches in movie theaters between reels; sponsored government-funded feature films depicting life on the front lines; and staged celebrity-studded rallies to promote the sale of war bonds. CPI writers and artists worked closely with government agencies such as the Food Administration and the Selective Service, as well as private organizations like the YMCA and the Red Cross, in creating patriotic campaigns in support of the war.

HOW WOULD you contrast the different kind of patriotic appeals made by *Pershing's Crusaders, Americans All,* and *And They Thought We Couldn't Fight?* Which of these posters do you think makes the most compelling case for supporting the war? How do the artists portray gender differences as part of a visual strategy for winning the war?

The Division of Pictorial Publicity, headed by the popular artist Charles Dana Gibson, churned out posters and illustrations designed to encourage military enlistment, food conservation, war bond buying, and contributions for overseas victims of war.

The posters generally defined the war as a clear struggle between good and evil, in which American democracy and freedom opposed German militarism and despotism. Artists used a wide range of visual themes to illustrate these stark contrasts. World War I posters drew upon traditional ideas about gender differences (men as soldiers, women as nurturers), but they also illustrated the new wartime expectations of women working outside the home in support of the war effort. Appeals to American patriotism cutting across lines of ethnic and religious difference were common, as was the demonizing of the German enemy. And just as the wartime economy blurred the boundaries between public and private enterprises, businesses adapted patriotic appeals to their own advertising.

Creel aptly titled the memoir of his war experience *How We Advertised America.* The three images here show the range of war propaganda

• **Seeing History.** This feature helps students use visual culture for making sense of the past. These carefully chosen images, with critical thinking questions for interpretation, include a broad array of fine art, drawings, political cartoons, advertisements, and photographs. Encouraged to look at the image with an analytical eye, students will think critically about how visual sources can illuminate their understanding of American history and the important role visuals play in our knowledge of the past.

• **Interpreting the Past.** This special feature, which appears at the end of selected chapters, provide documents and images on a key event or topic to help students see how historians understand and interpret the past. A critical thinking question provides students with the opportunity to analyze how these historical records illuminate this event or topic.

Democratic Roots in New England Soil

The Puritans of New England were less than democratic in both beliefs and goals. Contrary to popular myth, they did not migrate to the New World to establish religious freedom. They were seeking to establish a religious utopia to serve as what Governor John Winthrop called a "light upon a hill" for the world

WHY COULD New England society move from a firm condemnation of democracy to embracing the basic ideals that would lead to the Declaration of Independence and the Constitution of 1787?

to emulate. They forbid the establishment of other religious doctrine, especially the Quakers and Roman Catholic faith. In Puritan communities nonconformist behavior was looked upon with deep suspicion, especially if it was religious in nature.

However, the Puritans unknowingly planted the seeds for the very democracy that they viewed as an abomination of the purity of God's social order. In the Mayflower Compact, Puritan separatists agreed to a governmental covenant that allowed for majority rule and later established the idea of the town meeting. The charter of the Massachusetts Bay Colony provided for the elections of governors, colonial legislatures, and a General Court. Puritan customs forbid church ministers from serving in public office, an early version of separation of Church and State. Most important of all, the Puritans required that all church members be able to read and interpret the Bible. This emphasis upon the individual and his right to interpret the Bible, within certain doctrinal limits, without the intercession of a priest or minister would lead to political consequences.

A hundred years later, the political seeds they planted would bear democratic fruit. ■

MAYFLOWER COMPACT, 1620

IN THE NAME OF GOD, AMEN. We, whose names are underwritten, the Loyal Subjects of our dread Sovereign Lord King James, by the Grace of God, of Great Britain, France, and Ireland, King, Defender of the Faith, &c. Having undertaken for the Glory of God, and Advancement of the Christian Faith, and the Honour of our King and Country, a Voyage to plant the first Colony in the northern Parts of Virginia; Do by these Presents, solemnly and mutually, in the Presence of God and one another, covenant and combine ourselves together into a civil Body Politick, for our better Ordering and Preservation, and Furtherance of the Ends aforesaid; And by Virtue hereof do enact, constitute, and frame, such just and equal Laws, Ordinances, Acts, Constitutions, and Officers, from time to time, as shall be thought most meet and convenient for the general Good of the Colony; unto which we promise all due Submission and Obedience. IN WITNESS whereof we have hereunto subscribed our names at Cape-Cod the eleventh of

November, in the Reign of our Sovereign Lord King James, of England, France, and Ireland, the eighteenth, and of Scotland the fifty-fourth, Anno Domini; 1620. ■

The Signing of the *Mayflower Compact* a painting by E. Percy Moran shows the historic ceremonial signing on November 21, 1620 below the deck of the Mayflower. ➤

FUNDAMENTAL ORDERS OF CONNECTICUT (1639)
It is Ordered, sentenced, and decreed, that there shall be yearly two General Assemblies or Courts, the one the second Thursday in April, the other the second Thursday in September following; the first shall be called the Court of Election, wherein shall be yearly chosen from time to time, so many Magistrates and other public Officers as shall be found requisite: Whereof one to be chosen Governor for the year ensuing and until another be chosen, and no other Magistrate to be chosen for more than one year: provided always there be six chosen besides the Governor, which being chosen and sworn according to an Oath recorded for that purpose, shall have the power to administer justice according to the Laws here established. . . .

It is Ordered, sentenced, and decreed, that the election of the aforesaid Magistrates shall be in this manner: every person present and qualified for choice shall bring in (to the person deputed to receive them) one single paper with the name of him written in it whom he desires to have Governor, and that he that hath the greatest number of papers shall be Governor for that year. And the rest of the Magistrates or public officers to be chosen in this manner: the Secretary for the time being shall first read the names of all that are to be put to choice and then shall severally nominate them distinctly, and every one that would have the person nominated to be chosen shall bring in one single paper written upon, and he that would not have him chosen shall bring in a blank; and every one that hath more written papers than blanks shall be a Magistrate for that year. . . .

It is Ordered, sentenced, and decreed, that no person be chosen Governor above once in two years, and that the Governor be always a member of some approved Congregation. . . .

FUNDAMENTAL AGREEMENT, OR ORIGINAL CONSTITUTION OF THE COLONY OF NEW HAVEN (1639)
Query II. WHEREAS there was a covenant solemnly made by the whole assembly of free planters of this plantation, the first day of extraordinary humiliation, which we had

after we came together, that as in matters that concern the gathering and ordering of a church, so likewise in all public officers which concern civil order, as choice of magistrates and officers, making and repealing laws, dividing allotments of inheritance, and all things of like nature, we would all of us be ordered by those rules which the scripture holds forth to US; this covenant was called a plantation covenant, to distinguish it from a church covenant, which could not at that time be made a church not being then gathered, but was deferred till a church might be gathered, according to GOD. It was demanded whether all the free planters do hold themselves bound by that covenant, in all businesses of that nature which are expressed in the covenant, to submit themselves to be ordered by the rules held forth in the scripture. . . . ■

The wooden Old Ship Meeting House in Hingham, Massachusetts hosted the annual town meeting where Puritans voted and openly debated town policy. ➤

Here individuals of all nations are melted into a new race of men, whose labours and posterity will one day cause great changes in the world.
—Hector St. John Crèvecœur

Congress voting on the issue of independence.

8
THE NEW NATION
1786–1800

Hear the Audio
Hear the audio files for Chapter 8 at www.myhistorylab.com.

HOW DID economic conditions in the years after the Revolution lead to calls for fundamental political change?

HOW DID Americans differ in their views of the new Constitution, and how were those differences reflected in the struggle to achieve ratification?

HOW DID Washington's administration lay the foundation for the subsequent development of American politics and government?

HOW AND why did the first American political parties emerge?

WHAT DID Americans read in the early decades of the Republic?

• *Out of Many* offers **an engaging visual presentation** to pique—and retain—student interest. The text is packed with **stunning visuals** including chapter openers that highlight key events in the chapter. **Chapter opening questions** provide an overview and guide to the important concepts students need to learn.

• **Critical thinking questions** from the chapter opener are repeated in the margins at each major section of the chapter to promote critical reading.

• **Quick reviews** help students review selected topics as they go through the chapter.

• **Overview tables.** Overview tables provide students with a summary of complex issues.

Read the Document
William Penn, Description of Pennsylvania (1681) at www.myhistorylab.com

---

QUICK REVIEW

Pennsylvania

• Territory west of the Delaware River granted to William Penn in 1681.

• Penn supervised the establishment of Philadelphia in 1682.

• Penn, a Quaker, saw the colony as a "holy experiment."

WHAT LED to violent conflict between Indians and colonists?

Frame of Government William Penn's constitution for Pennsylvania

---

Penn, King Charles issued to [...] Delaware River. The next year, Penn [...] port of Philadelphia.

Penn wanted this colony to be a "holy experiment [...] drafted in 1682, he included guarantees of religious freedom, civil liberty [...] resentation. He also attempted to deal fairly with the native peoples, refusing to permit colonization to begin until settlement rights were negotiated and lands purchased. Although relations between Pennsylvania and Indian peoples later soured, during Penn's lifetime his reputation for fair dealing led a number of native groups to resettle in the Quaker colony.

During the first two decades of Pennsylvania's settlement, nearly 20,000 settlers spread agricultural communities from the banks of the Delaware to the fertile interior valleys. In the eighteenth century Pennsylvania would be known as America's breadbasket, and Philadelphia would become North America's most important port. In 1704 Penn approved the creation of a separate colony called Delaware for the governance of the counties near the mouth of the river formerly controlled first by the Swedes and then the Dutch.

CONFLICT AND WAR

Pennsylvania's ability to maintain peaceful relations with the Indians proved the great exception. The last quarter of the seventeenth century became a time of great violence throughout the colonial regions of the continent, mostly because of the expansion of European settlement (see Map 3.5).

---

16 **CHAPTER 1** A CONTINENT OF VILLAGES, TO 1500

OVERVIEW	Origins of Some Indian Tribal Names	
Cherokee	A corruption of the Choctaw *chiluk-ki*, meaning "cave people," an allusion to the many caves in the Cherokee homeland in the highlands of present-day Georgia. The Cherokees called themselves *Ani-Yun-Wiya*, or the "real people."	
Cheyenne	From the Sioux *Sha-hiyena*, "people of strange speech." The Cheyennes of the Northern Plains called themselves *Dzi-tsistas*, meaning "our people."	
Hopi	A shortening of the name the Hopis of northern Arizona use for themselves, *Hópitu*, which means "peaceful ones."	
Mohawk	From the Algonquian *Mohawaúuck*, meaning "man-eaters." The Mohawks of the upper Hudson Valley in New York called themselves *Kaniengehaga*, "people of the place of the flint."	
Pawnee	From the Pawnee term *paríki*, which describes a distinctive style of dressing the hair with paint and fat to make it stand erect like a horn. The Pawnees, whose homeland was the Platte River valley in present-day Nebraska, called themselves *Chahiksichahiks*, "men of men."	

during the 1720s and 1730s, Prime Minister [...] from war with other mercantilist powers. Earlier in [...] Britain against Spain and France (known as the War of the Sp[...] **Queen Anne's War** in America) had ended in a significant Britis[...] Utrecht in 1713. France was forced to cede Acadia, Newfoundland, [...] Great Britain in exchange for guarantees of security for the French-speak[...] those provinces. Spain was forced to open its American ports to British traders, who [...] also granted the exclusive right to supply slaves to the Spanish colonies.

Despite continuing tensions with Spain and France, Walpole saw considerable advantages in peace. For more than fifteen years Walpole prevailed over militant factions in the House of Commons that demanded complete elimination of Spanish competition in the Americas. But in 1739, at their urging, a one-eared sea captain by the name of Robert Jenkins testified about the indignities suffered by British merchant sailors at the hands of Spanish authorities in Caribbean ports. In a dramatic flourish, Jenkins produced a dried and withered ear, which he claimed the Spanish had cut from his head. The public outrage that followed forced Walpole to agree to a war of Caribbean conquest known as the War of Jenkins's Ear.

Walpole thought war was a mistake, and he was right. The only success of the war for the British came when the Georgia militia blocked a Spanish invasion from Florida in 1742. The war ended with no territorial gains on either side.

The war with Spain merged into a war with France that began in 1744. Known as **King George's War** in America (the War of the Austrian Succession in Europe), it began with a French invasion of their former colony of Acadia, which the British had renamed Nova Scotia. Indian and Canadian raids again devastated the border towns of New England and New York, and hundreds of British subjects were killed or captured. In return, New England forces attacked and conquered the great French fortress at Louisbourg. But Great Britain fared less well in the European fighting, and the war ended in stalemate with the return of all territory.

THE COLONIAL ECONOMY

Despite the resumption of warfare, the colonial economy continued to operate to the great benefit of planters, merchants, and white colonists in general. Southern slave owners made healthy profits on the sale of their commodities. Pennsylvania, New York, and New England, and increasingly the Chesapeake as well, produced grain, flour, meat, and dairy products. None of these was included in the list of **enumerated goods** and could be sold freely abroad. Most of this trade was carried in New England ships.

Queen Anne's War American phase (1702–1713) of Europe's War of the Spanish Succession.

King George's War The third Anglo-French war in North America (1744–1748), part of the European conflict known as the War of the Austrian Succession.

enumerated goods Items produced in the colonies and enumerated in acts of Parliament that could be legally shipped from the colony of origin only to specified locations.

• **In-text glossary.** A marginal glossary provides definitions of key terms and concepts, which are then listed at the end of the chapter for review.

MAP 16.4
The Turning Point, 1863 In June, Lee boldly struck north into Maryland and Pennsylvania, hoping for a victory that would cause Britain and France to demand a negotiated peace on Confederate terms. Instead, he lost the hard-fought battle of Gettysburg, July 1–3. The very next day, Grant's long siege of Vicksburg succeeded. These two great Fourth of July victories turned the tide in favor of the Union. The Confederates never again mounted a major offensive. Total Union control of the Mississippi now exposed the Lower South to attack.

WHAT WAS Lee hoping to achieve with his campaign northward and why was his defeat at Gettysburg the war's turning point?

✛ Read the Document
John Dooley, Passages from His Journal (1863) at www.myhistorylab.com

◉ See the Map
The Civil War, Part II: 1863–1865 at www.myhistorylab.com

that caught the Union troops by surprise. Chancellorsville was a great Confederate victory. However, Confederate losses were also great: 13,000 men, representing more than 20 percent of Lee's army.

Though weakened, Lee moved north into Maryland and Pennsylvania. His purpose was as much political as military: he hoped that a great Confederate victory would lead Britain and France to intervene in the war and demand a negotiated peace. The ensuing Battle of Gettysburg, July 1–3, 1863, was another horrible slaughter. When the battle was over, Lee retreated from the field, leaving more than one-third of his army behind—28,000 men killed, wounded, or missing. Lee's great gamble had failed; he never again mounted a major offensive (see Map 16.4).

The next day, July 4, 1863, Ulysses S. Grant took Vicksburg, Mississippi, after a costly siege. The combined news of Gettysburg and Vicksburg dissuaded Britain and France from recognizing the Confederacy and checked the Northern peace movement. It also tightened the North's grip on the South, for the Union now controlled the entire Mississippi River. In November, Generals Grant and Sherman broke the Confederate hold on Chattanooga, Tennessee, thereby opening the way to Atlanta.

GRANT AND SHERMAN

In March 1864, President Lincoln called Grant east and appointed him general-in-chief of all the Union forces. Lincoln's critics were appalled. Grant was an uncouth Westerner (like the president) and (unlike the president) was rumored to have a drinking problem. Lincoln replied that if he knew the general's brand of whiskey, he would send a barrel of it to every commander in the Union army.

Grant devised a plan of strangulation and annihilation. While he took on Lee in northern Virginia, he sent General William Tecumseh Sherman to defeat the Confederate Army of Tennessee, which was defending the approach to Atlanta. Both Grant and Sherman exemplified the new kind of warfare. They aimed to inflict maximum damage on the fabric of Southern life, hoping that the South would choose to surrender rather than face total destruction. This decision to broaden the war so that it directly affected civilians was new in American military history and prefigured the total wars of the twentieth century.

The most famous example of the new strategy of total war was General Sherman's 1864 march through Georgia. Sherman captured Atlanta on September 2, 1864. In November, Sherman set out to march the 285 miles to the coastal city of Savannah, living off the land and destroying everything in his path. His military purpose was to cut off Mississippi, Alabama, and Georgia from the rest of the Confederacy. But his second purpose, openly stated, was to "make war so terrible" to the people of the South, to "make them so sick of war that generations would pass away before they would again appeal to it."

Terrifying to white Southern civilians, Sherman was initially hostile to black Southerners as well. In the interests of speed and efficiency, his army turned away many of the 18,000 slaves who flocked to it in Georgia, causing a number to be recaptured and

• **NEW MyHistoryLab Icons.** Throughout each chapter, icons refer students to primary source documents, maps, videos, and activities from the MyHistoryLab website that relate directly to specific topics within the chapter.

THE CIVIL WAR, 1861–1865 **CHAPTER 16** **409**

myhistorylab Connections

Reinforce what you learned in this chapter by studying the many documents,
images, maps, review tools, and videos available at www.myhistorylab.com.

Read and Review

✓● Study and Review Chapter 16

●●● Read the Document

U.S. Sanitary Commission, Sketch of Its Purposes (1864)

Homestead Act of 1862

Elizabeth Keckley, Four Years in the White House (1868)

Abraham Lincoln to Horace Greeley (1862)

Clara Barton, Memoirs about Medical Life at the Battlefield (1862)

An African American Soldier Writes to the President Appealing for Equality in 1863

A Civil War Nurse Writes of Conditions of Freed Slaves (1864)

The New York Times Prints Opinion on the New York Draft Riots in 1863

John Dooley, Passages from His Journal (1863)

William T. Sherman, The March through Georgia (1875)

👁 See the Map

The Civil War, Part I: 1861–1862

The Civil War, Part II: 1863–1865

Research and Explore

●●● Read the Document

A Nation Divided: The Civil War

Exploring America: Fort Pillow Massacre

Profiles
Judah Benjamin
Louisa Schuyler

((●● Hear the Audio

Free at Last

When This Cruel War Is Over

📷 Watch the Video

The Civil War

What Caused the Civil War?

The Meaning of the Civil War for Americans

((●● Hear the Audio

Hear the audio files for Chapter 16 at
www.myhistorylab.com.

• **NEW MyHistoryLab Connections.** A list of documents, images, maps, activities, and videos available online at **www.myhistorylab.com** that relate to the specific content in each chapter. For a full description of the MyHistoryLab website for *Out of Many* see page xxxix.

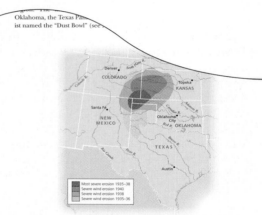

gion. The
Oklahoma, the Texas Pan
ist named the "Dust Bowl" (see

MAP 24.2
The Dust Bowl, 1935–40 This map shows the extent of the Dust Bowl in the southern Great Plains. Federal
programs designed to improve soil conservation, water management, and farming practices could not prevent
a mass exodus of hundreds of thousands out of the Great Plains.

Patriot aWERE the reasons for this ecological disaster and why was it particularly
Native peoples in the region?
political independence,

but Indian fears of Americ
rhetoric of natural rights and t
tribes that engaged in the fightin

British officials marshaled
Choctaws, and Chickasaws in th
from the British arsenal at Pensa
in 1781. The consequence was a
backcountry. In the summer of
by the warrior chief Dragging Ca
of American settlements. It requ
tia companies managed to drive

Among the Iroquois of New
(Thayendanegea) succeeded in b
British camp, although he was op
Tuscaroras, who supported the P
Loyalist forces raided the no
Pennsylvania. In retaliation an
homelands in 1779. Supported
Americans destroyed dozens of
of crops. For the first time since t
before, the Iroquois were fighting

Across the mountains, th
alliance under the British at De
warriors south against pioneer
Kentucky that had been founde
1763. Virginian George Rogers C
dition of Kentucky militia again
Illinois country, which were con

• **Photos and Illustrations.** The abundant illustrations in *Out of Many* include extensive captions that treat the images as visual primary source documents from the American past, describing their source and explaining their significance. In addition, the **Seeing History** feature in each chapter highlights a stunning visual and introduces students to the importance of visual documents in the study of history.

●●● Read the Document
Joseph Brant (Thayendanegea) at
www.myhistorylab.com

Joseph Brant, the brilliant chief of the Mohawks who sided with Great
Britain during the Revolution, in a 1786 painting by the American
artist Gilbert Stuart. After the Treaty of Paris, Brant led a large faction of Iroquois people north into British Canada, where they established a separate Iroquois Confederacy.

• **Chronologies, Review Questions, and Key Terms.** A chronology at the end of each chapter helps students build a framework of key events. Review questions at the end of chapters help students review, reinforce, and retain the material in each chapter and encourage them to relate the material to broader issues in American history. The list of key terms defined throughout the chapter serve as a review of specific concepts in the chapter.

CHRONOLOGY

1441	African slaves first brought to Portugal	1712	Slave uprising in New York City
1619	First Africans brought to Virginia	1713	Peace of Utrecht
1655	English seize Jamaica	1721–48	Robert Walpole leads British cabinet
1662	Virginia law makes slavery hereditary	1729	Natchez Rebellion in French Louisiana
1672	Royal African Company organized	1739	Stono Rebellion in South Carolina
1691	Virginia prohibits interracial sexual contact	1739–43	War of Jenkins's Ear
1698	Britain opens the slave trade to all its merchants	1741	Africans executed in New York for conspiracy
1699	Spanish declare Florida a refuge for escaped slaves	1744–48	King George's War
1702	South Carolinians burn St. Augustine	1752	Georgia officially opened to slavery
1705	Virginia Slave Code established	1770s	Peak period of the English colonies' slave trade
1706	French and Spanish navies bombard Charles Town	1808	Importation of slaves into the United States ends
1710	English capture Port Royal in Acadia		

CONCLUSION

During the eighteenth century, hundreds of thousands of Africans were kidnapped from their homes, marched to the African coast, and packed into ships for up to three months before arriving in British North America. They provided the labor that made colonialism profitable. Southern planters, northern merchants, and especially British traders and capitalists benefited greatly from the commerce in slave-produced crops. That prosperity trickled down to the ordinary white colonists of British North America. Mercantilism was a system designed to channel colonial wealth produced by slaves to the nation-state, but as long as profits remained high, the British tended to wink at colonists' violations of mercantilist regulations. In short, slavery was fundamental to the operation of the British empire in North America.

REVIEW QUESTIONS

1. Trace the development of the system of slavery and discuss the way it became entrenched in the Americas.

2. Describe the effects of the slave trade both on enslaved Africans and on the economic and political life of Africa.

3. Describe the process of acculturation involved in becoming an African American. In what ways did slaves "Africanize" the South?

4. Explain the connection between the institution of slavery and the building of a commercial empire.

5. In what ways did colonial policy encourage the growth of racism?

KEY TERMS

Enumerated goods (p. 91)
The Great Awakening (p. 85)
King George's War (p. 91)
Mercantilism (p. 89)

FOR INSTRUCTORS AND STUDENTS

Supplements for Instructors	Supplements for Students
myhistorylab www.myhistorylab.com **Save TIME. Improve Results.** MyHistoryLab provides a wealth of resources geared to meet the diverse teaching and learning needs of today's instructors and students. (See page xxxix for a description of the MyHistoryLab features.)	**myhistorylab** www.myhistorylab.com **Save TIME. Improve Results.** MyHistoryLab's many accessible tools will encourage you to read your text and help you improve your grade in your course. (See page xxxix for a description of the MyHistoryLab features.)
Instructor's Resource Center www.pearsonhighered.com/irc This website provides instructors with additional text-specific resources that can be downloaded for classroom use. Resources include the Instructor's Resource Manual, PowerPoint presentations, and the test item file. Register online for access to the resources for *Out of Many*.	***American Stories: Biographies in United States History*** This collection of sixty-two biographies provides insight into the lives and contributions of key figures as well as ordinary citizens to American history. Introductions, pre-reading questions, and suggested resources helps students connect the relevance of these individuals to historical events. Volume 1 **ISBN-10: 0131826549 ISBN-13: 9780131826540** Volume 2 **ISBN-10: 0131826530 ISBN-13: 9780131826533**
Instructor's Resource Manual Available at the Instructor's Resource Center for download, **www.pearsonhighered.com/irc**, the Instructor's Resource Manual contains chapter outlines, detailed chapter overviews, lecture outlines, topics for discussion, and information about audio-visual resources.	**Library of American Biography Series** www.pearsonhighered .com/educator/series/Library-of-American-Biography/10493.page Pearson's renowned series of biographies spotlighting figures who had a significant impact on American history. Included in the series are Edmund Morgan's *The Puritan Dilemma: The Story of John Winthrop*, B. Davis Edmund's *Tecumseh and the Quest for Indian Leadership*, J. William T. Youngs, *Eleanor Roosevelt: A Personal and Public Life*, and John R. M. Wilson's *Jackie Robinson and the American Dilemma*.
Test Item File Available at the Instructor's Resource Center for download, **www.pearsonhighered.com/irc**, the Test Item File contains more than 2,000 multiple-choice, identification, matching, true-false, and essay test questions.	**Penguin Valuepacks** www.pearsonhighered.com/penguin A variety of Penguin-Putnam texts is available at discounted prices when bundled with *Out of Many, 7/e*. Texts include Benjamin Franklin's *Autobiography and Other Writings*, Nathaniel Hawthorne's *The Scarlet Letter*, Thomas Jefferson's *Notes on the State of Virginia*, and George Orwell's *1984*.
PowerPoint Presentations Available at the Instructor's Resource Center for download, **www.pearsonhighered.com/irc**, the PowerPoints contain chapter outlines and full-color images of maps and art.	***A Short Guide to Writing About History, 7/e*** Written by Richard Marius, late of Harvard University, and Melvin E. Page, Eastern Tennessee State University, this engaging and practical text explores the writing and researching processes, identifies different modes of historical writing, including argument, and concludes with guidelines for improving style. **ISBN-10: 0205673708; ISBN-13: 9780205673704**
MyTest Available at **www.pearsonmytest.com**, MyTest is a powerful assessment generation program that helps instructors easily create and print quizzes and exams. Questions and tests can be authored online, allowing instructors ultimate flexibility and the ability to efficiently manage assessments anytime, anywhere! Instructors can easily access existing questions and edit, create, and store using simple drag-and-drop and Word-like controls.	***Longman American History Atlas*** This full-color historical atlas designed especially for college students is a valuable reference tool and visual guide to American history. This atlas includes maps covering the scope of American history from the lives of the Native Americans to the 1990s. Produced by a renowned cartographic firm and a team of respected historians, the *Longman American History Atlas* will enhance any American history survey course. **ISBN: 0321004868; ISBN-13: 9780321004864**
Retrieving the American Past Reader Program Available through the Pearson Custom Library (**www.pearsoncustom.com, keyword search I rtap**), the *Retrieving the American Past* (RTAP) program lets you create a textbook or reader that meets your needs and the needs of your course. RTAP gives you the freedom and flexibility to add chapters from several best-selling Pearson textbooks, in addition to *The American Journey, 5/e* and/or 100 topical reading units written by the History Department of Ohio State University, all under one cover. Choose the content you want to teach in depth, in the sequence you want, at the price you want your students to pay.	

PEARSON myhistorylab™

Save TIME. Improve Results.

MyHistoryLab is a dynamic website that provides a wealth of resources geared to meet the diverse teaching and learning needs of today's instructors and students. MyHistoryLab's many accessible tools will encourage students to read their text and help them improve their grade in their course.

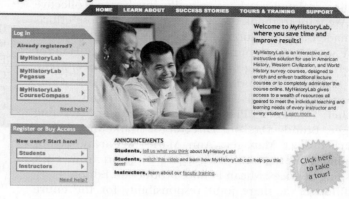

Features of MyHistoryLab

- **Pearson eText**—An e-book version of *Out of Many* is included in MyHistoryLab. Just like the printed text, students can highlight and add their own notes as they read the book online.
- **Audio Files**—Full audio of the entire text is included to suit the varied learning styles of today's students. In addition there are audio clips of speeches, readings, and music that provide another engaging way to experience history.
- **Pre-test, Post-tests, and Chapter Reviews**—Students can take quizzes to test their knowledge of chapter content and to review for exams.
- **Text and Visual Documents**—Over 1,500 primary source documents, images, and maps are available organized by chapter in the text. Primary source documents are also available in the MyHistoryLibrary and can be searched by author, title, theme, and topic. Many of these documents include critical thinking questions.
- **History Bookshelf**—Students may read, download, or print 100 of the most commonly assigned history works like Homer's *The Iliad* or Machiavelli's *The Prince*.
- **Lecture and Archival Videos**—Lectures by leading scholars on provocative topics give students a critical look at key points in history. Videos of speeches, news footage, key historical events, and other archival video take students back to the moment in history.
- **MySearchLab**—This website provides students access to a number of reliable sources for online research, as well as clear guidance on the research and writing process.
- **Gradebook**—Students can follow their own progress and instructors can monitor the work of the entire class. Automated grading of quizzes and assignments helps both instructors and students save time and monitor their results throughout the course.

NEW In-text References to MyHistoryLab Resources

Read, View, See, Watch, Hear, Study, and Review Icons integrated in the text connect resources on MyHistoryLab to specific topics within the chapters. The icons are not exhaustive; many more resources are available than those highlighted in the book, but the icons draw attention to some of the most high-interest resources available on MyHistoryLab.

Read the **Document** Primary and secondary source documents on compelling topics such as *Brown* v. *Board of Education of Topeka, Kansas* and Engel, Address by a Haymarket Anarchist enhance topics discussed in each chapter.

View the **Image** Photographs, fine art, and artifacts, provide students with a visual perspective on topics within the chapters, underscoring the role of visuals in understanding the past.

See the **Map** Atlas and interactive maps present both a broad overview and a detailed examination of historical developments.

Watch the **Video** Video lectures highlight topics ranging from Columbus to Lincoln to Obama, engaging students on both historical and contemporary topics. Also included are archival videos, such as footage of Ellis Island immigrants in 1903 and the Kennedy-Nixon debate.

Hear the **Audio** For each chapter there are audio files of the text, speeches, readings, and other audio material, such as "Battle Hymn of the Republic" and "The Star Spangled Banner" that will enrich students' experience of social and cultural history.

Study and **Review** MyHistoryLab provides a wealth of practice quizzes, tests, flashcards, and other study resources available to students online.

NEW MyHistoryLab Connections

At the end of each chapter, a new section, MyHistoryLab Connections, provides a list of the references within the chapter and additional documents, maps, videos, or additional resources that relate to the content of the chapter.

ACKNOWLEDGMENTS

In the years it has taken to bring *Out of Many* from idea to reality and to improve it in successive editions, we have often been reminded that although writing history sometimes feels like isolated work, it actually involves a collective effort. We want to thank the dozens of people whose efforts have made the publication of this book possible.

We wish to thank our many friends at Prentice Hall for their efforts in creating the seventh edition of *Out of Many*, Brief Edition: Yolanda de Rooy, President; Craig Campanella, Editorial Director; Charlyce Jones Owen, Publisher; Maureen Prado Roberts, Senior Marketing Manager; Brandy Dawson, Director of Marketing; Cheryl Keenan, Project Manager; Ann Marie McCarthy, Senior Managing Editor; Maria Lange, Art Director; from GEX Publishing Services: Micah Petillo, Production Editor.

Although we share joint responsibility for the entire book, the chapters were individually authored: John Mack Faragher wrote Chapters 1–8; Susan Armitage wrote Chapters 9–16; Mari Jo Buhle wrote Chapters 18–20, 25–26, 29; and Daniel Czitrom wrote Chapters 17, 21–24, 27–28. For this edition Buhle and Czitrom co-authored Chapters 30–31.

Each of us depended on a great deal of support and assistance with the research and writing that went into this book. We want to thank Kathryn Abbott, Nan Boyd, Krista Comer, Jennifer Cote, Crista DeLuzio, Keith Edgerton, Carol Frost, Jesse Hoffnung Garskof, Pailin Gaither, Jane Gerhard, Todd Gernes, Mark Krasovic, Daniel Lanpher, Melani McAlister, Rebecca McKenna, Cristiane Mitchell, J. C. Mutchler, Keith Peterson, Alan Pinkham, Tricia Rose, Gina Rourke, Jessica Shubow, Gordon P. Utz Jr., Maura Young, Teresa Bill, Gill Frank, and Naoko Shibusawa. Our families and close friends have been supportive and ever so patient over the many years we have devoted to this project. But we want especially to thank Paul Buhle, Meryl Fingrutd, Bob Greene, and Michele Hoffnung.

John Mack Faragher   John Mack Faragher is Arthur Unobskey Professor of American History and director of the Howard R. Lamar Center for the Study of Frontiers and Borders at Yale University. Born in Arizona and raised in southern California, he received his B.A. at the University of California, Riverside, and his Ph.D. at Yale University. He is the author of *Women and Men on the Overland Trail* (1979), *Sugar Creek: Life on the Illinois Prairie* (1986), *Daniel Boone: The Life and Legend of an American Pioneer* (1992), *The American West: A New Interpretive History* (2000), and *A Great and Noble Scheme: The Tragic Story of the Expulsion of the French Acadians from their American Homeland* (2005).

Daniel Czitrom   Daniel Czitrom is Professor of History at Mount Holyoke College. Born and raised in New York City, he received his B.A. from the State University of New York at Binghamton and his M.A. and Ph.D. from the University of Wisconsin, Madison. He is the author of *Media and the American Mind: From Morse to McLuhan* (1982), which won the First Books Award of the American Historical Association and has been translated into Spanish and Chinese. He is co-author of *Rediscovering Jacob Riis: Exposure Journalism and Photography in Turn of the Century New York* (2008). He has served as a historical consultant and featured on-camera commentator for several documentary film projects, including the PBS productions *New York: A Documentary Film; American Photography: A Century of Images;* and *The Great Transatlantic Cable.* He currently serves as a Distinguished Lecturer for the Organization of American Historians.

MARI JO BUHLE   Mari Jo Buhle is William R. Kenan, Jr. University Professor *Emerita* of American Civilization and History at Brown University, specializing in American women's history. She received her B.A. from the University of Illinois, Urbana-Champaign, and her Ph.D. from the University of Wisconsin, Madison. She is the author of *Women and American Socialism, 1870–1920* (1981) and *Feminism and Its Discontents: A Century of Struggle with Psychoanalysis* (1998). She is also coeditor of the *Encyclopedia of the American Left,* (second edition, 1998). Professor Buhle held a fellowship (1991–1996) from the John D. and Catherine T. MacArthur Foundation. She is currently an Honorary Fellow of the History Department at the University of Wisconsin, Madison.

Susan H. Armitage   Susan H. Armitage is Professor of History and Women's Studies, *Emerita*, at Washington State University, where she was a Claudius O. and Mary R. Johnson Distinguished Professor. She earned her Ph.D. from the London School of Economics and Political Science. Among her many publications on western women's history are three coedited books, *The Women's West* (1987), *So Much To Be Done: Women on the Mining and Ranching Frontier* (1991), and *Writing the Range: Race, Class, and Culture in the Women's West* (1997). She served as editor of the feminist journal *Frontiers* from 1996 to 2002. Her most recent publication, coedited with Laurie Mercier, is *Speaking History: Oral Histories of the American Past, 1865–Present* (2009).

One of the most characteristic features of our country is its astounding variety. The American people include the descendants of native Indians; colonial Europeans of British, French, and Spanish background; Africans; and migrants from virtually every country and continent. Indeed, at the beginning of the new century the United States is absorbing a flood of immigrants from Latin America and Asia that rivals the great tide of people from eastern and southern Europe one hundred years before. What's more, our country is one of the world's most spacious, sprawling across than 3.6 million square miles of territory. The struggle to meld a single nation out of our many far-flung communities is what much of American history is all about. That is the story told in this book.

Every human society is made up of communities. A community is a set of relationships linking men, women, and their families to a coherent social whole that is more than the sum of its parts. In a community people develop the capacity for unified action. In a community people learn, often through trial and error, how to transform and adapt to their environment.

The sentiment that binds the members of a community together is the mother of group consciousness and ethnic identity. In the making of history, communities are far more important than even the greatest of leaders, for the community is the institution most capable of passing a distinctive historical tradition to future generations.

William Sidney Mount (1807–1868) *California News* 1850. Oil on canvas. The Long Island Museum of American Art, History and Carriages.

Gift of Mr. and Mrs. Ward Melville, 1955.

Harvey Dinnerstein, *Underground, Together* 1996, oil on canvas, 90" × 107".
Photograph courtesy of Gerold Wunderlich & Co., New York, NY.

Communities bind people together in multiple ways. They can be as small as local neighborhoods, in which people maintain face-to-face relations, or as large as the nation itself. This book examines American history from the perspective of community life—an ever-widening frame that has included larger and larger groups of Americans.

Networks of kinship and friendship, and connections across generations and among families, establish the bonds essential to community life. Shared feelings about values and history establish the basis for common identity. In communities, people find the power to act collectively in their own interest. But American communities frequently took shape as a result of serious conflicts among groups, and within communities there was often significant fighting among competing groups or classes. Thus the term *community,* as we use it here, includes conflict and discord as well as harmony and agreement.

For decades Americans have complained about the "loss of community." But community has not disappeared—it has been continuously reinvented. Until the late eighteenth century, community was defined primarily by space and local geography. But in the nineteenth century communities were reshaped by new and powerful historical forces such as the marketplace, industrialization, the corporation,

mass immigration, mass media, and the growth of the nation-state. In the twentieth century, Americans struggled to balance commitments to multiple communities. These were defined not simply by local spatial arrangements, but by categories as varied as race and ethnicity, occupation, political affiliation, and consumer preference.

The "American Communities" vignettes that open each chapter reflect these transformations. Most of the vignettes in the pre–Civil War chapters focus on geographically defined communities, such as the ancient Indian city at Cahokia, or the experiment in industrial urban planning in early nineteenth-century Lowell, Massachusetts. Post–Civil War chapters explore different and more modern kinds of communities. In the 1920s, movies and radio offered communities of identification with dreams of freedom, material success, upward mobility, youth and beauty. In the 1950s, rock 'n' roll music helped germinate a new national community of teenagers, with profound effects on the culture of the entire country in the second half of the twentieth century. In the late 1970s, fear of nuclear accidents like the one at Three Mile Island brought concerned citizens together in communities around the country and encouraged a national movement opposing nuclear power.

The title for our book was suggested by the Latin phrase selected by John Adams, Benjamin Franklin, and Thomas Jefferson for the Great Seal of the United States: *E Pluribus Unum*—"Out of Many Comes Unity." These men understood that unity could not be imposed by a powerful central authority but had to develop out of mutual respect among Americans of different backgrounds. The revolutionary leadership expressed the hope that such respect could grow on the basis of a remarkable proposition: "We hold these truths to be self-evident, that all men are created equal; that they are endowed by their Creator with certain unalienable rights; that among these are life, liberty, and the pursuit of happiness." The national government of the United States would preserve local and state authority but would guarantee individual rights. The nation would be strengthened by guarantees of difference.

"Out of Many" comes strength. That is the promise of America and the premise of this book. The underlying dialectic of American history, we believe, is that as a people we must locate our national unity in the celebration of the differences that exist among us; these differences can be our strength, as long as we affirm the promise of the Declaration. Protecting the "right to be different," in other words, is absolutely fundamental to the continued existence of democracy, and that right is best protected by the existence of strong and vital communities. We are bound together as a nation by the ideal of local and cultural differences protected by our common commitment to the values of the American Revolution.

Today those values are endangered by those who use the tactics of mass terror. In the wake of the September 11, 2001 attack on the United States, and with the continuing threat of biological, chemical, or even nuclear assaults, Americans can not afford to lose faith in our historic vision. The thousands of victims buried in the smoking ruins of the World Trade Center included people from dozens of different ethnic and national groups. The United States is a multicultural and transnational society. We must rededicate ourselves to the protection and defense of the promise of diversity and unity.

Our history demonstrates that the promise has always been problematic. Centrifugal forces have been powerful in the American past, and at times the country seemed about to fracture into its component parts. Our transformation from a collection of groups and regions into a nation was marked by painful and often violent struggles. Our past is filled with conflicts between Indians and colonists, masters and slaves, Patriots and Loyalists, Northerners and Southerners, Easterners and Westerners, capitalists and workers, and sometimes the government and the people. War can bring out our best, but it can also bring out our worst. During World War II thousands of Japanese American citizens were deprived of their rights and locked up in isolated detention centers because of their ethnic background.

Thomas Satterwhite Noble, *Last Sale of Slaves on the Courthouse Steps*, 1860, oil on canvas, Missouri Historical Society.

Americans often appear to be little more than a contentious collection of peoples with conflicting interests, divided by region and background, race and class.

Our most influential leaders have also sometimes suffered a crisis of faith in the American project of "liberty and justice for all." Thomas Jefferson not only believed in the inferiority of African Americans but feared that immigrants from outside the Anglo-American tradition might "warp and bias" the development of the nation "and render it a heterogeneous, incoherent, distracted mass." We have not always lived up to the American promise and there is a dark side to our history. It took the bloodiest war in American history to secure the human rights of African Americans, and the struggle for full equality for all our citizens has yet to be won. During the great influx of immigrants in the early twentieth century, fears much like Jefferson's led to movements to Americanize the foreign born by forcing them, in the words of one leader, "to give up the languages, customs, and methods of life which they have brought with them across the ocean, and adopt instead the language, habits, and customs of this country, and the general standards and ways of American living." Similar thinking motivated Congress at various times to bar the immigration of Africans, Asians, and other people of color into the country, and to force assimilation on American Indians by denying them the freedom to practice their religion or even to speak their own language. Such calls for restrictive unity resound in our own day.

But other Americans have argued for a more fulsome version of Americanization. "What is the American, this new man?" asked the French immigrant Michel Crévecoeur in 1782. "A strange mixture of blood which you will find in no other country." In America, he wrote, "individuals of all nations are melted into a new race of men." A century later Crévecoeur was echoed by historian Frederick Jackson Turner, who believed that "in the crucible of the frontier, the immigrants were Americanized, liberated, and fused into a mixed race, English in neither nationality nor characteristics. The process has gone on from the early days to our own."

The process by which diverse communities have come to share a set of common American values is one of the most fundamental aspects of our history. It did not occur, however, because of compulsory Americanization programs, but because of free public education, popular participation in democratic politics, and the impact of popular culture. Contemporary America does have a common culture: we share a commitment to freedom of thought and expression, we join in the aspirations to own our own homes and send our children to college, we laugh at the same television programs or video clips on YouTube.

To a degree that too few Americans appreciate, this common culture resulted from a complicated process of mutual discovery that took place when different ethnic and regional groups encountered one another. Consider just one small and unique aspect of our culture: the barbecue. Americans have been barbecuing since before the beginning of written history. Early settlers adopted this technique of cooking from the Indians—the word itself comes from a native term for a framework of sticks over a fire on which meat was slowly cooked. Colonists typically barbecued pork, fed on Indian corn. African slaves lent their own touch by introducing the use of spicy sauces. The ritual that is a part of nearly every American family's Fourth of July silently celebrates the heritage of diversity that went into making our common culture.

The American educator John Dewey recognized this diversity early in the last century. "The genuine American, the typical American, is himself a hyphenated character," he declared, "international and interracial in his make-up." It was up to all Americans, Dewey argued, "to see to it that the hyphen connects instead of separates." We, the authors of *Out of Many,* endorse Dewey's perspective. "Creation comes from the impact of diversity," the American philosopher Horace Kallen wrote about the same time. We also endorse Kallen's vision of the American promise: "A democracy of nationalities, cooperating voluntarily and autonomously through common institutions, . . . a multiplicity in a unity, an orchestration of mankind." And now, let the music begin.

Out of Many

Native Americans build thatch houses beside a massive pyramid in *Community Life at Cahokia* by Michael Hampshire.

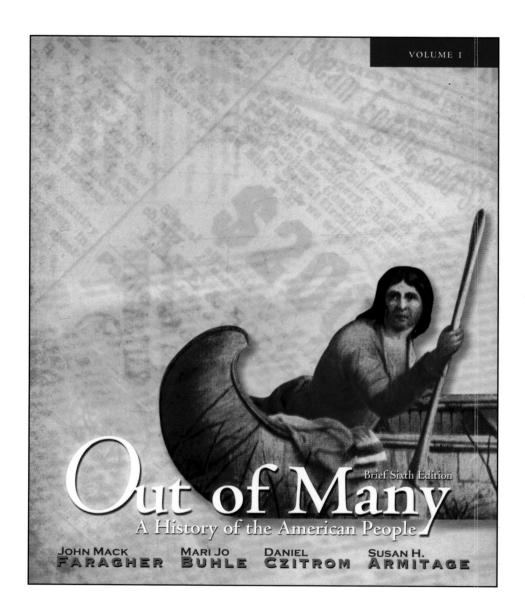

To order, please request
VOLUME 1
Chapters 1-17

ISBN-10: 0-205-01063-6 | ISBN-13: 978-0-205-01063-9

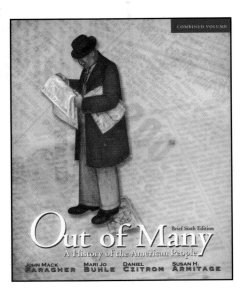

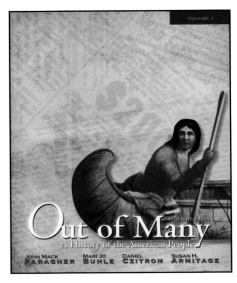

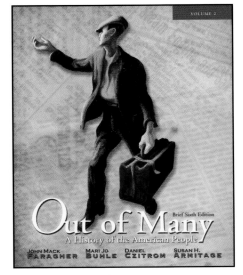

COMBINED VOLUME
Chapters 1-31
ISBN-10: 0-205-01064-4
ISBN-13: 978-0-205-01064-6

VOLUME 1
Chapters 1-17
ISBN-10: 0-205-01063-6
ISBN-13: 978-0-205-01063-9

VOLUME 2
Chapters 17-31
ISBN-10: 0-205-01062-8
ISBN-13: 978-0-205-01062-2

1

A CONTINENT OF VILLAGES

TO 1500

((•─[Hear th**dio**

Hear the audio for Chapter 1 at **www.myhistorylab.com**.

WHAT ENTS led to the migration of Asian peoples into North Ameri

WHAT ERE the consequences of the development of farming for native c nities?

WHAT NDS of agricultural societies developed in North America?

WHA MPORTANT differences were there between Indian societies i Southwest, South, and Northeast on the eve of colonization?

AMERICAN COMUNITIES

Cahokia: Thirteenth-Century Life on the Mississippi

As the sun rose over the rich floodplain, the people of the riverbank city set about their daily tasks. Some went to shops where they manufactured tools, pots, and luxury items—goods destined to be exchanged in the far corners of the continent. Others left their densely populated neighborhoods for the outlying countryside, where they worked the fields that fed the city. From almost any point people could see the great temple that rose from the city center.

The Indian residents of this thirteenth-century city lived and worked on the east banks of the Mississippi River, across from present-day St. Louis, a place known today as **Cahokia**. In the thirteenth century, Cahokia was an urban cluster of 20,000 or 30,000 people. Its farm fields were abundant with corn, beans, and squash. The temple, a huge earthwork pyramid, covered fifteen acres at its base and rose as high as a ten-story building.

The vast urban complex of Cahokia, which at its height stretched six miles along the Mississippi River, flourished from the tenth to the fourteenth century. Its residents were not nomadic hunters but farmers, participants in a complex agricultural culture that archaeologists term "Mississippian." Hundreds of acres of crops fed the people of Cahokia, the largest urban community north of the Aztec civilization of central Mexico. Moreover, Cahokia stood at the center of a long-distance trading system that linked it to other Indian communities over a vast area. Copper came from Lake Superior, mica from the southern Appalachians, and conch shells from the Atlantic coast. Cahokia's specialized artisans were renowned the manufacture of high-quality flint hoes, which were exported throughout the Mississippi Valley.

Evidence suggests that Cahokia was a city-state supported by tribute taxation. Like the awe-inspiring public works of other early societies in other parts of the world, most notably the pyramids of ancient Egypt and the acropolis of Athens, the temple mound of Cahokia was intended to showcase its wealth and power. The mounds and other colossal public works at Cahokia were the monuments of a society ruled by a class of elite leaders. From their residences atop the mound, priests and chiefs looked down on their subjects both literally and figuratively.

The long story of North America before European colonization reveals that the native inhabitants developed a great variety of societies. Beginning as migrant hunting and gathering bands, they found ways to fine-tune their subsistence strategies to fit environmental possibilities and limitations.

Communities in the highlands of Mexico invented systems of farming that spread to all the regions where cultivation was possible. Not only the Aztecs of Mexico and the Mayans of Central America but also communities in the Southwest and the Mississippi Valley constructed densely settled urban civilizations. North America before colonization was, as historian Howard R. Lamar phrases it, "a continent of villages," a land with thousands of communities.

Cahokia

Cahokia   One of the largest urban centers created by Mississippian peoples, containing 30,000 residents in 1250.

THE FIRST AMERICAN SETTLERS

"Why do you call us Indians?" a Massachusetts native complained to Puritan missionary John Eliot in 1646. Christopher Columbus, who mistook the Taino people of the Caribbean for the people of the East Indies, called them "**Indios**." Within a short time this Spanish word had passed into English as "Indians" and was commonly used to refer to all the native peoples of the Americas. Today anthropologists sometimes employ the term "Amerindians," and others use "Native Americans." But in the United States most of the descendants of the original inhabitants refer to themselves as "Indian people."

WHO ARE THE INDIAN PEOPLE?

At the time of their first contacts with Europeans at the beginning of the sixteenth century, the inhabitants of the Western Hemisphere represented over 2,000 separate cultures, spoke several hundred different languages, and made their livings in scores of different environments. Just as the term "European" includes many nations, so the term "Indian" covers an enormous diversity among the peoples of the Americas.

No single physical type characterized all the peoples of the Americas. Although most had straight, black hair and dark, almond-shaped eyes, their skin color ranged from mahogany to light brown. Few fit the "redskin" descriptions used by North American colonists of the eighteenth and nineteenth centuries. Indeed, it was only when Europeans had compared Indian peoples with natives of other continents, such as Africans, that they seemed similar enough to be classified as a group.

Once Europeans realized that the Americas were in fact a "New World," rather than part of the Asian continent, a debate began over how people might have moved there from Europe and Asia, where (according to the Bible) God had created the first man and woman. In 1590, the Spanish Jesuit missionary Joseph de Acosta reasoned that because Old World animals were present in the Americas, they must have crossed by a land bridge that could have been used by humans as well.

MIGRATION FROM ASIA

Acosta was the first to propose the Asian migration hypothesis that is widely accepted today. Siberian and American Indian populations suggest that migrants to North America began leaving Asia approximately 30,000 years ago (see Map 1.1).

The migration was possible because during the last Ice Age, from 70,000 to 10,000 years ago, huge glaciers locked up massive volumes of water, and sea levels were as much as 300 feet lower than they are today. Asia and North America, now separated by the Bering Strait, were joined by a huge subcontinent of ice-free, treeless grassland, which geologists have named **Beringia**. Summers there were warm, and winters were cold but almost snow free, so there was no glaciation. It was a perfect environment for large mammals—mammoth and mastodon, bison, horse, reindeer, camel, and saiga (a goat-like antelope). Small bands of Siberian hunter-gatherers were surely attracted by these animal populations.

Access to the interior of North America, however, was blocked by huge ice sheets covering much of what is today Canada. How did the migrants get through those 2,000 miles of deep ice? The standard hypothesis is that with the warming of the climate and the end of the Ice Age, about 13,000 BCE (before the common era), glacial melting

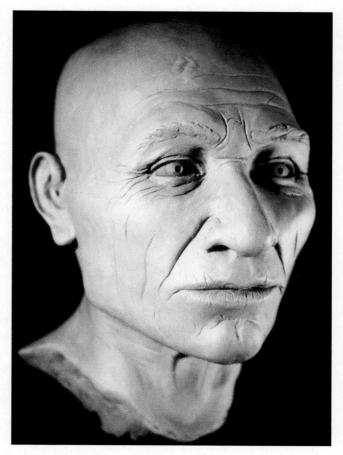

A forensic artist reconstructed this bust from the skull of "Kennewick Man," whose skeletal remains were discovered along the Columbia River in 1996. Scientific testing suggested that the remains were more than 9,000 years old.

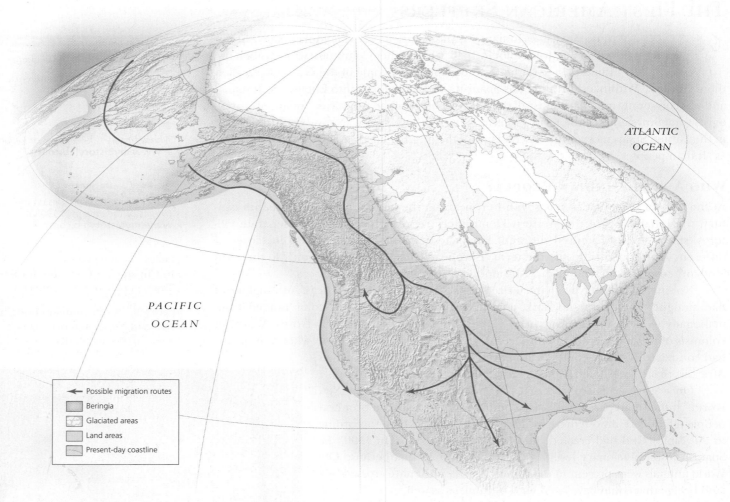

ATLANTIC OCEAN

PACIFIC OCEAN

← Possible migration routes
▢ Beringia
▢ Glaciated areas
▢ Land areas
▭ Present-day coastline

MAP 1.1
Migration Routes from Asia to America   During the Ice Age, Asia and North America were joined where the Bering Strait is today, forming a migration route for hunting peoples. Either by boat along the coast, or through a narrow corridor between the huge northern glaciers, these migrants began making their way to the heartland of the continent as much as 30,000 years ago.

WHAT GEOGRAPHICAL features shaped the dispersal of Asian migrants throughout the Americas?

created an ice-free corridor—an original "Pan-American Highway"—along the eastern front range of the Rocky Mountains. Using this thoroughfare, the hunters of big game reached the Great Plains as early as 11,000 BCE.

Recently, however, new archaeological finds along the Pacific coast of North and South America have complicated this hypothesis. Radiocarbon analysis of remains discovered at several newly excavated human sites suggested dates of 12,000 BCE or earlier. The most spectacular find, at Monte Verde in southern Chile, produced striking evidence of tool making, house building, and rock painting conservatively dated at 12,500 BCE. A number of archaeologists believe that the people who founded these settlements moved south in boats along a coastal route—an ancient "Pacific Coast Highway."

There were two later migrations into North America. About 5000 BCE the **Athapascan** people moved across Beringia and began to settle the forests in the

Athapascan   A people that began to settle the forests in the northwestern area of North America around 5000 BCE.

northwestern area of the continent. Eventually groups of Athapascan speakers, the ancestors of the Navajos and Apaches, migrated across the Great Plains to the Southwest. A third and final migration began about 3000 BCE, long after Beringia had disappeared under rising seas, when a maritime hunting people crossed the Bering Strait in small boats. The Inuits (also known as the Eskimos) colonized the polar coasts of the Arctic, the Yupiks the coast of southwestern Alaska, and the Aleuts the Aleutian Islands (which are named for them).

While scientists debate the timing and mapping of these various migrations, many Indian people hold to oral traditions that say they have always lived in North America. Every culture has its origin stories, offering explanations of the customs and beliefs of the group. A number of scholars believe these origin stories may shed light on ancient history. Could these stories preserve a memory of the changes at the end of the Ice Age?

THE CLOVIS CULTURE: THE FIRST ENVIRONMENTAL ADAPTATION

The tools found at the earliest North American archaeological sites, crude stone or bone choppers and scrapers, are similar to artifacts from the same period found in Europe or Asia. About 11,000 years ago, however, ancient Americans developed a much more sophisticated style of making fluted blades and lance points, a tradition named "Clovis," after the location of the initial discovery near Clovis, New Mexico, in 1926. In the years since, archaeologists have unearthed Clovis stone tools at sites throughout the continent all dating within 1,000 or 2,000 years of one another, suggesting that the Clovis technology spread quickly throughout the continent.

The evidence suggests that Clovis bands were mobile communities of foragers numbering perhaps thirty to fifty individuals from several interrelated families. They returned to the same hunting camps year after year, migrating seasonally within territories of several hundred square miles. Camps found throughout the continent overlooked watering places that would attract game. Clovis blades have been found amid the remains of mammoth, camel, horse, giant armadillo, and sloth.

The global warming trend that ended the Ice Age dramatically altered the North American climate. About 15,000 years ago the giant continental glaciers began to melt and the northern latitudes were colonized by plants, animals, and humans. Meltwater created the lake and river systems of today and raised the level of the surrounding seas, not only flooding Beringia but also vast stretches of the Atlantic and Gulf coasts, creating fertile tidal pools and offshore fishing banks.

NEW WAYS OF LIVING ON THE LAND

These huge transformations produced new patterns of wind, rainfall, and temperature, reshaping the ecology of the entire continent and gradually producing the distinct North American regions of today (see Map 1.2). The great integrating force of a single continental climate faded, and with its passing the continental Clovis culture fragmented into a number of different regional patterns.

The retreat of the glaciers led to new ways of finding food: hunting in the Arctic, foraging in the arid deserts, fishing along the coasts, hunting and gathering in the forests. These developments took place roughly 10,000 to 2,500 years ago, during what archaeologists call the **Archaic period**.

These Clovis points are typical of thousands that archaeologists have found at sites all over the continent, dating from a period about 12,000 years ago. When inserted in a spear shaft, these three- to six-inch fluted points made effective weapons for hunting mammoth and other big game. The ancient craftsmen who made these points often took advantage of the unique qualities of the stone they were working to enhance their aesthetic beauty.

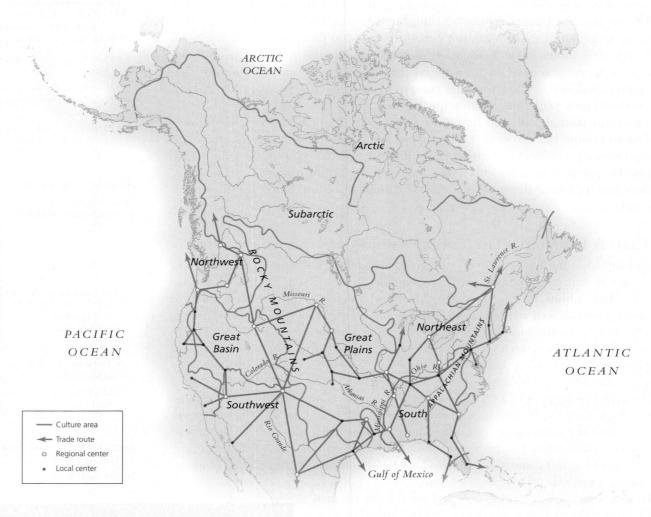

See the Map

The First Americans: Location of Major Indian Groups and Culture Areas in the 1600s at **www.myhistorylab.com**

MAP 1.2

Native North American Culture Areas and Trade Networks, ca. 1400 CE   All peoples must adjust their diet, shelter, and other material aspects of their lives to the physical conditions of the world around them. By considering the ways in which Indian peoples developed distinct cultures and adapted to their environments, anthropologists developed the concept of "culture areas." They divide the continent into nine fundamental regions that have greatly influenced the history of North America over the past 10,000 years. Just as regions shaped the lifeways and history of Indian peoples, after the coming of the Europeans they nurtured the development of regional American cultures. By determining the origin of artifacts found at ancient sites, historians have devised a conjectural map of Indian trade networks. Among large regional centers and smaller local ones, trade connected Indian peoples of many different communities and regions.

HOW MIGHT the diversity of climates in North America have shaped Indian trade patterns?

QUICK REVIEW

Hunting the Bison

* Climate shift resulted in the extinction of many large New World animals.

* As other large-mammal populations declined, hunters concentrated on bison herds.

* The growing complexity of Indian communities was reflected in bison hunting strategies.

Hunting Traditions   One of the most important effects of this massive climatic shift was the stress it placed on the big-game animals best suited to an Ice Age environment. The archaeological record documents the extinction of thirty-two classes of large New World mammals. Changing climatic conditions lowered the reproduction and survival rates of these large mammals, forcing hunting bands to intensify their hunting.

As the other large-mammal populations declined, hunters on the Great Plains concentrated on the herds of American bison (known more familiarly as buffalo). To hunt these animals, people needed a weapon. In archaeological sites dating from about 10,000 years ago, a new style of tool is found mingled with animal remains. This technology, named "Folsom" (for the site of the first major find near Folsom, New Mexico) was a refinement of the Clovis culture that featured more delicate but deadlier spear points. Hunters probably hurled the lances to which these points were attached with wooden spear-throwers, attaining far greater momentum than possible using their arms alone.

These archaeological finds suggest the growing complexity of early Indian communities. Hunters frequently stampeded herds of bison into canyon traps or over cliffs. At one such kill site in southeastern Colorado, dated at about 6500 BCE, archaeologists uncovered the remains of nearly 200 bison that had been slaughtered and then systematically butchered on a single occasion. Such tasks required a sophisticated division of labor among dozens of men and women and the cooperation of a number of communities. Taking food in such great quantities also suggests a knowledge of basic preservation techniques.

Desert Culture   In the Great Basin, the warming trend created a desert where once there had been enormous inland seas. Here Indian people developed what anthropologists call "**Desert culture**," a way of life based on the pursuit of small game and the intensified foraging of plant foods. Small communities of desert foragers migrated seasonally within a small range.

Archaeologists today find the artifacts of desert foragers in the caves and rock shelters in which they lived. In addition to stone tools, there are objects of wood, hide, and fiber, wonderfully preserved for thousands of years in the dry climate.

The innovative practices of Desert culture gradually spread from the Great Basin to the Great Plains and the Southwest, where foraging for plant foods began to supplement hunting. About 6,000 years ago, these techniques were carried to California, where communities developed economies capable of supporting some of the densest populations and the first permanently settled villages in North America. Another dynamic center developed along the coast of the Pacific Northwest, where Indian communities developed a way of life based on the abundance of fish and sea mammals. Densely populated and permanently settled communities developed there as well.

Forest Efficiency   There were similar trends east of the Mississippi. In the centuries prior to colonization and settlement by Europeans, the whole of eastern North America was a vast forest. Communities of native people achieved a comfortable and secure life by developing a sophisticated knowledge of the rich and diverse available resources, a principle anthropologists term "**forest efficiency**."

Archaeological sites in the East suggest that during the late Archaic period community populations grew and settlements became increasingly permanent, providing convincing evidence of the practicality of forest efficiency. The different roles of men and women were reflected in the artifacts these peoples buried with their dead: axes, fishhooks, and animal bones with males; nut-cracking stones, beads, and pestles with females.

When, in 1927, archaeologists at Folsom, New Mexico, uncovered this dramatic example of a projectile point embedded in the ribs of a long-extinct species of bison, it was the first proof that Indians had been in North America for many thousands of years.
Courtesy of the Denver Museum of Nature and Science.

QUICK REVIEW

Forest Living

⦁ Eastern North America a vast forest.

⦁ Indian communities took advantage of rich forest resources.

⦁ Indians developed settled forest communities.

Desert culture   A way of life based on hunting small game and the foraging of plant foods.

forest efficiency   Creation of a comfortable life through the development of a sophisticated knowledge of available resources.

THE DEVELOPMENT OF FARMING

WHAT WERE the consequences of the development of farming for native communities?

Hear the **Audio**
Ritual of the Maize
at **www.myhistorylab.com**

Mesoamerica The region stretching from central Mexico to Central America.

Aztecs A warrior people who dominated the Valley of Mexico from 1100–1521.

At the end of the Stone Age, communities in different regions of the world independently created systems of farming, each based on a unique staple crop: rice in Southeast Asia, wheat in the Middle East, potatoes in the Andean highlands of South America, and maize (what Americans call "corn") in Mexico. The dynamic center of this development in North America was in the highlands of Mexico, from which the new technology spread north and east.

ORIGINS IN MEXICO

Archaeological evidence suggests that plant cultivation in the highlands of central Mexico began about 5,000 years ago. Ancient Mexicans developed crops that responded well to human care and produced larger quantities of food in a limited space than did plants growing in the wild. Maize was particularly productive.

As farming became increasingly important, it radically reshaped social life. Farming provided not only the incentive for larger families (more workers for the fields) but also the means to feed them. People became less mobile, built more substantial residences near their crops, and developed more effective means of storage. Villages grew into towns and eventually into large, densely settled communities. Autumn harvests had to be stored during winter months, and the storage and distribution of food had to be managed. The division of labor increased with the appearance of specialists like toolmakers, craft workers, administrators, priests, and rulers.

By 1000 BCE urban communities governed by permanent bureaucracies had begun to form in **Mesoamerica**, the region stretching from central Mexico to Central America. By the beginning of the first millennium CE (common era), highly productive farming was supporting complex urban civilizations in the Valley of Mexico (the location of present-day Mexico City), the Yucatan Peninsula, and other parts of Mesoamerica. Like many of the ancient civilizations of Asia and the Mediterranean, these Mesoamerican civilizations were characterized by the concentration of wealth and power in the hands of an elite class of priests and rulers, the construction of temples and other public structures, and the development of systems of mathematics and astronomy and several forms of hieroglyphic writing. These civilizations also engaged in warfare between states and practiced ritual human sacrifice.

The great city of Teotihuacan in the Valley of Mexico, which emerged about 100 BCE, had a population of as many as 200,000 at the height of its power around 500 CE. Teotihuacan's leaders controlled an elaborate state-sponsored trading system that stretched from present-day Arizona to Central America and may have included coastal shipping connections with the civilizations of Peru. Teotihuacan began to decline in the sixth century, and by the eighth century it was mostly abandoned. A new empire, that of the Toltecs, dominated central Mexico from the tenth to the twelfth centuries. By the fourteenth century a people known as the **Aztecs**, migrants from the north, had settled in the Valley of Mexico and begun a dramatic expansion into a formidable imperial power. By the early fifteenth century an estimated 200,000 people lived in the Aztec capital, Tenochtitlán, making it one of the largest cities in the world.

The Mayan peoples of the Yucatan Peninsula developed a group of competing city-states that flourished from about 300 BCE until 900 CE. Their achievements included advanced writing and calendar systems and a sophisticated knowledge of mathematics.

Mesoamerican maize cultivation, as illustrated by an Aztec artist for the *Florentine Codex*, a book prepared several decades after the Spanish conquest. The peoples of Mesoamerica developed a greater variety of cultivated crops than those found in any other region in the world, and their agricultural productivity helped sustain one of the world's great civilizations.

Image #1739-3, courtesy the Library, American Museum of Natural History.

INCREASING SOCIAL COMPLEXITY

In a few areas, farming truly did result in a revolutionary change in Indian communities, producing urban civilizations like those in Mesoamerica or on the banks of the Mississippi at Cahokia. It is likely that among the first social transformations was the development of significantly more elaborate systems of kinship. Greater population density prompted families to group themselves into clans, and separate clans gradually became responsible for different social, political, or ritual functions. Clans may have been an important mechanism for binding together the people of several communities into larger social units based on ethnic, linguistic, and territorial unity. These "tribes" were headed by leaders or chiefs from honored clans, often advised by councils of elders.

Chiefs' primary functions were the supervision of the economy, the collection and storage of the harvest, and the distribution of food to the clans. Wealth inequalities were kept in check by redistribution according to principles of sharing similar to those operating in foraging communities. Nowhere in North America did Indian cultures develop a concept of the private ownership of land or other resources, which were usually considered the common resource of the people and were worked collectively.

Indian communities practiced a rather strict division of labor according to gender. In foraging communities, hunting was generally men's work, while the gathering of food and the maintenance of home-base camps were the responsibility of women. The development of farming may have challenged that pattern. Where hunting remained an important activity, women took responsibility for the growing of crops. But in areas like Mexico, where communities were almost totally dependent on cultivated crops for their survival, both men and women worked the fields.

In most North American Indian farming communities, women and men belonged to separate social groupings, each with its own rituals and lore. Membership in these gender societies was one of the most important elements of a person's identity. Marriage ties, on the other hand, were relatively weak, and in most Indian communities divorce was a simple matter.

Farming communities were far more complex than foraging communities, but they were also less stable. Growing populations demanded increasingly large surpluses of food, and this need often led to social conflict and warfare. Moreover, farming systems were especially vulnerable to changes in climate, such as drought, as well as to crises of their own making, such as soil depletion or erosion.

THE RESISTED REVOLUTION

Some scholars describe the transition to farming as a revolution. Their argument is that farming offered such obvious advantages that communities rushed to adopt it. But there is very little evidence to support the notion that farming was a clearly superior way of life. Anthropologists have demonstrated that farmers work considerably longer and harder than do foragers. Moreover, farmers depend on a relatively narrow selection of plants and animals for food and are more vulnerable to famine.

Moreover, ignorance of cultivation was never the reason communities failed to take up farming. All foraging cultures understand a great deal about plant reproduction and take steps to ensure the availability of their preferred food sources. Cultures in different regions assessed the relative advantages and disadvantages of adopting farming. In California and the Pacific Northwest, acorn gathering or salmon fishing made the cultivation of food crops seem a waste of time. In the Great Basin, there were attempts to farm but without much success. Before the invention of modern irrigation systems, which require sophisticated engineering, only the Archaic Desert culture could prevail in this harsh environment.

The creation of man and woman depicted on a pot (dated about 1000 CE) from the ancient villages of the Mimbres River of southwestern New Mexico, the area of Mogollon culture. Mimbres pottery is renowned for its spirited artistry. Such artifacts were usually intended as grave goods to honor the dead.

Mimbres black on white bowl, with painted representations of man and woman under a blanket. Grant County, New Mexico. Diam. 26.7 cm. Courtesy National Museum of the American Indian, Smithsonian Institution, 24/3198.

QUICK REVIEW

Indian Agrarian Society

- Families grouped themselves in clans which, in turn, were grouped in tribes.
- Chiefs supervised economic activities.
- No concept of private ownership of land.
- Strict division of labor according to gender.

In the neighboring Southwest, however, farming resolved certain ecological dilemmas and transformed the way of life. Like the development of more sophisticated traditions of tool manufacture, farming represented another stage in *economic intensification* (like the advance in tool making represented by Clovis technology) that kept populations and available resources in balance. It seems that where the climate favored it, people tended to adopt farming as a way of increasing the production of food, thus continuing the Archaic tradition of squeezing as much productivity as they could from their environment.

FARMING IN EARLY NORTH AMERICA

WHAT KINDS of agricultural societies developed in North America?

Maize farming spread north from Mexico into the area now part of the United States in the first millennium BCE. Over time maize was adapted to a range of climates and its cultivation spread to all the temperate regions.

FARMERS OF THE SOUTHWEST

Farming communities began to emerge in the arid Southwest during the first millennium BCE. Among the first to develop a settled farming way of life was a culture known to archaeologists as Mogollon. These people farmed maize, beans, squash, and constructed ingenious food storage pits in permanent village sites along what is today the southern Arizona–New Mexico border. Those pits may have been the precursors of what southwestern peoples today call kivas, sites of community religious rituals.

During the same centuries, a culture known as Hohokam flourished in the region along the floodplain of the Salt and Gila Rivers in southern Arizona. The Hohokam, who lived in farming villages, built and maintained the first irrigation system in America north of Mexico, channeling river water through 500 miles of canals to water desert fields of maize, beans, squash, tobacco, and cotton. Hohokam culture shared many traits with Mesoamerican civilization to the south, including platform mounds for religious ceremonies and large courts for ball playing.

THE ANASAZIS

The best-known ancient farming culture of the Southwest is the Anasazi, which developed around the first century CE in the Four Corners area, where the states of Arizona, New Mexico, Utah, and Colorado meet on the great plateau of the Colorado River. Around 750 CE, possibly in response to population pressure and an increasingly dry climate, the residents of communities there began shifting from pit-house villages to densely populated, multistoried apartment complexes that the Spanish invaders called "pueblos."

Anasazi culture extended over a very large area. The sites of more than 25,000 Anasazi communities are known in New Mexico alone. The most prominent center was Pueblo Bonito in Chaco Canyon. Completed in the twelfth century, this complex of 700 interconnected rooms is a monument to the Anasazi golden age.

Cliff Palace, at Mesa Verde National Park in southwest Colorado, was created 900 years ago when the Anasazis left the mesa tops and moved into more secure and inaccessible cliff dwellings. Facing southwest, the building gained heat from the rays of the low afternoon sun in winter, and overhanging rock protected the structure from rain, snow, and the hot midday summer sun. The numerous round kivas, each covered with a flat roof originally, suggest that Cliff Palace may have had a ceremonial importance.

The Anasazis faced a major challenge in the thirteenth and fourteenth centuries. The arid climate became even drier, and growing populations had to redouble their efforts to improve food production. A devastating drought from 1276 to 1293 resulted in repeated crop failures and eventual famine. The ecological crisis was heightened by the arrival in the fourteenth century of Athapascan migrants, ancestors of the Navajos and the Apaches. Athapascans raided Anasazi farming communities, taking food, goods, and possibly slaves. Gradually Anasazi communities abandoned the Four Corners area altogether, most resettling along the Rio Grande, joining with local residents to form the Pueblo communities that were living there when the Spanish arrived.

FARMERS OF THE EASTERN WOODLANDS

Archaeologists date the beginning of the farming culture of eastern North America, known as Woodland culture, from the first appearances of pottery in the region about 3,000 years ago. Woodland culture was based on a sophisticated way of life that combined gathering and hunting with the cultivation of a few local crops.

Woodland people began cultivating maize during the first millennium CE, but even before that they had begun to adopt an increasingly settled existence and a more complex social organization, evidenced by complex earthen constructions. Around 1000 BCE, at a place called Poverty Point in northeastern Louisiana, residents erected a remarkable series of concentric semicircular earthen mounds covering an area about a mile square.

Mound building was also a characteristic activity of the peoples living in the Ohio Valley during this period. The people of a culture known as Adena lived in semi permanent villages and constructed large burial mounds during the first millennium BCE. They were succeeded by a culture called Hopewell. Hopewell chiefs mobilized an elaborate trade network, acquiring obsidian from the Rocky Mountains, copper from the Great Lakes, mica from the Appalachians, and shells from the Gulf Coast. Hopewell artisans converted these materials into goods that played an important role in trade and were used to adorn the dead in their impressive graves.

MISSISSIPPIAN SOCIETY

The Hopewell culture collapsed in the fifth century CE, perhaps as a result of an ecological crisis brought on by shifting climate patterns. Over the next several centuries, however, a number of important technological innovations were introduced in the East. The bow and arrow, developed first on the Great Plains, appeared east of the Mississippi in about the seventh century, greatly increasing the efficiency of hunting. At about the same time maize farming spread widely through the East. A shift from digging sticks to flint hoes also took place about this time, further increasing the productive potential of maize farming.

On the basis of these innovations, a powerful new culture known as Mississippian arose in the seventh or eighth century CE. The peoples of Mississippian culture were farmers living in permanent community sites along the floodplains of the Mississippi Valley. Cahokia was the largest and most spectacular, with its monumental temple mounds, its residential

The Great Serpent Mound in southern Ohio, the shape of an uncoiling snake more than 1,300 feet long, is the largest effigy earthwork in the world. Monumental public works like these suggest the high degree of social organization of the Mississippian people.

This bottle in the shape of a nursing mother (dated about 1300 BCE) was found at a Mississippian site. Historians can only speculate about the thoughts and feelings of the Mississippians, but such works of art are testimonials to the universal human emotion of maternal affection.

"Nursing Mother Effigy Bottle." From the Whelpley Collection at the St. Louis Science Center. Photograph © 1985 the Detroit Institute of Arts/The Bridgeman Art Library, NY.

neighborhoods, and its surrounding farmlands. But there were dozens of other urban communities, each with thousands of residents.

THE POLITICS OF WARFARE AND VIOLENCE

These centers, linked by the Mississippi River and its many tributaries, became the earliest city-states north of Mexico, hierarchical chiefdoms that extended political control over the farmers of the surrounding countryside (see Map 1.2 for an illustration of trade networks). With continued population growth, these cities engaged in vigorous and probably violent competition for the limited space along the rivers. It may have been the need for more orderly ways of allocating territories that stimulated the evolution of political hierarchies. The tasks of preventing local conflict, storing large food surpluses, and redistributing foodstuffs from farmers to artisans and elites required a leadership class with the power to command.

Mississippian culture reached its height between the eleventh and thirteenth centuries CE, the same period in which the Anasazi culture constructed its desert cities. Both groups adapted to their own environment the technology that was spreading northward from Mexico. Both developed impressive artistic traditions, and their feats of engineering reflect the beginnings of science and technology. They were complex societies characterized by urbanism, social stratification, craft specialization, and regional trade.

Organized violence was probably rare among hunting bands, which could seldom manage more than a small raid against an enemy. Certain hunting peoples, though, such as the southward-moving Athapascans, must have engaged in systematic raiding of settled farming communities. Warfare was also common among farming confederacies fighting to gain additional lands for cultivation.

The archaeological remains of Cahokia reveal that during the thirteenth and fourteenth centuries the residents enclosed the central sections of their city with a heavy log stockade. There must have been a great deal of violent warfare with other nearby communities. Also during this period, numerous towns were formed throughout the river valleys of the Mississippi, each based on the domination of farming countrysides by metropolitan centers. Eventually conditions in the upper Mississippi Valley deteriorated so badly that Cahokia and many other sites were abandoned altogether, and as the cities collapsed, people relocated in smaller, decentralized communities. Among the peoples of the South, however, Mississippian patterns continued into the period of colonization.

CULTURAL REGIONS OF NORTH AMERICA ON THE EVE OF COLONIZATION

WHAT IMPORTANT differences were there between Indian societies in the Southwest, South, and Northeast on the eve of colonization?

An appreciation of the ways human cultures adapted to geography and climate is fundamental to an understanding of American history, for just as regions shaped the development of Indian cultures in the centuries before the arrival of Europeans, so they continued to influence the character of American life in the centuries thereafter.

In order to understand the impact of regions on Indian cultures, anthropologists divide North America into several distinct "culture areas" within which groups shared a significant number of cultural traits: Arctic, Subarctic, Great Basin, Great Plains, California, Northwest, Plateau, Southwest, South, and Northeast.

THE POPULATION OF INDIAN AMERICA

Determining the size of the precolonial population of the Americas is a tricky business, and estimates vary greatly, but there seems to be general agreement among historical demographers that the population of the North American continent (excluding Mesoamerica) numbered between 5 and 10 million at the time of the first European voyages of discovery. The population of the Western Hemisphere as a whole may have numbered 50 million or more, the same order of magnitude as Europe's population at the time.

Population varied tremendously by cultural region (see Map 1.2). Although the cultural regions of the Arctic, Subarctic, Great Basin, and Great Plains made up more than half the physical space of the continent, they were inhabited by only a small fraction of the native population. Those regions were home to scattered bands who continued to practice the Archaic economy. Hunting and gathering continued in California as well, although the population there grew large and dense because of the region's natural abundance. In the Pacific Northwest, abundant salmon fisheries supported large populations concentrated in permanent villages. The people of the Plateau also made their living by fishing, although their communities were not as large or as concentrated.

The largest populations of the continent were concentrated in the farming regions of the Southwest, South, and Northeast. These were the areas in which European explorers, conquerors, and colonists concentrated their first efforts, and they deserve more detailed examination (see Map 1.3).

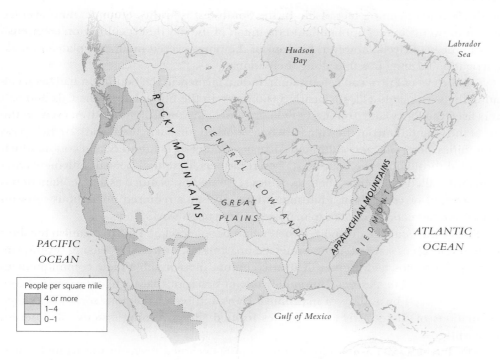

MAP 1.3

Population Density of Indian Societies in the Fifteenth Century   Based on what is called the "carrying capacity" of different subsistence strategies—the population density they could support—historical demographers have mapped the hypothetical population density of Indian societies in the fifteenth century, before the era of European colonization. Populations were densest in farming societies or in coastal areas with marine resources and sparsest in extreme environments like the Great Basin.

WHAT WERE the key factors in determining population density?

OVERVIEW | Origins of Some Indian Tribal Names

Cherokee	A corruption of the Choctaw *chiluk-ki*, meaning "cave people," an allusion to the many caves in the Cherokee homeland in the highlands of present-day Georgia. The Cherokees called themselves *Ani-Yun-Wiya*, or the "real people."
Cheyenne	From the Sioux *Sha-hiyena*, "people of strange speech." The Cheyennes of the Northern Plains called themselves *Dzi-tsistas*, meaning "our people."
Hopi	A shortening of the name the Hopis of northern Arizona use for themselves, *Hópitu*, which means "peaceful ones."
Mohawk	From the Algonquian *Mohawaúuck*, meaning "man-eaters." The Mohawks of the upper Hudson Valley in New York called themselves *Kaniengehaga*, "people of the place of the flint."
Pawnee	From the Pawnee term *paríki*, which describes a distinctive style of dressing the hair with paint and fat to make it stand erect like a horn. The Pawnees, whose homeland was the Platte River valley in present-day Nebraska, called themselves *Chahiksichahiks*, "men of men."

THE SOUTHWEST

The single overwhelming fact of life in the Southwest is aridity. Summer rains average only ten to twenty inches annually, and on much of the dry desert cultivation is impossible. A number of rivers, however, flow out of the pine-covered mountain plateaus, making irrigation farming possible along their courses.

On the eve of European colonization, Indian farmers in the Southwest had been cultivating their irrigated fields for nearly 3,000 years. In the floodplain of the Gila and Salt Rivers lived the Pimas and Tohono O'Odhams and along the Colorado River, even on the floor of the Grand Canyon, the Yuman peoples worked small irrigated fields. In their oasis communities, desert farmers cultivated corn, beans, squash, sunflowers, and cotton, which they traded throughout the Southwest. Desert farmers lived in dispersed settlements that the Spanish called **rancherias**, their dwellings separated by as much as a mile. Rancherias were governed by councils of adult men whose decisions required unanimous consent, although a headman was chosen to manage the irrigation works.

East of the Grand Canyon lived the Pueblo peoples, named by the Spanish for their unique dwellings of stacked, interconnected apartments. Although speaking several languages, the Pueblos had a great deal in common, most notably their commitment to communal village life. A strict communal code of behavior that regulated personal conduct was enforced by a maze of matrilineal clans and secret religious societies; unique combinations of these clans and societies formed the governing systems of different Pueblo villages.

The Pueblos inhabit the oldest continuously occupied towns in the United States. The village of Oraibi, Arizona, dates from the twelfth century, when the Hopis ("peaceful ones") founded it in the isolated central mesas of the Colorado Plateau. Using dry-farming methods and drought-resistant plants, the Hopis produced rich harvests of corn and squash amid shifting sand dunes.

The Athapascans, more recent immigrants to the Southwest, also lived in the arid deserts and mountains. They hunted and foraged, traded meat and medicinal herbs with farmers, and often raided and plundered these same villages and rancherias. One group of Athapascans, the Apaches, continued to maintain their

rancherias Dispersed settlements of Indian farmers in the Southwest.

An Early European Image of Native Americans

From the very beginning of Europeans' contact with native American peoples, they depicted Indians as savages rather than as peoples with complex cultures. This woodcut by German artist Johann Froschauer was included in a 1505 German edition of Amerigo Vespucci's account of his voyage to the New World in 1499, and is among the very first images of Native Americans published. The image is a complete fantasy, lacking any ethnographic authenticity. Indians gather for a feast on the beach. The caption in the original publication read, in part: "The people are naked, handsome, brown, well-shaped in body. . . . No one has anything, but all things are in common. And the men have as wives those who please them, be they mothers, sisters, or friends; therein they make no distinction. They also fight with each other; and they eat each other, even those who are slain, and hang the flesh of them in the smoke." A cannibalized body is being devoured. A couple is kissing. Women display their breasts. The image sent a powerful message: that some of the strongest taboos of Europeans—nakedness, sexual promiscuity, and cannibalism—were practiced by the people of the New World. It is an unrelentingly negative picture. The arrival of European vessels in the background of the image suggests that all this was about to change. Images like these continued to dominate the depiction of Indians for the next 400 years, and were used as justifications for conquest. ∎

HOW ARE European stereotypes of savage people conveyed visually in this image?

nomadic ways. But another group, known as the Navajos, gradually adopted the farming and handicraft skills of their Pueblo neighbors.

THE SOUTH

The South enjoys a mild, moist climate with short winters and long summers, ideal for farming. In the sixteenth century, large populations of Indian peoples farmed this rich land, fishing or hunting local fauna to supplement their diets. They lived in communities ranging from villages of twenty or so dwellings to large towns of a thousand or more inhabitants (see Map 1.4).

Mississippian cultural patterns continued among many of the peoples of the South. Along waterways, many farming towns were organized into chiefdoms. Because most of

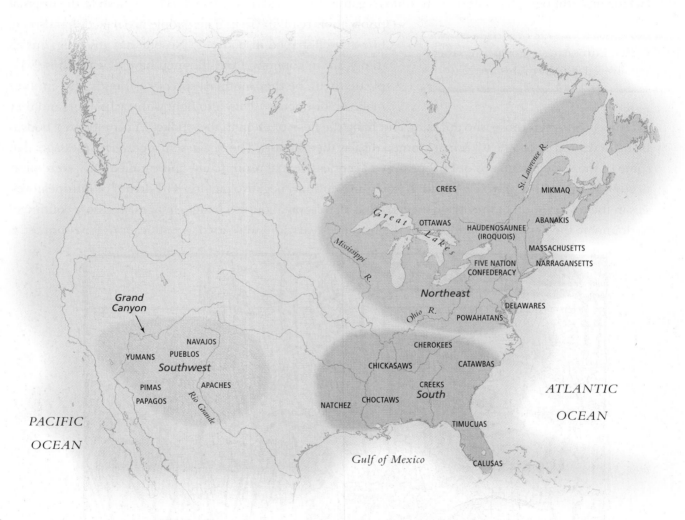

MAP 1.4

Indian Groups in the Areas of First Contact   The Southwest was populated by desert farmers like the Pimas, Tohono O'Odhams, Yumans, and Pueblos, as well as by nomadic hunters and raiders like the Apaches and Navajos. On the eve of colonization, the Indian societies of the South shared many traits of the complex Mississippian farming culture. The Indians of the Northeast were mostly village peoples. In the fifteenth century, five Iroquois groups—the Mohawks, Oneidas, Onondagas, Cayugas, and Senecas—joined together to form the Iroquois Five Nation Confederacy.

HOW DID geography help define the major Indian cultural groups?

these groups were decimated by disease in the first years of colonization, they are poorly documented. Archaeologists have excavated sites on the east bank of the Mississippi, in what is now Arkansas, inhabited by the Caddo people. The evidence suggests that in the fifteenth century they lived in complex ranked communities, built monumental temple mounds, and counted a population of more than 200,000. There is historical evidence about the Natchez, who survived into the eighteenth century before being defeated and dispersed in a war with the French. They too lived on the Mississippi, on the opposite bank from the Caddos, where they farmed the rich floodplains. The Natchez were also a ranked society, with a small group of nobility ruling over the majority.

These chiefdoms were rather unstable. Under the pressure of climate change, population growth, and warfare, many were weakened and others collapsed. As a result, thousands of people left behind the grand mounds and earthworks and migrated to the woodlands and hill country, where they took up hunting and foraging, returning to the tried and true methods of "forest efficiency." They formed communities and banded together in confederacies, which were less centralized and more egalitarian than the Mississippian chiefdoms and would prove considerably more resilient to conquest.

Among the most prominent of these new ethnic groups were a people in present-day Mississippi and Alabama who came to be known as the Choctaws. Another group in

"The New Queen Being Taken to the King,"** an engraving copied from a drawing by Jacques LeMoyne, an early French colonist of Florida, and published by the German Theodor de Bry in 1591. The communities of Florida were hierarchical, with classes and hereditary chiefs, some of whom were women. Here, LeMoyne depicted a "queen" being carried on an ornamental litter by men of rank.

Neg. No. 324281, Photographed by Rota, Engraving by DeBry. American Museum of Natural History Library.

western Tennessee became known as the Chickasaws, and another people in Georgia later became known as the Creeks. On the mountain plateaus lived the Cherokees, the single largest confederacy, which included more than sixty towns. For these groups, farming was somewhat less important, hunting somewhat more so. There were no ruling classes or kings, and leaders included women as well as men. Councils of elderly men governed the confederacies but were joined by clan matrons for annual meetings at the central council house.

THE NORTHEAST

The Northeast, the colder sector of the eastern woodlands, has a varied geography of coastal plains and mountain highlands, great rivers, lakes, and valleys. In the first millennium CE, farming became the main support of the Indian economy in those places where the growing season was long enough to bring a crop of corn to maturity. In such areas of the Northeast, along the coasts and in the river valleys, Indian populations were large and dense (see Map 1.4).

•••Read the Document

Iroquois Creation Story
at **www.myhistorylab.com**

The Iroquois of present-day Ontario and upstate New York have lived in the Northeast for at least 4,500 years and were among the first northeastern peoples to adopt cultivation. Iroquois women produced crops sufficient to support up to fifty longhouses, each occupied by a large matrilineal extended family. Typically, these villages were surrounded by substantial wooden walls or palisades, clear evidence of conflict and warfare.

Population growth and the resulting intensification of farming in Iroquoia stimulated the development of chiefdoms there as it did elsewhere. By the eleventh century, several centers of population had coalesced from east to west across upstate New York. These were the five Iroquois chiefdoms or nations: the Mohawks, Oneidas, Onondagas, Cayugas, and Senecas. Oral histories collected from Iroquois speakers during the nineteenth century remember this as an era of persistent violence, possibly the consequence of conflicts over territory.

•••Read the Document

Profile: *Hiawatha (Deganawida)*
at **www.myhistorylab.com**

•••Read the Document

*Dekanawida Myth & the Achievement of
Iroquois Unity* at **www.myhistorylab.com**

To control this violence, the five nations established a confederacy. According to Iroquois oral history, Chief Deganawida, speaking through the great orator Hiawatha, convinced the five nations to agree to prohibit warfare with each other, replacing revenge with payment and gift exchange. Iroquois legend refers to Deganawida "blocking out the sun" as a demonstration of his powers.

The Iroquois called their confederacy Haudenosaunee, meaning "people of the longhouse." Each nation, they said, occupied a separate hearth but acknowledged a common mother. As in the longhouse, women played important roles in the confederacy, choosing male leaders who would represent their lineages and chiefdom on the Iroquois council. The confederacy suppressed violence among its members but did not hesitate to encourage war against neighboring Iroquoian speakers, such as the Hurons or the Eries, who constructed defensive confederacies of their own at about the same time.

The other major language group of the Northeast was Algonquian, whose speakers divided among at least fifty distinct cultures. The Algonquian peoples north of the Great Lakes

This Hiawatha wampum belt of the Haudenosaunee or Iroquois Five Nation Confederacy is exquisitely constructed of nearly 7,000 purple and white drilled shell beads, woven together with buckskin thongs and hemp thread. It is a ceremonial artifact, a symbol of the unity of the five Iroquois nations. With the central tree or heart pointed up, the first two squares on the right represent the Mohawk and Oneida, the tree stands for the Onondaga, where the council met, and the third and fourth squares stand for the Cayuga and Seneca nations. The belt itself dates from the early eighteenth century, but the design is thought to have originated with the confederacy itself, perhaps in the twelfth century CE.

CHRONOLOGY

30,000 BCE	First humans populate Beringia	**200 BCE–400 CE**	Hopewell culture flourishes
13,000 BCE	Global warming trend begins	**650**	Bow and arrow, flint hoes, and Northern Flint corn in the Northeast
12,500 BCE	Monte Verde site in southern Chile flourishes		
10,000 BCE	Clovis technology	**775–1150**	Hohokam culture flourishes
9000 BCE	Extinction of big-game animals	**1000**	Tobacco in use throughout North America
8000 BCE	Beginning of the Archaic period	**1142**	Founding of Haudenosaunee Confederacy
7000 BCE	First cultivation of plants in the Mexican highlands	**1150**	Founding of Hopi village of Oraibi, oldest continuously occupied town in the United States
5000 BCE	Athapascan migration to America begins		
4000 BCE	First settled communities along the Pacific coast	**1200**	High point of Mississippian and Anasazi cultures
3000 BCE	Inuit, Yupik, and Aleut migrations begin	**1276**	Severe drought begins in the Southwest
1500–1000 BCE	Maize and other Mexican crops introduced into the Southwest	**1300**	Arrival of Athapascans in the Southwest
1000 BCE	First urban communities in Mexico		

and in northern New England were hunters and foragers, organized into bands with loose ethnic affiliations. Several of these peoples were the first to become involved in the fur trade with European newcomers. Among the Algonquians of the Atlantic coast from present-day Massachusetts south to Virginia, as well as among those in the Ohio Valley, farming led to the development of settlements as densely populated as those of the Iroquois.

In contrast to the Iroquois, most Algonquian peoples were patrilineal. In general, they lived in less extensive dwellings and in smaller villages, often without palisade fortifications. Although Algonquian communities were relatively autonomous, they began to form confederacies during the fifteenth and sixteenth centuries.

CONCLUSION

Over the thousands of years that elapsed between the initial settlement of North America and the arrival of Europeans at the end of the fifteenth century, Indian peoples developed dozens of distinctive cultures, each fine-tuned to the geographic and climatic possibilities and limitations of their environments. The ruins of the ancient city of Cahokia provide dramatic evidence that North America was not the "virgin" continent Europeans proclaimed it to be. Indians had transformed the natural world, making it into a human landscape.

"Columbus did not discover a new world," writes historian J. H. Perry, "he established contact between two worlds, both already old." North America had a rich history, one that European colonists did not understand and that later generations of Americans have too frequently ignored. The colonists and settlers who came to take the land encountered thousands of Indian communities with deep roots and vibrant traditions. In the confrontation that followed, Indian communities called on their own traditions and their own gods to help them defend their homelands.

QUICK REVIEW

The Northeast

- Varied geography of plains, mountains, rivers, lakes, and valleys.
- The Iroquois have lived in the region for 4,500 years.
- Population growth and intensification of farming led to the development of chiefdoms.

Read the Document

Thomas Harriot, *The Algonquian Peoples of the Atlantic Coast* (1588) at **www.myhistorylab.com**

REVIEW QUESTIONS

1. List the evidence for the hypothesis that the Americas were settled by migrants from Asia.

2. Discuss the impact of environmental change and human hunting on the big-game populations of North America.

3. Review the principal regions of the North American continent and the human adaptations that made social life possible in each of them.

4. Define the concept of "forest efficiency." How does it help to illuminate the major development of the Archaic period?

5. Why did the development of farming lead to increasing social complexity? Discuss the reasons why organized political activity began in farming societies.

6. What were the hunting and agrarian traditions? In what ways did the religious beliefs of Indian peoples reflect their environmental adaptations?

7. What factors led to the organization of the Iroquois Five Nation Confederacy?

KEY TERMS

Cahokia (p. 4)
Indios (p. 5)
Beringia (p. 5)
Athapascan (p. 6)
Desert culture (p. 9)

Forest Efficiency (p. 9)
Archaic period (p. 7)
Mesoamerica (p. 10)
Aztecs (p. 10)
Rancherias (p. 16)

myhistorylab Connections

PEARSON

Reinforce what you learned in this chapter by studying the many documents, images, maps, review tools, and videos available at www.myhistorylab.com.

Read and Review

✓● Study and Review **Chapter 1**

●●● Read the Document

Pima Creation Story

Dekanawida Myth & the Achievement of Iroquois Unity

Iroquois Creation Story

Ottawa Origins Story (recorded ca. 1720)

The Story of the Creation of the World, Told by a Zuñi Priest in 1885

Thomas Harriot, The Algonquian Peoples of the Atlantic Coast (1588)

José de Acosta, Speculations on the Origins of the Indians (1590)

👁 See the Map

The First Americans: Location of Major Indian Groups and Culture Areas in the 1600s

Pre-Columbian Societies of the Americas

Research and Explore

●●● Read the Document

Exploring America: America and the Horse

Whose History Is It?: Images of Indians

Profiles
  Trickster
  Hiawatha (Deganawida)

History Bookshelf: *Bartolome de las Casas,* Brief Account of the Devastation of the Indies *(1542)*

((●● Hear the Audio *Ritual of the Maize*

((●● Hear the Audio

Hear the audio files for Chapter 1 at
www.myhistorylab.com.

Our lord and king it is true that the strange people have come to the shores of the great sea . . .
—Miguel Leon-Portilla

The French, under the command of Jean Ribault, discover the River of May (St Johns River) in Florida on 1 May 1562: colored engraving, 1591, by Theodor de Bry after a now lost drawing by Jacques Le Moyne de Morgues. The Granger Collection.

2

WHEN WORLDS COLLIDE

1492–1590

((•●─[**Hear** the **Audio**

Hear the audio files for Chapter 2 at **www.myhistorylab.com**.

HOW DID social change in Europe contribute to European expansion overseas?

HOW DID the Spanish invasion transform the Americas?

WHAT IMPORTANT differences were there between Spanish, English, and French patterns of colonization?

AMERICAN COMMUNITIES

The English at Roanoke

IT WAS LATE AUGUST 1590 WHEN THE ENGLISH VESSELS ARRIVED AT ROANOKE Island, off the coast of present-day North Carolina. Governor John White was returning to the first English community established in America. He had left three years before, sailing home to appeal for additional support. He was extremely anxious about the fate of the colonists, including his daughter, son-in-law, and granddaughter Virginia Dare, the first English child born in the New World. Rowing ashore, he found the colonists' houses "taken down," their possessions "spoiled and scattered about." Looking around, White noticed a word carved on a nearby tree trunk: "CROATOAN," the name of a friendly Indian village some fifty miles south. White reassured himself that his people awaited him at Croatoan and returned to his vessel, anxious to rescue them.

The Roanoke settlement had been sponsored by Sir Walter Raleigh, a wealthy English adventurer. In 1584 Raleigh sponsored a small group of adventurers who first landed on the island the Indians called Roanoke. The men found the coastal region densely populated and were entertained by a local chief named Wingina. To Wingina, the English were potential allies in his struggle to extend authority over more villages, and he granted the men permission to plan a large English settlement. He even sent two of his leading men, Manteo and Wanchese, back to England to help prepare the enterprise. When the Englishmen returned in 1585 to establish the colony of Virginia, (christened in honor of England's virgin queen, Elizabeth I), the two Indians offered Wingina conflicting reports. Manteo, from the village of Croatoan, argued that English technology made these men powerful allies. But Wanchese told of the disturbing inequalities he had seen among the English and warned his chief of the potential brutality of these men. He rightly suspected their intentions, for Raleigh's plans for a profitable colony were based on the expectation of exploiting the Indians.

After building a rough fort on the island, the English requested supplies and received from Wingina. But as fall turned to winter and his own stores diminished, Wingina grew weary of their persistent demands. He was also stunned by the new diseases the English brought. In the spring Wingina ran out of patience. Before the Indians could act, however, the Englishmen caught wind of the rising hostility and in a surprise attack in May 1586 they killed several leaders, including Wingina. Leaving his head on a stake, they fled back to England.

Two of the colonists, John White and Thomas Harriot, who had spent their time exploring the physical and human world of the coast and recording their findings in notes and sketches, were appalled by the turn of events. Back in England, Harriot, believing the attack unnecessary, argued for the possibility that the Indians, "through discreet dealing" might yet come to "honor, obey, fear and love us." White proposed a new plan for a colony of genuine settlers, families who would attempt to live in harmony with the natives.

In 1587, with Raleigh's financial support, John White returned to Virginia as governor of a new colony of 117 men, women, and children. Arriving at Roanoke, White found himself among Indians who had already been completely alienated, and within a month, one of the colonists had been shot full of arrows. White's counterattack only increased the Indians' resolve to expel the intruders. The colonists begged White to sail home in their only seaworthy vessel to ask Raleigh for additional support. He left reluctantly, arriving in England just as war began with Spain.

After three long and anxious years, Governor White now found the settlement destroyed, and the colonists gone. He returned to his vessel eager to leave for the village of Croatoan. But within minutes a great storm blew up, and the captain told White they had to sail for deeper waters. White would never glimpse the shores of America again. The English settlers of Roanoke became "The Lost Colony," their disappearance and ultimate fate one of the enduring mysteries of colonial history.

Blinded by their desire for immediate rewards, the colonists wasted the opportunity presented by the natives' initial welcome. But the Roanoke story also says something about the importance of community in the first attempts at colonization. There is some evidence to suggest that the so-called lost colonists lived out the rest of their lives as residents of Indian villages. Virginia Dare and other English children may have been adopted by Indian families, grown up and taken Indian spouses, in the process creating the first mixed community of English and Indians in North America.

European colonists came to the Americas for a variety of reasons, but high on their list of priorities were plunder and profit. The invasion of America often included terrible violence, as well as frequent possibilities for accommodation and cooperation between natives and newcomers. The invasion also introduced mortal epidemic diseases that devastated native communities. The encounter of communities at Roanoke was, in numerous ways, a template for New World colonization.

Roanoke

The Expansion of Europe

Roanoke and other European colonial settlements of the sixteenth century came in the wake of Christopher Columbus's voyage of 1492. The connection with America established by Columbus had earthshaking consequences. Within a generation, the exchanges of peoples, crops, animals, and germs had transformed the world. The key to understanding these remarkable events is the transformation of Europe during the several centuries preceding the voyage of Columbus.

HOW DID social and religious change in Europe contribute to European expansion overseas?

Western Europe before Columbus

Western Europe was an agricultural society: most Europeans lived in family households clustered in farming villages. During the late Middle Ages there were great advances in agricultural technology. From the eleventh to the fourteenth centuries the quantity of land under cultivation in western Europe more than doubled. During the same period the population nearly tripled.

Europe was a world of social contrasts, characterized by a social system historians call "feudalism." The land was divided into hundreds of small territories, each ruled by a family of lords that held a monopoly of wealth and power. Feudal lords commanded labor service from peasants and tribute in the form of crops. They were the main beneficiaries of medieval economic expansion.

Western Europe was officially Christian, united under the authority of the Roman Catholic Church. The Catholic Church was one of the most powerful feudal landowners in Europe. It insisted on its dogmas and actively persecuted heretics, nonbelievers, and devotees of older "pagan" religions.

For the great majority of Europeans, living conditions were harsh. Most rural people survived on bread and porridge, supplemented with vegetables and an occasional piece of meat or fish. Infectious diseases abounded and famines periodically ravaged the countryside. In the fourteenth century, for example, a series of crop failures resulted in widespread starvation and death. This episode prepared the way for the so-called Black Death, a widespread epidemic of bubonic plague that swept in from Asia and wiped out a third of Europe's population between 1347 and 1353.

Strengthened by the technological developments of the Middle Ages, Europe's agricultural economy quickly recovered. By 1500 the population had rebounded to its former high of 65 million.

QUICK REVIEW

European Society

- European states were hierarchical.
- Most Europeans were peasant farmers.
- Medieval economic growth mostly benefited wealthy landowners.

The Merchant Class and the Renaissance

The economic growth of the late Middle Ages was accompanied by the expansion of commerce, especially the trade in basic goods such as minerals, salt, timber, fish, cereals, wool, and wine. Commercial expansion stimulated the growth of markets and towns.

The heart of this dynamic European commercialism lay in the city-states of Italy. During the late Middle Ages, the cities of Venice, Genoa, and Pisa seized control of Mediterranean trade. The merchants of these cities became the principal outfitters of the Crusades, a series of great military expeditions promoted by the Catholic Church to recover Palestine from the Muslims. With the conquest of Jerusalem at the end of the eleventh century, the silk and spice trades of Asia were delivered into the hands of Italian merchants. Asian civilization also supplied a number of technical innovations that further propelled European economic growth. From China alone came the compass, gunpowder, and use of movable type in printing.

A French peasant labors in the field before a spectacular castle in a page taken from the illuminated manuscript *Tres Riches Heures*, made in the fifteenth century for the duc de Berry. In 1580 the essayist Montaigne talked with several American Indians at the French court who "noticed among us some men gorged to the full with things of every sort while their other halves were beggars at their doors, emaciated with hunger and poverty" and "found it strange that these poverty-stricken halves should suffer such injustice, and that they did not take the others by the throat or set fire to their houses."

Renaissance   The intellectual and artistic flowering in Europe during the fourteenth, fifteenth, and sixteenth centuries sparked by a revival of interest in classical antiquity.

Contact with Muslim civilization provided access to important ancient texts, long lost in Europe but preserved in the great libraries of the Muslim world. The revived interest in classical antiquity triggered a period of intellectual and artistic flowering from the fourteenth to sixteenth centuries that later generations called the **Renaissance**. The revolution in communication made possible by the printing press, the beginning of regular postal service, and the growth of universities helped spread Renaissance ideas throughout the elite circles of Europe.

The Renaissance celebrated human possibility. This human-centered perspective was part of what became known as humanism, in which life on Earth took precedence over the afterlife of the soul. This outlook was a critical component of the inquisitive and acquisitive spirit that motivated the exploration of the Americas.

THE NEW MONARCHIES

The Renaissance began amid the ruins of the plague. Famine and disease led to violence, as groups battled for their share of a shrinking economy. A series of peasant rebellions culminated in the great English Peasants' Revolt of 1381. Warfare among the nobility weakened and greatly reduced the power of the landed classes, and the Catholic Church was seriously destabilized by an internal struggle between French and Italian factions.

It was during this period of social and political chaos that the monarchs of western Europe began to replace the lords as the new centers of power. They built their legitimacy by promising internal order as they unified their realms (see Map 2.1). They built royal bureaucracies and standing armies and navies. In many cases, the new monarchs found support among the increasingly wealthy merchants, who in return sought lucrative royal contracts and trading monopolies. This alliance between commerce and political power was another important development that prepared the way for European expansion.

THE PORTUGUESE VOYAGES

Portugal became the first of the new Renaissance kingdoms to send out explorers on voyages to distant lands. Lisbon, the principal port on the sea route between the Mediterranean and northwestern Europe, was a bustling, cosmopolitan city with large enclaves of Italian merchants. By 1385 the local merchant community had grown powerful enough to place João I, their favorite, on the throne. João had ambitious plans to establish a Portuguese trading empire.

A central figure in this development was the king's son, Prince Henry, known to later generations as "the Navigator." Prince Henry established an academy of eminent geographers, instrument makers, shipbuilders, and seamen. Studying the seafaring traditions of Asia and the Muslim world, Prince Henry's experts incorporated them into the design of a new ship called the *caravel*, faster and better-handling than any ship previously known in Europe. They promoted the use of Arab instruments for astronomical calculation. With such innovations, Europeans became the masters of the world's seas.

MAP 2.1

Western Europe in the Fifteenth Century   By the middle of the century, the monarchs of western Europe had unified their realms and begun to build royal bureaucracies and standing armies and navies. These states, all with extensive Atlantic coastlines, sponsored the voyages that inaugurated the era of European colonization.

WHY WERE some European states better positioned for colonizing than others?

The Portuguese explored the Atlantic coast of northwestern Africa for direct access to the lucrative gold and slave trades of that continent. By the time of Prince Henry's death in 1460, they had colonized the Atlantic islands of the Azores and the Madeiras and founded bases along the West African "Gold Coast." In 1488 Portuguese captain Bartholomeu Días rounded the southern tip of Africa, and ten years later Vasco da Gama, with the aid of Arab pilots, reached India. The Portuguese eventually built strategic trading forts along the coasts of Africa, India, Indonesia, and China, and gained control of much of the Asian spice trade. Most important for the history of the Americas, the Portuguese established the Atlantic slave trade. (For a full discussion of slavery, see Chapter 4.)

COLUMBUS REACHES THE AMERICAS

In 1476, Christopher Columbus, a young Genoan sailor, joined his brother in Lisbon, where he became a seafaring merchant for Italian traders. He developed the simple idea of opening a new route to the Indies by sailing west across the Atlantic Ocean. Such a venture would require royal backing, but when he approached the various monarchs of Europe with his idea, their advisers rejected his plan, pointing out that

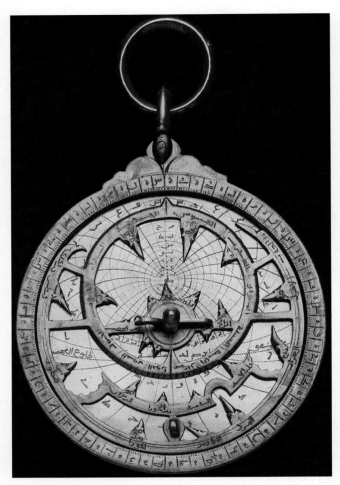

The astrolabe, an instrument used for determining the precise position of heavenly bodies, was introduced into early modern Europe by the Arabs. This is one of the earliest examples, an intricately engraved brass astrolabe produced by a master craftsman in Syria in the thirteenth century.

© National Maritime Museum Picture Library, London, England. Neg. #E5555-3.

Read the Document

From The Journal of Christopher Columbus (1492) at
www.myhistorylab.com

Watch the Video

What Is Columbus's Legacy? at
www.myhistorylab.com

Reconquista The long struggle (ending in 1492) during which Spanish Christians reconquered the Iberian peninsula from Muslim occupiers.

his calculation of the distance to Asia was much too short. They were right: Columbus was wrong. But it turned out to be an error of monumental good fortune.

Columbus finally sold his plan to the monarchs of Castile and Aragon, Isabel and Ferdinand. These two had just completed the **Reconquista**, a centuries-long struggle between Catholics and Muslims that ended Muslim rule in Spain. The Catholic monarchs of Spain were eager for new lands to conquer, and observing the successful Portuguese push to the south along the west coast of Africa, they became interested in opening lucrative trade routes of their own to the Indies.

Columbus called his undertaking "the Enterprise of the Indies," which suggests his commercial hopes. But his mission was more than commercial. One of his prime goals was to "occupy" the islands he found, establishing title for Spain by the right of occupancy. Like the adventurers who later established the first English colony at Roanoke, Columbus's objectives were starkly imperial.

Columbus's three vessels reached the Bahamas in October 1492. But Columbus believed he was in the Indies, somewhere near the Asian mainland. He explored the northern island coasts of Cuba and Hispaniola before heading home, fortuitously catching the westerly winds that blow from the American coast toward Europe north of the tropics. Perhaps Columbus's most important discovery was the clockwise circulation of the Atlantic winds and currents that would carry thousands of European ships back and forth to the Americas.

Leading Columbus's triumphal procession to the royal court were half a dozen Taíno Indians. "Should your majesties command it," Columbus told the monarchs, "all the inhabitants could be made slaves." Moreover, he reported, "there are many spices and great mines of gold and of other metals." In fact, none of the Eastern spices familiar to Europeans grew in the Caribbean and there were only small quantities of alluvial gold in the riverbeds of the islands. Nonetheless, Columbus reported that he had left a small force behind in a rough fort on the northern coast of Hispaniola to explore for gold.

The enthusiastic monarchs financed a return convoy of seventeen vessels and 1,500 men that sailed in late 1493 to begin the systematic colonization of the islands. Like the later English colonists at Roanoke, Columbus expected the Indians would provide the necessary labor. But returning to Hispaniola, Columbus found his fort in ruins and his men all killed by the Taínos. Columbus directed his men to attack and destroy the nearby Taíno villages, enslaving the inhabitants and demanding tribute in gold.

Columbus's voyages were a disaster for the Taínos. The combined effects of warfare, famine, and demoralization resulted in the collapse of their society. Numbering perhaps 300,000 in 1492, they were reduced to fewer than 30,000 within fifteen years, and by the 1520s had been effectively eliminated as a people.

Columbus made two additional voyages to the Caribbean, both characterized by the same obsessive searching for gold and violent raiding for slaves. He died in Spain in 1506, still convinced he had opened a new way to Asia.

Columbus bids farewell to the monarchs Isabel and Ferdinand at the port of Palos in August 1492, illustrated in a copperplate engraving published in 1594 by Theodore de Bry of Frankfort. While armed men are ferried out to the vessels, three accountants in a room directly above the monarchs count out the gold to fund the journey.

THE SPANISH IN THE AMERICAS

Long before the English attempted to plant their first colony at Roanoke, the Spanish had created a huge and wealthy empire in the Americas. They created a caste system, in which a small minority of settlers and their offspring controlled the lives and labor of millions of Indian and African workers. But it was also a society in which colonists, Indians, and Africans mixed to form a new people.

HOW DID the Spanish invasion transform the Americas?

THE INVASION OF AMERICA

The first stages of the Spanish invasion of America included frightful violence. Armies marched across the Caribbean islands, plundering and killing. Columbus and his successors established an institution known as the *encomienda*, in which Indians were compelled to labor in the service of Spanish lords. In practice it amounted to little more than slavery. Faced with labor shortages, slavers raided the Bahamas and soon depopulated them of native people. The depletion of gold on Hispaniola led to the invasion of the islands of Puerto Rico and Jamaica in 1508, then Cuba in 1511. Meanwhile, rumors of wealthy native societies to the west led to scores of probing expeditions (see Map 2.2). The Spanish invasion of Central America began in 1511, and two years later Vasco Núñez de Balboa crossed the Isthmus of Panama to the Pacific Ocean. In 1517, Spaniards landed on the coast of Mexico, and within a year they made contact with the Aztec empire (see Chapter 1).

Hernán Cortés landed on the Mexican coast in 1519 with armed troops. Within two years he overthrew the Aztec empire, a spectacular military accomplishment that has few parallels in the annals of conquest. Cortés skillfully exploited the resentment of the many peoples who lived under Aztec domination, forging Spanish–Indian alliances that became a model for the subsequent European colonization of the Americas. Here, as at Roanoke and dozens of other sites of European invasion, colonizers found Indians eager for allies to support them in their conflicts with other Indians. Even so, the Aztecs succeeded in driving the Spaniards from Tenochtitlán,

Read the **Document**
Exploring America: Exploitation of the Americas at **www.myhistorylab.com**

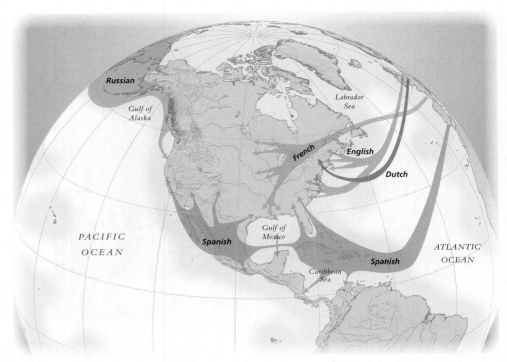

MAP 2.2

The Invasion of America In the sixteenth century, the Spanish first invaded the Caribbean and used it to stage their successive wars of conquest in North and South America. In the seventeenth century, the French, English, and Dutch invaded the Atlantic coast. The Russians, sailing across the northern Pacific, mounted the last of the colonial invasions in the eighteenth century.

WHAT IMPORTANT differences were there between Spanish, English, and French patterns of colonization?

QUICK REVIEW

Cortés and the Aztecs

• Hernán Cortés arrived in Mexico in 1519.

• Cortés exploited resentment toward the Aztecs to overthrow their empire.

• Smallpox outbreaks undermined the Aztecs' ability to resist the Spanish.

then put up a bitter and prolonged defense when Cortés returned with tens of thousands of Indian allies to besiege the capital. In the meantime, however, the Aztecs suffered a devastating epidemic of smallpox that killed thousands and undermined their ability to resist. In the aftermath of conquest, the Spanish plundered Aztec society, providing the Catholic monarchs with wealth beyond their wildest imagining.

THE DESTRUCTION OF THE INDIES

The Indian peoples of the Americas resisted Spanish conquest with determination, but most proved a poor match for mounted warriors with steel swords. The Carib people (for whom the Caribbean Sea is named) successfully defended the outermost islands until the end of the sixteenth century, and the nomadic tribes of arid northern Mexico, known collectively as the Chichimecs, proved equally difficult to subdue.

Some Europeans protested the horrors of the conquest. In 1511 the Catholic priest Antonio de Montesinos condemned the violence in a sermon delivered to colonists on Hispaniola. In the congregation was Bartolomé de las Casas, a man who had participated in the plunder of Cuba. Renouncing his own wealth, las Casas entered the priesthood and dedicated his life to the protection of the Indians. Long before the world recognized the concept of universal human rights, las Casas was proclaiming that "the entire human race is one."

In his brilliant history of the conquest, *The Destruction of the Indies* (1552), las Casas blamed the Spanish for cruelties resulting in millions of Indian deaths—in effect he

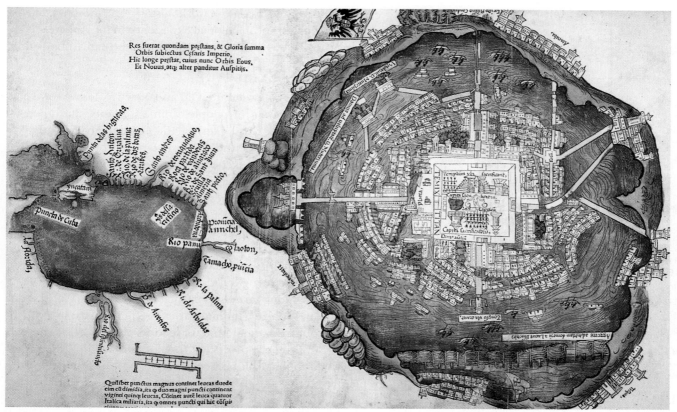

This map of Tenochtitlán, published in 1524 and attributed to the celebrated engraver Albrecht Dürer, shows the city before its destruction, with the principal Aztec temples in the main square, causeways connecting the city to the mainland, and an aqueduct supplying fresh water. The information on this map must have come from Aztec sources, as did much of the intelligence Cortés relied on for the Spanish conquest.

accused them of genocide. Although later scholars disputed las Casas's estimates of huge population losses, recent demographic studies suggest he was more right than wrong. The destruction of the Taínos on Hispaniola was repeated elsewhere.

THE VIRGIN SOIL EPIDEMICS

Las Casas was incorrect, however, in attributing most of these Indian deaths to warfare. Although lethal violence cost thousands of lives, and thousands more starved because their economies were destroyed, the primary cause of the drastic reduction in native populations was epidemic disease—influenza, plague, smallpox, measles, and typhus. Indian peoples lacked the antibodies necessary to protect them from European germs and viruses. Such devastating outbreaks of disease, striking for the first time against a completely unprotected population, are known as "virgin soil epidemics." Smallpox made its first appearance in America in 1518. The epidemic hit Mexico in 1520, destroying the Aztecs and preparing the way for their conquest, then spreading along the Indian trade network. In 1524 it strategically weakened the Inca civilization of the Andes eight years before their empire was conquered by Francisco Pizarro. Spanish chroniclers wrote that this single epidemic killed half the native Americans it touched. Disease was the secret weapon of the Spanish, and it helps explain their extraordinary success.

Warfare, famine, lower birthrates, and epidemic disease knocked the native population of the Americas into a downward spiral that was not reversed until the twentieth century (see Figure 2.1). By that time native population had fallen by more than 90 percent. It was

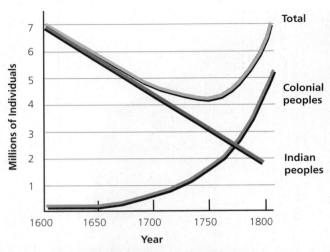

Figure 2.1 North America's Indian and Colonial Populations in the Seventeenth and Eighteenth Centuries
The primary factor in the decimation of native peoples was epidemic disease, brought to the New World from the Old. In the eighteenth century, the colonial population overtook North America's Indian populations.

Historical Statistics of the United States (Washington, DC: Government Printing Office, 1976), 8, 1168; Russell Thornton, *American Indian Holocaust and Survival* (Norman: University of Oklahoma Press, 1987), 32.

the greatest demographic disaster in world history. The most notable difference between the European colonial experience in the Americas compared to Africa or Asia was this radical reduction in the native population.

THE COLUMBIAN EXCHANGE

The passage of diseases between the Old and New Worlds was one part of the large-scale exchange of people, animals, plants, and goods— what the historian Alfred Crosby terms "the Columbian Exchange"— that marks the beginning of the modern era of world history (see Map 2.3). The most obvious exchange was the vast influx into Europe of the precious metals plundered from the Aztec and Incan empires of the New World. Silver from mines the Spanish discovered and operated with Indian labor in Mexico and Peru tripled the amount of silver coin circulating in Europe between 1500 and 1550, then tripled it again before 1600. The result of so much new coin in circulation was runaway inflation, which stimulated commerce and raised profits but lowered the standard of living for most people.

Of even greater long-term importance were the New World crops brought to Europe. Maize (Indian corn), became a staple crop in Mediterranean countries, the dominant feed for livestock elsewhere in Europe, and the primary provision for the slave ships of Africa. Potatoes provided the margin between famine and subsistence for the peasant peoples of northern Europe and Ireland.

Although the Spanish failed to locate valuable spices such as black pepper or cloves in the New World, new tropical crops more than compensated. Tobacco, first introduced to Europe about 1550 as a cure for disease, was soon in wide use as a stimulant. American vanilla and chocolate both became highly valued. American cotton proved far superior to Asian varieties for the production of cheap textiles. Each of these native plants—along with tropical transplants from the Old World to America, with sugar, rice, and coffee being the most important—supplied the basis for important new industries and markets that altered the course of world history.

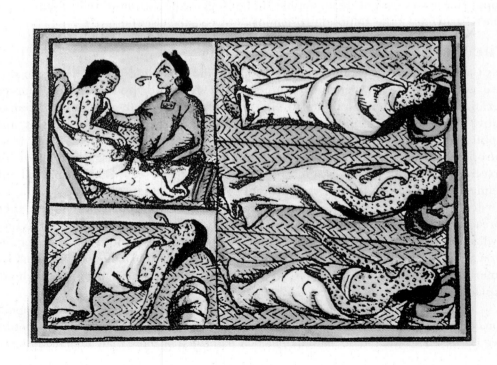

This drawing of victims of the smallpox epidemic that struck the Aztec capital of Tenochtitlán in 1520 is taken from the *Florentine Codex*, a postconquest history written and illustrated by Aztec scribes. "There came amongst us a great sickness, a general plague," reads the account, "killing vast numbers of people. It covered many all over with sores: on the face, on the head, on the chest, everywhere. . . . The sores were so terrible that the victims could not lie face down, nor on their backs, nor move from one side to the other. And when they tried to move even a little, they cried out in agony."

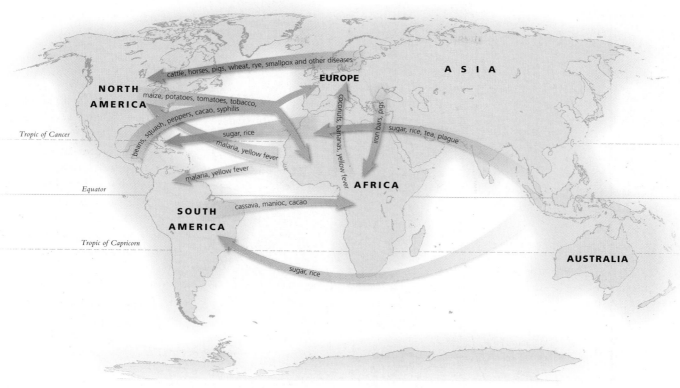

MAP 2.3

The Columbian Exchange   Europeans voyaging between Europe, Africa, Asia, and the Americas in the fifteenth and sixteenth centuries began a vast intercontinental movement of plants, animals, and diseases that shaped the course of modern history. New World corn and potatoes became staple foods in Africa and Europe, while Eurasian and African diseases such as smallpox, malaria, and yellow fever devastated native communities in the Western Hemisphere.

WHAT WERE the most important exports from Europe and Africa to the Americas? What were the most important exports from the Americas to Europe and Africa?

Columbus introduced domesticated animals into Hispaniola and Cuba, and livestock were later transported to Mexico. The movement of Spanish settlement northward through Mexico was greatly aided by an advancing wave of livestock, for grazing animals did serious damage to native fields and forests. In the seventeenth century, horses reached the Great Plains of North America, where they eventually transformed the lives of the nomadic hunting Indians (see Chapter 5).

THE SPANISH IN NORTH AMERICA

Ponce de León, governor of Puerto Rico, was the first Spanish conquistador to attempt to extend the Spanish conquest to North America (see Map 2.4). In search of slaves, he made his first landing on the mainland coast, which he named Florida, in 1513. Warriors from the powerful Indian chiefdoms there beat back this and several other attempts at invasion, and in 1521 succeeded in killing de León. Seven years later, another Spanish attempt to colonize Florida, under the command of Pánfilo de Narváez, also ended in disaster. Most of Narváez's men were lost in a shipwreck, but a small group of them survived, living and wandering for several years among the native peoples of the Gulf Coast. One of these castaways, Alvar Núñez Cabeza de Vaca, published an account of his adventures in which he repeated rumors of a North American empire known as Cíbola, with golden cities "larger than the city of Mexico."

●●●—[Read the Document

Alvar Núñez Cabeza de Vaca, "Indians of the Rio Grande" (1528-1536) at
www.myhistorylab.com

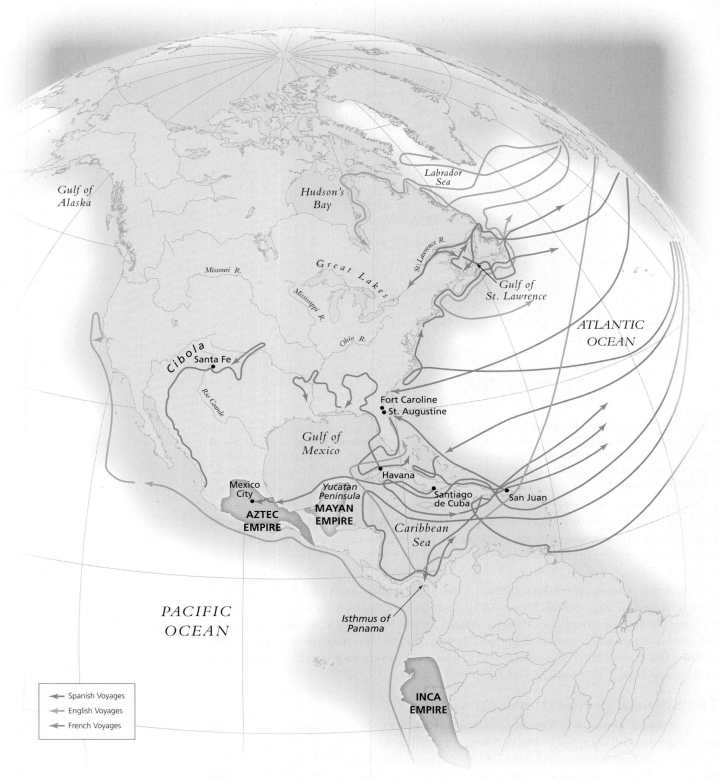

MAP 2.4

European Exploration, 1492–1591 By the mid-sixteenth century, Europeans had explored most of the Atlantic coast of North America and penetrated into the interior in the disastrous expeditions of de Soto and Coronado.

WHAT MOTIVES were behind European efforts to push their expansion into the interior of North America?

Cabeza de Vaca's report inspired Hernán de Soto to lead an expedition into North America. Landing in Florida in 1539 with over 700 men, de Soto pushed hundreds of miles through the heavily populated South, commandeering food and slaves from the Mississippian towns in his path. Moving westward, his expedition was twice mauled by powerful native armies and reduced by half. When he reached the Mississippi, he was met by a great flotilla of 200 vessels said to have come down river from a great city to the west. The Spaniards crossed the river and pushed westward through present-day Arkansas, but failing to find the great city, returned to the Mississippi. There de Soto fell sick and died. Some 300 dispirited survivors eventually made it back to Mexico on rafts. The native peoples of the South had successfully turned back Spanish invasion. But de Soto had introduced epidemic disease, which over the next several years drastically depopulated and undermined the Mississippian chiefdoms of the South.

In the same year of 1539, Spanish officials in Mexico launched a second attempt to conquer North America, this one aimed at the Southwest. Francisco Vásquez de Coronado led the expedition, passing through the settlements of Piman Indians near the present border of the United States and Mexico and finally reaching the Pueblo villages along the Rio Grande. The initial resistance of the Pueblo people was quickly quashed. From the Rio Grande, Coronado sent out expeditions in all directions in search of the legendary golden cities of Cíbola. He led his army as far north as the Great Plains, but found no gold. For the next fifty years Spain would lose all interest in the Southwest.

THE SPANISH NEW WORLD EMPIRE

A century after Columbus, some 250,000 European immigrants, most of them Spaniards, had settled in the Americas. Another 125,000 Africans had been forcibly resettled as slaves on the Spanish plantations of the Caribbean, as well as on the Portuguese plantations of Brazil. Most of the Spanish settlers lived in the more than 200 urban communities founded during the conquest.

Spanish women came to America as early as Columbus's second expedition, but over the course of the sixteenth century they made up only about 10 percent of the immigrants. Most male colonists married or cohabited with Indian or African women, and the result was what some historians call "a frontier of inclusion," a frontier society characterized by a great deal of mixing between male colonists and native or African women, with the corresponding growth of large mixed-ancestry groups that the Spanish labeled *mestizos* and *mulattoes*. Mixed-ancestry people quickly became the majority population in the mainland Spanish American empire.

The New World colonies of Spain made up one of the largest and most powerful empires in world history. In theory the empire operated as a highly centralized and bureaucratic system. But the Council of the Indies, the advisers of the Spanish king who made all the laws and regulations for the empire, was located far away in Spain. What looked in the abstract like a centrally administered empire was in fact a fragmented collection of colonial regions that tolerated a great deal of local decision making.

NORTHERN EXPLORATIONS AND ENCOUNTERS

When the Spanish empire was at the height of its power in the sixteenth century, the merchants and monarchs of other European seafaring states began looking across the Atlantic for opportunities of their own (see Map 2.4). France was first to sponsor expeditions to the New World in the early sixteenth century. The French first attempted to plant settlements on the coasts of Brazil and Florida, but Spanish opposition forced them to concentrate on the North Atlantic. England did not develop its own plans to colonize North America until the second half of the sixteenth century.

WHAT IMPORTANT differences were there between Spanish, English, and French patterns of colonization?

TRADE, NOT CONQUEST: FISH AND FURS

Long before France and England made attempts to found colonies, European fishermen were exploiting the coastal North American waters of the North Atlantic. By 1500, hundreds of ships and thousands of sailors were sailing annually to the Grand Banks, fishing for cod.

The first European voyages of exploration in the North Atlantic used the talents of these experienced European sailors and fishermen. With a crew from Bristol, England, Genovese explorer Giovanni Caboto (or John Cabot) reached Labrador in 1497, but the English did little to follow up on his voyage. In 1524, Tuscan captain Giovanni da Verrazano, sailing for the French, explored the North American coast from Cape Fear (North Carolina) to the Penobscot River (Maine). Encouraged by his report, the French crown commissioned captain Jacques Cartier to locate a "Northwest Passage" to the Indies. In a series of voyages undertaken in 1534, 1535, and 1541, Cartier failed to locate such a passage but became the first European to explore the St. Lawrence River, which led to the Great Lakes, and provided easy access to the Ohio and Mississippi rivers. Cartier's exploration established France's imperial claim to the lands of Canada and provided the French with an incomparable geographic advantage over other colonial powers.

Contacts in the northern woodlands between northern Europeans and Indians were quite different than those of the tropics, and were based on commerce rather than conquest. The natives immediately appreciated the usefulness of textiles, glass, copper, and ironware. Europeans were interested in the fur coats of the Indians. The growing population of the late Middle Ages had so depleted European wild game that the price of furs had risen beyond the reach of most people. Thus, the North American fur trade filled an important demand and produced high profits.

The fur trade would continue to play an important role in the Atlantic economy for the next three centuries. The trade, however, also had familiar negative consequences. European epidemic disease soon followed in the wake of the traders, and violent warfare broke out between tribes over access to hunting grounds. Moreover, as European-manufactured goods, such as metal knives, kettles, and firearms, became essential to their way of life, Indians grew dependent upon European suppliers.

By the end of the sixteenth century over a thousand European ships were trading for furs each year along the northern Atlantic coast. Within a few years the French

●●●—Read the Document

Jacques Cartier on Meeting the Mi'kmaq Indians (1534) at **www.myhistorylab.com**

A Mi'kmaq Indian petroglyph or rock carving depicting a European vessel and crew, photographed in 1946 at Kejimkujik National Park, Nova Scotia, by Arthur and Olive Kelsall, who traced the lines of the image with white ink to enhance the contrast. The vessel appears to be a small pinnace with lanteen sails, similar to those used by French merchants and explorers in the early seventeenth century. Living along the southern shore of the Gulf of Saint Lawrence and on the Acadian peninsula, the Mi'kmaq were among the first natives in North America to establish contact with European traders, and understanding immediately the value of iron and textiles, they soon developed a system of coastal barter.

would attempt to monopolize the northern trade by planting colonies along the coast and on the St. Lawrence. The first French colonies in North America, however, were planted farther south by a group of French Protestant religious dissenters known as the Huguenots.

THE PROTESTANT REFORMATION AND THE FIRST FRENCH COLONIES

The **Protestant Reformation**—the religious revolt against the Roman Catholic Church—began in 1517 when German priest Martin Luther publicized his differences with Rome. Luther declared that eternal salvation was a gift from God and not related to works or service to the Catholic Church. His position fit into a climate of widespread dissatisfaction with the power and prosperity of the Catholic Church. Luther soon was attracting followers all over northwestern Europe, and just as soon, Catholic authorities were working to quash his movement. One of Luther's most prominent converts was Jean Chauvin (known to English speakers as John Calvin), a young theology student in Paris.

In 1533, as the persecution of **Protestants** intensified, Calvin fled France, eventually taking up residence in Geneva, Switzerland, where civic leaders had renounced the Catholic Church and expelled the city's bishop. Working with those leaders, Calvin established a Protestant theocracy in Geneva. His followers in France, known as

This watercolor depicts the friendly relations between the Timucuas of coastal Florida and the colonists of the short-lived French colony of Fort Caroline. The Timucuas hoped that the French would help defend them against the Spanish, who plundered the coast in pursuit of Indian slaves.

Jacques Le Moyne, *Rene de Loudonniere and Chief Athore*, 1564. Gouache and metallic pigments on vellum. Print Collection, The New York Public Library, New York. The New York Public Library/Art Resource, NY.

Huguenots   French Protestant religious dissenters who planted the first French colonies in North America.

Huguenots, largely came from the urban middle class but also included a portion of the nobility, those opposed to the central authority of the Catholic monarch. In 1560 the French crown successfully defeated a plot among powerful Huguenots to seize royal power, inaugurating nearly forty years of violent religious conflict in France.

The first French colonies developed as attempts to establish a religious refuge in the New World for Huguenots. In 1562 French naval officer Jean Ribault and a group of 150 Huguenots from Normandy landed on Parris Island, near present-day Beaufort, South Carolina. Ribault soon returned to France for supplies, where he was caught up in the religious wars. The colonists nearly starved and were forced to resort to cannibalism before being rescued by a passing English ship. In 1564, Ribault and his followers established a second Huguenot colony, Fort Caroline, on the St. Johns River of Florida, south of present-day Jacksonville.

The Spanish were alarmed by these moves. In 1565 King Philip II of Spain sent Don Pedro Menéndez de Avilés, captain general of the Indies, to crush the Huguenots. After founding a settlement south of Fort Caroline at a place called St. Augustine, he marched his men overland through the swamps, surprising the Huguenots from the rear. "I put Jean Ribault and all the rest of them to the knife," Menéndez wrote triumphantly to the king. To prevent further French incursions the Spanish built massive Castillo San Marcos (still standing) and established a garrison at St. Augustine, which has the distinction of being the oldest continuously occupied European city in North America.

SOCIAL CHANGE IN SIXTEENTH-CENTURY ENGLAND

The English movement across the Atlantic, like the French, was tied to social change at home. Perhaps most important were changes in the economy. As prices for goods rose steeply—the result of New World inflation—English landlords, their rents fixed by custom, sought ways to increase their incomes. Seeking profits in the woolen trade, many converted the common pasturage used by tenants into grazing land for sheep, dislocating large numbers of farmers. Between 1500 and 1650 a third of all the common lands

Elizabeth I, thought to be the work of court artist George Gower in 1588. The queen places her hand on the globe, covering North America, symbolizing England's ambitions there. Through the open windows, we see the battle against the Spanish Armada in 1588 and the destruction of the Spanish ships in a providential storm, which the Queen interpreted as an act of divine intervention.

Elizabeth I, Armada portrait, c. 1588 (oil on panel) by English School (C16th) Private Collection/The Bridgeman Art Library, London/New York.

A Watercolor from the First Algonquian–English Encounter

Some of the first accurate images of the native inhabitants of North America were produced by the artist John White during his stay in 1585 at the first English colony in North America, at Roanoke Island on North Carolina's Outer Banks. Two years later White would become governor of the famous "Lost Colony." This image of an Indian mother and daughter illustrates the care White brought to the task of recording as fully as possible the Indians' way of life. The woman wears an apron-skirt of fringed deerskin, its borders edged with white beads, and a woven beadwork necklace. The body decorations on her face and upper arms are tattooed. One of her arms rests in a sling, an unusual posture, something quite unique to this culture. In the other hand she holds an empty gourd container for carrying water. The little girl holds an English wooden doll, a gift from White, and it seems to greatly please her. In the written account that accompanied White's images, Thomas Harriot wrote that all the Indian girls "are greatly delighted with puppetts and babes which were brought out of England" as gifts of exchange. Historic images bear close observation, for it is often small details like this one that are most revealing. ∎

IN WHAT ways does this image document John White's powers of observation?

in England were "enclosed" in this way. Deprived of their livelihoods, thousands of families left their traditional rural homes and sought employment in English cities. The roads were crowded with homeless people.

Sixteenth-century England also became deeply involved in the Protestant Reformation. There great public resentment in England over the vast properties owned by the church and the loss of revenue to Rome. When the pope refused to grant King Henry VIII (reigned 1509–47) an annulment of his marriage to Catherine of Aragon, daughter of Ferdinand and Isabel of Spain, the king exploited this popular mood. Taking up the cause of reform in 1534, he declared himself head of a separate Church of England.

Henry was succeeded by his young and sickly son Edward VI (reigned 1547–53), who soon died. Next in succession was Edward's Catholic half-sister Mary (reigned 1553–1558), who persecuted and martyred hundreds of English Protestants (gaining her the nickname "Bloody Mary") and married Philip II of Spain, self-declared defender of the Catholic faith. With Mary's premature death, however, her Protestant half-sister Elizabeth I (reigned 1558–1603) reversed course, tolerating a variety of perspectives within the English church. Spain's monarch, Mary's widower, head of the most powerful empire in the world, vowed to overthrow Elizabeth.

Fearing Spanish subversion on the neighboring Catholic island of Ireland, Elizabeth urged enterprising supporters such as Walter Raleigh and his half-brother Humphrey Gilbert to subdue the Irish Catholics and settle homeless English families on their land. During the 1560s, Raleigh, Humphrey, and many other commanders invaded the island and viciously attacked the Irish, forcing them to retreat beyond a frontier line of English settlement along the coast. The English considered the Irish an inferior race, and the notion that civilized people could not mix with such "savages" was an assumption English colonists would carry with them to the Americas.

EARLY ENGLISH EFFORTS IN THE AMERICAS

England's first ventures in the New World were made against the backdrop of its conflict with Spain. In 1562, John Hawkins violated Spanish regulations by transporting a load of African slaves to the Caribbean, bringing back valuable tropical goods. (For a full discussion of the slave trade, see Chapter 4.) The Spanish attacked Hawkins on another of his voyages in 1567, an event English privateers such as Francis Drake used as an excuse for launching a series of devastating and lucrative raids against Spanish New World ports and fleets.

A consensus soon developed among Elizabeth's closest advisers that the time had come to enter the competition for American colonies. Elizabeth authorized several private attempts at exploration and colonization. In the late 1570s, Martin Frobisher conducted three voyages of exploration in the North Atlantic. Next Gilbert and Raleigh, fresh from the Irish wars, planned the first true colonizing ventures. In 1583 Gilbert sailed with a flotilla of ships from Plymouth and landed at St. John's Bay, Newfoundland. He claimed the territory for his queen, but Gilbert's ship was lost, however, on the return voyage.

Following his brother's death, Raleigh moved to establish a colony to the south, in the more hospitable climate of the mid-Atlantic coast. The Roanoke enterprise of 1584–1587 seemed far more promising than Gilbert's, but it too failed. In contrast to the French, who concentrated on commerce, the English attempted to dominate and conquer the natives, drawing on their Irish experience. The most positive legacy of the Roanoke experience was the work of Thomas Harriot and John White, who mapped the area, surveyed its commercial potential, and observed the Indian inhabitants. Harriot's *A Briefe and True Report of the Newfound Land of Virginia* (1588) provided the single most accurate description of North American Indians at the moment of their contact with Europeans.

QUICK REVIEW

Religion and Monarchy

- Henry VIII (r. 1509–1547): Broke with the Catholic Church.
- Edward IV (r. 1547–1553): Strong Protestant.
- Mary I (r. 1558–1603): Attempted to return England to Catholicism.
- Elizabeth I (r. 1558–1603): Sought to end religious turmoil by establishing moderate Protantism.

CHRONOLOGY

1000	Norse settlement at L'Anse aux Meadows	1534	Jacques Cartier first explores the St. Lawrence River
1347–53	Black Death in Europe	1539–40	Hernán de Soto and Francisco Vásquez de Coronado expeditions
1381	English Peasants' Revolt		
1488	Bartolomeu Días sails around the African continent	1550	Tobacco introduced to Europe
1492	Christopher Columbus first arrives in the Caribbean	1552	Bartolomé de las Casas's *Destruction of the Indies* published
1494	Treaty of Tordesillas		
1497	John Cabot explores Newfoundland	1558	Elizabeth I of England begins her reign
1500	High point of the Renaissance	1562	Huguenot colony planted along the mid-Atlantic coast
1508	Spanish invade Puerto Rico		
1513	Juan Ponce de León lands in Florida	1565	St. Augustine founded
1514	Bartolomé de las Casas begins preaching against the conquest	1583	Humphrey Gilbert attempts to plant a colony in Newfoundland
1516	Smallpox introduced to the New World	1584–87	Walter Raleigh's colony on Roanoke Island
1517	Martin Luther breaks with the Roman Catholic Church	1588	English defeat the Spanish Armada
1519	Hernán Cortés lands in Mexico	1590	John White returns to find Roanoke colony abandoned

Philip II was outraged at the English incursions. He had authorized the destruction of the French colony in Florida, and now he committed himself to smashing England. In 1588, he sent a fleet of 130 ships carrying 30,000 men to invade the British Isles. Countered by the English navy and frustrated by an ill-timed storm that the English chose to interpret as an act of divine intervention, the Spanish Armada foundered. The Spanish monopoly of the New World had been broken in the English Channel.

CONCLUSION

The era of European colonization in the Americas opened with Columbus's voyage in 1492. The subsequent Spanish invasion of America had catastrophic consequences for the Indian peoples of the Caribbean, Mesoamerica, and beyond. Wars of conquest and dispossession, and especially the introduction of epidemic disease, took an enormous toll in human life. Civilizations collapsed and whole cultures disappeared. Amidst this destruction, the Spanish succeeded in constructing the world's most powerful empire through the use of forced labor.

Inspired by the Spanish success, the French and the English sought to plant colonies on the coast of North America in the second half of the century, but neither succeeded in establishing lasting communities. Meanwhile, a very different kind of colonial encounter, one based on commerce rather than conquest, was taking place along the coasts of northeastern North America. Early in the next century the French would turn this development to their advantage.

The English would move in a different direction. The colony of Roanoke in the land the English called Virginia failed because of the imperial assumptions and the brutal behavior of the first colonists toward the native residents. The experience might have suggested the importance and necessity of "discreet dealing" with native peoples. But instead the English would put their Irish experience to use, pioneering an altogether new kind of American colonialism.

REVIEW QUESTIONS

1. Discuss the roles played by the rising merchant class, the new monarchies, Renaissance humanism, and the Reformation in the development of European colonialism.

2. Define a "frontier of inclusion." In what ways does this description apply to the Spanish empire in the Americas?

3. Make a list of the major exchanges that took place between the Old World and the New World in the centuries following the European invasion of America. Discuss some of the effects these exchanges had on the course of modern history.

4. In what ways did colonial contact in the Northeast differ from contacts in the Caribbean and Mexico?

5. In what ways might the English experience in Ireland have shaped expectations about American colonization?

KEY TERMS

Huguenots (p. 40)
Protestant Reformation (p. 39)
Protestants (p. 39)

Reconquista (p. 30)
Renaissance (p. 28)

PEARSON myhistorylab Connections

Reinforce what you learned in this chapter by studying the many documents, images, maps, review tools, and videos available at www.myhistorylab.com.

Read and Review

✓•─ Study and Review **Chapter 2**

•:•─ Read the Document

From The Journal of Christopher Columbus (1492)

Christopher Columbus, Letter to Luis de Sant' Angel (1493)

Alvar Núñez Cabeza de Vaca, "Indians of the Rio Grande" (1528–36)

Jacques Cartier on Meeting the Mi'kmaq Indians (1534)

Mi'kmaq Chief's Observations of the French (1691)

Bartolomè de Las Casas, "Of the Island of Hispaniola" (1542)

Research and Explore

•:•─ Read the Document

Exploring America: Exploitation of the Americas

Cultures Meet: Europeans View the New World

Profiles
Virginia Dare
Bartolomè de Las Casas

◉─ Watch the Video

How Should We Think of Columbus?

What Is Columbus's Legacy?

((•●─ **Hear** the **Audio**

Hear the audio files for Chapter 2 at
www.myhistorylab.com.

These seventeen ships . . . made a long, a troublesome, and costly voyage . . . with contrary winds after they set sail, and so scattered with mist and tempests that few of them arrived together . . .
—Thomas Dudley, March 28, 1631

Pueblo de Taos, New Mexico. The Beinecke Rare Book Library and Manuscript Library.

Matoaks als Rebecka daughter to the mighty Prince
Powhatan Emperour of Attanoughkomouck als Virginia
converted and baptized in the Christian faith and
Wife to the worll Mr Tho: Rolff.

3

PLANTING COLONIES IN NORTH AMERICA
1588–1701

((•─┤**Hear** the **Audio**

Hear the audio files for Chapter 3 at **www.myhistorylab.com**.

WHAT WERE relations between Indians and Europeans like in New Spain, New France, and New Netherlands?

HOW DID tobacco cultivation shape English colonization in the Chesapeake?

WHAT WERE the social and political values of Puritanism and how did religious dissent shape the history of the New England colonies?

WHAT ROLE did the crown play in the founding of English colonies after 1660?

WHAT LED to violent conflict between Indians and colonists?

1588 | 1701

AMERICAN COMMUNITIES
Communities and Diversity in Seventeenth-Century Santa Fé

IT WAS A HOT AUGUST DAY IN 1680 WHEN THE FRANTIC MESSENGERS RODE into the small mission outpost of El Paso with the news that the Pueblo Indians to the north had risen in revolt. More than 400 Spanish colonists had been killed. Two thousand survivors huddled inside the Palace of Governors in Santa Fé, surrounded by 3,000 angry warriors.

Spanish colonists had been in New Mexico for a century. Franciscan priests from Mexico came first, in the 1580s, followed by a military expedition in search of precious metals. The goals of the colonists were stark. The Pueblos at first resisted, but in the face of Spanish armed might, they were forced to give in.

Colonization took a tremendous toll on them. Epidemic disease, striking in successive waves, claimed thousands of lives. Taxes, tribute, and labor service left Pueblo storehouses empty, and starving times came much more frequently. Nomadic Apache neighbors, mounted on stolen Spanish horses, raided their villages with increasing frequency. From 1610 to 1680 the number of Pueblo communities fell by more than half, and their population plummeted by two-thirds.

Over the decades thousands of Pueblos had accepted Christianity, but in the face of a devastating drought in the 1670s, there was a revival of their traditional religious rituals. Outraged Franciscan missionaries invaded the underground *kivas*, destroyed sacred Indian artifacts, and publicly humiliated holy men. In 1675 the Spanish governor rounded up religious leaders from many villages, publicly executed three of them, and whipped the others. One of those men, Popé of San Juan Pueblo, vowed to overthrow the regime. During the next several years he and other rebel leaders organized a conspiracy among more than twenty Pueblo communities.

In Santa Fé, the survivors of the Indian attack managed to escape, but left the city in the rebels' hands. Santa Fé became the capital of a Pueblo confederacy led by Popé. He forced Christian Indians "to plunge into the rivers" to wash away the taint of baptism and ordered the destruction of everything Spanish. Getting rid of Jesus was one thing, but the rest was harder. Horses and sheep, fruit trees and wheat, new tools and new crafts—these things the Pueblos found useful. They also found that they missed the support of the Spanish in their struggle against the Apaches. With chaos mounting, Popé was deposed in 1690.

In 1692, a Spanish force under Governor Diego de Vargas returned to New Mexico in an attempt to reestablish the colonial regime. Some communities welcomed him while others resisted. In 1696 there was another attempt at revolt, but Vargas crushed it with overwhelming force. The Spanish succeeded in their reconquest, but they seemed to have learned something in the process. They began to practice greater restraint, curtailing efforts to suppress Indian religious practices and protecting Indian economic rights. This, in turn, enabled the Pueblos to accept their authority. New Mexico remained a Spanish colony. But in the aftermath of the Pueblo Revolt, the governing principle was accommodation.

Thus did the Spanish in New Mexico and elsewhere seek to include native peoples as subjects of the king and communicants of the Church. Because the French developed a commercial empire, they too came to rely on a policy of native inclusion. In New England, Virginia, and Carolina, however, where English settlers developed agricultural colonies, the policy was one of exclusion. Indians were pushed to the periphery. These differences help explain the very different histories of the three principal colonial empires in North America.

Santa Fé

THE SPANISH, THE FRENCH, AND THE DUTCH IN NORTH AMERICA

At the beginning of the seventeenth century the Spanish controlled the only colonial outposts on the North American mainland, a series of forts along the Florida coast to protect the convoys carrying wealth from their New World colonies to Spain. During the first two decades of the new century, however, the Spanish, French, Dutch, and English were all drawn into planting far more substantial colonies in North America.

NEW MEXICO

After the 1539 expedition of Francisco Vásquez de Coronado failed to turn up fabled cities of gold, Spanish interest in the Southwest faded. The densely settled farming communities of the Pueblos did attract missionaries, however, and by the 1580s the Franciscans were at work there. Soon rumors drifted back to Mexico City of rich mines along the Rio Grande. In 1598, Juan de Oñate, the son of a wealthy mining family of New Spain, financed an expedition made up of Indians and *mestizos* (people of mixed Indian and European ancestry) with the purpose of mining both gold and souls.

Moving north into the upper Rio Grande Valley, Oñate encountered varying degrees of resistance. His siege at Acoma ended with his forces laying waste to the town, killing 800 men, women, and children. All surviving warriors had one of their feet severed, and more than 500 people were enslaved. In 1606 Spanish authorities in Mexico recalled Oñate for his failure to locate the fabled gold mines. The church, however, convinced the Spanish monarchy to subsidize New Mexico as a special missionary colony. In 1609, a new governor founded the capital of Santa Fé, and from this base the Franciscan missionaries penetrated all the surrounding Indian villages (see Map 3.1).

The colonial economy of New Mexico was never very prosperous. Spanish expectations, never very high, were even lower after the Pueblo Revolt and the

WHAT WERE relations between Indians and Europeans like in New Spain, New France, and New Netherlands?

●◆●⌐**Read** the **Document**

Don Juan de Oñate, Letter from New Mexico to the Viceroy (1599) at **www.myhistorylab.com**

Acoma Pueblo, the "sky city," was founded in the thirteenth century and is one of the oldest continuously inhabited sites in the United States. In 1598, Juan de Oñate attacked and laid waste to the pueblo, killing some 800 inhabitants and enslaving another 500.

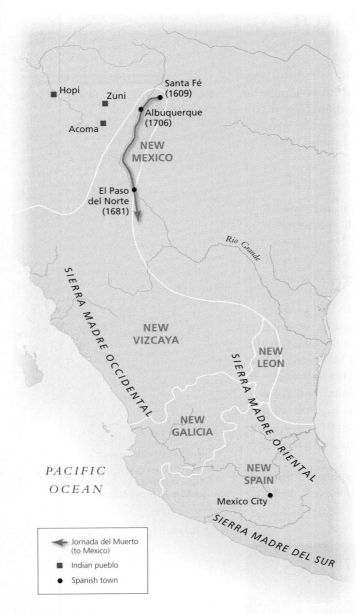

MAP 3.1

New Mexico in the Seventeenth Century By the end of the seventeenth century, New Mexico numbered 3,000 colonial settlers in several towns, surrounded by an estimated 50,000 Pueblo Indians living in some fifty farming villages. The isolation and sense of danger among the Hispanic settlers are evident in their name for the road linking the colony with New Spain, *Jornada del Muerto*, "Road of Death."

HOW DID New Mexico's isolation shape its development?

coureurs de bois French for "woods runner," an independent fur trader in New France.

reconquest. Very few newcomers came from Mexico. Population growth was almost entirely the result of marriages between colonial men and Indian women. New Mexico was a "frontier of inclusion."

NEW FRANCE

In the early seventeenth century the French devised a strategy to monopolize the northern fur trade. In 1605 Samuel de Champlain founded the settlement of Québec on the St. Lawrence River at a site where he could intercept the traffic in furs. He forged an alliance with the Huron Indians, who controlled access to the rich fur grounds of the Great Lakes, and in 1609 and 1610 joined them in making war on their traditional enemies, the Five Nation Iroquois Confederacy. Champlain sent agents and traders to live among native peoples, where they learned native languages and customs, and directed the flow of furs to Québec.

Thousands of Frenchmen went to New France as *engagés* ("hired men") in the fur trade or the fishery, but nine out of ten returned to France when the term of their service ended. The French might have populated their American empire with willing Huguenot religious dissenters, but the state resolved that New France would be exclusively Catholic. As a result, the population grew very slowly, reaching a total of only 15,000 colonists by 1700. Rather than facing the Atlantic, the communities of Canada tended to look westward toward the continental interior. It was typical for the sons of habitants to take to the woods, working as independent traders or **coureurs de bois**, paid agents of the fur companies. Most eventually returned to their home communities, but others married Indian women and raised mixed-ancestry families in distant Indian villages. French traders were living on the Great Lakes as early as the 1620s, and both missionaries and traders were exploring the upper Mississippi River by the 1670s. In 1681–82, fur-trade commandant Robert Sieur de La Salle navigated the mighty river to its mouth on the Gulf of Mexico and claimed its entire watershed for France (see Map 3.2).

Thus, the French, like the Spanish, established a frontier of inclusion in North America. But in other ways the two colonial systems were quite different. The Spanish program was the conquest of native peoples and their exploitation as a labor force in mining, farming, or livestock raising. The French, on the other hand, lacking sufficient manpower to do otherwise, sought to build an empire through alliance and commerce with independent Indian nations. There were also important differences between Spanish and French missionary efforts. Unlike Franciscans in New Mexico, who insisted that natives must accept European cultural norms as part of their conversion, Jesuit missionaries in New France learned native languages and attempted to understand native customs, in an effort to introduce Christianity as a part of the existing Indian way of life.

MAP 3.2

New France in the Seventeenth Century By the late seventeenth century, French settlements were spread from the town of Port Royal in Acadia to the post and mission at Sault Ste. Marie on the Great Lakes. But the heart of New France comprised the communities stretching along the St. Lawrence River between the towns of Québec and Montreal.

WHAT FACTORS did the French consider when placing their settlements?

NEW NETHERLAND

The United Provinces of the Netherlands, commonly known as Holland, was only a fraction of the size of France, but in the sixteenth century it became the center of Europe's economic transformation. Amsterdam became the site of the world's first stock exchange and investment banks. Dutch investors built the largest commercial fleet in Europe.

Early in the seventeenth century the United Netherlands organized two great monopolies, the Dutch East India Company and the Dutch West India Company, combining naval military might and commercial strength in campaigns to seize the maritime trade of Asia and the Atlantic. Backed by powerful armed vessels, Dutch traders constructed a series of trading posts in China, Indonesia, India, Africa, Brazil, the Caribbean, and North America, making Holland into the world's greatest commercial power. The Dutch first established themselves in North America with the explorations of Henry Hudson in 1609, and within a few years had founded settlements on the Hudson River at Fort Orange (today's Albany) and at New Amsterdam on Manhattan Island. In the 1640s the Dutch also succeeded in overwhelming a small colony of Swedes planted by a Swedish company on the lower Delaware River in 1637, incorporating that region as well into their sphere of influence (see Map 3.3).

Seeking to match French success in the fur trade, the Dutch West India Company negotiated a commercial alliance with the Five Nation Iroquois Confederacy. The Iroquois soon launched a campaign to make themselves into the strategic middlemen of the fur trade. Beginning in the 1640s the Iroquois conducted a series of military expeditions against their northern, western, and southern neighbors, known as the **Beaver Wars**. They attacked and dispersed the Hurons, who had long controlled the flow of furs from the Great Lakes to their French allies.

QUICK REVIEW

New Netherland

- United Province of the Netherlands played a key role in sixteenth-century Europe's economy.
- The Dutch established trading outposts throughout the Americas.
- Dutch expansion led by the Dutch East India Company and the Dutch West India Company.

Beaver Wars Series of bloody conflicts, occurring between 1640s and 1680s, during which the Iroquois fought the French for control of the fur trade in the east and the Great Lakes region.

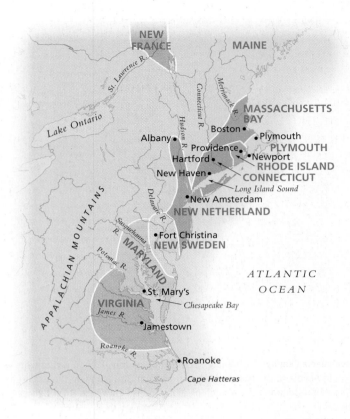

MAP 3.3
European Colonies of the Atlantic Coast, 1607–39 Virginia, on Chesapeake Bay, was the first English colony in North America, but by the mid-seventeenth century, Virginia was joined by settlements of Scandinavians on the Delaware River and Dutch on the Hudson River, as well as English religious dissenters in New England. The territories indicated here reflect the vague boundaries of the early colonies.

HOW MANY European nations had established colonies on the Atlantic coast by the middle of the seventeenth century?

THE CHESAPEAKE: VIRGINIA AND MARYLAND

England first attempted to plant colonies in North America during the 1580s in Newfoundland and at Roanoke Island in present-day North Carolina (see Chapter 2). Both attempts were dramatic failures. England's war with Spain (1588–1604) suspended further efforts, but thereafter the English once again turned to the Americas.

JAMESTOWN AND THE POWHATAN CONFEDERACY

In 1607, a group of London investors known as the **Virginia Company** sent a small convoy of vessels to Chesapeake Bay, where a hundred men built a fort they named Jamestown in honor of King James I (reigned 1603–25). It was destined to become the first permanent English settlement in North America.

The Chesapeake was already home to an estimated 14,000 Indian inhabitants. The village communities of the Chesapeake were united in a politically sophisticated union known as the **Powhatan Confederacy**, led by a powerful chief named Wahunsonacook, whom the Jamestown colonists called "King Powhatan" (a little like calling James I "King England"). Powhatan's feelings about Europeans were mixed. He knew they could mean trouble. Still, Powhatan was eager to forge an alliance with these people from across the

---

HOW DID tobacco cultivation shape English colonization in the Chesapeake?

Read the **Document**

Exploring America: Jamestown at
www.myhistorylab.com

Virginia Company A group of London investors who sent ships to Chesapeake Bay in 1607.

Powhatan Confederacy A village of communities of the Chesapeake united under Chief Wahunsonacook, who was called King Powhatan by the colonists.

sea to obtain access to supplies of metal tools and weapons. As was the case elsewhere in the Americas, Indians attempted to use Europeans to pursue ends of their own.

The Jamestown colonists had come to find gold and a passage to the Indies, and failing at both they spent their time gambling and drinking. They survived only because of Powhatan's help. But as more colonists arrived from England and demands for food multiplied, Powhatan realized that the English had come not as traders but as invaders, and withdrew his support. During the terrible winter of 1609–10 more than 400 colonists starved and a number resorted to cannibalism. Of the 500 colonists at Jamestown in the fall, only 60 remained alive by the spring.

Determined to prevail, the Virginia Company sent out a large additional force of men, women, and livestock, committing itself to a protracted war against the Indians. The grim fighting persisted until 1613, when the English captured one of Powhatan's favorite daughters, Matoaka, a girl of about fifteen whom the colonists knew by her nickname, Pocahontas. Eager for the return of his child, and worn down by violence and disease, the next year Powhatan accepted a treaty of peace. The peace was sealed by the marriage of Pocahontas to John Rolfe, one of the leading colonists.

For a brief moment it seemed the English too might move in the direction of a society of inclusion. In 1617 Rolfe traveled with his wife and son to England but Pocahontas fell ill and died there. Crushed by the news, Powhatan abdicated in favor of his brother Opechancanough before dying of despair. Economic and social developments, however, were already pushing Virginia in the direction of a frontier of exclusion.

TOBACCO, EXPANSION, AND WARFARE

The Virginia colonists struggled to find the "merchantable commodity" that would secure the economic viability of the colony. They finally found it in tobacco. By the 1610s a craze for smoking had created strong demand for the product. Pocahontas's husband John Rolfe developed a mild hybrid variety, and soon the first commercial shipments reached England. Tobacco provided the Virginia Company with the first returns on its investment.

Questions of land and labor would dominate the history of colonial Virginia. Tobacco cultivation required a great deal of hand labor, and it quickly exhausted the soil. The Virginia Company instituted a program of "headright grants," awards of large plantations to wealthy colonists who agreed to transport workers from England at their own cost. Because thousands of English families were being thrown off the land (see Chapter 2), many were attracted to Virginia. Thus, English colonization took a different turn from the Spanish, who mostly sent male colonists. Moreover, the English concentration on plantation agriculture contrasted with the French emphasis on trade. With little need to incorporate Indians into the colony as workers or marriage partners, the English pushed natives out. Virginia became a "frontier of exclusion."

Pressed for additional lands on which to grow tobacco, Chief Opechancanough decided on an assault that would expel the English for good. He encouraged a cultural revival under the guidance of a native shaman named Nemattanew, who instructed his followers to reject the English and their ways, much as Popé would do among the Pueblos. Opechancanough's uprising, which began on Good Friday, March 22, 1622, completely surprised the English, claiming the lives of 347 colonists, nearly a third of Virginia's colonial population. The attack stretched into a ten-year war of attrition with horrors committed by both sides.

Read the Document
Remarks by Chief Powhatan to John Smith (ca. 1609) at **www.myhistorylab.com**

Read the Document
John Smith, "The Starving Time" (1624) at **www.myhistorylab.com**

Read the Document
Profiles: Pocohantas at **www.myhistorylab.com**

QUICK REVIEW

Powhatan, Indian Leader

- Chief of a confederacy of about thirty tribes.
- Initially eager to ally with the English.
- Changed his policy in response to incessant English demands.
- Lost war with the English after the kidnapping of his daughter Pocahontas.

This illustration, from John Smith's memoirs (1624), was engraved by the artist Robert Vaughn. Seizing Chief Opechancanough, Powhatan's brother, by the scalplock, Smith attempts to obtain needed supplies from the Indians. Opechancanough later succeeded Powhatan and ruled the Chesapeake Algonquian Confederacy for a quarter century.

The French Intervene in Native Warfare

This illustration, taken from Samuel de Champlain's 1613 account of the founding of New France, depicts him joining a Huron attack on the Iroquois on July 30, 1609. The French sought to build a commercial empire by allying with the powerful Huron confederacy to control access to the great fur grounds of the West. The image depicts the moment when Champlain fired his arquebus (a muzzle-loading firearm), killing two of the Iroquois leaders. After this confrontation, the Iroquois formed an alliance of their own with the Dutch, who founded a trading colony on the Hudson River. The contrast between the heavily armored Frenchmen and the naked Indians was part of the convention of depicting "civilized" and "savage" nations. The palm trees in the background of this drawing suggest that it was not executed by an eyewitness, but rather by an illustrator more familiar with South American scenes. ■

WHAT KIND of relationship between Europeans and Indians is depicted in this image?

The Powhatans finally sued for peace in 1632. In the meantime, however, the war had bankrupted the Virginia Company. In 1624 England converted Virginia into a royal colony with civil authorities appointed by the crown, although property-owning colonists continued to elect representatives to the colony's **House of Burgesses**, created in 1619 in an attempt to encourage immigration. As a result of continuous emigration from England by 1640 the number of colonists had reached approximately 10,000 (see Figure 3.1). Now the English outnumbered the Powhatans, who were decimated by violence and disease.

In 1644 Opechancanough organized a final desperate revolt in which more than 500 colonists were killed. But the next year the Virginians crushed the Powhatans, capturing and executing their leader. A formal treaty granted the Indians a number of small reserved territories.

Read the **Document**

The Charter of Maryland (1632) at **www.myhistorylab.com**

House of Burgesses The legislature of colonial Virginia. First organized in 1619, it was the first institution of representative government in the English colonies.

MARYLAND

In 1632, King Charles I (reigned 1625–49) granted 10 million acres at the northern end of Chesapeake Bay to the Calvert family, the Lords Baltimore, important Catholic supporters of the English monarchy. The Calverts named their colony Maryland, in honor of the king's wife, and in 1634 sent the first party of colonists to found the settlement of St. Mary's near the mouth of the Potomac River. Two features distinguished Maryland from Virginia. First, it was a "proprietary" colony in which the Calvert family held the sole power to appoint civil officers and was sole owner of all the land, which they planned to carve into feudal manors providing them with rents. Second, the Calvert family encouraged settlement by Catholics, a persecuted minority in seventeenth-century England. In fact, Maryland became the only English colony in North America with a substantial Catholic minority.

Yet Maryland quickly became much like neighboring Virginia. The tobacco plantation economy created pressures for labor and land that could not be met by the Calverts' original feudal plans. In 1640, the colony adopted the system of headright grants previously

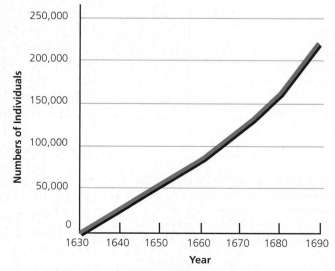

Figure 3.1 Population Growth of the British Colonies in the Seventeenth Century
The British colonial population grew steadily through the century, then increased sharply in the closing decade as a result of the new settlements of the proprietary colonies.

developed in Virginia, and settlements of independent planters quickly spread out on both sides of Chesapeake Bay. By the 1670s, Maryland's English population numbered more than 15,000.

COMMUNITY LIFE IN THE CHESAPEAKE

At least three-quarters of the English migrants to the Chesapeake came as **indentured servants**. In exchange for the cost of their transportation to the New World, men and women contracted to labor for a master for a fixed term. Most were young, unskilled males, who served for two to seven years, but some were skilled craftsmen, unmarried women, or even orphan children.

African slaves were first introduced to the Chesapeake in 1619, but slaves were more expensive than servants, and as late as 1680 they made up less than 7 percent of the population. In the hard-driving economy of the Chesapeake, however, masters treated servants as cruelly as they treated slaves. Because of the high mortality resulting from epidemics of typhus and malaria, approximately two of every five servants died during the term of their indenture. Indentured labor may not have been slavery, but this may have seemed like a distinction without a difference (see Chapter 4 for a full discussion of slavery).

Many indentured servants who survived their terms and were able to raise the price of passage quickly returned to England. Those who remained became eligible for "freedom dues"—clothing, tools, a gun, or a spinning wheel to help them get started on their own. They often headed west in the hope of cutting a farm from the forest.

Because most emigrants were men, whether free or indentured, free unmarried women often married as soon as they arrived. Their scarcity provided women with certain advantages. Shrewd widows bargained for a remarriage agreement that gave them a larger share of the estate than what was set by common law. But because of high mortality rates, family size was smaller and kinship bonds—one of the most important components of community—were weaker than in England.

English visitors often remarked on the crude conditions of community life. Prosperous planters, investing everything in tobacco production, lived in rough wooden dwellings. On the western edge of the settlements, freed servants lived with their families in shacks, huts, or even caves. Colonists spread across the countryside in search of new tobacco lands, creating dispersed settlements with hardly any towns. Before 1650 there were few community institutions such as schools and churches.

Nevertheless, the Chesapeake was a growing region. By the end of the seventeenth century the combined population of the Maryland and Virginia colonies was nearly 90,000. In contrast to the colonists of New France, who were developing a distinctive identity because of their connections with native peoples, the English residents of the Chesapeake maintained close emotional ties to the mother country.

THE NEW ENGLAND COLONIES

Both in climate and in geography, the northern coast of North America was far different from the Chesapeake. "Merchantable commodities" such as tobacco could not be produced there, and thus it was far less favored for investment and settlement. Instead, the region became a haven for Protestant dissenters from England, who gave the colonies of the north a distinctive character of their own (see Map 3.3).

PURITANISM

Most English men and women continued to practice a Christianity little different from traditional Catholicism. But the English followers of John Calvin, known as **Puritans** because they wished to purify and reform the English church from within, grew

indentured servants Individuals who contracted to serve a master for a period of four to seven years in return for payment of the servant's passage to America.

Puritans Individuals who believed that Queen Elizabeth's reforms of the Church of England had not gone far enough in improving the church. Puritans led the settlement of Massachusetts Bay Colony.

increasingly influential during the last years of Elizabeth's reign at the end of the six-teenth century. James I abandoned Queen Elizabeth's policy of religious tolerance. His persecution of the Puritans, however, merely stiffened their resolve and turned them toward open political opposition. James's son and successor, Charles I (reigned 1625–49), was heavily criticized by the increasingly vocal Puritan minority for marrying a French Roman Catholic princess and supporting "High Church" policies, emphasiz-ing the authority of the clerical hierarchy and traditional forms of worship. In 1629, determined to rule without these troublesome opponents, Charles dismissed Parliament and launched a campaign of repression against the Puritans. This political turmoil provided the context for the migration of thousands of English Protestants to New England.

PLYMOUTH COLONY

The first English colony in New England was founded by a group of religious dissenters known to later generations as the Pilgrims. One group moved to Holland in 1609, but fearful that tolerant and secular Dutch society was seducing their children, they decided on emigration to North America. Backed by the Virginia Company of London and led by tradesman William Bradford, 102 people sailed from England on the *Mayflower* in September 1620.

The little group, mostly families but including a substantial number of single men hired by the investors, arrived in Massachusetts Bay at a site the English called Plymouth. Soon the hired men began to grumble about being excluded from decision making, and to reassure them Bradford drafted an agreement by which all the male members of the expedition did "covenant and combine together into a civil body politic." The Mayflower Compact was the first document of self-government in North America.

Nearly half the colonists perished over the first winter. Like the earlier settlers of Roanoke and Jamestown, however, they were rescued by Indians. Massasoit, the *sachem*, or chief, of the Pokanokets, offered the newcomers food and advice in return for an alliance against his enemies, the Narragansetts. It was the familiar pattern of Indians attempting to incorporate European colonists into their own world.

The Pilgrims supported themselves by farming, but like all colonies Plymouth needed a source of revenue, in their case in order to pay off their English investors. The foundation of their commercial economy was the cod fishery in the rich coastal banks of the Atlantic. With this revenue the Pilgrims were able to establish a self-sufficient community.

THE MASSACHUSETTS BAY COLONY

In England, the political climate of the late 1620s convinced growing numbers of influ-ential Puritans that the only way to protect their congregations was by emigration. In 1629 a royal charter was granted to a group of wealthy Puritans who called their enter-prise the **Massachusetts Bay Company**, and an advance force of 200 settlers left for North America.

The colonists hoped to establish what John Winthrop, their leader and first gover-nor, called "a city on a hill," a New England model of reform for old England. In this they differed from the Pilgrims, who never considered returning. Between 1629 and 1643 some 20,000 individuals relocated to Massachusetts, establishing the port town of Boston and ringing it with towns.

In 1629 Puritan leaders transferred company operations from England to Massachusetts, and within a few years had transformed the company into a civil gov-ernment. The original charter established a General Court composed of a governor and his deputy, a board of magistrates (or advisers), and the members of the corpora-tion, known as freemen. In 1632, Governor Winthrop and his advisers declared that all the male heads of households in Massachusetts, who were also church members, were freemen. Two years later, the freemen secured their right to select delegates to represent the towns in drafting the laws of the colony. These delegates and the magistrates later became the colony's two legislative houses.

DISSENT AND NEW COMMUNITIES

The Puritans immigrated to North America in order to practice their variety of Christianity. But like the Pilgrims they had little tolerance for religious difference. Doctrinal disagreements among them often led to the establishment of new colonies. In 1636 Thomas Hooker, minister of the congregation at Cambridge, after objecting to the Massachusetts policy of restricting male suffrage to church members, led his followers west to the Connecticut River, where they founded the town of Hartford. The same year Roger Williams, the minister at Salem, was banished from Massachusetts for advocating religious tolerance. With a group of his followers, Williams immigrated to the country surrounding Narragansett Bay.

In 1637 Anne Hutchinson, the brilliant and outspoken wife of a Puritan merchant, criticized a number of Boston ministers. Their concentration on good works, she argued, led people to believe they could earn their way to heaven. Hutchinson was called before the General Court, and in an extraordinary hearing was reprimanded, excommunicated, and banished. She and a group of followers relocated to the Williams colony on Narragansett Bay.

To protect the dissenters in his settlement from Puritan interference, Williams won royal charters in 1644 and 1663 establishing the independent colony of Rhode Island with guarantees of self-government and complete religious liberty.

Governor John Winthrop, a portrait painted by an unknown artist, about 1640. Winthrop was first elected governor of Massachusetts Bay Colony in 1629 and reelected a total of twelve times.

QUICK REVIEW

Early Dissenters

- Thomas Hooker: Objected to restrictions on male suffrage.
- Anne Hutchinson: Voiced theological disagreements with Boston ministers.
- Roger Williams: Advocated religious toleration.

INDIANS AND PURITANS

The Indian communities of southern New England discovered soon after the arrival of the Pilgrims and the Puritans that these colonists were quite different from the French and Dutch traders who had preceded them. Although the fur trade was an important part of the economy of Plymouth and Massachusetts, the principal concern of the colonists was the acquisition of Indian land for their growing settlements.

Most Puritans believed they had the right to take what they considered "unused" lands from the Indians, that is, lands not used in the English. Potential conflicts among settlers over title, however, made it necessary to obtain original deeds from Indians, and the English used a variety of tactics to pressure leaders into relinquishing all claim to specified properties. Colonists allowed livestock to graze in native fields, destroying their subsistence. They fined Indians for violations of English law, such as working on the Sabbath, and demanded land as payment. They made deals with corrupt Indian leaders. Meanwhile epidemic disease continued to devastate Indian villages. Disorganized and demoralized, many coastal native communities not only gave up their lands but also placed themselves under the protection of the English.

By the late 1630s only a few tribes in southern New England retained the power to challenge Puritan expansion. The Pequots, who lived along the shores of Long Island Sound near the mouth of the Connecticut River, were one of the most powerful. In 1637, Puritan leaders pressured the Pequots' traditional enemies, the Narragansetts of present-day Rhode Island, to join them in waging war on the Pequots. Narragansett warriors and English troops attacked the main Pequot village, burning the houses and killing most of their slumbering residents. The indiscriminate slaughter shocked the Narragansetts, who condemned the English way of war. It was "too furious and slays too many," they declared.

THE ECONOMY: NEW ENGLAND MERCHANTS

In England, the dispute between King Charles I and the Puritans in Parliament escalated into armed conflict in 1642. Several years of revolutionary confrontation finally led to Charles's arrest, his execution in 1649, and the creation of an English Commonwealth, headed by the Puritan military leader Oliver Cromwell. Because the Puritans were on the victorious side in the English civil war, they no longer had the same incentive to migrate to New England. A number of colonists returned to England.

New England's economy had depended on the sale of supplies and land to arriving immigrants, but this market collapsed as the migration tailed off. Puritan merchants turned to the flourishing fishery, shipping cod (in addition to lumber and farm products) to the West Indies, where they bartered for sugar, molasses, and rum. By midcentury New England had constructed a commercial

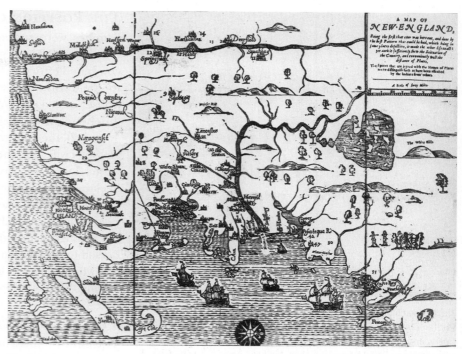

The first map printed in the English colonies, this view of New England was published in Boston in 1677. With north oriented to the right, it looks west from Massachusetts Bay, the two vertical black lines indicating the approximate boundaries of the Commonwealth of Massachusetts. The territory west of Rhode Island is noted as an Indian stronghold, the homelands of the Narragansett, Pequot, and Nipmuck peoples.

fleet of more than 300 vessels, and by the end of the century Boston had become the third largest English commercial center in the Atlantic (after London and Bristol). The development of a diversified economy provided New England with important long-term strength and offered a striking contrast with the specialized fur-trade economy of New France.

COMMUNITY AND FAMILY IN NEW ENGLAND

Pilgrims and Puritans stressed the importance of well-ordered communities. The Massachusetts General Court, the governing body of the colony, granted townships to a group of proprietors, the leaders of a congregation wishing to settle new lands. These men then distributed fields, pasture, and woodlands in quantities proportional to the social status of the recipient, with wealthy families receiving more than others. The Puritans believed that social hierarchy was ordained by God and made for well-ordered communities. Settlers typically clustered their dwellings in a central village, near the meetinghouse that served as both church and civic center. Clustered settlements and strong communities distinguished New England from the dispersed and weak communities of the Chesapeake.

The ideal Puritan family was also well ordered. Parents often participated in the choice of mates for their offspring, and children typically married in the order of their births. But well-disciplined children also needed education. In 1647 the Massachusetts General Court required that towns with 50 families or more support a public school; those with 100 families were to establish a grammar school instructing students in Latin, knowledge of which was required for admission to Harvard College, founded in 1636. The Puritan colony of Connecticut enacted similar requirements.

By the mid-seventeenth century, New England men boasted the highest rates of literacy in North America and much of Europe. Because girls were excluded from grammar schools, however, women's literacy remained relatively low.

The Mason children, by an unknown Boston artist, ca. 1670. These Puritan children—David, Joanna, and Abigail Mason—are dressed in finery, an indication of the wealth and prominence of their family. The cane in young David's hand indicates his position as the male heir, while the rose held by Abigail is a symbol of childhood innocence.

The Freake-Gibbs Painter (American, Active 1670), "David, Joanna, and Abigail Mason," 1670. Oil on canvas, 39 ½ × 42 ½ in.; Frame: 42 ¾ × 45 ½ × 1 ½ in. Fine Arts Museums of San Francisco, Gift of Mr. and Mrs. John D. Rockefeller 3rd to The Fine Arts Museums of San Francisco, 1979.7.3.

●●●–[Read the Document
The Examination and Confession of Ann Foster at Salem (1692) at
www.myhistorylab.com

●●●–[Read the Document
Exploring America: Witches in the American Imagination at
www.myhistorylab.com

WHAT ROLE did the crown play in the founding of English colonies after 1660?

proprietary colony A colony created when the English monarch granted a huge tract of land to an individual or group of individuals, who became "lords proprietor."

THE POSITION OF WOMEN

Families were supposed to operate as "little commonwealths," with everyone working cooperatively. The domestic economy required the combined efforts of husband and wife. Men were generally responsible for fieldwork, women for the work of the household, garden, hen-house, and dairy. Women managed a rich array of tasks, and some independently traded garden products, milk, and eggs.

Still, the cultural ideal was the subordination of women to men. "I am but a wife, and therefore it is sufficient for me to follow my husband," wrote Lucy Winthrop Downing, and her brother John Winthrop declared that "a true wife accounts her subjection her honor and freedom." Married women could not make contracts, own property, vote, or hold office. A typical woman, marrying in her early twenties and surviving through her forties, could expect to bear eight children and devote herself to husband and family. Wives who failed to have children, or widows who were economically independent, aroused significant suspicion among their neighbors.

THE SALEM WITCH TRIALS

The cultural mistrust of women came to the surface most notably in periodic witchcraft scares. During the seventeenth century, according to one historian, 342 New England women were accused by their neighbors of witchcraft. The majority of the accused were unmarried, childless, widowed, or had reputations in their communities for assertiveness and independence. In the vast majority of cases, the charges were dismissed by authorities as baseless. In the infamous 1692 case of Salem, Massachusetts, however, the whole community was thrown into a panic of accusations when a group of girls claimed that they had been bewitched by a number of old women. Before the colonial governor finally called a halt to the persecutions in 1693, twenty people had been tried, condemned, and executed.

The Salem witchcraft scare may have reflected social tensions that found their outlet through an attack on people perceived as outsiders. Salem was a booming commercial port, but while some residents were prospering, others were not. Most of the victims came from the commercial eastern end of town, the majority of their accusers from the economically stagnant western side. Most of the accused also came from Anglican, Quaker, or Baptist families. Finally, a majority of the victims were old women, suspect because they lived alone, without the guidance of men.

By the time of the witchcraft crisis New England's population was rapidly approaching 100,000. Massachusetts (which absorbed Plymouth colony in 1691) was the residence of considerably more than half this number, most concentrated in communities surrounding the port of Boston, although others were planted as far west as the Connecticut River Valley and as far north as the coast of Maine (not separated from Massachusetts until 1820). Connecticut claimed 26,000 residents, Rhode Island about 6,000, and New Hampshire, set off as a royal colony in 1680, another 5,000.

THE PROPRIETARY COLONIES

Oliver Cromwell died in 1658 and two years later Parliament, anxious for stability, restored the Stuart monarchy, placing on the throne Charles II (reigned 1660–85), eldest son of the deposed king. Charles took an active interest in North America, establishing several new **proprietary colonies** on the model of Maryland (see Map 3.4).

THE CAROLINAS

Charles II issued the first of his charters in 1663, establishing a new colony called Carolina, which stretched along the Atlantic coast from Virginia south to the northern limits of Spanish Florida. Virginians had already begun moving into the northern part of this territory, and in 1664 the Carolina proprietors appointed a governor and created a popularly elected assembly. By 1700 North Carolina, as it became known, included 11,000 small farmers and large tobacco planters.

Settlement farther south began in 1670 with the founding of coastal Charles Town (renamed Charleston in 1783). Most South Carolina settlers came from the sugar colony of Barbados, a Caribbean colony founded by the English in 1627. Hundreds of Barbadian planters relocated to South Carolina with their slaves during the last quarter of the seventeenth century. By 1700 South Carolina's population was more than 6,000, including some 3,000 enslaved Africans. (For a complete discussion of slavery see Chapter 4.)

NEW YORK AND NEW JERSEY

Charles also coveted the lucrative Dutch colony of New Netherland. In response to the growth of New England's population and its merchant economy, the Dutch West India Company changed course in the 1640s. Shifting from the French model to the English, it began sponsoring the immigration of European settlers to the Hudson River Valley, seeking to develop the colony as a diversified supply center for the West Indies. In 1651, Parliament passed a Trade and Navigation Act that barred Dutch vessels from English colonial possessions. This led to an inconclusive naval war between the two nations from 1652 to 1654. Ten years later the two powers clashed once again, leading to a second Anglo-Dutch war. In September 1664 a small English fleet sailed into Manhattan harbor and forced the surrender of New Amsterdam without firing a shot. When the war ended with an inconclusive peace in 1667, the English were left in possession. Holland briefly regained control during a third and final conflict from 1672 to 1674, but the English won the war and won possession of the colony in the peace negotiations.

Charles II issued a proprietary charter granting the former Dutch colony to his brother James, the Duke of York, renaming it New York in his honor. Otherwise the English did little to disturb the existing order. Ethnically and linguistically diversified, and accommodating a wide range of religious sects, New York society was the most heterogeneous in North America. In 1665, the communities of the Delaware Valley were split off as the proprietary colony of New Jersey. By the end of the century more than 33,000 residents lived in these two colonies.

THE FOUNDING OF PENNSYLVANIA

In 1676, the proprietary rights to the western portion of New Jersey were sold to a group of English religious dissenters, including William Penn. A member of the Society of Friends (known popularly as the **Quakers**), Penn intended to make the colony a haven for religious toleration and pacifism. Penn was the son of a wealthy and influential English admiral who was a close adviser to the king. In 1681, to settle a large debt he owed Admiral

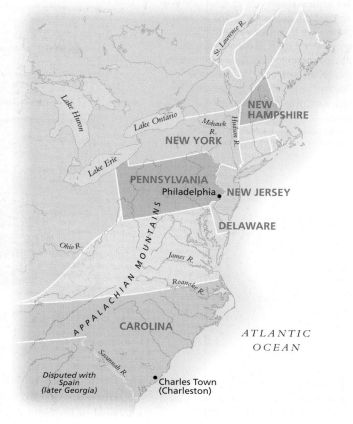

MAP 3.4

The Proprietary Colonies   After the restoration of the Stuart monarchy in 1660, King Charles II of England created the new proprietary colonies of Carolina, New York, Pennsylvania, and New Jersey. New Hampshire was set off as a royal colony in 1680, and in 1704, the lower counties of Pennsylvania became the colony of Delaware.

COMPARE THIS map with Map 3.3 (European Colonies of the Atlantic Cost, 1607–39). How had the political landscape changed since 1639?

Quakers   Members of the Society of Friends, a radical religious group that arose in the mid-seventeenth century. Quakers rejected formal theology, focusing instead on the Holy Spirit that dwelt within them.

The earliest known view of New Amsterdam, published in 1651. Indian traders are shown arriving with their goods in a dugout canoe of distinctive design known to have been produced by the native people of Long Island Sound. Twenty-five years after its founding, the Dutch settlement still occupied only the lower tip of Manhattan Island.

Fort New Amsterdam, New York, 1651. Engraving. Collection of The New-York Historical Society, 77354d.

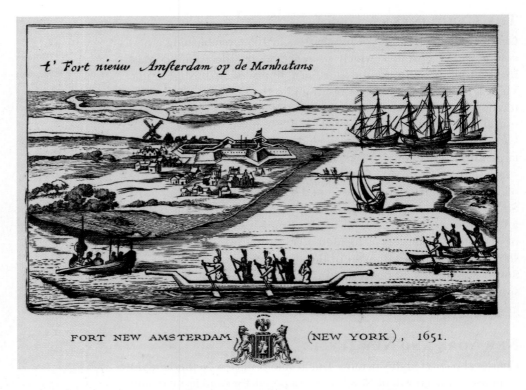

FORT NEW AMSTERDAM (NEW YORK), 1651.

◆◆▶ Read the Document

William Penn, Description of Pennsylvania (1681) at **www.myhistorylab.com**

Penn, King Charles issued to his son a proprietary grant to a huge territory west of the Delaware River. The next year, Penn sailed to America and supervised the laying out of the port of Philadelphia.

Penn wanted this colony to be a "holy experiment." In his first **Frame of Government**, drafted in 1682, he included guarantees of religious freedom, civil liberties, and elected representation. He also attempted to deal fairly with the native peoples, refusing to permit colonization to begin until settlement rights were negotiated and lands purchased. Although relations between Pennsylvania and Indian peoples later soured, during Penn's lifetime his reputation for fair dealing led a number of native groups to resettle in the Quaker colony.

During the first two decades of Pennsylvania's settlement, nearly 20,000 settlers spread agricultural communities from the banks of the Delaware to the fertile interior valleys. In the eighteenth century Pennsylvania would be known as America's breadbasket, and Philadelphia would become North America's most important port. In 1704 Penn approved the creation of a separate colony called Delaware for the governance of the counties near the mouth of the river formerly controlled first by the Swedes and then the Dutch.

CONFLICT AND WAR

Pennsylvania's ability to maintain peaceful relations with the Indians proved the great exception. The last quarter of the seventeenth century became a time of great violence throughout the colonial regions of the continent, mostly because of the expansion of European settlement (see Map 3.5).

KING PHILIP'S WAR

In New England, nearly forty years of peace followed the **Pequot War** of 1637. Natives and colonists lived in close, if tense, contact. Several Puritan ministers began to preach to the Indians, and some 2,000 native converts eventually relocated to Christian communities known as "praying towns." But there remained several independent tribes, including the

---

QUICK REVIEW

Pennsylvania

◆ Territory west of the Delaware River granted to William Penn in 1681.

◆ Penn supervised the establishment of Philadelphia in 1682.

◆ Penn, a Quaker, saw the colony as a "holy experiment."

WHAT LED to violent conflict between Indians and colonists?

Frame of Government William Penn's constitution for Pennsylvania which included a provision allowing for religious freedom.

Pequot War Conflict between English settlers and Pequot Indians over control of land and trade in eastern Connecticut.

Pokanokets, the Narragansetts, and the Abenakis of northern New England. The extraordinary expansion of the colonial population, and the increasing hunger for land, created inexorable pressures for expansion into their territories.

The Pokanokets, whose homeland lay between Rhode Island and Plymouth, were led by the sachem Metacom, whom the English called King Philip. Metacom had been raised among English colonists and educated in their schools. He operated on the assumption that his people had a future in the English colonial world but was gradually forced to conclude that the colonists had no room for the Pokanokets. In 1671 the colonial authorities of Plymouth pressured Metacom into granting them sovereign authority over his homeland. This humiliation convinced him that he had to break the half-century alliance with Plymouth and take up armed resistance. The Puritan colonies, meanwhile, prepared for a war of conquest.

War came in the spring of 1675, after Plymouth magistrates arrested and executed three Pokanoket men for the murder of a Christian Indian. Metacom appealed to the Narragansetts for a defensive alliance, which the New England colonies interpreted as an act of aggression. They sent armed forces into Pokanoket and Narragansett country, attacking and burning a number of villages. Soon all New England was engulfed in what became known as King Philip's War.

At first things went well for the Indians. They forced the abandonment of English settlements on the Connecticut River and torched towns less than twenty miles from Boston. By the beginning of 1676, however, their campaign was collapsing. A combined colonial army defeated a large Indian force in a battle known as the Great Swamp Fight in Narragansett country. Metacom led his men and fled west to the border with New York where he appealed for support from the Iroquois. But instead of helping, the Iroquois attacked, forcing Metacom back to Pokanoket territory, where colonists annihilated his army in August 1676. Metacom's severed head was mounted on a pike at Plymouth.

In attacking the Pequots, the Iroquois were motivated by interests of their own casting themselves as powerful intermediaries between other tribes and the English. In a series of negotiations conducted at Albany in 1677, the Iroquois Confederacy and the colony of New York created an alliance known as the **Covenant Chain**. It envisioned Iroquois dominance over all other tribes, thus putting New York in an economically and politically dominant position among the other colonies.

An estimated 4,000 natives and 2,000 colonists died during the war, and dozens of native and colonial towns lay in ruins. Calculated in the number of lives lost, King Philip's War was the most destructive Indian–colonist conflict in early American history.

BACON'S REBELLION AND SOUTHERN CONFLICTS

While King Philip's War raged in New England, another English–Indian confrontation took shape in the Chesapeake and mutated into civil war. By the 1670s Indian communities residing on the frontier of the colony were under assault by colonists in search of new tobacco lands. The hunger for new lands came from established planters with lands reaching exhaustion but also from former servants who had served out their indentures. Governor William Berkeley ruled in alliance with the big planters, who feared landless freemen even more than they did Indians. In 1670 the Burgesses had enacted legislation restricting the suffrage to property owners; nevertheless, every man still had to pay taxes. Smoldering class antagonism thus added to the volatile mix. When in 1675 the governor declined to send the

MAP 3.5

Spread of Settlement: British Colonies, 1650–1700 The spread of settlement in the English colonies in the late seventeenth century created the conditions for a number of violent conflicts, including King Philip's War, Bacon's Rebellion, and King William's War.

WHAT FACTORS were behind the spread of British settlement in the second half of the seventeenth century?

QUICK REVIEW

King Philip's War

- King Philip's War broke out in 1675.
- Conflict between Wampanoags and settlers led to war.
- Thousands of settlers and Indians died in the fighting.

Covenant Chain   An alliance between the Iroquois Confederacy and the colony of New York which sought to establish Iroquois dominance over all other tribes.

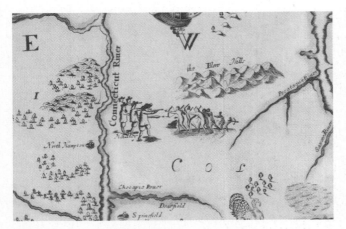

Indians and New Englanders skirmish during King Philip's War in a detail from John Seller's "A Mapp of New England," published immediately after the war.

militia against the Indians, colonists under the leadership of wealthy backcountry planter Nathaniel Bacon embarked on unauthorized raids. Bacon became a hero to former servants, and although Berkeley fumed, he ordered the first elections in many years in an attempt to appease the people. The new assembly restored the suffrage to freemen without property.

But Berkeley's move backfired when Bacon went further, demanding the death or removal of all Indians from the colony as well as an end to the rule of aristocratic "grandees" and "parasites." Berkeley fled across the Chesapeake, Bacon seized control. Soon thereafter, however, the rebel leader came down with dysentery. He died and the rebellion collapsed. Berkeley returned, reestablished control, and ordered the execution of Bacon's lieutenants.

Backcountry men in the Albermarle region of North Carolina staged a similar revolt in 1677, an episode known as **Culpeper's Rebellion**. They overthrew the established government and held power for two years before the proprietors reestablished authority. These rebellions revealed the power of class antagonism, but they also suggested that the Indians could play the role of convenient scapegoats.

Colonial officials in South Carolina seemed to be paying attention. They encouraged Indians allied with the colony—Yamasees, Creeks, Cherokees, and Chickasaws—to wage war on tribes affiliated with rival colonial powers. In addition to opening new lands for settlement, the brutal fighting resulted in the capture of many thousands of Indians who were sold into slavery. These wars continued into the first quarter of the eighteenth century.

THE GLORIOUS REVOLUTION IN AMERICA

Dynastic change in England was another factor in the violence in North America. After Charles II died in 1685, his brother and successor, James II (reigned 1685–88), began a concerted effort to strengthen royal control over the colonies. The New York assembly, considered particularly troublesome, was abolished and all power placed in the hands of the colony's royal governor. In the other colonies governors challenged the authority of assemblies. The king annulled the charter governments of New England, New York, and New Jersey and combined them into a single supercolony known as the Dominion of New England. Edmund Andros, appointed royal governor, imposed Anglican forms of worship in Puritan areas and overthrew long-standing traditions of local autonomy.

James ruled England in the same imperious style. He was a practicing Catholic, and his appointment of Catholics to high positions of state added to rising discontent and protest. The last straw was the birth of a royal son in 1688. Fearing the establishment of a Catholic dynasty, Parliamentary leaders deposed James and replaced him with his Protestant daughter Mary, who was married to William of Orange, hereditary head of state of the Netherlands. The relatively nonviolent "Glorious Revolution," as it came to be known, included a Bill of Rights, issued by the new monarchs at the insistence of Parliament, in which they promised to respect traditional civil liberties, to summon and consult with Parliament annually, and to enforce and administer its legislation. In essence, England had become a "constitutional monarchy."

In North America, news of the Glorious Revolution sparked a series of colonial rebellions against the authorities set in place by King James. In the spring of 1689, Governor Andros was arrested and deported. The Boston uprising inspired another in New York led by merchant Jacob Leisler. Rebels seized control of the city and called for the formation of a new legislature. In Maryland, rumors of a Catholic plot led to the overthrow of the proprietary rule of the Calvert family by an insurgent group calling itself the Protestant Association.

Culpeper's Rebellion The overthrow of the established government in the Albermarle region of North Carolina by backcountry men in 1677.

CHRONOLOGY

1598	Juan de Oñate leads Spanish into New Mexico	1660	Stuart monarchy restored, Charles II becomes king
1607	English found Jamestown	1675	King Philip's War
1608	French found Québec		Bacon's Rebellion
1609	Spanish found Santa Fé	1680	Pueblo Revolt
1620	Pilgrim emigration	1681–82	Robert Sieur de La Salle explores the Mississippi
1622	Indian uprising in Virginia	1688	The Glorious Revolution
1625	Jesuit missionaries arrive in New France	1689	King William's War
1629	Puritans begin settlement of Massachusetts Bay	1696	Spanish reconquest of the Pueblos completed
1637	Pequot War	1701	English impose royal governments on all colonies but Massachusetts, Connecticut, and Pennsylvania
1649	Charles I executed		

The new regime in London carefully measured its response to these uprisings. When Jacob Leisler attempted to prevent the landing of the king's troops in New York, he was arrested, tried, and executed. But William and Mary also consented to the breakup of the Dominion of New England and the termination of proprietary rule in Maryland. All the affected colonies quickly revived their assemblies and returned to their tradition of self-government. The monarchs strengthened royal authority, however, by decreeing that henceforth Massachusetts, New York, and Maryland would be royal colonies.

KING WILLIAM'S WAR

The year 1689 also marked the beginning of nearly seventy-five years of armed conflict between English and French forces for control of the North American interior. The Iroquois–English Covenant Chain alliance challenged New France's fur-trade empire, and in response the French pressed farther west in search of commercial opportunities. In the far north, the English countered with the establishment of Hudson's Bay Company, a royal fur-trade monopoly that sought to exploit the watershed of the great northern bay.

The competition in the colonies was part of a larger conflict between England and France over the European balance of power. Armed conflict in what is known as the War of the Grand Alliance began in Europe in 1688 and spread to the colonies, where it was known as **King William's War** (for the new king of England). The inconclusive war ended in 1697 with an equally inconclusive peace. War between England and France, however, would resume only five years later.

The persistent violence of the last quarter of the seventeenth century greatly concerned English authorities, who began to fear the loss of their North American possessions by outside attack or internal disorder. In 1701 the English Board of Trade converted the remaining charter and proprietary colonies into royal ones. Eventually William Penn succeeded in regaining private control of Pennsylvania, and Rhode Island and Connecticut won reinstatement of their charter governments. But the most lasting result of this quarter-century of turmoil was the tightening of English control over its North American colonies.

CONCLUSION

By 1700 the human landscape of the Southwest, the South, and the Northeast had been transformed. More than a quarter million migrants from the Old World had come to North America, the great majority of them to the English colonies.

King William's War The first of a series of colonial struggles between England and France, these conflicts occur principally on the frontiers of northern New England and New York between 1689 and 1697.

Indian societies had been disrupted, depopulated, and in some cases destroyed. The violence that flared during the last quarter of the seventeenth century was a measure of the cost of empire. Indian people resisted colonial rule in New Mexico, New England, and the Chesapeake.

Like King Philip's War and Bacon's Rebellion, the Pueblo Revolt was an episode of great violence and destruction. Yet it resulted in a long period of accommodation between the Pueblos and the Spanish colonists. The English colonists, however, took a different lesson from the violent conflicts in their colonies. They renewed their commitment to establishing communities of exclusion with ominous implications for the future of relations between colonists and natives.

REVIEW QUESTIONS

1. Using examples drawn from this chapter, discuss the differences between colonizing "frontiers of inclusion" and "exclusion."

2. What factors turned England's Chesapeake colony of Virginia from stark failure to brilliant success?

3. Discuss the role of religious dissent in the founding of the first New England colonies and in stimulating the creation of others.

4. Compare and contrast William Penn's policy with respect to Indian tribes with the policies of other English settlers, in the Chesapeake and New England, and with the policies of the Spanish, the French, and the Dutch.

5. What were the principal causes of colonial violence and warfare of the late seventeenth century?

KEY TERMS

Beaver Wars (p. 51)
Coureurs de bois (p. 50)
Covenant Chain (p. 63)
Culpeper's Rebellion (p. 64)
Frame of Government (p. 62)
House of Burgesses (p. 55)
Indentured Servants (p. 56)
King William's War (p. 65)

Massachusetts Bay Company (p. 57)
Pequot War (p. 62)
Powhatan Confederacy (p. 52)
Proprietary colony (p. 60)
Puritans (p. 56)
Quakers (p. 61)
Virginia Company (p. 52)

PEARSON
myhistorylab Connections

Reinforce what you learned in this chapter by studying the many documents,
images, maps, review tools, and videos available at www.myhistorylab.com.

Read and Review

✓• Study and Review Chapter 3

•••• Read the Document

*Don Juan de Oñate, Letter from New Mexico to
the Viceroy (1599)*

*Remarks by Chief Powhatan to John Smith
(ca. 1609)*

John Smith, "The Starving Time" (1624)

The Charter of Maryland (1632)

*Agreement between the Settlers at New
Plymouth (Mayflower Compact) (1620)*

*John Winthrop, A Model of Christian
Charity (1630)*

*The Examination and Confession of Ann Foster
at Salem (1692)*

Ann Putnam's Deposition (1692)

William Penn, Description of Pennsylvania (1681)

👁• See the Map

The Colonies to 1740

French America, 1608–1763

Research and Explore

•••• Read the Document

Exploring America: Jamestown

*Exploring America: Witches in the American
Imagination*

Profiles
Pocahontas
John Winthrop

History Bookshelf: *William Bradford,* Of
Plymouth Plantation *(1650)*

((•• Hear the Audio

Hear the audio files for Chapter 3 at
www.myhistorylab.com.

Democratic Roots in New England Soil

The Puritans of New England were less than democratic in both beliefs and goals. Contrary to popular myth, they did not migrate to the New World to establish religious freedom. They were seeking to establish a religious utopia to serve as what Governor John Winthrop called a "light upon a hill" for the world to emulate. They forbid the establishment of other religious doctrine, especially the Quakers and Roman Catholic faith. In Puritan communities nonconformist behavior was looked upon with deep suspicion, especially if it was religious in nature.

WHY COULD New England society move from a firm condemnation of democracy to embracing the basic ideals that would lead to the Declaration of Independence and the Constitution of 1787?

However, the Puritans unknowingly planted the seeds for the very democracy that they viewed as an abomination of the purity of God's social order. In the Mayflower Compact, Puritan separatists agreed to a governmental covenant that allowed for majority rule and later established the idea of the town meeting. The charter of the Massachusetts Bay Colony provided for the elections of governors, colonial legislatures, and a General Court. Puritan customs forbid church ministers from serving in public office, an early version of separation of Church and State. Most important of all, the Puritans required that all church members be able to read and interpret the Bible. This emphasis upon the individual and his right to interpret the Bible, within certain doctrinal limits, without the intercession of a priest or minister would lead to political consequences.

A hundred years later, the political seeds they planted would bear democratic fruit.■

MAYFLOWER COMPACT, 1620

IN THE NAME OF GOD, AMEN. We, whose names are underwritten, the Loyal Subjects of our dread Sovereign Lord King James, by the Grace of God, of Great Britain, France, and Ireland, King, Defender of the Faith, &c. Having undertaken for the Glory of God, and Advancement of the Christian Faith, and the Honour of our King and Country, a Voyage to plant the first Colony in the northern Parts of Virginia; Do by these Presents, solemnly and mutually, in the Presence of God and one another, covenant and combine ourselves together into a civil Body Politick, for our better Ordering and Preservation, and Furtherance of the Ends aforesaid: And by Virtue hereof do enact, constitute, and frame, such just and equal Laws, Ordinances, Acts, Constitutions, and Officers, from time to time, as shall be thought most meet and convenient for the general Good of the Colony; unto which we promise all due Submission and Obedience. IN WITNESS whereof we have hereunto subscribed our names at Cape-Cod the eleventh of November, in the Reign of our Sovereign Lord King James, of England, France, and Ireland, the eighteenth, and of Scotland the fifty-fourth, Anno Domini; 1620.■

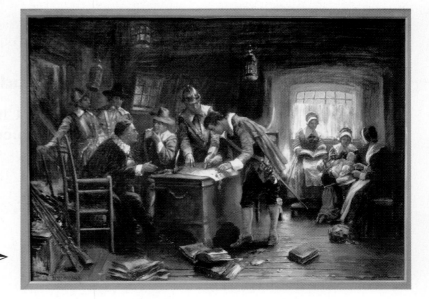

The Signing of the *Mayflower Compact* a painting by ➤ E. Percy Moran shows the historic ceremonial signing on November 21, 1620 below the deck of the Mayflower.

FUNDAMENTAL ORDERS OF CONNECTICUT (1639)

It is Ordered, sentenced, and decreed, that there shall be yearly two General Assemblies or Courts, the one the second Thursday in April, the other the second Thursday in September following; the first shall be called the Court of Election, wherein shall be yearly chosen from time to time, so many Magistrates and other public Officers as shall be found requisite: Whereof one to be chosen Governor for the year ensuing and until another be chosen, and no other Magistrate to be chosen for more than one year: provided always there be six chosen besides the Governor, which being chosen and sworn according to an Oath recorded for that purpose, shall have the power to administer justice according to the Laws here established. . . .

It is Ordered, sentenced, and decreed, that the election of the aforesaid Magistrates shall be in this manner: every person present and qualified for choice shall bring in (to the person deputed to receive them) one single paper with the name of him written in it whom he desires to have Governor, and that he that hath the greatest number of papers shall be Governor for that year. And the rest of the Magistrates or public officers to be chosen in this manner: the Secretary for the time being shall first read the names of all that are to be put to choice and then shall severally nominate them distinctly, and every one that would have the person nominated to be chosen shall bring in one single paper written upon, and he that would not have him chosen shall bring in a blank; and every one that hath more written papers than blanks shall be a Magistrate for that year. . . .

It is Ordered, sentenced, and decreed, that no person be chosen Governor above once in two years, and that the Governor be always a member of some approved Congregation. . . .

FUNDAMENTAL AGREEMENT, OR ORIGINAL CONSTITUTION OF THE COLONY OF NEW HAVEN (1639)

Query II. WHEREAS there was a covenant solemnly made by the whole assembly of free planters of this plantation, the first day of extraordinary humiliation, which we had after we came together, that as in matters that concern the gathering and ordering of a church, so likewise in all public officers which concern civil order, as choice of magistrates and officers, making and repealing laws, dividing allotments of inheritance, and all things of like nature, we would all of us be ordered by those rules which the scripture holds forth to US; this covenant was called a plantation covenant, to distinguish it from a church covenant. which could not at that time be made a church not being then gathered, but was deferred till a church might be gathered, according to GOD. It was demanded whether all the free planters do hold themselves bound by that covenant, in all businesses of that nature which are expressed in the covenant, to submit themselves to be ordered by the rules held forth in the scripture. . . . ∎

The wooden Old Ship Meeting House in Hingham, Massachusetts hosted the annual town meeting where Puritans voted and openly debated town policy.

The first object that saluted my eyes when I arrived on the coast was the sea, and a slave ship, which was then riding at anchor, and waiting for its cargo.

—*from* The Interesting Life of Olaudah Equiano

4

SLAVERY AND EMPIRE
1441–1770

 Hear the **Audio**

Hear the audio files for Chapter 4 at **www.myhistorylab.com**.

WHAT LED to the growth of the African slave trade?

WHAT WERE the major components of the African slave trade?

HOW AND why did slave societies emerge in North America?

HOW DID African slaves create a distinct African American culture?

HOW DID slavery fuel the economic development of Europe and the American colonies in the seventeenth and eighteenth centuries?

HOW DID slavery shape southern colonial society?

1441 | 1770

AMERICAN COMMUNITIES

Rebellion in Stono, South Carolina

On September 9, 1739, a group of twenty slaves gathered on the banks of the Stono River, twenty miles south of Charles Town, South Carolina. Led by an Angolan known in some accounts as Jemmy, in others as Cato, the slaves made their way to Hutchinson's general store in the hamlet of Stono Bridge. They killed the two storekeepers, ransacked the place, and arming themselves with firearms and ammunition, set off for Florida, where the Spanish governor had issued a proclamation promising freedom for all runaway British slaves. They made no attempt to hide themselves but marched boldly to the beat of drummers and shouts of "Liberty!" As they made their way through the swampy countryside, dozens of slaves joined the marchers, women and children as well as men. They plundered and burned the homes of planters and pursued and killed almost every white person they encountered along the way. According to the official government report of the incident, a total of twenty-three whites lost their lives.

Word of the rebellion quickly spread throughout the planter community, and soon a heavily armed and mounted posse was hot on the rebels' trail. Late in the afternoon, near the crossing of the Edisto River, the posse overtook them. The rebel band, grown to nearly a hundred strong, had halted in a field. The planters surrounded the field, then opened fire, killing two dozen slaves and scattering the rest. Over the next few weeks the remaining fugitives were tracked down and killed by Indian allies of the South Carolina colony. A total of forty-five or fifty African Americans died. Thus ended the Stono Rebellion, the most violent slave uprising of the colonial period.

That slaves would rise up with the odds so stacked against them was a sign of their desperation. Most of these men and women were West Africans who had endured the shock of enslavement. On the rice plantations of low-country South Carolina, they suffered from overwork, poor diet, minimal clothing, and inadequate housing. Colonial laws permitted masters to discipline and punish harshly and indiscriminately. Slaves were whipped, confined in irons, mutilated, sold away, even murdered.

That slaves would rise up was also a sign of their community. The Stono Rebellion required the kind of careful organization possible only with the social trust and confidence built by community ties. Plantation slaves married, raised children, and constructed kinship networks. They passed on African names and traditions and created new ones. We know almost nothing about the central group of conspirators in the Stono Rebellion, but very likely they were leaders of the emerging local African American community.

The history of slavery in early America includes some of the most troubling stories from our past, among them the horrid misery of the Atlantic slave trade, the shocking plunder of Africa, the use of forced labor for the production of sugar and other tropical commodities, and the foundational profits of empire. The conflicts of European nations over the access to and control of this shameful commerce led directly to colonial wars of great devastation. Yet amid this history are also stories of the making of African American families, kin networks, and communities under the most difficult of all imaginable circumstances.

Stono, SC

THE BEGINNINGS OF AFRICAN SLAVERY

One of the goals of Portuguese expansion in the fifteenth century was to gain access to the lucrative West African trade in gold, ivory, textiles, and slaves previously dominated by the Moors of northern Africa. By the mid-fifteenth century, the Portuguese were shipping a thousand or more slaves each year from Africa. Most were sent to labor on the sugar plantations on the Portuguese island colony of Madeira, which lies off the northern African coast.

WHAT LED to the growth of the African slave trade?

SUGAR AND SLAVERY

Sugar and slaves had gone together since Italian merchants of the fourteenth century set up the first modern sugar plantations on islands in the Mediterranean. Columbus introduced sugar to Hispaniola on his second voyage, and plantations were soon in operation there. Because the Indian population had been devastated by warfare and disease, colonists imported African slaves as laborers. Meanwhile, the Portuguese, aided by Dutch financiers, created a center of sugar production in their Brazilian colony that became a model for the efficient and brutal exploitation of African labor. By 1600, at least 25,000 enslaved Africans were laboring on plantations in Hispaniola and Brazil.

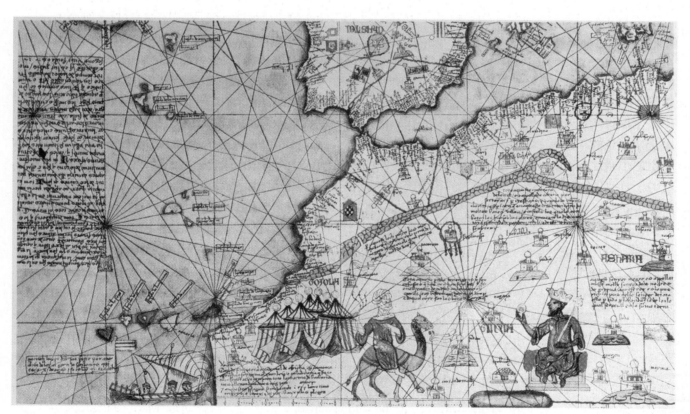

A portion of the *Catalan Atlas*, a magnificent map presented to the king of France in 1381 by his cousin, the king of Aragon, showing Iberia and north Africa, with the Straits of Gibralter connecting the Atlantic Ocean to the Mediterranean Sea. A depiction of Mansa Musa (1312–37), ruler of the Muslim kingdom of Mali, is bottom right. The accompanying inscription describes Musa as "the richest, the most noble lord in all this region on account of the abundance of gold that is gathered in his land." He holds what was thought to be the world's largest gold nugget. Under Musa's reign, Timbuktu became a capital of world renown.

African slaves operate a sugar mill on the Spanish island colony of Hispaniola, illustated in a copperplate engraving published by Theodore de Bry in 1595. Columbus introduced sugar on his second voyage, and plantations were soon in operation. Because the native population was devastated by warfare and disease, colonists imported African slaves as laborers.

Skilled at finance and commerce, the Dutch greatly expanded the European market for sugar, converting it from a luxury item for the rich to a staple for ordinary people. Once the demand for sugar and its profitability had been demonstrated, England and France began seeking West Indian sugar colonies of their own. By the 1640s, English Barbados and French Martinique had become highly profitable sugar colonies. In 1655 the English seized the island of Jamaica from the Spanish, and by 1670 the French had established effective control over the western portion of Hispaniola, which they renamed Saint Domingue (present-day Haiti). By then, Caribbean sugar and slavery had become the centerpiece of the European colonial system.

WEST AFRICANS

The men and women whose labor made these colonies so profitable came from the long-established societies and local communities of West Africa. In the sixteenth century more than a hundred different peoples lived along the coast of West Africa. In the north were the Wolofs, Mandingos, Hausas, Ashantis, and Yorubas; to the south the Ibos, Sekes, Bakongos, and Mbundus.

West African societies were based on sophisticated farming systems many thousands of years old. Farming sustained large populations and thriving networks of commerce, and in some areas kingdoms and states developed. Along the upper Niger River, towns such as Timbuktu developed into trading centers. There were a number of lesser states and kingdoms along the coast, and it was with these that the Portuguese first bargained for Africans who could be sold as slaves.

Varieties of household slavery were common in West African societies, although slaves there were often treated as subordinate members of the family. They were allowed to marry, and their children were born When African merchants sold the first slaves to the Portuguese, they may have thought that European slavery would be similar. Yet the West African familiarity with "unfree" labor made it possible for African and European traders to begin the trade in human merchandise.

THE AFRICAN SLAVE TRADE

The movement of Africans across the Atlantic to the Americas was the largest forced migration in world history (see Map 4.1). More than 12.5 million people were crowed on vessels and transported. This makes Africans the single largest group of people to come to the Americas before the nineteenth century, outnumbering European migrants of the same period by a ratio of six to one. The Atlantic slave trade began with the Portuguese in the fifteenth century and did not end in the United States until 1807, and it continued elsewhere in the Americas until 1867. It is one of the most brutal chapters in the story of America.

WHAT WERE the major components of the African slave trade?

◄●▶ **Read** the **Document**

Alexander Falconbridge, The African Slave Trade (1788) at **www.myhistorylab.com**

A GLOBAL ENTERPRISE

Approximately 10.5 million Africans arrived in the Americas during the four-century history of the slave trade. Ninety percent of them went directly to areas of sugar production—nearly half to the Caribbean, and more than 40 percent to Portuguese

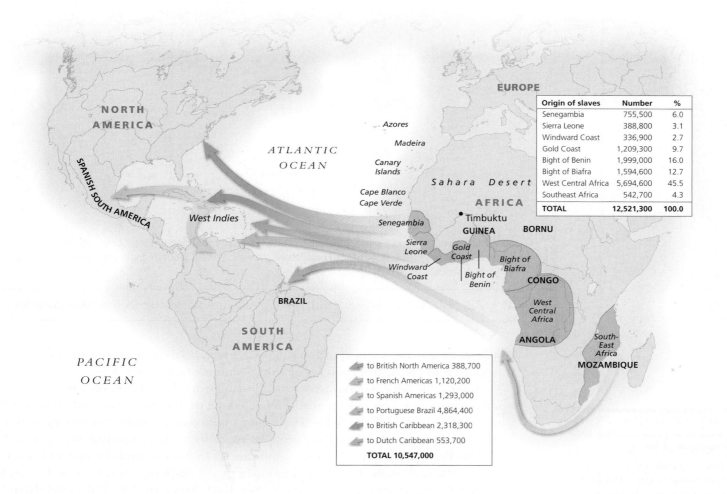

Origin of slaves	Number	%
Senegambia	755,500	6.0
Sierra Leone	388,800	3.1
Windward Coast	336,900	2.7
Gold Coast	1,209,300	9.7
Bight of Benin	1,999,000	16.0
Bight of Biafra	1,594,600	12.7
West Central Africa	5,694,600	45.5
Southeast Africa	542,700	4.3
TOTAL	**12,521,300**	**100.0**

to British North America 388,700
to French Americas 1,120,200
to Spanish Americas 1,293,000
to Portuguese Brazil 4,864,400
to British Caribbean 2,318,300
to Dutch Caribbean 553,700
TOTAL 10,547,000

MAP 4.1
The African Slave Trade   The enslaved men, women, and children transported to the Americas came from West Africa, the majority from the lower Niger River (called the Slave Coast) and the region of the Congo and Angola.

WHERE IN the Americas were most African slaves sent? Why?

MAP 4.2

Slave Colonies of the Seventeenth and Eighteenth Centuries By the eighteenth century, the system of slavery had created societies with large African populations throughout the Caribbean and along the southern coast of North America.

WHAT REGIONS in eighteenth-century America can be described as "slave societies"?

Brazil. A much smaller proportion, about 1 in every 25 transported Africans were transported to the British colonies of North America (see Figure 4.1).

Among the Africans transported to the Americas, men generally outnumbered women two to one. This ratio probably reflected the preferences of plantation masters, who wanted workers for the fields. The majority were young people, between the ages of fifteen and thirty. Nearly every ethnic group in West Africa was represented among them.

The Portuguese were the most important slave traders until the end of the sixteenth century, when the Dutch and English began to challenge their control. England became the largest slave-trading nation after 1640. From 1650 to 1807 English and Anglo-American vessels carried half of all the slaves from Africa to the Americas. The Dutch, the French, and especially the Portuguese, however, continued to play important roles (see Map 4.2).

The European presence in Africa generally was confined to coastal outposts and the slave trade was a collaboration between European or American and African traders.

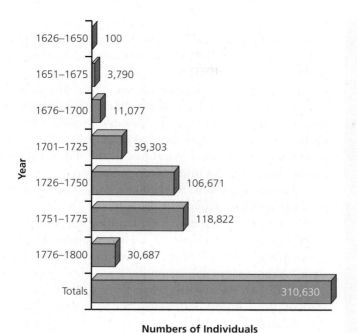

Figure 4.1 Africans Imported to Mainland British North America, 1626–1800
These statistics, generated by the computer database of all documented transAtlantic slave voyages, demonstrate the rising importance of the slave trade in the British mainland North American colonies.

Voyages: The Trans-Atlantic Slave Trade Database. http://www.slavevoyages.org (accessed 2010).

Dependent on the favor of local rulers, many colonial slave traders lived permanently in coastal forts and married African women, reinforcing their commercial ties with kinship relations. In many areas their mixed-ancestry children and grandchildren became prominent players in the slave trade. Continuing the practice of the Portuguese, the grim business of slave raiding was left to the Africans themselves.

THE SHOCK OF ENSLAVEMENT

Most Africans were enslaved through warfare. Sometimes large armies launched massive attacks, burning whole towns, killing many and enslaving others. More common were smaller raids in which a group of armed men attacked at nightfall, seized everyone within reach, then escaped with their captives. Capture and enslavement was an unparalleled shock. Venture Smith, an African born in Guinea in 1729, was eight years old when he was captured. After many years in North American slavery, he still vividly recalled the attack on his village, the torture and murder of his father, and the long march of his people to the coast. "The shocking scene is to this day fresh in my mind," he wrote, "and I have often been overcome while thinking on it."

On the coast, European traders and African raiders assembled their captives. Prisoners waited in dark dungeons or in open pens. To lessen the possibility of collective resistance, traders split up families and ethnic groups. Captains carefully inspected each man and woman, and those selected for transport were branded on the back or buttocks with the mark of the buyer.

THE MIDDLE PASSAGE

English sailors christened the voyage of slave vessels across the Atlantic from Africa to America as the "**Middle Passage**," that is, the middle part of the trading triangle linking Europe to Africa, Africa to America, and America back to Europe. From holding areas on the coast, crews rowed small groups of slaves to the waiting transports and packed them into shelves below deck only six feet long by two and a half feet high. "Rammed like herring in a barrel," wrote one observer, slaves were "chained to each other hand and foot, and stowed so close, that they were not allowed above a foot and a half for each in breadth." People were forced to sleep "spoon fashion," and the tossing of the ship

Middle Passage   The voyage between West Africa and the New World slave colonies.

Portrait of Olaudah *Equiano*, by an unknown English artist, ca. 1780. His autobiography, *The Interesting Narrative of the Life of Olaudah Equiano* (1789), was published in numerous editions, translated into several languages, and became the prototype for dozens of other slave narratives in the nineteenth century. In the book, Equiano described his capture in west Africa in 1756, when he was eleven years old, his "middle passage" voyage to America, and his eventual purchase by an English sea captain. After ten years as a slave, Equiano succeeded in purchasing his freedom and dedicated himself thereafter to the antislavery cause.

Royal Albert Memorial Museum, Exeter, Devon, UK/Bridgeman Art Library.

knocked them about so violently that the skin over their elbows sometimes was worn to the bone from scraping on the planks. One vessel designed to carry 450 slaves regularly crossed the Atlantic tightly packed with more than 600.

Their holds filled with human cargo, the transports headed up the African coast to Cape Verde where they caught the trade winds blowing toward America. A favorable voyage from Senegambia to Barbados might be accomplished in as little as three weeks, but a ship from Guinea or Angola, becalmed in the doldrums or driven back by storms, might take as much as three months.

Most voyages were marked by a daily routine. In the morning the crew opened the hatch and brought the captives on deck, attaching their leg irons to a great chain running the length of the bulwarks. After a breakfast of beans the crew commanded men and women to jump up and down, a bizarre session of exercise known as "dancing the slave." A day spent chained on deck was concluded by a second bland meal and then the stowing away. During the night, according to one seaman, there issued from below "a howling melancholy noise, expressive of extreme anguish."

Among the horrors of the voyage was the absence of any adequate sanitation. Crews were supposed to swab the holds daily, but so sickening was the task that it was rarely performed, and the captives were left to wallow in their own wastes. According to Atlantic sailors, they could "smell a slaver five miles downwind." In these conditions many captives sickened and died.

Other captives contracted infectious diseases, and those exacted the greatest toll. Dysentery, known as the "flux," was common. Frequent shipboard epidemics of smallpox, measles, and yellow fever added to the misery. One comparative study of trans-oceanic voyages during the colonial period found that mortality on slave vessels was significantly higher than on the ships of migrating colonists, indentured servants, or even convict laborers. The consensus among historians is that approximately one of every seven transported Africans perished during the Middle Passage.

The unwilling voyagers offered plenty of resistance. As long as ships were still within sight of the African coast, hope remained alive and the danger of revolt was great. One historian found evidence of hundreds of slave revolts at sea, and estimates that insurrections occurred on one of every ten trans-Atlantic slaving voyages. Once on the open sea, however, the captives' resistance took more desperate form. Captains took the precaution of spreading netting along the sides of their ships to prevent suicides.

As the vessels approached their destination, crews prepared the human cargo for market. All but the most rebellious were freed from their chains and allowed to wash themselves and move about the deck. But the toll of the Middle Passage was difficult to disguise. One observer described a disembarking group as "walking skeletons covered over with a piece of tanned leather."

Some cargoes were destined for a single wealthy planter or consigned to a merchant who sold the captives in return for a commission. In other cases the captain himself was responsible. Buyers painstakingly examined the Africans, who once again suffered the indignity of probing eyes and poking fingers. In ports such as Charles Town in South Carolina, sales were generally made by auction or by a cruel method known as the scramble: with prices fixed in advance the Africans were driven into a corral, and on cue the buyers would rush in among them, grabbing their pick.

•⬤•–Read the Document

Olaudah Equiano, The Middle Passage
(1788) at **www.myhistorylab.com**

Slaves below deck on the Portugese vessel *Albaroz*, a sketch made by Lt. Francis Meynell of the British Navy shortly after his warship captured the slaver in 1845. Slaves were "stowed so close, that they were not allowed above a foot and a half for each in breadth," wrote one observer. This practice of "tight packing," which originated in the fifteenth century, continued to the end of the trade in the late 1860s.

POLITICAL AND ECONOMIC EFFECTS ON AFRICA

Africa began the sixteenth century with genuine independence. But as surely as Europe and America grew stronger as a result of the transport of captive Africans, so Africa grew weaker by their loss. For every individual taken captive, at least another died in the chronic slave raiding. Death and destruction spread deep into the African interior. Coastal slave-trading kingdoms drew slaves from central Africa. Many of the new states became little more than machines for supplying captives to European traders, and a "gun-slave cycle" pushed them into a destructive arms race with each other. Soldiers captured in these wars were themselves enslaved.

More serious still was the long-term stagnation of the West African economy. Labor was drawn away from productive activities while imported consumer goods stifled local manufacturing. African traders were expert at driving a hard bargain for slaves, but even when they appeared to get the best of the exchange, the ultimate advantage lay with the Europeans, who received wealth-producing workers in return for mere consumer goods. This political, economic, and cultural demoralization prepared the way for the European colonization of Africa in the nineteenth century.

HOW AND why did slave societies emerge in North America?

Africans herded from a slave ship to a corral where they were to be sold by the cruel method known as "the scramble," buyers rushing in and grabbing their pick. An engraving by William Blake in John Gabriel Stedman, *Narrative of a Five Years' Expedition Against the Revolted Negroes of Surinam* (1796).

THE DEVELOPMENT OF NORTH AMERICAN SLAVE SOCIETIES

New World slavery was nearly two centuries old before it became an important system of labor in North America. There were slaves in all the British colonies of the seventeenth century, but as late as 1700 they accounted for less than 12 percent of the colonial population. During the eighteenth century, however, slavery expanded greatly, and by 1770 there were 460,000 Africans and African Americans in British North America, making up more than 20 percent of the population (see Figure 4.2).

SLAVERY COMES TO NORTH AMERICA

The first Africans arrived in Virginia in 1619. But because slaves generally cost twice as much as indentured servants , they had little economic benefit for planters. Consequently, seventeenth-century Chesapeake planters employed far more indentured servants than slaves. The African proportion of the Chesapeake population did grow, but slowly, from 2 percent in 1630 to 7 percent in 1670. Servants and the small number of slaves worked together, ate and slept in common quarters, and often developed intimate relationships. The Chesapeake was what one historian has termed a "society with slaves," a society in which slavery was one form of labor among several.

Under these circumstances the status of black Virginians could be ambiguous. An interesting case illustrates the point. In 1654, the African John Castor complained in a local court that "he came unto Virginia for seven or eight years of indenture, yet Anthony Johnson his Master had kept him his servant seven years longer than he should or ought." Johnson claimed that "he had the Negro for his life." The court decided in the master's favor. But strange to say, Johnson himself was a man of African descent. He had arrived in Virginia as a slave in 1621, but by hiring himself out during his free time had earned enough to gain freedom for himself and his family. Seventeenth-century Virginia records reveal that some Africans acquired farms, servants, and slaves of their own. Moreover, sexual relations among Africans, Indians, and Europeans produced a sizable group of free people of mixed ancestry, known as mulattoes. It was only later that dark skin came automatically to mean slavery, segregation, and the absence of the rights of freemen.

During the last quarter of the seventeenth century, however, the Chesapeake developed into a "slave society," a place where slavery was the dominant form of labor. Among several developments, perhaps most important was the sharp decline in the number of indentured servants migrating to the Chesapeake. The incentive had been the availability of land after the term of service, but by midcentury most of the arable land was already in the hands of the planter elite. Bacon's and Culpeper's rebellions (see Chapter 3) offered examples of the violent potential of the land crisis. They also suggested how much serious trouble servants and former servants could make for planters. After Bacon's Rebellion, English immigrants turned away from the Chesapeake to colonies such as Pennsylvania, where there was more land and more opportunity.

The British Royal African Company, which began to import slaves directly to North America in the 1670s, was more than happy to supply the planters' need for labor. By 1700 there were 5,000 slaves in Virginia, and the proportion of the Chesapeake population of African descent stood at more than 22 percent.

Slavery had no English legal precedent, no laws or traditions allowing for lifetime enslavement or for making that status inheritable. So as the proportions of slaves in the colonial population gradually rose, colonists wrote slavery into law, a process best observed in the case of Virginia. In 1662 the planter assembly declared that henceforth children would be "bond or free only according to the condition of the mother." Five years later they passed a law that Christian baptism could no longer alter conditions of servitude. Thus, two important avenues to freedom were closed. The colony then gave masters the right to administer life-threatening violence, declaring in 1669 that the death of a slave

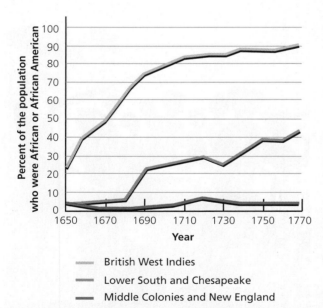

Figure 4.2 Africans as a Percentage of Total Population of the British Colonies, 1650–1770
Although the proportion of Africans and African Americans was never as high in the South as in the Caribbean, the ethnic structure of the South diverged radically from that of the North during the eighteenth century.

Time on the Cross: The Economics of American Negro Slavery, by Robert William Fogel and Stanley L. Engerman. Copyright © 1974 by Robert William Fogel and Stanley L. Engerman. Used by permission of W. W. Norton & Company, Inc.

during punishment "shall not be accounted felony." Such rules accumulated piecemeal until 1705, when Virginia gathered them into a comprehensive slave code that became a model for other colonies.

Thus, slavery was institutionalized just as the Atlantic slave trade reached flood tide in the eighteenth century. In the single decade of 1701 to 1710 more Africans were imported into North America than the entire previous century. The English colonies were primed for an unprecedented growth of plantation slavery.

THE TOBACCO COLONIES

During the eighteenth century the European demand for tobacco increased more than tenfold, and it was supplied largely by increased production in the Chesapeake region. Tobacco was far and away the single most important commodity produced in eighteenth-century North America, accounting for more than a quarter of the value of all colonial exports.

The expansion of tobacco production could not have taken place without a corresponding growth in the size of the slave labor force. Unlike sugar, tobacco did not require large plantations and could be produced successfully on small farms. But the crop demanded a great deal of hand labor and close attention. As tobacco production expanded, slaveholding became widespread. By 1770 more than a quarter million slaves labored in the colonies of the Upper South (Maryland, Virginia, and North Carolina), and because of the exploding market for tobacco, their numbers expanded at about double the rate of the general population.

Shipments of what were known as "saltwater slaves," direct from Africa, accounted for much of this growth. But natural increase was even more important. In the Caribbean and Brazil, where profits from sugar were extremely high, many planters literally worked their slaves to death, replenishing them with a constant stream of new arrivals from Africa. In the Chesapeake, however, significantly lower profits led tobacco planters to pay more attention to the health of their labor force, establishing work routines that were not as deadly. Moreover, food supplies were more plentiful in North America and slaves better fed, making them more resistant to disease.

As a consequence, in the 1730s the slave population of the Chesapeake was the first in the Western Hemisphere to achieve self-sustained growth. Natural increase gradually balanced the sex ratio among slaves, another encouragement to population growth. By the 1750s, about 80 percent of Chesapeake slaves were "country-born."

THE LOWER SOUTH

The Chesapeake did not become a slave society until almost a century after its founding. South Carolina, however, was a slave society from the beginning. The most valuable part of the early Carolina economy was the Indian slave trade. Practicing a strategy of divide and conquer, using Indian tribes to fight one another, Carolinians established a trade in Indian captives during the 1670s. By the early eighteenth century more than 12,000 mission Indians from Florida had been captured and sold into slavery and thousands more killed or dispersed.

In the early eighteenth century, however, planter preference turned toward African rather than Indian slaves. Rice production had become the most dynamic sector of the South Carolina economy, and their experience in agriculture made West Africans much preferred as rice workers. Another important crop was added to the mix in the 1740s when West Indian indigo, used to make blue dye for the textile industry, was successfully adapted to the low-country climate. Rice grew in the lowlands, but indigo could be cultivated on high ground, and with different seasonal growing patterns, planters were able to harmonize their production. Rice and indigo became two of the most valuable commodities exported from the mainland colonies of North America. The boom in these two crops

●●●─Read the **Document**

Of the Servants and Slaves in Virginia (1705) at **www.myhistorylab.com**

QUICK REVIEW

Growth of Slavery

◆ Slavery grew rapidly in the South.

◆ The use of slaves made economic sense on tobacco and rice plantations.

◆ Northern slaves worked as servants, craftsmen, and day laborers.

Artist Thomas Coram painted this image of Mulberry Plantation, near Charleston, South Carolina, about 1800. The cabins of the slaves line the path to the mansion. Their steep roofs, an architectural feature introduced in America by enslaved African builders, kept living quarters cool by allowing the heat to rise and dissipate in the rafters.

Thomas Coram, "View of Mulberry Street, House and Street." Oil on paper, 10 × 17.6 cm. Gibbes Museum of Art/Carolina Art Association. 68.18.01.

Read the Document

James Oglethorpe, Establishing the Colony of Georgia (1733) at www.myhistorylab.com

QUICK REVIEW

Slavery in the Lower South

- Indian slavery prominent in early Carolina economy.
- Boom in rice and indigo production depended on African slaves.
- 1770: African Americans make up 80 percent of population of South Carolina and Georgia coast.

depended on the growth of African slavery. Before the international slave trade to the United States was ended in 1808, at least 100,000 slaves landed in South Carolina.

By the 1740s many of these arriving Africans were being taken to Georgia, a colony created by an act of the English Parliament in 1732. Its leader, James Edward Oglethorpe, hoped to establish a buffer against Spanish invasion from Florida and make the colony a haven for poor British farmers who could sell their products in the markets of South Carolina. Under Oglethorpe's influence, Parliament agreed to prohibit slavery in Georgia. But soon Georgia's coastal regions were being colonized by South Carolina rice planters and their slaves. By the time Oglethorpe and Georgia's trustees opened their colony to slavery in 1752, the Georgia coast had already become an extension of the Carolina low-country slave system.

By 1770 nearly 90,000 African Americans made up about 80 percent of the coastal population of South Carolina and Georgia. The African American communities of the Lower South had achieved self-sustained growth by the middle of the eighteenth century, a generation later than those in the Chesapeake.

SLAVERY IN THE SPANISH COLONIES

Slavery was basic to the Spanish colonial labor system, yet doubts about the enslavement of Africans were raised by both church and crown. The papacy denounced slavery as a violation of Christian principles. But the institution remained intact, and later in the eighteenth century, when sugar production expanded in Cuba, the slave system there turned as brutal as any in the history of the Americas.

The character of slavery in the Spanish colonies varied with local conditions. One of the most benign forms operated in Florida. In many Florida settlements, the conditions of servitude more resembled the household slavery common in African communities than the plantation slavery of South Carolina and Georgia. In 1699, in an attempt to undermine the English colonies of the Lower South, Spanish authorities declared Florida a refuge for escaped slaves, offering free land to any fugitive who would help defend the colony. Over the next half century, refugee Indians and fugitive Africans established many communities in the countryside surrounding St. Augustine. By 1763, 3,000 African Americans, a quarter of them free, made up 25 percent of St. Augustine's population.

In New Mexico, the Spanish depended on Indian slavery. In the sixteenth century the colonial governor sent Indian slaves to the mines of Mexico. The enslavement of Indians was one of the causes of the **Pueblo Revolt** (see Chapter 3). In the aftermath of the revolt the Spanish became much more cautious in their treatment of the Pueblos, who were officially considered Catholics. But they participated in a robust trade in captured and enslaved "infidel Indians," mostly nomadic people from the Great Plains, employing them as house servants and fieldworkers.

SLAVERY IN FRENCH LOUISIANA

Slavery was also important in Louisiana, the colony founded by the French in the lower Mississippi Valley. The French Company of the Indies imported some 6,000 African slaves, and planters invested in tobacco and indigo plantations along the river banks north of New Orleans. This was the country of the Natchez Indians, who greatly resented the French intrusion. In 1729 the Natchez joined forces with rebellious slaves in an armed uprising. The Natchez Rebellion claimed the lives of more than 200 French settlers, 10 percent of the population. Planters elsewhere did everything they could to pit Indians and Africans against one another, employing Indians as slave-catchers, as they did after the Stono Rebellion. An alliance of slaves and Indians was the greatest of all planter fears. The French colonial militia put down the rebellion with brutal force, crushing and dispersing the Natchez people in the process.

Bitter memories of the Natchez Rebellion kept the Louisiana French from committing themselves totally to slavery. In 1750 African slaves amounted to less than a third of the colonial population of 10,000. It was not until the end of the century that the colony of Louisiana became an important North American slave society.

SLAVERY IN THE NORTH

None of the northern colonies could be characterized as slave societies, but slavery was an important form of labor in a number of localities. During the eighteenth century it grew increasingly significant in the commercial farming regions of southeast Pennsylvania, central New Jersey, and Long Island, areas where slaves made up about 10 percent of rural residents. In Rhode Island—a center of the slave trade—large gangs of slaves were used in cattle and dairy operations, and the proportion of slaves in the population reached nearly a third.

Slavery was common in all northern port cities, including Boston. Slave ownership was nearly universal among the wealthy and ordinary among craftsmen and professionals. By 1750 slaves, along with small populations of free blacks, made up 15 to 20 percent of the residents of Boston, New York City, and Philadelphia.

The Quakers of Pennsylvania and New Jersey, many of whom kept slaves, were the first colonists to voice antislavery sentiment. In 1715, John Hepburn of New Jersey published the first North American critique of slavery, but his was a lonely voice. By midcentury, however, there was a significant antislavery movement among Quakers. In 1758 the Philadelphia Friends Meeting voted to condemn slavery and urged masters to voluntarily free their slaves. But it was not until the Revolution that antislavery attitudes became more widespread in the northern colonies.

Pueblo Revolt Rebellion in 1680 of Pueblo Indians in New Mexico against their Spanish overlords.

HOW DID African slaves create a distinct African American culture?

Hear the Audio
On Being Brought from Africa to America
at **www.myhistorylab.com**

AFRICAN TO AFRICAN AMERICAN

African men and women from dozens of ethnic groups, representing many different languages, religions, and customs, were transported across the Atlantic without any of their cultural possessions. In America they were subjected to the control of masters intent on maximizing their work and minimizing their liberty. Nevertheless, African Americans carved out lives of their own with a degree of independence. Their African heritage was not erased; it provided them with a fundamental outlook, the basis for a common identity.

Africans transported to North America arrived during the eighteenth century joined a rapidly growing population of country-born slaves or "creoles." The perspective of creoles was shaped by their having grown up under slavery, and that perspective helped them to determine which elements of African culture they would incorporate into the emerging culture of the African American community. That community was formed out of the relationship between creoles and Africans, and between slaves and their European masters.

THE DAILY LIFE OF SLAVES

Slaves did the work that made plantation colonies so profitable. As an agricultural people, Africans, both women and men, were accustomed to the routines of field labor. Most slaves were field hands, and even domestic servants labored in the fields when necessary. Masters provided their workers with rude clothing, sufficient in the summer but nearly always inadequate in the winter.

On small plantations and farms, typical in the tobacco country of the Chesapeake, Africans might work side by side with their owners and, depending on the character of the master, might enjoy a standard of living not too different from that of other family members. The work was more demanding and living conditions far worse on the great rice and indigo plantations of the Lower South, where slaves usually lived separately from the master in their own quarters. But large plantations, with large numbers of slaves, created a concentration of population that made for more resilient African American communities.

FAMILIES AND COMMUNITIES

The family was the most important institution for the development of community and culture, but **slave codes** did not provide for legal slave marriages—that would have contradicted the master's freedom to dispose of his property as he saw fit. Planters commonly separated families by sale or bequest, dividing husbands from wives and even separating mothers from children. Ball never saw her again. Later, after he had grown and married, his master sold him to a rice planter in Georgia. "My heart died away within me," Ball remembered vividly. "I felt incapable of weeping or speaking, and in my despair I laughed loudly." On his journey south he dreamed his wife and children were "beseeching and imploring my master on their knees."

Despite the odds against them, however, slaves in both the Chesapeake and the Lower South created the families that were essential for the development of African American culture. On large plantations throughout the southern colonies, travelers found Africans living in family households. In the Lower South, where there were greater concentrations of slaves on the rice plantations, husbands and wives often lived together in the slave quarters. On the smaller plantations of the Upper South, men frequently married women from neighboring farms, and with the permission of both owners visited their families in the evenings or on Sundays.

Emotional ties to particular places, connections between the generations, and relations of kinship and friendship linking neighboring plantations and farms were the foundation stones of African American community life. Kinship was especially important. African American parents encouraged their children to use family terms in addressing

slave codes A series of laws passed mainly in the Southern colonies in the late seventeenth and early eighteenth centuries to defend the status of slaves and codify the denial of basic civil rights to them.

QUICK REVIEW

Slave Society

- Traces of African culture remained in slave society.
- Labor consumed most of slave's time.
- Kinship played a key role in solidifying African American communities.

unrelated persons: "auntie" or "uncle" became a respectful way of addressing older men and women, "brother" and "sister" affectionate terms for age mates. This may have been one of the first devices enslaved Africans used to humanize the world of slavery.

AFRICAN AMERICAN CULTURE

The eighteenth century was the formative period in the development of the African American community, for it was then that the high birthrate and the growing numbers of country-born provided the necessary stability for the evolution of culture. The emergence of distinctive patterns in music and dance, religion, and oral tradition illustrate the resilience of the human spirit under bondage as well as the successful struggle of African Americans to create a spiritually sustaining culture of their own.

Eighteenth-century masters were reluctant to allow their slaves to become Christians, fearing that baptism would open the way to claims of freedom or give Africans dangerous notions of universal brotherhood and equality with masters. The majority of black southerners before the American Revolution practiced some form of African religion. Large numbers of African Americans were not converted to Christianity until **The Great Awakening**, which swept across the South just before the American Revolution (see Chapter 5).

One crucial area of religious practice concerned the rituals of death and burial. African Americans often decorated graves with shells and pottery, an old African custom. African Americans generally believed that the spirits of their dead would return to Africa. The burial ceremony, which included African dances and songs, was often held at night to keep it secret from masters, who objected to the continuation of African traditions. As slaves from different backgrounds joined together in such ceremonies, they were beginning the process of cultural unification.

Music and dance may have formed the foundation of African American culture, coming even before a common language. Many Africans were accomplished players of stringed instruments and drums, and their style featured improvisation and rhythmic complexity, elements that would become prominent in African American music. In America, slaves re-created African instruments such as the banjo, and mastered the European violin and guitar.

One of the most important developments of the eighteenth century was the invention of an African American language. An English traveler during the 1770s complained he could not understand Virginia slaves who spoke "a mixed dialect between the Guinea and English." But such a language made it possible for country-born and "saltwater" Africans to communicate. Creole languages were a transitional phenomenon, gradually giving way to distinctive forms of black English, although in certain isolated areas, such as the sea islands of the Carolinas and Georgia, they persisted into the twentieth century.

THE AFRICANIZATION OF THE SOUTH

The African American community often looked to recently arrived Africans for religious leadership and medical magic. Throughout the South, many whites had as much faith in slave conjurers and herb doctors as the slaves did themselves, and slaves won fame for their healing powers. This was one of many ways in which white and black southerners came to share a common culture. Acculturation was by no means a one-way street; English men and women in the South were also being Africanized.

Slaves worked in the kitchens of their masters and thus introduced an African style of cooking into colonial diets already transformed by Indian crops. African American culinary arts are responsible for such southern culinary specialties as barbecue, fried chicken, black-eyed peas, and collard greens. In Louisiana a combination of African, French, and Indian elements produced a distinguished American regional cuisine, exemplified by gumbos (soups) and jambalayas (stews).

((•―Hear the **Audio**
"Ghana: Ewe-Atsiagbekor" from Roots of Black Music in America at **www.myhistorylab.com**

The Great Awakening Tremendous religious revival in colonial America striking first in the Middle Colonies and New England in the 1740s and then spreading to the southern colonies.

A Musical Celebration in the Slave Quarters

This anonymous watercolor, discovered in South Carolina, dates from the last quarter of the eighteenth century. It offers a wonderfully detailed depiction of Africans or African Americans gathered together in the slave quarters, celebrating with music. This is clearly a community celebration, involving several families. Seated on the right, two men play instruments that suggest continuity with the African heritage. One plucks on something that looks like a banjo, and indeed, the banjo can be traced back to West Africa. "The instrument proper to them," Thomas Jefferson wrote of his slaves, "is the banjar, which they brought hither from Africa." The other man plays a drum that resembles the gudugudu, a small wooden kettledrum from Nigeria played with two long, thin rawhide sticks. The dancing man with the carved stick may indicate that this is a wedding ceremony that involves jumping the broom, a custom that may have originated in Africa, although versions of it were practiced in medieval Europe as well. One planter's description of a slave dance seems to fit this scene: the men leading the women in "a slow shuffling gait, edging along by some unseen exertion of the feet, from one side to the other—sometimes courtesying down and remaining in that posture while the edging motion from one side to the other continued." The women, he wrote, "always carried a handkerchief held at arm's length, which was waved in a graceful motion to and fro as she moved." The painting is a tribute to the celebration of life amidst adversity. ■

WHY DO you think the plantation master is omitted from this painting?

Mutual acculturation was also evident in many aspects of material culture. Southern basket weaving used Indian techniques and African designs. Woodcarving often featured African motifs. The West African iron-working tradition was evident throughout the South, especially in the ornamentation of the homes of Charles Town and New Orleans.

Even more important were less tangible aspects of culture. Slave mothers nursed white children as well as their own. As one English observer wrote, "each child has its [black] Momma, whose gestures and accent it will necessarily copy, for children, we all know, are imitative beings." In this way many Africanisms passed into the English language of the South: goober (peanut), yam (sweet potato), banjo, okay, tote, buddy.

VIOLENCE AND RESISTANCE

Slavery was made possible by the threat and reality of violence. The only way to make slaves work, Virginia planter Robert "King" Carter instructed his overseer, was "to make them stand in fear." Humane slave masters like George Washington did not wish to be harsh. He sought, as he wrote it, "tranquility with a certain income." But the tranquility of Mount Vernon rested on the threat of violence. Washington ordered his overseers to carefully monitor the work of the slaves and punish their offenses with regular whippings. Even the most cultured plantation owners thought nothing about floggings of fifty or seventy-five lashes.

Yet African Americans demonstrated a resisting spirit. In their day-to-day existence they often refused to cooperate: they malingered, they mistreated animals and broke tools, they

Fugitive slaves flee through the swamps in Thomas Moran's *The Slave Hunt* (1862). Many slaves ran away from their masters, and colonial newspapers included notices urging readers to be on the lookout for them. Some fled in groups or collected together in isolated communities called "maroon" colonies, located in inaccessible swamps and woods.

Thomas Moran (American, 1837–1926), "Slave Hunt, Dismal Swamp, Virginia," 1862. Gift of Laura A. Clubb, 1947.8.44. ©2008 The Philbrook Museum of Art, Inc.,Tulsa, Oklahoma.

wantonly destroyed the master's property. An analysis of hundreds of eighteenth-century advertisements for runaways concludes that 80 percent were young men in their twenties, suggesting that flight was an option mostly exercised by unattached males.

Runaways sometimes collected together in isolated and hidden communities called "maroons." Slaves who escaped from South Carolina or Georgia into Spanish Florida created maroon communities among the Creek Indians there. Maroons also lay hidden in the backcountry of the Lower South, and although they were less common in the Upper South, there were a number of them in the Great Dismal Swamp, the coastal region between Virginia and North Carolina.

The most direct form of resistance was revolt. The first notable slave uprising of the colonial era occurred in New York City in 1712. Twenty-three Africans armed themselves with guns, swords, daggers, and hatchets, killed nine colonists, and burned several buildings before being surrounded by the militia. Six of the conspirators committed suicide rather than surrender. Thirteen were hanged, another was starved to death in chains, another broken on the wheel, and three more burned at the stake. In 1741, New York authorities uncovered what they believed was another conspiracy. Thirteen black leaders were burned alive, eighteen more hanged, and eighty sold and shipped off to the West Indies. A family of colonists and a Catholic priest, accused of providing weapons, were also executed.

A series of small rebellions and rumors of large ones in Virginia during the 1720s culminated in the Chesapeake Rebellion of 1730, the largest slave uprising of the colonial period. Several hundred slaves assembled in Norfolk and Princess Anne counties where they chose commanders for their "insurrection." More than 300 escaped en masse into the Dismal Swamp. Hunted down by Indians in the employ of the colony, their community was soon destroyed. Twenty-nine leaders were executed and the rest were returned to their masters.

In the Lower South, where slaves were a majority of the population, there were isolated but violent uprisings in 1704, 1720, and 1730. In 1738 a series of revolts broke out in South Carolina and Georgia. These prepared the way for the **Stono Rebellion** of 1739 (see the Introduction), the most violent slave rebellion of the colonial period. In the aftermath of Stono several similar uprisings were quickly crushed by planters.

Wherever masters held slaves, fears of uprisings persisted. But compared with such slave colonies as Jamaica, Guiana, or Brazil, there were relatively few revolts in North America. The conditions favoring revolt (large African majorities, brutal exploitation with correspondingly low survival rates, little acculturation, and geographic isolation) prevailed only in some areas of the Lower South. Indeed, the very success of African Americans in British North America at establishing families, communities, and a culture of their own inevitably made them less likely to take the risks that rebellions required.

QUICK REVIEW

Resistance to Slavery

- Refusal to cooperate or destruction of property.
- Running away and establishing fugitive communities.
- Revolting.

HOW DID slavery fuel the economic development of Europe and the American colonies in the seventeenth and eighteenth centuries?

Stono Rebellion One of the largest and most violent slave uprisings during the Colonial Period that occurred in Stono, South Carolina.

SLAVERY AND THE ECONOMICS OF EMPIRE

The British slave colonies—the sugar plantations of the West Indies, the tobacco plantations of the Chesapeake, and the rice and indigo plantations of the Lower South—accounted for 95 percent of exports from the Americas to Great Britain from 1714 to the eve of the American Revolution. Moreover, there was the prime economic importance of the slave trade itself, which one eighteenth-century economist described as the "foundation" of the British economy. The labor of African slaves was largely responsible for the economic success of the British Empire in the Americas. New World slavery contributed enormously to the growth and development of the Old World economy. and was responsible for the capital formation that made possible the beginnings of the industrial economy.

SLAVERY: FOUNDATION OF THE BRITISH ECONOMY

Slavery contributed to the economic development of Great Britain in three principal ways. First, it generated enormous profits.

Profits derived from the triangular trade in slaves, plantation products, and manufactured goods (see Map 4.3) furnished from 21 to 35 percent of Great Britain's fixed capital formation in the eighteenth century. This capital funded the first modern banks and insurance companies and, through loans and investments, found its way into a wide range of economic activities. Merchant capitalists were prominent investors in the expansion of the merchant marine, the improvement of harbors, and the construction of canals.

Second, slave colonies in the Caribbean supplied 69 percent of the raw cotton for British textile mills, the earliest sector of industrial development. The demand for cotton would eventually lead to the development of the cotton gin and the rise of cotton plantations in the United States (see Chapter 11).

Third, slavery provided an enormous stimulus to the growth of manufacturing by creating a huge colonial market for exports. From 1700 to 1740, the growth in American and African demand for manufactured goods (principally textiles, metal products, and ship's wares) accounted for nearly 70 percent of the expansion of British exports.

The multiplier effects of these activities are best seen in the growth of English ports such as Liverpool and Bristol. There African and American commerce provided employment for ships' crews, dockmen, construction

Eighteenth-century ships being unloaded of their colonial cargoes on London's Old Custom House Quay. Most of the goods imported into England from the American colonies were produced by slave labor.
Samuel Scott, "Old Custom House Quay" Collection. V&A IMAGES, THE VICTORIA AND ALBERT MUSEUM, LONDON.

workers, traders, shopkeepers, lawyers, clerks, factory workers, and officials of all ranks down to the humblest employees of the custom house. In the countryside surrounding Liverpool and elsewhere, capital acquired through slavery was invested in the new industrial methods of producing cotton textiles, the beginning of the Industrial Revolution.

THE POLITICS OF MERCANTILISM

Imperial officials argued that colonies existed solely for the benefit of the mother country. To ensure that the wealth generated by colonies benefited their own nation-state, imperialists created a system of regulations that became known as "**mercantilism.**" The essence of mercantilist policy was the political control of the economy by the state. The monarchy and Parliament established a uniform national monetary system, regulated wages, subsidized agriculture and manufacturing, and protected themselves from foreign competition by erecting tariff barriers. Britain also sought to organize and control colonial trade to the maximum advantage of its own shippers, merchants, manufacturers, and bureaucrats.

mercantilism Economic system whereby the government intervenes in the economy for the purpose of increasing national wealth.

MAP 4.3

Triangular Trade Across the Atlantic   The pattern of commerce among Europe, Africa, and the Americas became known as the "triangular trade." Sailors called the voyage of slave ships from Africa to America the "Middle Passage" because it formed the crucial middle section of this trading triangle.

HOW WERE Europe, Africa, and America linked together by commerce?

The mercantilists viewed the economy as a "zero-sum game," in which total economic gains were equal to total losses. The essence of the competition between states, the mercantilists argued, was the struggle to acquire and hoard the fixed amount of wealth that existed in the world.

BRITISH COLONIAL REGULATION

Acting on mercantilist principles, Parliament passed a series of Navigation Acts between 1651 and 1696, creating the legal and institutional structure of Britain's eighteenth-century colonial system. The acts defined the colonies as both suppliers of raw materials and as markets for English manufactured goods. Merchants from other nations were forbidden from doing business in the English colonies, and colonial commodities were required to be transported in English vessels.

The regulations specified a list of "enumerated commodities" that could be shipped to England only. Those included the products of the southern slave colonies (sugar, molasses, rum, tobacco, rice, and indigo), those of the northern Indian trade (furs, pelts, and skins), and those essential for supplying the shipping industry (pine masts, tar, pitch, resin, and turpentine). The bulk of these products was not destined for English consumption but was exported elsewhere at great profit.

England also placed limitations on colonial enterprises that might compete with those at home. A series of enactments—including the Wool Act of 1699, the Hat Act of 1732, and the Iron Act of 1750—forbade the manufacture of those products in the colonies. Moreover, colonial assemblies were forbidden to impose tariffs on English imports as a way to protect colonial industries. Banking was disallowed, local coinage prohibited, and the export of coin from England forbidden.

Between 1700 and 1760 the quantity of goods exported from the colonies to the mother country rose 165 percent, while imports from Britain to North America increased by more than 400 percent. In part because of the lax enforcement, but mostly because the system operated to the profit of colonial merchants, colonists complained very little about the operation of the mercantilist system before the 1760s. It seemed that everyone was getting rich off the labor of slaves—except the slaves, of course.

WARS FOR EMPIRE

During the 1720s and 1730s, Prime Minister Robert Walpole steered Great Britain away from war with other mercantilist powers. Earlier in the century, a war pitting Great Britain against Spain and France (known as the War of the Spanish Succession in Europe, **Queen Anne's War** in America) had ended in a significant British victory. In the Peace of Utrecht in 1713. France was forced to cede Acadia, Newfoundland, and Hudson Bay to Great Britain in exchange for guarantees of security for the French-speaking residents of those provinces. Spain was forced to open its American ports to British traders, who were also granted the exclusive right to supply slaves to the Spanish colonies.

Despite continuing tensions with Spain and France, Walpole saw considerable advantages in peace. For more than fifteen years Walpole prevailed over militant factions in the House of Commons that demanded complete elimination of Spanish competition in the Americas. But in 1739, at their urging, a one-eared sea captain by the name of Robert Jenkins testified about the indignities suffered by British merchant sailors at the hands of Spanish authorities in Caribbean ports. In a dramatic flourish, Jenkins produced a dried and withered ear, which he claimed the Spanish had cut from his head. The public outrage that followed forced Walpole to agree to a war of Caribbean conquest known as the War of Jenkins's Ear.

Walpole thought war was a mistake, and he was right. The only success of the war for the British came when the Georgia militia blocked a Spanish invasion from Florida in 1742. The war ended with no territorial gains on either side.

The war with Spain merged into a war with France that began in 1744. Known as **King George's War** in America (the War of the Austrian Succession in Europe), it began with a French invasion of their former colony of Acadia, which the British had renamed Nova Scotia. Indian and Canadian raids again devastated the border towns of New England and New York, and hundreds of British subjects were killed or captured. In return, New England forces attacked and conquered the great French fortress at Louisbourg. But Great Britain fared less well in the European fighting, and the war ended in stalemate with the return of all territory.

THE COLONIAL ECONOMY

Despite the resumption of warfare, the colonial economy continued to operate to the great benefit of planters, merchants, and white colonists in general. Southern slave owners made healthy profits on the sale of their commodities. Pennsylvania, New York, and New England, and increasingly the Chesapeake as well, produced grain, flour, meat, and dairy products. None of these was included in the list of **enumerated goods** and could be sold freely abroad. Most of this trade was carried in New England ships.

Queen Anne's War   American phase (1702–1713) of Europe's War of the Spanish Succession.

King George's War   The third Anglo-French war in North America (1744–1748), part of the European conflict known as the War of the Austrian Succession.

enumerated goods   Items produced in the colonies and enumerated in acts of Parliament that could be legally shipped from the colony of origin only to specified locations.

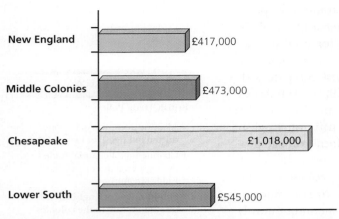

Figure 4.3 Value of Colonial Exports by Region, Annual Average, 1768–72
With tobacco, rice, grain, and indigo, the Chesapeake and Lower South accounted for nearly two-thirds of colonial exports in the years preceding the American Revolution.

Shipping, Maritime Trade and the Economic Development of Colonial America, James J. Shepherd, and Gary M. Walton, Eds. Copyright © 1972 Cambridge University Press. Reprinted with the permission of Cambridge University Press.

QUICK REVIEW

Colonial Exports

◆ Chesapeake colonies: tobacco.

◆ South Carolina: rice and indigo.

◆ Middle colonies: wheat.

HOW DID slavery shape southern colonial society?

◆◆◆ Read the Document

Whose History Is It?: The Living Legacy of Slavery at **www.myhistorylab.com**

The greatest benefits for the port cities of the North came from their commercial relationship to the slave colonies (see Figure 4.3). In addition to entering the slave trade itself, New England merchants began to make inroads into the export trade of the West Indian colonies. In the Caribbean northern merchants blatantly ignored mercantilist laws and British authorities made little effort to enforce them. In violation of Spanish, French, and Dutch regulations prohibiting foreign trade, New Englanders traded foodstuffs for sugar in foreign colonies. By 1750, more than sixty distilleries in Massachusetts were exporting more than 2 million gallons of rum, most of it produced from molasses obtained illegally. Because the restrictive rules and regulations enacted by Britain for its colonies were not enforced, the merchants and manufacturers of the port cities of the North prospered.

By the mid-eighteenth century, the Chesapeake and Lower South regions were major exporters of tobacco, rice, and indigo to Europe, and the middle colonies were major exporters of grain. The carrying trade in the products of slave labor made it possible for the northern and middle colonies to earn the income necessary to purchase British imports despite the lack of valuable products from their own regions. Gradually, the commercial economies of the Northeast and the South were becoming integrated. The port cities of the North became pivots in the expanding trade network linking slave plantations with Atlantic markets. This trade provided northern merchants with the capital that financed commercial growth and development in their cities and the surrounding countryside. Slavery thus contributed to the growth of a score of northern port cities, forming an indirect but essential part of their economies.

SLAVERY, PROSPERITY, AND FREEDOM

The prosperity of the eighteenth-century plantation economy thus improved the living conditions for the residents of northern cities as well as for a large segment of the white population of the South, providing them with the opportunity for a kind of freedom unknown in the previous century. The price of this prosperity and freedom, however, was the enslavement and exploitation of millions of Africans and African Americans.

THE SOCIAL STRUCTURE OF THE SLAVE COLONIES

Slavery produced a highly stratified class society. At the summit of power stood an elite of wealthy planters who held more than half the cultivated land and over 60 percent of the wealth. Although there was no formal colonial aristocracy—no royal recognition of social rank—the landed elite of the slave colonies sought to present itself as one. Binding themselves together through strategic marriage alliances and carefully crafted business dealings, they made up what one historian calls an "interlocking directorate."

The typical wealthy Virginia planter of the eighteenth century lived in a Tidewater county, owned several thousand acres of prime farmland and more than a hundred slaves, resided in a luxurious plantation mansion, and possessed an estate valued at more than £10,000. Elected to the House of Burgesses and forming the group from which the magistrates and counselors of the colony were chosen, these "first families of Virginia" constituted a self-perpetuating governing class. A similar elite ruled the Lower South, although wealthy landowners spent little time on their plantations. They lived instead in fashionable Charles Town, where they made up a close-knit group who controlled the colonial government.

A considerable distance separated this elite from typical southern landowners. About half the adult white males were small planters and farmers. But while the gap between rich and middling colonists grew larger during the eighteenth century, the prosperity of the plantation economy created generally favorable conditions for the landowning class as a whole. Slave ownership, for example, became widespread among this group during the eighteenth century. In Virginia at midcentury, 45 percent of heads of household held one to four slaves and even poorer farmers kept one or two.

Despite the prosperity that accompanied slavery, however, a substantial number of white colonists owned no land or slaves at all. Some rented land or worked as tenant farmers, some hired out as overseers or farm workers, and still others were indentured servants. Throughout the plantation region, landless men constituted about 40 percent of the population. A New England visitor found a "much greater disparity between the rich and poor in Virginia" than at home.

WHITE SKIN PRIVILEGE

But all the white colonists of eighteenth-century North America shared the privileged status of their color. In the early seventeenth century, there had been more diversity in views about race. For some, black skin was thought to be a sign of God's curse. "The blackness of the Negroes," one Englishman argued, "proceedeth of some natural infection." But not everyone shared those views. "I can't think there is any intrinsic value in one colour more than another," another Englishman remarked, "nor that white is better than black, only we think it so because we are so."

As slavery became increasingly important, however, Virginia officials took considerable care to create legal distinctions between the status of colonists and that of Africans. Beginning in 1670, free Africans were prohibited from owning Christian servants. Ten years later, another law declared that any African, free or slave, who struck a Christian would receive thirty lashes on his bare back. One of the most important measures was designed to suppress intimate interracial contacts between white servants and enslaved Africans. A 1691 act established severe penalties for interracial sexual relationships.

Such penalties were rarely applied to masters who had sexual relations with their slave women and relationships between free whites and enslaved blacks produced a large mixed-ancestry group known as mulattoes. The majority of them were slaves. A minority, the children of European women and African men, were free. According to a Maryland census of 1755, more than 60 percent of the mulattoes of that colony were slaves. But mulattoes also made up three-quarters of the small free African American population. This group, numbering about 4,000 in the 1770s, was denied the right to vote, to hold office, or to testify in court—all on the basis of racial background. Denied the status of citizenship enjoyed by even the poorest white men, free blacks were an outcast group who raised the status of white colonials by contrast. Racial distinctions were a constant reminder of the freedom of white colonists and the debasement of all blacks, slave or free.

RUN away from the subscriber in *Albemarle*, a Mulatto slave called *Sandy*, about 35 years of age, his stature is rather low, inclining to corpulence, and his complexion light; he is a shoemaker by trade, in which he uses his left hand principally, can do coarse carpenters work, and is something of a horse jockey; he is greatly addicted to drink, and when drunk is insolent and disorderly, in his conversation he swears much, and in his behaviour is artful and knavish. He took with him a white horse, much scarred with traces, of which it is expected he will endeavour to dispose; he also carried his shoemakers tools, and will probably endeavour to get employment that way. Whoever conveys the said slave to me, in *Albemarle*, shall have 40 s. reward, if taken up within the county, 4 l. if elsewhere within the colony, and 10 l. if in any other colony. from

THOMAS JEFFERSON.

Thomas Jefferson placed this advertisement in the *Virginia Gazette* on September 14, 1769. Americans need to seriously consider the historical relationship between the prosperity and freedom of white people and the oppression and exploitation of Africans and African Americans.

CHRONOLOGY

1441	African slaves first brought to Portugal	**1712**	Slave uprising in New York City
1619	First Africans brought to Virginia	**1713**	Peace of Utrecht
1655	English seize Jamaica	**1721–48**	Robert Walpole leads British cabinet
1662	Virginia law makes slavery hereditary	**1729**	Natchez Rebellion in French Louisiana
1672	Royal African Company organized	**1739**	Stono Rebellion in South Carolina
1691	Virginia prohibits interracial sexual contact	**1739–43**	War of Jenkins's Ear
1698	Britain opens the slave trade to all its merchants	**1741**	Africans executed in New York for conspiracy
1699	Spanish declare Florida a refuge for escaped slaves	**1744–48**	King George's War
1702	South Carolinians burn St. Augustine	**1752**	Georgia officially opened to slavery
1705	Virginia Slave Code established	**1770s**	Peak period of the English colonies' slave trade
1706	French and Spanish navies bombard Charles Town	**1808**	Importation of slaves into the United States ends
1710	English capture Port Royal in Acadia		

CONCLUSION

During the eighteenth century, hundreds of thousands of Africans were kidnapped from their homes, marched to the African coast, and packed into ships for up to three months before arriving in British North America. They provided the labor that made colonialism profitable. Southern planters, northern merchants, and especially British traders and capitalists benefited greatly from the commerce in slave-produced crops. That prosperity trickled down to the ordinary white colonists of British North America. Mercantilism was a system designed to channel colonial wealth produced by slaves to the nation-state, but as long as profits remained high, the British tended to wink at colonists' violations of mercantilist regulations. In short, slavery was fundamental to the operation of the British empire in North America.

REVIEW QUESTIONS

1. Trace the development of the system of slavery and discuss the way it became entrenched in the Americas.

2. Describe the effects of the slave trade both on enslaved Africans and on the economic and political life of Africa.

3. Describe the process of acculturation involved in becoming an African American. In what ways did slaves "Africanize" the South?

4. Explain the connection between the institution of slavery and the building of a commercial empire.

5. In what ways did colonial policy encourage the growth of racism?

KEY TERMS

Enumerated goods (p. 91)

The Great Awakening (p. 85)

King George's War (p. 91)

Mercantilism (p. 89)

PEARSON
myhistorylab Connections

Reinforce what you learned in this chapter by studying the many documents, images, maps, review tools, and videos available at www.myhistorylab.com.

Read and Review

✓●—Study and Review Chapter 4

●●●—Read the Document

Alexander Falconbridge, The African Slave Trade (1788)

Olaudah Equiano, The Middle Passage (1788)

Of the Servants and Slaves in Virginia (1705)

James Oglethorpe, Establishing the Colony of Georgia (1733)

Runaway Notices from the South Carolina Gazette (1732 and 1737)

James Oglethorpe, The Stono Rebellion (1739)

👁—See the Map *African Slave Trade, 1500–1870*

((●—Hear the Audio

On Being Brought from Africa to America

"Ghana: Ewe-Atsiagbekor" from Roots of Black Music in America

Research and Explore

●●●—Read the Document

Exploring America: Racism in American History

Profiles
 Olaudah Equiano
 John Woolman

Whose History Is It?: The Living Legacy of Slavery

History Bookshelf: *Olaudah Equiano, The Interesting Narrative of the Life of Olaudah Equiano (1791)*

Watson and the Shark: Reading the Representation of Race

((●—Hear the Audio

"Ghana: Ewe-Atsiagbekor" from Roots of Black Music in America

Phillis Wheatley, On Being Brought from Africa to America

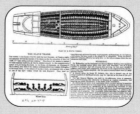

((●—**Hear the Audio**

Hear the audio files for Chapter 4 at
www.myhistorylab.com.

*Mr. Lawrence, Be pleased to send me
a geenteel sute of Cloaths made of superfine
broad Cloth handsomely chosen...*

—*George Washington, April, 26, 1763*

The Old State House, historic Philadelphia, Pennsylvania in the
late 1700s. Hand colored engraving. North Wind Pictures.

5

The Cultures of Colonial North America

1700–1780

(((●─[Hear the Audio

Hear the audio files for Chapter 5 at **www.myhistorylab.com**.

WHAT EXPLAINS the regional diversity of colonial North America?

HOW DID colonial and European social and political patterns differ?

WHAT WERE the most important cultural trends in eighteenth-century British North America?

AMERICAN COMMUNITIES

The Revival of Religion and Community in Northampton

IN 1734 JONATHAN EDWARDS, MINISTER OF THE PURITAN CHURCH IN Northampton, a rural town on the Connecticut River in western Massachusetts, rose before his congregation and began to preach. His words were frightening: "God will crush you under his feet without mercy, He will crush out your blood and make it fly, and it shall be sprinkled on His garments." Such torments would continue for "millions of millions of ages," and there could be no hope of relief from hell's fires.

"Before the sermon was done," one Northampton parishioner later recalled, "there was a great moaning and crying through the whole house—What shall I do to be saved?—I am going to Hell!—Oh what shall I do for Christ?" Sarah Edwards, the minister's wife, lost "all ability to stand or speak," sometimes jerking involuntarily. Religious fervor swept through the community, and church membership increased. A few years later an even greater revival known as the Great Awakening swept through all the colonies and plunged Northampton into turmoil once again. Important underlying issues prepared the ground for these religious revivals. They reflected the tensions that had arisen in the maturing communities of the colonies in which frontier opportunity was giving way to class inequity.

Founded in 1654 on the site of an Algonquian village, Northampton had grown from the original 50 households to more than 200 by the time of the 1734 revival. The last of the community's land had been parceled out to its residents. With the French and their Indian allies barring movement northward, and the colony of New York to the west, there was little opportunity for young men. Meanwhile, a small elite of well-to-do families controlled a disproportionately large share of local real estate. From their ranks came the majority of the officials of local and county government, as well as the ministers and elders of the Puritan congregations.

By the time Edwards became pastor in 1729, the authority and influence of the church had declined greatly from the heyday of Puritan power in the seventeenth century. The congregation adopted rules allowing church membership without evidence of a conversion experience. Some families simply fell away. The congregation built a new meetinghouse, scrapping the old seating plan in which people were sorted by age and sex in favor of a new one ranking families according to wealth. It was an important symbol of change. The Northampton community, Edwards believed, had been divided into "two parties," the rich and the envious.

Many of the town's young people faced a bleak future. The tight supply of real estate meant that most couples were forced to postpone marriage until they were in their late twenties. In the meantime they continued to live with their parents, and there were growing discipline problems in Northampton homes. Restless young people of both sexes began to meet together at nightly "frolics." This group became Edwards's special constituency. The revival of religious enthusiasm began during special services he directed at them, but it was the same everywhere throughout the British colonies. Young people in their early twenties played the most important role in the movement to restore religious enthusiasm. Edwards and other revival preachers called for a return to the Calvinist traditions of the Puritan faith, criticizing what they saw as the growing materialism, joining the rising generation in questioning the order of the world into which they had been born.

The disaffection of young people with the social and economic conditions of the mid-eighteenth century created the conditions for the Great Awakening, but the revival remained a religious event. The social order in Northampton was challenged, but it remained intact. The town's elite had always been uncomfortable with the message Edwards preached, and when the fervor died down, as it inevitably did, they succeeded in voting him out. The turmoil in Northampton subsided, yet the tensions remained.

Rising tensions were typical in many of the colonial communities of British North America. Things went on much as they had in the French and Spanish colonies. But in British colonial communities a growing population meant narrowing opportunities for the ownership of local land, creating strong pressure for expansion into Indian homelands. Expanding economies led to increasing class inequality. Meanwhile, new secular and rationalist ways of thinking challenged traditional values. Simmering social conflict set the stage for religious and cultural turmoil.

Northampton, MA

NORTH AMERICAN REGIONS

American history too often is written as if only the British colonists really mattered. It is an error residents of the British colonies could not afford to make. Most critically, there was Indian America. In the mid-eighteenth century Indian peoples retained their majority in North America (see Table 5.1). From the fringes of colonial societies to the native heart of the continent, thousands of native communities, despite being deeply affected by the spread of colonial cultures, remained firmly in control of their homelands.

Neither could British colonists afford to ignore their colonial competitors. North and west of the English-speaking enclaves along the Atlantic coast, French-speaking communities were clustered along the St. Lawrence and scattered down the Mississippi to the Gulf of Mexico. South and west, isolated Spanish-speaking communities of the northern Spanish borderlands stretched from Florida to Texas and on to California. There were impressive similarities among these colonial communities, representing a continuation in the New World of Old World traditions and beliefs, customs, and institutions. But there was also a general pattern of European adaptation to American conditions (see Map 5.1).

WHAT EXPLAINS the regional diversity of colonial North America?

MAP 5.1

Regions in Eighteenth-Century North America   By the middle of the eighteenth century, European colonists had established a number of distinctive colonial regions in North America. The northern periphery of New Spain, the oldest and most prosperous European colony, stretched from Baja California to eastern Texas, then jumped to the settlements on the northern end of the Florida peninsula; cattle ranching was the dominant way of life in this thinly populated region. New France was like a great crescent, extending from the plantation communities along the Mississippi near New Orleans to the French colonial communities along the St. Lawrence; in between were isolated settlements and forts connected only by the extensive French trading network.

WHAT STEPS did Spain take to reinforce and expand its holdings in North America in the eighteenth century?

TABLE 5.1

Population of North America in 1750

Region	Population
New France	70,000
New England	400,000
New York	100,000
Pennsylvania	230,000
Chesapeake	390,000
Lower South	100,000
Backcountry	100,000
Northern New Spain	20,000
Indian America	1,500,000
TOTAL	2,910,000

Exploring America: *America and the Horse* at **www.myhistorylab.com**

A portrait of the Delaware chief Tishcohan by Gustavus Hesselius, painted in 1735. In his purse of chipmunk hide is a clay pipe, a common item of the Indian trade. Tishcohan was one of the Delaware leaders forced by Pennsylvania authorities into signing a fraudulent land deal that reversed that colony's history of fair dealing with Indians over land. He moved west to the Ohio River as settlers poured into his former homeland.

Gustavus Hesselius, *Tishcohan*, Native American Portrait, 1735. Courtesy of the Historical Society of Pennsylvania Collection, Atwater Kent Museum of Philadelphia.

INDIAN AMERICA

After two centuries of European colonization, Indian peoples had adapted and changed. They incorporated firearms and metal tools and learned to build their homes of logs. They participated enthusiastically in the fur trade. But in the process they became dependent on European commerce. "The clothes we wear, we cannot make ourselves, they are made for us," a Cherokee chief lamented. "We cannot make our guns. Every necessary thing in life we must have from the White People."

Yet Indian peoples continued to assert a proud independence and demonstrated considerable skill in playing colonial powers against each other. In 1701 the Iroquois, allies of the British, signed a treaty of neutrality with the French. Exploiting the vulnerabilities of these two powers, the Iroquois Confederacy became a major power broker during the first half of the eighteenth century. In the Lower South native peoples found similar room to maneuver between the competing interests of Britain, France, and Spain.

But native leaders confronted enormous difficulties. In the eastern portion of the continent the preeminent concern was the tremendous growth of the population in the British colonies and especially the movement of settlers westward. Meanwhile, Indian communities continued to suffer from long-term population decline as the result of epidemic Old World diseases. Historical demographers estimate that from a high of 7 to 10 million north of Mexico in 1500, the native population had fallen to around a million by 1800.

Other changes offered opportunity. By the early eighteenth century, Indians on the southern fringe of the Great Plains had acquired horses from Spanish colonists in New Mexico (see Map 5.2). Horses enabled Indian hunters to exploit the buffalo herds much more efficiently, and on the basis of this more productive economy peoples like the Comanches, Cheyennes, and Sioux built distinctive and elaborate nomadic cultures. Great numbers of Indian peoples moved onto the plains during the eighteenth century, pulled by this new way of life and pushed by colonial invasions and disruptions radiating southwest from Canada and north from the Spanish borderlands. The invention of nomadic Plains Indian culture was another of the dramatic cultural innovations of the eighteenth century.

THE SPANISH BORDERLANDS

In the mid-eighteenth century the region now known as the Sunbelt formed the periphery of the largest and most prosperous European colony on the North American continent, the viceroyalty of New Spain, with a population of approximately 1 million Spanish-speaking inhabitants and 2 million Indians. New Spain's northern provinces of Florida, Texas, New Mexico, and California, however, were far removed from New Spain's capital, Mexico City. Officials who oversaw these colonies thought of them as buffer zones, protecting New Spain from the expanding empires of Spain's rivals. Compared to the dynamic changes going on in the English colonies, society in the Spanish borderland was relatively static.

In Florida fierce fighting with the British and their Indian allies had reduced the Spanish presence to little more than the forts of St. Augustine on the Atlantic and Pensacola on the Gulf of Mexico, each surrounded by small colonized territories populated with the families of Spanish troops. In their weakened condition, the Spanish had no choice but to establish cooperative relations with the Creek and Seminole Indians who dominated the region, as well as hundreds of African American runaways who fled to Florida. In 1750 Florida included a growing mestizo population and a considerable number of free African Americans and Hispanicized Indians from the old missions.

Nearly 2,000 miles to the west, New Mexico was similarly isolated from the mainstream of New Spain. In 1750 New Mexico included some 20,000 Pueblo Indians (their numbers greatly reduced by disease) and perhaps 10,000 mestizo colonists. The prosperity of these colonists, who supported themselves with subsistence agriculture, was severely limited by a restrictive colonial economic policy that required them to exchange their wool, pottery, and buffalo hides for imported goods at unfavorable rates. But unlike the population of Florida, that of colonial New Mexico was gradually expanding, as settlers left the original colonial outposts along the upper Rio Grande to follow the valleys and streams leading north and east.

Concerned about the expansion of other colonial empires, the Spanish founded several new northern outposts in the eighteenth century. French activity in the Mississippi Valley prompted authorities to establish a number of military posts or presidios on the fringes of Louisiana and in 1716 to begin the construction of a string of Franciscan missions among the Indian peoples of Texas. By 1750 the settlement of San Antonio had become the center of a developing frontier province known as Tejas (Texas). New colonial outposts were also founded west of New Mexico in what is today southern Arizona.

In 1769, acting on rumors of Russian expansion in the north Pacific (for a discussion of Russian America, see Chapter 9), officials in Mexico City ordered Gaspar de Portolá, governor of what is today Baja California, to establish a Spanish presence along the Pacific coast to the north. With Portolá were Franciscan missionaries led by Junípero Serra, president of the missions in Baja. Over the next fifty years the number of California settlements grew to include twenty-one missions and a half-dozen presidios and pueblos (towns).

The Spanish plan for California called for converting the natives to Catholicism, subjecting them to the rule of the crown, and putting them to work raising the subsistence necessary for a small civil and military establishment that would hold the province against colonial rivals. The first contacts between Franciscans and natives were not

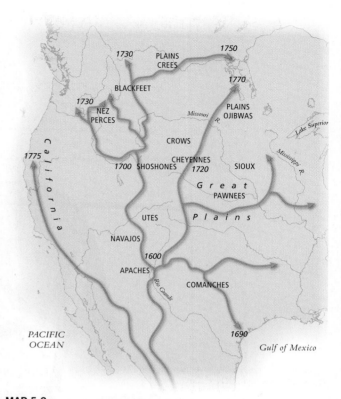

MAP 5.2

Growing Use of the Horse by Plains Indians   In the seventeenth and eighteenth centuries, Spanish settlers introduced horses into their New Mexican colony. Through trading and raiding, horses spread northward in streams both west and east of the Rocky Mountains. The horse, whose genetic ancestor had been native to the American continent in pre-Archaic times, offered the Indian peoples of the Great Plains the opportunity to create a distinctive hunting and warrior culture.

HOW DID the spread of the horse transform Indian lifestyles?

A mounted Soldado de Cuera (Leather-Coated Soldier), a watercolor by Ramón de Murillo, c. 1803. Thick leather coats offered protection from Indian arrows for the cavalry posted to the northern frontiers of eighteenth-century New Spain.

encouraging, but numerous native families were attracted by offerings of food and clothing, by new tools and crafts, and by fascination with the spiritual power of the newcomers. Gradually the Spanish built a flourishing local economy based on irrigated farming and livestock raising.

Indians were not forced to join the missions, but once they did so they were not permitted to leave. The Franciscan missionaries resorted to cruel and sometimes violent means of controlling their Indian subjects, including shackles, solitary confinement, and whipping posts. Resistance developed early. In 1775, the natives at San Diego rose up and killed several priests, and over the years several other missions experienced similar revolts. But Spanish soldiers suppressed the uprisings. Another form of protest was flight. Soldiers hunted down the runaways and brought many back. Aggressive tribes in the hills and deserts, however, often proved even more threatening than the Spanish, so many Indians remained at the missions despite the harsh discipline. Overwork, inadequate nutrition, overcrowding, poor sanitation, and epidemic disease contributed to death rates that exceeded birthrates. During the period of the mission system, the native population of coastal California fell by 74 percent.

Throughout the Spanish borderlands the Catholic Church played a dominant role in community life. Religion was no private affair but a deadly serious business dividing nations into warring camps, and the Spanish considered themselves the special protectors of the traditions of Rome. There was no tradition of religious dissent. Certain of the truth of their "right and perfect way," the Spanish could see no reason for tolerating the errors of others.

THE FRENCH CRESCENT

In France, as in Spain, church and state were closely interwoven. During the seventeenth century the chief ministers to the French monarchy, Cardinal Richelieu and his successor Cardinal Mazarin, laid out a fundamentally Catholic imperial policy. In 1674 church and state collaborated in establishing the bishopric of Québec, which founded local seminaries, oversaw the appointment and review of priests, and laid the foundation of the resolutely Catholic culture of New France. Jesuit missionaries, meanwhile, continued to carry Catholicism deep into the continent.

The French sent few colonists to New France, but by natural increase the population rose from fewer than 15,000 in 1700 to more than 70,000 by 1750. The French used their trade and alliance network to establish colonies, military posts, and settlements that extended in a great crescent from the mouth of the St. Lawrence River southwest through the Great Lakes, then down the Mississippi River to the Gulf of Mexico (see Map 5.3). After the loss in 1713 of the maritime colony of Acadia to the British (see Chapter 4), French authorities constructed the great port and fortress of Louisbourg on Ile Royale (Cape Breton Island) to guard the northern approach to New France. The southern approach was protected by French troops at the port of New Orleans in Louisiana. Between these two points, the French laid a thin colonial veneer, the beginning of what they planned as a great commercial empire that would confine the Protestant British to the Atlantic coastline.

At the heart of the French empire in North America were the communities of farmers or habitants that stretched along the banks of the St. Lawrence between the provincial capital of Québec and the fur trade center of Montreal. There were also farming communities in the Illinois country, supplying wheat to sugar plantations in Louisiana. By the 1750s, those plantations, extending along the Mississippi from Natchez and Baton Rouge to New Orleans, had become the most profitable French enterprise in North America.

Among the most distinctive French stamps on the North American landscape were the "long lots" stretching back from the rivers, providing each settler a share of good bottomland to farm and frontage on the waterways, the "interstate highway system" of the French Crescent. Long lots were laid out along the Mississippi River in Louisiana

The Church of San Xavier del Bac, constructed in the late eighteenth century, is located a few miles south of the city of Tucson, where Jesuit Father Eusebio Kino founded a mission among the Pima Indians in 1700. Known as the White Dove of the Desert, it is acclaimed as the most striking example of Spanish colonial architecture in the United States.

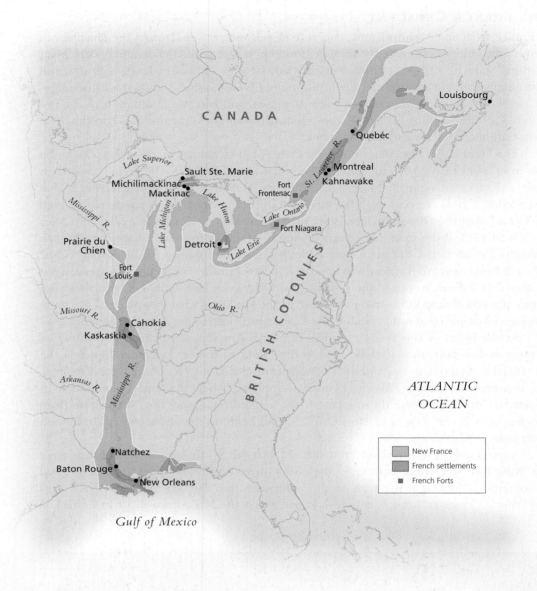

MAP 5.3

The French Crescent The French empire in North America was based on a series of alliances and trade relations with Indian nations linking a great crescent of colonies, settlements, and outposts that extended from the mouth of the St. Lawrence River, through the Great Lakes, and down the Mississippi River to the Gulf of Mexico. In 1713, Acadia was ceded to the British, but the French established the fortress of Louisbourg to anchor the eastern end of the crescent.

WHAT GEOGRAPHIC rationale might have been behind French decisions to convert native peoples to Catholic Christianity?

and Illinois and at the strategic passages of the Great Lakes. Detroit, the most important of those, was a stockaded town with a military garrison, a small administrative center, several stores, a Catholic church, and 100 households of métis (French for mestizo) families. Farmers worked the land along the Detroit River, not far from communities inhabited by several thousand Indians from the Ottawa, Potawatomi, and Huron tribes.

Communities of this sort, combining both European and native American elements, were in the tradition of the inclusive frontier. Detroit looked like "an old French village," said one observer, except that its houses were "mostly covered with bark," in Indian style. Detroit had much of the character of a mixed community. Family and kinship were cast in the Indian pattern, yet the people focused their activities on commerce and overwhelmingly identified themselves as Catholics.

NEW ENGLAND

Just as New Spain and New France had their official church, so too did the inhabitants of New England. Rather than the centralized authority of the Catholic hierarchy, however, communities in New England (except Rhode Island) were governed by Puritan congregations. Adult male church members constituted the freemen of the town, so there was very little distinction between religious and secular authority. At the town meeting the freemen chose their minister, voted on his salary, and elected local men to offices ranging from town clerk to animal warden.

The Puritan tradition was a curious mix of freedom and repression. Although local communities had considerable autonomy, they were tightly bound by the religious restrictions. Puritan authorities banned and exiled Anglicans, Baptists, Quakers, and other dissidents. Quakers who returned to Massachusetts to preach their pacifist faith were branded with "H" for heretic, had their tongues bored with hot irons, or had their ears cut off. Between 1659 and 1661 four Quakers were executed for proselytizing.

Soon after the last of these executions King Charles II, newly placed on the throne, ordered a stop to religious persecution in Massachusetts. Several years later Roger Williams, whose Rhode Island colony had no established religion, made one of the first formal arguments for religious toleration. "Forced worship," Williams wrote in 1670, "stinks in God's nostrils." The new climate of opinion was best expressed by English political philosopher John Locke in "A Letter Concerning Tolerance," written in 1689. Churches were voluntary societies, Locke argued, and could gain genuine converts only through persuasion. The state, he asserted, had no legitimate concern with religious belief. That same year Parliament passed the **Act of Toleration**, granting religious freedom to Protestant dissenters (but not to Catholics). In 1700, under pressure from English authorities, Massachusetts and Connecticut reluctantly permitted other Protestant denominations to meet openly, although Puritan congregations continued to be supported officially through taxation.

By then New Englanders were less concerned with religious conformity than with the problem of land. As population grew, groups of residents left established towns, "hiving off" to form new congregations and towns elsewhere. By the 1730s, Puritan communities had taken up most of the available land of Massachusetts, Connecticut, and Rhode Island, leaving only a few isolated reservations for small communities of Pequots, Narragansetts, and Wampanoags. Northern Algonquians allied with the French in Québec maintained a defensive barrier that prevented expansion northward. New England had reached the limit of its land supply.

THE MIDDLE COLONIES

In striking contrast to the ethnically homogeneous colonies of Connecticut and Massachusetts, populated almost entirely by English families, New York featured one of the most ethnically diverse populations on the continent. At midcentury, society along the lower Hudson River, including the counties in northern New Jersey, was a veritable

The persistence of French colonial long lots in the pattern of modern landholding is clear in this enhanced satellite photograph of the Mississippi River near New Orleans. Long lots, the characteristic form of property holding in New France, were designed to offer as many settlers as possible a share of good bottomland as well as a frontage on the waterways, which served as the basic transportation network.

Act of Toleration Act passed in 1661 by King Charles II ordering a stop to religious persecution in Massachusetts.

This view of the Philadelphia waterfront, painted about 1720, conveys the impression of a city firmly anchored to maritime commerce. The long, narrow canvas was probably intended for display over the mantel of a public room.

Peter Cooper, *The South East Prospect of the City of Philadelphia*, ca. 1720. The Library Company of Philadelphia.

mosaic of ethnic communities, including the Dutch of Flatbush, the Huguenots of New Rochelle, the Flemish of Bergen, and the Scots of Perth Amboy. African Americans, both slave and free, constituted more than 15 percent of the population of the lower Hudson. Puritan, Baptist, Quaker, and Catholic congregations worshiped without legal hindrance, and in New York City, several hundred Jewish families built North America's first synagogue in 1730.

Although New York City grew by leaps and bounds in the eighteenth century, the colony as a whole was less attractive to immigrants than neighboring Pennsylvania. The New York elite who owned the rich lands and great manors along the upper Hudson chose to rent to tenants rather than to sell, but Pennsylvania's proprietors were willing to sell land to anyone who could pay the modest prices. The region along the Delaware River—encompassing not only Pennsylvania but New Jersey, Delaware, and the northern portion of Maryland—grew more dramatically than any other in North America during the eighteenth century. Immigration played the dominant role in achieving the astonishing annual growth rate of nearly 4 percent. Farmers and merchants were soon exporting abundant produce through the prosperous port at Philadelphia.

The Quakers quickly became a minority, but unlike the Puritans they were generally comfortable with religious and ethnic pluralism. Many of the founders of the Society of Friends had been imprisoned for their beliefs in pre-Restoration England, and they were determined to prevent a repetition of this injustice in their own province. This was a perspective well suited to the ethnically and religiously diverse population of the colony.

The institutions of government were another pillar of community organization. Colonial officials appointed justices of the peace who provided judicial authority for the countryside. Property-owning farmers chose their own local officials. Country communities were bound together by kinship bonds as well as economic relations between neighbors. These communities were more loosely bound than those of New England. Rates of mobility were considerably higher, with about half the population moving on during any given decade. Because land was sold in individual lots rather than in communal parcels, farmers tended to disperse themselves over the open countryside. The individual settlement pattern of Pennsylvania would provide the basic model for American expansion across the continent.

THE BACKCOUNTRY

By 1750 Pennsylvania's exploding population had pushed beyond the first range of the Appalachian highlands (see Map 5.4). Settlers moved southwest, through western Maryland and down the valley of the Shenandoah River into western Virginia. Although they hoped to become commercial farmers, these families began more modestly, planting Indian corn and raising hogs, hunting in the woods for meat and furs, and building log cabins (see Seeing History).

The movement into the Pennsylvania and Virginia backcountry that began during the 1720s was the first of the great pioneer treks that would take white pioneers into the continental interior. Many, perhaps most, of these pioneers held no legal title to the lands they occupied. To the Delawares and Shawnees, who had been pushed into the interior, or the Cherokees, who occupied the Appalachian highlands to the south, these settlers presented a new and deadly threat. Rising fears and resentments over this expanding population triggered much eighteenth-century violence.

THE SOUTH

The Chesapeake and the Lower South were triracial societies, with intermingled communities of white colonists and black slaves, along with substantial Indian communities living on the fringes of colonial settlement. Much of the population growth of the region resulted from the forced migration of enslaved Africans, who by 1750 made up 40 percent of the population. Specializing in rice, tobacco, and other commercial crops, these colonies were overwhelmingly rural. Farms and plantations were dispersed across the countryside, and villages or towns were few.

English authorities established the Church of England as the state religion in the Chesapeake colonies. Residents paid taxes to support the church and were required to attend services. Yet the Anglican establishment was internally weak. It maintained neither a colonial bishop nor local institutions for training clergy.

Along the rice coast, the dominant social institution was the large plantation. Rice cultivation required heavy capital investment. Consequently, only men of means could undertake it. By midcentury established rice plantations typically were dominated by a large main house, generally located on a spot of high ground overlooking the fields. Nearby, but a world apart, were the rough wooden cabins that were the slave quarters.

Because tobacco, unlike rice, could be grown profitably in small plots, the Chesapeake included a greater variety of farmers and a correspondingly diverse landscape. The poorest farmers lived in wooden cabins little better than the shacks of the slaves. More prosperous farm families lived with two or three slaves in houses that nevertheless were considerably smaller than the substantial homes of New England.

Compared to the Lower South, where there was almost no community life outside the plantation, the Chesapeake boasted well-developed neighborhoods constructed from kinship networks and economic connections. The most important community institution was the county court, which held both executive and judicial power. On court day white people of all ranks held a great gathering that included public business, horse racing, and perhaps a barbecue. The gentleman justices of the county, appointed by the governor, included the heads of the elite planter families. These men in turn selected the grand jury, composed of substantial freeholders. One of the most significant bonding forces in this free white population was a growing sense of racial solidarity in response to the increasing proportion of African slaves dispersed throughout the neighborhoods.

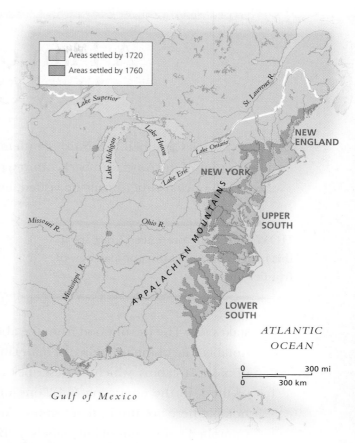

MAP 5.4

Spread of Settlement: Movement into the Backcountry, 1720–60   The spread of settlement from 1720 to 1760 shows the movement of population into the backcountry during the midcentury.

HOW DID the movement into the backcountry affect the relations among colonists, Indians, and English authorities?

A Plan of an American New Cleared Farm

Patrick Campbell, a Scottish gentleman traveler, included this delightful plate in the account of his tour of the American backcountry, published in 1793. The illustration provides a composite view of the raw frontier farms he visited, entirely typical of the eighteenth century. Note the way the pioneers hacked out their farms from the forest, leaving stumps standing in the fields. See how they fenced their fields to keep out livestock, which were allowed to forage freely. The engraving illustrates four different types of fencing: plain log (marked 4), worm fence made of split poles (5), post-and-rail (6), and Virginia rail fence of crossed stakes (7). The use of wood from the abundant forest was an essential economic strategy. Campbell was notably free of the prejudice of many British visitors to the frontier, but he could not disguise his scorn of pioneer cabins, which he described as "miserable little hovels covered with bark." He included one of them in the engraving (14), one of the first illustrations of a log cabin to appear in print. Also notable here are the Indian canoes, one poled by a man, the other paddled by two women with what Campbell's note mistakenly labels a "Babose." Campbell made the entire trip with his own hunting dog, seen in the front of the canoe on the left. Note also the wonderful little "Indian dog" (15). ■

HOW DOES the presence of Indians in this image contradict the popular view of frontier life?

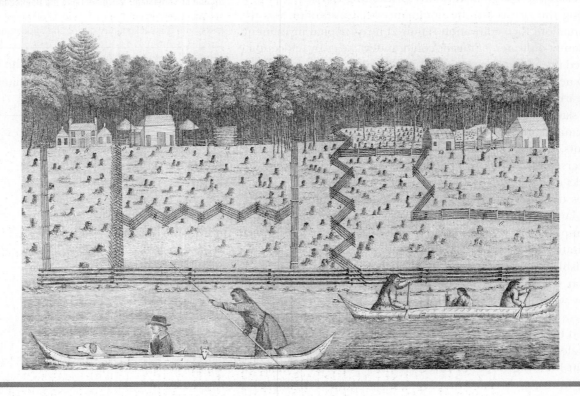

SOCIAL AND POLITICAL PATTERNS

Despite important similarities among the colonial regions of North America, during the eighteenth century the trajectory of the British colonies began to diverge sharply from that of the French and Spanish. Immigration, economic growth, and provincial political struggles all pushed British colonists in a radically new direction.

HOW DID colonial and European social and political patterns differ?

THE PERSISTENCE OF TRADITIONAL CULTURE IN THE NEW WORLD

In each of the regional North American societies, family and kinship, the church, and the local community were the most significant factors in everyday life. In this regard, Northampton was typical of settlement communities all over the continent. Everywhere colonists tended to live much as people had lived in European homeland communities at the time the colonies were settled. Nostalgia for Europe helped to fix a conservative colonial attitude toward culture.

These were oral cultures, depending on the transmission of information by the spoken rather than the printed word. North American colonial folk cultures, traditional and suspicious of change, preserved an essentially medieval worldview. The rhythms of life were regulated by the hours of sunlight and the seasons of the year. They farmed with simple tools, and drought, flood, or pestilence might quickly sweep away their efforts. Experience told them that the natural world imposed limitations within which men and women had to learn to live.

These were also communal cultures. In Quebéc, villagers worked side by side to repair the roads. In New Mexico they collectively maintained the irrigation ditches. In New England they gathered in town meetings to decide the dates when common fields were to be plowed, sowed, and harvested. For most North American colonists of the mid-eighteenth century, the community was more important than the individual.

Most colonists continued the traditional European occupation of working the land. Commercial agriculture was practiced on slave plantations, of course. And it also developed in some areas of the northern colonies, such as fertile southeastern Pennsylvania—which became known as the breadbasket of North America—and in the rural districts surrounding colonial cities. The majority of North American farmers, however, grew crops and raised livestock for their own needs or for local barter, and communities were largely self-sufficient. For most colonial farmers, the primary goal was ownership of land and the assurance that children and descendants would be able to settle on lands nearby.

Colonial cities, by contrast, were centers of commerce. Artisans and craftsmen worked at their trades full time, organizing themselves according to the European craft system. A young man who wished to pursue a trade served several years as an apprentice, working in exchange for learning the skills and secrets of the craft. After completing his apprenticeship, the young craftsman sought employment in a shop, often necessitating his migration to some other area, thus becoming a "journeyman." Most craftsmen remained at the journeyman level for the whole of their careers. But by building a good name and carefully saving, a journeyman hoped to become a master craftsman, opening his own shop and employing journeymen and apprentices of his own.

There were few opportunities for women outside the household. By law, husbands held managerial rights over family property, but widows received support in the form of a one-third lifetime interest, known as "dower," in a deceased husband's real estate (the rest of the estate being divided among the heirs). In certain occupations, such as printing (which had a tradition of employing women), widows succeeded their husbands in business.

Read the **Document**

An Older Businessman Advises a Young One (1748) at **www.myhistorylab.com**

QUICK REVIEW

Key Aspects of Early Colonial Culture

♦ Family and kinship.

♦ Church and religion.

♦ Local community.

A spinner and potter from *The Book of Trades*, an eighteenth-century British survey of the crafts practiced in colonial America. In colonial cities, artisans organized themselves into the traditional European craft system with apprentices, journeymen, and masters. There were few opportunities for the employment of women outside the household, but women sometimes earned income by establishing sidelines as mid-wives or spinners.

THE FRONTIER HERITAGE

The colonial societies of eighteenth-century North America also shared a set of assumptions originating in their common frontier heritage. European colonists came from Old World societies in which land was scarce and monopolized by property-owning elites. They settled in a continent where, for the most part, land was abundant and cheap. The widespread and general expectation of property ownership was the most important cultural distinction between North America and Europe.

This expectation led to rising popular demands in all the colonial regions of the continent that land be taken from the Indian inhabitants and opened to colonial settlement. The majority of colonists—whether British, Spanish, or French—endorsed the violence directed against Indian peoples as an essential aspect of colonial life. This attitude was as true of inclusive as exclusive societies, with the difference that in the former, native peoples were incorporated into colonial society, while in the latter, tribes were pushed from the frontier.

American historians once tied the existence of this "free land" directly to the development of democracy. But the frontier heritage encouraged the popular acceptance of forced labor, a system that was anything but democratic. Labor was the key to prosperity, and it was in short supply throughout the colonies. In a land where free men and women could work for themselves on their own plot of ground, there was little incentive to work for wages. The use of forced labor was one of the few ways a landowner could secure an agricultural workforce.

POPULATION GROWTH AND IMMIGRATION

All the colonial regions of North America experienced unprecedented growth in the eighteenth century. In 1700, there were 290,000 colonists north of Mexico; fifty years later they had grown to approximately 1.3 million, an average annual growth rate of about 3 percent. Preindustrial societies typically grew at rates of less than 1 percent per year, approximately the pace of Europe's expansion in the eighteenth century.

High fertility and low mortality played important roles. Colonial women typically bore seven or more children during their childbearing years. And blessed with an abundance of food, colonists enjoyed generally good health and relatively low mortality. But the British colonies grew far more rapidly than those of France or Spain (see Figure 5.1). It was immigration that made the difference. Fearful of depleting their population at home, the Spanish severely limited the migration of their own subjects and absolutely forbade the immigration of foreigners. Dedicated to keeping their colonies exclusively Catholic, the French ignored the desire of Protestant Huguenots to emigrate. But the English dispatched an estimated 400,000 of their own countrymen to populate their North American colonies during the seventeenth and eighteenth centuries.

Moreover, the British were the only colonial power to encourage the immigration of foreign nationals. William Penn was the first colonial official to promote the

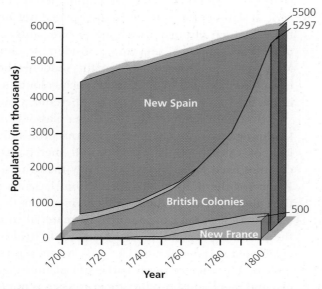

Figure 5.1 Estimated Total Population of New Spain, New France, and the British North American Colonies, 1700–1800
Although the populations of all three North American colonial empires grew in the eighteenth century, the explosive growth of the British colonies was unmatched.

Historical Statistics of the United States (Washington, DC: Government Printing Office, 1976), 1168.

immigration of Europeans, in the 1680s sending agents to recruit settlers in Holland, France, and the German principalities along the Rhine River. Soon the leaders of other British colonies were emulating his success.

Early in the century, a number of British colonies enacted liberal naturalization laws that allowed immigrants who professed Protestantism and swore allegiance to the British crown to become free "denizens," with all the privileges of natural-born subjects. In 1740 Parliament extended these provisions to all the British colonies by enacting a general naturalization law.

Trans-Atlantic migration made for colonies characterized by extraordinary ethnic diversity (see Map 5.5 and Figure 5.2). First there were the Africans, the largest group to come to North America in the colonial period, larger even than the English. Forced relocation brought an estimated 600,000 to the colonies before the official end of the slave trade to the United States in 1807. Then there was the massive emigration from the northern British Isles. Squeezed by economic hardship, an estimated 150,000 Highland Scots and Protestant Irish from the Ulster region of northern Ireland (known as the "Scots-Irish") emigrated in the eighteenth century. German speakers were next in importance, at least 125,000 of them settling in the colonies.

SOCIAL CLASS

North American society was not aristocratic in the European fashion, but neither was it without social hierarchy. In New France, landowning seigneurs (lords) claimed privileges similar to those enjoyed by their aristocratic counterparts at home. In New Spain the official criterion for status was racial purity. *Españoles* (Spaniards), also known as *gente de razon* (literally, "people of reason"), occupied the top rung of the social ladder, with mestizos, mulattoes, and others on descending levels, with Indians and African slaves at the bottom. In the isolated northern borderlands, however, such distinctions tended to blur, with castas (persons of mixed background) enjoying considerably more opportunity. Mestizos who acquired land might suddenly be reclassified as españoles. Even so, Spanish and French colonial societies were cut in the style of the Old World, with its hereditary ranks and titles.

In the British colonies the upper class was made up of large landowners, merchants, and prosperous professionals. Despite the lack of titles, wealthy planters and merchants of the British colonies lived far more extravagantly than the seigneurs of New France or the dons of the Spanish borderlands. What separated the culture of class in the British colonies from that of New France or New Mexico was not so much the material conditions of life as the prevailing attitude toward social rank. British North America celebrated social mobility. The class system was remarkably open, and the entrance of newly successful planters, commercial farmers, and merchants into the upper ranks was not only possible but also common.

There was also a large and impoverished lower class in the British colonies. Slaves, bound servants, and poor laboring families made up 40 percent or more of the population. For them the standard of living did not rise above bare subsistence. African

MAP 5.5

Ethnic Groups in Eighteenth-Century British North America   The first federal census, taken in 1790, revealed remarkable ethnic diversity. New England was filled with people from the British Isles, but the rest of the colonies were a patchwork. Most states had at least three different ethnic groups within their borders, and although the English and Scots-Irish were heavily represented in all colonies, in some they had strong competition from Germans (eastern and southern Pennsylvania) and from African peoples (Virginia and South Carolina).

IN WHAT areas were Scots and Scots-Irish most heavily concentrated? Why?

Map legend:
- English and Welsh
- Scots, Scots-Irish
- Dutch
- German and Swiss
- African (slaves)

American slaves stood apart from the gains in the standard of living enjoyed by immigrants from Europe. Their lives in America had been degraded beyond measure from the conditions that had prevailed in their native lands.

The feature of the class system most often commented on by eighteenth-century observers was not the character or composition of the lower ranks, but rather the size and strength of the middle class, a rank entirely absent in the colonies of France and Spain. More than half the population of the British colonies, and nearly 70 percent of all white settlers, might have been so classified. Most were landowning farmers of small to moderate means, but the group also included artisans, craftsmen, and small shopkeepers. The colonial middle class enjoyed a standard of living higher than that of the great majority of people in England and Europe.

ECONOMIC GROWTH AND ECONOMIC INEQUALITY

One of the most important differences among North American colonial regions in the eighteenth century was the economic stagnation of New France and New Spain compared with the impressive economic growth of the British colonies. Weighed down by royal bureaucracies and regulations, the communities of the French Crescent and New Spain never evidenced much prosperity. In eighteenth-century British North America, by contrast, per capita production grew at an annual rate of 0.5 percent. As economic growth increased the size of the economic pie, most middle- and upper-class British Americans began to enjoy improved living conditions. Improving standards of living and open access to land encouraged British colonists to see theirs as a society where hard work and savings could translate into prosperity, thus producing an upward spiral of economic growth.

At the same time, economic growth produced increasing social inequality (see Table 5.2). In the commercial cities, for example, prosperity was accompanied by a concentration of assets in the hands of wealthy families. In Boston and Philadelphia at the beginning of the century, the wealthiest 10 percent of households owned about half of the taxable property; by midcentury their share had risen to more than 65 percent. In the commercial farming region of Chester County in southeastern Pennsylvania, the holdings of the wealthiest 10 percent of households increased more modestly, from 24 percent of taxable property in 1700 to 30 percent in 1750, but the share owned by the poorest third fell from 17 percent to 6 percent. The general standard of living may have been rising, but the rich were getting richer and the poor poorer. The greatest concentrations of wealth occurred in the cities and in regions dominated by commercial farming, while the greatest economic equality was found in areas of self-sufficient farming.

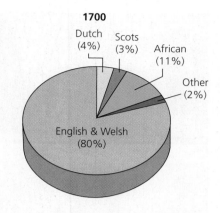

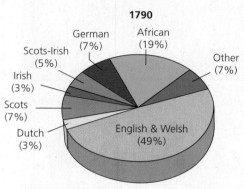

Figure 5.2 The Ancestry of the British Colonial Population
The legacy of eighteenth-century immigration to the British colonies was a population of unprecedented ethnic diversity.

"The European Ancestry of the United States Population," by Thomas L. Purvis. *William and Mary Quarterly* 61 (1984): 85–101. Reprinted by permission of the *William and Mary Quarterly*.

Read the Document
A Boston Woman Writes about Her Trip to New York (1704) at
www.myhistorylab.com

QUICK REVIEW

Poverty in the Colonies
- Gap between rich and poor widened in the eighteenth century.
- The trend was most pronounced in cities.
- Poverty led to homelessness and added to the pressure for westward migration.

TABLE 5.2

Wealth Held by Richest 10 Percent of Population in British Colonial America, 1770

Region	North	South
Frontier	33	40
Rural subsistence farming	35	45
Rural commercial farming	45	65
Cities	60	65
Overall	45	55

Jackson Turner Main, *The Social Structure of Revolutionary America* (Princeton, NJ: Princeton University Press, 1965), 276n.

Español con India. Mestizo.

Mestizo con Española. Castizo.

Castizo con Española. Español.

Español con Mora. Mulato.

5

6

Mulato con Española. Morisco.

Morisco con Española. Chino.

7

Chino con India. Salta atras.

Salta atras con Mulata. Lobo.

An eighteenth-century genre painting from New Spain showing various racial *castas*, the result of ethnic mixing.

WHAT WERE the most important cultural trends in eighteenth-century British North America?

Another eighteenth-century trend, however, stymied upward economic mobility in the countryside. As population grew and as generations succeeded one another in older settlements, all the available land eventually was taken up. Under the pressure of increased demand, land prices rose beyond the reach of families of modest means. And as a family's land was divided among the heirs of the second and third generations, parcels became ever smaller and more intensively farmed. Eventually, the soil was exhausted. This pattern was most pronounced in New England. The region saw increases in the number of landless poor, as well as the disturbing appearance of what were called the "strolling poor," homeless people who traveled from town to town looking for work or simply a handout. In other regions, land shortages in the older settlements almost inevitably prompted people to move to the frontier in search of cheap or free land.

COLONIAL POLITICS

The administration of the Spanish and French colonies was highly centralized. French Canada was ruled by a superior council. New Spain was governed by the Council of the Indies, which sat in Spain, with the viceroy in Mexico City exercising direct executive authority over all political affairs. Although local communities had informal independence, these highly bureaucratized and centralized governments left little room for the development of vigorous traditions of self-government.

The situation in the British colonies was quite different. During the early eighteenth century the British government of Prime Minister Robert Walpole assumed that a decentralized administration would best accomplish the nation's economic goals. With the exception of Connecticut and Rhode Island, both of which retained their charters and continued to choose their own governors, the colonies were administered by royally appointed governors. But taxation and spending continued to be controlled by elected assemblies. The right to vote was restricted to men with property. Yet the proportion of adult white males who qualified approached 50 percent in the British colonies. Proportionally, the electorate of the British colonies was the largest in the world.

That did not mean that the colonies were democratic. The basic principle of order in eighteenth-century British culture was the ideal of deference to natural hierarchy. Members of subordinate groups, such as women, non-English immigrants, African American slaves, servants, and Indians, were not allowed to vote or hold public office. Moreover, for the most part, the men who did vote nearly always chose wealthy landowners, planters, or merchants to serve as their leaders.

To educated British colonists the word "democracy" implied rule by the mob. Yet over the century there was an important trend toward stronger institutions of representative government. By midcentury most colonial assemblies in British North America had achieved considerable power over provincial affairs, sharing authority with governors. Because the assemblies controlled the finances of government—the "purse strings"—most royal governors were unable to resist this trend.

THE CULTURAL TRANSFORMATION OF BRITISH NORTH AMERICA

The same ships that transported European immigrants and European goods across the Atlantic could also transport new ways of thinking that historians call "the Enlightenment." Inspired by the sixteenth- and seventeenth-century revolution in scientific thought represented by giants such as Copernicus, Galileo, Descartes, and Newton, intellectuals in Europe and Great Britain became advocates for the power of human reason rather than spiritual revelation as the sole way of discovering natural law. They sought to establish an authoritative canon of logic, ethics, and aesthetics, as well as political philosophy. In the

1690s, for example, Englishman John Locke proposed that individuals were endowed with inalienable rights to life, liberty, and property and that the state existed to protect those rights.

In New Spain and New France colonial officials worked diligently to suppress such challenging ideas and writings. Cultural censorship in the French and Spanish colonies was effective because literacy was confined to a tiny minority of elite men. In the British colonies, by contrast, literacy was widespread. British colonial officials made little attempt at cultural censorship, and as a result these new ideas sparked a cultural transformation in eighteenth-century British North America.

THE ENLIGHTENMENT CHALLENGE

The **Enlightenment** is a simple label for a complex movement encompassing many different thinkers with many different ideas. But Enlightenment writers shared some things in common. They were optimistic about the ability of the rational human mind to discover the natural laws that were thought to govern the physical world and human affairs. Coupled with their commitment to reason was their belief in progress. These themes were in stark contrast with the traditional emphasis of folk culture on the unfathomable mysteries of God and nature and the inevitability of human failure and disorder.

Such thinking was most attractive to the British colonial elite, families experiencing rising prosperity. This group had good reason to believe in progress. They sent their sons to colonial colleges, the focal point for the dissemination of Enlightenment ideas. Harvard, established in 1636, remained the only institution of higher education in British America until 1693, when Anglicans established the College of William and Mary at Williamsburg. Puritans in Connecticut, believing Harvard was too liberal, founded Yale College in 1701. The curricula of these colleges, modeled on those of Oxford and Cambridge in England, were designed to train ministers, but gradually each institution changed to curricula influenced by Enlightenment thinking. By the 1730s students were studying Newton and reading Locke, as well as other British Enlightenment texts.

The tastes of ordinary readers ran to traditional rather than Enlightenment fare. The best-selling book of the colonial era, not surprisingly, was the Bible. But in second place was a unique American literary form, the captivity narrative. The genre originated with the appearance of The Sovereignty and Goodness of God (1682), Mary Rowlandson's tale of her captivity among Indians during King Philip's War. Another popular literary genre was the almanac, a combination calendar, astrological guide, sourcebook of medical advice, and farming tips that largely reflected the concerns of traditional folk culture.

Such reading material was supplemented by newspapers. By the mid-eighteenth century there were more than twenty newspapers in the British colonies. These papers did not employ reporters but instead depended on official government announcements, travelers' and correspondents' reports, and articles reprinted from other sources. Most literate people had access to them, and they were often read aloud in local taverns, making their information available to all within hearing.

A mixture of traditional and Enlightenment views characterized the thinking of many colonial intellectuals. Jonathan Edwards of Northampton offers a good example. Edwards sought to defend traditional Calvinist doctrine, but he did so by employing the concepts of Enlightenment thought, in which he was very well read. Worrying, however, that the new thinking tended toward a philosophy of materialism, Edwards argued that natural law revealed the harmony of God's creation.

A DECLINE IN RELIGIOUS DEVOTION

As Enlightenment thinking gradually gained in popularity, religious commitment seemed to decline, much as Edwards feared. In the South, by the 1730s, only one adult in fifteen was affiliated with a church. The Anglican establishment in the Chesapeake and the Lower South was institutionally feeble, its ministers uninspiring, and many families "unchurched."

Enlightenment Intellectual movement stressing the importance of reason and the existence of discoverable natural laws.

Puritan churches in New England also suffered declining membership and falling attendance, and ministers began to warn of Puritanism's "declension." By the second decade of the eighteenth century only one in five New Englanders belonged to an established congregation. And among the churched, an increasing number began to question the **Calvinist theology of election**, the belief that salvation was the result of God's sovereign decree, that only a small number of men and women would be the recipients of God's grace. Many turned instead to the view that people had a natural ability to accept God's grace by developing their faith and doing good works.

The dispute between advocates of free will and determinism was ancient, but the idea that men and women were not helpless pawns but rational beings who could actively shape their own destinies was strengthened by Enlightenment thinking. It became a force at Harvard and Yale in the first quarter of the eighteenth century, and soon a generation of ministers with more liberal ideas were taking positions in New England churches. Their ideas appealed to the same men and women attracted to Enlightenment thinking, those experiencing rising prosperity and social improvement. Among ordinary people in the countryside, however, especially among those in communities with narrowing opportunities, there was a good deal of opposition to these unorthodox ideas.

THE GREAT AWAKENING

The first stirrings of a movement challenging the rationalist approach to religion occurred during the 1730s, most notably in the revival sparked by Edwards in Northampton. Edwards was a committed Calvinist and used his charged preaching style to attack liberal theology. But there was more to this movement than the power of a single preacher. Similar revivals soon broke out in other New England communities, as well as among German Lutherans and Scots-Irish Presbyterians in Pennsylvania. Not all the revivalists were Calvinists. Some promoted a theology that emphasized human choice. But the common thread was a complaint of "spiritual coldness," of ministers whose sermons read like rational dissertations. People clamored for preaching that was more emotional.

These local revivals became an intercolonial phenomenon thanks to the preaching of George Whitefield, an evangelical Anglican minister from England, who in 1738 made the first of several tours of the colonies. By all accounts, his preaching had a powerful effect. Even Benjamin Franklin, a religious skeptic, wrote of the "extraordinary influence of his oratory" after attending an outdoor service in Philadelphia where 30,000 people crowded the streets to hear him preach.

This widespread colonial revival of religion, which later generations called **The Great Awakening**, was an American version of the second phase of the Protestant Reformation (see Chapter 2). Religious leaders condemned the laxity, decadence, and bureaucracy of established Protestantism and sought to reinvigorate it with renewed piety and purity. People undergoing the economic and social stresses of the age, unsure about their ability to find land, marry, and participate in the promise of a growing economy found relief in religious enthusiasm.

Among Presbyterians, open conflict broke out between the revivalists and the old guard, and in some regions the church hierarchy divided into separate organizations. In New England, where these factions were known as the **New Lights** and the **Old Lights**, the two sides accused each other of heresy. New Lights railed against liberal theology as a "rationalist heresy" and called for a revival of Calvinism. Old Lights condemned emotional enthusiasm as a "lawless heresy." Itinerant preachers appeared in the countryside, stirring up trouble. Many congregations split into feuding factions, and ministers found themselves challenged by their newly awakened parishioners.

The revivals began somewhat later in the South, first developing in the mid-1740s, reaching full impact in the 1760s. They affected not only white southerners but also for the first time introduced many slaves to Christianity. Baptist churches of the

---

◦◦◦─[Read the Document

Jonathan Edwards, Sinners in the Hands of an Angry God (1741) at **www.myhistorylab.com**

◦◦◦─[Read the Document

Benjamin Franklin on George Whitefield (1771) at **www.myhistorylab.com**

◦◦◦─[Read the Document

Exploring America: The Great Awakening at **www.myhistorylab.com**

Calvinist theology of election   Belief that salvation was the result of God's sovereign decree and that few people would receive God's grace.

The Great Awakening   North American religious revival in the middle of the eighteenth century.

New Lights   People who experienced conversion during the revivals of the Great Awakening.

Old Lights   Religious faction that condemned emotional enthusiasm as part of the heresy of believing in a personal and direct relationship with God outside the order of the church.

South in the era of the American Revolution included members of both races and featured spontaneous preaching by slaves as well as masters. In the nineteenth century white and black Christians would go their separate ways, but the joint experience of the eighteenth-century Awakening shaped the religious cultures of both groups.

Many other "unchurched" colonists were brought back to Protestantism by revivalism. But a careful examination of statistics suggests that the proportion of church members in the general population did not increase during the middle decades of the century. While the number of churches more than doubled from 1740 to 1780, the colonial population grew even faster, increasing threefold. The greatest impact was on families already associated with congregations. Before the Awakening, attendance at church had been mostly an adult affair, but throughout the colonies the revival of religion had its deepest effects on young people, who flocked to church in greater numbers than ever before. Church membership previously had been concentrated among women, leading Cotton Mather, for one, to speculate that perhaps women were indeed more godly. But men were particularly affected by the revival of religion, and their attendance and membership rose.

THE POLITICS OF REVIVALISM

Revivalism appealed most of all to groups that felt bypassed by the economic and cultural development of the British colonies during the first half of the eighteenth century. The New Lights tended to draw their greatest strength from small farmers and less prosperous craftsmen. Many members of the upper class and the comfortable "middling sort" viewed the excesses of revivalism as indications of anarchy, and they became even more committed to rational religion.

Revivalism sometimes had political implications. In Connecticut, for example, Old Lights politicized the religious dispute by passing a series of laws in the General Assembly designed to suppress revivalism. Judges sympathetic to New Light views were thrown off the bench, and others were denied their elected seats in the assembly. The arrogance of these actions was met with popular outrage: by the 1760s the Connecticut New Lights had organized themselves politically and, in what amounted to a political rebellion, succeeded in turning the Old Lights out of office. New Light politicians would provide the leadership for the American Revolution in Connecticut.

Such direct connections between religion and politics were rare. There can be little doubt, however, that for many people revivalism offered the first opportunity to participate actively in public debate and public action that affected the direction of their lives. Choices about religious styles, ministers, and doctrine were thrown open for public discourse, and ordinary people began to believe that their opinions actually counted for something. Underlying the debate over these issues were insecurities about warfare, economic growth, and the development of colonial society. Revivalism empowered ordinary people to question their leaders, an experience that would prove critical in the political struggles to come.

Baptism by Full *Immersion in the Schuylkill River of Pennsylvania*, an engraving by Henry Dawkins illustrating events in the history of American Baptists, was published in Philadelphia in 1770. With calls for renewed piety and purity, the Great Awakening reinvigorated American Protestantism. The Baptists preached an egalitarian message, and their congregations in the South often included both white and black Protestants.

Henry Dawkins, *Baptismal Ceremony Beside the Schuykill*. Engraving, 1770. John Carter Brown Library at Brown University.

CHRONOLOGY

1636	Harvard College founded	1716	Spanish begin construction of Texas missions
1674	Bishopric of Quebéc established	1732	Franklin begins publishing *Poor Richard's Almanac*
1680s	William Penn begins recruiting settlers from the European continent	1738	George Whitefield first tours the colonies
		1740s	Great Awakening gets under way in the Northeast
1682	Mary Rowlandson's *The Sovereignty and Goodness of God*	1740	Parliament passes a naturalization law for the colonies
1689	Toleration Act passed by Parliament	1746	College of New Jersey (Princeton University) founded
1690s	Beginnings of Jesuit missions in Arizona		
1693	College of William and Mary founded	1760s	Great Awakening achieves full impact in the South
1700s	Plains Indians begin adoption of the horse	1769	Spanish colonization of California begins
1701	Yale College founded; Iroquois sign treaty of neutrality with France	1775	Indian revolt at San Diego
		1781	Los Angeles founded

CONCLUSION

By the middle of the eighteenth century a number of distinct colonial regions had emerged in North America, all of them with rising populations demanding that more land be seized from the Indians. Some colonies attempted to ensure homogeneity, whereas others embraced diversity. Within the British colonies, New England in particular seemed bound to the past, whereas the middle colonies and the backcountry pointed the way toward pluralism and expansion. These developments placed them in direct competition with the expansionist plans of the French and at odds with Indian peoples committed to the defense of their homelands.

The economic development of the British colonies introduced new social and cultural tensions that led to the Great Awakening, a massive revival of religion that was the first transcolonial event in American history. Beginning in small communities like Northampton, Massachusetts, the revivals affected thousands of people, leading to a renewal of religious passions. Rather than resuscitating old traditions, however, the Awakening seemed to point people toward a more active role in their own political futures.

REVIEW QUESTIONS

1. What were the principal colonial regions of North America? Discuss their similarities and their differences. Contrast the development of their political systems.

2. Why did the Spanish and the French close their colonies to immigration? Why did the British open their colonies? How do you explain the ethnic homogeneity of New England and the ethnic pluralism of New York and Pennsylvania?

3. What were the principal trends in the history of Indian America in the eighteenth century?

4. Discuss the development of class differences in the Spanish, French, and British colonies in the eighteenth century.

5. Discuss the effects of the Great Awakening on the subsequent history of the British colonies.

KEY TERMS

Act of Toleration (p. 105)
Calvinist theology of election (p. 116)
Enlightenment (p. 115)

The Great Awakening (p. 116)
New Lights (p. 116)
Old Lights (p. 116)

Reinforce what you learned in this chapter by studying the many documents,
images, maps, review tools, and videos available at www.myhistorylab.com.

Read and Review

✓•—Study and Review **Chapter 5**

•••—Read the Document

An Older Businessman Advises a Young One (1748)

A Boston Woman Writes about Her Trip to New York (1704)

Jonathan Edwards, Sinners in the Hands of an Angry God (1741)

Benjamin Franklin on George Whitefield (1771)

👁—See the Map **Colonial Products**

Research and Explore

•••—Read the Document

Exploring America: America and the Horse

Exploring America: The Great Awakening

Profiles
Martha Ballard
Benjamin Franklin

History Bookshelf: The Autobiography of Benjamin Franklin *(1788)*

▶—Watch the Video *Chief Plenty Coups, Crow*

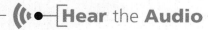 **Hear** the **Audio**

Hear the audio files for Chapter 5 at
www.myhistorylab.com.

My dear Jack, All the Provinces [are]
arming and Training in the same Manner,
for they are all determined to die or be Free . . .
—Eliza Farmer, June 28, 1775

Chaplain Jacob Duché leads the first prayer
in the First Continental Congress at
Carpenter's Hall, Philadelphia,
September 1774; mezzotint, 1848.

6

FROM EMPIRE TO INDEPENDENCE
1750–1776

((•─┤Hear the **Audio**

Hear the audio files for Chapter 6 at **www.myhistorylab.com**.

HOW DID the Seven Years' War change the relationship between the British government and its colonial subjects in North America?

WHAT FACTORS led to the growth of American nationalism in the 1760s?

HOW DID political and economic problems in Britain contribute to unrest in the colonies?

WHAT STEPS did Britain take to punish Massachusetts for the colonists' acts of resistance?

WHAT EVENTS led the second Continental Congress to declare independence?

1750   1776

AMERICAN COMMUNITIES

The First Continental Congress Begins to Shape a National Political Community

THE OPENING OF THE FIRST CONTINENTAL CONGRESS, HELD IN Philadelphia in September 1774, did not bode well. One of the delegates moved that the session open with prayer, but others objected. John Adams's cousin and fellow Massachusetts delegate Samuel Adams leapt to his feet. He was no bigot, he proclaimed, and was willing to hear a prayer "from any gentleman of piety and virtue who was at the same time a friend to his country." Putting aside their religious differences, the delegates agreed to ask a local clergyman to give the invocation. He took as his text the Thirty-fifth Psalm: "Plead my cause, O Lord, with them that strive with me; fight against them that fight against me."

The incident highlights the most important task confronting the First Continental Congress—strengthening their common cause without compromising their local identities. The delegates represented distinct colonies with traditions and histories as different as those of separate countries. Moreover, these lawyers, merchants, and planters, leaders in their respective colonies, were strangers to one another.

Britain's North American colonies enjoyed considerable prosperity during the first half of the eighteenth century. So in 1765 British authorities thought it only fair that colonists shoulder some of the expense of the late great war for empire—the Seven Years' War—during which Great Britain soundly defeated France and forced the cession of the French North American colonies. But the new taxes and trade restrictions inspired resistance among the colonists. By the opening session of the First Continental Congress, peaceful protest had escalated into violent riot, and in an attempt to force the colonists to acknowledge the power of Parliament to make laws binding them "in all cases whatsoever," the British had proclaimed a series of repressive measures, including the closure of ports in Massachusetts and the suspension of that colony's elected government. In this atmosphere of crisis, most of the colonial assemblies elected delegates for a "Continental Congress" to map out a coordinated response.

Despite their differences, during seven weeks of deliberations the delegates succeeded in forging an agreement on the principles and policies they would follow in this, the most serious crisis in the history of the British North American colonies. At the outset they resolved that each colony would have one vote, thereby committing themselves to the preservation of provincial autonomy. Their most vexing problems they sent to committees, whose members could sound each other out without committing themselves on the public record. They added to their daily routine dinners, parties, and much late-night tavern-hopping. And in so doing they began to construct a community of interest and friendship among themselves. These were the first tentative steps toward the creation of an American national political community.

Patrick Henry, a Virginia delegate strongly committed to American independence, was exuberant by the time the Congress adjourned in late October. "The distinctions between Virginians, Pennsylvanians, New Yorkers, and New Englanders, are no more," he declared. "I am not a Virginian, but an American." He exaggerated the unity. It remained very much a work in progress. Local, provincial, and regional differences would continue to clash. But Henry voiced an important hope.

In its attempt to force the colonists to pay a share of the costs of empire through taxation, Great Britain had sparked a revolt of both elite and ordinary colonists. The road to a shared community of interest among British colonists, distinguishing them from the mother country, was marked by milestones with legendary names: the Stamp Act, the Boston Massacre, the Tea Party, the Intolerable Acts. The violent events that would follow the First Continental Congress—the first clash of arms at Lexington and Concord, the siege of Boston, and the Battle of Bunker Hill—would lead to a second session of the Congress. Reluctantly at first, then enthusiastically, the delegates would move toward independence. The difficult months and years of warfare would sorely test the imagined community of the united colonies, and the differences among them would frequently threaten to abort the nation being born. But the sessions of the First Continental Congress marked the moment when Americans first began the struggle to overcome local differences in pursuit of national goals.

Philadelphia

THE SEVEN YEARS' WAR IN AMERICA

Leaders of the British colonies made an early attempt at cooperation in 1754, when representatives from New England, New York, Pennsylvania, and Maryland met to consider a joint approach to military challenges from the French and their Indian allies. Even as the delegates met the first shots were fired in a great global war for empire pitting Great Britain (and Prussia) against the combined might of France, Spain, and Austria. In North America this would be the final and most destructive armed conflict between the British and the French empires. Ultimately the war would decide the future of the vast region between the Appalachian Mountains and the Mississippi River. It would also lay the groundwork for the conflict between the British and the colonists that led to the American Revolution.

HOW DID the Seven Years' War change the relationship between the British government and its colonial subjects in North America?

THE ALBANY CONFERENCE OF 1754

The British Board of Trade convened the 1754 meeting in the New York town of Albany on the Hudson River. They wanted the colonies to consider a collective response to the continuing conflict with New France and the Indians of the interior. High on the agenda was the negotiation of a settlement with the leaders of the Iroquois Confederacy, who had grown impatient with colonial land grabbing. But as the negotiations began, behind the scenes real estate developers were bribing minor Iroquois chiefs, affixing their signatures on a "deed" for an enormous tract of land in Pennsylvania, and turning the meeting into a vehicle for the very abuses the British sought to correct. Angered by these manipulations, the official Iroquois delegation walked out of the conference refusing all offers to join a British alliance.

Despite this failure, the **Albany Conference** succeeded in adopting the "**Plan of Union**" put forward by Benjamin Franklin, a delegate from Pennsylvania. Franklin's proposal would have placed Indian affairs, western settlement, and other items of mutual interest under the authority of a grand council composed of representatives elected by the colonial assemblies and led by a British-appointed president. British authorities, however, were suspicious of the plan, fearing it would create a powerful entity they would have difficulty controlling. They had nothing to fear, for all the colonies rejected the Albany Plan of Union, fearful of losing their autonomy. The absence of cooperation would prove one of the greatest weaknesses during the subsequent war with the French.

Albany Conference   A 1754 meeting, held in Albany, NY, between the British and leaders of the Iroquois Confederacy.

Plan of Union   Plan put forward by Benjamin Franklin in 1754 calling for an intercolonial union to manage defense and Indian affairs. The plan was rejected by participants at the Albany Congress.

FRANCE VS. BRITAIN IN AMERICA

There were three violent flash points in the conflict between Great Britain and France for control of North America. First was the northern Atlantic coast, the ragged boundary between New France and New England. In 1713 France had ceded this region, known as Acadia, to the British, who called it Nova Scotia. To protect the ocean approach to their colonial heartland, the French constructed the port and fortress of Louisbourg on Cape Breton Island. In 1745, during King George's War, New Englanders captured Louisbourg, but the French reclaimed it upon the settlement of that conflict in 1748 (see Chapter 4). In 1749 the British established a large naval facility at Halifax in Nova Scotia, but worried about the loyalty of the 18,000 French-speaking Acadians of the province.

The second flash point was the border region between New France and New York, extending from Niagara Falls to Lake Champlain, where Canadians and New Yorkers were rivals for the lucrative Indian trade. The French, who found it difficult to compete

This woodcut cartoon, created by Benjamin Franklin, was published in his newspaper, the *Pennsylvania Gazette*, on May 9, 1754. It accompanied Franklin's editorial about the "disunited state" of the colonies on the eve of the French and Indian War, and helped make his point about the need for unity. It plays on the superstition that a snake that had been cut into pieces would come back to life if the pieces were put back together before sunset. The cartoon was reprinted widely, and used again, more than twenty years later, during the Revolutionary War.

The Library Company of Philadelphia

against superior English goods, resorted instead to military might, garrisoning fortifications on Lake George and at Niagara. In this zone the strategic advantage was held by the Iroquois Confederacy.

The third area of conflict was the Ohio country, the trans-Appalachian region bisected by the Ohio River. The rich lands along the Ohio were a prime target of British land speculators and backcountry settlers, whom the French feared would overrun their isolated outposts and threaten their entire Mississippi trading empire. To reinforce their claim, in 1749 the French sent a heavily armed force down the Ohio River to ward off the British, and in 1752 they attempted to expel all British traders from the region. Then, in 1753, French Canadian troops began the construction of a line of forts running south from Lake Erie to the headwaters of the Ohio River. In a direct challenge to the French claims in the West, the British government issued a royal charter for more than 200,000 acres to the Ohio Company, organized by London and Virginia investors.

The Indian peoples of the Ohio country had interests of their own to defend. In addition to native inhabitants, the region had become a refuge for Indian peoples who had fled the British seaborne colonies. Most of the Indians of the Ohio country opposed further British expansion and wished to make the Appalachians into a defensive wall. Meanwhile the Iroquois Confederacy continued the game of playing the British against the French. In the South the Creeks (and to a lesser extent the Cherokees and Choctaws) attempted to carve out a similar balancing role for themselves among the British in the Lower South, the French in Louisiana, and the Spanish in Florida.

FRONTIER WARFARE

As the delegates to the Albany Conference conducted their business, they received news of the first clash with the French. Colonel George Washington, a young militia officer sent by the governor of Virginia to expel the French from the upper Ohio, had been forced to surrender his troops to a French Canadian force. The French now commanded the interior country from Fort Duquesne at the "Forks of the Ohio," the junction of the Allegheny and Monongahela Rivers.

Taking up the challenge, in 1755 the British launched an effort to strike the French in all three zones. An army of New England militiamen succeeded in capturing two important French forts on the northern border of Nova Scotia. The British then began the systematic removal of the Acadian inhabitants. A substantial number of the Acadians ended up in Louisiana, where they became known as "Cajuns."

Elsewhere the British military campaigns failed miserably. In northern New York a large colonial force was repulsed by the French. And on July 9, 1755, Major General Edward Braddock's 1,500 British troops were ambushed and destroyed by a much smaller force of 600 confederated Indian fighters supported by a mere 30 French Canadians. It was the worst military defeat of a British army during the eighteenth century.

Full-scale warfare between Great Britain (supported by Prussia) and France (supported by Spain) began the next year, 1756. This was truly a global war, fought in Europe, Asia, and America, and known to history as the Seven Years' War (or the **French and Indian War** in America) (see Map 6.1).The first two years were a near catastrophe for Great Britain. In the face of a string of French victories, the lack of colonial cooperation greatly hampered the British attempt to mount a counterattack. When British commanders tried to exert direct control over provincial troops, they succeeded only in angering local authorities.

THE CONQUEST OF CANADA

In 1757 William Pitt, an enthusiastic advocate of British expansion, became prime minister of Great Britain. Pitt committed himself to the conquest of Canada and the final elimination of French competition in North America. He dispatched over 20,000 regular

👁‑**See** the **Map**
The Seven Years' War at
www.myhistorylab.com

French and Indian War The last of the Anglo-French colonial wars (1754–1763) and the first in which fighting began in North America. The war ended with France's defeat. Also known as the Seven Years' War.

MAP 6.1

The War for Empire in North America, 1754–1763   The Seven Years' War in America (also known as the French and Indian War) was fought in three principal areas: Nova Scotia and what was then Acadia, the frontier between New France and New York, and the upper Ohio River—gateway to the Old Northwest.

HOW DID the British turn the tide of war in their favor? Which victories were most important to their ultimate success?

British troops across the Atlantic. In combination with colonial militias, Pitt massed more than 50,000 troops against Canada.

The British were also effective at attracting Indian support. In 1758, at a conference with representatives of the Iroquois and the Ohio Indians held in the Pennsylvania town of Easton, British officials promised to establish "clear and fixed boundaries" between English settlements and Indian lands. This succeeded in neutralizing a good deal of the Indian support for the French.

Thus did Pitt succeed in reversing the course of the war. Regular and provincial forces captured the French fortress of Louisbourg in July 1758, setting the stage for the invasion of New France. A month later a force of New Englanders captured the strategic French fort of Oswego on Lake Ontario, thereby preventing the Canadians from resupplying their western posts. Encouraged by British promises, increasing numbers

Treaty of Paris The formal end to British hostilities against France and Spain in February 1763.

of Indians deserted the French. The last of the French forts in northern New York fell in 1759.

British forces now converged on French Canada. In 1759 colonial and British troops, under General James Wolfe, arrived at Québec City. In an epic battle fought on the Plains of Abraham before the city walls, more than 2,000 British, French, American, and Canadian men lost their lives, including both Wolfe and the Marquis de Montcalm, the French commander. The British army prevailed and Québec fell. The next year another British force moved up the Hudson and conquered Montreal. Its fall marked the end of the French empire in America.

In the final two years of the war the British swept French ships from the seas, conquered the Spanish colony of Cuba, captured the Spanish Philippines, and achieved dominance in India. In the 1763 **Treaty of Paris**, France lost all its possessions on the North American mainland, ceding to Great Britain all its claims east of the Mississippi, with the exception of New Orleans, which Britain agreed that France would pass to Spain, along with other French claims to the huge trans-Mississippi region. In exchange for the return of its Caribbean and Pacific colonies, Spain ceded Florida to Britain. Three centuries of European imperial rivalry in eastern North America ended with complete victory for the British Empire (see Map 6.2).

The death of General James Wolfe at the conclusion of the battle in which the British captured Québec in 1759 became the subject of American artist Benjamin West's most famous painting, which was exhibited to tremendous acclaim in London in 1770.

Benjamin West (1738–1820), "The Death of General Wolfe," 1770. Oil on canvas, 152.6 × 214.5 cm. Transfer from the Canadian War Memorials, 1921 (Gift of the 2nd Duke of Westminster, Eaton Hall, Cheshire, 1918). National Gallery of Canada, Ottawa, Ontario.

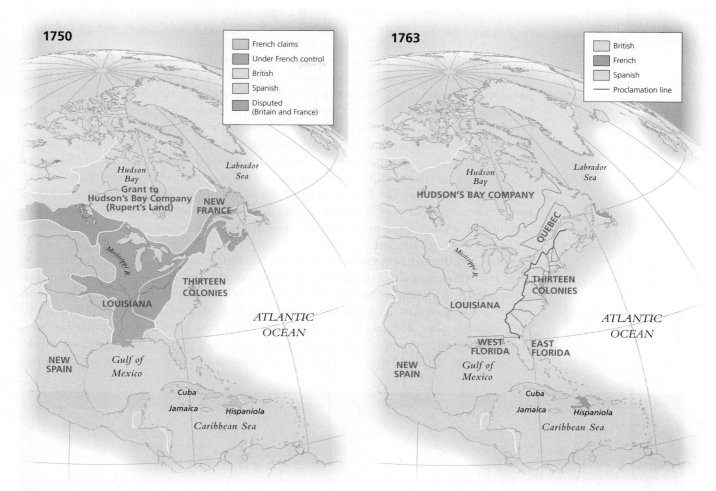

MAP 6.2

European Claims in North America, 1750 and 1763   As a result of the British victory in the Seven Years' War, the map of colonial claims in North America was fundamentally transformed.

HOW DID the balance of power in North America change between 1750 and 1763?

THE STRUGGLE FOR THE WEST

The Ohio Indians were shocked when told of the French cession. A new set of British policies soon shocked them even more. The French and the British had long used gift-giving as a way of gaining favor with Indians. But in one of his first official acts, General Jeffery Amherst, British military governor of the western region, banned presents to Indian chiefs and tribes. Not only were Indians angered by Amherst's policy, but they were also frustrated by his refusal to supply them with the ammunition they needed for hunting. Many were left destitute.

In this climate, hundreds of Ohio Indians became disciples of an Indian visionary named Neolin ("The Enlightened One"), known to the English as the Delaware Prophet. The core of Neolin's teaching was that Indians had been corrupted by European ways and needed to purify themselves by returning to their traditions and preparing for a holy war. In the spring of 1763 a confederacy of tribes inspired by Neolin's ideas laid plans for a coordinated attack on British frontier posts. The principal leader of this resistance was an Ottawa chief named Pontiac. In May 1763 Pontiac's alliance simultaneously attacked

Royal Proclamation of 1763 Royal proclamation declaring the trans-Appalachian region to be "Indian Country."

all the British posts in the West, destroying eight of them, but failing to take the key forts at Niagara, Detroit, and the forks of the Ohio River (Fort Pitt). Pontiac and his followers fought on for another year, but most Indians sued for peace.

They were encouraged by the announcement of the British **Royal Proclamation of 1763**, which in keeping with the promise made in the Treaty of Easton declared the trans-Appalachian region to be "Indian Country," reserved as a homeland for the Indian nations. British settlers had expected that the removal of the French threat would allow them to move into the West, but under the terms of the royal Proclamation specific authorization from the crown was now required for any movement onto protected Indian lands. In an act emblematic of the anger backcountry settlers felt about these restrictions, in December 1763 a mob of backcountry Pennsylvanians, calling themselves "the Paxton Boys," butchered twenty Christian Indians at the small village of Conestoga on the Susquehanna River. When colonial authorities attempted to arrest the murderers, 600 frontiersmen marched on Philadelphia in protest. Negotiations led by Benjamin Franklin helped prevent a bloody confrontation.

In fact, the British proved unable and ultimately unwilling to prevent the westward migration that was a dynamic part of the colonization of British North America. In response to demands by settlers and speculators, British authorities were soon pressing the Iroquois and Cherokees for cessions of land in Indian Country. No longer able to play off rival colonial powers, Indians were reduced to a choice between compliance and resistance. Weakened by the recent war, they chose to sign away lands. In the Treaty of Hard Labor in 1768, the Cherokees ceded a vast tract on the upper

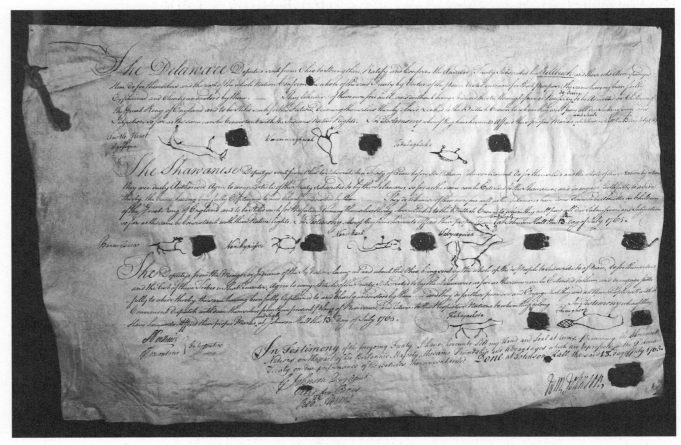

A treaty between the Delaware, Shawnee, and Mingo (western Iroquois) Indians and Great Britain, July 13, 1765, at the conclusion of the Indian uprising known as Pontiac's Rebellion. The Indian chiefs signed with pictographs symbolizing their clans, each notarized with an official wax seal.

Tennessee River, where British settlers had already planted communities. In the Treaty of Fort Stanwix, signed the same year, the Iroquois gave up their claim to the Ohio Valley, hoping thereby to deflect English settlement away from their own homeland in New York.

The individual colonies were even more aggressive. Locked in a dispute with Pennsylvania about jurisdiction in the Ohio country, in 1773 Virginia governor John Murray, Earl of Dunmore, sent a force to occupy Fort Pitt. In 1774, in an attempt to gain legitimacy for his dispute with Pennsylvania, Dunmore provoked a frontier war with the Shawnees. After dealing them a humiliating defeat, Dunmore forced them to cede the upper Ohio River Valley to Virginia. The continuing struggle for the West would be an important issue in the coming Revolutionary struggle.

THE EMERGENCE OF AMERICAN NATIONALISM

No colonial power of the mid-eighteenth century could match Britain in projecting imperial power over the face of the globe. During the years following its victory in the Seven Years' War, Britain turned confidently to the reorganization of its North American empire. The new colonial policy plunged British authorities into a new and ultimately more threatening conflict with the colonists, who had begun to develop a sense of a separate identity.

WHAT FACTORS led to the growth of American nationalism in the 1760s?

AN AMERICAN IDENTITY

Despite the anger of frontier settlers over the Proclamation of 1763, the conclusion of the Seven Years' War left most colonists proud of their place in the British Empire. But many people had begun to note important contrasts between themselves and the mother country. The arrival of thousands of British troops raised the problem of where to house them. British commanders demanded they be quartered in private homes. British subjects at home were protected against such demands by an act of Parliament, but that protection had expressly not been extended to the colonies.

Americans who were thrown into contact with regular British troops were shocked by their profanity, lewdness, and violence. They were equally shocked by the swift and terrible punishment inflicted by aristocratic officers to keep those men in line. A Massachusetts militiaman wrote of witnessing the punishment of two soldiers sentenced to eight hundred lashes apiece. "The flesh appeared to be entirely whipped from their shoulders, and they hung as mute and motionless as though they had long since been deprived of life." Men who witnessed such scenes found it easy to believe the danger of British "slavery."

Colonial forces, by contrast, were composed of volunteer companies. Militia officers were moderate in the administration of punishment, knowing they had to maintain the enthusiasm of their troops. Discipline thus fell considerably below the standards to which British officers were accustomed. "Riff-raff," one British general labeled colonial troops, "the lowest dregs of the people, both officers and men." Americans believed British scorn blinded them to the important role played by the colonists in the Seven Years' War. It was during the Seven Years' War that many colonists began to view themselves as having an identity distinct from the British.

The Seven Years' War also strengthened a sense of intercolonial unity among the colonists. Farm boys who never before had ventured outside the communities of their birth fought in distant regions with men from other colonies. Such experiences reinforced a developing sense of national community. This sentiment built on previous developments, including the growth of intercolonial commerce, which involved the movement of people as well as goods.

THE PRESS, POLITICS, AND REPUBLICANISM

One of the most important means of intercolonial communication was the weekly newspaper. Early in the century the colonial press had functioned as a mouthpiece for British officialdom. But a bold stroke for freedom of the press was struck in 1735 when a New York City jury acquitted editor John Peter Zenger of seditious libel after he printed antigovernment articles. Newspapers became a lively means of public discourse, and by 1760 more than twenty weekly papers were being published in the British colonies.

The papers carried an increasing amount of colonial news. Editors began to look at events from what they called a "continental" perspective. This trend accelerated during the Seven Years' War, when communities demanded news of the distant places where their men were fighting. Thus did the war promote a new spirit of nationalism and a wider notion of community. Editors began using the term "American" to denote the common identity of British colonists.

Colonial editors frequently reprinted writings by British authors, including poems by Alexander Pope, satiric essays by Jonathan Swift, and political philosophy by

A protest against the Stamp Act from newspaper editor William Bradford, publisher of the *Pennsylvania Journal and Weekly Advertiser*. Bradford decorated his masthead with skull and crossbones, and in the bottom right corner included a satiric version of "the fatal Stamp," also with skull and crossbones.

OVERVIEW | Eleven British Measures That Led to Revolution

Year	Legislation	
1764	Sugar Act	Placed prohibitive duty on imported sugar; provided for greater regulation of American shipping to suppress smuggling
1765	Stamp Act	Required the purchase of specially embossed paper for newspapers, legal documents, licenses, insurance policies, ships' papers, and playing cards; struck at printers, lawyers, tavern owners, and other influential colonists. Repealed in 1766
1766	Declaratory Act	Asserted the authority of Parliament to make laws binding the colonies "in all cases whatsoever"
1767	Townshend Revenue Acts	Placed import duties, collectible before goods entered colonial markets, on many commodities including lead, glass, paper, and tea. Repealed in 1770
1773	Tea Act	Gave the British East India Company a monopoly on all tea imports to America, hitting at American merchants
1774	Coercive or Intolerable Acts	
	Boston Port Bill	Closed Boston Harbor
	Massachusetts Government Act	Annulled the Massachusetts colonial charter
	Administration of Justice Act	Protected British officials from colonial courts by sending them home for trial if arrested
	Quartering Act	Legalized the housing of British troops in private homes
	Québec Act	Created a highly centralized government for Canada

John Locke. They also frequently reprinted political essays by British republicans, who warned of the growing threat to liberty posed by the unchecked exercise of state power. Some essayists suggested that a conspiracy existed among European monarchs, aristocrats, and Catholics to quash liberty and reinstitute tyranny. These ideas came to define a political consensus in the British colonies, a point of view that came to be called "**republicanism**."

Republicanism asserted that state power, by its very nature, was antithetical to liberty and, consequently, had to be limited; that the authority of rulers should be conditional rather than absolute; and that the people had an inherent right to withdraw their support from the government if it did not fulfill their expectations, and organize a new one. The best guarantee of good government, republicans argued, was a broad distribution of power to the people, who could not only select their own leaders but also vote them out of office. The theory of republican government relied on the virtue of the people, on their willingness to make the stability and justice of the political community their first priority. But that kind of virtue was possible only for an "independent" population in control of its own affairs.

This was a political theory that fit well with the circumstances of American life, with its wide base of property ownership, its tradition of representative assemblies, and its history of struggle with royal authority. Contrast the assumptions of republicans with those of British monarchists, who argued that the good society was one in which a strong state, controlled by a hereditary elite, kept a vicious and unruly people in line.

QUICK REVIEW

Republican Principles

- Power is antithetical to liberty and had to be limited.
- The authority of rulers was conditional, not absolute.
- The people had the right to withdraw their support from an unsatisfactory government and form a new one.
- The best guarantee of good government was the broad distribution of power to the people.

republicanism A complex, changing body of ideas, values, and assumptions that influenced American political behavior during the eighteenth and nineteenth centuries.

Sugar Act Law passed in 1764 to raise revenue in the American colonies. It lowered the duty from 6 pence to 3 pence per gallon on foreign molasses imported into the colonies and increased the restrictions on colonial commerce.

Stamp Act Law passed by Parliament in 1765 to raise revenue in America by requiring taxed, stamped paper for legal documents, publications, and playing cards.

virtual representation The notion that parliamentary members represented the interests of the nation as a whole, not those of the particular district that elected them.

•••▸|Read the Document

James Otis, The Rights of the British Colonies Asserted and Proved (1763) at **www.myhistorylab.com**

Samuel Adams, a second cousin of John Adams, was a leader of the Boston radicals and an organizer of the Sons of Liberty. The artist of this portrait, John Singleton Copley, was known for setting his subjects in the midst of everyday objects; here he portrays Adams in a middle-class suit with the charter guaranteeing the liberties of Boston's freemen.

John Singleton Copley (1738–1815), "Samuel Adams," ca. 1772. Oil on canvas, 49 ½ × 39 ½ in. (125.7 cm × 100.3 cm). Deposited by the City of Boston, 30.76c. Courtesy, Museum of Fine Arts, Boston. Reproduced with permission. ©2000 Museum of Fine Arts, Boston. All Rights Reserved.

THE SUGAR AND STAMP ACTS

The emerging sense of American political identity was soon tested by British measures designed to raise revenue in the colonies. At the conclusion of the Seven Years' War the British decided to keep 10,000 regular troops stationed in North America. The cost of maintaining this force added to the enormous debt run up during the fighting. In 1764 Prime Minister George Grenville decided to obtain the needed revenue from American colonists. Parliament passed a measure known as the **Sugar Act**, which placed a tariff on sugar imported into the colonies.

Anticipating that American importers would attempt to avoid the duty by smuggling, Parliament also broad ened the jurisdiction of the vice-admiralty court at Halifax, which had jurisdiction over customs cases. Both merchants and artisans viewed the Sugar Act as a threat to their livelihoods, and there were public protests in many port towns. The residents of Boston were especially vocal. The town meeting proposed a boycott of certain English imports, and the tactic of nonimportation soon spread to other port towns.

James Otis, a brilliant Massachusetts lawyer, became one of the first Americans to give voice to these protests, striking a number of themes that were repeated many times over the next fifteen years. Every man, Otis declared, in rhetoric lifted directly from the Great Awakening, "was an independent sovereign, subject to no law but the law written on his heart and revealed to him by his Maker." No government, he argued, using the logic of British republicanism, could rightfully deprive a man of the right "to his life, his liberty, and his property." Otis's most memorable phrase would echo throughout the subsequent decade: "Taxation without representation is tyranny."

THE STAMP ACT CRISIS

Ignoring American protests, in early 1765 Grenville pushed through a considerably more sweeping revenue measure known as the **Stamp Act**. This legislation required the purchase of specially embossed paper for all newspapers, legal documents, licenses, insurance policies, ships' papers, even dice and playing cards. It affected nearly every colonial resident in one way or another.

The American reaction to the Stamp Act during the summer and autumn of 1765 created a crisis of unprecedented proportions. Many colonists complained of being "miserably burdened and oppressed with taxes." But constitutional objections had more importance over the long term. Although colonial male property owners elected their own assemblies, they could not vote in British elections and had no representatives in Parliament. The British government argued that colonists were still subject to the acts of Parliament because of what they termed "**virtual representation**."

Americans were unconvinced. They argued instead for "actual representation," emphasizing the direct relationship that should exist between the people and their political leaders. Just such constitutional issues were emphasized in the Virginia Stamp Act Resolutions, written by Patrick Henry, a passionate young backcountry lawyer and member of the House of Burgesses. Although Henry's colleagues rejected the most radical of his resolutions, all of them were reprinted in the colonial press. By the end of 1765 the assemblies of eight other colonies had approved similar measures denouncing the Stamp Act and proclaiming their support of "no taxation without representation."

The most violent protests took place in Boston. The city's elite had prospered over the previous decade, but conditions for workers and the poor had worsened. Ordinary Bostonians were resentful. Their discontent was channeled by Samuel Adams, the son of a brewer, who became a powerful local politician. In the late summer of 1765 he and his associates organized a protest of Boston workingmen. On August 14 a large crowd assembled near Boston Common, and in an old elm, known as the "Liberty Tree," strung up effigies of several British officials, including Boston's stamp distributor, Andrew Oliver. The restless crowd then invaded and vandalized Oliver's office as well as his home. Soon thereafter, Oliver resigned his commission. Several days later another mob broke into the mansion of Thomas Hutchinson, lieutenant governor of the colony.

During the fall and winter, urban crowds protested in port towns from Halifax in the north to Savannah in the south (see Map 6.3). Growing alarmed at the rising potential for violence, merchants, lawyers, and respectable craftsmen gained control of the resistance

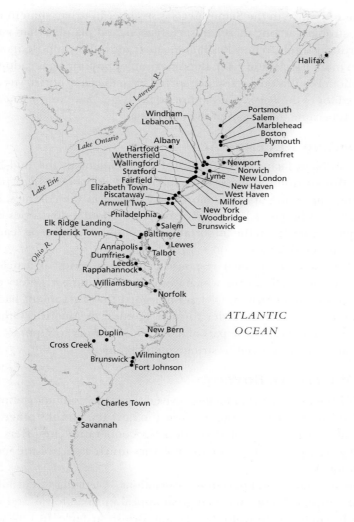

MAP 6.3
Demonstrations against the Stamp Act, 1765 From Halifax in the North to Savannah in the South, popular demonstrations against the Stamp Act forced the resignation of British tax officials. The propaganda of 1765 even reached the breakfast table, emblazoned on teapots.

WHY WERE the demonstrations concentrated in the coastal areas of New England and the Middle colonies?

movement. Calling themselves the **Sons of Liberty**, these leaders encouraged more moderate forms of protest, such as circulating petitions and publishing pamphlets. There were few repetitions of mob attacks, but by the end of 1765 almost all the stamp distributors had resigned or fled, making it impossible for Britain to enforce the Stamp Act. Pressured by British merchants, who worried over the effects of the growing **nonimportation movement** among the colonists, in March 1766 Parliament repealed the Stamp Act and reduced the duties under the Sugar Act.

Overlooked, however, was the fact that Parliament coupled repeal with what was termed a "Declaratory Act," affirming its full authority to make laws binding the colonies "in all cases whatsoever." The Declaratory Act signaled that the conflict between the mother country and the colonies had not been resolved but merely postponed.

"Save Your Money and Save Your Country"

Colonial resistance to the Stamp Act was stronger in urban than in rural communities, stronger among merchants, craftsmen, and planters than among farmers and frontiersmen. When Parliament next moved to impose its will, as it had promised to do in the **Declaratory Act**, the American opposition again adopted the tactic of nonimportation. But this time resistance spread from the cities and towns into the countryside. As the editor of the *Boston Gazette* phrased the issue, "Save your money and you save your country." It became the slogan of the movement.

The Townshend Revenue Acts

The foremost problem facing the new British government in the mid-1760s was the national debt. Britain suffered massive unemployment, riots over high prices, and tax protests. Fearing opposition at home more than protest in the colonies, in June 1767, Chancellor of the Exchequer Charles Townshend proposed a new series of **Townshend Revenue Acts** placing tariffs on the importation of commodities such as lead, glass, paint, paper, and tea into the colonies.

The most influential colonial response came in a series of articles by wealthy Philadelphia lawyer John Dickinson, which were reprinted in nearly every colonial newspaper. Posing as a humble farmer, Dickinson argued that Parliament had no constitutional authority to tax goods in order to raise revenue in America. Other Americans warned that the Revenue Acts were part of a British conspiracy to suppress American liberties. Their fears were reinforced by stringent enforcement.

An Early Political Boycott

In October 1767 the Boston town meeting revived the tactic nonimportation, drawing up a long list of British products to boycott. Over the next few months other port cities set up nonimportation campaigns of their own. Uncooperative importers and retailers became the object of protesters. Coercion was very much a part of the movement, and there was occasional violence.

Protestors formed "nonimportation associations," pledging to curtail luxuries and stimulate local industry. These aims had great appeal in small towns and rural districts, which previously had been uninvolved in the anti-British struggle. In 1768 and 1769 colonial newspapers paid a great deal of attention to women's support for the boycott. Groups of women, some calling themselves Daughters of Liberty, organized spinning and weaving bees to produce homespun for local consumption. Other women renounced silks and satins and pledged to stop serving tea to their husbands.

Nonimportation was greatly strengthened in May 1769 when the Virginia House of Burgesses enacted the first provincial legislation banning the importation of goods

---

HOW DID political and economic problems in Britain contribute to unrest in the colonies?

◄●➜ Read the Document

John Dickinson, from Letters from a Farmer in Pennsylvania (1768) at **www.myhistorylab.com**

Sons of Liberty Secret organizations in the colonies formed to oppose the Stamp Act.

nonimportation movement A tactical means of putting economic pressure on Britain by refusing to buy its exports to the colonies.

Declaratory Act Law passed in 1776 to accompany repeal of the Stamp Act that stated that Parliament had the authority to legislate for the colonies "in all cases whatsoever."

Townshend Revenue Acts Act of Parliament, passed in 1767, imposing duties on colonial tea, lead, paint, paper, and glass.

enumerated in the Townshend Acts. Over the next few months all the colonies but New Hampshire enacted similar legislation. Because of these efforts, the value of colonial imports from Britain declined by 41 percent over the next year.

THE MASSACHUSETTS CIRCULAR LETTER

Boston and Massachusetts were at the center of the agitation over the Townshend Revenue Acts. In February 1768 the Massachusetts House of Representatives approved a letter drawn up by Samuel Adams and addressed to the speakers of the other colonial assemblies. The letter denounced the Revenue Acts, attacked the British plan to make royal officials independent of colonial assemblies, and urged the colonies to find a way to "harmonize with each other." Massachusetts governor Francis Bernard condemned the document for stirring up rebellion and dissolved the legislature. In Britain, Lord Hillsborough, secretary of state for the colonies, ordered each royal governor in America to dissolve his colony's assembly if it should endorse the letter. Before this demand reached America, the assemblies of New Hampshire, New Jersey, and Connecticut had commended Massachusetts. Virginia, moreover, had issued a circular letter encouraging a "hearty union" among the colonies and urging common action against the British measures.

Throughout this crisis there were rumors and threats of mob rule in Boston. Because customs agents pressed on smugglers and honest traders alike, they enraged merchants, seamen, and dockworkers, some of whom resorted to attacks on customs officers. In September, the Boston town meeting called on the people to arm themselves and issued an invitation for all the colony's towns to send delegates to a provincial convention. Although a number of delegates made threats of armed resistance, they received little support and the convention broke up in chaos. Fearful of insurrection, on October 1, 1768, the British occupied Boston with infantry and artillery regiments. This action added greatly to the growing tensions.

THE BOSTON MASSACRE

The British troops stationed in the colonies were the object of scorn and hostility over the next two years and there were a number of violent confrontations. A persistent source of conflict was the competition between troops and townsmen over jobs. Soldiers were permitted to work on their days off-duty, thus competing with poor day laborers. In early March 1770 a British soldier walked into a Boston ropewalk in search of a job. "You can clean my shithouse," the scornful owner told him. The soldier later returned with some of his friends and a small riot resulted. Over the next few days sporadic fighting between soldiers and townsmen continued in the streets between the wharf and the Common, where the soldiers were encamped. Finally, on the evening of March 5, 1770, a crowd at the Customs House began taunting a guard. A captain and a company of seven soldiers went to his rescue, only to be pelted with snowballs and stones. Suddenly someone shouted "Fire!" and the frightened soldiers shot indiscriminately into the crowd. Five men fell dead and six were wounded, two of them mortally. What became known as "the **Boston Massacre**" was soon infamous throughout the colonies. For many colonists the incident was a disturbing reminder of the extent to which relations with the mother country had deteriorated. During the next two years many people found themselves pulling back from the brink.

The growth of American resistance was slowed as well by the news that Parliament had repealed most of the Revenue Acts. In the climate of apprehension and confusion, there were few celebrations of the repeal, and the nonimportation associations almost immediately collapsed. The parliamentary retreat on the question of duties, like the earlier repeal of the Stamp Act, was accompanied by a face-saving measure—retention of the tax on tea.

Read the Document

Boston Gazette *Description of the Boston Massacre (1770)* at **www.myhistorylab.com**

Boston Massacre   After months of increasing friction between townspeople and the British troops stationed in the city, on March 5, 1770, British troops fired on American civilians in Boston.

In Paul Revere's version of the Boston Massacre, issued three weeks after the incident, the British fire an organized volley into a crowd of unresisting civilians. Revere's print—which he plagiarized from another Boston engraver—was historically inaccurate but enormously effective propaganda. It hung in so many Patriot homes that the judge hearing the murder trial of these British soldiers warned the jury not to be swayed by "the prints exhibited in our houses."

FROM RESISTANCE TO REBELLION

WHAT STEPS did Britain take to punish Massachusetts for the colonists' acts of resistance?

There was a lull in the American controversy during the early 1770s, but the situation turned violent once again in 1773, when Parliament infuriated the Americans by passing an ill-advised tax on tea. The tax pushed the colonists onto a fast track from resistance to outright rebellion.

COMMITTEES OF CORRESPONDENCE

In June 1772, Governor Hutchinson of Massachusetts announced that henceforth his salary and those of other royally appointed officials would be paid by the crown. In effect, this made the executive and judiciary branches of the colony's government independent of control by elected representatives. In October, the Boston town meeting appointed a committee of correspondence to communicate with other communities regarding this challenge.

In March 1773 the Virginia House of Burgesses appointed a standing committee of correspondence "to obtain the most early and authentic intelligence" of British actions affecting America, "and to keep up and maintain a correspondence and communication with our sister colonies." The Virginia committee served as a model for the other colonies, and within a year all but Pennsylvania (where conservatives were in control of the legislature) had created committees of their own. The committees of correspondence became the principal channel for sharing information, shaping public opinion, and building cooperation among the colonies before the opening meeting of the First Continental Congress in 1774.

The information most damaging to British influence came from the radicals in Boston. In June 1773 the Boston committee circulated a set of confidential letters from Governor Hutchinson to the ministry in Britain. The letters revealed the governor's call for "an abridgement of what are called English liberties" in the colonies. His statement appeared to be the "smoking gun" of the conspiracy theory, and it created a torrent of anger against the British and their officials in the colonies.

THE BOSTON TEA PARTY

It was in this context that the colonists received the news that Parliament had passed the **Tea Act**. As a result of the Townshend duties the market for tea in the colonies had collapsed. The British East India Company, the sole agent of British power in India, was on the brink of bankruptcy. Parliament considered it too big to fail, and devised a scheme to offer tea to Americans at prices that would tempt even the most patriotic drinker. The radicals argued that this was merely a device to make palatable the payment of unconstitutional taxes and further evidence of the British effort to seduce and corrupt the colonists.

In October 1773 a mass meeting in Philadelphia denounced anyone importing the tea as "an enemy of his country." A group calling itself "the Committee for Tarring and Feathering" published a broadside threatening captains whose ships carried British tea. The Philadelphia consignees resigned in terror. Similar protests in New York City forced resignations there as well. The town meeting in Boston soon passed resolutions patterned on those of Philadelphia.

The first of three tea ships arrived in Boston Harbor late in November. On the evening of December 16, 1773, 5,000 people crowded into the Old South Church to hear the captain of one of the vessels report to Sam Adams that Governor Hutchinson had issued orders that the ship was to remain docked at the wharf. "This meeting can do nothing more to save the country," Adams declared. This was the signal for a disciplined group of fifty or sixty men to march to the wharf. Dressed as Indians and cheered on by Boston's citizens, they boarded the ships and dumped into the harbor some forty-five tons of tea, valued at £18,000.

Boston's was the first tea party, and other incidents of property destruction soon followed. But it was the initial action in Boston that infuriated the British. The government became convinced that something had to be done about the rebellious colony of Massachusetts.

Boston Tea Party   Incident that occurred on December 16, 1773, in which Bostonians, disguised as Indians, destroyed £18,000 worth of tea belonging to the British East India Company in order to prevent payment of the duty on it.

Tea Act   Act of Parliament that permitted the East India Company to sell through agents in America without paying the duty customarily collected in Britain, thus reducing the retail price.

Read the **Document**

John Andrew to William Barrell, Boston Tea Party (1773) at **www.myhistorylab.com**

The Bostonians Paying the Excise-Man, or Tarring and Feathering

Political cartoons played an important role in the public controversy leading to the American Revolution. This print, published in London in 1774 and sold on the streets for a few pennies, depicts the violent attack of a Boston mob on customs commissioner John Malcolm several weeks after the "Tea Party." Malcolm, an ardent Loyalist, had been the frequent target of protests. In January 1774 he struck a prominent Patriot activist on the head with his cane, seriously injuring him. That night a mob dragged Malcolm from his house and covered him with tar and feathers, a ritual of public humiliation. Hot tar produced painful blistering of the skin, and the effort to remove it made the condition worse. The feathers made the victim into an object of ridicule. Hauled to the Liberty Tree in Boston Common, Malcolm was threatened with hanging if he did not apologize and renounce his commission. When he did he was allowed to return home. The pro-Loyalist print includes a number of telling details. Malcolm is attacked by a group that includes a leather-aproned artisan. A broadside announcing the Stamp Act is posted upside down on the Liberty Tree. A hangman's noose dangles from a branch. The Boston Tea Party takes place in the background. In the foreground is a tar bucket and a pole topped by a "liberty cap," a symbol of freedom adopted by American protesters (and later an icon of the French Revolution). These details were intended to mock the Americans. But when the print found its way to North America it was embraced by Patriots and became an enduring American favorite. In the nineteenth century it was reprinted as a celebration of the righteous violence of the Revolution. ■

HOW COULD this image, intended to ridicule and shame the American patriots, have been embraced and celebrated by them?

The Bostonian's Paying the EXCISE-MAN, or TARRING & FEATHERING
Plate I.

THE INTOLERABLE ACTS

During the spring of 1774 an angry Parliament passed a series of acts—officially called the **Coercive Acts** but known by Americans as the **Intolerable Acts**—calculated to punish the colony of Massachusetts and strengthen the British hand. The Boston Port Bill prohibited the loading or unloading of ships in any part of Boston Harbor until the town fully compensated the East India Company and the customs service for the destroyed tea. The Massachusetts Government Act annulled the colonial charter, shifted authority and control to the crown at all levels of government, and terminated the long history of self-rule by communities in the colony of Massachusetts.

Additional measures affected the other colonies and encouraged them to see themselves in league with Massachusetts. The Administration of Justice Act protected British officials from colonial courts, thereby encouraging them to pursue the work of suppression. Those accused of committing capital crimes while putting down riots or collecting revenue—as in the Boston Massacre—were now to be sent to England for trial. The **Quartering Act** legalized the housing of troops at public expense not only in taverns and abandoned buildings but also in occupied dwellings and private homes.

Finally, in the **Québec Act**, the British authorized a permanent government for the territory taken from France during the Seven Years' War: a strictly anti-republican government with an appointed council (see Map 6.4). The act also granted religious toleration to

MAP 6.4

The Québec Act of 1774 With the Québec Act, Britain created a centralized colonial government for Canada and extended that colony's administrative control south west to the Ohio River, invalidating the sea-to-sea boundaries of many colonial charters.

HOW DID the boundaries set by the Québec Act of 1774 contribute to rising tensions between the colonists and imperial authorities?

Coercive Acts Legislation passed by Parliament in 1774; included the Boston Port Act, the Massachusetts Government Act, the Administration of Justice Act, and the Quartering Act of 1774.

Intolerable Acts American term for the Coercive Acts and the Quebec Act.

Quartering Act Acts of Parliament requiring colonial legislatures to provide supplies and quarters for the troops stationed in America.

Québec Act Law passed by Parliament in 1774 that provided an appointed government for Canada, enlarged the boundaries of Quebec, and confirmed the privileges of the Catholic Church.

First Continental Congress Meeting of delegates from most of the colonies held in 1774 in response to the Coercive Acts.

the Roman Catholic Church and upheld the Church's traditional right to collect tithes, in effect endorsing Catholicism as the state religion of Québec. To the American colonists it seemed a frightening preview of what imperial authorities had in store for them, and it confirmed the contention of the committees of correspondence that there was a British plot to destroy American liberty. In May General Thomas Gage arrived in Boston to replace Hutchinson as governor.

THE FIRST CONTINENTAL CONGRESS

It was amid this crisis that town meetings and colonial assemblies alike chose representatives for the **First Continental Congress**. The delegates who arrived in Philadelphia in September 1774 included the most important leaders of the American cause. Cousins Samuel and John Adams from Massachusetts were joined by Patrick Henry and George Washington of Virginia and Christopher Gadsden of South Carolina. Many of the delegates were conservatives, including John Dickinson and Joseph Galloway of Philadelphia, and John Jay and James Duane from New York.

After one of their first debates, the delegates passed a "Declaration and Resolves," asserting that all the colonists sprang from a common tradition and enjoyed rights guaranteed "by the immutable laws of nature, the principles of the English constitution, and the several charters or compacts" of their provinces. Thirteen acts of Parliament, passed since 1763, were declared in violation of these rights. Until these acts were repealed, the delegates declared, they were imposing a set of sanctions against the British. These included not only the nonimportation and nonconsumption of British goods but a prohibition on the export of colonial commodities to Britain or its other colonies.

To enforce these sanctions, the Continental Congress urged that "a committee be chosen in every county, city, and town, by those who are qualified to vote for representatives in the legislature, whose business it shall be attentively to observe the conduct of all persons." Known as "Committees of Observation and Safety," these groups took over the functions of local government throughout the colonies. In addition to providing government, the committees also scrutinized the activities of fellow citizens, suppressed the expression of Loyalist opinion, and practiced other forms of coercion. Throughout the colonies the Committees formed a bridge between the old colonial administrations and the revolutionary governments organized over the next few years. Committees began to link localities together in the cause of a wider American community.

LEXINGTON AND CONCORD

On September 1, 1774, General Gage sent troops to seize stores of gunpowder and arms from several storehouses on the outskirts of Boston. In response, the Massachusetts House of Representatives, calling itself the Provincial Congress, created a Committee of Safety, empowered to call up the militia. On October 15 the Committee authorized the creation of special units, to be known as "Minutemen," who stood ready to be called at a moment's notice. The armed militia of the towns and communities surrounding Boston now opposed the British army, quartered in the city. Worrying that his forces were insufficient to suppress the rebellion, Gage wrote to London to request reinforcements. The stalemate continued throughout the fall and winter as he awaited instructions.

British monarch George III (reigned 1760–1820) believed the time for war had come. "The New England Governments are in a State of Rebellion," he wrote, and "blows must decide whether they are to be subject to this Country or independent." In Virginia, at almost the same moment, Patrick Henry, predicting that hostilities soon would begin, made his choice clear. "Is life so dear, or peace so sweet, as to be purchased at the price of chains and slavery? . . . I know not what course others may take, but as for me give me

QUICK REVIEW

Congressional Response to the Intolerable Acts

◆ All agreed that Acts were unconstitutional.

◆ Sought to impose economic sanctions on Britain.

◆ Urged the creation of Committees of Observation and Safety.

Read the Document

Patrick Henry, "Give Me Liberty or Give Me Death" (1775) at **www.myhistorylab.com**

liberty or give me death!" Three weeks later, on April 14, 1775, General Gage received instructions to immediately strike against the Massachusetts militia.

On the evening of April 18, Gage ordered 700 troops to Concord, some miles outside Boston, to take possession of the armory there. Learning of the operation, the Boston Committee dispatched two men, Paul Revere and William Dawes, to alert the militia of the countryside. By the time the British forces had reached Lexington, midway to their destination, some seventy armed minutemen were assembled on the green in the center of town. They were disorganized and confused. No order to fire was given, but suddenly shots rang out spontaneously. Eight Americans were killed, ten wounded.

The British marched on to Concord where they burned a small quantity of supplies and cut down a liberty pole. Meanwhile, news of the deaths at Lexington had spread throughout the surrounding countryside, and the militia companies from communities from miles around converged on the town. At a Concord bridge they encountered the enemy and opened fire. Three regular soldiers were killed, the first British casualties. Seeing that their men were greatly outnumbered by Massachusetts militia, British officers immediately ordered a return to Boston, but at many points along the way they were subjected to withering fire. By the time the British force finally reached the city, 73 soldiers had been killed and 202 wounded (see Map 6.5). The engagement forecast what would be a central problem for the British: they would be forced to fight an armed population defending their own communities against outsiders.

MAP 6.5

The First Engagements of the Revolution   The first military engagements of the American Revolution took place in the spring of 1775 in the countryside surrounding Boston.

WHAT SPARKED the clashes at Lexington and Concord?

Read the Document

Joseph Warren, "Account of the Battle of Lexington" (1775) at **www.myhistorylab.com**

British soldiers fire upon Massachusetts militia at Lexington, the first of four hand-colored engravings included in Amos Doolittle's *View of the Battle of Lexington and Concord* (1775). It is the only contemporary pictorial record of the events of April 19, 1775, from an American point of view. Doolittle, a Connecticut silversmith, traveled to the site of the conflict in the weeks afterward, and his engravings are based on first-hand observation. Important buildings, individuals, or groups of people are keyed to a legend that explains what is happening. Doolittle intended his prints to be informative in the same sense as a photograph in a modern newspaper.

Deciding for Independence

WHAT EVENTS led the second Continental Congress to declare independence?

Throughout the colonies community militia companies mobilized for war. At Boston, thousands of militiamen besieged the city, leaving the British no escape but by sea. Meanwhile, delegates from twelve colonies converged again on Philadelphia.

The Second Continental Congress

The Second Continental Congress, which opened on May 10, 1775, included representatives from twelve of the British colonies on the mainland of North America. Few conservatives or Loyalists were among them. Georgia, unrepresented at the First Continental Congress, remained absent at the opening of the Second. It depended heavily on British subsidies, and its leaders were cautious, fearing both slave and Indian uprisings. But the political balance soon shifted in favor of the radicals in Georgia, and by the end of the summer the colony had sent delegates to Philadelphia.

On May 15 the representatives resolved to put the colonies in a state of defense but were divided on how best to do it. They lacked the power and the funds to raise and supply an army. John Adams made the winning proposal that they simply designate as a Continental Army the militia forces besieging Boston. In order to emphasize their national aspirations, they decided to select a man from the South to command those New England forces. On June 15 Thomas Jefferson and Adams nominated George Washington to be commander-in-chief, and he was elected by acclaim. On June 22, the Congress voted to finance the army with an issue of $2 million in bills of credit, backed by the good faith of the "Confederated Colonies."

During the early summer of 1775 the Congress began to move cautiously toward independence. On July 5, 1775, the delegates passed the so-called "Olive Branch Petition," written by John Dickinson of Pennsylvania, in which they professed their attachment to King George and begged him to prevent further hostilities so that there might be an accommodation. The next day they approved a "Declaration of the Causes and Necessities of Taking Up Arms," written by Jefferson and Dickinson. In this the delegates adopted a harsher tone, resolving "to die freemen rather than to live slaves."

Canada and the Spanish Borderlands

In one of their first acts, delegates to the Continental Congress called on "the oppressed inhabitants of Canada" to join in the struggle for "common liberty." French Canadians felt little sympathy for the British, but the Americans were traditional enemies, much feared because of their aggressive expansionism. Indeed, when the Canadians failed to respond positively and immediately, the Congress reversed itself and voted to authorize a military expedition against Québec to eliminate any possibility of a British invasion from that quarter. This set a course toward the development of the separate nations of the United States and Canada.

In the British island colonies, there was at first considerable sympathy for the American struggle. The legislative assemblies of Jamaica, Grenada, and Barbados declared themselves in accord with the Continental Congress. But the British navy prevented them from sending representatives. The island colonies would remain aloof from the imperial crisis, largely because the colonists there were dependent on a British military presence to guard against slave revolts.

Things at first seemed more promising in Nova Scotia (not then a part of Canada), where many New Englanders had relocated after the expulsion of the Acadians. There had been Stamp Act demonstrations in Halifax, and when the British attempted to recruit among the Nova Scotians for soldiers to serve in Boston, one community responded that since "almost all of us [were] born in New England, [we are] divided betwixt natural affection to our nearest relations and good faith and friendship to our

QUICK REVIEW

The Second Continental Congress

- Opened on May 10, 1775.
- May 15: Congress resolved to put the colonies in a state of defense.
- June 15: George Washington nominated to be commander-in-chief.

king and country." The British naval stronghold at Halifax, however, secured the province for the empire. Large contingents of British troops also kept Florida (which Britain had divided into two colonies, East and West Florida) solidly in the empire.

In Cuba, some 3,000 exiled Spanish Floridians, who had fled there in 1763 rather than live under British rule, now clamored for Spain to take advantage of the situation and retake their homeland. Many of them were active supporters of American independence. Spanish colonial authorities, who also administered the newly acquired colony of Louisiana, were conflicted. They certainly felt no solidarity with the cause of the American rebels, whom they thought threatened the idea of monarchy and empire. But with painful memories of the British invasion of Havana in 1763, they looked forward to the prospect of taking revenge on their traditional enemy, as well as regaining control of the Floridas and eliminating the British threat to their Mexican and Caribbean colonies.

In 1775 Spain publicly declared itself neutral but secretly searched for an opportunity to support the Americans. The Spanish government eventually approved a plan to sell arms and ammunition to the rebels, turning Havana and New Orleans into important supply centers for the Americans.

FIGHTING IN THE NORTH AND SOUTH

Violent conflict took place between British forces and American rebels in both the northern and southern colonies in 1775 and early 1776. On the evening of May 10, 1775, a small force of armed New Englanders jointly commanded by Ethan Allen of Vermont and Benedict Arnold of Connecticut, surprised the British garrison at Fort Ticonderoga on Lake Champlain. With great effort, the Americans hauled the fort's cannon overland to be used in the siege of Boston.

At Boston, the British reinforced Gage's forces, and by the middle of June had approximately 6,500 soldiers in the city. They were besieged by more than 10,000 New England militia. Fearing a move by Gage to occupy the heights south of town, the Americans made a countermove, occupying the Charlestown peninsula on the north. Gage decided on a frontal assault to dislodge them. In bloody fighting at Breed's and Bunker Hill, the British overran the Americans, killing 140 men, but not before suffering over a thousand casualties of their own, including 226 dead. The fierce patriotic reaction in England to this enormous loss ended any possibility of a last-minute reconciliation. In August 1775 King George refused to hear the Olive Branch Petition and issued a royal proclamation declaring the colonists in "open and avowed rebellion."

> **Read** the **Document**
>
> *Royal Proclamation of Rebellion (1775)* at **www.myhistorylab.com**

In June Congress assembled an expeditionary force against Canada. One thousand Americans moved north up the Hudson River corridor, and in November General Richard Montgomery forced the capitulation of Montreal. In the meantime Colonel Benedict Arnold set out from Massachusetts with another American army and joined Montgomery outside the walls of Québec. But the American assault failed to take the city. By the summer of 1776 the Americans had been forced back from Canada.

There were successes elsewhere. In the South local militias decisively defeated the Loyalist forces of Virginia's Governor Dunmore, who alienated the planter class by promising freedom to any slave who would fight with the British. The next month the North Carolina rebel militia crushed a Loyalist force at the Battle of Moore's Creek Bridge near Wilmington, ending British plans for an invasion there. The British elected to attack Charles Town, but an American force turned back the assault. It would be more than two years before the British would try to invade the South again. At Boston, Washington installed the British artillery captured at Fort Ticonderoga on the heights south of town, placing the city and harbor within cannon range. In March 1776 the British sailed out of Boston Harbor heading northeast to Halifax, accompanied by at least a thousand American Loyalists.

NO TURNING BACK

Any hope of reconciliation died with the mounting casualties. The Second Continental Congress, rapidly assuming the role of a general government for all the colonies, now called the states, reconvened in Philadelphia in September 1775. Although the Congress continued to disclaim any intention of denying the sovereignty of the king, it now moved to organize an American navy, and declared British vessels open to capture. The Congress took further steps toward independence when it authorized contacts with foreign powers through its agents in Europe. In the spring of 1776 France joined Spain in approving the shipping of supplies to the rebellious provinces. The Continental Congress then declared colonial ports open to the trade of all nations but Britain.

But the emotional ties to Great Britain proved difficult to break. Help arrived in January 1776 in the form of a pamphlet entitled *Common Sense*, written by Thomas Paine, a radical Englishman recently arrived in Philadelphia. For years Americans had defended their actions as consistent with British tradition. But Paine argued that the British system rested on "the base remains of two ancient tyrannies," aristocracy and monarchy, neither of which was appropriate for America. Paine placed the blame for the oppression of the colonists on the shoulders of George III. *Common Sense* was the single most important piece of writing during the Revolutionary era, selling more than 100,000 copies within a few months of its publication. It reshaped popular thinking and put independence squarely on the agenda.

In April, the North Carolina convention became the first to empower its delegates to the Continental Congress to vote for independence. In May the Congress voted to recommend that the individual states move as quickly as possible toward the adoption of state constitutions. In the preamble to this statement John Adams wrote that "the exercise of every kind of authority under the said crown should be totally suppressed." This sent a strong signal that the delegates were on the verge of approving a momentous declaration.

THE DECLARATION OF INDEPENDENCE

On June 7, 1776, Richard Henry Lee of Virginia offered the first motion for independence: After some debate, a vote was postponed until July, but a committee composed of John Adams, Thomas Jefferson, Benjamin Franklin, Roger Sherman of Connecticut, and

Read the **Document**

History Bookshelf: *Thomas Paine, Common Sense (1776)* at **www.myhistorylab.com**

The Connecticut artist John Trumbull painted *The Battle of Bunker Hill* in 1785, the first of a series that earned him the informal title of "the Painter of the Revolution." Trumbull was careful to research the details of his paintings but composed them in the grand style of historical romance. In the early nineteenth century, he repainted this work and three other Revolutionary scenes for the rotunda of the Capitol in Washington, DC.

CHRONOLOGY

1713	France cedes Acadia to Britain		**1764**	Sugar Act
1745	New Englanders capture Louisbourg		**1765**	Stamp Act and Stamp Act Congress
1749	French send an expeditionary force down the Ohio River		**1766**	Declaratory Act
			1767	Townshend Revenue Acts
1753	French begin building forts from Lake Erie to the Ohio		**1768**	Treaties of Hard Labor and Fort Stanwix
1754	Albany Conference		**1770**	Boston Massacre
1755	British General Edward Braddock defeated by a combined force of French and Indians		**1772**	First Committee of Correspondence organized in Boston
	Britain expels Acadians from Nova Scotia		**1773**	Tea Act
1756	Seven Years' War begins in Europe			Boston Tea Party
1757	William Pitt becomes prime minister		**1774**	Intolerable Acts
1758	Louisbourg captured by the British for the second time			First Continental Congress
				Dunmore's War
1759	British capture Québec		**1775**	Fighting begins at Lexington and Concord
1763	Treaty of Paris			Second Continental Congress
	Pontiac's uprising		**1776**	Americans invade Canada
	Proclamation of 1763 creates "Indian Country"			Thomas Paine's *Common Sense*
	Paxton Boys massacre			Declaration of Independence

Robert Livingston of New York was asked to prepare a draft declaration of American independence. The committee assigned the writing of a first draft to Jefferson.

The intervening time allowed the delegates to debate and receive instructions from their state conventions. By the end of the month all the states but New York had authorized a vote for independence, and when the question came up for debate again on July 1, there was a large majority in support. The final vote, taken on July 2, was twelve in favor of independence, none against, with New York abstaining. The delegates then turned to the Declaration itself and made a number of changes in Jefferson's draft, striking out, for example, a long passage condemning slavery.

The first section of the Declaration expressed the highest ideals of the delegates:

> We hold these truths to be self-evident, that all men are created equal, that they are endowed by their creator with certain unalienable rights, that among these are life, liberty, and the pursuit of happiness. That to secure these rights, governments are instituted among men, deriving their just powers from the consent of the governed. That whenever any form of government becomes destructive of these ends, it is the right of the people to alter or to abolish it, and to institute a new government, laying its foundation on such principles, and organizing its powers in such form, as to them shall seem most likely to effect their safety and happiness.

There was very little debate over this extraordinary statement. The delegates, mostly men of wealth and position, realized that the coming struggle for independence would require the steady support of ordinary people, and thus they asserted this great

Read the Document

Thomas Jefferson, "Original Rough Draught" of the Declaration of Independence (1776) at **www.myhistorylab.com**

principle of equality and the right of revolution. There was little debate about the implications or the potential consequences. The statement of principles would resonate throughout subsequent American history. The ideal of equality would inspire the poor as well as the wealthy, women as well as men, blacks as well as whites.

It was the final section of the Declaration, however, that may have contained the most meaning for the delegates themselves: "And for the support of this declaration, with a firm reliance on the Protection of Divine Providence, we mutually pledge to each other our Lives, our Fortunes, and our sacred Honor." By voting for independence, these men were not only proclaiming a belief in their newly conceived national community, they were also committing treason against their king and empire. They would be condemned as traitors, hunted as criminals, and might stand on the scaffold in payment for their actions. On July 4, 1776, the Declaration of Independence was adopted without dissent.

CONCLUSION

Great Britain emerged from the Seven Years' War as the dominant power in North America. Yet despite its attempts at strict regulation and determination of the course of events in its colonies, it faced consistent resistance. The British underestimated the political consensus that existed among the colonists about the importance of republican government. They also underestimated the ability of the colonists to inform one another, to work together, and to build the bonds of national community cutting across boundaries of ethnicity, region, and economic condition. Through newspapers, pamphlets, committees of correspondence, community organizations, and group protest, the colonists discovered the concerns they shared, and in so doing fostered a new American identity. Without that identity it would have been difficult for them to consent to the treasonous act of declaring independence, especially when the independence they sought was from an international power that dominated much of the globe.

REVIEW QUESTIONS

1. How did overwhelming British success in the Seven Years' War lead to an imperial crisis in British North America?

2. Outline the changes in British policy toward the colonies from 1750 to 1776.

3. Trace the developing sense of an American national community over this same period.

4. What were the principal events leading to the beginning of armed conflict at Lexington and Concord?

5. How were the ideals of American republicanism expressed in the Declaration of Independence?

KEY TERMS

Albany Conference (p. 123)

Boston Massacre (p. 135)

Boston Tea Party (p. 137)

Coercive Acts (p. 139)

Declaratory Act (p. 134)

First Continental Congress (p. 140)

French and Indian War (p. 124)

Intolerable Acts (p. 139)

Nonimportation movement (p. 134)

Plan of Union (p. 123)

Quartering Act (p. 139)

Québec Act (p. 139)

Republicanism (p. 131)

Royal Proclamation of 1763 (p. 128)

 **Connections**

Reinforce what you learned in this chapter by studying the many documents,
images, maps, review tools, and videos available at www.myhistorylab.com.

Read and Review

✓● Study and Review Chapter 6

●● Read the Document

Benjamin Franklin, Testimony against the Stamp Act (1766)

Otis, The Rights of the British Colonies Asserted and Proved (1763)

The Stamp Act Crisis

John Dickinson, from Letters from a Farmer in Pennsylvania (1768)

Boston Gazette Description of the Boston Massacre (1770)

John Andrew to William Barrell, Boston Tea Party (1773)

Patrick Henry, "Give Me Liberty or Give Me Death" (1775)

Joseph Warren, "Account of the Battle of Lexington" (1775)

Royal Proclamation of Rebellion (1775)

Thomas Jefferson, "Original Rough Draught" of the Declaration of Independence (1776)

◉ See the Map *The Seven Years' War*

Research and Explore

●● Read the Document

Exploring America: The Stamp Act

Profiles
Samuel Adams
Thomas Hutchinson

History Bookshelf: *Thomas Paine,* Common Sense *(1776)*

The Connecticut Peddler

◉ Watch the Video *The Revolution*

 **Hear** the **Audio**

Hear the audio files for Chapter 6 at
www.myhistorylab.com.

These are the times that try men's souls. . .
—Thomas Paine

UNITE OR DIE

The surrender of Lord Cornwallis at Yorktown on October 19, 1781, led to the British decision to withdraw from the war. Cornwallis, who claimed to be ill, absented himself from the ceremony and is not in the picture. Washington, who is astride the horse under the American flag, designated General Benjamin Lincoln (on the white horse in the center) as the one to accept the submission of a subordinate British officer. John Trumbull, who painted The Battle of Bunker Hill and some three hundred other scenes from the Revolutionary War, finished this painting while he was in London about fifteen years after the events depicted. A large copy of the work now hangs in the rotunda of the United States Capitol in Washington, D.C. Source: Surrender of Lord Cornwallis at Yorktown, by John Trumbull (American, 1756–1843). Oil on canvas, 20 7/8 × 30 5/8 in.

7

THE AMERICAN REVOLUTION
1776–1786

((•—[**Hear** the **Audio**

Hear the audio files for Chapter 7 at **www.myhistorylab.com**.

HOW DID the Americans win the war for independence?

WHAT KIND of government was created by the Articles of Confederation?

HOW DID political debate in America change in the years after 1774?

1786

1776

AMERICAN COMMUNITIES
A National Community Evolves at Valley Forge

A DRUM ROLL ANNOUNCED THE DAWN OF A COLD JANUARY MORNING IN 1778. Along a two-mile line of rude log cabins, doors opened and the ragged men of the Continental Army stepped out onto the frozen ground of Valley Forge. The reek of unwashed bodies and foul straw filled the air. "No bread, no soldier!" The chant began as a barely audible murmur, then was picked up by men all along the line. "No bread, no soldier! No bread, no soldier!" At last the chanting grew so loud it could be heard at General Washington's headquarters, a mile away. The 11,000 men of the American army were surviving on little more than "firecake," a mixture of flour and water baked hard before the fire. Two thousand men were without shoes; others were without blankets and had to sit up all night about the fires to keep from freezing.

After suffering a series of shattering defeats at the hands of a British force nearly twice their number, the soldiers of the Continental Army straggled into its winter headquarters at Valley Forge, some twenty miles northwest of Philadelphia, only to find themselves at the mercy of indifferent local suppliers. Congress refused to pay the exorbitant rates demanded by contractors for food and clothing. Local farmers preferred to deal with the British, who paid in pounds sterling rather than depreciated Continental currency.

The 11,000 men of the Continental Army were divided into sixteen brigades composed of regiments from the individual states. Many were drawn from the ranks of the poor and disadvantaged. They included landless tenant farmers, indentured servants, and nearly a thousand African Americans, both slave and free. A majority of the men came from rural districts or small towns, places where precautions regarding sanitation were unnecessary. Every thaw that winter revealed ground covered with "much filth and nastiness," and officers ordered sentinels to fire on any man "easing himself elsewhere than at the vaults." Such conditions bred infectious epidemic diseases like typhoid that spread quickly among men already weakened by malnutrition, dysentery, and exposure. Some 2,500 men died that winter.

Yet the army that marched out of Valley Forge five months later was considerably stronger for its experience there. The men of the Continental Army spent the late winter and spring drilling under the strict discipline of Friedrich Wilhelm Augustus von Steuben, a Prussian officer who came to America to volunteer for the American cause. They were already resilient and tough; now they learned how to fight as a unit.

But most important were the bonds forged among the men. Thrown together under the most trying of circumstances, men from different localities and ethnic backgrounds found a common identity in their struggle. On May Day they celebrated the end of winter and the coming of spring by raising maypoles before the cabins of each state regiment. Led by a sergeant decked out as King Tammany, the great Delaware chief of American folklore, and accompanied by thirteen honor guards representing each of the states, the men paraded through camp, pausing at each maypole to dance together. It was a ritual of their new sense of national community.

To some American Patriots—as the supporters of the Revolution called themselves—the European-style Continental Army betrayed the revolutionary ideals of the citizen-soldier and the autonomy of local communities. Washington argued strongly, however, that the Revolution could not be won without a national army insulated from politics and able to withstand shifts in the popular mood. Moreover, during the critical period of the nation's founding, the Continental Army acted as a popular democratic force, counterbalancing the conservatism of the new republic's elite leadership. The national spirit built at places like Valley Forge sustained the fighting men through years of war and provided momentum for the long process of forging a national political system out of the persistent localism of American politics. The soldiers of the Continental Army were among the first of their countrymen to think of themselves as Americans.

The Revolutionary years were characterized by warfare not only between armed American and British forces but also between Patriots and Loyalists, settlers and Indians, masters and slaves. Jealous of their autonomy, the individual colonies shaped a weak central government that just barely managed to keep them unified. The glue that held Americans together during this long struggle was the sense of national community that emerged in places like Valley Forge during the winter of 1777.

Valley Forge

THE WAR FOR INDEPENDENCE

At the beginning of the Revolution, the British had the world's best-equipped and most disciplined army, as well as a navy that was unopposed in American waters. But this overwhelming force encouraged them to greatly underestimate the American capacity to fight. With a native officer corps and considerable experience in the colonial wars of the eighteenth century, Patriot forces proved formidable. The British also misperceived the sources of the conflict. Seeing the rebellion as the work of a small group of conspirators, they defined their objective as defeating this Patriot opposition. They believed that in the wake of a military victory they could easily reassert political control. But the geography of eastern North America offered no single vital center whose conquest would end the war. When the British succeeded in defeating the **Patriots** in one area, resistance would spring up in another. The key factor in the outcome of the war for independence was popular support for the American cause.

THE PATRIOT FORCES

Most American men of fighting age had to face the call to arms. From a population of approximately 350,000 eligible men, more than 200,000 saw action. About half served in the **Continental Army** under Washington's command, the other half in militia companies.

These militias—armed bodies of men drawn from local communities—proved important in the defense of their own areas, for they had homes as well as local reputations to protect. But the Revolution was not won by such citizen-soldiers. In the exuberant days of 1776, many Patriots hoped that militias alone could win the war against the British. But serving short terms of enlistment, often with officers of their own choosing, militiamen resisted discipline. Indeed, in the face of battle, militia companies during the Revolution demonstrated appalling rates of desertion.

The final victory resulted primarily from the steady struggle of the Continental Army. Washington and his officers wanted a force that could directly engage the British, and from the beginning of the war, he argued that victory could be won only with a full commitment to a truly national army. His views conflicted with popular fears of a standing army. Swayed by such fears, Congress initially refused to invoke a draft or mandate army enlistments exceeding one year.

But the failings of the militias in the early battles of the war sobered Congress, and it responded with greatly enlarged state quotas for the Continental Army and terms of service that lasted for the duration of the conflict. To spur enlistment, Congress offered bounties, regular wages, and promises of free land after victory. By the spring of 1777, Washington's army had grown to nearly 9,000 men.

A wide chasm separated the officer corps from the rank and file in the Continental Army. Officers came from propertied and socially prominent families and considered themselves gentlemen, while enlisted men came mainly from the economically deprived and socially marginal elements of the population.

The New England militia companies that made up the original core of the Continental Army included a small number of African

HOW DID the Americans win the war for independence?

Watch the Video
The American Revolution as Different Americans Saw It at **www.myhistorylab.com**

Read the Document
Proclamation of Lord Dunmore (1775) at **www.myhistorylab.com**

Patriots   British colonists who favored independence from Britain.

Continental Army   The regular or professional army authorized by the Second Continental Congress and commanded by General George Washington during the Revolutionary War.

Jean Baptiste Antoine de Verger, a French officer serving with the Continental Army, made these watercolors of American soldiers during the Revolution. Some 200,000 men saw action, including at least 5,000 African Americans; more than half of these troops served with the Continental Army.

Loyalists British colonists who opposed independence from Britain.

Tories A derisive term applied to Loyalists in America who supported the king and Parliament just before and during the American Revolution.

••►[Read the **Document**

Letter from a Revolutionary War Soldier (1776) at **www.myhistorylab.com**

The TORY'S Day of JUDGMENT.

A Patriot mob torments Loyalists in this print published during the Revolution. One favorite punishment was the "grand Tory ride," in which a crowd hauled the victim through the streets astride a fence rail. In another, men were stripped to "buff and breeches" and their naked flesh coated liberally with heated tar and feathers.

Americans. But in late 1775, under pressure from southern delegates, the Continental Congress barred them from enlistment. What changed this policy was the British promise of liberty for all slaves who fought for the crown, first offered by Virginia's royal governor John Murray, Earl of Dunmore. Thousands of slaves fled their masters and enlisted, forcing the states of the Upper South to admit free persons of color and even slaves into the ranks. By war's end, at least 5,000 African Americans had served in Patriot militias or the Continental Army, and in the Upper South some slaves won their freedom through military service. In the Lower South, however, where the numerical superiority of slaves inspired fears of rebellion among whites, there was no similar movement.

The Continental Army played an important political role during the war. At a time when Americans identified most strongly with their local communities or their states, the Continental Army, through experiences like the Valley Forge winter, evolved into a powerful force for nationalist sentiment. Over 100,000 men from every state served in the Continental Army, contributing mightily to the unity of purpose that was essential to the process of nation making.

THE TOLL OF WAR

The best estimate is that 25,324 American men died in the fighting, approximately 6,800 from wounds suffered in battle, most of the rest from the effects of disease. But since these numbers include only the major battles, the total death toll must have been considerably higher. The Continental Army experienced the heaviest casualty rates, losses in some regiments approaching 40 percent. Indeed, the casualty rate overall was higher than in any other American conflict except the Civil War. In New England and the Mid-Atlantic states the war claimed few civilian lives, for it was confined largely to direct engagements between armies. In the South and backcountry, however, where Patriot and Loyalist militias waged violent and often vicious campaigns, there were many noncombatant casualties. There are no overall statistics for Loyalist casualties, but British forces suffered at least 10,000 killed or wounded in the major battles of the war.

THE LOYALISTS

Not all Americans were Patriots. Between a fifth and a third of the population, somewhere between a half a million and a million people, remained loyal to the British crown. They called themselves **Loyalists** but were known to Patriots as **Tories**, the popular name for the conservative party in England, traditionally supporters of the king's authority over that of Parliament.

A large proportion of the Loyalists were relatively recent migrants to the colonies, born in England, Scotland, or Ireland. Others, such as royal officeholders or Anglican clergymen, were dependent on the British government for their salaries. Many Loyalists were men of conservative temperament, fearful of political or social upheaval. Loyalists were particularly strong in some colonies. They were nearly a majority in New York. In Georgia, Loyalists made up such a large majority that the colony would probably have abandoned the revolutionary movement had the British not surrendered at Yorktown in 1781.

Patriots passed state treason acts that prohibited speaking or writing against the Revolution. They also punished Loyalists by issuing bills of attainder, a legal process (later made illegal by the United States

Constitution) by means of which Loyalists were deprived of civil rights and property. In some areas, notably New York, South Carolina, Massachusetts, and Pennsylvania, Loyalists faced mob violence.

The British strategy for suppressing the Revolution depended on mobilizing the Loyalists, as many as 50,000 of whom took up arms for Great Britain. Many joined Loyalist militias or engaged in irregular warfare, especially in the Lower South.

As many as 80,000 Loyalists fled the country during and after the Revolution. Many went to England or the British West Indies, but the largest number settled in the northern British colonies that would later become the nation of Canada. Some 4,000 former slaves who fought for the British settled near Halifax in Nova Scotia, where they formed the largest independent black community outside Africa. Most Loyalists were unhappy exiles. "I earnestly wish to spend the remainder of my days in America," William Pepperell, formerly of Maine, wrote from London in 1778. "I love the country. I love the people." Despite their disagreement with the Patriots on essential political questions, they remained Americans, and they mourned the loss of their country.

Among those exiles was the most infamous American supporter of the British cause, Benedict Arnold. Arnold was a hero of the early battles of the Revolution on the Patriot side (see Chapter 6), but in 1779, resentful of what he perceived to be humiliating assignments and rank below his station, he became a paid informer of the British. In 1780 Patriots uncovered Arnold's plot to betray the strategic post of West Point, which he commanded. He fled to the British, who paid him a handsome stipend and pension. Arnold moved to London after the war, where he died in 1801, impoverished and unknown.

WOMEN AND THE WAR

As men marched off to war, women across the colonies assumed the management of farms and businesses. Some women participated even more directly in Patriot politics. Mercy Otis Warren, sister of the Massachusetts leader James Otis, turned her home into a center of Patriot political activity and published a series of satires supporting the American cause and scorning the Loyalists. Thousands of women volunteered to support the war effort by working as seamstresses, nurses, even spies.

Thousands of women also traveled with the armies of both sides. Some camp followers were prostitutes, but most were wives, nurses, cooks, and laundresses. In sharp contrast to the wives of officers who rode in coaches or wagons and were put up in the best available housing, working women were consigned to the back of the line with the baggage.

These women not only shared the hardships of the soldiers but also were on the battlefields bringing water, food, and supplies to the front lines under withering cannon and musket fire and nursing the wounded and dying. The Continental Congress and state legislatures awarded pensions to numerous women wounded in battle. According to one estimate, several hundred women dressed themselves as men and enlisted. One of them, Deborah Sampson of Massachusetts, was the subject of a sensational biography after the war and became the first American woman to embark on a lecture tour.

THE CAMPAIGN FOR NEW YORK AND NEW JERSEY

During the winter of 1775–76, the British developed a strategic plan for the war. From his base at Halifax, Sir William Howe would take his army to New York City, which the British navy would protect. From there Howe was to drive north along the Hudson, while another British

Constitution The written document providing for a new central government of the United States.

Profile: *Mercy Otis Warren* at **www.myhistorylab.com**

John Singleton Copley's portrait of Mercy Otis Warren captured her at the age of thirty-six, in 1765. During the Revolution, her home in Boston was a center of Patriot political activity.

MAP 7.1
Campaign for New York and New Jersey, 1775–77

WHY DID the British concentrate their early efforts on New York and New Jersey?

⊙ See the **Map**

The American Revolution at
www.myhistorylab.com

••• Read the **Document**

*Exploring America: Exploring the
Geography of the American Revolution* at
www.myhistorylab.com

QUICK REVIEW

Victories at Trenton and Princeton

♦ 1776: a series of defeats devastated the Continental Army.

♦ Christmas night 1776: Washington crosses the Delaware and launches a surprise attack.

♦ Victories at Trenton and Princeton revive the American cause.

army marched south from Canada. The two armies would converge at Albany, cutting New England off from the rest of the colonies, then turn eastward. Washington, in command of Patriot forces at Boston, shifted his forces southward toward New York in the spring of 1776.

In early July, as Congress adopted the Declaration of Independence, the British began their operation by landing 32,000 troops on Staten Island. The Patriots set up fortified positions across the harbor in Brooklyn. In late August the British attacked, inflicting heavy casualties. The Battle of Long Island ended in disaster for the Patriots, and they were forced to withdraw across the East River to Manhattan.

The British then offered Congress an opportunity to negotiate, and on September 6, Benjamin Franklin, John Adams, and Edward Rutledge met with General Howe and his brother, Admiral Richard Howe. But the meeting broke up when the Howes demanded repeal of the Declaration of Independence. Six days later, the British invaded Manhattan, and only a desperate American stand at Harlem Heights prevented the destruction of a large portion of the Patriot army. In a series of battles over the next few months, they forced Washington back at White Plains and overran the American posts of Fort Washington and Fort Lee, on the Hudson River. By November, the Americans were fleeing south across New Jersey (see Map 7.1).

With morale desperately low, whole militia companies deserted. American resistance seemed to be collapsing. But rather than fall back farther, Washington decided to risk a counterattack. On Christmas night 1776, he led 2,400 troops back across the Delaware, and the next morning defeated the Hessian forces in a surprise attack on their headquarters at Trenton, New Jersey. The Americans inflicted further heavy losses on the British at Princeton, then drove them all the way back to the environs of New York City.

These victories had little strategic importance, but they salvaged American morale. As Washington settled into winter headquarters at Morristown, he realized he had to pursue a defensive strategy, avoiding direct confrontations with the British while checking their advances and hurting them wherever possible. The most important thing would be the survival of the Continental Army.

THE NORTHERN CAMPAIGNS OF 1777

The fighting with American forces prevented Howe from moving north up the Hudson River, and the British advance southward from Canada was stalled by American resistance at Lake Champlain. In 1777, however, the British decided to replay their strategy. From Canada they dispatched General John Burgoyne with nearly 8,000 British and allied German troops. Howe was to move his force from New York, first taking the city of Philadelphia, the seat of the Continental Congress, and then moving north to meet Burgoyne (see Map 7.2).

Fort Ticonderoga fell to Burgoyne on July 6, but by August the general found himself bogged down and harassed by Patriot militias. After several defeats in September at the hands of an American army commanded by General Horatio Gates, Burgoyne retreated to Saratoga. There he was surrounded by a considerably larger force of Americans, and on October 18 he surrendered his army. It would be the biggest British defeat until Yorktown, decisive because it forced the nations of Europe to recognize that the Americans had a chance to win their Revolution.

The Americans were less successful against Howe. A force of 15,000 British troops left New York in July and landed a month later at the northern end of Chesapeake Bay. In September, at Brandywine Creek outside Philadelphia, the British outflanked the Americans, inflicting heavy casualties and forcing a retreat. Ten days later they routed the

Americans a second time, clearing the way for the British occupation of Philadelphia on September 26.

After this campaign, the Continentals headed into winter quarters at Valley Forge, the bitterness of their defeats muted somewhat by news of Burgoyne's surrender at Saratoga. The British had possession of Philadelphia, the most important city in North America, but it would prove of little strategic value to them. The Continental Congress continued to function, so the unified effort suffered little disruption. At the end of two years of fighting, despite numerous military victories, the British strategy for suppressing the Revolution had been a failure.

A GLOBAL CONFLICT

During these two years of fighting, the Americans were sustained by loans from France and Spain, traditional enemies of Great Britain. Both saw an opportunity to win back North American territories lost as a result of the Seven Years' War. Seeking more support, the Continental Congress sent a diplomatic delegation to Paris headed by Benjamin Franklin. The French longed to weaken the British Empire any way they could and were inclined to support the Americans. But they were reluctant to encourage a republican revolution against monarchy and colonialism.

The American victory at Saratoga, and the fear that Great Britain might enter into negotiations with the revolutionaries, persuaded the French to recognize American independence in December 1777. In the treaty signed by the two nations the French pledged to "maintain effectually the liberty, sovereignty, and independence" of the United States, while the United States promised to recognize French acquisitions of British island colonies in the West Indies.

Americans also found much support in the Netherlands. Although officially allied with Great Britain, the Dutch maintained a position of neutrality and opened secret negotiations with the Americans for a treaty of trade and friendship. The Dutch became the second European nation to recognize the United States and its financiers became the most important source of loans for the new nation.

Spain had entered the war in 1779. As early as 1775, Spanish officials in New Orleans were providing substantial ammunition and provisions for American forts in the West. But unlike France and the Netherlands, the Spanish refused to establish a formal alliance with the United States. They viewed the Revolution as an opportunity to regain Florida from the British and extend their control of the Mississippi Valley, but they feared the threat the Americans would pose to New Spain.

Thus, the Spanish pursued an independent strategy against the British, seizing the weakly defended Mississippi River towns of Natchez and Baton Rouge in 1779, and winning the important Gulf ports of Mobile in 1780 and Pensacola in 1781. Alarmed by the quick spread of American settlements west of the Appalachians, the Spanish sent an expedition into the

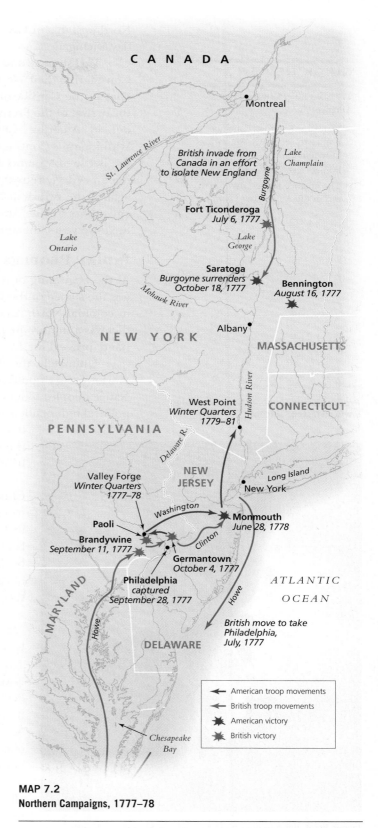

MAP 7.2
Northern Campaigns, 1777–78

WHAT STRATEGY did the British pursue in the North in 1777? What did they hope to accomplish by moving troops towards New York from both the north and the south?

Northwest that in 1781 succeeded in taking the minor British post of St. Joseph, in present-day Michigan.

With France and Spain now in the war, the British rethought their military strategy. Considering their West Indies sugar colonies at risk, they shipped 5,000 troops from New York to the Caribbean, where they succeeded in beating back a French attack. Fearing the arrival of the French fleet along the North American coast, the new British commander in America, General Henry Clinton, evacuated Philadelphia in June 1778. Washington's Continentals, fresh out of Valley Forge, went in hot pursuit. On June 28, at the Battle of Monmouth, the British blunted the American drive and succeeded in making an orderly retreat to New York City. After a failed American-French joint campaign against the British at Newport, Rhode Island, Washington decided on a defensive strategy. Although the Americans enjoyed several small successes in the Northeast over the next two years, the war there went into a stalemate.

INDIAN PEOPLES AND THE REVOLUTION IN THE WEST

At the beginning of the conflict, both sides looked for Indian support. Most important was the stance of the Iroquois Confederacy, long one of the most potent political forces in colonial North America. A delegation from Congress told the Iroquois that the conflict was a "family quarrel" and urged them to keep out of it. British agents, on the other hand, pressed the Iroquois to unite against the Americans.

Ultimately, the British proved more persuasive. It became clear to Indians that a Patriot victory would mean the extension of American settlements into their homelands. Native peoples fought in the Revolution for some of the same reasons Patriots did—for political independence, cultural integrity, and the protection of their land and property—but Indian fears of American expansion led them to oppose the Patriot rhetoric of natural rights and the equality of all men. Almost all the tribes that engaged in the fighting did so on the side of the British.

British officials marshaled the support of Cherokees, Creeks, Choctaws, and Chickasaws in the South, supplying them with arms from the British arsenal at Pensacola until it was seized by the Spanish in 1781. The consequence was a ferocious Indian war in the southern backcountry. In the summer of 1776 a large number of Cherokees, led by the warrior chief Dragging Canoe (Tsiyu-Gunsini), attacked dozens of American settlements. It required hard fighting before Patriot militia companies managed to drive the Cherokees into the mountains.

Among the Iroquois of New York, the Mohawk leader Joseph Brant (Thayendanegea) succeeded in bringing most Iroquois warriors into the British camp, although he was opposed by the chiefs of the Oneidas and Tuscaroras, who supported the Patriots. In 1777 and 1778, Iroquois and Loyalist forces raided the northern frontiers of New York and Pennsylvania. In retaliation an American army invaded the Iroquois homelands in 1779. Supported by Oneida and Tuscarora warriors, the Americans destroyed dozens of western villages and thousands of acres of crops. For the first time since the birth of their confederacy centuries before, the Iroquois were fighting each other (see Map 7.3).

Across the mountains, the Ohio Indians formed an effective alliance under the British at Detroit, and in 1777 and 1778 they sent warriors south against pioneer communities in western Virginia and Kentucky that had been founded in defiance of the Proclamation of 1763. Virginian George Rogers Clark countered by organizing an expedition of Kentucky militia against the old French settlements in the Illinois country, which were controlled by the British. They succeeded

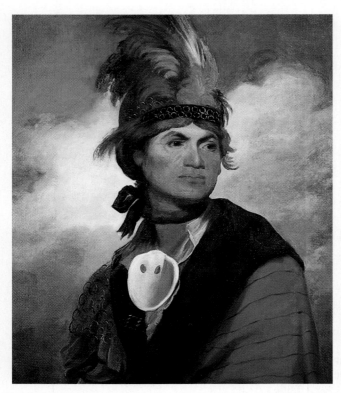

Joseph Brant, the brilliant chief of the Mohawks who sided with Great Britain during the Revolution, in a 1786 painting by the American artist Gilbert Stuart. After the Treaty of Paris, Brant led a large faction of Iroquois people north into British Canada, where they established a separate Iroquois Confederacy.

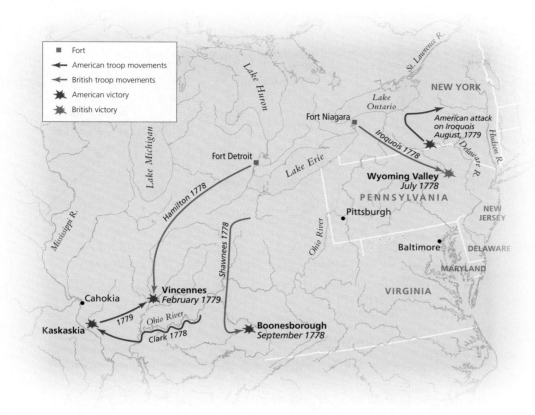

MAP 7.3
Fighting in the West, 1778–79

WHAT ROLE did Indian peoples play in the fighting in the West?

in taking the British post at Kaskaskia in the summer of 1778, and in early 1779, they captured Colonel Henry Hamilton, British commander in the West.

But Clark lacked the strength to attack the strategic British garrison at Detroit. Coordinating his Iroquois forces with those in Ohio, Brant mounted a new set of offensives that cast a shadow over Clark's successes. Raids back and forth across the Ohio River by Indians and Americans claimed hundreds of lives over the next three years. The war in the West would not end with the conclusion of hostilities in the East. With barely a pause, the fighting in the trans-Appalachian West between Americans and Indians would continue for another two decades.

THE WAR IN THE SOUTH

The most important fighting of the Revolution took place in the South (see Map 7.4). General Clinton regained the initiative for Britain in December 1778 by sending a force from New York against Georgia, the weakest of the colonies. The British crushed the Patriot militia at Savannah and began to organize the Loyalists in an effort to reclaim the colony. Encouraged by their success in Georgia, the British decided to apply the lessons learned there throughout the South. This involved a fundamental change from a strategy of military conquest to one of pacification. Territory would be retaken step by step, then handed over to Loyalists who would reassert the crown's authority.

In October 1779 Clinton evacuated Rhode Island, the last British stronghold in New England, and proceeded with 8,000 troops for a campaign against Charleston.

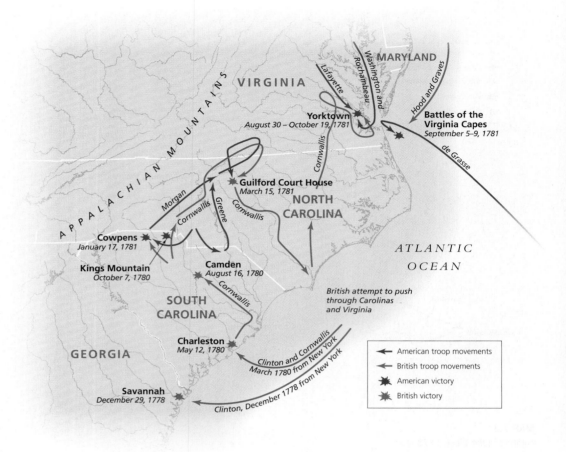

MAP 7.4
Fighting in the South, 1778–81

WHAT WAS the British strategy in the South? How did it differ from earlier British strategies?

Outflanking the American defenders, he forced the surrender of more than 5,000 troops in May. It was the most significant American defeat of the war. Patriot resistance collapsed in the Lower South.

The southern campaign was marked by vicious fighting between partisan militias of Patriots and Loyalists. The violence peaked in September 1780 with Cornwallis's invasion of North Carolina, where the Patriots were stronger and better organized. There the British found their southern strategy untenable: plundering towns and farms in order to feed the army in the interior had the effect of producing angry support for the Patriots. In October at Kings Mountain. Patriot sharpshooters outflanked and destroyed a Loyalist force, and in January 1781, Loyalists were again defeated at the Battle of the Cowpens, not far from Kings Mountain.

Into 1781 the Continentals and Patriot militias waged what General Greene called a fugitive war of hit and run against the British. Finally in the summer of 1781, deciding he would not be able to hold the Carolinas as long as Virginia remained a base of support and supply for the Americans, Cornwallis led his army north to Yorktown on the Chesapeake. The British withdrawal from North Carolina allowed Greene to reestablish Patriot control of the Lower South.

In 1845 Artist William Ranney depicted a famous moment during the Battle of Cowpens that took place in January 1781. Lieutenant Colonel William Washington, leader of the Patriot cavalry and a relative of George Washington, was attacked by a squadron of British dragoons. As Washington was about to be cut down, he was saved by his servant William Ball, who fired a pistol that wounded the attacker. Nothing more is known about Ball, but he was one of a number of African Americans who fought on the Patriot side in the battle.

William Ranney, *The Battle of Cowpens*. Oil on canvas. Photo by Sam Holland. Courtesy South Carolina State House.

THE YORKTOWN SURRENDER

While the British raged through the South, the stalemate continued in the Northeast. In the summer of 1780, taking advantage of the British evacuation of Rhode Island, the French landed 5,000 troops at Newport. But it was not until the spring of 1781 that the French commander, General Rochambeau, risked joining his force to Washington's Continentals north of New York City. In August Washington learned that the French Caribbean fleet was headed for the Chesapeake. If he and Rochambeau could move their troops south, they might lock up Cornwallis in his camp at Yorktown. Leaving a small force behind as a decoy, they marched their 16,000 men overland to the Virginia shore in little more than a month.

The maneuver was a complete success. The French and Americans surrounded and besieged the British encampment. French and American heavy artillery hammered the British until the middle of October. After the failure of a planned retreat across the York River, Cornwallis opened negotiations for the surrender of his army. Two days later, on October 19, 1781, between lines of victorious American and French soldiers, the British troops came out from their trenches to surrender. Everyone was aware that it was an event of incalculable importance, but few guessed it was the end of the war. The British still controlled New York.

In London a month later Lord North received the news "as he would have taken a ball in the breast," the colonial secretary reported. The American Revolution had turned

QUICK REVIEW

Yorktown

- American and French forces surround British encampment.
- British General Cornwallis forced to surrender his army.
- Defeat forced the British to accept American independence.

The Surrender of Lord Cornwallis

Seeing History

American artist John Trumbull displayed a preliminary version of *Surrender of Lord Cornwallis* in 1797 along with three other history paintings of the Revolution, including his depiction of the signing of the Declaration of Independence, the surrender of General Burgoyne at Saratoga, and the resignation of General Washington from his military commission at the war's conclusion. Young Trumbull had been an officer in the Continental Army and served for a time as Washington's aide-de-camp, but he had not been at Yorktown. By that time he was in London studying with the American expatriate artist Benjamin West. This painting was done in the heroic style of nationalist art popular at the time in Great Britain and Europe. Trumbull was at pains to get the details right. He visited Yorktown to sketch the landscape and traveled across the United States and France to capture the likenesses of the senior American and French officers, including Washington and Rochambeau, shown lining the two sides, colors flying, as the British troops file by. But Trumbull was criticized by the public for getting one detail appallingly wrong. He depicted Cornwallis on horseback in the center, when in fact the British commander was not present at the ceremony but was sulking in his tent. Trumbull corrected his error by changing the color of the central figure's uniform from red to blue, thereby turning Cornwallis into General Benjamin Lincoln, who is seen reaching for the sword in the possession of the British second-in-command, General Charles O'Hara. In 1817 the Senate commissioned Trumbull to repaint his Revolutionary scenes for placement in the Rotunda of the Capitol. ■

IN WHAT ways does Trumbull create a heroic painting by the arrangement of his subjects?

into war with France and Spain, and British fortunes were at low ebb in India, the West Indies, Florida, and the Mediterranean. The cost of the war was enormous, and there was little support for it among either the British public or the members of Parliament. George III wished to press on, but North submitted his resignation, and in March 1782 the king was forced to offer the office of prime minister to Charles Watson-Wentworth, Lord Rockingham, who long had favored granting the Americans their independence.

THE UNITED STATES IN CONGRESS ASSEMBLED

The Articles of Confederation, the first written constitution of the United States, created a national government of sharply limited powers. This arrangement reflected the concerns of people fighting to free themselves from a coercive central government. But the weak Confederation government had a difficult time forging the unity and assembling the resources necessary to fight the war and win the peace.

THE ARTICLES OF CONFEDERATION

The debate over confederation that took place in the Continental Congress during 1776 made it clear that delegates favoring a loose union of autonomous states outnumbered those who wanted a strong central government. A consensus finally emerged in 1777, and the "**Articles of Confederation**" were formally adopted by the Continental Congress in November and sent to the states for ratification. The Articles created a national assembly, called the Congress, in which each state had a single vote. Delegates, selected annually in a manner determined by the individual state legislatures, could serve no more than three years out of six. A presiding president, elected annually by Congress, was eligible to hold office no more than one year out of three. Votes would be decided by a simple majority of the states, except for major questions, which would require the agreement of nine states.

Congress was granted national authority in the conduct of foreign affairs, matters of war and peace, and maintenance of the armed forces. It could raise loans, issue bills of credit, establish a coinage, and regulate trade with Indian peoples, and it was to be the final authority in jurisdictional disputes between states. Lacking the power to tax citizens directly, however, the national government was to apportion its financial burdens among the states according to the extent of their surveyed land. The Articles explicitly guaranteed the sovereignty of the individual states, reserving to them all powers not expressly delegated to Congress. The Articles of Confederation thus created a national government of specific yet sharply circumscribed powers.

The legislatures of twelve states soon voted in favor of the Articles, but final ratification was held up for more than three years by the state of Maryland. Representing the interests of states without claims to lands west of the Appalachians, Maryland demanded that states cede to Congress their western claims, the new nation's most valuable resource, for "the good of the whole" (see Map 7.5). During the subsequent stalemate, Congress agreed to conduct business under the terms of the unratified document. It was 1781 before Virginia, the state with the largest western claims, broke the logjam by agreeing to the cession. Maryland then ratified the Articles of Confederation, and in March they took effect.

FINANCING THE WAR

Lacking the authority to levy direct taxes, Congress financed the Revolution through grants and loans from friendly foreign powers and by issuing paper currency. The total foreign subsidy by the end of the war approached $9 million, but this was not enough to back the circulating Continental currency that Congress authorized, the face value of

WHAT KIND of government was created by the Articles of Confederation?

Read the **Document**
The Articles of Confederation (1777) at **www.myhistorylab.com**

QUICK REVIEW

Powers of the Central Government under the Articles of Confederation

- No national judiciary.
- No separate executive branch.
- Congress sole national authority.
- No Congressional authority to raise troops or impose taxes.

See the **Map**
Western Land Claims Ceded by the States at **www.myhistorylab.com**

Read the **Document**
Congress Decides What to Do with the Western Lands (1785) at **www.myhistorylab.com**

Articles of Confederation Written document setting up the loose confederation of states that comprised the first national government of the United States.

MAP 7.5

State Claims to Western Lands The ratification of the Articles of Confederation in 1781 awaited settlement of the western claims of eight states. Vermont, claimed by New Hampshire and New York, was not made a state until 1791, after disputes were settled the previous year. The territory north of the Ohio River was claimed in whole or in part by Virginia, New York, Connecticut, and Massachusetts. All of them had ceded their claims by 1786, except for Connecticut, which had claimed an area just south of Lake Erie, known as the Western Reserve; Connecticut ceded this land in 1800. The territory south of the Ohio was claimed by Virginia, North Carolina, South Carolina, and Georgia; in 1802, the latter became the last state to cede its claims.

HOW DID the ceding of such claims shape the course of American expansion to the West?

which amounted to $200 million. In an attempt to retire this currency, Congress called on the states to raise taxes, payable in Continental dollars. But most of the states were unwilling to do this. In fact, most had resorted to printing currency of their own, estimated at a face value of another $200 million by war's end. The result of this expansion in the money supply was the rapid depreciation of Continental currency. By the time Robert Morris, one of the wealthiest merchants in the country, became secretary of finance in May 1781, Continental currency had ceased to circulate.

Morris was able to turn things around. He persuaded Congress to charter a "Bank of North America" located in Philadelphia, the first private commercial bank in the United States. Into its vaults he deposited large quantities of gold and silver coin and bills of exchange obtained through loans from Holland and France. He then issued new paper currency backed by this treasure. Once he established confidence in the bank, Morris was able to supply the Continental Army through private contracts. He also began making interest payments on the debt, which in 1783 was estimated at $30 million.

NEGOTIATING INDEPENDENCE

Peace talks between the United States and Great Britain opened in July 1782 when Benjamin Franklin sat down with the British emissary in Paris. The fundamental demand was recognition of American independence and withdrawal of British forces. American

See the Map

Territorial Claims in Eastern America after Treaty of Paris at
www.myhistorylab.com

negotiators were instructed to press for the largest territorial limits possible, as well as guarantees of American rights to fish North Atlantic waters. As for its French ally, Congress instructed the commissioners to be guided by friendly advice, but also by "knowledge of our interests, and by your own discretion, in which we repose the fullest confidence." The French were not happy with this, and partly as a result of French pressure, in June 1781 Congress issued a new set of instructions. The commissioners were to settle merely for a grant of independence and withdrawal of troops and to be subject to the guidance and control of the French in the negotiations.

Ben Franklin, John Jay, and John Adams, the peace commissioners in Paris, were well aware of French attempts to manipulate the outcome of negotiations and place limits on American power. In violation of both Congressional instructions and treaty obligations to France, they signed a preliminary treaty with Britain in November 1782 without consulting the French. In the treaty, Britain acknowledged the United States as "free, sovereign & independent" and agreed to withdraw its troops from all forts within American territory "with all convenient speed." The American commissioners pressed the British for Canada but settled for western territorial boundaries extending to the Mississippi (see Map 7.6) with unencumbered navigation of the river. All in all, it was an astounding coup for the Americans.

The preliminary treaty confronted France with an accomplished fact. When French diplomats criticized the American commissioners, they responded by hinting that resistance to the treaty provisions could result in a British–American alliance. Thereupon France quickly made an agreement of its own with the British.

Spain did not participate in the negotiations with the Americans. But having waged a successful campaign against the British on the Mississippi and the Gulf Coast, its government issued a claim of sovereignty over much of the trans-Appalachian territory granted to the United States by Great Britain. Spain arranged a separate peace with Great Britain, in which it won the return of Florida. The final Treaty of Paris—actually a series of separate agreements among the United States, Great Britain, France, and Spain—was signed at Versailles on September 3, 1783.

THE CRISIS OF DEMOBILIZATION

In 1778 Continental officers had won from Congress a promise of life pensions at half pay in exchange for enlistment for the duration of the war. By 1783, however, Congress had still not made any specific provisions for officers' pensions. With peace at hand, the officers began to fear that the army would be disbanded before the problem was resolved, and they would lose whatever power they had to pressure Congress. In January 1783, a group of prominent senior officers petitioned Congress, demanding that pensions be converted to a bonus equal to five years of full pay. Despite barely veiled threats of military intervention, Congress rejected their petition.

With the backing of congressional nationalists, a group of army officers associated with General Horatio Gates circulated a letter arguing for direct military intervention and calling a meeting of the officer corps at Newburgh. But General Washington, on whom the officers counted for support, criticized the meeting as "disorderly" and called an official meeting of his own (see Communities in Conflict). There was enormous tension as

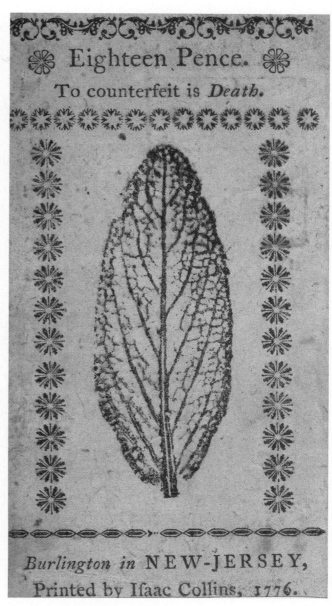

The Continental Congress printed currency to finance the Revolution. Because of widespread counterfeiting, engravers attempted to incorporate complex designs, like the unique vein structure in the leaf on this eighteen-pence note. In case that wasn't enough, the engraver of this note also included the warning: "To counterfeit is Death."

QUICK REVIEW

Treaty of Paris

- Signed September 3, 1783.
- United States got virtually everything it sought at peace talks.
- Treaty addressed important economic issues, but said nothing about slavery.

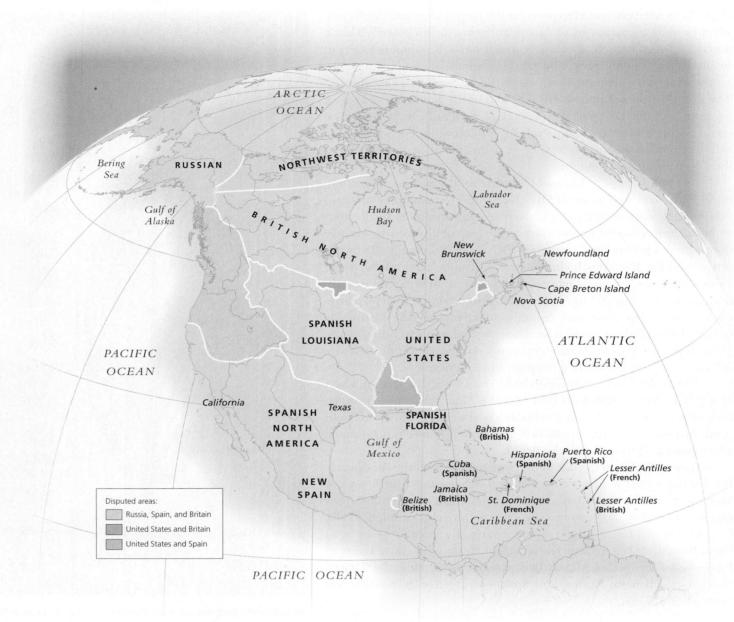

MAP 7.6
North America After the Treaty of Paris, 1783   The map of European and American claims to North America was radically altered by the results of the American Revolution.

HOW DID the Treaty of Paris alter the balance of power in North America?

the officers assembled on March 15, 1783. Washington strode into the room and mounted the platform. Turning his back in disdain on Gates, he delivered an address from memory condemning the circular letter. After he left, the officers adopted resolutions rejecting intervention, and a week later, on Washington's urging, Congress converted the promised pensions to bonuses.

Washington's role in this crisis was one of his greatest contributions to the nation. At stake was nothing less than the possibility of a military coup at the very moment of victory. The American Revolution was the first of many successful colonial revolutions, and in hindsight it is clear that post independence military rule was a common outcome in many of them. In December 1783 Washington resigned his commission as general of the army despite calls for him to remain. There is little doubt he could have assumed the role of an American dictator. Instead, by his actions and example, the principle of military subordination to civil authority was firmly established.

As for the common soldiers, they wanted simply to be discharged. In May 1783, Congress voted the soldiers three months' pay as a bonus and instructed Washington to begin dismissing them. By the beginning of 1784, the Continental Army had shrunk to no more than a few hundred men.

THE PROBLEM OF THE WEST

Even during the Revolution thousands of Americans migrated westward, and after the war settlers poured over the mountains and down the Ohio River. Thousands of Americans pressed against the Indian country north of the Ohio River, and destructive violence continued along the frontier. British troops continued to occupy posts in the Great Lakes region and encouraged Indian attacks on vulnerable settlements. Spain refused to accept the territorial settlement of the Treaty of Paris and closed the port of New Orleans to Americans, effectively blockading the Mississippi River. Westerners who saw that route as their primary access to markets were outraged.

John Jay, appointed secretary for foreign affairs by the Confederation Congress in 1784, attempted to negotiate with the British for their complete withdrawal but was told that was not possible until all outstanding debts from before the war were settled. Jay also negotiated with the Spanish for guarantees of territorial sovereignty and commercial relations, but they insisted that the Americans relinquish free navigation of the Mississippi. Congress would approve no treaty under those conditions, and some frustrated Westerners considered leaving the Confederation.

In 1784, Congress took up the problem of extending national authority over the West. Legislation was drafted, principally by Thomas Jefferson, providing for "Government for the Western Territory." The legislation proposed a remarkably republican colonial policy. The western public domain would be divided into states, fully the equals of the original thirteen, with Congressional guarantees of self-government and republican institutions. Once the population of a territory numbered 20,000, the residents could call a convention and establish a constitution and government of their own choosing. And once the population grew to equal that of the smallest of the original thirteen states, the territory could petition for statehood, provided it agreed to remain forever a member of the Confederation. Congress accepted these proposals but rejected by a vote of seven to six Jefferson's clause forever prohibiting slavery in the West.

Passed the following year, the **Land Ordinance of 1785** provided for the survey and sale of western lands. The Land Ordinance created an ordered system of survey, dividing the land into townships composed of thirty-six sections of one square mile (640 acres) each. Jefferson argued that land ought to be given away to actual settlers. But, eager to establish a revenue base for the government, Congress provided for the auction of public lands for not less than one dollar per acre.

In the treaties of Fort Stanwix in 1784 and Fort McIntosh in 1785, congressional commissioners forced the Iroquois and a number of

Land Ordinance of 1785 Act passed by Congress under the Articles of Confederation that created the grid system of surveys by which all subsequent public land was made available for sale.

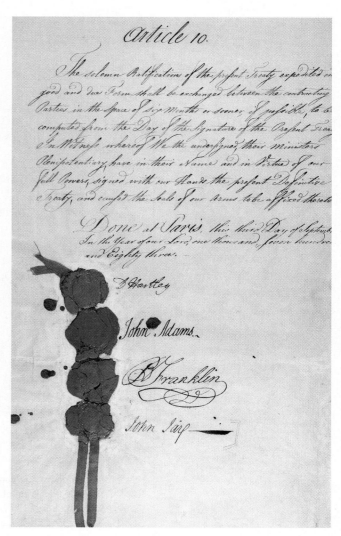

The last page of the Treaty of Paris, signed in Paris on September 3, 1783, by David Hartley for Great Britain, and for the United States by John Adams, Benjamin Franklin, and John Jay.

Ohio tribes, respectively, to cede portions of their territory in what is now eastern Ohio. These treaties were not the result of negotiation but intimidation. The commissioners dictated the terms by seizing hostages and forcing compliance. Surveyors were immediately sent west to divide up the land. The first surveyed lands did not come onto the market until the fall of 1788, and in the meantime Congress, desperate for revenue, sold a tract of more than 1.5 million acres to the Ohio Company, a new consortium of land speculators, for a million dollars. Thousands of Westerners chose not to wait for the official opening of the public lands north of the Ohio River but simply settled illegally by making squatters' claims. In 1785 Congress raised troops and evicted many of them, but once the troops departed the squatters returned. The persistence of this problem convinced many congressmen to revise Jefferson's democratic territorial plan.

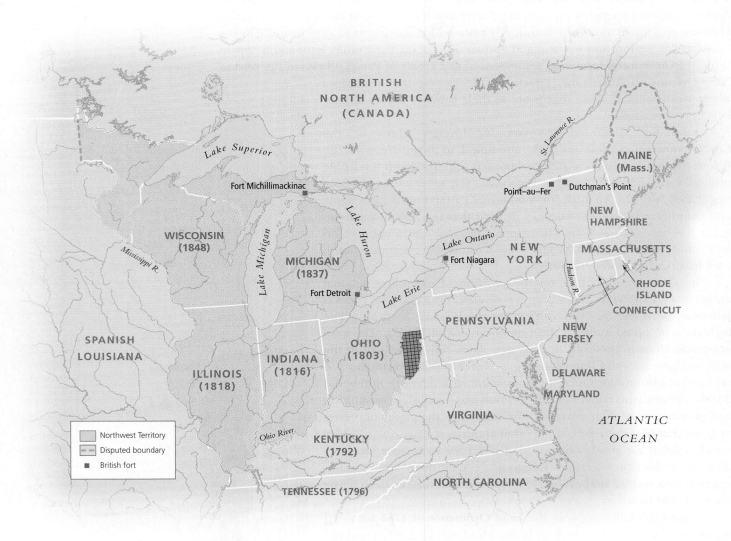

MAP 7.7
The Northwest Territory and the Land Survey System of the United States   The Land Ordinance of 1785 created an ordered system of survey (revised by the Northwest Ordinance of 1787), dividing the land into townships and sections.

IN WHAT ways did the Northwest Ordinance affect the admission of new states into the Union? What were the consequences for western lands?

In the **Northwest Ordinance of 1787**, Congress established a system of government for the territory north of the Ohio (see Map 7.7). Three to five states were to be carved from the giant Northwest Territory. Slavery was prohibited. But the initial guarantee of self-government in Jefferson's plan was replaced by a congressionally appointed governor and court of judges. Once the free white male population of the territory had grown to 5,000, these citizens would be permitted to choose an assembly, but the governor had the power of absolute veto on all territorial legislation. National interest would be imposed on the local western communities.

The creation of the land system of the United States was the major achievement of the Confederation government. But there were other important accomplishments. Under the Articles of Confederation, Congress led the country through the Revolution and its commissioners negotiated the terms of a comprehensive peace treaty. And by organizing the departments of war, foreign affairs, finance, and the post office, the Confederation government created the beginnings of a national bureaucracy.

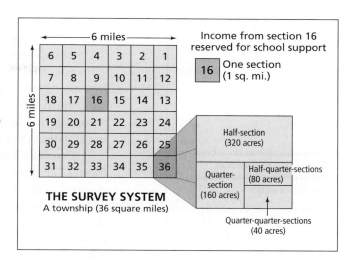

THE SURVEY SYSTEM
A township (36 square miles)

Income from section 16 reserved for school support

One section (1 sq. mi.)

Half-section (320 acres)

Quarter-section (160 acres)

Half-quarter-sections (80 acres)

Quarter-quarter-sections (40 acres)

REVOLUTIONARY POLITICS IN THE STATES

Despite the accomplishments of the Confederation, most Americans were focused on the governments of their own states. The national government was distant and had relatively little effect on people's lives. Social and political identity was located in local communities and states rather than the American nation. The states were the setting for the most important political struggles of the Confederation period.

HOW DID political debate in America change in the years after 1774?

A NEW DEMOCRATIC IDEOLOGY

The political mobilization that took place in 1774 and 1775 greatly broadened political participation. Mass meetings in which ordinary people expressed their opinions, voted, and gained political experience were common not only in the cities but in small towns and rural communities as well. During these years a greater proportion of the population began to participate in elections. Compared with the colonial assemblies, the new state legislatures included more men from rural and western districts—farmers and artisans as well as lawyers, merchants, and large landowners.

This transformation was accompanied by a dramatic shift in the content of political debate. During the colonial period, when only the upper classes were truly engaged in the political process, the principal argument followed the lines of the traditional Tory and Whig divide in Great Britain. The Tory position, taken by colonial officials, was that colonial governments were simply convenient instruments of royal prerogative, serving at the king's pleasure. The Whig position, adopted by colonial elites who sought to preserve and increase their own power, emphasized the need for a government balancing the power of a governor with an upper house and an assembly. As a result of the Revolution, the Tory position lost all legitimacy and the Whig position was challenged by farmers, artisans, and ordinary people armed with a new and radical democratic ideology. The spectrum of politics shifted to the left.

THE FIRST STATE CONSTITUTIONS

One of the first post-Revolution debates focused on an appropriate governmental structure for the new states. The thinking of democrats was indicated by the title of a New England pamphlet of 1776: *The People the Best Governors*. The ideal form of government, according to Democrats, was the community or town meeting, in which the people set their own tax

Northwest Ordinance of 1787
Legislation that prohibited slavery in the Northwest Territories and provided the model for the incorporation of future territories into the union as co-equal states.

rates, created a militia, controlled their own schools and churches, and regulated the local economy. State government was necessary only for coordination among communities.

Conservative Americans took up the Whig argument of the need for balanced government. The "unthinking many," wrote a conservative pamphleteer, should be checked by a strong executive and an upper house. Both of these would be insulated from popular control by property qualifications and long terms in office. The greatest danger, according to conservatives, was the possibility of majority tyranny, which might lead to the violation of property rights and dictatorship.

Fourteen states—the original thirteen plus Vermont, an independent republic from 1777 until 1791—adopted constitutions between 1776 and 1780. Each of those charters reflected a particular political alignment. Pennsylvania was the first state to adopt a radically democratic constitution, with a unicameral assembly elected annually by all free male taxpayers. North Carolina, Georgia, and Vermont followed the Pennsylvania model. At the other extreme, South Carolina and Maryland created a conservative set of institutions designed to keep citizens and rulers as far apart as possible. The other states adopted constitutional systems somewhere in the middle.

DECLARATIONS OF RIGHTS

One of the most important innovations of the state constitutions were the guarantees of rights patterned on the Virginia "Declaration of Rights" of June 1776. Written by George Mason, the fifteen articles of the Virginia Declaration declared, among other things, that sovereignty resided in the people, that government was the servant of the people, and that the people had the "right to reform, alter, or abolish" that government. There were guarantees of due process and trial by jury in criminal prosecutions, as well as prohibitions against excessive bail and "cruel and unusual punishment." Freedom of the press was guaranteed and the people were assured of "the free exercise of religion, according to the dictates of conscience."

Eight state constitutions included a general declaration of rights; others incorporated specific guarantees. A number of states proclaimed the right of the people to engage in free speech and free assembly, to instruct their representatives, and to petition for the redress of grievances—rights either inadvertently or deliberately omitted from Virginia's declaration. These declarations were important precedents for the **Bill of Rights**, the first ten amendments to the federal Constitution of 1789.

THE SPIRIT OF REFORM

The political upheaval of the Revolution raised the possibility of other reforms in American society. The New Jersey constitution of 1776 enfranchised both male and female property owners. Because married women could own no property in their own names, only single women voted in New Jersey, but large numbers of them participated in elections and spoke out on political issues. There were male protests of this "irregular" situation, and in 1807 the legislature passed a law explicitly limiting the right to vote to "free white male citizens."

The New Jersey controversy was something of an anomaly, yet women's participation in the Revolution wrought subtle but important changes. In the aftermath of the Revolution, there was evidence of increasing sympathy in the courts for women's property rights and fairer treatment of women's petitions for divorce. And the postwar years witnessed an increase in opportunities for women seeking an education.

The most steadfast reformer of the day was Thomas Jefferson. In 1776 he introduced a bill in the Virginia legislature abolishing entail (restriction of inheritance to particular heirs in order that landed property remain undivided) and primogeniture (the inheritance of all the family property by the firstborn son), legal customs long in effect in aristocratic England that Jefferson believed had no place in a Republican society.

Bill of Rights   A written summary of inalienable rights and liberties.

Jefferson's reform of inheritance law passed and had a dramatic effect. By 1798, every state had followed Virginia's lead.

Jefferson's other notable success was his **Bill for Establishing Religious Freedom**. He considered it one of his greatest accomplishments. At the beginning of the Revolution, there were established churches—denominations officially supported and funded by the government—in nine of the thirteen colonies. Many Anglican clergymen harbored Loyalist sympathies, and as part of an anti-Loyalist backlash, New York, Maryland, the Carolinas, and Georgia had little difficulty passing acts that disestablished the Anglican Church. In Virginia, however, many planters viewed Anglicanism as a bulwark against Baptist and Methodist democratic thinkers, resulting in bitter and protracted opposition to Jefferson's bill. It did not pass until 1786.

New England Congregationalists proved even more resistant to change. Although Massachusetts, New Hampshire, and Connecticut allowed dissenting churches to receive tax support, they maintained the official relationship between church and state well into the nineteenth century. Other states, despite disestablishment, retained certain religious tests in their legal codes.

AFRICAN AMERICANS AND THE REVOLUTION

For most African Americans there was little to celebrate, for the American victory guaranteed the continuation of slavery as an institution. Few people were surprised when thousands of black fighters and their families departed with the Loyalists and the British at the end of the war, settling in the West Indies, Canada, and Africa. Most of these refugees were fugitive slaves rather than committed Loyalists. were recaptured, but most left the country with the British.

There was an obvious contradiction in waging a war for liberty while continuing to support the institution of slavery. The contradiction was not lost on Washington, who during the Revolution began to agonize over the morality of slavery. He was not alone. Revolutionary idealism, in combination with a shift away from tobacco farming, weakened the commitment of many Chesapeake planters to the slave system. After the Revolution, a sizable number of Virginians granted freedom to their slaves, and there was a small but important movement to encourage gradual emancipation by convincing masters to free their slaves in their wills.

Bill for Establishing Religious Freedom A bill authored by Thomas Jefferson establishing religious freedom in Virginia.

This portrait of the African American poet Phyllis Wheatley was included in the collection of her work published in London in 1773 when she was only twenty years old. Kidnapped in Africa when a girl, then purchased off the Boston docks, she was more like a daughter than a slave to the Wheatley family. She later married and lived as a free woman of color before her untimely death in 1784.

George Washington was one of them, making a will that not only freed several hundred slaves upon his death but also included an elaborate plan for apprenticeship and tenancy for the able-bodied, and lodging and pensions for the aged. Planters in the Lower South, however, heavily dependent as they were on slave labor, resisted the growing calls for an end to slavery. Between 1776 and 1786 all the states but South Carolina and Georgia prohibited or heavily taxed the international slave trade, and this issue became an important point of conflict at the **Constitutional Convention** in 1787 (see Chapter 8).

Perhaps the most important result of this development was the growth of the free African American population. From a few thousand in 1750, their number grew to more than 200,000 by the end of the century. The increase was most notable in the Upper South. The free black population of Virginia, for example, grew from fewer than 2,000 in 1780 to more than 20,000 in 1800. Largely excluded from the institutions of white Americans, the African American community now had enough strength to establish schools, churches, and other institutions of its own. At first, this development was opposed by whites. In Williamsburg, Virginia, for instance, the leader of a black congregation was seized and whipped when he attempted to gain recognition from the Baptist Association. But by the 1790s the Williamsburg African Church had grown to over 500 members, and the Baptist Association reluctantly recognized it.

In the North, slavery was first abolished in the state constitution of Vermont in 1777, in Massachusetts in 1780, and New Hampshire in 1784. Pennsylvania, Connecticut, and Rhode Island adopted systems of gradual emancipation during these years, freeing the children of slaves at birth. By 1804, every northern state had provided for abolition or gradual emancipation, although as late as 1810, 30,000 African Americans remained enslaved in the North.

During the era of the Revolution, a small group of African American writers rose to prominence. Benjamin Banneker, born free in Maryland, where he received an

Constitutional Convention
Convention of delegates from the colonies that first met to organize resistance to the Intolerable Acts.

CHRONOLOGY

1775	Lord Dunmore, royal governor of Virginia, appeals to slaves to support Britain
1776	July: Declaration of Independence
	August: Battle of Long Island initiates retreat of Continental Army
	September: British land on Manhattan Island
	December: George Washington counterattacks at Trenton
1777	Slavery abolished in Vermont
	September: British General William Howe captures Philadelphia
	October: British General John Burgoyne surrenders at Saratoga
	November: Continentals settle into winter quarters at Valley Forge
	December: France recognizes American independence
1778	June: France enters the war
	June: Battle of Monmouth hastens British retreat to New York
	July: George Rogers Clark captures Kaskaskia
	December: British capture Savannah

1779	Spain enters the war
1780	February: British land at Charleston
	July: French land at Newport
	September: British General Charles Cornwallis invades North Carolina
1781	March: Articles of Confederation ratified
	May: Robert Morris appointed secretary of finance
	October: Cornwallis surrenders at Yorktown
1782	Peace talks begin
1783	March: Washington mediates issue of officer pensions
	September: Treaty of Paris signed
	November: British evacuate New York
1784	Treaty of Fort Stanwix
	Postwar depression begins
1785	Land Ordinance of 1785
	Treaty of Fort McIntosh
1786	Jefferson's Bill for Establishing Religious Freedom

education, became one of the most accomplished mathematicians and astronomers of late eighteenth-century America. In the 1790s, he published a popular almanac that both white and black Americans consulted. Jupiter Hammon, a New York slave, took up contemporary issues in his poems and essays. But the most famous African American writer was Phyllis Wheatley, who came to public attention when her *Poems on Various Subjects, Religious and Moral* appeared in London in 1773, while she was still serving as a domestic slave in Boston. Kidnapped in Africa as a young girl and converted to Christianity during the Great Awakening, Wheatley wrote poems combining piety with a concern for her people. Writing to the Mohegan Indian minister Samuel Occom in 1774, Wheatley penned a line that not only applied to African Americans but also to all Americans struggling to be free. "In every human breast God has implanted a principle, which we call love of freedom; it is impatient of oppression, and pants for deliverance. The same principle lives in us."

QUICK REVIEW

African Americans and the Revolution

◆ Revolutionary principles sparked some to challenges slavery.

◆ More than 50,000 slaves gained freedom as result of the war.

◆ 1800 free black population reached 100,000.

((•—Hear the Audio

Phyllis Wheatly, On Being Brought from Africa to America at
www.myhistorylab.com

CONCLUSION

The Revolution was a tumultuous era, marked by violent conflict between Patriots and Loyalists, masters and slaves, settlers and Indian peoples. The advocates of independence emerged successfully, largely because of their ability to pull together and consolidate their identification with the national community, an identity that emerged from national institutions like the Continental Army during periods of trial like the Valley Forge winter. Fearful of the power of central authority, however, Americans created a relatively weak national government. People identified strongly with their local and state communities, and these governments became the site for most of the struggles over political direction that characterized the Revolution and its immediate aftermath. But not all problems, it turned out, could be solved locally. Within a very few years, the nation would sink into a serious economic depression that sorely tested the resources of local communities. By the mid-1780s, many American nationalists were increasingly uncertain about the future of the nation.

REVIEW QUESTIONS

1. Assess the relative strengths of the Patriots and the Loyalists in the American Revolution.

2. What roles did Indian peoples and African Americans play in the Revolution?

3. Describe the structure of the Articles of Confederation. What were its strengths and weaknesses?

4. How did the Revolution affect politics within the states?

5. What was the effect of the Revolution on African Americans?

KEY TERMS

Articles of Confederation (p. 161)
Bill for Establishing Religious Freedom (p. 169)
Bill of Rights (p. 168)
Constitution (p. 153)
Continental Army (p. 151)

Constitutional Convention (p. 170)
Land Ordinance of 1785 (p. 165)
Loyalists (p. 152)
Northwest Ordinance of 1787 (p. 167)
Patriots (p. 151)
Tories (p. 152)

PEARSON myhistorylab Connections

Reinforce what you learned in this chapter by studying the many documents,
images, maps, review tools, and videos available at www.myhistorylab.com.

Read and Review

✓●—Study and Review **Chapter 7**

●●●—Read the Document

Proclamation of Lord Dunmore (1775)

Letter from a Revolutionary War Soldier (1776)

The Articles of Confederation (1777)

Congress Decides What to Do with the Western Lands (1785)

👁—See the Map

Revolutionary War: Northern Theater, 1775-1780

The American Revolution

Western Land Claims Ceded by the States

Territorial Claims in Eastern America after Treaty of Paris

Research and Explore

●●●—Read the Document

Exploring America: Exploring the Geography of the American Revolution

Profiles
  Joseph Brant
    (Thayendanegea)
  Mercy Otis Warren

History Bookshelf
  Phillis Wheatley, Religious and Moral Poems (1773)
  Thomas Paine, Crisis Papers (1776)

((●—Hear the Audio *Phillis Wheatley, On Being Brought from Africa to America*

●●●—Watch the Video

The War for Independence

The American Revolution as Different Americans Saw It

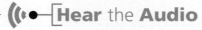

((●—Hear the Audio

Hear the audio files for Chapter 7 at
www.myhistorylab.com.

*Here individuals of all nations
are melted into a new race of men,
whose labours and posterity will one day
cause great changes in the world.*
—Hector St. John Crèvecoeur

Congress voting on the issue of independence.

8

THE NEW NATION
1786–1800

((•─[Hear the Audio

Hear the audio files for Chapter 8 at **www.myhistorylab.com**.

HOW DID economic conditions in the years after the Revolution lead to calls for fundamental political change?

HOW DID Americans differ in their views of the new Constitution, and how were those differences reflected in the struggle to achieve ratification?

HOW DID Washington's administration lay the foundation for the subsequent development of American politics and government?

HOW AND why did the first American political parties emerge?

WHAT DID Americans read in the early decades of the Republic?

1800

1786

AMERICAN COMMUNITIES
A Rural Massachusetts Community Rises in Defense of Liberty

SEVERAL HUNDRED FARMERS FROM THE TOWN OF PELHAM AND SCORES OF other rural communities in western Massachusetts converged on the courthouse in Northampton, the county seat, before sunrise on Tuesday, August 29, 1786. They arrived armed and in military formation, the men's tricorner hats festooned with sprigs of evergreen, symbols of freedom frequently worn by Yankee soldiers during the War for Independence. At least a third of the men and virtually all their officers were veterans. The country was in the midst of an economic depression that had hit farm communities particularly hard. Two-thirds of the men who marched on Northampton had been sued for debt, and many had spent time in debtor's prison. Dozens of rural towns petitioned the state government for relief, but not only did the merchant-dominated legislature reject their pleas, it raised the property tax in order to pay off the enormous debt the state had accumulated during the Revolution.

The farmers decided to take matters into their own hands. When outsiders threatened a man's property, they argued, the community had the right, indeed the duty, to rise up in defense. During the Revolution, armed men had marched on the courts, shutting down the operation of government, and now they were doing it again. The judges of the Northampton court had no choice but to shut down, and that success led to similar actions in many other Massachusetts counties.

This uprising quickly became known as Shays' Rebellion, named for Daniel Shays, a decorated Revolutionary officer and one of the leaders from the town of Pelham. Although rebellion was most widespread in the state of Massachusetts, similar disorders occurred in the country districts of New Hampshire, Vermont, Pennsylvania, Maryland, and Virginia. Conservatives around the country were thrown into panic. The rebels, wrote Secretary of War Henry Knox to George Washington, planned to seize the property of the wealthy and redistribute it to the poor. Washington shared Knox's concerns and worried that rebellion threatened to break out everywhere.

Washington and other conservative leaders saw Shays' Rebellion as a class conflict pitting poor against rich, debtor against creditor. Yet the residents of Pelham and other rural towns acted in common, without regard to rank or property. Big farmers and small farmers alike marched on the county court. They came from tight-knit communities, bound together by family and kinship. Whether well-to-do or poor, they considered themselves "husbandmen," and they directed their protest against "outsiders," the urban residents of Boston and other coastal towns.

The crisis in Massachusetts ended when a militia force raised in the eastern part of the state, and financed by the great merchants, marched west and crushed the Shaysites in January 1787. Daniel Shays fled the state and never returned. Fifteen of the leaders were tried and sentenced to death. Two were hanged before the remainder were pardoned, and some four thousand other farmers temporarily lost their right to vote, to sit on juries, or to hold office. Yet many of them considered their rebellion a success. The next year Massachusetts voters rejected the old governor and elected a new legislature, which passed a moratorium on debts and cut taxes to only 10 percent of what they had been.

Shays' Rebellion was the most prominent of hundreds of protests, uprisings, and revolts across the United States focusing on the hard times caused by the economic depression. But the most important consequence of this unrest was not relief for the poor and distressed. Rather it was the effect they had on conservative nationalists unhappy with the distribution of power between the states and national governments under the Articles of Confederation. In the aftermath of Shays' Rebellion, they acquired a new determination to create a stronger national government.

The economic and political crisis of the 1780s would lead to the Constitutional Convention and a new charter for a national state. It would be enthusiastically supported by many, passionately opposed by many others. Its ratification would bring a new and stronger government to power, headed by the leaders of the Revolution. Before the end of the century, that government would lay the groundwork for the longest-lived democratic republic in the world.

Pelham

THE CRISIS OF THE 1780S

The depression of the mid-1780s and the political protests it generated were instrumental in the development of strong nationalist sentiment among elite circles. In the aftermath of Shays' Rebellion, these sentiments coalesced into a powerful political movement dedicated to strengthening the national government.

HOW DID economic conditions in the years after the Revolution lead to calls for fundamental political change?

THE ECONOMIC CRISIS

The economic crisis that produced Shays' Rebellion had its origins in the Revolution. The shortage of goods resulting from the British blockade, the demand for supplies by the army and the militias, and the flood of paper currency issued by the Confederation Congress and the states combined to create the worst inflation in American history. By 1781, Congress had issued more than $190 million in currency (see Figure 8.1). Most of this paper money ended up in the hands of merchants who had paid only a fraction of its face value.

After the war ended, inflation gave way to depression. Political revolution could not alter economic realities: the independent United States continued to be a supplier of raw materials and an importer of manufactured products, and Great Britain remained the country's most important trading partner. In 1784, British merchants began dumping goods in the American market, offering easy terms of credit. But the production of exportable goods had been drastically reduced by the fighting, and thus the trade deficit with Britain soared (see Figure 8.2). The deficit acted like a magnet, drawing hard currency from American accounts, leaving the country with little silver or gold coin in circulation. Commercial banks insisted on the repayment of old loans and refused to issue new ones. By the end of 1784, the country had fallen into the grip of economic depression.

The depression struck while the nation was attempting to dig out from the huge mountain of debt incurred during the Revolution. Not allowed to raise taxes on its own, the Confederation Congress requisitioned the states for the funds necessary for debt repayment. The states in turn taxed their residents. At a time when there was almost no money in circulation, ordinary Americans feared being crushed by the burden of private debt and public taxes. The economic problem became a political problem.

STATE REMEDIES

In the states, radicals called for regulation of the economy. The most controversial remedies were those designed to relieve the burden on debtors and ordinary taxpayers. Farmers and debtors pressed their state governments for legal tender laws, which required creditors to accept a state's paper currency at face value (rather than depreciated market value) for all debts public and private. Despite the opposition of creditors, seven states enacted such laws. For the most part, these were modest programs that worked rather well, caused little depreciation, and did not result in the problems creditors feared.

Some states erected high tariff barriers to curb imports and protect domestic industries. But foreign shippers found it easy to avoid these duties simply by unloading their cargo in states without tariffs and distributing the goods by overland transport. To be effective, commercial regulations had to be national. Local sentiment had to give way to the unity of a national community.

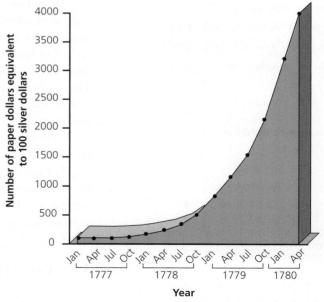

Figure 8.1 Postwar Inflation, 1777–80: The Depreciation of Continental Currency

The flood of Continental currency issued by Congress, and the shortage of goods resulting from the British blockade, combined to create the worst inflation Americans have ever experienced. Things of no value were said to be "not worth a Continental."

From "How Much Is That in Real Money?" *Proceedings of the American Antiquarian Society*, N.S. 102 (1992): 297–359. Copyright © 1992 American Antiquarian Society. Courtesy of American Antiquarian Society. Used by permission.

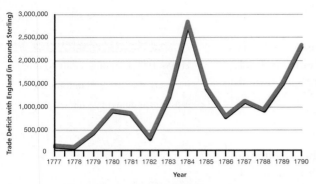

Figure 8.2 The Trade Deficit with Great Britain
The American trade deficit with Great Britain rose dramatically with the conclusion of the Revolution.

Historical Statistics of the United States (Washington, DC: Government Printing Office, 1976), 1176.

TOWARD A NEW NATIONAL GOVERNMENT

In 1786 the legislature of Virginia invited all the states to appoint delegates to a convention where they might consider political remedies for the economic crisis. The meeting, held in Annapolis, Maryland, in September, was sparsely attended (only twelve delegates from five states), but the men shared their alarm over the rebellion that was simultaneously taking place in Massachusetts, and the possibility of others like it.

Convinced of the absolute necessity of strengthening the national government, the **Annapolis convention** passed a resolution requesting that the Confederation Congress call on all the states to send delegates to a national convention that they might "render the constitution of the federal government adequate to the exigencies of the union." A few weeks later, with some reluctance, the Congress voted to endorse a convention to be held in Philadelphia in May 1787, "for the sole and express purpose of revising the Articles of Confederation."

Conservatives had in mind more than simply a revision of the Articles, however. They looked forward to a considerably strengthened national government. Believing that the consolidation of power in a strong central government would better serve their interests as merchants, bankers, and planters, the conservatives hid their motives behind the call for revision of the Articles.

THE NEW CONSTITUTION

In late May 1787, a few weeks after the suppression of Shays' Rebellion, fifty-five men from twelve states (a newly elected radical government in Rhode Island refusing to send a delegation) assembled at the Pennsylvania State House in Philadelphia. Twenty-nine of the delegates were college educated, thirty-four were lawyers, twenty-four had served in Congress, and twenty-one were veterans of the officer corps of the Continental Army. At least nineteen owned slaves, and there were also land speculators and merchants. There were no ordinary farmers or artisans and, of course, no women, African Americans, or Indians. The Constitution was framed by white men who represented America's social and economic elite.

These men were patriots, however, and committed to republicanism: that government must rest on the consent of the governed, and that the authority of rulers must be conditional on popular support. (For a discussion of republicanism see Chapter 6.) But they were not Democrats. They believed that the country already suffered from too much democracy. They feared that ordinary people, if given ready access to power, would enact policies against the interests of the privileged classes and, thus, the nation as a whole. The specter of Shays' Rebellion hung over the proceedings.

THE CONSTITUTIONAL CONVENTION

On their first day of work, the delegates agreed to vote by states, as was the procedure of Congress. They chose Washington to chair the meeting. Although the sessions were closed to the public, James Madison, a young, conservative Virginian took voluminous daily minutes that provide the best record of the proceedings. Madison and his fellow Virginians had drafted what became known as the **Virginia Plan**. Presented to the convention shortly after it convened, their plan set the agenda for the convention.

The Virginia Plan proposed scrapping the Articles of Confederation in favor of a "consolidated government" with the power to tax and to enforce its laws directly rather than through the states. The Virginia Plan would have reduced the states to little more

---

HOW DID Americans differ in their views of the new Constitution, and how were those differences reflected in the struggle to achieve ratification?

●●–Read the **Document**
The United States Constitution (1789) at **www.myhistorylab.com**

●●–Read the **Document**
James Madison, The Virginia (or Randolph) Plan (1787) at **www.myhistorylab.com**

Annapolis Convention Conference of state delegates at Annapolis, Maryland, that issued a call in September 1786 for a convention to meet at Philadelphia to consider fundamental changes.

Virginia Plan Proposal calling for a national legislature in which the states would be represented according to population.

George Washington presides over a session of the Constitutional Convention meeting in Philadelphia's State House (now known as Independence Hall) in an engraving of 1799.

than administrative institutions, something like counties. There would be a bicameral national legislature with all seats apportioned by population; members of the House of Representatives would be elected by popular vote, but members of the Senate chosen indirectly by state legislators, insulating them from democratic pressure. The Senate would lead, controlling foreign affairs and the appointment of officials. An appointed chief executive and a national judiciary would together form a Council of Revision having the power to veto both national and state legislation.

The main opposition to the Virginia Plan came from the delegates of the small states who feared being swallowed up by the large ones. After two weeks of debate, William Paterson of New Jersey introduced an alternative that became known as the **New Jersey Plan**. This plan also proposed increasing the powers of the central government but retained the single-house Congress of the Confederation government in which the states were equally represented. After much debate, the delegates finally agreed to what has been called the **Great Compromise**. Representation would be proportional to population in the House, with equal representation to each of the states in the Senate. The compromise allowed for the creation of a strong national government while still providing an important role for the states.

Part of this Great Compromise was a second fundamental agreement between North and South. Southern delegates wanted protections for slavery. They wanted provision for the mandatory return of fugitive southern slaves from the free northern states. To boost their power in Congress, they wanted slaves counted for the purpose of determining a state's proportional representation but excluded from the apportioning of taxes. Northern delegates, who wanted a central government with the power to regulate commerce, agreed to count five slaves as the equivalent of three free men—the so-called "three-fifths rule"—in exchange for southern support for a "commerce clause," providing the federal government with the power to regulate commerce with foreign nations, among the several states, and with Indian tribes. After bitter debate the delegates also

Watch the Video
Slavery and the Constitution at
www.myhistorylab.com

New Jersey Plan Proposal of the New Jersey delegation for a strengthened national government in which all states would have an equal representation in a unicameral legislature.

Great Compromise Plan proposed at the 1787 Constitutional Convention for creating a national bicameral legislature in which all states would be equally represented in the Senate and proportionally represented in the House.

Federalists Supporters of the Constitution who favored its ratification.

Anti-Federalists Opponents of the Constitution in the debate over its ratification.

QUICK REVIEW

Central Government Under the Constitution

- More powerful than Congress under the Articles of Confederation.
- Establishment of strong single person executive.
- Establishment of the Supreme Court.
- Expanded economic powers for Congress.

◆◆◆ Read the Document

Exploring America: Ratifying the Constitution at **www.myhistorylab.com**

agreed to include a provision preventing any federal restriction on the importation of slaves for twenty years.

There was still much to decide regarding the other branches of government. Madison's Council of Revision was scratched in favor of a strong federal judiciary with the implicit power to declare unconstitutional acts of Congress. There were demands for a powerful chief executive with veto power to check the legislature. To keep the president independent, the delegates decided he should be elected rather than appointed by the Congress, as was the procedure under the Articles of Confederation. But fearing that ordinary voters would never "be sufficiently informed" to select wisely, they insulated the process from popular choice by creating the electoral college. Voters in the states would not actually vote for president. Rather, each state would select a slate of "electors" equal in number to the state's total representation in the House and Senate. Following the general election, the electors in each state would meet to cast their ballots and elect the president.

The delegates voted their approval on September 17, 1787, and transmitted the document to the Confederation Congress, agreeing that it would become operative after ratification by nine states. A number of congressmen were outraged that the convention had exceeded its charge of simply modifying the Articles, but Congress agreed to issue a call for a special ratifying convention in each of the states.

RATIFYING THE NEW CONSTITUTION

The supporters of the new Constitution immediately adopted the name **Federalists** to describe themselves. Their opponents had to content themselves with the negative label **Anti-Federalists** (see Map 8.1). The critics of the Constitution were by no means a unified

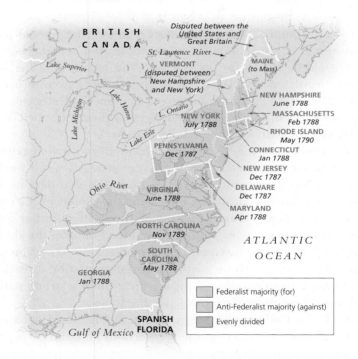

MAP 8.1

The Ratification of the Constitution, 1787–90 The distribution of the vote for the ratification of the Constitution demonstrated its wide support in sections of the country linked to the commercial economy and its disapproval in more remote and backcountry sections. (Note that Maine remained a part of Massachusetts until admitted as a separate state in 1820.)

WHERE WAS support for the Constitution strongest? Where was it weakest? Why?

group. But most believed it granted far too much power to the central government, weakening the autonomy of local communities and states.

Elections to select delegates for the state ratification conventions. The alignment of forces generally broke down along the lines laid down during the fights over economic issues in the years since the Revolution. An agrarian-localist versus commercial-cosmopolitan alignment characterized most of the states. The most critical convention took place in Massachusetts in early 1788. Five states—Delaware, Pennsylvania, New Jersey, Georgia, and Connecticut—had already voted to ratify, but the states with the strongest Anti-Federalist movements had yet to convene. If the Constitution lost in Massachusetts, its fate would be in great danger.

At the Massachusetts convention, the opponents of ratification enjoyed a small majority. But several important Anti-Federalist leaders, including Governor John Hancock and Revolutionary leader Samuel Adams, were swayed by the enthusiastic support for the Constitution among Boston's townspeople, whose livelihoods were tied to the commercial economy. On February 16, the convention voted narrowly in favor of ratification. Rhode Island rejected the Constitution in March, but Maryland and South Carolina approved it in April and May. On June 21, 1788, New Hampshire became the ninth state to ratify. The Constitution was now the law of the land.

New York, Virginia, and North Carolina were left with the decision of whether to join the new Union. Anti-Federalist support was strong in these states. North Carolina voted to reject. (It would reconsider and join the next year, followed by a still reluctant Rhode Island in 1790.) In New York the delegates were moved to vote their support by a threat from New York City to secede from the state and join the Union separately if the state convention failed to ratify. The Virginia convention was almost evenly divided, but promises to amend the Constitution to protect the people from the potential abuses of the federal government persuaded enough delegates to produce a victory for the Constitution. The promise of such a "Bill of Rights" was important in the ratification vote of five of the states.

THE BILL OF RIGHTS

Anti-Federalist delegates in numerous state ratification conventions had proposed a grab bag of over 200 potential amendments protecting the rights of the people against the power of the central government. In June 1789, James Madison, elected to the first Congress as a representative from Virginia, set about transforming these proposed amendments into a coherent series of proposals. Congress approved twelve and sent them to the states, and ten survived the ratification process to become the **Bill of Rights** in 1791.

The First Amendment prohibited Congress from establishing an official religion and provided for the freedom of assembly. It also ensured freedom of speech, a free press, and the right of petition. The other amendments guaranteed the right to bear arms, to limit the government's power to quarter troops in private homes, and to restrain the government from unreasonable searches or seizures; they guaranteed the traditional legal rights under the common law, including the prohibition of double jeopardy, the right

Bill of Rights The first ten amendments to the Constitution.

Read the **Document**
The Debates in the Federal Convention of 1787 at **www.myhistorylab.com**

Read the **Document**
The Bill of Rights (1789) at **www.myhistorylab.com**

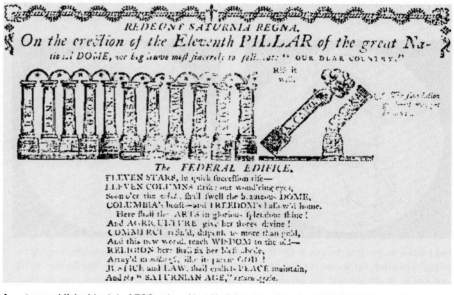

A cartoon published in July 1788, when New York became the eleventh state to ratify the Constitution. After initially voting to reject, North Carolina soon reconsidered, but radical and still reluctant Rhode Island did not join the Union until 1790.

The Federal Edifice "On the Erection of the Eleventh Pillar," caricature from the "Massachusetts Centinal, August 2, 1788. Neg. #33959. Collection of The New-York Historical Society.

HOW DID Washington's administration lay the foundation the subsequent development of American politics and government?

Judiciary Act of 1789 Act of Congress that implemented the judiciary clause of the Constitution by establishing the Supreme Court and a system of lower federal courts.

judicial review A power implied in the Constitution that gives federal courts the right to review and determine the constitutionality of acts passed by Congress and state legislatures.

not to be compelled to testify against oneself, and due process of law before life, liberty, or property could be taken away. Finally, the unenumerated rights of the people were protected, and the powers not delegated to the federal government were reserved to the states.

THE FIRST FEDERAL ADMINISTRATION

Ratification of the Constitution was followed in the fall of 1788 by the first federal elections for Congress and the presidency, and in the spring of 1789 the new federal government assumed power in the temporary capital of New York City. The inauguration of George Washington as the first president of the United States took place on April 30. Reelected without opposition in 1792, Washington served until 1797. The first years under the new federal Constitution were especially important for the future because they shaped the structure of the American nation-state in ways that would be enormously significant for later generations.

THE WASHINGTON PRESIDENCY

Congress quickly moved to establish departments to run the affairs of state, and Washington soon appointed Thomas Jefferson as secretary of state, Alexander Hamilton as secretary of the treasury, Henry Knox as secretary of war (continuing in the position he held under the Confederation government), and Edmund Randolph as attorney general. The president consulted each of these men regularly and during his first term met with them as a group to discuss matters of policy. By the end of Washington's presidency the secretaries had coalesced in what came to be known as the cabinet, an institution that has survived to the present despite the absence of constitutional authority. Washington understood the importance of national unity, and in his style of leadership, his consultations, and his appointments he sought to achieve a balance of conflicting political perspectives and sectional interests. His intentions would be sorely tested during the eight years of his administration.

THE FEDERAL JUDICIARY

The most important piece of legislation to emerge from the first session of Congress was the **Judiciary Act of 1789**, implementing the judicial clause of the Constitution, which empowered Congress to set the number of justices on the Supreme Court and create a system of federal courts. The act established a High Court of six justices (increased to nine in 1869) and established circuit and district federal courts. Strong nationalists argued for a powerful federal legal system that would provide a uniform code of civil and criminal justice throughout the country. But the localists in Congress, intent on preserving local community autonomy, successfully fought to retain the various bodies of law that had developed in the states. The act gave federal courts limited original jurisdiction, restricting them mostly to appeals from state courts. But it established the principle of federal **judicial review** of state legislation, despite the silence of the Constitution on this point.

Two coins from the first decade of the federal republic illustrate political controversies of the period. The Washington cent was proposed by Treasury Secretary Alexander Hamilton in 1792, in the hope of enhancing popular respect for the new government by having the president's bust impressed on coins in the manner of European kings. But after long debate, Congress defeated the plan, the opponents claiming it smacked of monarchy. The Liberty coin, issued by the Mint of the United States in 1795, when under the authority of Secretary of State Thomas Jefferson, features Liberty wearing a liberty cap and bearing a marked resemblance to the French Revolutionary icon Marianne.

HAMILTON'S FISCAL PROGRAM

Fiscal and economic affairs were important in the new government. It was, after all, the economic crisis and the resulting unrest in episodes like Shays' Rebellion that had provided the momentum for the new Constitution. Lacking revenue and facing the massive national debt run up during the Revolution, the government took power in a condition of virtual bankruptcy.

Treasury Secretary Hamilton took on the task of reorganizing the nation's finances. In 1790 he submitted a "Report on the Public Credit," recommending the federal "redemption" at full value of the national debt owed to foreign and domestic creditors, as well as the "assumption" of the obligations accumulated by the states during the previous fifteen years. Congress readily agreed to settle the $11 million owed to foreign creditors but balked at the redemption of the domestic debt of $42 million and the assumption of the state debts of another $25 million. Hamilton proposed issuing new interest-bearing government bonds that would be exchanged for the full face value of all the notes, warrants, and securities the government had distributed during the Revolution.

Thousands of veterans had been rewarded for their service with warrants for land or money, but as they waited for Congress to mark out the territory or provide the funding, many had been forced by necessity to sell to speculators at deep discounts. Hamilton's proposal, his colleague James Madison objected, would result in windfall profits for speculators and create a permanent federal debt. Hamilton did not dispute these claims but instead argued that they were good things. The creation of a federal debt by the issue of securities would give the government the ability to finance national projects or provide for national defense in the event of war, and the possession of those securities in the hands of a wealthy class of citizens would offer a guarantee for the government's stability. There was even greater congressional opposition to Hamilton's proposal for the assumption of state debts. Some states (mostly in the South) had already arranged to pay off their debts, whereas others (mostly in the North) had not, so the plan seemed to reward the insolvent and punish the thrifty. Congress remained deadlocked on these issues for six months, until congressmen from Pennsylvania and Virginia arranged a compromise.

Final agreement, however, was stalled by a sectional dispute over the location of the new national capital. Southerners supported Washington's desire to plant it on the Potomac River, but Northerners argued for Philadelphia. In return for Madison's pledge to obtain enough southern votes to pass Hamilton's debt assumption plan, northern congressmen agreed to a location for the new federal district on the boundary of Virginia and Maryland.

Hamilton now proposed a second component of his fiscal program, the establishment of a Bank of the United States. The bank, a public corporation funded by private capital, would serve as the depository of government funds and the fiscal agent of the Treasury. Congress narrowly approved it, but Madison's opposition raised doubts in the president's mind about the constitutionality of the measure, and Washington solicited the opinion of his cabinet. Jefferson took a "strict constructionist" position, arguing that the powers of the federal government must be limited to those specifically enumerated in the Constitution. Hamilton, on the other hand, reasoned that the Constitution "implied" the power to use whatever means were "necessary and proper" to carry out its enumerated powers, the "loose constructionist" position. Persuaded by Hamilton's opinion, Washington signed the bill, and the bank went into operation in 1791.

The final component of Hamilton's fiscal program, outlined in his famous "Report on Manufactures," was an ambitious plan, involving the use of government securities as investment capital for "infant industries" and high protective tariffs to encourage the

Alexander Hamilton (ca. 1804) by John Trumbull. Although Hamilton's fiscal program was controversial, it restored the financial health of the United States.

Read the Document

Alexander Hamilton, An Opinion on the Constitutionality of an Act to Establish a Bank (1791) at **www.myhistorylab.com**

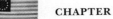

development of an industrial economy. This last component of Hamilton's program failed to gain sufficient support to become law. Many of Hamilton's specific proposals for increased tariff protection, however, became part of the revision of duties that took place in 1792. Moreover, his fiscal program as a whole dramatically restored the financial health of the United States.

The Federalist political coalition, forged during the ratification of the Constitution, was sorely strained by these debates over fiscal policy. By the middle of 1792, Jefferson—representing southern agrarians—and Hamilton—speaking for northern capitalists—were locked in a full-scale feud within the administration. Hamilton stated the difference clearly when he wrote that "one side appears to believe that there is a serious plot to overturn the State governments, and substitute a monarchy to the present republican system," while "the other side firmly believes that there is a serious plot to overturn the general government and elevate the separate powers of the States upon its ruins."

Distressed by these political disputes, Washington considered retiring at the end of his first term, but both factions encouraged him to remain in office to bridge their differences. The factions did contest the vice presidency. In December 1792 Washington was reelected by unanimous vote in the electoral college, but incumbent Vice President John Adams was only narrowly returned to office. It was an indication of things to come.

AMERICAN FOREIGN POLICY

The conflict between Hamilton and Jefferson grew even bitterer over the issue of American foreign policy. The commanding event of the Atlantic world during the 1790s was the French Revolution, which broke out in 1789. Most Americans enthusiastically welcomed the fall of the French monarchy. But with the inauguration of the Reign of Terror in 1793, which claimed the lives of hundreds of aristocrats and politicians upon the guillotine, American conservatives began to voice their opposition. The execution of King Louis XVI in January 1793 and the outbreak of war between revolutionary France and monarchical Great Britain a few weeks later firmly divided American opinion.

Most at issue was whether the Franco-American alliance of 1778 required the United States to support France in its war with Britain. All of Washington's cabinet agreed on the importance of American neutrality. Jefferson believed it highly unlikely that the French would call upon the Americans to honor the 1778 treaty and that the administration should simply wait and see. But Hamilton argued that so great was the danger of American involvement in the war that Washington should immediately declare the treaty "temporarily and provisionally suspended."

These disagreements revealed two contrasting perspectives on the course the United States should chart in international waters. Hamilton and the nationalists believed in the necessity of an accommodation with Great Britain, the most important trading partner of the United States and the world's greatest naval power. Jefferson, Madison, and their supporters, on the other hand, looked for more international independence, less connection with the British, and thus closer relations with Britain's traditional rival, France. They pinned their hopes for the future on American western expansion.

The debate in the United States grew hotter with the arrival in early 1793 of French ambassador Edmond Genêt. Large crowds of supporters greeted him throughout the nation, and Genêt solicited contributions and distributed commissions authorizing American privateering raids against the British. Knowing he must act before "Citizen" Genêt (as the ambassador was popularly known) compromised American sovereignty and involved the United States in a war with Britain, Washington issued a proclamation of neutrality on April 22, 1793.

Hamilton's supporters applauded the president, but Jefferson's friends were outraged. Throughout the country, activists sympathetic to France organized Democratic Societies, political clubs modeled after the Sons of Liberty. Society members corresponded with each other, campaigned on behalf of candidates, and lobbied with congressmen.

Citizen Genêt miscalculated, however, alienating even his supporters, when he demanded that Washington call Congress into special session to debate neutrality. Jefferson, previously a confidant of the ambassador, now denounced Genêt as "hotheaded" and "indecent towards the President." But his words came too late to save his reputation with Washington, and at the end of 1793 Jefferson left the administration. The continuing upheaval in France soon swept Genêt's party from power and he was recalled, but fearing the guillotine, he claimed sanctuary and remained in the United States. During his time in the limelight, however, Genêt had furthered the division of the Federalist coalition into two factions, one identifying with Washington, Hamilton, and conservative principles, the other supporting Jefferson, Madison, democracy, and the French Revolution.

THE UNITED STATES AND THE INDIAN PEOPLES

One of the most pressing problems of the Washington presidency concerned the West. The American attempt to treat western Indian tribes as conquered peoples after the Revolution had resulted only in further violence and warfare. In the Northwest Ordinance of 1787 (see Chapter 7), the Confederation Congress abandoned that course for a new approach. "The utmost good faith shall always be observed towards the Indians," the ordinance read. "Their lands and property shall never be taken from them without their consent." Yet the ordinance was premised on the survey and sale to American settlers of Indian land north of the Ohio River and the creation of new state governments. The ordinance pointed in wildly contradictory directions.

The new federal government continued to pursue this inconsistent policy. In 1790 Congress passed the **Intercourse Act**. In an attempt to clarify the vexing problem of Indian sovereignty, the act declared public treaties between the United States and the Indian nations the only legal means of obtaining Indian land. Treaty making, thus,

Intercourse Act Passed in 1790, this law regulated trade and intercourse with the Indian tribes and declared public treaties between the United States and Indian nations the only means of obtaining Indian lands.

Little Turtle, a war chief of the Miami tribe of the Ohio Valley, led a large pan-Indian army to victory over the Americans in 1790 and 1791. After his forces were defeated at the Battle of Fallen Timbers in 1794, he became a friend of the United States. This lithograph is a copy of an oil portrait, which no longer survives, by the artist Gilbert Stuart.

Little Turtle, or Mich-i-kin-i-qua, Miami War Chief, Conqueror of Harmar and St. Clair. Lithograph made from a portrait painted in 1797 by Gilbert Stuart. Indiana Historical Society Library (negative no. C2584).

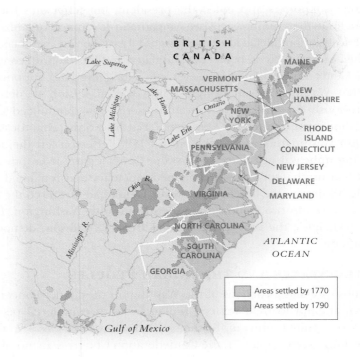

MAP 8.2
Spread of Settlement: The Backcountry Expands, 1770–90 From 1770 to 1790, American settlement moved across the Appalachians for the first time. The Ohio Valley became the focus of bitter warfare between Indians and settlers.

WHERE WAS new settlement concentrated in the 1780s?

became the procedure for establishing and maintaining relations with Indian nations. To eliminate the abuses of unscrupulous traders, the act also created a federal licensing system, and subsequent legislation authorized the creation of subsidized trading houses, or "factories," where Indians could obtain manufactured goods at reasonable prices. These provisions indicated the best intentions of the Washington administration.

On the other hand, one of the federal government's highest priorities was the acquisition of western Indian land to support a growing population of farmers (see Map 8.2). The federal government, in fact, was unable to control the flood of settlers coming down the Ohio River. An American expeditionary force was sent to evict squatters from Indian land, but inevitably the troops ended up protecting settlers and fighting Indians. In defense of their homelands, villages of Shawnees, Delawares, and other Indian peoples confederated with the Miamis under their war chief Little Turtle. In the fall of 1790 Little Turtle lured federal forces led by General Josiah Harmar into the confederacy's stronghold in Ohio and badly mauled them. In November 1791 the confederation inflicted an even more disastrous defeat on a large American force under General Arthur St. Clair. More than 900 Americans were killed or wounded, making this the worst defeat of an army by Indians in North American history (see Seeing History).

SPANISH FLORIDA AND BRITISH CANADA

The position of the United States in the West was made even more precarious by the hostility of Spain and Great Britain, which controlled the adjoining territories. Under the dynamic leadership of King Carlos III and his able ministers, Spain introduced liberal reforms to revitalize the rule-bound bureaucracy of its American empire. As a result the

The Columbian Tragedy

Broadsides—large sheets printed on one side, suitable for posting—were an important medium of popular communication in the late eighteenth and early nineteenth centuries. This one, lamenting the disastrous defeat of an American expeditionary force at the hands of the Ohio Indian confederacy in 1791 in which more than 900 Americans were killed or wounded, was published in Boston and sold throughout New England for the price of six cents. The struggle against the Ohio Indian confederacy was one of the most critical issues

WHY WOULD Americans purchase this broadside and display it in their homes?

during Washington's presidency. Across the top are the names of the officers killed in battle, each accompanied by the icon of a black coffin. On the left is a woodcut of Major-General Richard Butler, the highest-ranking officer to die, and beneath it an Indian warrior alongside a skull and crossbones. On the right is a crude representation of the battleground. As one contemporary critic put it, all the images are "of the commonest description," yet the broadside survives in a number of copies, indicating that it probably sold quite well. The broadside did double duty—as both memorial for the dead and protest against the incompetence of the army's leaders. Most of the broadside is devoted to a mournful ballad that nevertheless concludes that the nation will ultimately prevail because "the *Lord* is on our side." ■

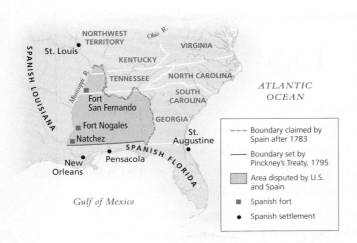

MAP 8.3

Spanish Claims to American Territory, 1783–95   Before 1795, the Spanish claimed the American territory of the Old Southwest and barred Americans from access to the port of New Orleans, effectively closing the Mississippi River. This dispute was settled by Pinckney's Treaty in 1795.

WHERE WAS the southern boundary of the United States set under the terms of Pinckney's Treaty? Why might Spain have insisted that it be set above New Orleans?

economy of New Spain grew rapidly in the 1780s. Moreover, Spain had reasserted itself in North America, acquiring the French claims to Louisiana before the end of the Seven Years' War, expanding into California, seizing the Gulf Coast during the American Revolution, and regaining Florida from Britain in the Treaty of Paris in 1783. Spain claimed for itself much of the territory that today makes up the states of Tennessee, Alabama, and Mississippi and pursued a policy designed to block the continued expansion of the United States (see Map 8.3).

Spain's anti-American policy in the West had several facets. Controlling both sides of the lower Mississippi, the Spanish closed the river to American shipping, making it impossible for western American farmers to market their crops through the port of New Orleans. They also sought to create a barrier to American settlement by promoting immigration to Louisiana and Florida. They succeeded in attracting several thousand Acadians, whom the British had deported from Nova Scotia during the Seven Years' War. Reassembling their distinctive communities in the bayou country of Louisiana, these emigrants became known as the Cajuns. But otherwise, the Spanish had little success with immigration and relied mostly on creating a barrier of pro-Spanish Indian nations in the lower Mississippi Valley. In the early 1790s the Spanish attempted to extend their control of the Mississippi River by constructing two new forts at sites that would later become the river cities of Vicksburg and Memphis.

North of the Ohio River, the situation was much the same. Thousands of Loyalists had fled the United States in the aftermath of the Revolution and settled north of lakes Ontario and Erie. In 1791 the British Parliament passed the Canada Act, creating the province of Upper Canada (later renamed Ontario) and granting the Loyalists limited self-government. To protect this province, British troops remained at a number of posts within American territory, such as Detroit, where they supplied arms to the Indian nations, in hopes of creating a buffer to American expansion.

THE CRISES OF 1794

These conditions laid the groundwork for the gravest crisis of Washington's presidency in 1794. In the West, the inability of the federal government to subdue the Indians, eliminate the British from the northern fur trade, or arrange with the Spanish for unencumbered use of the Mississippi River stirred frontiersmen to loud protest. Secret agents for Great Britain and Spain sought to entice American settlers to quit the Union and join themselves to Canada or Florida. In the Atlantic, Great Britain declared a blockade of France and its colonies in the West Indies, and by early 1794 the Royal Navy had confiscated the cargoes of more than 250 American ships, threatening hundreds of merchants with ruin.

To make matters worse a rebellion broke out among farmers in western Pennsylvania in the summer of 1794. To produce needed revenue, Congress had placed an excise tax on the distillation of whiskey, which many farm families produced from their surpluses of corn. Throughout rural America, farmers protested that the new tax ran counter to the principles of the Revolution. "Internal taxes upon consumption," declared the citizens of Mingo Creek, in western Pennsylvania, are "most dangerous to the civil rights of freemen, and must in the end destroy the liberties of every country in which they are introduced." Protest turned to riot when the Mingo Creek militia attempted to seize the tax collector, and several of their number were killed in the confrontation.

The "**Whiskey Rebellion**" came at a time when Washington considered the nation to be under siege. The combination of Indian attack, international intrigue, and domestic

Whiskey Rebellion   Armed uprising in 1794 by farmers in western Pennsylvania who attempted to prevent the collection of the excise tax on whiskey.

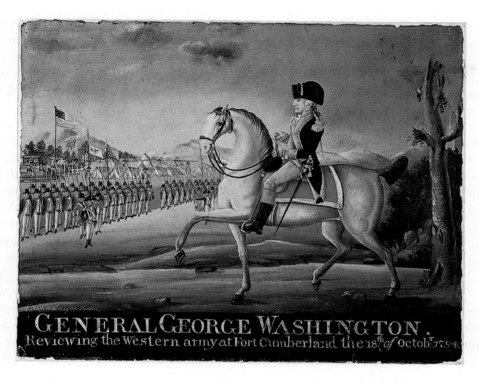

GENERAL GEORGE WASHINGTON.
Reviewing the Western army at Fort Cumberland the 18.ᵗʰ of Octobᵣ 1794.

insurrection, he believed, posed the greatest threat to the nation since the Revolution. He called up a federal army of 13,000 men and ordered the occupation of western Pennsylvania. Federal troops dragged protesting farmers from their beds and confined them to open pens, where they remained for days in the freezing rain. Authorities arrested twenty people, and a judge convicted two of treason. The protests gradually died down and Washington pardoned the felons, sparing their lives. The president overreacted, for there was no organized insurrection in western Pennsylvania. Nevertheless, his mobilization of federal military power was a dramatic demonstration of his commitment to the preservation of the Union, the protection of the western boundary, and the supremacy of the national over the local community.

Washington's action was reinforced by an American victory against the western Indian confederacy. Following the disastrous defeat of St. Clair by Little Turtle, the president directed General Anthony Wayne to lead a greatly strengthened American force to secure the Northwest. At the Battle of Fallen Timbers, fought in northern Ohio on August 20, 1794, Wayne crushed the Indians. This American victory set the stage for the **Treaty of Greenville** in 1795, in which the representatives of twelve Indian nations ceded a huge territory encompassing most of present-day Ohio, much of Indiana, and other enclaves in the Northwest.

SETTLING DISPUTES WITH BRITAIN AND SPAIN

The strengthened American position in the West encouraged the British finally to settle their dispute with the United States so that they might concentrate on defeating republican France. Washington dispatched Chief Justice John Jay to London to arrange a settlement with the British, and in November 1794 Jay and his British counterpart signed an agreement providing for British withdrawal from American soil by 1796, for limited American trade with British colonies, and for "most-favored-nation" status (meaning that each nation would enjoy terms of trade equal to the best terms accorded any other nation).

Jay's Treaty enshrined Hamilton's conception of American neutrality. Hamilton's opponents, on the other hand, were enraged at what they considered an accommodation with the British at the expense of the French. Moreover, Southerners were alienated by

◆●◆⊣Read the Document

George Washington, Proclamation Regarding the Whiskey Rebellion (1794) at **www.myhistorylab.com**

Treaty of Greenville Treaty of 1795 in which Native Americans in the Old Northwest were forced to cede most of the present state of Ohio to the United States.

Jay's Treaty Treaty with Britain negotiated in 1794 in which the United States made major concessions to avert a war over the British seizure of American ships.

Jay's failure to negotiate compensation for masters whose slaves had fled to the British during the Revolution. Throughout the country opponents of the treaty organized protests and demonstrations. Nevertheless, the Senate, dominated by supporters of Hamilton, ratified the agreement in June 1795. In the House, a coalition of southerners, westerners, and friends of France attempted to stall the treaty by threatening to withhold the necessary appropriations.

The deadlock continued until late in the year, when word arrived that the Spanish had abandoned their claims to the territory south of the Ohio River. Spain had declared war on revolutionary France but quickly suffered a humiliating defeat. Fearing the loss of its American empire, the Spanish found it expedient to come to an agreement with the Americans. In 1795 American envoy Thomas Pinckney negotiated a treaty setting the international boundary at the 31st parallel (the southern boundary of Mississippi and Alabama) and opening the Mississippi to American shipping. This treaty was compatible with the Jeffersonian conception of empire, and congressmen from the South and West were delighted with its terms. Administration supporters, however, demanded that the House agree in the matter of Jay's Treaty before the Senate would approve Pinckney's.

With the ratification of these important treaties, the United States established its sovereignty over the land west of the Appalachians and opened to American commerce a vast market extending from Atlantic ports to the Mississippi Valley. From a political stand-point, however, the events of 1794 and 1795 brought Washington down from his pedestal. Vilified by the opposition press, sick of politics, and longing to return to private life, Washington rejected the idea of a third term.

WASHINGTON'S FAREWELL ADDRESS

During the last months of his term, Washington published a "Farewell Address" to the nation. He extolled the benefits of the federal government and praised the financial stability that had resulted from Hamilton's policy. In the best-remembered portion of the address, he urged that the United States seek commercial connections with all nations but "have with them as little political connection as possible." Looking forward, he expressed great concern about the growing acrimony between political factions, which, he argued, "agitates the community with ill-founded jealousies and false alarms, . . . and opens the door to foreign influence and corruption."

FEDERALISTS AND DEMOCRATIC-REPUBLICANS

HOW AND why did the first American political parties emerge?

The framers of the Constitution envisioned a one-party state in which partisan distinctions would be muted by patriotism and public virtue. Despite the intentions of the framers, in the twelve years between the ratification of the Constitution and the federal election of 1800, political parties became a fundamental part of the American system of government.

THE RISE OF POLITICAL PARTIES

Evident in the debates and votes of Congress from 1789 to 1795 was a series of shifting coalitions. These coalitions first began to polarize into opposing political factions during the debate over Jay's Treaty in 1795, when agrarians, westerners, southerners, and supporters of France came together in opposition. By the time of the election of 1796, the factions had taken names for themselves. Hamilton's supporters continued to claim the mantle of Federalism. But Jefferson's supporters christened themselves Republicans, suggesting by implication that the Federalists were really monarchists at heart. (Historians use the term "Democratic-Republicans" to distinguish them from the modern Republican Party, founded in 1854.) The two political factions played a fitful role in the

OVERVIEW | The First American Party System

Federalist Party	Organized by figures in the Washington administration who were in favor of a strong federal government, friendship with the British, and opposition to the French Revolution; its power base was among merchants, property owners, and urban workers tied to the commercial economy. A minority party after 1800, it was regionally strong only in New England.
Democratic-Republican Party	Arose as the opposition to the Federalists; its adherents were in favor of limiting federal power; they were sympathetic to the French Revolution and hostile to Great Britain; the party drew strength from southern planters and northern farmers and was the majority party after 1800.

presidential election of 1796, which pitted Vice President John Adams against Thomas Jefferson. Adams was victorious, but in accordance with the Constitution the vice presidency went to the candidate with the second-highest total, and that was Jefferson. The new administration was born divided.

THE ADAMS PRESIDENCY

Adams was put in the difficult situation of facing a political opposition led by his own vice president. He nevertheless attempted to conduct his presidency along the lines laid down by Washington and retained most of the former president's appointees.

On the other hand, Adams benefited from rising tensions between the United States and France. Angered by Jay's Treaty, the French suspended diplomatic relations with the United States at the end of 1796 and inaugurated a tough new policy toward American shipping, seizing American vessels and confiscating their cargoes. Hoping to resolve the crisis, Adams sent an American delegation to France. But in dispatches sent back to the United States, the envoys reported that three agents of the French foreign ministry had demanded a bribe before any negotiations could begin. Skeptical Republicans demanded the release of the dispatches, which Adams agreed to in 1798, substituting the letters X, Y, Z for the names of the French agents. The documents upheld Adams's case and proved a major liability for the Republicans, sparking powerful anti-French sentiment throughout the country. The **XYZ Affair**, as it became known, sent Adams's popularity soaring.

THE ALIEN AND SEDITION ACTS

During the spring of 1798 Adams and the Federalists prepared the country for war with France. Congress authorized tripling the size of the army, and Washington came out of retirement to command the force. Fears of a French invasion declined after word arrived of a British naval victory over the French at Aboukir Bay in Egypt in August 1798, but what became known as the "**Quasi-War**" between France and the United States continued.

The Democratic-Republicans contested the Federalist war measures and began for the first time to act as a genuine opposition party, complete with caucuses, floor leaders, and partisan discipline. The more effective the Republicans became as an opposition, the more treasonous they appeared in the eyes of the Federalists. Disagreement with the administration was misconstrued by the Federalists as opposition to the state itself.

In the summer of 1798 the Federalist majority in Congress, with the acquiescence of President Adams, passed four acts severely limiting both freedom of speech and the freedom of the press and threatening the liberty of foreigners in the United States. The Naturalization Act extended the period of residence required for citizenship from five to fourteen years. The **Alien Act** and the Alien Enemies Act authorized the president to order the imprisonment or deportation of suspected aliens during wartime. Finally, the **Sedition Act** provided heavy fines and imprisonment for anyone convicted of writing,

XYZ Affair Diplomatic incident in 1798 in which Americans were outraged by the demand of the French for a bribe as a condition for negotiating with American diplomats.

Quasi-War Undeclared naval war of 1797 to 1800 between the United States and France.

Alien Act Act passed by Congress in 1798 that authorized the president to imprison or deport suspected aliens during wartime.

Sedition Act An act passed by Congress in 1798 that provided fines for anyone convicted of writing, publishing, or speaking out against the government or its officers.

In this contemporary cartoon, *Congressional Pugilists, Congress Hall in Philadelphia, February 15, 1798*, Roger Griswold, a Connecticut Federalist, uses his cane to attack Matthew Lyon, a Vermont Democratic-Republican, who retaliates with fire tongs.

Collection of The New-York Historical Society, Neg. #33995.

publishing, or speaking anything of "a false, scandalous and malicious" nature against the government or any of its officers.

The Federalists intended these repressive laws as weapons to defeat the Democratic-Republicans. They prosecuted dissent by indicting leading opposition newspaper editors and writers, fining and imprisoning at least twenty-five of them.

In response to these four acts, Madison and Jefferson anonymously authored resolutions, passed by the Virginia and Kentucky legislatures, declaring the Constitution a compact among sovereign states and advocating the power of the states to "nullify" unconstitutional laws. When threatened with overbearing central authority, they argued, the states had the right to go their own way. The Virginia and Kentucky Resolves, as they were known, would later be used to justify the secession of the Southern states at the beginning of the Civil War.

THE REVOLUTION OF 1800

In 1799 the French convinced President Adams that they were willing to settle their dispute with the United States when they released seized American ships and requested negotiations. But conservative Federalists continued to beat the drums of war. When Federalists in Congress attempted to block the negotiations, Adams threatened to resign and turn the government over to Vice President Jefferson. Adams considered the settlement of this conflict with France to be one of the greatest accomplishments of his career.

The presidential campaign of 1800 was the first to be contested by two disciplined political parties. Caucuses of congressmen nominated respective slates: Adams and Charles Cotesworth Pinckney of South Carolina for the Federalists, Jefferson and Aaron Burr of New York for the Republicans. Both tickets thus represented attempts at sectional balance. The Democratic-Republicans presented themselves as the party of traditional agrarian purity, of liberty and **states' rights**. They were optimistic, convinced they were riding the wave of the future. The Federalists, divided over foreign policy and embittered, waged a defensive struggle for strong central government and public order.

Adams won in New England but elsewhere was overwhelmed (see Map 8.4). Jefferson called it "the Revolution of 1800." Party discipline was so effective, in fact, that it created a constitutional crisis. By casting all their ballots for Jefferson and Burr, Republican electors thoughtlessly produced a tie vote, thus forcing the election into the lame duck House of Representatives controlled by the Federalists. Given a last chance to decide the election,

●**•**●┤**Read** the **Document**

The Alien and Sedition Acts (1798) at **www.myhistorylab.com**

QUICK REVIEW

Presidential Election of 1800

◆ Federalists could not overcome internal divisions.

◆ First election in which Federalists and Republicans acted as national parties.

◆ Both parties aimed at sectional balance in their tickets.

states' rights Favoring the rights of individual states over rights claimed by the national government.

Federalist representatives attempted to cut a deal with Burr. Although Burr refused, he also declined to withdraw his name from consideration. Finally, on the thirty-fifth ballot the Federalists arranged with their opponents to elect Jefferson without any of them having to vote in his favor. Afterward, Congress passed and the states ratified the Twelfth Amendment, creating separate ballots for president and vice president in time for the next presidential election.

DEMOCRATIC POLITICAL CULTURE

Accompanying the rise of partisan politics was a transformation in popular political participation. Consider the custom of celebrating Independence Day. At the beginning of the 1790s, in many communities, the day featured demonstrations of military prowess by veteran officers, followed by banquets for leaders. Relatively few Americans played a direct role. But during the political controversies of the decade, a tradition of popular celebration developed. People took to the streets, set off fireworks, erected liberty poles, and listened to readings of the preamble of the Declaration of Independence.

There was a corresponding increase in the **suffrage**. In 1789 state regulations limited the franchise to a small percentage of the adult population. Women, African Americans, and Indians could not vote, but neither could a third to a half of all free adult males, who were excluded by tax-paying or property-owning requirements. Moreover, even among the eligible, the turnout was generally low.

The situation changed with the increasing competition between Democratic-Republicans and Federalists. Popular pressure resulted in the introduction of universal white manhood suffrage in four states by 1800 and the reduction of property requirements in others. Thus was inaugurated a movement that would sweep the nation over the next quarter century. As a consequence, voter turnout increased in all the states. The growth of popular interest in politics was a transformation as important as the peaceful transition from Federalists to Democratic-Republicans in national government.

Electoral Vote (%)	
THOMAS JEFFERSON (Jeffersonian Republican)	73 (53)
JOHN ADAMS (Federalist)	65 (47)

MAP 8.4

The Election of 1800   In the presidential election of 1800, Democratic-Republican victories in New York and the divided vote in Pennsylvania threw the election to Jefferson. The combination of the South and these crucial Middle States would keep the Democratic-Republicans in control of the federal government for the next generation.

WHERE WERE the Federalists strongest in 1800? Where were the Democratic Republicans strongest?

suffrage The right to vote in a political election.

The presidential election of 1800 was the first to feature campaign advertising. "T. Jefferson, President of the United States of America; John Adams—no more," reads the streamer on this election banner, illustrated with an American eagle and a portrait of Jefferson. This was mild rhetoric in a campaign characterized by wild charges. The Republicans labeled Adams a warmonger and a monarchist, while the Federalists denounced Jefferson as an atheist, Jacobin, and sexual libertine.

CHRONOLOGY

1786	Shays' Rebellion
	Annapolis Convention
1787	Constitutional Convention
1787–88	*The Federalist Papers* published
1788	Constitution ratified
	First federal elections
1789	President George Washington inaugurated in New York City
	Judiciary Act
	French Revolution begins
1790	Agreement on site on the Potomac River for the nation's capital
	Indian Intercourse Act
	Judith Sargent Murray publishes "On the Equality of the Sexes"
1791	Bill of Rights ratified
	Bank of the United States chartered
	Alexander Hamilton's "Report on Manufactures"
	Ohio Indians defeat General Arthur St. Clair's army
1792	Washington reelected

1793	England and France at war; America reaps trade windfall
	Citizen Genêt affair
	President Washington proclaims American neutrality in Europe
	Supreme Court asserts itself as final authority in *Chisholm* v. *Georgia*
1794	Whiskey Rebellion
	Battle of Fallen Timbers
	Jay's Treaty with the British concluded
1795	Pinckney's Treaty negotiated with the Spanish
	Treaty of Greenville
1796	President Washington's Farewell Address
	John Adams elected president
1797–98	French seize American ships
1798	XYZ Affair
	"Quasi-War" with France
	Alien and Sedition Acts
	Kentucky and Virginia Resolves
1800	Convention of 1800
	Thomas Jefferson elected president
	Mason Locke Weems publishes *Life of Washington*

"THE RISING GLORY OF AMERICA"

WHAT DID Americans read in the early decades of the Republic?

In 1771, Philip Freneau and Hugh Henry Brackenridge addressed their graduating class at Princeton on "The Rising Glory of America." Thus far American contributions to learning and the arts had been slim, they admitted, but they were boundlessly optimistic about the potential of their country. Indeed, judged against the creative work of the colonial period, the Revolutionary generation accomplished a great deal in their effort to build a national culture.

THE LIBERTY OF THE PRESS

●•●—Read the Document
Exploring America: The Partisan Press at
www.myhistorylab.com

At the beginning of the Revolution in 1775, there were thirty-seven weekly or semiweekly newspapers in the thirteen colonies. By 1789, the number of papers in the United States had grown to ninety-two. Relative to population, there were more newspapers in the United States than in any other country in the world—a reflection of the remarkably high literacy rate of the American people. In New England, almost 90 percent of the population could read, and even on the frontier about two-thirds of the males were literate. During the political controversy of the 1790s, the press became the principal medium of Federalist and Democratic-Republican opinion, and papers came to be identified by their politics.

The prosecutions under the Sedition Act, however, threatened to curb the further development of the media, and in their opposition to these measures Democratic-Republicans played an important role in establishing the principle of a free press. In his first inaugural address, Jefferson championed freedom of expression. "Error of opinion may be tolerated," he declared, "where reason is left free to combat it." During his presidency, the Alien and Sedition Acts, which had justified the suppression of political opinion, were repealed or allowed to expire.

BOOKS, BOOKS, BOOKS

During the post-Revolutionary years there was an enormous outpouring of American publications. In the cities the number of bookstores grew in response to the demand for reading matter. Perhaps even more significant was the appearance in the countryside of numerous book peddlers who supplied farm households with Bibles, gazettes, almanacs, sermons, and political pamphlets. One of them wrote that he found his customers "uninformed, their minds bitter, and their manners savage," but they cried out for "books, books, books!"

Some of the most interesting American books of the postwar years examined the developing American character. The French emigrant Michel-Guillaume Jean de Crevecoeur, in *Letters from an American Farmer* (1782), proposed that the American, a product of many cultures, was a "new man" with ideas new to the world. John Filson, the author of *The Discovery, Settlement, and Present State of Kentucke* (1784), presented the narrative of one such new man, the Kentucky pioneer Daniel Boone. In doing so, he took an important step toward the creation of that most American of literary genres, the western.

But for Americans, the most important "new man" was George Washington. Mason Locke Weems's short biography of the first president became the new nation's first best-seller. Weems's *Life of Washington* (1800) introduced a series of popular and completely fabricated anecdotes, including the story of young Washington and the cherry tree. Although Washington had in fact become a partisan leader of the Federalists during his second term, Weems presented him as a unifying figure for the political culture of the new nation, and that was the way he would be remembered.

WOMEN ON THE INTELLECTUAL SCENE

One of the most interesting literary trends of the 1790s was the growing demand for books appealing to women readers. Susanna Haswell Rowson's *Charlotte Temple* (1791) and Hannah Webster Foster's *The Coquette* (1797), tales of seduction and abandonment were extremely popular. The young republic thus marked the first dramatic appearance of women writers and women readers. Although women's literacy rates continued lower than men's, they rose steadily as girls joined boys in common schools. This increase was one of the most important social legacies of the democratic struggles of the Revolutionary era.

Some writers argued that the new republican order ought to provide new roles for women as well as for men. The first avowed feminist in American history was Judith Sargent Murray, who publicly stated her belief that women "should be taught to depend on their own efforts, for the procurement of an establishment in life." Her essay "On the Equality of the Sexes," written in 1779 and published in 1790, threw down a bold challenge to men. "Yes, ye lordly, ye haughty sex," she wrote, "our souls are by nature equal to yours," and predicted that American women would commence "a new era in female history." Federalists listened to

Judith Sargent Murray, a portrait by John Singleton Copley, completed in 1771. Born into an elite merchant family in Gloucester, Massachusetts, she became a wife and mother but also a poet, essayist, playwright, novelist, and historian. In 1779 she published an essay on the equality of the sexes that distinguished her as the first avowed feminist in American history.

John Singleton Copley (1738–1815), "Portrait of Mrs. John Stevens (Judith Sargent, later Mrs. John Murray)," 1770–72. Commissioned on the occasion of her first marriage, at age eighteen. Oil on canvas, 50 × 40 in. Daniel J. Terra Art Acquisition Endowment Fund, 2000.6. © Terra Foundation for American Art, Chicago / Art Resource, New York.

such opinions with horror. "Women of masculine minds," one Boston minister sneered, "have generally masculine manners."

There seemed to be general agreement among all parties, however, that the time had come for women to be better educated. Republican institutions of self-government were widely thought to depend on the wisdom and self-discipline of the American people. Civic virtue, so indispensable for the republic, needed to be taught at home. By placing her learning at the service of her family, the "republican mother" was spared the criticism leveled at independent-minded women such as Murray. "A woman will have more commendation in being the mother of heroes," wrote one Federalist, "than in setting up, Amazon-like, for a heroine herself." Thus were women provided the opportunity to be not simply "helpmates" but also people "learned and wise." But they were also expected to be content with a narrow role, not to wish for fuller participation in the American experiment.

CONCLUSION

During the last years of the eighteenth century, the United States adopted a new constitution and established a new national government. It repaid the debt run up during the Revolution and made peace with adversaries abroad and Indian peoples at home. Americans began to learn how to channel their disagreements into political struggle. The new government, born in the economic and political crisis that surrounded Shays' Rebellion, had withstood a first decade of stress, but tensions would continue to divide the people. At the beginning of the new century, it remained uncertain whether the new nation would find a way to control and channel the energies of an expanding people.

REVIEW QUESTIONS

1. Discuss the conflicting ideals of local and national authority in the debate over the Constitution.

2. What were the major crises faced by the Washington and Adams administrations?

3. Describe the roles of Madison and Hamilton in the formation of the first American political parties.

4. What did Jefferson mean when he talked of "the Revolution of 1800"?

5. Discuss the contributions of the Revolutionary generation to the construction of a national culture.

KEY TERMS

Alien Act (p. 191)
Annapolis Convention (p. 178)
Anti-Federalists (p. 180)
Bill of Rights (p. 181)
Federalists (p. 180)
Great Compromise (p. 179)
Intercourse Act (p. 185)
Jay's Treaty (p. 189)
Judicial review (p. 182)
Judiciary Act of 1789 (p. 182)

New Jersey Plan (p. 179)
Quasi-War (p. 191)
Sedition Act (p. 191)
States' rights (p. 192)
Suffrage (p. 193)
Treaty of Greenville (p. 189)
Virginia Plan (p. 178)
Whiskey Rebellion (p. 188)
XYZ Affair (p. 191)

PEARSON myhistorylab Connections

Reinforce what you learned in this chapter by studying the many documents, images, maps, review tools, and videos available at www.myhistorylab.com.

Read and Review

✓● Study and Review **Chapter 8**

●●● Read the Document

The United States Constitution (1789)

James Madison, The Virginia (or Randolph) Plan (1787)

The Debates in the Federal Convention of 1787

The Bill of Rights (1789)

Alexander Hamilton, An Opinion on the Constitutionality of an Act to Establish a Bank (1791)

George Washington, Proclamation Regarding the Whiskey Rebellion (1794)

The Alien and Sedition Acts (1798)

James Madison Defends the Constitution (1788)

Patrick Henry against Ratification of the Constitution (1788)

A Free African American Petitions the Government for Emancipation of All Slaves (1777)

⊙● See the Map *The Ratification of the Constitution, 1787–90*

Research and Explore

●●● Read the Document

Are you an Anti-Federalist?

Exploring America: The Partisan Press

Exploring America: Ratification of the Constitution

Profiles
Matthew Lyon
Charles Wilson Peale

History Bookshelf: Alexander Hamilton, John Jay, and James Madison, The Federalist Papers (1787–1788)

●● Watch the Video *Slavery and the Constitution*

((●● Hear the Audio

Hear the audio files for Chapter 8 at
www.myhistorylab.com.

Since I started this letter we have been in a state of continual alarm, and now I have time to write only two or three lines to ask you to tell Papa that we are alive, in good health, and I hope safe from danger . . .
—Rosalie E. Calvert–August 30, 1814

"Burning of the White House" by Leslie Saalburg.

9

AN EMPIRE FOR LIBERTY
1790–1824

((•─┤Hear the **Audio**

Hear the audio files for Chapter 9 at **www.myhistorylab.com**.

WITH WHAT other nations did the United States share North America in the decades after independence?

WHAT WERE the most important strengths of the American economy in the early 1800s?

HOW DID Jefferson's political philosophy shape his administration's policies?

WHAT FACTORS led to conflict between the United States and its European rivals in the Americas?

WHAT WERE the consequences of the War of 1812?

WHAT WERE the causes and consequences of early nineteenth-century American expansion?

1790 | 1824

AMERICAN COMMUNITIES
Expansion Touches Mandan Villages on the Upper Missouri

IN MID-OCTOBER 1804, NEWS ARRIVED AT THE MANDAN VILLAGES ALONG the the upper Missouri River, that an American military party led by Meriwether Lewis and William Clark was coming up the river. The principal chiefs, hoping for expanded trade and support against their enemies the Sioux, welcomed these first American visitors with an enthusiastic dance and gifts of food.

Since the fourteenth century, when they had migrated from the East, the Mandans had lived along the Missouri, on the edge of the Great Plains in what is now North Dakota. Mandan men hunted buffalo and Mandan women kept storage pits full with abundant crops grown on the fertile soil of the river bottomlands. The Mandan villages were also the central marketplace of the northern Plains; at trading time in late summer they filled with Crows, Assiniboins, Cheyennes, Kiowas, and Arapahoes. Well before any of these people, or those of other tribes, had met a European, they were trading in kettles, knives, and guns acquired from the French and English to the east, and leatherwork, glassware, and horses acquired from the Spanish in the Southwest.

Lewis and Clark had been sent by President Thomas Jefferson to survey the Louisiana Purchase and to find an overland route to the Pacific Ocean. They were also instructed to inform the Indians that they now owed loyalty—and trade—to the American government, thereby challenging British economic control over the lucrative North American fur trade. Meeting with the village chiefs, the Americans offered the Mandans a military and economic alliance. His people would like nothing better, responded Chief Black Cat, for the Mandans had fallen on hard times over the past decade. [Some twenty years earlier], "the smallpox destroyed the greater part of the nation," the chief said. "All the nations before this malady [were] afraid of them, [but] after they were reduced, the Sioux and other Indians waged war, and killed a great many."

The Americans spent the winter with the Mandans, joining in their communal life and establishing firm and friendly relations with them. Lewis and Clark spent many hours acquiring important geographic information from the Mandans, who drew charts and maps showing the course of the Missouri, the ranges of the Rocky Mountains, and places where one could cross the Continental Divide. The information provided by the Mandans and other Indian peoples to the west was vital to the success of the expedition. Lewis and Clark's "voyage of discovery" depended largely on the willingness of Indian peoples to share their knowledge of the land with the Americans.

In need of interpreters who could help them communicate with other Indian communities on their way, the Americans hired several multilingual Frenchmen who lived with the Mandans. They also acquired the services of Sacajawea, the fifteen-year-old Lemhi Shoshone wife of one of the Frenchmen, who became the only woman to join the westward journey. The presence of Sacajawea and her baby son was a signal, as Clark noted, to "all the Indians as to our friendly intentions"; everyone knew that women and children did not go on war parties.

The party left the Mandan villages in March. After an arduous journey across the Rockies, the party reached the Pacific Ocean at the mouth of the Columbia River, where they spent the winter. Overdue and feared lost, they returned in triumph to St. Louis in September 1806. Before long the Americans had established Fort Clark at the Mandan villages, giving American traders a base for challenging British dominance of the western fur trade.

The permanent American presence brought increased contact, and with it much more disease. In 1837, a terrible smallpox epidemic carried away the vast majority of the Mandans, reducing the population to fewer than 150.

Mandan Villages

In sending Lewis and Clark on their "voyage of discovery" to claim the land and the loyalty of the Mandans and other western Indian communities, President Jefferson was motivated by his vision of an expanding American republic of self-sufficient farmers. During his and succeeding presidencies, expansion became a key element of national policy and pride. Yet, as the experience of the Mandans showed, what Jefferson viewed as enlargement of "the empire for liberty" had a dark side—the destruction, from disease and coerced displacement, of the communities created by America's first peoples.

In the first quarter of the nineteenth century, the young American nation was preoccupied with defining its place on the North American continent and in the larger world of independent nations. At the same time that America found opportunities in world trade and in territorial expansion, it encountered international opposition from Britain and resistance at home from hard-pressed Indian nations. This chapter describes the ways in which, through war and diplomacy, the United States defined and controlled the nation's expanded boundaries, a vital step in building a sense of national identity and community.

North American Communities From Coast to Coast

In spite of the political turmoil of the 1790s, the young United States entered the new century full of national pride and energy. But the larger issue, America's place in the world, was still uncertain, beginning with its situation on the North American continent (see Map 9.1).

WITH WHAT powers did the United States share North America in the decades after independence?

MAP 9.1

North America in 1800   In 1800, the new United States of America shared the North American continent with territories held by the European powers: British Canada, French Louisiana (secretly ceded that year to France by Spain), Spanish Florida, Spanish Mexico, and Russian Alaska, expanding southward along the Pacific Coast. Few people could have imagined that by 1850, the United States would span the continent. But the American settlers who had crossed the Appalachians to the Ohio River Valley were already convinced that opportunity lay in the West.

WHAT OBSTACLES were there to American westward expansion in 1800?

THE NEW NATION

The United States of America in 1800 seemed much like it had been before the American Revolution: a loosely-connected group of scattered states clinging to the Atlantic seaboard. Two-thirds of the young nation's people still lived within fifty miles of the Atlantic coast. Most people lived on farms or in small towns. Because they rarely traveled far from home, peoples' horizons were limited and local. The exception was the Atlantic seaports which looked outward to the world. Although only 3 percent of the nation's population lived in cities, the Atlantic ports continued to dominate the nation economically and politically.

Nevertheless, the new nation was already transforming itself: between 1790 and 1800, the American population grew from 3.9 million to 5.3 million. Growth by migration was greatest in the trans-Appalachian West, a region that was already home to approximately 100,000 Indians. Soon, expansion was to transform the nation, but in 1800 the United States of America was a new and weak country sharing a continent with the potentially hostile colonies of most of the world's great powers.

TO THE NORTH: BRITISH NORTH AMERICA AND RUSSIAN AMERICA

Although Britain had lost its war to keep the American colonies, it kept a firm grasp on British North America, which had once been French Canada (see Chapter 6). In 1800, its heart remained the former French colony of Quebec. Most of the rest of the settlers elsewhere were American, many of them Loyalists driven out at the time of the Revolution.

British North America dominated the continental fur trade and the great succession of waterways—the St. Lawrence River, the Great Lakes, and the rivers beyond—that made it possible. Britain was on friendly terms with many of the native peoples north and south of the border who were part of the fur trade. This economic grip was a challenge and frustration to many westward-moving Americans.

Russian settlement of what is now Alaska posed another potential threat to the United States. Alaska was an extension of the Russian conquest of Siberia, which was driven by the fur trade as well. By the 1750s, Russian and Siberian fur trappers, known as *promyshleniki*, were shipping a steady supply of furs from Russian America.

The Russians sometimes took furs by force, holding whole villages hostage and brutalizing the native Inuit and Aleut peoples. After the Aleut Revolt of 1766, the Russian authorities promised to end the abuse, but by 1800, the pre-contact population of 25,000 Aleuts had been greatly reduced. At the same time, sexual relations and intermarriage between fur trappers and Aleut women created a large group of Russian creoles who assumed an increasingly prominent position in the Alaskan fur trade as navigators, explorers, clerks, and traders.

The Russian-American Company, chartered by the tsar in 1799, set up American headquarters in Sitka, only to have their first fortress destroyed in the Tlingit Revolt of 1802. The Russians reestablished Sitka by force in 1804, and over the next generation, they reached south along the Pacific Coast, cooperating with the Spanish in California at Fort Ross and also with Hudson's Bay officials at Fort Vancouver in Oregon Country.

This view shows Sitka, the center of Russian activities in Alaska, in 1827. Russian architectural styles and building techniques are apparent in the Church of St. Michael the Archangel in the right background, contrasting with the Asian and Indian origins of most of Sitka's inhabitants.

To the West and South: The Spanish Empire, Haiti, and the Caribbean

Spain posed the greatest threat to the United States because it possessed most of North and South America. Mexico City, with a population of 200,000, was by far the largest city on the continent. But Spanish control crumbled rapidly in the 1790s. Tensions mounted between the Spanish-born *peninsulares* high officials and bureaucrats, and the native-born *criollos* of Spanish descent, who chafed at their subordination, especially after the success of the American Revolution. In the 1790s, there were two abortive criollo conspiracies on behalf of independence in Mexico City alone. Furthermore, none of New Spain's northern provinces thrived. In all of the older settlements—San Antonio, Santa Fé, and Tucson—only a handful of persons of Spanish descent lived among a preponderantly native population.

In 1769, in their last effort to protect their rich colony of Mexico, the Spanish established a chain of twenty-one missions in Alta California that stretched north from San Diego (1769) to Sonoma (1823). Despite Spain's desire to seal its territory from commerce with other nations, a brisk but illegal trade in otter skins, hides, and tallow developed between the United States and California.

American traders were making inroads on Spanish-held territory along the Mississippi River as well. New Orleans, acquired by Spain from France at the end of the Seven Years' War in 1763, was becoming a thriving international port. Every year, a greater proportion of products for the New Orleans trade was supplied by Americans living some distance up the Mississippi River. Pinckney's 1795 treaty with Spain guaranteed Americans free navigation of the Mississippi River and the right to deposit goods at the port of New Orleans. Nevertheless, Americans were uncomfortably aware that the city's crucial location at the mouth of the Mississippi meant that whatever foreign nation possessed New Orleans had the power to choke off the flourishing trade in the vast Mississippi Valley river system.

More than 600 miles north was the small trading town of St. Louis, founded by the New Orleans trader Pierre Laclède in 1763. By 1800, the town had fewer than a thousand residents, three-quarters of whom were involved in the Indian trade of the Missouri River. Spanish officials tried to supervise that trade, but real control rested in the hands of the Laclèdes and other French traders.

The Caribbean posed a racial challenge to the United States. The rich sugar-producing island colonies of Spain, France, and Britain provided 80 to 90 percent of the European supply of sugar. All the sugar plantations used enslaved Africans as the labor force. Thus, they shared with the slaveholding American South a distinctive Afro–North American society that cut across national boundaries. This world was jolted in 1791 by the revolt of black slaves in Saint-Domingue, France's richest colony. Under the leadership of Toussaint L'Ouverture, the former colony, renamed Haiti, became North America's first independent black nation. Its existence struck fear into the hearts of white slave owners at the same time that it served as a beacon of hope to the enslaved.

Trans-Appalachia

Within the United States itself, the region of greatest growth was territory west of the Appalachian Mountains, and it was this area that was most affected by fears of continuing British influence on Indian peoples. By 1800, about 500,000 people had found rich and fertile land along the Ohio River system. Soon there was enough population for statehood. Kentucky (1792) and Tennessee (1796) were the first trans-Appalachian states admitted to the Union.

Cincinnati, strategically situated 450 miles downstream from Pittsburgh, was a particularly dramatic example of the rapid community growth and development that characterized the trans-Appalachian region. Founded in 1788, Cincinnati began life as a military fort, defending settlers from resistance by Shawnee and Miami Indians. After the battle of Fallen Timbers broke Indian resistance in 1794, Cincinnati became the point of

---

QUICK REVIEW

European Colonies in the Early Nineteenth Century

- Spain: challenged in its efforts to control New Spain and the Caribbean.
- Britain: government of Canada reflected lessons learned in the colonies.
- Russia: rapidly expanding presence centered on Alaska and the Northwest.

The launching of a ship from Becket's Shipyard in Essex, Massachusetts, in 1802. Shipbuilding was a major New England industry and, as this picture shows, a launching was a community event.

departure for immigrants arriving by the Ohio River on their way to settle the interior of the Old Northwest: Ohio, Indiana, and Illinois. In 1800, Cincinnati had a population of about 750 people. By 1810, it had tripled in size.

Cincinnati merchants were soon shipping farm goods from the fertile Miami Valley down the Ohio–Mississippi River system to New Orleans, 1,500 miles away. River hazards like snags and sandbars made the downriver trip by barge or keelboat hazardous, and the return trip upriver was slow, more than three months from New Orleans to Cincinnati. Nevertheless, river traffic increased yearly, and control of New Orleans became a key concern of western farmers and merchants.

A National Economy

WHAT WERE the most important strengths of the American economy in the early 1800s?

Concern about New Orleans illustrates the new nation's weak position in international trade. In 1800, the United States was a producer of raw materials. It faced the same challenge that developing nations confront today. At the mercy of fluctuating world commodity prices they cannot control, such countries have great difficulty protecting themselves from economic dominance by stronger, more established nations.

Cotton and the Economy of the Young Republic

In 1800, the United States was predominantly rural and agricultural. According to the census, 94 of 100 Americans lived in communities of fewer than 2,500 people, and four of five families farmed the land. Crops were grown for subsistence (home use) rather than for sale.

Commodities such as whiskey and hogs (both easy to transport) provided small and irregular cash incomes or items for barter. As late as 1820, only 20 percent of the produce of American farms was consumed outside the local community.

The situation was different in the South, where plantation agriculture based on enslaved African workers was both commercial and international. The demand for cotton was growing rapidly in response to the boom in the industrial production of textiles in England and Europe, but extracting the seeds from the fibers of the variety of cotton that grew best in the southern interior required an enormous investment of labor. The cotton gin, which mechanized this process, was invented in 1793; soon cotton, and the slave labor system that produced it, assumed a commanding place in southern life and in the foreign trade of the United States. The essential contribution of cotton to the nation's economy was the most important social and political reality of the early nineteenth century.

In 1790, however, increasing foreign demand for American goods and services hardly seemed likely. Britain and France both excluded Americans from their lucrative West Indian trade and taxed American ships with discriminatory duties. It was difficult to be independent in a world dominated by great powers.

NEUTRAL SHIPPING IN A WORLD AT WAR

Despite these restrictions on American commerce, the strong shipping trade begun during the colonial era and centered in the Atlantic ports became a major asset in the 1790s, when events in Europe provided America with extraordinary opportunities. The French Revolution, which began in 1789, initiated nearly twenty-five years of warfare between Britain and France. American ships carried European goods that could no longer be transported on British ships without danger of French attack (and vice versa). Because America was neutral, its merchants had the legal right to import European goods and promptly reexport them to other European countries. In spite of British and French efforts to prevent the practice (see Chapter 8), reexports amounted to half of the profits in the booming shipping trade (see Figure 9.1).

The vigorous international shipping trade had dramatic effects within the United States. The active American participation in international trade fostered a strong and diversified shipbuilding industry. As a result, the coastal cities all grew substantially from 1790 to 1820. This rapid urbanization was a sign of real economic growth, for it reflected expanding opportunities in the cities. Moreover, the rapid growth of cities stimulated farmers to produce the food to feed the new urban dwellers.

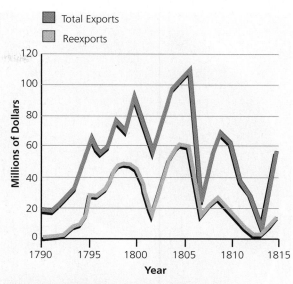

Figure 9.1 American Export Trade, 1790–1815
This graph shows how completely the American shipping boom was tied to European events. Exports, half of which were reexports, surged when Britain and France were at war and America could take advantage of its neutral status. Exports slumped in the brief period of European peace from 1803 to 1805 and plunged following the Embargo Act of 1807 and the outbreak of the War of 1812.

QUICK REVIEW

Growth of American Trade: 1793–1807

- French Revolution initiated renewed period of warfare between France and Britain.
- American merchants wanted to supply both sides.
- Expansion of trade led to development of shipbuilding industry and growth of coastal cities.

THE JEFFERSON PRESIDENCY

At noon on March 4, 1801, Thomas Jefferson walked from his modest boarding-house through the streets of the new federal city of Washington to the unfinished Capitol. George Washington and John Adams had ridden in decorated carriages to their inaugurals. Jefferson, although accepting a military honor guard, demonstrated by his actions that he rejected the elaborate, quasi-monarchical style of the two Federalist presidents and (to his mind) their autocratic style of government as well.

Jefferson's inauguration as the third president of the United States was a momentous occasion in American history, for it marked the peaceful transition from one political party, the Federalists, to their rivals, the Jeffersonian Republicans. Beginning in an atmosphere of exceptional political bitterness, Jefferson's presidency was to demonstrate that a strongly led party system could shape national policy without leading either to dictatorship or to revolt.

HOW DID Jefferson's political philosophy shape his administration's policies?

Read the **Document**

Margaret Bayard Smith, Reflections upon Meeting Jefferson (1809) at **www.myhistorylab.com**

Tall, ungainly, and diffident in manner, Thomas Jefferson was nonetheless a man of genius: an architect, naturalist, philosopher, and politician. His political philosophy, republican agrarianism, exemplified Jefferson's hopes for America in the efforts of the ordinary farmer. As he said, "those who labor in the earth are the chosen people of God."

REPUBLICAN AGRARIANISM

Jefferson brought to the presidency a clearly defined political philosophy. Behind all the events of his administration (1801–09) was a clear set of beliefs that embodied Jefferson's interpretation of the meaning of republicanism for Americans.

Jefferson's years as ambassador to France in the 1780s were particularly important in shaping his political thinking. Recoiling from the extremes of wealth and poverty he saw there, he came to believe that it was impossible for Europe to achieve a just society that could guarantee to most of its members the "life, liberty and . . . pursuit of happiness" of which he had written in the Declaration of Independence. Only America, he believed, provided fertile earth for the true citizenship necessary to a republican form of government. What America had, and Europe lacked, was room to grow.

Jefferson's thinking about growth was directly influenced by Englishman Thomas Malthus's *Essay on the Principle of Population*, published in 1798. Warning of an impending population explosion, Malthus predicted that unless population growth was checked, misery and poverty would soon be widespread throughout Europe and even, Malthus warned, in America. Although America had one of the fastest rates of population growth in the world, close to 40 percent per decade. Thomas Jefferson was not worried. He used Malthus to underline the opportunity created by America's vast land resources. The Malthusian prediction need not trouble the United States, Jefferson said, as long as the country kept expanding.

Jefferson envisaged a nation of small family farms clustered together in rural communities—an agrarian republic. He believed that only a nation of roughly equal yeoman farmers, each secure in his own possessions and not dependent on someone else for his livelihood, would exhibit the concern for the community good that was essential in a republic.

Jefferson's vision of an expanding agrarian republic remains to this day one of our most compelling ideas about America's uniqueness and special destiny. But expansionism contained some negative aspects. The lure of the western lands fostered constant mobility and dissatisfaction rather than the stable, settled communities Jefferson envisaged. Expansionism caused environmental damage, in particular soil exhaustion—a consequence of abandoning old lands, rather than conserving them, and moving on to new ones. Expansionism encouraged the spread of plantations based on slave labor in the South (see Chapter 10). Finally, it bred a ruthlessness toward Indian peoples, who were pushed out of the way for white settlement or were devastated by the diseases that accompanied European trade and contact. Jefferson's agrarianism thus bred some of the best and some of the worst traits of the developing nation.

JEFFERSON'S GOVERNMENT

Thomas Jefferson came to office determined to reverse the Federalist policies of the 1790s and to ensure an agrarian "republic of virtue." Accordingly, he proposed a program of "simplicity and frugality," promising to cut all internal taxes, to reduce the size of the army, the navy, and the government staff, and to eliminate the entire national debt inherited from the Federalists. He kept all of these promises. This diminishment of government was a key matter of republican principle to Jefferson. If his ideal yeoman farmer was to be a truly self-governing citizen, the federal government must not, Jefferson believed, be either large or powerful.

This 1800 watercolor by William Russell Birch shows the original Capitol building. This simple rectangular structure is a far cry from the imposing domed structure we recognize today, yet it was typical of the modest beginnings of the nation's capital city.

Perhaps one reason for Jefferson's success was that the federal government he headed was small and unimportant by today's standards. For instance, Jefferson found only 130 federal officials in Washington. The national government's main service to ordinary people was mail delivery, and already in 1800 there were persistent complaints about the slowness, unreliability, and expense of the Postal Service! Everything else—law and order, education, welfare, road maintenance, economic control—rested with state or local governments. Power and political loyalty were still local, not national.

AN INDEPENDENT JUDICIARY

Although determined to reverse Federalist fiscal policies, Jefferson was much more moderate concerning Federalist officeholders. He resisted demands by other Jeffersonian Republicans that all Federalist officeholders be replaced with party loyalists. During his term of office, Jefferson allowed 132 Federalists to remain at their posts, while placing Jeffersonian Republicans in 158 other posts.

Jefferson's restraint, however, had its limits. In the last days of the Adams administration, the Federalist-dominated Congress passed several acts that created new judgeships and other positions within the federal judiciary. Jeffersonian Republicans feared that the losing Federalist Party was trying to politicize the judiciary by appointing Federalists who would use their positions to strengthen the powers of the federal government, a policy the Jeffersonians opposed. In one of his last acts in office, President Adams appointed Federalists—quickly dubbed the "midnight judges"—to these new positions. William Marbury, whom President Adams had appointed justice of the peace for Washington, DC, and three other appointees sued James Madison, Jefferson's secretary of state, to receive their commissions for their offices. Before the case came to trial,

Read the **Document**

Supreme Court Retains Right to Overrule Legislation (1803) at **www.myhistorylab.com**

QUICK REVIEW

Marbury v. Madison (1803)

◆ Case sparked by Jefferson's refusal to recognize Adams's "midnight judges."

◆ Justice Marshall ruled that the duty of the courts was "to say what the law is."

◆ Ruling made the Supreme Court a powerful nationalizing force.

Read the **Document**

Exploring America: Continentalism at **www.myhistorylab.com**

Marbury v. Madison Supreme Court decision of 1803 that created the precedent of judicial review by ruling as unconstitutional part of the Judiciary Act of 1789.

however, Congress, controlled by Jeffersonian Republicans, repealed the acts. This case, *Marbury* v. *Madison*, provoked a landmark decision from the U.S. Supreme Court.

At issue was a fundamental constitutional point: Was the judiciary independent of politics? In his celebrated 1803 decision in *Marbury* v. *Madison*, Chief Justice John Marshall ruled that Marbury was entitled to his commission but that the Supreme Court did not have the power to force the executive branch to give it to him. At first glance, Jefferson's government appeared to have won the battle. But in the long run, Marshall established the principle that only the federal judiciary could "say what the law is," thus unequivocally defending the independence of the judiciary and the principle of judicial review. This was a vital step in realizing the three-way balance of power among the branches of the federal government—executive (president), legislative (Congress), and judiciary (courts)—envisaged in the Constitution. Equally important, during his long tenure in office (1801–35), Chief Justice Marshall consistently led the Supreme Court in a series of decisions that favored the federal government over state governments (see Chapter 12). Under Marshall's direction, the Supreme Court became a powerful nationalizing force, often to the dismay of defenders of states' rights.

OPPORTUNITY: THE LOUISIANA PURCHASE

In 1800, the United States was a new and fragile democracy in a world dominated by two contending great powers: Britain and France, who were almost continuously at war from 1789 (the French Revolution) until 1815, when Napoleon Bonaparte was defeated at the battle of Waterloo. Jefferson, who had once ardently supported the goals of the French Revolution, viewed Napoleon's ambitions with increasing apprehension. He feared a resumption of the political animosity of the 1790s, when Federalists and Jeffersonian Republicans had so bitterly disagreed on policy toward France (see Chapter 8).

In his planning for battles with the British, Napoleon looked at the Caribbean, where he planned to reconquer Haiti and use the rich profits from sugar to finance his European wars. As a first step, in 1800, France secretly reacquired the Louisiana Territory from Spain, which had held the region since 1763. Napoleon planned to use Louisiana to grow food for sugar-producing Haiti, to counterbalance the British in Canada, and to check any American expansion that might threaten Spain's North American colonies. In 1802, he launched the plan by sending an army of 30,000 to reconquer Haiti.

In 1801, when President Jefferson first learned of the French–Spanish secret agreement about Louisiana, he was concerned about the threat to American commerce on the Mississippi River. In fact, in 1802, the Spanish commander at New Orleans (the French had not yet taken formal control) closed the port to American shippers. As Jefferson feared, Federalists in Congress clamored for military action to reopen the port. Jefferson was willing to fight for American commerce, but he decided to try diplomacy first.

In the summer of 1802, Jefferson instructed Robert Livingston, the American ambassador to France, to try to buy New Orleans and the surrounding area. The initial bargaining went badly, but suddenly, in early 1803, Napoleon was ready to sell. His army of 30,000 men had been forced to withdraw from Haiti, defeated by yellow fever and by an army of former slaves led by Toussaint L'Ouverture. In need of money for European military campaigns, Napoleon suddenly offered the entire Louisiana Territory, including the crucial port of New Orleans, to the Americans for $15 million. In an age when it took at least two months for messages to cross the Atlantic, special American envoy James Monroe and Ambassador Livingston could not wait to consult Jefferson. They seized the opportunity: they bought the entire Louisiana Territory from Napoleon in Paris in April 1803. Overnight, the size of the United States more than doubled. It was the largest peaceful acquisition of territory in U.S. history.

At home, Jefferson suffered brief qualms. The Constitution did not authorize the president to purchase territory, and Jefferson had always rigidly insisted on a limited interpretation of executive rights. However, the prize was too rich to pass up. Jefferson now argued that Louisiana was vital to the nation's republican future. "By enlarging the empire of liberty," Jefferson wrote, "we . . . provide new sources of renovation, should its principles, at any time, degenerate, in those portions of our country which gave them birth." In other words, expansion was essential to liberty. But for African American slaves and Native Americans, the Louisiana Purchase simply increased the scope of their enslavement and destruction. By 1850, four of the six states in the Louisiana Purchase had entered the Union as slave states (see Chapter 10), and Indian Territory, envisaged by Jefferson as a distant refuge for beleaguered eastern Indian peoples, was surrounded by new settlements (see Chapter 15). No matter how noble Jefferson's rhetoric, neither African Americans nor American Indians shared in his "empire of liberty" (see Map 9.2).

See the Map
Louisiana Purchase at
www.myhistorylab.com

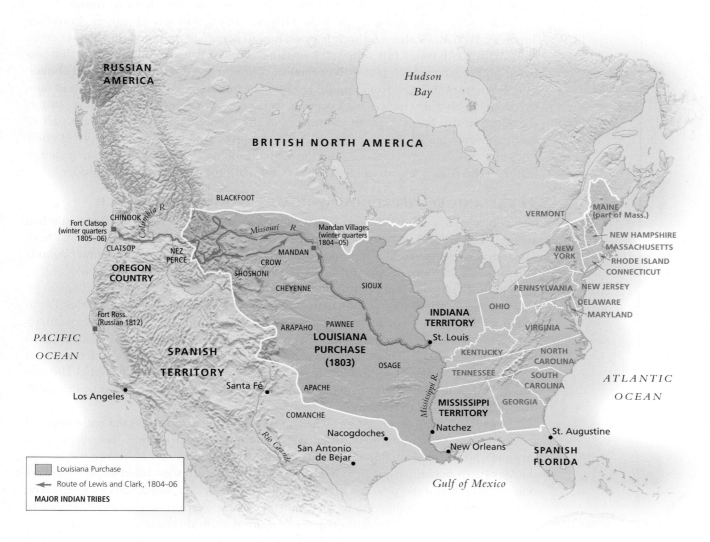

MAP 9.2
Louisiana Purchase The Louisiana Purchase of 1803, the largest peaceful acquisition of territory in U.S. history, more than doubled the size of the nation. The Lewis and Clark expedition (1804–06) was the first to survey and document the natural and human richness of the area. The American sense of expansiveness and continental destiny owes much to the extraordinary opportunity provided by the Louisiana Purchase.

WHAT KEY geographic features dictated the route taken across the continent by the Lewis and Clark expedition?

INCORPORATING LOUISIANA

The immediate issue following the Louisiana Purchase was how to treat the French and Spanish inhabitants of the Louisiana Territory. In 1803, when the region that is now the state of Louisiana became American property, it had a racially and ethnically diverse population of 43,000 people, of whom only 6,000 were American. French and French-speaking people were numerically and culturally dominant, especially in the city of New Orleans. In addition to the French, New Orleans population included Germans, Spanish, Irish, Americans and native born Creoles (persons of French descent). Two-thirds of the non-white half of the population were slaves, while the remainder were "free persons of color," who under French law enjoyed legal rights equal to those of white people, and there was a sizable number of Indians as well. The incorporation of Louisiana into the American federal system thus posed a novel challenge to the many different communities involved, with differing results.

The U.S. representative in New Orleans and governor of Lower Louisiana Territory, William Claiborne, slowly learned how to negotiate with the French and Creole elite. With Claiborne's full support, Louisiana adopted a legal code in 1808 that was based on French civil law rather than English common law. This was not a small concession. French law differed from English law in many fundamental respects, such as in family property, in inheritance, and even in contracts, which were much more strictly regulated in the French system. Remnants of the French legal system remain part of Louisiana state law to this day. The losers in the process were the free people of color whose legal rights were curtailed, and the Caddo Indians, in particular, who struggled to maintain the region known as the Neutral Ground on the Texas–Louisiana border.

TEXAS AND THE STRUGGLE FOR MEXICAN INDEPENDENCE

Spain objected in vain to Napoleon's 1803 sale of Louisiana to America. For years, Spain had attempted to seal off its rich colony of Mexico from commerce with other nations. Now, American Louisiana shared a vague and disputed boundary (including the Neutral Ground) with Mexico's northern province of Texas, which was already coveted by some Americans.

Soon Napoleon brought turmoil to all of Mexico. In 1808, having invaded Spain, he installed his brother Joseph Bonaparte as king, forcing Spain's king, Charles IV, to renounce his throne. For the next six years, as warfare convulsed Spain, the country's long-prized New World empire slipped away. Mexico, divided between royalists loyal to Spain and populists seeking social and economic justice for mestizos and Indians, edged toward independence. Two populist revolts—one in 1810 led by Father Miguel Hidalgo and the other in 1813 led by Father José María Morelos—were suppressed by the royalists, who executed both revolutionary leaders.

In 1812, a small force, led by Mexican republican Bernardo Gutiérrez but composed mostly of American adventurers, invaded Texas, captured San Antonio, assassinated the provincial governor Manuel Salcedo, and declared Texas independent. A year later, however, the Mexican republicans were defeated by a royalist army, which then killed suspected collaborators and pillaged the province so thoroughly that the local economy was devastated. The Mexican population declined to fewer than 2,000. These circumstances seemed, at least to some Americans, to offer yet another opportunity for expansion. For years Louisiana seethed with rumors of American plots to invade Texas and set up a separate nation.

RENEWED IMPERIAL RIVALRY IN NORTH AMERICA

WHAT FACTORS led to conflict between the United States and its European rivals in the Americas?

Fresh from the triumph of the Louisiana Purchase, Jefferson scored a major victory over the Federalist Charles Cotesworth Pinckney in the presidential election of 1804, garnering 162 electoral votes to Pinckney's 14. However, Jefferson's second term was fraught with fruitless efforts to remain neutral in the ongoing struggle between Britain and France.

PROBLEMS WITH NEUTRAL RIGHTS

In his first inaugural address in 1801, Jefferson had announced a foreign policy of "peace, commerce, and honest friendship with all nations, entangling alliances with none." This was a difficult policy to pursue after 1803, when the Napoleonic Wars resumed. The United States, trying to profit from trade with both Britain and France, was caught in the middle. Beginning in 1805, the British targeted the American reexport trade between the Caribbean and France by seizing American ships that were bringing French West Indian goods to Europe. Angry Americans viewed these seizures as violations of their rights as shippers of a neutral nation.

An even more contentious issue arose from the substantial desertion rate of British sailors. Many deserters promptly signed up on American ships, where they drew better pay and sometimes obtained false naturalization papers as well. Soon the British were stopping American merchant vessels and removing any man they believed to be British, regardless of his papers. At least 6,000 innocent American citizens suffered forced impressment into the British navy from 1803 to 1812. In 1807, impressment turned bloody when the British ship *Leopard* stopped the American ship *Chesapeake* in American territorial waters and demanded to search for deserters. When the American captain refused, the *Leopard* opened fire, killing three men. An indignant public protested British interference and the death of innocent sailors.

THE EMBARGO ACT

Jefferson insisted on America's right as a neutral nation to ship goods to Europe. He first tried diplomatic protests, then negotiations, and finally threats, all to no avail. In 1806, Congress passed the Non-Importation Act, hoping that a boycott of British goods, which had worked so well during the Revolutionary War, would be effective once again. It was not. Finally, in desperation, Jefferson imposed the **Embargo Act** in December 1807. This act forbade American ships from sailing to any foreign port, thereby cutting off all exports as well as imports. The intent of the act was to force both Britain and France to recognize neutral rights by depriving them of American-shipped raw materials.

But the results were a disaster for American trade. The commerce of the new nation, which Jefferson himself had done so much to promote, came to a standstill. Exports fell sharply, and the nation was driven into a deep depression. There was widespread evasion of the embargo, and smuggling flourished. Pointing out that the American navy's weakness was due largely to the deep cuts Jefferson had inflicted on it, the Federalists sprang to life with a campaign of outspoken opposition, and they found a ready audience in New England, the area hardest hit by the embargo.

MADISON AND THE FAILURE OF "PEACEABLE COERCION"

In this troubled atmosphere, Thomas Jefferson despondently ended his second term, acknowledging the failure of what he called "peaceable coercion." He was followed in office by his friend and colleague James Madison of Virginia. Although Madison defeated the Federalist candidate—again Charles Cotesworth Pinckney—by 122 electoral votes to 47, Pinckney's share of the votes was three times what it had been in 1804.

Ironically, the Embargo Act had almost no effect on its intended victims. The French used the embargo as a pretext for seizing American ships, claiming they must be British ships in disguise. The British, in the absence of American competition, developed new markets for their goods in South America. In March 1809, Congress admitted failure, and the Embargo Act was repealed. But the struggle to remain neutral in the confrontation between the European giants continued. The next two years saw passage of several acts—among them the Non-Intercourse Act of 1809 and Macon's Bill Number 2 in 1810—that unsuccessfully attempted to prohibit trade with Britain and France unless they ceased their hostile treatment of U.S. shipping. Frustration with the ineffectiveness of government policy mounted.

Embargo Act Act passed by Congress in 1807 prohibiting American ships from leaving for any foreign port.

A CONTRADICTORY INDIAN POLICY

The United States faced other conflicts besides those with Britain and France over neutral shipping rights. In the West, the powerful Indian nations of the Ohio Valley were determined to resist the wave of expansion that had carried thousands of white settlers onto their lands.

According to the Indian Intercourse Act of 1790, the United States could not simply seize Indian land; it could only acquire it when the Indians ceded it by treaty. But this policy conflicted with the harsh reality of westward expansion. Commonly, settlers pushed ahead of treaty boundaries. When Indian peoples resisted the invasion of their lands, the pioneers fought back and called for military protection. Defeat of an Indian people led to further land cessions. The result for the Indians was a relentless cycle of invasion, resistance, and defeat.

Thomas Jefferson was deeply concerned with the fate of the western Indian peoples. Convinced that Indians had to give up hunting in favor of the yeoman-farmer lifestyle he so favored for all Americans, Jefferson directed the governors of the Northwest Territories to "promote energetically" his vision for civilizing the Indians, which included Christianizing them and teaching them to read. Many Indian peoples actively resisted these efforts at conversion (see Communities in Conflict). In addition, Jefferson's Indian civilization plan was never fully supported by territorial governors and settlers.

After the Louisiana Purchase, Jefferson offered traditionalist Indian groups new lands west of the Mississippi River, where they could live undisturbed by white settlers. But he failed to consider the pace of westward expansion. In fact, Jefferson's Indian policy, because it did nothing to slow down the ever-accelerating westward expansion, offered little hope to Indian peoples. The alternatives they faced were stark: acculturation, removal, or extinction.

INDIAN ALTERNATIVES

There was no escape from white encroachment. Between 1801 and 1809, William Henry Harrison, governor of Indiana Territory, concluded fifteen treaties with the Delawares, Potawatomis, Miamis, and other tribes. These treaties opened eastern Michigan, southern Indiana, and most of Illinois to white settlement and forced the Indians onto ever-smaller reservations. Many of these treaties were obtained by coercion, bribery, and outright trickery, and most Indians did not accept them.

The Shawnees, a seminomadic hunting and farming tribe of the Ohio Valley, had resisted white settlement in Kentucky and Ohio since the 1750s. Anthony Wayne's decisive defeat of the Indian confederacy led by Little Turtle at Fallen Timbers (1794) and the continuing pressure of American settlement, however, had left the Shawnees divided. One group, about one quarter of the total, led by Black Hoof, tried to retain tribal homelands by accepting acculturation directed by government officials and missionaries. The rest of the tribe tried to maintain traditional ways. The vast majority broke into small bands and moved west of the Mississippi. One small group of militant Shawnees, however, led by the warrior Tecumseh, refused to move west and embarked on a **pan-Indian resistance movement** that rapidly became famous.

In 1805, Tecumseh's brother, Tenskwatawa, known as The Prophet, began preaching a message of Indian revitalization: a rejection of all contact with the Americans, including the use of American alcohol, clothing, and trade goods, and a return to traditional practices of hunting and farming. If the Northwest Indians returned to traditional ways, Tenskwatawa promised, "the land will be overturned so that all the white people will be covered and you alone shall inhabit the land." Tecumseh succeeded in molding his brother's religious following into a powerful pan-Indian military resistance movement. With each new treaty that Harrison concluded, Tecumseh gained new followers among the Northwest Confederation tribes. Significantly, he also had the support of the British,

•••−[Read the **Document**

Profile: *Tenskwatawa* at
www.myhistorylab.com

pan-Indian military resistance movement   Movement calling for the political and cultural unification of Indian tribes in the late eighteenth and early nineteenth centuries.

(left) Tecumseh, a Shawnee military leader, and (right) his brother Tenskwatawa, a religious leader called The Prophet, led a pan-Indian revitalization and resistance movement that posed a serious threat to American westward expansion. Tecumseh traveled widely, attempting to build a military alliance on his brother's spiritual message. He achieved considerable success in the Old Northwest but less in the Old Southwest, where many Indian peoples put their faith in accommodation. Tecumseh's death at the Battle of the Thames (1813) and British abandonment of their Shawnee allies at the end of the War of 1812 brought an end to organized Indian resistance in the Old Northwest.

(right) 1830. Oil on canvas. 29 × 24 in. (73.7 × 60.9 cm) Location: Smithsonian American Art Museum, Washington, DC, U.S.A.

who, after 1807, began sending food and guns to him, and who promised an alliance with the Indians if war broke out between Britain and America.

Tecumseh's pan-Indian strategy was at first primarily defensive, aimed at preventing further westward expansion. But after the Treaty of Fort Wayne in 1809, in which the United States gained 3 million acres of Delaware and Potawatomi land in Indiana, Tecumseh moved from passive to active resistance. Confronting Harrison directly, Tecumseh argued that the land belonged to the larger community of all the Indian peoples; no one tribe could give away the common property of all. He then warned that any surveyors or settlers who ventured into the 3 million acres would risk their lives.

Tecumseh took his message of common land ownership and military resistance to all the Indian peoples of the Northwest Confederacy. He was not uniformly successful, even among the Shawnees. Black Hoof, for example, refused to join. Tecumseh also recruited, with mixed success, among the tribes south of the Ohio River (see Map 9.3).

In November 1811, while Tecumseh was still recruiting among the southern tribes, Harrison marched to the pan-Indian village of Tippecanoe with 1,000 soldiers. In the battle that followed, the Americans inflicted about 150 Indian casualties, while sustaining about as many themselves. Although Harrison claimed victory, the truth was far different. Dispersed from Tippecanoe, Tecumseh's angry followers fell on American settlements in Indiana and southern Michigan, killing many pioneers and forcing the rest to flee to fortified towns. Tecumseh himself entered into a formal alliance with the British. For western settlers, the Indian threat was greater than ever.

⊙ See the **Map**

Native American Removal at **www.myhistorylab.com**

MAP 9.3

Indian Removals and Resistance, 1790–1814   American westward expansion put relentless pressure on the Indian nations in the trans-Appalachian South and West. The trans-Appalachian region was marked by constant displacement and warfare from the time of the earliest settlements in Kentucky in the 1780s to the War of 1812. Tecumseh's Alliance in the Old Northwest (1809–11) and the Creek Rebellion in the Old Southwest (1813–14) were the culminating struggles in Indian resistance to the American invasion of the trans-Appalachian region. Indian resistance was a major reason for the War of 1812.

WHERE WAS Indian resistance concentrated? Why?

THE WAR OF 1812

Many Westerners blamed the British for Tecumseh's attacks on pioneer settlements in the Northwest. British support of western Indians and the long-standing difficulties over neutral shipping rights were the two grievances cited by President Madison when he asked Congress for a declaration of war against Britain on June 1, 1812. Congress obliged him on June 18. But the war had other, more general causes as well.

THE WAR HAWKS

A rising young generation of political leaders, first elected to Congress in 1810, strongly resented the continuing influence of Britain on American affairs. These **War Hawks**, who included such future leaders as Henry Clay of Kentucky and John C. Calhoun of South

War Hawks   Members of Congress, predominantly from the South and West, who aggressively pushed for a war against Britain after their election in 1810.

Carolina, were young Jeffersonian Republicans from the West and South. Eager to assert independence from England once and for all, these young men saw themselves finishing the job begun by the aging revolutionary generation. They also wanted to occupy Florida to prevent runaway slaves from seeking refuge with the Seminole Indians. Westerners wanted to invade Canada, hoping thereby to end threats from British-backed Indians in the Northwest, such as Tecumseh and his followers. As resentments against England and frustrations over border issues merged, the pressure for war—always a strong force for national unity—mounted.

Unaware that the British, seriously hurt by the American trade embargo, were about to adopt a more conciliatory policy, President James Madison yielded to the War Hawks' clamor for action in June 1812. His declaration of war was passed by a divided Congress, with all the Federalists voting against the war. The vote was sectional, with New England and the Middle States in opposition and the West and South strongly prowar. Thus, the United States entered the **War of 1812** more deeply divided along sectional lines than during any other foreign war in American history.

As a result of Jefferson's economizing, the American army and navy were small and weak. At sea, the British navy quickly established a strong blockade, harassing coastal shipping along the Atlantic seaboard and attacking coastal settlements at will. In the most humiliating attack, the British burned Washington in the summer of 1814, forcing the president and Congress to flee. There were a few American naval successes. The American frigate *Constitution*, known as "Old Ironsides," destroyed two British men-of-war, the *Guerrière* and the *Java*, in classic naval battles, but these failed to lift the British blockade (see Map 9.4).

THE CAMPAIGNS AGAINST THE NORTHERN AND SOUTHERN INDIANS

The American goal of expansion fared badly as well. Americans envisaged a quick victory over sparsely populated British Canada that would destroy British support for Tecumseh and his Northwest Indian allies, but instead the British–Indian alliance defeated them (see Seeing History). In July 1812, an American foray into western Canada was repulsed. A joint British and Indian force went on, in August, to capture Detroit and Fort Dearborn (site of Chicago). In September 1813, at the battle of Put-in-Bay, Captain Oliver H. Perry established

War of 1812 War fought between the United States and Britain from June 1812 to January 1815 largely over British restrictions on American shipping.

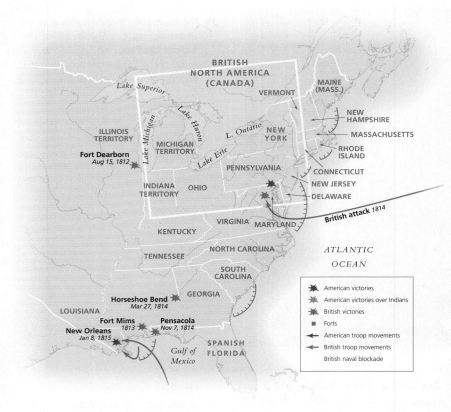

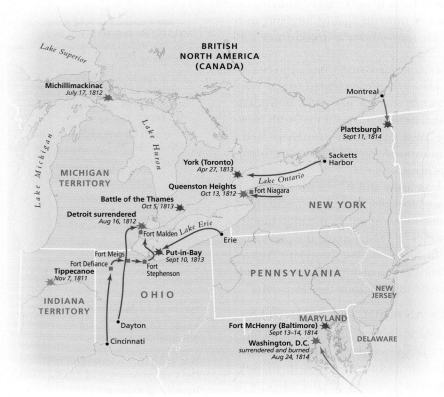

MAP 9.4

The War of 1812 On land, the War of 1812 was fought to define the nation's boundaries. In the North, where military action was most intense, American armies attacked British forts in the Great Lakes region with little success, and several invasions of Canada failed. In the South, the Battle of New Orleans made a national hero of Andrew Jackson, but it occurred after the peace treaty had been signed. On the sea, with the exception of Oliver Perry's victory in the Great Lakes, Britain's dominance was so complete and its blockade so effective that British troops were able to invade the Chesapeake and burn the capital of the United States.

WHAT ROLE did British naval power play in the War of 1812?

American control over Lake Erie, leading to the recapture of Detroit by William Henry Harrison. Assisted by naval forces commanded by Perry, Harrison defeated British and Indian defenders in the battle of the Thames in October 1813. Among those slain in the battle was Tecumseh, fighting on the British side. Later attempts by the United States to invade Canada in the Niagara area failed, but so too did British attempts to invade the United States in the same area.

In the South, warfare similar to that waged against Tecumseh's pan-Indian resistance movement in the Northwest dramatically affected the southern Indian peoples. The first of the Indian peoples to battle the Americans were the Creeks. When white settlers began to occupy Indian lands in northwestern Georgia and central Alabama early in the nineteenth century, the Creeks, like the Shawnees in the Northwest, were divided in their response. Although many Creek bands argued for accommodation, a group known as the Red Sticks was determined to fight. During the War of 1812, the Red Sticks, allied with the British and Spanish, fought not only the Americans but also other Indian groups.

In August 1813, the Red Sticks attacked Fort Mims on the Alabama River, killing more than 500 Americans and mixed-race Creeks who had gathered there for safety. Led by Andrew Jackson, troops from the Tennessee and Kentucky militias combined with the Creeks' traditional foes—the Cherokees, Choctaws, and Chickasaws—to exact revenge. At the battle of Horseshoe Bend in March 1814, the Creeks were trapped between American cannon fire and their Indian enemies: more than 800 were killed, more than in any other battle in the history of Indian–white warfare.

"A Scene on the Frontiers as Practiced by the 'Humane' British and their 'Worthy' Allies"

This American cartoon, published during the War of 1812, shows a British officer paying for a scalp from an Indian, while another man is shown in the act of scalping a dead American soldier. The cartoon may have been prompted by an actual event: the offer of bounties for scalps made by British Colonel Proctor at Fort Dearborn (Chicago) in August 1815. In any case, the cartoon mocking the "humane" British and their "worthy allies" was intended to spur "Columbia's Sons" to avenge "Your Country's wrongs."

THIS CARTOON relied on popular fears of Indians and resentment of the British that existed long before the War of 1812. In what way did these familiar images contribute to the American war effort?

The figures in the cartoon are familiar types dating back to before the American Revolution: the fat British officer, the dead American victims, and the Indians with their scalping knives. What made the cartoon effective in the War of 1812? Was it the familiar scenario? The sarcastic jibe at the "humane" British? The long-held fear of "savage" Indians? How did the cartoon mobilize these familiar feelings to support the war? ∎

nullification A constitutional doctrine holding that a state has a legal right to declare a national law null and void within its borders.

Treaty of Ghent Treaty signed in December 1814 between the United States and Britain that ended the War of 1812.

At the end of the Creek War in 1814, Jackson demanded huge land concessions from the Creeks: 23 million acres, or more than half the Creek domain. The Treaty of Fort Jackson (1814) confirming these land concessions earned Jackson his Indian name, Sharp Knife. In early 1815 (after the peace treaty had been signed but before news of it arrived in America), Andrew Jackson achieved his best-known victory, an improbable win over veteran British troops in the Battle of New Orleans.

ENDING THE WAR: THE HARTFORD CONVENTION AND THE TREATY OF GHENT

America's occasional successes failed to diminish the angry opposition of New England Federalists to the War of 1812. That opposition culminated in the Hartford Convention of 1814, where Federalist representatives from the five New England states met to discuss their grievances. At first the air was full of talk of secession from the Union, but soon cooler heads prevailed. The convention did insist, however, that a state had the right "to interpose its authority" to protect its citizens against unconstitutional federal laws. This **nullification** doctrine was not new; Madison and Jefferson had proposed it in the Virginia and Kentucky Resolves opposing the Alien and Sedition Acts in 1798 (see Chapter 8). In any event, the nullification threat from Hartford was ignored, for peace with Britain was announced as delegates from the convention made their way to Washington to deliver their message to Congress.

By 1814, the long Napoleonic Wars in Europe were slowly drawing to a close, and the British decided to end their war with the Americans. The peace treaty, after months of hard negotiation, was signed at Ghent, Belgium, on Christmas Eve in 1814. Like the war itself, the treaty was inconclusive. The major issues of impressment and neutral rights were not mentioned, but the British did agree to evacuate their western posts, and late in the negotiations they abandoned their insistence on a buffer state for neutral Indian peoples in the Northwest.

For all its international inconsequence, the war did have an important effect on national morale. Andrew Jackson's victory at New Orleans allowed Americans to believe that they had defeated the British. It would be more accurate to say that by not losing the war the Americans had ended their own feelings of colonial dependency. Equally important, they convinced the British government to stop thinking of America as its colony.

The only clear losers of the war were the northwestern Indian nations and their southern allies. With the death of Tecumseh at the Battle of the Thames in 1813 and the defeat of the southern Creeks in 1814, the last hope of a united Indian resistance to white expansion perished forever. Britain's abandonment of its Indian allies in the **Treaty of Ghent** sealed their fate. By 1815, American settlers were on their way west again.

DEFINING THE BOUNDARIES

With the War of 1812 behind them, Americans turned, more seriously than ever before, to the tasks of expansion and national development. The so-called Era of Good Feelings (1817–23) found politicians largely in agreement on a national agenda, and a string of diplomatic achievements forged by John Quincy Adams gave the nation sharper definition. But the limits to expansion also became clear: the Panic of 1819 showed the dangers in economic growth, and the Missouri Crisis laid bare the sectional split that attended westward expansion.

WHAT WERE the causes and consequences of early nineteenth-century American expansion?

ANOTHER WESTWARD SURGE

The end of the War of 1812 was followed by a westward surge to the Mississippi River that populated the Old Northwest (Ohio, Indiana, Illinois, Michigan, and Wisconsin) and the Old Southwest (western Georgia, Alabama, Mississippi, and Louisiana). The extent of the population redistribution was dramatic: in 1790, about 95 percent of the nation's population had lived in states bordering the Atlantic Ocean; by 1820 fully 25 percent of the population lived west of the Appalachians (see Map 9.5).

What accounted for this extraordinary westward surge? There were both push and pull factors. Between 1800 and 1820, the nation's population almost doubled, increasing from 5.3 million to 9.6 million. Overpopulated farmland in all of the seaboard states pushed farmers off the land, while new land pulled them westward. The defeat and removal of Indians in the War of 1812 was another important pull factor. The most important pull factor, however, was the attractive price of western land. The Land Ordinance of 1785 priced western lands too high for all but speculators and the wealthy (see Chapter 7), but subsequent realities had slowly forced Congress to enact land laws more favorable to the small farmer.

The major migration routes west favored cultural transplantation. Because of lateral westward movement, Northerners tended to migrate to the Old Northwest, Southerners to the Old Southwest. Except in southern Ohio and parts of Kentucky and Tennessee, there was very little contact among regional cultures. New Englanders carried their values and lifestyles directly west and settled largely with their own communities; Southerners did the same (see Map 9.5).

One section of northern Ohio along Lake Erie, for example, had been Connecticut's western land claim since the days of its colonial charter. Rather than give up the land when the Northwest Territory was established in 1787, Connecticut held onto the Western Reserve (as it was known) and encouraged its citizens to move there. Group settlement was common and New Englanders brought to the Western Reserve their religion (Congregational), their love of learning (tiny Norwalk soon boasted a three-story academy), and their adamant opposition to slavery.

Western migration in the South was very different. On this frontier, the people clearing the land were African American slaves creating plantations not for themelves but for their owners. After the War of 1812, as cotton growing expanded, hopeful slave owners from older parts of the South (Virginia, North and South Carolina, Georgia) flooded into the region. The migration was like a gold rush, characterized by high hopes, land speculation, and riches—for a few. Most of the white settlers in the Old Southwest were small farm families who did not own slaves, but they hoped to, for ownership of slaves was the means to wealth. More than half of the migrants to the Old Southwest after 1812 were enslaved African Americans. This involuntary migration of slaves tore African American families apart at the same time that white families

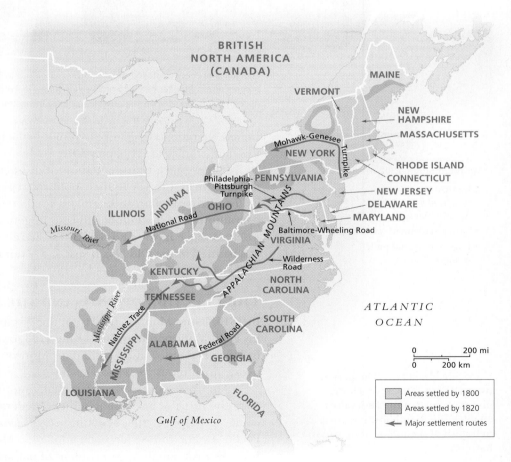

MAP 9.5

Spread of Settlement: Westward Surge, 1800–1820   Within a period of twenty years, a quarter of the nation's population had moved west of the Appalachian Mountains. The westward surge was a dynamic source of American optimism.

HOW DID westward movement vary by region between 1800 and 1820?

The hopes of every westward migrant are exemplified in this series of four illustrations imagining inevitable progress from pioneer cabin to prosperous farm. The illustrations, "The Pioneer Settler and His Progress," appeared in a booster history advertising land in western New York.

QUICK REVIEW

Westward Surge, 1800–1820

◆ By 1820 25 percent of the population lived west of the Appalachians.

◆ Group settlement was common.

◆ Lure of new land pulled farmers west.

Era of Good Feelings The period from 1817 to 1823 in which the disappearance of the Federalists enabled the Republicans to govern in a spirit of seemingly nonpartisan harmony.

American System The program of government subsidies favored by Henry Clay and his followers to promote American economic growth and protect domestic manufacturers from foreign competition.

viewed migration as a chance to replicate the lifestyle and values of older southern states on this new frontier (see Chapter 10).

The western transplantation of distinctive regional cultures explains why the West did not form a third, unified political region. Although there were common western issues—in particular, the demand for better roads and other transportation routes—communities in the Old Northwest, in general, shared New England political attitudes, whereas those in the Old Southwest shared southern attitudes. Then too, while slavery was banned in the Old Northwest, it was not in the Old Southwest, thus sowing the seeds of the sectionalism to come.

THE ELECTION OF 1816 AND THE ERA OF GOOD FEELINGS

In 1816, James Monroe, the last of the Virginia Dynasty, was easily elected president over his Federalist opponent Rufus King (183 to 34 electoral votes). This was the last election in which Federalists ran a candidate. Monroe had no opponent in 1820 and was reelected nearly unanimously (231 to 1).

Monroe's politics reflected changing times. When he visited Boston, as recently as 1815 the heart of a secession-minded Federalist region, he received an enthusiastic welcome, prompting the Federalist *Columbian Centinel* to proclaim an "**Era of Good Feelings**." The phrase has been applied to Monroe's presidency (1817–25) ever since.

Monroe sought a government of national unity, and he chose men from North and South, Jeffersonian Republicans and Federalists, for his cabinet. He selected John Quincy Adams, a former Federalist, as his secretary of state, virtually assuring that Adams, like his father, would become president. To balance Adams, Monroe picked John C. Calhoun of South Carolina, a prominent War Hawk, as secretary of war. And Monroe supported the **American System**, a program of national economic development that became identified with westerner Henry Clay, Speaker of the House of Representatives.

In supporting the American System, Monroe broke with Jefferson's agrarianism to embrace much of the Federalist program for economic development, including the chartering of a national bank, a tax on imported goods to protect American manufacturers, and a national system of roads and canals. The support that Monroe gave to these ideas following the War of 1812 was a crucial sign of the dynamism of the American commercial economy. Many Republicans now acknowledged that the federal government had a role to play in fostering the economic and commercial conditions in which both yeoman farmer and merchant could succeed.

In 1816, Congress chartered the Second Bank of the United States for twenty years. The bank was a private institution supported by some of the nation's wealthiest men with whom the government cooperated. The bank was expected to provide the large-scale financing that the smaller state banks could not handle and to create a strong national currency. Because they feared the economic power of rich men, Jeffersonian Republicans had allowed the charter of the original Bank of the United States, founded in 1791, to expire in 1811. The Republican about-face in 1816 was a sign that the strength of commercial interests had grown to rival that of farmers, whose distrust for central banks persisted.

The **Tariff of 1816** was the first substantial protective tariff in American history. In 1815, British manufacturers, who had been excluded for eight years (from the Embargo Act of 1807 to the end of the War of 1812), flooded the U.S. market with their products. American manufacturers complained that the British were dumping goods below cost in order to prevent the growth of American industries. Congress responded with a tariff on imported woolens and cottons, on iron, leather, hats, paper, and sugar.

The third item in the American System, funding for roads and canals was more controversial. Monroe supported genuinely national (that is, interstate) projects such as the National Road from Cumberland, Maryland, to Vandalia, Illinois. Congressmen, however, aware of the urgent need to improve transportation in general, and sensing the political advantages from directing funds to their districts, proposed spending federal money on local projects. Monroe vetoed such local proposals, believing them to be unconstitutional.

Monroe's support for measures initially identified with his political opposition was an indicator of his realism. The three aspects of the American System—bank, tariff, roads—were all parts of the basic infrastructure that the American economy needed in order to develop. Briefly, during the Era of Good Feelings, politicians agreed about the need for all three. Later, each would be a source of heated partisan argument.

The Diplomacy of John Quincy Adams

The diplomatic achievements of the Era of Good Feelings were due almost entirely to the efforts of one man, John Quincy Adams, Monroe's secretary of state. Adams set himself the task of tidying up the borders of the United States. Two accords with Britain—the **Rush-Bagot Treaty** of 1817 and the Convention of 1818—fixed the border between the United States and Canada at the 49th parallel and resolved conflicting U.S. and British claims to Oregon with an agreement to occupy it jointly for ten (eventually twenty) years.

Adams's major diplomatic accomplishment was the Adams-Onís or Transcontinental Treaty of 1819, in which he skillfully wrested concessions from the faltering Spanish empire. Adams convinced Spain not only to cede Florida but also to drop all previous claims it had to the Louisiana Territory and Oregon. In return, the United States relinquished claims on Texas and assumed responsibility for the $5 million in claims that U.S. citizens had against Spain.

Finally, Adams picked his way through the remarkable changes occurring in Latin America, developing the policy that bears his president's name, the **Monroe Doctrine**. The United States was the first country outside Latin America to recognize the independence

Tariff of 1816 A tax imposed by Congress on imported goods.

Rush-Bagot Treaty of 1817 Treaty between the United States and Britain that effectively demilitarized the Great Lakes by sharply limiting the number of ships each power could station on them.

Monroe Doctrine Declaration by President James Monroe in 1823 that the Western Hemisphere was to be closed off to further European colonization and that the United States would not interfere in the internal affairs of European nations.

•••—Read the Document

The President Addresses the Union (1823) at **www.myhistorylab.com**

of Spain's former colonies. When the European powers (France, Austria, Russia, and Prussia) began to talk of a plan to help Spain recover the lost colonies, the British proposed a British-American declaration against European intervention in the hemisphere. Others might have been flattered by an approach from the British empire, but Adams would have none of it. Showing the national pride that was so characteristic of the era, Adams insisted on an independent American policy. He therefore drafted for the president the hemispheric policy that the United States has followed ever since.

On December 2, 1823, the president presented the Monroe Doctrine to Congress. He called for the end of colonization of the Western Hemisphere by European nations. Intervention by European powers in the affairs of the independent New World nations would be considered by the United States a danger to its own peace and safety. Finally, Monroe pledged that the United States would not interfere in the affairs of European countries or in the affairs of their remaining New World colonies.

All of this was a very loud bark from a very small dog. In 1823, the United States lacked the military and economic force to back up its grand statement. In fact, what kept the European powers out of Latin America was British opposition to European intervention, enforced by the Royal Navy. The Monroe Doctrine was, however, useful in Adams's last diplomatic achievement, the Convention of 1824, in which Russia gave up its claim to the Oregon Territory and accepted 54°40' north latitude as the southern border of Russian America. Thus, Adams had contained another possible threat to American continental expansion (see Map 9.6).

In the short space of twenty years, the position of the United States on the North American continent had been transformed. Not only was America a much larger nation, but also the Spanish presence was much diminished, Russian expansion on the West Coast contained, and peace prevailed with Britain. This string of diplomatic achievements represented a great personal triumph for the stubborn, principled John Quincy Adams. A committed nationalist and expansionist, he showed that reason and diplomacy were in some circumstances more effective than force. Adams's diplomatic achievements were a fitting end to the period dominated by the Virginia Dynasty, the trio of enlightened revolutionaries who did so much to shape the new nation.

THE PANIC OF 1819

Across this impressive record of political and economic nation building fell the shadow of the Panic of 1819. A delayed reaction to the end of the War of 1812 and the Napoleonic Wars, the panic forced Americans to come to terms with their economic place in a peaceful world. As British merchant ships resumed trade on routes they had abandoned during the wars, the American shipping boom ended. And as European farm production recovered from the wars, the international demand for American foodstuffs declined and American farmers and shippers suffered.

Domestic economic conditions made matters worse. The western land boom that began in 1815 turned into a speculative frenzy. This was not the first—or the last—speculative boom in western lands. But it ended like all the rest—with a sharp contraction of credit, begun on this occasion by the Second Bank of the United States, which in 1819 forced state banks to foreclose on many bad loans. Many small farmers were ruined, and they blamed the faraway Bank of the United States for their troubles. In the 1830s, Andrew Jackson would build a political movement on their resentment.

Urban workers lost their jobs as international trade declined and as manufacturers failed because of competition from British imports. As they lobbied for local relief, many workers became deeply involved in urban politics, where they could express their resentment against the merchants and owners who had laid them off. Thus developed another component of Andrew Jackson's new political coalition.

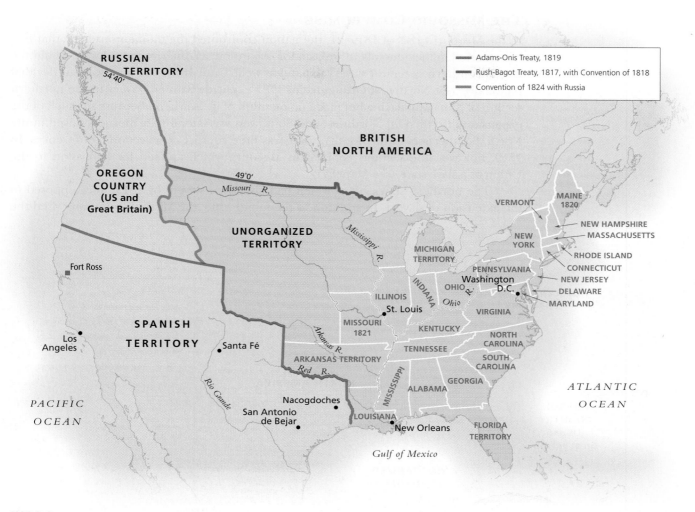

MAP 9.6

John Quincy Adams's Border Treaties   John Quincy Adams, secretary of state in the Monroe administration (1817–25), solidified the nation's boundaries in several treaties with Britain and Spain. The Rush-Bagot Treaty of 1817 and the Conventions of 1818 and 1824 settled the northern boundary with Canada and the terms of a joint occupancy of Oregon. The Adams-Onís Treaty of 1819 added Florida to the United States and settled the disputed border between the American Louisiana Territory and Spanish possessions in the West.

WHAT AGREEMENTS were reached in the treaties signed by John Quincy Adams to settle U.S. borders?

Another confrontation arose over the tariff. Southern planters, hurt by a decline in the price of cotton, began to actively protest the protective tariff, which kept the price of imported goods high even when cotton prices were low. Manufacturers, hurt by British competition, lobbied for even higher rates, which they achieved in 1824 over southern protests. Southerners then began to express doubts about the fairness of a political system in which they were always outvoted.

The Panic of 1819 was a symbol of this transitional time. It showed how far the country had moved since 1800, from Jefferson's republic of yeoman farmers toward a nation dominated by commerce. And the anger and resentment expressed by the groups harmed by the depression—farmers, urban workers, and southern planters—were portents of the politics of the upcoming Jackson era.

THE MISSOURI COMPROMISE

In the Missouri Crisis of 1819–21, the nation confronted the momentous issue that had been buried in the general enthusiasm for expansion: as America moved west, would the largely southern system of slavery expand as well? Until 1819, this question was decided regionally. The Northwest Ordinance of 1787 explicitly banned slavery in the northern section of trans-Appalachia but made no mention of it elsewhere. Because so much of the expansion into the Old Northwest and Southwest was lateral (Northerners stayed in the North, Southerners in the South), there was little conflict over sectional differences. In 1819, however, the sections collided in Missouri, which applied for admission to the Union as a slave state (see Map 9.7).

The northern states, all of which had abolished slavery by 1819, were opposed to the extension of slavery. In addition to the moral issue, the Missouri question raised the

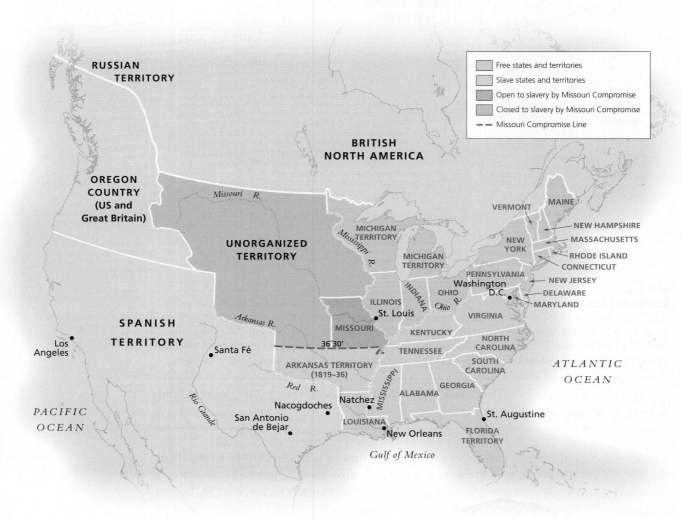

MAP 9.7

The Missouri Compromise Before the Missouri Compromise of 1820, the Ohio River was the dividing line between the free states of the Old Northwest and the slaveholding states of the Old Southwest. The compromise stipulated that Missouri would enter the Union as a slave state (balanced by Maine, a free state), but slavery would be prohibited in the Louisiana Territory north of 36°30' (Missouri's southern boundary). This awkward compromise lasted until 1846, when the Mexican-American War reopened the issue of the expansion of slavery.

HOW DID westward expansion create added pressure to resolve the question of slavery?

CHRONOLOGY

1800	Thomas Jefferson elected president
1802	Russian-American Company headquarters established at Sitka, Alaska
	First Barbary War begins
1803	Louisiana Purchase
	Marbury v. *Madison*
	Ohio admitted to the Union
1804	Lewis and Clark expedition leaves St. Louis
	Vice President Aaron Burr kills Alexander Hamilton in a duel
	Thomas Jefferson reelected president
1807	*Chesapeake–Leopard* incident
	Embargo Act
	Former Vice President Aaron Burr tried for treason but acquitted
1808	James Madison elected president
1809	Tecumseh forms military alliance among Northwest Confederacy peoples
1811	Battle of Tippecanoe

1812	War of 1812 begins
	James Madison reelected president
	Louisiana admitted to the Union
1814	Treaty of Ghent
1815	Battle of New Orleans
1816	James Monroe elected president
	Congress charters Second Bank of the United States
	Indiana admitted to the Union
1817	Mississippi admitted to the Union
1818	Illinois admitted to the Union
1819	Panic of 1819
	Adams-Onís Treaty
	Alabama admitted to the Union
1819–20	Missouri Crisis and Compromise
1820	James Monroe reelected president
	Maine admitted to the Union
1821	Missouri admitted to the Union as a slave state
1823	Monroe Doctrine

political issue of sectional balance. Northern politicians did not want to admit another slave state. To do so would tip the balance of power in the Senate, where the 1819 count of slave and free states was eleven apiece. For their part, Southerners believed they needed an advantage in the Senate; because of faster population growth in the North, they were already outnumbered (105 to 81) in the House of Representatives.

But above all, Southerners did not believe Congress had the power to limit the expansion of slavery. Slavery, in southern eyes, was a question of property and, therefore, a matter for state rather than federal legislation. Thus, from the very beginning, the expansion of slavery exposed vital constitutional issues.

In 1819, Representative James Tallmadge Jr. of New York began more than a year of congressional controversy when he demanded that Missouri agree to the gradual end of slavery as the price of entering the Union. At first, the general public paid little attention, but religious reformers (Quakers prominent among them) organized a number of antislavery rallies in northern cities that made politicians take notice. Former Federalists in the North who had seen their party destroyed by the achievements of Jefferson and his successors in the Virginia Dynasty eagerly seized on the Missouri issue. This was the first time that the growing northern reform impulse had intersected with sectional politics. It was also the first time that southern threats of secession were made openly in Congress.

In 1820, Congress achieved compromise over the sectional differences. Henry Clay forged the first of the many agreements that were to earn him the title of "the Great Pacificator" (peacemaker). The **Missouri Compromise** maintained the balance between free and slave states: Maine (which had been part of Massachusetts) was admitted as a free state in 1820 and Missouri as a slave state in the following year. A policy was also enacted

Missouri Compromise Sectional compromise in Congress in 1820 that admitted Missouri to the Union as a slave state and Maine as a free state and prohibited slavery in the northern Louisiana Purchase territory.

with respect to slavery in the rest of the Louisiana Purchase: slavery was prohibited north of 36°30′ north latitude—the southern boundary of Missouri—and permitted south of that line. This meant that the vast majority of the Louisiana Territory would be free. In reality, then, the Missouri Compromise could be only a temporary solution, because it left open the question of how the balance between slave and free states would be maintained. But the Compromise did have one immediate effect: Southerners now realized that slavery was under attack and quickly built new arguments to defend it (see Chapter 10).

CONCLUSION

In complex ways a developing economy, geographical expansion, and even a minor war helped shape American unity. Local, small, settled, face-to-face communities in both the North and the South began to send their more mobile, expectant members to new occupations in urban centers or west to form new settlements.

The westward population movement dramatically changed the political landscape and Americans' view of themselves. But expansion did not create the "empire for liberty" that Thomas Jefferson had hoped for. While expansion did indeed create economic opportunity, it also displaced and destroyed Indian communities such as the Mandans, the Shawnee, and many others. And it also created an even greater denial of liberty, as we shall see in the next chapter, in a greatly expanded community tied to cotton and to the slave labor that produced it.

REVIEW QUESTIONS

1. What economic and political problems did the United States face as a new nation in a world dominated by war between Britain and France? How successful were the efforts by the Jefferson, Madison, and Monroe administrations to solve these problems?

2. The anti-European cast of Jefferson's republican agrarianism made it appealing to many Americans who wished to believe in their nation's uniqueness, but how realistic was it?

3. Some Federalists opposed the Louisiana Purchase, warning of the dangers of westward expansion. What are arguments for and against expansion?

4. What contradictions in American Indian policy did the confrontations between Tecumseh's alliance and soldiers and settlers in the Old Northwest reveal? Can you suggest solutions to these contradictions?

5. What did the War of 1812 accomplish?

6. What were the issues that made it impossible for the Era of Good Feelings to last?

KEY TERMS

American System (p. 220)
Embargo Act (p. 211)
Era of Good Feelings (p. 220)
Marbury v. *Madison* (p. 208)
Missouri Compromise (p. 225)
Monroe Doctrine (p. 221)
Nullification (p. 218)

Pan-Indian military resistance movement (p. 212)
Rush-Bagot Treaty of 1817 (p. 221)
Tariff of 1816 (p. 221)
Treaty of Ghent (p. 218)
War Hawks (p. 214)
War of 1812 (p. 215)

PEARSON
myhistorylab Connections

Reinforce what you learned in this chapter by studying the many documents, images, maps, review tools, and videos available at www.myhistorylab.com.

Read and Review

✓● Study and Review Chapter 9

●●● Read the Document

Thomas Jefferson to Meriweather Lewis (1803)

Supreme Court Retains Right to Overrule Legislation (1803)

Constitutionality of the Louisiana Purchase (1803)

Lewis and Clark Meet the Shoshone (1805)

Margaret Bayard Smith, Reflections upon Meeting Jefferson (1809)

A War Hawk Speaks About the British (1811)

Indian Hostilities (1812)

"The Western Country" Letter in Niles Weekly Register

The President Addresses the Union (1823)

👁 See the Map

Louisiana Purchase

Native American Removal

The War of 1812

Research and Explore

●●● Read the Document

Exploring America: Continentalism

Whose History Is It?: In the Footsteps of Lewis and Clark

Profiles
Dolley Madison
Tenskwatawa

((●● Hear the Audio

Jefferson and Liberty

The Star Spangled Banner

●● Watch the Video Lewis and Clark: What Were They Trying to Accomplish?

((●● Hear the Audio

Hear the audio files for Chapter 9 at
www.myhistorylab.com.

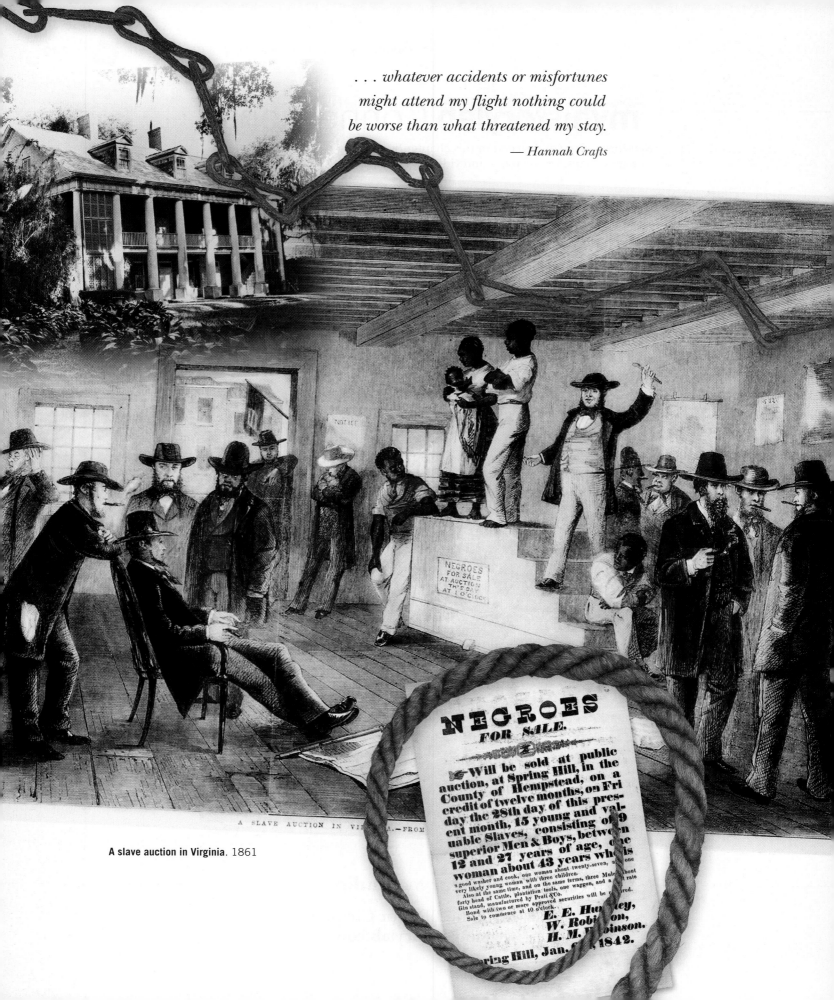

. . . whatever accidents or misfortunes might attend my flight nothing could be worse than what threatened my stay.

— *Hannah Crafts*

A slave auction in Virginia. 1861

10

THE SOUTH AND SLAVERY

1790s–1850s

((•—[Hear the Audio

Hear the audio files for Chapter 10 at **www.myhistorylab.com**.

HOW DID attitudes in the South toward slavery change after the invention of the cotton gin?

WHAT WAS life like for the typical slave in the American South?

HOW DID African Americans endure and resist slavery?

WHAT WERE the values of yeoman farmers?

WHO MADE up the planter elite?

WHAT PROSLAVERY arguments were developed in the first half of the nineteenth century?

AMERICAN COMMUNITIES
Cotton Communities
in the Old Southwest

IN 1834, SAMUEL TOWNES OF SOUTH CAROLINA CAUGHT "ALABAMA FEVER." Restive under what seemed to him excessive demands from his large and well-connected family, Samuel moved, with his slaves, to Perry County, Alabama, a newly opened part of the Old Southwest suitable for growing cotton. There he practiced law in the village of Marion, bought a plantation on the banks of the Cahaba River, and acquired ten to fifteen more slaves. Almost all of Samuel's new workers were bought on credit, which was plentiful at this "flush time" of high cotton prices and rich new land just coming into cultivation. Samuel's desire for wealth caused him to drive his slaves very hard, demanding that his overseer "whip them like the devil" to pick more cotton.

The Panic of 1837 devastated Samuel's ambitions. As the price of cotton fell to seven cents a pound, banks demanded repayment of their generous loans. Samuel sold some slaves, rented out the labor of others, but he was forced to ask for loans from the family he had been so eager to escape. In 1844 his plantation was sold at auction. Three years later, his health failed, and he and his wife Joanna returned to South Carolina and the charity of kinfolk.

The rapid westward expansion of cotton cultivation exposed the undeveloped state of community formation among the southern elite. The plantation form of agriculture, which had been the rule in the South since its earliest days, meant that cities were few and community institutions like churches and schools were rare. Slave-owning families depended almost entirely on kinship networks for assistance (and the obligations that Samuel Townes wished to avoid) and for sociability. Families who moved west like the Townes's frequently found themselves lost without their customary family connections.

What of the slaves that Samuel brought with him? Once part of a larger Townes family group in South Carolina, the slaves that Samuel owned were separated from their kinfolk permanently and had to adjust to living with a number of newly purchased slaves in Alabama. Most of the new slaves were bought as individuals and were usually still in their teens or even younger. Young male slaves were favored for the backbreaking work of cutting trees and clearing land for cultivation. Owners eager to clear land rapidly and make quick profits often drove the clearing crews at an unmerciful pace. And, as Samuel Townes had, they attempted to impose strict discipline and a rapid pace on the work gangs that planted, hoed, and harvested cotton.

Only long-practiced African American community-building strategies saved these young transported slaves from complete isolation. Beginning in the earliest days of slavery, Africans from many different tribes built their own communities by using the language of kinship (for example, "brother," "sister," "uncle," "aunt," and "child") to encompass everyone in new imagined families. On one hand, the cultivation of cotton required many workers, thus creating the conditions necessary for large slave communities in the Old Southwest. On the other hand, because the price of cotton was unstable, probably many shared the experience of the Townes slaves, who were sold again when the plantation failed.

Thus, the new land in the Old Southwest that appeared to offer so much opportunity for owners bred tensions caused by forcible sale and migration, by the organization and pace of cotton cultivation, and by the owners' often violent efforts to control their slaves in a new region where community bonds were undeveloped. For planters and slaves alike, migration broke long-standing family ties that were the most common form of community throughout the South.

In the first half of the nineteenth century, world demand for cotton transformed the South, promoting rapid expansion and unprecedented prosperity. But it also tied the South to a slave system that was inherently unstable and violent. Although southern slave owners frequently talked about their plantations as communities and their slaves as family, the slave system was not one community but two with the strengths of the slave community largely invisible to the owners.

Marion, AL

KING COTTON AND SOUTHERN EXPANSION

S lavery had long dominated southern life. African American slaves grew the great export crops of the colonial period, tobacco, rice, and indigo. Briefly, in the early days of American independence, the slave system waned, only to be revived by the immense profitability of cotton in a newly industrializing world. Cotton became the dominant crop in a rapidly expanding South that more than doubled in size (see Map 10.1), and as it expanded, attitudes toward slavery hardened.

HOW DID attitudes in the South toward slavery change after the invention of the cotton gin?

COTTON AND EXPANSION INTO THE OLD SOUTHWEST

Short-staple cotton had long been recognized as a crop ideally suited to southern soils and growing conditions. But it had one major drawback: the seeds were so difficult to remove from the lint that it took an entire day to hand-clean a single pound of cotton. The invention in 1793 of the cotton gin, the result of collaboration between Eli Whitney and Catherine Greene, made cotton growing profitable. With the cotton gin, it was possible to clean more than fifty pounds of cotton a day. Soon large and small planters in the inland regions of Georgia and South Carolina had begun to grow cotton. By 1811, this area was producing 60 million pounds of cotton a year and exporting most of it to England.

Other areas of the South quickly followed South Carolina and Georgia into cotton production. New land was needed because cotton growing rapidly depleted the soil. The profits to be made from cotton growing drew a rush of southern farmers into the so-called black belt—an area stretching through western Georgia, Alabama, and Mississippi that was blessed with exceptionally fertile soil. Following the War of 1812, Southerners were seized by "Alabama Fever." In one of the swiftest migrations in American history, white

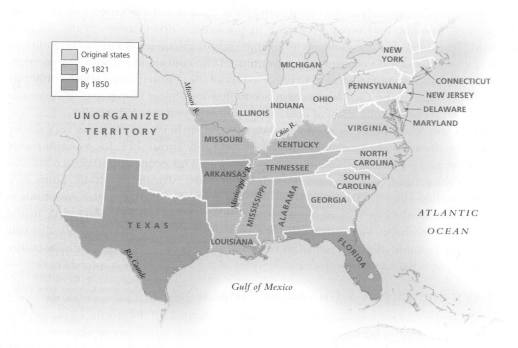

MAP 10.1

The South Expands, 1790–1850   This map shows the dramatic effect cotton production had on southern expansion. From the original six states of 1790, westward expansion, fueled by the search for new cotton lands, added another six states by 1821 and three more by 1850.

See the **Map**

United States Territorial Expansion in the 1850s at **www.myhistorylab.com**

WHAT NEW states were established as a direct result of the search for new cotton lands?

This model of Eli Whitney's cotton gin, invented in 1793, was a simple device with huge consequences. It transformed the South, condemned millions of African Americans to slavery, and was the largest source of American economic growth before 1860.

Southerners and their slaves flooded into western Georgia and the areas that would become Alabama and Mississippi (the Old Southwest).

Like the simultaneous expansion into the Old Northwest, settlement of the Old Southwest took place at the expense of the region's Indian population (see Chapter 9). Beginning with the defeat of the Creeks at Horseshoe Bend in 1814 and ending with the Cherokee forced migration along the "Trail of Tears" in 1838, the Five Civilized Tribes—the Cherokees, Chickasaws, Choctaws, Creeks, and Seminoles—were forced to give up their lands and move to Indian Territory (see Chapter 11).

Following the "Alabama Fever" of 1816–20, several later surges of southern expansion (1832–38, and again in the mid-1850s) carried cotton planting over the Mississippi River into Louisiana and deep into Texas. In the minds of the mobile, enterprising Southerners who sought their fortunes in the West, cotton profits and expansion went hand in hand. But the expansion of cotton meant the expansion of slavery.

SLAVERY THE MAINSPRING—AGAIN

The export of cotton from the South was the dynamic force in the developing American economy in the 1790–1840 period. Just as the international slave trade had been the dynamic force in the Atlantic economy of the eighteenth century (see Chapter 4), southern slavery financed northern industrial development in the nineteenth century.

The rapid growth of cotton production was an international phenomenon, prompted by events occurring far from the American South. The insatiable demand for cotton was a result of the technological and social changes that we know today as the **Industrial Revolution**. Beginning early in the eighteenth century, a series of inventions resulted in the mechanized spinning and weaving of cloth in the world's first factories in the north of England. The ability of these factories to produce unprecedented amounts of cotton cloth revolutionized the world economy. The invention of the cotton gin came at just the right time. British textile manufacturers were eager to buy all the cotton that the South could produce. By the time of the Civil War, cotton accounted for almost 60 percent of American exports, representing a total value of nearly $200 million a year (see Figure 10.1).

The connection between southern slavery and northern industry was very direct. Most mercantile services associated with the cotton trade (insurance, for example) were in northern hands and, significantly, so was shipping. This economic structure was not new. In colonial times, New England ships dominated the African slave trade. Some New England families—like the Browns of Providence who made fortunes in the slave trade—invested some of their profits in the new technology of textile manufacturing in the 1790s. Other merchants—such as the Boston Associates who financed the cotton textile mills at Lowell—made their money from cotton shipping and brokerage. Thus, as cotton boomed, it provided capital for the new factories of the North (see Chapter 12).

A SLAVE SOCIETY IN A CHANGING WORLD

In the flush of freedom following the American Revolution, all the northern states abolished slavery or passed laws for gradual emancipation, and a number of slave owners in the Upper South freed their slaves (see Chapter 7). Thomas Jefferson, ever the optimist, claimed that "a total emancipation with the consent of the masters" could not be too far in the future.

Attitudes toward slavery rapidly changed following the invention of the cotton gin in 1793 and the realization of the riches to be made from cotton. As the production of cotton climbed higher every year in response to a seemingly inexhaustible international demand, so too did the demand for slaves and the conviction of Southerners that slavery

QUICK REVIEW

The Economics of Slavery

◆ Worldwide demand for cotton supported slavery.

◆ Export of cotton a dynamic part of American economy.

◆ Northern industry directly connected to slavery.

Read **the Document**

Thomas Jefferson, Notes on Virginia (1787) at **www.myhistorylab.com**

Industrial Revolution Revolution in the means and organization of production.

was an economic necessity. Figures from the international slave trade in the decade before it was banned demonstrate this conclusively: nearly 75,000 new slaves were imported from Africa in 1800–1808, more than any other decade's total in the entire history of American slavery. Yet at the same time Southerners continued to argue that slavery was a problem that they themselves would someday resolve. Opinions and interference from the North were unwelcome.

As had been true since colonial times, the centrality of slavery to the economy and the need to keep slaves under firm control required the South to become a slave society, rather than merely a society with slaves, as had been the case in the North. What this meant was that one particular form of social relationship, that of master and slave (one dominant, the other subordinate), became the model for all relationships, including personal interactions between white husbands and wives as well as interactions in politics and at work. The profitability of cotton reconfirmed this model and extended it far beyond its original boundaries, thus creating a different kind of society in the South than the one emerging in the North.

At a time when the North was experiencing the greatest spurt of urban growth in the nation's history (see Chapter 13), most of the South remained rural. The agrarian ideal, bolstered by the cotton boom, encouraged the antiurban and anticommercial sentiments of many white Southerners. The South also lagged behind the North in industrialization and in canals and railroads (see Chapter 12). Southern capital was tied up in land and slaves, and Southerners, buoyed by the world's insatiable demand for cotton, saw no reason to invest in economically risky railroads, canals, and factories.

Other changes, however, could not be so easily ignored. Nationwide, the slave states were losing their political dominance because their population was not keeping pace with that of the North and the Northwest. Equally alarming, outside the South, antislavery sentiment was growing rapidly. The South felt increasingly hemmed in by northern opposition to the expansion of slavery.

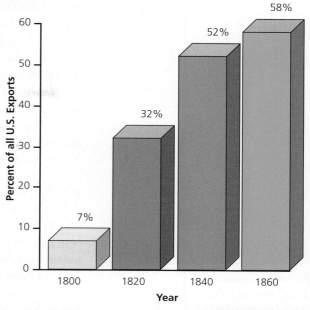

Figure 10.1 Cotton Exports as a Percentage of All U.S. Exports, 1800–1860
One consequence of the growth of cotton production was its importance in international trade. The growing share of the export market and the great value (nearly $200 million in 1860) led southern slave owners to assert that "Cotton is King." They believed that the importance of cotton to the national economy entitled the South to a commanding voice in national policy.

From *Atlas of Antebellum Southern Agriculture*, by Sam B. Hilliard. (Baton Rouge: Louisiana State University Press, 1984), pp. 67–71. Copyright © 1984 Louisiana State University Press. Reprinted by permission.

●◦●─ **Read** the **Document**
State Laws Govern Slavery (1824) at
www.myhistorylab.com

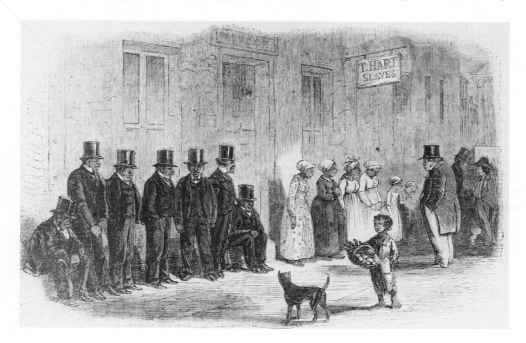

This engraving from *Harper's Weekly* shows slaves, dressed in new clothing, lined up outside a New Orleans slave pen for inspection by potential buyers before the actual auction began. They were often threatened with punishment if they did not present a good appearance and manner that would fetch a high price.

THE SECOND MIDDLE PASSAGE: THE INTERNAL SLAVE TRADE

The cotton boom caused a huge increase in the domestic slave trade. Plantation owners in the Upper South (Delaware, Kentucky, Maryland, Virginia, and Tennessee) sold their slaves to meet the demand for labor in the new and expanding cotton-growing regions of the Old Southwest. Cumulatively, between 1820 and 1860, nearly 50 percent of the slave population of the Upper South took part against their will in southern expansion (see Map 10.2).

More slaves—an estimated 1 million—were uprooted by this internal slave trade and enforced migration in the early nineteenth century than were brought to North America during the entire time the international slave trade was legal (see Chapter 4).

Purchased by slave traders from owners in the Upper South, slaves were gathered together in notorious "slave pens" in places like Richmond and Charleston and then moved south by train or boat. Often slaves moved on foot, chained together in groups of fifty or more known as "coffles." Arriving at a central market in the Lower South like Natchez, New Orleans, or Mobile, the slaves, after being carefully inspected by potential buyers, were sold at auction to the highest bidder (see Map 10.3).

In New Orleans, in the streets outside large slave pens near the French Quarter, thousands of slaves were displayed and sold each year. Dressed in new clothes provided by the traders and exhorted by the traders to walk, run, and otherwise show their stamina, slaves were presented to buyers. For their part, suspicious buyers poked, prodded, and frequently stripped male and female slaves to be sure they were as healthy as the traders claimed. Most slaves were sold as individuals: buyers rarely responded to pleas to buy an "extra" slave to keep a family together.

◦●▸ Read the Document

A Slave Tells of His Sale at Auction (1848)
at **www.myhistorylab.com**

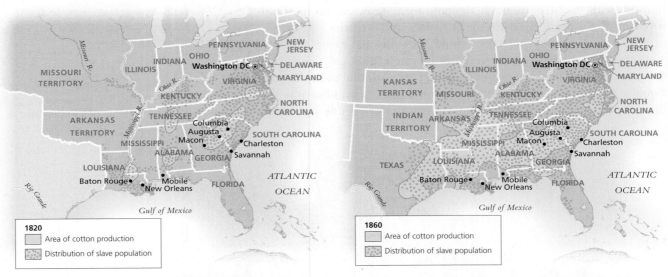

MAP 10.2

Cotton Production and the Slave Population, 1820–60 In the forty years from 1820–60, cotton production grew dramatically in both quantity and extent. Rapid westward expansion meant that by 1860 cotton production was concentrated in the black belt (so called for its rich soils) in the Lower South. As cotton production moved west and south, so did the enslaved African American population that produced it, causing a dramatic rise in the internal slave trade.

From *Atlas of Antebellum Southern Agriculture*, by Sam B. Hilliard. (Baton Rouge: Louisiana State University Press, 1984), pp. 67–71. Copyright © 1984 Louisiana State University Press. Reprinted by permission.

WHY WAS the increasing dominance of cotton cultivation in the Lower South accompanied by a growing concentration of slaves in that region?

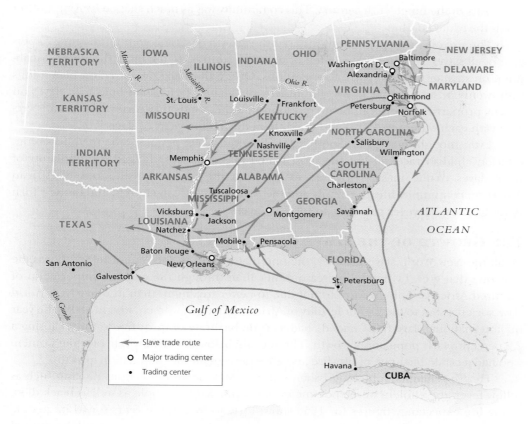

MAP 10.3

Internal Slave Trade, 1820–60   Between 1820 and 1860, nearly 50 percent of the slave population of the Upper South was sold to labor on the cotton plantations of the Lower South. This map shows the various routes by which they were "sold down the river," shipped by boat or marched south.

From *Historical Atlas of the United States* (Washington, DC: National Geographic Society, 1988). Copyright © 1988 National Geographic Society. Reprinted by permission.

WHAT AGRICULTURAL trends help explain the relative decline of slavery in the Upper South?

THE AFRICAN AMERICAN COMMUNITY

Surely no group in American history has faced a harder job of community building than the black people of the antebellum South. Living in intimate, daily contact with their oppressors, African Americans nevertheless created an enduring culture of their own, a culture that had far-reaching and lasting influence on all of southern life and American society as a whole (see Chapter 4).

WHAT WAS life like for the typical slave in the American South?

THE MATURE AMERICAN SLAVE SYSTEM

On January 1, 1808, the United States ended its participation in the international slave trade. Although a small number of slaves continued to be smuggled in from Africa, the growth of the slave labor force depended primarily on natural increase—that is, through births within the slave population. The slave population, estimated at 700,000 in 1790, grew to more than 4 million in 1860. A distinctive African American slave community, which had first emerged in the eighteenth century (see Chapter 4), expanded dramatically in the early years of the nineteenth century. This community was as much shaped by King Cotton as was the white South.

The size of cotton plantations fostered the growth of slave communities: now 75 percent of all slaves lived in groups of ten or more, in contrast to the more dispersed distribution on smaller farms in earlier generations. Over half of all slaves lived on plantations with twenty or more other slaves, and others, on smaller farms, had links with slaves on nearby properties. There can be no question that the bonds that African Americans created with each other were what sustained them during the years of slavery.

Even though most white Southerners believed black people to be members of an inferior, childish race, all but the most brutal masters acknowledged the humanity of their slaves. White masters learned to live with the two key institutions of African American community life: the family and the African American church, and in their turn slaves learned, however painfully, to survive slavery.

THE GROWTH OF THE SLAVE COMMUNITY

Of all the New World slave societies, the one that existed in the American South was the only one that grew by natural increase rather than through the constant importation of captured Africans. This growth was not due to better treatment than in other New World slave societies, but to the higher fertility of African American women, who in 1808 (the year the international slave trade ended) had a crude birthrate of thirty-five to forty, causing a 2.2 percent yearly population growth. This was still below the fertility rate of white women, who had a crude birthrate of fifty-five and a 2.9 percent annual population growth.

Health remained a lifelong issue for slaves. Malaria and infectious diseases such as yellow fever and cholera were endemic in the South. White people as well as black died, as the life expectancy figures for 1850 show: forty to forty-three years for white people and thirty to thirty-three years for African Americans. Slaves were more at risk because of the circumstances of slave life: poor housing, poor diet, and constant, usually heavy, work. Sickness was chronic: 20 percent or more of the slave labor force on most plantations were sick at any one time. Because of the poor medical knowledge of the time, slave owners failed to realize that adequate diet, warm housing, and basic sanitation might have prevented the pneumonia and dysentery that killed or weakened many slaves and that exacted an especially high toll on children under five, who died at twice the rate of their white counterparts.

FROM CRADLE TO GRAVE

Slavery was a lifelong labor system, and the constant and inescapable issue between master and slave was how much work the slave would—or could be forced to—do. Southern white slave owners claimed that by housing, feeding, and clothing their slaves from infancy to death they were acting more humanely than northern industrialists who employed people only during their working years. But in spite of occasional instances of **manumission**—the freeing of a slave—the child born of a slave was destined to remain a slave.

Children lived with their parents (or with their mother if the father was a slave on another farm or plantation) in housing provided by the owner. Husband and wife cooperated in loving and sheltering their children and teaching them survival skills. From birth to about age seven, slave children played with one another and with white children, observing and learning how to survive. They saw the penalties: black adults, perhaps their own parents, whipped for disobedience; black women, perhaps their own sisters, violated by white men. And they might see one or both parents sold away as punishment or for financial gain. They would also see signs of white benevolence: special treats for children at holidays, appeals to loyalty from the master or mistress, perhaps friendship with a white child.

Of course, black children had no schooling of any kind; in most of the southern states, it was against the law to teach a slave to read. Instead of learning to read, most

Manumission   The freeing of a slave.

children learned slave ways of getting along: apparent acquiescence to white demands, pilfering, malingering, incomprehension, sabotage, and other methods of slowing the relentless work pace. Many white Southerners genuinely believed that their slaves were both less intelligent and more loyal than they really were. Frederick Douglass, whose fearless leadership of the abolitionist movement made him the most famous African American of his time, wryly noted, "As the master studies to keep the slave ignorant, the slave is cunning enough to make the master think he succeeds."

Whatever their particular childhood circumstances, at age twelve, slaves were considered full grown and put to work in the fields or in their designated occupation.

FIELD WORK AND THE GANG SYSTEM

In 1850, 55 percent of all slaves were engaged in cotton growing. Another 20 percent labored to produce other crops: tobacco (10 percent), rice, sugar, and hemp. About 15 percent of all slaves were domestic servants, and the remaining 10 percent worked in mining, lumbering, industry, and construction (see Figure 10.2).

The field workers, 75 percent of all slaves, both male and female, were most directly affected by the **gang system** employed on cotton plantations (as well as in tobacco and sugar). Cotton was a crop that demanded nearly year-round labor. Owners divided their slaves into gangs of twenty to twenty-five, a communal labor pattern reminiscent of parts of Africa, but with a crucial difference—these workers were supervised by overseers with whips. On most plantations, slaves were expected to be on their way to the fields as soon as it was light. Work continued till noon, and after an hour or so for lunch and rest, the slaves worked until nearly dark. Work days were shorter in the winter, perhaps only ten hours.

Work was tedious in the hot and humid southern fields, and the overseer's whip was never far away. Cotton growing was hard and demanding work demanding real skill: plowing and planting, chopping weeds with a heavy hoe, and picking the ripe cotton from the stiff and scratchy bolls, at the rate of 150 pounds a day. Slaves aged fast under this regime. Poor diet and heavy labor undermined health. When they were too old to work, they took on other tasks within the black community, such as caring for young children.

HOUSE SERVANTS AND SKILLED WORKERS

In the eighteenth century, as profits from slavery grew, slave owners diverted an increasing proportion of slave labor from the fields to the house service necessary to sustain their rich lifestyles. By one calculation, fully one-third of the female slaves in Virginia worked as house servants by 1800, but the figures were much lower in the newly opened cotton lands in the West.

At first glance, working in the big house might seem to have been preferable to working in the fields. Physically, it was much less demanding, and house slaves were often better fed and clothed. They also had much more access to information, for white people, accustomed to servants and generally confident of their loyalty, often forgot their presence and spoke among themselves about matters of interest to the slaves.

From the point of view of the slave, the most unpleasant thing about being a house servant (or the single slave of a small owner) was the constant presence of white people. There was no escape from white supervision. Many slaves who were personal maids and children's nurses were required to live in the big house and rarely saw their own families. Cooks and other house servants were exposed to the tempers and whims of all members

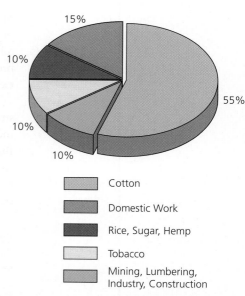

Figure 10.2 Distribution of Slave Labor, 1850

Cotton

Domestic Work

Rice, Sugar, Hemp

Tobacco

Mining, Lumbering, Industry, Construction

In 1850, 55 percent of all slaves worked in cotton, 10 percent in tobacco, and another 10 percent in rice, sugar, and hemp. Ten percent worked in mining, lumbering, industry, and construction, and 15 percent worked as domestic servants. Slave labor was not generally used to grow corn, the staple crop of the yeoman farmer.

◆●◆—Read the **Document**

Frances Ann Kemble, Journal of a Residence on a Georgia Plantation (1838) at **www.myhistorylab.com**

Gang System   The organization and supervision of slave field hands into working teams on Southern plantations.

Thomas Jefferson used this revolving bookstand with five adjustable bookrests at Monticello. It was built of walnut in 1810 by slaves from the plantation whom Jefferson had directed to be trained as skilled carpenters.

of the white family, including the children, who prepared themselves for lives of mastery by practicing giving orders to slaves many times their own age. And house servants, more than any others, were forced to act grateful and ingratiating. An escaped slave, Jermain Loguen, recalled with distaste the charade of "servile bows and counterfeit smiles . . . and other false expressions of gladness" with which he placated his master and mistress.

A small number of slaves were skilled workers: weavers, seamstresses, carpenters, blacksmiths, and mechanics. More slave men than women achieved skilled status (partly because many jobs considered appropriate for women, like cooking, were not thought of as skilled). Black people worked as lumberjacks, as miners, as deckhands and stokers on Mississippi riverboats, as stevedores loading cotton on the docks of Charleston, Savannah, and New Orleans, and sometimes as workers in the handful of southern factories. Because slaves were their masters' property, the wages of the slave belonged to the owner, not the slave.

The extent to which slaves made up the laboring class was most apparent in cities. In part because the South failed to attract as much immigrant labor as the North, southern cities offered both enslaved and free black people opportunities in skilled occupations such as blacksmithing and carpentering that free African Americans in the North were denied.

SLAVE FAMILIES

As had been true in the eighteenth century, families remained essential to African American culture (see Chapter 4). No southern state recognized slave marriages in law, but masters encouraged marriage among their slaves, believing it made the men less rebellious, and because they were eager for the slave women to have children. Whatever marriages meant to the masters, to slaves they were a haven of love and intimacy in a cruel world and the basis of the African American community. Husbands and wives had a chance, in their own cabins, to live their own lives among loved ones. The relationship between slave husband and wife was different from that of the white husband and wife. The master–slave system dictated that the white marriage be unequal, for the man had to be dominant and the woman dependent and submissive. Slave marriages were ironically more equal, for husband and wife were both powerless within the slave system.

Marriage was more than a haven from cruelty: it was the foundation of community. Family meant continuity. Parents made great efforts to teach their children the family history and to surround them with a supportive and protective kinship network. The strength of these ties is shown by the many husbands, wives, children, and parents who searched for each other after the Civil War when slavery came to an end. Observing African Americans' postwar migrations, a Freedmen's Bureau agent commented that "every mother's son among them seemed to be in search of his mother; every mother in search of her children."

Given the vast size of the internal slave trade, fear of separation was constant—and real. One in every five slave marriages was broken, and one in every three children sold away from their families. In the face of constant separation, slave communities attempted to act like larger families. Following practices developed early in slavery, children were taught to respect and learn from all the elders, to call all adults of a certain

Slave quarters built by slave owners, like these pictured on a South Carolina plantation, provided more than basic shelter. Slave quarters were the center of the African American community life that developed during slavery.

Collection of The New-York Historical Society. Photograph by G.N. Barnard, Bagoe Collection, ca. 1865, negative number 48169.

age "aunt" or "uncle," and to call children of their own age "brother" or "sister" (see Chapter 4). Thus, in the absence of their own family, separated children could quickly find a place and a source of comfort in the slave community to which they had been sold.

This emphasis on family and on kinship networks had an even more fundamental purpose. The kinship of the entire community, where old people were respected and young ones cared for, represented a conscious rejection of white paternalism. The slaves' ability, in the most difficult of situations, to structure a community that expressed their values, not those of their masters, was extraordinary. Equally remarkable was the way in which African Americans reshaped Christianity to serve their needs.

FREEDOM AND RESISTANCE

Whatever their dreams, most slaves knew they would never escape. Almost all successful escapes in the nineteenth century (approximately a thousand a year) were from the Upper South (Delaware, Maryland, Virginia, Kentucky, and Missouri). A slave in the Lower South or the Southwest simply had too far to go to reach freedom. That meant that ways to endure and to resist became all the more important.

AFRICAN AMERICAN RELIGION

Black Christianity was an enabling religion: it helped slaves to survive, not as passive victims of white tyranny but as active opponents of an oppressive system that they daily protested in small but meaningful ways. In their faith, African Americans expressed a spiritual freedom that white people could not destroy.

HOW DID African Americans endure and resist slavery?

African cultural patterns persisted in the preference for night funerals and for solemn pageantry and song, as depicted in British artist John Antrobus's *Plantation Burial*, ca. 1860. Like other African American customs, the community care of the dead contained an implied rebuke to the masters' care of the living slaves.

John Antrobus, *Plantation Burial*. Oil painting. The Historic New Orleans Collection. #1960.46.

The Second Great Awakening
Religious revival among black and white Southerners in the 1790s.

●◆●─Read the Document
Slave Culture Documented in Song (1867) at **www.myhistorylab.com**

QUICK REVIEW

Religion and Slavery

- A variety of African religions survived in America.
- The Great Awakening introduced many slaves to Christianity.
- Most planters tried to control the religious life of their slaves.

●◆●─Read the Document
Runaway Slave Advertisements (1838–1839) at **www.myhistorylab.com**

Harriet Tubman was 40 years old when this photograph (later hand-tinted) was taken. Already famous for her daring rescues, she gained further fame by serving as a scout, spy, and nurse during the Civil War.

African religions managed to survive from the earliest days of slavery in forms that white people considered as "superstition" or "folk belief." Religious ceremonies survived, too, in late-night gatherings deep in the woods where the sound of drumming, singing, and dancing could not reach white ears (see Chapter 4). In the nineteenth century, these African traditions allowed African Americans to reshape white Christianity into their own distinctive faith that expressed their deep resistance to slavery.

The Great Awakening, which swept the South after the 1760s, introduced many slaves to Christianity, often in mixed congregations with white people (see Chapter 5). The transformation was completed by **The Second Great Awakening**, which took root among black and white Southerners in the 1790s. The number of African American converts, preachers, and lay teachers grew rapidly, and a distinctive form of Christianity took shape. Free African Americans founded their own independent churches and denominations. The first African American Baptist and Methodist churches were founded in Philadelphia in 1794 by the Reverend Absalom Jones and the Reverend Richard Allen. In 1816, the Reverend Allen joined with African American ministers from other cities to form the African Methodist Episcopal (AME) denomination.

Many southern slave owners expected Christianity to make their slaves obedient and peaceful. Forbidding their slaves to hold their own religious gatherings, owners insisted that their slaves attend white church services. On many plantations, slaves attended religious services with their masters every Sunday, sitting quietly in the back of the church or in the balcony, as the minister preached messages justifying slavery and urging obedience. But at night, away from white eyes, they held their own prayer meetings.

African Americans found in Christianity a powerful vehicle to express their longings for freedom and justice. In churches and in spontaneous religious expressions, the black community made Christianity its own. Fusing Christian texts with African elements of group activity, such as the circle dance, the call-and-response pattern, and, above all, group singing, black people created a unique community religion full of emotion, enthusiasm, and protest.

OTHER KINDS OF RESISTANCE

The rapid geographical spread of cotton introduced a new source of tension and resistance into the slave–master relationship. White Southerners did everything they could to prevent escapes and rebellions. Slave patrols were a common sight on southern roads: any black person without a pass from his or her master was captured (usually roughly) and returned home to certain punishment. But despite almost certain recapture, slaves continued to flee and to help others do the same. Escaped slave Harriet Tubman of Maryland, who made twelve rescue missions freeing sixty to seventy slaves in all, had extraordinary determination and skill. As a female runaway, she was unusual, too: most escapees were young men, for women often had small children they were unable to take and unwilling to leave behind.

Much more common was the practice of "running away nearby." Slaves who knew they could not reach freedom still frequently demonstrated their desire for liberty or their discontent over mistreatment by taking unauthorized leave from their plantation. Hidden in nearby forests or swamps, provided with food smuggled by other slaves from the plantation, the runaway might return home after a week or so, often to rather mild punishment.

SLAVE REVOLTS

The ultimate resistance, however, was the slave revolt. Southern history was dotted with stories of former slave conspiracies and rumors of current plots (see Chapter 4). Every white Southerner knew about the last-minute failure of Gabriel Prosser's insurrection in Richmond in 1800 and the chance discovery of Denmark Vesey's plot in Charleston in 1822. But when in 1831, Nat Turner actually started a rebellion in which a number of white people were killed, southern fears were greatly magnified.

A literate man, Nat Turner was a lay preacher, but he was also a slave. It was Turner's intelligence and strong religious commitment that made him a leader in the slave community. Turner began plotting his revolt after a religious vision in which he saw "white spirits and black spirits engaged in battle"; "the sun was darkened—the thunder rolled in the Heavens, and blood flowed in streams."

Turner and five other slaves struck on the night of August 20, 1831. Moving from plantation to plantation and killing a total of fifty-five white people, the rebels numbered sixty by the next morning, when they fled from a group of armed white men. More than forty blacks were executed after the revolt, including Turner, who was captured accidentally after he had hidden for two months in the woods.

Gabriel's Rebellion, the Denmark Vesey plot, and Nat Turner's revolt were the most prominent examples of organized slave resistance, but they were far from the only ones. Conspiracies and actual or rumored slave resistance began in colonial times (see Chapter 4) and never ceased. These plots exposed the truth white Southerners preferred to ignore: only force kept Africans and African Americans enslaved, and because no system of control could ever be total, white Southerners could never be completely safe from the possibility of revolt.

FREE AFRICAN AMERICANS

Another source of white disquiet was the growing number of free African Americans. By 1860, nearly 250,000 free black people lived in the South. For most, freedom dated from before 1800, when antislavery feeling among slave owners in the Upper South was widespread and cotton cultivation had yet to boom.

After 1830, manumission was virtually impossible throughout the South. In the 1830s, state legislatures tightened **black codes**—laws concerning free black people. Free African Americans could not carry firearms, could not purchase slaves (unless they were members of their own family), and were liable to the criminal penalties meted out to slaves (that is, whippings and summary judgments without a jury trial). They could not testify against whites, hold office, vote, or serve in the militia. In other words, except for

This drawing shows the moment, almost two months after the failure of his famous and bloody slave revolt, when Nat Turner was accidentally discovered in the woods near his home plantation. Turner's cool murder of his owner and methodical organization of his revolt deeply frightened many white Southerners.

⊷ Read the Document

The Confession of Nat Turner (1831) at
www.myhistorylab.com

Black codes   Laws passed by states and municipalities denying many rights of citizenship to free black people.

One of the ways Charleston attempted to control its African American population was to require all slaves to wear badges showing their occupation. After 1848, free black people also had to wear badges, which were decorated, ironically, with a liberty cap.

the right to own property, free blacks had no civil rights. White people increasingly feared the influence free black people might have on slaves, for free African Americans were a living challenge to the slave system. Their very existence disproved the basic southern equations of white equals free, and black equals slave. No one believed more fervently in those equations than the South's largest population group, white people who did not own slaves.

THE WHITE MAJORITY

WHAT WERE the values of yeoman farmers?

The pervasive influence of the slave system in the South is reflected in the startling contrast of two facts: two-thirds of all Southerners did not own slaves, yet slave owners dominated the social and political life of the region. Although slave owners occupied the most productive land, the poor white people and small farmers occupied the rest of the rural land, and a small middle class lived in the cities of the South.

POOR WHITE PEOPLE

From 30 to 50 percent of all southern white people were landless, a proportion similar to that in the North. But the existence of slavery limited the opportunities for poor white people. Slaves made up the permanent, stable workforce in agriculture and in many skilled trades. Many poor white people led highly transient lives in search of work, such as farm labor at harvest time, which was only temporary. Others were tenant farmers working under share-tenancy arrangements that kept them in debt to the landowner.

Relationships between poor whites and black slaves were complex. White men and women often worked side by side with black slaves in the fields and were socially and sexually intimate with enslaved and free African Americans. White people engaged in clandestine trade to supply slaves with items like liquor that slave owners prohibited, helped slaves to escape, and even (in an 1835 Mississippi case) were executed for their participation in planning a slave revolt. At the same time, the majority of poor white people insisted, sometimes violently, on their racial superiority over blacks. For their part, many African American slaves, better dressed, better nourished, and healthier, dismissed them as "poor white trash." But the fact was that the difficult lives of poor whites served to blur the crucial racial distinction between independent whites and supposedly inferior, dependent black people on which the system of slavery rested.

SOUTHERN "PLAIN FOLK"

The word "**yeoman**," originally a British term for a farmer who works his own land, is often applied to independent farmers of the South, most of whom lived on family-sized farms. Southerners themselves referred to them as "plain folk." Although yeoman farmers sometimes owned a few slaves, in general they and their families worked their land by themselves. Typical of the yeoman-farmer community was northwestern Georgia, once home to the Creeks and Cherokees, but now populated by communities of small farmers who grew enough vegetables to feed their families, including corn, which they either ate themselves or fed to hogs. In addition, these farmers raised enough cotton every year to bring in a little cash. At least 60 percent owned their own farms.

Just as elsewhere in the South, family was the mainstay of community. Farm men and women depended on their relatives and neighbors for assistance in large farm tasks such as planing, harvesting, and construction. Farmers repaid this help and obtained needed goods through complex systems of barter with other members of the community. One of the key items in the community barter system was the labor of slaves, who were frequently loaned out to neighbors by small slave owners to fulfill an obligation to another farmer.

yeoman Independent farmers of the South, most of whom lived on family-sized farms.

Where yeomen and large slave owners lived side by side, as in the Georgia black belt where cotton was the major crop, slavery again provided a link between the rich and the "plain folk." Large plantation owners often bought food for their slaves from small local farmers, ground the latter's corn in the plantation mill, ginned their cotton, and transported and marketed it as well. But although planters and much smaller yeomen were part of a larger community network, in the black belt the large slave owners were clearly dominant. Only in their own up-country communities did yeomen feel truly independent.

Many southern yeomen lived apart from large slaveholders in the up-country regions where plantation agriculture was unsuitable. The very high value southern yeomen placed on freedom grew directly from their own experience as self-sufficient property-owning farmers in small, family-based communities, and from the absolute, patriarchal control they exercised over their own wives and children. This was a way of life that southern "plain folk" were determined to preserve. It made them resistant to the economic opportunities and challenges that capitalism and industrialization posed for northern farmers, which southern yeomen perceived as encroachments on their freedom.

Yeoman farmer Robert Smith, who owned 11 slaves and 800 acres, was much wealthier than most other yeoman, but like them he conducted a mixed farming and grazing operation. Today, the Tullie Smith house and its many outbuildings is preserved as a living history farm at the Atlanta History Center as a reminder to visitors that yeoman farms were much more common in Georgia than large single-crop plantations.

The irony was that the freedom yeomen so prized rested on slavery. Slavery meant that all white people, rich and poor, were equal in the sense that they were all free. This belief in white skin privilege had begun in the eighteenth century as slavery became the answer to the South's labor problem (see Chapter 4). The democratization of politics in the early nineteenth century and the enactment of nearly universal white manhood suffrage perpetuated the belief in white skin privilege, even though the gap between rich and poor white people was widening.

THE MIDDLING RANKS

In the predominantly rural South, cities provided a home for a small commercial middle class of merchants, bankers, factors (agents), and lawyers on whom the agricultural economy depended to sell its produce to a world market. Adding to them small businessmen such as shopkeepers, teachers, doctors and ministers, the professional class as a whole made up about ten percent of the population. Urban growth lagged far behind the North, but increased rapidly in the 1840s and the 1850s. Although many scorned the "backwardness" of the plantation elite and yeoman farmers, these middle class Southerners were not abolitionists. Indeed, most believed that the slave system was essential to maintaining social peace as industrialization went forward.

Many southern planters scorned members of the commercial middle class because they had to please their suppliers and customers and thus lacked, in planter's eyes, true independence. This was an attitude strikingly different from that in the North, where the commercial acumen of the middle class was increasingly valued (see Chapter 12).

> ### QUICK REVIEW
>
> **Yeoman Farmers**
>
> - Most independent farmers in the South lived on family farms.
> - Farmers formed tight networks of friends and family.
> - Slavery linked large planters and yeoman farmers.

PLANTERS

WHO MADE up the planter elite?

Remarkably few slave owners fit the popular stereotype of the rich and leisured plantation owner with hundreds of acres of land and hundreds of slaves. Only 36 percent of southern white people owned slaves in 1830, and only 2.5 percent owned fifty slaves or more. Just as yeomen and poor whites were diverse, so, too, were southern slave owners (see Figure 10.3).

SMALL SLAVE OWNERS

The largest group of slave owners was small yeomen taking the step from subsistence agriculture to commercial production. To do this in the South's agricultural economy, they had to own slaves. But getting a secure footing on the bottom rung of the slave-owner ladder was very difficult. In good economic times, the owner might buy a new slave or two, but a poor crop or a downturn in cotton prices could wipe out his gains and force him to sell all of his slaves. The roller-coaster economy of the early nineteenth century did not help matters, and the Panic of 1837 was a serious setback to many small farmers.

For a smaller group of slave owners, the economic struggle was not so hard. Middle-class professional men frequently managed to become large slave owners because they already had capital (the pay from their professions) to invest in land and slaves. These owners were the most likely to own skilled slaves—carpenters, blacksmiths, and other artisans—and to rent them out for profit. By steady accumulation, the most successful members of this middle class were able to buy their way into the slave-owning elite and to confirm that position by marrying their sons or daughters into the aristocracy.

THE PLANTER ELITE

The slave-owning elite, those 2.5 percent who owned fifty slaves or more, enjoyed the prestige, the political leadership, and the lifestyle to which many white Southerners aspired. Almost all great slave owners inherited their wealth. They were rarely self-made men, although most tried to add to the land and slaves they had inherited. Men of wealth and property had led southern politics since colonial times. Increasingly after 1820, as universal manhood suffrage spread, planters had to learn how to appeal to the popular vote, but most never acquired "the common touch." The smaller slave owners, not the great planters, formed a clear majority in every southern state legislature.

The eastern seaboard had first given rise to a class of rich planters in the colonial period. As Southerners and slave owning spread westward, membership in the elite broadened to include the new wealth of Alabama, Mississippi, Louisiana, and Texas. Natchez, on the Mississippi River, became so wealthy that its rich planters were popularly called "nabobs" (from a Hindi word for Europeans who had amassed fabulous wealth in India).

CREATING A PLANTATION IDEOLOGY

Many wealthy planters, especially those on new lands in the Old Southwest, lived in isolation on their plantations with their families and slaves. The small new planter elite consciously worked to create and maintain a distinctive lifestyle that was modeled on that of the English aristocracy, as Southerners understood it. This entailed a large estate, a spacious, elegant mansion, and lavish hospitality. For men, the gentlemanly lifestyle meant immersion in masculine activities such as hunting, soldiering, or politics, and a touchy concern with "honor" that could lead to duels and other acts of bravado. Women of the slave-owning elite, in contrast, were expected to be gentle, charming, and always welcoming of relatives, friends, and other guests.

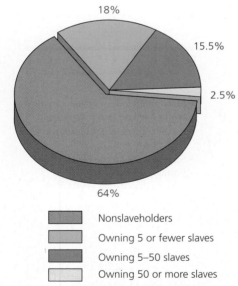

18%

15.5%

2.5%

64%

- Nonslaveholders
- Owning 5 or fewer slaves
- Owning 5–50 slaves
- Owning 50 or more slaves

Figure 10.3 Slaveholding and Class Structure in the South, 1830

The great majority of the southern white population was yeoman farmers. In 1830, slave owners made up only 36 percent of the southern white population; owners of more than fifty slaves constituted a tiny 2.5 percent. Yet they and the others who were middling planters dominated politics, retaining the support of yeomen who prized their freedom as white men above class-based politics.

U.S. Bureau of the Census.

The economic reality of plantation life was that large numbers of black slaves had to be forced to work to produce the wealth that supported the planters' gracious lifestyle. Each plantation aimed to be self-sufficient, producing not only the cash crop but also most of the food and clothing for both slaves and family. There were stables full of horses for plowing, transportation, and show. There were livestock and vegetable gardens to be tended, and carpentry, blacksmithing, weaving, and sewing to be done. A large plantation was an enterprise that required many hands, many skills, and a lot of management. Large plantation owners might have overseers or black drivers to supervise field work, but frequently they themselves had direct financial control of daily operations.

Plantation mistresses spent most of their lives tending "family" members—including slaves—in illness and in childbirth, and supervising their slaves' performance of such daily tasks as cooking, housecleaning, weaving, and sewing. In addition, the plantation mistress often had to spend hours, even days, of behind-the-scenes preparation for the crowds of guests she was expected to welcome in her role as elegant and gracious hostess.

Many southern women also suffered deeply from their isolation from friends and kin. Sometimes the isolation of life on rural plantations could be overcome by long visits, but women with many small children and extensive responsibilities found it difficult to leave. Plantation masters, on the other hand, often traveled widely for political and business reasons. John C. Calhoun, for example, spent much less time than his wife on the family plantation, Fort Hill. He spent years in Washington as a politician, while Floride Calhoun, who had accompanied him in his early career, remained at Fort Hill after the first five of their ten children were born.

The planter elite developed a paternalistic ideology to justify their rigorous insistence on the master–slave relationship. According to this ideology, each plantation was a family composed of both black and white. The master, as head of the plantation, was head of the family, and the mistress was his "helpmate." The master was obligated to provide for all of his family, both black and white, and to treat them with humanity. In return, slaves were to work properly and do as they were told, as children would. Most elite slave owners spoke of their position of privilege as a duty and a burden. Convinced of their own benevolence, slave owners expected not only obedience but also gratitude from all members of their great "families."

COERCION AND VIOLENCE

There were generous and benevolent masters, but most large slave owners believed that constant discipline and coercion were necessary to make slaves work hard (see Seeing History). Some slave owners used their slaves with great brutality. Owners who killed slaves were occasionally brought to trial (and usually acquitted), but no legal action was taken in the much more frequent cases of excessive punishment, general abuse, and rape. All southern slave owners, not just those who experienced the special tensions of new and isolated plantations in the Old Southwest, were engaged in a constant battle of wills with their slaves that owners frequently resolved by violence.

One of the most common violations of the paternalistic code of behavior (and of southern law) was the sexual abuse of female slaves by their masters. Usually, masters forcibly raped

Read the **Document**

Overseer's Report from Chicora Wood Plantation (1858) at **www.myhistorylab.com**

QUICK REVIEW

Plantation Mistresses

- Mistresses ran the household staff.
- Mistresses were responsible for arrangements for visitors.
- Husbands were usually the real authority on the plantation.

SCENE ON A COTTON PLANTATION. GATHERING COTTON.

The gang system used in cotton cultivation necessitated overseers to keep the gang at work. Hence scenes like this where slaves work hard to pick and bale cotton while white overseers with whips stand lazily.

"Gordon under Medical Inspection"

This horrifying image of the badly scarred back of a former slave named Gordon appeared in *Harper's Weekly* in July 1863. He was an escaped slave who entered Union lines in Baton Rouge in March 1863, arriving in the bedraggled condition shown on the left. Under medical examination, he revealed the scars from a whipping three months earlier. As the third picture shows, he promptly joined the Union Army.

AFTER VIEWING this image, how seriously would you consider claims that southern slavery was a benign, paternalistic system?

Although abolitionist literature frequently described brutal whippings endured by slaves, few people in the North can have seen such graphic examples before the publication of this article in 1863. A photographic image of "The Scourged Back" is one of the earliest examples of the impact of photography as propaganda. Since that time, the picture of Gordon's back has frequently been used to illustrate the violence of the slave system. There is no question that whipping was a frequent punishment in the slaveholding South and that masters, mistresses, and overseers, in fits of temper, whipped harshly. Although we do not know if Gordon's scars were representative, the image makes it impossible to deny the reality of brutality in the slave system. ■

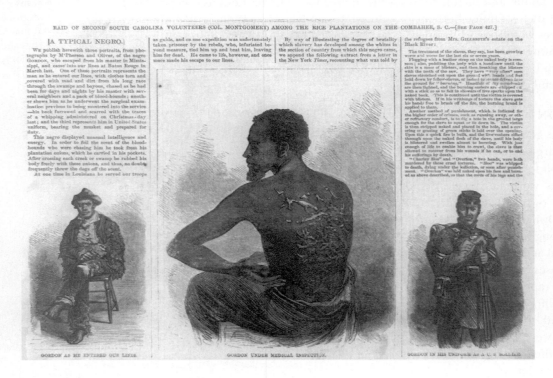

their women slaves at will, and slave women had little hope of defending themselves from these attacks. Occasionally long-term intimate relationships between masters and slaves developed, such as the one that apparently existed between Thomas Jefferson and Sally Hemmings.

It was rare for slave owners to publicly acknowledge fathering slave children or to free these children, and black women and their families were helpless to protest their treatment. Equally silenced was the master's wife, who for reasons of modesty as well as her subordinate position was not supposed to notice either her husband's infidelity or his flagrant crossing of the color lines.

Perhaps as common but veiled by the gentle female stereotype was the daily violence practiced by plantation mistresses. House servants bore the brunt of the brunt of petty and persistent punishment by their mistresses, and personal servants often suffered mental cruelty. Although on every plantation black women served as nursemaids to white children and as lifelong maids to white women, there are few historical examples of genuine sympathy between women across racial lines. Few white women seemed to realize the sadness, frustration and despair often experienced by their lifelong maids, who were forced to leave their own husbands and children to serve their mistresses as they married and moved to new homes. Years later many former slaves remembered their mistresses as being kinder than their masters, but fully a third of such accounts mention cruel whippings and other punishments by women.

An owner could do what he chose on his plantation, and his sons and daughters grew up expecting to do likewise. Unchecked power is always dangerous, and it is not surprising that it was frequently misused, often in the name of "discipline." Perhaps the most surprising thing about the southern slave system is how much humanity survived despite the intolerable conditions. For that, most of the credit goes not to white paternalism, but to African Americans and the communities they created under slavery.

THE DEFENSE OF SLAVERY

66 "Slavery informs all our modes of life, all our habits of thought, lies at the basis of our social existence, and of our political faith," announced South Carolina planter William Henry Trescot in 1850, explaining why the South would secede from the Union before giving up slavery. Slavery bound white and black Southerners together in tortuous ways that eventually led, as Trescot had warned, to the Civil War. Population figures tell much of the story of the complex relationship between whites and blacks: of the 12 million people who lived in the South in 1860, 4 million were slaves. These sheer numbers of African Americans reinforced white people's perpetual fears of black retaliation for the violence exercised by the slave master. Every rumor of slave revolts, real or imagined, kept those fears alive.

WHAT PROSLAVERY arguments were developed in the first half of the nineteenth century?

DEVELOPING PROSLAVERY ARGUMENTS

Once the cotton boom began in the 1790s, Southerners increasingly sought to justify slavery. They found justifications for slavery in the Bible and in the histories of Greece and Rome, both slave-owning societies. The strongest defense was a legal one: the Constitution allowed slavery. Though never specifically mentioned in the final document, slavery had been a major issue between North and South at the Constitutional Convention in 1787. In the end, the delegates agreed that seats in the House of Representatives would be apportioned by counting all of the white population and three-fifths of the black people (Article I, Section 2, Paragraph 3); they included a clause requiring the return of runaway slaves who had crossed state lines (Article IV, Section 2, Paragraph 3); and they agreed that Congress could not abolish the international slave

trade for twenty years (Article I, Section 9, Paragraph 1). There was absolutely no question: the Constitution did recognize slavery. Just as important, but unwritten, was the implicit understanding in 1787 that slavery was a sectional problem that Southern politicians, not the federal government, would work to eliminate. That unvoiced agreement, of course, occurred before cotton became the South's economic mainspring.

The Missouri Crisis of 1819–20 deeply alarmed most Southerners, who were shocked by the evidence of widespread antislavery feeling in the North, and northern willingness to intervene in southern politics. South Carolinians viewed **Denmark Vesey's conspiracy**, occurring only two years after the Missouri debate, as an example of the harm that irresponsible northern antislavery talk could cause. In the wake of the Vesey conspiracy, Charlestonians turned their fear and anger outward by attempting to seal off the city from dangerous outside influences. In December 1822, the South Carolina legislature passed a bill requiring that all black seamen be seized and jailed while their ships were in Charleston harbor.

After **Nat Turner's revolt** in 1831, Governor John Floyd of Virginia blamed the uprising on "Yankee peddlers and traders" who supposedly told slaves that "all men were born free and equal." Thus, northern antislavery opinion and the fear of slave uprisings were firmly linked in southern minds. This extreme reaction, which Northerners viewed as paranoid, stemmed from the basic nature of a slave society: *anything* that challenged the master–slave relationship was viewed as a basic threat to the entire system.

AFTER NAT TURNER

In 1831, the South began to close ranks in defense of slavery. Several factors contributed to this regional solidarity. Nat Turner's revolt was important, linked as it was in the minds of many Southerners with antislavery agitation from the North. Militant abolitionist William Lloyd Garrison began publishing the *Liberator*, the newspaper that was to become the leading antislavery organ, in 1831. The British gave notice that they would soon abolish slavery on the sugar plantations of the West Indies, an action that seemed to many Southerners much too close to home. Emancipation for West Indian slaves came in 1834. Finally, 1831 was the year before the Nullification Crisis (see Chapter 11) was resolved.

Although the other southern states did not support the hotheaded South Carolinians who called for secession, they did sympathize with the argument that the federal government had no right to interfere with a state's special interest (namely, slavery). Following the crisis, other southern states joined with South Carolina in the belief that the only effective way to prevent other federal encroachment was through the militant and vehement defense of slavery.

In the 1830s, southern states began to barricade themselves against "outside" antislavery propaganda. In 1835, a crowd broke into a Charleston post office, made off with bundles of antislavery literature, and set an enormous bonfire to fervent state and regional acclaim. By 1835, every southern legislature had tightened its laws concerning control of slaves. For example, they tried to blunt the effect of abolitionist literature by passing laws forbidding slaves to learn how to read. In only three border states— Kentucky, Tennessee, and Maryland—did slave literacy remain legal. By 1860, it is estimated, only 5 percent of all slaves could read. Slaves were forbidden to gather for dances, religious services, or any kind of organized social activity without a white person present. They were forbidden to have whiskey because it might encourage them toward revolt. The penalty for plotting insurrection was death. Other laws made manumission illegal and placed even more restrictions on the lives of free black people. In many areas, slave patrols were augmented and became more vigilant in restricting African American movement and communication between plantations.

In 1836, Southerners introduced a "gag rule" in Washington to prevent congressional consideration of abolitionist petitions. Attempts were made to stifle all open

Denmark Vesey's conspiracy   The most carefully devised slave revolt in which rebels planned to seize control of Charleston in 1822 and escape to freedom in Haiti, a free black republic, but they were betrayed by other slaves, and seventy-five conspirators were executed.

Nat Turner's Revolt   Uprising of slaves in Southampton County, Virginia, in the summer of 1831 led by Nat Turner that resulted in the death of fifty-five white people.

debate about slavery within the South; dissenters were pressured to remain silent or to leave. A few, such as James G. Birney and Sarah and Angelina Grimké of South Carolina, left for the North to act on their antislavery convictions, but most chose silence.

In addition to fueling fears of slave rebellions, the growing abolitionist sentiment of the 1830s raised the worry that southern opportunities for expansion would be cut off. Southern politicians painted melodramatic pictures of a beleaguered white South hemmed in on all sides by "fanatic" antislavery states. At home, Southerners were forced to contemplate what might happen when they had "to let loose among them, freed from the wholesome restraints of patriarchal authority . . . an idle, worthless, profligate set of free negroes" whom they feared would "prowl the . . . streets at night and [haunt] the woods during the day armed with whatever weapons they could lay their hands on."

Finally, southern apologists moved beyond defensiveness to develop proslavery arguments. One of the first to do this was James Henry Hammond, elected a South Carolina congressman in 1834. In 1836, Hammond delivered a major address to Congress in which he denied that slavery was evil. Rather, he claimed, it had produced "the highest toned, the purest, best organization of society that has ever existed on the face of the earth." In 1838, Senator John C. Calhoun of South Carolina took the argument a step further by claiming that slavery was "the most safe and stable basis for free institutions in the world" because it subordinated an "inferior" race to benevolent white paternalists devoted to their wellbeing and moral improvement. In 1858, another southern spokesman, George Fitzhugh, asserted that "the negro slaves of the South are the happiest, and, in some sense, the freest people in the world" because all the responsibility for their care was borne by concerned white masters. Fitzhugh contrasted southern paternalism with the heartless individualism that ruled the lives of northern "wage slaves."

CHANGES IN THE SOUTH

In spite of these defensive and repressive proslavery measures, which made the South seem monolithic in northern eyes, there were some surprising indicators of dissent. One protest occurred in the Virginia state legislature in 1832, when nonslaveholding delegates, alarmed by the Nat Turner rebellion, forced a two-week debate on the merits of gradual abolition. In the final vote, abolition was defeated seventy-three to fifty-eight. Although the subject was never raised again, this debate was a startling indicator of frequently unvoiced doubts about slavery that existed in the South.

But slavery was not a static system. From the 1830s on, financial changes increasingly underlined class differences among southern whites. It was much harder to become a slaveholder: from 1830 to 1860, slave owners declined from 36 to 25 percent of the population. In 1860, the average slaveholder was ten times as wealthy as the average nonslaveholder. A major reason for the shrinking number of slave owners and their increased wealth was the rapidly increasing price of slaves: a "prime field hand" was worth more than $1,500 in 1855. Such prices caused the internal slave trade to flourish: during the 1850s, slave owners from the Upper South sold some 250,000 slaves to the Lower South for handsome profits. By 1850, in the Chesapeake (Virginia, Maryland, and Delaware), where American slavery had its origin, the percentage of slave owners had fallen to 28 percent, while the comparable figures for Louisiana and Mississippi were 45 percent. Agriculture was diversifying in the Upper South, while the plantation system flourished in the Lower South, as indicated by the fact that 85 percent of the great planters with more than a hundred slaves lived there. Such differences in the extent of slaveholding between the Upper and Lower South threatened regional political unity (see Map 10.4).

Another alarming trend was the disintegration of the slave system in southern cities. The number of urban slaves greatly decreased because plantation owners deeply distrusted the effect of cities on the institution of slavery. Urban slaves led much more

Read the Document

George Fitzhugh, Slavery Justified (1854)
at **www.myhistorylab.com**

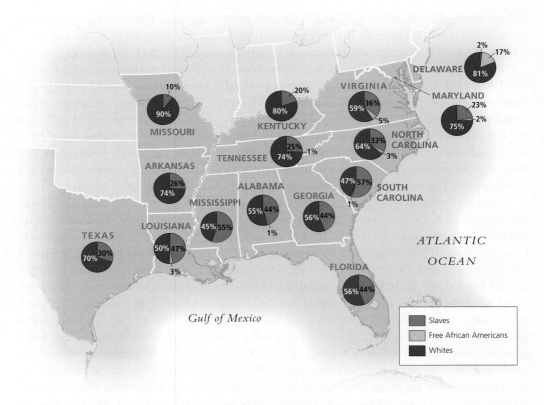

MAP 10.4

Population Patterns in the South, 1850 In South Carolina and Mississippi, the enslaved African American population outnumbered the white population; in four other Lower South states, the percentage was above 40 percent. These ratios frightened many white Southerners. White people also feared the free black population, though only three states in the Upper South and Louisiana had free black populations of over 3 percent. Six states had free black populations that were so small (less than 1 percent) as to be statistically insignificant.

WHERE WERE the greatest concentrations of African Americans? How would you explain the patterns the map reveals?

informed lives than rural ones and were often in daily contact with free blacks and urban poor whites. Many slaves were hired out and a number even hired out their own time, making them nearly indistinguishable from northern "free labor." Other urban slaves worked in commercial and industrial enterprises in jobs that were nearly indistinguishable from those of whites. Planters viewed all of these changes with suspicion, yet they also had to acknowledge that southern cities were successful and bustling centers of commerce.

Economic changes adversely affected poor whites and yeomen as well. Increased commercialization of agriculture (other than cotton) led to higher land prices that made it harder for poor whites to buy or rent land. Extensive railroad building in up-country regions during the boom of the 1850s ended the isolation of many yeomen, exposing them for the first time to the temptations and dangers of the market economy. While slave owners grew increasingly worried about threats from the abolitionist and capitalist North, yeomen worried about local threats to their independence from banks, railroads, and activist state governments. In North Carolina, disputes between slave owners and nonslaveholders erupted in print in 1857, when Hinton Helper published an attack on slavery in a book titled *The Impending Crisis*. His protest was an indicator of the growing tensions between the haves and the have-nots in the South. Equally significant, though,

CHRONOLOGY

1790s	The Second Great Awakening
	Black Baptist and African Methodist Episcopal churches founded
1793	Cotton gin invented
1800	Gabriel Prosser's revolt discovered in Virginia
1806	Virginia tightens law on manumission of slaves
1808	Congress prohibits U.S. participation in the international slave trade
1816–20	"Alabama Fever": migration to the Old Southwest
1819–20	Missouri Crisis
1822	Denmark Vesey's conspiracy in Charleston
1831	Nat Turner's revolt in Virginia
	William Lloyd Garrison begins publishing an antislavery newspaper, the *Liberator*
1832	Nullification Crisis
1832–38	"Flush Times": second wave of westward expansion
1832	Virginia legislature debates and defeats a measure for gradual emancipation
1834	Britain frees slaves throughout the empire, including in its Caribbean colonies
1835	Charleston crowd burns abolitionist literature
	Tightening of black codes completed by southern legislatures
1836	Congress passes "gag rule" to prevent discussion of antislavery petitions
	James Henry Hammond announces to Congress that slavery is not evil
1846	William Gregg opens model textile mill at Graniteville, South Carolina
1854	George Fitzhugh publishes *Sociology for the South*, a defense of slavery
1857	Hinton Helper publishes *The Impending Crisis*, an attack on slavery
1858	James Henry Hammond's "King Cotton" speech

Helper's book was published in New York, where he was forced to move once his views became known.

In spite of these signs of tension and dissent, the main lines of the southern argument were drawn in the 1830s and remained fixed thereafter. The defense of slavery stifled debate within the South, prevented a search for alternative labor systems, and narrowed the possibility of cooperation in national politics. In time, it made compromise impossible.

CONCLUSION

The amazing growth of cotton production after 1793 transformed the South and the nation. Physically, the South expanded explosively westward: in all, seven southern states were admitted to the Union between 1800 and 1845. Cotton production fastened the slave system of labor upon the region. Although the international slave trade was abolished in 1808, the internal slave trade flourished, with devastating effects on African American families. Nationally, the profitable cotton trade fueled economic development and provided much of the original capital for the infant factory system of the North. Cotton production was based on the labor of African American slaves, who built strong communities under extremely difficult circumstances. The cohesion of African American families and the powerful faith of African American Christianity were the key community elements that bred a spirit of endurance and resistance. White Southerners, two-thirds of whom did not own slaves, denied their real dependence on slave labor by claiming equality in white skin privilege, while slave owners boasted of their own paternalism. But the extreme fear generated by a handful of slave revolts and the growing number of free African Americans in many areas gave the lie to white claims of benevolence. In the 1830s, the South defensively closed ranks against real and perceived threats to the slave system. In this sense, the white South was nearly as trapped as the African American slaves they claimed to control. And in its growing concern for the defense of the slave system, the South's role in national politics became more rigid, as we shall see in the next chapter.

REVIEW QUESTIONS

1. How did cotton production after 1793 transform the social and political history of the South? How did the rest of the nation benefit? In what way was it an "international phenomenon"?

2. What were the two key institutions of the African American slave community? How did they function, and what beliefs did they express?

3. The circumstances of two groups—poor whites and free African Americans—put them outside the dominant southern equations of white equals free and black equals slave. Analyze the difficulty each group encountered in the slave-owning South.

4. Who were the yeoman farmers? What was their interest in slavery?

5. Southern slaveholders claimed that their paternalism justified their ownership of slaves, but paternalism implied obligations as well as privileges. How well do you think slaveholders lived up to their paternalistic obligations?

6. How did slave owners justify slavery? How did their defense change over time?

KEY TERMS

Black codes (p. 241)
Denmark Vesey's conspiracy (p. 248)
Gang System (p. 237)
Industrial Revolution (p. 232)

Manumission (p. 236)
Nat Turner's Revolt (p. 248)
The Second Great Awakening (p. 240)
Yeoman (p. 242)

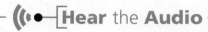
myhistorylab Connections

Reinforce what you learned in this chapter by studying the many documents, images, maps, review tools, and videos available at www.myhistorylab.com.

Read and Review

✓● [Study and Review Chapter 10

●●● [Read the Document

Thomas Jefferson, Notes on Virginia (1787)

State Laws Govern Slavery (1824)

A Slave Tells of His Sale at Auction (1848)

Frances E.W. Harper, The Slave Auction (1854)

Frances Ann Kemble, Journal of a Residence on a Georgia Plantation (1838)

A Catechism for Slaves (1854)

Slave Culture Documented in Song (1867)

Runaway Slave Advertisements (1838–1839)

The Confession of Nat Turner (1831)

Overseer's Report from Chicora Wood Plantation (1858)

George Fitzhugh, Slavery Justified (1854)

👁 [See the Map *United States Territorial Expansion in the 1850s*

Research and Explore

●●● [Read the Document

Exploring America: Alexis de Tocqueville

Profiles
  Hinton Rowan Helper
  Harriet Jacobs

[Watch the Video *The Plantation System*

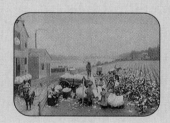

(((●● [**Hear** the **Audio**

Hear the audio files for Chapter 10 at
www.myhistorylab.com.

I blush for my country when I see such things, and I often tremble with apprehension that our Constitution will not long withstand the current which threatens to overwhelm it . . .

—Benjamin B. French, September 1828

Andrew Jackson speaking to a crowd after his election. Politics in the olden time— General Jackson, President-elect, on his way to Washington.

11

THE GROWTH OF DEMOCRACY
1824–1840

((•—[**Hear** the **Audio**

Hear the audio files for Chapter 11 at **www.myhistorylab.com**.

WHAT WERE the consequences of the expansion of suffrage to include the majority of adult white males?

WHAT STEPS did Andrew Jackson take to strengthen the executive branch of the federal government?

WHAT WERE Andrew Jackson's most important policy objectives?

HOW DID the Second Party System differ from the First Party System?

HOW DID Americans create their own cultural identity in the first half of the nineteenth century?

AMERICAN COMMUNITIES
A Political Community Abandons
Deference for Democracy

PHILADELPHIA HAD LONG BEEN A STRONGHOLD OF CRAFT ASSOCIATIONS FOR skilled workers. Their organizations, and their parades and celebrations, were recognized parts of the urban community. Pennsylvania enfranchised all men who were taxpayers in 1776, enabling many of Philadelphia's skilled workers to vote, but they were willing to follow the leadership of the city's political elite. This was the accepted rule of republican government as understood by leaders such as Thomas Jefferson: an independent and virtuous people willingly deferred to wealthy and enlightened leaders who would govern in the public interest. In reality, most states limited the vote to property owners, and so many ordinary men had little choice but to accept the decisions of the wealthy.

By the 1820s, the lives of workers in Philadelphia had changed. As the Market Revolution transformed the economy, many skilled workers lost their independence and became wage earners in factories owned by others. Members of urban workers' associations realized that their own economic interests were different from those of the owners. In other states, where many men gained the vote for the first time in the 1820s, a similar process of identifying common interests at odds with the traditional political elite was also underway. The spread of universal manhood suffrage marked the transition from traditional deferential politics to democracy.

In 1827, the British-born shoemaker William Heighton urged his fellow workers in Philadelphia to band together and form their own political party to press for issues of direct concern to workingmen, including the ten-hour day, free public education for their children, the end of imprisonment for debt, and curbing the powers of banks. Until producers (by which he meant both urban workers and rural farmers) united and formed their own political party, Heighton warned, politicians would continue to ignore their concerns.

In response to Heighton's call, the Philadelphia Working Men's Party was formed in 1828 and elected a slate of local officials as well as voting for Andrew Jackson for president. Andrew Jackson, who was so untraditional that at first national politicians did not take him seriously as a candidate, perfectly personified the new democratic mood and its animosity toward what was often termed "the monied aristocracy."

Thus, when a committee of the Philadelphia Working Men's Party attacked the banking system in 1829, Andrew Jackson paid attention. Their report decried the control by wealthy men of banks and of the paper money each bank issued (there was no national government-controlled currency until 1862). This fear of the threat to democracy from a moneyed aristocracy was common among voters in rural areas of the South and West as well as in urban areas. Jackson not only understood this public resentment, but he also shared it. In 1832 he had Philadelphia's workers and others in mind when, speaking for "the humble members of society—the farmers, mechanics and laborers," he refused to renew the charter of the Bank of the United States and thereby instigated the events that we call the **Bank War**.

The Philadelphia Working Men's Party did not last very long. Nevertheless, its brief history is significant for marking the end of traditional ideas about a unitary local political community and the transition to the more diverse and contentious community of competing interests that has characterized American democracy ever since. But it also set some limits. Politicians were quick to note that most Americans were uncomfortable with President Jackson's use of the language of class warfare in his veto message. Henceforth, whatever the competing interests might be, appeal to resentment alone was rarely successful. Rather, politicians sought to create national coalitions of voters with similar interests, creating new and more democratic political communities than had existed before.

Cahokia

Bank War   The political struggle between President Andrew Jackson and the supporters of the Second Bank of the United States.

THE NEW DEMOCRATIC POLITICS IN NORTH AMERICA

The early years of the nineteenth century were a time of extraordinary growth and change, not only for the United States but for all the countries of North America as well. Seen in continental perspective, the American embrace of popular democracy was unusual. Elsewhere, crises over popular rights dominated.

WHAT WERE the consequences of the expansion of suffrage to include the majority of adult white males?

STRUGGLES OVER POPULAR RIGHTS: MEXICO, THE CARIBBEAN, CANADA

In 1821, after eleven years of revolts (see Chapter 9), Mexico achieved its independence from Spain. Briefly united under the leadership of Colonel Agustin de Iturbide, Mexico declared itself a constitutional monarchy that promised equality for everyone—peninsulares, criollos, mestizos, and Indians alike. But because Spanish colonial rule had left a legacy of deep social divisions, the initial unity was short-lived. Iturbide reigned as Emperor of Mexico for little more than a year before he was overthrown by a military junta and later executed as a traitor. A series of weak presidents repeatedly invoked emergency powers and relied on the army, as they attempted to revive a faltering economy and reconcile the differences between competing groups and interests. The unresolved issue of elite versus popular rule continued to undermine the hope for unity, popular rights, and stable government in an independent Mexico.

The independence of Haiti in 1804 (see Chapter 9) set the pattern for events in many other Caribbean islands in subsequent years. Independence destroyed the sugar industry, for freed slaves asserted their popular rights by refusing to perform the killing labor demanded of them on sugar plantations. The British Caribbean islands were racked with revolts, the largest occurring on Barbados in 1816 and on Jamaica in 1831. In response the British Parliament abolished slavery in all British colonies in 1834. As in Haiti, sugar production then plunged. Economic collapse following emancipation destroyed the political authority of local white elites, forcing the British government to impose direct rule. This sequence of events—revolt, emancipation, economic collapse, loss of local political autonomy—was closely observed by slave owners in the American South and made them fear for their own futures.

Still a third crisis of popular rights occurred in British North America. In 1837, both Upper and Lower Canada rebelled against the limited representative government that the British government had imposed in the Constitutional Act of 1791. By far the most serious revolt was in predominantly French Lower Canada. In 1840, Britain abolished the local government of Lower Canada and joined it to Upper Canada in a union that most French Canadians opposed and in which they were a minority. In his report to the British government, Lord Durham announced that the purpose of union was to end the ethnic enmity between British and French by forcing the latter to assimilate and "abandon their vain hopes of nationality."

In comparison to these experiences, the rapid spread of suffrage in the United States and the growth of a democratic political culture seemed all the more extraordinary. But after a brilliant start, in the 1850s the United States, like its neighbors, foundered on a basic sectional difference—slavery—that not even political democracy could reconcile (see Chapter 15).

THE EXPANSION AND LIMITS OF SUFFRAGE

Before 1800, most of the original thirteen states had limited the vote to property owners or taxpayers, thereby excluding about half of the white male population. Westward expansion changed the nature of American politics by undermining the traditional authority structures in the older states (see Map 11.1).

MAP 11.1

Population Trends: Westward Expansion, 1830 Westward population movement, only a trickle in 1800, had become a flood by 1830. Between 1800 and 1830, the U.S. white and African American population more than doubled (from 5.3 million to 12.9 million), but the trans-Appalachian population grew tenfold (from 370,000 to 3.7 million). By 1830, more than a third of the nation's inhabitants lived west of the original thirteen states.

WHAT AREAS drew the densest concentrations of new settlers? Why?

Most of the new states extended the right to vote to all white males over the age of twenty-one. Vermont led the way in 1791, followed by Kentucky in 1792. Tennessee (1796) and Ohio (1803) entered with low taxpayer qualifications that approached universal suffrage. By 1820, most of the older states had followed suit. By 1840, more than 90 percent of adult white males in the nation could vote. And they could vote for more officials: governors and (most important) presidential electors were now elected by direct vote, rather than chosen by small groups of state legislators.

Universal white manhood suffrage, of course, was far from true universal suffrage: the right to vote remained barred to most of the nation's free African American males and to women of any race. Only in five New England states (Maine, New Hampshire, Vermont, Massachusetts, and Rhode Island) could free African American men vote before 1865. In the rest of the northern states, the right of free African American men to vote was restricted to only the most affluent property owners. Free African American men were denied the vote in the all of the new western states and of course, all free black men were prohibited from voting in the slave states of the South (see Figure 11.1).

What accounted for this nearly universal denial of voting rights to free black men? Racism accounted for much of it, an attitude that was strengthened by the backlash against the extremely controversial abolitionist movement of the 1830s and 1840s (see Chapter 13). In addition, as party lines hardened, northern Democrats, the party most closely aligned with the slave South, opposed enfranchising African American men who were almost certain to vote for their opponents. Above all, it was a sign of the growing influence that the southern slave system cast over all of American politics.

The denial of suffrage to white women stemmed from the traditional patriarchal belief that men headed households and represented the interests of all household members. Even wealthy single women who lived alone were considered subordinate to male relatives and denied the right to vote. Although unable to vote, women of the upper classes had long played important informal roles in national politics, especially in Washington, D.C. At the local level as well, women—often the wives of leading citizens—were accustomed to engaging informally in politics through their benevolent groups. These groups, often church related, had since colonial times not only provided charity to the poor but also raised money to support basic community institutions such as schools, churches, and libraries, in effect setting community priorities in the process.

Although the extension of suffrage to all classes of white men seemed to indicate that women had no role in public affairs, in fact women's informal involvement in politics grew along with the increasing pace of political activity. At the same time, however, as "manhood" rather than property became the qualification for voting, men began to ignore women's customary political activity and to regard their participation as inappropriate. Thus, in a period famous for democratization and "the rise of the common man," the exclusion of important groups—African American men and women of all races—marked the limits of liberalization.

THE ELECTION OF 1824

The 1824 election marked a dramatic end to the political truce that James Monroe had established in 1817 and to the idea of leadership by a small nonpartisan political elite. Five candidates, all of them members of the Republican Party, ran for president in the elections of 1824: William H. Crawford of Georgia, Secretary of State John Quincy Adams of Massachusetts, Henry

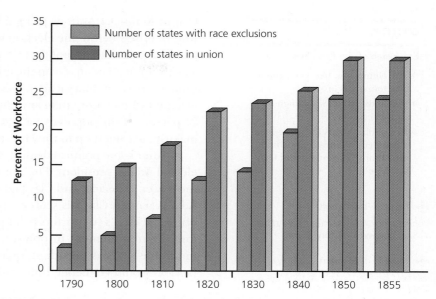

Figure 11.1 Race Exclusions for Suffrage, 1790–1855
This graph shows that as the number of states increased so did the percentage that excluded African American men from voting. None of the states that entered the Union after 1819 allowed African American suffrage.

From *The Right to Vote*, by Alexander Keyssar. Copyright © 2009 Alexander Keyssar. Reprinted by permission of Basic Books, a member of the Perseus Books Group.

Read the **Document**
A Legal Scholar Opposes Spreading the Vote (1821) at **www.myhistorylab.com**

This well-known painting by George Caleb Bingham, *Stump Speaking*, shows a group of men (and boys and dogs) of all social classes brought together by their common interest in politics.

George Caleb Bingham (American, 1811–1879), *Stump Speaking*, 1853–54. Oil on canvas, 42 ½ × 58 in. Saint Louis Art Museum, Gift of Bank of America.

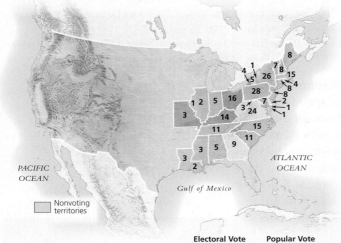

	Electoral Vote (%)	Popular Vote (%)
Andrew Jackson	99 (38)	153,544 (43)
JOHN QUINCY ADAMS	84 (32)	108,740 (31)
William H. Crawford	41 (16)	46,618 (13)
Henry Clay	37 (14)	47,136 (13)

MAP 11.2

The Election of 1824 The presidential vote of 1824 was clearly sectional. John Quincy Adams carried his native New England and little else, Henry Clay carried only his own state of Kentucky and two adjoining states, and Crawford's appeal was limited to Virginia and Georgia. Only Andrew Jackson moved beyond the regional support of the Old Southwest to wider appeal and the greatest number of electoral votes. Because no candidate had a majority, however, the election was thrown into the House of Representatives, which chose Adams.

HOW DID Jackson escape the sectional restraints that limited the appeal of his opponents?

Clay of Kentucky, Andrew Jackson of Tennessee, and John C. Calhoun of South Carolina, who withdrew before the election to run for vice president. Jackson's record as a legislator was lackluster, and his political views unknown, and he was not a member of the elite political group that had made up the governing class since 1790. However, owing to his national reputation as a military leader, Jackson won 43 percent of the popular vote and ninety-nine electoral votes—more than any other candidate. The runner-up, John Quincy Adams, won 31 percent of the popular vote and eighty-four electoral votes. But neither had an electoral majority, leaving it up to the House of Representatives to pick the winner.

After some political dealing, Henry Clay threw his support to Adams, and the House elected Adams president. This was customary and proper: the Constitution gave the House the power to decide, and Clay had every right to advise his followers how to vote. But when Adams named Clay his secretary of state, the traditional stepping-stone to the highest office, Jackson's supporters promptly accused them of a "corrupt bargain." Popular opinion, the new element in politics, supported Jackson. John Quincy Adams served four miserable years as president, marked by few legislative accomplishments, knowing that Jackson would challenge him, and win, in 1828 (see Map 11.2).

THE NEW POPULAR DEMOCRATIC CULTURE

In 1834, the French visitor Michel Chevalier witnessed a mile-long nighttime parade in support of Andrew Jackson. Stunned by what he saw, Chevalier wrote, "These scenes belong to history. They are the episodes of a wondrous epic which will bequeath a lasting memory to posterity, that of the coming of democracy." Mass campaigns—huge political rallies, parades, and candidates with wide "name recognition," such as military heroes—were the hallmarks of the new popular democratic culture. So were less savory customs, such as the distribution of lavish food and (especially) drink at polling places, which frequently turned elections into rowdy, brawling occasions. The spirit that motivated the new mass politics was democratic pride in participation. And as the election of 1824 showed, along with the spread of universal male suffrage went a change in popular attitudes that spelled the end of the customary dominance of small political elites. However, the new mass of voters was quickly absorbed into a new political structure. New national parties that superseded sectional interests emerged: to succeed, they had to appeal to the interests of a diverse range of voters.

In New York State, master political tactician Martin Van Buren forged a tightly organized, broad-based political group nicknamed the Albany Regency that wrested political control away from the former elite. In doing so, he became a major architect of the new democratic politics of mass participation. In other states, a Virginia group known as the Richmond Junto, the Nashville Junto in Tennessee, and New Hampshire's Concord Regency all aspired to the same discipline and control. Coordinated by Van Buren, they formed the coalition that nearly elected Andrew Jackson president in 1824.

One of the keys to their success was their use of newspapers to reach a broad audience. The number of newspapers soared from 376 in 1810 to 1,200 in 1835. This rise paralleled the growth of interest in politics, for most newspapers were published by political parties and were openly partisan. Packed with articles that today would be considered libelous and scandalous, newspapers were entertaining and popular reading, and they rapidly became a key part of democratic popular culture (see Figure 11.2).

The new politics appealed to new voters by placing great emphasis on participation and party loyalty. One way for ordinary citizens to show their loyalty was to turn out for parades. Political processions were huge affairs, marked by the often spontaneous participation of men carrying badges and party regalia, banners and placards, and portraits of the candidates, accompanied by bands, fireworks, and the shouting and singing of party slogans and songs. In effect, political parties functioned as giant national men's clubs. They made politics an immediate and engrossing topic of conversation and argument for men of all walks of life. In this sense, the political party was the political manifestation of a wider social impulse toward community (see Figure 11.3).

THE ELECTION OF 1828

The election of 1828 was the first to demonstrate the power and effectiveness of the new popular democratic culture and party system. With the help of Martin Van Buren, his campaign manager, Andrew Jackson rode the wave of the new democratic politics to the presidency. Voter turnout in 1828 was more than twice that of 1824. Jackson's party, the Democratic-Republicans (they soon dropped "Republicans" and became simply the **Democrats**), spoke the language of democracy, and they opposed the special privilege personified for them by President John Quincy Adams and his National Republican (as distinguished from the earlier Jeffersonian Republican) Party. Jackson's supporters, playing on popular resentment of a wealthy political elite, portrayed the campaign as a contest between "the democracy of the country, on the one hand, and a lordly purse-proud aristocracy on the other." In their turn, Adams's supporters depicted Jackson as an illiterate backwoodsman, a murderer, and an adulterer. Jackson's running mate for vice president was John C. Calhoun of South Carolina. Although this choice assured Jackson of valuable southern support, it also illustrated the transitional nature of politics, for Calhoun was at the time of the election serving as vice president to John Quincy Adams, Jackson's opponent. That Calhoun was easily able to lend his support to a rival faction was a holdover from the old elite and

Politics, abetted by the publication of inexpensive party newspapers, was a great topic of conversation among men in early nineteenth-century America, as Richard Caton Woodville's 1845 painting *Politics in an Oyster House* suggests.

Richard Caton Woodville, *Politics in an Oyster House*, 1848. Oil on canvas. The Walters Art Museum, Baltimore.

Democrats   Political party formed in the 1820s under the leadership of Andrew Jackson; favored states' rights and a limited role for the federal government.

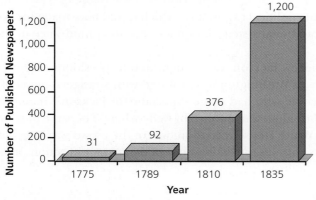

Figure 11.2 The Burgeoning of Newspapers
Newspapers have a long history in the United States. Even before the American Revolution, the colonies boasted thirty-seven newspapers, and within little more than a decade, that number had nearly tripled. Toward the end of the century, however, the number of newspapers expanded rapidly, by 1835 numbering more than thirty times that of 1775.

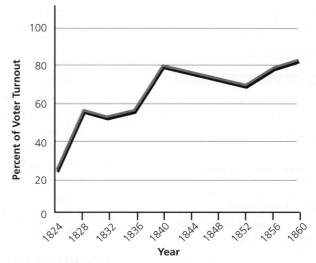

Figure 11.3 Pre–Civil War Voter Turnout
The turnout of voters in presidential elections more than doubled from 1824 to 1828, the year Andrew Jackson was first elected. Turnout surged to 80 percent in 1840, the year the Whigs triumphed. The extension of suffrage to all white men, and heated competition between two political parties with nationwide membership, turned presidential election campaigns into events with great popular appeal.

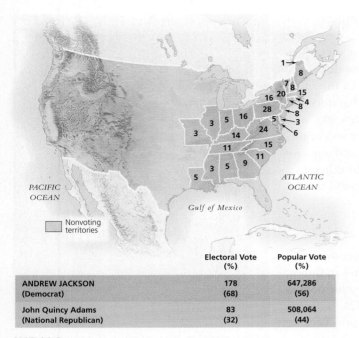

	Electoral Vote (%)	Popular Vote (%)
ANDREW JACKSON (Democrat)	178 (68)	647,286 (56)
John Quincy Adams (National Republican)	83 (32)	508,064 (44)

MAP 11.3
The Election of 1828 Andrew Jackson's victory in 1828 was the first success of the new national party system. The coalition of state parties that elected him was national, not regional. Although his support was strongest in the South and West, his ability to carry Pennsylvania and parts of New York demonstrated his national appeal.

IN WHAT regions did Jackson gain strength between 1824 and 1828 ?

Read the **Document**

Ballad of General Jackson and the Six Militia Men (1827) at
www.myhistorylab.com

WHAT STEPS did Andrew Jackson take to strengthen the executive branch of the federal government?

QUICK REVIEW

Jackson's Inauguration

- Westerners and common people crowded into Washington for the inauguration.
- Jackson's brief address was a raucous affair.
- The crowd at the White House was large and disorderly.

personal politics that would soon be impossible in the new democratic political system.

Jackson won 56 percent of the popular vote (well over 80 percent in much of the South and West) and a decisive electoral majority of 178 votes to Adams's 83. The vote was interpreted as a victory for the common man. But the most important thing about Jackson's victory was the coalition that achieved it. The new democratically based political organizations—the Richmond and Nashville juntos, the Albany and Concord regencies, with help from Calhoun's organization in South Carolina—worked together to elect him. Popular appeal, which Jackson the military hero certainly possessed, was not enough to ensure victory. To be truly national, a party had to create and maintain a coalition of North, South, and West. The Democrats were the first to do this (see Map 11.3).

THE JACKSON PRESIDENCY

Andrew Jackson's election ushered in a new era in American politics, an era that historians have called the "Age of the Common Man." Jackson himself, however, was no common man: he was a military hero, a rich slave owner, and an imperious and decidedly undemocratic personality. Yet he had a mass appeal to ordinary people, unmatched by earlier presidents. The secret to Jackson's extraordinary appeal lies in the changing nature of American society. Jackson was the first to respond to the ways in which westward expansion and the extension of the suffrage were changing politics at the national as well as the local and state levels.

A POPULAR PRESIDENT

Jackson was born in 1767 and raised in North Carolina. As a young man without wealth or family support, he moved west to Nashville, Tennessee, in 1788. There he made his career as a lawyer and his considerable wealth as a slave-owning planter. He first became a national hero with his underdog win against the British in the Battle of New Orleans in 1815. The fact that he had little political experience, which would have made his nomination impossible under the traditional system of politics, was not a hindrance in the new age of popular politics.

On March 4, 1829, Andrew Jackson was inaugurated as president of the United States. The small community of Washington was crowded with strangers, many of them Westerners and common people who had come especially for Jackson's inauguration. After the ceremony the new president was mobbed by well-wishers. The same unrestrained enthusiasm was evident at a White House reception, where the crowd was large and disorderly (see Seeing History). This was the exuberance of democracy in action. It marked something new in American politics.

A STRONG EXECUTIVE

Jackson's personal style quickly stripped national politics of the polite and gentlemanly aura of cooperation it had acquired during the Era of Good Feelings. Jackson had played rough all his life, and he relished controversy. His administration (1829–37) had plenty of it. Andrew Jackson dominated his administration. Except for Martin Van Buren, whom he appointed secretary of state, he mostly ignored the heads of government departments who made up his official cabinet. Instead he consulted with an informal group, dubbed the "Kitchen Cabinet," made up of Van Buren and old western friends.

President's Levee, or all Creation Going to the White House

ntil 1829, presidential inaugurations had been small, polite, and ceremonial occasions. Andrew Jackson's popularity, however, brought a horde of well-wishers to Washington for his inaugural. "Thousands and thousands of people, without distinction of rank," reported Washington resident Margaret Bayard Smith, "collected in an immense mass round the Capitol, silent, orderly and tranquil," to watch Jackson's swearing-in. But afterwards, when the crowd followed Jackson to an open house at the White House, says Smith, "what a scene did we witness! . . . a rabble, a mob of boys, negros, women, children, scrambling, fighting, romping. What a pity what a pity." Her consternation was echoed by many respectable people who feared that "the reign of King Mob" had begun.

DOES IT matter that the details are not correct?

This famous illustration of the raucous crowd at the White House reception is by the British caricature artist Robert Cruikshank. It was probably first shown, along with other pictures, in a London printmaker's window display in 1829, with copies sold for two shillings. For the British, amusement came from the fact that American democracy so quickly turned into a rowdy mob, just as the British had always predicted.

Cruikshank was not in Washington at the time of Jackson's inaugural. At best, the details of the illustration are based on accounts provided to him by others or perhaps simply invented. Nevertheless, the illustration captures the mood of the celebrating crowd. ■

263

This anti-Jackson "coffin bill" from the election of 1828 accuses Jackson of murder because he ordered three men executed for desertion during the War of 1812.

Jackson freely used the tools of his office to strengthen the executive branch of government at the expense of the legislature and judiciary. By using the veto more frequently than all previous presidents combined (twelve vetoes compared with nine by the first six presidents), Jackson forced Congress to constantly consider his opinions. Even more important, Jackson's "negative activism" restricted federal activity (see Chapter 9). Only his strong and popular leadership made this sharp change of direction possible.

THE NATION'S LEADER VERSUS SECTIONAL SPOKESMEN

Despite his western origins, Jackson was a genuinely national figure. He believed that the president, who symbolized the popular will of the people, ought to dominate the government. This was new. Voters were much more accustomed to thinking of politics in sectional terms. Jackson faced a Congress full of strong and immensely popular sectional figures. Three stood out: Southerner John C. Calhoun, Northerner Daniel Webster, and Westerner Henry Clay.

Intense, dogmatic, and uncompromising, John C. Calhoun of South Carolina was identified with southern interests, first and foremost among which was the preservation and expansion of slavery. As the South's minority position in Congress became clear over the years, Calhoun's defense of southern economic interests and slavery became more and more rigid. Not for nothing did he earn his nickname the "Cast-Iron Man."

Senator Daniel Webster of Massachusetts was the outstanding orator of the age. Large, dark, and stern, Webster delivered his speeches in a deep, booming voice that, listeners said, "shook the world." Webster became the main spokesman for the new northern commercial interests, supporting a high protective tariff, a national bank, and a strong federal government.

In contrast with the other two, Henry Clay of Kentucky, spokesman of the West, was charming, witty, and always eager to forge political compromises. Clay held the powerful position of Speaker of the House of Representatives from 1811 to 1825 and later served several terms in the Senate. Well known for his ability to make a deal—he was known as "the Great Pacificator" (compromiser)—Clay worked to incorporate western desires for cheap and good transportation into national politics. It was he who promoted the national plan for economic development known as the American System: a national bank, a protective tariff, and the use of substantial federal funds for internal improvements such as roads, canals, and railroads (see Chapter 9). Clay might well have forged a political alliance between the North and the West if not for the policies of President Jackson, his fellow Westerner and greatest rival.

The prominence and popularity of these three politicians show that sectional interests remained strong even under a president as determined as Jackson to override them and disrupt "politics as usual" by imposing his own personal style. Nothing showed the power of sectional interests more clearly than the unprecedented confrontation provoked by South Carolina in Jackson's first term, the Nullification Crisis.

THE NULLIFICATION CRISIS

The crisis raised the fundamental question concerning national unity in a federal system: What was the correct balance between local interests—the rights of the states—and the powers of the central government? Because the Constitution deliberately left the federal structure ambiguous, all sectional disagreements automatically became constitutional issues that carried a threat to national unity.

The political issue that came to symbolize the divergent economic interests of North and South was the protective tariff that placed a duty (or surcharge) on imported goods.

Three Great Sectional Leaders. The years of Jackson's presidency were also notable for the prominence of regional spokesmen, among them John C. Calhoun (left), who spoke for the South and slavery, Henry Clay (center) who spoke for the West, and Daniel Webster (right), who represented northern business. Clay's great personal charm is captured in this 1824 portrait, contrasting with Calhoun's dour expression and Webster's stern image.

(center) Matthew H. Joulett (1788–1827), *Henry Clay*, c. 1824. Oil on panel. (attr. to Jouett) © Chicago Historical Society, Chicago, USA.

The first substantial tariff was enacted in 1816 after northern manufacturing interests clamored for protection from the ruthless British competition that followed the War of 1812 (see Chapter 9). As a group, wealthy southern planters were opposed to tariffs, both because duties raised the cost of the luxury goods they imported from Europe and because they feared that American tariffs would cause other countries to retaliate with tariffs against southern cotton.

As the North industrialized and new industries demanded protection, tariff bills in 1824 and 1828 raised rates still higher and protected more items. Southerners protested, but they were outvoted in Congress by northern and western representatives. The 1828 tariff, nicknamed the "Tariff of Abominations," was a special target of southern anger because Jackson's supporters in Congress had passed it, over southern objections, in order to increase northern support for him in the presidential campaign of that year. Southern opponents of the tariff insisted that it was not a truly national measure but rather a sectional one that helped only some groups while harming others. Thus, they claimed, it was unconstitutional because it violated the rights of some of the states.

South Carolina, Calhoun's home state, reacted the most forcefully to the Tariff of 1828. Of the older southern states, South Carolina had been the hardest hit by the opening of the new cotton lands in the Old Southwest, which had drained both population and commerce from the state. To these economic woes were added the first real fears about national attitudes toward slavery.

South Carolinians were shaken by the news that the British Parliament, bowing to popular pressure at home, was planning to emancipate all the slaves in the British West Indies. If Congress had the power to impose tariffs that were harmful to some states, South Carolinians asked, what would prevent it from enacting legislation like Britain's, depriving Southerners of their slaves and, thus, of their livelihood? In this sense, although the Nullification Crisis was about the tariff, it was also about the greatest of all sectional issues, slavery.

Read the **Document**
Proclamation Concerning Nullification (1832) at **www.myhistorylab.com**

Nullification Crisis   Sectional crisis in the early 1830s in which a states' rights party in South Carolina attempted to nullify federal law.

The result of these fears was a renewed interest in the doctrine of nullification, a topic that became the subject of widespread discussion in South Carolina. The doctrine upheld the right of a state to declare a federal law null and void and to refuse to enforce it within the state. South Carolinian John C. Calhoun wrote a widely circulated defense of the doctrine, the *Exposition and Protest*, in 1828.

Where Calhoun saw nullification as a safeguard of the rights of the minority, Jackson saw it as a threat to national unity. The president and the vice president were thus in open disagreement on a matter of crucial national importance. The outcome was inevitable: Calhoun lost all influence with Jackson, and two years later, he took the unusual step of resigning the vice presidency. Martin Van Buren was elected to the office for Jackson's second term. Calhoun became a senator from South Carolina, and in that capacity, participated in the last act of the nullification drama.

In 1832, the nullification controversy became a full-blown crisis. In passing the Tariff of 1832, Congress retained high taxes on woolens, iron, and hemp, although it reduced duties on other items. South Carolina responded with a special convention and an Ordinance of Nullification, in which it rejected the tariff and refused to collect the taxes it required. The state further issued a call for a volunteer militia and threatened to secede from the Union if Jackson used force against it. Jackson responded by obtaining from Congress a Force Bill authorizing the federal government to collect the tariff in South Carolina at gunpoint if necessary. Intimidated, the other southern states refused to follow South Carolina's lead. More quietly, Jackson also asked Congress to revise the tariff, which it did, passing the Tariff Act of 1833. The South Carolina legislature, unwilling to act without the support of other southern states, quickly accepted this face-saving compromise.

Read the Document

An American Senator Opposes Nullification, (1830) at **www.myhistorylab.com**

The **Nullification Crisis** was the most serious threat to national unity that the United States had ever experienced. South Carolinians, by threatening to secede, had forced concessions on a matter they believed of vital economic importance. They—and a number of other Southerners—believed that the resolution of the crisis illustrated the success of their uncompromising tactics.

CHANGING THE COURSE OF GOVERNMENT

WHAT WERE Andrew Jackson's most important policy objectives?

As Martin Van Buren later recalled, Jackson came to the presidency with a clear agenda: "First, the removal of the Indians from the vicinity of the white population and their settlement beyond the Mississippi. Second, to put a stop to the abuses of the Federal government in regard to internal improvements [and] Third, to oppose as well the existing re-incorporation of the existing National Bank." As Jackson enacted his agenda, which he believed expressed the popular will, he changed the course of the federal government as decisively as Jefferson had during his presidency (see Chapter 9). But the opposition that Jackson evoked also revealed the limits of presidential authority in an age of democratic politics.

INDIAN REMOVAL

The official policy of the U.S. government from the time of Jefferson's administration was to promote the assimilation of Indian peoples by encouraging them to adopt white ways. In addition, Jefferson offered the alternative of removal from settled areas in the East to the new Indian Territory west of the Mississippi River. At the end of the War of 1812, the federal government signed removal treaties with a number of Indian nations of the Old Northwest, thereby opening up large tracts of land for white settlement (see Chapter 9). In the Southwest, however, the Five Southern Tribes—the Cherokees, Chickasaws, Choctaws, Creeks, and Seminoles—remained.

By the 1830s, under constant pressure from settlers, each of the five southern tribes had ceded most of its lands, but sizable self-governing groups lived in Georgia, Alabama,

Mississippi, and Florida. All of these (except the Seminoles) had moved far in the direction of coexistence with whites.

The Cherokees took the most extensive steps to adopt white ways. Their tribal lands in northwestern Georgia boasted prosperous farms, businesses, grain and lumber mills, and even plantations with black slaves. Intermarriage with whites and African Americans had produced an influential group of mixed-bloods within the Cherokee nation, some of whom were eager to accept white ways.

Despite the evidence of the Cherokees' successful adaptation to the dominant white culture, in the 1820s, the legislatures of Georgia, Alabama, and Mississippi, responding to pressures from land-hungry whites, voted to invalidate federal treaties granting special self-governing status to Indian lands. Because the federal government, not the states, bore responsibility for Indian policy, these state actions constituted a sectional challenge to federal authority. In this instance, however, the resisting states had presidential support. Jackson was committed to a federal policy of wholesale removal of the southern Indian tribes.

In 1830, at President Jackson's urging, the U.S. Congress passed the hotly debated **Indian Removal Act**, which appropriated funds for relocation, by force if necessary. When Jackson increased the pressure by sending federal officials to negotiate removal treaties with the southern tribes, most reluctantly signed and prepared to move. The Cherokees, however took their case to court. At first they seemed to have won: in *Cherokee Nation* v. *Georgia* (1831) and *Worcester* v. *Georgia* (1832), Chief Justice John Marshall ruled that the Cherokees, though not a state or a foreign nation, were a "domestic dependent nation" that could not be forced by the state of Georgia to give up its land against its will. Ignoring the decision, Jackson continued his support for removal.

Although some Seminole bands mounted a successful resistance war in the Florida Everglades, the majority of Seminoles and members of other tribes were much less fortunate: most of the Choctaws moved west in 1830; the last of the Creeks were forcibly moved by the military in 1836, and the Chickasaws a year later. And in 1838, in the last and most infamous removal, resisting Cherokees were driven west to Oklahoma along what came to be known as the "**Trail of Tears**." Perhaps a quarter of the 16,000 Cherokees died along the way (see Map 11.4).

Another futile effort to resist removal, the Black Hawk "war," occurred in the Old Northwest. In 1832, Sauk and Fox Indians, led by Black Hawk, attempted to move back to their old tribal grounds in Illinois following removal, but settlers saw the move as an invasion and demanded military protection. Federal troops chased the Black Hawk band to Wisconsin, where more than 300 Indians died in a final battle, and Black Hawk himself was taken prisoner. As in the South, the last of the remaining Indians east of the Mississippi were removed by the end of the 1830s.

Indian removal was a deeply divisive national issue. President Jackson's policies undoubtedly expressed the opinion of most Southerners and Westerners. But northern opinion, led by Protestant missionaries and reform groups, was strongly opposed. Among the groups mobilized in protest were members of female benevolent societies who had a direct interest in the issue, for they had long raised money to support missionary activities aimed at assimilating, not removing, American Indians. Now, they joined together to organize the first national female petition drive. In the end, the protest failed, but by the barest of margins: the Indian Removal Act passed the House of Representatives by only three votes (out of 200).

In contrast to the lesson of the Nullification Crisis, Jackson's policy on Indian removal showed how unfair majority rule could be when the minority was not strong enough to force a compromise. But just as South Carolinians were emboldened by the success of their resistance, benevolent women were encouraged by their intervention in national politics and soon focused their petitioning skills on another cause, abolition (see Chapter 13).

Read the Document

Memorial of the Cherokee Nation (1830) at **www.myhistorylab.com**

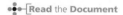

QUICK REVIEW

Georgia and the Cherokees

♦ Georgia stole the Creek Indians' land in 1825.

♦ Georgia moved against Cherokees in 1828, stripping them of all legal rights.

♦ Stage was set for Indian Removal Act.

Read the Document

A Choctaw Chief Bids Farewell (1832) at **www.myhistorylab.com**

See the Map

Native American Land Cessions to 1829 at **www.myhistorylab.com**

Indian Removal Act   President Andrew Jackson's measure that allowed state officials to override federal protection of Native Americans.

Trail of Tears   The forced march in 1838 of the Cherokee Indians from their homelands in Georgia to the Indian Territory in the West.

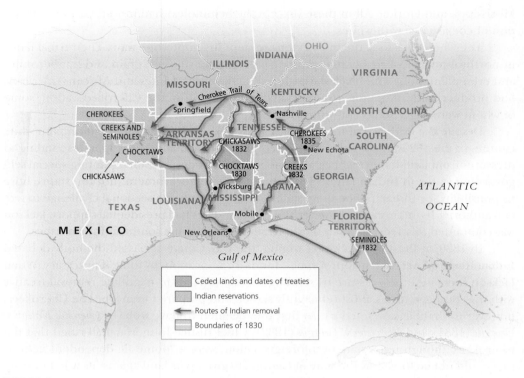

MAP 11.4

Southern Indian Cessions and Removals, 1830s Pressure on the five major southern Indian peoples—the Cherokees, Chickasaws, Choctaws, Creeks, and Seminoles—that began during the War of 1812 culminated with their removal in the 1830s. Some groups from every tribe ceded their southern homelands peacefully and moved to the newly established Indian Territory west of Arkansas and Missouri. Some, like the Seminoles, resisted by force. Others, like the Cherokees, resisted in the courts, but finally lost when President Andrew Jackson refused to enforce a Supreme Court decision in their favor. The Cherokees, the last to move, were forcibly removed by the U.S. Army along the "Trail of Tears" in 1838.

WHAT DOES this map tell you about the connection between the expansion of cotton cultivation and Indian removal?

INTERNAL IMPROVEMENTS

Because Jackson was a Westerner, his supporters expected him to recognize the nation's urgent need for better transportation and to provide federal funding for internal improvements, especially in the West. Jackson's veto of the Maysville Road Bill of 1830 was, therefore, one of his most unexpected actions. Jackson argued that federal funding for extensive and expensive transportation measures was unconstitutional because it infringed on the "reserved powers" the Constitution left to the states. He also had the satisfaction of defeating a measure central to the American System proposed by his western rival, Henry Clay.

Internal improvements were a part of Clay's American System (which had been supported by the Monroe and Adams administrations) that envisaged the national government as planner and administrator of a coordinated policy to encourage economic growth and foster the development of a national market. But since 1816, it had proved impossible to propose a nationally funded transportation plan that satisfied everyone. Jackson ended most of the debate over internal improvements by refusing federal funds for all but the most obviously interstate projects (such as the National Road).

But the country still needed a basic infrastructure of roads, canals, and railroads to tie the national economy together. Without federal funding and planning, the initiative passed to private developers, who turned to individual states. The states actually spent more than the federal government on internal improvements, with a fivefold increase from 1820 to 1840 (from $26 million to $108 million). States and towns, especially in newly populated areas of the West, competed in giving land, subsidies, and other forms of encouragement to road, canal, and railroad companies to provide transportation to their particular localities.

FEDERAL AND STATE SUPPORT FOR PRIVATE ENTERPRISE

At the same time that funding for internal improvements passed to the states, a series of decisions by federal courts asserted broad federal powers over interstate commerce. The effect of these decisions, contradictorily, was to vastly encourage commercial enterprise by limiting the regulatory power of the states at the same time that they were putting up most of the money for the new transportation network. By preventing states from interfering with interstate commerce, the courts encouraged development by assuring entrepreneurs the freedom and security to operate in the risky new national market.

Two key decisions were handed down by Chief Justice John Marshall (who had been on the bench since 1801). In *Dartmouth College* v. *Woodward* (1819), the Supreme Court prevented states from interfering in contracts, and in *Gibbons* v. *Ogden* (1824), it enjoined the State of New York from giving a monopoly over a steamboat line to Robert Fulton, inventor of the vessel. Although Fulton's invention was protected by a federal patent, its commercial application was not. Patenting thus encouraged technology, but not at the expense of competition. A decision handed down by Marshall's successor, Roger Taney, *Charles River Bridge* v. *Warren Bridge* (1837), again supported economic opportunity by denying a monopoly.

At the state level, another crucial commercial protection was the passage of laws concerning incorporation of businesses that had grown too large for individual proprietorship, family ownership, or limited partnership. Businesses that needed to raise large amounts of capital by attracting many investors found the contractual protections provided by incorporation to be essential. The protection investors wanted most was limited liability—the assurance that they would lose no more than what they had invested in a corporation if it were sued or went bankrupt. The net effect of state incorporation laws was to encourage large-scale economic activity and to hasten the commercialization of rural areas, both crucial aspects of the Market Revolution (see Chapter 12).

THE BANK WAR

In the case of internal improvements, Jackson rejected, on behalf of popular democracy, the notion of coordinated economic planning by the government. His rejection set up the conditions for a speculative frenzy. Precisely the same result occurred in his epic battle with the Second Bank of the United States.

In 1816, Congress had granted a twenty-year charter to the Second Bank of the United States. The Bank was owned by private investors, with the U.S. government holding only one-fifth of the shares. With thirty branches, it was the nation's largest and performed a variety of functions, the most important of which was the control it exercised over state banks. Because state banks tended to issue more paper money than they could back with hard currency, the Bank always demanded repayment of its loans to them in hard currency. This policy forced state banks to maintain adequate reserves and restricted speculative activities. In times of recession, the Bank eased the pressure on state banks, demanding only partial payment in coin. Thus, the Bank acted as a currency stabilizer by helping to control the money supply.

The concept of a strong national bank controlled by wealthy investors, not the federal government, was supported by the majority of the nation's merchants and businessmen. Nevertheless, the Bank had many opponents. Both western farmers and urban workers had bitter memories of the Panic of 1819, which the Bank had caused (at least

"King Andrew." This Whig cartoon, published at the height of the Bank War, depicted Jackson as an absolute monarch trampling on the Constitution. The caption asked "Shall he reign over us, or shall the PEOPLE RULE?"

●●●—Read the **Document**

Andrew Jackson, Veto of the Bank Bill (1832) at **www.myhistorylab.com**

QUICK REVIEW

Jackson and the Bank of the United States

◆ Jackson, and most Westerners, distrusted banks.

◆ Jackson vetoed rechartering of the Bank of the United States.

◆ Struggle over future of Bank ended with victory for Jackson.

Whigs The name used by advocates of colonial resistance to British measures during the 1760s and 1770s.

in part) by sharply cutting back on available credit. Many ordinary people believed that a system based on paper currency would be manipulated by bankers—the "monied aristocracy"—in selfish and dangerous ways. Among those who held that opinion was Andrew Jackson, who had hated and feared banks ever since the 1790s, when he had lost a great deal of money in a speculative venture.

Early in his administration, Jackson hastened to tell Nicholas Biddle, the director of the Bank: "I do not dislike your Bank any more than all banks." By 1832, Jackson's opinion had changed, and he and Biddle were locked in a personal conflict that harmed not only the national economy but also the reputations of both men. Biddle, urged on by Henry Clay and Daniel Webster, precipitated the conflict by making early application for rechartering the Bank. Congress approved the application in July 1832. Jackson immediately decided on a stinging veto, announcing to Van Buren, "The bank . . . is trying to kill me, but I will kill it!"

And kill it he did that same July, with one of the strongest veto messages in American history. Asserting that the Bank's "exclusive privileges" were benefiting only the rich, Jackson claimed to speak for the "humble members of society—the farmers, mechanics and laborers" and to oppose injustice and inequality. Jackson's veto message was a great popular success, and it set the terms for the presidential election of 1832. Henry Clay, the nominee of the anti-Jackson forces, lost the battle for popular opinion. Democrats successfully painted Clay as the defender of the Bank and of privilege. Clay's defeat was decisive: he drew only forty-nine electoral votes to Jackson's 219.

Although the election was a triumph for Jackson, the Bank War continued because Jackson decided to kill the Bank by transferring its $10 million in government deposits to favored state banks ("pet banks," critics called them). Cabinet members objected, as did the Senate, but Jackson responded that the election had given him a popular mandate to act against the Bank. Short of impeachment, there was nothing Congress could do to prevent Jackson from acting on his expansive—and novel—interpretation of presidential powers.

Jackson's refusal to renew the charter of the Second Bank of the United States had lasting economic and political consequences. Economically, it inaugurated the economic policy known as *laissez-faire*, where decision-making power rests with commercial interests, not with government. Politically, it so infuriated Jackson's opponents that they formed a permanent opposition party. It was from the heat of the Bank War that the now characteristic American two-party system emerged.

WHIGS, VAN BUREN, AND THE PANIC OF 1837

In 1833, as the government withdrew its deposits, Nicholas Biddle, the Bank's director, counterattacked by calling in the Bank's commercial loans, thereby causing a sharp panic and recession in the winter of 1833–34. Merchants, businessmen, and southern planters were all furious—at Jackson. His opponents, only a loose coalition up to this time, coalesced into a formal opposition party that called itself the **Whigs**. Evoking the memory of the Patriots who had resisted King George III in the American Revolution, the new party called on everyone to resist tyrannical "King Andrew."

Vice President Martin Van Buren, Jackson's designated successor, won the presidential election of 1836 because the Whigs ran four sectional candidates, hoping their combined votes would deny Van Buren a majority and force the election into the House of Representatives. The strategy failed, but not by much. Their near success showed them that the basis for a united national opposition did exist. In 1840, the Whigs would prove that they had learned this lesson.

Meanwhile, the consequences of the Bank War continued. The recession of 1833–34 was followed by a wild speculative boom, caused as much by foreign investors as by the expiration of the Bank. Many new state banks were chartered that were eager to give loans, the price of cotton rose rapidly, and speculation in western lands was feverish. A government surplus of $37 million distributed to the states in 1836 made the inflationary pressures worse. Jackson became alarmed at the widespread use of paper money (which he blamed for the inflation), and in July 1836, he issued the **Specie Circular**, announcing that the government would accept payment for public lands only in hard currency. At the same time, foreign investors, especially British banks, affected by a world recession, called in their American loans. The sharp contraction of credit led to the Panic of 1837 and a six-year recession, the worst the American economy had yet known.

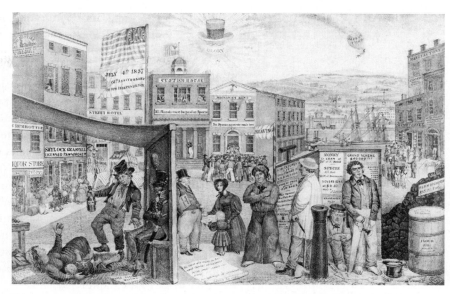

This contemporary cartoon bitterly depicts the terrible effects of the Panic of 1837 on ordinary people—bank failures, unemployment, drunkenness, and destitution—which the artist links to the insistence of the rich on payment in specie (as Jackson had required in the Species Circular of 1836). Over the scene waves the American flag, accompanied by the ironic message, "61st Anniversary of Our Independence."

In 1837, some 800 banks suspended business, refusing to pay out any of their $150 million in deposits. The collapse of the banking system led to business closures and outright failures. Nationwide, the unemployment rate reached more than 10 percent. The Panic of 1837 lasted six long years, causing widespread misery. Not until 1843 did the economy show signs of recovery.

In 1837 the federal government did nothing to aid victims of economic recession. No banks were bailed out, no bank depositors were saved by federal insurance, no laid-off workers got unemployment payments. Nor did the government undertake any public works projects or pump money into the economy. All of these steps, today seen as essential to prevent economic collapse and to alleviate human suffering, were unheard of then.

Martin Van Buren (quickly nicknamed "Van Ruin") spent a dismal four years in the White House presiding over bank failures, bankruptcies, and massive unemployment. Van Buren, who lacked Jackson's compelling personality, could find no remedies to the depression. His misfortune gave the opposition party, the newly formed Whigs, its opportunity.

THE SECOND AMERICAN PARTY SYSTEM

The First American Party System, the confrontation between the Federalists and the Jeffersonian Republicans that began in the 1790s, had been widely viewed at the time as an unfortunate factional squabble (see Chapter 8). By the 1830s, with the expansion of suffrage, attitudes had changed. The political struggles of the Jackson era, coupled with the dramatic social changes caused by expansion and economic growth, created the basic pattern of American politics: two major parties, each with at least some appeal among voters of all social classes and in all sections of the country. That pattern, which we call the "**Second American Party System**," continues to this day.

WHIGS AND DEMOCRATS

There were genuine differences between the Whigs and the Democrats, but they were not sectional differences. Instead, the two parties reflected just-emerging class and cultural differences. The Democrats had inherited Thomas Jefferson's belief in the democratic

HOW DID the Second Party System differ from the First Party System?

Specie Circular Proclamation issued by President Andrew Jackson in 1836 stipulating that only gold or silver could be used as payment for public land.

Second American Party System The basic pattern of American politics of two parties, each with appeal among voters of all social voters and in all sections of the country.

rights of the small, independent yeoman farmer. They had nationwide appeal, especially in the South and West, the most rural regions. As a result of Jackson's presidency, Democrats came to be identified with independence and a distaste for interference, whether from the government or from economic monopolies such as the Bank of the United States. They favored expansion, Indian removal, and the freedom to do as they chose on the frontier. Most Democratic voters were opposed to the rapid social and economic changes of the 1830s and 1840s.

The Whigs were themselves often the initiators and beneficiaries of economic change and were more receptive to it. Heirs of the Federalist belief in the importance of a strong federal role in the national economy (see Chapter 8), they supported Henry Clay's American System: a strong central government, the Bank of the United States, a protective tariff, and internal improvements. Many Whigs were members of evangelical reforming denominations. Whigs favored government intervention in both economic and social affairs, calling for education and social reforms, such as temperance, that aimed to improve the ordinary citizen. The Whigs' greatest strength was in New England and the northern part of the West (the Old Northwest), the areas most affected by commercial agriculture and factory work (see Chapter 13).

Yet neither party was monolithic. As has continued to be true of American political parties, both the Democrats and the Whigs were a coalition of interests affected by local and regional factors. Although Jackson's appeal was strongest in the rural South and West, the Democrats also appealed to some workers in Philadelphia and other northern cities because they shared with Democrats from other regions a dislike of big business. On the other hand, a number of southern planters with close ties to merchant and banking interests were attracted to the Whig policy of a strong federal role in economic development, though they were less active than many northern Whigs in advocating sweeping social reform.

THE CAMPAIGN OF 1840

In 1840, the Whigs set out to beat the Democrats at their own game, nominating a man as much like Andrew Jackson as possible, the aging Indian fighter William Henry Harrison, former governor of the Indiana Territory from 1801 to 1812. In an effort to duplicate Jackson's winning appeal to the South as well as the West, the Whigs balanced the ticket by nominating a Southerner, John Tyler, for vice president. The Whigs reached out to ordinary people with torchlight parades, barbecues, songs, coonskin caps, bottomless jugs of hard cider, and claims that Martin Van Buren, Harrison's hapless opponent, was a man of privilege and aristocratic tastes.

The Whig campaign tactics, added to the popular anger at Van Buren because of the continuing depression, gave Harrison a sweeping electoral victory, 234 votes to 60. Even more remarkable, the campaign achieved the greatest voter turnout up to that time (and rarely equaled since): 80 percent (see Map 11.5).

THE WHIG VICTORY TURNS TO LOSS: THE TYLER PRESIDENCY

Although the Whig victory of 1840 was a milestone in American politics, the triumph of Whig principles was short-lived. William Henry Harrison, who was sixty-eight, died of pneumonia a month after his inauguration. For the first time in American history, the

QUICK REVIEW

William Henry Harrison of Ohio

- Indian fighter and former governor of the Indian Territory.
- Hero of War of 1812.
- Selected John Tyler of Virginia as his running mate.

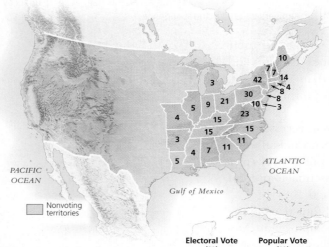

	Electoral Vote (%)	Popular Vote (%)
WILLIAM HENRY HARRISON (Whig)	234 (80)	1,275,016 (53)
Martin Van Buren (Democrat)	60 (20)	1,129,102 (47)

MAP 11.5

The Election of 1840 The Whigs triumphed in the election of 1840 by beating the Democrats at their own game. Whigs could expect to do well in the commercializing areas of New England and the Old Northwest, but their adopted strategy of popular campaigning worked well in the largely rural South and West as well, contributing to Harrison's victory. The Whigs' choice of John Tyler as vice presidential candidate, another strategy designed to appeal to southern voters, backfired when Harrison died and Tyler, who did not share Whig principles, became America's first vice president to succeed to the presidency.

WHAT POLICIES and tactics made Whig success in the South possible?

OVERVIEW | The Second American Party System

Democrats	First organized to elect Andrew Jackson to the presidency in 1828. The Democratic Party spoke for Jeffersonian democracy, expansion, and the freedom of the "common man" from interference from government or from financial monopolies like the Bank of the United States. It found its power base in the rural South and West and among some northern urban workers. The Democratic Party was the majority party from 1828 to 1860.
Whigs	Organized in opposition to Andrew Jackson in the early 1830s. Heir to Federalism, the Whig Party favored a strong role for the national government in the economy (for example, it promoted Henry Clay's American System) and supported active social reform. Its power base lay in the North and Old Northwest among voters who benefited from increased commercialization and among some southern planters and urban merchants. The Whigs won the elections of 1840 and 1848.

vice president stepped up to the presidency. Not for the last time, important differences between the dead president and his successor reshaped the direction of American politics. John Tyler of Virginia, quickly nicknamed "His Accidency," was a former Democrat who had left the party because he disagreed with Jackson's autocratic style. The Whigs had sought him primarily for his sectional appeal and had not inquired too closely into his political opinions, which turned out to be anti-Whig as well as anti-Jackson.

President Tyler vetoed a series of bills embodying all the elements of Henry Clay's American System: tariffs, internal improvements, a new Bank of the United States. In exasperation, congressional Whigs forced Tyler out of the party, and his entire cabinet of Whigs resigned. To replace them, Tyler appointed former Democrats like himself. Thus, the Whig triumph of 1840, one of the clearest victories in American electoral politics, was negated by the stalemate between Tyler and the Whig majority in Congress. The Whigs were to win only one more election, that of 1848.

AMERICAN ARTS AND LETTERS

Jackson's presidency was a defining moment in the development of an American identity. His combination of western belligerency and combative individualism was the strongest statement of American distinctiveness since Thomas Jefferson's agrarianism. Did Jackson speak for all of America? The Whigs did not think so. And the definitions of American identity that were beginning to emerge in popular culture and in intellectual circles were more complex than the message coming from the White House. Throughout the nation, however, there was a widespread interest in information and literature of all kinds. The Age of the Common Man would prove to be the period when American writers and painters found the national themes that allowed them to produce the first distinctively American literature and art.

POPULAR CULTURES AND THE SPREAD OF THE WRITTEN WORD

The print revolution, described earlier in connection with political parties, had effects far beyond politics. Newspapers and pamphlets fostered a variety of popular cultures. For western readers, the Crockett almanacs offered a mix of humorous stories and tall tales attributed to Davy Crockett (the boisterous Tennessee "roarer" who died defending the Alamo in 1836). In New York City, the immensely popular "penny papers" (so called from their price) that began appearing in 1833 fostered a distinctive urban culture. These papers, with lurid headlines such as "Double Suicide" and "Secret Tryst," fed the same popular appetite for scandal as did other popular publications. Throughout the country, religious literature was still most widely read, but a small

HOW DID Americans create their own cultural identity in the first half of the nineteenth century?

Read the **Document**
Davy Crockett, Advice to Politicians (1833) at **www.myhistorylab.com**

QUICK REVIEW

The Print Revolution

♦ 1826: First use of steam-powered press in the United States.

♦ Greatest growth was in newspapers.

♦ Newspapers and pamphlets fostered a variety of popular cultures.

middle-class audience existed for literary magazines and, among women especially, for sentimental magazines and novels.

Accompanying all these changes in print communication was an invention that outsped them all: the telegraph, so innovative that its inventor spent years fruitlessly seeking private funds to back its application. Finally, with financing from the federal government, Samuel F. B. Morse sent his first message from Washington to Baltimore in 1844. Soon messages in Morse code would be transmitted instantaneously across the continent. The timeliness of information available to the individual, from important national news to the next train's arrival time, vastly increased. Distant events gained new and exciting immediacy. Everyone's horizon and sense of community were widened.

CREATING A NATIONAL AMERICAN CULTURE

In a famous essay in the *Edinburgh Review* in 1820, Sidney Smith bitingly inquired, "In the four quarters of the globe, who reads an American book? or goes to an American play? or looks at an American picture or statue? What does the world yet owe to American physicians or surgeons? What new substances have their chemists discovered?" The answer was nothing—yet.

In the early years of the nineteenth century, eastern seaboard cities actively built the cultural foundation that would nurture American art and literature. Philadelphia's American Philosophical Society, founded by Benjamin Franklin in 1743, boasted a distinguished roster of scientists. Culturally, Boston ran a close second to Philadelphia. Southern cities were much less successful in supporting culture. Charleston had a Literary and Philosophical Society (founded in 1814), but the widely dispersed residences of the southern elite made urban cultural institutions difficult to sustain. Thus, unwittingly, the South ceded cultural leadership to the North.

The cultural picture was much spottier in the West. A few cities, such as Lexington, Kentucky, and Cincinnati, Ohio, had civic cultural institutions, and some transplanted New Englanders maintained connections with New England culture. But most pioneers were at best uninterested and at worst actively hostile to traditional literary culture. This was neither from lack of literacy nor from a failure to read. Newspaper and religious journals both had large readerships in the West. The frontier emphasis on the practical was hard to distinguish from anti-intellectualism.

Thus, in the early part of the nineteenth century, the gap between the intellectual and cultural horizons of a wealthy Bostonian and a frontier farmer in Michigan widened. Part of the unfinished task of building a national society was the creation of a national culture that could fill this gap. For writers and artists, the challenge was to find distinctively American themes.

Asher Durand, a member of the Hudson River School of landscape painting, produced this work, *Kindred Spirits*, as a tribute to Thomas Cole, the leader of the school. Cole is one of the figures depicted standing in a romantic wilderness.

Asher Brown Durand, *Kindred Spirits*, 1849. Oil on canvas, 44 × 36 in. Collection of the New York Public Library, Astor, Lenox and Tilden Foundations.

CHRONOLOGY

1819	*Dartmouth College* v. *Woodward*
1821	Mexican independence from Spain
1824	*Gibbons* v. *Ogden*
	John Quincy Adams elected president by the House of Representatives
1826	First American use of the steam-powered printing press
1828	Congress passes "Tariff of Abominations"
	Andrew Jackson elected president
	John C. Calhoun publishes *Exposition and Protest* anonymously
1830	Jackson vetoes Maysville Road Bill
	Congress passes Indian Removal Act
1832	Nullification Crisis begins
	Jackson vetoes renewal of Bank of the United States charter
	Jackson reelected president
1833	General Antonio Lopez de Santa Anna elected president of Mexico
1834	Whig Party organized
	British abolish slavery in their Caribbean colonies
1836	Jackson issues Specie Circular
	Martin Van Buren elected president
1837	*Charles River Bridge* v. *Warren Bridge*
	Revolts against Britain in Upper and Lower Canada
	Ralph Waldo Emerson first presents "The American Scholar"
	Panic of 1837
1838	Cherokee removal along the "Trail of Tears"
1840	Whig William Henry Harrison elected president
	Act of Union merges Upper and Lower Canada
1841	John Tyler assumes presidency at the death of President Harrison

Of the eastern cities, New York produced the first widely recognized American writers. In 1819, Washington Irving published *The Sketch Book*, thus immortalizing Rip Van Winkle and the Headless Horseman. Within a few years, James Fenimore Cooper's Leatherstocking novels (of which *The Last of the Mohicans*, published in 1826, is the best known) established the experience of westward expansion, of which the conquest of the Indians was a vital part, as a serious and distinctive American literary theme.

It was New England, however, that claimed to be the forge of American cultural independence from Europe. As Ralph Waldo Emerson proclaimed in "The American Scholar," a lecture he delivered in 1837 to the Harvard faculty, "Our day of dependence, our long apprenticeship to the learning of other lands, draws to a close." Immensely popular, Emerson gave more than 1,500 lectures in twenty states between 1833 and 1860. "The American Scholar," his most famous lecture, carried a message of cultural self-sufficiency that Americans were eager to hear.

Read the **Document**

Exploring America: American Art at **www.myhistorylab.com**

ARTISTS AND BUILDERS

Artists were as successful as novelists in finding American themes. Thomas Cole, who came to America from England in 1818, painted American scenes in the style of the British romantic school of landscape painting. Cole founded the Hudson River school of American painting, a style and subject matter frankly nationalistic in tone.

The western painters—realists such as Karl Bodmer and George Catlin as well as the romantics who followed them, like Albert Bierstadt and Thomas Moran—drew on the dramatic western landscape and its peoples. Their art was an important contribution to the American sense of the land and to the nation's identity.

The haste and transience of American life are nowhere as obvious as in the architectural record of this era, which is sparse. In general, Americans were in too much of a hurry to build for the future, and in balloon-frame construction, they found the perfect

technique for the present. Balloon-frame structures—which consist of a basic frame of wooden studs fastened with crosspieces top and bottom—could be put up quickly, cheaply, and without the help of a skilled carpenter. The four-room balloon-frame house, affordable to many who could not have paid for a traditionally built dwelling, became standard in that decade. This was indeed housing for the common man and his family.

CONCLUSION

Andrew Jackson's presidency witnessed the building of a strong national party system based on nearly universal white manhood suffrage. Sectionalism and localism seemed to have been replaced by a more national consciousness that was clearly expressed in the two national political parties, the Whigs and the Democrats. The Second American Party System created new democratic political communities united by common political opinions and often mobilized by common political resentments.

Culturally, American writers and artists began to establish a distinctive American identity in the arts. But as the key battles of the Jackson presidency—the Nullification Crisis, Indian removal, and the Bank War—showed, the forces of sectionalism resisted the strong nationalizing tendencies of the era. Equally clearly, popular political opinion, once aroused, was not always as controllable as politicians may have wished. As the next chapter will show, economic developments in the North were beginning to create a very different society and electorate from that of the slave South or the rural West.

REVIEW QUESTIONS

1. What reasons might a person of the 1820s and 1830s give for opposing universal white manhood suffrage? Suffrage for free African American men? For women of all races?

2. Opponents believed that Andrew Jackson was unsuited in both political experience and temperament to be president of the United States, yet his presidency is considered one of the most influential in American history. Why?

3. Both the Nullification Crisis and Indian removal raised the constitutional issue of the rights of a minority in a nation governed by majority rule. What rights, in your opinion, does a minority have, and what kinds of laws are necessary to defend those rights?

4. Why was the issue of government support for internal improvements so controversial? What *is* the appropriate role for government in economic development?

5. What were the key differences between Whigs and Democrats? What did each party stand for? Who were their supporters? What were the links between each party's programs and party supporters?

6. What distinctive American themes did the writers, artists, and builders of the 1820s and 1830s express in their works? Are they still considered American themes today?

KEY TERMS

Bank War (p. 256)

Democrats (p. 261)

Indian Removal Act (p. 267)

Nullification Crisis (p. 266)

Second American Party System (p. 271)

Specie Circular (p. 271)

Trail of Tears (p. 267)

Whigs (p. 270)

myhistorylab Connections

Reinforce what you learned in this chapter by studying the many documents, images, maps, review tools, and videos available at www.myhistorylab.com.

Read and Review

✓● Study and Review Chapter 11

●●● Read the Document

A Legal Scholar Opposes Spreading the Vote (1821)

An American Senator Opposes Nullification (1830)

A Choctaw Chief Bids Farewell (1832)

Black Hawk, from "The Life of Black Hawk" (1833)

Michel Chevalier, Society, Manner and Politics in the U.S. (1834)

Ballad of General Jackson and the Six Militia Men (1827)

Proclamation Concerning Nullification (1832)

Memorial of the Cherokee Nation (1830)

John Quincy Adams, Inaugural Address (1825)

Treaty with the Sioux and Other Tribes (1825)

Andrew Jackson, Veto of the Bank Bill (1832)

Alexis de Tocqueville, Democracy in America (1835)

The Force Bill (1833)

Davy Crockett, Advice to Politicians (1833)

👁 See the Map *Native American Land Cessions to 1829*

Research and Explore

●●● Read the Document

Exploring America: American Art

Profile
Davy Crockett

((●● Hear the Audio

Hear the audio files for Chapter 11 at
www.myhistorylab.com.

Jacksonian Democracy and American Politics

H istorians have referred to the years of Jackson's presidency as the Age of the Common Man and the Rise of Democracy. Perhaps this does carry a little too much elaboration with it, but the time of Andrew Jackson was a period of great ferment and change. The Second Great Awakening was stirring the religious and reform values of American citizens. The rise of the second two party system was creating both conflict and confrontation in American politics. The issues of national tariffs and slavery were beginning to divide the states and the slow movement toward civil war was becoming clearly apparent.

TO WHAT degree was the election of 1824 a turning point in American political history? Considering the role of the common man, changes in party operations and campaign tactics, and the growing influence of political patronage, how did the events initiated in that election change American politics between 1824 and 1840?

John Adams, Andrew Jackson, and Henry Clay and the election of 1824 comprise a turning point in U.S. politics. With a field of four candidates, the election for president was thrown to the U.S. House of Representatives where Henry Clay was the Speaker of the House and had heavy influence upon the vote of the members of that chamber. After Adams was elected over Jackson, who had the largest share of popular votes, Adams appointed Clay as the Secretary of State, then seen as a stepping stone to the presidency. Jackson's supporters immediately screamed "corrupt bargain" and the campaign of 1828 was underway before Adams was even inaugurated. Jackson's people coalesced into the Democratic party. Adams' followers became the National Republicans, later evolving into the Whigs. ∎

Henry Clay

JOHN QUINCY ADAMS, A "CORRUPT BARGAIN" OR POLITICS AS USUAL? (1824)

9TH. . . . Mr. Clay came at six, and spent the evening with me in a long conversation explanatory of the past and prospective of the future. He said that the time was drawing near when the choice must be made in the House of Representatives of a President from the three candidates presented by the electoral colleges; that he had been much urged and solicited with regard to the part in that transaction that he should take, and had not been five minutes landed at his lodgings before he had been applied to by a friend of Mr. Crawford's, in a manner so gross that it had disgusted him; that some of my friends also, disclaiming, indeed, to have any authority from me, had repeatedly applied to him, directly or indirectly, urging considerations personal to himself as motives to his cause. He had thought it best to reserve for sometime his determination to himself: first, to give a decent time for his own funeral solemnities as a candidate; and, secondly, to prepare and predispose all his friends to a state of neutrality between the three candidates who would be before the House, so that they might be free ultimately to take that course which might be most conducive to the public interest. The time had now come at which he might be explicit in his communication with me, and he had for that purpose asked this confidential interview. He wished me, as far as I might think proper, to satisfy him with regard to some principles of great public importance, but without any personal considerations for himself. In the question to come before the House between General Jackson, Mr. Crawford, and myself, he had no hesitation in saying that his preference would be for me. ∎

Charles Francis Adams, ed. Memoirs of John Quincy Adams, 12 Volumes (Philadelphia: J. B. Lippincott & Co., 1875)

Presidential Candidates and Political Parties, 1788–1840

IN THE slightly more than fifty years covered in this list, some parties flourished and some died. Some parties rose up to replace earlier parties and some changed into a new political alliance with a different name and evolved political goals.

1788	George Washington – No Party Designation John Adams – No Party Designation
1792	George Washington – No Party Designation John Adams – No Party Designation George Clinton – No Party Designation
1796	John Adams – Federalist Thomas Jefferson – Democratic-Republican Thomas Pinckney – Federalist Aaron Burr – Democratic-Republican
1800	Thomas Jefferson – Democratic-Republican Aaron Burr – Democratic-Republican John Adams – Federalist Charles C. Pinckney – Federalist
1804	Thomas Jefferson – Democratic-Republican Charles C. Pinckney – Federalist
1808	James Madison – Democratic-Republican Charles C. Pinckney – Federalist George Clinton – Democratic-Republican
1812	James Madison – Democratic-Republican Dewitt Clinton – Federalist
1816	James Monroe – Democratic-Republican Rufus King – Federalist
1820	James Monroe – Democratic-Republican John Q. Adams – Independent Republican
1824	John Q. Adams – Democratic-Republican Andrew Jackson – Democratic-Republican William H. Crawford – Democratic-Republican Henry Clay – Democratic-Republican
1828	Andrew Jackson – Democratic John Q. Adams – National Republican
1832	Andrew Jackson – Democratic Henry Clay – National Republican William Wirt – Anti-Masonic John Floyd – National Republican
1836	Martin Van Buren – Democratic William H. Harrison – Whig Hugh L. White – Whig Daniel Webster – Whig W.P. Mangum – Whig
1840	William H. Harrison – Whig Martin Van Buren – Democratic. ∎

Senator William Marcy

SENATOR WILLIAM Marcy gave the name "spoils system" to the practice of awarding political office to the supporters of your own party once you had won control of either state or federal government. His famous statement on the floor of the U.S. Senate: "When they are contending for victory, they avow the intention of enjoying it. If they are defeated, they expect to retire from office. If they are successful, they claim as matter of right the advantages of success. They see nothing wrong in the rule that to the victors belong the spoils of the enemy." This principal had been used heavily in the states of New York and Pennsylvania where Marcy engaged brutally in applying the practice. It was not until Jackson's election in 1828 the spoils system was introduced at the federal level. Previous presidents had been circumspect in removing federal office servers from their jobs. Washington had removed only 9 in two terms; Adams had removed 9 in one term. After the Federalists were defeated in 1800 and the Democratic Republicans took office, Jefferson refused to utilize the spoils system and removed only 39 federal office holders in two terms. Madison then dropped only 5 in two terms, Monroe removed only 9 in two terms, and John Q. Adams fired only 2 in one administration. This changed in 1829 when Jackson removed a total of 734 federal office holders in a single year of his first administration. The age of the spoils system had arrived. The Democrats clearly used the spoils system to their advantage. How did the other political parties respond to this concept?

◄ William Learned Marcy (1786–1857). American political leader. Steel engraving, 19th century.

ANDREW JACKSON, STATE OF THE UNION MESSAGE TO CONGRESS, DECEMBER 8, 1829

…The duties of all public officers are, or at least admit of being made, so plain and simple that men of intelligence may readily qualify themselves for their performance; and I can not but believe that more is lost by the long continuance of men in office than is generally to be gained by their experience. I submit, therefore, to your consideration whether the efficiency of the Government would not be promoted and official industry and integrity better secured by a general extension of the law which limits appointments to four years. ∎

Now if rights are founded on the nature of moral being, then the mere circumstance of sex does not give to man higher rights and responsibilities, than to woman. To suppose that it does, would be to deny the self-evident truth, that the physical constitution is the mere instrument of the moral nature.

—Angelina Emily Grimké, October 2, 1837

The Merrimack textile mills with boarding houses, Middlesex Company Woolen Mills, Lowell, Massachusetts.

12

INDUSTRY AND THE NORTH
1790s–1840s

((•●—[**Hear** the **Audio**

Hear the audio files for Chapter 12 at **www.myhistorylab.com**.

WHAT WERE the effects of the transportation revolution?

WHAT WAS the market revolution?

HOW DID a new wave of migrants from the North re-shape life in the Old Northwest?

HOW DID the market revolution change the lives of ordinary people?

WHAT VALUES were promoted by the new middle class?

AMERICAN COMMUNITIES

Women Factory Workers Form a Community in Lowell, Massachusetts

IN THE 1820s AND 1830s, YOUNG FARM WOMEN FROM ALL OVER NEW England flocked to Lowell, Massachusetts, to work a twelve-hour day in one of the first cotton textile factories in America. Living six to eight to a room in nearby boardinghouses, the women of Lowell earned an average of $3 a week. Some also attended inexpensive nighttime lectures or classes. Lowell, considered a model factory town, drew worldwide attention. As one admirer of its educated workers said, Lowell was less a factory than a "philanthropic manu-facturing college." The Boston investors who financed Lowell were businessmen, not philanthropists, but they wanted to keep Lowell free of the dirt, poverty, and social disorder that made English fac-tory towns notorious.

Their choice of young women as factory workers seemed shockingly unconventional. In the 1820s and 1830s, young unmar-ried women simply did not live alone; they lived and worked with their parents until they married. In these years of growth and west-ward expansion, however, America was chronically short of labor, and the Lowell manufacturers were shrewd enough to realize that young farm women were an untapped labor force. To attract respectable young women, Lowell offered supervision both on the job and at home, with strict rules of conduct, compulsory religious services, cultural opportunities such as concerts and lectures, and cash wages.

When they first arrived in Lowell, the young women were often bewildered by the large numbers of townspeople and embarrassed by their own rural clothing and country ways. The air of the mill was hot, humid, full of cotton lint, and the noise of the machinery was constant. It was company policy for senior women to train the newcomers, and often sisters or neighbors who had preceded them to the mill helped them adjust to their new surroundings and work routines.

Textile mills ran on a rigid work schedule with fines or penal-ties imposed on latecomers and slackers. Power-driven machinery operated at a sustained, uniform pace throughout every mill; human workers had to learn to do the same. This precise work schedule represented the single largest change from preindustrial work habits, and it was the hardest adjustment for the workers.

Why did young farm women come to Lowell? Some worked out of need, but most regarded Lowell as an opportunity: an escape from rural isolation and from parental supervision, a chance to save for a dowry, or to pay for an education. As writer Lucy Larcom, one of the most famous workers, said, the women who came to Lowell sought "an opening into freer life." Working side by side and living with six to twelve other women, some of whom might be relatives or friends from home, the Lowell women built a close, supportive com-munity for themselves.

The success of Lowell was short-lived. In the 1830s, facing com-petition and poor economic conditions, the owners imposed wage cuts and work speedups that their workforce did not take lightly. Despite the system of paternalistic control at the mills, the close bonds the women forged gave them the courage and solidarity to "turn out" in spontaneous protests, which were, however, unsuccessful in revers-ing the wage cuts. By 1850, the "philanthropic manufactur-ing college" was no more. The original Lowell workforce of New England farm girls had been largely replaced by poor Irish immigrants of both sexes, who earned much less than their predeces-sors. Now Lowell was simply another mill town.

The history of Lowell epitomizes the process by which the North (New England and the Middle Atlantic states) industrialized. A society com-posed largely of self-sufficient farm families changed to one of urban wage earners. Large factories were not common until the 1880s, but long before that decade, most workers had already experienced a fundamental change in their working patterns. Once under way, the market revolu-tion changed how people worked, how they thought, and how they lived: the very basis of community. In the early years of the nineteenth century, northern communities led this transformation, fostering atti-tudes far different from those prevalent in the agrarian South.

Lowell

•••◖ **Read** the **Document**

A Week at the Mill (1845)
at **www.myhistorylab.com**

THE TRANSPORTATION REVOLUTION

Between 1800 and 1840, the United States experienced truly revolutionary improvements in transportation. More than any other development, these improvements encouraged Americans to look beyond their local communities to broader ones and to foster the enterprising commercial spirit for which they became so widely known (see Map 12.1).

WHAT WERE the effects of the transportation revolution?

ROADS

In 1800, travel by road was difficult for much of the year. Mud in the spring, dust in the summer, and snow in the winter all made travel by horseback or carriage uncomfortable, slow, and sometimes dangerous. Localities and states tried to improve local roads or contracted with private turnpike companies to build, maintain, and collect tolls on important stretches of road. In general, however, local roads remained poor. The federal government demonstrated its commitment to the improvement of interregional transportation by funding the National Road in 1808. Stretching from Cumberland, Maryland, to Vandalia, Illinois, almost at the Mississippi River, by 1839, the National Road tied the East and the West together and helped to foster a national community.

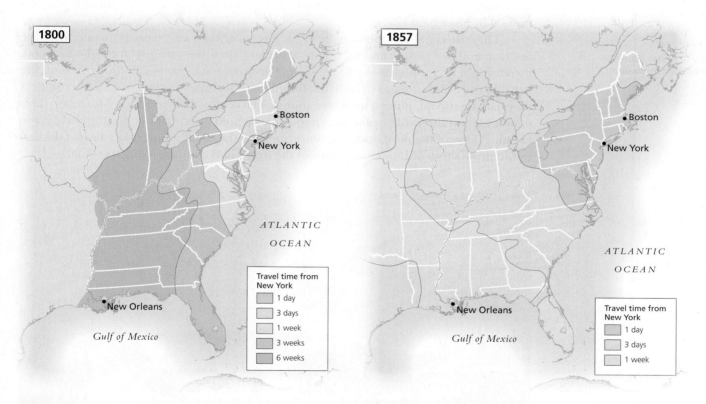

MAP 12.1

Travel Times, 1800 and 1857 The transportation revolution dramatically reduced travel times and vastly expanded everyone's horizons. Improved roads, canals, and the introduction of steamboats and railroads made it easier for Americans to move and made even those who did not move less isolated. Better transportation linked the developing West to the eastern seaboard and fostered a sense of national identity and pride.

HOW DID the federal government's funding of the National Road affect life in the United States?

CANALS AND STEAMBOATS

However much they helped the movement of people, the National Road and other roads were unsatisfactory in a commercial sense. Shipments of bulky goods like grain were too slow and expensive by road. Waterborne transportation was much cheaper and still the major commercial link among the Atlantic seaboard states and in the Mississippi–Ohio River system. But before the 1820s, most water routes were north–south or coastal (Boston to Charleston, for example); east–west links were urgently needed. Canals turned out to be the answer.

The Erie Canal was the brainchild of New York governor DeWitt Clinton, who envisioned a link between New York City and the Great Lakes through the Hudson River, and a 364-mile-long canal stretching from Albany to Buffalo. Despite considerable public skepticism, Clinton convinced the New York legislature to approve a bond issue for the canal, and investors (New York and British merchants) subscribed to the tune of $7 million, an immense sum for the day.

Building the canal was a vast engineering and construction challenge. In the early stages, nearby farmers worked for $8 a month, but when malaria hit the workforce in the summer of 1819, many went home. They were replaced by 3,000 Irish contract laborers, who were much more expensive—50 cents a day plus room and board—but more reliable (if they survived). The importation of foreign contract labor for this job was a portent of the future. Much of the heavy construction work on later canals and railroads was performed by immigrant labor.

The Erie canal was the wonder of the age, providing easy passage to and from the interior, both for people and for goods. It drew settlers like a magnet from the East and, increasingly, from overseas: by 1830, some 50,000 people a year were moving west on the canal to the rich farmland of Indiana, Illinois, and territory farther west. Earlier settlers now had a national, indeed an international, market for their produce. Moreover, farm families along the canal began purchasing household goods and cloth, formerly made at home. One of the most dramatic illustrations of the canal's impact was a rapid decline in the production of homespun cloth in the towns and counties along its route.

The Erie Canal bustled with commerce almost from the moment of its opening in 1825. Five boats are shown waiting their turn to enter the lock that will raise each of them to the next level of the canal.

Collection of The New-York Historical Society, Negative # 34684.

Towns along the canal—Utica, Rochester, Buffalo—became instant cities, each an important commercial center in its own right. Perhaps the greatest beneficiary was New York City, which quickly established a commercial and financial supremacy no other American city could match. The Erie Canal decisively turned New York's merchants away from Europe and toward America's own heartland, building both interstate commerce and a feeling of community.

The phenomenal success of the Erie Canal prompted other states to construct similar waterways to tap the rich interior market. Between 1820 and 1840, $200 million was invested in canal building. No other waterway achieved the success of the Erie. Nevertheless, the spurt of canal building ended the geographical isolation of much of the country.

An even more important improvement in water transportation, especially in the American interior, was the steamboat. Robert Fulton first demonstrated the commercial feasibility of steamboats in 1807, and they were soon operating in the East. Steamboats transformed commerce on the country's great inland river system: the Ohio, the Mississippi, the Missouri, and their tributaries. Steamboats were extremely dangerous, however; boiler explosions, fires, and sinkings were common, leading to one of the first public demands for regulation of private enterprise in 1838.

The increased river- and canal-borne trade, like the New England shipping boom of a generation earlier, stimulated urban growth and all kinds of commerce. Cities such as Cincinnati, already notable for its rapid growth, experienced a new economic surge. A frontier outpost in 1790, Cincinnati was by the 1830s a center of steamboat manufacture and machine tool production as well as a central shipping point for food for the southern market.

RAILROADS

Remarkable as all these transportation changes were, the most remarkable was still to come. Railroads, new in 1830 (when the Baltimore and Ohio Railroad opened with thirteen miles of track), grew to an astounding 31,000 miles by 1860. By that date, New England and the Old Northwest had laid a dense network of rails, and several lines had reached west beyond the Mississippi. The South, the least industrialized section of the nation, had fewer railroads.

THE EFFECTS OF THE TRANSPORTATION REVOLUTION

The new ease of transportation fueled economic growth by making distant markets accessible. The startling successes of innovations such as canals and railroads attracted large capital investments, including significant amounts from foreign investors ($500 million between 1790 and 1861), which fueled further growth.

Every east–west road, canal, and railroad helped to reorient Americans away from the Atlantic and toward the heartland. This new focus was decisive in the creation of national pride and identity. The transportation revolution fostered an optimistic, risk-taking mentality in the United States that stimulated invention and innovation. More than anything, the transportation revolution allowed people to move with unaccustomed ease. Transportation improvements linked Americans in larger communities of interest, beyond the local communities in which they lived. And improved transportation made possible the larger market on which commercialization and industrialization depended (see Map 12.2).

This Currier and Ives print of 1849, *The Express Train*, captures the popular awe at the speed and wonder of the new technology. This "express" probably traveled no more than thirty miles per hour.

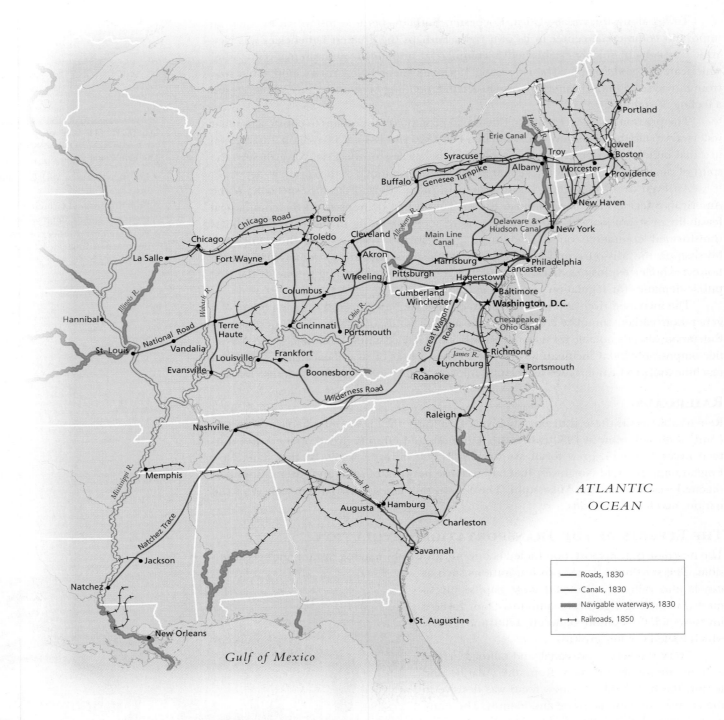

MAP 12.2

Commercial Links: Rivers, Canals, Roads, 1830, and Rail Lines, 1850 By 1830, the United States was tied together by a network of roads, canals, and rivers. This transportation revolution fostered a great burst of commercial activity and economic growth. Transportation improvements accelerated the commercialization of agriculture by getting farmers' products to wider, nonlocal markets. Access to wider markets likewise encouraged new textile and other manufacturers to increase their scale of production. By 1850, another revolutionary mode of transportation, the railroad, had emerged as a vital link to the transportation infrastructure.

HOW DID the transportation revolution of the mid-nineteenth century fuel the American economy?

THE MARKET REVOLUTION

The **market revolution**, the most fundamental change American communities had ever experienced, was the outcome of three interrelated developments: the rapid improvements in transportation just described, commercialization, and industrialization. Commercialization involved the replacement of household self-sufficiency and barter with the production of goods for a cash market. And industrialization involved the use of power-driven machinery to produce goods once made by hand.

THE ACCUMULATION OF CAPITAL

In the northern states, the business community was composed largely of merchants in the seaboard cities: Boston, Providence, New York City, Philadelphia, and Baltimore. Many had made substantial profits in the international shipping boom period from 1790 to 1807 (as discussed in Chapter 9). Such extraordinary opportunities attracted enterprising people. John Jacob Astor, who had arrived penniless from Germany in 1784, made his first fortune in the fur trade. Astor made a second fortune in New York real estate, and when he retired in 1834 with $25 million, he was reputed to be the wealthiest man in America.

When the early years of the nineteenth century posed difficulties for international trade, some of the nation's wealthiest men turned to local investments. In Providence, Rhode Island, Moses Brown and his son-in-law William Almy began to invest some of the profits the Brown family had reaped from a worldwide trade in iron, candles, rum, and African slaves in the new manufacture of cotton textiles. Cincinnati merchants banded together to finance the building of the first steamboats to operate on the Ohio River.

Much of the capital for the new investments came from banks. An astonishing amount of capital, however, was raised through family connections. In the late eighteenth century, members of the business communities in the seaboard cities had begun to consolidate their position and property by intermarriage. In Boston, such a strong community developed that when Francis Cabot Lowell needed $300,000 in 1813 to build the world's first automated cotton mill in Waltham, Massachusetts (the prototype of the Lowell mills), he had only to turn to his family network.

Southern cotton provided the capital for continuing development. Because Northerners built the nation's ships, controlled the shipping trade, and provided the nation's banking, insurance, and financial services, the astounding growth in southern cotton exports enriched northern merchants almost as much as southern planters. Although imperfectly understood at the time, the truth is that the development of northern industry was paid for by southern cotton produced by enslaved African American labor. The surprising wealth that cotton brought to southern planters fostered the market revolution.

Finally, the willingness of American merchants to "think big" and risk their money in the development of a large domestic market was caused in part by American nationalism. Their confidence in a future that did not yet exist was not simply a sober economic calculation but an assertion of pride in the potential of this new and expanding nation.

THE PUTTING-OUT SYSTEM

Initially, the American business community invested not in machinery and factories, but in the "**putting-out system**" of home manufacture. In this significant departure from preindustrial work, people still produced goods at home, but under the direction of a merchant, who "put out" the raw materials to them, paid them a certain sum per finished piece, and sold the completed item to a distant market. A look at the shoe industry in Lynn, Massachusetts, shows how the putting-out system transformed American manufacturing.

Long a major center of the shoe industry, Lynn, in 1800, produced 400,000 pairs of shoes—enough for every fifth person in the country. Skilled craftsmen in Lynn controlled production through the traditional system of apprenticeship. Apprentices lived with the

---

WHAT WAS the market revolution?

Watch the **Video**
Nineteenth-Century Industrialization at **www.myhistorylab.com**

market revolution The outcome of three interrelated developments: rapid improvements in transportation, commercialization, and industrialization.

putting-out system Production of goods in private homes under the supervision of a merchant who "put out" the raw materials, paid a certain sum per finished piece, and sold the completed item to a distant market.

This carved and painted figure, designed as a whirligig and trade sign, shows a woman at a spinning wheel. Until the transportation revolution made commercial cloth widely available, spinning was one of the most time-consuming tasks that women and young girls did at home.

QUICK REVIEW

Apprenticeship System

◆ Trades were controlled through a system of apprenticeship.

◆ Apprentices learned their craft over a three-to-seven-year period.

◆ Apprentices usually lived with the master craftsman overseeing their training.

QUICK REVIEW

The Putting-Out System

◆ Production of goods at home under the supervision of a merchant.

◆ Lynn, Massachusetts used putting-out system to become a center of the shoe industry.

◆ System gave control of production to merchant capitalists.

HOW DID a new wave of migrants from the North re-shape life in the Old Northwest?

master craftsman and were treated like members of the family. Commonly, apprentices became journeymen craftsmen, working for wages in the shops of master craftsmen until they had enough capital to set up shop for themselves. Although production of shoes in Lynn increased yearly from 1780 to 1810 as markets widened, shoes continued to be manufactured in traditional ways.

The investment of merchant capital in the shoe business changed everything. In Lynn, a small group of Quaker shopkeepers and merchants, connected by family, religious, and business ties, took the lead in reorganizing the trade. Financed by the bank they founded in 1814, Lynn capitalists like Micajah Pratt built large, two-story central workshops. Pratt employed a few skilled craftsmen to cut leather for shoes, but he put out the rest of the shoemaking to less-skilled workers who were no longer connected by family ties. Putting-out workers were paid on a piecework basis, much less than a master craftsman or a journeyman. Gradually the putting-out system and central workshops replaced artisans' shops. Some artisans became wealthy owners of workshops, but most became wage earners, and the apprenticeship system eventually disappeared.

The putting-out system moved the control of production from the individual artisan households to the merchant capitalists, who could now control labor costs, production goals, and shoe styles to fit certain markets. For example, the Lynn trade quickly monopolized the market for cheap boots for southern slaves and western farmers, leaving workshops in other cities to produce shoes for wealthier customers. This specialization of the national market—indeed, even thinking in terms of a national market—was new. Additionally, the owner of the business controlled the workers and could cut back or expand the labor force as economic and marketplace conditions warranted.

While the central workshop system prevailed in Lynn and in urban centers like New York City, the putting-out system also fostered a more dispersed form of home production. By 1810, there were an estimated 2,500 so-called outwork weavers in New England, operating handlooms in their own homes. Other crafts that rapidly became organized according to the putting-out system were flax and wool spinning, straw braiding, glove making, and the knitting of stockings.

THE SPREAD OF COMMERCIAL MARKETS

Although the putting-out system meant a loss of independence for artisans such as those in Lynn, Massachusetts, New England farm families liked it. From their point of view, the work could easily be combined with domestic work, and the pay was a new source of income that they could use to purchase mass-produced goods rather than spend the time required to make those things themselves. In this way farm families moved away from the local barter system and into a larger market economy.

Commercialization, or the replacement of barter by a cash economy, did not happen immediately or uniformly throughout the nation. Fixed prices for goods produced by the new principles of specialization and division of labor appeared first along established trade routes. Rural areas in established sections of the country that were remote from trade routes continued in traditional ways (see Seeing History). Strikingly, however, western farming frontiers were commercial from the very start. The existence of a cash market was an important spur to westward expansion.

THE YANKEE WEST

Every advance in transportation made it easier for farmers to get their produce to market. Improvements in agricultural machinery increased the amount of acreage a farmer could cultivate. These two developments, added to the availability of rich,

Industrialization and Rural Life

At first glance, this looks like a typical rural landscape of the well-known genre known as pastoral painting. But look again: what is the locomotive doing there? Its presence must have been a shock to the first viewers, who were familiar with pastoral landscapes but unfamiliar with new inventions like the steam locomotive in this setting. To appreciate its novelty, contrast this painting to the Currier and Ives print in *The Express Train* on p. 285.

WHY DO you think the railroad company chose Inness, known for his landscapes, to paint the picture? What kind of statement about the relationship between industrialization and rural life does the painting make?

George Inness was an American artist who specialized in painting settled and cultivated eastern landscapes. This painting was commissioned by the president of the Delaware Lackawanna and Western Railroad to mark its opening. Inness rose to the challenge of blending a locomotive, double tracks (foreground) and the roundhouse (background) into a rural landscape. However, the railroad committee was not satisfied, demanding that he show all four company locomotives (three are in the background) and that the letters *D.L.&W* be painted on the side of the nearest one. At first Inness refused on artistic grounds, but being in need of money, he finally agreed. The painting is thus one of the first American examples of a "fine art" advertisement. Even at this early date, there was conflict between the demands of art and those of the advertiser. ■

LeRoy Ireland, *The Works of George Inness, An Illustrated Catalogue Raisonne* (Austin: University of Texas Press, 1965), p. 28.

inexpensive land in the heartland, dramatically changed the Old Northwest. The sudden change from subsistence to commercial agriculture in the Old Northwest is a particularly vivid example of the impact of transportation changes and commercialization.

NEW ROUTES WEST

The impact of the transportation revolution on the Old Northwest was startling. Settlement of the region, ongoing since the 1790s, vastly accelerated and shifted. Before 1830, most migrants had traveled by the Pennsylvania Turnpike or the National Road to settle in the southern part of the region. In the 1830s, after the opening of the Erie Canal, migrants from New England streamed into northern Ohio, Illinois, Indiana, southern Wisconsin, and Michigan and began to reach into Iowa. By 1850 the population of the Old Northwest almost quadrupled.

Migrants of New England origin (Yankees) accounted for at least 40 percent of the population, and they brought with them a distinctive culture that stressed community building. New Englanders immediately established schools, churches, and town government in their new locations. Southern migrants, like their counterparts who migrated to the Old Southwest, were much more likely to rely on kinship ties rather than found community institutions, except for churches. Yankees were different from Southerners in another way: they welcomed commercial agriculture.

COMMERCIAL AGRICULTURE IN THE OLD NORTHWEST

The long period of subsistence farming that had characterized colonial New England and the early Ohio Valley frontier before 1830 was superseded by commercial agriculture stimulated by the transportation revolution and by government policy. The easy terms of federal land sales were an important inducement: terms eased from an initial rate of $2.00 per acre for a minimum of 320 acres in 1800 to $1.25 an acre for 80 acres in 1820. Still, this was too much for most settlers to pay all at once and many settlers relied on credit.

The very need for cash to purchase land involved western settlers in commercial agriculture from the beginning. Farmers, and the towns and cities that grew up to supply them, needed access to markets for their crops. Local residents clamored for the canals and railroads that tied the individual farm into national and international commercial networks. Commercial agriculture in turn encouraged regional specialization. The constant opening of new farmland encouraged mobility: prepared to move on when the price was right, many Yankee farmers regarded their farmland not as a permanent investment but as a speculation. This too marked a difference from colonial and southern attitudes in which permanent ownership of farms, with enough to land to endow one's sons, had always been the goal.

New tools made western farmers unusually productive. Steel plows and seed drills aided productivity, but the most remarkable innovation was Cyrus McCormick's reaper, patented in 1834. Previously, harvesting had depended on manpower alone. A man could cut two or three acres of wheat a day, but with the horse-drawn reaper, he could cut twelve acres. Western farmers rushed to buy the new machines, confident that increased production would rapidly pay for them. In most years, their confidence was justified. But in bad years, farmers found that their new levels of debt could mean failure and foreclosure. They were richer but more economically vulnerable than they had been before.

Thus, within a few short years the Old Northwest became the nation's agricultural heartland. In 1859, the region produced 46 percent of the nation's wheat and 33 percent of its corn. Moreover, a steadily

This advertisement contrasts farmers harvesting traditionally with a sickle compared to the speed of the mechanized McCormick reaper.

increasing amount was exported to foreign markets. While Southerners boasted in 1858 that "Cotton is note the problem of consistent capitalization King," in fact the Old Northwest, not the South, had become the export heart of the national economy.

TRANSPORTATION CHANGES AFFECT WESTERN CITIES

The changing fortunes of the region's major cities demonstrate the dramatic effects of improvements in transportation. Before 1830, Ohioans shipped corn and hogs first by flatboat and later by steamboat down the Ohio and Mississippi Rivers to New Orleans. Cincinnati, the center of the Ohio trade, earned the nickname "Porkopolis" because of the importance of its slaughterhouses.

After 1830, with the opening of the Erie Canal and canals in Ohio and Illinois, St. Louis became the distribution point for the flood of goods New York merchants sent westward via the canal system. St. Louis became a magnet for migration: in 1849, the year of the California gold rush (see Chapter 14), 60,000 people passed through the city and surprisingly one third of them stayed.

After 1840, with the impact of railroads, the region's distribution system changed again, causing Chicago to grow at an incredible rate. By 1860, it had reached a population of 100,000 and, although still smaller than Cincinnati and St. Louis, was clearly destined to become the nation's east–west hub (see Map 12.3).

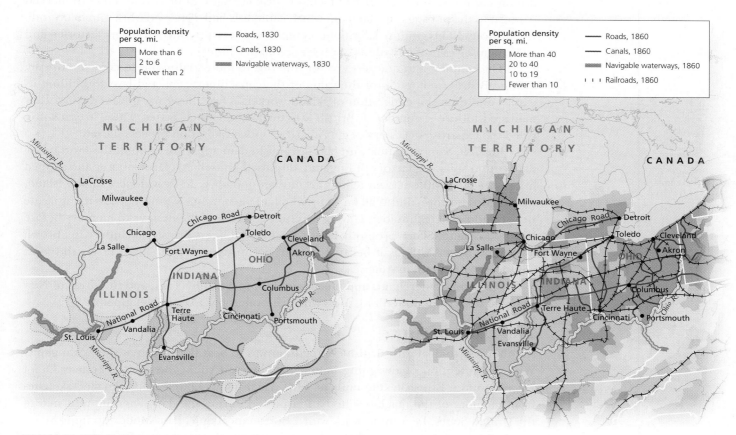

MAP 12.3A AND 12.3B

Commercial Links: The Old Northwest, 1830, 1860   After 1825, the Erie Canal brought streams of migrants to the upper parts of the Old Northwest, where they quickly built roads, canals, and railroads. These maps illustrate the changes in transportation that made their commercial agriculture possible.

WHAT EFFECT did the opening of various canals, including the Erie Canal, have on cities such as St. Louis, Chicago, and New Orleans?

The loser in this economic redistribution was New Orleans. As early as 1853, only 30 percent of Old Northwest produce was shipped via New Orleans, while 60 percent was exported via the Erie Canal. Railroads increased the disparity, while at the same time they provided easy transportation to New Englanders who wanted to move west. These new transportation links tied the Old Northwest to New York and New England economically and politically, creating, as one southerner bitterly commented, a "universal Yankee nation" that was a huge factor in the sectional disputes and eventual civil war that were to come (see Chapter 15).

INDUSTRIALIZATION BEGINS

The most dramatic single aspect of the market revolution was industrialization. Even in its earliest stages, industrialization changed the nature of work itself.

BRITISH TECHNOLOGY AND AMERICAN INDUSTRIALIZATION

It was the third component of the market revolution, industrialization, that brought the greatest changes to personal lives. Begun in Britain in the eighteenth century, industrialization was the result of a series of technological changes in the textile trade. In marked contrast to the putting-out system, in which capitalists had dispersed work into many individual households, industrialization required workers to concentrate in factories and pace themselves to the rhythms of power-driven machinery.

The simplest and quickest way for America to industrialize was to copy the British, but the British, well aware of the value of their machinery, enacted laws forbidding its export and even the emigration of skilled workers. Over the years, however, Americans managed to lure a number of British artisans to the United States. These artisans provided the expertise necessary to get America's industrialization process started.

In 1789, Samuel Slater, who had just finished an apprenticeship in the most up-to-date cotton spinning factory in England, disguised himself as a farm laborer and slipped out of England without even telling his mother good-bye. In Providence, Rhode Island, he met Moses Brown and William Almy, who had been trying without success to duplicate British industrial technology. Having carefully committed the designs to memory before leaving England, Slater promptly built copies of the latest British machinery for Brown and Almy. Slater Mill, as it became known, began operation in 1790. It was the most advanced cotton mill in America.

Many other merchants and mechanics followed Slater's lead, and the rivers of New England were soon dotted with mills wherever waterpower could be tapped.

THE LOWELL MILLS

Another way to deal with British competition was to beat the British at their own game. With the intention of designing better machinery, a young Bostonian, Francis Cabot Lowell, toured British textile mills in 1810. Each night, Lowell made detailed sketches from memory of the machines he had inspected during the day. When he returned to the United States, he went to work with a Boston mechanic, Paul Moody, to improve on the British models. Lowell and Moody not only made the machinery for spinning cotton more efficient, but they also invented a power loom. This was a great advance, for now all aspects of textile manufacture could be gathered together in the same factory. In 1814, Lowell opened the world's first integrated cotton mill in Waltham, near Boston. It was a great success: in 1815, the Boston Associates (Lowell's partners) made profits of 25 percent, and their efficiency allowed them to survive the intense British competition following the War of 1812. Many smaller New England mills did not survive.

HOW DID industrialization change the nature of work in early nineteenth-century America?

The Boston Associates took the lesson to heart, and when they moved their enterprise to a new location in 1823, they thought big. They built an entire town at the junction of the Concord and Merrimack Rivers. The new industrial community boasted six mills and company housing for all the workers. In 1826, the town had 2,500 inhabitants; ten years later the population was 17,000 (see Map 12.4).

FAMILY MILLS

Lowell was unique. Much more common in the early days of industrialization were small rural spinning mills, built on swiftly running streams near existing farm communities. Because the owners of smaller mills often hired entire families, their operations came to be called family mills. Children aged eight to twelve, whose customary job was "doffing" (changing) bobbins on the spinning machines, made up 50 percent of the workforce. Women and men each made up about 25 percent of the workforce, but men had the most skilled and best-paid jobs.

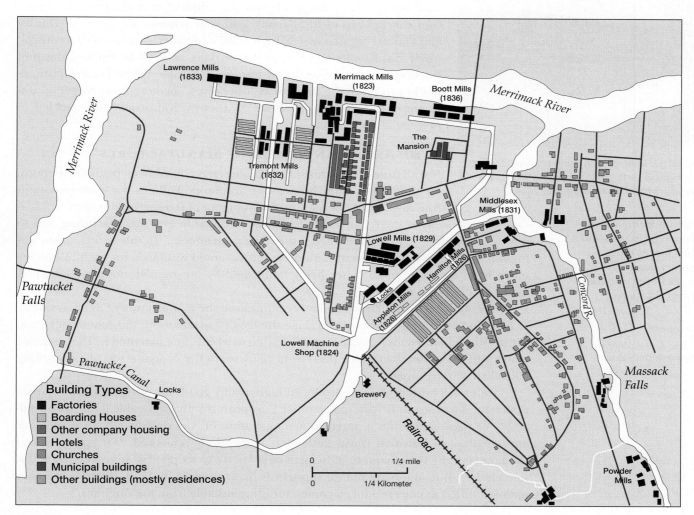

MAP 12.4

Lowell, Massachusetts, 1832   This town plan of Lowell, Massachusetts, in 1832, illustrates the comprehensive relationship the owners envisaged between the factories and the workforce. The mills are located on the Merrimack River, while nearby are the boardinghouses for the single young female workers, row houses for the male mechanics and their families, and houses for the overseers. Somewhat farther away is the mansion of the company agent.

WHAT DOES this town plan tell you about the vision and goals of the town planners?

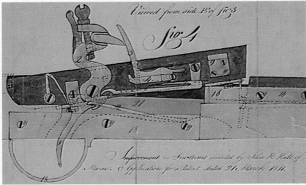

In 1816, Connecticut gunsmith Simeon North produced the first gun with interchangeable parts. North's invention formed the basis of the American system of manufactures.

American system A technique of production pioneered in the United States in the first half of the nineteenth century that relied on precision manufacturing with the use of interchangeable parts.

●●●—[Read the **Document**

Employers Advertise for Help Wanted in the 1820s at **www.myhistorylab.com**

Relations between these small rural mill communities and the surrounding farming communities were often difficult, as the history of the towns of Dudley and Oxford, Massachusetts, shows. Samuel Slater built three small mill communities near these towns in the early years of the nineteenth century. Each consisted of a small factory, a store, and cottages and a boardinghouse for workers. Most of Slater's workers came from outside the Dudley–Oxford area. They were a mixed group—single young farm women of the kind Lowell attracted, the poor and destitute, and workers from other factories looking for better conditions. They rarely stayed long.

Slater's mills also provided a substantial amount of work for local people, putting out to them both the initial cleaning of the raw cotton and the much more lucrative weaving of the spun yarn. Nevertheless, relations between Slater and his workers on one side and the farmers and shopkeepers of the Dudley and Oxford communities on the other were stormy. They disagreed over the building of mill dams, over taxes, over the upkeep of local roads, and over schools. Residents of Dudley and Oxford became increasingly hostile to Slater's authoritarian control. Their dislike carried over to the workers as well. Disdaining the mill workers for their poverty and transiency, people in the rural communities began referring to them as "operatives," making them somehow different in their work roles from themselves. Industrial work thus led to new social distinctions.

"THE AMERICAN SYSTEM OF MANUFACTURES"

Not all American industrial technology was copied from British inventions, for there were many homegrown inventors. Perhaps the most important American invention was the development of standardized parts.

The concept of interchangeable parts, realized first in gun manufacturing, was so unusual that the British soon dubbed it the "**American system.**" In this system, a gun was broken down into its component parts and an exact mold was made for each. All pieces made from the same mold (after being hand filed by inexpensive unskilled laborers) matched a uniform standard.

Standardized production quickly revolutionized the manufacture of items as simple as nails and as complicated as clocks. Like the factory system itself, the American system spread slowly. For example, Isaac Singer's sewing machine, first patented in 1851, was not made with fully interchangeable parts until 1873, when the company was already selling 230,000 machines a year.

American businesses mass-produced high-quality goods for ordinary people earlier than manufacturers in Britain or any other European country were able to do. The availability of these goods was a practical demonstration of American beliefs in democracy and equality. As historian David Potter has perceptively remarked, "European radical thought is prone to demand that the man of property be stripped of his carriage and his fine clothes. But American radical thought is likely to insist, instead, that the ordinary man is entitled to mass-produced copies, indistinguishable from the originals."

FROM ARTISAN TO WORKER

HOW DID the market revolution change the lives of ordinary people?

The changes wrought by the market revolution had major and lasting effects on ordinary Americans. The proportion of wage laborers in the nation's labor force rose from 12 percent in 1800 to 40 percent by 1860. Most of these workers were employed in the North, and almost half were women, performing piecework in their homes. The young farm woman who worked at Lowell for a year or two, then returned home; the master craftsman in Lynn who expanded his shop with the aid of merchant capital; the home weaver who prospered on outwork from Slater's mill—all were participating, often unknowingly, in fundamental personal and social changes.

PREINDUSTRIAL WAYS OF WORKING

When Lowell began operation, 97 percent of all Americans still lived on farms, and most work was done in or near the home. Work was slow, unscheduled, and task oriented. People did their jobs as they needed to be done, along with the daily household routine. "Home" and "work" were not separate locations or activities but were intermixed. Likewise, in urban areas, skilled craftsmen organized the apprenticeship system in the family-learning model, training apprentices who became journeymen and skilled workers in turn.

In both rural and urban settings, working families were organized along strictly patriarchal lines. The man had unquestioned authority to direct the lives and work of family members and apprentices and to decide on occupations for his sons and marriages for his daughters. His wife had many crucial responsibilities, but in all these duties she was subject to the direction of her husband. Men were heads of families and bosses of artisanal shops.

MECHANIZATION AND GENDER

The apprenticeship system was destroyed by the immense increase in productivity made possible by the principles of division of labor and specialization. For example, in New York by the mid-1820s, tailors and shoemakers were teaching apprentices only a few simple operations, using them as helpers. In almost every trade, apprentices no longer lived with the master's family, and their parents received cash payment for the child's work. Thus, in effect, the apprenticeship system was replaced by child labor.

Industrialization posed a further threat to the status and independence of skilled male workers. In trade after trade, mechanization meant that most tasks could be performed by unskilled labor. By 1850, in New York City, many formerly skilled trades, including shoemaking, weaving, silversmithing, pottery making, and cabinetmaking, were filled with unskilled, low-paid workers who did one specialized operation or tended machinery. Many former artisans were reduced to performing wage labor for others. Because women were so frequently hired in the putting-out system, male workers began to oppose female participation in the workforce, fearing that it would lower their own wages.

These fears appeared to be confirmed by the experience of women in the new garment industry, which emerged in the 1820s. In New York City, employers began hiring women to sew ready-made clothing. Most women performed this work at low piecework rates in their homes. Soon the low pay and seasonal nature of the industry became notorious. Overcrowding of the market led to low wages. Women were pushed into the garment trade because they were barred from many occupations considered inappropriate for them, and the oversupply of workers led to wage cutting. To make matters worse, most people believed that "respectable" women did not do factory work (Lowell in its "model" years was the exception that proved the rule), and this disparagement fostered low pay and poor working conditions.

Manufacturers in the garment trade made their profits not from efficient production but by obtaining intensive labor for very low wages. The invention of the sewing machine only made

Read the **Document**
Exploring America: Machinery at **www.myhistorylab.com**

Read the **Document**
Female Industrial Association (1825) at **www.myhistorylab.com**

QUICK REVIEW

Women in the Workforce

- Industrialization threatened skilled male workers.
- Mechanization created opportunities for women to work outside the home.
- The growing garment industry of the 1820s depended on cheap female labor.

This illustration of seamstresses at work, from *Sartain's Union Magazine*, January 1851, shows an early abuse created by the market revolution. Women workers were crowded into just a few occupations, thereby allowing owners to offer very low wages for very long hours of work. The women in this illustration appear to be gathered together in a central workshop, where they had each other for company. Many other women sewed alone at home, often for even lower wages.

**Read the Document**

A New England Factory Issues Regulations for Workers in 1825 at www.myhistorylab.com

matters worse. Manufacturers dropped their piecework rates, and some women found themselves working fifteen to eighteen hours a day, producing more than they ever had but earning the same pay.

TIME, WORK, AND LEISURE

Preindustrial work had a flexibility that factory work did not. Factory workers gradually adjusted to having their lives regulated by the sound of the factory bell, but they did not necessarily become the docile "hands" the owners wanted. Absenteeism was common, accounting for about 15 percent of working hours, and there was much pilfering. Workers were beginning to think of themselves as a separate community whose interests differed from those of owners.

Another adjustment required by the constant pace was that time now had to be divided into two separate activities—work and leisure. In preindustrial times, work and leisure were blended for farmers and artisans. The place of work—often the home—and the pace made it possible to stop and have a chat or a friendly drink with a visitor. Now, however, the separation of home and workplace and the pace of production not only squeezed the fun out of the long workday but also left a smaller proportion of time for leisure activities.

For many workingmen, the favored spot for after-hours and Sunday leisure became the local tavern. Community-wide celebrations and casual sociability, still common in rural areas, began to be replaced in cities by spectator sports and by popular entertainments. Some of these diversions, such as plays and horse racing, appealed to all social classes, but others, like parades, rowdy dance halls, and tavern games like quoits and ninepins were favored working-class amusements. The effect of these changes was to make working-class amusements more distinct, and visible, than they had been before.

FREE LABOR

Another effect of the market revolution was the transformation of a largely barter system into cash payments. For workers, this change was both unsettling and liberating. On the minus side, workers were no longer part of a settled, orderly, and familiar community. On the plus side, they were now free to labor wherever they could, at whatever wages their skills or their bargaining power could command. That workers took their freedom seriously is evidenced by the very high rate of turnover—50 percent a year—in the New England textile mills.

But if moving on was a sign of increased freedom of opportunity for some workers, for others it was an unwanted consequence of the market revolution. In New England, for example, many quite prosperous artisans and farmers faced disruptive competition from factory goods and western commercial agriculture. They could remain where they were only if they were willing to become factory workers or, in the case of farmers, to move west and try to become successful commercial farmers themselves.

At the heart of this industrializing economy was the notion of free labor. Originally, "free" referred to individual economic choice—that is, to the right of workers to move to another job. But "free labor" soon came to encompass as well the range of attitudes—hard work, self-discipline, and a striving for economic independence—that were necessary for success in a competitive, industrializing economy. These were profoundly new and individualistic attitudes.

The spread of the factory system and of the ideology of free labor soon became an issue in the growing political battle between the North and the South over slavery. Southern defenders of slavery compared

TIME TABLE OF THE LOWELL MILLS,

To take effect on and after Oct. 21st, 1851.

The Standard time being that of the meridian of Lowell, as shown by the regulator clock of JOSEPH RAYNES, 43 Central Street

	From 1st to 10th inclusive.				From 11th to 20th inclusive.				From 21st to last day of month.			
	1st Bell	2d Bell	3d Bell	Eve.Bell	1st Bell	2d Bell	3d Bell	Eve.Bell	1st Bell	2d Bell	3d Bell	Eve.Bell.
January,	5.00	6.00	6.50	*7.30	5.00	6 00	6.50	*7.30	5.00	6.00	6.50	*7.30
February,	4.30	5.30	6.40	*7.30	4.30	5.30	6.25	*7.30	4.30	5.30	6.15	*7.30
March,	5.40	6.00		*7.30	5.20	5.40		*7.30	5.05	5.25		6.35
April,	4.45	5.05		6.45	4.30	4.50		6.55	4.30	4.50		7.00
May,	4 30	4.50		7·00	4.30	4.50		7.00	4.30	4.50		7 00
June,	"	"		"	"	"		"	"	"		"
July,	"	"		"	"	"		"	"	"		"
August,	"	"		"	"	"		"	"	"		"
September,	4.40	5.00		6.45	4.50	5.10		6.30	5.00	5.20		*7.30
October,	5.10	5.30		*7.30	5.20	5.40		*7.30	5.35	5.55		*7.30
November,	4.30	5.30	6.10	*7.30	4.30	5.30	6.20	*7.30	5.00	6.00	6.35	*7.30
December,	5.00	6.00	6.45	*7.30	5.00	6.00	6.50	*7.30	5.00	6·00	6.50	*7.30

* Excepting on Saturdays from Sept. 21st to March 20th inclusive, when it is rung at 20 minutes after sunset.

YARD GATES,

Will be opened at ringing of last morning bell, of meal bells, and of evening bells; and kept open Ten minutes.

MILL GATES.

Commence hoisting Mill Gates, Two minutes before commencing work.

WORK COMMENCES,

At Ten minutes after last morning bell, and at Ten minutes after bell which "rings in" from Meals.

BREAKFAST BELLS.

During March "Ring out".........at....7.30 a. m.........."Ring in" at 8:05 a. m.
April 1st to Sept. 20th inclusive.....at....7 00 " " .... " " at 7.35 " "
Sept. 21st to Oct. 31st inclusive....at....7.30 " " .... " " at 8.05 " "
Remainder of year work commences after Breakfast.

DINNER BELLS.

" Ring out"...... ....12.30 p. m........."Ring in".... 1.05 p. m.

In all cases, the *first* stroke of the bell is considered as marking the time.

This timetable from the Lowell Mills illustrates the elaborate time schedules that the cotton textile mills expected their employees to meet. For workers, it was difficult to adjust to the regimentation imposed by clock time, in contrast to the approximate times common to preindustrial work.

their cradle-to-grave responsibility to their slaves with northern employers' "heartless" treatment of their "wage slaves." Certainly the new northern employer assumed less responsibility for individual workers than had the traditional artisan. Moreover, northern employers felt no obligation to help or care for old or disabled workers. Southerners were right: this was a heartless system. But Northerners were also right: industrialization was certainly freer than the slave system, freer even than the hierarchical craft system, although it sometimes offered only the freedom to starve.

EARLY STRIKES

Rural women workers led some of the first strikes in American labor history. In 1824, in one of the first of these actions, women workers at a Pawtucket, Rhode Island, textile mill led their coworkers, female and male, out on strike to protest wage cuts and longer hours.

More famous were the strikes led by the women at the model mill at Lowell. The first serious trouble came in 1834, when 800 women participated in a spontaneous turnout to protest a wage cut of 25 percent. The owners were shocked and outraged by the strike, considering it both unfeminine and ungrateful. The workers, however, were bound together by a sense of sisterhood and were protesting not just the attack on their economic independence but also the blow to their position as "daughters of freemen still." Nevertheless, the wage cuts were enforced, as were more cuts in 1836, again in the face of a turnout. Many women simply packed their clothes in disgust and returned home to the family farm. Others who remained formed the New England Female Labor Reform Association in 1845, which promptly petitioned the Massachusetts legislature to enact a ten-hour workday. The Massachusetts legislature ignored the ten-hour-day proposal. But in 1847, legislators in New Hampshire, responding to a petition from women workers in Nashua, enacted the nation's first ten-hour-day law. Maine followed in 1848 and Pennsylvania in 1849.

Like these strikes, most turnouts by factory workers in the 1830s—male or female—were unsuccessful. Owners, claiming that increasing competition made wage cuts inevitable, were always able to find new workers who would work at lower wages. The preindustrial notion of a community of interest between owner and workers had broken down and workers, both female and male, began to band together to act on their own behalf.

THE NEW MIDDLE CLASS

The market revolution reached into every aspect of life, down to the most personal family decisions. As just described, it changed working life. The market revolution also fundamentally changed the social order, creating a new middle class with distinctive habits and beliefs.

WEALTH AND RANK

There had always been social divisions in America. Since the early colonial period, planters in the South and merchants in the North had comprised a wealthy elite. Somewhere below the elite but above the mass of people was the "middling sort": a small professional group that included lawyers, ministers, schoolteachers, doctors, public officials, some prosperous farmers, prosperous urban shop keepers and innkeepers, and a few wealthy artisans. Artisans and yeoman farmers made up another large group, and the laboring poor, consisting of ordinary laborers, servants, and marginal farmers, were below them. At the very bottom were the paupers—those dependent on public charity—and the enslaved. This was the "natural" social order that fixed most people in the social rank to which they were born.

The market revolution ended this stable and hierarchical social order, creating the dynamic and unstable one we recognize today: upper, middle, and working classes, whose members all share the hope of climbing as far up the social ladder as they can. This social

WHAT VALUES were promoted by the new middle class?

QUICK REVIEW

Class Consciousness

♦ Social class always existed in America.

♦ Market revolution downgraded some independent artisans and elevated others.

♦ New work patterns helped form distinctive attitudes of new middle class.

mobility was new. The expanding opportunities of the market revolution enriched the already rich: by the 1840s, the top 1 percent of the population owned about 40 percent of the nation's wealth. At the other extreme, fully one-third of the population possessed little more than the clothes they wore and some loose change. The major transformation came in the lives of the "middling sort."

The market revolution downgraded many independent artisans. Formerly independent artisans or farmers (or, more frequently, their children) joined the rapidly growing ranks of managers and white-collar workers such as accountants, bank tellers, clerks, bookkeepers, and insurance agents. These new white-collar workers owed not only their jobs but also their lifestyles to the new structure and organization of industry. The new economic order demanded certain habits and attitudes of workers: sobriety, responsibility, steadiness, and hard work. Inevitably, employers found themselves not only enforcing these new standards but also adopting them themselves.

RELIGION AND PERSONAL LIFE

Religion, which had undergone dramatic changes since the 1790s, played a key role in the emergence of the new attitudes. The Second Great Awakening had supplanted the orderly and intellectual Puritan religion of early New England. The new evangelical religious spirit, which stressed the achievement of salvation through personal faith, was more democratic and more enthusiastic than the earlier faith. The concept of original sin, the cornerstone of Puritan belief, was replaced by the optimistic belief that a willingness to be saved was enough to ensure salvation. Conversion and repentance were no longer private, because they now took place in huge revival meetings in which an entire congregation focused on the sinners about to be saved and where group support actively encouraged individual conversion. The converted bore a heavy personal responsibility to demonstrate their faith in their own daily lives through morally respectable behavior. In this way, the new religious feeling fostered individualism and self-discipline.

The Second Great Awakening had its greatest initial success on the western frontier in the 1790s, but by the 1820s, evangelical religion was reaching a new audience: the people whose lives were being changed by the market revolution and who needed help in adjusting to the demands made by the new economic conditions. In 1825, in Utica, New York, and in other towns along the recently opened Erie Canal, evangelist Charles G. Finney began a series of dramatic revival meetings. His spellbinding message reached both rich and poor, converting members of all classes to the new evangelistic religion.

Middle-class women in particular carried Finney's message by prayer and pleading to the men of their families, who found that evangelism's stress on self-discipline and individual achievement helped them adjust to new business conditions. The enthusiasm and optimism of evangelism aided what was often a profound personal transformation in the face of the market's stringent new demands. Moreover, it gave businessmen a basis for demanding the same behavior from their workers. Businessmen now argued that traditional paternalism had no role in the new business world. Because achievement depended on individual character, each worker was responsible for making his own way.

THE NEW MIDDLE-CLASS FAMILY

The economic changes of the market revolution reshaped family roles, first in the middle class and eventually throughout the entire society. When the master craftsman became a small manufacturer, or the small subsistence farmer began to manage a large-scale commercial operation, production moved away from both the family home and its members. Husbands and fathers became managers of paid workers—or workers themselves—and although they were still considered the heads of their households, they spent most of the day away from their homes and families. The husband was no longer the undisputed head of a family unit that combined work and personal life. Their wives, on the other

Read the Document

Charles Finney, What a Revival of Religion Is (1835) at **www.myhistorylab.com**

hand, remained at home, where they were still responsible for cooking, cleaning, and other domestic tasks but no longer contributed directly to what had previously been the family enterprise. Instead, women took on a new responsibility, that of providing a quiet, well-ordered, and relaxing refuge from the pressures of the industrial world.

Catharine Beecher's *A Treatise on Domestic Economy*, first published in 1841, became the standard housekeeping guide for a generation of middle-class American women. In it, Beecher combined innovative ideas for household design with medical information, child-rearing advice, recipes, and numerous discussions of the mother's moral role in the family. The book clearly filled a need: for many pioneer women, it was the only book besides the Bible that they carried west with them.

As the work roles of middle-class men and women diverged, so did social attitudes about appropriate male and female characteristics and behavior. Men were expected to be steady, industrious, responsible, and painstakingly attentive to their business. They had little choice: in the competitive, uncertain, and rapidly changing business conditions of the early nineteenth century, these qualities were essential for men who hoped to hold their existing positions or to get ahead. In contrast, women were expected to be nurturing, gentle, kind, moral, and selflessly devoted to their families. They were expected to operate within the "woman's sphere"—the home.

The maintenance or achievement of a middle-class lifestyle required the joint efforts of husband and wife. More cooperation between them was called for than in the preindustrial, patriarchal family. The nature of the new, companionate marriage that evolved in response to the market revolution was reflected most clearly in decisions concerning children. Middle-class couples had fewer children than did their predecessors. The dramatic fall in the birthrate during the nineteenth century (from an average of seven children per woman in 1800 to five in 1860) is evidence of conscious decisions about family limitation, first by members of the new middle class and later by working-class families. Few couples used mechanical methods of contraception. Instead, people used birth control methods that relied on mutual consent: coitus interruptus (withdrawal before climax), the rhythm method (intercourse only during the woman's infertile period), and, most often, abstinence or infrequent intercourse.

When mutual efforts at birth control failed, married women often sought a surgical abortion, a new technique that was much more reliable than the folk remedies women had always shared among themselves. Surgical abortions were widely advertised after 1830, and widely used, especially by middle-class married women seeking to limit family size. The rising rate of abortion by married women prompted the first legal bans; by 1860, twenty states had outlawed the practice.

Accompanying the interest in family limitation was a redefinition of sexuality. Doctors generally recommended that sexual urges be controlled, but they believed that men would have much more difficulty exercising such control than women, partly because they also believed that women were uninterested in sex. Medical manuals of the period suggested that it was the task of middle-class women to help their husbands and sons restrain their sexuality by appealing to their higher, moral natures. Although it is always difficult to measure the extent to which the suggestions in advice books were applied in actual practice, it seems that many middle-class women accepted this new and limited definition of their sexuality because of the desire to limit the number of their pregnancies.

•••⌐Read the Document

Catharine Beecher, from A Treatise on Domestic Economy (1841) at **www.myhistorylab.com**

This middle-class family group, painted in 1840, illustrates the new importance of children and of the mother–child bond.

Frederick Spencer, *Family Group*, 1840. © Francis G. Mayer/CORBIS.

MIDDLE-CLASS CHILDREN

Child rearing had been shared in the preindustrial household, boys learning farming or craft skills from their fathers while girls learned domestic skills from their mothers. The children of the new middle class, however, needed a new kind of upbringing, one that involved a long period of nurturing in the beliefs and personal habits necessary for success. Mothers assumed primary responsibility for this training, in part because fathers were too busy but also because people believed that women's superior qualities of gentleness, morality, and loving watchfulness were essential to the task.

Fathers retained a strong role in major decisions concerning children, but mothers commonly turned to other women for advice on daily matters. Through their churches, women formed maternal associations for help in raising their children to be religious and responsible. In Utica, New York, for example, these extremely popular organizations enabled women to form strong networks sustained by mutual advice and by publications such as *Mother's Magazine*, issued by the Presbyterian Church, and *Mother's Monthly Journal*, put out by the Baptists.

Middle-class status required another sharp break with tradition. As late as 1855, artisanal families expected all children over fifteen years to work. Middle-class families, in contrast, sacrificed to keep their sons in school or in training for their chosen professions, and they often housed and fed their sons until the young men had "established" themselves financially and could marry. Mothers took the lead in an important informal activity: making sure their children had friends and contacts that would be useful when they were old enough to consider careers and marriage.

Contrary to the growing myth of the self-made man, middle-class success was not a matter of individual achievement. Instead it was usually based on a family strategy in which fathers provided the money and mothers the nurturance. The reorganization of the family described in this section was successful: from its shelter and support emerged generations of ambitious, responsible, and individualistic middle-class men. But although boys were trained for success, this was not an acceptable goal for their sisters. Women were trained to be the silent "support system" that undergirded male success.

SENTIMENTALISM AND TRANSCENDENTALISM

Just as factory workers were forced by the nature of their work to develop new attitudes, so too the new middle class adopted attitudes that suited its new social roles. Two new "isms" soon emerged: sentimentalism, which appealed particularly to women, and transcendentalism, which encouraged men to a new self-reliance.

The individualistic competitiveness brought by the market revolution caused women of the new middle class to place extraordinary emphasis on sincerity and feeling. So-called sentimentalism sprang from nostalgia for the imagined trust and security of the familiar, face-to-face life of the preindustrial village. Middle-class women were expected to counteract the impersonality and hypocrisy of the business world by the example of their own morality and sincere feeling.

Although sentimentalism originally sprang from genuine fear of the dangers individualism posed to community trust, it rapidly hardened into a rigid code of etiquette for all occasions. Moments of genuine and deep feeling, such as death, were smothered in elaborate rules concerning condolences, expressions of grief, and appropriate clothing. A widow, for example, was expected to wear "deep mourning" for a year—dresses of dull black fabrics and black bonnets covered with long, thick black veils—and in the following year "half mourning"—shiny black silk

Read the **Document**
Mother's Magazine (1934) at
www.myhistorylab.com

Read the **Document**
A New England Woman Describes the Responsibilities of American Women in 1847 at **www.myhistorylab.com**

Emerson's romantic glorification of nature included the notion of himself as a "transparent eyeball," as he wrote in "Nature" in 1836. This caricature of Emerson is from "Illustrations of the New Philosophy" by Christopher Pearce Cranch.

CHRONOLOGY

1790	Samuel Slater's first mill opens in Rhode Island		**1823**	Lowell mills open
1798	Eli Whitney contracts with the federal government for 10,000 rifles, which he undertakes to produce with interchangeable parts		**1824**	John Hall successfully achieves interchangeable parts at Harpers Ferry armory
				Women lead strike at Pawtucket textile mill
1810	Francis Cabot Lowell tours British textile factories		**1825**	Erie Canal opens
	First steamboat on the Ohio River		**1830**	Baltimore and Ohio Railroad opens
1812	Micajah Pratt begins his own shoe business in Lynn, Massachusetts			Charles G. Finney's Rochester revivals
1813	Francis Cabot Lowell raises $300,000 to build his first cotton textile factory at Waltham, Massachusetts		**1833**	National Road completed to Columbus, Ohio
			1834	First strike at Lowell mills
1815	War of 1812 ends; British competition in manufactures resumes			Cyrus McCormick patents the McCormick reaper
1817	Erie Canal construction begins		**1837**	John Deere invents steel plow
1818	National Road completed to Wheeling, Virginia (now West Virginia)		**1841**	Catharine Beecher's *A Treatise on Domestic Economy* published
1820s	Large-scale outwork networks develop in New England		**1845**	New England Female Reform Association formed

dresses, perhaps with trim of gray, violet, or white, and hats without veils. Thus, sentimentalism rapidly became concerned not with feelings but with social codes. Transformed into a set of rules about genteel manners to cover all occasions, sentimentalism itself became a mark of middle-class status. And it became one of the tasks of the middle-class woman to make sure her family conformed to the social code and associated only with other respectable families. In this way, women forged and enforced the distinctive social behavior of the new middle class.

As the new middle class conformed to the rules of sentimental behavior, it also sought a more general intellectual reassurance. Middle-class men, in particular, needed to feel comfortable about their public assertions of individualism and self-interest. One source of reassurance was the philosophy of transcendentalism and its well-known spokesman, Ralph Waldo Emerson. Famous as a writer and lecturer, Emerson popularized transcendentalism, a romantic philosophical theory claiming that there was an ideal, intuitive reality transcending ordinary life. The best place to achieve that individual intuition of the Universal Being, Emerson suggested, was not in church or in society but alone in the natural world. As he wrote in "Nature" (1836), "Standing on the bare ground—my head bathed by the blithe air, and uplifted into infinite space—all mean egotism vanishes. I become a transparent Eyeball; I am nothing; I see all; the currents of the Universal Being circulate through me; I am part and parcel of God." The same assertion of individualism rang through Emerson's stirring polemic "Self-Reliance" (1841). Announcing "Whoso would be a man, must be a nonconformist," Emerson urged that "Nothing is at last sacred but the integrity of your own mind." Inspirational but down-to-earth, Emerson was just the philosopher to inspire young businessmen of the 1830s and 1840s to achieve success in a responsible manner.

Emerson's younger friend, Henry David Thoreau, pushed the implications of individualism further than the more conventional Emerson. Determined to live the transcendental ideal of association with nature, Thoreau lived in solitude in a primitive cabin for two years at Walden Pond, near Concord, Massachusetts, confronting "the essential facts

Read the Document

Henry David Thoreau, Walden (1854) at **www.myhistorylab.com**

of life." His experience was the basis for *Walden* (1854), a penetrating criticism of the spiritual cost of the market revolution. Denouncing the materialism that led "the mass of men [to] lead lives of quiet desperation," Thoreau recommended a simple life of subsistence living that left time for spiritual thought.

Margaret Fuller, perhaps the most intellectually gifted of the transcendental circle, was patronized by Emerson because she was a woman. She expressed her sense of women's wasted potential in her pathbreaking work *Woman in the Nineteenth Century* (1845). Intellectually and emotionally, however, Fuller achieved liberation only when she moved to Europe and participated in the liberal Italian revolution of 1848. The romantic destiny she sought was tragically fulfilled when she, her Italian husband, and their child died in a shipwreck off the New York coast as they returned to America in 1850.

Although Thoreau and Fuller were too radical for many readers, Emerson's version of the romantic philosophy of transcendentalism, seemingly so at odds with the competitive and impersonal spirit of the market revolution, was in fact an essential component of it. Individualism, or, as Emerson called it, self-reliance, was at the heart of the personal transformation required by the market revolution. Sentimentalism, transcendentalism, and evangelical religion all helped the new middle class to forge values and beliefs that were appropriate to their social roles.

CONCLUSION

The three transformations of the market revolution—improvements in transportation, commercialization, and industrialization—changed the ways people worked, and in time, changed how they thought.

For most people, the changes were gradual. Until midcentury, the lives of rural people were still determined largely by community events, although the spread of democratic politics and the availability of newspapers and other printed material increased their connection to a larger world. Wage earners made up only 40 percent of the working population in 1860, and factory workers made up an even smaller percentage.

The new middle class was most dramatically affected by the market revolution. All aspects of life, including intimate matters of family organization, gender roles, and the number and raising of children, changed. New values—evangelical religion, sentimentalism, and transcendentalism—helped the members of the new middle class in their adjustment. As the next chapter describes, the nation's cities were the first arena where old and new values collided.

REVIEW QUESTIONS

1. What changes in preindustrial life and work were caused by the market revolution?

2. This chapter argues that when people begin doing new kinds of work, their beliefs and attitudes change. Give three examples of such changes described in the chapter. Can you think of other examples?

3. Discuss the opinion offered by historian David Potter that mass production has been an important democratizing force in American politics. Do you agree? Why or why not?

4. Consider the portrait of the nineteenth-century middle-class family offered in this chapter and imagine yourself as a member of such a family. What new aspects of family relations would you welcome? Which would be difficult? Why?

KEY TERMS

American system (p. 294)   **Putting-out system** (p. 287)
Market revolution (p. 287)

myhistory̌lab Connections

Reinforce what you learned in this chapter by studying the many documents,
images, maps, review tools, and videos available at www.myhistorylab.com.

Read and Review

✓•⎯⎡Study and Review Chapter 12

•⎯⎡Read the Document

A Week at the Mill (1845)

Extract from Albany Daily Advertiser (1819)

Employers Advertise for Help Wanted in the 1820s

Hodgdon Family Letters Regarding Life in the Mills (1840)

A New England Factory Issues Regulations for Workers in 1825

Female Industrial Association (1825)

Charles Finney, What a Revival of Religion Is (1835)

A New England Woman Describes the Responsibilities of American Women in 1847

Catharine Beecher, from A Treatise on Domestic Economy (1841)

Mother's Magazine (1934)

Henry David Thoreau, Walden (1854)

👁•⎡See the Map

Expanding America and Internal Improvements

Commercial Links: Rivers, Canals, Roads, 1830, and Rail Lines, 1850

Research and Explore

•⎯⎡Read the Document

Exploring America: Machinery

Profiles
  DeWitt Clinton
  Charles and Lydia Finney
  Samuel Slater

((•⎯⎡Hear the Audio *The Erie Canal*

•⎯⎡Watch the Video

Nineteenth-Century Industrialization

Railroads and Expansion

Hear the audio files for Chapter 12 at
www.myhistorylab.com.

The Second Great Awakening and Religious Diversity in America

One of the reasons that separation of church and state has worked so well in the United States is the wide diversity of religious affiliations within the American population. From the beginning of English colonial efforts to the time of the American Revolution, this happy scenario was not necessarily present. In the northern colonies the Congregationalist Church was the established state religion among Puritan settlers. In the middle and southern colonies the Anglican Church or Church of England was the established church.

THE SECOND Great Awakening (1800–1830s) led to the creation of many new religious affiliations and an increased diversity within American religious life. How has this growing diversity impacted American society.

In 1801 the Danbury Baptist Association wrote a letter to newly elected President Thomas Jefferson complaining that the dominant Congregationalist sect in Connecticut was threatening to legislate against them and called for religious freedom. Jefferson responded with a letter outlining what we now call the separation of church and state.

Religious diversity grew slowly in the early years of the American colonies and nation. The First Great Awakening of the 1730s and 1740s strengthened the Presbyterian, Baptist, and Methodist churches in their quest to attract the followers of the Congregationalist and Anglican churches and create diversity of American religions. The Second Great Awakening created even greater diversity. ■

Rev. Charles G. Finney – 1839

CHARLES GRANDISON FINNEY, *LECTURES ON THE REVIVAL OF RELIGION*, 1835

I WOULD say nothing to undervalue, or lead you to undervalue a thorough education for ministers. But I do not call that a thorough education, which they get in our colleges and seminaries. It does not fit them for their work.... Those fathers who have the training of our young ministers are good men, but they are ancient men, men of another age and different stamp from what is needed in these days of excitement, when the church and world are rising to new thought and action. Those dear fathers will not, I suppose, see this; and will perhaps think hard of me for saying it; but it is the cause of Christ. ■

FROM *AUTOBIOGRAPHY OF PETER CARTWRIGHT, THE BACKWOODS PREACHER*

The revival, or "camp meeting," was the signal event of the Second Great Awakening.
Somewhere between 1800 and 1801, in the upper part of Kentucky, at a memorable place called "Cane Ridge," there was appointed a sacramental meeting by some of the Presbyterian ministers, at which meeting, seemingly unexpected by ministers or people, the mighty power of God was displayed in a very extraordinary manner; many were moved to tears, and bitter and loud crying for mercy. The meeting was protracted for weeks. Ministers of almost all denominations flocked in from far and near. The meeting was kept up by night and day. Thousands heard of the mighty work, and came on

foot, on horseback, in carriages and wagons. It was supposed that there were in attendance at times during the meeting from twelve to twenty-five thousand people. Hundreds fell prostrate under the mighty power of God, as men slain in battle. Stands were erected in the woods from which preachers of different Churches proclaimed repentance toward God and faith in our Lord Jesus Christ, and it was supposed, by eye and ear witnesses, that between one and two thousand souls were happily and powerfully converted to God during the meeting.

SIMPLE GIFTS

'Tis the gift to be simple, 'tis the gift to be free,

'Tis the gift to come down where
we ought to be,

And when we find ourselves in the place just right,

'Twill be in the valley of love and delight.

When true simplicity is gain'd,

To bow and to bend we shan't be asham'd,

To turn, turn will be our delight,

Till by turning, turning we come round right.

A Religious camp meeting, ca. 1839

"*Simple Gifts*" is a Shaker quick dance or dancing song used in worship services. The hymn was written by Elder Joseph Brackett Jr. in 1848. Although they originated much earlier than the Second Great Awakening, the Shakers benefited from the diversity and growth of religious movements during the first decades of the 19th century. Shakers lived a communal, celibate lifestyle. Men and women lived in separate quarters, used separate stairs, and sat on opposite sides of the room during worship. Their devotions included rituals of trembling, shouting, dancing, shaking, singing, and speaking in unknown tongues. By the end of the 19th century the Shakers were practically extinct. ■

CHURCH OF JESUS CHRIST OF LATTER-DAY SAINTS

Founded in 1830 in New York by Joseph Smith, Jr., the Church of Jesus Christ of Latter-day Saints is based upon the Book of Mormon. Smith moved his followers to Missouri in the 1830's where controversy and persecution resulted in the Mormon War of 1838 after which the governor of the state ordered Smith to move his church elsewhere. Smith settled his people in Illinois and built the town of Navuoo. Mormon practices led to more persecution and the murder of Smith in 1844. Leadership of the church was taken over by Brigham Young who led his followers out of Illinois to the Mexican territories in Utah in 1846. The Mormon Church continued to thrive in Utah and the Southwest and in the 20th century has become one of the faster growing denominations in the U.S. ■

A Shaker Dance, Joseph Becker, *Frank Leslie's Illustrated Newspaper*, 1873

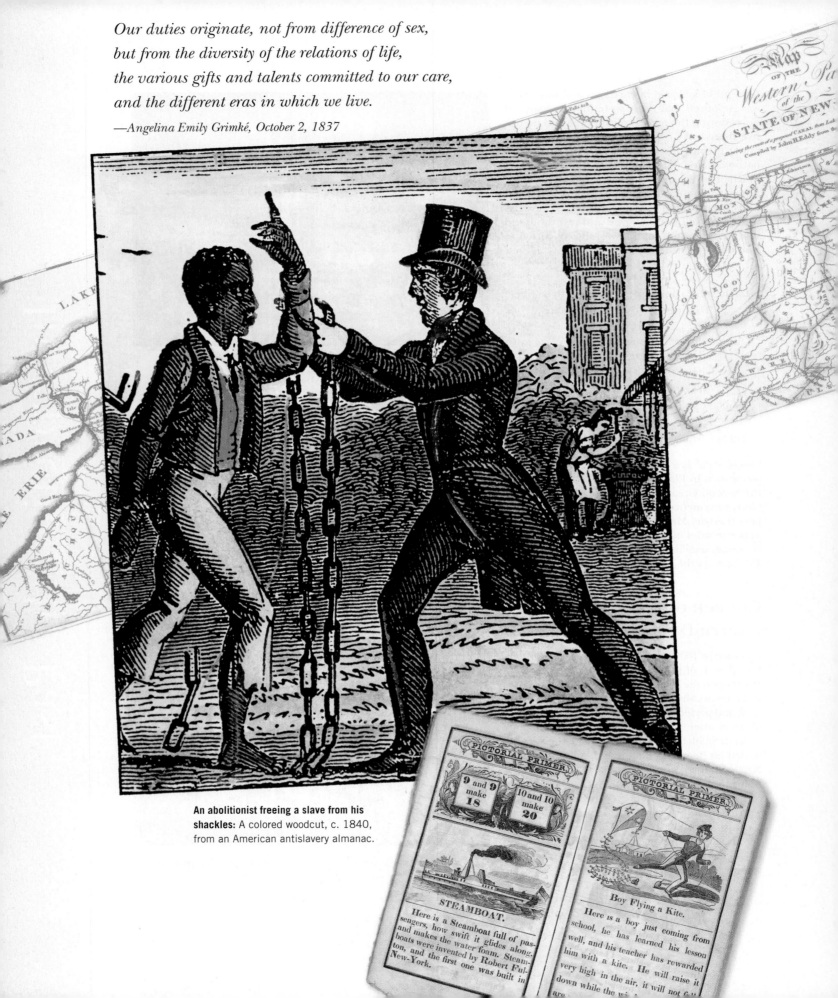

Our duties originate, not from difference of sex,
but from the diversity of the relations of life,
the various gifts and talents committed to our care,
and the different eras in which we live.
—Angelina Emily Grimké, October 2, 1837

An abolitionist freeing a slave from his shackles: A colored woodcut, c. 1840, from an American antislavery almanac.

13

MEETING THE CHALLENGES OF THE NEW AGE

IMMIGRATION, URBANIZATION, SOCIAL REFORM
1820s–1850s

((•─┤Hear the Audio

Hear the audio files for Chapter 13 at **www.myhistorylab.com**.

WHO IMMIGRATED to America in the first half of the nineteenth century and where did they settle?

HOW DID immigration change American cities in the first half of the nineteenth century?

WHAT FACTORS contributed to emergence of social reform movements in the 1820s and 1830s?

WHAT GROUPS worked to end slavery in the 1820s and 1830s?

WHAT CONNECTIONS were there between the women's rights movement and previous movements for social reform?

AMERICAN COMMUNITIES
Women Reformers of Seneca Falls Respond to the Market Revolution

IN THE SUMMER OF 1848, CHARLOTTE WOODWARD, A NINETEEN-YEAR-OLD glove maker who did outwork in her rural home, saw a small advertisement in an upstate New York newspaper announcing a "convention to discuss the social, civil, and religious condition and rights of woman," to be held at Seneca Falls. Woodward persuaded six friends to join her in the forty-mile journey to the convention. "At first we travelled quite alone," she recalled. "But before we had gone many miles we came on other wagon-loads of women, bound in the same direction. As we reached different crossroads we saw wagons coming from every part of the country, and long before we reached Seneca Falls we were a procession."

To the surprise of the convention organizers, almost 300 people—men as well as women—attended the two-day meeting, which focused on the **Declaration of Sentiments**. "We hold these truths to be self-evident," it announced: "That all men and women are created equal." As the Declaration of Independence detailed the oppressions King George III had imposed on the colonists, the Declaration of Sentiments detailed, in a series of resolutions, the oppressions men had imposed on women. Men had deprived women of legal rights, of the right to own their own property, of custody of their children in cases of divorce, of the right to higher education, of full participation in religious worship and activity, and of the right to vote.

> ● ●─ Read the Document
>
> *Elizabeth Cady Stanton, Declaration of Sentiments (1848)* at **www.myhistorylab.com**

The attendees approved all the resolutions unanimously but the last, which a minority found too radical. Buoyed by the success of this first women's rights convention, the group promptly planned another convention to reach new supporters and develop strategies to implement their resolutions.

The struggle for women's rights was only one of many reform movements that emerged in the United States in the wake of the economic and social disruptions of the market revolution that deeply affected regions like Seneca Falls. A farming frontier in 1800, it had been drawn into national commerce in 1828, when it was reached by an offshoot of the Erie Canal. It was drawn even further into the modern age when the railroad arrived in 1841. Swamped by newcomers (among them a growing number of poor Irish Catholics), the inhabitants of Seneca Falls struggled to maintain a sense of community. They formed volunteer organizations of all kinds—religious, civic, social, educational, and recreational. And they became active participants in reform movements seeking to counteract the effects of industrialization, rapid growth, and the influx of newcomers.

Many reformers belonged to liberal religious groups with wide social perspectives. Perhaps a third of those attending the women's rights convention, for example, were members of the Wesleyan Methodist Society of Seneca Falls, which had broken with the national Methodist organization because it would not take a strong stand against slavery. Another quarter was Progressive Quakers of the nearby town of Waterloo, who had broken with their national organization for the same reason. Seneca Falls had been the site of a "Temperance Reformation" in the early 1840s, and many attendees at the Women's Rights convention were also active in the temperance movement, a more limited but extremely popular reform cause dedicated to promoting abstinence from alcohol.

The idea for the Women's Rights convention emerged during a meeting in early July 1848 between Lucretia Mott, a Philadelphia Quaker and the nation's best-known woman reformer, and Elizabeth Cady Stanton of Seneca Falls, wife of a well-known antislavery orator. As the two spoke of the changes that would be necessary to allow women to care for their families but have energy left over to reform "the wrongs of society," the idea of a women's rights convention was born. The women's rights movement that took shape from this convention proved exceptionally long-lasting. Stanton, soon to form a working partnership with former temperance worker Susan B. Anthony, devoted the rest of her life to women's rights.

But what of Charlotte Woodward, a local farm girl, unaware of the national reform community? Why was she there? In this age of hopefulness and change, she wanted a better life for herself. She was motivated, she said, by "all the hours that I sat and sewed gloves for a miserable pittance, which, after it was earned, could never be mine." By law and custom, her father, as head of the household, was entitled to her wages. The reforming women of Seneca Falls, grouped together on behalf of social improvement, had found in the first women's rights convention a way to speak for the needs of working women such as Charlotte Woodward.

All over the North, in communities like Seneca Falls as well as in cities like New York, Americans gathered together in reform organizations to try to solve the problems that the market revolution posed for work, family life, personal and social values, and urban growth. Through these organizations, local women and men became participants in wider communities of social concern, but in spite of their best efforts, they were rarely able to settle the issues that had brought them together. The aspirations of some, among them women, free blacks, and immigrants, clashed with the social control agendas of other groups. In this fervent atmosphere of reform, many problems were raised but few were resolved.

IMMIGRATION AND THE CITY

Although the market revolution affected all aspects of American life, nowhere was its impact so noticeable as in the cities. And it was primarily in cities that the startlingly large number of new immigrants clustered.

THE GROWTH OF CITIES

The market revolution dramatically increased the size of America's cities. The proportion of America's population living in cities increased from only 7 percent in 1820 to almost 20 percent in 1860, a rate of growth greater than at any other time in the country's history. The nation's four largest cities, the Atlantic seaports of New York, Philadelphia, Baltimore, and Boston, all grew at least 25 percent each decade between 1800 and 1860, and often much more. New York, which grew from 60,000 in 1800 to 202,600 in 1830 and to more than 1 million in 1860, emerged as the nation's most populous city, its largest port, and its financial center.

Another result of the market revolution was the appearance of "instant" cities at critical points on the new transportation network. Utica, New York, once a frontier trading post, was transformed by the opening of the Erie Canal into a commercial and manufacturing center. Chicago, on the shores of Lake Michigan, was transformed by the coming of the railroad into a major junction for water and rail transport. By the 1850s, the city had become a hub of trade boasting grain storage facilities, slaughterhouses, and warehouses of all kinds. By 1860 Chicago had a population of over 100,000, making it the nation's eighth largest city (see Figure 13.1).

WHO IMMIGRATED to America in the first half of the nineteenth century and where did they settle?

QUICK REVIEW

"Instant" Cities

- Utica, New York transformed by opening of Erie Canal.
- Railroad made growth of Chicago possible.
- Chicago's population reached 100,000 in 1860.

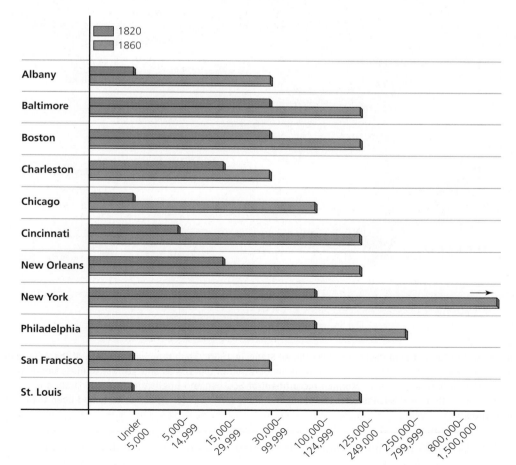

Figure 13.1 Urban Growth, 1820–60

From *Immigrant Life in New York City, 1825–1863* by Robert Ernst. Copyright 1994 by Syracuse University Press. Reprinted by permission.

Declaration of Sentiments The resolutions passed at the Seneca Falls Convention in 1848 calling for full female equality, including the right to vote.

PATTERNS OF IMMIGRATION

One of the key aspects of urban growth was a surge in immigration to the United States that began in the 1820s and accelerated dramatically after 1830. The proportion of immigrants in the population jumped from 1.6 percent in the 1820s to 11.2 percent in 1860. In the nation's cities, the proportion was vastly larger: by 1860, nearly half of New York's population (48 percent) was foreign-born (see Map 13.1).

Most of the immigrants to the United States during this period came from Ireland and Germany. Political unrest and poor economic conditions in Germany and the catastrophic Potato Famine of 1845–49 in Ireland were responsible for an enormous surge in immigration from those countries between 1845 and 1854. The starving, desperate "Famine Irish" who crowded into eastern seaports were America's first large refugee group. Between them, the Germans and the Irish represented the largest influx of non-English immigrants the country had known. Most of the Irish and half of the Germans were Catholics, an unwelcome novelty that provoked a nativist backlash among some

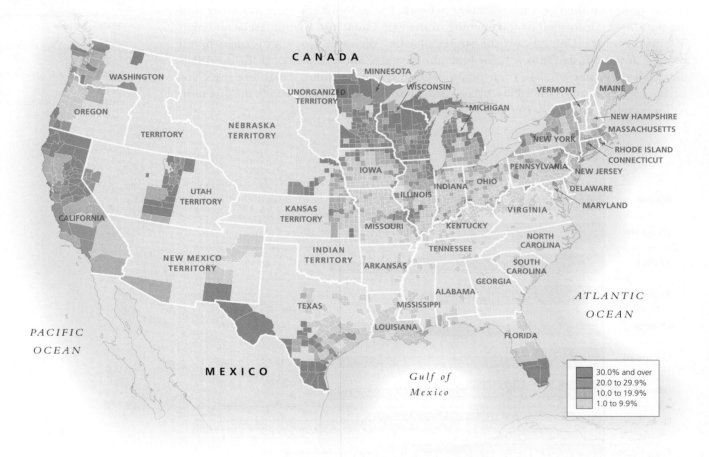

MAP 13.1

Distribution of Foreign-Born Residents of the United States in 1860 The ethnic composition of the American population was increased by Irish and German immigration in the 1840s and 1850s, Chinese immigration to the California gold rush, Mormon recruitment of Scottish and English followers to Utah, and the reclassification of Mexicans after the Mexican-American War as foreigners in what had been their own lands.

WHERE DID most immigrants to the United States in the first half of the nineteenth century settle? Why?

Protestant Americans, including many leaders of national reform movements (see Chapter 15).

It would be a mistake, however, to think that immigration was unwelcome to everyone. Industries needed workers, and western states, among them Wisconsin, Iowa, and Minnesota, actively advertised in Europe for settlers. Many of the changes in industry and transportation that accompanied the market revolution would have been impossible without immigrant labor.

Few immigrants found life in the United States pleasant or easy. In addition to the psychological difficulties of leaving a home and familiar ways behind, most immigrants endured harsh living and working conditions. America's cities were unprepared for the social problems posed by large numbers of immigrants.

IRISH IMMIGRATION

The first major immigrant wave to test American cities was caused by the catastrophic Irish Potato Famine of 1845–49. Throughout Ireland, many native Irish subsisted on small landholdings and a diet of potatoes while working as laborers on British-owned farms. In 1845 Ireland's green fields of potato plants turned black with blight. The British government could not cope with the scale of the disaster. The Irish had two choices: starve or leave. One million people died, and another 1.5 million emigrated, the majority to the United States. Lacking the money to go inland and begin farming, Irish immigrants remained in the cities. Crowded together in miserable housing, desperate for work at any wages, foreign in their religion and pastimes, tenaciously nationalistic and bitterly anti-British, they created ethnic enclaves of a kind new to American cities.

The largest numbers of Irish came to New York, which managed to absorb them. But Boston, a much smaller and more homogeneous city, was overwhelmed by the Irish influx. By 1850, a quarter of Boston's population was Irish, most of them recent immigrants. Boston, the home of Puritanism and the center of American intellectualism, did not welcome illiterate Irish Catholic peasants. All over the city, in places of business and in homes normally eager for domestic servants, the signs went up: "No Irish Need Apply."

GERMAN IMMIGRATION

The nineteenth-century immigration of Germans began somewhat later and more slowly than that of the Irish, but by 1854 it had surpassed the Irish influx. The typical German immigrant was a small farmer or artisan dislodged by the same market forces at work in America: the industrialization of production and consolidation, and the commercialization of farming. There was also a small group of middle-class liberal intellectuals who left the German states (Germany was not yet a unified nation) after 1848 when attempts at revolution had failed.

On the whole, German migrants were not as poor as the Irish, and they could afford to move out of the East Coast seaports to other locations. Many Germans made their way up the Mississippi and Ohio valleys, where they settled in Pittsburgh, Cincinnati, St. Louis, and Milwaukee and on farms in Ohio, Indiana, Missouri, and Texas. Few Germans settled either in northeastern cities or in the South.

German agricultural communities took a distinctive form that fostered cultural continuity. Immigrants formed predominantly German towns by clustering, or taking up adjoining land. A small cluster could support German churches, German-language schools, and German customs and thereby attract other Germans, some directly from Europe and some from other parts of the United States. Non-German neighbors often sold out and moved on, but the Germans stayed and improved the land so they could pass it on to the next generation.

♦♦♦ Read the Document

Irish Laborers Get an Endorsement in 1833 at **www.myhistorylab.com**

Samuel Waugh's *The Bay and Harbor of New York*, painted in 1855, Castle Garden, New York's first official center for immigrants, receiving a boatload of newcomers from Ireland and perhaps from Germany. Note the anti-Irish caricatures, including the trunk on the right labeled "Pat Murfy for Ameriky." A Chinese junk rides at anchor in the harbor, a reminder that not all immigration in this period was from Europe.

THE CHINESE IN CALIFORNIA

Another area attracting immigrants was Gold Rush California, which drew, among others, numbers of Chinese (see Chapter 14). The Chinese who came to California worked in the mines, mostly as independent prospectors. By the mid-1860s, Chinese workers made up 90 percent of the laborers building the Central Pacific Railroad, replacing more expensive white laborers and sowing the seeds of the long-lasting hostility of American workers toward Chinese. In the meantime, however, San Francisco's Chinatown, the oldest Chinese ethnic enclave in America, became a well-established, thriving community and a refuge in times of anti-Chinese violence.

ETHNIC NEIGHBORHOODS

Ethnic neighborhoods were not limited to the Chinese. Almost all new immigrants preferred to live in neighborhoods where they could find not only family ties and familiar ways but also community support as they learned how to survive in new surroundings. Irish immigrants created their own communities in Boston and New York, their major destinations. They raised the money to erect Catholic churches with Irish priests. They established parochial schools with Irish nuns as teachers. They formed mutual aid societies based on kinship or town of origin in Ireland. Men and women formed religious and social clubs, lodges, and brotherhoods and their female auxiliaries. This dense network of associations served the same purpose that social welfare organizations do today: providing help in time of need and offering companionship in a hostile environment.

Germans who settled in urban areas also built their own ethnic enclaves in which they sought to duplicate the rich cultural life of their homeland. Like the Irish, the Germans formed groups and societies to provide mutual support. Partly because their communities were more prosperous than those of the Irish, the Germans also formed a network of leisure organizations: singing societies, debating and political clubs, concert halls, theaters, *turnvereins* (gymnastics associations), and beer gardens. They published German-language newspapers as well.

Many native-born Americans, however, viewed ethnic neighborhoods with deep suspicion. The *Boston American* expressed the sentiments of many in 1837 when it remarked:

> Our foreign population are too much in the habit of retaining their own national usages, of associating too exclusively with each other, and living in groups together. It would be the part of wisdom, to ABANDON AT ONCE ALL USAGES AND ASSOCIATIONS WHICH MARK THEM AS FOREIGNERS, and to become in feeling and custom, as well as in privileges and rights, citizens of the United States.

URBAN PROBLEMS

It was within the new urban environment, with its stimulating and frightening confusion of rapid growth, occupational and ethnic change, and economic competition, that new American political and social forms began to emerge.

NEW LIVING PATTERNS IN THE CITIES

The preindustrial cities of eighteenth-century America had been small and compact "walking cities," in which people, rich and poor, lived near their work in a dense, small-scale housing pattern that fostered neighborliness and the mingling of social classes. The growth caused by immigration changed the character of urban life by sharpening class differences.

Even though per capita income in America is estimated to have doubled between 1800 and 1850, the gap between rich and poor was glaringly apparent in the nation's cities. Differences in income affected every aspect of urban life. Very poor families (about 70 percent of the urban population), including almost all new immigrants, performed unskilled labor, lived in cheap rented housing, moved frequently, and depended on more

HOW DID immigration change American cities in the first half of the nineteenth century?

THE FIVE POINTS IN 1859
Crossing of Baxter (late Orange) Park (late Cross) & Worth (late Anthony) Sts.

The Five Points neighborhood in lower Manhattan illustrates the segregated housing patterns that emerged as New York City experienced rapid growth. Immigrants, free African Americans, the poor, and criminals were crowded together in New York's most notorious slum, while wealthier people moved to more prosperous neighborhoods.

than one income to survive. Artisans and skilled workers with incomes of $500 or more could live adequately, though often in cramped quarters that also served as their shops. A middle-class family with an income of more than $1,000 a year (about 25 percent of the population) could live comfortably in a house of four to six rooms. The very rich (about 3 percent) built mansions and large town houses. In the summer, they left the cities for country estates or homes at seaside resorts.

Early nineteenth-century cities lacked municipal water supplies, sewers, and garbage collection. As a consequence, every American city suffered epidemics of sanitation-related diseases such as yellow fever, cholera, and typhus. For example, Philadelphia's yellow fever epidemic of 1793 caused 4,000 deaths and stopped all business with the outside world for more than a month.

Yet the cities were slow to take action. Mostly, this was due to poor understanding of the links between sanitation and disease, but expense was also a factor. Neither New York nor Boston had a public water system until the 1840s. Garbage collection remained a private service, and cities charged property owners for the costs of sewers, water mains, and street paving. Poorer areas of the cities could not afford the costs. When disease struck, wealthier people simply left the cities, leaving the poor to suffer.

Lack of municipal services encouraged residential segregation. Richer people clustered in neighborhoods that had the new amenities. By the 1850s, the middle class began to escape cities completely by moving to the new "streetcar suburbs," named for the new mode of urban transportation that connected these nearby areas to the city itself.

As the middle class left the city, the poor clustered in bad neighborhoods that became known as slums. With the influx of European immigrants after 1830, middle-class Americans increasingly saw slums as the home of strange and foreign people who deserved less than American-born citizens did. In this way, residential patterns came to embody larger issues of class and citizenship. Even disease itself was blamed on immigrants. As banker John Pintard reasoned in 1832, the cholera epidemic of that year must be God's judgment on "the lower classes of intemperate dissolute and filthy people huddled together like swine in their polluted habitations."

ETHNICITY IN URBAN POPULAR CULTURE

Immigrants to American cities contributed to a new urban popular culture, with New York, the largest city, leading the way. In the period 1820–60, New York experienced the replacement of artisanal labor by wagework, two serious depressions (1837–43 and 1857), and a vast influx of immigrant labor (see Figure 13.2).

In response to these pressures, working-class amusements became rougher and rowdier. Taverns that served as neighborhood centers of drink and sociability were also frequent centers of brawls and riots.

Irish immigrants, in particular, faced not only employment discrimination but also persistent cultural denigration. It was common for newspapers of the time to caricature the Irish as monkeys, similar to the way cartoonists portrayed African Americans. The Irish response,

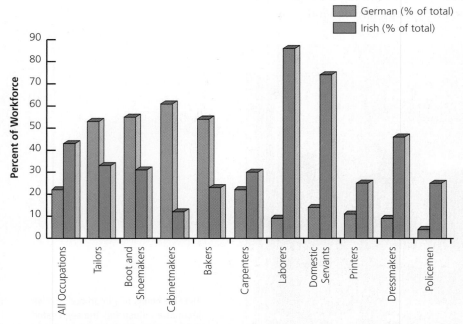

Figure 13.2 Participation of Irish and German Immigrants in the New York City Workforce for Selected Occupations, 1855

This chart shows the impact of the new immigrants on the New York's workforce, and the dramatic difference between groups. German workers predominate in the skilled trades, while the Irish are clustered in low-skilled, low paying occupations.

From *The Alcoholic Republic: An American Tradition*, by W. J. Rorabaugh, copyright © 1979 by Oxford University Press, Inc. Used by permission of Oxford University Press, Inc.

which was to insist on their "whiteness," played itself out in urban popular culture in violence and mockery. In the popular blackface minstrel shows, white actors (often Irish) blacked their faces and entertained audiences with songs, dances, theatrical skits, and antiblack political jokes.

THE LABOR MOVEMENT AND URBAN POLITICS

By the 1830s, the status of artisans and independent craftsmen in the nation's cities had deteriorated. Members of urban workers' associations, increasingly angry over their declining status in the economic and social order, became active defenders of working-class interests in their cities.

Urban worker protest against changing conditions first took the form of party politics. The Workingmen's Party was founded in Philadelphia in 1827, and chapters quickly formed in New York and Boston as well. The "Workies" campaigned for the ten-hour day and the preservation of the small artisanal shop. Jacksonian Democrats were quick to pick up on some of their themes, attracting many Workingmen's votes in 1832, the year Andrew Jackson campaigned against the "monster" Bank of the United States (see Chapter 11).

For their part, the Whigs wooed workers by assuring them that Henry Clay's American System, and tariff protection in particular, would be good for the economy and for workers' jobs. Nevertheless, neither major political party really spoke to the primary need of workers—for well-paid, stable jobs that assured them independence and respect. Unsatisfied with the response of political parties, workers turned to labor organization to achieve their goals.

Between 1833 and 1837, a wave of strikes in New York City cut the remaining ties between master craftsmen and the journeymen who worked for them. In 1833, journeymen carpenters struck for higher wages. Workers in fifteen other trades came to their support, and within a month the strike was won. The same year, representatives from nine different craft groups formed the General Trades Union (GTU) of New York. By 1834, similar groups had sprung up in over a dozen cities—Boston, Louisville, and Cincinnati among them. In 1834 representatives of several local GTUs organized the National Trades Union (NTU).

Employers fought back against workers' organizations. In Cincinnati and elsewhere, employers prevailed upon police to arrest strikers even when no violence had occurred. In another case, New York employers took striking journeymen tailors to court in 1836. Judge Ogden Edwards pronounced the strikers guilty of conspiracy and declared unions un-American. The GTU responded with a mass rally at which Judge Edwards was burned in effigy.

A year later, stunned by the effects of the Panic of 1837, the GTU collapsed. The founding of these general unions, a visible sign of a class-based community of interest

IRISH EMIGRANT.

Patrick, (just landing.) "By my Sowl, you're black, old fellow! How long have ye bin here?"

Nigger, (imitatng the brogue.) "Jist three months, my honey!"

Pat. "By the powers, I'll go back to Tipperary in a jiffy! I'd not be so black as that fur all the whiskey in Roscrea!"

This cartoon encounter between a newly arrived Irishman and an African American expresses the fear of many immigrants that they would be treated like blacks and denied the privileges of whiteness.

•••─ Read the Document

Preamble of the Mechanics Union of Trade Associations (1827) at **www.myhistorylab.com**

P.T. Barnum's Famous "Curiosity:" General Tom Thumb

Seeing History

Phineas T. Barnum opened Barnum's American Museum in New York City in 1842 exhibiting human and animal "curiosities" with inimitable showmanship that was an artful mix of fact and fiction. For example it was a fact that "General" Tom Thumb, one of Barnum's most famous exhibits, was midget who stood 25 inches tall and weighed 15 pounds. But he was not a general: he was a carefully-coached four-year-old boy when Barnum first started exhibiting him in 1842, claiming that he was eleven years old.

BARNUM'S MIXTURE of fact and fiction was regularly denounced as "humbug," but audiences flocked to his shows. Why? What drew them?

His real name was Charles Stratton; his father had agreed that Barnum could exhibit his son for $3.00 a week.

Onstage, the tiny general was an instant success. Singing, dancing, and portraying characters as varied as Napoleon, a Scottish highlander, and Cupid, Tom Thumb enjoyed a long, happy, and profitable career under Barnum's tutelage. As a child, he met and performed for Queen Victoria of England. As an adult (he grew to 40 inches) he and his wife (another midget employed by Barnum named Lavinia Warren) were guests of President and Mrs. Lincoln at the White House. He and Barnum enjoyed a long friendship, and Thumb never expressed any feelings of resentment.

Many of Barnum's exhibits *were* outright hoaxes (for example The Feejee Mermaid, and General Washington's nurse who claimed to be 161 years old) but many were persons with physical anomalies (Siamese twins, giants, bearded women, fat boys, and so on) or "exotics" from little-known cultural groups like a family from Burma who appeared "half-naked" in American eyes. ■

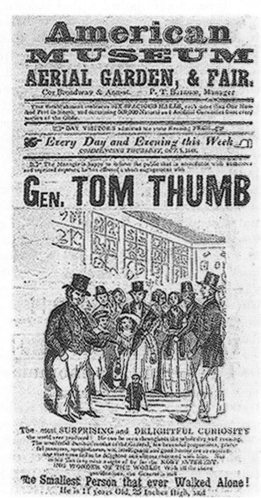

among workers, is generally considered to mark the beginning of the American labor movement. However, the early unions included only white men in skilled trades, who made up only a small percentage of all workers. The majority of workers—men in unskilled occupations, all free African Americans, and all women—were excluded.

Although workers were unable to create strong unions or stable political parties that spoke for their economic interests, they were a vital factor in urban politics. As America's cities experienced unprecedented growth, the electorate mushroomed. In New York, for example, the number of voters grew from 20,000 in 1825 to 88,900 in 1855. Furthermore, by 1855 half of the voters were foreign-born. Irish-dominated districts quickly became Democratic Party strongholds. Germans, who were less active politically than the Irish, nevertheless voted heavily for the new Republican Party in the 1850s. Between them, these two new blocs of immigrant voters destroyed the Whig Party that had controlled New York politics before the immigrants arrived.

In New York City, the **Tammany Society**, begun in the 1780s as a fraternal organization of artisans, slowly evolved into the key organization of the new mass politics. Tammany, which was affiliated with the national Democratic Party, reached voters by using many of the techniques of mass appeal made popular earlier by craft organizations—parades, rallies, popular songs, and party newspapers.

CIVIC ORDER

The challenges to middle-class respectability posed by new immigrants and unruly workers were fostered and publicized by the immensely popular "penny papers," which began publication in 1833, and by the rapidly growing number of political papers. This exuberant urban popular culture was unquestionably a part of the same new democratic political spirit that led to the great upsurge in political participation discussed in Chapter 11.

Working-class use of the streets for parades, celebrations, and marches was an established aspect of urban life and perhaps nowhere so much a part of the city as in New Orleans. There, African American bands played in funeral processions, and dances drawing hundreds of slaves were regularly held in Congo Square, while elsewhere Choctaw Indians drummed and respectable middle-class men rang cowbells as they took part in rowdy street serenades in response to unpopular events.

In New York, the prosperous classes were increasingly frightened by the urban poor and by working-class rowdyism. New York City's tradition of New Year's Eve "frolics," in which laborers, apprentices, and other members of the lower classes paraded through the streets playing drums, trumpets, whistles, and other noisemakers, was an example. By 1828, the revelry had been taken over by gangs of young workers from the lower classes, who marched through the city, overturning carts, breaking windows, obstructing traffic, and harassing middle-class citizens. In the following year, the city government banned the traditional New Year's Eve parade.

New York City's first response in the 1820s and 1830s to increasing civic disorder was to hire more city watchmen and to augment them with constables and marshals. When riots occurred, the militia was called, and deaths were increasingly common as they forcibly restrained mobs. Finally, in 1845, the city created a permanent police force with a mandate to keep the poor in order. Southern cities, because of fear of slave disorder, had police forces much earlier: by the 1820s, New Orleans, Charleston, and Savannah had armed and uniformed city guards who patrolled in military fashion.

But even with police forces in place, the pressures of rapid urbanization, immigration, and the market revolution proved to be too much for America's cities. Beginning in the 1830s, a series of urban riots broke out against the two poorest urban groups: Catholics and free black people. As if their miserable living conditions were not enough, Irish immigrants were met with virulent anti-Catholicism. In 1834, rioters burned an

Tammany Society   A fraternal organization of artisans begun in the 1780s that evolved into a key organization of the new mass politics in New York City.

By 1855, half the voters in New York City were foreign-born. This 1858 engraving of an Irish bar in the Five Points area appeared in the influential *Harper's Weekly*. It expressed the temperance reformers' dislike of immigrants and their drinking habits and the dismay of political reformers that immigrant saloons and taverns were such effective organizing centers for urban political machines.

Ursuline convent in Charlestown, Massachusetts; in 1844, a Philadelphia mob attacked priests and nuns and vandalized Catholic churches; in 1854, a mob destroyed an Irish neighborhood in Lawrence, Massachusetts. But the most common targets of urban violence were free African Americans.

FREE AFRICAN AMERICANS IN THE CITIES

By 1860, there were nearly half a million free African Americans in the United States, constituting about 11 percent of the country's total black population. More than half of all free African Americans lived in the North, mostly in cities, where they competed with immigrants and native-born poor white people for jobs as day laborers and domestic servants. Their relative social position is reflected in statistics on per capita annual income in Boston in the 1850s: $91 for black people and $131 for Irish immigrants compared to $872 for the population at large.

Free African Americans in northern cities faced residential segregation, pervasive job discrimination, segregated public schools, and severe limitations on their civil rights. In addition to these legal restrictions, there were matters of custom: African Americans of all economic classes endured daily affronts, such as exclusion from public concerts, lectures, and libraries, and segregation or exclusion from public transportation.

In common with Irish and German immigrants, African Americans created defenses against the hostile larger society by building their own community structures. They formed associations for aiding the poorest members of the community, for self-improvement, and for socializing. African American communities supported their own newspapers. The major community organization was the black Baptist or African

Methodist Episcopal (AME) church, which served, as one historian put it, as "a place of worship, a social and cultural center, a political meeting place, a hiding place for fugitives, a training ground for potential community leaders, and one of the few places where blacks could express their true feelings."

Employment prospects for black men deteriorated from 1820 to 1850. Those who had held jobs as skilled artisans were forced from their positions, and their sons denied apprenticeships, by white mechanics and craftsmen who were themselves suffering from the effects of the market revolution. Limited to day labor, African Americans found themselves in direct competition with the new immigrants, especially the Irish, for jobs. One of the few occupations to remain open to them was that of seaman. More than 20 percent of all American sailors in 1850 were black, and over the years, their ranks included an increasing number of runaway slaves. Mothers, wives, and daughters worked as domestic servants (in competition with Irishwomen), washerwomen, and seamstresses.

Free African Americans remained committed to their enslaved brethren in the South. In New York, for example, black communities rioted four times—in 1801, 1819, 1826, and 1832—against slave catchers taking escaped slaves back to slavery. But even more frequently, free African Americans were themselves targets of urban violence. An 1829 riot in Cincinnati sent a thousand black people fleeing to Canada in fear for their lives; a three-day riot in Providence in 1831 destroyed an African American district; an 1834 New York riot destroyed a black church, a school, and a dozen homes. Philadelphia was repeatedly rocked by antiblack riots in the period between 1820 and 1859. Urban riots of all kinds had cost 125 lives by 1840, and more than 1,000 by 1860.

This appealing portrait of a musician, *The Bone Player*, evokes the prevalent stereotype of African Americans as innately musical, but it also clearly portrays a man who is proud of his talent.

William Sidney Morris (American, 1807–1868), *The Bone Player*, 1856. Oil on canvas, 91.76 × 73.98 cm (36⅛ × 29⅛ in.). Courtesy, Museum of Fine Arts, Boston. Bequest of Martha C. Karolik for the M. and M. Karolik Collection of American Paintings. 48.46 Reproduced with permission. Photograph © 2006 Museum of Fine Arts, Boston. All Rights Reserved.

SOCIAL REFORM MOVEMENTS

The passion for reform that had become such an important part of the new middle-class thinking was focused on the problems of the nation's cities. As the opening of this chapter describes, the earliest response to the dislocations caused by the market revolution was community based and voluntary. The reform message was, however, vastly amplified by inventions such as the steam printing press, which made it possible to publish reform literature in great volume. Soon there were national networks of reform groups.

WHAT FACTORS contributed to emergence of social reform movements in the 1820s and 1830s?

RELIGION, REFORM, AND SOCIAL CONTROL

Evangelical religion was fundamental to social reform. Men and women who had been converted to the enthusiastic new faith assumed personal responsibility for making changes in their own lives. Personal reform quickly led to social reform. Religious converts were encouraged in their social activism by such leading revivalists as Charles G. Finney, who preached a doctrine of "perfectionism," claiming it was possible for all Christians to personally understand and live by God's will and thereby become "as perfect as God." Furthermore, Finney predicted, "the complete reformation of the whole world" could be achieved if only enough converts put their efforts into moral reform.

Much of America was swept by this reform-minded religious fervor, and it was the new middle class that set the agenda. Reform efforts arose from the recognition that the traditional methods of small-scale local relief were no longer adequate. In colonial times, families had housed and cared for the ill or incapacitated. Small local almshouses and prisons had housed the poor and the criminal. Reformers now realized that large cities had to make large-scale provisions for social misfits and that institutional rather than private efforts were needed.

A second characteristic of the reform movements was a belief in the basic goodness of human nature. All reformers believed that the condition of the unfortunate—the poor, the insane, the criminal—would improve in a wholesome environment. Thus, insane asylums were built in rural areas, away from the noise and stress of the cities, and orphanages had strict rules that were meant to encourage discipline and self-reliance. Prison reform carried this sentiment to the extreme. On the theory that bad social influences were largely responsible for crime, some "model" prisons completely isolated prisoners from one another, making them eat, sleep, work, and do required Bible reading in their own cells.

A third characteristic of the reform movements was their moralistic dogmatism. Reformers were certain they knew what was right and were determined to see their improvements enacted. It was a short step from developing individual self-discipline to imposing discipline on others. The reforms that were proposed thus took the form of social controls. Lazy, sinful, intemperate, or unfit members of society were to be reformed for their own good, whether they wanted to be or not. This attitude was bound to cause controversy; by no means did all Americans share the reformers' beliefs, nor did those for whom it was intended always take kindly to being the targets of the reformers' concern.

Indeed, some aspects of the social reform movements were harmful. The evangelical Protestantism of the reformers promoted a dangerous hostility to Catholic immigrants that repeatedly led to urban riots. The temperance movement, in particular, targeted immigrants. The reformers thus helped to promote the virulent nativism that infected American politics between 1840 and 1860 (see Chapter 15).

Regional and national reform organizations quickly grew from local projects to deal with social problems such as drinking, prostitution, mental illness, and crime. In 1828, for example, Congregationalist minister Lyman Beecher joined other ministers in forming a General Union for Promoting the Observance of the Christian Sabbath; the aim was to prevent business on Sundays. To achieve its goals, the General Union adopted the same methods used by political parties: lobbying, petition drives, fundraising, and special publications.

In effect, Beecher and similar reformers engaged in political action but remained aloof from direct electoral politics, stressing their religious mission. In any case, **sabbatarianism** was controversial. Workingmen were angered when the General Union forced the Sunday closure of their favorite taverns and were quick to vote against the Whigs, the party perceived to be most sympathetic to reform thinking. Other reforms likewise muddied the distinction between political and social activity. It is not surprising that women, who were barred from electoral politics but not from moral and social activism, were major supporters of reform.

EDUCATION AND WOMEN TEACHERS

Women became deeply involved in reform movements through their churches. It was they who did most of the fundraising for the home missionary societies that were beginning to send the evangelical message worldwide. Nearly every church had a maternal association, where mothers gathered to discuss ways to raise their children as true Christians. These associations reflected a new and more positive definition of childhood. The Puritans had believed that children were born sinful and that their wills had to be broken before they could become godly. Early schools reflected these beliefs: teaching was by rote, and punishment was harsh and physical. Educational reformers, however,

Read the **Document**

Noted Educator Speaks on Public Schooling in 1848 at **www.myhistorylab.com**

Sabbatarianism Reform movement that aimed to prevent business on Sundays.

Winslow Homer's famous painting, *The Country School* (1871), illustrates the central role of young women in education. Homer's painting is both affectionate and realistic, showing the idealism of the young teacher at the same time showing the barefoot condition of many of her pupils.

tended to believe that children were born innocent and needed gentle nurturing and encouragement if they were to flourish. At home, mothers began to play the central role in child rearing. Outside the home, women helped spread the new public education pioneered by Horace Mann, secretary of the Massachusetts State Board of Education.

In 1827, Massachusetts pioneered compulsory education by legislating that public schools be supported by public taxes. Uniformity in curriculum and teacher training, and the grading of classes by ability—measures pioneered by Horace Mann in the 1830s—quickly caught on in other states. In the North and West (the South lagged far behind), more and more children went to school, and more and more teachers, usually young single women, were hired to teach them. By 1850, women were dominant in primary school teaching, which had come to be regarded as an acceptable occupation for educated young women during the few years between their own schooling and marriage.

The spread of public education created the first real career opportunity for women. The great champion of teacher training for women was Catharine Beecher, who clearly saw her efforts as part of the larger work of establishing "the moral government of God." Arguing that women's moral and nurturing nature ideally suited them to be teachers, Beecher campaigned tirelessly on their behalf.

TEMPERANCE

Reformers believed not only that children could be molded but also that adults could change. The largest reform organization of the period, the **American Society for the Promotion of Temperance**, founded in 1826, boasted more than 200,000 members by the mid-1830s. Dominated by evangelicals, local chapters used revival methods—lurid temperance tracts detailing the evils of alcohol, large prayer and song meetings, and heavy group pressure—to encourage young men to "take the pledge" not to drink. Here again, women played an important role (see Figure 13.3).

Excessive drinking was a national problem, and it appears to have been mostly a masculine one, for respectable women did not drink in public. Men drank hard cider and liquor—whiskey, rum—in abundance. Traditionally, drinking had been a basic part of men's working lives. It concluded occasions as formal as the signing of a contract and accompanied such informal activities as card games. Drink was a staple offering at political speeches, rallies, and elections. In the old artisanal workshops, drinking had been a customary pastime. Much of the drinking was well within the bounds of sociability, but the widespread use must have encouraged drunkenness.

Watch the Video
Who Was Horace Mann and Why Are So Many Schools Named After Him? at **www.myhistorylab.com**

QUICK REVIEW

Women and Reform

◆ Women often became involved in reform through their churches.

◆ Maternal associations focused on raising children as true Christians.

◆ Women were involved in nearly all areas of reform.

Temperance Reform movement originating in the 1820s that sought to eliminate the consumption of alcohol.

American Society for the Promotion of Temperance Largest reform organization of its time dedicated to ending the sale and consumption of alcoholic beverages.

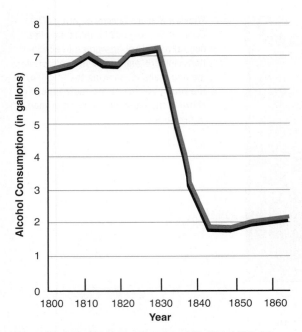

Figure 13.3 Per Capita Consumption of Alcohol, 1800–60
The underlying cause of the dramatic fall in alcohol consumption during the 1830s was the changing nature of work brought about by the market revolution. Contributing factors were the shock of the Panic of 1837 and the untiring efforts of temperance reformers.

W. J. Rorabaugh, *The Alcoholic Republic: An American Tradition* (New York: Oxford University Press, 1979).

**Watch the Video**

Drinking and the Temperance Movement in Nineteenth-Century America at **www.myhistorylab.com**

Female Moral Reform Society
Antiprostitution group founded by evangelical women in New York in 1834.

There were many reasons to support temperance. Heavy-drinking men hurt their families economically by spending their wages on drink. Excessive drinking also led to violence and crime, both within the family and in the larger society.

But there were other reasons. The new middle class, preoccupied with respectability, morality, and efficiency, found the old easygoing drinking ways unacceptable. Temperance became a social and political issue. Whigs, who embraced the new morality, favored it; Democrats, who in northern cities consisted increasingly of immigrant workers, were opposed. Both German and Irish immigrants valued the social drinking that occurred in beer gardens and saloons and were hostile to temperance reform.

The Panic of 1837 affected the temperance movement. Whereas most temperance crusaders in the 1820s had been members of the middle class, the long depression of 1837–43 prompted artisans and skilled workers to give up or at least cut down substantially on drinking. Forming associations known as Washington Temperance Societies, these workers spread the word that temperance was the workingman's best chance to survive economically and to maintain his independence. Their wives, gathered together in Martha Washington Societies, were frequently even more committed to temperance than their husbands. By the mid-1840s, alcohol consumption had been more than halved, to less than two gallons per capita, about the level of today.

MORAL REFORM, ASYLUMS, AND PRISONS

Alcohol was not the only "social evil" that reform groups attacked. Another was prostitution, which was common in the nation's port cities. The customary approach of evangelical reformers was to "rescue" prostitutes, offering them the salvation of religion, prayer, and temporary shelter. The success rate was not very high. Nevertheless, campaigns against prostitution, generally organized by women, continued throughout the nineteenth century.

One of the earliest and most effective antiprostitution groups was the **Female Moral Reform Society**. Founded by evangelical women in New York in 1834, it boasted 445 affiliates throughout the country by 1840. The societies quickly realized that prostitution was not as much a moral as an economic issue and moved to organize charity and work for poor women and orphans. They also took direct action against the patrons of prostitutes by printing their names in local papers and then successfully lobbied the New York state legislature for criminal penalties against the male clients as well as the women themselves.

Another dramatic example of reform was the asylum movement, spearheaded by the evangelist Dorothea Dix. In 1843, Dix horrified the Massachusetts state legislature with the results of her several years of study of the conditions to which insane women were subjected. Dix's efforts led to the establishment of a state asylum for the insane in Massachusetts and to similar institutions in other states. By 1860, twenty-eight states had public institutions for the insane.

Other reformers were active in related causes, such as prison reform and the establishment of orphanages, homes of refuge, and hospitals. Model penitentiaries were built in Auburn and Ossining (known as "Sing Sing"), New York, and in Philadelphia and Pittsburgh. Characterized by strict order and discipline, these prisons were supposed to reform rather than simply incarcerate their inmates, but their regimes of silence and isolation caused despair more often than rehabilitation.

UTOPIANISM AND MORMONISM

Amid all the political activism and reform fervor of the 1830s, a few people chose to escape into utopian communities and new religions. The upstate New York area along the Erie Canal was the seedbed for this movement, just as it was for evangelical revivals

THE DRUNKARDS PROGRESS.
FROM THE FIRST GLASS TO THE GRAVE.

This Currier and Ives lithograph, *The Drunkard's Progress*, dramatically conveys the message that the first glass leads the drinker inevitably to alcoholism and finally to the grave, while his wife and child (shown under the arch) suffer.

and reform movements like the **Seneca Falls convention**. The area was so notable for its reform enthusiasm that it has been called "the Burned-Over District," a reference to the waves of reform that swept through like forest fires (see Map 13.2).

Apocalyptic religions tend to spring up in places experiencing rapid social change. The Erie Canal region, which experienced the full impact of the market revolution in the early nineteenth century, was such a place. A second catalyst is hard times, and the prolonged depression that began with the Panic of 1837 led some people to embrace a belief in imminent catastrophe. The Millerites (named for their founder, William Miller) believed that the Second Coming of Christ would occur on October 22, 1843. When the Day of Judgment did not take place as expected, most of Miller's followers drifted away. But a small group persisted. Revising their expectations, they formed the core of the Seventh-Day Adventist faith, which is still active today.

The **Shakers**, founded by "Mother" Ann Lee in 1774, were the oldest utopian group. An offshoot of the Quakers, the Shakers espoused a radical social philosophy that called for the abolition of the traditional family in favor of a family of brothers and sisters joined in equal fellowship. Despite its insistence on celibacy, the Shaker movement grew between 1820 and 1830, eventually reaching twenty settlements in eight states with a total membership of 6,000. In contrast, another utopian community, the Oneida Community, became notorious for its sexual freedom. Founded by John Humphrey Noyes in 1848, members of the Oneida community practiced "complex marriage," a system of highly regulated group sexual activity. These practices gave the sect a notorious reputation as a den of "free love" and "socialism," preventing Noyes from increasing its membership beyond 200.

Still other forthrightly socialist communities flourished briefly. New Harmony, Indiana, founded by the famous Scottish industrialist Robert Owen in 1825, was to be a manufacturing community without poverty and unemployment. The community survived only three years. The rapid failure of these socialist communities was due largely to inadequate planning and organization.

The most successful of the nineteenth-century communitarian movements was also a product of the Burned-Over District. In 1830, Joseph Smith founded the Church of Jesus Christ of Latter-Day Saints, based on the teachings of the Book of Mormon, which he claimed to have received from an angel in a vision. Initially **Mormonism**, as the new

See the Map
Utopian Communities before the Civil War at **www.myhistorylab.com**

Read the Document
Visit to the Shakers, Lowell Offering (1841) at **www.myhistorylab.com**

Read the Document
O. A. Brownson, Brook Farm (1842) at **www.myhistorylab.com**

Seneca Falls convention   The first convention for women's equality in legal rights, held in upstate New York in 1848.

Shakers   The followers of Mother Ann Lee, who preached a religion of strict celibacy and communal living.

Mormonism   The doctrines based on the Book of Mormon, taught by Joseph Smith and the succeeding prophets and leaders of the Church.

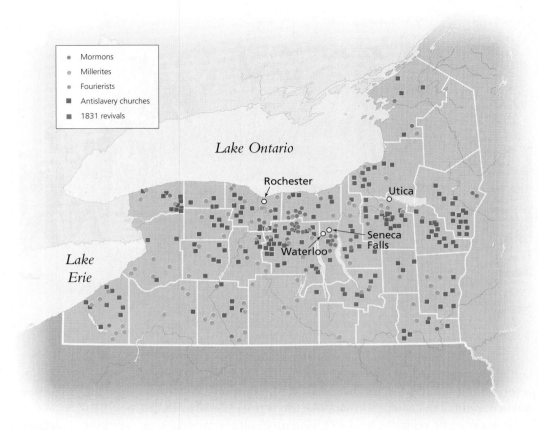

MAP 13.2
Reform Movements in the Burned-Over District The so-called Burned-Over District, the region of New York State most changed by the opening of the Erie Canal, was a seedbed of religious and reform movements. The Mormon Church originated there and utopian groups and sects like the Millerites and the Fourierists thrived. Charles G. Finney held some of his most successful evangelical revivals in the district. Antislavery feeling was common in the region, and the women's rights movement began at Seneca Falls.

Reprinted from *Whitney R. Cross, The Burned-Over District: The Social and Intellectual History of Enthusiastic Religion in Western New York, 1800–1850.* Copyright © 1950 by Cornell University. Used with permission of the publisher, Cornell University Press.

WHAT EXPLAINS the high concentration of reform movements in the Burned-Over District?

religion became known, seemed little different from the many other new religious groups and utopian communities of the time. But under Smith, it rapidly gained distinction for its extraordinary unity. Close cooperation and hard work made the Mormon community successful, attracting both new followers and the animosity of neighbors, who resented Mormon exclusiveness and economic success.

The Mormons were harassed in New York and driven west to Ohio and then Missouri. Finally they seemed to find an ideal home in Nauvoo, Illinois, where in 1839 they built a model community, achieving almost complete self-government and isolation from non-Mormon neighbors. But in 1844, dissension within the community over Joseph Smith's new doctrine of polygamy (marriage between one man and more than one woman simultaneously) gave outsiders a chance to intervene. Smith and his brother were arrested peacefully but were killed by a mob from which their jailers failed to protect them. The beleaguered Mormon community decided to move beyond reach of harm. Led by Brigham Young, the Mormons migrated in 1846 to the Great Salt Lake in present-day Utah. Their hopes of isolation were dashed, however, by the California Gold Rush of 1849 (see Chapter 14).

ANTISLAVERY AND ABOLITIONISM

The antislavery feeling that was to play such an important role in the politics of the 1840s and 1850s also had its roots in the religious reform movements that began in the 1820s and 1830s. Three groups—free African Americans, Quakers, and militant white reformers—worked to bring an end to slavery, but each in different ways. Their efforts eventually turned a minor reform movement into the dominant political issue of the day.

AFRICAN AMERICANS AGAINST SLAVERY

For free African Americans, the resistance to slavery was fundamental; organized antislavery groups dated to the 1790s. By 1830, there were at least fifty African American abolitionist societies in the North. These organizations held yearly national conventions, where famous African American abolitionists such as Frederick Douglass, Harriet Tubman, and Sojourner Truth spoke. The first African American newspaper, founded in 1827 by John Russwurm and Samuel Cornish, announced its antislavery position in its title, *Freedom's Journal*, and its position in the famous opening lines of the first issue: "for too long others have spoken for us."

In 1829, David Walker, a free African American in Boston, wrote a widely distributed pamphlet, *Appeal to the Colored Citizens of the World*, that encouraged slave rebellion. White Southerners blamed pamphlets such as these and the militant articles of African American journalists for stirring up trouble among southern slaves and, in particular, for Nat Turner's revolt in 1831. The vehemence of white southern reaction testifies to the courage of that handful of determined free African Americans who persisted in speaking for their enslaved brothers and sisters long before most white Northerners even noticed.

THE AMERICAN COLONIZATION SOCIETY

The first national attempt to "solve" the problem of slavery was a plan for gradual emancipation of slaves (with compensation to their owners) and their resettlement in Africa. This plan was the work of the **American Colonization Society**, formed in 1817 by northern religious reformers (Quakers prominent among them) and a number of southern slave owners, most from the Upper South and the border states. The American Colonization Society was remarkably ineffective; by 1830, it had managed to send only 1,400 black people to a colony in Liberia, West Africa. The reaction of free African Americans to the prospect of resettlement was emphatic: "We are natives of this country," an African American minister in New York pointed out. Then he added bitterly, "We only ask that we be treated as well as foreigners."

WHITE ABOLITIONISTS

The third and best-known group of antislavery reformers was headed by William Lloyd Garrison. In 1831, deeply influenced by black activists, Garrison broke with the gradualist persuaders of the American Colonization Society and began publishing his own paper, the *Liberator*. Garrison's new "immediatist" tactic was to mount a sweeping crusade condemning slavery as sinful and demanding its immediate abolition. In reality, Garrison did not expect that all slaves would be freed immediately, but he did want and expect everyone to acknowledge the immorality of slavery. On the other hand, Garrison took the truly radical step of demanding full social equality for African Americans, referring to them individually as "a man and a brother" and "a woman and a sister." Garrison's determination electrified the antislavery movement, but his inability to compromise limited his effectiveness as a leader.

Garrison's moral vehemence radicalized northern antislavery religious groups. Theodore Weld, an evangelical minister, joined Garrison in 1833 in forming the American

WHAT GROUPS worked to end slavery in the 1820s and 1830s?

◆◆-Read the **Document**
National Convention of Colored People, Report on Abolition (1847) at **www.myhistorylab.com**

◆◆-Read the **Document**
An African American Abolitionist Advocates Racial Action in 1829 at **www.myhistorylab.com**

QUICK REVIEW

The American Colonization Society

- Formed in 1817 with the goal of resettling slaves in Africa.
- Members included Northern religious reformers and some Southern slave owners.
- By 1830, the Society had only managed to send 1,400 people to Liberia, West Africa.

◆◆-Read the **Document**
William Lloyd Garrison, First Issue of the Liberator (1831) at **www.myhistorylab.com**

American Colonization Society Organization founded in 1817 by antislavery reformers, that called for gradual emancipation and the removal of freed blacks to Africa.

Anti-Slavery Society. The following year, Weld encouraged a group of students at Lane Theological Seminary in Cincinnati to form an antislavery society. When the seminary's president, Lyman Beecher, sought to suppress it, the students moved en masse to Oberlin College in northern Ohio, where they were joined by revivalist Charles Finney, who became president of the college. Oberlin soon became known as the most liberal college in the country, not only for its antislavery stance but for its acceptance of African American students and of women students as well.

Moral horror over slavery deeply engaged many Northerners in the abolitionist movement. They flocked to hear firsthand accounts of slavery by Frederick Douglass and Sojourner Truth and by the white sisters from South Carolina, Angelina and Sarah Grimké. Northerners eagerly read slave narratives and books such as Theodore Weld's 1839 treatise *American Slavery As It Is* (based in part on the recollections of Angelina Grimké, whom Weld had married), which provided graphic details of abuse under slavery.

The style of abolitionist writings and speeches was similar to the oratorical style of the religious revivalists. Northern abolitionists believed that a full description of the evils of slavery would force southern slave owners to confront their wrongdoing and lead to a true act of repentance—freeing their slaves. They were confrontational, denunciatory, and personal in their message, much like the evangelical preachers. Southerners, however, regarded abolitionist attacks as libelous and abusive.

Abolitionists adopted another tactic of revivalists and temperance workers when, to enhance their powers of persuasion, they began to publish great numbers of antislavery tracts. In 1835 alone, they mailed more than a million pieces of antislavery literature to southern states. This tactic also drew a backlash: southern legislatures banned abolitionist literature, encouraged the harassment and abuse of anyone distributing it, and looked the other way when proslavery mobs seized and burned it. Most serious, the majority of southern states reacted by toughening laws concerning emancipation, freedom of movement, and all aspects of slave behavior. Hoping to prevent the spread of the abolitionist message, most southern states reinforced laws making it a crime to teach a slave how to read. Ironically, then, the immediate impact of abolitionism in the South was to stifle dissent and make the lives of slaves harder.

Even in the North, controversy over abolitionism was common. Some places were prone to anti-abolitionist violence. The Ohio Valley, settled largely by Southerners, was one such place, as were northern cities experiencing the strains of rapid growth, such as Philadelphia. Immigrant Irish, who found themselves pitted against free black people for jobs, were often violently anti-abolitionist. A tactic that abolitionists borrowed from revivalists—holding large and emotional meetings—opened the door to mob action. Crowds of people often disrupted such meetings, especially those addressed by Theodore Weld, whose oratorical style earned him the title of "the Most Mobbed Man in the United States."

ABOLITIONISM AND POLITICS

Abolitionism began as a social movement but soon intersected with sectional interests and became a national political issue. In the 1830s, massive abolitionist petition drives gathered a total of nearly 700,000 petitions requesting the abolition of slavery and the slave trade in the District of Columbia but were rebuffed by Congress. At southern insistence and with President Andrew Jackson's approval, Congress passed a "gag rule" in 1836 that prohibited discussion of antislavery petitions.

Many Northerners viewed the gag rule and censorship of the mail as alarming threats to free speech. First among them was Massachusetts representative John Quincy Adams, the only former president ever to serve in Congress after leaving the executive branch. Adams so publicly and persistently denounced the gag rule as a violation of the constitutional right to petition that it was repealed in 1844. Less well-known Northerners, like the thousands of women who canvassed their neighborhoods with petitions, made personal commitments to abolitionism that they did not intend to abandon.

John Quincy Adams was also a key figure in the abolitionists' one undoubted victory, the fight to free the fifty-three slaves on the Spanish ship *Amistad* and return them to Africa. Although the Africans successfully mutinied against the *Amistad*'s crew in 1839, when the ship was found in American waters, a legal battle over their "ownership" ensued, during which the Africans themselves were held in jail. The legal fight went all the way to the Supreme Court, where Adams won the case for the *Amistad* defendants against the American government, which supported the Spanish claim.

Although abolitionist groups raised the nation's emotional temperature, they failed to achieve the moral unity they had hoped for, and they began to splinter. Frederick Douglass and William Lloyd Garrison parted ways when Douglass, refusing to be limited to a simple recital of his life as a slave, began to make specific suggestions for improvements in the lives of free African Americans. When Douglass chose the path of political action, Garrison denounced him as "ungrateful."

Douglass and other free African Americans worked under persistent discrimination, even from antislavery whites; some of the latter refused to hire black people or to meet with them as equals. While many white reformers eagerly pressed for civil equality for African Americans, they did not accept the idea of social equality. On the other hand, black and white "stations" worked closely in the risky enterprise of passing fugitive

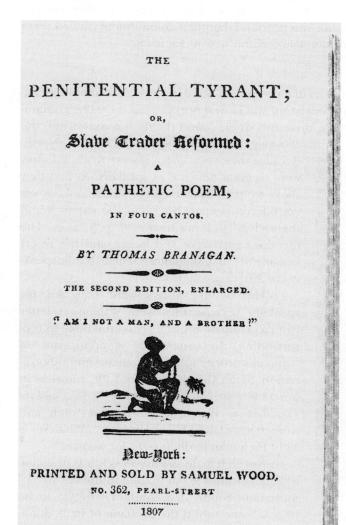

The different dates of these two widely used antislavery images are important. The title page of Thomas Branagan's 1807 book includes an already commonly used image at the time of a male slave. The engraving of a chained female slave was made by Patrick Reason, a black artist, in 1835. The accompanying message saying "Am I Not a Woman and a Sister?" spoke particularly to white female abolitionists in the North, who were just becoming active in antislavery movements in the 1830s.

Liberty Party   The first antislavery political party, formed in 1840.

slaves north over the famous Underground Railroad, as the various routes by which slaves made their way to freedom were called. Contrary to abolitionist legend, however, it was free African Americans, rather than white people, who played the major part in helping the fugitives.

In 1840, the abolitionist movement formally split. The majority moved toward party politics (which Garrison abhorred), founding the **Liberty Party** and choosing James G. Birney as their presidential candidate. Thus, the abolitionist movement, which began as an effort at moral reform, took its first major step into politics, and this step in turn led to the formation of the Republican Party in the 1850s and to the Civil War (see Chapter 15).

For one particular group of antislavery reformers, the abolitionist movement opened up new possibilities for action. Through their participation in antislavery activity, some women came to a vivid realization of the social constraints on their activism.

THE WOMEN'S RIGHTS MOVEMENT

WHAT CONNECTIONS were there between the women's rights movement and previous movements for social reform?

Watch the **Video**
The Women's Rights Movement in Nineteenth-Century America at **www.myhistorylab.com**

Read the **Document**
Exploring America: Angelina Grimké at **www.myhistorylab.com**

American women, without the vote or a role in party politics, found a field of activity in social reform movements. The majority of women did not participate in these activities, for they were fully occupied with housekeeping and child rearing. A few women—mostly members of the new middle class, who could afford servants—had the time and energy to look beyond their immediate tasks. Touched by the religious revival, these women enthusiastically joined reform movements. Led thereby to challenge social restrictions, some, such as the Grimké sisters, found that their commitment carried them beyond the limits of what was considered acceptable activity for women.

THE GRIMKÉ SISTERS

Sarah and Angelina Grimké, members of a prominent South Carolina slaveholding family, rejected slavery out of religious conviction and moved north to join a Quaker community near Philadelphia. In the 1830s, these two sisters found themselves drawn into the growing antislavery agitation in the North. Because they knew about slavery firsthand, they were in great demand as speakers. At first they spoke to "parlor meetings" of women only, as was considered proper. But soon the sisters found themselves speaking to mixed gatherings. The meetings got larger and larger, and the sisters became the first well-known female public speakers in America.

The Grimké sisters were criticized for speaking because they were women. A letter from a group of ministers cited the Bible in reprimanding the sisters for stepping out of "woman's proper sphere" of silence and subordination. Sarah Grimké answered the ministers in her 1838 *Letters on the Equality of the Sexes and the Condition of Women*, claiming that "men and women were CREATED EQUAL. . . . Whatever is right for a man to do, is right for woman."

Not all female assertiveness was as dramatic as Sarah Grimké's, but women in the antislavery movement found it a constant struggle to be heard. Some solved the problem of male dominance by forming their own groups, like the

A CONVENTION OF HEMMERS AND STITCHERS HELD AT LYNN, FEB. 28, FOR ADOPTING A LIST OF PRICES; MRS. E. HALL, PRESIDING.—(See page 284.)

Women's gatherings, like the first women's rights convention in Seneca Falls in 1848, and this meeting of strikers in Lynn in 1860, were indicators of widespread female activism.

CHRONOLOGY

1817	American Colonization Society founded
1820s	Shaker colonies grow
1825	New Harmony founded, fails three years later
1826	American Society for the Promotion of Temperance founded
1827	Workingmen's Party founded in Philadelphia
	Freedom's Journal begins publication
	Public school movement begins in Massachusetts
1829	David Walker's *Appeal to the Colored Citizens of the World* is published
1830	Joseph Smith founds Church of Jesus Christ of Latter-Day Saints (Mormon Church)
	Charles G. Finney's revivals in Rochester
1831	William Lloyd Garrison begins publishing antislavery newspaper, the *Liberator*
1832	Immigration begins to increase
1833	American Anti-Slavery Society founded by William Lloyd Garrison and Theodore Weld
1834	First Female Moral Reform Society founded in New York
	National Trades Union formed
1836	Congress passes "gag rule" to prevent discussion of antislavery petitions

1837	Antislavery editor Elijah P. Lovejoy killed
	Angelina Grimké addresses Massachusetts legislature
	Sarah Grimké writes *Letters on the Equality of the Sexes and the Condition of Women*
	Panic begins seven-year depression
1839	Theodore Weld publishes *American Slavery As It Is*
1840s	New York and Boston complete public water systems
1840	Liberty Party founded
1843	Millerites await the end of the world
	Dorothea Dix spearheads asylum reform movement
1844	Mormon leader Joseph Smith killed by mob
1845	New York creates city police force
	Beginning of Irish Potato Famine and mass Irish immigration into the United States
1846	Mormons begin migration to the Great Salt Lake
1848	Women's Rights Convention at Seneca Falls
	John Noyes founds Oneida Community

Philadelphia Female Anti-Slavery Society. In the antislavery movement and other reform groups as well, men accorded women a secondary role, even when—as was frequently the case—women constituted a majority of the members.

WOMEN'S RIGHTS

The Seneca Falls Convention of 1848, the first women's rights convention in American history, was an outgrowth of almost twenty years of female activity in social reform. As described in the chapter opener, the long agenda of rights was drawn directly from the discrimination many women had experienced in social reform groups. Every year after 1848, women gathered to hold women's rights conventions and to work for political, legal, and social equality. Over the years, in response to persistent lobbying, states passed property laws more favorable to women, and altered divorce laws to allow women to retain custody of children. Teaching positions in higher education opened up to women, as did jobs in some other occupations, and women gained the vote in some states, beginning with Wyoming Territory in 1869. In 1920, seventy-two years after universal woman suffrage was first proposed at Seneca Falls, a woman's right to vote was at last guaranteed in the Nineteenth Amendment to the Constitution.

Historians have only recently realized how much the reform movements of this "Age of the Common Man" were due to the efforts of the "common woman." Women played a vital role in all the social movements of the day. In doing so, they implicitly

Read the Document

Sojourner Truth, Address to Woman's Rights Convention (1851) at **www.myhistorylab.com**

QUICK REVIEW

Seneca Falls Convention

- 1848: First women's rights convention in American history.
- Every year after 1848 conventions gathered to work for equality.
- Efforts resulted in political and legal advances.

challenged the popular notion of separate spheres for men and women—the public world for him, home and family for her. The reforms discussed in this chapter show clearly that women reformers believed they had a right and a duty to propose solutions for the moral and social problems of the day. Empowered by their own religious beliefs and activism, the Seneca Falls reformers spoke for all American women when they demanded an end to the unfair restrictions they suffered as women.

CONCLUSION

Beginning in the 1820s, the market revolution changed the size and social order of America's preindustrial cities and towns. Immigration, dramatically rapid population growth, and changes in working life and class structure created a host of new urban problems ranging from sanitation to civic order. These changes occurred so rapidly that they seemed overwhelming. Former face-to-face methods of social control no longer worked. To fill the gap, new kinds of associations—the political party, the religious crusade, the reform cause, the union movement—sprang up. These associations were new manifestations of the deep human desire for social connection, for continuity, and—especially in the growing cities—for social order. A striking aspect of these associations was the uncompromising nature of the attitudes and beliefs on which they were based. Most groups were formed of like-minded people who wanted to impose their will on others. Such intolerance boded ill for the future. If political parties, religious bodies, and reform groups were to splinter along sectional lines (as happened in the 1850s), political compromise would be very difficult. In the meantime, however, Americans came to terms with the market revolution by engaging in a passion for improvement. As a perceptive foreign observer, Francis Grund noted, "Americans love their country not as it is but as it will be."

REVIEW QUESTIONS

1. What impact did the new immigration of the 1840s and 1850s have on American cities?

2. Why did urbanization produce so many problems?

3. What motivated the social reformers of the period? Were they benevolent helpers or dictatorial social controllers? Study several reform causes and discuss similarities and differences among them.

4. Abolitionism differed little from other reforms in its tactics, but the effects of antislavery activism were politically explosive. Why was this so?

5. Women were active members of almost every reform group. What reasons might women have given for their unusual degree of participation?

KEY TERMS

American Colonization Society (p. 325)
American Society for the Promotion of Temperance (p. 321)
Declaration of Sentiments (p. 309)
Female Moral Reform Society (p. 322)
Liberty Party (p. 328)

Mormonism (p. 323)
Sabbatarianism (p. 320)
Seneca Falls convention (p. 323)
Shakers (p. 323)
Tammany Society (p. 317)
Temperance (p. 321)

PEARSON myhistorylab™ Connections

Reinforce what you learned in this chapter by studying the many documents,
images, maps, review tools, and videos available at www.myhistorylab.com.

Read and Review

✓• Study and Review Chapter 13

•••• Read the Document

*Elizabeth Cady Stanton, Declaration of
Sentiments (1848)*

Irish Laborers Get an Endorsement in 1833

*Preamble of the Mechanics Union of Trade
Associations (1827)*

*Noted Educator Speaks on Public Schooling
in 1848*

Visit to the Shakers, Lowell Offering (1841)

O. A. Brownson, Brook Farm (1842)

*An African American Abolitionist Advocates
Racial Action in 1829*

*William Lloyd Garrison, First Issue of the
Liberator (1831)*

*Sojourner Truth, Address to Woman's Rights
Convention (1851)*

*National Convention of Colored People, Report
on Abolition (1847)*

👁 See the Map Utopian Communities before the
Civil War

Research and Explore

•••• Read the Document

Exploring America: Angelina Grimké

Profiles
Mother Ann Lee
Walt Whitman

▶ Watch the Video

Religious Troublemakers of the 19th Century

*Drinking and the Temperance Movement in
Nineteenth-Century America*

*Who Was Horace Mann and Why Are So Many
Schools Named After Him?*

*The Women's Rights Movement in Nineteenth-
Century America*

((•• Hear the Audio

Hear the audio files for Chapter 13 at
www.myhistorylab.com.

They immigrate constantly, hardly no one to prevent them, and take possession of the location that best suits them without either asking leave or going through any formality other than that of building their homes.
—José Maria Sánchez

Albert Bierstadt (1830–1902), *The Oregon Trail* **(oil on canvas).**

Private Collection/Bridgeman Art Library International Ltd., New York

Butler Institute of American Art, Youngstown, OH, USA/Gift of Joseph G. Butler III 1946/Bridgeman Art Library.

14

The Territorial Expansion of the United States

1830s–1850s

((•—[Hear the **Audio**

Hear the audio files for Chapter 14 at **www.myhistorylab.com**.

WHAT ROLE did the federal government play in the exploration of the West?

WHAT WERE the major similarities and differences between the Oregon, Texas, and California frontiers?

WHAT WERE the most important consequences of the Mexican-American War?

HOW DID the gold rush of 1849 change California?

WHAT KEY factors explain the outcome of the election of 1848?

AMERICAN COMMUNITIES

Texans and Tejanos
"Remember the Alamo!"

FOR THIRTEEN DAYS IN FEBRUARY AND MARCH 1836, A FORCE OF 187 Texans held the mission fortress known as the Alamo against a siege by 5,000 Mexican troops under General Antonio López de Santa Anna, president of Mexico. Santa Anna had come north to subdue rebellious Texas, the northernmost part of the Mexican province of Coahuila y Tejas, and to place it under central authority. On March 6 he ordered a final assault, and in brutal fighting that claimed over 1,500 Mexican lives, his army took the mission. All the defenders were killed, including Commander William Travis and the well-known frontiersmen Jim Bowie and Davy Crockett. It was a crushing defeat for the Texans. But the cry "Remember the Alamo!" rallied their remaining forces, which, less than two months later, routed the Mexican army and forced Santa Anna to grant Texas independence from Mexico.

But memory is selective: within a generation of the uprising, few remembered that many Tejanos, Spanish-speaking people born in Texas, had joined with American settlers fighting for Texas independence. During the 1820s, the Mexican government had authorized several American colonies, concentrated in the central and eastern portions of the huge Texas territory. These settler communities consisted mostly of farmers from the Mississippi Valley, who introduced slavery and cotton growing to the rich soil of coastal and upland Texas.

Although there was relatively little contact between the Americans and Tejanos, their leaders interacted in San Antonio, the center of regional government. The Tejano elite, enthusiastic about American plans for the economic development of Texas, welcomed the American immigrants. Many Americans married into elite Tejano families, who hoped that by thus assimilating and sharing power with the Americans, they could not only maintain but also strengthen their community.

The Mexican state, however, was politically and socially unstable during these first years after its successful revolt against Spain in 1821. Liberals favored a loose federal union, conservatives a strong central state. Most Tejanos supported the liberal side in the struggle. When, in 1828, the conservative centralists came to power in Mexico City and decided the Americans had too much influence in Texas, many Tejanos rose up with the Americans in opposition.

As Santa Anna's army approached from the south, Juan Nepomuceno Seguín, one of the leaders of the San Antonio community, recruited a company of Tejano volunteers and joined the American force inside the walls of the Alamo. During the siege, Commander Travis sent Seguín and some of his men for reinforcements. Seguín returned from his unsuccessful mission to find the burned bodies of the Alamo defenders, including seven San Antonio Tejanos. *"Texas será*

libre!" ("Texas shall be free!") Seguín called out as he directed the burial of the Alamo defenders. In April, Seguín led a regiment of Tejanos in the decisive battle of San Jacinto that won independence for Texas.

Read the Document

A Tejano Describes the Beginning of the Texas Revolution in 1835–36 at **www.myhistorylab.com**

Pleased with independence, Tejanos played an important political role in the new Republic of Texas at first. The liberal Lorenzo de Zavala was chosen vice president, and Seguín became the mayor of San Antonio. But soon things began to change, illustrating a recurring pattern in the American occupation of new lands—a striking shift in the relations between different cultures in frontier areas. Most commonly, in the initial stage newcomers blended with native peoples, creating a "frontier of inclusion." Outnumbered Americans adapted to local societies as a matter of simple survival.

A second stage occurred when the number of Americans increased and they began occupying more and more land or, as in California, "rushing" in great numbers to mine gold, overrunning native communities. This unstable period usually resulted in warfare along with rapidly growing hostility and racial prejudice—all of which were largely absent in earlier days.

A third stage of stable settlement occurred when the native community had been completely "removed" or isolated. In this "frontier of exclusion," racial mixing was rare. In Texas, American settlers—initially invited in by Mexicans and Tejanos—developed an anti-Mexican passion, regarding all Spanish speakers as their Mexican enemies rather than their Tejano allies. Tejanos were attacked and forced from their homes; some of their villages were burned to the ground.

Spanish-speaking communities in Texas, and later in New Mexico and California, like the communities of Indians throughout the West, became conquered peoples. "White folks and Mexicans were never made to live together," a Texas woman told a traveler a few years after the revolution. "The Mexicans had no business here," she said, and the Americans might "just have to get together and drive them all out of the country."

For Americans, westward expansion has always meant the establishment of American communities in new territory. In the nineteenth century, this establishment was marked by an intolerance of diversity. Frontiers in Oregon, Texas, and California differed in their details, but the movement from inclusion to exclusion occurred everywhere: as communities were established, the "other" people were either removed, as in the case of American Indians, or subjected, as with the Tejanos. This is one example of how the word "community" has had different meanings at different times in American history.

San Antonio

EXPLORING THE WEST

There seemed to be no stopping the expansion of the American people. By 1840, they had occupied all of the land east of the Mississippi River and had organized all of it (except for Florida and Wisconsin) into states. Less than sixty years after the United States gained its independence, the majority of its population lived west of the original thirteen states.

The speed and success of this expansion were a source of deep national pride that whetted appetites for further expansion. Many Americans looked eagerly westward to the vast unsettled reaches of the Louisiana Purchase: to Texas, Santa Fé, to trade with Mexico, and even to the Far West, where New England sea captains had been trading for furs since the 1780s. By 1848, the United States had gained all of these coveted western lands. This chapter examines the way the United States became a continental nation, forming many frontier communities in the process.

WHAT ROLE did the federal government play in the exploration of the West?

THE FUR TRADE

The fur trade was an important spur to exploration on the North American continent. In the 1670s, the British Hudson's Bay Company and its French Canadian rival, Montreal's North West Company, began exploring beyond the Great Lakes in the Canadian West in search of beaver pelts. Indeed, Alexander Mackenzie of the North West Company reached the Pacific Ocean in 1793, becoming the first European to make a transcontinental crossing of North America. Traders and trappers for both companies depended on the goodwill and cooperation of the native peoples of the region. From the marriages of European men with native women arose a distinctive mixed-race group, the "métis" (French for "mixed").

Not until the 1820s were American companies able to challenge British dominance of the trans-Mississippi fur trade. In 1824, William Henry Ashley of the Rocky Mountain Fur Company instituted the "rendezvous" system. This was a yearly trade fair, held deep in the Rocky Mountains, to which trappers brought their catch of furs. The fur rendezvous was a boisterous, polyglot, many-day affair at which trappers of many nationalities—Americans and Indian peoples, French Canadians, and métis, as well as Mexicans from Santa Fé and Taos—gathered to trade, drink, and gamble.

Most American trappers, like the British and French before them, sought accommodation and friendship with Indian peoples: nearly half of them contracted long-lasting marriages with Indian women, who not only helped in the trapping and curing of furs but also acted as vital diplomatic links between the white and Indian worlds.

For all its adventure, the American fur trade was short-lived. By the 1840s, the population of beaver in western streams was virtually destroyed, and the day of the mountain man was over. But with daring journeys like that of Jedediah Smith, the first American to enter California over the Sierra Nevada Mountains, the mountain men had helped forge a clear picture of western geography. Soon permanent settlers would follow the trails they had blazed.

GOVERNMENT-SPONSORED EXPLORATION

Following the lead of fur trade explorers, the federal government played a major role in the exploration and development of the U.S. West. The exploratory and scientific aspects of the Lewis and Clark expedition in 1804–06 set a precedent for many government-financed quasi-military expeditions. In 1806 and 1807, Lieutenant Zebulon Pike led an expedition to the Rocky Mountains in Colorado. Major Stephen Long's exploration and mapping of the Great Plains in the years 1819–20 was part of a show of force meant to frighten British fur trappers out of the West. Then, in 1843 and 1844, another military explorer, John C. Frémont, mapped the overland trails to Oregon and California. In the 1850s, the Pacific Railroad surveys explored possible transcontinental railroad routes (see Map 14.1).

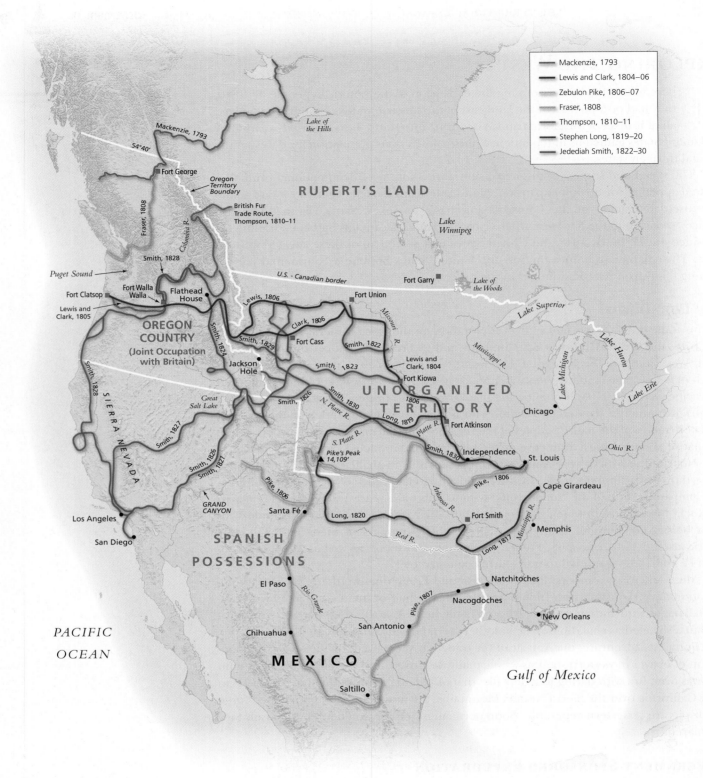

MAP 14.1

Exploration of the Continent, 1804–30 Members of British fur trading companies like Alexander Mackenzie and David Thompson led the way in exploration. Lewis and Clark's "voyage of discovery" of 1804–06 was the first of many U.S. government-sponsored western military expeditions. Lieutenant Zebulon Pike crossed the Great Plains in 1806, followed by Major Stephen Long in 1819–20. Meanwhile, American fur trappers, among them the much-traveled Jedediah Smith, became well acquainted with the Far West as they hunted beaver for their pelts.

WHAT ROLE did the routes taken by major expeditions westward between 1804 and 1830 play in shaping United States policy in the West?

The artist Alfred Jacob Miller, a careful observer of the western fur trade, shows a mountain man and his Indian wife in his 1837 *Bourgeois Walker and His Wife*. Walker and his wife worked together to trap and prepare beaver pelts for market, as did other European men and their Indian wives.

Alfred Jacob Miller, *Bourgeois Walker and His Wife*, 1837. Watercolor. 37.1940.78. The Walters Art Museum, Baltimore.

In the wake of the pathfinders came hundreds of government geologists and botanists as well as the surveyors who mapped and plotted the West for settlement according to the Land Ordinance of 1785. The basic pattern of land survey and sale established by these measures (see Chapter 7) was followed all the way to the Pacific Ocean. The federal government sold the western public lands at low prices. The federal government also shouldered the expense of Indian removal by making long-term commitments to compensate the Indian people themselves and supporting the forts and soldiers whose task was to maintain peace between settlers and Indian peoples in newly opened areas.

EXPANSION AND INDIAN POLICY

In the early decades of the nineteenth century, eastern Indian tribes were removed from their homelands to Indian Territory (present-day Oklahoma, Kansas, and Nebraska), a region widely regarded as unfarmable and popularly known as the Great American Desert. The justification for this western removal, as Thomas Jefferson had explained early in the century, was the creation of a space where Indian people could live undisturbed by white people while they slowly adjusted to "civilized" ways. But the government officials who negotiated the removals failed to predict the tremendous speed at which white people would settle the West (see Map 14.2).

Encroachment on Indian Territory was not long in coming. The territory was crossed by the **Santa Fé Trail**, established in 1821; in the 1840s, the northern part was crossed by the heavily traveled Overland Trails to California, Oregon, and the Mormon community in Utah. In 1854, the government abolished the northern half of Indian Territory, establishing the Kansas and Nebraska Territories in its place and opening them to immediate white settlement. The tribes of the area—the Potawatomis, Wyandots, Kickapoos, Sauks, Foxes, Delawares, Shawnees, Kaskaskias, Peorias, Piankashaws, Weas, Miamis, Omahas, Otos, and Missouris—signed treaties accepting either vastly reduced reservations or allotments. Those who accepted allotments—sections of private land—often sold them, under pressure, to white people. Thus, many of the Indian people who had hoped for independence and escape from white pressures in Indian Territory lost both their autonomy and their tribal identity.

The people in the southern part of Indian Territory, in what is now Oklahoma, fared somewhat better. Those members of the southern tribes—the Cherokees, Chickasaws,

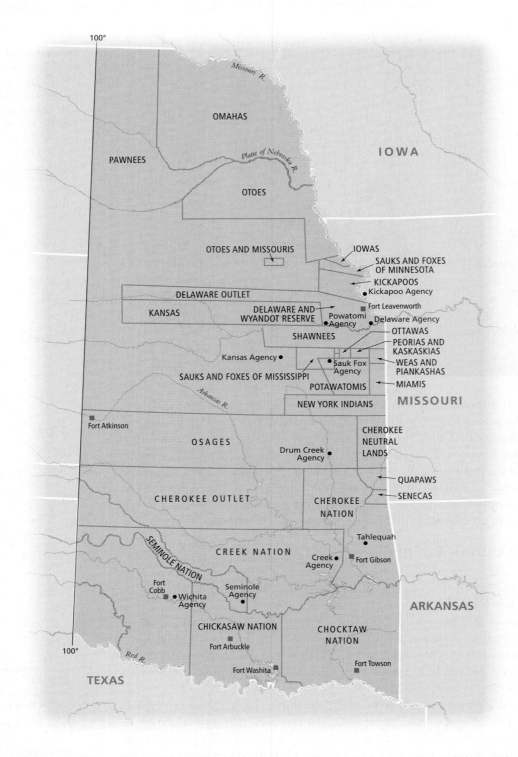

MAP 14.2

Indian Territory before the Kansas-Nebraska Act of 1854 Indian Territory lay west of Arkansas, Missouri, and Iowa and east of Mexican Territory. Most of the Indian peoples who lived there in the 1830s and the 1840s had been "removed" from east of the Mississippi River. The southern part (now Oklahoma) was inhabited by peoples from the Old Southwest: the Cherokees, Chickasaws, Choctaws, Creeks, and Seminoles. North of that in what is now Kansas and Nebraska lived peoples who had been removed from the Old Northwest. All these Indian peoples had trouble adjusting not only to a new climate and a new way of life but also to the close proximity of some Indian tribes who were their traditional enemies.

WHY DID the United States chose to designate this region as Indian Territory? Why did the establishment of Indian Territory fail to eliminate conflict between Indians and white settlers?

Choctaws, Creeks, and Seminoles—who had survived the trauma of forcible removal from the Southeast in the 1830s, quickly created impressive new communities. Until after the Civil War, these southern tribes were able to withstand outside pressures and remain the self-governing communities that treaties had assured them they would be.

THE POLITICS OF EXPANSION

America's rapid expansion had many consequences, but perhaps the most significant was that it reinforced Americans' sense of themselves as pioneering people. Ever since the time of Daniel Boone, venturing into the wilderness has held a special place in the American imagination and been seen almost as a right.

MANIFEST DESTINY, AN EXPANSIONIST IDEOLOGY

How did Americans justify their restless expansionism? After all, the United States was already a very large country with much undeveloped land. To push beyond existing boundaries was to risk war with Great Britain, which claimed the Pacific Northwest, and with Mexico, which held what is now Texas, New Mexico, Arizona, Utah, Nevada, California, and part of Colorado. Undertaking such a conquest required a rationale.

In 1845, newspaperman John O'Sullivan provided it. It was, he wrote, "our **manifest destiny** to overspread the continent allotted by Providence for the free development of our yearly multiplying millions." Sullivan argued that Americans had a God-given right to bring the benefits of American democracy to other, more backward peoples—meaning Mexicans and Indians—by force, if necessary. The notion of manifest destiny summed up the powerful combination of pride in what America had achieved and missionary zeal and racist attitudes toward other peoples that lay behind the thinking of many expansionists.

Expansionism was deeply tied to national politics. O'Sullivan was not a neutral observer: he was the editor of the *Democratic Review*, a party newspaper. Most Democrats were wholehearted supporters of expansion, whereas many Whigs (especially in the North) opposed it. Whigs welcomed most of the changes brought by industrialization but advocated strong government policies that would guide growth and development within the country's existing boundaries. They feared (correctly, as it turned out) that expansion would raise the contentious issue of the extension of slavery to new territories.

On the other hand, many Democrats feared the industrialization that the Whigs welcomed. Where the Whigs saw economic progress, Democrats saw economic depression (the Panic of 1837 was the worst the nation had experienced), uncontrolled urban growth, and growing social unrest. For many Democrats, the answer to the nation's social ills was to continue to follow Thomas Jefferson's vision of establishing agriculture in the new territories in order to counterbalance industrialization. Another factor in the political struggle over expansion in the 1840s was that many Democrats were Southerners, for whom the continual expansion of cotton-growing lands was a matter of social faith as well as economic necessity.

These were politicians' reasons. The average farmer moved west for many other reasons: land hunger, national pride, plain and simple curiosity, and a sense of adventure.

THE OVERLAND TRAILS

The 2,000-mile trip on the Overland Trails from the banks of the Missouri River to Oregon and California usually took seven months, sometimes more. Travel was slow, dangerous, tedious, and exhausting. Forced to lighten their loads as animals died and winter weather threatened, pioneers often arrived at their destinations with little food and few belongings. They faced the prospect of being, in the poignant and much-used biblical phrase, "strangers in a strange land." Yet despite the risks, settlers streamed west: 5,000 to Oregon by 1845 and about 3,000 to California by 1848 (before the discovery of gold) (see Map 14.3).

Pioneers had many motives for making the trip. Glowing reports from Oregon's Willamette Valley, for example, seemed to promise economic opportunity and healthy

---

WHAT WERE the major similarities and differences between the Oregon, Texas, and California frontiers?

◆●➤ **Read** the **Document**

A Newspaper Man Declares the "Manifest Destiny" of the United States in 1845 at **www.myhistorylab.com**

QUICK REVIEW

Manifest Destiny

◆ Proponents of manifest destiny believed white Americans had a God-given right to expansion.

◆ Doctrine operated as a self-serving justification for territorial aggrandizement.

◆ Manifest destiny associated with Democratic party.

◆●➤ **Read** the **Document**

Francis Parkman, The Oregon Trail (1847) at **www.myhistorylab.com**

---

manifest destiny   Doctrine, first expressed in 1845, that the expansion of white Americans across the continent was inevitable and ordained by God.

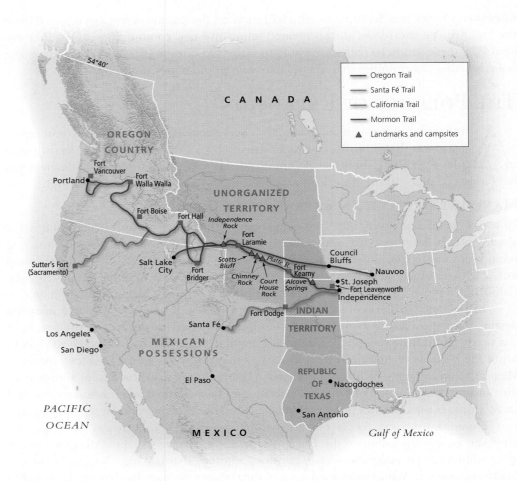

MAP 14.3

The Overland Trails, 1840 All the great trails west started at the Missouri River. The Oregon, California, and Mormon Trails followed the Platte River into Wyoming, crossed South Pass, and divided in western Wyoming. The much harsher Santa Fé Trail stretched 900 miles southwest across the Great Plains. All of the trails crossed Indian Territory and, to greater or lesser extent, Mexican possessions as well.

WHAT DANGERS did settlers face as they followed the overland trails?

Read the Document
Elizabeth Dixon Smith Geer, Oregon Trail Journal (1847, 1848) at
www.myhistorylab.com

surroundings, an alluring combination to farmers in the malaria-prone Midwest who had been hard hit by the Panic of 1837. But rational motives do not tell the whole story. Many men were motivated by a sense of adventure, by a desire to experience the unknown.

Few pioneers traveled alone, partly because they feared Indian attack but largely because they needed help fording rivers or crossing mountains with heavy wagons. Most Oregon pioneers traveled with their families but usually also joined a larger group, forming a "train." Often the men of the wagon train drew up semimilitary constitutions, electing a leader. In essence, all pioneers—men, women, and children— were part of a new, westward-moving community in which they had to accept both the advantages and disadvantages of community membership.

Wagon trains started westward as soon as the prairies were green (thus ensuring feed for the livestock). Slowly, at a rate of about fifteen miles a day, the wagon trains moved west until they reached Oregon or California. In addition to tedium and exhaustion, wagon trains were beset by such trail hazards as illness and accident. Danger from Indian attack, which all pioneers feared, was actually very small. In contrast, cholera killed at least a thousand people a year in 1849 and in the early 1850s, when it was common along sections of

FERRIAGE of the PLATTE.
above the mouth of Deer Ck.
July 20, 1849

J. Goldsborough Bruff, one of thousands who rushed to California for gold in 1849, sketched several wagons being ferried over the Platte River. The need for individuals to cooperate is obvious. Less obvious in this sketch is the danger: men and livestock often drowned trying to ford western rivers.

the trail along the Platte River. Spread by contaminated water, cholera caused vomiting and diarrhea, which in turn led to extreme dehydration and death, often in one night.

In the afflicted regions, trailside graves were a frequent and grim sight. Drownings were not uncommon, nor were accidental ax wounds or shootings, and children sometimes fell out of wagons and were run over. The members of the wagon train community provided support for survivors: men helped widows drive their wagons onward, women nursed and tended babies whose mothers were dead.

By 1860, almost 300,000 people had traveled the Overland Trails to Oregon or California. Ruts from the wagon wheels can be seen in a number of places along the route even today. In 1869, the completion of the transcontinental railroad marked the end of the wagon train era (see Figure 14.1).

OREGON

The American settlement of Oregon provides a capsule example of the stages of frontier development. The first contacts between the region's Indian peoples and Europeans were commercial. Spanish, British, Russian, and American ships traded for sea otter skins from the 1780s to about 1810. Subsequently, land-based groups scoured the region for beaver skins as well. In this first "frontier of inclusion" there were frequent contacts, many of them sexual, between Indians and Europeans.

Both Great Britain and the United States claimed the Oregon Country by right of discovery, but in the Convention of 1818, the two nations agreed to occupy it jointly, postponing a final decision on its disposition. In reality, the British clearly dominated the region. In 1824, the Hudson's Bay Company consolidated Britain's position by establishing a major fur trading post at Fort Vancouver, on the banks of the Columbia River. Like all fur-trading ventures, the post exemplified the racial mixing of a "frontier of inclusion." Fort Vancouver housed a polyglot population of eastern Indians (Delawares and

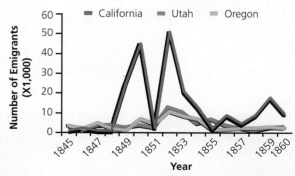

Figure 14.1 Overland Emigration to Oregon, California, and Utah, 1840–60

Before 1849, the westward migration consisted primarily of family groups going to Oregon or Utah. The discovery of gold in California dramatically changed the migration: through 1854, most migrants were single men "rushing" to California, which remained the favored destination up until 1860. Over the twenty-year period from 1840 to 1860, the Overland Trails were transformed from difficult and dangerous routes to well-marked and well-served thorough-fares.

From *The Plains Across: The Overland Emigrants and the Trans-Mississippi West, 1840-60.* Copyright 1979 by Board of Trustees of the University of Illinois. Used with permission of the University of Illinois Press.

Oregon Trail Overland trail of more than two thousand miles that carried American settlers from the Midwest to new settlements in Oregon, California, and Utah.

Iroquois), local Chinook Indians, French and métis from Canada, British traders, and Hawaiians. But the effect of the fur trade on native tribes in Oregon was catastrophic; suffering the fate of all Indian peoples after their initial contact with Europeans, they were decimated by European diseases.

The first permanent European settlers in Oregon were retired fur trappers and their Indian wives and families. The next to arrive were Protestant and Catholic missionaries. Their efforts met with little success. Epidemics had taken the lives of many of the region's peoples, and those who were left were disinclined to give up their nomadic life and settle down as the missionaries wanted them to do.

Finally, in the 1840s, came the Midwest farmers who would make up the majority of Oregon's permanent settlers, carried on the wave of enthusiasm known as "Oregon fever" and lured by free land and patriotism. By 1845, Oregon boasted 5,000 American settlers, most of them living in the Willamette Valley and laying claim to lands to which they had as yet no legal right, because neither Britain nor the United States had concluded land treaties with Oregon's Indian peoples. Their arrival signaled Oregon's transition away from a "frontier of inclusion."

Joint occupancy of Oregon by the Americans and the British continued until 1846. Initially, a peaceful outcome seemed doubtful. In his campaign for president in 1844, President James K. Polk coined the slogan "Fifty-four Forty or Fight," suggesting that the United States would go to war if it didn't get control of all the territory south of 54°40' north latitude, the border between Russian Alaska and British Canada. Once elected, however, Polk was willing to compromise. In June 1846, Britain and the United States concluded a treaty establishing the 49th parallel as the U.S.–Canada border but leaving the island of Vancouver in British hands. Oregon's Donation Land Claim Act of 1850 codified the practice of giving 320 acres to each white male aged eighteen or over and 640 acres to each married couple to settle in the territory (African Americans, Hawaiians, and American Indians were excluded).

The white settlers realized that they had to forge strong community bonds if they hoped to survive on their distant frontier. Cooperation and mutual aid were the rule. Until well into the 1850s, residents organized yearly parties that traveled back along the last stretches of the **Oregon Trail** to help straggling parties making their way to the territory. Kinship networks were strong and vital: many pioneers came to join family who had migrated before them. Food sharing and mutual labor were essential in the early years when crop and livestock loss to weather or natural predators was common. Help, even to total strangers, was customary in times of illness or death.

Relations with the small and unthreatening disease-thinned local Indian tribes were generally peaceful until 1847, when Cayuse Indians killed the missionaries Marcus and Narcissa Whitman. Their deaths triggered a

This view of Fort Vancouver on the Columbia River in the 1840s shows established agriculture and thriving commerce, indicated by the large sailing ship on the river, which is probably the Hudson's Bay Company yearly supply ship from England. It was a scene like this that led Narcissa Whitman to call Fort Vancouver "the New York of the Pacific."

series of "wars" against the remaining native people. A "frontier of exclusion" had been achieved. Nonetheless, the process by which Oregon became part of the United States (it was admitted as a state in 1859) was relatively peaceful, especially when compared with American expansion into the Spanish provinces of New Mexico and Texas.

Tejanos Persons of Spanish or Mexican descent born in Texas.

THE SANTA FÉ TRADE

Commerce with Santa Fé, first settled by colonists from Mexico in 1609, and the center of the Spanish frontier province of New Mexico, had long been desired by American traders. But Spain had forcefully resisted American penetration.

When Mexico gained its independence from Spain in 1821, this exclusionary policy changed. American traders were now welcome in Santa Fé, but the trip over the legendary Santa Fé Trail from Independence, Missouri, was a forbidding 900 miles of arid plains, deserts, and mountains. On the Santa Fé Trail, unlike the Oregon Trail, there was serious danger of Indian attack, for neither the Comanches nor the Apaches of the southern high plains tolerated trespassers. In 1825, Congress voted federal protection for the Santa Fé Trail, even though much of it lay in Mexican territory. By the 1840s, a few hundred American trappers and traders (called *extranjeros*, or "foreigners") lived permanently in New Mexico. In Santa Fé, some American merchants married daughters of important local families, suggesting the start of the inclusive stage of frontier contact.

Settlements and trading posts soon grew up along the long Santa Fé Trail. One of the most famous was Bent's Fort, on the Arkansas River in what is now eastern Colorado, which did a brisk trade in beaver skins and buffalo robes. Like most trading posts, it had a multiethnic population. This racially mixed existence was characteristic of all early trading frontiers, but another western frontier, the American agricultural settlement in Texas, was different from the start.

MEXICAN TEXAS

In 1821, when Mexico gained its independence from Spain, there were 2,240 Tejano (Spanish-speaking) residents of Texas. Established in 1716 as a buffer against possible French attack on New Spain, the main Texas settlements of Nacogdoches, Goliad, and San Antonio remained small, far-flung frontier outposts (see Chapter 5). Communities were organized around three centers: missions and *presidios* (forts), which formed the nuclei of towns, and the large cattle-raising ranchos on which rural living depended. Most **Tejanos** were small farmers or common laborers who led hardscrabble frontier lives. But all Tejanos, rich and poor, faced the constant threat of raids by Comanche Indians.

Legendary warriors, the Comanches raided the small Texas settlements at will and even struck deep into Mexico itself. The nomadic Comanches followed the immense buffalo herds on which they depended for food and clothing. Their relentless raids on the Texas settlements rose from a determination to hold onto this rich buffalo territory, for the buffalo provided all that they wanted. They had no interest in being converted by mission priests or incorporated into mixed-race trading communities.

Painted by George Catlin in about 1834, this scene, *Commanche Village Life*, shows how the everyday life of the Comanches was tied to buffalo. The women in the foreground are scraping buffalo hide, and buffalo meat can be seen drying on racks. The men and boys may be planning their next buffalo hunt.

AMERICANS IN TEXAS

In 1821, seeking to increase the strength of its buffer zone between the heart of Mexico and the marauding Comanches, the Mexican government granted Moses Austin of Missouri an area of 18,000 square miles within the territory of Texas. Moses died shortly thereafter, and the grant was taken up by his son Stephen F. Austin, who became the first American *empresario* (land agent). From the beginning, the American settlement of Texas differed markedly from that of other frontiers. Elsewhere, Americans frequently settled on land to which Indian peoples still held title, or, as in the case of Oregon, they occupied lands to which other countries also made claim. In contrast, the Texas settlement was fully legal: Austin and other **empresarios** owned their lands as a result of formal contracts with the Mexican government. In exchange, Austin agreed that he and his colonists would become Mexican citizens and would adopt the Catholic religion. It is difficult to say which of these two provisions was the more remarkable, for most nineteenth-century Americans defined their Americanness in terms of citizenship and the Protestant religion.

As settlers for his land, Austin chose instead prosperous southern slave owners eager to expand the lands devoted to cotton. Soon Americans (including African American slaves, to whose presence the Mexican government turned a blind eye) outnumbered Tejanos by nearly two to one: in 1830, there were an estimated 7,000 Americans and 4,000 Tejanos living in Texas.

The Austin settlement of 1821 was followed by others, twenty-six in all, concentrating in the fertile river bottoms of eastern and south central Texas. These large settlements were highly organized farming enterprises whose principal crop was cotton, grown by African American slave labor and sold in the international market. By the early 1830s, Americans in Texas, ignoring the border between Mexican Texas and the United States, were sending an estimated $500,000 worth of goods (mostly cotton) yearly to New Orleans for export.

Austin's colonists and those who settled later were predominantly Southerners who viewed Texas as a natural extension of the cotton frontier in Mississippi and Louisiana. These settlers created "**enclaves**" (self-contained communities) that had little contact with Tejanos or Indian peoples. In fact, although they lived in Mexican territory, most Americans never bothered to learn Spanish. Nor, in spite of Austin's promises, did they become Mexican citizens or adopt the Catholic religion. Like the immigrants who flooded into East Coast cities (see Chapter 13), the Americans in Texas were immigrants to another country—but one to which they did not intend to adapt.

For a brief period, Texas was big enough to hold three communities: Comanche, Tejano, and American. The nomadic Comanches rode the high plains of northern and western Texas, raiding settlements primarily for horses. The Tejanos maintained their ranchos and missions mostly in the South, while American farmers occupied the eastern and south central sections.

The balance among the three communities in Texas was broken in 1828, when centrists gained control of the government in Mexico City and, in a dramatic shift of policy, decided to exercise firm control over the northern province. As the Mexican government restricted American immigration, outlawed slavery, levied customs duties and taxes, and planned other measures, Americans seethed and talked of rebellion. Bolstering their cause were as many as 20,000 additional Americans, many of them openly expansionist, who flooded into Texas after 1830. These most recent settlers did not intend to become Mexican citizens. Instead, they planned to take over Texas.

Between 1830 and 1836, the mood on both the Mexican and the American-Texan sides became more belligerent. In the fall of 1835, war finally broke out, and a volunteer American and Tejano army assembled. After the disastrous defeat at the **Alamo** described in the chapter opener, Mexican general and president Antonio López de Santa Anna led his army in pursuit of the remaining army of American and Tejano volunteers commanded by General Sam Houston.

empresarios   Agents who received a land grant from the Spanish or Mexican government in return for organizing settlements.

enclave   Self-contained community.

Alamo   Franciscan mission at San Antonio, Texas that was the site in 1836 of a siege and massacre of Texans by Mexican troops.

On April 21, 1836, at the San Jacinto River in eastern Texas, Santa Anna thought he had Houston trapped at last. Confident of victory against the exhausted Texans, Santa Anna's army rested in the afternoon, failing even to post sentries. Although Houston advised against it, Houston's men voted to attack immediately rather than wait till the next morning. Shouting "Remember the Alamo!" for the first time, the Texans completely surprised their opponents and won an overwhelming victory. On May 14, 1836, Santa Anna signed a treaty fixing the southern boundary of the newly independent Republic of Texas at the Rio Grande. The Mexican Congress, however, repudiated the treaty and refused to recognize Texan independence (see Map 14.4).

THE REPUBLIC OF TEXAS

The Republic of Texas was unexpectedly rebuffed in another quarter as well. The U.S. Congress refused to grant it statehood when, in 1837, Texas applied for admission to the Union. Petitions opposing the admission of a fourteenth slave state (there were then thirteen free states) poured into Congress. Congress debated and ultimately dropped the Texas application.

The unresolved conflict with Mexico put heavy stress on American–Tejano relations. As before, ambitious Anglos married into the Tejano elite, which made it easier for those Tejano families to adjust to the changes in law and commerce that the Americans quickly enacted. But following a temporary recapture of San Antonio by Mexican forces in 1842, positions hardened. Many more of the Tejano elite fled to Mexico, and Americans discussed banishing or imprisoning all Tejanos until the border issue was settled. This was, of course, impossible. Culturally, San Antonio remained a Mexican city long after the Americans had declared independence. The Americans in the Republic of Texas were struggling to reconcile American ideals of democracy with the reality of subordinating those with a prior claim, the Tejanos, to the status of a conquered people.

American control over the other Texas residents, the Indians, was also slow in coming. The Comanches still rode the high plains of northern and western Texas. West of the Rio Grande, equally fierce Apache bands were in control. Not until after the Civil War and major campaigns by the U.S. Army were these fierce Indian tribes conquered.

Texans continued to press for annexation to the United States, while at the same time seeking recognition and support from Great Britain. The idea of an independent and expansionist republic on its southern border that might gain the support of America's traditional enemy alarmed many Americans. Annexation thus became an urgent matter of national politics. This issue also added to the troubles of a governing Whig Party that was already deeply divided by the policies of John Tyler, who had become president by default when William Harrison died in office (see Chapter 11). Tyler raised the issue of annexation in 1844, hoping thereby to ensure his reelection, but the strategy backfired. Presenting the annexation treaty to Congress, Secretary of State John Calhoun awakened sectional fears by connecting Texas with the urgent need of southern slave owners to extend slavery.

In a storm of antislavery protest, Whigs rejected the treaty proposed by their own president and ejected Tyler himself from the party. In his place, they chose Henry Clay as their presidential candidate. Clay took a noncommittal stance on Texas, favoring annexation, but only if Mexico approved. Since Mexico's emphatic disapproval was well known, Clay's position was widely interpreted as a politician's effort not to alienate voters on either side of the fence.

In contrast, in the Democratic Party, wholehearted and outspoken expansionists seized control. Sweeping aside their own senior politician, Van Buren, who like Clay tried to remain uncommitted, the Democrats nominated their first "dark horse" candidate, James K. Polk of Tennessee. Democrats enthusiastically endorsed Polk's platform, which called for "the re-occupation of Oregon and the re-annexation of Texas at the earliest practicable period."

•••• Read the Document

Whose History Is It: Remembering the Alamo at **www.myhistorylab.com**

Watch the Video

The Annexation of Texas at **www.myhistorylab.com**

MAP 14.4

Texas: From Mexican Province to U.S. State   In the space of twenty years, Texas changed shape three times. Initially part of the Mexican province of Coahuila y Tejas, it became the Republic of Texas in 1836, following the Texas Revolt, and was annexed to the United States in that form in 1845. Finally, in the Compromise of 1850 following the Mexican-American War, it took its present shape.

WHERE DID most of the American settlers in Texas come from? How did the origins of American Texans shape the region's history and development?

Polk won the 1844 election by a narrow margin. Nevertheless, the 1844 election was widely interpreted as a mandate for expansion. Thereupon, John Tyler, in one of his last actions as president, pushed through Congress a joint resolution (which did not require the two-thirds approval by the Senate necessary for treaties) for the annexation of Texas. When Texas entered the Union in December 1845, it was the twenty-eighth state and the fifteenth slave state.

THE MEXICAN-AMERICAN WAR

WHAT WERE the most important consequences of the Mexican-American War?

James K. Polk lived up to his expansive campaign promises. In 1846, he peacefully added Oregon south of the 49th parallel to the United States; in 1848, following the Mexican-American War, he acquired Mexico's northern provinces of California and New Mexico as well. Thus, with the annexation of Texas, the United States, in the short space of three years, had added 1.5 million square miles of territory, an increase of nearly 70 percent.

ORIGINS OF THE WAR

In the spring of 1846, just as the controversy over Oregon was drawing to a peaceful conclusion, tensions with Mexico grew more serious. Because the United States supported the Texas claim of all land north of the Rio Grande, it became embroiled in a border dispute with Mexico. In June 1845, Polk sent General Zachary Taylor to Texas, and by October a force of 3,500 Americans was on the Nueces River with orders to defend Texas in the event of a Mexican invasion.

Polk had something bigger than border protection in mind. He coveted the continent clear to the Pacific Ocean. At the same time that he sent Taylor to Texas, Polk secretly instructed the Pacific naval squadron to seize the California ports if Mexico declared war. He also wrote the American consul in Monterey, Thomas Larkin, that a peaceful takeover of California by its residents—Spanish Mexicans and Americans alike—would not be unwelcome.

Meanwhile, in November 1845, Polk sent a secret envoy, John Slidell, to Mexico with an offer of $30 million or more for the Rio Grande border in Texas and Mexico's provinces of New Mexico and California. When the Mexican government refused even to receive Slidell. Polk ordered General Taylor and his forces south to the Rio Grande, into the territory that Mexicans claimed as their soil. In April 1846, a brief skirmish between American and Mexican soldiers broke out in the disputed zone. Polk seized on the event as a pretext for war, and on May 13, 1846, Congress declared war on Mexico (see Map 14.5).

MR. POLK'S WAR

From the beginning, the **Mexican-American War** was politically divisive. Whig critics in Congress questioned Polk's account of the border incident. They accused the president of misleading Congress and of maneuvering the country into an unnecessary war. As the Mexican-American War dragged on and casualties and costs mounted, opposition increased, especially among northern antislavery Whigs. Many Northerners asked why Polk had been willing to settle for only a part of Oregon but was so eager to pursue a war for slave territory. Thus, expansionist dreams served to fuel sectional antagonisms.

The northern states witnessed both mass and individual protests against the war. In Massachusetts, the legislature passed a resolution condemning Polk's declaration of war as unconstitutional, and philosopher–writer Henry David Thoreau went to jail rather than pay the taxes he believed would support the war effort. (Thoreau's dramatic gesture was undercut by his aunt, who paid his fine after he had spent only one night in jail.) Thoreau then wrote his classic essay "Civil Disobedience," justifying the individual's moral duty to oppose an immoral government.

Polk assumed the overall planning of the war's strategy. By his personal attention to the coordination of civilian political goals and military requirements, Polk gave a new and expanded definition to the role of the president as commander in chief during wartime. By the end of 1846, the northern provinces that Polk had coveted were secured, but

LANDING OF THE AMERICAN FORCES UNDER GENL SCOTT
AT VERA CRUZ MARCH 9TH 1847

General Winfield Scott's amphibious attack on the Mexican coastal city of Veracruz in March 1847 was greeted with wide popular acclaim in the United States. It was the first successful amphibious attack in U.S. military history. Popular interest in the battles of the Mexican-American War was fed by illustrations such as this in newspapers and magazines.

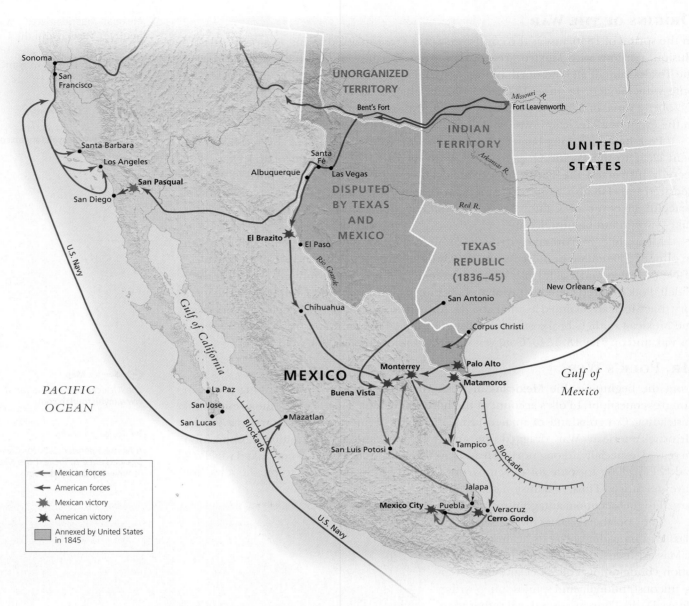

MAP 14.5

The Mexican-American War, 1846–48   The Mexican-American War began with an advance by U.S. forces into the disputed area between the Nueces River and the Rio Grande in Texas. The war's major battles were fought by General Zachary Taylor in northern Mexico and General Winfield Scott in Veracruz and Mexico City. Meanwhile Colonel Stephen Kearny secured New Mexico and, with the help of the U.S. Navy and John C. Frémont's troops, California.

QUICK REVIEW

War with Mexico

- Polk sought a war that would give United States control of California.
- Mexico fought hard but could not match American military.
- Treaty of Guadalupe Hidalgo (1848): Mexico gave up claim to Texas north of Rio Grande, Alta California, and New Mexico.

WHAT DOES the American military strategy tell you about Polk's war aims?

contrary to his expectations, Mexico refused to negotiate. In February 1847, General Santa Anna attacked American troops led by General Taylor at Buena Vista but was repulsed by Taylor's small force. A month later, in March 1847, General Winfield Scott captured the coastal city of Veracruz. These victories were to be the last easy victories of the war. It took Scott six months of brutal fighting against stubborn Mexican resistance on the battlefield and harassing guerrilla raids to force his way to Mexico City. American troops reacted bitterly to their high casualty rates, retaliating against Mexican citizens with acts of murder, robbery, and rape. In September, Scott took Mexico City, and Mexican resistance came to an end.

With the American army went a special envoy, Nicholas Trist, who delivered Polk's terms for peace. In the Treaty of Guadalupe Hidalgo, signed February 2, 1848, Mexico ceded its northern provinces of California and New Mexico (which included present-day Arizona, Utah, Nevada, and part of Colorado) and accepted the Rio Grande as the boundary of Texas. The United States agreed to pay Mexico $15 million and assume about $2 million in individual claims against that nation.

When Trist returned to Washington with the treaty, however, Polk was furious. He had actually recalled Trist after Scott's sweeping victory, intending to send a new envoy with greater demands, but Trist had ignored the recall order. "All Mexico!" had become the phrase widely used by those in favor of further expansion, Polk among them. But two very different groups opposed further expansion. The first group, composed of northern Whigs, included such notables as Ralph Waldo Emerson, who grimly warned, United States will conquer Mexico, but it will be as the man swallows arsenic, which brings him down in turn. Mexico will poison us." The second group was composed of Southerners who realized that Mexicans could not be kept as conquered people but would have to be offered territorial government as Louisiana had been offered in 1804. Senator John C. Calhoun of South Carolina, leading the opposition, warned against admitting "colored and mixed-breed" Mexicans "on an equality with people of the United States." Bowing to these political protests, Polk reluctantly accepted the treaty. A later addition, the $10 million Gadsden Purchase of parts of present-day New Mexico and Arizona, added another 30,000 square miles to the United States in 1853 (see Map 14.6).

THE PRESS AND POPULAR WAR ENTHUSIASM

The Mexican-American War was the first war in which regular, on-the-scene reporting caught the mass of ordinary citizens up in the war's daily events. Thanks to the recently invented telegraph, newspapers could get the latest news from their reporters, who were among the world's first war correspondents. For the first time in American history, accounts by journalists, and not the opinions of politicians, became the major shapers of popular attitudes toward a war. From beginning to end, news of the war stirred unprecedented popular excitement (see Seeing History).

The reports from the battlefield united Americans in a new way: they became part of a temporary but highly emotional community linked by newsprint and buttressed by public gatherings. Exciting, sobering, and terrible, war news had a deep hold on the popular imagination. It was a lesson newspaper publishers never forgot.

MAP 14.6

Territory Added, 1845–53 James K. Polk was elected president in 1844 on an expansionist platform. He lived up to most of his campaign rhetoric by gaining the Oregon Country (to the 49th parallel) peacefully from the British, Texas by the presidential action of his predecessor John Tyler, and present-day California, Arizona, Nevada, Utah, New Mexico, and part of Colorado by war with Mexico. In the short space of three years, the size of the United States grew by 70 percent. In 1853, the Gadsden Purchase added another 30,000 square miles.

WHAT FUTURE did southerners imagine for the American West? What about northerners?

CALIFORNIA AND THE GOLD RUSH

In the early 1840s, California was inhabited by many seminomadic Indian tribes whose people numbered approximately 50,000. There were also some 7,000 *Californios*, descendants of the Spanish-Mexican pioneers who had begun to settle in 1769. Even American annexation at the end of the Mexican-American War changed little for the handful of Americans on this remote frontier. But then came the gold rush of 1849, which changed California permanently.

HOW DID the gold rush of 1849 change California?

Californios   Californians of Spanish descent.

War News from Mexico

The unprecedented immediacy of the news reporting from the battlefields of the Mexican-American War, transmitted for the first time by telegraph, is captured in this painting by the American artist Richard Caton Woodville, painted in 1848 (the year the war ended). Woodville was one of a number of genre painters who enlivened their depictions of everyday life and ordinary people by focusing on political debates or dramatic moments like the one shown here.

Almost every aspect of this painting is political commentary. The central figure in the painting is standing on the porch of the American Hotel reading the latest war news to the crowd of men gathered around him from a cheap "penny paper" full of sensational stories, war news, and lithographs of battle scenes from the war. Although the audience seems deeply engaged, the range of expressions reminds the viewer that the war was very divisive, with many antislavery Northerners in outright opposition. The placement of the African American man at a lower level on the step is a clear statement of his exclusion from political participation. Don't overlook the woman leaning out of the window on the right side of the painting. She too is excluded from politics but is obviously just as interested and concerned as the men. Woodville's inclusion of the black child in a white smock seems to be an ambiguous statement about the impact of the Mexican-American War on slavery. ■

ARE YOU surprised at the extent of political commentary in this painting? Are paintings an appropriate media for political opinion?

Richard Caton Woodville, *War News from Mexico*, Oil on canvas. Manovgian Foundation on loan to the National Gallery of Art, Washington, DC. © Board of Trustees, National Gallery of Art, Washington.

RUSSIAN–CALIFORNIO TRADE

The first outsiders to penetrate the isolation of Spanish California were not Americans but Russians. Evading Spanish regulations, Californios traded with the Russian American Fur Company in Sitka, Alaska. A mutually beneficial barter of California food for iron tools and woven cloth from Russia was established in 1806. This arrangement became even brisker after the Russians settled Fort Ross (near present-day Mendocino) in 1812.

When Mexico became independent in 1821, Californios continued their special relationship with the Russians. However, agricultural productivity declined after 1832, when the Mexican government ordered the secularization of the California missions, and the Russians turned to the Hudson's Bay Company in the Pacific Northwest for their food supply. In 1841, they sold Fort Ross, and the Russian–Californio connection came to an end.

EARLY AMERICAN SETTLEMENT

Johann Augustus Sutter, a Swiss who had settled in California in 1839, becoming a Mexican citizen, served as a focal point for American settlement in the 1840s. Sutter held a land grant in the Sacramento Valley. At the center of his holdings was Sutter's Fort. In the 1840s, Sutter offered valuable support to the handful of American overlanders who chose California over Oregon. Most of these Americans, keenly aware that they were interlopers in Mexican territory, settled near Sutter in California's Central Valley, away from the Californio clustered along the coast.

In June 1846, these Americans banded together at Sonoma in the Bear Flag Revolt (so called because their flag bore a bear emblem), declaring independence from Mexico. The American takeover of California was not confirmed until the Treaty of Guadalupe Hidalgo in 1848.

GOLD!

In January 1848, carpenter James Marshall noticed small flakes of gold in the millrace at Sutter's Mill (present-day Coloma). Soon he and all the rest of John Sutter's employees were panning for gold in California's streams. But not until the autumn of 1848 did the East Coast hear the first rumors about the discovery of gold in California. When the reports were confirmed in November, thousands left farms and jobs and headed west, by land and by sea, to make their fortune. Later known as "forty-niners" for the year the gold rush began in earnest, these people came from all parts of the United States—and indeed, from all over the world. They transformed what had been a quiet ranching paradise into a teeming and tumultuous community in search of wealth.

Eighty percent of the forty-niners were Americans. The second largest group of migrants was from nearby Mexico and the western coast of Latin America (13 percent). The remainder came from Europe and Asia (see Figure 14.2).

The presence of Chinese miners surprised many Americans. Several hundred Chinese arrived in California in 1849 and 1850, and in 1852 more than 20,000 landed in San Francisco. Most came, like the Americans, as temporary sojourners, intending to return home as soon as they made some money. Again, like most of the American miners, the majority of Chinese were men who left their wives at home. Chinese miners soon became a familiar sight in the gold fields, as did the presence of "Chinatowns." The

Richard Henry Dana, Two Years before the Mast (1840) at **www.myhistorylab.com**

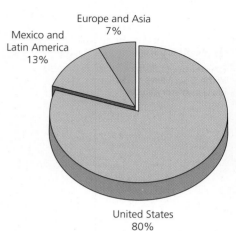

Europe and Asia 7%

Mexico and Latin America 13%

United States 80%

Figure 14.2 Where the Forty-Niners Came From
Americans drawn to the California gold rush of 1849 encountered a more diverse population than most had previously known. Nearly as novel to them as the 20 percent from foreign countries was the regional variety from within the United States itself.

Chinese first came to California in 1849 attracted by the gold rush. Frequently, however, they were forced off their claims by intolerant whites. Rather than enjoy an equal chance in the goldfields, they were often forced to work as servants or in other menial occupations.

Chinese quickly aroused American hostility. A special tax was imposed on foreign miners in 1852, and in the 1870s, Chinese immigration was sharply curtailed.

In 1849, as the gold rush began in earnest, San Francisco, the major entry port and supply point, sprang to life. From a settlement of 1,000 in 1848, it grew to a city of 35,000 in 1850. This surge suggested that the real money to be made in California was not in panning for gold but in feeding, clothing, housing, provisioning, and entertaining the miners. The white population of California jumped from an estimated pre–gold rush figure of 11,000 to more than 100,000 by 1852. California was admitted into the Union as a state in 1850.

MINING CAMPS

As had occurred in San Francisco, most mining camps boomed almost instantly to life, but unlike San Francisco, they were empty again within a few years. They were generally dirty and dreary places. Most miners lived in tents or hovels and led a cheerless, uncomfortable, and unhealthy existence, especially during the long, rainy winter months, with few distractions apart from the saloon, the gambling hall, and the prostitute's bed (see Map 14.7). Partly because few people put any effort into building communities—they were too busy

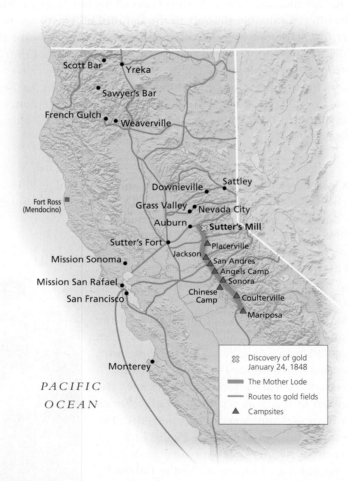

MAP 14.7

California in the Gold Rush This map shows the major gold camps along the mother lode in the western foothills of the Sierra Nevada Mountains. Gold seekers reached the camps by crossing the Sierra Nevada near Placerville on the Overland Trail or by sea via San Francisco. The main area of Spanish-Mexican settlement, the coastal region between Monterey and Los Angeles, was remote from the goldfields.

From *The Historical Atlas of California* by Warren A. Beck and Ynez Hasse. Copyright 1974 University of Oklahoma Press. Reprinted by permission.

WHERE DID the miners come from? How did their arrival change California?

seeking gold—violence was endemic in mining areas, and much of it was racial. Discrimination, especially against Chinese, Mexicans, and African Americans, was common.

Most miners were young, unmarried, and unsuccessful. Only a small percentage ever struck it rich in California. Gold deposits that were accessible with pick and shovel were soon exhausted, and the deeper deposits required capital and machinery. Increasingly, those who stayed on in California had to give up the status of independent miners and become wage earners for large mining concerns.

By the mid-1850s, the immediate effects of the gold rush had passed. California had a booming population, a thriving agriculture, and a corporate mining industry. The gold rush also left California with a population that was larger, more affluent, and (in urban San Francisco) more culturally sophisticated than that in other newly settled territories. And it was significantly more multicultural than the rest of the nation, for many of the Chinese and Mexicans, as well as immigrants from many European countries, remained in California after the gold rush subsided. But the gold rush left some permanent scars: the virtual extermination of the California Indian peoples, the dispossession of many Californios who were legally deprived of their land grants, and the growth of racial animosity toward the Chinese in particular.

THE POLITICS OF MANIFEST DESTINY

In three short years, from 1845 to 1848, the territory of the United States grew an incredible 70 percent, and a continental nation took shape. This expansion, pushed by economic desires and feelings of American cultural superiority, led directly to the emergence of the divisive issue of slavery as the dominant issue in national politics.

THE WILMOT PROVISO

In 1846, almost all the northern members of the Whig Party opposed Democratic president James Polk's belligerent expansionism on antislavery grounds. Northern Whigs correctly feared that expansion would reopen the issue of slavery in the territories. But the outpouring of popular enthusiasm for the Mexican-American War convinced most Whig congressmen that they needed to vote military appropriations for the war in spite of their misgivings.

Ironically, it was not the Whigs but a Democratic congressman from Pennsylvania, David Wilmot, who opened the door to sectional controversy over expansion. In August 1846, only a few short months after the beginning of the Mexican-American War, Wilmot proposed, in an amendment to a military appropriations bill, that slavery be banned in all the territories acquired from Mexico. In the debate and voting that followed, something new and ominous occurred: southern Whigs joined southern Democrats to vote against the measure, while Northerners of both parties supported it. Sectional interest had triumphed over party loyalty. Wilmot's Proviso triggered the first breakdown of the national party system and reopened the debate about the place of slavery in the future of the nation.

The **Wilmot Proviso** was so controversial that it was deleted from the necessary military appropriations bills during the Mexican-American War. But in 1848, following the Treaty of Guadalupe Hidalgo, the question of the expansion of slavery could no longer be avoided or postponed. Antislavery advocates from the North argued with proslavery Southerners in a debate that was much more prolonged and bitter than in the Missouri Crisis debate of 1819. Civility quickly wore thin: threats were uttered and fistfights broke out on the floor of the House of Representatives.

THE FREE-SOIL MOVEMENT

Why did David Wilmot propose this controversial measure? Wilmot, a northern Democrat, was propelled not by ideology but by the pressure of practical politics. The dramatic rise of the **Liberty Party**, founded in 1840 by abolitionists, threatened to take votes away from both the Whig and the Democratic parties.

WHAT KEY factors explain the outcome of the election of 1848?

Wilmot Proviso The amendment offered by Pennsylvania Democrat David Wilmot in 1846 which stipulated that "as an express and fundamental condition to the acquisition of any territory from the Republic of Mexico . . . neither slavery nor involuntary servitude shall ever exist in any part of said territory."

Liberty Party The first antislavery political party, formed in 1840.

OVERVIEW | Expansion Causes the First Splits in the Second American Party System

1844	Whigs reject President John Tyler's move to annex Texas and expel him from the Whig Party.
	Southern Democrats choose expansionist James K. Polk as their presidential candidate, passing over Martin Van Buren, who is against expansion.
	Liberty Party runs abolitionist James Birney for president, attracting northern antislavery Whigs.
1846	The Wilmot Proviso, proposing to ban slavery in the territories that might be gained in the Mexican-American War, splits both parties: southern Whigs and Democrats oppose the measure; northern Whigs and Democrats support it.
1848	The new Free-Soil Party runs northern Democrat Martin Van Buren for president, gaining 10 percent of the vote from abolitionists, antislavery Whigs, and some northern Democrats. This strong showing by a third party causes Democrat Lewis Cass to lose the electoral votes of New York and Pennsylvania, allowing the Whig Zachary Taylor to win.

The Liberty Party took an uncompromising stance against slavery. The party proposed to prohibit the admission of slave states to the Union, end slavery in the District of Columbia, and abolish the interstate slave trade. Liberty Party members also favored denying office to all slaveholders. Liberty Party doctrine was too uncompromising for the mass of northern voters, who immediately realized that the southern states would leave the Union before accepting it. Still, many Northerners opposed slavery. From this sentiment, the Free-Soil Party was born.

The free-soil argument was a calculated adjustment of abolitionist principles to practical politics. It shifted the focus from the question of the morality of slavery to the ways in which slavery posed a threat to northern expansion. The free-soil doctrine thus established a direct link between expansion, which most Americans supported, and sectional politics.

Free-soilers were willing to allow slavery to continue in the existing slave states because they supported the Union, not because they approved of slavery. They were unwilling, however, to allow the extension of slavery to new and unorganized territory. If the South were successful in extending slavery, they argued, northern farmers who moved west would find themselves competing at an economic disadvantage with large planters using slave labor. Free-soilers also insisted that the northern values of freedom and individualism would be destroyed if the slave-based southern labor system were allowed to spread.

Many free-soilers really meant "anti-black" when they said "antislavery." They proposed to ban all African American people from the new territories. William Lloyd Garrison promptly denounced the free-soil doctrine as "whitemanism," a racist effort to make the territories white. There was much truth to his charge: most Northerners were unwilling to consider social equality for African Americans, free or slave. Banning all black people from the western territories seemed a simple solution.

THE ELECTION OF 1848

A swirl of emotions—pride, expansionism, sectionalism, abolitionism, free-soil sentiment—surrounded the election of 1848. The issues raised by the Wilmot Proviso remained to be resolved, and every candidate had to have an answer to the question of whether slavery should be admitted in the new territories.

Lewis Cass of Michigan, the Democratic nominee for president (Polk, in poor health, declined to run for a second term), proposed to apply the doctrine of **popular sovereignty** to the crucial slave–free issue. Popular sovereignty was based on the accepted constitutional principle that decisions about slavery (like, for example, rules about suffrage) should be made at the state rather than the national level. In reality, popular sovereignty was an admission of the national failure to resolve sectional differences. It simply shifted decision making on the crucial issue of the expansion of slavery from national politicians to the members of territorial and state legislatures.

Moreover, the doctrine of popular sovereignty was deliberately vague about when a territory would choose its status. Would it do so during the territorial stage or at the point of applying for statehood? Clearly, this question was crucial, for no slave owner would invest in new land if the territory could later be declared free, and no abolitionist would move to a territory that was destined to become a slave state. Cass hoped his ambiguity on this point would win him votes in both North and South.

For their part, the Whigs passed over perennial candidate Henry Clay and turned to a war hero, General Zachary Taylor. Taylor, a Louisiana slaveholder, refused to take a position on the Wilmot Proviso, allowing both northern and southern voters to hope that he agreed with them.

The deliberate vagueness of the two major candidates displeased many northern voters. An uneasy mixture of disaffected Democrats and Whigs joined former Liberty Party voters to support the candidate of the Free-Soil Party, former president Martin Van Buren. In the end, Van Buren garnered 10 percent of the vote (all in the North). The vote for the Free-Soil Party cost Cass the electoral votes of New York and Pennsylvania, and General Zachary Taylor won the election with only 47 percent of the popular vote.

CONCLUSION

In the decade of the 1840s, westward expansion took many forms, from relatively peaceful settlement in Oregon, to war with Mexico over Texas, to the overwhelming numbers of gold rushers who changed California forever. Most of these frontiers—in Oregon, New Mexico, and California—began as frontiers of inclusion, in which small numbers of Americans were eager for trade, accommodation, and intermarriage with the original inhabitants. Texas, with its agricultural enclaves, was the exception to this pattern. Yet on every frontier, as the number of American settlers increased, so did the sentiment for exclusion, so that by 1850, whatever their origins, the far-flung American continental settlements were more similar than different, and the success of manifest destiny seemed overwhelming.

The election of 1848, virtually a referendum on manifest destiny, yielded ironic results. James K. Polk, who presided over the unprecedented expansion, did not run for a second term and, thus, the Democratic Party gained no electoral victory to match the military one. The electorate that had been so thrilled by the war news voted for a war hero—who led the anti-expansionist Whig Party. The election was decided by Martin Van Buren, the Free-Soil candidate who voiced the sentiments of the abolitionists, a reform group that had been insignificant just a few years before. The amazing expansion achieved by the Mexican-American War—America's manifest destiny—made the United States a continental nation but stirred up the issue that was to tear it apart. Sectional rivalries and fears now dominated every aspect of politics. Expansion, once a force for unity, now divided the nation into Northerners and Southerners, who could not agree on the community they shared—the federal Union.

popular sovereignty   A solution to the slavery crisis suggested by Michigan senator Lewis Cass by which territorial residents, not Congress, would decide slavery's fate.

CHRONOLOGY

1609	First Spanish settlement in New Mexico
1670s	British and French Canadians begin fur trade in western Canada
1716	First Spanish settlements in Texas
1769	First Spanish settlement in California
1780s	New England ships begin sea otter trade in Pacific Northwest
1793	Alexander Mackenzie of the North West Company reaches the Pacific Ocean.
1803	Louisiana Purchase
1804–06	Lewis and Clark expedition
1806	Russian–Californio trade begins
1806–07	Zebulon Pike's expedition across the Great Plains to the Rocky Mountains
1819–20	Stephen Long's expedition across the Great Plains
1821	Hudson's Bay Company gains dominance of western fur trade
	Mexico seizes independence from Spain
	Santa Fé Trail opens, soon protected by U.S. military
	Stephen F. Austin becomes first American empresario in Texas
1824	First fur rendezvous sponsored by Rocky Mountain Fur Company
	Hudson's Bay Company establishes Fort Vancouver in Oregon Country
1830	Indian Removal Act moves eastern Indians to Indian Territory
1833–34	Prince Maximilian and artist Karl Bodmer visit Plains Indians
1834	Jason Lee establishes first mission in Oregon Country
1835	Texas revolts against Mexico
1836	Battles of the Alamo and San Jacinto
	Republic of Texas formed
1843–44	John C. Frémont maps trails to Oregon and California
1844	Democrat James K. Polk elected president on an expansionist platform
1845	Texas annexed to the United States as a slave state
	John O'Sullivan coins the phrase "manifest destiny"
1846	Oregon question settled peacefully with Britain
	Mexican-American War begins
	Bear Flag Revolt in California
	Wilmot Proviso
1847	Cayuse War begins in Oregon
	Americans win battles of Buena Vista, Veracruz, and Mexico City
1848	Treaty of Guadalupe Hidalgo
	Free-Soil Party captures 10 percent of the popular vote in the North
	General Zachary Taylor, a Whig, elected president
1849	California gold rush

REVIEW QUESTIONS

1. Define and discuss the concept of manifest destiny.

2. Trace the different ways in which the frontiers in Oregon, Texas, and California moved from frontiers of inclusion to frontiers of exclusion.

3. Take different sides (Whig and Democrat) and debate the issues raised by the Mexican-American War.

4. The California gold rush was an unprecedented scramble for riches. What were its effects on its participants, on California, and on the nation as a whole?

5. Referring to Chapter 13, compare the positions of the Liberty Party and the Free-Soil Party. Examine the factors that made the free-soil doctrine politically so acceptable and abolitionism so controversial.

KEY TERMS

Alamo (p. 344)
Californios (p. 349)
Empresarios (p. 344)
Enclave (p. 344)
Liberty Party (p. 353)
Manifest Destiny (p. 339)

Mexican-American War (p. 347)
Oregon Trail (p. 342)
Popular sovereignty (p. 355)
Santa Fé Trail (p. 337)
Tejanos (p. 343)
Wilmot Proviso (p. 353)

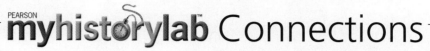

myhistorylab Connections

Reinforce what you learned in this chapter by studying the many documents,
images, maps, review tools, and videos available at www.myhistorylab.com.

Read and Review

✓ Study and Review Chapter 14

Read the Document

*A Tejano Describes the Beginning of the Texas
Revolution in 1835–36*

*William Barret Travis, Letter from the
Alamo (1836)*

*A Newspaper Man Declares the "Manifest
Destiny" of the United States in 1845*

Francis Parkman, The Oregon Trail (1847)

*Elizabeth Dixon Smith Geer, Oregon Trail Journal
(1847, 1848)*

Mariah and Stephen King to Their Family (1846)

James K. Polk, First Inaugural Address (1845)

*Richard Henry Dana, Two Years before the
Mast (1840)*

*Edward Gould Buffum, from Six Months in the
Gold Mines (1850)*

Hear the Audio *A New Englander Calls for Civil
Disobedience to Protest the Mexican War*

See the Map *The Mexican-American War*

Research and Explore

Read the Document

Exploring America: The Unwelcome Mat

Whose History Is It: Remembering the Alamo

Profiles
  Jim Beckwourth
  Juan Seguin

Watch the Video *The Annexation of Texas*

Hear the audio files for Chapter 14 at
www.myhistorylab.com.

This horror, this nightmare abomination!
Can it be in my country! It lies like lead on
my heart, it shadows my life with sorrow . . .
— *Harriet Beecher Stowe, December 16, 1852*

Grand procession of Wide-Awakes at New York on the evening
of October 3, 1860.

15

THE COMING CRISIS
THE 1850S

((•—Hear the Audio

Hear the audio files for Chapter 15 at **www.myhistorylab.com**.

HOW DID expansion shape how Americans saw themselves as a nation in 1850?

WHY DID expansion lead to increasing sectional division in the 1850s?

WHAT EXPLAINS the end of the Second American Party System and the rise of the Republican Party?

WHAT EVENTS helped propel the country towards Civil War in the late 1850s?

WHY DID the South secede following the Republican Party victory in the election of 1860?

1850s

AMERICAN COMMUNITIES

Illinois Communities
Debate Slavery

ON SEVEN OCCASIONS THROUGH THE LATE SUMMER AND AUTUMN OF 1858, in seven small Illinois towns, thousands of farmers and townspeople put aside their daily routines and converged on their local town green. Entertained by brass bands and pageantry, they waited impatiently for the main event, the chance to take part in the Lincoln–Douglas debate on the most urgent question of the day—slavery.

The decade-long effort to solve the problem of the future of slavery had failed. For most of this time, Washington politicians trying to build broad national parties with policies acceptable to voters in both the North and the South had done their best not to talk about slavery. That the Lincoln–Douglas debates were devoted to one issue alone—slavery and the future of the Union—showed how serious matters had become.

Democratic Senator Stephen A. Douglas of Illinois and his Republican challenger, Springfield lawyer Abraham Lincoln, presented their views in three hours of closely reasoned argument. But they did not speak alone. Cheers, boos, groans, and shouted questions from active, engaged listeners punctuated all seven of the now famous confrontations between the two men. Thus, the Lincoln–Douglas debates were community events in which Illinois citizens took part. Some individuals were proslavery, some antislavery, and many were undecided, but all were agreed that democratic politics gave them the means to air their opinions, to resolve their differences, and to assess the candidates who were running for a Senate seat from Illinois.

Stephen Douglas was the leading Democratic contender for the 1860 presidential nomination, but first he had to win reelection to the Illinois seat he had held in the U.S. Senate for twelve years. His vote against allowing slavery in Kansas had alienated him from the strong southern wing of his own party. Because the crisis of the Union was so severe and Douglas's role so pivotal, his reelection campaign clearly previewed the 1860 presidential election. For the sake of its future, the Republican Party had to field a strong opponent: it found its candidate in Abraham Lincoln.

Lincoln had represented Illinois in the House of Representatives in the 1840s but had lost political support in 1848 because he had opposed the Mexican-American War. Developing a prosperous law practice, he had been an influential member of the Illinois Republican Party since its founding in 1856. Although he had entered political life as a Whig, Lincoln was radicalized by the issue of the extension of slavery. Even though his wife's family were

Kentucky slave owners, Lincoln's commitment to freedom and his resistance to the spread of slavery had now become absolute.

Douglas had many strengths going into the debates. He spoke for the Union, he claimed, pointing out that the Democratic Party was a national party whereas the Republican Party was only sectional. He repeatedly appealed to the racism of much of his audience. Calling his opponent a "Black Republican," he implied that Lincoln and his party favored the social equality of whites and blacks, even race mixing.

Lincoln did not believe in the social equality of the races, but he did believe wholeheartedly that slavery was a moral wrong. Pledging the Republican Party to the "ultimate extinction" of slavery, Lincoln continually warned that Douglas's position would lead to the opposite result: the spread of slavery everywhere.

The first of the seven debates, held in Ottawa, in northern Illinois, on Saturday, August 21, 1858, showed not only the seriousness but also the exuberance of the democratic politics of the time. By early morning, the town was jammed with people. By one o'clock, the town square was filled to overflowing, and the debate enthralled an estimated 12,000 people. Ottawa was pro-Republican, and the audience heckled Douglas unmercifully. But as the debates moved south in the state, where Democrats predominated, the tables were turned, and Lincoln sometimes had to plead for a chance to be heard.

Read the Document

The Lincoln-Douglas Debates (1858) at **www.myhistorylab.com**

—Illinois

Although Douglas won the 1858 senatorial election in Illinois, the acclaim that Lincoln gained in the famous debates helped establish the Republicans' claim to be the only party capable of stopping the spread of slavery and made Lincoln himself a strong contender for the Republican presidential nomination in 1860. But the true winners of the Lincoln–Douglas debates were the people of Illinois who gathered peacefully to discuss the most serious issue of their time.

The Lincoln–Douglas debates are famous for their demonstration of the widespread public belief in commonality and community to resolve disagreements. Unfortunately, differences that could be resolved through conversation and friendship in the local community were less easy to resolve at the national level. In the highly charged and highly public political atmosphere of Congress, politicians struggled in vain to find compromises to hold the national community together.

AMERICA IN 1850

The swift victory in the Mexican-American War bolstered American national pride and self-confidence. Certainly, the America of 1850 was a very different nation from the republic of 1800. Geographic expansion, population increase, economic development, and the changes wrought by the market revolution had transformed the struggling new nation. Economically, culturally, and politically Americans had forged a strong sense of national identity.

HOW DID expansion shape how Americans saw themselves as a nation in 1850?

EXPANSION AND GROWTH

America was now a much larger nation than it had been in 1800. Through war and diplomacy, the country had more than tripled in size from 890,000 to 3 million square miles. Its population had increased enormously from 5.3 million in 1800 to more than 23 million. Comprising just sixteen states in 1800, America in 1850 had thirty-one states, and more than half of the population lived west of the Appalachians. America's cities had undergone the most rapid half century of growth they were ever to experience (see Map 15.1).

MAP 15.1
U.S. Population and Settlement, 1850 By 1850, the United States was a continental nation. Its people, whom Thomas Jefferson had once thought would not reach the Mississippi River for forty generations, had not only passed the river but also leapfrogged to the West Coast. In comparison to the America of 1800 (see Map 9.1 on p. 222), the growth was astounding.

WHERE WERE the areas of densest population west of the Mississippi River? What explains these pockets of concentrated population?

This poster advertises *Uncle Tom's Cabin*, the best-selling novel by Harriet Beecher Stowe. The poignant story of long-suffering African American slaves had an immense impact on Northern popular opinion, swaying it decisively against slavery. In that respect, the poster's boast, "The Greatest Book of the Age," was correct.

Watch the Video
Harriet Beecher Stowe and the Making of Uncle Tom's Cabin *at*
www.myhistorylab.com

Read the Document
A New England Writer Portrays Slavery in 1852 at **www.myhistorylab.com**

America was also much richer: it is estimated that real per capita income doubled between 1800 and 1850. Southern cotton, which had contributed so much to American economic growth, continued to be the nation's principal export, but it was no longer the major influence on the domestic economy. The growth of manufacturing in the Northeast and the rapid opening up of rich farmlands in the Midwest had serious domestic implications. As the South's share of responsibility for economic growth waned, so did its political importance. Thus, the very success of the United States both in geographic expansion and in economic development served to undermine the role of the South in national politics and to hasten the day of open conflict between the slave South and the free-labor North and Midwest.

POLITICS, CULTURE, AND NATIONAL IDENTITY

The notion of "manifest destiny" first expressed in the expansionist fervor of the 1840s was based on a widespread belief among Americans in the superiority of their democracy. This belief was a unifying theme in a growing sense of national identity and the new middle-class values, institutions, and culture that supported it. Since the turn of the century, American writers had struggled to find distinctive American themes, and these efforts bore fruit in the 1850s in the burst of creative activity termed the "American Renaissance."

During the American Renaissance, American writers pioneered new literary forms. Nathaniel Hawthorne raised the short story to a distinctive American literary form. Poets like Walt Whitman and Emily Dickinson experimented with unrhymed and "off-rhyme" verse. Henry David Thoreau published *Walden* in 1854, a searching meditation on the cost to the individual of the loss of contact with nature that was a consequence of the market revolution.

Indeed, although the midcentury popular mood was one of self-congratulation, most of the writers of the American Renaissance were social critics. In *The Scarlet Letter* (1850) and *The House of the Seven Gables* (1851), Nathaniel Hawthorne brilliantly exposed the repressive and hypocritical aspects of Puritan New England in the colonial period and the often impossible moral choices faced by individuals. Herman Melville, in his great work *Moby-Dick* (1851), used the story of Captain Ahab's obsessive search for the white whale to write a profound study of the nature of good and evil and a critique of American society in the 1850s. The strongest social critique, however, was Frederick Douglass's starkly simple autobiography, *Narrative of the Life of Frederick Douglass* (1845), which told of his brutal life as a slave.

The most successful American novel of the mid-nineteenth century was also about the great issue of the day—slavery. In writing *Uncle Tom's Cabin*, Harriet Beecher Stowe combined the literary style of the popular women's domestic novels of the time with vivid details of slavery culled from firsthand accounts by northern abolitionists and escaped slaves.

Published in 1851, it was a runaway best seller. More than 300,000 copies were sold in the first year, and within ten years, the book had sold more than 2 million copies, becoming the all-time American best seller in proportion to population. *Uncle Tom's Cabin* was more than a heart-tugging story: it was a call to action. In 1863, when Harriet Beecher Stowe was introduced to Abraham Lincoln, the president is said to have remarked, "So you're the little woman who wrote the book that made this great war!"

CRACKS IN NATIONAL UNITY

The year 1850 opened to the most serious political crisis the United States had ever known. The issue raised by the 1846 Wilmot Proviso—whether slavery should be extended to the new territories—could no longer be ignored (see Chapter 14). Furthermore, California, made rich and populous by the gold rush, applied for statehood in 1850, thereby reopening the issue of the balance between slave and free states.

THE COMPROMISE OF 1850

The **Compromise of 1850** was actually five separate bills (lacking a majority for a comprehensive measure), embodying three separate compromises.

First, California was admitted as a free state, but the status of the remaining former Mexican possessions was left to be decided by **popular sovereignty** (a vote of the territory's inhabitants) when they applied for statehood. The result was, for the time being, fifteen slave states and sixteen free states. Second, Texas (a slave state) was required to cede land to New Mexico Territory (free or slave status undecided). In return, the federal government assumed $10 million of debts Texas had incurred before it became a state. Finally, the slave trade, but not slavery itself, was ended in the District of Columbia, but a stronger fugitive slave law, to be enforced in all states, was enacted (see Map 15.2).

Jubilation and relief greeted the news that compromise had been achieved, but analysis of the votes on the five bills that made up the compromise revealed no consistent majority. The sectional splits within each party that had existed before the compromise remained.

POLITICAL PARTIES SPLIT OVER SLAVERY

The Second American Party System, forged in the great controversies of Andrew Jackson's presidency (see Chapter 11), was a national party system. At a time when the ordinary person still had very strong sectional loyalties, the mass political party created a national community of like-minded voters. Yet, by the election of 1848, sectional interests were eroding the political "glue" in both parties.

Political splits were preceded by divisions in other social institutions. Disagreements about slavery had already split the country's great religious organizations into northern and southern groups: the Presbyterians in 1837, the Methodists in 1844, and the Baptists in 1845. Theodore Weld, the abolitionist leader, saw these splits as inevitable: "Events . . . have for years been silently but without a moment's pause, settling the basis of two great parties, the nucleus of one slavery, of the other, freedom."

WHY DID expansion lead to increasing sectional division in the 1850s?

Read the **Document**
Daniel Webster, Speech to the U.S. Senate (1850) at **www.myhistorylab.com**

Compromise of 1850 The four-step compromise which admitted California as a free state, allowed the residents of the New Mexico and Utah territories to decide the slavery issue for themselves, ended the slave trade in the District of Columbia, and passed a new fugitive slave law.

popular sovereignty A solution to the slavery crisis suggested by Michigan senator Lewis Cass by which territorial residents, not Congress, would decide slavery's fate.

OVERVIEW | The Great Sectional Compromises

Year	Compromise	Description
1820	**Missouri Compromise**	Admits Missouri to the Union as a slave state and Maine as a free state; prohibits slavery in the rest of the Louisiana Purchase Territory north of 36°30′. Territory Covered: The entire territory of the Louisiana Purchase, exclusive of the state of Louisiana, which had been admitted to the Union in 1812.
1850	**Compromise of 1850**	Admits California to the Union as a free state, settles the borders of Texas (a slave state); sets no conditions concerning slavery for the rest of the territory acquired from Mexico. Enacts national Fugitive Slave Law. Territory Covered: The territory that had been part of Mexico before the end of the Mexican-American War and the Treaty of Guadalupe Hidalgo (1848): part of Texas, California, Utah Territory (now Utah, Nevada, and part of Colorado), and New Mexico Territory (now New Mexico and Arizona).

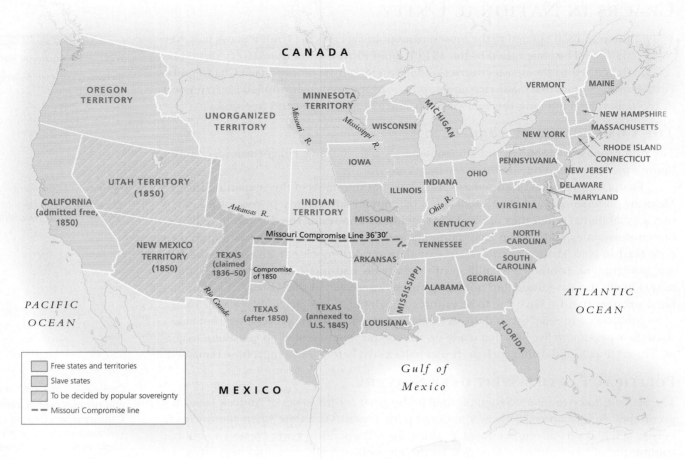

See the Map

The Compromise of 1850 at
www.myhistorylab.com

MAP 15.2
The Compromise of 1850 The Compromise of 1850, messier and more awkward than the Missouri Compromise of 1820, reflected heightened sectional tensions. California was admitted as a free state, the borders of Texas were settled, and the status of the rest of the former Mexican territory was left to be decided later by popular sovereignty. No consistent majority voted for the five separate bills that made up the compromise.

HOW DID the Compromise of 1850 affect the political balance between free and slave states?

CONGRESSIONAL DIVISIONS

In the midst of the debate that preceded the Compromise of 1850, President Zachary Taylor died of acute gastroenteritis. A bluff military man, Taylor had been prepared to follow Andrew Jackson's precedent during the Nullification Crisis of 1832 and simply demand that Southern dissidents compromise. Vice President Millard Fillmore, who assumed the presidency, was a much weaker man who did not seize the opportunity for presidential action.

And Southerners, personified by John C. Calhoun, were unwilling to compromise. Calhoun insisted that Congress did not have a constitutional right to prohibit slavery in the territories. The territories, he said, were the common property of all the states, North and South, and slave owners had a constitutional right to the protection of their property wherever they moved.

Calhoun's position on the territories quickly became Southern dogma: anything less than full access to the territories was unconstitutional. As Congressman Robert Toombs of Georgia put the case in 1850, the choice was stark: "Give us our just rights and we are ready to stand by the Union. Refuse [them] and for one, I will strike for independence."

The Southern threat to secede confirmed for many Northerners the warnings of antislavery leaders that they were endangered by a menacing "slave power." Liberty Party leader James Birney, in a speech in 1844, was the first to add this phrase to the nation's political vocabulary. "The slave power," Birney explained, was a group of aristocratic slave owners who conspired to control the federal government, posing a danger to free speech and free institutions throughout the nation.

The defensive Southern political strategies of the 1850s convinced an increasing number of Northern voters that "the slave power" did in fact exist. The long-standing proslavery strategy of maintaining supremacy in the Senate by having at least as many slave as free states admitted to the Union (a plan that required slavery expansion) now looked like a conspiracy by sectional interests to control national politics.

In 1850, the three men who had long represented America's three major regions attempted to resolve the political crisis brought on by the application of California for statehood. Henry Clay is speaking; John C. Calhoun stands second from right; and Daniel Webster is seated at the left, with his head in his hand. Both Clay and Webster were ill, and Calhoun died before the Compromise of 1850 was arranged by a younger group of politicians led by Stephen A. Douglas.

TWO COMMUNITIES, TWO PERSPECTIVES

Ironically, it was their common commitment to expansion that made the argument between Northerners and Southerners so irreconcilable. Southerners had been the strongest supporters of the Mexican-American War. On the other hand, although many Northern Whigs had opposed the Mexican-American War, most did so for antislavery reasons, not because they opposed expansion. Basically, both North and South believed in manifest destiny, but each on its own terms.

Similarly, both North and South used the language of basic rights and liberties in the debate over expansion. But free-soilers were speaking of personal liberty, whereas Southerners meant their right to own a particular kind of property (slaves) and to maintain a way of life based on the possession of that property. In defending its own rights, each side had taken measures that infringed on the rights of the other.

By 1850, North and South had created fixed stereotypes of the other. To antislavery Northerners, the South was an economic backwater dominated by a small slave-owning aristocracy that lived off the profits of forced labor and deprived poor whites of their democratic rights and the fruits of honest work.

Things looked very different through Southern eyes. Far from being economically backward, the South, through its export of cotton, was, according to Southerners, the great engine of national economic growth from which the North benefited. Slavery was not only a blessing to an inferior race but also the cornerstone of democracy, for it ensured the freedom and independence of all white men without entailing the bitter class divisions that marked the North. Slave owners accused Northern manufacturers of hypocrisy for practicing "wage slavery" without the paternal benevolence they claimed to bestow on their slaves.

By the early 1850s, these vastly different visions of the North and the South—the result of many years of political controversy—had become fixed, and the chances of national reconciliation increasingly slim. Over the course of the decade, many Americans came to believe that the place of slavery in the nation's life had to be permanently settled. And they

QUICK REVIEW

Regional Stereotypes

◆ Northern perspective: South an economic backwater dominated by immoral slave owners.

◆ Southern perspective: North a beneficiary of cotton industry dominated by hypocritical manufacturers.

◆ By 1850s stereotypes were fixed in many people's minds.

increasingly wondered whether their two sectional communities—one slave, one free—could continue to be part of a unitary national one.

In the country as a whole, the feeling was that the Compromise of 1850 had solved the question of slavery in the territories. But many Southerners felt that their only real gain in the contested compromise was the Fugitive Slave Law, which quickly turned out to be an inflammatory measure.

THE FUGITIVE SLAVE LAW

Northerners had long been appalled by professional slave catchers, who zealously seized African Americans in the North and took them south into slavery again. Most abhorrent in Northern eyes was that captured black people were at the mercy of slave catchers because they had no legal right to defend themselves. In more than one case, a free African American was captured in his own community and helplessly shipped into slavery.

As a result of stories like this, nine Northern states passed personal liberty laws between 1842 and 1850, serving notice that they would not cooperate with federal recapture efforts. These laws enraged Southerners, who had long been convinced that all Northerners, not just abolitionists, were actively hindering efforts to reclaim their escaped slaves.

The **Fugitive Slave Law**, enacted in 1850, dramatically increased the power of slave owners to capture escaped slaves. The full authority of the federal government now supported slave owners, and although fugitives were guaranteed a hearing before a federal commissioner, they were not allowed to testify on their own behalf. Furthermore, the new law imposed federal penalties on citizens who protected or assisted fugitives or who did not cooperate in their return. A number of free Northern blacks, estimated at 30,000 to 40,000, emigrated to Canada to avoid the possibility of capture.

In Boston, the center of the American abolitionist movement, reaction to the Fugitive Slave Law was fierce. In the most famous Boston case, a biracial group of armed abolitionists stormed the federal courthouse in 1854 in an attempt to save escaped slave Anthony Burns. The rescue effort failed, and a federal deputy marshal was killed. President Pierce sent marines, cavalry, and artillery to Boston to reinforce the guard over Burns and ordered a federal ship to be ready to deliver the fugitive back into slavery. When the effort by defense lawyers to argue for Burns's freedom failed, Burns was marched to the docks through streets lined with sorrowing abolitionists. Buildings were shrouded in black and draped with American flags hanging upside down, while bells tolled as if for a funeral. The Burns case radicalized many Northerners. Conservative Whig George Hilliard wrote to a friend, "When it was all over, and I was left alone in my office, I put my face in my hands and wept. I could do nothing less."

In this volatile atmosphere, escaped African Americans wrote and lectured bravely on behalf of freedom. Frederick Douglass, the most famous and eloquent of the fugitive slaves, spoke out fearlessly in support of armed resistance. Harriet Jacobs, who escaped to the North after seven years in hiding in the South, wrote bitterly in her *Incidents in the Life of a Slave Girl* (1861) that "I was, in fact, a slave in New York, as subject to slave laws as I had been in a slave state . . . I had been chased during half my life, and it seemed as if the chase was never to end."

The Fugitive Slave Law made slavery national and forced Northern communities to confront the full meaning of slavery. Although most people were still unwilling to grant social equality to the free African Americans who lived in the Northern states, more and

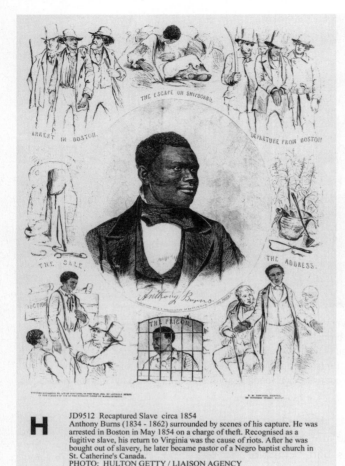

JD9512 Recaptured Slave circa 1854
Anthony Burns (1834 - 1862) surrounded by scenes of his capture. He was arrested in Boston in May 1854 on a charge of theft. Recognised as a fugitive slave, his return to Virginia was the cause of riots. After he was bought out of slavery, he later became pastor of a Negro baptist church in St. Catherine's Canada.
PHOTO: HULTON GETTY / LIAISON AGENCY

Escaped slave Anthony Burns, shown here surrounded by scenes of his capture in 1854, was the cause of Boston's greatest protest against the Fugitive Slave Law. The injustice of his trial and shipment back to the South converted many Bostonians to the antislavery cause.

Read the **Document**

Benjamin Drew, from Narratives of Fugitive Slaves in Canada (1855) at **www.myhistorylab.com**

Read the **Document**

Exploring America: Anthony Burns at **www.myhistorylab.com**

Read the **Document**

Harriet Jacobs, Incidents in the Life of a Slave Girl (1861) at **www.myhistorylab.com**

Fugitive Slave Law   Part of the Compromise of 1850 that required the authorities in the North to assist Southern slave catchers and return runaway slaves to their owners.

more had come to believe that the institution of slavery was wrong. Northern protests against the Fugitive Slave Law bred suspicion in the South and encouraged secessionist thinking. These new currents of public opinion were reflected in the election of 1852.

THE ELECTION OF 1852

The first sign of the weakening of the national party system in 1852 was the difficulty both parties experienced at their nominating conventions. After fifty-two ballots General Winfield Scott, rather than the sitting President Fillmore, was nominated. Many Southern Whigs were permanently alienated by the choice; although Whigs were still elected to Congress from the South, their loyalty to the national party was strained to the breaking point. The Whigs never again fielded a presidential candidate.

The Democrats had a wider variety of candidates: Lewis Cass of popular sovereignty fame; Stephen Douglas, architect of the Compromise of 1850; and James Buchanan, described as a "northern man with southern principles." Cass, Douglas, and Buchanan competed for forty-nine ballots, each strong enough to block the others but not strong enough to win. Finally, the party turned to a handsome, affable nonentity, Franklin Pierce of New Hampshire, who was thought to have Southern sympathies. Uniting on a platform pledging "faithful execution" of all parts of the Compromise of 1850, including the Fugitive Slave Law, Democrats polled well in the South and in the North. Most Democrats who had voted for the Free-Soil Party in 1848 voted for Pierce. So, in record numbers, did immigrant Irish and German voters, who were eligible for citizenship after three years' residence. The strong immigrant vote for Pierce was a sign of the strength of Democratic Party organizations in Northern cities.

"YOUNG AMERICA": THE POLITICS OF EXPANSION

Pierce entered the White House in 1853 on a wave of good feeling. This goodwill was soon strained by Pierce's support for the expansionist adventures of the "Young America" movement.

The "Young America" movement began as a group of writers and politicians in the New York Democratic Party who believed in the democratic and nationalistic promise of "manifest destiny." Young America expansionists had glanced covetously southward to Cuba and Central America since the end of the Mexican-American War. During the Pierce administration, several private "filibusters" (from the Spanish *filibustero*, meaning an "adventurer" or "pirate") invaded Caribbean and Central American countries, usually with the declared intention of extending slave territory.

The Pierce administration, not directly involved in the filibustering, *was* deeply involved in an effort to obtain Cuba. In 1854, Pierce authorized his minister to Spain, Pierre Soulé, to try to force the unwilling Spanish to sell Cuba for $130 million. Soulé met in Ostend, Belgium, with the American ministers to France and England, John Mason and James Buchanan, to compose the offer, which was a mixture of cajolements and threats. This document, which became known as the Ostend Manifesto, was supposed to be secret but was soon leaked to the press. Deeply embarrassed, the Pierce administration was forced to repudiate it.

The complicity between the Pierce administration and proslavery expansionists was foolhardy and lost the Northern goodwill with which it had begun. The sectional crisis that preceded the Compromise of 1850 had made obvious the danger of reopening the territorial issue. Ironically, it was not the Young America expansionists but the prime mover of the Compromise of 1850, Stephen A. Douglas, who reignited the sectional struggle over slavery expansion.

CAUTION!!
COLORED PEOPLE
OF BOSTON, ONE & ALL,

You are hereby respectfully CAUTIONED and advised, to avoid conversing with the

Watchmen and Police Officers
of Boston,

For since the recent ORDER OF THE MAYOR & ALDERMEN, they are empowered to act as

KIDNAPPERS
AND
Slave Catchers,

And they have already been actually employed in KIDNAPPING, CATCHING, AND KEEPING SLAVES. Therefore, if you value your LIBERTY, and the *Welfare of the Fugitives* among you, **Shun** them in every possible manner, as so many *HOUNDS* on the track of the most unfortunate of your race.

Keep a Sharp Look Out for
KIDNAPPERS, and have
TOP EYE open.
APRIL 24, 1851.

This handbill warning free African Americans of danger circulated in Boston following the first of the infamous recaptures under the Fugitive Slave Law, that of Thomas Sims in 1851.

THE CRISIS OF THE NATIONAL PARTY SYSTEM

In 1854, Douglas introduced the Kansas-Nebraska Act, proposing to open those lands that had been the northern part of Indian Territory to American settlers under the principle of popular sovereignty. He thereby reopened the question of slavery in the territories. Douglas knew he was taking a political risk, but he believed he could satisfy both his expansionist aims and his presidential ambitions. He was wrong: he pushed the national party system into crisis, first killing the Whigs and then destroying the Democrats.

THE KANSAS-NEBRASKA ACT

In a stunning example of the expansionist pressures generated by the market revolution, Stephen Douglas introduced the **Kansas-Nebraska Act** to further the construction of a transcontinental railroad. Douglas wanted the rail line to terminate in Chicago, in his own state of Illinois, rather than in the rival St. Louis, but for that to happen, the land west of Iowa and Missouri had to be organized into territories (the first step toward statehood). To get Congress to agree to the organization of the territories, however, Douglas needed the votes of Southern Democrats, who were unwilling to support him unless the territories were open to slavery.

Douglas thought he was solving his problem by proposing that the status of slavery in the new territories be governed by the principle of popular sovereignty. Douglas thought Southerners would support his bill because of its popular sovereignty provision and Northerners because it favored a northern route for the transcontinental railroad. Douglas chose also to downplay the price he had to pay for Southern support—by allowing the possibility of slavery in the new territories, his bill in effect repealed the Missouri Compromise of 1820, which barred slavery north of latitude 36°30' (see Map 15.3).

The Kansas-Nebraska bill passed, but it badly strained the major political parties. Southern Whigs voted with Southern Democrats in favor of the measure; Northern Whigs rejected it absolutely, creating an irreconcilable split that left Whigs unable to field a presidential candidate in 1856. The damage to the Democratic Party was almost as great. In the congressional elections of 1854, Northern Democrats lost two-thirds of their seats, giving the Southern Democrats the dominant voice both in Congress and within the party. Douglas had committed one of the greatest miscalculations in American political history.

In Kansas in 1854, hasty treaties were concluded with the Indian tribes who owned the land. Some, such as the Kickapoos, Shawnees, Sauks, and Foxes, agreed to relocate to small reservations. Others, like the Delawares, Weas, and Iowas, agreed to sell their lands to whites. Still others, such as the Cheyennes and Sioux, kept the western part of Kansas Territory (now Colorado)—until gold was discovered there in 1859. Once the treaties were signed, both proslavery and antislavery white settlers began to pour in, and the battle was on.

"BLEEDING KANSAS"

The first to claim land in Kansas were residents of nearby Missouri, itself a slave state. Missourians took up land claims, established proslavery strongholds such as the towns of Leavenworth, Kickapoo, and Atchison, and repeatedly and blatantly swamped Kansas elections with Missouri votes. In 1855, in the second of several notoriously fraudulent elections, 6,307 ballots were cast in a territory that had fewer than 3,000 eligible voters. Most of the proslavery votes were cast by "border ruffians," as they proudly called themselves, from Missouri.

Northerners quickly responded. The first party of New Englanders arrived in the summer of 1854 and established the free-soil town of Lawrence. More than a thousand

Kansas-Nebraska Act Law passed in 1854 creating the Kansas and Nebraska Territories but leaving the question of slavery open to residents, thereby repealing the Missouri Compromise.

Bleeding Kansas Violence between pro- and antislavery forces in Kansas Territory after the passage of the Kansas-Nebraska Act in 1854.

MAP 15.3

The Kansas-Nebraska Act, 1854   The Kansas-Nebraska Act, proposed by Steven A. Douglas in 1854, opened the central and northern Great Plains to settlement. The act had two major faults: it robbed Indian peoples of half the territory guaranteed to them by treaty and, because it repealed the Missouri Compromise line, it opened up the lands to warring proslavery and antislavery factions.

See the **Map**
The Kansas-Nebraska Act at
www.myhistorylab.com

WHY WAS Steven Douglas so intent on opening up the central and northern Great Plains to settlement?

others had joined them by the following summer. Many Northern migrants were free-soilers, and many were religious reformers as well.

Kansas soon became a bloody battleground as the two factions struggled to secure the mandate of "popular sovereignty." Free-soilers in Lawrence received shipments of heavy crates, innocuously marked "BOOKS" but actually containing Sharps repeating rifles, sent by eastern supporters. For their part, the border ruffians called for reinforcements. Senator David Atchison of Missouri exhorted Alabamans: "Let your young men come forth to Missouri and Kansas! Let them come well armed!"

In the summer of 1856, these lethal preparations exploded into open warfare. First, proslavery forces burned and looted the town of Lawrence. In retaliation, a grim old man named John Brown led his sons in a raid on the proslavery settlers of Pottawatomie Creek, killing five unarmed people. A wave of violence ensued. Armed bands roamed the countryside, and burnings and killings became commonplace. Peaceful residents of large sections of rural Kansas were repeatedly forced to flee to the safety of military forts when rumors of one or another armed band reached them.

Lawrence, the center of free-soil sentiment in Kansas, was burned and looted
by proslavery opponents in 1856. Events
like this, perpetrated by pro- and antislavery forces alike, earned the territory
the name, "Bleeding Kansas."

The rest of the nation watched in horror as the residents of Kansas slaughtered
each other in the pursuit of sectional goals. Americans' pride in their nation's great
achievements was threatened by the endless violence in one small part—but a part that
increasingly seemed to represent the divisions of the whole.

THE POLITICS OF NATIVISM

The violence in Kansas was echoed by increasing violence in the nation's cities. Violence
marred the elections of 1854 and 1856 in New York, and there were serious disturbances in
New Orleans and elsewhere. In Chicago, riots started in 1855, when the mayor attempted to
close the saloons on Sunday. German workingmen joined by Irishmen and Swedes paraded
in protest and were met by 200 men of the National Guard, militia, and special police. The
ensuing "Lager Beer Riots" ended with the imposition of martial law on the entire city.

This urban violence, like that in Kansas, was caused by the breakdown of the two-party
system. The breakup of the Whig Party left a political vacuum that was filled by one of the
strongest bursts of nativism, or anti-immigrant feeling, in American history, and by the rapid
growth of the new American Party, which formed in 1850 to give political expression to
nativism. The new party was in part a reaction to the Democratic Party's success in capturing
the support of the rapidly growing population of mostly Catholic foreign-born voters.

The reformist and individualistic attitudes of many Whigs inclined them toward
nativism. Many Whigs disapproved of the new immigrants because they were poor,
Catholic, and often disdainful of the temperance movement. Moreover, nativist Whigs
held immigration to be solely responsible for the increases in crime and the rising cost of
relief for the poor that accompanied the astoundingly rapid urban growth of the 1830s
and 1840s (see Chapter 13).

Nativism drew former Whigs, especially young men in white-collar and skilled
blue-collar occupations, to the new American Party. At the core of the party were several
secret fraternal societies open only to native-born Protestants. When questioned about
their beliefs, party members maintained secrecy by answering, "I know nothing"—
hence, the popular name for American Party members, the **Know-Nothings**. Publicly,

Know-Nothings Name given to the
anti-immigrant party formed from
the wreckage of the Whig Party and
some disaffected Northern
democrats in 1854.

Brooks Beats Sumner

In a violent episode on the floor of the U.S. Senate in 1856, Senator Charles Sumner of Massachusetts suffered permanent injury when Congressman Preston Brooks of South Carolina beat him so hard with his cane that it broke. A few days earlier, Sumner had given an insulting anti-slavery speech in which he had singled out for ridicule Senator Andrew Butler of South Carolina. Senator Butler was Preston Brooks's uncle; in Brooks's mind, he was simply avenging an intolerable affront to his uncle's honor.

So far had the behavioral codes of North and South diverged that each man found his own action perfectly justifiable and the action of the other outrageous. Their attitudes were mirrored in their respective sections. Protest rallies were held in most northern cities; Sumner himself received sympathy letters from hundreds of strangers, all expressing indignation, as one writer put it, over "the most foul, most damnable and dastardly attack," and sympathetic illustrations like this one appeared in northern papers. In contrast, southern newspapers almost unanimously supported Brooks, regarding it as a well-deserved whipping for an intolerable insult. A group of Charleston merchants even bought Brooks a new cane inscribed: "Hit him again." ■

IS VIOLENCE always a threat to democracy? Are there situations where it is justified? Is this one of those occasions?

SOUTHERN CHIVALRY — ARGUMENT versus CLUB'S.

This nighttime meeting of supporters of the Know-Nothing Party in New York City was dramatically spotlighted by a new device borrowed from the theater, an incandescent calcium light, popularly called a limelight.

the party proposed a twenty-one-year residency requirement before foreigners could vote and a head tax that would "restrain the most worthless and vicious of foreign emigrants from debarking on our shores."

Know-Nothings scored startling victories in Northern state elections in 1854, winning control of the legislature in Massachusetts and polling 40 percent of the vote in Pennsylvania. But in the 1850s, no party could ignore slavery, and in 1855, the American Party split into Northern (antislavery) and Southern (proslavery) wings. Soon after this split, many people who had voted for the Know-Nothings shifted their support to another new party, one that combined many characteristics of the Whigs with a westward-looking, expansionist, free-soil policy. This was the Republican Party, founded in 1854.

THE REPUBLICAN PARTY AND THE ELECTION OF 1856

Supporters of the Republican Party included many former Northern Whigs who opposed slavery absolutely, many Free-Soil Party supporters who opposed the expansion of slavery but were willing to tolerate it in the South, and many Northern reformers concerned about temperance and Catholicism. The Republicans also attracted the economic core of the old Whig Party—the merchants and industrialists who wanted a strong national government to promote economic growth by supporting a protective tariff, transportation improvements, and cheap land for western farmers.

The immediate question facing the nation in 1856 was which new party, the Know-Nothings or the Republicans, would emerge the stronger. But the more important question was whether the Democratic Party could hold together. The two strongest contenders for the Democratic nomination were President Pierce and Stephen A. Douglas. Douglas had proposed the Kansas-Nebraska Act and Pierce had actively supported it. Both men, therefore, had the support of the southern wing of the party. But it was precisely their support of this act that made Northerners oppose both of them. The

Republican Party   Party that emerged in the 1850s in the aftermath of the bitter controversy over the Kansas-Nebraska Act, consisting of former Whigs, some Northern Democrats, and many Know-Nothings.

Kansas-Nebraska Act's divisive effect on the Democratic Party now became clear: no one who had voted on the bill, either for or against, could satisfy both wings of the party. A compromise candidate was found in James Buchanan of Pennsylvania, the "northern man with southern principles." Luckily for him, he had been ambassador to Great Britain at the time of the Kansas-Nebraska Act and, thus, had not had to commit himself.

The election of 1856 appeared to be a three-way contest that pitted Buchanan against explorer John C.Frémont of the Republican Party and the American (Know-Nothing) Party's candidate, former president Millard Fillmore (see Map 15.4).

In fact, the election was two separate contests, one in the North and one in the South. The Northern race was between Buchanan and Frémont, the Southern one between Buchanan and Fillmore. Fillmore attracted more than 40 percent of the vote in ten slave states. Frémont decisively defeated Buchanan in the North, winning eleven of sixteen free states. Buchanan, however, won the election with only 45 percent of the popular vote, because he was the only national candidate. But the Republicans, after studying the election returns, claimed "victorious defeat," for they realized that in 1860, the addition of just two more northern states to their total would mean victory. Furthermore, the Republican Party had clearly defeated the American Party in the battle to win designation as a major party. These were grounds for great optimism—and great concern—for the Republican Party was a sectional, rather than a national, party; it drew almost all its support from the North. Southerners viewed its very existence as an attack on their vital interests. Thus, the rapid rise of the Republicans posed a growing threat to national unity.

THE DIFFERENCES DEEPEN

Although James Buchanan firmly believed that he alone could hold together a nation so split by hatred and violence, his self-confidence outran his abilities. He was so deeply indebted to the strong southern wing of the Democratic Party that he could not take the impartial actions necessary to heal "Bleeding Kansas." And his support for a momentous prosouthern decision by the Supreme Court further aggravated sectional differences.

THE *DRED SCOTT* DECISION

Dred Scott v. *Sandford* was decided on March 6, 1857, two days after James Buchanan was sworn in as president. Dred Scott had been a slave all his life. His owner, army surgeon John Emerson, had taken Scott on his military assignments during the 1830s to Illinois (a free state) and Wisconsin Territory (a free territory, north of the Missouri Compromise line). During that time, Scott married another slave, Harriet, and their daughter Eliza was born in free territory. Emerson and the Scotts then returned to Missouri (a slave state) and there, in 1846, Dred Scott sued for his freedom and that of his wife and his daughter born in Wisconsin Territory (who as women had no legal standing of their own) on the grounds that residence in free lands had made them free. It took eleven years for the case to reach the Supreme Court.

The Court declared the Missouri Compromise unconstitutional. Chief Justice Roger B. Taney, speaking for the majority, asserted that the federal government had no

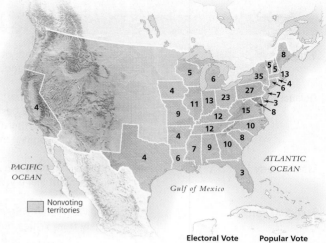

	Electoral Vote (%)	Popular Vote (%)
JAMES BUCHANAN (Democrat)	174 (59)	1,832,955 (45)
John C. Frémont (Republican)	114 (39)	1,339,932 (33)
Millard Fillmore (American)	8 (3)	871,731 (22)

MAP 15.4

The Election of 1856   Because three parties contested the 1856 election, Democrat James Buchanan was a minority president. Although Buchanan alone had national support, Republican John Frémont won most of the free states, and Millard Fillmore of the American Party gained 40 percent of the vote in most of the slave states.

WHAT DOES this map tell you about the political weakness of Buchanan? What groups, if any, constituted his core political support?

WHAT EVENTS helped propel the country towards Civil War in the late 1850s?

OVERVIEW | Political Parties Split and Realign

Whig Party	Ran its last presidential candidate in 1852. The candidate, General Winfield Scott, alienated many Southern Whigs, and the party was so split it could not field a candidate in 1856.
Democratic Party	Remained a national party through 1856, but Buchanan's actions as president made Southern domination of the party so clear that many Northern Democrats were alienated. Stephen Douglas, running as a Northern Democrat in 1860, won 29 percent of the popular vote; John Breckinridge, running as a Southern Democrat, won 18 percent.
Liberty Party	Antislavery party; ran James G. Birney for president in 1844. He won 62,000 votes, largely from Northern antislavery Whigs.
Free-Soil Party	Ran Martin Van Buren, former Democratic president, in 1848. Gained 10 percent of the popular vote, largely from Whigs but also from some Northern Democrats.
American (Know-Nothing) Party	Nativist party made striking gains in 1854 congressional elections, attracting both Northern and Southern Whigs. In 1856, its presidential candidate, Millard Fillmore, won 21 percent of the popular vote.
Republican Party	Founded in 1854. Attracted many Northern Whigs and Northern Democrats. Presidential candidate John C. Frémont won 33 percent of the popular vote in 1856; in 1860, Abraham Lincoln won 40 percent and was elected in a four-way race.

Watch the **Video**

Dred Scott and the Crises that Led to the Civil War at **www.myhistorylab.com**

right to interfere with the free movement of property throughout the territories. He then dismissed the *Dred Scott* case on the grounds that only citizens could bring suits before federal courts and that black people—slave or free—were not citizens. With this bold judicial intervention into the most heated issue of the day, Taney intended to settle the controversy over the expansion of slavery once and for all. Instead, he inflamed the conflict.

The response to the ruling was sectional. Southerners expressed great satisfaction and strong support for the Court. The *Georgia Constitutionalist* announced, "Southern opinion upon the subject of southern slavery . . . is now the supreme law of the land . . . and opposition to southern opinion upon this subject is now opposition to the Constitution, and morally treason against the Government."

Northerners disagreed. Many were so troubled by the *Dred Scott* decision that, for the first time, they found themselves seriously questioning the power of the Supreme Court to establish the "law of the land." The New York legislature passed a resolution declaring that the Supreme Court had lost the confidence and respect of the people of that state.

For the Republican Party, the *Dred Scott* decision represented a formidable challenge. By invalidating the Missouri Compromise, the decision swept away the free-soil foundation of the party. But to directly challenge a Supreme Court decision was a weighty matter. The most sensational Republican counterattack—made by both Abraham Lincoln and William Seward—was the accusation that President Buchanan had conspired with the Southern Supreme Court justices to subvert the American political system by withholding the decision until after the presidential election. Lincoln also raised the frightening possibility that "the next *Dred Scott* decision" would legalize slavery even in free states that abhorred it. President Buchanan's response to events in Kansas, including the drafting of a proslavery constitution, also stoked sectional antagonisms.

QUICK REVIEW

The *Dred Scott* Decision

- 1857 attempt by Supreme Court to solve the political controversy over slavery.
- Court ruled that slaves were property and government could not restrain free movement of property.
- Decision invalidated the Missouri Compromise.

Dred Scott **decision**   Supreme Court ruling, in a lawsuit brought by Dred Scott, a slave demanding his freedom based on his residence in a free state, that slaves could not be U.S. citizens and that Congress had no jurisdiction over slavery in the territories.

THE LECOMPTON CONSTITUTION

In Kansas, the doctrine of popular sovereignty led to continuing civil strife and the political travesty of two territorial governments. The first election of officers to a territorial government in 1855 produced a lopsided proslavery outcome that was clearly the result of illegal voting by Missouri border ruffians. Free-soilers protested by forming their own government, giving Kansas both a proslavery territorial legislature in Lecompton and a free-soil government in Topeka.

Free-soil voters boycotted a June 1857 election of representatives to a convention called to write a constitution for the territory once it reached statehood. As a result, the convention had a proslavery majority that wrote the proslavery **Lecompton constitution** and then applied to Congress for admission to the Union under its terms. Buchanan, in the single most disastrous mistake of his administration, endorsed the proslavery constitution, because he feared the loss of the support of Southern Democrats. It seemed that Kansas would enter the Union as a sixteenth slave state, making the number of slave and free states equal.

Unexpected congressional opposition came from none other than Stephen Douglas, author of the legislation that had begun the Kansas troubles in 1854. Now, in 1857, in what was surely the bravest step of his political career, Douglas opposed the Lecompton constitution on the grounds that it violated the principle of popular sovereignty. He insisted that the Lecompton constitution must be voted on by Kansas voters in honest elections. Defying James Buchanan, the president of his own party, Douglas voted with the majority in Congress in April 1858 to refuse admission to Kansas under the Lecompton constitution. In a new referendum, the people of Kansas also rejected the Lecompton constitution, 11,300 to 1,788. Kansas was finally admitted as a free state in January 1861.

The defeat of the Lecompton constitution did not come easily. There was more bloodshed in Kansas. There was more violence in Congress: a free-for-all involving almost thirty congressmen broke out in the House late one night after an exchange of insults between Republicans and Southern Democrats. And the Democratic Party was breaking apart. Douglas had intended to preserve the Democrats as a national party, but instead he lost the support of the southern wing.

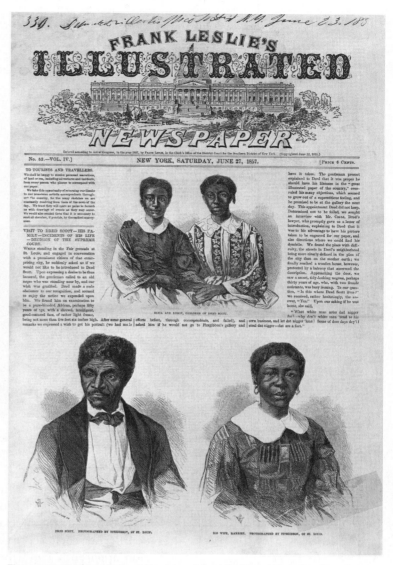

These sympathetic portraits of Harriet and Dred Scott and their daughters in 1857 helped to shape the Northern reaction to the Supreme Court's decision that denied the Scotts' claim to freedom. The infamous *Dred Scott* decision was intended to resolve the issue of slavery expansion but instead heightened angry feelings in both North and South.

THE PANIC OF 1857

Adding to the growing political tensions was the short, but sharp, depression of 1857 and 1858. Technology played a part. In August 1857, the failure of an Ohio investment house—the kind of event that had formerly taken weeks to be widely known—was the subject of a news story flashed immediately over telegraph wires to Wall Street and other financial markets. A wave of panic selling ensued, leading to business failures and slowdowns that threw thousands out of work. The major cause of the panic was a sharp, but temporary, downturn in agricultural exports to Britain, and recovery was well under way by early 1859.

Because it affected cotton exports less than northern exports, the **Panic of 1857** was less harmful to the South than to the North. Southerners took this as proof of the superiority of their economic system to the free-labor system of the North. It seemed that all matters of political discussion were being drawn into the sectional dispute. The next step toward disunion was an act of violence perpetrated by the grim abolitionist from Kansas, John Brown.

Lecompton constitution Proslavery draft written in 1857 by Kansas territorial delegates elected under questionable circumstances; it was rejected by two governors, supported by President Buchanan, and decisively defeated by Congress.

Panic of 1857 Banking crisis that caused a credit crunch in the North; it was less severe in the South, where high cotton prices spurred a quick recovery.

In a contemporary engraving, John Brown and his followers are shown trapped inside the armory at Harpers Ferry in October 1859. Captured, tried, and executed, Brown was regarded as a martyr in the North and a terrorist in the South.

WHY DID the South secede following the Republican Party victory in the election of 1860?

JOHN BROWN'S RAID

In the heated political mood of the late 1850s, some improbable people became heroes. None was more improbable than John Brown, the self-appointed avenger who had slaughtered unarmed proslavery men in Kansas in 1856. In 1859, Brown proposed a wild scheme to raid the South and start a general slave uprising. Significantly, free African Americans—among them Frederick Douglass—did not support Brown, thinking his plan to raid the federal arsenal at Harpers Ferry, Virginia, was doomed to failure. They were right. On October 16, 1859, Brown led a group of twenty-two white and African American men against the arsenal. In less than a day, the raid was over. Eight of Brown's men (including two of his sons) were dead, no slaves had joined the fight, and Brown himself was captured. Moving quickly to prevent a lynching by local mobs, the state of Virginia tried and convicted Brown (while he was still weak from the wounds of battle) of treason, murder, and fomenting insurrection.

Brown's death by hanging on December 2, 1859, was marked throughout northern communities with public rites of mourning not seen since the death of George Washington. Church bells tolled, buildings were draped in black, ministers preached sermons, prayer meetings were held, abolitionists issued eulogies. Naturally, not all Northerners supported Brown's action. But many people, while rejecting Brown's raid, increasingly supported the antislavery cause that he represented.

Brown's raid shocked the South because it aroused the fear of slave rebellion. Southerners believed that Northern abolitionists were provoking slave revolts, a suspicion apparently confirmed when documents captured at Harpers Ferry revealed that Brown had the financial support of half a dozen members of the Northern elite. These "Secret Six"—Gerrit Smith, George Stearns, Franklin Sanborn, Thomas Wentworth Higginson, Theodore Parker, and Samuel Gridley Howe—had been willing to finance armed attacks on the slave system.

Even more shocking to Southerners than the raid itself was the extent of Northern mourning for Brown's death. Although the Republican Party disavowed Brown's actions, Southerners simply did not believe the party's statements. Senator Robert Toombs of Georgia warned that the South would "never permit this Federal government to pass into the traitorous hands of the Black Republican party." Talk of secession as the only possible response became common throughout the South.

THE SOUTH SECEDES

By 1860, sectional differences had caused one national party, the Whigs, to collapse. The second national party, the Democrats, stood on the brink of dissolution. Not only the politicians but also ordinary people in both the North and the South were coming to believe there was no way to avoid what in 1858 William Seward (once a Whig, now a Republican) had called an "irrepressible conflict."

OVERVIEW | The Irrepressible Conflict

1776	Declaration of Independence	Thomas Jefferson's denunciation of slavery deleted from the final version.
1787	Northwest Ordinance	Slavery prohibited in the Northwest Territory (north of the Ohio River).
1787	Constitution	Slavery unmentioned but acknowledged in Article I, Section 2, counting three-fifths of all African Americans, slave and free, in a state's population; and in Article I, Section 9, which barred Congress from prohibiting the international slave trade for twenty years.
1803	Louisiana Purchase	Louisiana admitted as a slave state in 1812; no decision about the rest of Louisiana Purchase.
1820	Missouri Compromise	Missouri admitted as a slave state, but slavery prohibited in Louisiana Purchase north of 36°30'.
1846	Wilmot Proviso	Proposal to prohibit slavery in territory that might be gained in Mexican-American War causes splits in national parties.
1850	Compromise of 1850	California admitted as free state; Texas (already admitted in 1845) is a slave state; the rest of Mexican Cession to be decided by popular sovereignty. Ends the slave trade in the District of Columbia, but a stronger Fugitive Slave Law, leading to a number of violent recaptures, arouses Northern antislavery opinion.
1854	Kansas-Nebraska Act	At the urging of Stephen A. Douglas, Congress opens Kansas and Nebraska Territories for settlement under popular sovereignty. Open warfare between proslavery and antislavery factions breaks out in Kansas.
1857	Lecompton Constitution	President James Buchanan's decision to admit Kansas to the Union with a proslavery constitution is defeated in Congress.
1857	*Dred Scott* Decision	The Supreme Court's denial of Dred Scott's case for freedom is welcomed in the South, condemned in the North. After years of avoidance by politicians, slavery and the future of the Union is the sole topic of the debates.
1858	The Lincoln–Douglas Debates	The first open, extended debate between leading politicians about the place of slavery in the Union.
1859	John Brown's Raid and Execution	Northern support for John Brown shocks the South.
1860	Democratic Party Nominating Conventions	The Democrats are unable to agree on a candidate; two candidates, one Northern (Stephen A. Douglas) and one Southern (John C. Breckinridge) split the party and the vote, thus allowing Republican Abraham Lincoln to win.

THE ELECTION OF 1860

The split of the Democratic Party into northern and southern wings that had occurred during President Buchanan's tenure became official at the Democratic nominating conventions in 1860. The party convened first in Charleston, South Carolina, the center of secessionist agitation. Although Stephen Douglas had the support of the plurality of delegates, he did not have the two-thirds majority necessary for nomination. As the price of their support, Southerners insisted that Douglas support a federal slave code—a guarantee that slavery would be protected in the territories. Douglas could not agree without violating his own belief in popular sovereignty and losing his Northern support. After ten days, fifty-nine ballots, and two Southern walkouts, the convention ended where it had begun: deadlocked.

Constitutional Union Party National party formed in 1860, mainly by former Whigs, that emphasized allegiance to the Union and strict enforcement of all national legislation.

In June, the Democrats met again in Baltimore. The Douglasites, recognizing the need for a united party, were eager to compromise wherever they could, but most Southern Democrats were not. More than a third of the delegates bolted. Later, holding a convention of their own, they nominated Buchanan's vice president, John C. Breckinridge of Kentucky. The remaining two-thirds of the Democrats nominated Douglas, but everyone knew that a Republican victory was inevitable. To make matters worse, some Southern Whigs joined with some border-state nativists to form the **Constitutional Union Party**, which nominated John Bell of Tennessee.

Republican strategy was built on the lessons of the 1856 "victorious defeat." The Republicans planned to carry all the states Frémont had won, plus Pennsylvania, Illinois, and Indiana. The two leading Republican contenders were Senator William H. Seward of New York and Abraham Lincoln of Illinois. Seward, the party's best-known figure, had enemies among party moderates, who thought he was too radical, and among nativists with whom he had clashed in the New York Whig Party. Lincoln, on the other hand, appeared new, impressive, more moderate than Seward, and certain to carry Illinois. Lincoln won the nomination on the third ballot.

The election of 1860 presented voters with one of the clearest choices in American history. On the key issue of slavery, Breckinridge supported its extension to the territories; Lincoln stood firmly for its exclusion. Douglas attempted to hold the middle ground with his principle of popular sovereignty; Bell vaguely favored compromise as well.

The Republicans did not campaign in the South; Breckinridge did not campaign in the North. Each side was, therefore, free to believe the worst about the other. The mood in the Deep South was close to mass hysteria. Rumors of slave revolts—in Texas, Alabama, and South Carolina—swept the region, and vigilance committees sprang up to counter the supposed threat. In the South Carolina up-country, the question of secession dominated races for the state legislature. Candidates, such as A. S. Wallace of York, who advocated "patriotic forbearance" if Lincoln won, were soundly defeated. The very passion and excitement of the election campaign moved Southerners toward extremism.

The election of 1860 produced the second highest voter turnout in U.S. history (81.2 percent, topped only by 81.8 percent in 1876). The election turned out to be two regional contests: Breckinridge versus Bell in the South, Lincoln versus Douglas in the North. Breckinridge carried eleven slave states with 18 percent of the popular vote; Bell carried Virginia, Tennessee, and Kentucky with 13 percent of the popular vote. Lincoln won all eighteen of the free states (he split New Jersey with Douglas) and almost 40 percent of the popular vote. Douglas carried only Missouri but gained nearly 30 percent of the popular vote. Lincoln's electoral vote total was overwhelming: 180 to a combined 123 for the other three candidates. But although Lincoln had won 54 percent of the vote in the northern states, his name had not even appeared on the ballot in ten southern states. The true winner of the 1860 election was sectionalism (see Map 15.5).

	Electoral Vote (%)	Popular Vote (%)
ABRAHAM LINCOLN (Republican)	180 (59)	1,865,593 (40)
John C. Breckinridge (Southern Democrat)	72 (24)	848,356 (18)
John Bell (Constitutional Union)	39 (13)	592,906 (13)
Stephen A. Douglas (Northern Democrat)	12 (4)	1,382,713 (29)
States that Republicans lost in 1856, won in 1860		

MAP 15.5

The Election of 1860 The election of 1860 was a sectional election. Lincoln won no votes in the South, Breckinridge none in the North. The contest in the North was between Lincoln and Douglas, and although Lincoln swept the electoral vote, Douglas's popular vote was uncomfortably close. The large number of Northern Democratic voters opposed to Lincoln was a source of political trouble for him during the Civil War.

WHAT DO the results of the election of 1860 tell us about support for Lincoln in the North on the eve of the Civil War?

THE SOUTH LEAVES THE UNION

The results of the election shocked Southerners. They were humiliated and frightened by the prospect of becoming a permanent minority in a political system dominated by a party pledged to the elimination of slavery. In Southern eyes, the Republican triumph meant they would become unequal partners in the federal enterprise, their way of life (the slave system) existing on borrowed time.

The governors of South Carolina, Alabama, and Mississippi, each of whom had committed his state to secession if Lincoln were elected, immediately issued calls for special state conventions. At the same time, calls went out to southern communities to form vigilance committees and volunteer militia companies. Cooperationists (the term used for those opposed to immediate secession) were either intimidated into silence or simply left behind by the speed of events.

On December 20, 1860, a state convention in South Carolina voted unanimously to secede from the Union. In the weeks that followed, conventions in six other southern states (Mississippi, Florida, Alabama, Georgia, Louisiana, and Texas) followed suit, with the support, on average, of 80 percent of their delegates. There was genuine division of opinion in the Deep South, especially in Georgia and Alabama, along customary up-country–low-country lines. Yeoman farmers who did not own slaves and workers in the cities of the South were most likely to favor compromise with the North. But secessionists constantly reminded both groups that the Republican victory would lead to the emancipation of the slaves and the end of white privilege. And all Southerners, most of whom were deeply loyal to their state and region, believed that Northerners threatened their way of life. Throughout the South, secession occurred because Southerners no longer believed they had a choice.

In every state that seceded, celebrations broke out as the decisiveness of action replaced the long years of anxiety and tension. People danced in the streets, most believing the North had no choice but to accept secession peacefully. They ignored the fact that eight other slave states—Delaware, Maryland, Kentucky, Missouri, Virginia, North Carolina, Tennessee, and Arkansas—had not acted, though the latter four states did secede after war broke out (see Map 15.6).

Just as Republicans had miscalculated in thinking Southern threats a mere bluff, so secessionists now miscalculated in believing they would be able to leave the Union in peace.

THE NORTH'S POLITICAL OPTIONS

What should the North do? President Buchanan, indecisive as always, did nothing. The decision thus rested with Abraham Lincoln, even before he officially became president. One possibility was compromise, and many proposals were suggested Lincoln cautiously refused them all, making it clear that he would not compromise on the extension of slavery, which was the South's key demand. He hoped, by appearing firm but moderate, to discourage additional southern states from seceding, while giving pro-Union Southerners time to organize. He succeeded in his first aim but not in the second. Lincoln and most of the Republican Party had seriously overestimated the strength of pro-Union sentiment in the South.

A second possibility, suggested by Horace Greeley of the *New York Tribune*, was to let the seven seceding states "go in peace." This is what many secessionists expected, but too many Northerners—including Lincoln himself—believed in the Union for this to happen. At stake, for Lincoln and others, was all the accumulated American pride in the federal government as a model for democracies the world over.

The third possibility was force, and this was the crux of the dilemma. Although he believed their action was wrong, Lincoln was loath to go to war to force the seceding states back into the Union. On the other hand, he refused to give up federal powers over military forts and customs posts in the South. These were precisely the powers the seceding states had to command if they were to function as an independent nation. A confrontation was bound to come.

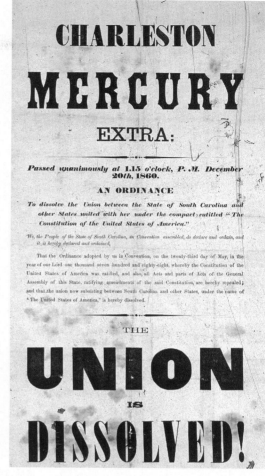

This special edition of the *Charleston Mercury* was issued on December 20, 1860, the day South Carolina voted to secede from the Union.

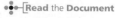

Read the Document

South Carolina Declaration of the Causes of Secession (1860) at **www.myhistorylab.com**

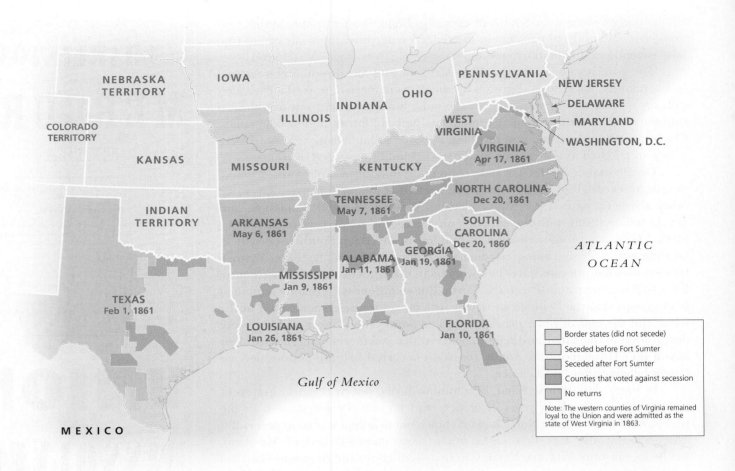

MAP 15.6

The South Secedes The southern states that would constitute the Confederacy seceded in two stages. The states of the Lower South seceded before Lincoln took office. Arkansas and three states of the Upper South—Virginia, North Carolina, and Tennessee—waited until after the South fired on Fort Sumter. And four border slave states—Delaware, Maryland, Kentucky, and Missouri—chose not to secede. Every southern state (except South Carolina) was divided on the issue of secession, generally along up-country–low-country lines. In Virginia, this division was so extreme that West Virginia split off to become a separate nonslave state admitted to the Union in 1863.

WHY WERE some states quicker to secede than others?

ESTABLISHMENT OF THE CONFEDERACY

In February, delegates from the seven seceding states met in Montgomery, Alabama, and created the Confederate States of America. They wrote a constitution that was identical to the Constitution of the United States, with a few crucial exceptions: it strongly supported states' rights and made the abolition of slavery practically impossible. These two clauses did much to define the Confederate enterprise. It was difficult to avoid the conclusion that the new Confederacy was defined by the Southern dependence on slave labor.

The Montgomery convention chose Jefferson Davis of Mississippi as president and Alexander Stephens of Georgia as vice president of the new nation. Both men were known as moderates. Davis, a slave owner who had been a general in the Mexican-American War and secretary of war in the Pierce administration, and who was currently a senator from Mississippi, had expressed his own uncertainties by retaining his Senate seat for two weeks after Mississippi seceded. Stephens, a former leader in the Whig Party, had

CHRONOLOGY

1820	Missouri Compromise
1828–32	Nullification Crisis
1846	Wilmot Proviso
1848	Treaty of Guadalupe Hidalgo ends Mexican-American War
	Zachary Taylor elected president
	Free-Soil Party formed
1849	California and Utah seek admission to the Union as free states
1850	Compromise of 1850
	California admitted as a free state
	American (Know-Nothing) Party formed
	Zachary Taylor dies; Millard Fillmore becomes president
1851	North reacts to Fugitive Slave Law
	Harriet Beecher Stowe's *Uncle Tom's Cabin* published
1852	Franklin Pierce elected president
1854	Ostend Manifesto
	Kansas-Nebraska Act
	Treaties with Indians in northern part of Indian Territory renegotiated
	Republican Party formed as Whig Party dissolves

1855	William Walker leads his first filibustering expedition to Nicaragua
1856	Burning and looting of Lawrence, Kansas
	John Brown leads Pottawatomie massacre
	Attack on Senator Charles Sumner
	James Buchanan elected president
1857	*Dred Scott* decision
	President Buchanan accepts proslavery Lecompton constitution in Kansas
	Panic of 1857
1858	Congress rejects Lecompton constitution
	Lincoln–Douglas debates
1859	John Brown's raid on Harpers Ferry
1860	Four parties run presidential candidates
	Abraham Lincoln elected president
	South Carolina secedes from Union
1861	Six other Deep South states secede
	Confederate States of America formed
	Lincoln takes office

been a cooperationist delegate to Georgia's convention, where he urged that secession not be undertaken hastily.

The choice of moderates was deliberate, for the strategy of the new Confederate state was to argue that secession was a normal, responsible, and expectable course of action, and nothing for the North to get upset about. This was the theme that President Jefferson Davis of the **Confederate States of America** struck in his Inaugural Address, delivered to a crowd of 10,000 from the steps of the State Capitol at Montgomery, Alabama, on February 18, 1861. "We have changed the constituent parts," Davis said, "but not the system of our Government." Secession was a legal and peaceful step that, Davis said, quoting from the Declaration of Independence, "illustrates the American idea that governments rest on the consent of the governed . . . and that it is the right of the people to alter or abolish them at will whenever they become destructive of the ends for which they were established."

LINCOLN'S INAUGURATION

The country as a whole waited to see what Abraham Lincoln would do, which at first appeared to be very little. In Springfield, Lincoln refused to issue public statements before his inaugural (although he sent many private messages to Congress and to key military officers), for fear of making a delicate situation worse. Eastern intellectuals, already suspicious of a mere "prairie lawyer," were not impressed. These signs of moderation and

Confederate States of America
Nation proclaimed in Montgomery, Alabama, in February 1861, after the seven states of the Lower South seceded from the United States.

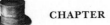

caution did not appeal to an American public with a penchant for electing military heroes. Americans wanted leadership and action.

Lincoln continued, however, to offer nonbelligerent firmness and moderation. And at the end of his Inaugural Address on March 4, 1861, as he stood ringed by federal troops called out in case of a Confederate attack, the new president offered unexpected eloquence:

> I am loath to close. We are not enemies, but friends. We must not be enemies. Though passion may have strained, it must not break our bonds of affection. The mystic chords of memory, stretching from every battlefield, and patriot grave, to every living heart and hearthstone, all over this broad land, will yet swell the chorus of the Union, when again touched, as surely they will be, by the better angels of our nature.

CONCLUSION

Americans had much to boast about in 1850. Their nation was vastly larger, richer, and more powerful than it had been in 1800. But the issue of slavery was slowly dividing the North and the South, two communities with similar origins and many common bonds. The following decade was marked by frantic efforts at political compromise, beginning with the Compromise of 1850, continuing with the Kansas-Nebraska Act of 1854, and culminating in the Supreme Court's 1859 decision in the *Dred Scott* case. Increasingly, the ordinary people of the two regions demanded resolution of the crisis. The two great parties of the Second American Party System, the Democrats and the Whigs, unable to find a solution, were destroyed. Two new sectional parties—the Republican Party and a Southern party devoted to the defense of slavery—fought the 1860 election, but Southerners refused to accept the national verdict. Politics had failed: the issue of slavery was irreconcilable. The only remaining recourse was war. But although Americans were divided, they were still one people. That made the war, when it came, all the more terrible.

REVIEW QUESTIONS

1. What aspects of the remarkable economic development of the United States in the first half of the nineteenth century contributed to the sectional crisis of the 1850s?

2. How might the violent efforts by abolitionists to free escaped slaves who had been recaptured and the federal armed enforcement of the Fugitive Slave Law have been viewed differently by northern merchants (the so-called Cotton Whigs), Irish immigrants, and abolitionists?

3. Consider the course of events in "Bloody Kansas" from Douglas's Kansas-Nebraska Act to the congressional rejection of the Lecompton constitution. Were these events the inevitable result of the political impasse in Washington, or could other decisions have been made that would have changed the outcome?

4. The nativism of the 1850s that surfaced so strongly in the Know-Nothing Party was eclipsed by the crisis over slavery. But nativist sentiment has been a recurring theme in American politics. Discuss why it was strong in the 1850s and why it has emerged periodically since then.

5. Evaluate the character and actions of John Brown. Was he the hero proclaimed by Northern supporters or the terrorist condemned by the South?

6. Imagine that you lived in Illinois, home state to both Douglas and Lincoln, in 1860. How would you have voted in the presidential election, and why?

KEY TERMS

Bleeding Kansas (p. 368)
Compromise of 1850 (p. 363)
Confederate States of America (p. 381)
Constitutional Union Party (p. 378)
Dred Scott **decision** (p. 374)
Fugitive Slave Law (p. 366)

Kansas-Nebraska Act (p. 368)
Know-Nothings (p. 370)
Lecompton constitution (p. 375)
Panic of 1857 (p. 375)
Popular sovereignty (p. 363)
Republican Party (p. 372)

PEARSON
myhistorylab Connections

Reinforce what you learned in this chapter by studying the many documents,
images, maps, review tools, and videos available at www.myhistorylab.com.

Read and Review

✓●—|Study and Review Chapter 15

•:•—|Read the Document

The Lincoln-Douglas Debates of 1858

A New England Writer Portrays Slavery in 1852

Daniel Webster, Speech to the U.S. Senate (1850)

*Benjamin Drew, from Narratives of Fugitive
Slaves in Canada (1855)*

*Harriet Jacobs, Incidents in the Life of a Slave
Girl (1861)*

Opinion of the Supreme Court for Dred Scott *v.
Sanford (1857)*

*An Abolitionist Is Given the Death Sentence
in 1859*

John Brown's Address before Sentencing (1859)

*South Carolina Declaration of the Causes of
Secession (1860)*

◉—|See the Map

The Compromise of 1850

The Kansas-Nebraska Act

Research and Explore

•:•—|Read the Document

Exploring America: Anthony Burns

Profiles
*Dred and Harriet Scott
John Brown*

◉—|Watch the Video

Dred Scott and the Crises that Led to the Civil War

*Harriet Beecher Stowe and the Making of Uncle
Tom's Cabin*

((•●—|**Hear** the **Audio**

Hear the audio files for Chapter 15 at
www.myhistorylab.com.

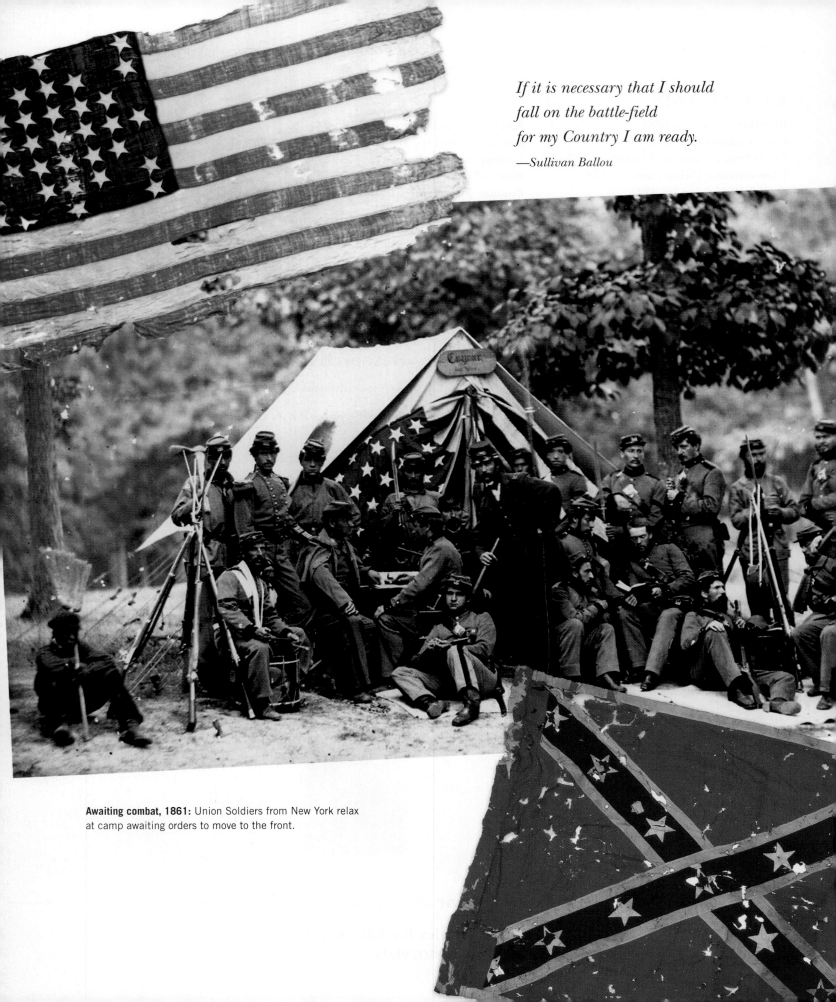

If it is necessary that I should fall on the battle-field for my Country I am ready.
—Sullivan Ballou

Awaiting combat, 1861: Union Soldiers from New York relax at camp awaiting orders to move to the front.

16

THE CIVIL WAR
1861–1865

((•—|**Hear** the **Audio**

Hear the audio files for Chapter 16 at **www.myhistorylab.com**.

WHAT ADVANTAGES did the North possess at the outset of the Civil War?

WHAT CHALLENGES did Abraham Lincoln and Jefferson Davis face as they attempted to unify their people and lead in war?

WHAT SUCCESSES did the South enjoy in the early years of the war and how were they achieved?

HOW DID the Emancipation Proclamation change the nature of the war?

WHAT IMPACT did the war have on the political, economic, and social life of the North and the South?

HOW DID Grant and Sherman turn the tide of the war?

1861 | 1865

AMERICAN COMMUNITIES
Mother Bickerdyke Connects
Northern Communities to Their Boys at War

IN MAY 1861, THE REVEREND EDWARD BEECHER READ A DISTURBING LETTER to his Galesburg, Illinois, congregation. Two months earlier, Galesburg had sent 500 of its young men off to join the Union army. They had not yet been in battle. Yet, the letter reported, an alarming number were dying of diseases caused by inadequate food, medical care, and sanitation at the crowded military camp in Cairo, Illinois.

The shocked and grieving members of Beecher's congregation quickly decided to send not only supplies but also one of their number to inspect the conditions at the Cairo camp and to take action. In spite of warnings that army regulations excluded women from encampments, the congregation voted to send their most qualified member, Mary Ann Bickerdyke, a middle-aged widow who made her living as a "botanic physician." This simple gesture of community concern launched a remarkable Civil War career.

Once in Cairo, "Mother" Bickerdyke, as she was called, immediately set to work cleaning the hospital tents and the soldiers themselves, and finding and cooking nourishing food for them. The hospital director, who resented her interference, ordered her to leave, but she continued her work. When he reported her to the commanding officer, General Benjamin Prentiss, she quickly convinced the general to let her stay.

A plainspoken, hardworking woman, totally unfazed by rank or tender masculine egos, Mother Bickerdyke single-mindedly devoted herself to what she called "the Lord's work." The ordinary soldiers loved her; wise generals supported her. Once, when an indignant officer's wife complained about Bickerdyke's rudeness, General William Tecumseh Sherman joked, "You've picked the one person around here who outranks me. If you want to lodge a complaint against her, you'll have to take it to President Lincoln."

Other communities all over the North rallied to make up for the Army's shortcomings with supplies and assistance. By their actions, Mother Bickerdyke and others like her exposed the War Department's inability to meet the needs of the nation's first mass army. The efforts of women on the local level—for example, to make clothing for men from their communities who had gone off to the war—quickly took on national dimensions. The Women's Central Association of Relief (WCAR), whose organizers were mostly reformers in the abolitionist, temperance, and education movements, eventually had 7,000 chapters throughout the North. Its volunteers raised funds, made and collected food, clothes,

medicine, bandages, and more than 250,000 quilts and comforters, and sent them to army camps and hospitals. All told, association chapters supplied an estimated $15 million worth of goods to the Union troops.

In June 1861, responding to requests by officials of the WCAR for formal recognition of the organization, President Abraham Lincoln created the United States Sanitary Commission and gave it the power to investigate and advise the Medical Bureau. The commission's more than 500 "sanitary inspectors" (usually men) instructed soldiers in such matters as water supply, placement of latrines, and safe cooking.

Read the Document
U.S. Sanitary Commission, Sketch of Its Purposes (1864) at **www.myhistorylab.com**

In 1862 Mother Bickerdyke became an official agent of "the Sanitary," as it was known. Mother Bickerdyke was an unequaled fundraiser. In speaking tours throughout Illinois, she touched her female listeners with moving stories of wounded boys whom she had cared for as if they were her own sons. Her words to men were more forceful. It was a man's business to fight, she said. If he was too old or ill to fight with a gun, he should fight with his dollars. With the help of Bickerdyke's blunt appeals, the Sanitary raised $50 million for the Union war effort.

As the Civil War continued, Mother Bickerdyke became a key figure in the medical support for General Ulysses S. Grant's campaigns along the Mississippi River. She was with the army at Shiloh, and as Grant slowly fought his way to Vicksburg, she set up convalescent hospitals in Memphis. Grant authorized her to commandeer any army wagons she needed to transport supplies. On the civilian side, the Sanitary Commission authorized her to draw on its supply depots in Memphis, Cairo, Chicago, and elsewhere. In a practical sense a vital "middlewoman" between the home front and the battlefield, she was also, in a symbolic and emotional sense, a stand-in for all mothers who had sent their sons to war.

The Civil War was a national tragedy, ripping apart the political fabric of the country and causing more casualties than any other war in the nation's history. The death toll of approximately 620,000 exceeded the number of dead in all the other wars from the Revolution through the Vietnam War. Yet in another sense, it was a community triumph. Local communities directly supported and sustained their soldiers on a massive scale in unprecedented ways. As national unity failed, the strength of local communities, symbolized by Mother Bickerdyke, endured.

COMMUNITIES MOBILIZE FOR WAR

A neutral observer in March 1861 might have seen ominous similarities. Two nations—the United States of America and the Confederate States of America—each blamed the other for the breakup of the Union. Two new presidents—Abraham Lincoln and Jefferson Davis—each faced the challenging task of building and maintaining national unity. Two regions—North and South—scorned each other and boasted of their own superiority. But the most important similarity was not yet apparent: both sides were unprepared for the ordeal that lay ahead.

FORT SUMTER: THE WAR BEGINS

Fort Sumter, a federal military installation, sat on an island at the entrance to Charleston harbor. So long as it remained in Union hands, Charleston, the center of secessionist sentiment, would be immobilized. With the fort dangerously low on supplies, Lincoln had to decide whether to abandon it or risk the fight that might ensue if he ordered it resupplied. On April 6, 1861, Lincoln took cautious and careful action, notifying the governor of South Carolina that he was sending a relief force to the fort carrying only food and no military supplies. Now the decision rested with Jefferson Davis, who opted for decisive action. On April 10, he ordered General P. G. T. Beauregard to demand the surrender of Fort Sumter and to attack it if the garrison did not comply. On April 12, Beauregard opened fire. Two days later, the defenders surrendered.

Even before the attack on Fort Sumter, the Confederate Congress had authorized a volunteer army of 100,000 men to serve for twelve months. Men flocked to enlist, and their communities sent them off in ceremonies featuring bands, bonfires, and belligerent oratory. The cry of "On to Washington!" was raised throughout the South, and orators confidently predicted that the city would be captured and the war concluded within sixty days.

The "thunderclap of Sumter" startled the North into an angry response. The apathy and uncertainty that had prevailed since Lincoln's election disappeared, to be replaced by strong feelings of patriotism. On April 15, Lincoln issued a proclamation calling for 75,000 state militiamen to serve in the federal army for ninety days. Enlistment offices were swamped with enthusiastic volunteers. Free African Americans, among the most eager to serve, were turned away: this was not yet a war for or by black people.

The mobilization in Chester, Pennsylvania, was typical of the Northern response to the outbreak of war. A patriotic rally was held at which a company of volunteers (the first of many from the region) were mustered into the Ninth Regiment of Pennsylvania Volunteers. Companies of home guards were organized by the men who remained behind. Within a month, the women of Chester had organized a countywide system of war relief. Such relief organizations emerged in every community, North and South, that sent soldiers off to the Civil War. These organizations not only played a vital role in supplying the troops, but they also maintained the human, local link on which so many soldiers depended. In this sense, every American community accompanied its young men to war.

THE BORDER STATES

The first secession, between December 20, 1860, and February 1, 1861, had taken seven Deep South states out of the Union. Now, in April, the firing on Fort Sumter and Lincoln's call for state militias forced the other Southern states to take sides. Four states of the Upper South (Virginia, Arkansas, Tennessee, and North Carolina) joined the original seven in April and May 1861.

Still undecided was the loyalty of the northernmost tier of slave-owning states: Missouri, Kentucky, Maryland, and Delaware. Each controlled vital strategic assets. Missouri not only bordered the Mississippi River but also controlled the routes to the west. Kentucky controlled the Ohio River. The main railroad link with the West ran through Maryland and the hill region of western Virginia (which split from Virginia to become the free state of West

WHAT ADVANTAGES did the North possess at the outset of the Civil War?

Watch the Video
What Caused the Civil War? at
www.myhistorylab.com

This Currier and Ives lithograph shows the opening moment of the Civil War. On April 12, 1861, Confederate General P.G.T. Beauregard ordered the shelling of Fort Sumter in Charleston harbor. Two days later, Union Major Robert Anderson surrendered, and mobilization began for what turned out to be the most devastating war in American history.

Virginia in 1863). Delaware controlled access to Philadelphia. Finally, were Maryland to secede, the nation's capital would be completely surrounded by Confederate territory.

Delaware was loyal to the Union (less than 2 percent of its population were slaves), but Maryland's loyalty was divided, as an ugly incident on April 19 showed. When the Sixth Massachusetts Regiment marched through Baltimore, a hostile crowd of 10,000 Southern sympathizers pelted the troops with bricks, paving stones, and bullets. Finally, in desperation, the troops fired on the crowd, killing twelve people and wounding others. In retaliation, Southern sympathizers burned the railroad bridges to the North and destroyed the telegraph line to Washington.

In response Lincoln stationed Union troops along Maryland's crucial railroads, declared martial law in Baltimore, and arrested the suspected ringleaders of the pro-Confederate mob and held them without trial. The arrests in Maryland were the first of a number of violations of basic civil rights during the war, all of which the president justified on the basis of national security.

An even bloodier division occurred in Missouri. The proslavery governor and most of the legislature fled to Arkansas, where they declared a Confederate state government in exile, while Unionists remained in control in St. Louis. Consequently, Missouri was plagued by guerrilla battles throughout the war. In Kentucky, division took the form of a huge illegal trade with the Confederacy through neighboring Tennessee.

That Delaware, Maryland, Missouri, and Kentucky chose to stay in the Union was a severe blow to the Confederacy. Among them, the four states could have added 45 percent to the white population and military manpower of the Confederacy and 80 percent to its manufacturing capacity.

THE BATTLE OF BULL RUN

Once sides had been chosen and the initial flush of enthusiasm had passed, the nature of the war, and the mistaken notions about it, soon became clear. The event that shattered the illusions was the First Battle of Bull Run, at Bull Run Creek near Manassas in Virginia in July 1861. A Union army of 35,000 men marched south, crying "On to Richmond!" So lighthearted and unprepared was the Washington community that the troops were accompanied not only by journalists but also by a crowd of politicians and sightseers. At first the Union troops held their ground against the 25,000 Confederate troops commanded by General P. G. T. Beauregard. But when 2,300 fresh Confederate troops arrived as reinforcements, the untrained Northern troops broke ranks. Soldiers and civilians alike retreated in disarray all the way to Washington.

THE RELATIVE STRENGTHS OF NORTH AND SOUTH

Bull Run was sobering—and prophetic. The Civil War was the most lethal military conflict in American history. It claimed the lives of nearly 620,000 soldiers, more than the First and Second World Wars combined. One out of every four soldiers who fought in the war never returned home.

Overall, in terms of both population and productive capacity, the Union seemed to have a commanding edge over the Confederacy. The North had two and a half times the South's population and enjoyed an even greater advantage in industrial capacity (nine

QUICK REVIEW

The First Battle of Bull Run

- July 1861: Beauregard (Confederacy) and McDowell (Union) meet at Manassas.
- Confederate troops repulse a strong Union attack.
- Battle foreshadowed war to come.

times that of the South). The North produced almost all of the nation's firearms (97 percent), had 71 percent of its railroad mileage, and produced 94 percent of its cloth and 90 percent of its footwear. These advantages were ultimately to prove decisive. But in the short term, the South had important assets to counter the advantage of the North (see Figure 16.1).

The first was the nature of the struggle. For the South, this was a defensive war, in which the basic principle of the defense of home and community united almost all white citizens, regardless of their views about slavery. The North would have to invade the South and then control it against guerrilla opposition in order to win.

Second, the military disparity was less extreme than it appeared. Although the North had manpower, its troops were mostly untrained. Moreover, the South, because of its tradition of honor and belligerence, appeared to have an advantage in military leaders, the most notable of which was Robert E. Lee.

Finally, it was widely believed that slavery would work to the South's advantage, for slaves could continue to do the vital plantation work while their masters went off to war. But above all, the South had the weapon of cotton. Because of the crucial role of cotton in industrialization, Southerners were confident that the British and French need for Southern cotton would soon bring those countries to recognize the Confederacy as a separate nation.

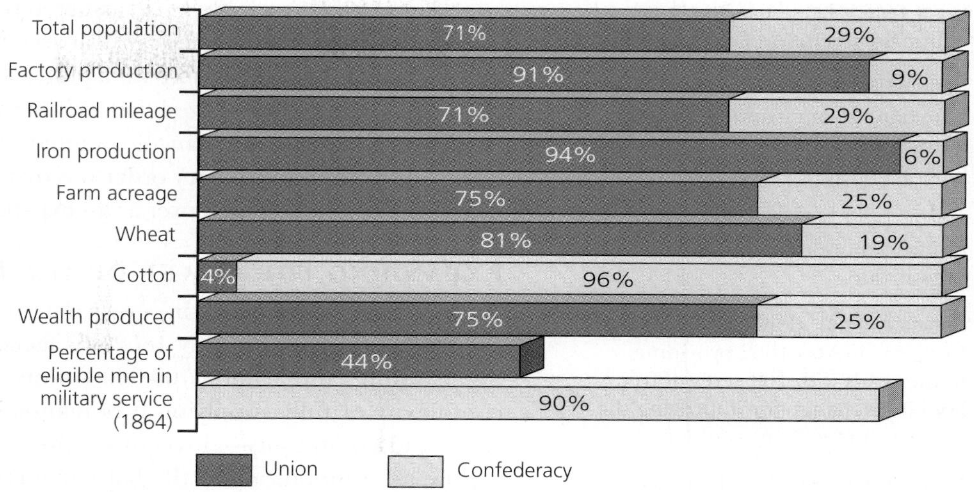

Figure 16.1 Comparative Resources, North and South, 1861
As this chart shows, the North far surpassed the South in the resources necessary to support a large, long war. Initially, however, these strengths made little difference in a struggle that began as a traditional war of maneuver in which the South held the defensive advantage. Only slowly did the Civil War become a modern war in which all the resources of society, including the property and lives of civilians, were mobilized for battle.

From *The Times Atlas of World History* Copyright © 1978, Hammond. Reprinted by permission of the publisher.

QUICK REVIEW

Northern Advantages

- Two and a half times the South's population.
- North controlled much of nation's industrial capacity.
- Could field a much larger army.

The Governments Organize for War

The Civil War forced the federal government to assume powers unimaginable just a few years before. Abraham Lincoln took as his primary task leading and unifying the nation in his role as commander in chief. He found the challenge almost insurmountable. Jefferson Davis's challenge was even greater. He had to create a Confederate nation out of a loose grouping of eleven states, each believing strongly in states' rights.

Lincoln Takes Charge

Lincoln's first task as president was to assert control over his own cabinet. Most unusually, Lincoln chose to include in his cabinet several men who had been his rivals for the presidential nomination, among them Secretary of State William Seward and Treasury Secretary Salmon P. Chase. That the Republican Party was a not-quite-jelled mix of former Whigs, abolitionists, moderate free-soilers, and even some prowar Democrats made Lincoln's task as party leader much more difficult than it might otherwise have been.

After the fall of Fort Sumter, military necessity prompted Lincoln to call up the state militias, order a naval blockade of the South, and vastly expand the military budget. Military necessity—the need to hold the border states—likewise prompted other early actions, such as the suspension of *habeas corpus* and the acceptance of Kentucky's ambiguous neutrality. The president also repudiated an unauthorized declaration issued by General John C. Frémont, military commander in Missouri, in August 1861 that would have freed Missouri's slaves. Lincoln feared that such an action would lead to the secession of Kentucky and Maryland.

WHAT CHALLENGES did Abraham Lincoln and Jefferson Davis face as they attempted to unify their people and lead in war?

Legal Tender Act   Act creating a national currency in February 1862.

National Bank Act   Act prohibiting state banks from issuing their own notes and forcing them to apply for federal charters.

Morrill Tariff Act   Act that raised tariffs to more than double their prewar rate.

Homestead Act   Law passed by Congress in May 1862 providing homesteads with 160 acres of free land in exchange for improving the land within five years of the grant.

Morrill Land Grant Act   Law passed by Congress in July 1862 awarding proceeds from the sale of public lands to the states for the establishment of agricultural and mechanical colleges.

Read the **Document**

Homestead Act of 1862 at
www.myhistorylab.com

This photograph, taken a month before his inauguration, shows Lincoln looking presidential. It was clearly intended to reassure a public still doubtful about his abilities.

Although James K. Polk had assumed responsibility for overall American military strategy during the Mexican-American War (see Chapter 14), Lincoln was the first president to act as commander in chief in both a practical and a symbolic way. He actively directed military policy, because he realized that a civil war presented problems different from those of a foreign war of conquest. Lincoln wanted above all to persuade the South to rejoin the Union, and his every military order was dictated by the hope of eventual reconciliation. At the same time, he presided over a vast expansion of the powers of the federal government.

EXPANDING THE POWER OF THE FEDERAL GOVERNMENT

The greatest expansion in government power during the war was in the War Department, which by early 1862 was faced with the unprecedented challenge of feeding, clothing, and arming 700,000 Union soldiers. The size of the Union army and the complexity of fully supplying it demanded constant efforts at all levels—government, state, and community—throughout the war. Thus, in the matter of procurement and supply, as in mobilization, the battlefront was related to the home front on a scale that Americans had not previously experienced.

The need for money for the vast war effort was pressing. Treasury Secretary Chase worked closely with Congress to develop ways to finance the war. With the help of Philadelphia financier Jay Cooke, the Treasury used patriotic appeals to sell war bonds to ordinary people in amounts as small as $50. By the war's end, the United States had borrowed $2.6 billion for the war effort, the first example in American history of the mass financing of war.

Most radical of all was Chase's decision to print and distribute Treasury notes (paper money). Until then, the money in circulation had been a mixture of coins and state bank notes issued by 1,500 different state banks. The **Legal Tender Act** of February 1862 created a national currency. In 1863, Congress passed the **National Bank Act**, which prohibited state banks from issuing their own notes and forced them to apply for federal charters. The switch to a national currency was widely recognized as a major step toward centralization of economic power in the hands of the federal government. Such a measure would have been unthinkable if Southern Democrats had still been part of the national government. The absence of Southern Democrats also made possible passage of a number of Republican economic measures not directly related to the war.

Although the outbreak of war overshadowed everything else, the Republican Party in Congress was determined to fulfill its campaign pledge of a comprehensive program of economic development. Republicans quickly passed the **Morrill Tariff Act** (1861); by 1864, this and subsequent measures had raised tariffs to more than double their prewar rate. In 1862 and 1864, Congress created two federally chartered railroad companies, the Union Pacific and Central Pacific, to build a transcontinental railroad. The **Homestead Act** (1862) gave 160 acres of public land to any citizen who agreed to live on the land for five years, improve it by building a house and cultivating some of the land, and pay a small fee. The **Morrill Land Grant Act** (1862) gave states public land that would allow them to finance land-grant colleges offering education to ordinary citizens in practical skills such as agriculture, engineering, and military science. Coupled with this act, the establishment of a federal Department of Agriculture in 1862 gave American farmers a big push toward modern commercial agriculture.

DIPLOMATIC OBJECTIVES

To Secretary of State William Seward fell the job of making sure that Britain and France did not extend diplomatic recognition to the Confederacy. Although Southerners had been certain that King Cotton would gain them European support, they were wrong. British public opinion, which had strongly supported the abolition of slavery within the British Empire in the 1830s, would not now countenance the recognition of a new nation based on slavery. British cotton manufacturers found economic alternatives, first using up their backlog of Southern cotton and then turning to Egypt and India for new supplies. In spite of Union protests, however, both Britain and France did allow Confederate vessels to use their ports, and British shipyards sold six ships to the Confederacy. But in 1863, when the Confederacy commissioned Britain's Laird shipyard to build two iron-clad ships with pointed prows for ramming Union ships, the Union threatened war, and the British government made sure that the Laird ironclads were never delivered.

In 1861, a bankrupt Mexico suffered conquest by France. This was a serious violation of Mexican independence, just the kind of European intervention the Monroe Doctrine had been formulated to prevent (see Chapter 9). Mexican forces repelled the French troops on May 5, 1862. Ever since, Mexico has celebrated *El Cinco de Mayo*, although France eventually prevailed and installed the Austrian archduke Maximilian as emperor.

Fearing that France might recognize the Confederacy or invade Texas, Seward had to content himself with refusing to recognize the new Mexican government. Although the goal of Seward's diplomacy—preventing recognition of the Confederacy by the European powers—was always clear, its achievement was uncertain for more than two years. Northern fears and Southern hopes seesawed with the fortunes of battle. Not until the victories at Vicksburg and Gettysburg in July 1863 could Seward be reasonably confident of success.

JEFFERSON DAVIS TRIES TO UNIFY THE CONFEDERACY

Although Jefferson Davis had held national cabinet rank (as secretary of war under President Franklin Pierce), had experience as an administrator, and was a former military man, he was unable to hold the Confederacy together. Perhaps no one could have.

Davis's first cabinet of six men, appointed in February 1861, included a representative from each of the states of the first secession except Mississippi, which was represented by Davis himself. This careful attention to the equality of the states pointed to the fundamental problem Davis was unable to overcome. A shared belief in states' rights—that is, in their own autonomy—was a poor basis on which to build a unified nation. Although Davis saw the need for unity, he was unable to impose it. Soon his style of leadership—micromanagement—angered his generals, alienated cabinet members, and gave Southern governors reason to resist his orders.

CONTRADICTIONS OF SOUTHERN NATIONALISM

The failure of "cotton diplomacy" was a crushing blow. White Southerners were stunned that Britain and France would not recognize their claim to independence. For the first two years of the war, plantations continued to grow cotton, but the South withheld it from market, in the hope that lack of raw material for their textile mills would lead the British and French to recognize the Confederacy. In 1862, when the Confederacy ended the embargo and began to ship its great surplus, the world price of cotton plunged. Then too, the Union naval blockade, weak at first, began to take effect. Cotton turned out to be not so powerful a diplomatic weapon after all.

Perhaps the greatest Southern failure was in the area of finances. At first, the Confederate government tried to raise money from the states, but governors refused to impose new taxes. By the time uniform taxes were levied in 1863, it was too

This painting by William C. Washington, *Jackson Entering the City of Winchester*, shows the dashing Confederate General "Stonewall" Jackson saving the Virginia town from Union capture in 1862. Jackson and other Confederate generals evoked fierce loyalty to the Confederacy. Unfortunately, by the time this victory was commemorated, Jackson himself was dead from wounds caused by friendly fire at the Battle of Chancellorsville in May of 1863.

William Washington, *Stonewall Jackson Entering the City of Winchester, Virginia*. Oil painting. Valentine Museum Library, Richmond, Virginia.

late. Heavy borrowing and the printing of great sums of paper money produced runaway inflation. Inflation, in turn, caused incalculable damage to morale and prospects for unity.

After the initial surge of volunteers, enlistment in the military fell off, as it did in the North also. In April 1862, the Confederate Congress passed the first draft law in American history, and the Union Congress followed suit in March 1863. The Southern law declared that all able-bodied men between eighteen and thirty-five were eligible for three years of military service. As in the North, purchase of substitutes was allowed. The most disliked part of the draft law was a provision exempting one white man on each plantation with twenty or more slaves. This provision not only seemed to disprove the earlier claim that slavery freed white men to fight, but also it aroused class resentments. A bitter phrase of the time complained, "It's a rich man's war but a poor man's fight."

The inequitable draft was only one of many things that convinced the ordinary people of the South that this was a war for privileged slave owners, not for them. With its leaders and citizens fearing (perhaps correctly) that centralization would destroy what was distinctively Southern, the Confederacy was unable to mobilize the resources—financial, human, and otherwise—that might have prevented its destruction by Northern armies.

THE FIGHTING THROUGH 1862

Just as political decisions were often driven by military necessity, the basic Northern and Southern military strategies were affected by political considerations as much as by military ones. The initial policy of limited war, thought to be the best route to ultimate reconciliation, ran into difficulties because of the public's impatience for victories. But victories, as the mounting slaughter made clear, were not easy to achieve.

WHAT SUCCESSES did the South enjoy in the early years of the war and how were they achieved?

The contrast between the hope and valor of these young Southern volunteer soldiers, photographed shortly before the First Battle of Bull Run, and the later advertisements for substitutes (at right), is marked. Southern exemptions for slave owners and lavish payment for substitutes increasingly bred resentment among the ordinary people of the South.

Cook Collection. Valentine Museum Library/Richmond History Center.

SUBSTITUTE NOTICES.

WANTED—A SUBSTITUTE for a conscript, to serve during the war. Any good man over the age of 35 years, not a resident of Virginia, or a foreigner, may hear of a good situation by calling at Mr. GEORGE BAGBY'S office, Shockoe Slip, to-day, between the hours of 9 and 11 A. M.   [jy 9—1t*]   A COUNTRYMAN.

WANTED—Two SUBSTITUTES—one for artillery, the other for infantry or cavalry service. Also, to sell, a trained, thoroughbred cavalry HORSE. Apply to   DR. BROOCKS, Corner Main and 12th streets, or to   T. T. BROOCKS, jy 9—3t*   Petersburg, Va.

WANTED—Immediately, a SUBSTITUTE. A man over 35 years old, or under 18, can get a good price by making immediate application to Room No. 50, Monument Hotel, or by addressing "J. W.," through Richmond P. O.   jy 9—1t*

WANTED—A SUBSTITUTE, to go into the 24th North Carolina State troops, for which a liberal price will be paid. Apply to me at Dispatch office this evening at 4 o'clock P. M. jy 9—1t*   R. R. MOORE.

WANTED—A SUBSTITUTE, to go in a first-rate Georgia company of infantry, under the heroic Jackson. A gentleman whose health is impaired, will give a fair price for a substitute. Apply immediately at ROOM, No. 13, Post-Office Department, third story, between the hours of 10 and 3 o'clock.   jy 9—6t*

WANTED—Two SUBSTITUTES for the war. A good bonus will be given. None need apply except those exempt from Conscript. Apply to-day at   GEORGE I. HERRING'S, jy 9—1t*   Grocery store, No. 56 Main st.

THE WAR IN NORTHERN VIRGINIA

The initial Northern strategy, dubbed by critics the Anaconda Plan (after the constrictor snake), envisaged slowly squeezing the South with a blockade at sea and on the Mississippi River. The plan avoided invasion and conquest in the hope that a strained South would recognize the inevitability of defeat and thus surrender. Lincoln accepted the basics of the plan, but public clamor for a fight pushed him to agree to the disastrous Battle of Bull Run and then to a major buildup of Union troops in northern Virginia under General George B. McClellan (see Map 16.1).

In March 1862, after almost a year spent drilling the raw Union recruits and after repeated exhortations by an impatient Lincoln, McClellan committed 120,000 troops to what became known as the **Peninsular campaign**. The objective was to capture Richmond, the Confederate capital. McClellan had his troops and their supplies ferried in 400 ships from Washington to Fortress Monroe, near the mouth of the James River, an effort that took three weeks. Inching up the James Peninsula toward Richmond, he tried to avoid battle, hoping his overwhelming numbers would convince the South to surrender.

In a series of battles known as the Seven Days, Robert E. Lee boldly counterattacked, repeatedly catching McClellan off guard. Taking heavy losses as well as inflicting them, Lee drove McClellan back. In August, Lee routed another Union army, commanded by

Peninsular campaign   Union offensive led by McClellan with the objective of capturing Richmond.

MAP 16.1

Overall Strategy of the Civil War The initial Northern strategy for subduing the South entailed strangling it by a blockade at sea and obtaining control of the Mississippi River. But at the end of 1862, it was clear that the South's defensive strategy could only be broken by the invasion of Southern territory. In 1864, Sherman's "March to the Sea" and Grant's hammering tactics in northern Virginia brought the war home to the South. Lee's surrender to Grant at Appomattox Courthouse on April 9, 1865, ended the bloodiest war in the nation's history.

HOW DID the military strategies of the North and the South reflect each side's larger goals?

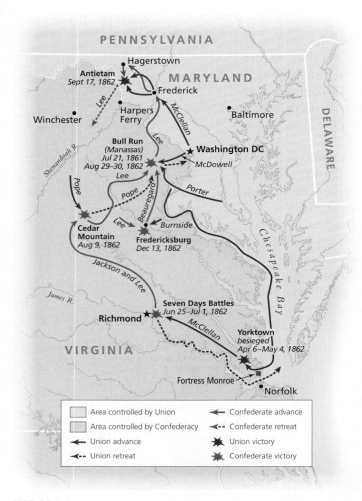

MAP 16.2
Major Battles in the East, 1861–62   Northern Virginia was the most crucial and the most constant theater of battle. The prizes were the two opposing capitals, Washington and Richmond, only 70 miles apart. By the summer of 1862, George B. McClellan, famously cautious, had achieved only stalemate in the Peninsular campaign. He did, however, turn back Robert E. Lee at Antietam in September.

WHAT WAS the Anaconda Plan? Why did it fail?

See the **Map**
The Civil War, Part I: 1861–1862 at
www.myhistorylab.com

General John Pope, at the Second Battle of Bull Rull (Second Manassas). Lincoln, alarmed at the threat to Washington and disappointed by McClellan's inaction, ordered him to abandon the Peninsular campaign and return to the capital.

Jefferson Davis, like Abraham Lincoln, was an active commander in chief. And like Lincoln, he responded to a public that clamored for more action than a strictly defensive war entailed. After the Seven Days victories, Davis supported a Confederate march into Maryland. But in the brutal battle of Antietam on September 17, 1862, McClellan's army checked Lee's advance. Lee retreated to Virginia, inflicting terrible losses on Northern troops at Fredericksburg when they again made a thrust toward Richmond in December 1862. The war in northern Virginia was stalemated (see Map 16.2).

SHILOH AND THE WAR FOR THE MISSISSIPPI

Although most public attention was focused on the fighting in Virginia, battles in Tennessee and along the Mississippi River proved to be the key to eventual Union victory. The rising military figure in the West was Ulysses S. Grant. In February 1862, Grant captured Fort Henry and Fort Donelson, on the Tennessee and Cumberland Rivers, establishing Union control of much of Tennessee and forcing Confederate troops to retreat into northern Mississippi.

Moving south, Grant met a Confederate force commanded by General Albert Sidney Johnston at Shiloh Church in April 1862. Seriously outnumbered on the first day, Grant's forces were reinforced by the arrival of troops under the command of General Don Carlos Buell. After two days of bitter and bloody fighting in the rain, the Confederates withdrew. The losses on both sides were enormous: the North lost 13,000 men, the South 11,000, including General Johnston, who bled to death. Nevertheless, Union forces kept moving, capturing Memphis in June and beginning a campaign to eventually capture Vicksburg, "the Gibraltar of the Mississippi." Earlier that year, naval forces under Admiral David Farragut had captured New Orleans and by the end of 1862, it was clearly only a matter of time before the entire Mississippi River would be in Union hands. Arkansas, Louisiana, and Texas would then be cut off from the rest of the Confederacy (see Map 16.3).

THE WAR IN THE TRANS–MISSISSIPPI WEST

Although only one western state, Texas, seceded from the Union, the Civil War was fought in small ways in many parts of the West. The just-announced discovery of gold in Colorado impelled the Confederacy to attempt to capture it. Texans mounted an attack on New Mexico, which they had long coveted, and kept their eyes on the larger prizes of Arizona and California. A Confederate force led by General Henry H. Sibley occupied Santa Fé and Albuquerque early in 1862 without resistance, thus posing a serious threat to the entire Southwest. Confederate hopes were dashed, however, by a group of 950 miners and adventurers organized into the first Colorado Volunteer Infantry Regiment. After an epic march of 400 miles from Denver, the Colorado militia stopped the unsuspecting Confederate troops in the Battle of Glorieta Pass on March 26–28, 1862. This dashing action, coupled with the efforts of California militias to safeguard

Arizona and Utah from seizure by Confederate sympathizers, secured the Far West for the Union.

Other military action in the West was less decisive. The chronic fighting along the Kansas–Missouri border was brutal and included attacks on civilians. Another civil war took place in Indian Territory, south of Kansas. The southern Indian tribes who had been removed there from the Old Southwest in the 1830s included many who were still bitter over the horrors of their removal by federal troops, and they sympathized with the Confederacy. The Confederacy actively sought Indian support by offering Indian people representation in the Confederate Congress. Consequently, many Indians fought for the South. Union victories at Pea Ridge (in northwestern Arkansas) in 1862 and near Fort Gibson (in Indian Territory) in 1863 secured the area for the Union. After the Civil War, the victorious federal government used the tribes' wartime support for the Confederacy as a justification for demanding further land cessions.

Elsewhere in the West, other groups of Indians found themselves caught up in the wider war. An uprising by the Santee Sioux in Minnesota occurred in August 1862. Alarmed whites, certain that the uprising was a Confederate plot, ignored legitimate Sioux grievances and responded in kind to Sioux ferocity. In little more than a month, 500 to 800 white settlers and an even greater number of Sioux were killed. Thirty-eight Indians were hanged in a mass execution in Mankato on December 26, 1862, and subsequently all Sioux were expelled from Minnesota. In 1863, U.S. Army Colonel Kit Carson invaded Navajo country in Arizona in retaliation for Indian raids on U.S. troops. Eight thousand Navajos were forced on the brutal "Long Walk" to Bosque Redondo on the Pecos River in New Mexico, where they were held prisoner until 1868.

The hostilities in the West showed that no part of the country, and none of its inhabitants, could remain untouched by the Civil War.

THE NAVAL WAR

The Union's naval blockade of the South, intended to cut off commerce between the Confederacy and the rest of the world, was initially unsuccessful. Southern blockade runners evaded Union ships with ease: only an estimated one-eighth of all Confederate shipping was stopped in 1862. Beginning in 1863, however, as the Union navy became larger, the blockade began to take effect. In 1864, a third of the blockade runners were captured, and in 1865, half of them. As a result, fewer and fewer supplies reached the South.

For the Union, the most successful naval operation in the first two years of the war was not the blockade but the seizing of exposed coastal areas. The Sea Islands of South Carolina were taken, as were some of the North Carolina islands and Fort Pulaski, which commanded the harbor of Savannah, Georgia. Most damaging to the South was the capture of New Orleans.

THE BLACK RESPONSE

The capture of Port Royal in the South Carolina Sea Islands in 1861 was important for another reason. Whites fled at the Union advance, but 10,000 slaves greeted the troops with jubilation. Union troops had unwittingly freed these slaves in advance of any official Union policy on the status of slaves in captured territory.

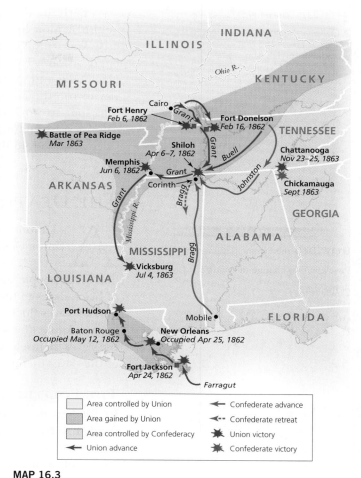

MAP 16.3

Major Battles in the Interior, 1862–63   Ulysses S. Grant waged a mobile war, winning at Fort Henry and Fort Donelson in Tennessee in February 1862, at Shiloh in April, and capturing Memphis in June. He then laid siege to Vicksburg, as Admiral David Farragut captured New Orleans and began to advance up the Mississippi River.

WHAT ROLE did Indians Play in the Fighting in the West?

•••⌐Read the Document

A Civil War Nurse Writes of Conditions of Freed Slaves (1864) at
www.myhistorylab.com

Early in the war, an irate Southerner who saw three of his slaves disappear behind Union lines at Fortress Monroe, Virginia, demanded the return of his property. The Union commander, refused, declaring that the escaped slaves were "contraband of war." Two days later, eight runaway slaves appeared; the next day, fifty-nine black men and women arrived at the fort. Union commanders had found an effective way to rob the South of its basic workforce. The "contrabands," as they were known, were put to work building fortifications and doing other useful work in Northern camps. Washington, DC, became a refuge for contraband blacks, who crowded into the capital to join the free black people who lived there.

THE DEATH OF SLAVERY

HOW DID the Emancipation Proclamation change the nature of the war?

As Union troops drove deeper into the South, the black response grew. When Union General William Tecumseh Sherman marched his army through Georgia in 1864, 18,000 slaves flocked to the Union lines. By the war's end, nearly a million black people had "voted with their feet" for the Union. The overwhelming response of black slaves to the Union advance changed the nature of the war. As increasing numbers of slaves flocked to Union lines, the conclusion that the South refused to face was unmistakable: the southern war to defend the slave system did not have the support of the slaves themselves. Any Northern policy that ignored the issue of slavery and the wishes of the slaves themselves was unrealistic.

THE POLITICS OF EMANCIPATION

In 1862, as the issue of slavery loomed ever larger, Abraham Lincoln, acutely aware of divided Northern opinion, inched his way toward a declaration of emancipation. Lincoln was correct to be worried about opinion in the North. Before the war, within the Republican Party, only a small group of abolitionists had favored freeing the slaves. Most Republicans were more concerned about the expansion of slavery than they were about the lives of slaves themselves. For their part, most Northern Democrats were openly antiblack. There was also the question of what would become of slaves who were freed. Northern Democrats effectively played on racial fears in the 1862 congressional elections, warning that freed slaves would pour into northern cities and take jobs from white laborers.

•••⌐Read the Document

Abraham Lincoln to Horace Greeley (1862) at **www.myhistorylab.com**

((•━⌐Hear the Audio

Free at Last at **www.myhistorylab.com**

Nevertheless, the necessities of war demanded that Lincoln adopt a policy to end slavery. Following the Union victory at Antietam in September 1862, Lincoln issued a preliminary decree: unless the rebellious states returned to the Union by January 1, 1863, he would declare their slaves "forever free." Thus, the freedom of black people became part of the struggle. Frederick Douglass, the voice of black America, wrote, "We shout for joy that we live to record this righteous decree."

On January 1, 1863, Lincoln duly issued the final **Emancipation Proclamation**, which turned out to be less than sweeping. The proclamation freed the slaves in the areas of rebellion—the areas the Union did not control—but specifically exempted slaves in the border states and in former Confederate areas conquered by the Union. Lincoln's purpose was to meet the abolitionist demand for a war against slavery while not losing the support of conservatives, especially in the border states.

QUICK REVIEW

The Emancipation Proclamation

◆ Freed slaves in the areas of rebellion, but not in areas under Union control.

◆ An attempt to satisfy both abolitionists and conservatives.

◆ Proclamation met with mixed response in the North.

Nonetheless, one group greeted the Emancipation Proclamation with open celebration. On New Year's Day, hundreds of African Americans gathered outside the White House and cheered the president. Free African Americans predicted that the news would encourage Southern slaves either to flee to Union lines or refuse to work for their masters. Both of these things were already happening as African Americans seized on wartime changes to reshape white–black relations in the South. In one sense, then, the Emancipation Proclamation simply gave a name to a process already in motion.

Emancipation Proclamation   Decree announced by President Abraham Lincoln in September 1862 and formally issued on January 1, 1863, freeing slaves in all Confederate states still in rebellion.

Abolitionists set about moving Lincoln beyond his careful stance in the Emancipation Proclamation. Reformers such as Elizabeth Cady Stanton and Susan B. Anthony lobbied and petitioned for a constitutional amendment outlawing slavery. Congress, at Lincoln's urging, approved and sent to the states a statement banning slavery throughout the United States. Quickly ratified by the Union states in 1865, the statement became the **Thirteenth Amendment** to the Constitution. Lincoln's firm support for this amendment is a good indicator of his true feelings about slavery.

BLACK FIGHTING MEN

As part of the Emancipation Proclamation, Lincoln gave his support for the first time to the recruitment of black soldiers. Early in the war, eager black volunteers had been turned away. Many, like Robert Fitzgerald, a free African American from Pennsylvania, found other ways to serve the Union cause. Fitzgerald first drove a wagon and mule for the Quartermaster Corps, and later served in the Union navy. After the Emancipation Proclamation, Fitzgerald enlisted in the Fifth Massachusetts Cavalry, a regiment that, like all the units in which black soldiers served, was 100 percent African American but commanded by white officers (see Seeing History).

In Fitzgerald's company of eighty-three men, half came from slave states and had run away to enlist; the other half came mostly from the North but also from Canada, the West Indies, and France. Other regiments had volunteers from Africa. The proportion of volunteers from the loyal border states (where slavery was still legal) was upwards of 25 percent—a lethal blow to the slave system in those states. Black volunteers, eager and willing to fight, made up 10 percent of the Union army. Nearly 200,000 African Americans (one out of every five black males in the nation) served in the Union army or navy. A fifth of them—37,000—died defending their own freedom and the Union.

This dramatic illustration shows the text of the Emancipation Proclamation and Abraham Lincoln, flanked by the allegorical figures of Justice and Liberty. The glorification of Lincoln as "The Great Emancipator" has obscured the record of his cautious actions before January 1, 1863.

Military service was something no black man could take lightly. African American soldiers faced prejudice within the army and had to prove themselves in battle. Moreover, the Confederates hated and feared African American troops and threatened to treat any captured black soldier as an escaped slave subject to execution. On at least one occasion, the threats were carried out. In 1864, Confederate soldiers massacred 262 black soldiers at Fort Pillow, Tennessee, after they had surrendered.

Another extraordinary part of the story of the African American soldiers was their reception by black people in the South, who were overjoyed at the sight of black Union soldiers, many of them former slaves themselves. As his regiment entered Wilmington, North Carolina, one soldier wrote, "Men and women, old and young, were running throughout the streets, shouting and praising God. We could then truly see what we have been fighting for."

African American soldiers were not treated equally by the Union army. They were segregated in camp, given the worst jobs, and paid less than white soldiers. Although they might not be able to do much about the other kinds of discrimination, the men of the Fifty-fourth Massachusetts found an unusual way to protest their unequal pay: they refused to accept it, preferring to serve the army for free until it decided to treat them as

QUICK REVIEW

African American Soldiers

- Lincoln supported recruitment of black soldiers as part of the Emancipation Proclamation.
- Nearly 200,000 African Americans served in the Union army.
- 37,000 African Americans died defending their freedom and the Union.

Thirteenth Amendment
Constitutional amendment ratified in 1865 that freed all slaves throughout the United States.

Come and Join Us Brothers

This is a recruitment poster for the Massachusetts 54th Infantry regiment, one of the first official black regiments in the U.S. Army. Organized in March 1863, the 600-man unit led the charge against Fort Wagner, South Carolina, in July, resulting in 116 deaths, including that of the white commanding officer, Colonel Robert Gould Shaw, and many casualties. The bravery of the recruits at Fort Wagner and in other battles changed the minds of many Union officers, who had previously disparaged the fighting abilities of African Americans.

FREDERICK DOUGLASS said, "Once let the black man get upon his person the brass letters, U.S., let him get an eagle on his button and a musket on his shoulder and bullets in his pocket," Douglass continued, and "there is no power on earth that can deny that he has earned the right to citizenship." Was Douglass right?

A general belief in African American inferiority was rampant in the North, but the army service of black men made a dent in white racism. Massachusetts enacted the first law forbidding discrimination against African Americans in public facilities. Some major cities, among them San Francisco, Cincinnati, Cleveland, and New York, desegregated their streetcars. Some states—Ohio, California, Illinois—repealed statutes that had barred black people from testifying in court or serving on juries. ∎

COME AND JOIN US BROTHERS.

PUBLISHED BY THE SUPERVISORY COMMITTEE FOR RECRUITING COLORED REGIMENTS
1210 CHESTNUT ST. PHILADELPHIA.

E. Sachse and Company, "The Shackle Broken by the Genius of Freedom," Baltimore, Md.; 1874, Chicago Historical Society.

free men. The protest was effective; in June 1864, the War Department equalized the wages of black and white soldiers.

THE FRONT LINES AND THE HOME FRONT

Civil War soldiers wrote millions of letters home, more proportionally than in any American war. Their letters and the ones they received in return were links between the front lines and the home front, between the soldiers and their home communities. They are a testament to the patriotism of both Union and Confederate troops, for the story they tell is frequently one of slaughter and horror.

THE TOLL OF WAR

Civil War battles were appallingly deadly (see Figure 16.2). One reason was technology: improved weapons, particularly modern rifles, had much greater range and accuracy than the smooth-bore muskets they replaced. As Ulysses Grant observed, "At a distance of a few hundred yards, a man could fire at you all day [with a musket] without your finding out."

Civil War generals, however, were slow to adjust to this new reality. Almost all Union and Confederate generals remained committed to the conventional military doctrine of massed infantry offensives that they had learned in their military classes at West Point. Part of this strategy had been to "soften up" a defensive line with artillery before an infantry assault, but now the range of the new rifles made artillery itself vulnerable to attack. As a result, generals relied less on "softening up" than on immense numbers of infantrymen, hoping that enough of them would survive the withering rifle fire to overwhelm the enemy line.

Medical ignorance was another factor in the casualty rate. Because the use of antiseptic procedures was in its infancy, men often died because minor wounds became infected. Disease was an even more frequent killer, taking twice as many men as were lost in battle. The overcrowded and unsanitary conditions of many camps were breeding grounds for smallpox, dysentery, typhoid, pneumonia, and, in the summer, malaria.

Both North and South were completely unprepared to handle the supply and health needs of their large armies. Twenty-four hours after the battle of Shiloh, most of the wounded still lay on the field in the rain. Many died of exposure; some, unable to help themselves, drowned. There was no overall system for recording the war dead, or for their burial. Relatives were often forced to travel to battlefields to search, frequently in vain, for the bodies of their loved ones. Nor were the combatants prepared to deal with masses of war prisoners, as the shocking example of the Confederate prison camp at Andersonville in northern Georgia

•◦•─[Read the **Document**

An African American Soldier Writes to the President Appealing for Equality in 1863 at **www.myhistorylab.com**

WHAT IMPACT did the war have on the political, economic, and social life of the North and the South?

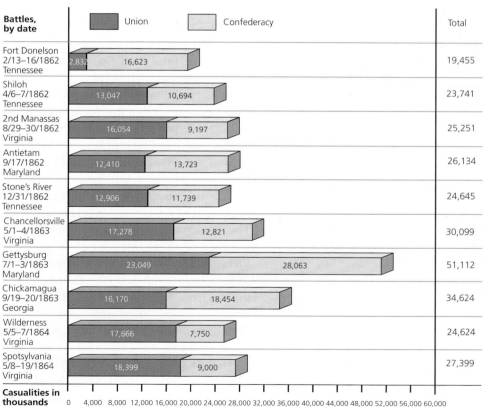

Figure 16.2 The Casualties Mount Up

This chart of the ten costliest battles of the Civil War shows the relentless toll of casualties (killed, wounded, missing, captured) on both the Union and Confederate sides.

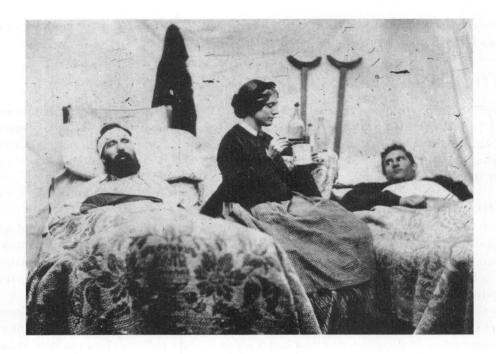

Read the **Document**

Clara Barton, Memoirs about Medical Life at the Battlefield (1862) at
www.myhistorylab.com

demonstrated. Andersonville was an open stockade with no shade or shelter, erected early in 1864 to hold 10,000 Northern prisoners. But by midsummer, it held 33,000. During the worst weeks of that summer, 100 prisoners died of disease, exposure, or malnutrition each day.

ARMY NURSES

Under the pressure of wartime necessity, and over the objections of most army doctors—who resented the challenge to their authority from people no different than their daughters or wives—women became army nurses. Hospital nursing, previously considered a job only disreputable women would undertake, now became a suitable vocation for middle-class women. Under the leadership of veteran reformer Dorothea Dix of the asylum movement, and in cooperation with the Sanitary Commission (and with the vocal support of Mother Bickerdyke), by the war's end more than 3,000 Northern women had worked as paid army nurses and many more as volunteers. Although women had made important advances, most army nurses and medical support staff were men.

Southern women were also active in nursing and otherwise aiding soldiers, though the South never boasted a single large-scale organization like the Sanitary Commission. The women of Richmond volunteered when they found the war on their doorstep in the summer of 1862. During the Seven Days Battles, thousands of wounded poured into Richmond; many died in the streets, because there was no room for them in hospitals. Richmond women first established informal "roadside hospitals" to meet the need, and their activities expanded from there. As in the North, middle-class women at first faced strong resistance from army doctors and even their own families, who believed that a field hospital was "no place for a refined lady."

THE LIFE OF THE COMMON SOLDIER

The conditions experienced by the eager young volunteers of the Union and Confederate armies included massive, terrifying, and bloody battles, apparently unending, with no sign of victory in sight. Soldiers suffered from the uncertainty of supply, which left troops, especially in the South, without uniforms, tents, and sometimes even food. They endured long marches over muddy, rutted roads while carrying packs weighing fifty or sixty pounds. Disease was rampant in their dirty, verminous, and unsanitary camps. Hospitals were so dreadful that more men left them dead than alive. As a result, desertion was common: an estimated one of every nine Confederate soldiers and one of every seven Union soldiers deserted.

WARTIME POLITICS

In the earliest days of the war, Northerners had joined together in support of the war effort. Democrat Stephen A. Douglas, Lincoln's defeated rival, paid a visit to the White House to offer Lincoln his support, then traveled home to Illinois, where he addressed a huge rally of Democrats in Chicago: "There can be no neutrals in this war, only patriots—or traitors!" By 1862, Democrats had split into two factions: the War Democrats and the Peace Democrats, derogatorily called "**Copperheads**" (from the poisonous snake).

Despite the split in the party in 1860 and the secession of the South, the Democratic Party remained a powerful force in Northern politics. Its united opposition to the emancipation of slaves explains much of Lincoln's equivocal action on this issue. But the Peace Democrats went far beyond opposition to emancipation, denouncing the draft, martial law, and the high-handed actions of "King Abraham."

The leader of the Copperheads, Clement Vallandigham, a former Ohio congressman, advocated an armistice and a negotiated peace that would "look only to the welfare, peace and safety of the white race, without reference to the effect that settlement may have on the African." Western Democrats, he threatened, might form their own union with the South. Indeed, in the fall and winter of 1862–63 rumors swirled that the Northwest was ready to secede. Lincoln could not afford to take these threats and rumors lightly.

In 1862, Lincoln proclaimed that all people who discouraged enlistments in the army or otherwise engaged in disloyal practices would be subject to martial law. More than 13,000 people, most of them deserters and war profiteers, were arrested, tried in military courts, and imprisoned. One of them was Vallandigham himself, who courted arrest but was denied the chance of martyrdom when Lincoln exiled him to the Confederacy rather than to jail.

Lincoln also faced challenges from the radical faction of his own party. As the war continued, the Radicals gained strength: it was they who pushed for emancipation in the early days of the war and for harsh treatment of the defeated South after it ended. The most troublesome Radical was Salmon P. Chase, who in December 1862 caused a cabinet crisis when he encouraged Senate Republicans to complain that Secretary of State William Seward was "lukewarm" in his support for emancipation.

ECONOMIC AND SOCIAL STRAINS ON THE NORTH

Wartime needs caused a surge in Northern economic growth, but the gains were unequally distributed. Early in the war, some industries suffered: textile manufacturers could not get cotton, and shoe factories that had made cheap shoes for slaves were without a market. But other industries boomed—boot making, shipbuilding, and the manufacture of woolen goods such as blankets and uniforms, to give just three examples. Coal mining expanded, as did ironmaking. Agricultural goods were in great demand, promoting further mechanization of farming.

Meeting wartime needs enriched some people honestly, but speculators and profiteers also flourished, as they have in every war. By the end of the war, government contracts had exceeded $1 billion. Not all of this business was free from corruption. New wealth was evident in every northern city.

For most people, however, the war brought the day-to-day hardship of inflation. During the four years of the war, the North suffered an inflation rate of 80 percent, or nearly 15 percent a year. This annual rate, three times what is generally considered tolerable, did much to inflame social tensions. Wages rose only half as much as prices, and

Copperheads   A term Republicans applied to Northern war dissenters and those suspected of aiding the Confederate cause during the Civil War.

workers responded by joining unions and striking. Manufacturers hired strikebreakers (many of whom were African Americans, women, or immigrants) and formed organizations of their own to prevent further unionization and to blacklist union organizers. The formation of large-scale organizations, fostered by wartime demand, laid the groundwork for the national battle between workers and manufacturers that would dominate the last part of the nineteenth century.

Another major source of social tension was conscription. The Union introduced a draft in March 1863. Especially unpopular was a provision in the draft law that allowed the hiring of substitutes or the payment of a commutation fee of $300. Substitution had been accepted in all previous European and American wars. It was so common that President Lincoln, though overage, tried to set an example by paying for a substitute himself. The Democratic Party, however, made substitution an inflammatory issue. Pointing out that $300 was almost a year's wages for an unskilled laborer, they appealed to popular resentment by calling the draft law "aristocratic legislation" and to fear, by running headlines such as "Three Hundred Dollars or Your Life."

As practiced in the local communities, conscription was indeed often marred by favoritism and prejudice. Local officials called up many more poor than rich men and selected a higher proportion of immigrants than nonimmigrants. In reality, however, only 7 percent of all men called to serve actually did so. Nevertheless, by 1863, many Northern urban workers believed that the slogan "a rich man's war but a poor man's fight," though coined in the South, applied to them as well.

THE NEW YORK CITY DRAFT RIOTS

In the spring of 1863, there were protests against the draft throughout the North. Riots and disturbances broke out in many cities, and several federal enrollment officers were killed. The greatest trouble occurred in New York City between July 13 and July 16, 1863, where a wave of working-class looting, fighting, and lynching claimed the lives of 105 people, many of them African American.

The riots had several causes. Anger at the draft and racial prejudice were what most contemporaries saw. From a historical perspective, however, the riots were at least as much about the urban growth and tensions described in Chapter 13. The Civil War made urban problems worse and heightened the visible contrast between the lives of the rich and those of the poor. These tensions exploded in the summer of 1863.

Ironically, African American men, a favorite target of the rioters' anger, were a major force in easing the national crisis over the draft. Though they had been barred from service until 1863, in the later stages of the war African American volunteers filled much of the manpower gap that the controversial draft was meant to address.

THE FAILURE OF SOUTHERN NATIONALISM

The war brought even greater changes to the South. As in the North, war needs led to expansion and centralization of government control over the economy. The expansion of government brought sudden urbanization, a new experience for the predominantly rural South. Because of the need for military manpower, a good part of the Confederate bureaucracy consisted of women, who were referred to as "government girls." All

A black man is lynched during the New York City Draft Riots in July 1863. Free black people and their institutions were major victims of the worst rioting in American history until then. The riots were more than a protest against the draft; they were also an outburst of frustration over urban problems that had been festering for decades.

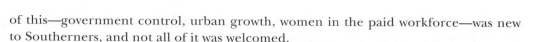

of this—government control, urban growth, women in the paid workforce—was new to Southerners, and not all of it was welcomed.

Even more than in the North, the voracious need for soldiers fostered class antagonisms. When small yeoman farmers went off to war, their wives and families struggled to farm on their own, without the help of mechanization, which they could not afford, and without the help of slaves, which they had never owned. But wealthy men could be exempted from the draft if they had more than twenty slaves. Furthermore, many upper-class Southerners—at least 50,000—avoided military service by paying liberally for substitutes. Worst of all was the starvation. The North's blockade and the breakdown of the South's transportation system restricted the availability of food in the South, and these problems were vastly magnified by runaway inflation. Speculation and hoarding by the rich made matters even worse. In the spring of 1863, food riots broke out in four Georgia cities (Atlanta among them) and in North Carolina.

Increasingly, the ordinary people of the South, preoccupied with staying alive, refused to pay taxes, to provide food, or to serve in the army. Soldiers were drawn home by the desperation of their families as well as by the discouraging course of the war. By January 1865, the desertion rate had climbed to 8 percent a month.

At the same time, the life of the Southern ruling class was irrevocably altered by the changing nature of slavery. By the end of the war, one-quarter of all slaves had fled to the Union lines, and those who remained often stood in a different relationship to their owners. As white masters and overseers left to join the army, white women were left behind on the plantation to cope with shortages, grow crops, and manage the labor of slaves. Slaves increasingly made their own decisions about when and how they would work, and they refused to accept the punishments that would have accompanied this insubordination in prewar years. One black woman, implored by her mistress not to reveal the location of a trunk of money and silver plate when the invading Yankees arrived, looked her in the eye and said, "Mistress, I can't lie over that; you bought that silver plate when you sold my three children."

Peace movements in the South were motivated by a confused mixture of realism, war weariness, and the animosity of those who supported states' rights and opposed Jefferson Davis. Peace sentiment was especially strong in North Carolina, where more than a hundred public meetings in support of negotiations were held in the summer of 1863. Davis would have none of it, and he commanded enough votes in the Confederate Congress to enforce his will and to suggest that peace sentiment was traitorous.

THE TIDE TURNS

As Lincoln's timing of the Emancipation Proclamation showed, by 1863 the nature of the war was changing. The proclamation freeing the slaves struck directly at the Southern home front and the civilian workforce. That same year, the nature of the battlefield war changed as well. The Civil War became the first total war.

HOW DID Grant and Sherman turn the tide of the war?

THE TURNING POINT OF 1863

For the Union army, 1863 opened with stalemate in the East and slow and costly progress in the West. For the South, 1863 represented its highest hopes for military success and for diplomatic recognition by Britain or France.

Attempting to break the stalemate in northern Virginia, General Joseph Hooker and a Union army of 130,000 men attacked a Confederate army half that size at Chancellorsville in May. In response, Robert E. Lee daringly divided his forces, sending General Thomas "Stonewall" Jackson and 30,000 men on a day-long flanking movement

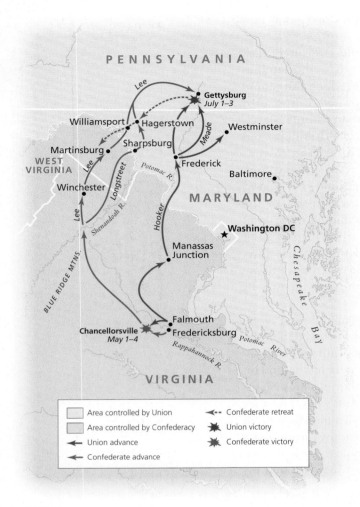

MAP 16.4

The Turning Point, 1863 In June, Lee boldly struck north into Maryland and Pennsylvania, hoping for a victory that would cause Britain and France to demand a negotiated peace on Confederate terms. Instead, he lost the hard-fought battle of Gettysburg, July 1–3. The very next day, Grant's long siege of Vicksburg succeeded. These two great Fourth of July victories turned the tide in favor of the Union. The Confederates never again mounted a major offensive. Total Union control of the Mississippi now exposed the Lower South to attack.

WHAT WAS Lee hoping to achieve with his campaign northward and why was his defeat at Gettysburg the war's turning point?

⊙ See the **Map**

The Civil War, Part II: 1863–1865 at **www.myhistorylab.com**

•:•• Read the **Document**

John Dooley, Passages from His Journal (1863) at **www.myhistorylab.com**

that caught the Union troops by surprise. Chancellorsville was a great Confederate victory. However, Confederate losses were also great: 13,000 men, representing more than 20 percent of Lee's army.

Though weakened, Lee moved north into Maryland and Pennsylvania. His purpose was as much political as military: he hoped that a great Confederate victory would lead Britain and France to intervene in the war and demand a negotiated peace. The ensuing Battle of Gettysburg, July 1–3, 1863, was another horrible slaughter. When the battle was over, Lee retreated from the field, leaving more than one-third of his army behind— 28,000 men killed, wounded, or missing. Lee's great gamble had failed; he never again mounted a major offensive (see Map 16.4).

The next day, July 4, 1863, Ulysses S. Grant took Vicksburg, Mississippi, after a costly siege. The combined news of Gettysburg and Vicksburg dissuaded Britain and France from recognizing the Confederacy and checked the Northern peace movement. It also tightened the North's grip on the South, for the Union now controlled the entire Mississippi River. In November, Generals Grant and Sherman broke the Confederate hold on Chattanooga, Tennessee, thereby opening the way to Atlanta.

GRANT AND SHERMAN

In March 1864, President Lincoln called Grant east and appointed him general-in-chief of all the Union forces. Lincoln's critics were appalled. Grant was an uncouth Westerner (like the president) and (unlike the president) was rumored to have a drinking problem. Lincoln replied that if he knew the general's brand of whiskey, he would send a barrel of it to every commander in the Union army.

Grant devised a plan of strangulation and annihilation. While he took on Lee in northern Virginia, he sent General William Tecumseh Sherman to defeat the Confederate Army of Tennessee, which was defending the approach to Atlanta. Both Grant and Sherman exemplified the new kind of warfare. They aimed to inflict maximum damage on the fabric of Southern life, hoping that the South would choose to surrender rather than face total destruction. This decision to broaden the war so that it directly affected civilians was new in American military history and prefigured the total wars of the twentieth century.

The most famous example of the new strategy of total war was General Sherman's 1864 march through Georgia. Sherman captured Atlanta on September 2, 1864. In November, Sherman set out to march the 285 miles to the coastal city of Savannah, living off the land and destroying everything in his path. His military purpose was to cut off Mississippi, Alabama, and Georgia from the rest of the Confederacy. But his second purpose, openly stated, was to "make war so terrible" to the people of the South, to "make them so sick of war that generations would pass away before they would again appeal to it."

Terrifying to white Southern civilians, Sherman was initially hostile to black Southerners as well. In the interests of speed and efficiency, his army turned away many of the 18,000 slaves who flocked to it in Georgia, causing a number to be recaptured and reenslaved. This callous action caused such a scandal in Washington that Secretary of War Edwin Stanton arranged a special meeting in Georgia with Sherman and twenty African American ministers who spoke for the freed slaves. The result was Sherman's Special Field Order 15, issued in January 1865. He set aside more than 400,000 acres of Confederate land to be given to the freed slaves in forty-acre parcels. This was war of a kind that white Southerners had never imagined.

THE 1864 ELECTION

The war complicated the 1864 presidential election. Lincoln was renominated during a period when the war was going badly. Opposed by the Radicals, who thought he was too conciliatory toward the South, and by Republican conservatives, who disapproved of the Emancipation Proclamation, Lincoln had little support within his own party.

This striking photograph by Thomas C. Roche shows a dead Confederate soldier, killed at Petersburg on April 3, 1865, only six days before the surrender at Appomattox. The new medium of photography conveyed the horror of the war with a gruesome reality to the American public.

In contrast, the Democrats had an appealing candidate: General George McClellan, a war hero who was known to be sympathetic to the South. Democrats played shamelessly on the racist fears of the urban working class, accusing Republicans of being "negro-lovers" and warning that racial mixing lay ahead.

A deeply depressed Lincoln fully expected to lose the election. Lincoln's political fortunes changed, however, when Sherman captured Atlanta on September 2. Jubilation swept the North and Lincoln won the election with 55 percent of the popular vote. The election was important evidence of Northern support for Lincoln's policy of unconditional surrender for the South. There would be no negotiated peace; the war would continue.

NEARING THE END

As Sherman devastated the lower South, Grant was locked in struggle with Lee in northern Virginia. Grant eventually hammered Lee into submission but at enormous cost. Lee had learned the art of defensive warfare, and he inflicted heavy losses on the Union army in a succession of bloody encounters in the spring and summer of 1864: almost 18,000 at the battle of the Wilderness, more than 8,000 at Spotsylvania, and 12,000 at Cold Harbor.

Despite these losses, rather than pulling back after his failed assaults, Grant kept moving south, finally settling in for a prolonged siege of Lee's forces at Petersburg. The North's great advantage in population finally began to tell. There were more Union soldiers to replace those lost in battle, but there were no more white Confederates (see Map 16.5).

In desperation, the South turned to what had hitherto been unthinkable: arming slaves to serve as soldiers in the Confederate army. But—and this was the bitter irony—the African American soldiers and their families would have to be promised freedom or they would desert to the Union at the first chance they had. Even though Davis's proposal had the support of General Robert E. Lee, the Confederate Congress balked at first. Finally, on March 13, the Confederate Congress authorized a draft of black soldiers—without mentioning freedom. Although two regiments of African American soldiers were immediately organized in Richmond, it was too late.

By the spring of 1865, public support for the war simply disintegrated in the South. Starvation, inflation, dissension, and the prospect of military defeat were too much. In

QUICK REVIEW

Grant's Strategy

- Better coordination of Union effort and the application of steady pressure.
- The waging of nonstop warfare.
- Grant's plan worked in the long run, but at a high cost.

Read the **Document**

William T. Sherman, The March through Georgia (1875) at **www.myhistorylab.com**

Hear the **Audio**

When This Cruel War Is Over at **www.myhistorylab.com**

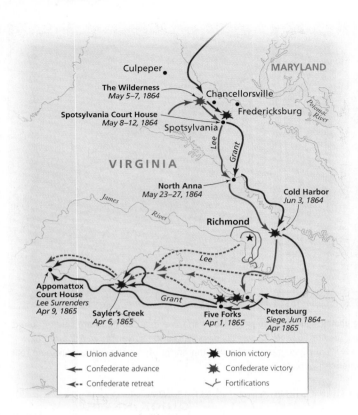

MAP 16.5

The Final Battles in Virginia, 1864–65   In the war's final phase early in 1865, Sherman closed one arm of a pincers by marching north from Savannah, while Grant attacked Lee's last defensive positions in Petersburg and Richmond. Lee retreated from them on April 2 and surrendered at Appomattox Court House on April 9, 1865.

WHAT DESPERATE measures did the South resort to as the war came to an end?

Watch the Video

The Meaning of the Civil War for Americans at **www.myhistorylab.com**

February, Jefferson Davis sent his vice president, Alexander Stephens, to negotiate terms at a peace conference at Hampton Roads. Lincoln would not countenance anything less than full surrender, although he did offer gradual emancipation with compensation for slave owners. Davis, however, insisted on Southern independence at all costs. Consequently, the Hampton Roads conference failed and Southern resistance faded away.

APPOMATTOX

In the spring of 1865, Lee and his remaining troops, still held Petersburg and Richmond. Starving, short of ammunition, and losing men in battle or to desertion every day, Lee retreated from Petersburg on April 2. The Confederate government fled Richmond, stripping and burning the city. Seven days later, Lee and his 25,000 troops surrendered to Grant at Appomattox Court House. Grant treated Lee with great respect and set a historic precedent by giving the Confederate troops parole. This meant they could not subsequently be prosecuted for treason. Grant then sent the starving army on its way with three days' rations for every man. Jefferson Davis, who had hoped to set up a new government in Texas, was captured in Georgia on May 10. The war was finally over.

DEATH OF A PRESIDENT

Lincoln had only the briefest time to savor the victory. On the night of April 14, President and Mrs. Lincoln went to Ford's Theater in Washington. There Lincoln was shot at point-blank range by John Wilkes Booth, a Confederate sympathizer. He died the next day. After a week of observances in Washington, Lincoln's coffin was loaded on a funeral train that slowly carried him back to Springfield. All along the railroad route, day and night, in small towns and large, people gathered to see the train pass and to pay

The 55th Massachusetts Colored Regiment is shown entering Charleston, February 21, 1865, greeted by happy crowds of African Americans. For white Charlestonians, the sight of victorious black troops in the cockpit of the Confederacy was devastating.

PEARSON **myhistorylab** Connections

Reinforce what you learned in this chapter by studying the many documents,
images, maps, review tools, and videos available at www.myhistorylab.com.

Read and Review

✓●⎯ **Study** and **Review** Chapter 16

⠿●⎯ **Read** the **Document**

U.S. Sanitary Commission, Sketch of Its Purposes (1864)

Homestead Act of 1862

Elizabeth Keckley, Four Years in the White House (1868)

Abraham Lincoln to Horace Greeley (1862)

Clara Barton, Memoirs about Medical Life at the Battlefield (1862)

An African American Soldier Writes to the President Appealing for Equality in 1863

A Civil War Nurse Writes of Conditions of Freed Slaves (1864)

The New York Times Prints Opinion on the New York Draft Riots in 1863

John Dooley, Passages from His Journal (1863)

William T. Sherman, The March through Georgia (1875)

👁⎯ **See** the **Map**

The Civil War, Part I: 1861–1862

The Civil War, Part II: 1863–1865

Research and Explore

⠿●⎯ **Read** the **Document**

A Nation Divided: The Civil War

Exploring America: Fort Pillow Massacre

Profiles
  Judah Benjamin
  Louisa Schuyler

((●⎯ **Hear** the **Audio**

Free at Last

When This Cruel War Is Over

🎦⎯ **Watch** the **Video**

The Civil War

What Caused the Civil War?

The Meaning of the Civil War for Americans

((●⎯ **Hear** the **Audio**

Hear the audio files for Chapter 16 at
www.myhistorylab.com.

The war passed from words to stones which the white children began to hurl at the colored. Several colored children were hurt and, as they had not resented the rock throwing . . . , the white children became more aggressive and abusive.

— T. Thomas Fortune, *from* Norfolk Journal and Guide, *1866*

Theodor Kaufmann (1814–1896), *On to Liberty*, 1867. Oil on canvas, 36 × 56 in (91.4 × 142.2 cm). Runaway slaves escaping through the woods. Art Resource/Metropolitan Museum of Art.

CHRONOLOGY

1861 March: Morrill Tariff Act

April: Fort Sumter falls; war begins

April: Mobilization begins

April–May: Virginia, Arkansas, Tennessee, and North Carolina secede

June: United States Sanitary Commission established

July: First Battle of Bull Run

December: French troops arrive in Mexico, followed by British and Spanish forces in January

1862 February: Legal Tender Act

February: Battles of Fort Henry and Fort Donelson

March: Battle of Pea Ridge

March: Battle of the *Monitor* and the *Merrimack* (renamed the *Virginia*)

March–August: George B. McClellan's Peninsular campaign

March: Battle of Glorieta Pass

April: Battle of Shiloh

April: Confederate Conscription Act

April: David Farragut captures New Orleans

May: *El Cinqo de Mayo*: Mexican troops repel French invaders

May: Homestead Act

June–July: Seven Days Battles

July: Pacific Railway Act

July: Morrill Land Grant Act

August: Santee Sioux Uprising, Minnesota

September: Battle of Antietam

December: Battle of Fredericksburg

1863 January: Emancipation Proclamation

February: National Bank Act

March: Draft introduced in the North

March: Colonel Kit Carson sends 8,000 Navajos on the "Long Walk" to Bosque Redondo, New Mexico Territory

April: Richmond bread riot

May: Battle of Chancellorsville

June: French occupy Mexico City

July: Battle of Gettysburg

July: Surrender of Vicksburg

July: New York City Draft Riots

November: Battle of Chattanooga

November: Union troops capture Brownsville, Texas

1864 March: Ulysses S. Grant becomes general-in-chief of Union forces

April: Fort Pillow massacre

May: Battle of the Wilderness

May: Battle of Spotsylvania

June: Battle of Cold Harbor

June: Maximilian becomes Emperor of Mexico

September: Atlanta falls

October: St. Albans incident

November: Abraham Lincoln reelected president

November–December: William Tecumseh Sherman's march to the sea

1865 April: Richmond falls

April: Robert E. Lee surrenders at Appomattox

April: Lincoln assassinated

December: Thirteenth Amendment to the Constitution becomes law

their last respects. At that moment, the Washington community and the larger Union community were one and the same.

The nation as a whole was left with Lincoln's vision for the coming peace, expressed in the unforgettable words of his Second Inaugural Address:

> With malice toward none, with charity for all, with firmness in the right as God gives us to see the right, let us strive on to finish the work we are in, to bind up the nation's wounds, to care for him who shall have borne the battle and for his widow and his orphan, to do all which may achieve and cherish a just and lasting peace among ourselves and with all nations.

CONCLUSION

In 1865, a divided people were forcibly reunited by battle. Their nation, the United States of America, had been permanently changed by civil war. Devastating losses among the young men of the country—the greatest such losses the nation was ever to suffer—would affect not only their families but also all of postwar society. Politically, the deepest irony of the Civil War was that only by fighting it had America become completely a nation. For it was the war that broke down local isolation. Ordinary citizens in local communities, North and South, developed a national perspective as they sent their sons and brothers to be soldiers, their daughters to be nurses and teachers. Then, too, the federal government, vastly strengthened by wartime necessity, reached the lives of ordinary citizens more than ever before. The question now was whether this strengthened but divided national community, forged in battle, could create a just peace.

REVIEW QUESTIONS

1. At the outset of the Civil War, what were the relative advantages of the North and the South, and how did they affect the final outcome?

2. In the absence of the Southern Democrats, in the early 1860s, the new Republican Congress was able to pass a number of party measures with little opposition. What do these measures tell you about the historical roots of the Republican Party? More generally, how do you think we should view legislation passed in the absence of the customary opposition, debate, and compromise?

3. The greatest problem facing Jefferson Davis and the Confederacy was the need to develop a true feeling of nationalism. Can the failure of this effort be blamed on Davis's weakness as a leader alone, or are there other causes?

4. In what ways can it be said that the actions of African Americans, both slave and free, came to determine the course of the Civil War?

5. Wars always have unexpected consequences. List some of those consequences both for soldiers and for civilians in the North and in the South.

6. Today Abraham Lincoln is considered one of our greatest presidents, but he did not enjoy such approval at the time. List and evaluate some of the contemporary criticisms of Lincoln.

KEY TERMS

Copperheads (p. 401)
Emancipation Proclamation (p. 396)
Homestead Act (p. 390)
Legal Tender Act (p. 390)
Morrill Land Grant Act (p. 390)

Morrill Tariff Act (p. 390)
National Bank Act (p. 390)
Peninsular campaign (p. 393)
Thirteenth Amendment (p. 397)

VOLUME 2

Brief Sixth Edition

Out of Many
A History of the American People

JOHN MACK FARAGHER   MARI JO BUHLE   DANIEL CZITROM   SUSAN H. ARMITAGE

To order, please request
VOLUME 2
Chapters 17-31
ISBN-10: 0-205-01062-8 | ISBN-13: 978-0-205-01062-2

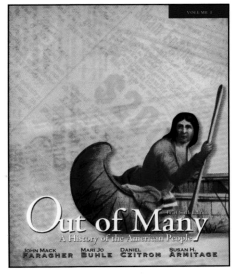

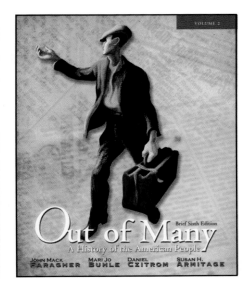

COMBINED VOLUME
Chapters 1-31
ISBN-10: 0-205-01064-4
ISBN-13: 978-0-205-01064-6

VOLUME 1
Chapters 1-17
ISBN-10: 0-205-01063-6
ISBN-13: 978-0-205-01063-9

VOLUME 2
Chapters 17-31
ISBN-10: 0-205-01062-8
ISBN-13: 978-0-205-01062-2

17

RECONSTRUCTION
1863–1877

((•—[**Hear** the **Audio**

Hear the audio files for Chapter 17 at **www.myhistorylab.com**.

WHAT WERE the competing political plans for reconstructing the defeated Confederacy?

WHAT WERE the most important changes in the lives of African Americans in the years immediately following the war?

HOW SUCCESSFUL were Southern Republicans in reshaping southern society and government?

HOW DID the northern political landscape change in the decades after the Civil War?

1877

1863

AMERICAN COMMUNITIES
Hale County, Alabama: From Slavery to Freedom in a Black Belt Community

ON A BRIGHT SATURDAY MORNING IN MAY 1867, 4,000 FORMER SLAVES streamed into the town of Greensboro, bustling seat of Hale County in west-central Alabama. They came to hear speeches from two delegates to a recent freedmen's convention in Mobile and to find out about the political status of black people under the Reconstruction Act just passed by Congress. Tensions mounted as military authorities began supervising voter registration for elections to the upcoming constitutional convention that would rewrite the laws of Alabama. On June 13, John Orrick, a local white, confronted Alex Webb, a politically active freedman, on the streets of Greensboro. Webb had recently been appointed a voter registrar for the district. Orrick swore he would never be registered by a black man and shot Webb dead. Hundreds of armed and angry freedmen formed a posse to search for Orrick but failed to find him. Galvanized by Webb's murder, 500 local freedmen formed a chapter of the Union League, the Republican Party's organizational arm in the South. The chapter functioned as both a militia company and a forum to agitate for political rights.

Violent political encounters between black people and white people were common in southern communities in the wake of the Civil War. Communities throughout the South struggled over the meaning of freedom in ways that reflected their particular circumstances. The black–white ratio in individual communities varied enormously. In some places, the Union army had been a strong presence during the war, hastening the collapse of the slave system and encouraging experiments in free labor. Other areas had remained relatively untouched by the fighting. In some areas, small farms prevailed; in others, including Hale County, large plantations dominated economic and political life.

West-central Alabama had emerged as a fertile center of cotton production just two decades before the Civil War. There, African Americans, as throughout the South's black belt, constituted more than three-quarters of the population. With the arrival of federal troops in the spring of 1865, African Americans in Hale County, like their counterparts elsewhere, began to challenge the traditional organization of plantation labor.

Above all, freed people wanted more autonomy. Overseers and owners grudgingly allowed them to work the land "in families," letting them choose their own supervisors and find their own provisions. The result was a shift from the gang labor characteristic of the antebellum period, in which large groups of slaves worked under the harsh and constant supervision of white overseers, to the sharecropping system, in which African American families worked small plots of land in exchange for a small share of the crop.

Only a small fraction—perhaps 15 percent—of African American families were fortunate enough to be able to buy land. The majority settled for some version of sharecropping, while others managed to rent land from owners, becoming tenant farmers. Still, planters throughout Hale County had to change the old routines of plantation labor. Local African Americans also organized politically. In 1866, Congress had passed the Civil Rights Act and sent the Fourteenth Amendment to the Constitution to the states for ratification; both promised full citizenship rights to former slaves. Hale County freedmen used their new political power to press for better labor contracts, demand greater autonomy for the black workforce, and agitate for the more radical goal of land confiscation and redistribution. Two Hale County former slaves, Brister Reese and James K. Green, won election to the Alabama state legislature in 1869.

It was not long before these economic and political gains prompted a white counterattack. In the spring of 1868, the Ku Klux Klan—a secret organization devoted to terrorizing and intimidating African Americans and their white Republican allies—came to Hale County. Klansmen flogged, beat, and murdered freed people. They intimidated voters and silenced political activists. Planters used Klan terror to dissuade former slaves from leaving plantations or organizing for higher wages. With the passage of the Ku Klux Klan Act in 1871, the federal government cracked down on the Klan, breaking its power temporarily in parts of the former Confederacy. But no serious effort was made to stop Klan terror in the west Alabama black belt, and planters there succeeded in reestablishing much of their social and political control.

The events in Hale County illustrate the struggles that beset communities throughout the South during the Reconstruction era after the Civil War. The destruction of slavery and the Confederacy forced African Americans and white people to renegotiate their old roles. These community battles both shaped and were shaped by the victorious and newly expansive federal government in Washington. But the new arrangements of both political power sharing and the organization of labor had to be worked out within local communities.

Greensboro

The Politics of Reconstruction

When General Robert E. Lee's men stacked their guns at Appomattox, the bloodiest war in American history ended. More than 600,000 soldiers had died during the four years of fighting. Although President Abraham Lincoln insisted early on that the purpose of the war was to preserve the Union, by 1863 it had evolved as well into a struggle for African American liberation. Indeed, the political, economic, and moral issues posed by slavery were the root cause of the Civil War, and the war ultimately destroyed slavery, although not racism, once and for all.

The Civil War also settled the constitutional crisis provoked by the secession of the Confederacy and its justification in appeals to states' rights. The old notion of the United States as a voluntary union of sovereign states gave way to the new reality of a single nation, in which the federal government took precedence over the individual states. The key historical developments of the Reconstruction era revolved around precisely how the newly strengthened national government would define its relationship with the defeated Confederate states and the 4 million newly freed slaves.

The Defeated South

The white South paid an extremely high price for secession, war, and defeat. In addition to the battlefield casualties, much of the best agricultural land was laid waste. Many towns and cities were in ruins. By 1865, the South's most precious commodities, cotton and African American slaves, no longer were measures of wealth and prestige. Retreating Confederates destroyed most of the South's cotton to prevent its capture by federal troops. What remained was confiscated by Union agents as contraband of war. The former slaves, many of whom had fled to Union lines during the latter stages of the war, were determined to chart their own course in the reconstructed South as free men and women.

Emancipation proved the bitterest pill for white Southerners to swallow, especially the planter elite. Conquered and degraded, and in their view robbed of their slave property, white people responded by regarding African Americans, more than ever, as inferior to themselves. The specter of political power and social equality for African Americans made racial order the consuming passion of most white Southerners during the Reconstruction years. In fact, racism can be seen as one of the major forces driving Reconstruction and, ultimately, undermining it.

Abraham Lincoln's Plan

By late 1863, Union military victories had convinced President Lincoln of the need to fashion a plan for the reconstruction of the South (see Chapter 16). Lincoln based his reconstruction program on bringing the seceded states back into the Union as quickly as possible. His Proclamation of Amnesty and Reconstruction of December 1863 offered "full pardon" and the restoration of property, not including slaves, to white Southerners willing to swear an oath of allegiance to the United States and its laws, including the Emancipation Proclamation. Prominent Confederate military and civil leaders were excluded from Lincoln's offer, though he indicated that he would freely pardon them.

The president also proposed that when the number of any Confederate state's voters who took the oath of allegiance reached 10 percent of the number who had voted in the election of 1860, this group could establish a state government that Lincoln would recognize as legitimate. Fundamental to this Ten Percent Plan was that the reconstructed governments accept the abolition of slavery.

Lincoln's amnesty proclamation angered those Republicans—known as **Radical Republicans**—who advocated not only equal rights for the freedmen but also a tougher stance toward the white South. In July 1864, Senator Benjamin F. Wade of Ohio and

WHAT WERE the competing political plans for reconstructing the defeated Confederacy?

Read the Document

Confederate Song, "I'm a Good Old Rebel" (1866) at **www.myhistorylab.com**

Radical Republicans   A shifting group of Republican congressmen, usually a substantial minority, who favored the abolition of slavery from the beginning of the Civil War and later advocated harsh treatment of the defeated South.

"Decorating the Graves of Rebel Soldiers," *Harper's Weekly*, August 17, 1867. After the Civil War, both Southerners and Northerners created public mourning ceremonies honoring fallen soldiers. Women led the memorial movement in the South that, by establishing cemeteries and erecting monuments, offered the first cultural expression of the Confederate tradition. This engraving depicts citizens of Richmond, Virginia, decorating thousands of Confederate graves with flowers at the Hollywood Memorial Cemetery on the James River. A local women's group raised enough funds to transfer over 16,000 Confederate dead from northern cemeteries for reburial in Richmond.

Congressman Henry W. Davis of Maryland, both Radicals, proposed a harsher alternative to the Ten Percent Plan. The Wade–Davis bill required 50 percent of a seceding state's white male citizens to take a loyalty oath before elections could be held for a convention to rewrite the state's constitution. The Radical Republicans saw reconstruction as a chance to effect a fundamental transformation of southern society. They thus wanted to delay the process until war's end and to limit participation to a small number of southern Unionists. Lincoln viewed Reconstruction as part of the larger effort to win the war and abolish slavery. He wanted to weaken the Confederacy by creating new state governments that could win broad support from southern white people. The Wade–Davis bill threatened his efforts to build political consensus within the southern states. Lincoln, therefore, pocket-vetoed the bill by refusing to sign it within ten days of the adjournment of Congress.

As Union armies occupied parts of the South, commanders improvised a variety of arrangements involving confiscated plantations and the African American labor force. For example, in 1862 General Benjamin F. Butler began a policy of transforming slaves on Louisiana sugar plantations into wage laborers under the close supervision of occupying federal troops. Butler's policy required slaves to remain on the estates of loyal planters, where they would receive wages according to a fixed schedule, as well as food and medical care for the aged and sick. In January 1865, General William T. Sherman issued **Special Field Order 15**, setting aside the Sea Islands off the

Special Field Order 15 Order by General William T. Sherman in January 1865 to set aside abandoned land along the southern Atlantic coast for forty-acre grants to freedmen; rescinded by President Andrew Johnson later that year.

Georgia coast and a portion of the South Carolina Lowcountry rice fields for the exclusive settlement of freed people. Each family would receive forty acres of land and the loan of mules from the army—the origin, perhaps, of the famous call for "forty acres and a mule" that would soon capture the imagination of African Americans throughout the South.

Conflicts within the Republican Party prevented the development of a systematic land distribution program. Still, Lincoln and the Republican Congress supported other measures to aid the emancipated slaves. In March 1865 Congress established the Freedmen's Bureau. Along with providing food, clothing, and fuel to destitute former slaves, the bureau was charged with supervising and managing "all the abandoned lands in the South and the control of all subjects relating to refugees and freedmen." The act that established the bureau also stated that forty acres of abandoned or confiscated land could be leased to freed slaves or white Unionists, who would have an option to purchase after three years.

On the evening of April 14, 1865, while attending the theater in Washington, President Lincoln was shot and killed by John Wilkes Booth. At the time of his assassination, Lincoln's reconstruction policy remained unsettled and incomplete. The specifics of postwar Reconstruction now had to be hammered out by a new president, Andrew Johnson of Tennessee.

Photography pioneer Timothy O'Sullivan took this portrait of a multigenerational African American family on the J. J. Smith plantation in Beaufort, South Carolina, in 1862. Many white plantation owners in the area had fled, allowing slaves like these to begin an early transition to freedom before the end of the Civil War.

ANDREW JOHNSON AND PRESIDENTIAL RECONSTRUCTION

Andrew Johnson, a Democrat and former slaveholder, was the only southern member of the U.S. Senate to remain loyal to the Union. In 1862, Lincoln appointed Johnson to the difficult post of military governor of Tennessee. There he successfully began wartime Reconstruction and cultivated Unionist support in the mountainous eastern districts of that state.

In 1864, the Republicans, in an appeal to northern and border state "**War Democrats**," nominated Johnson for vice president. In the immediate aftermath of Lincoln's murder, however, Johnson appeared to side with those Radical Republicans who sought to treat the South as a conquered territory. But this impression quickly faded as the new president's policies unfolded. Johnson defined Reconstruction as the province of the executive, not the legislative branch, and he planned to restore the Union as quickly as possible. He blamed individual Southerners—the planter elite—rather than entire states for leading the South down the disastrous road to secession. In line with this philosophy, Johnson outlined mild terms for reentry to the Union.

In the spring of 1865, Johnson granted amnesty and pardon, including restoration of property rights except slaves, to all Confederates who pledged loyalty to the Union and support for emancipation. Fourteen classes of Southerners, mostly major Confederate officials and wealthy landowners, were excluded. But these men could apply individually for presidential pardons. (During his tenure Johnson pardoned roughly 90 percent of those who applied.) Significantly, Johnson instituted this plan while Congress was not in session.

By the autumn of 1865, ten of the eleven Confederate states claimed to have met Johnson's requirements to reenter the Union. On December 6, 1865, the president declared the "restoration" of the Union virtually complete. But a serious division within the federal government was taking shape, for the Congress was not about to allow the president free rein in determining the conditions of southern readmission.

◆◆-Read the Document

Carl Schurz, Report on the Condition of the South (1865) at **www.myhistorylab.com**

War Democrats   Those from the North and the border states who broke with the Democratic Party and supported Abraham Lincoln's military policies during the Civil War.

QUICK REVIEW

Johnson's Reconstruction Plan

- ◆ Johnson extended pardons to Southerners who swore an oath of allegiance.
- ◆ He restored property rights to Southerners who swore an oath of allegiance.
- ◆ His plan had nothing to say about the voting and civil rights of former slaves.

FREE LABOR AND THE RADICAL REPUBLICAN VISION

Most Radicals were men whose careers had been shaped by the slavery controversy. One of the most effective rhetorical weapons used against slavery and its spread had been the ideal of a society based upon free labor. The model of free individuals, competing equally in the labor market and enjoying equal political rights, and the possibility of social and economic mobility, formed the core of this worldview.

Radicals now looked to reconstruct southern society along these same lines, backed by the power of the national government. They argued that once free labor, universal education, and equal rights were implanted in the South, that region would be able to share in the North's material wealth, progress, and social mobility. In the most far-reaching proposal, Representative Thaddeus Stevens of Pennsylvania called for the confiscation of 400 million acres belonging to the wealthiest 10 percent of Southerners to be redistributed to black and white yeomen and northern land buyers. "The whole fabric of Southern society must be changed," Stevens told Pennsylvania Republicans in September 1865, "and never can it be done if this opportunity is lost. How can republican institutions, free schools, free churches, free social intercourse exist in a mingled community of nabobs and serfs?"

Northern Republicans were especially outraged by the stringent "**black codes**" passed by South Carolina, Mississippi, Louisiana, and other states. These were designed to restrict the freedom of the black labor force and keep freed people as close to slave status as possible. Laborers who left their jobs before contracts expired would forfeit wages already earned and be subject to arrest by any white citizen. Vagrancy, very broadly defined, was punishable by fines and involuntary plantation labor. Apprenticeship clauses obliged black children to work without pay for employers. Some states attempted to bar African Americans from land ownership. Other laws specifically denied African Americans equality with white people in civil rights, excluding them from juries and prohibiting interracial marriages.

The Radicals, although not a majority of their party, were joined by moderate Republicans as growing numbers of Northerners grew suspicious of white southern

---

···⟦Read the Document

Mississippi Black Code (1865) at
www.myhistorylab.com

black codes   Laws passed by states and municipalities denying many rights of citizenship to free black people before the Civil War.

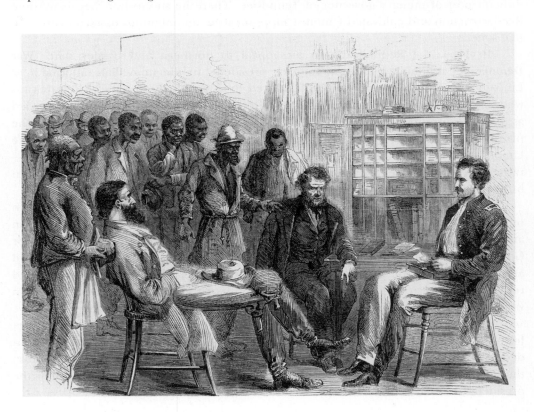

"Office of the Freedmen's Bureau, Memphis, Tennessee," *Harper's Weekly*, June 2, 1866. Established by Congress in 1865, the Freedmen's Bureau provided economic, educational, and legal assistance to former slaves in the post–Civil War years. Bureau agents were often called on to settle disputes between black and white Southerners over wages, labor contracts, political rights, and violence. Although most southern whites only grudgingly acknowledged the bureau's legitimacy, freed people gained important legal and psychological support through testimony at public hearings like this one.

intransigence and the denial of political rights to freedmen. When Congress convened in December 1865, the large Republican majority prevented the seating of the white Southerners elected to Congress under President Johnson's provisional state governments. Republicans also established the Joint Committee on Reconstruction to investigate conditions in the South.

In the spring of 1866, Congress passed two important bills designed to aid African Americans. The landmark **Civil Rights bill**, which bestowed full citizenship on African Americans, overturned the 1857 *Dred Scott* decision and the black codes. Under this bill, African Americans acquired "full and equal benefit of all laws and proceedings for the security of person and property as is enjoyed by white citizens."

Congress also voted to enlarge the scope of the **Freedmen's Bureau**, empowering it to build schools and pay teachers, and also to establish courts to prosecute those charged with depriving African Americans of their civil rights. The bureau achieved important, if limited, success in aiding African Americans. Bureau-run schools helped lay the foundation for southern public education. The bureau's network of courts allowed freed people to bring suits against white people in disputes involving violence, nonpayment of wages, or unfair division of crops.

But an angry President Johnson vetoed both of these bills. In opposing the Civil Rights bill, Johnson denounced the assertion of national power to protect African American civil rights, claiming it was a "stride toward centralization, and the concentration of all legislative powers in the national Government." But Johnson's intemperate attacks on the Radicals united moderate and Radical Republicans and they succeeded in overriding the vetoes.

In June 1866, fearful that the Civil Rights Act might be declared unconstitutional, and eager to settle the basis for the seating of southern representatives, Congress passed the Fourteenth Amendment. The amendment defined national citizenship to include former slaves and prohibited the states from violating the privileges of citizens without due process of law. It also empowered Congress to reduce the representation of any state that denied suffrage to males over twenty-one. Republicans adopted the Fourteenth Amendment as their platform for the 1866 congressional elections and suggested that southern states would have to ratify it as a condition of readmission. President Johnson, meanwhile, campaigned in support of conservative Democratic and Republican candidates. His unrestrained speeches often degenerated into harangues, alienating many voters and aiding the Republican cause.

For their part, the Republicans skillfully portrayed Johnson and northern Democrats as disloyal and white Southerners as unregenerate. Republicans began an effective campaign tradition known as "waving the bloody shirt"—reminding northern voters of the hundreds of thousands of Yankee soldiers left dead or maimed by the war. In the November 1866 elections, the Republicans increased their majority in both the House and the Senate and gained control of all the northern states. The stage was now set for a battle between the president and Congress.

CONGRESSIONAL RECONSTRUCTION AND THE IMPEACHMENT CRISIS

In March 1867, Congress passed the **First Reconstruction Act** over Johnson's veto. This act divided the South into five military districts subject to martial law. To achieve restoration, southern states were first required to call new constitutional conventions, elected by universal manhood suffrage. Once these states had drafted new constitutions, guaranteed African American voting rights, and ratified the Fourteenth Amendment, they were eligible for readmission to the Union. Supplementary legislation, also passed over the president's veto, invalidated the provisional governments established by Johnson, empowered the military to administer voter registration, and required an oath of loyalty to the United States (see Map 17.1).

Civil Rights Bill   The 1866 act that gave full citizenship to African Americans.

Freedmen's Bureau   Agency established by Congress in March 1865 to provide social, educational, and economic services, advice, and protection to former slaves and destitute whites; lasted seven years.

Congressional Reconstruction   Name given to the period 1867–1870 when the Republican-dominated Congress controlled Reconstruction-era policy.

First Reconstruction Act   1877 act that divided the South into five military districts subject to martial law.

QUICK REVIEW

Key Components of the Radical Agenda

♦ Free labor.
♦ Universal education.
♦ Equal rights.

⊙ **See** the **Map**
Reconstruction at **www.myhistorylab.com**

Tenure of Office Act Act stipulating that any officeholder appointed by the president with the Senate's advice and consent could not be removed until the Senate had approved a successor.

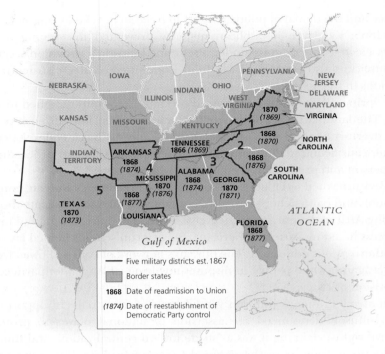

MAP 17.1

Reconstruction of the South, 1866–77 Dates for the readmission of former Confederate states to the Union and the return of Democrats to power varied according to the specific political situations in those states.

WHAT LED to the establishment of military districts in the South? How did white southerners resist northern efforts at reconstruction?

Congress also passed several laws aimed at limiting Johnson's power. One of these, the **Tenure of Office Act**, stipulated that any officeholder appointed by the president with the Senate's advice and consent could not be removed until the Senate had approved a successor. In this way, congressional leaders could protect Republicans, such as Secretary of War Edwin M. Stanton, entrusted with implementing Congressional Reconstruction. In August 1867, with Congress adjourned, Johnson challenged the Tenure of Office Act by suspending Stanton and appointing General Ulysses S. Grant interim secretary of war. In January 1868, when the Senate overruled Stanton's suspension, Grant broke openly with Johnson and vacated the office. Stanton resumed his position and barricaded himself in his office when Johnson attempted to remove him once again.

Outraged by Johnson's relentless obstructionism, and seizing upon his violation of the Tenure of Office Act as a pretext, moderate and Radical Republicans in the House of Representatives again joined forces and voted to impeach the president on February 24, 1868. To ensure the support of moderate Republicans, the articles of impeachment focused on violations of the Tenure of Office Act. Left unstated were the Republicans' real reasons for wanting the president removed: Johnson's political views and his opposition to the Reconstruction Acts.

An influential group of moderate Senate Republicans feared the damage a conviction might do to the constitutional separation of powers. They also worried about the political and economic policies that might be pursued by Benjamin Wade, the president pro tem of the Senate and a leader of the Radical Republicans, who, because there was no vice president, would succeed to the presidency if Johnson were removed from office. Behind the scenes during his Senate trial, Johnson agreed to abide by the Reconstruction

Acts. In May, the Senate voted 35 for conviction, 19 for acquittal—one vote shy of the two-thirds necessary for removal from office. Johnson's narrow acquittal established the precedent that only criminal actions by a president—not political disagreements—warranted removal from office.

THE ELECTION OF 1868

By the summer of 1868, seven former Confederate states (Alabama, Arkansas, Florida, Louisiana, North Carolina, South Carolina, and Tennessee) had ratified the revised constitutions, elected Republican governments, and ratified the Fourteenth Amendment. They had thereby earned readmission to the Union. In 1868 Republicans nominated Ulysses S. Grant, the North's foremost military hero, as their nominee for President. Totally lacking in political experience, Grant admitted, after receiving the nomination, that he had been forced into it in spite of himself.

Significantly, at the very moment that the South was being forced to enfranchise former slaves as a prerequisite for readmission to the Union, the Republicans rejected a campaign plank endorsing black suffrage in the North. The Democrats, determined to reverse Congressional Reconstruction, nominated Horatio Seymour, former governor of New York and a longtime foe of emancipation and supporter of states' rights.

The **Ku Klux Klan** emerged as a potent instrument of terror (see the opening of this chapter). Klan violence enabled the Democrats to carry Georgia and Louisiana, but it ultimately cost the Democrats votes in the North. In the final tally, Grant carried twenty-six of the thirty-four states for an Electoral College victory of 214 to 80. The Republicans also retained large majorities in both houses of Congress.

In February 1869, Congress passed the **Fifteenth Amendment**, providing that "the right of citizens of the United States to vote shall not be denied or abridged on account of race, color, or previous condition of servitude." To enhance the chances of ratification, Congress required the four remaining unreconstructed states—Mississippi, Georgia,

Ku Klux Klan   Perhaps the most prominent of the vigilante groups that terrorized black people in the South during Reconstruction era, founded by the Confederate veterans in 1866.

Fifteenth Amendment   Passed by Congress in 1869, guaranteed the right of American men to vote, regardless of race.

◆◆◆ Read the Document

History Bookshelf: *Ulysses S. Grant, Memoirs (1886)* at **www.myhistorylab.com**

The Fifteenth Amendment, ratified in 1870, stipulated that the right to vote could not be denied "on account of race, color, or previous condition of servitude." This illustration expressed the optimism and hopes of African Americans generated by this consitutional landmark aimed at protecting black political rights. Note the various political figures (Abraham Lincoln, John Brown, Frederick Douglass) and movements (abolitionism, black education) invoked here, providing a sense of how the amendment ended a long historical struggle.

Texas, and Virginia—to ratify both the Fourteenth and Fifteenth Amendments before readmission. They did so and rejoined the Union in early 1870. The Fifteenth Amendment was ratified in February 1870. In the narrow sense of simply readmitting the former Confederate states to the Union, Reconstruction was complete.

WOMAN SUFFRAGE AND RECONSTRUCTION

Many women's rights advocates had long been active in the abolitionist movement. The Fourteenth and Fifteenth Amendments, which granted citizenship and the vote to freedmen, both inspired and frustrated these activists. Throughout the nation, the old abolitionist organizations and the Republican Party emphasized passage of the Fourteenth and Fifteenth Amendments and withdrew funds and support from the cause of woman suffrage. Disagreements over these amendments divided suffragists for decades.

The radical wing, led by Elizabeth Cady Stanton and Susan B. Anthony, opposed the Fifteenth Amendment, arguing that ratification would establish an "aristocracy of sex," enfranchising all men while leaving women without political privileges. They argued for a Sixteenth Amendment that would secure the vote for women. Other women's rights activists, including Lucy Stone and Frederick Douglass, asserted that "this hour belongs to the Negro." They feared a debate over woman suffrage at the national level would jeopardize passage of the two amendments. By 1869 woman suffragists had split into two competing organizations: the moderate American Woman Suffrage

This contemporary colored engraving depicts a meeting of the National Woman Suffrage Association in Chicago, c.1870. The suffrage campaign attracted many middle class women into political activism for the first time.

OVERVIEW | Reconstruction Amendments to the Constitution, 1865–1870

Amendment and Date Passed by Congress	Main Provisions	Ratification Process (3/4 of all States Including Ex-Confederate States Required)
13 (January 1865)	• Prohibited slavery in the United States	December 1865 (27 states, including 8 southern states)
14 (June 1866)	• Conferred national citizenship on all persons born or naturalized in the United States • Reduced state representation in Congress proportionally for any state disfranchising male citizens • Denied former Confederates the right to hold state or national office • Repudiated Confederate debt	July 1868 (after Congress made ratification a prerequisite for readmission of ex-Confederate states to the Union)
15 (February 1869)	• Prohibited denial of suffrage because of race, color, or previous condition of servitude	March 1870 (ratification required for readmission of Virginia, Texas, Mississippi, and Georgia)

Association (AWSA), which sought the support of men, and the more radical all-female National Woman Suffrage Association (NWSA) (see Chapter 13).

Although women did not win the vote in this period, they did establish an independent suffrage movement that eventually drew millions of women into political life. The NWSA in particular demonstrated that self-government and democratic participation in the public sphere were crucial for women's emancipation.

THE MEANING OF FREEDOM

For nearly 4 million slaves, freedom arrived in various ways in different parts of the South. In many areas, slavery had collapsed long before Lee's surrender at Appomattox. In regions far removed from the presence of federal troops, African Americans did not learn of slavery's end until the spring of 1865. But regardless of specific regional circumstances, the meaning of "freedom" would be contested for years to come. The deep desire for independence from white control formed the underlying aspiration of newly freed slaves. For their part, most southern white people sought to restrict the boundaries of that independence. As former slaves struggled to establish autonomy, they built on the twin pillars of slave culture—the family and the church—to consolidate and expand African American institutions and thereby laid the foundation for the modern African American community.

WHAT WERE the most important changes in the lives of African Americans in the years immediately following the war?

MOVING ABOUT

The first impulse of many emancipated slaves was to test their freedom. The simplest, most obvious way to do this involved leaving home. Throughout the summer and fall of 1865, observers in the South noted enormous numbers of freed people on the move. Yet

Read the Document
Jourdon Anderson to His Former Master (1865) at **www.myhistorylab.com**

many who left their old neighborhoods returned soon afterward to seek work in the general vicinity or even on the plantation they had left. Many wanted to separate themselves from former owners, but not from familial ties and friendships. Others moved away altogether, seeking jobs in nearby towns and cities. Between 1865 and 1870, the African American population of the South's ten largest cities doubled, while the white population increased by only 10 percent.

Disgruntled planters had difficulty accepting African American independence. Many could not understand why so many former slaves wanted to leave, despite urgent pleas to continue working at the old place. The deference and humility white people expected from African Americans could no longer be taken for granted. Indeed, many freed people went out of their way to reject the old subservience. Moving about freely was one way of doing this, as was refusing to tip one's hat to white people, ignoring former masters or mistresses in the streets, and refusing to step aside on sidewalks.

AFRICAN AMERICAN FAMILIES, CHURCHES, AND SCHOOLS

Emancipation allowed freed people to strengthen family ties. For many former slaves, freedom meant the opportunity to find long-lost family members. To track down these relatives, freed people trekked to faraway places, put ads in newspapers, sought the help of Freedmen's Bureau agents, and questioned anyone who might have information about loved ones. Thousands of African American couples who had lived together under slavery streamed to military and civilian authorities and demanded to be legally

An overflow congregation crowds into Richmond's First African Baptist Church in 1874. Despite their poverty, freed people struggled to save money, buy land, and erect new buildings as they organized hundreds of new black churches during Reconstruction. As the most important African American institution outside the family, the black church, in addition to tending to spiritual needs, played a key role in the educational and political life of the community.

married. By 1870, the two-parent household was the norm for a large majority of African Americans.

For many freed people, the attempt to find lost relatives dragged on for years. Searches often proved frustrating, exhausting, and ultimately disappointing. Some "reunions" ended painfully with the discovery that spouses had found new partners and started new families.

Emancipation brought changes to gender roles within the African American family as well. By serving in the Union army, African American men played a more direct role than women in the fight for freedom. In the political sphere, black men could now serve on juries, vote, and hold office; black women, like their white counterparts, could not. Freedmen's Bureau agents designated the husband as household head and established lower wage scales for women laborers. African American editors, preachers, and politicians regularly quoted the biblical injunction that wives submit to their husbands.

African American men asserted their male authority, denied under slavery, by insisting their wives work at home instead of in the fields. African American women generally wanted to devote more time than they had under slavery to caring for their children and to performing such domestic chores as cooking, sewing, gardening, and laundering. Yet African American women continued to work outside the home, engaging in seasonal field labor for wages or working a family's rented plot. Most rural black families barely eked out a living and, thus, the labor of every family member was essential to survival.

The creation of separate African American churches proved the most lasting and important element of the energetic institution building that went on in postemancipation years. Before the Civil War, southern Protestant churches had relegated slaves and free African Americans to second-class membership. Even in larger cities, where all-black congregations sometimes built their own churches, the law required white pastors.

In communities around the South, African Americans now pooled their resources to buy land and build their own churches. Churches became the center not only for religious life but also for many other activities that defined the African American community: schools, picnics, festivals, and political meetings. The church became the first social institution fully controlled by African Americans. In nearly every community, ministers, respected for their speaking and organizational skills, were among the most influential leaders. By 1877, the great majority of black Southerners had withdrawn from white-dominated churches, with most African American Christians belonging to black Baptist or Methodist churches.

The rapid spread of schools reflected African Americans' thirst for self-improvement. Southern states had prohibited education for slaves. But many free black people managed to attend school, and a few slaves had been able to educate themselves. Still, over 90 percent of the South's adult African American population was illiterate in 1860. Access to education thus became a central part of the meaning of freedom.

African American communities received important educational aid from outside organizations. By 1869, the Freedmen's Bureau was supervising nearly 3,000 schools serving over 150,000 students throughout the South. Over half of the roughly 3,300 teachers in these schools were African Americans, many of whom had been free before the Civil War. Other teachers included dedicated northern white women, volunteers sponsored by the American Missionary Association (AMA). The bureau and the AMA also assisted in the founding of several black colleges, including Tougaloo, Hampton, and Fisk, designed to train black teachers. Black self-help proved crucial to the education effort. Throughout the South in 1865 and 1866, African Americans raised money to build schoolhouses, buy supplies, and pay teachers. Black artisans donated labor for construction, and black families offered room and board to teachers.

LAND AND LABOR AFTER SLAVERY

Most newly emancipated African Americans aspired to quit the plantations and to make new lives for themselves. Some freed people did find jobs in railroad building, mining, ranching, or construction work. Others raised subsistence crops and tended vegetable gardens as squatters. White planters, however, tried to retain African Americans as permanent agricultural laborers and restricting the employment of former slaves was an important goal of the black codes.

The majority of African Americans hoped to become self-sufficient farmers. Many former slaves believed they were entitled to the land they had worked throughout their lives. But by 1866, the federal government had already pulled back from the various wartime experiments involving the breaking up of large plantations and the leasing of small plots to individual families. President Johnson directed General Howard of the Freedmen's Bureau to evict tens of thousands of freed people settled on confiscated and abandoned land in southeastern Virginia, southern Louisiana, and the Georgia and South Carolina Lowcountry.

In communities throughout the South, freed people and their former masters negotiated new arrangements for organizing agricultural labor. In Hale County, Alabama, for example, local black farmhands contracted to work on Henry Watson's plantation in 1866 deserted him when they angrily discovered that their small share of the crop left them in debt. Local Union League activists encouraged newly freed slaves to remain independent of white farmers, and political agitation for freedmen's rights encouraged them to push for better working conditions as well. Yet few owners would sell or even rent land to blacks. Watson, desperate for field hands, finally agreed to subdivide his plantation and rent it to freedmen, who would work under their own supervision without overseers. By 1868, Watson was convinced that black farmers made good tenants; like many other landowners, he grudgingly accepted greater independence for black families in exchange for a more stable labor force (see Map 17.2).

By the late 1860s, **sharecropping** and tenant farming had emerged as the dominant form of working the land. Sharecropping represented a compromise between planters and former slaves. Under sharecropping arrangements that were usually very detailed, individual families contracted with landowners to be responsible for a specific plot. Large plantations were thus broken into family-sized farms. Generally, sharecropper families received one-third of the year's crop if the owner furnished implements, seed, and draft animals or one-half if they provided their own supplies. African Americans preferred sharecropping to gang labor, as it allowed families to set their own hours and tasks and offered freedom from white supervision and control. For planters, the system stabilized the workforce by requiring sharecroppers to remain until the harvest and to employ all family members. It also offered a way around the chronic shortage of cash and credit that plagued the postwar South.

THE ORIGINS OF AFRICAN AMERICAN POLITICS

Hundreds of African American delegates, selected by local meetings or churches, attended statewide political conventions held throughout the South in 1865 and 1866. Convention debates sometimes reflected the tensions within African American communities, such as friction between poorer former slaves and better-off free black people, or between lighter- and darker-skinned African Americans. But most of these state gatherings concentrated on passing resolutions on issues that united all African Americans. The central concerns were suffrage and equality before the law.

The passage of the First Reconstruction Act in 1867 encouraged even more political activity among African Americans. The military started registering the South's electorate, ultimately enrolling approximately 735,000 black and 635,000 white voters in the

●●●─[Read the Document

A Sharecrop Contract (1882) at
www.myhistorylab.com

sharecropping   Labor system that evolved during and after Reconstruction whereby landowners furnished laborers with a house, farm animals, and tools and advanced credit in exchange for a share of the laborers' crop.

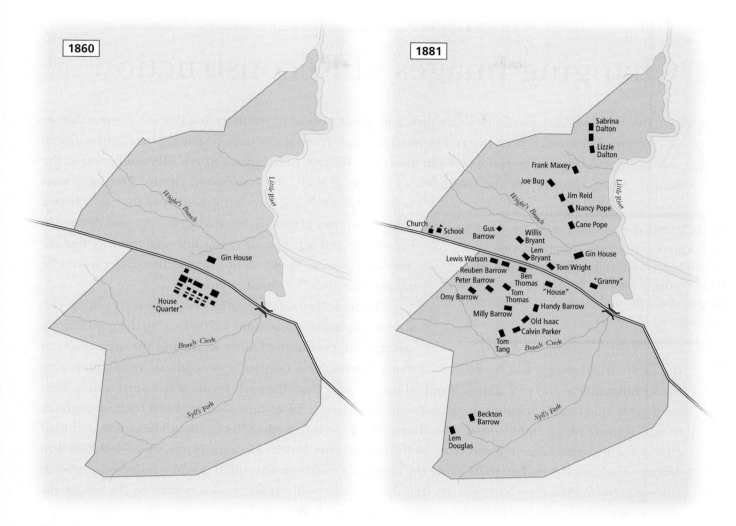

MAP 17.2

The Barrow Plantation, Oglethorpe County, Georgia, 1860 and 1881 (approx. 2,000 acres) These two maps, based on drawings from *Scribner's Monthly*, April 1881, show some of the changes brought by emancipation. In 1860, the plantation's entire black population lived in the communal slave quarters, right next to the white master's house. In 1881, black sharecropper and tenant families lived on individual plots, spread out across the land. The former slaves had also built their own school and church.

IN WHAT states was sharecropping the most prevalent? In what states was it least prevalent? What explains the patterns you note?

ten unreconstructed states. Five states—Alabama, Florida, Louisiana, Mississippi, and South Carolina—had black electoral majorities. Fewer than half the registered white voters participated in the elections for state constitutional conventions in 1867 and 1868. In contrast, four-fifths of the registered black voters cast ballots in these elections. Much of this new African American political activism was channeled through local Union League chapters throughout the South.

Begun during the war as a northern, largely white middle-class patriotic club, the **Union League** now became the political voice of the former slaves. Union League chapters brought together local African Americans, soldiers, and Freedmen's Bureau agents to demand the vote and an end to legal discrimination against African Americans. It brought out African American voters, instructed freedmen in the rights and duties of citizenship,

Union League Republican party organizations in Northern cities that became an important organizing device among freedmen in Southern cities after 1865.

Changing Images of Reconstruction

After the Civil War, northern journalists and illustrators went south to describe Reconstruction in action. They took a keen interest in how the newly freed slaves were reshaping local and national politics. A drawing by *Harper's Weekly* illustrator William L. Sheppard titled "Electioneering in the South" clearly approved of the freedmen's exercise of their new citizenship rights. "Does any man seriously doubt," the caption asked, "whether it is better for this vast population to be sinking deeper and deeper in ignorance and servility, or rising into general intelligence and self-respect? They can not be pariahs; they can not be peons; they must be slaves or citizens."

HOW DOES the portrayal of the larger African American community in "Electioneering in the South" reflect the political point being made? What do the caricatures in "The Ignorant Vote" suggest about Reconstruction era ideas about the meaning of "whiteness"?

Thomas Nast was the nation's best-known political cartoonist during the 1860s and 1870s. During the Civil War he strongly supported the Union cause and the aspirations of the newly freed slaves. But by 1876, like many Northerners originally sympathetic to guaranteeing blacks full political and civil rights, Nast had turned away from the early ideals of Reconstruction. Nast used grotesque racial caricature to depict southern African Americans and northern Irish immigrants as undeserving of the right to vote. The aftermath of the disputed 1876 presidential election included charges of widespread vote fraud from both Republicans and Democrats. Nast's view—published in *Harper's Weekly* in December 1876, while the election's outcome was still in doubt—reflected concerns among many middle-class Northerners that the nation's political system was tainted by the manipulation of "ignorant" voters in both the South and the North. ■

"The First Vote," *Harper's Weekly*, November 16, 1867, reflected the optimism felt by much of the northern public as former slaves began to vote for the first time. The caption noted that freedmen went to the ballot box "not with expressions of exultation or of defiance of their old masters and present opponents depicted on their countenances, but looking serious and solemn and determined."

and promoted Republican candidates. Not surprisingly, newly enfranchised freedmen voted Republican and formed the core of the Republican Party in the South. For most ordinary African Americans, politics was inseparable from economic issues, especially the land question. Grassroots political organizations frequently intervened in local disputes with planters over the terms of labor contracts. African American political groups closely followed the congressional debates over Reconstruction policy and agitated for land confiscation and distribution. Perhaps most important, politics was the only arena where black and white Southerners might engage each other on an equal basis.

●●●–**Read** the **Document**

Address from the Colored Citizens of Norfolk, VA (1865) at **www.myhistorylab.com**

SOUTHERN POLITICS AND SOCIETY

By the summer of 1868, when the South had returned to the Union, the majority of Republicans believed the task of Reconstruction to be finished. Most Republican congressmen were moderates, conceiving Reconstruction in limited terms. They rejected radical calls for confiscation and redistribution of land, as well as permanent military rule of the South. The Reconstruction Acts of 1867 and 1868 laid out the requirements for the readmission of southern states, along with the procedures for forming and electing new governments. Yet over the next decade, the political structure created in the southern states proved too restricted and fragile to sustain itself.

HOW SUCCESSFUL were Southern Republicans in reshaping southern society and government?

SOUTHERN REPUBLICANS

Three major groups composed the fledgling Republican coalition in the postwar South. African American voters made up a large majority of southern Republicans throughout the Reconstruction era. Yet African Americans outnumbered whites in only three southern states; Republicans would have to attract white support to win elections and sustain power.

A second group consisted of white Northerners, derisively called "**carpetbaggers**" by native white Southerners. Most were veterans of the Union army who stayed in the South after the war. Others included Freedmen's Bureau agents and businessmen who had invested capital in cotton plantations and other enterprises. Although they made up a tiny percentage of the population, carpetbaggers played a disproportionately large role in southern politics. They won a large share of Reconstruction offices, particularly in Florida, South Carolina, and Louisiana and in areas with large African American constituencies.

The third major group of southern Republicans was the native whites pejoratively termed "**scalawags**." They had even more diverse backgrounds and motives than the northern-born Republicans. Some were prominent prewar Whigs who saw the Republican Party as their best chance to regain political influence. Others viewed the party as an agent of modernization and economic expansion. Loyalists during the war and traditional enemies of the planter elite (most were small farmers), these white Southerners looked to the Republican Party for help in settling old scores and relief from debt and wartime devastation.

Southern Republicanism also reflected prewar political divisions. Its influence was greatest in those regions that had long resisted the political and economic power of the plantation elite. Thus, southern Republicans could dominate the mountainous areas of western North Carolina, eastern Tennessee, northern Georgia, and southwestern Virginia as much as Democrats controlled other areas. Yet few white Southerners identified with the political and economic aspirations of African Americans. Moderate elements more concerned with maintaining white control of the party, and encouraging economic investment in the region, outnumbered and defeated "confiscation radicals" who focused on obtaining land for African Americans.

RECONSTRUCTING THE STATES: A MIXED RECORD

With the old Confederate leaders barred from political participation, and with carpetbaggers and newly enfranchised African Americans representing many of the plantation districts, Republicans managed to dominate the ten southern constitutional conventions from 1867 to 1869. Most of these conventions produced constitutions that expanded democracy and the public role of the state. In 1868, only three years after the end of the war, Republicans came to power in most of the southern states. By 1869, new constitutions had been ratified in all the old Confederate states.

Republican governments in the South faced a continual crisis of legitimacy that limited their ability to legislate change. They had to balance reform against the need to gain acceptance, especially by white Southerners. Their achievements were thus mixed. In the realm of race relations there was a clear thrust toward equal rights and against discrimination. Republican legislatures followed up the federal Civil Rights Act of 1866 with various antidiscrimination clauses in new constitutions and laws prescribing harsh penalties for civil rights violations.

Segregation, though, became the norm in public school systems. African American leaders often accepted segregation because they feared that insistence on integrated education would jeopardize funding for the new school systems. Segregation in railroad cars and other public places was more objectionable. By the early 1870s, as black influence

carpetbaggers Northern transplants to the South, many of whom were Union soldiers who stayed in the South after the war.

scalawags Southern whites, mainly small landowning farmers and well-off merchants and planters, who supported the Southern Republican party during Reconstruction.

and assertiveness grew, laws guaranteeing equal access to transportation and public accommodation were passed in many states. By and large, though, such civil rights laws were difficult to enforce in local communities.

In economic matters, Republican governments failed to fulfill African Americans' hopes of obtaining land. Republicans tried to weaken the plantation system and promote black ownership by raising taxes on land. Yet even when state governments seized land for nonpayment of taxes, the property was never used to help create black homesteads.

Republican leaders envisioned promoting northern-style capitalist development— factories, large towns, and diversified agriculture—through state aid. Much Republican state lawmaking was devoted to encouraging railroad construction. But in spite of all the new laws, it proved impossible to attract significant amounts of northern and European investment capital. The obsession with railroads withdrew resources from education and other programs. As in the North, it also opened the doors to widespread corruption and bribery of public officials. Railroad failures eroded public confidence in the Republicans' ability to govern.

WHITE RESISTANCE AND "REDEMPTION"

The emergence of a Republican Party in the reconstructed South brought two parties, but not a two-party system, to the region. The opponents of Reconstruction, the Democrats, refused to acknowledge Republicans' right to participate in southern political life. Republicans were split between those who urged conciliation in an effort to gain

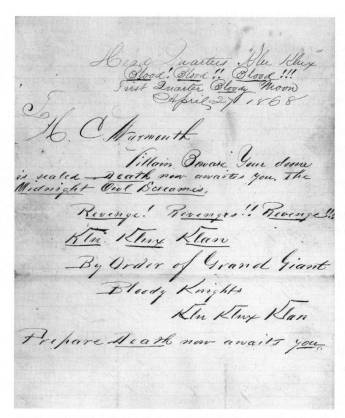

The Ku Klux Klan emerged as a potent political and social force during Reconstruction, terrorizing freed people and their white allies. An 1868 Klan warning threatens Louisiana governor Henry C. Warmoth with death. Warmoth, an Illinois-born "carpetbagger," was the state's first Republican governor. Two Alabama Klansmen, photographed in 1868, wear white hoods to hide their identities.

white acceptance and those who emphasized consolidating the party under the protection of the military.

From its founding in 1868 through the early 1870s, the Ku Klux Klan waged an ongoing terrorist campaign against Reconstruction governments and local leaders. Just as the institution of slavery had depended on violence and the threat of violence, the Klan acted as a kind of guerrilla military force in the service of the Democratic Party, the planter class, and all those who sought the restoration of white supremacy.

In October 1870, after Republicans carried Laurens County in South Carolina, bands of white people drove 150 African Americans from their homes and murdered thirteen white and black Republican activists. In March 1871, three African Americans were arrested in Meridian, Mississippi, for giving "incendiary" speeches. At their court hearing, Klansmen killed two of the defendants and the Republican judge, and thirty more African Americans were murdered in a day of rioting. The single bloodiest episode of Reconstruction era violence took place in Colfax, Louisiana, on Easter Sunday 1873. Nearly 100 African Americans were murdered after they failed to hold a besieged courthouse during a contested election.

Southern Republicans looked to Washington for help. In 1870 and 1871, Congress passed three Enforcement Acts designed to counter racial terrorism. The most sweeping measure was the Ku Klux Klan Act of April 1871, which made the violent infringement of civil and political rights a federal crime punishable by the national government. By the election of 1872, the federal government's intervention had helped break the Klan and restore a semblance of law and order.

The Civil Rights Act of 1875 outlawed racial discrimination in theaters, hotels, railroads, and other public places. But the law proved more an assertion of principle than a direct federal intervention in southern affairs. Enforcement required African Americans to take their cases to the federal courts, a costly and time-consuming procedure.

As wartime idealism faded, northern Republicans became less inclined toward direct intervention in southern affairs. They had enough trouble retaining political control in the North. In 1874, the Democrats gained a majority in the House of Representatives for the first time since 1856. Key northern states also began to fall to the Democrats. Northern Republicans slowly abandoned the freedmen and their white allies in the South. Southern Democrats were also able to exploit a deepening fiscal crisis by blaming Republicans for excessive extension of public credit and the sharp increase in tax rates.

Gradually, conservative Democrats "redeemed" one state after another. Virginia and Tennessee led the way in 1869, North Carolina in 1870, Georgia in 1871, Texas in 1873, and Alabama and Arkansas in 1874. In Mississippi, white conservatives employed violence and intimidation to wrest control in 1875 and "redeemed" the state the following year. Republican infighting in Louisiana in 1873 and 1874 led to a series of contested election results, including bloody clashes between black militia and armed whites, and finally to "redemption" by the Democrats in 1877.

Several Supreme Court rulings involving the Fourteenth and Fifteenth Amendments effectively constrained federal protection of African American civil rights. In the so-called **Slaughterhouse cases** of 1873, the Court issued its first ruling on the Fourteenth Amendment. In its ruling, the Court separated national citizenship from state citizenship and declared that most of the rights that Americans enjoyed on a daily basis—freedom of speech, fair trials, the right to sit on juries, protection from unreasonable searches, and the right to vote—were under the control of state law. The ruling in effect denied the original intent of the Fourteenth Amendment—to protect against state infringement of national citizenship rights as spelled out in the Bill of Rights.

Three other decisions curtailed federal protection of black civil rights. In *United States* v. *Reese* (1876) and *United States* v. *Cruikshank* (1876), the Court restricted congressional

Slaughterhouse cases Group of cases resulting in one sweeping decision by the U.S. Supreme Court in 1873 that contradicted the intent of the Fourteenth Amendment by decreeing that most citizenship rights remained under state, not federal, control.

power to enforce the Ku Klux Klan Act. Future prosecution would depend on the states rather than on federal authorities. In these rulings, the Court held that the Fourteenth Amendment extended the federal power to protect civil rights only in cases involving discrimination by states; discrimination by individuals or groups was not covered. The Court also ruled that the Fifteenth Amendment did not guarantee a citizen's right to vote; it only barred certain specific grounds for denying suffrage—"race; color, or previous condition of servitude." This interpretation opened the door for southern states to disenfranchise African Americans for allegedly nonracial reasons.

Finally, in the 1883 Civil Rights Cases decision, the Court declared the Civil Rights Act of 1875 unconstitutional, holding that the Fourteenth Amendment gave Congress the power to outlaw discrimination by states but not by private individuals. The majority opinion held that black people must no longer "be the special favorite of the laws." Together, these Supreme Court decisions marked the end of federal attempts to protect African American rights until well into the next century.

KING COTTON: SHARECROPPERS, TENANTS, AND THE SOUTHERN ENVIRONMENT

The Republicans' vision of a "New South" remade along the lines of the northern economy failed to materialize. Instead, the South declined into the country's poorest agricultural region. In the post–Civil War years, "King Cotton" expanded its realm, as greater numbers of small white farmers found themselves forced to switch from subsistence crops to growing cotton for the market (see Map 17.3).

QUICK REVIEW

The End of Federal Intervention: Key Supreme Court Cases

◆ Slaughterhouse cases (1873).
◆ *United States* v. *Reese* (1876).
◆ *United States* v. *Cruikshank* (1876).
◆ Civil Rights Cases (1883).

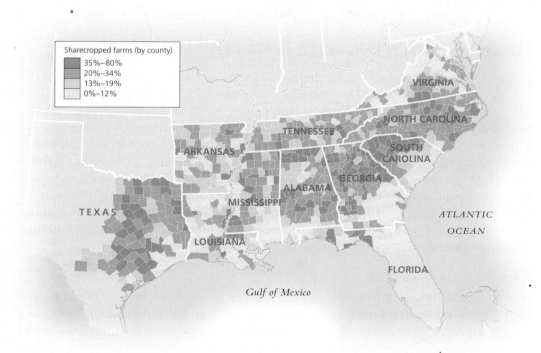

Sharecropped farms (by county)
- 35%–80%
- 20%–34%
- 13%–19%
- 0%–12%

MAP 17.3
Southern Sharecropping and the Cotton Belt, 1880 The economic depression of the 1870s forced increasing numbers of southern farmers, both white and black, into sharecropping arrangements. Sharecropping was most pervasive in the cotton belt regions of South Carolina, Georgia, Alabama, Mississippi, and eastern Texas.

HOW DID this new form of labor affect the lives of former slaves?

A chronic shortage of capital and banking institutions made local merchants and planters the sole source of credit. They advanced loans and supplies to small owners, tenant farmers, and sharecroppers in exchange for a lien, or claim, on the year's cotton crop. They often charged extremely high interest rates on advances, while marking up the prices of the goods sold in their stores. At the end of the year, sharecroppers and tenants found themselves deep in debt to stores for seed, supplies, and clothing.

As the "crop lien" system spread, and as more and more farmers turned to cotton growing as the only way to obtain credit, expanding production depressed prices. Competition from new cotton centers in the world market, such as Egypt and India, accelerated the downward spiral. As cotton prices declined alarmingly, to roughly eleven cents per pound in 1875 to five cents by the early 1890s, per capita wealth in the South fell steadily, equaling only one-third that of the East, Midwest, or West by the 1890s. Small farmers caught up in a vicious cycle of low cotton prices, debt, and dwindling food crops found their old ideal of independence sacrificed to the cruel logic of the cotton market.

To obtain precious credit, most southern farmers, both black and white, found themselves forced to produce cotton for market and, thus, became enmeshed in the debt-ridden crop lien system. In traditional cotton-producing areas, especially the black belt, landless farmers growing cotton had replaced slaves growing cotton. In the Upcountry and newer areas of cultivation, cotton-dominated commercial agriculture, with landless tenants and sharecroppers as the main workforce, had replaced the more diversified subsistence economy of the antebellum era. These patterns hardened throughout the late nineteenth century. By 1900, over one-third of the white farmers and nearly three-quarters of the African American farmers in the cotton states were tenants or sharecroppers.

•◦•─Read the Document

James T. Rapier, Testimony Before U.S. Senate (1880) at **www.myhistorylab.com**

RECONSTRUCTING THE NORTH

Abraham Lincoln liked to cite his own rise as proof of the superiority of the northern system of "free labor" over slavery. "There is no permanent class of hired laborers amongst us," Lincoln asserted. "Twenty-five years ago, I was a hired laborer. The hired laborer of yesterday, labors on his own account today; and will hire others to labor for him tomorrow." But the triumph of the North brought with it fundamental changes in the economy, labor relations, and politics that brought Lincoln's vision into question. The spread of the factory system, the growth of large and powerful corporations, and the rapid expansion of capitalist enterprise all hastened the development of a large unskilled and routinized workforce. Rather than becoming independent producers, more and more workers found themselves consigned permanently to wage labor.

HOW DID the northern political landscape change in the decades after the Civil War?

THE AGE OF CAPITAL

In the decade following Appomattox, the North's economy continued the industrial boom begun during the Civil War. By 1873, America's industrial production had grown 75 percent over the 1865 level. Between 1860 and 1880, the number of wage earners in manufacturing and construction more than doubled, from 2 million to over 4 million. During the same period, nearly 3 million immigrants arrived in America, almost all of whom settled in the North and West.

The railroad business both symbolized and advanced the new industrial order. Shortly before the Civil War, enthusiasm mounted for a transcontinental line. Private companies took on the huge and expensive job of construction, but the federal government funded the project, providing the largest subsidy in American history.

The Union Pacific employed gangs of Irish American and African American workers to lay track heading west from Omaha. Meanwhile the Central Pacific, pushing east from California, had a tougher time finding workers, and began recruiting thousands of men from China. Some 12,000 Chinese laborers (about 90 percent of the workforce) bore the brunt of the difficult conditions in the Sierra Nevada where blizzards, landslides, and steep rock faces took an awful toll. But after completion of the transcontinental line threw thousands of Chinese railroad workers onto the California labor market, anti-Chinese agitation grew among western politicians and labor unions. In 1882, Congress passed the Chinese Exclusion Act, suspending any further Chinese immigration for ten years.

On May 10, 1869, Leland Stanford, the former governor of California and president of the Central Pacific Railroad, traveled to Promontory Point in Utah Territory to hammer a ceremonial golden spike, marking the finish of the first transcontinental line. Other railroads went up with less fanfare. The Southern Pacific, chartered by the state of California, stretched from San Francisco to Los Angeles, and on through Arizona and New Mexico to connections with New Orleans. The Atchison, Topeka, and Santa Fe reached the Pacific in 1887 by way of a southerly route across the Rocky Mountains. The Great Northern, one of the few lines financed by private capital, extended west from St. Paul, Minnesota, to Washington's Puget Sound.

Chinese immigrants, like these section gang workers, provided labor and skills critical to the successful completion of the first transcontinental railroad. This photo was taken in Promontory Point, Utah Territory, in 1869.

Railroad corporations became America's first big businesses. Railroads required huge outlays of investment capital, and their growth increased the economic power of banks and investment houses centered in Wall Street. Bankers often gained seats on the boards of directors of railroad companies, and their access to capital sometimes gave them the real control of the corporations. A small group of railroad executives, including Cornelius Vanderbilt, Jay Gould, Collis P. Huntington, and James J. Hill, amassed unheard-of fortunes.

Some of the nation's most prominent politicians routinely accepted railroad largesse. The worst scandal of the Grant administration grew out of corruption involving railroad promotion. As a way of diverting funds for the building of the Union Pacific Railroad, an inner circle of Union Pacific stockholders created the dummy Crédit Mobilier construction company. In return for political favors, a group of prominent Republicans received stock in the company. When the scandal broke in 1872, it politically ruined Vice President Schuyler Colfax and led to the censure of two congressmen.

Other industries also boomed in this period, especially those engaged in extracting minerals and processing natural resources. Railroad growth stimulated expansion in the production of coal, iron, stone, and lumber, and these also received significant government aid. For example, under the National Mineral Act of 1866, mining companies received millions of acres of free public land. Oil refining enjoyed a huge expansion in the 1860s and 1870s. As with railroads, an early period of fierce competition soon gave way to concentration. By the late 1870s, John D. Rockefeller's Standard Oil Company controlled almost 90 percent of the nation's oil-refining capacity.

LIBERAL REPUBLICANS AND THE ELECTION OF 1872

With the rapid growth of large-scale, capital-intensive enterprises, Republicans increasingly identified with the interests of business rather than the rights of freedmen or the antebellum ideology of "free labor." State Republican parties now organized themselves around the spoils of federal patronage rather than grand causes such as preserving the Union or ending slavery. Republicans had no monopoly on political scandal. In 1871 New York City newspapers reported the shocking story of how Democratic Party boss William M. Tweed and his friends had systematically stolen tens of millions from the city treasury. But to many the scandal represented only the most extreme case of the routine corruption that now plagued American political life.

By the end of President Grant's first term, a large number of disaffected Republicans sought an alternative. The **Liberal Republicans**, as they called themselves, emphasized the doctrines of classical economics. They called for a return to limited government, arguing that bribery, scandal, and high taxes all flowed from excessive state interference in the economy.

Liberal Republicans were also suspicious of expanding democracy. They believed that politics ought to be the province of "the best men"—educated and well-to-do men like themselves, devoted to the "science of government." They proposed civil service reform as the best way to break the hold of party machines on patronage.

Most Liberal Republicans opposed continued federal intervention in the South. The national government had done all it could for the former slaves; they must now take care of themselves. In the spring of 1872, a diverse collection of Liberal Republicans nominated Horace Greeley to run for president. A longtime foe of the Democratic Party, Greeley nonetheless won that party's presidential nomination as well.

Grant easily defeated Greeley, carrying every state in the North and winning 56 percent of the popular vote. But the 1872 election accelerated the trend toward federal

Liberal Republicans Disaffected Republicans that emphasized the doctrines of classical economics.

abandonment of African American citizenship rights. The Liberal Republicans quickly faded as an organized political force. But their ideas helped define a growing conservative consciousness among the northern public. Their agenda included retreat from the ideal of racial justice, hostility toward trade unions, suspicion of immigrant and working-class political power, celebration of competitive individualism, and opposition to government intervention in economic affairs.

THE DEPRESSION OF 1873

In the fall of 1873, the postwar boom came to an abrupt halt as a severe financial panic triggered a deep economic depression. The collapse resulted from commercial overexpansion, especially speculative investing in the nation's railroad system. Over the next two years more than 100 banks folded and 18,000 businesses shut their doors. The depression that began in 1873 lasted sixty-five months—the longest economic contraction in the nation's history until then.

The human toll was enormous. As factories began to close across the nation, the unemployment rate soared to about 15 percent. In many cities the jobless rate was much higher. Many thousands of men took to the road in search of work, and the "tramp" emerged as a new and menacing figure on the social landscape. Farmers were also hard hit by the depression. Agricultural output continued to grow, but prices and land values fell sharply. As prices for their crops fell, farmers had a more difficult time repaying their fixed loan obligations; many sank deeper into debt.

Mass meetings of workers in New York and other cities issued calls to government officials to create jobs through public works. But these appeals were rejected. Indeed, many business leaders and political figures denounced even meager efforts at charity. They saw the depression as a natural, if painful, part of the business cycle, one that would allow only the strongest enterprises (and workers) to survive. The depression of the 1870s prompted workers and farmers to question the old free-labor ideology that celebrated a harmony of interests in northern society. More people voiced anger at and distrust of large corporations that exercised great economic power from outside their communities.

THE ELECTORAL CRISIS OF 1876

With the economy mired in depression and the Grant administration weakened by scandals, Democrats looked forward to capturing the White House in 1876. Democrats nominated Governor Samuel J. Tilden of New York, who brought impeccable reform credentials to his candidacy. In 1871 he had helped expose and prosecute the "Tweed Ring" in New York City. As governor he had toppled the "Canal Ring," a graft-ridden scheme involving inflated contracts for repairs on the Erie Canal. In their platform, the Democrats linked the issue of corruption to an attack on Reconstruction policies. They blamed the Republicans for instituting "a corrupt centralism."

Republican nominee Rutherford B. Hayes, governor of Ohio, also sought the high ground. As a lawyer in Cincinnati he had defended runaway slaves. Later he had distinguished himself as a general in the Union army. Hayes promised, if elected, to support an efficient civil service system, to vigorously prosecute officials who betrayed the public trust, and to introduce a system of free universal education.

On an election day marred by widespread vote fraud and violent intimidation, Tilden received 250,000 more popular votes than Hayes. But Republicans refused to concede victory, challenging the vote totals in the electoral college. Tilden garnered 184 uncontested electoral votes, one shy of the majority required to win, while Hayes received 165 (see Map 17.4).

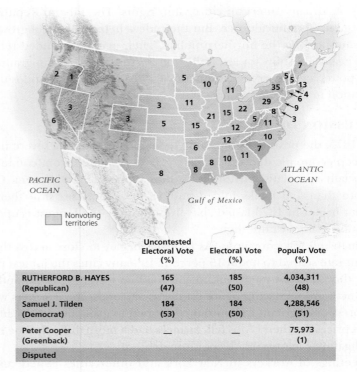

	Uncontested Electoral Vote (%)	Electoral Vote (%)	Popular Vote (%)
RUTHERFORD B. HAYES (Republican)	165 (47)	185 (50)	4,034,311 (48)
Samuel J. Tilden (Democrat)	184 (53)	184 (50)	4,288,546 (51)
Peter Cooper (Greenback)	—	—	75,973 (1)
Disputed			

MAP 17.4
The Election of 1876 The presidential election of 1876 left the nation without a clear-cut winner.

WHAT DOES this map tell us about the nature of sectional politics in 1876? What allowed Democrats to make inroads in the North?

The problem centered on twenty disputed votes from Florida, Louisiana, South Carolina, and Oregon. In each of the three southern states two sets of electoral votes were returned. In Oregon, which Hayes had unquestionably carried, the Democratic governor nevertheless replaced a disputed Republican elector with a Democrat.

The crisis was unprecedented. In January 1877, Congress moved to settle the deadlock, establishing an Electoral Commission composed of five senators, five representatives, and five Supreme Court justices; eight were Republicans and seven were Democrats. The commission voted along strict partisan lines to award all the contested electoral votes to Hayes. Outraged by this decision, Democratic congressmen threatened a filibuster to block Hayes's inauguration. Violence and stalemate were avoided when Democrats and Republicans struck a compromise in February. In return for Hayes's ascendance to the presidency, the Republicans promised to appropriate more money for southern internal improvements, to appoint a Southerner to Hayes's cabinet, and to pursue a policy of noninterference ("home rule") in southern affairs.

Shortly after assuming office, Hayes ordered removal of the remaining federal troops in Louisiana and South Carolina. Without this military presence to sustain them, the Republican governors of those two states quickly lost power to Democrats. "Home rule" meant Republican abandonment of freed people, Radicals, carpetbaggers, and scalawags. It also effectively nullified the Fourteenth and Fifteenth Amendments and the Civil Rights Act of 1866. The **Compromise of 1877** completed repudiation of the idea, born during the Civil War and pursued during Congressional Reconstruction, of a powerful federal government protecting the rights of all American citizens.

Compromise of 1877 The Congressional settling of the 1876 election which installed Republican Rutherford B. Hayes in the White House and gave Democrats control of all state governments in the South.

CHRONOLOGY

1865	Freedmen's Bureau established
	Abraham Lincoln assassinated
	Andrew Johnson begins Presidential Reconstruction
	Black codes begin to be enacted in southern states
	Thirteenth Amendment ratified
1866	Civil Rights Act passed
	Congress approves Fourteenth Amendment
	Ku Klux Klan founded
1867	Reconstruction Acts, passed over President Johnson's veto, begin
	Congressional Reconstruction
	Tenure of Office Act
	Southern states call constitutional conventions
1868	President Johnson impeached by the House but acquitted in Senate trial
	Fourteenth Amendment ratified
	Most Southern states readmitted to the Union
	Ulysses S. Grant elected president
1869	Congress approves Fifteenth Amendment
	Union Pacific and Central Pacific tracks meet at Promontory Point in Utah Territory
	Suffragists split into National Woman Suffrage Association and American Woman Suffrage Association
1870	Fifteenth Amendment ratified
1871	Ku Klux Klan Act passed
	"Tweed Ring" in New York City exposed
1872	Liberal Republicans break with Grant and Radicals, nominate Horace Greeley for president
	Crédit Mobilier scandal
	Grant reelected president
1873	Financial panic and beginning of economic depression
	Slaughterhouse Cases
1874	Democrats gain control of House for first time since 1856
1875	Civil Rights Act
1876	Disputed election between Samuel Tilden and Rutherford B. Hayes
1877	Electoral Commission elects Hayes president
	President Hayes dispatches federal troops to break Great Railroad Strike and withdraws last remaining federal troops from the South

CONCLUSION

Reconstruction succeeded in the limited political sense of reuniting a nation torn apart by the Civil War. The Radical Republican vision, emphasizing racial justice, equal civil and political rights guaranteed by the Fourteenth and Fifteenth Amendments, and a new southern economy organized around independent small farmers, never enjoyed the support of the majority of its party or the northern public. By 1877, the political force of these ideals was spent and the national retreat from them nearly complete.

The end of Reconstruction left the way open for the return of white domination in the South. The freed people's political and civil equality proved only temporary. It would take a "Second Reconstruction," the civil rights movement of the next century, to establish full black citizenship rights once and for all. The federal government's failure to pursue land reform left former slaves without the economic independence needed for full emancipation. Yet the newly autonomous black family, along with black-controlled churches, schools, and other social institutions, provided the foundations for the modern African

American community. If the federal government was not yet fully committed to protecting equal rights in local communities, the Reconstruction Era at least pointed to how that goal might be achieved. Even as the federal government retreated from the defense of equal rights for black people, it took a more aggressive stance as the protector of business interests. The Hayes administration responded decisively to one of the worst outbreaks of class violence in American history by dispatching federal troops to several northern cities to break the Great Railroad Strike of 1877. In the aftermath of Reconstruction, the struggle between capital and labor had clearly replaced "the southern question" as the number one political issue of the day. "The overwhelming labor question has dwarfed all other questions into nothing," wrote an Ohio Republican. "We have home questions enough to occupy attention now."

REVIEW QUESTIONS

1. How did various visions of a "reconstructed" South differ? How did these visions reflect the old political and social divisions that had led to the Civil War?

2. What key changes did emancipation make in the political and economic status of African Americans? Discuss the expansion of citizenship rights in the post–Civil War years. To what extent did women share in the gains made by African Americans?

3. What role did such institutions as the family, the church, the schools, and the political parties play in the African American transition to freedom?

4. How did white Southerners attempt to limit the freedom of former slaves? How did these efforts succeed, and how did they fail?

5. Evaluate the achievements and failures of Reconstruction governments in the southern states.

6. What were the crucial economic changes occurring in the North and South during the Reconstruction era?

KEY TERMS

Black codes (p. 416)
Carpetbaggers (p. 428)
Civil Rights Bill (p. 417)
Congressional Reconstruction (p. 417)
Compromise of 1877 (p. 436)
Fifteenth Amendment (p. 419)
First Reconstruction Act (p. 417)
Freedmen's Bureau (p. 417)
Ku Klux Klan (p. 419)

Liberal Republicans (p. 434)
Radical Republicans (p. 413)
Scalawags (p. 428)
Sharecropping (p. 424)
Slaughterhouse cases (p. 430)
Special Field Order 15 (p. 414)
Tenure of Office Act (p. 418)
Union League (p. 425)
War Democrats (p. 415)

PEARSON myhistorylab Connections

Reinforce what you learned in this chapter by studying the many documents, images, maps, review tools, and videos available at www.myhistorylab.com.

Read and Review

✓• Study and Review **Chapter 17**

•••• Read the Document

Confederate Song, "I'm a Good Old Rebel" (1866)

Carl Schurz, Report on the Condition of the South (1865)

Mississippi Black Code (1865)

Jourdon Anderson to His Former Master (1865)

A Sharecrop Contract (1882)

Address from the Colored Citizens of Norfolk, VA (1865)

James T. Rapier, Testimony Before U.S. Senate (1880)

👁 See the Map **Reconstruction**

Research and Explore

•••• Read the Document

Exploring America: Did Reconstruction Work for the Freed People?

Profiles
Tunis Campbell
Nathan Bedford Forrest

History Bookshelf: *Ulysses S. Grant, Memoirs (1886)*

Whose History Is it?: Flying the Stars and Bars: The Contested Meaning of the Confederate Flag

◉ Watch the Video

Reconstruction in Texas

The Promise and Failure of Reconstruction

Trials of Racial Identity in Nineteenth-Century America

((•• Hear the Audio

Hear the audio files for Chapter 17 at
www.myhistorylab.com.

Realities of Freedom

The Freedmen's Bureau established in 1865 by Congress provided freedmen with clothing, temporary shelter, food, and series of freedmen's schools across the South. Southern response was to fall into the use of terror to deter blacks from becoming economically independent using the agencies of groups like the Ku Klux Klan. Sharecropping, tenant farming, and peonage were insidious economic arrangements that placed whites and blacks in a form of economic slavery to large land holders in the South of the post-Civil War era.

The story of African Americans after the end of slavery is complex and varied. Some blacks attempted to seek out better places to establish their new lives while others remained in the security of the only home they had known as slaves. ■

FOLLOWING EMANCIPATION, what economic and social opportunities existed for African Americans in the United States? How did these opportunities change the lives of freedmen after the official end to slavery?

AN ACT TO ESTABLISH A BUREAU FOR THE RELIEF OF FREEDMEN AND REFUGEES, 1865

BE IT enacted, That there is hereby established in the War Department, to continue during the present war of rebellion, and for one year thereafter, a bureau of refugees, freedmen, and abandoned lands, to which shall be committed, as hereinafter provided, the supervision and management of all abandoned lands, and the control of all subjects relating to refugees and freedmen from rebel states, or from any district of country within the territory embraced in the operations of the army, under such rules and regulations as may be prescribed by the head of the bureau and approved by the President. The said bureau shall be under the management and control of a commissioner to be appointed by the President, by and with the advice and consent of the Senate... ■

◄ African-American family working together in the cotton fields.

When We Worked on Shares, We Couldn't Make Nothing

AFTER SLAVERY we had to get in before night too. If you didn't, Ku Klux would drive you in. They would come and visit you anyway. . . . When he got you good and scared he would drive on away. They would whip you if they would catch you out in the night time. . . .

I've forgot who it is that that told us that we was free. Somebody come and told us we're free now. I done forgot who it was.

After freedom, we worked on shares a while. Then we rented. When we worked on shares, we couldn't make nothing, just overalls and something to eat. Half went to the other man and you would destroy your half if you weren't careful. A man that didn't know how to count would always lose. He might lose anyhow. They didn't give no itemized statement. No, you just had to take their word. They never give you no details. They just say you owe so much. No matter how good account you kept, you had to go by their account and now, Brother, I'm tellin' you the truth about this. It's been that way for a long time. You had to take the white man's work on note, and everything. Anything you wanted, you could git if you were a good hand. You could git anything you wanted as long as you worked. If you didn't make no money, that's all right; they would advance you more. But

Share croppers and their families were evicted from the plantation they were working after being convicted of engaging in a conspiracy to retain their homes. This picture was taken just after the evictions before the families were moved into a tent colony.

you better not leave him, you better not try to leave and get caught. They'd keep you in debt. They were sharp. Christmas come, you could take up twenty dollar, in somethin' to eat and much as you wanted in whiskey. You could buy a gallon of whiskey. . . . Anything that kept you a slave because he was always right and you were always wrong it there was difference. If there was an argument, he would get mad and there would be a shooting take place. . . . ∎

Sharecrop Contract, 1882

TO EVERY one applying to rent land upon shares, the following conditions must be read, and agreed to.

To every 30 or 35 acres, I agree to furnish the team, plow, and farming implements, except cotton planters, and I do not agree to furnish a cart to every cropper. The croppers are to have half of the cotton, corn and fodder (and peas and pumpkins and potatoes if any are planted. . .

Croppers are to have no part or interest in the cotton seed raised from the crop planted and worked by them. No vine crops of any description, that is, no watermelons, muskmelons,…squashes or anything of that kind, except peas and pumpkins, and potatoes, are to be planted in the cotton or corn. All must work under my direction. All plantation work to be done by the croppers. . . .

For every mule or horse furnished by me there must be 1000 good sized rails…hauled, and the fence repaired as far as they will go, the fence to be torn down and put up from the bottom if I so direct. All croppers to haul rails and work on fence whenever I may order. Rails to be split when I may say. . . .

Each cropper must keep in good repair all bridges in his crop or over ditches that he has to clean out and when a bridge needs repairing that is outside of all their crops, then any one that I call on must repair it. . . .

No cropper to work off the plantation when there is any work to be done on the land he has rented, or when his work is needed by me or other croppers. Trees to be cut down on Orchard, House field & Evanson fences, leaving such as I may designate. . . . ∎

The two locomotives then moved up until they touched each other, . . .and at one p.m., under an almost cloudless sky, and in the presence of about one thousand one hundred people, the completion of the greatest railroad on earth was announced.

—*Andrew J. Russel, from* Frank Leslie's Illustrated Railroad, *June 5, 1869*

This engraving, showing passengers shooting buffalo from a train crossing the plains, suggests the often casual approach Americans took toward the Western Environment. The destruction of the buffalo herds, for both profit and "sport," also destroyed the basis of the Plains Indians' economy and culture.

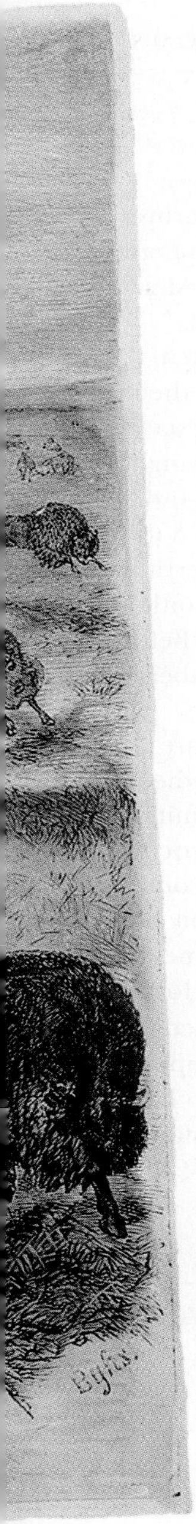

18

CONQUEST AND SURVIVAL
THE TRANS–MISSISSIPPI WEST, 1860–1900

((•—|Hear the Audio

Hear the audio files for Chapter 18 at **www.myhistorylab.com**.

HOW AND why did federal policy towards Indian peoples change in the decades following the Civil War?

HOW DID Americans exploit the West's natural resources in the second half of the nineteenth century?

WHAT LED to the growth of the cattle industry after the Civil War?

HOW DID the Great Plains become a center of American agriculture?

HOW DID agribusiness differ from more traditional forms of farming?

WHAT PLACE did the West hold in the national imagination?

WHAT KIND of Indian society did reformers envision?

AMERICAN COMMUNITIES
The Oklahoma Land Rush

DECADES AFTER THE EVENT, COWBOY EVAN G. BARNARD VIVIDLY RECALLED the preparations settlers made when Oklahoma territorial officials announced the biggest "land rush" in American history. "Thousands of people gathered along the border. . . . As the day for the race drew near, the settlers practiced running their horses and driving carts." Finally, the morning of April 22, 1889, arrived. "At ten o'clock people lined up . . . ready for the great race of their lives." Like many others, Barnard displayed his guns prominently on his hips, determined to discourage competitors from claiming the 160 acres of prime land that he intended to grab for himself.

Evan Barnard's story was one strand in the larger tale of the destruction and creation of communities in the trans–Mississippi West. In the 1830s, the federal government designated what was to become the state of Oklahoma as Indian Territory, reserved for the Five Civilized Tribes (Cherokees, Chickasaws, Choctaws, Creeks, and Seminoles) who had been forcibly removed from their eastern lands. All five tribes had reestablished themselves as sovereign republics in Indian Territory. The Cherokees and Choctaws became prosperous cotton growers. The Creeks managed large herds of hogs and cattle, and the Chickasaws grazed not only cattle but also sheep and goats on their open fields.

The Civil War, however, took a heavy toll on their success. Some tribes, slaveholders themselves, sided with the Confederacy; others with the Union. When the war ended, more than 10,000 people— nearly one-fifth of the population of Indian Territory—had died. To make matters worse, new treaties required the Five Civilized Tribes to cede the entire western half of the territory, including the former northern Indian territory of Nebraska and Kansas, for the resettlement of tribes from other regions. Western Oklahoma thereby became home to thousands of newly displaced peoples. Eventually, more than 80,000 tribespeople were living on twenty-one separate reservations in western Oklahoma, all governed by agents appointed by the federal government.

The opening of the unassigned far western district of Oklahoma, however, signaled the impending end of Indian sovereignty. Many non-Indians saw this almost 2-million-acre strip as a Promised Land, perfect for dividing into thousands of small farms. Moreover, the railroads, seeing the potential for lucrative commerce, put constant pressure on the federal government to open No Man's Land for settlement. In 1889, the U.S. Congress finally gave in.

Dramatic as it was, the land rush of 1889 was only one in a series of events that soon dispossessed Oklahoma's Indians of their remaining lands. First, the federal government broke up the estates held collectively by various tribes in western Oklahoma, assigning to individuals the standard 160-acre allotment and allowing non-Indian homesteaders to claim the rest. Then, in 1898, Congress passed the Curtis Act, which abolished tribal jurisdiction over all Indian Territory. Members of the former Indian nations were directed to dismantle their governments and abandon their estates (see Map 18.1). Before a decade had passed, tribespeople in Oklahoma were outnumbered by ten to one.

By this time, nearly one-quarter of the entire population of the United States lived west of the Mississippi River. Hundreds of new communities, supported primarily by cattle ranching, agriculture, mining, or other industries, had not only grown with the emerging national economy but also helped to shape it in the process. The newcomers had displaced communities that had formed centuries earlier. They also drastically transformed the physical landscape. Through their activities and the support of Easterners, the United States realized an ambition that John L. O'Sullivan had described in 1845 as the nation's "manifest destiny to overspread the continent" and remake it in a new image.

Indian Territory (Oklahoma)

INDIAN PEOPLES UNDER SIEGE

The Indians living west of the Mississippi River keenly felt the pressure of the gradual incorporation of the West into the American nation. California became a state in 1850, Oregon in 1859. In the next decades, Congress granted territorial status to Utah, New Mexico, Washington, Dakota, Colorado, Nevada, Arizona, Idaho, Montana, and Wyoming. The purchase of Alaska in 1867 added an area twice the size of Texas. The federal government made itself the custodian of these thinly settled regions, with appointed white governors supervising the transition from territorial status to statehood.

A series of events brought large numbers of white settlers into these new states and territories: the discovery of gold in California in 1848, the opening of western lands to homesteaders in 1862, and the completion of the transcontinental railroad in 1869. With competition for the land and its resources escalating into violent skirmishes and small wars, federal officials became determined to end tribal rule and bring Indians into the American mainstream.

HOW AND why did federal policy towards Indian peoples change in the decades following the Civil War?

INDIAN TERRITORY

Before the European colonists reached the New World, hundreds of tribes, totaling perhaps a million members, had occupied western lands for more than 20,000 years. The arrival of Europeans brought disease, religious conversion, and new patterns of commerce. But geographic isolation still gave many tribes a margin of survival unknown in the East. At the close of the Civil War, approximately 360,000 Indian peoples still lived in the trans–Mississippi West, the majority of them in the Great Plains.

The surviving tribes adapted to changing conditions. The Plains Indians learned to ride the horses and shoot the guns introduced by Spanish and British traders. The Pawnees migrated farther westward to evade encroaching non-Indian settlers, while the Sioux and the Comanches fought neighboring tribes to gain control of large stretches of the Great

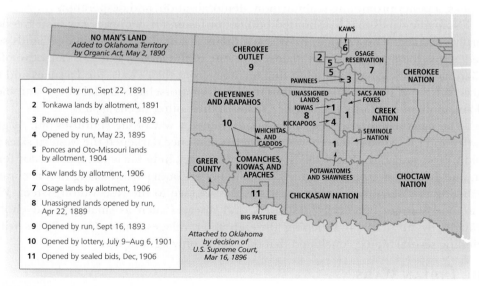

1 Opened by run, Sept 22, 1891
2 Tonkawa lands by allotment, 1891
3 Pawnee lands by allotment, 1892
4 Opened by run, May 23, 1895
5 Ponces and Oto-Missouri lands by allotment, 1904
6 Kaw lands by allotment, 1906
7 Osage lands by allotment, 1906
8 Unassigned lands opened by run, Apr 22, 1889
9 Opened by run, Sept 16, 1893
10 Opened by lottery, July 9–Aug 6, 1901
11 Opened by sealed bids, Dec, 1906

MAP 18.1
Oklahoma Territory Land openings to settlers came at different times, making new land available through various means.

From *Historical Atlas of Oklahoma* by Morris, Goins, McReynolds. Copyright © 1965 University of Oklahoma Press. Reprinted by permission.

WHAT WAS the impact of the land rush on Indian settlements?

Plains. The southwestern Hopis and Zunis, conquered earlier by the Spanish, continued to trade with the Mexicans who lived near them. Some tribes took dramatic steps toward accommodation with white ways. Even before they were uprooted and moved across the Mississippi River, the Cherokees had learned English, converted to Christianity, established a constitutional republic, and become a nation of farmers.

In 1830, Congress passed the Indian Removal Act (see Chapter 11), which provided funds to relocate all eastern tribes by force if necessary. The Cherokees challenged this legislation and the Supreme Court ruled in their favor. Ignoring the Court's decision, President Andrew Jackson forced many tribes to cede their land and remove to Indian Territory. There, it was believed, they might live undisturbed by whites and gradually adjust to "civilized" ways. But soon, the onslaught of white settlers, railroad entrepreneurs, and Gold Rush prospectors pressured tribes to cede millions of their acres to the United States. As demand for resources and land accelerated, the entire plan for a permanent Indian Territory fell apart.

THE RESERVATION POLICY AND THE SLAUGHTER OF THE BUFFALO

As early as the 1840s, officials had outlined a plan to subdue the intensifying rivalry over natural resources and land. Under the terms of their proposal, individual tribes would agree to live within clearly defined zones—reservations. In exchange, the Bureau of Indian Affairs would provide guidance, while U.S. military forces ensured protection. By the end of the 1850s, eight western reservations had been established (see Map 18.2).

Those tribes that moved to reservations often found provisions inadequate to their needs. The Medicine Lodge Treaty of 1867 assigned reservations in existing Indian Territory to Comanches, Plains (Kiowa) Apaches, Kiowas, Cheyennes, and Arapahoes, bringing these tribes together with Sioux, Shoshones, and Bannocks. All told, more than 100,000 people found themselves competing intensely for survival. Corrupt officials of the Bureau of Indian Affairs routinely diverted funds for their own use and reduced food supplies, a policy promoting malnutrition, demoralization, and desperation.

Nomadic tribes that had hunted buffalo, or bison, for centuries saw their freedom sharply curtailed. The Lakotas, or Western Sioux, a loose confederation of bands scattered across the northern Great Plains, were one of the largest and most adaptive of all Indian nations. Seizing buffalo-hunting territory from their rivals, the Pawnees and the Crows, the Sioux had learned to follow the herds on horseback. Buffalo meat and hides fed and clothed the Sioux and satisfied many of their other needs as well.

The mass slaughter of the buffalo undermined a way of life centuries old. As gunpowder and the railroad moved west, the herds that once darkened the western skies fell rapidly. Non-Indian traders avidly sought fur for coats, hide for leather, bones for fertilizer, and heads for trophies. Army commanders encouraged the slaughter, accurately predicting that starvation would break tribal resistance to the reservation system. With their food sources practically destroyed, and diseases such as smallpox and cholera (brought by fur traders) sweeping through their villages, many Great Plains tribes, including several Sioux, concluded that they could only fight or die.

THE INDIAN WARS

In 1864, large-scale war erupted. Having decided to terminate all treaties with tribes in eastern Colorado, territorial governor John Evans encouraged a group of white civilians, the Colorado Volunteers, to stage raids through Cheyenne campgrounds. On November 29, 1864, the Colorado Volunteers and soldiers attacked a Cheyenne campground at Sand Creek. While the Cheyenne chief Black Kettle held up a U.S. flag and a white truce banner, a group of 700 men, slaughtered as many as 200 Cheyennes, the majority elderly men, women, and children. They mutilated the corpses and took scalps back to Denver

QUICK REVIEW

White Migration and the Plains Indians

◆ Desire by whites for land led to violations of treaties.

◆ Buffalo were eliminated from tribal hunting grounds.

◆ Many Indian peoples decided they could only fight or die.

◆◆◆ Read the Document

Congressional Report on Sand Creek Massacre (1867) at **www.myhistorylab.com**

MAP 18.2

Major Indian Battles and Indian Reservations, 1860–1900   As commercial routes and white populations passed through and occupied Indian lands, warfare inevitably erupted. The displacement of Indians to reservations opened access by farmers, ranchers, and investors to natural resources and to markets.

WHERE WERE Indian reservations located? What explains the pattern of reservation sites this map reveals?

to exhibit as trophies. Months after the **Sand Creek Massacre**, bands of Cheyennes, Sioux, and Arapahoes were still retaliating, burning civilian outposts and sometimes killing whole families.

In 1851, believing the U.S. government would recognize their own rights of conquest over other Indian tribes, the Sioux relinquished large tracts of land as a demonstration of good faith. But within a decade, a mass invasion of miners and the construction of military forts along the Bozeman Trail in Wyoming, the Sioux's principal buffalo range, threw the tribe's future into doubt. During the **Great Sioux War** of 1865–67, the Oglala Sioux warrior Red Cloud fought the U.S. Army to a stalemate. The Treaty of Fort Laramie, signed in 1868, restored only a temporary peace to the region.

The **Treaty of Fort Laramie** granted the Sioux the right to occupy the Black Hills, or Paha Sapa, their sacred land, "as long as the grass shall grow," but the discovery of gold soon undermined this guarantee. Directed to map a site for a new fort and to quietly look for gold, Lieutenant Colonel George Armstrong Custer led an expedition to

Sand Creek Massacre   The near annihilation in 1864 of Black Kettle's Cheyenne band by Colorado troops under Colonel John Chivington's orders to "kill and scalp all, big and little."

Great Sioux War   From 1865 to 1867 the Oglala Sioux warrior Red Cloud waged war against the U.S. Army, forcing the U.S. to abandon its forts built on land relinquished to the government by the Sioux.

Treaty of Fort Laramie   The treaty acknowledging U.S. defeat in the Great Sioux War in 1868 and supposedly guaranteeing the Sioux perpetual land and hunting rights in South Dakota, Wyoming, and Montana.

This painting depicts the Battle of Sand Creek, fought in November 1864. Colorado militia volunteers, under Colonel John Chivington, led the deadly attack on the Cheyennes and their allies in southeastern Colorado Territory.

the Black Hills during the summer of 1874. Contrary to the plan, Custer broadcast his discovery of the precious ore. White prospectors soon overran the territory. Determined to fight for the right to this land, thousands of Sioux, Cheyenne, and Arapaho warriors moved into war camps during the summer of 1876 and prepared for battle (see Map 18.2).

After several months of skirmishes between the U.S. Army and Indian warriors, Lieutenant Colonel Custer decided to rush ahead to a site in Montana known to white soldiers as Little Bighorn. This foolhardy move offered the allied Cheyenne and Sioux warriors a perfect opportunity to cut off Custer's logistical and military support. On June 25, 1876, Cheyenne and Sioux warriors wiped out Custer and his ill-trained troops.

"Custer's Last Stand" gave Indian-haters the emotional ammunition to whip up public sentiment against the Indians. After Custer's defeat, Sitting Bull reportedly said, "Now they will never let us rest." The U.S. Army tracked down the disbanded Indian contingents one by one and forced them to surrender. In February 1877, Sioux leadership in the Indian Wars ended.

Among the last to strike out against the reservation system were the Apaches in the Southwest. Unable to tolerate the harsh conditions on the reservation, and angered by the encroachment of whites, some of the Apache bands returned to their old ways of seizing territory and stealing cattle. Pursued by the U.S. Army, the Apaches earned a reputation as intrepid warriors. Brilliant strategists like Geronimo and skilled horse-riding braves became legendary for lightning-swift raids against the white outposts in the rugged Arizona terrain.

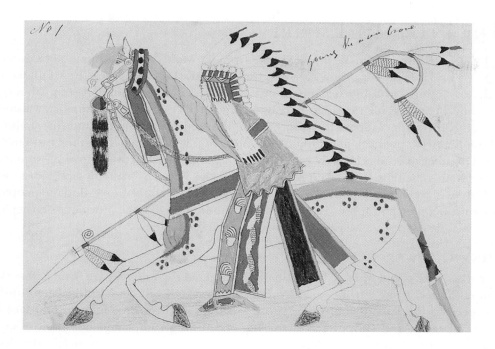

Kiowa Preparing for *a War Expedition*, ca. 1887. This sketch on paper was made by an Indian artist, Silverhorn, who had himself taken part in the final revolt of the Kiowas in 1874. He later became a medicine man and then served as a private in the U.S. Cavalry at Fort Sill, Oklahoma Territory.

Silverhorn (Native American), *Kiowa Preparing for a War Expedition*. From "Sketchbook," 1887. Graphite, ink, and crayon on paper. Collection of the McNay Art Museum, Gift of Mrs. Terrell Bartlett.

In 1874–75, the Kiowas and the Comanches, both powerful tribes, joined the Apaches in one of the bloodiest conflicts of the era, the Red River War. The U.S. Army ultimately prevailed, although less by military strategy than by new technologies of warfare and by denying Indians access to food. Small-scale warfare sputtered on until September 1886, when Geronimo, his band reduced to only ten people, finally surrendered, thereby ending the Indian Wars.

THE NEZ PERCES

For generations, the Nez Perces (Nimiipuu) had regarded themselves as good friends to white traders and settlers. But the discovery of gold on Nez Perce land in 1860 changed their relations with whites for the worse and also challenged their tribal identity. Pressed by prospectors and mining companies, U.S. government officials demanded, in the treaty of 1863, that the Nez Perces cede about nine-tenths of their holdings, at less than ten cents per acre. Some of the Nez Perce leaders agreed to the terms of the treaty, which had been fraudulently signed on behalf of the entire tribe, but others refused. Joseph, who became chief of the Wallowa band in 1871, held out. Only to avoid warfare did he agree to move his band to the small Lapwai Reservation in Idaho.

In 1877, Chief Joseph's band reluctantly set out from the Wallowa Valley. Along the way, some young members of another Indian band traveling with them rode away from camp to avenge the death of one of their own by killing several white settlers. Hoping to explain the situation, a Nez Perce truce team approached U.S. troops. The troops opened fire, and the Indian riders fired back, killing one-third of the soldiers. Outmaneuvering vengeful U.S. troops sent to intercept them, the 750 Nez Perce retreated for some 1,400 miles into Montana and Wyoming. U.S. troops finally trapped the Nez Perces in the Bear Paw Mountains of northern Montana, just thirty miles from the Canadian border. Suffering from hunger and cold, they surrendered.

The Nez Perces were sent to disease-ridden bottomland near Fort Leavenworth in Kansas and then to Oklahoma. The last remnants of Joseph's band were eventually deported to a non–Nez Perce reservation in Washington, where Chief Joseph died in 1904 of a broken heart, according to a reservation doctor, and where his descendants continue to live in exile to this day.

THE INTERNAL EMPIRE

HOW DID Americans exploit the West's natural resources in the second half of the nineteenth century?

👁 **See** the **Map**
Resources and Conflict in the West at **www.myhistorylab.com**

Watch the **Video**
The Real West Is an Urban West at **www.myhistorylab.com**

Read the **Document**
John Lester, Hydraulic Mining (1873) at **www.myhistorylab.com**

Determined to make their fortunes from the West's abundant natural resources, be it from copper in Arizona, timber in Washington, wheat in Montana, or oranges in California, numerous adventurers traveled west. As a group, they carried out the largest migration and greatest commercial expansion in American history.

But the settlers themselves also became the subjects of a huge "internal empire" whose financial, political, and industrial centers of power remained in the East. Only a small number of settlers actually struck it rich in the great extractive industries—mining, lumbering, ranching, and farming—that ruled the western economy and supported industrial development in the east. Meanwhile, older populations—Indian peoples, Hispanic peoples, and more recently settled communities like the Mormons—struggled to create places for themselves in this new expansionist order.

MINING TOWNS

The discovery of gold in California in 1848 attracted fortune seekers from across the United States, from Europe, and from as far away as Chile and China. Meanwhile, prospecting parties overran the territories, setting a pattern for intermittent rushes for gold, silver, and copper across the region. Mining camps and boomtowns soon dotted what had once been thinly settled regions and speeded the urban development of the West. The population of California alone jumped from 14,000 in 1848 to 223,856 just four years later. Mining soon brought the West into a vast global market for capital, commodities, and labor (see Map 18.3).

The mining industry quickly grew into a corporate enterprise. The most successful mine owners bought out the smaller claims and built an entire industry around their stakes. They found investors to finance their expansion and used the borrowed capital to purchase the latest in extractive technology. They gained access to timber to fortify their underground structures and water to feed the hydraulic pumps that washed down mountains. They built smelters to refine the crude ore into ingots and often financed railroads to transport the product to distant markets.

The mining corporations laid the basis for a new economy as well as an interim government and established many of the region's first white settlements. Before the advent of railroads, ore had to be brought out of, and supplies brought into, mining areas by boats, wagons, and mules traveling hundreds of miles over rough territory. The railroad made transportation of supplies and products easier and faster. The shipping trade meanwhile grew into an important industry of its own, employing thousands of merchants, peddlers, and sailors.

The many boomtowns, known as "Helldorados," flourished, if only temporarily, as ethnically diverse communities. Men

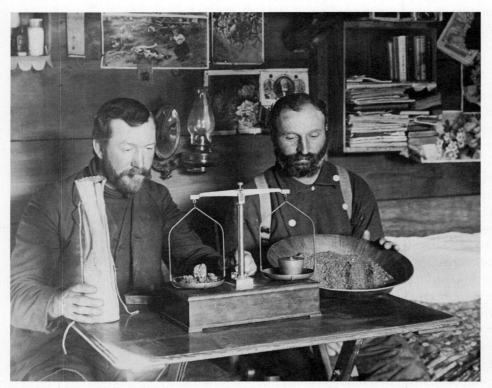

After news of the discovery of gold in the Klondike reached the United States in July 1897, tens of thousands of "stampeders," hoping to strike it rich, rushed to the Yukon Territory. Among them were more than twenty commercial photographers who made good livings selling photographs, such as this image of prospectors weighing gold nuggets. Many prospectors themselves also used roll film cameras and contributed to the production of thousands of photographs of their adventures.

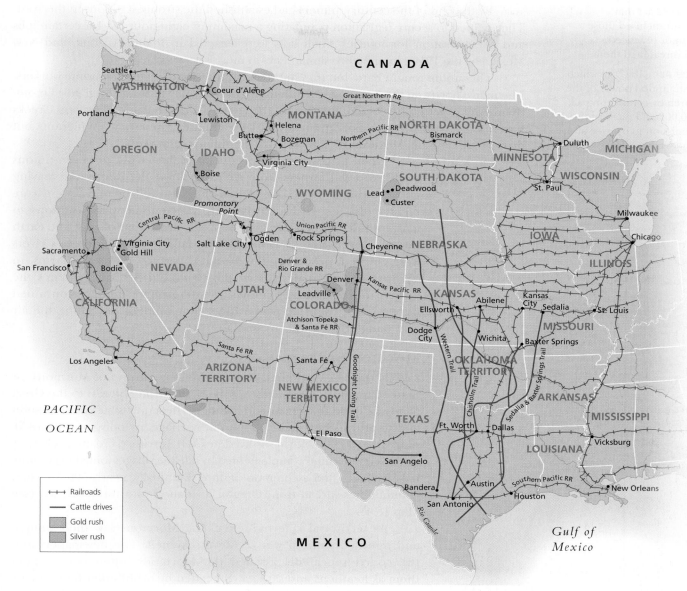

MAP 18.3

Railroad Routes, Cattle Trails, Gold and Silver Rushes, 1860–1900   By the end of the nineteenth century, the vast region of the West was crosscut by hundreds of lines of transportation and communication. The trade in precious metals and in cattle helped build a population almost constantly on the move, following the rushes for gold or the herds of cattle.

Encyclopedia of American Social History.

HOW DID the growth of railroads facilitate the growth of the mining and cattle industries?

outnumbered women by as much as ten to one, and very few lived with families or stayed very long. The town center was usually the saloon.

The western labor movement began in these camps, partly as a response to dangerous working conditions. In the hardrock mines of the 1870s, one of every thirty workers was disabled, and one of every eighty killed. Miners began to organize in the 1860s, demanding good pay for dangerous and life-shortening work.

QUICK REVIEW

Technology and Mining

- Mining began as an individual enterprise.
- Deeper mining required expensive equipment.
- As mining became more complex and costly, it came under corporate control.

Edmunds Act 1882 act that effectively disenfranchised those who believed in or practiced polygamy and threatened them.

Edmunds-Tucker Act 1887 act which destroyed the temporal power of the Mormon Church by confiscating all assets over $50,000 and establishing a federal commission to oversee all elections in the Utah territory.

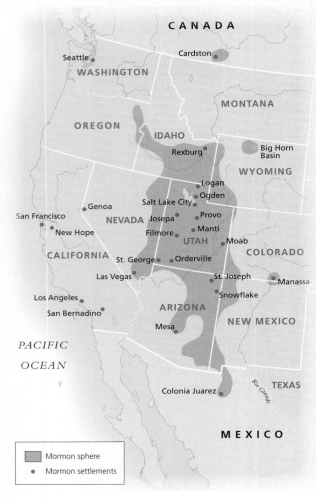

MAP 18.4

Mormon Cultural Diffusion, ca. 1883 Mormon settlements permeated many sparsely populated sections of Idaho, Nevada, Arizona, Wyoming, Colorado, and New Mexico. Built with church backing and the strong commitment of community members, they survived and even prospered in adverse climates.

"THE MORMON CULTURE REGION: STRATEGIES AND PATTERNS IN THE GEOGRAPHY OF THE AMERICAN WEST, 1847–1964" by Donald W. Meinig, from *The Annals of the Association of American Geographers* 55, no. 2, June 1965, reprinted by permission of the publisher (Taylor & Francis Group, http://www.informaworld.com).

WHAT IF any factors in the West provided a more conducive environment in which the Mormons could flourish?

By the end of the century, miners had established the strongest unions in the West. They helped to secure legislation mandating a maximum eight-hour day for certain jobs and compensation for injuries. Such laws were enacted in Idaho, Arizona, and New Mexico by the 1910s, long before similar laws in most Eastern states.

The unions fought hard, but they did so exclusively for the benefit of white workers. The native-born and the Irish and Cornish immigrants (from Cornwall, England) far outnumbered other groups before the turn of the century, when Italians, Slavs, and Greeks began to replace them. Labor unions eventually admitted these new immigrants but drove away Chinese, Mexican, Indian, and African American workers.

When prices and ore production fell sharply, not even unions could stop the owners from shutting down the mines and leaving ghost towns in their wake. Often they also left behind an environmental disaster. Hydraulic mining, which used water cannons to blast hillsides and expose gold deposits, drove tons of rock and earth into the rivers and canyons. By the late 1860s, California's rivers were clogged, producing floods that wiped out towns and farms. In 1893, Congress finally passed the Caminetti Act, giving states the power to regulate the mines. Underground mining continued unregulated, using up whole forests for timbers and filling the air with dangerous, sulfurous smoke.

MORMON SETTLEMENTS

Led by their new prophet, Brigham Young, a group of Mormons, or Latter-day Saints, migrated in 1846–47 from the Midwest to the Great Salt Lake Basin to form an independent theocratic state called Deseret and to affirm the sanctity of plural marriage, or polygamy. By 1870, more than 87,000 Mormons lived in Utah Territory, creating relatively sizable communities complemented by satellite villages joined to communal farmlands and a common pasture. Eventually, nearly 500 Mormon communities spread from Oregon to Idaho to northern Mexico (see Map 18.4).

As territorial rule tightened, the Mormons saw their unique and tightly organized way of life threatened. The newspapers and the courts repeatedly assailed the Mormons, often condemning them as heathens and savages. Preceded by prohibitory federal laws enacted in 1862 and 1874, the Supreme Court finally ruled against polygamy in the 1879 case of *United States* v. *Reynolds*. In 1882, Congress passed the **Edmunds Act**, which disfranchised those who believed in or practiced polygamy and threatened them with fines and imprisonment. More devastating was the **Edmunds-Tucker Act**, passed five years later, which effectively destroyed the temporal power of the Mormon Church by confiscating all assets over $50,000 and establishing a federal commission to oversee all elections in the territory. By the early 1890s, Mormon leaders officially renounced the practice of plural marriage.

Forced to abandon polygamy, Mormons gave up many other aspects of their distinctive communal life, including the common ownership of land. By the time Utah became a state in 1896, Mormon communities resembled in some ways the society that the original settlers had sought to escape. Nevertheless, they combined their religious cohesion with leadership in the expanding regional economy to become a major political force in the West.

MEXICAN BORDERLAND COMMUNITIES

The Treaty of Guadalupe Hidalgo, which ended the Mexican-American War in 1848, allowed the Hispanic people north of the Rio Grande to choose between immigrating to Mexico or staying in what was now the United States. But the new Mexican-American border did not sever communities that had been connected for centuries. What gradually emerged was an economically and socially interdependent zone, the Anglo-Hispanic borderlands linking the United States and Mexico.

For a time, the borderlands held out hope for a mutually beneficial interaction between Mexicanos and Anglos (as Mexicans called white Americans). A prosperous class of Hispanic landowners, with long-standing ties to Anglos through marriage, had established itself in cities like Albuquerque and Tucson. These Mexican elites, well integrated into the emerging national economy, continued to wield political power as ranchers, landlords, and real estate developers until the end of the century. They secured passage of bills for education in their regions and often served as superintendents of local schools. Several prominent merchants became territorial delegates to Congress.

The majority of Mexicans worked outside the commercial economy, farming and herding sheep for their own subsistence. With the Anglos came land closures as well as commercial expansion, prompted by railroad, mining, and timber industries. Many poor families found themselves crowded onto plots of land too small for subsistence farming. Many men turned to seasonal labor on the new Anglo-owned commercial farms. Others took jobs on the railroad or in the mines. Meanwhile, their wives and daughters moved to the new towns and cities in such numbers that by the end of the century Mexicanos had become a predominantly urban population, dependent on wages for survival.

Women were quickly drawn into the expanding network of market relations. They tried to make ends meet by selling produce from their backyard gardens; more often they worked as seamstresses or laundresses. Formerly at the center of a communal society, Mexicanas found themselves with fewer options in the cash economy. What wages they could earn fell below even the low sums paid to their husbands, and women lost status within both the family and community.

Mexican Americans in San Antonio continued to conduct their traditional market bazaar well after the incorporation of this region into the United States. Forced off the land and excluded from the better-paying jobs in the emerging regional economy, many Mexicanos, and especially women, sought to sell the products of their own handiwork for cash or for bartered food and clothing.

Thomas Allen, *Market Plaza*, 1878–1879. Oil on canvas, 26 × 39 ½. Witte Museum, San Antonio, Texas.

Hispanic-American Alliance
Organization formed to protect and fight for the rights of Spanish Americans.

Commercial expansion occasionally strained relations between Mexicanos and Anglos to the breaking point. Although the Treaty of Guadalupe Hidalgo formally guaranteed Mexicanos the "free enjoyment of their liberty and property," local Anglos often violated these provisions and, through fraud or coercion, took control of the land. The Sante Fe Ring, a group of lawyers, politicians, and land speculators, stole millions of acres from the public domain and grabbed over 80 percent of the Mexicano landholdings in New Mexico alone.

Mexicanos organized to reverse these trends or at least to limit the damage done to their communities. In the late 1880s, Las Gorras Blancas, a band of agrarian rebels in northern New Mexico, destroyed railroad ties and farm machinery and posted demands for justice on new fences enclosing Anglo farms and ranches that shut off grazing land. In 1890, Las Gorras turned from social banditry to political organization, forming *El Partido del Pueblo Unido* (The People's Party). Organized along similar lines, *El Alianzo Hispano-Americano* (The **Hispanic-American Alliance**) was formed "to protect and fight for the rights of Spanish Americans" through political action.

Despite many pressures, Mexicanos preserved much of their cultural heritage. The influx of new immigrants from Mexico helped to reinforce older ways. Beginning in the late 1870s, the policies of Porfirio Diaz, the president of Mexico from 1876 to 1911, brought deteriorating living conditions to the masses of poor people and prompted a migration northward that accelerated through the first decades of the twentieth century. These newcomers revitalized old customs and rituals associated with family and religion. Spanish language and Spanish place names continued to distinguish the Southwest.

THE OPEN RANGE

WHAT LED to the growth of the cattle industry after the Civil War?

The borderlands, especially the Mexican territory that became Texas in 1836, gave birth to the enormously profitable cattle industry. Texas longhorns numbered more than 5 million at the close of the Civil War and represented a potentially plentiful supply of beef for eastern consumers. Entrepreneurs such as Joseph G. McCoy began to build a spectacular cattle market in the eastern part of Kansas, where the Kansas Pacific Railroad provided crucial transportation links to slaughtering and packinghouses and commercial distributors in Kansas City, St. Louis, and Chicago.

THE LONG DRIVES

The great cattle drives depended on the cowboy, a seasonal or migrant worker. After the Civil War, cowboys rounded up herds of Texas cattle and drove them as much as 1,500 miles north to grazing ranches or to the stockyards where they were readied for shipping by rail to eastern markets. In return for his labor, the cowboy received at the best of times about $30 per month. Wages were usually paid in one lump sum at the end of a drive, a policy that encouraged cowboys to spend their money quickly and recklessly in the booming cattle towns. In the 1880s, when wages began to fall along with the price of beef, cowboys fought back by stealing cattle or by forming unions. In 1883, many Texas cowboys struck for higher wages; nearly all Wyoming cowboys struck in 1886.

Like other parts of the West, the cattle range was ethnically diverse. Mexican cowboys, or *vaqueros*, had worked the great herds before Texas became a state in 1845. During the peak of the cattle drives, between one-fifth and one-third of all workers were Indian, Mexican, or African American. Indian cowboys worked mainly on the northern plains and in Indian Territory; the *vaqueros* continued to work in the borderlands. African American cowboys worked primarily in Texas (see Seeing History). The majority of cowboys were white, and often former soldiers hoping to avoid the indoor work that prevailed in the cities.

Like the *vaqueros*, African American cowboys were highly skilled managers of cattle. Unlike Mexicans, they earned wages comparable to those paid to Anglos and, especially

QUICK REVIEW

Cattle Ranching

- Indian removal and the arrival of the railroad opened land for ranching.
- High profits in the industry attracted speculative capital and large companies.
- The industry collapsed in the 1880s due to overgrazing.

The Legendary Cowboy: Nat Love, Deadwood Dick

Nat Love was born a slave in 1854 and spent his childhood on a plantation in Tennessee. In 1907 he published a short autobiography, *The Life and Adventures of Nat Love, Better Known in the Cattle Country as "Deadwood Dick,"* recounting his "unusually adventurous" life during the decades after emancipation. He worked as a cowboy, a ranch hand, an Indian fighter, and a rodeo performer. His most famous episode occurred in the boomtown of Deadwood, South Dakota, where in 1876 he won a cowboy tournament. It began with a roping contest, in which Love roped, saddled, and mounted a mustang in just nine minutes, winning the almost unbelievably large prize of $200. In the second part of this competition, a shooting contest, Love once again came out on top, hitting the bull's-eye in ten out of twelve shots. He boasted that the miners and gam-

HOW DOES Nat Love fit into the legendary Wild West? How readily would you expect nineteenth-century readers of the *Deadwood Dick* dime novels to accept the hero's identity as a black man? How does Nat Love's identity as an African American line up with the image of the heroic cowboy in modern American popular culture?

blers who had gathered for the tournament were so awed that they called him "Deadwood Dick," a name he proudly claimed until his death in 1921.

That name became familiar to the many readers of Edward Wheeler's *Deadwood Dick* dime novels, and at least five of Love's contemporaries claimed to be that character. Wheeler published the first installment in this popular series in 1877 as *Deadwood Dick, the Prince of the Road, or, The Black Rider of the Black Hills.* It is said that Love's autobiography reads like a dime novel, packed with adventures that no historian has yet been able to authenticate.

The photograph illustrating Love's popular autobiography captures the standard image of the cowboy of the legendary Wild West—the chaps, firearm, and ammunition in the cartridge belt circling his waist, the tack on the floor (saddle, harness, rope), and the assertive body language. But in Love's case, the cowboy is a black man. ■

Read the Document

*Perspectives on the American Cowboy
(1884, 1886)* at **www.myhistorylab.com**

during the early years, worked in integrated drover parties. By the 1880s, as the center of the cattle industry shifted to the more settled regions around the northern ranches, African Americans were forced out, and they turned to other kinds of work.

THE SPORTING LIFE

In cattle towns as well as mining camps, saloons, gambling establishments, and dance halls were regular features. The hurdy-gurdy, a form of hand organ, supplied music for cowboys eager to spend their money and blow off steam after the long drive. Here they found dancing partners, often called hurdy-girls or hurdies. If they wanted to do more than dance, the cowboy and his partner could retreat to one of the small rooms for rent, which were often located at the rear of the building.

Although prostitution was illegal in most towns, the laws were rarely enforced until the end of the century, when reformers led campaigns to shut down the red-light districts. Like the cowboys who bought their services, most prostitutes were unmarried and in their teens or twenties. Often fed up with underpaid jobs in dress-making or domestic service, they found few alternatives to prostitution in the cattle towns, where the cost of food and lodging was notoriously high. Still, earnings in prostitution were slim, except during the cattle-shipping season when young men outnumbered women by as much as three to one. Injury or even death from violent clients, addiction to narcotics such as cocaine or morphine, and venereal disease were workaday dangers.

FRONTIER VIOLENCE AND RANGE WARS

The combination of prostitution, gambling, and drinking discouraged the formation of stable communities. Personal violence was notoriously commonplace on the streets and in the barrooms of cattle towns and mining camps populated mainly by young, single men. Many western towns such as Wichita outlawed the carrying of handguns, but enforcement usually lagged.

After the Civil War, violent crime, assault, and robbery rose sharply throughout the United States. In the West, the most prevalent crimes were horse theft and cattle rustling, which peaked during the height of the open range period and then fell back by the 1890s. Death by legal hanging or illegal lynching was the usual sentence.

The "range wars" of the 1880s and 1890s produced violent conflicts. By this time, both farmers and sheepherders were encroaching on the fields where cattle had once grazed freely. Sheep chew grass down to its roots, making it practically impossible to raise cattle on the same land. Farmers built fences to protect their crops and domestic livestock. Great cattle barons fought back by ordering cowboys to cut the new barbed-wire fences.

The cattle barons helped to bring about their own demise, but they did not go down quietly. Eager for greater profits, and often backed by foreign capital, they overstocked their herds, and eventually the cattle began to deplete the limited supply of grass. Finally, during 1885–87, a combination of summer drought and winter blizzards killed 90 percent of the cattle in the northern Plains. Many ranchers went bankrupt. Along the way, they often took out their grievances against the former cowboys who had gathered small herds for themselves. They charged these small ranchers with cattle rustling, taking them to court or, in some cases, rounding up lynching parties. As one historian has written, violence was "not a mere sideshow" but "an intrinsic part of western society."

As early as 1879, the local newspaper described Leadville, Colorado, as a town that never sleeps: "The dancing houses and liquoring shops are never shut. . . . The streets are full of drunken carousers taking the town." This photograph of a typical saloon was taken shortly before the silver mining town reached its peak, with a population topping 60,000 in 1893. That year, the repeal of the Sherman Silver Act forced thousands of out-of-work miners to search for jobs elsewhere in the West.

FARMING COMMUNITIES ON THE PLAINS

The first explorers who traveled through the Great Plains called the region "The Great Desert." Few trees blocked the blazing sun of summer or promised a supply of lumber for homes and fences. The occasional river or stream flowed with "muddy gruel" rather than pure, sweet water. Economically, the entire region appeared as hopelessly barren as it was vast. It took massive improvements in both transportation and farm technology—as well as unrelenting advertising and promotional campaigns—to open the Great Plains to widescale agriculture.

THE HOMESTEAD ACT

The **Homestead Act of 1862** offered the first incentive to prospective farmers. This act granted a quarter section (160 acres) of the public domain free to any settler who lived on the land for at least five years and improved it; or who could buy the land for $1.25 per acre after only six months' residence.

Although the Homestead Act did spark the largest migration in American history, only 10 percent of all settlers got their start under its terms, and nearly half of all homesteaders lost their claims. Rather than filing a homestead claim with the federal government, most settlers acquired their land outright. State governments and land companies usually held the most valuable land near transportation and markets, and the majority of farmers were willing to pay a hefty price for those benefits. The big-time land speculators did even better, plucking choice locations at bargain prices and selling high. And the railroads, which received land grants from the federal government, did best, selling off the holdings near their routes at top dollar.

POPULATING THE PLAINS

The rapid settlement of the West could not have taken place without the railroad. Although the Homestead Act offered prospective farmers free land, it was the railroad that promoted settlement, brought people to their new homes, and carried crops and cattle to eastern markets.

Unlike the railroads built before the Civil War, which followed the path of villages and towns, the western lines preceded settlement. Bringing people west became their top priority, and the railroad companies conducted aggressive promotional and marketing campaigns. Agents enticed Easterners and Europeans alike with long-term loans and free transportation by rail to distant points in the West. The railroads also sponsored land companies to sell parcels of their own huge allotments from the federal government. The National Land Company, founded in Chicago in 1869, alone organized sixteen colonies of mainly European immigrants in parts of Kansas and Colorado.

More than 2 million Europeans, many recruited by professional promoters, settled the Great Plains between 1870 and 1900. Some districts in Minnesota seemed to be virtual colonies of Sweden; others housed the largest number of Finns in the New World. Nebraska concentrated Germans, Swedes, Danes, and Czechs. But Germans outnumbered all other immigrants by far. A smaller portion of European immigrants reached Kansas, still fewer reached the territories to the south where Indian and Hispanic peoples and African Americans remained the major ethnic groups.

Traveling the huge distance with kin or members of their Old World villages meant immigrants formed tight-knit communities of their fellow travelers on the Great Plains. Many married only within their own group. Like many Mexicanos in the Southwest, several immigrant groups retained their languages well into the twentieth century, usually by sponsoring parochial school systems and publishing their own newspapers. A few groups closed their communities to outsiders.

HOW DID the Great Plains become a center of American agriculture?

QUICK REVIEW

The Homestead Act

- 1862 Act granted 160 acres to any settler who lived on land for five years and improved it.
- Achieved greatest success in the central and upper Midwest.
- Most settlers acquired their land outright, rather than filing a homestead claim.

Homestead Act of 1862 1862 act which granted a quarter section (160 acres) of the public domain free to any settler who lived on the land for at least five years and improved it.

In 1887, Lizzie Chrisman filed the first homestead claim on Lieban Creek in Custer County, Nebraska. Joined by her three sisters, she is shown here standing in front of her sod cabin. "Soddies," as these small houses were called, were constructed of stacked layers of cut prairie turf, which were eventually fortified by a thick network of roots. The roofs, often supported by timber, were usually covered with more sod, straw, and small branches.

Among the native-born settlers of the Great Plains, the largest number had migrated from states bordering the Mississippi River. Settling as individual families rather than as whole communities, they faced an exceptionally solitary life on the Great Plains. To stave off isolation, homesteaders sometimes built their homes on the adjoining corners of their homestead plots. Still, the prospect of improving their lives, which brought most homesteaders to the Great Plains in the first place, caused many families to keep seeking greener pastures. Mobility was so high that between one-third and one-half of all households pulled up stakes within a decade.

Communities eventually flourished in prosperous towns like Grand Island, Nebraska; Coffeyville, Kansas; and Fargo, North Dakota, that served the larger agricultural region. Built alongside the railroad, they grew into commercial centers, home to banking, medical, legal, and retail services. A social hierarchy based on education (for the handful of doctors and lawyers) and, more important, investment property (held mainly by railroad agents and bankers) governed relationships between individuals and families. Reinforced by family ties and religious and ethnic differences, this hierarchy often persisted across generations.

WORK, DAWN TO DUSK

Most farm families survived, and prospered if they could, through hard work, often from dawn to dusk. Men's activities in the fields tended to be seasonal, with heavy work during planting and harvest. At other times, their labor centered on construction or repair of buildings and on taking care of livestock. Women's activities were usually far more routine, week in and week out: cooking and canning of seasonal fruit and vegetables, washing, ironing, churning cream for butter, and keeping chickens for their eggs. Women tended to the young children, and they might occasionally take in boarders, usually young men working temporarily in railroad construction. Many women complained about the ceaseless drudgery, especially when they watched their husbands invest in farm equipment rather than in domestic appliances. Others relished the challenge.

Milking the cows, hauling water, and running errands to neighboring farms could be done by the children, once they had reached the age of nine or so. The "one-room school," where all grades learned together, taught the basics of literacy and arithmetic that a future farmer or commercial employee would require.

The harsh climate and unyielding soil nevertheless forced all but the most reclusive families to seek out friends and neighbors. Many hands were needed to clear the land for cultivation or for roadbeds, to raise houses and barns, or to bring in a harvest before a threatening storm. Neighbors might agree to work together haying, harvesting, and threshing grain. A well-to-do farmer might "rent" his threshing machine in exchange for a small cash fee and, for instance, three days' labor. His wife might barter her garden produce for her neighbor's bread and milk or for help during childbirth or illness. Women often combined work and leisure in quilting bees and sewing circles. Whole communities turned out for special events, such as the seasonal husking bees, which were organized mainly by women.

For many farmers, the soil simply would not yield a livelihood, and they often owed more money than they took in. Start-up costs, including the purchase of land and equipment, put many farmers deep in debt. Some lost their land altogether. By the turn of the century, more than one-third of all farmers in the United States were tenants on someone else's land.

No matter how hard the average farm family worked, again and again, foreclosures wiped out the small landowner through dips in commodity prices, bad decisions, natural disasters, or illness. The swift growth of rural population soon ended. Although writers and orators alike continued to celebrate the family farm as the source of virtue and economic well being, the hard reality of big money and political power told a far different story.

THE WORLD'S BREADBASKET

During the second half of the nineteenth century, commercial farmers employed the most advanced methods of agricultural production in the world. They brought huge numbers of acres under cultivation and used new technologies to achieve unprecedented levels of efficiency in the planting and harvesting of crops. As a result, farming became increasingly tied to international trade, and modern capitalism soon ruled western agriculture, as it did the mining and cattle industries.

HOW DID agribusiness differ from more traditional forms of farming?

NEW PRODUCTION TECHNOLOGIES

Only after the brush had been cleared and grasslands cut free of roots could the soil be prepared for planting. But the sod west of the Mississippi did not yield readily to cultivation and often broke the cast-iron plows typically used by eastern farmers. Farther west,

This "thirty-three horse team harvester" was photographed at the turn of the century in Walla Walla, Washington. Binding the grain into sheaves before it could hit the ground, the "harvester" cut, threshed, and stacked wheat in one single motion.

some farmers resorted to drills to plant seeds for crops such as wheat and oats. Even in the best locations the preliminary breaking, or "busting," of the sod required hard labor.

Agricultural productivity depended as much on new technology as on the farmers' hard labor. In 1837, John Deere designed his famous "singing plow," which easily turned prairie grasses under and turned up even highly compacted soils. Around the same time, Cyrus McCormick's reaper began to be used for cutting grain. The harvester, invented in the 1870s, drew the cut stalks upward to a platform where two men could bind them into sheaves; by the 1880s, an automatic knotter tied them together. The introduction of mechanized corn planters and mowing or raking machines for hay all but completed the technological arsenal (see Table 18.1). The improvements in the last half of the century allowed an average farmer to produce up to ten times more than was possible with the old implements.

Scientific study of soil, grain, and climate conditions was another factor in the record output. Through the **Morrill Act of 1862**, "land-grant" colleges acquired space for campuses in return for promising to institute agricultural programs. The Department of Agriculture, which attained cabinet-level status in 1889, and the Weather Bureau (transferred from the War Department in 1891) also made considerable contributions to farmers' knowledge. The federal Hatch Act of 1887, which created a series of state experimental stations, provided for basic agricultural research, especially in the areas of soil minerals and plant growth. Many states added their own agricultural stations, usually connected with state colleges and universities.

Nonetheless, nature often reigned over technological innovation and seemed in places to take revenge against these early successes. Summer heat burned out crops and ignited grass fires. Mountains of winter snows turned rivers into spring torrents that flooded fields; heavy fall rains washed crops away. Even good weather invited worms and flying insects to infest the crops. During the 1870s, grasshoppers in clouds a mile long ate everything organic, including tree bark and clothes.

CALIFORNIA AGRIBUSINESS

The new technology and scientific expertise favored the large, well-capitalized farmer over the small one. The trend toward large-scale or bonanza farming reached an apex in California, where farming as a business surpassed farming as a way of life. Bankers, railroad magnates, and other Anglos made rich by the gold rush took possession of the best farming land in the state. They introduced the latest technologies, built dams and canals, and invested huge amounts of capital, setting the pattern for the state's prosperous agribusiness. By the turn of the century, two-thirds of the state's arable land was in 1,000-acre farms.

QUICK REVIEW

Changes in Farming

- Increased emphasis on production for exchange.
- International demand for wheat supported wheat farming in U.S.
- New technology encouraged the consolidation of land into large farms.

Morrill Act of 1862 Act by which "land-grant" colleges acquired space for campuses in return for promising to institute agricultural programs.

TABLE 18.1

Machine Labor on the Farm, ca. 1880

Crop	Time Worked		Labor Cost	
	Hand	**Machine**	**Hand**	**Machine**
Wheat	61 hours	3 hours	$3.55	$0.66
Corn	39 hours	15 hours	3.62	1.51
Oats	66 hours	7 hours	3.73	1.07
Loose Hay	21 hours	4 hours	1.75	0.42
Baled Hay	35 hours	12 hours	3.06	1.29

This scale of production made California the national leader in wheat production by the mid-1880s. But the state also produced tons of fruits and vegetables. Large- and medium-sized growers, shrewdly combined in cooperative marketing associations during the 1870s and 1880s, used the new refrigerator cars to ship produce in large quantities to the East and to Europe.

By 1900, California had become the model for American agribusiness—not the home of self-sufficient homesteaders, but the showcase of heavily capitalized farm factories that employed a huge tenant and migrant workforce, including many Chinese. After the mines gave out and work on the transcontinental railroad ended, thousands of Chinese helped to bring new lands under cultivation. Chinese tenant farmers specialized in labor-intensive crops, such as vegetables and fruits, and peddled their crops door-to-door or sold them in roadside stands. Others worked in packing and preserving in all the major agricultural regions of the state. However, the Chinese, like the majority of field hands, rarely rose to the ranks of agricultural entrepreneurs. By the turn of the century, amid intense legislative battles over land and irrigation rights, it was clear that the rich and powerful dominated California agribusiness.

THE TOLL ON THE ENVIRONMENT

Viewing the land as a resource to command, the new inhabitants often looked past the existing flora and fauna toward a landscape remade strictly for commercial purposes. The changes they produced in some areas were nearly as cataclysmic as those that occurred during the Ice Age.

Farmers "improved" the land by introducing exotic plants and animals—that is, biological colonies indigenous to other regions and continents. Farmers also unintentionally introduced new varieties of weeds, insect pests, and rats.

Numerous species disappeared altogether or suffered drastic reduction. The grizzly bear, for example, an animal exclusive to the West, once could be found in large numbers from the Great Plains to California and throughout much of Alaska; by the early decades of the twentieth century, one nature writer estimated that only 800 survived. At the same time, the number of wolves declined from perhaps as many as 2 million to just 200,000. By the mid-1880s, no more than 5,000 buffalo survived in the entire United States.

The slaughter of the buffalo had a dramatic impact, not only on the fate of the species, but also on the grasslands of the Great Plains. Having killed off the giant herds, ranchers and farmers quickly shifted to cattle and sheep production. Unlike the roaming buffalo, these livestock did not range widely and soon devoured the native grasses down to their roots. With the ground cover destroyed, the soil eroded and became barren. By the end of the century, huge dust storms swept across the plains.

Large-scale commercial agriculture also took a heavy toll on inland waters. Before white settlement, rainfall had drained naturally into lakes and underground aquifers, and watering spots were abundant throughout the Great Plains. Farmers mechanically rerouted and dammed water to irrigate their crops, causing many bodies of water to disappear and the water table to drop significantly. In the 1870s, successful ranchers in California pressed for ever greater supplies of water and contracted Chinese work gangs to build the largest irrigation canal in the West. In 1887, the state of California formed irrigation districts, securing bond issues for the construction of canals, and other western states followed. But by the 1890s, irrigation had seemed to reach its limit without federal support. The Newlands or **National Reclamation Act** of 1902 added 1 million acres of irrigated land, and state irrigation districts added more than 10 million acres.

Although western state politicians and federal officials debated water rights for decades, they rarely considered the impact of water policies on the environment. Lake Tulare in California's Central Valley, for example, had occupied up to 760 square miles.

National Reclamation Act 1902 act which added 1 million acres of irrigated land to the United States.

General Land Revision Act of 1891
Act which gave the president the power to establish forest reserves to protect watersheds against the threats posed by lumbering, overgrazing, and forest fires.

Forest Management Act 1897 act which, along with the National Reclamation Act, set the federal government on the path of large-scale regulatory activities.

After farmers began to irrigate their land by tapping the rivers that fed Tulare, the lake shrank dramatically, covering a mere 36 square miles by the early twentieth century. Finally the lake disappeared entirely. The land left behind, now wholly dependent on irrigation, grew so alkaline in spots that it could no longer be used for agricultural purposes.

The need to maintain the water supply indirectly led to the creation of national forests and the Forest Service. Western farmers supported the **General Land Revision Act of 1891**, which gave the president the power to establish forest reserves to protect watersheds against the threats posed by lumbering, overgrazing, and forest fires. In the years that followed, President Benjamin Harrison established fifteen forest reserves exceeding 16 million acres, and President Grover Cleveland added more than 21 million acres. Only in 1897 did the secretary of the interior finally gain the authority to regulate the use of these reserves.

The **Forest Management Act** of 1897 and the National Reclamation Act of 1902 set the federal government on the path of large-scale regulatory activities. The Forest Service was established in 1905, and in 1907, forest reserves were transferred from the Department of the Interior to the Department of Agriculture. The federal government began to play an even larger role in economic development of the West, dealing mainly with corporate farmers and ranchers eager for improvements.

THE WESTERN LANDSCAPE

Throughout the nineteenth century, many Americans viewed western expansion as the nation's "manifest destiny," and just as many marveled at the region's natural and cultural wonders. The region and its peoples came to represent what was both unique and magnificent about the American landscape.

WHAT PLACE did the West hold in the national imagination?

NATURE'S MAJESTY

Artists, writers, and scientists soon built their reputations on what they saw and imagined. Scores of writers described spectacular, breathtaking natural sites like the Grand Tetons and High Sierras. Geologists, botanists, historians, and anthropologists toured the trans–Mississippi West in pursuit of new data. Landscape painters, particularly the group that became known as the Rocky Mountain School, also piqued the public's interest in western scenery.

The federal government set aside huge tracts of land as nature reserves. In 1864, Congress passed the Yosemite Act, which placed the spectacular cliffs and giant sequoias under the management of the State of California. In 1872, Congress named Yellowstone in the Rocky Mountains the first national park. Yosemite and Sequoia in California, Crater Lake in Oregon, Mount Rainier in Washington, and Glacier in Montana all became national parks between 1890 and 1910 (see Map 18.5).

•••┤Read the Document

History Bookshelf: *John Muir,* The Yosemite *(1890) at* **www.myhistorylab.com**

QUICK REVIEW

National Parks

- 1864: Congress passed the Yosemite Act placing area under management of state of California.
- 1872: Yellowstone named first national park.
- Five new national parks named between 1890 and 1910.

THE LEGENDARY WILD WEST

By the end of the century, many Americans imagined the West as a land of promise and opportunity and, above all, of excitement and adventure. Later President Theodore Roosevelt helped to promote this view. He wrote three books recounting his adventures in the West, claiming that they had instilled in him not only personal bravery and "hardihood" but also self-reliance. The West, Roosevelt insisted, meant "vigorous manhood."

The first "westerns," the "dime novels" that sold in the 1860s in editions of 50,000 or more, reflected the myths about the West. Edward Zane Carroll Judson's *Buffalo Bill, the King of the Border Men,* first published in 1869, spawned hundreds of other novels, thousands of stories, and an entire magazine devoted to Buffalo Bill.

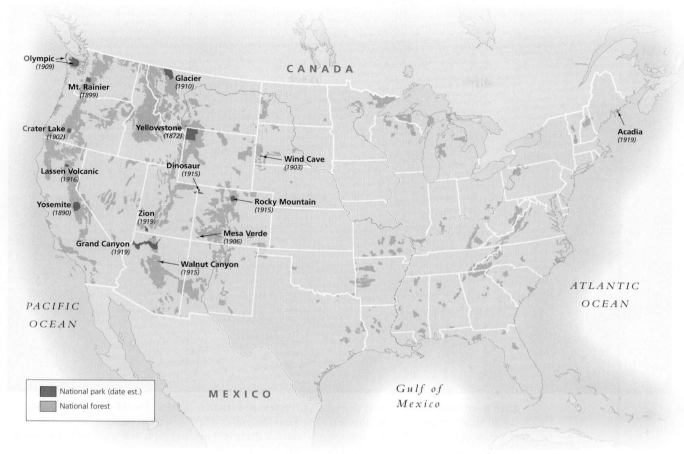

MAP 18.5

The Establishment of National Parks and Forests The setting aside of land for national parks saved large districts of the West from early commercial development and industrial degradation, setting a precedent for the later establishment of additional parks in economically marginal, but scenic, territory. The West, home to the vast majority of park space, became a principal site of tourism by the end of the nineteenth century.

WHY WERE many western parks and National Forests established before eastern ones?

Cowman Joseph McCoy staged Wild West shows in St. Louis and Chicago, where Texas cowboys entertained prospective buyers by roping calves and breaking horses. Many cowboys played up this imaginary role, dressing and talking to match the stories told about them.

In 1883, the former army scout and famed buffalo hunter William F. Cody hit upon the idea of an extravaganza that would bring the legendary West to those who could never experience it in person. "Buffalo Bill" Cody made sharpshooter Annie Oakley a star performer. Cody also hired chief Sitting Bull and other Sioux Indians and hundreds of cowboys to perform in mock stagecoach robberies and battles.

Cody's Wild West Show attracted masses of fairgoers at the World's Columbian Exposition, the spectacular celebration of the 400th anniversary of Columbus's landing in the New World held in Chicago in 1893. Less well attended but nonetheless significant was the annual meeting of the American Historical Association. At this meeting, Frederick Jackson Turner, a young historian at the University of Wisconsin, read a paper that, like Cody's Wild West Show, celebrated the West. "The Significance of the Frontier in American History" made a compelling argument that the continuous westward movement

Albert Bierstadt became one of the first artists to capture on enormous canvases the legendary vastness and rugged terrain of western mountains and wilderness. Many other artists joined Bierstadt to form the Rocky Mountain School. In time, the camera largely replaced the paintbrush, and most Americans formed an image of these majestic peaks from postcards and magazine illustrations.

Albert Bierstadt (1830–1902), *Among the Sierra Nevada Mountains, California,* 1868. Oil on canvas, 71 × 120 in. (183 × 305 cm). © Smithsonian American Art Museum, Washington, DC/Art Resource, Ny.

of settlement allowed Americans to develop new standards for democracy. Turner reasoned that each generation, in its move westward, mastered the "primitive conditions" and thereby developed a distinctive American character—"that coarseness and strength combined with acuteness and acquisitiveness; that practical inventive turn of mind, quick to find expedients; that masterful grasp of material things . . . that restless, nervous energy; that dominant individualism"—all of which encouraged democracy.

What became known as the "frontier thesis" also sounded a warning bell. The 1890 federal census revealed that the "free land" had been depleted, prompting Turner to conclude that the "closing" of the frontier marked the end of the formative period of American history.

THE "AMERICAN PRIMITIVE"

New technologies of graphic reproduction encouraged painters and photographers to circulate new images of Indian peoples. A young German American artist, Charles Schreyvogel depicted Indian warriors and U.S. cavalry fighting furiously but without blood and gore. Charles Russell, a genuine cowboy, painted the life he knew but also indulged in imaginary scenarios, producing paintings of buffalo hunts and first encounters between Indian peoples and white explorers.

Frederic Remington, the most famous of all the western artists, left Yale Art School to visit Montana in 1881, became a Kansas sheepherder and tavern owner, and then returned to painting. Painstakingly accurate in physical details, especially of horses, his paintings and popular magazine illustrations celebrated the "winning of the West" from the Indian peoples.

Photographers often produced highly nuanced portraits of Indian peoples. Dozens of early photographers from the Bureau of American Ethnology captured the gaze of noble tribespeople or showed them hard at work digging clams or grinding corn. President Theodore Roosevelt praised Edward Sheriff Curtis for vividly conveying tribal virtue. Generations later, in the 1960s and 1970s, Curtis's photographs again captured the imagination of western enthusiasts, who were unaware or unconcerned that Curtis often posed his subjects or retouched his photos to blur out any artifacts of white society.

Painters and photographers led the way for scholarly research on the various Indian societies. The early ethnographer and pioneer of fieldwork in anthropology Lewis Henry Morgan devoted his life to the study of Indian family or kinship patterns, mostly of eastern tribes such as the Iroquois, who adopted him into their Hawk Clan. In his major work, *Ancient Society*, published in 1877, he posited a universal process of social evolution leading from savagery to barbarism to civilization.

One of the most influential interpreters of the cultures of living tribespeople was the pioneering ethnographer Alice Cunningham Fletcher. In 1879, Fletcher met Susette (Bright Eyes) La Flesche of the Omaha tribe. Fletcher, then forty-two years old, accompanied La Flesche to Nebraska, telling the Omahas that she had come "to learn, if you will let me, something about your tribal organization, social customs, tribal rites, traditions and songs. Also to see if I can help you in any way." After transcribing hundreds of songs, Fletcher became well known as an expert on Omaha music. She also promoted assimilation through the allotment of individual claims to 160-acre homesteads, eked out of tribal lands, and helped to draft the model legislation that was enacted by Congress as the **Omaha Act of 1882**. As a founder of the American Anthropological Society and president of the American Folklore Society, she encouraged further study of Indian societies.

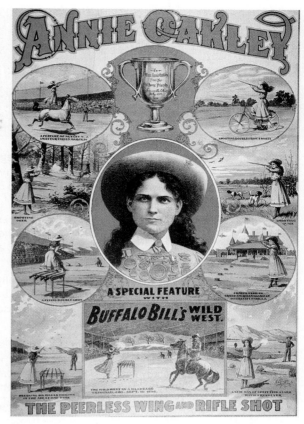

Born Phoebe Ann Moses in 1860, Annie Oakley was a star attraction in Buffalo Bill's Wild West show. Dubbed "Little Sure Shot" by Chief Sitting Bull, Oakley traveled with Cody's show for seventeen years. This poster from 1901 advertises her sharp-shooting talents.

THE TRANSFORMATION OF INDIAN SOCIETIES

In 1871, the U.S. government formally ended the treaty system, eclipsing but not completely abolishing the sovereignty of Indian nations. Still, the tribes persisted. Using a mixture of survival strategies from farming and trade to the leasing of reservation lands, they both adapted to changing conditions and maintained old traditions.

WHAT KIND of Indian society did reformers envision?

REFORM POLICY AND POLITICS

By 1880, many Indian tribes had been forcibly resettled on reservations, but few had adapted to white ways. For decades, reformers, mainly from the Protestant churches, had lobbied Congress for a program of salvation through assimilation, and they looked to the Board of Indian Commissioners, created in 1869, to carry out this mission. The board often succeeded in mediating conflicts among the various tribes crowded onto reservations but made far less headway in converting them to Christianity or transforming them into prosperous farming communities.

The majority of Indian peoples lived in poverty and misery, deprived of their traditional means of survival and, more often than not, subjected to fraud by corrupt government officials and private suppliers. Reformers who observed these conditions firsthand nevertheless remained unshaken in their belief that tribespeople must be raised out of

Omaha Act of 1882 Act which allowed the establishment of individual title to tribal lands.

OVERVIEW | Major Indian Treaties and Legislation of the Late Nineteenth Century

1863	Nez Perce Treaty	Signed illegally on behalf of the entire tribe, in which the Nez Perces abandoned 6 million acres of land in return for a small reservation in northeastern Oregon. Led to Nez Perce wars, which ended in 1877 with the surrender of Chief Joseph.
1867	Medicine Lodge Treaty	Assigned reservations in existing Indian Territory to Comanches, Plains (Kiowa), Apaches, Kiowas, Cheyennes, and Arapahoes, bringing these tribes together with Sioux, Shoshones, Bannocks, and Navajos.
1868	Treaty of Fort Laramie	Successfully ended Red Cloud's war by evacuating federal troops from Sioux Territory along the Bozeman Trail; additionally granted Sioux ownership of the western half of South Dakota and rights to use Powder River country in Wyoming and Montana.
1871		Congress declares end to treaty system.
1887	Dawes Severalty Act	Divided communal tribal land, granting the right to petition for citizenship to those Indians who accepted the individual land allotment of 160 acres. Successfully undermined sovereignty.

the darkness of ignorance into the light of civilization. Some conceded, however, that the reservation system might not be the best means to this end.

Unlike most Americans, who saw the conquest of the West as a means to national glory, some reformers were genuinely outraged by the government's continuous violation of treaty obligations and the military enforcement of the reservation policy. One of the most influential was Helen Hunt Jackson. In 1879, Jackson had attended a lecture in Hartford, Connecticut, by a chief of the Ponca tribe whose destitute people had been forced from their Dakota homeland. Heartstruck, Jackson lobbied former abolitionists such as Wendell Phillips to work for Indians' rights and she herself began to write against government policy. Her book-length exposé, *A Century of Dishonor*, published in 1881, detailed the plight of Indian peoples.

Jackson threw herself into the Indian Rights Association, an offshoot of the Women's National Indian Association (WNIA), which had been formed in 1874 to rally public support for a program of assimilation. The two organizations helped to place Protestant missionaries in the West to work to eradicate tribal customs as well as to convert Indian peoples to Christianity. According to the reformers' plans, men would now farm as well as hunt, while women would leave the fields to take care of home and children. Likewise, all communal practices would be abandoned in favor of individually owned homesteads, where families could develop in the "American" manner. Children, hair trimmed short, would be placed in boarding schools where, removed from their parents' influence, they would shed traditional values and cultural practices. By 1882, the WNIA had gathered 100,000 signatures on petitions urging Congress to phase out the reservation system, to establish universal education for Indian children, and to award title to 160 acres to any Indian individual willing to work the land.

The **Dawes Severalty Act**, passed by Congress in 1887, incorporated many of these measures and established federal Indian policy for decades to come. The act allowed the

Read the Document

Helen Hunt Jackson, from A Century of Dishonor (1881) at **www.myhistorylab.com**

Dawes Severalty Act An 1887 law terminating tribal ownership of land and allotting some parcels of land to individual Indians with the remainder opened for white settlement.

president to distribute land, not to tribes, but to individuals legally "severed" from their tribes. Those individuals who accepted the land allotment of 160 acres and agreed to allow the government to sell unallotted tribal lands (with some funds set aside for education) could petition to become citizens of the United States. A little over a decade after its enactment, many reformers believed that the Dawes Act had resolved the basis of the "Indian problem." Hollow Horn Bear, a Sioux chief, offered a different opinion, judging the Dawes Act to be "only another trick of the whites."

The Dawes Act successfully undermined tribal sovereignty but offered little compensation. Indian religions and sacred ceremonies were banned, the telling of legends and myths forbidden, and shaman and medicine men imprisoned or exiled for continuing their traditional practices. "Indian schools" forbade Indian languages, clothing styles, and even hair fashions.

These and other measures did little to integrate Indians into white society. Treated as savages, Indian children fled most white schools. Nor did adults receive much encouragement to become property holders. Government agencies allotted them inferior farmland, inadequate tools, and little training for agricultural self-sufficiency. Seeing scant advantage in assimilating, only a minority of adults dropped their tribal religion for Christianity or their communal ways for the accumulation of private property. Within the next forty years, the Indian peoples lost 60 percent of the reservation land remaining in 1887 and 66 percent of the land allotted to them as homesteaders. The tenets of the Dawes Act were not reversed until 1934. In that year, Congress passed the Indian Reorganization Act, which affirmed the integrity of Indian cultural institutions and returned some land to tribal ownership (see Chapter 24).

THE GHOST DANCE

After the passage of the Dawes Severalty Act, one more cycle of rebellion remained for the Sioux. In 1889, the Northern Paiute Wovoka had a vision during a total eclipse of the sun. In his vision, the Creator told him that if the Indian peoples learned to love each other, they would be granted a special place in the afterlife. The Creator also gave him the Ghost Dance, which the shaman performed for others and soon spread to other tribes. The Sioux, among others, elaborated Wovoka's prophecy into a religion of resistance. They came to believe that when the day of judgment came, all Indian peoples who had ever lived would return to their lost world and white peoples would vanish from the earth.

Many white settlers and federal officials feared the Ghost Dancers. After decades of Indian warfare, however, white Americans took the Ghost Dance as a warning of tribal retribution rather than a religious ceremony. As thousands of Sioux danced to exhaustion, local whites intolerantly demanded the practice be stopped. The U.S. Seventh Cavalry, led in part by survivors of the Battle of Little Bighorn, rushed to the Pine Ridge Reservation, and a group of the Sioux led by Big Foot, fearing mass murder, moved into hiding in the Badlands of South Dakota. After a skirmish, the great leader Sitting Bull and his young son lay dead.

The Seventh Cavalry pursued the Sioux Ghost Dancers and 300 undernourished Sioux, freezing and without horses, to Wounded Knee Creek on the Pine Ridge Reservation. There, on December 29, 1890, while the peace-seeking Big Foot, who had personally raised a white flag of surrender, lay dying of pneumonia, they were surrounded by soldiers armed with automatic guns. The U.S. troops expected the Sioux to surrender their few remaining weapons, but an accidental gunshot from one deaf brave who misunderstood the command caused panic on both sides.

Within minutes, 200 Sioux had been cut down and dozens of soldiers wounded, mostly by their own crossfire. For two hours soldiers continued to shoot at anything that moved—mostly women and children straggling away. Many of the injured froze to

The explorer John Wesley Powell led an expedition of ten men in 1869 to map the Colorado River, its tributaries, and its canyons. He became fascinated with the culture of the tribespeople he encountered and learned to speak the Ute language. In 1871–1872 Powell, accompanied by a photographer, remade the trip to the Grand Canyon, which he named. In this image, Powell appears alongside Tau-gue, Chief of the Paiutes, overlooking the Virgin River.

death in the snow; others were transported in open wagons and finally laid out on beds of hay under Christmas decorations at the Pine Ridge Episcopal Church. The massacre, which took place almost exactly 400 years after Columbus "discovered" the New World for Christian civilization, seemed to mark the final conquest of the continent's indigenous peoples.

ENDURANCE AND REJUVENATION

The most tenacious tribes were those occupying land rejected by white settlers or those distant from their new communities. Still, not even an insular, peaceful agricultural existence on semiarid, treeless terrain necessarily provided protection. Nor did a total willingness to peacefully accept white offers prevent attack.

The Pimas of Arizona, for instance, had a well-developed agricultural system adapted to a scarce supply of water, and they rarely warred with other tribes. After the arrival of white settlers, they integrated Christian symbolism into their religion, learned to speak English, and even fought with the U.S. cavalry against the Apaches. Still, the Pimas saw their lands stolen, their precious waterways diverted, and their families impoverished.

The similarly peaceful Yana tribes of California, hunters and gatherers rather than farmers, were even less fortunate. Suffering enslavement, prostitution, and multiple new diseases from white settlers, they faced near extinction within a generation. One Yana tribe, the Yahi, chose simply to disappear. For more than a decade, they lived in caves and avoided all contact with white settlers.

Many tribes found it difficult to survive in the proximity of white settlers. The Flatheads, for example, seemed to Indian commissioners in the Bitterroot region of Montana to be destined for quick assimilation. They had refused to join the Ghost Dance and had agreed to sell their rich tribal land and move to a new reservation. While waiting to be moved, however, the dispossessed Flatheads nearly starved. When they finally reached the new reservation in October 1891, the remaining 250 Flatheads put on their finest war paint and whooped and galloped their horses, firing guns in the air in celebration. Disappointment and tragedy lay ahead. The federal government drastically reduced the size of the reservation, using a large part of it to provide a national reserve for buffalo. Only handfuls of Flatheads, mostly elderly, continued to live together in pockets of rural poverty.

A majority of tribes, especially smaller ones, sooner or later reached numbers too low to maintain their collective existence. Intermarriage, although widely condemned by the white community, drew many young people outside their Indian communities. Some tribal leaders also deliberately chose a path toward assimilation. The Quapaws, for example, formally disbanded in the aftermath of the Dawes Severalty Act. The minority that managed to prosper in white society as tradespeople or farmers abandoned their language, religious customs, and traditional ways of life. Later generations petitioned the federal government and regained tribal status, established ceremonial grounds and cultural centers (or bingo halls), and built up one of the most durable powwows in the state. Even so, much of the tribal lore that had underpinned distinct identity had simply vanished.

For those tribes who remained on reservations, the aggressively assimilationist policies of the Office of Indian Affairs (OIA) challenged their traditional ways. The Southern Ute, for example, at one time hunted, fished, and gathered throughout a huge region spanning the Rocky Mountains and the Great Basin. In 1848, they began to sign a series of treaties in accord with the reservation policy of the U.S. government. Twenty years later, their territory had been reduced to approximately one-quarter of Colorado Territory, and in 1873, they had further relinquished about one-quarter of this land. After the passage of the Dawes Act, the U.S. government, pressured by white settlers, gave the tribe two choices: they could break up their communal land holdings and accept the 160 acres granted to the male heads of families, or they could maintain their tribal status and move to a reservation in Utah. The Utes were divided over the issue, but a considerable number chose to live on reservations under the administration of the OIA.

Under the terms of the Dawes Act, Southern Ute men and women endured continuous challenges to their egalitarian practices. The OIA assumed, for example, that Ute men would represent the tribe in all official matters, a policy that forced Ute women to petition the U.S. government to recognize their rights and concerns. Similarly, Ute women struggled to hold on to their roles as producers within the subsistence family economy against the efforts of the OIA agents to train them for homemaking alone. In the 1880s, the OIA established a matrons program to teach Ute women to create a "civilizing" home, which included new lessons about sanitation, home furnishings, and health care. But even fifty years later, some Ute preferred to live at least part of the year in a teepee in a multigenerational family, rather than in a private residence designed for a single married couple and their children.

A small minority of tribes, grown skillful in adapting to dramatically changing circumstances, managed to persist and even grow. Never numbering more than a few thousand people, during the late eighteenth century the Cheyennes found themselves caught geographically between aggressive tribes in the Great Lakes region and had migrated into the Missouri area, where they split into small village-sized communities. By the mid-nineteenth century, they had become expert horse traders on the Great Plains, well prepared to meet the massive influx of white settlers by shifting their location frequently. They avoided the worst of the pestilence that spread from the diseases white people carried and likewise survived widespread intermarriage with the Sioux in the 1860s and 1870s. Instructed to settle, many Cheyennes took up elements of the Christian religion and became farmers, also without losing their tribal identity. Punished by revenge-hungry soldiers after the battle of Little Bighorn, their lands repeatedly taken away, they still held on. The Cheyennes were survivors.

The Navajos experienced an extraordinary renewal, largely because they built a life in territory considered worthless by whites. Having migrated to the Southwest from the northwestern part of the continent perhaps 700 years earlier, the Diné ("the People"), as they called themselves, had already survived earlier invasions by the Spanish. In 1863, they had been conquered again through the cooperation of hostile tribes led by the famous Colonel Kit Carson. Their crops burned, their fruit trees destroyed, 8,000 Navajos were forced in the 300-mile "Long Walk" to the desolate Bosque Redondo reservation, where they nearly starved. Four years later, the Indian Bureau allowed the severely reduced tribe to return to a fraction of its former lands.

By 1880, the Navajos' population had returned to nearly what it had been before their conquest by white Americans. Quickly depleting the deer and antelope on their hemmed-in reservation, they had to rely on sheep alone as a food reserve during years of bad crops. With their wool rugs and blankets much in demand in the East, the Navajos increasingly turned to crafts, eventually including silver jewelry as well as weaving, to survive. Although living on the economic margin, they persevered to become the largest Indian nation in the United States.

The nearby Hopis, like the Navajos, survived by stubbornly clinging to lands unwanted by white settlers, and by adapting to drastically changing conditions. A famous tribe of "desert people," the Hopis had lived for centuries in their cliff cities. Their highly developed theological beliefs, peaceful social system, sand paintings, and kachina dolls interested many educated and influential whites. The resulting publicity helped them gather the public supporters and financial resources needed to fend off further threats to their reservations.

Fortunate northwestern tribes remained relatively isolated from white settlers until the early twentieth century, although they had begun trading with white visitors centuries earlier. Northwestern peoples relied largely on salmon and other resources of the region's rivers and bays. In potlatch ceremonies, leaders redistributed tribal wealth and maintained their personal status and the status of their tribe by giving lavish gifts to invited guests. Northwestern peoples also made intricate wood carvings, including commemorative "totem" poles that recorded their history and identified their regional status. Northwestern peoples maintained their cultural integrity in part through connections with kin in Canada, as did southern tribes with kin in Mexico. In Canada and Mexico, native populations suffered less pressure from new populations and retained more tribal authority than in the United States.

Indian nations approached their nadir as the nineteenth century came to a close. The descendants of the great pre-Columbian civilizations had been conquered by foreigners, their population reduced to fewer than 250,000. Under the pressure of assimilation, the remaining tribespeople became known to non-Indians as "the vanishing Americans." It would take several generations before Indian sovereignty experienced a resurgence.

CHRONOLOGY

1848	Treaty of Guadalupe Hidalgo
1853	Gadsden Purchase
1862	Homestead Act makes free land available
	Morrill Act authorizes "land-grant" colleges
1865–67	Great Sioux War
1866	Texas cattle drives begin
1867	Medicine Lodge Treaty established reservation system
	Alaska purchased
1869	Board of Indian Commissioners created
	Buffalo Bill, the King of the Border Men sets off "Wild West" publishing craze
1870s	Grasshopper attacks on the Great Plains
1872	Yellowstone National Park created
1874–75	Sioux battles in Black Hills of Dakotas
	Red River War
1876	Custer's Last Stand
1877	Defeat of the Nez Perces
1878	John Wesley Powell published *Report on the Lands of the Arid Region*
1881	Helen Hunt Jackson, *A Century of Dishonor*
1882	Edmunds Act outlaws polygamy
1885–87	Droughts and severe winters cause the collapse of the cattle boom
1887	Dawes Severalty Act
1890	Sioux Ghost Dance movement
	Massacre of Lakota Sioux at Wounded Knee
	Census Bureau announces the end of the frontier line
1893	Frederick Jackson Turner presents his "frontier thesis"
1897	Forest Management Act gives the federal government authority over forest reserves

Conclusion

Amid the land rush of April 22, 1889, the town of Guthrie, Oklahoma, was built, contemporaries liked to brag, not in a day but in a single afternoon, its population leaping from a dozen or so to 10,000 by sundown. Throughout the territory, new communities formed almost as rapidly and often displaced old ones. Farms and ranches owned by white settlers soon spread out across the vast countryside that earlier had been Indian Territory. This spectacular development of Oklahoma was, however, but one chapter in the history of the trans–Mississippi West as an internal empire.

The West, rich in natural resources, soon served the nation in supplying ore and timber for its expanding industries and agricultural products for the growing urban populations. Envisioning the West as a cornucopia whose boundless treasures would offer themselves to the willing pioneer, most of the new residents failed to calculate the odds against their making a prosperous livelihood as miners, farmers, or petty merchants. Nor could they appreciate the long-term consequences of the violence they brought with them from the battlefields of the Civil War to the far reaches of the West.

The new settlers adapted their political and legal systems, as well as many of their economic and cultural institutions, to western circumstances. Ironically though, even after statehood, they would still be only distant representatives of an empire whose financial, political, and industrial centers remained in the Northeast. They were often frustrated by their isolation and enraged at the federal regulations that governed them and at the eastern investors and lawyers who seemed poised on all sides to rob them of the fruits of their labor. Embittered Westerners, along with Southerners, would form the core of a nationwide discontent that would soon threaten to uproot the American political system.

REVIEW QUESTIONS

1. Discuss the role of federal legislation in accelerating and shaping the course of westward expansion.

2. How did the incorporation of western territories into the United States affect Indian nations such as the Sioux or the Nez Perce? Discuss the causes and consequences of the Indian Wars. Discuss the significance of reservation policy and the Dawes Severalty Act for tribal life.

3. What were some of the major technological advances in mining and in agriculture that promoted the development of the western economy?

4. Describe the unique features of Mexicano communities in the Southwest before and after the mass immigration of Anglos. How did changes in the economy affect the patterns of labor and the status of women in these communities?

5. What role did the Homestead Act play in western expansion? How did farm families on the Great Plains divide chores among their members? What factors determined the likelihood of economic success or failure?

6. Describe the responses of artists, naturalists, and conservationists to the western landscape. How did their photographs, paintings, and stories shape perceptions of the West in the East?

7. How can the history of the American West be told as the creation of new communities and the displacement of old communities?

KEY TERMS

Dawes Severalty Act (p. 466)

Edmunds Act (p. 452)

Edmunds-Tucker Act (p. 452)

Forest Management Act (p. 462)

General Land Revision Act of 1891 (p. 462)

Great Sioux War (p. 447)

Hispanic-American Alliance (p. 454)

Homestead Act of 1862 (p. 457)

Morrill Act of 1862 (p. 460)

National Reclamation Act (p. 461)

Omaha Act of 1882 (p. 465)

Sand Creek Massacre (p. 447)

Treaty of Fort Laramie (p. 447)

PEARSON

myhistorylab Connections

Reinforce what you learned in this chapter by studying the many documents, images, maps, review tools, and videos available at www.myhistorylab.com

Read and Review

✓●─┤Study and Review **Chapter 18**

●●●─┤Read the Document

Congressional Report on Sand Creek Massacre (1867)

John Lester, Hydraulic Mining (1873)

Elizabeth Cady Stanton Speaks to Mormon Women in Utah (1871)

Perspectives on the American Cowboy (1884, 1886)

Helen Hunt Jackson, from A Century of Dishonor (1881)

👁─┤See the Map *Resources and Conflict in the West*

Research and Explore

●●●─┤Read the Document

Exploring America: Dakota Sioux Conflict

Profiles
  George Armstrong Custer
  Helen Hunt Jackson

History Bookshelf: *John Muir,* The Yosemite *(1890)*

((●─┤Hear the Audio *Omaha Funeral Song*

((●●─┤Watch the Video

The Real West Is an Urban West

The Plains

──── ((●─┤**Hear** the **Audio** ────

Hear the audio files for Chapter 18 at
www.myhistorylab.com.

Here we had been taken to a lonely place;
. . . our things were taken away, our friends
separated from us; a man came to inspect us,
as if to ascertain our full value . . .
—*Mary Antin, from* The Promised Land

Noted urban photographer Lewis Hines captures the cramped working conditions
and child labor in this late nineteenth-century canning factory. Women and children
provided a cheap and efficient work force for labor-intensive industries.

19

PRODUCTION AND CONSUMPTION IN THE GILDED AGE

1865–1900

((•—[Hear the **Audio**

Hear the audio files for Chapter 19 at **www.myhistorylab.com**.

WHAT EXPLAINS the rise of big business in the late nineteenth century?

HOW DID American workers respond to the changing economic conditions of the late nineteenth century?

WHO BENEFITED the most from economic developments in the post-Reconstruction South? Why?

WHAT WAS life like in the industrial cities of late nineteenth-century America?

WHAT ACCOUNTS for the rise of a consumer society and how did various groups participate in its development?

HOW DID cultural developments in America's cities reflect larger social and economic tensions?

1865 | 1900

AMERICAN COMMUNITIES
Haymarket Square, Chicago, May 4, 1886

APPROXIMATELY 1,500 PEOPLE GATHERED FOR A MASS MEETING IN Haymarket Square to protest the brutality of the previous day, when Chicago police killed four strikers at the McCormick Reaper Works. The crowd listened peacefully as several speakers denounced the violence. Around 10:00 P.M. most headed for home, including the city's longtime mayor, Democrat Carter Harrison. According to newspaper reports, the crowd quickly dwindled to only 600 people. The final speaker, stone hauler Samuel Fielden, jumped up on the hay wagon that served as a makeshift stage and concluded on an ominous note. He warned that "war has been declared on us" and advised the crowd "to get hold of anything that will help you to resist the onslaught of the enemy and the usurper."

Within minutes, a column of 176 police marched down the street, pushing what remained of the crowd onto the wooden sidewalks and commanding them to disperse. Then, according to the city's leading newspaper, the *Tribune*, "something like a miniature rocket suddenly rose out of the crowd on the east sidewalk." The bomb exploded "with terrific force, shaking buildings on the street and creating havoc among the police." One policeman died immediately, provoking others to open fire into the scattering crowd. At the end of just a few minutes of chaos, seven policemen had received mortal wounds and as many as sixty more were injured, many in their own crossfire. Several civilians were killed, and dozens were injured.

Those who attended the rally were mainly disgruntled workers, recent immigrants from central and eastern Europe who had come to Chicago to take advantage of the city's growing industries. At the time of the rally, they were primarily determined to establish unions and a workday shorter than the customary ten or twelve hours.

Since early in the year, an eight-hour campaign had been sweeping the nation, with its center in Chicago. Workers and sympathetic consumers alike boycotted brands of beer, tobacco, bread, and other products made in longer-hour shops. With more than wages at stake, workers were joining unions and striking so often that the era became known as the "Great Upheaval." Their leaders responded to this upsurge by calling for a general strike across all industries on May 1, 1886.

A community of radical workers who had emigrated from Germany and settled in Chicago's near North Side made up the most militant contingent of the movement. They sought to establish a government of working people in place of politicians and corporate power. Writing in the *Arbeiter-Zeitung* (*Workers' Newspaper*), the local German-language newspaper, editor August Spies greeted May 1, hailed as "Emancipation Day," calling: "Workmen, let your watchword be: No compromise! Cowards to the Rear! Men to the front!"

On May Day, Spies helped to lead the spectacular parade of 80,000 men, women, and children up Michigan Avenue, Chicago's main street. A Saturday, the day passed peacefully. However, when the workweek resumed on Monday, May 3, the deadly confrontation of strikers and police at the McCormick Reaper Works set the stage for virtual class warfare.

Feelings of animosity on all sides intensified. In the days following the tragedy at Haymarket Square, Chicago police arrested hundreds of working people, rounded up known leaders, and searched their homes and detained them without warrants. Meanwhile, newspapers denounced them as "enemy forces" and the "scum" of Europe. Sentiment swung sharply against immigrants.

Ultimately, eight men were charged with incitement to murder. A jury of middle-class men pronounced all eight guilty despite the lack of evidence linking the defendants to the bombing. Three of the eight had not even been at Haymarket Square on the evening of May 4. The judge sentenced them to death by hanging.

At the other end of the social scale, the 1880s for middle- and upper-class Chicagoans was an era of unprecedented prosperity. Incorporated in 1837, the city boasted a population of 200,000—second only to New York—and dozens of new mass industries and vibrant new classes of consumers. Many of the workers in Chicago's industries, especially immigrants, could barely make ends meet. But thousands of better-off Chicagoans rushed to Marshall Field & Company to survey the ever-expanding range of goods in one of the finest department stores in the nation and a major source of pride for the city. Less affluent consumers could turn to less expensive goods offered by Chicago-based Montgomery Ward, the nation's first large-scale mail-order business.

By the final decades of the nineteenth century, the nation's eyes were fixed on Chicago because the city was marking the steps being taken by the nation as a whole. If class differences sharpened and led to violence, the rise in living standards provided a different, more appealing focus. The city with the most technologically advanced industries in the world seemed to be leading the way—but to what?

Chicago

THE RISE OF INDUSTRY, THE TRIUMPH OF BUSINESS

At the time of the Civil War, the typical American business firm was a small enterprise, owned and managed by a single family, and producing goods for a local or regional market. By the turn of the century, businesses depending on large-scale investments had organized as corporations and grown to unforeseen size. These mammoth firms could afford to mass-produce goods for national and even international markets. At the helm stood unimaginably wealthy men, powerful representatives of a new national business community, who led in the transformation of the United States from a rural to an urban industrial nation.

MECHANIZATION TAKES COMMAND

The Centennial Exposition of 1876, held in Philadelphia, celebrated not so much the American Revolution 100 years earlier as the industrial and technological promise of the century to come. The visiting emperor of Brazil spoke into an unfamiliar device on display and gasped, "My God, it talks!" The telephone, patented that year by Alexander Graham Bell, signaled the rise of the United States to world leadership in industrial technology.

The year 1876 also marked the opening of Thomas Alva Edison's laboratory in Menlo Park, New Jersey, one of the first devoted to industrial research. Three years later, his team produced an incandescent lamp. By 1882, the Edison Electric Light Company had launched its service in New York City's financial district. Electricity revolutionized both urban life and industry.

The second industrial revolution (1871–1914) proceeded at a pace that was not only unprecedented but also previously unimaginable. In 1865, the annual production of goods was estimated at $2 billion; by 1900, it stood at $13 billion, transforming the United States from fourth to first in the world in terms of productivity.

A major force behind economic growth was the vast transcontinental railroad, completed in 1869. The construction of additional major rail lines in the 1880s and 1890s completed the most extensive transportation network in the world. Railroads linked cities in every state and served as nationwide distributors of goods. Freight trains carried the natural resources, such as iron, coal, and minerals, that supplied the raw materials for industry, as well as food and other commodities for the growing urban populations (see Map 19.1).

No factor was more important in promoting economic growth than the application of new technologies to increase the productivity of labor and the volume of goods. Machines, factory managers, and workers together created a system of continuous production by which more could be made—and faster—than anywhere else on earth. Higher productivity depended not only on machinery and technology but also on economies of scale and speed, reorganization of factory labor and business management, and the unparalleled growth of a market for goods of all kinds.

New systems of mass production replaced wasteful and often chaotic practices and speeded up the delivery of finished goods. In the 1860s, meatpackers set up one of the earliest

In 1887, Thomas Alva Edison (1847–1931), shown here with the phonograph, moved his laboratory from Menlo Park to West Orange, New Jersey. There, he invented the alkaline storage battery, the phonograph, and the kinetoscope, the first machine to allow one person at a time to view motion pictures.

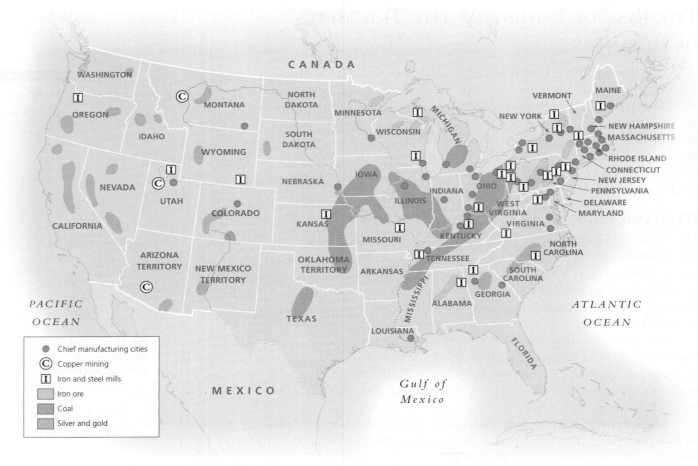

MAP 19.1

Patterns of Industry, 1900   Industrial manufacturing concentrated in the Northeast and Midwest, whereas the raw materials for production came mostly from other parts of the nation.

HOW DID industrialization in the Northeast impact other regions of the country?

QUICK REVIEW

The Second Industrial Revolution

- 1865: $2 billion annual production of goods.
- 1900: $13 billion annual production of goods.
- Revolutions in technology and transportation made growth possible.

production lines. Sometimes the invention of a single machine could instantly transform production, mechanizing every stage from processing the raw material to packaging the product. The cigarette-making machine, patented in 1881, could produce more than 7,000 cigarettes per hour, replacing the worker who at best made 3,000 per day. After a few more improvements, fifteen machines could meet the total demand for American cigarettes. Within a generation, continuous production—the assembly line—became standard in most areas of manufacturing, revolutionizing the making of furniture, cloth, grain products, soap, and canned goods; the refining, distilling, and processing of animal and vegetable fats; and eventually, the manufacture of automobiles.

EXPANDING THE MARKET FOR GOODS

To distribute the growing volume of goods and to create a dependable market, businesses demanded new techniques of merchandising on a national and, in some cases, international scale. For generations, legions of sellers, or "drummers," had worked their routes, pushing goods to individual buyers and local retail stores. After the Civil War, the appearance of mail-order houses, which accompanied the consolidation of the railroad lines and the expansion of the postal system, helped to get new products to consumers.

Growing directly out of these services, the successful Chicago-based mail-order houses drew rural and urban consumers into a common marketplace. Sears, Roebuck and Company and Montgomery Ward offered an enormous variety of goods, from shoes to buggies to gasoline stoves and cream separators.

Chain stores achieved similar economies of scale. By 1900, a half-dozen grocery chains had sprung up. Frank and Charles Woolworth, for example, offered inexpensive variety goods in five-and-ten-cent stores. Other chains selling drugs, costume jewelry, shoes, cigars, and furniture soon appeared, offering a greater selection of goods and lower prices than the small, independent stores.

Opening shortly after the Civil War, department stores began to take up much of the business formerly enjoyed by specialty shops, offering a spectrum of services that included restaurants, restrooms, ticket agencies, nurseries, reading rooms, and post offices. By the close of the century, the names of Marshall Field of Chicago, Filene's of Boston, The Emporium of San Francisco, Wanamaker's of Philadelphia, and Macy's of New York came to represent the splendors of those great cities as well as the apex of mass retailing.

Advertising lured customers to the department stores, the chains, and the independent neighborhood stores. The advertising revolution began in 1869, when Francis Wayland Ayer founded the earliest advertising agency. With the help of this new sales tool, gross revenues of retailers raced upward from $8 million in 1860 to $102 million in 1900.

INTEGRATION, COMBINATION, AND MERGER

Businesses grew in two distinct, if overlapping, ways. Through *vertical integration*, a firm gained control of production at every step of the way—from raw materials through processing to the transporting and merchandising of the finished items. In 1899, the United Fruit Company began to build a network of wholesale houses in the United States, and within two years it had opened distribution centers in twenty-one major cities. Eventually, it controlled an elaborate system of Central American plantations and temperature-controlled shipping and storage facilities for its highly perishable bananas.

The second means of growth, *horizontal combination*, entailed gaining control of the market for a single product. The most famous case was the Standard Oil Company, founded by John D. Rockefeller in 1870. Operating out of Cleveland, Rockefeller first secured preferential rates from railroads eager to ensure a steady supply of oil. He then convinced or coerced other local oil operators to sell their stock to him. The Standard Oil Trust, established in 1882, controlled over 90 percent of the nation's oil-refining industry (see Seeing History).

In 1890, Congress passed the Sherman Antitrust Act to restore competition by encouraging small business and outlawing "every . . . combination . . . in restraint of trade or commerce." Ironically, the courts interpreted the law in ways that inhibited the organization of trade unions and actually helped the consolidation of business. More than 2,600 firms vanished between 1898 and 1902 alone.

THE GOSPEL OF WEALTH

Ninety percent of the nation's business leaders were Protestant, and the majority attended church services regularly. They attributed their personal achievement to hard work and perseverance and made these the principal tenets of a new faith that imbued the pursuit of wealth with old-time religious zeal.

vertical integration The consolidation of numerous production functions, from the extraction of the raw materials to the distribution and marketing of the finished products, under the direction of one firm.

horizontal combination The merger of competitors in the same industry.

The Standard Oil Company

John D. Rockefeller, who formed the Standard Oil Company in 1870, sought to control all aspects of the industry, from the transportation of crude oil to the marketing and distribution of the final products. By the end of the decade, after making shrewd deals with the railroads and underselling his rivals, he managed to control 90 percent of the oil-refining industry. To further consolidate his interests, in 1882 Rockefeller created the Standard Oil Trust, which, by integrating both vertically and horizontally, became a model for other corporations and an inspiration for critical commentary and antitrust legislation.

WHAT DOES this cartoon tell us about Rockefeller's reputation at the turn of the twentieth century? What does it suggest about Americans' feelings about the trusts?

Rockefeller's best-known critic was Ida Tarbell. In 1904 she published *The History of the Standard Oil Company*, first in serial form in the popular *McClure's Magazine* and later as a book. Tarbell's muckraking exposé attracted a great deal of attention. Even more popular were political cartoons depicting Rockefeller's stranglehold on the entire oil industry. *Puck* magazine, which was founded in 1871 by Joseph Keppler, an immigrant from Austria, held up Rockefeller and his company to ridicule. This cartoon, published in *Puck* in 1904, shows Standard Oil as a sinister octopus, wrapping its arms around the White House and Congress as well as workers and even the denizens of Wall Street. In 1911, in response to an antitrust suit, the Supreme Court ordered the company to break up. The modern corporations Exxon, Mobil, Chevron, Amoco, and Sohio (some of which have merged) all descended from Rockefeller's Standard Oil. ■

This engraving of steel manufacturing at Andrew Carnegie's plant in 1886 features a Bessemer Converter, which converts molten pig iron into steel. The process was named after Sir Henry Bessemer of Sheffield, England, who first patented the process in 1855.

One version of this "**gospel of wealth**" justified the ruthless behavior of the entrepreneurs who accumulated unprecedented wealth and power through shady deals and conspiracies. Speculator Jay Gould, known in the popular press as the "Worst Man in the World," rose quickly from his modest origins through a series of unsavory financial maneuvers.

Speculation in railroads proved to be Gould's forte. He took over the Erie Railroad, paying off New York legislators to get the state to finance its expansion, and he acquired the U.S. Express Company by pressuring and tricking its stockholders. When threatened with arrest, Gould sold off his shares for $9 million and moved on to the Union Pacific, where he cut wages, precipitated strikes, and manipulated elections in the western and Plains states.

Andrew Carnegie—the "Richest Man in the World"—offered a strikingly different model. Carnegie built an empire in steel. A genius at vertical integration, he undercut his competitors by using the latest technology and designing his own system of cost analysis.

gospel of wealth Thesis that hard work and perseverance lead to wealth, implying that poverty is a character flaw.

●:●─ Read the Document

Andrew Carnegie, Wealth at
www.myhistorylab.com

By 1900, Carnegie managed the most efficient steel mills in the world, which accounted for one-third of the nation's output.

Carnegie was well known as a civic leader. From one point of view, he was a factory despot who underpaid his employees and ruthlessly managed their working conditions. But to the patrons of the public libraries, art museums, concert halls, colleges, and universities that he funded, Carnegie appeared to be the single greatest philanthropist of the age. Late in his life, he outlined his personal philosophy in a popular essay, *The Gospel of Wealth* (1889), explaining that "there is no genuine, praiseworthy success in life if you are not honest, truthful, and fair-dealing." By the time he died, he had given away his massive personal fortune.

Whether following the rough road of Gould or the smooth path of Carnegie, the business community worked together to fashion the new conservative ideology of social Darwinism, which purportedly explained, and justified, why some Americans grew rich while others remained poor. Grafted on the biological theory of evolution propounded by Charles Darwin, social Darwinism raised the principle of the "survival of the fittest" as an ideal for modern society. In 1883, the Yale professor William Graham Sumner published an essay entitled *What Social Classes Owe to Each Other*, wherein he argued that only a few individuals were capable of putting aside selfish pleasures to produce the capital needed to drive the emerging industrial economy and, moreover, they were fully deserving of their great fortunes. In contrast, the vast majority, too lazy or profligate to rise above poverty, deserved their own miserable fates. To tamper with this "natural" order by establishing welfare programs to help the poor or redistributing wealth in any way would be hazardous to society.

LABOR IN THE AGE OF BIG BUSINESS

HOW DID American workers respond to the changing economic conditions of the late nineteenth century?

Like the gospel of wealth, the "gospel of work" affirmed the dignity of production and the importance of individual initiative. But unlike business leaders, the philosophers of American working people did not believe in riches as the proof of civic virtue or in the lust for power as the driving force of progress. On the contrary, they contended that a hard day's work should be the badge of all responsible citizens.

Behind the "gospel of work" stood the reality of the rising industrial order. The impact of the new order on the lives of working people would be nothing less than revolutionary. Increasingly, Americans made their livelihoods by producing, not for their own subsistence, but exclusively for the market, and they earned wages in return for their labor. Big business thus found its mirror image in the labor movement spawned by the consolidation of the wage system.

THE WAGE SYSTEM

The accelerating growth of industry, especially the steady mechanization of production, dramatically changed employer–employee relations and created new categories of workers. For most craft workers, the new system destroyed long-standing practices and chipped away at their customary autonomy. Managers constantly supervised workers and set the pace of production and rate of payment. In addition, new, faster machinery made many skills obsolete. In the woodworking trades, highly skilled cabinetmakers, who for generations had brought their own tools to the factory, were largely replaced with "green hands"—immigrants, including many women—who with only minimal training and close supervision could operate new woodworking machines at the cheaper rates of pay.

Not all trades conformed to this pattern. The garment industry, for example, grew at a very fast pace in New York, Boston, Chicago, Philadelphia, Cleveland, and

St. Louis, but retained older systems of labor along with the new. The highly mechanized factories employed hundreds of thousands of young immigrant women, while the outwork system, established well before the Civil War, contracted ever-larger numbers of families to work in their homes on sewing machines or by hand.

Industrial expansion also offered new opportunities for women to work outside the home, and many young women fled the family farm for the factory. African American and immigrant women found employment in trades least affected by technological advances, such as domestic service. In contrast, English-speaking white women moved into the better-paying clerical and sales positions in the rapidly expanding business sector. After the typewriter and telephone came into widespread use in the 1890s, the number of women employed in office work rose even faster. At the turn of the century, 8.6 million women worked outside their homes—nearly triple the number in 1870.

In contrast, African American men found themselves excluded from many fields. In Cleveland, for example, the number of black carpenters declined after 1870, just as the number of construction jobs grew. African American men were also systematically driven from restaurant service and barred from newer trades that European immigrants secured for themselves.

Discriminatory or exclusionary practices fell hardest on workers recruited earlier from China. From the 1860s on, many Chinese established laundries and restaurants in West Coast cities where they were viewed as potential competitors by both white workers and proprietors of small businesses. A potent and racist anti-Chinese movement organized to protest "cheap" Chinese labor and to demand a halt to Chinese immigration. During the nationwide depression of the 1870s, white rioters insistently called for deportation measures and razed Chinese neighborhoods. In 1882, Congress passed the **Chinese Exclusion Act**, which restricted Chinese immigration by barring laborers, limited the civil rights of resident Chinese, and forbade their naturalization.

For even the best-placed wage earners, the new workplace could be unhealthy, even dangerous. Factory owners often failed to mark high-voltage wires, locked fire doors, and allowed the emission of toxic fumes. Moreover, machines ran faster in American factories than anywhere else in the world, and workers who could not keep up or suffered serious injury found themselves without a job.

Even under less hazardous conditions, workers complained about the tedium of performing repetitive tasks for many hours each day. Although federal employees had been granted the eight-hour day in 1868, most workers still toiled upward of ten to twelve hours. Nor could glamour be found in the work of saleswomen in the elegant department stores. Clerks could not sit down, despite workdays as long as sixteen hours in the busy season, or hold "unnecessary conversations" with customers or other clerks. Despite these disadvantages, most women preferred sales and manufacturing jobs to domestic service.

Moreover, steady employment was rare. Between 1866 and 1897, fourteen years of prosperity stood against seventeen years of hard times. The major depressions of 1873–79 and 1893–97 were the worst in the nation's history up to that time. Three "minor" recessions (1866–67, 1883–85, and 1890–91) did not seem insignificant to the millions who lost their jobs.

E PLURIBUS UNUM (EXCEPT THE CHINESE).

Thomas Nast (1840–1902), the most famous political cartoonist of the late nineteenth century, used his art to comment on pressing political issues, such as the plight of former slaves during Reconstruction, the evils of machine politics, and the rivalry between the national political parties. His drawings were made into wood engravings that were then printed in newspapers and popular magazines. In this cartoon, published in *Harper's Weekly,* April 1, 1882, Nast shows America welcoming all immigrants except Chinese.

◆◆◆ Read the Document

Chinese Exclusion Act (1882) at **www.myhistorylab.com**

Chinese Exclusion Act   Act which suspended Chinese immigration, limited the civil rights of resident Chinese, and forbade their naturalization.

Knights of Labor Labor union founded in 1869 that included skilled and unskilled workers irrespective of race or gender.

THE KNIGHTS OF LABOR

The **Knights of Labor**, founded by a group of Philadelphia garment cutters in 1869, grew to become the largest labor organization in the nineteenth century. Led by Terence V. Powderly, the order sought to bring together wage earners, regardless of skill. The Knights endorsed a variety of reform measures—the restriction of child labor, a graduated income tax, more land set aside for homesteading, the abolition of contract labor, and monetary reform—to offset the power of the industrialists. They believed that the "producing classes," once freed from the grip of corporate monopoly and the curses of ignorance and alcohol, would transform the United States into a genuinely democratic society.

The Knights sought to overturn the wage system and, as an alternative, they promoted producers' cooperatives. In these factories, workers collectively made all decisions on prices charged for goods and shared all the profits. Local assemblies launched thousands of small coops. Successful for a time, most cooperatives could not compete against the heavily capitalized enterprises and ultimately failed.

For women, the Knights of Labor created a special department within the organization "to investigate the abuses to which our sex is subjected by unscrupulous employers, to agitate the principles which our Order teaches of equal pay for equal work and the abolition of child labor." At the 1886 convention, delegates approved this plan, and Powderly appointed knit-goods worker Leonora M. Barry general investigator. With perhaps 65,000 women members at its peak, the Knights ran daycare centers and occasionally even set up cooperative kitchens.

The Knights reached their peak in 1886 during the great campaign for a shorter workday with 700,000 members. The Knights welcomed workers usually excluded by other unions. Nearly 3,000 women formed their own "ladies assemblies" or joined mixed locals. The Knights also organized African American workers mainly in separate assemblies within the organization. Chinese workers, however, were barred from membership.

The Haymarket affair in Chicago, where the Knights were headquartered, virtually crushed the organization. Local employers' associations successfully pooled funds to rid their factories of troublesome organizers. By 1890, membership had declined to less than 100,000. The wage system had triumphed.

QUICK REVIEW

The Knights of Labor

- Founded in 1869 by Philadelphia garment cutters.
- Knights promoted economic cooperation.
- Reached their peak during campaign for eight-hour work day.

At the 1886 General Assembly of the Knights of Labor, which met in Richmond, Virginia, sixteen women attended as delegates. Elizabeth Rodgers, the first woman in Chicago to join the Knights and the first woman to serve as a master workman in a district assembly, attended with her two-week-old daughter. The convention established a Department of Women's Work and appointed Leonora M. Barry, a hosiery worker, as general investigator.

THE AMERICAN FEDERATION OF LABOR

The events of 1886 also signaled the rise of a very different kind of organization, the **American Federation of Labor** (AFL). Unlike the Knights, the AFL accepted the wage system. The AFL sought recognition of its union status to bargain with employers for better working conditions, higher wages, and shorter hours. In return, it offered compliant firms the benefit of amenable day-to-day relations with the most highly skilled wage earners. Only if companies refused to bargain in good faith would union members resort to strikes.

The new federation, with twelve national unions and 140,000 affiliated members in 1886, rapidly pushed ahead of the rival Knights by organizing craft workers. AFL president Samuel Gompers disregarded unskilled workers, racial minorities, and immigrants, believing they were impossible to organize and even unworthy of membership.

While Gompers advanced the interests of the "aristocrats of labor," the rank-and-file often pursued broader aims. Chicago's Central Labor Federation, for example, worked closely with urban reformers. Finding allies among women's clubs and church groups, within the state legislature, and even among some socially minded members of the business community, they cultivated an atmosphere of civic responsibility. The Illinois Factory Investigation Act of 1893 offered evidence of their hard work and patience: under its terms, unionists secured funds from the state legislature to monitor working conditions and, particularly, to improve the terrible conditions under which women and children worked in sweatshops.

Although the AFL represented only a small minority of working Americans—about 10 percent at the end of the century—local unions often played important roles in their communities. They may not have been able to slow the steady advance of mass production, but AFL members managed to make their presence felt. Local politicians courted their votes, and Labor Day, first celebrated in the 1880s, became a national holiday in 1894.

Read the Document

Profile: Samuel Gompers at
www.myhistorylab.com

THE NEW SOUTH

Physically and financially devastated by the war, the South remained economically stagnant, its per capita wealth only 27 percent of that of the northeastern states. While a few urban centers moved very slowly into the era of modern industry, the countryside receded into greater isolation and poverty. The southern economy in general was held back by dependence on northern finance capital, continued reliance on cotton production, and the legacy of slavery.

WHO BENEFITED the most from economic developments in the post-Reconstruction South? Why?

AN INTERNAL COLONY

In the 1870s, a vocal and powerful new group of Southerners headed by Henry Woodfin Grady, editor of the *Atlanta Constitution*, insisted that the region enjoyed a great potential in its abundant natural resources of coal, iron, turpentine, tobacco, and lumber. Grady and his peers envisioned a "New South" where modern textile mills operated efficiently and profitably, close to the expansive fields of cotton, and a plentiful and cheap supply of labor, unrestricted by unions or by legal limitations on the employment of children. Arguing against those planters who hoped to rejuvenate the agricultural economy by cultivating a few staple crops, this group forcefully promoted industrial development and welcomed northern investors.

Northern investors secured huge concessions from southern state legislatures, including land, forest, and mineral rights and large tax exemptions. Exploiting the incentives, railroad companies laid more than 22,000 miles of new track, connecting the region to national markets and creating new cities. By 1890, a score of large railroad companies, centered mainly in New York, owned more than half of all the track in the South.

Read the Document

William D. Grady, The New South (1887)
at **www.myhistorylab.com**

American Federation of Labor (AFL) Union formed in 1886 that organized skilled workers along craft lines and emphasized a few workplace issues rather than a broad social program.

Northerners also employed various means to protect their investments from southern competition. By the late 1870s, southern merchants, with help from foreign investors, had begun to run iron factories around Birmingham, Alabama. Southern iron production was soon encroaching on the northeastern market. To stave off this competition, Andrew Carnegie ordered the railroads to charge higher freight fees to Birmingham's iron producers. After the turn of the century, the U.S. Steel Corporation simply bought out the local merchants and took over much of Birmingham's production.

The production of cotton textiles followed a similar course. Powerful merchants and large landowners, realizing that they could make high profits by controlling the cotton crop from field to factory, promoted the vertical integration of the cotton industry. The number of mills in the South grew from 161 in 1880 to 400 in 1900. Southern investors supplied large amounts of the capital for the industrial expansion and technological improvements. The latest machines ran the new mills, and the South boasted the first factory fully equipped with electricity.

Recognizing the potential for great profit, many New England mill owners moved their operations to the South. By the 1920s, northern investors held much of the South's wealth, including the major textile mills, but returned through employment or social services only a small share of the profits to the region's people.

Beyond iron or steel and textiles, southern industry remained largely extractive and, like the South itself, rural. For the most part, southern enterprises mainly produced raw materials for consumption or use in the North, thereby perpetuating the economic imbalance between the sections.

The governing role of capital investments from outside the region reinforced long-standing relationships. Even rapid industrialization—in iron, railroads, and textiles—did not carry the same consequences engendered in the North. The rise of the New South reinforced, rather than diminished, the region's status as the nation's internal colony.

SOUTHERN LABOR

The advance of southern industry did little to improve the working lives of most African Americans, who made up more than one-third of the region's population. Although the majority continued to work in agriculture, large numbers found jobs in industries such as the railroad. In booming cities like Atlanta, they even gained skilled positions as brick-layers, carpenters, and painters. For the most part, however, African Americans were limited to unskilled, low-paying jobs. Nearly all African American women who earned wages did so as household workers.

Most trade unions refused membership to black workers. Only at rare moments did southern workers unite across racial lines. In the 1880s, the Knights of Labor briefly organized both black and white workers. But when white politicians and local newspapers began to raise the specter of black domination, the Knights were forced to retreat. Across the region, their assemblies collapsed. Other unions remained the exclusive preserve of white skilled workers.

Wages throughout the South were low for both black and white workers. Southern textile workers' wages were barely half those of New Englanders. Black men earned at or below the poverty line of $300 per year, while black women rarely earned more than $120 and white women about $220 annually. The poorest paid workers were children, the mainstay of southern mill labor.

As industry expanded throughout the nation, so, too, did the number of children earning wages. This was especially so in the South. In 1896, only one in twenty Massachusetts mill workers was younger than sixteen, but one in four North Carolina cotton mill operatives was that age or younger. Traditions rooted in the agricultural economy reinforced the practice of using the labor of all family members, even the very young. Seasonal labor, such as picking crops or grinding sugarcane, put families on the move, making formal education all but impossible. Not until well into the twentieth century did compulsory school attendance laws effectively restrict child labor in the South.

A system of convict labor also thrived in the South. African Americans constituted up to 90 percent of the convict workforce. Transported and housed like animals—chained together by day and confined in portable cages at night—these workers suffered high mortality rates. White politicians expressed pride in what they called the "good roads movement"—the chief use of convict labor—as proof of regional progress.

THE TRANSFORMATION OF PIEDMONT COMMUNITIES

The impact of modern industry was nowhere greater than in the Piedmont, the region extending from southern Virginia and the central Carolinas into northern Alabama and Georgia. After 1870, long-established farms and plantations gave way to railroad tracks, textile factories, numerous mill villages, and a few sizable cities. Once the South's backcountry, the Piedmont surpassed New England in the production of yarn and cloth to stand first in the world.

A typical mill community was made up of rows of single-family houses, a small school, several churches, a company-owned store, and the home of the superintendent, who governed everyone's affairs. It was not unknown for a superintendent to prowl the neighborhood to see which families burned their lanterns past nine o'clock at night and, finding a violator, to knock on the door and tell the offenders to go to bed. Millworkers frequently complained that they had no private life at all.

Mill superintendents also relied on schoolteachers and clergy to set the tone of community life. They hired and paid the salaries of Baptist and Methodist ministers to preach a faith encouraging workers to be thrifty, orderly, temperate, and hardworking. The schools, similarly subsidized by the company, reinforced the lesson of moral and social discipline required of industrial life and encouraged students to follow their parents into the mill. It was mainly young children between six and eight years old who attended school. When more hands were needed in the mill, superintendents plucked out those youngsters and sent them to join their older brothers and sisters who were already at work.

The processing of raw tobacco employed thousands of African American women, who sorted, stripped, stemmed, and hung tobacco leaves as part of the redrying process. After mechanization was introduced, white women took jobs as cigarette rollers, but black women kept the worst, most monotonous jobs in the tobacco factories. The women shown in this photograph are stemming tobacco in a Virginia factory while their white male supervisor oversees their labor.

THE INDUSTRIAL CITY

Before the Civil War, manufacturing had centered in the countryside, in new factory towns such as Lowell, Massachusetts, and Troy, New York. By the end of the nineteenth century, 90 percent of all manufacturing took place in cities. The metropolis stood at the center of the growing industrial economy, a magnet drawing raw material, capital, and labor, and a key distribution point for manufactured goods throughout the nation and worldwide. The industrial city became the home of nearly 20 million immigrants, mainly the so-called "new immigrants" from southern and eastern Europe, who hoped to escape famine, political upheaval, or religious persecution in their homelands or simply make a better life for themselves and their families.

WHAT WAS life like in the industrial cities of late nineteenth-century America?

POPULATING THE CITY

The population of cities grew at double the rate of the nation's population as a whole. In 1860, only sixteen cities had more than 50,000 residents. By 1890, one-third of all Americans were city dwellers (see Table 19.1).

Many of the new city dwellers had migrated from rural communities within the United States. Between 1870 and 1910, an average of nearly 7,000 African Americans moved north each year, hoping to escape the poverty and oppression in the South and to find better-paying jobs. By the end of the century, nearly 80 percent of African Americans in the North lived in urban areas.

The major source of urban growth in the late nineteenth century were immigrants and their children. Most of those in the first wave of immigration, before the Civil War, had settled in the countryside. In contrast, the so-called new immigrants, who came primarily from eastern and southern Europe, populated the industrial cities. By the turn of the century, Chicago had more Germans than all but a few German cities and more Poles than most Polish cities; New York had more Italians than a handful of the largest Italian cities, and Boston had nearly as many Irish as Dublin. In almost every group except the Irish, men outnumbered women (see Map 19.2).

Like rural migrants, immigrants headed for the American city to take advantage of the expanding opportunities for employment. While many hoped to build a new home in the land of plenty, many others intended to work hard, save money, and return to their families in the Old Country. In the 1880s, for example, nearly half of all Italian, Greek, and Serbian men returned to their native lands. Others could not return to their homelands or did not wish to. Jews, for instance, had emigrated to escape persecution in Russia and Russian-dominated Polish and Romanian lands.

Of all groups, Jews had the most experience with urban life. Forbidden to own land in most parts of Europe and boxed into *shtetls* (villages), Jews had also formed thriving urban communities in Vilna, Berlin, London, and Vienna. Many had worked in garment manufacturing and followed a path to American cities like New York, Rochester, Philadelphia, or Chicago where the needle trades flourished.

Other groups, the majority coming from rural parts of Europe, sought out their kinfolk in American cities, where they could most easily find housing and employment. Bohemians settled largely in Chicago, Pittsburgh, and Cleveland. French Canadians emigrated from Quebec and settled almost exclusively in New England and upper New York State. Cubans, themselves often first- or second-generation immigrants from Spain, moved to Ybor City, a section of Tampa, Florida, to work in cigar factories. Italians, the most numerous among the new immigrants, settled mainly in northeastern cities, laying railroad track, excavating subways, and erecting buildings.

QUICK REVIEW

Big Cities

- Cities grew at double the rate of the nation as a whole.
- Immigrants and their children were the major source of urban population growth.
- After the Civil War, most new immigrants settled in cities.

• • ◦ Read the Document

Exploring America: French-Canadian Controversy at **www.myhistorylab.com**

TABLE 19.1

A Growing Urban Population

	1870	1880	1890	1900
U.S. population	35,558,000	50,156,000	62,947,000	75,995,000
Urban population	9,902,000	14,130,000	22,106,000	30,160,000
Percent urban	25.7	28.2	35.1	39.7
Percent rural	74.3	71.8	64.9	60.3

Note that during each decade, the U.S. population as a whole grew between 20 and 30 percent. Figures in the table have been rounded to the nearest thousand.

From *The Gilded Age* edited by Charles W. Calhoun. © 1996. Reprinted by permission of Rowman & Littlefield.

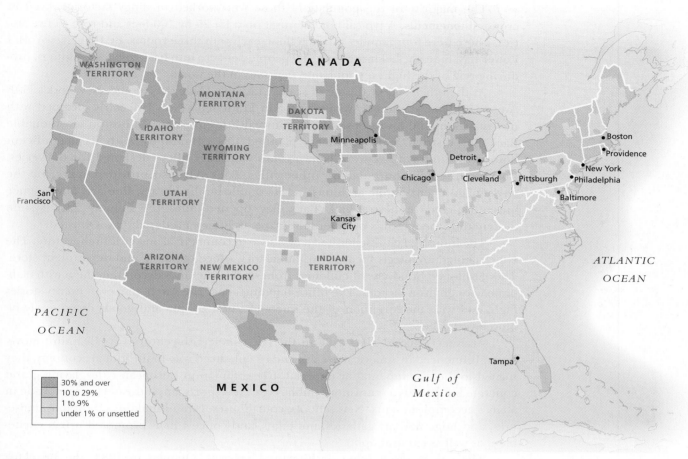

MAP 19.2

Population of Foreign Birth by Region, 1880   European immigrants after the Civil War settled primarily in the industrial districts of the northern Midwest and parts of the Northeast. French Canadians continued to settle in Maine, Cubans in Florida, and Mexicans in the Southwest, where earlier immigrants had established thriving communities.

From LORD. *Historical Atlas of the United States*, 1E. © 1962 Wadsworth, a part of Cengage Learning, Inc. Reproduced by permission. www.cengage.com/permission.

WHAT REGION attracted the fewest immigrants? Why?

Resettlement in an American city did not necessarily mark the end of the immigrants' travels. Newcomers, both native-born and immigrants, moved frequently from one neighborhood to another and from one city to another. As manufacturing advanced outward from the city center, working populations followed.

THE URBAN LANDSCAPE

Faced with a population explosion and an unprecedented building boom, the cities encouraged the creation of many beautiful and useful structures, including commercial offices, sumptuous homes, and efficient public services. At the same time, open space decreased as builders leveled hills, filled ponds, and pulled down any farms or houses in the way. Factories often occupied the best sites, typically near waterways, where goods could be easily transported and chemical wastes dumped. City officials usually lacked any master plan, save the idea of endless expansion.

The majority of the population, those who worked in dingy factories, lived in crowded **tenements**. A typical tenement sat on a lot 25 by 100 feet and rose to five stories. There were four families on each floor, each with three rooms. By 1890, New York's Lower East Side packed more than 700 people per acre into back-to-back buildings, producing one of the highest population densities in the world.

At the other end of the social scale, Chicago's Michigan Avenue, New York's Fifth Avenue, St. Paul's Summit Avenue, and San Francisco's Nob Hill fairly gleamed with new mansions and townhouses. Commonwealth Avenue marked Boston's fashionable Back Bay district. State engineers planned this community, with its magnificent boulevard, uniform five-story brownstones, and back alleys designed for deliveries. Like wealthy neighborhoods in other cities, Back Bay also provided space for the city's magnificent public architecture: its stately public library, fine arts and science museums, and orchestra hall. Back Bay opened onto the Fenway Park system designed by the nation's premier landscape architect, Frederick Law Olmsted.

The industrial city established a new style of commercial and civic architecture. The era's talented architects focused on the factory, office building, and department store. They fashioned hundreds of buildings from steel, sometimes decorating them with elaborate wrought-iron facades. The office building could rise seven, ten, even twenty stories high, and with the invention of the safety elevator, people and goods could easily be moved vertically.

Architects played a key role in the late nineteenth-century City Beautiful movement. Influenced by American wealth and its enhanced role in the global economy, they turned to the monumental or imperial style common in European cities, laying grand concrete boulevards at enormous public cost. New sports amphitheaters spread pride in a city's accomplishments. New schools, courthouses, capitol buildings, hospitals, museums, and huge new art galleries, museums, and concert halls promoted urban excitement as well as cultural uplift.

The city inspired other architectural marvels. Opened in 1883, the Brooklyn Bridge won wide acclaim as the most original American construction. Designed by John Roebling and his son Washington Roebling, the bridge was considered an aesthetic and practical wonder. The Brooklyn Bridge also helped to speed the transformation of rural townships into suburban communities.

Like the railroad, but on a smaller scale, streetcars and elevated railroads changed business dramatically, because they moved traffic of many different kinds—information, people, and goods—faster and farther than before. In 1902, New York opened its subway system, which would grow to become the largest in the nation.

THE CITY AND THE ENVIRONMENT

By making it possible for a great number of workers to live in communities distant from their place of employment, mass transportation allowed the metropolitan region to grow dramatically. Suburbs sprang up outside the major cities, offering many professional workers quiet residential retreats from the city's busy and increasingly polluted downtown.

Electric trolleys eliminated the tons of waste from horsecars that had for decades fouled city streets. The new rail systems also increased congestion and created new safety hazards for pedestrians. During the 1890s, 600 people were killed each year by Chicago's trains. Elevated trains, designed to avoid these problems, placed entire communities under the shadow of noisy and rickety wooden platforms.

Modern water and sewer systems constituted a hidden city of pipes and wires, mirroring the growth of the visible city above ground. These advances, which brought indoor plumbing to most homes, did not, however, eradicate serious environmental or health problems. Most cities continued to dump sewage into nearby bodies of water.

tenements   Four- to six-story residential dwellings, once common in New York, built on tiny lots without regard to providing ventilation or light.

In his watercolor *The Bowery at Night*, painted in 1885, W. Louis Sonntag Jr. shows a New York City scene transformed by electric light. Electricity transformed the city in other ways as well, as seen in the electric streetcars and elevated railroad.

Moreover, most municipal governments established separate clean-water systems through the use of reservoirs rather than outlawing upriver dumping by factories.

The unrestricted burning of coal to fuel the railroads and to heat factories and homes after 1880 greatly intensified urban air pollution. Noise levels continued to rise in the most compacted living and industrial areas. Overcrowded conditions and inadequate sanitary facilities bred tuberculosis, smallpox, and scarlet fever, among other contagious diseases. Only after the turn of the century, amid an intensive campaign against municipal corruption, did laws and administrative practices address the serious problems of public health (see Chapter 21).

Meanwhile, the distance between the city and the countryside narrowed. Naturalists had hoped for large open spaces—a buffer zone—to preserve farmland and wild areas, protect future water supplies, and diminish regional air pollution. But soon the industrial landscape invaded the countryside. Nearby rural lands not destined for private housing or commercial development became sites for water treatment and sewage plants, garbage dumps, and graveyards—services essential to the city's growing population.

THE RISE OF CONSUMER SOCIETY

The growth of industry and the spread of cities promoted—and depended on—the consumption of mass-produced goods. During the final third of the nineteenth century, the standard of living climbed, although unevenly and erratically. Real wages (pay in relation to the cost of living) rose, fostering improvements in nutrition, clothing, and housing. Meanwhile, prices dropped. More and cheaper products came into the reach of all but the very poor. Although many Americans continued to acknowledge the moral value of hard work, thrift, and self-sacrifice, the explosion of consumer goods and services promoted sweeping changes in behavior and beliefs, although in vastly and increasingly different ways.

WHAT ACCOUNTS for the rise of a consumer society and how did various groups participate in its development?

View the **Image**

Residence of Andrew Carnegie at
www.myhistorylab.com

"CONSPICUOUS CONSUMPTION"

Labeled the "**Gilded Age**" by humorist and social critic Mark Twain, the era following the Civil War favored the growth of a new business class that pursued both money and leisure and formed national networks to consolidate their power. Business leaders built diverse stock portfolios and often served simultaneously on the boards of several corporations. Similarly, they intertwined their interests by joining the same religious, charitable, athletic, and professional societies.

According to economist and social critic Thorstein Veblen, the rich had created a new style of "**conspicuous consumption**." The Chicago mansion of real estate tycoon Potter Palmer, for example, was constructed without exterior doorknobs. Not only could no one enter uninvited, but a visitor's calling card supposedly passed through the hands of twenty-seven servants before admittance was allowed. The women who oversaw these elaborate households served as measures of their husbands' status, according to Veblen, by adorning themselves in jewels, furs, and dresses of the latest Paris design.

Toward the end of the century, the wealthy added a dramatic public dimension to the "high life." New York's Waldorf-Astoria hotel, which opened in 1897, incorporated the grandeur of European royalty but with an important difference. Because rich Americans wanted to be watched, the elegantly appointed corridors and restaurants were visible to the public through huge windows. The New York rich also established a unique custom to welcome the New Year: they opened wide the curtains of their Fifth Avenue mansions so that passersby could marvel at the elegant decor.

The wealthy became the leading patrons of the arts as well as the chief procurers of art treasures from Europe and Asia. They provided the bulk of funds for the new symphonies, operas, and ballet companies, which soon rivaled those of Continental Europe.

Read the **Document**

History Bookshelf: *Veblen,* Theory
of the Leisure Class at
www.myhistorylab.com

SELF-IMPROVEMENT AND THE MIDDLE CLASS

A new middle class, very different from its predecessor, formed during the last half of the century. The older middle class comprised the owners or superintendents of small businesses, doctors, lawyers, teachers, and ministers and their families. The new middle class included these professionals but also the growing number of salaried employees— the managers, technicians, clerks, and engineers who worked in the complex web of corporations and government.

By the end of the century, many middle-class families were nestled in suburban retreats far from the noise, filth, and dangers of the city. This peaceful domestic setting, with its manicured lawns and well-placed shrubs, afforded both privacy and rejuvenation as well as the separation of business from leisure and the breadwinner from his family for most of the day. Assisted by modern transportation systems, men often traveled one to two hours each day, five or six days a week, to their city offices and back again.

Middle-class women devoted a large part of their day to care of the home. Improvements in the kitchen stove, such as the conversion from wood fuel to gas, saved a lot of time. Yet, simultaneously, with the widespread circulation of cookbooks and recipes in newspapers and magazines, as well as the availability of new foods, the preparation of meals became more complex and time-consuming. New devices such as the eggbeater speeded some familiar tasks, but the era's fancy culinary practices offset any gains in saving time. Similarly, the new carpet sweepers surpassed the broom in efficiency, but the fashionable high-napped carpeting demanded more care. Thus, rather than diminishing with technological innovation, household work expanded to fill the time available.

By the end of the century, though, middle-class women had added shopping to their list of household chores. They took charge of the household budget and purchased

Gilded Age Term applied to late nineteenth-century America that refers to the shallow display and worship of wealth characteristic of that period.

conspicuous consumption Highly visible displays of wealth and consumption.

an ever-expanding range of machine-made goods, packaged foods, manufactured clothing, and personal luxuries. With the rise of department stores, which catered specifically to them, shopping combined work and pleasure and became a major pastime for women.

Almost exclusively white, Anglo-Saxon, and Protestant, the new middle class embraced "culture" not for purposes of conspicuous consumption but as a means of self-improvement. Whole families visited the new museums and art galleries. The middle class also provided the bulk of patrons for the new public libraries.

Middle-class families applied the same standards to their leisure activities. What one sporting-goods entrepreneur rightly called the "gospel of exercise" involved men and women in calisthenics and outdoor activities, not so much for pleasure as for physical and mental discipline. Hiking was a favorite among both men and women. Soon men and women began camping out, with almost enough amenities to re-create a middle-class home in the woods. Roller-skating and ice-skating took place in specially designed rinks in almost every major town. By the 1890s, the "safety" bicycle had also been marketed. It replaced the large-wheel variety, which was difficult to keep upright. A good-quality "bike" cost $100 and, like the piano, was a symbol of middle-class status.

Leisure became the special province of middle-class childhood. Removed from factories and shops and freed from many domestic chores, children enjoyed creative play and physical activity. The toy market boomed, and lower printing prices helped children's literature flourish. Uplifting classics such as *Little Women* and *Black Beauty* were popular.

LIFE IN THE STREETS

Immigrants often weighed the material abundance they found in the United States against their memories of the Old Country. One could "live better" here, but only by working much harder. In letters home, immigrants described the riches of the new

Read the Document

Frances E. Willard, On Riding the Bicycle (1895) at **www.myhistorylab.com**

QUICK REVIEW

The New Middle Class

♦ Middle-class women devoted a large portion of their day to housework.

♦ The new middle class embraced "culture" as means of self-improvement.

♦ Leisure activities reflected middle-class values.

The intersection of Orchard and Hester Streets on New York's Lower East Side, photographed ca. 1905. Unlike the middle classes, who worked and played hidden away in offices and private homes, the Jewish lower-class immigrants who lived and worked in this neighborhood spent the greater part of their lives on the streets.

country but warned friends and relatives not to send weaklings, who would surely die of stress and strain amid the alien and intense commercialism of American society.

Many newcomers, having little choice about their place of residence, were concentrated in urban districts marked off by racial or ethnic lines. In San Francisco, city ordinances prevented Chinese from operating laundries in most of the city's neighborhoods, and the city's schools excluded their children. In Los Angeles and San Antonio, Mexicans lived in distinctive barrios. In most cities, African American families were similarly compelled to remain in the dingiest, most crime-ridden, and dangerous sections of town.

The working-class home did not necessarily ensure privacy or offer protection from the dangers of the outside world. In the tenements, families often shared their rooms with other families or paying boarders. During the summer heat, adults, children, and boarders alike competed for a sleeping place on the fire escape or roof, and throughout the year, noise resounded through paper-thin walls.

The working-class home involved women and children in routines of household labor without the aid of new mechanical devices. In addition to cooking and cleaning, women used their cramped domestic space for work that provided a small income. They gathered their children—and their husbands after a hard day's labor—to sew garments, wrap cigars, string beads, or paint vases for a contractor who paid them by the piece. And they cooked and cleaned for the boarders whose rent supplemented the family income.

Despite working people's slim resources, their combined buying power created new and important markets for consumer goods. Several leading clothing manufacturers specialized in inexpensive ready-to-wear items, usually copied from patterns designed for wealthier consumers but constructed hastily from flimsy materials. Patent medicines for ailments caused by working long periods in cramped conditions sold well in working-class communities, where money for doctors was scarce.

The close quarters of the urban neighborhood allowed immigrants to preserve many Old World customs. In immigrant communities such as Chicago's German North Side, Pittsburgh's Poletown, New York's Lower East Side, or San Francisco's Chinatown, people usually spoke their native language while visiting friends and relatives. No organization was as important as the fraternal society, which sponsored social clubs and provided insurance benefits. Immigrants also re-created Old World religious institutions such as the temple, church, or synagogue, or secular institutions such as German family-style saloons or Russian Jewish tearooms. Chinese theaters, in inexpensive daily and nightly performances, presented dramas depicting historical events or explicating moral teachings and thereby preserved much of Chinese native culture. Immigrants also replicated their native cuisine and married, baptized children, and buried their dead according to Old World customs.

In the cosmopolitan cities, immigrants, by being innovative entrepreneurs as well as the best customers, helped to shape the emerging popular culture. German immigrants, for example, created Tin Pan Alley, the center of the popular music industry. They also became the first promoters of ragtime. Created by African American and Creole bands, ragtime captivated the teenage offspring of immigrants who rushed to the new dance halls.

When developers realized that "wholesome fun" for the masses could pay better than upper-class leisure or lower-class vice, in 1895 they decided to transform Coney Island into a magnificent seaside park filled with ingenious amusements such as water slides, mechanized horse races, carousels, roller coasters, and fun houses. At Coney Island or at Riverview, Chicago's oldest amusement park, located on the city's North Side, millions of working-class people enjoyed cheap thrills that offset the hardships of their working lives.

CULTURES IN CONFLICT, CULTURE IN COMMON

Just as the changes in production fostered conflict in the forms of strikes and workers' protests, so, too, did the accompanying changes in the daily life of the community. Competing claims to the resources of the new urban, industrial society, such as public schools and urban parks, became more intense as the century moved to a close.

HOW DID cultural developments in America's cities reflect larger social and economic tensions?

EDUCATION

Business and civic leaders realized that the welfare of society depended on an educated population, one possessing the skills and knowledge required to keep both industry and government running. In the last three decades of the nineteenth century, the idea of universal free schooling, at least for white children, took hold. Kindergartens in particular flourished.

Public high schools, which were rare before the Civil War, also increased in number, from 160 in 1870 to 6,000 by the end of the century. Despite this spectacular growth, which was concentrated in urban industrial areas, as late as 1890 only 4 percent of children between the ages of fourteen and seventeen were enrolled in school, the majority of them girls planning to become teachers or office workers (see Figure 19.1). Most high schools continued to serve mainly the middle class.

Higher education also expanded along several lines. Agricultural colleges formed earlier in the century developed into institutes of technology and took their places alongside the prestigious liberal arts colleges. To extend learning to the "industrial classes," the Morrill Federal Land Grant Act of 1862 funded a system of state colleges and universities for teaching agriculture and mechanics "without excluding other scientific and classic studies."

Read the **Document**
Morrill Act (1862) at
www.myhistorylab.com

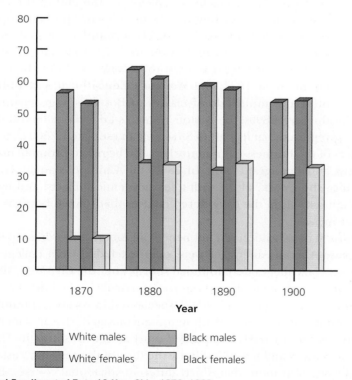

Year

White males   Black males
White females   Black females

Figure 19.1 School Enrollment of 5- to 19-Year-Olds, 1870–1900
In the final decades of the nineteenth century, elementary and high school enrollments grew across the board, but especially so for children of color and for girls.

U.S. Department of Commerce, Bureau of the Census, *Historical Statistics of the United States, Colonial Times to 1970.* U.S. Department of Education, Office of Educational Research and Improvement.

George Washington Carver (1864–1943), who was born into slavery, had been invited by Booker T. Washington to direct agricultural research at the Tuskegee Institute in Alabama. A leader in development of agriculture in the New South, Carver promoted crop diversification to rejuvenate soil that was depleted by the continuous planting of cotton. He also encouraged the cultivation of alternative, high-protein crops such as peanuts and soybeans. He designed his programs in sustainable agriculture mainly for African American farmers and sharecroppers rather than for commercial purposes.

QUICK REVIEW

Public Education

♦ 1870: 160 public high schools.

♦ 1900: 6,000 public high schools.

♦ Expansion of public education benefited women

Women's Educational and Industrial Union Boston organization offering classes to wage-earning women.

Meanwhile, established private institutions like Harvard, Yale, Princeton, and Columbia grew with the help of huge endowments from business leaders. By 1900, sixty-three Catholic colleges were serving mainly the children of immigrants from Ireland and eastern and southern Europe. Still, while the overall number of colleges and universities grew from 563 in 1870 to nearly 1,000 by 1910, only 3 percent of the college-age population took advantage of these new opportunities. One of the most important developments occurred in the area of research and graduate studies. By the end of the century, several American universities offered advanced degrees in the arts and sciences.

This expansion benefited women, who previously had little access to higher education. After the Civil War, a number of women's colleges were founded, beginning in 1865 with Vassar, which set the academic standard for the remainder of the century. By the end of the century, 125 women's colleges offered a first-rate education comparable to that given to men at Harvard, Yale, or Princeton. Meanwhile, coeducation grew at an even faster rate; by 1890, 47 percent of the nation's colleges and universities admitted women. The proportion of women college students changed dramatically. Women constituted 21 percent of undergraduate enrollments in 1870, 32 percent in 1880, and 40 percent in 1910.

An even greater number of women enrolled in vocational courses. Normal schools, which offered one- or two-year programs for women who planned to become elementary school teachers, developed a collegiate character after the Civil War and had become accredited state teachers' colleges by the end of the century. Other institutions, many founded by middle-class philanthropists, also prepared women for vocations. For example, the first training school for nurses opened in Boston in 1873, followed in 1879 by a diet kitchen that taught women to become cooks in the city's hospitals. Founded in 1877, the **Women's Educational and Industrial Union** offered a multitude of classes to Boston's wage-earning women. In the early 1890s, the Boston Women's Educational and Industrial Union reported that its staff of 83 served an estimated 1,500 clients per day.

The leaders of the business community had also begun to promote manual training for working-class and immigrant boys. In 1884, the Chicago Manual Training School opened, teaching "shop work" along with a few academic subjects, and by 1895, all elementary and high schools in the city offered courses that trained boys for future jobs in industry and business.

The expansion of education did not benefit all Americans or benefit them all in the same way. Because African Americans were often excluded from colleges attended by white students, special colleges were founded shortly after the Civil War. All-black Atlanta and Fisk Universities both soon offered rigorous curricula in the liberal arts. Other institutions, such as Hampton, founded in 1868, specialized in vocational training, mainly in manual trades. Educator Booker T. Washington encouraged African Americans to strive for practical instruction. In 1881, he founded the Tuskegee Institute in Alabama to provide industrial education and moral uplift. By the turn of the century, Tuskegee enrolled 1,400 men and women in more than thirty different vocational courses. Black colleges, including Tuskegee, trained so many teachers that by the century's end, the majority of black schools were staffed by African Americans.

The nation's educational system was becoming more inclusive and yet more differentiated. The majority of children attended school for several years or more. At the same time, students were tracked—by race, gender, and class—to fill particular roles in an industrial society.

LEISURE AND PUBLIC SPACE

Most large cities set aside open land for leisure-time use by residents. New York's Central Park opened for ice-skating in 1858, providing a model for urban park systems across the United States. In 1869, planners in Chicago secured funds to create a citywide park system and within a few years, Lincoln Park, on the city's north side, was attracting crowds of nearly 30,000 on Sundays. These parks were rolling expanses, cut across by streams and pathways and footbridges and set off by groves of trees, ornamental shrubs, and neat flower gardens. According to the designers' vision, the urban middle class might find here a respite from the stresses of modern life. To ensure this possibility, posted regulations forbade many activities, ranging from walking on the grass to gambling, picnicking, or ball playing without permission.

The working classes had their own ideas about the use of parks and open land in their communities. Trapped in overcrowded tenements or congested neighborhoods, they wanted space for sports, picnics, and lovers' trysts. Young people openly defied ordinances that prohibited play on the grassy knolls, while their elders routinely voted against municipal bonds that did not include funds for more recreational space.

Eventually, most park administrators set aside some sections for playgrounds and athletic fields and others for public gardens and band shells. Yet intermittent conflicts erupted. The Worcester, Massachusetts, park system, for example, allowed sports leagues to schedule events but prohibited pickup games. This policy gave city officials more control over the use of the park for outdoor recreation but at the same time forced many ball-playing boys into the streets. When working-class parents protested, city officials responded by instituting programs of supervised play.

Public drinking of alcoholic beverages, especially on Sunday, provoked similar disputes. Although civil leaders hoped to discourage Sunday drinking by sponsoring alternative events, such as free organ recitals and other concerts, many working people, especially beer-loving German immigrants, continued to treat Sunday as their one day of relaxation. In Chicago, when not riding the streetcars to the many beer gardens and taverns that thrived on the outskirts, Germans gathered in large numbers for picnics in the city's parks.

Toward the end of the century, many park administrators relaxed the rules and expanded the range of permitted activities. By that time, large numbers of the middle class had become sports enthusiasts and pressured municipal governments to turn meadowlands into tennis courts and golfing greens. In the 1890s, bicycling brought many women into the parks. Still, not all city residents enjoyed these facilities. Officials in St. Louis, for example, barred African Americans from the city's grand Forest Park and set aside the smaller Tandy Park for their use.

NATIONAL PASTIMES

Toward the end of the century, the younger members of the urban middle class had begun to find common ground in lower-class pastimes, especially ragtime music. Introduced to many Northerners by the African American composer Scott Joplin at the Chicago World's Fair of 1893, "rag" quickly became the staple of entertainment in the new cabarets and nightclubs.

Vaudeville, the most popular form of commercial entertainment since the 1880s, also bridged middle- and working-class tastes. Drawing on a variety-show tradition, "vaude" became a big business that made ethnic and racial stereotypes and the daily frustrations of city life into major topics of amusement. Vaudeville palaces attracted huge, "respectable" crowds that sampled between twenty and thirty dramatic, musical, and comedy acts averaging fifteen minutes each.

Sports, however, outdistanced all other commercial entertainments in appealing to all kinds of fans and managing to create a sense of national community. No doubt the most popular parks in the United States were the baseball fields. Baseball clubs formed in many cities, and shortly after the Civil War, traveling teams with regular schedules made baseball a professional sport. The formation of the National League in 1876 encouraged other spectator sports, but for generations baseball remained the most popular.

Baseball, like many other sports, soon became incorporated into the larger business economy. In Chicago, local merchants, such as Marshall Field, supported teams, and by the end of the 1860s there were more than fifty company-sponsored teams playing in the local leagues. By 1870, a Chicago Board of Trade team emerged as the city's first professional club, the White Stockings. The White Stockings soon succeeded in recruiting a star pitcher from the Boston Red Stockings, Albert Spalding, who eventually became manager and then president of the team. Spalding also came to see baseball as a source of multiple profits. He procured the exclusive rights to manufacture the official ball and the rule book, while producing large varieties of other sporting equipment. Meanwhile, he built impressive baseball parks in Chicago, with seating for 10,000.

Spalding also succeeded in tightening the rules of participation in the sport. In 1879, he dictated the "reserve clause," which prevented players from negotiating a better deal and leaving the team that originally signed them. He encouraged his player-manager "Cap" Anson to forbid the White Stockings from playing against any team with

BOSTON NATIONAL BLOOMER GIRL'S BASE BALL CLUB. L. J. GALBREATH, Originator and Owner.

By the 1890s, Bloomer Girls baseball teams had organized in many parts of the country. To fill out a season, many of these clubs played against men's teams. To fill out a lineup, many of these women's clubs included male players, who at first wore wigs and women's clothing. By the early twentieth century, when this photograph was taken, men played openly in regulation uniforms. The last Bloomer Girl club disbanded in the 1930s. This photograph shows the Boston club with owner L. J. Galbreath.

CHRONOLOGY

1862	Morrill Act authorizes "land-grant" colleges	1883	William Graham Sumner published the social Darwinist classic *What Social Classes Owe to Each Other*
1869	Knights of Labor founded		
1870	Standard Oil founded	1886	Campaigns for eight-hour workday peak
1873	Financial panic brings severe depression		Haymarket riot and massacre discredit the Knights of Labor
1876	Baseball's National League founded		American Federation of Labor founded
	Alexander Graham Bell patents the telephone	1889	Andrew Carnegie's *The Gospel of Wealth* recommends honesty and fair dealing
1879	Thomas Edison invents the incandescent bulb	1890	Sherman Antitrust Act passed
	Depression ends	1893	Stock market panic precipitates severe depression
1881	Tuskegee Institute founded	1895	Coney Island opens
1882	Peak of immigration to the United States (1.2 million) in the nineteenth century	1901	U.S. Steel Corporation formed
	Chinese Exclusion Act passed		
	Standard Oil Trust founded		

an African American member. The firing of Moses "Fleet" Walker, an African American, from the Cincinnati Red Stockings in 1884 marked the first time the color line had been drawn in a major professional sport. Effectively excluded, African Americans organized their own traveling teams. In the 1920s, they formed the Negro Leagues, which produced some of the nation's finest ball players.

As attendance continued to grow, the enthusiasm for baseball straddled major social divisions, bringing together Americans of many backgrounds, if only on a limited basis. By the end of the century, no section of the daily newspaper drew more readers than the sports pages. Although it interested relatively few women, sports news riveted the attention of men from all social classes. Loyalty to the "home team" helped to create an urban identity, while individual players became national heroes.

CONCLUSION

By the end of the nineteenth century, industry and the growing cities had opened a new world for Americans. Fresh from Europe or from the native countryside, ordinary urban dwellers struggled to form communities of fellow newcomers through both work and leisure, in the factory, the neighborhood, the ballpark, and the public school. Meanwhile, their "betters," the wealthy and the new middle class, made and executed the decisions of industry and marketing, established the era's grand civic institutions, and set the tone for high fashion and art. Rich and poor alike shared many aspects of the new order. Yet inequality not only persisted but also increased and prompted new antagonisms.

The Haymarket tragedy highlighted the often strained relationships between Chicago's immigrant working population and civic leaders, precipitating violence, which included the public hanging of four of the eight men brought to trial, including August Spies. Although the new governor of Illinois, Peter Altgeld, pardoned the three who had their sentences commuted to life in prison, his attempt at amelioration did not signal a shift in the political climate. In the 1890s, hopes for a peaceful reconciliation of these tensions had worn thin, and the lure of an overseas empire appeared as one of the few goals that held together a suffering and divided nation.

REVIEW QUESTIONS

1. Discuss the sources of economic growth in the decades after the Civil War. Historians often refer to this period as the era of the "second industrial revolution." Do you agree with this description?

2. Describe the impact of new technologies and new forms of production on the routines of industrial workers. How did these changes affect African American and women workers in particular? What role did trade unions play in this process?

3. Discuss the role of northern capital in the development of the New South. How did the rise of industry affect the lives of rural Southerners? Analyze these changes from the point of view of African Americans.

4. How did urban life change during the Gilded Age? How did economic development affect residential patterns? How did the middle class aspire to live during the Gilded Age? How did their lifestyles compare with those of working-class urbanites?

5. How did the American educational system change to prepare children for their adult roles in the new industrial economy?

6. How did the rise of organized sports and commercial amusements reflect and shape social divisions at the end of the century? Which groups were affected most (or least) by new leisure activities?

KEY TERMS

American Federation of Labor (AFL) (p. 485)
Chinese Exclusion Act (p. 483)
Conspicuous consumption (p. 492)
Gilded Age (p. 492)
Gospel of wealth (p. 481)

Horizontal combination (p. 479)
Knights of Labor (p. 484)
Tenements (p. 490)
Vertical integration (p. 479)
Women's Educational and Industrial Union (p. 496)

myhistorẙlab Connections

Reinforce what you learned in this chapter by studying the many documents, images, maps, review tools, and videos available at www.myhistorylab.com.

Read and Review

✓•⎯Study and Review **Chapter 19**

•••⎯Read the Document

Thomas Edison, *The Success of the Electric Light (1880)*

Andrew Carnegie, *Wealth*

Chinese Exclusion Act *(1882)*

William D. Grady, *The New South (1887)*

Frances E. Willard, *On Riding the Bicycle (1895)*

Morrill Act *(1862)*

•⊙•⎯View the Image *Residence of Andrew Carnegie*

Research and Explore

•••⎯Read the Document

Exploring America: French Canadian Controversy

Industrializing America: Life and Labor in Smokestack America

History Bookshelf: Veblen, Theory of the Leisure Class

Profiles
  Samuel Gompers
  Thomas Edison

((•⎯Hear the Audio

Hear the audio files for Chapter 19 at
www.myhistorylab.com.

Destruction of the battleship Maine in Havana harbor.

20

DEMOCRACY AND EMPIRE
1870–1900

((•—[Hear the Audio

Hear the audio files for Chapter 20 at **www.myhistorylab.com**.

WHAT FACTORS contributed to the growth of government in the late nineteenth century?

WHAT ROLE did farmers and workers organizations play in the politics of the 1880s and 1890s?

HOW DID the depression that began in 1893 threaten the existing political system?

IN WHAT ways did the election of 1896 represent a turning point in U.S. political history?

HOW DID proponents of imperialism justify colonization?

HOW DID the Spanish-American War change the place of the United States in world affairs?

AMERICAN COMMUNITIES
The Annexation of Hawai'i

ON JANUARY 17, 1891, LILI'UOKALANI SUCCEEDED HER BROTHER, KING Kalakaua, to become the queen of Hawai'i. Raised a Christian and fluent in English, the fifty-two-year-old monarch was nevertheless intensely loyal to the Hawaiian people and to their language and customs. This allegiance—and her strong opposition to a movement to annex Hawai'i to the United States—brought her downfall. On January 17, 1893, the queen was deposed in a plot carried out by an American diplomat and his coconspirators.

This event followed more than a half century of intense economic and diplomatic maneuvering by the United States and other nations. Both American and British missionaries, who had arrived in the 1820s to convert Hawaiians to Christianity, had bought up huge parcels of land and grown into a large and powerful community of planters. The missionaries in turn encouraged American businesses to buy into the sugar plantations, and by 1875, U.S. corporations dominated the sugar trade. Hawai'i was beginning to appear, in the opinion of Secretary of State James G. Blaine, to be "an outlying district of the state of California," and he pushed for formal annexation.

In 1888, American planters forced on the weak King Kalakaua a new constitution that severely limited his power and established wealth and property qualifications for voting. This so-called Bayonet Constitution, because it implied the use of U.S. arms to implement it, allowed noncitizens, Europeans as well as Americans, to vote, but denied the right of suffrage to poor native Hawaiians and the Chinese and Japanese who had come to work in the sugar fields.

The white planters had secured a constitutional government that was closely allied to their economic interests—until King Kalakaua died in 1891. After ascending to the throne, Queen Lili'uokalani struck back. She decided she must empower native Hawaiians and limit the political influence of the white elite and noncitizens.

The U.S.-led annexation forces first denounced the queen for attempting to abrogate the Bayonet Constitution and then welcomed Blaine's decision to send in U.S. troops to protect American lives and property. Lili'uokalani was deposed and a new provisional government installed. Sanford B. Dole stepped in as the president of the new provisional government of Hawai'i, now a protectorate of the United States.

Lili'uokalani called on President Cleveland to recognize her authority as "the constitutional sovereign of the Hawaiian Islands" and to reinstate her as queen. After investigating the situation, Cleveland agreed and ordered Lili'uokalani's reinstatement.

Ironically, Dole, who had been a major force for annexation, countered by refusing to recognize the right of the U.S. president "to interfere in our domestic affairs." On July 3, 1894, he proclaimed Hawai'i an independent republic, with himself retaining the office of present.

After Lili'uokalani's supporters attempted an unsuccessful military uprising in 1895, the deposed queen was arrested, tried by a military tribunal, and convicted of misprision of treason (having knowledge of treason but not informing the authorities). She was fined and sentenced to a five-year term in prison at hard labor, although Dole allowed her to serve a shorter sentence under "house arrest."

President Cleveland later declared privately that he was "ashamed of the whole affair" and refused to listen to arguments for annexation. But he was powerless to stop the process before William McKinley succeeded him as president in 1896. Although more than a hundred members of Congress voted against annexation, an improper joint resolution passed to annex Hawai'i. In 1900, at McKinley's urging, Hawai'i became a territory. The people of Hawai'i were never consulted about this momentous change in their national identity.

Many Americans had long viewed Hawai'i as a stepping-stone to vast Asian markets, and by the 1890s they were determined to acquire the island nation to extend the reach of the United States beyond the continent. Domestic unrest increased pressures for overseas expansion. "American factories are making more than the American people can use; American soil is producing more than they can consume," declared Senator Albert J. Beveridge, Republican from Indiana. "[T]he trade of the world must and shall be ours." Others had different reasons for expanding the national boundaries, and a sizable number of Americans strongly opposed all such ventures. Nevertheless, the century closed on the heels of a war with Spain that won for the United States a swatch of new possessions that extended halfway around the world, from Puerto Rico to the Philippines.

The path to empire was paved with major changes in government and the party system. As the 1890s culminated in the acquisition of new territories, the United States also witnessed a decisive realignment of the party system. Voters not only changed affiliations that had been in place since the Civil War, but also waged significant challenges to the two-party system at the local, regional, and national levels. While Queen Lili'uokalani was trying to regain control of her government, a mass political movement was forming in the United States to revive the nation's own democratic impulse.

Oahu

Toward a National Governing Class

The basic structure of government changed dramatically in the last quarter of the nineteenth century. Mirroring the fast-growing economy, public administration expanded at all levels—municipal, county, state, and federal—and took on greater responsibility for regulating society, especially market and property relations. Moreover, the expansion of government at home, particularly its increasing oversight of commerce, laid the foundation for economic and territorial expansion abroad.

Reformers mobilized to rein in corruption and to promote both efficiency and professionalism in the multiplying structures of government. Meanwhile, some notable politicians acted to benefit directly, competing with one another for control of the new mechanisms of power. A lot was at stake.

WHAT FACTORS contributed to the growth of government in the late nineteenth century?

The Growth of Government

Before the Civil War, local governments attended mainly to the promotion and regulation of trade and relied on private enterprise to supply vital services such as fire protection and public access to water. Cities gradually introduced professional police and firefighting forces and began to finance expanding school systems, public libraries, roads, and parks, an expansion requiring huge increases in local taxation. State governments grew in tandem, consolidating oversight of banking, transportation systems such as the railroads, and major enterprises such as the construction of dams and canals.

At the national level, mobilization for the Civil War and Reconstruction had demanded an unprecedented degree of resources and their coordination, as both revenues and administrative bureaucracy grew quickly. After the war, the federal government as a whole continued to expand under the weight of new tasks and responsibilities. The federal bureaucracy soon doubled, from about 50,000 employees in 1871 to 100,000 only a decade later.

The modern apparatus of departments, bureaus, and cabinets took shape amid this upswing. The Department of the Interior, created in 1849, grew into the largest and most important federal office other than the Post Office. Through its authority, the federal government was the chief landowner in the West. The Department of the Treasury, responsible for collecting federal taxes and customs as well as printing money and stamps, quadrupled in size from 1873 to 1900.

Regulatory agencies sprung up: foremost was the **Interstate Commerce Commission (ICC)**. The ICC was created in 1887 to bring order to the growing patchwork of state laws concerning railroads. The five-member commission appointed by the president approved freight and passenger rates set by the railroads. The ICC remained weak during that period, its rate-setting policies usually voided by the Supreme Court. But the activities of the ICC set a precedent for future regulation of trade as well as for positive government, making rules for business while superseding state laws with federal power—that is, for the intervention of the federal government into the affairs of private enterprise.

The Machinery of Politics

Only gradually did Republicans and Democrats adapt to the demands of government expansion. The Republican Party continued to run on its Civil War record, pointing to its achievements in reuniting the nation and in passing new reform legislation. Democrats, by contrast, sought to reduce the influence of the federal government, slash expenditures, repeal legislation, and protect states' rights. While Republicans held on to their longtime constituencies, Democrats gathered support from southern white voters and immigrants newly naturalized in the North.

Interstate Commerce Commission (ICC) The 1887 law that expanded federal power over business by prohibiting pooling and discriminatory rates by railroads and establishing the first federal regulatory agency, the Interstate Commerce Commission.

Presidents in the last quarter of the century—Rutherford B. Hayes (1877–81), James A. Garfield (1881), Chester A. Arthur (1881–85), Grover Cleveland (1885–89), Benjamin Harrison (1889–93), and Cleveland again (1893–97)—lacked luster. Democrats usually held a majority in the House and Republicans a majority in the Senate. With neither party sufficiently strong to govern effectively, Congress passed little legislation before 1890.

One major political issue that separated the two parties was the tariff. Manufacturing regions, especially the Northeast, favored a protective policy, while the southern and western agricultural regions opposed high tariffs as unfair to farmers and ranchers who had to pay the steep fees on imported necessities. Democrats, with a stronghold among southern voters, argued for sharp reductions in the tariff as a way to save the rural economy and to give a boost to workers. Republicans, who represented mainly business interests, raised tariffs to new levels on a wide array of goods during the Civil War and retained high tariffs as long as they held power.

In 1888, Grover Cleveland, with his running mate, Allen G. Thurman, led a spirited campaign for reelection to the presidency. Although he played up his strong record on civil service reform and tariff reduction, Cleveland, an incumbent, lost the election to his Republican challenger, Benjamin Harrison. Cleveland tallied the greatest number of popular votes, but Harrison easily won in the Electoral College by a margin of 233 to 168. In this lithograph campaign poster, the Democratic ticket invokes the legacy of Thomas Jefferson and the patriotism of Uncle Sam.

Despite differences over the tariff, the Democratic and Republican parties both operated mainly as state or local organizations, and by the 1870s, partisan politics had become a full-time occupation, with local elections usually held every two years. Election paraphernalia—leaflets or pamphlets, banners, hats, flags, buttons, inscribed playing cards, or clay pipes featuring a likeness of a candidate's face or the party symbol—became a major expense for both parties. And voters did turn out. During the last quarter of the century, participation in presidential elections peaked at nearly 80 percent of those eligible to vote.

The rising costs of maintaining local organizations and orchestrating mammoth campaigns drove party leaders to seek ever-larger sources of revenue. Winners often seized and added to the "spoils" of office through an elaborate system of payoffs and patronage. At the time, few politicians or business leaders regarded these practices as unethical.

At the local level, where a combination of ethnicity, race, and religion determined party loyalty, powerful bosses and political machines dominated both parties. Democrats William Marcy Tweed of New York's powerful political organization, Tammany Hall, and Michael "Hinky Dink" Kenna of Chicago, specialized in giving municipal jobs to loyal voters and holiday food baskets to their families.

A large number of federal jobs, meanwhile, changed hands each time the presidency passed from one party to another. More than 50 percent of all federal jobs were patronage positions—nearly 56,000 in 1881—jobs that could be awarded to loyal supporters as part of the "spoils" of the "victor."

Upon taking office, President James Garfield encountered loyal Republicans "lying in wait" for him "like vultures for a wounded bison." His colleagues in Congress were no less besieged. Observers estimated that decisions about patronage filled one-third of their time. Garfield himself served as president for only four months before being mortally wounded by a disappointed office seeker, an event that prompted his successor, Chester A. Arthur, to encourage reform of the civil service system.

THE SPOILS SYSTEM AND CIVIL SERVICE REFORM

In January 1883, a bipartisan congressional majority passed the **Pendleton Civil Service Reform Act**. This measure allowed the president to create, with Senate approval, a three-person commission to draw up a set of guidelines for executive and legislative appointments. The commission established a system of standards for various federal jobs and instituted "open, competitive examinations for testing the fitness of applicants for public service." The Pendleton Act also barred political candidates from funding their campaigns by assessing a "tax" on the salaries of holders of party-sponsored government jobs.

Although patronage did not disappear entirely, many departments of the federal government took on a professional character. At the same time, the federal judiciary began to act more aggressively to establish the parameters of government. With the Circuit Courts of Appeals Act of 1891, Congress granted the U.S. Supreme Court the right to review all cases at will. Despite these reforms, many observers still viewed government as a sinkhole of self-interest and corruption.

FARMERS AND WORKERS ORGANIZE THEIR COMMUNITIES

Farmers and workers began to build regional as well as national organizations to oppose, as a Nebraska newspaper put it, "the wealthy and powerful classes who want the control of government to plunder the people." By the 1890s, farmers and workers had formed a mass movement that presented the most significant challenge to the

Pendleton Civil Service Reform Act
A law of 1883 that reformed the spoils system by prohibiting government workers from making political contributions and creating the Civil Service Commission to oversee their appointment on the basis of merit rather than politics.

View the Image

Nast Cartoon: Boss Tweed at **www.myhistorylab.com**

QUICK REVIEW

Civil Service Reform

♦ Reform movement led by Senator George H. Pendleton.

♦ Pendleton Civil Service Reform Act passed in 1883.

♦ Act created commission to reform and professionalize civil service.

WHAT ROLE did farmers and workers organizations play in the politics of the 1880s and 1890s?

Populism A mass movement of the 1890s formed on the basis of the Southern Farmers' Alliance and other reform organizations.

Grange The National Grange of the Patrons of Husbandry, a national organization of farm owners formed after the Civil War.

two-party system since the Civil War—**Populism**—and pledged themselves to restore the reins of government to "the hands of the people."

THE GRANGE

In 1867, white farmers in the Midwest formed the Patrons of Husbandry for their own "social, intellectual, and moral improvement." Led by Oliver H. Kelley, this fraternal society resembled the secretive Masonic order but admitted women. Whole families staffed a complex array of offices and engaged in mysterious rituals involving passwords, flags, songs, and costumes. In many farming communities, the headquarters of the local chapter, known as the **Grange** (a word for "farm"), became the main social center.

The Granger movement spread rapidly, especially in areas where farmers were experiencing their greatest hardships. Great Plains farmers barely survived the blizzards, grasshopper infestations, and droughts of the early 1870s. Meanwhile, farmers throughout the trans–Mississippi West and the South watched the prices for grains and cotton fall year by year in the face of growing competition from foreign producers (see Figure 20.1). Membership soon swelled to more than 775,000 in a network of 20,000 local chapters.

The symbols chosen by Grange artists represented their faith that all social value could be traced to honest labor and most of all to the work of the entire farm family. The hardworking American required only the enlightenment offered by the Grange to build a better community.

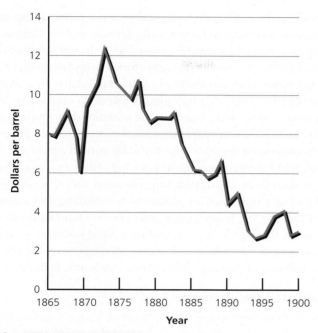

Figure 20.1 Falling Price of Wheat Flour, 1865–1900
The falling price of wheat was often offset by increased productivity, giving farmers a steady, if not higher, income. Nevertheless, in the short term, farmers often carried more debt and faced greater risk, both of which were factors in sparking the populists' protest by the end of the century.

Grangers blamed hard times on a band of "thieves in the night"—especially railroads and banks—that charged exorbitant fees for service. They mounted their greatest assault on the railroad corporations. By bribing state legislators, railroads enjoyed a highly discriminatory rate policy, commonly charging farmers more to ship their crops short distances than over long hauls. In 1874, several midwestern states responded to pressure and passed a series of so-called **Granger laws** establishing maximum shipping rates. Grangers also complained to their lawmakers about the price-fixing policies of grain wholesalers and operators of grain elevators. In 1873, the Illinois legislature passed a Warehouse Act establishing maximum rates for storing grains.

Determined to buy less and produce more, Grangers created a vast array of cooperative enterprises for both the purchase of supplies and the marketing of crops. They established local grain elevators, set up retail stores, and even manufactured some of their own farm machinery. Grangers ran banks as well as fraternal life and fire insurance companies.

The deepening depression of the late 1870s wiped out most of these cooperative programs, and Grange membership soon fell. In the mid-1880s, the Supreme Court overturned most of the key legislation regulating railroads. Despite these setbacks, the Patrons of Husbandry had nonetheless effectively promoted the idea of an activist government with primary responsibility to its producer-citizens. This idea would remain at the heart of farmer-worker protest movements until the end of the century.

THE FARMERS' ALLIANCE

Agrarian unrest did not end with the downward turn of the Grange, but instead moved south. The falling price of cotton underscored the need for action, and farmers organized in communities where both poverty and the crop-lien system prevailed. In the 1880s, the **Southern Farmers' Alliance** established cooperative stores complemented by the cooperative merchandising of crops, becoming a viable alternative to the capitalist marketplace—if only temporarily.

Granger laws   State laws enacted in the Midwest in the 1870s that regulated rates charged by railroads, grain elevator operators, and other middlemen.

Southern Farmers' Alliance   The largest of several organizations that formed in the post-Reconstruction South to advance the interests of beleaguered small farmers.

Great Uprising of 1877
Unsuccessful railroad strike to protest wage cuts and the use of federal troops against strikers; the first nationwide work stoppage in American history.

The Northern Farmers' Alliance took shape in the Great Plains states, drawing on larger organizations in Minnesota, Nebraska, Iowa, Kansas, and the Dakota Territory. During 1886 and 1887, summer drought followed winter blizzards and ice storms, reducing wheat harvests by one-third on the plains. Locusts and chinch bugs ate much of the rest. As if this were not enough, prices for wheat on the world market fell sharply for what little remained.

In 1889, the regional organizations joined forces to create the National Farmers' Alliance and Industrial Union. Within a year, the combined movement claimed 3 million white members. Excluded from the all-white chapters, the Colored Farmers' Alliance and Cooperative Union organized separately and quickly spread across the South.

The Grangers had rarely put up candidates for office. In comparison, the Farmers' Alliance had few reservations about entering electoral races. At the end of the 1880s, regional alliances put up candidates on platforms demanding state ownership of the railroads, a graduated income tax, lower tariffs, restriction of land ownership to citizens, and easier access to money through "the free and unlimited coinage of silver." By 1890, the alliances had won several local and state elections, gained control of the Nebraska legislature, and held the balance of power in Minnesota and South Dakota.

WORKERS SEARCH FOR POWER

Before the end of the century, more than 6 million workers would strike in industries ranging from New England textiles to southern tobacco factories to western mines. Although most of these strikes ended in failure, they showed that workers were ready to spell out their grievances in a direct and dramatic manner. They also suggested how strongly many townspeople, including merchants who depended on workers' wages, would support local strikes and turn them into community uprisings (see Map 20.1).

While the Farmers' Alliance put up candidates in the South and Plains states, workers launched labor parties in dozens of industrial towns and cities. In the late 1880s, labor parties won seats on many city councils and state legislatures. The Milwaukee People's Party elected the mayor, a state senator, six assemblymen, and one member of Congress. In smaller industrial towns where workers outnumbered the middle classes, labor parties did especially well.

The victories of local labor parties caught the attention of farmers, who began to weigh their prospects for a political alliance with discontented urban workers. For the

The Great Uprising of 1877, which began as a strike of railroad workers, spread rapidly to communities along the railroad routes. Angry crowds defied the armed militia and the vigilantes hired to disperse them. In Philadelphia, for example, strikers set fire to the downtown, destroying many buildings before federal troops were brought in to stop them. More than a hundred people died before the strike ended, and the railroad corporations suffered a $10 million loss in property.

MAP 20.1

Strikes by State, 1880 Most strikes after the Uprising of 1877 could be traced to organized trades, concentrated in the manufacturing districts of the Northeast and Midwest.

From *Geographical Inquiry and American Historical Problems*, edited by Earl Carville. (Stanford, CA: Stanford University Press, 1992). Originally published in the *Third Annual Report of the Commissioner of Labor*, 1887.

WHERE WERE strikes least common? Why?

1888 presidential election, they formed a coalition to sponsor the Union Labor Party, which ran on a plank of government ownership of the railroads. The new party made no headway against the two-party system, polling little more than 1 percent of the vote. Still, the successes in local communities nurtured hopes for a viable political alliance of the "producing classes," rural as well as urban.

WOMEN BUILD ALLIANCES

Women activists helped build both the labor and agrarian protest movements while campaigning for their own rights as citizens.

The Grangers issued a charter to a local chapter only when women were well represented on its rolls, and in the 1870s, delegates to its conventions routinely gave speeches endorsing woman suffrage. In both the Northern and Southern Farmers' Alliances, women made up perhaps one-quarter of the membership, and several advanced through the ranks to become leading speakers and organizers.

Women in both the Knights of Labor and the Farmers' Alliance found their greatest leader in Frances E. Willard, the most famous woman of the nineteenth century and a shrewd politician in her own right. Willard argued that women, who guarded their families' physical and spiritual welfare, should play a similar role outside their homes. From 1878 until her death in 1897, she presided over the **Woman's Christian Temperance Union (WCTU)**. Most numerous in the Midwest, WCTU members preached total abstinence from the consumption of alcohol, but ultimately endorsed Willard's "do everything" agenda. By the 1880s, the most militant branches were campaigning for an activist government and demanding an overhaul of the prison system, the eradication of prostitution, changes in

Read the Document

Frances E. Willard on the Reorganization of Government (1891) at **www.myhistorylab.com**

Woman's Christian Temperance Union (WCTU) Women's organization whose members visited schools to educate children about the evils of alcohol, addressed prisoners, and blanketed men's meetings with literature.

Frances E. Willard (1839–1898) became a full-time activist for the national Woman's Christian Temperance Union (WCTU) in 1874. From 1879 until her death, she served as president, pushing the organization to expand its interests beyond temperance under the rubric of her "do-everything" policy. Under her leadership, the WCTU established 39 departments promoting a wide array of reform causes ranging from the establishment of free kindergartens to the prohibition of the manufacture of cigarettes.

Read the Document

The People's Party Platform (1892) at **www.myhistorylab.com**

HOW DID the depression that began in 1893 threaten the existing political system?

the age of consent, and even the elimination of the wage system. By 1890, she had mobilized nearly 200,000 paid members into the largest organization of women in the world.

Willard understood that for women to participate in politics they needed the right to vote. Under her leadership, the WCTU grew into the major force for woman suffrage. In Iowa, Nebraska, Colorado, and especially Kansas, agitation for the right to vote provided a political bridge among women in the WCTU, Farmers' Alliance, Knights of Labor, and various local suffrage societies. The most active members were affiliated with several organizations or, in some cases, with all.

POPULISM AND THE PEOPLE'S PARTY

In December 1890, the Farmers' Alliance called a meeting at Ocala, Florida, to press for the creation of a national third party. This was a risky proposition because the Southern Alliance hoped to capture control of the Democratic Party, whereas many farmers in the Plains states and African Americans nearly everywhere voted Republican. In some areas, however, the Farmers' Alliance established an independent third party, put up full slates of candidates for local elections, won majorities in state legislatures, and even sent a representative to Congress. Reviewing these successes, delegates at Ocala decided to push ahead and form a national party, and they appealed to other farm, labor, and reform organizations to join them.

In February 1892, 1,300 representatives from the Farmers' Alliance, the Knights of Labor, and the Colored Farmers' Alliance, among others, met in St. Louis. The new People's Party called for government ownership of railroads, banks, and telegraph lines, prohibition of large landholding companies, a graduated income tax, an eight-hour workday, and restriction of immigration. The most ambitious plan called for the national government to build local warehouses—"subtreasuries"—where farmers could store their crops until prices reached acceptable levels. The People's Party convened again in Omaha in July 1892 and nominated James Baird Weaver of Iowa for president.

The Populists, as supporters of the People's Party styled themselves, quickly became a major factor in American politics. Although Democrat Grover Cleveland regained the presidency in 1892 (he had previously served from 1885 to 1889), Populists scored a string of local victories. They elected three governors, ten representatives to Congress, and five senators. Despite poor showings among urban workers east of the Mississippi, Populists looked forward to the next round of state elections in 1894. But the great test would come with the presidential election in 1896.

THE CRISIS OF THE 1890S

A series of events in the 1890s shook the confidence of many citizens in the reigning political system. But nothing was more unsettling than the severe economic depression that consumed the nation and lasted for five years. Many feared—while others hoped—that the entire political system would topple.

FINANCIAL COLLAPSE AND DEPRESSION

By the spring of 1893, the nation was drawn into a depression that had been plaguing European nations since the late 1880s. The European market for imported goods, including those manufactured in the United States, sharply contracted. Financial panic in England spread across the Atlantic, as British investors began to sell off their American stocks to obtain funds. Other factors—tight credit, falling agricultural prices, a weak banking system, and overexpansion, especially in railroad construction—all helped to bring about the collapse of the U.S. economy. The business boom of nearly two decades ended, and the entire economy ground to a halt. The new century arrived before prosperity returned.

In many cities, unemployment rates reached 25 percent. Tens of thousands "rode the rails" or went "on the tramp" to look for work, hoping that their luck might change in a new city or town. Vagrancy laws (enacted during the 1870s) forced many without homes into prison. Inadequate diets prompted a rise in communicable diseases, such as tuberculosis and pellagra. Unable to buy food, clothes, or household items, many families learned to survive with the barest minimum.

As the depression deepened, so did demands on the federal government for positive action. Populist Jacob Sechler Coxey decided to gather the masses of unemployed into a huge army and then to march to Washington, DC. Coxey proposed that Congress fund a public works program to give jobs to the unemployed. On Easter Sunday, 1894, Coxey left Massillon, Ohio, with several hundred followers. Meanwhile, brigades from across the country joined his "petition in boots." Only 600 men and women reached the nation's capital, where the police first clubbed and then arrested the leaders for trespassing on the grass. "**Coxey's Army**" quickly disbanded, but not before voicing the public's expectation of federal responsibility for the welfare of its citizens, especially in times of crisis.

STRIKES: COEUR D'ALENE, HOMESTEAD, AND PULLMAN

Even before the onset of the depression, the conflict between labor and capital had escalated to the brink of civil war. In the 1890s, three major strikes dramatized the extent of collusion between the corporations and government. In each case, state or federal troops were deployed to crush the labor uprising, providing a vivid lesson to workers on the growing role of government in this era.

Wage cuts in the silver and lead mines of northern Idaho led to one of the most bitter conflicts of the decade. To put a brake on organized labor, mine owners had formed a "**protective association**," and in March 1892, they announced a wage cut throughout

Coxey's Army A protest march of unemployed workers, led by Populist businessman Jacob Coxey, demanding inflation and a public works program during the depression of the 1890s.

protective association Organizations formed by mine owners in response to the formation of labor unions.

●●●―Read the Document
Jacob Coxey, Address of Protest (1894) at **www.myhistorylab.com**

After five weeks, the main body of Coxey's Army reached Washington, DC, where on May 1, 1894, the leaders were immediately arrested for trespassing on government property. Fifty years later, on May 1, 1944, the ninety-year-old Coxey finally gave his speech advocating public works programs on the steps of the nation's capitol.

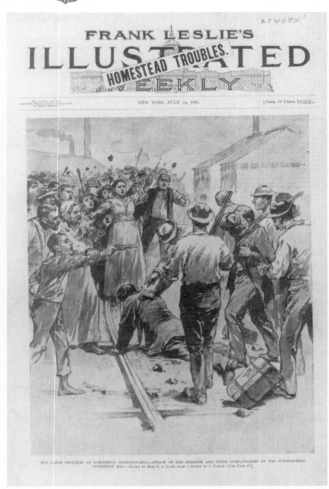

FRANK LESLIE'S
ILLUSTRATED
HOMESTEAD TROUBLES.
WEEKLY

NEW YORK, JULY 14, 1892.

THE LABOR TROUBLES AT HOMESTEAD PENNSYLVANIA—ATTACK OF THE STRIKERS AND THEIR SYMPATHIZERS ON THE SURRENDERED PINKERTON MEN.

The popular magazine *Frank Leslie's* published this illustration of workers and their families confronting the private security force brought in to break the strike at the Carnegie Steel Company in Homestead, Pennsylvania, in July 1892.

Read the **Document**

Exploring America: Homestead Strike of 1892 at **www.myhistorylab.com**

View the **Image**

Homestead Strikers Surrendering at **www.myhistorylab.com**

the Coeur d'Alene district. After the miners' union refused to accept the cut, the owners locked out all union members and brought in strikebreakers ("scab" laborers) by the trainload. Unionists tried peaceful methods of protest. But after three months of stalemate, they loaded a railcar with explosives and blew up a mine. The governor proclaimed martial law and dispatched a combined state-federal force of about 1,500 troops, who broke the strike. But the miners' union survived, and most members became active in the Populist Party, which at the next session of the Idaho legislature allied with Democrats to cut back all appropriations to the National Guard.

At Homestead, Pennsylvania, members of the Amalgamated Iron, Steel and Tin Workers, the most powerful union of the AFL, had carved out an admirable position for themselves in the Carnegie Steel Company. Well paid and proud of their skills, the unionists customarily directed their unskilled helpers without undue influence of company supervisors. Determined to gain control over every stage of production, however, Carnegie and his partner, Henry C. Frick, decided not only to lower wages but also to break the union.

In 1892, when Amalgamated's contract expired, Frick announced a drastic wage cut. When Homestead's city government refused to assign police to disperse the strikers, Frick dispatched a barge carrying a private army. Gunfire broke out and continued throughout the day. Finally, the governor stepped in and sent the Pennsylvania National Guard to restore order, and Carnegie's factory reopened with strikebreakers doing the work.

After four months, the union was forced to concede a crushing defeat, not only for itself, but, in effect, for all steelworkers. The Carnegie Company reduced its workforce by 25 percent, lengthened the workday, and cut wages 25 percent for those who remained on the job. Within a decade, every major steel company operated without union interference.

Pullman, Illinois, just south of Chicago, had been constructed as a model industrial community. Its creator and proprietor, George M. Pullman, had manufactured luxurious "sleeping cars" for railroads since 1881. He built his company as a self-contained community, with the factory at the center. The Pullman Palace Car Company deducted rent, library fees, and grocery bills from each worker's weekly wages. In good times, workers enjoyed a decent livelihood, although many resented Pullman's autocratic control of their daily affairs.

When times grew hard, the company cut wages by as much as one-half, in some cases down to less than $1 a day. Charges for food and rent remained unchanged. Furthermore, factory supervisors sought to make up for declining profits by driving workers to produce more. In May 1894, workers voted to strike.

Pullman workers found their champion in Eugene V. Debs, who had recently formed the American Railway Union (ARU) to bring railroad workers across the continent into one organization. Debs advised caution, but delegates to an ARU convention voted to support a nationwide boycott of all Pullman cars. This action soon turned into a sympathy strike by railroad workers across the country.

At first, the Pullman strike at first produced little violence. ARU officials urged strikers to ignore all provocations and hold their ground peacefully. But Richard C. Olney, a former railroad lawyer, used his current office as attorney general to issue a blanket injunction against the strike. On July 4, President Cleveland sent army units to Chicago, over the objections of pro-labor Illinois governor John Peter Altgeld. After a bitter confrontation that left thirteen people dead and more than fifty wounded, the army dispersed the strikers. For the next week, railroad workers in twenty-six other states resisted federal troops, and a dozen more people were killed. On July 17, the strike finally ended when federal marshals arrested Debs and other leaders.

Debs concluded that the labor movement could not regain its dignity without seizing the reigns of government. He came out of jail committed to the ideals of socialism, and in 1898 helped to form a political party dedicated to its principles.

THE SOCIAL GOSPEL

"What is socialism?" Debs once asked. "Merely Christianity in action. It recognizes the equality in men." During the 1890s, especially as hard times spread across the nation, a growing number of Protestants and Catholics came close to sharing Debs's perspective.

Social gospel ministers called on the government to be more responsible toward its most impoverished and unprotected citizens. Supporting labor's right to organize and, if necessary, to strike, they petitioned government officials to regulate corporations and place a limit on profits. Washington Gladden, a Congregationalist minister, warned that if churches continued to ignore pressing social problems, they would devolve into institutions whose sole purpose was to preserve obscure rituals and superstitions. He addressed his most important book, *Applied Christianity* (1886), to the nation's business leaders, imploring them to return to Christ's teachings.

Catholic clergy, doctrinally more inclined than Protestants to accept poverty as a natural condition, joined the social gospel movement in smaller numbers. Many of their parishioners, especially Polish and Irish Americans, however, allied with the labor movement, finding solace in Pope Leo XIII's encyclical *Rerum Novarum* (1891), which endorsed the right of workers to form trade unions.

Women guided the social gospel movement in their communities. Since the early part of the nineteenth century, middle-class women in northern cities had formed numerous voluntary associations to improve the conditions of the poor and destitute. In the 1890s, women activists revived this legacy and responded to the plight of the poor and dispossessed. At the forefront of this movement was the Young Women's Christian Association (YWCA), which by 1900 had more than 600 local chapters. The "Y" sponsored a range of services for needy Christian women, ranging from homes for the elderly and for unmarried mothers to elaborate programs of vocational instruction and physical fitness. Meanwhile, Catholic laywomen and nuns served the poor women of their faith, operating numerous schools, hospitals, and orphanages.

Affiliated principally with the Baptist Church, African American women sponsored dozens of self-help programs and, in addition, emphasized the importance of education to racial uplift. Excluded by the whites-only policy of the YWCA in most localities, they organized their own chapters and branched out to form nurseries, orphanages, hospitals, and nursing homes.

POLITICS OF REFORM, POLITICS OF ORDER

The severe hardships of the 1890s, following a quarter century of popular unrest, pushed economic issues to the forefront of politics. Voters were more than ready for a change. As a consequence, the presidential election of 1896, considered a turning point in American politics, marked a dramatic realignment. The election also sanctioned the popular call for a stronger government and, ultimately, established a clear link between domestic problems and overseas markets.

Read the Document

Eugene V. Debs, The Outlook for Socialism in America (1900) at **www.myhistorylab.com**

QUICK REVIEW

The Social Gospel

♦ Growing number of clergy called for reconciliation of social reality with Christian ideals.

♦ Catholics joined social gospel movement in smaller numbers than Protestants.

♦ Women played key roles in the movement.

IN WHAT ways did the election of 1896 represent a turning point in U.S. political history?

Interpreting the Past: *Currency Reform, pp. 530–531*

THE FREE SILVER ISSUE

For generations, farmers had advocated "soft" currency, that is, an increase in the money supply that would loosen credit. During the Civil War, the federal government took decisive action, replacing state bank notes with a national paper currency. Then in 1873, the Coinage Act tightened the money supply by eliminating silver from circulation. This measure actually had little real impact on the economy but opened the door to yet more tinkering.

Farmers readily approved the **Sherman Silver Purchase Act** of 1890, which directed the Treasury to increase the amount of currency coined from silver mined in the West and also permitted the U.S. government to print paper currency backed by silver. In turn, Westerners, who stood to benefit most from this reform, agreed to support the McKinley Tariff of 1890, which, by establishing the highest import duties yet on foreign goods, pleased the business community.

Following the crash of 1893, President Cleveland concluded that the economic crisis was "largely the result of financial policy . . . embodied in unwise laws" and insisted that only the gold standard could pull the nation out of the depression. By exerting intense pressure on congressional Democrats, Cleveland succeeded in repealing the Sherman Act in October 1893, but not without ruining his chances for renomination.

The midterm elections of 1894 brought the largest shift in congressional power in American history: the Republicans gained 117 seats, while the Democrats lost 113. The "Silver Democrats" of Cleveland's own party vowed revenge and began to look to the Populists, mainly Westerners and farmers who favored "**free silver**," that is, the unlimited coinage of silver. Republicans confidently began to prepare for the presidential election of 1896, warming to what they called the "battle of the standards."

POPULISM'S LAST CAMPAIGNS

As Populists prepared for the 1896 presidential campaign, they found themselves at a crossroad: what were they to do with the growing popularity of the Democratic candidate, William Jennings Bryan? A spellbinding orator, Bryan won a congressional seat in 1890. After seizing the Populist slogan "Equal Rights to All, Special Privilege to None," the thirty-six-year-old lawyer from Nebraska became a major contender for president of the United States.

Bryan won back many disaffected Democrats by championing free silver. For two years before the 1896 election, he wooed potential voters in a speaking tour that took him to every state in the nation. Pouring new life into his divided party, Bryan pushed Silver Democrats to the forefront.

At the 1896 party convention, Bryan delivered what became one of the most famous speeches in American political history. Spreading his arms to suggest the crucified Christ figure, he pledged to resist all demands for a gold standard by saying, "You shall not press down upon the brow of labor this crown of thorns, you shall not crucify mankind upon a cross of gold." The next day, Bryan carried the Democratic presidential nomination.

The Populists realized that by nominating Bryan, the Democrats had stolen their thunder. They also feared that the growing emphasis on currency would overshadow their more important planks calling for government ownership of the nation's railroads and communications systems. As the date of their own convention approached, delegates divided over strategy: they could endorse Bryan and give up their independent status, or they could run an independent campaign and risk splitting the silver vote.

In the end, Populists nominated Bryan for president and one of their own, Georgian Tom Watson, for vice president. Most of the state Democratic Party organizations, however, refused to put the "fusion" ticket on the ballot, and Bryan and his Democratic running mate Arthur Sewall simply ignored the Populist campaign.

● ► Read the Document

Profile: *William Jennings Bryan* at **www.myhistorylab.com**

● ► Read the Document

William Jennings Bryan, "Cross of Gold" Speech (1896) at **www.myhistorylab.com**

Sherman Silver Purchase Act 1890 act which directed the Treasury to increase the amount of currency coined from silver mined in the West and also permitted the U.S. government to print paper currency backed by the silver.

free silver Philosophy that the government should expand the money supply by purchasing and coining all the silver offered to it.

THE REPUBLICAN TRIUMPH

Republicans anticipated an easy victory in 1896, but Bryan's nomination, as party stalwart Mark Hanna warned, "changed everything." Luckily, they had their own handsome, knowledgeable, courteous, and ruthless candidate, Civil War veteran William McKinley.

The Republican campaign, in terms of sheer expense and skill of coordination, outdid all previous campaigns and established a precedent for future presidential elections. Hanna guided a strategy that outspent Bryan more than ten to one. Fearful that the silver issue would divide their own ranks, Republicans stepped around it while emphasizing the tariff. Delivering a hard-hitting negative campaign, they consistently cast Bryan as a naysayer.

McKinley triumphed in the most important presidential election since Reconstruction. Bryan managed to win 46 percent of the popular vote, but failed to carry the Midwest, West Coast, or Upper South (see Map 20.2). The Populist following, already divided and now further disillusioned, dwindled away.

Once in office, McKinley strengthened the executive branch and actively promoted a mixture of probusiness and expansionist measures. He supported the Dingley Tariff of 1897, which raised import duties to an all-time high. In 1897, McKinley also encouraged Congress to create the United States Industrial Commission, which would plan business regulation; in 1898, he promoted a bankruptcy act that eased the financial situation of small businesses; and he proposed the Erdman Act of the same year, which established a system of arbitration to avoid rail strikes. The Supreme Court ruled in concert with the president, finding eighteen railways in violation of antitrust laws, and granting states the right to regulate hours of labor under certain circumstances. In 1900, McKinley settled the currency issue by overseeing the passage of the Gold Standard Act.

McKinley's triumphs ended the popular challenge to the nation's governing system. With prosperity returning by the end of the century and nationalism rising swiftly, McKinley easily won re-election in the 1900 presidential campaign. With news of his second triumph, stock prices on Wall Street skyrocketed.

This Republican campaign poster of 1896 depicts William McKinley standing on sound money and promising a revival of prosperity. The depression of the 1890s shifted the electorate into the Republican column.

NATIVISM AND JIM CROW

Campaign rhetoric aside, McKinley and Bryan had differed only slightly on the major problems facing the nation in the 1890s. Neither Bryan nor McKinley addressed the escalation of racism and **nativism** (anti-immigrant feeling) throughout the nation.

Toward the end of the century, many political observers noted, the nation's patriotic fervor took on a strongly nationalistic and antiforeign tone. Striking workers and their employers alike tended to blame "foreigners" for the hard times. Semisecret organizations such as the American Protective Association sprang up to defend American institutions.

In the South, local and state governments codified racist ideology by passing discriminatory and segregationist legislation, which became known as Jim Crow laws. By the end of the century, "**Jim Crow**" referred to the customs of **segregation** that were becoming secured by legislation throughout the South. State after state in the South enacted new legislation to cover facilities such as restaurants, public transportation, and even drinking fountains. Signs reading "White Only" and "Colored" appeared over theaters, parks, rooming houses, and toilets.

nativism Favoring the interests and culture of native-born inhabitants over those of immigrants.

Jim Crow laws Segregation laws that became widespread in the South during the 1890s.

segregation A system of racial control that separated the races, initially by custom but increasingly by law during and after Reconstruction.

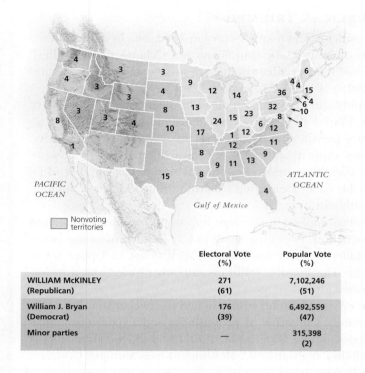

	Electoral Vote (%)	Popular Vote (%)
WILLIAM McKINLEY (Republican)	271 (61)	7,102,246 (51)
William J. Bryan (Democrat)	176 (39)	6,492,559 (47)
Minor parties	—	315,398 (2)

MAP 20.2

Election of 1896   Democratic candidate William Jennings Bryan carried most of rural America but could not overcome Republican William McKinley's stronghold in the populous industrial states.

WHAT DOES this map reveal about regional divisions in American politics in 1896?

Plessy v. *Ferguson*   Supreme Court decision holding that Louisiana's railroad segregation law did not violate the Constitution as long as the railroads or the state provided equal accommodations.

Grandfather clauses   Rules that required potential voters to demonstrate that their grandfathers had been eligible to vote; used in some Southern states after 1890 to limit the black electorate.

The United States Supreme Court upheld the new discriminatory legislation. Its decisions in the *Civil Rights Cases* (1883) overturned the Civil Rights Act of 1875; in *Plessy* v. *Ferguson* (1896), the Court upheld a Louisiana state law formally segregating railroad passenger cars on the basis of the "separate but equal" doctrine.

This ruling established the legal rationale for segregation, in the North as well as the South, for the next fifty years. In *Cumming* v. *Richmond County Board of Education* (1899), the Court allowed separate schools for blacks and whites, even where facilities for African American children did not exist. This ruling reverberated in other parts of the country. For example, a year later, in 1900, the New Orleans school board decided to eliminate all schools for black children beyond the fifth grade, reasoning that African Americans needed only minimal education to fit them for menial jobs "to which they are best suited and seem ordained by the proper fitness of things."

Southern states enacted new literacy tests and property qualifications for voting. Loopholes permitted poor whites to vote, except where they threatened the Democratic Party's rule. "**Grandfather clauses**," invented in Louisiana, exempted from all restrictions those who had been entitled to vote on January 1, 1867, together with their sons and grandsons, a measure that effectively enfranchised whites while barring African Americans. In 1898, the Supreme Court ruled that poll taxes and literacy requirements were a proper means of restricting the ballot to "qualified" voters. By this time, only 5 percent of the southern black electorate voted, and African Americans were barred from public office and jury service (see Figure 20.2).

Racial violence escalated. Race riots broke out in small towns like Rosewood, Florida, and Phoenix, South Carolina, and in large cities like New Orleans and Tulsa. In November 1898, in Wilmington, North Carolina, where a dozen African Americans had ridden out the last waves of the Populist insurgency to win appointments to minor political offices, a group of white opponents organized to root them out and ultimately staged a violent coup, restoring white rule and forcing black leaders to leave. As many as 100 African Americans were killed in what came to be known as the Wilmington massacre.

Not only race riots, but also thousands of lynchings took place. Mobs often burned or dismembered victims to drag out their agony and entertain the crowd of onlookers. Announced in local newspapers, lynchings in the 1890s became public spectacles for entire white families, and railroads sometimes offered special excursion rates for travel to these events.

Antilynching became the one-woman crusade of Ida B. Wells, the young editor of a black newspaper in Memphis. After three local black businessmen were lynched in 1892, Wells vigorously denounced the outrage, blaming the white business competitors of the victims. Local whites destroyed her press and forced Wells to leave the city. She then launched an international movement against lynching, lecturing across the country and in Europe, demanding an end to the silence about this barbaric crime. Her work also inspired the growth of a black women's club movement. The National Association of Colored Women, founded in 1896, took up the antilynching cause and also fought to protect black women from sexual exploitation by white men.

Few white reformers rallied to defend African Americans. Even the National American Woman Suffrage Association, in an attempt to appease its southern members at its 1899 convention, voted down a resolution condemning racial segregation in public facilities. More than a few Americans had come to believe that their future welfare hinged on white supremacy, not only in their own country but across the globe as well.

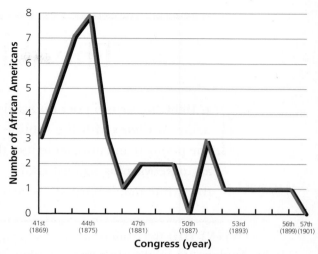

Figure 20.2 African American Representation in Congress, 1867–1900
Black men served in the U.S. Congress from 1870 until 1900. All were Republicans.

THE PATH TO IMPERIALISM

Many Americans attributed the economic crisis of 1893–97 not simply to the collapse of the railroads and banks but also to basic structural problems: an overbuilt economy and an insufficient domestic market for goods. To find new markets for American goods, many Americans looked abroad.

HOW DID proponents of imperialism justify colonization?

ALL THE WORLD'S A FAIR

The World's Columbian Exposition, held in Chicago, commemorated the four hundredth anniversary of Columbus's landing with "an exhibition of the progress of civilization in the New World." On May Day 1893, less than two months after the nation's economy had collapsed, crowds began to flock to the fair.

The section known as "The White City" celebrated the achievements of American business in the global economy. Agriculture Hall showcased the production of corn, wheat, and other crops and featured a gigantic globe encircled by samples of American-manufactured farm machinery. Another building housed a model of a canal cut across Nicaragua, suggesting the ease with which American traders might reach Asian markets if transport ships could travel directly from the Caribbean to the Pacific.

In contrast to the White City was the Midway, a strip nearly a mile long and more than 600 feet wide that offered entertainment. The new, spectacular Ferris wheel, designed to rival the Eiffel Tower of Paris, was the largest attraction. But the Midway also offered amusement in the form of "displays" of "uncivilized" people from foreign lands.

One enormous sideshow re-created Turkish bazaars and South Sea island huts. There were Javanese carpenters, Dahomean drummers, Egyptian swordsmen, and Hungarian

The White Man's Burden

In 1899, the British poet Rudyard Kipling published "The White Man's Burden" in the American magazine *McClure's* with the subtitle "The United States and the Philippine Islands." Some interpreted the poem as an endorsement of the U.S. imperialist ventures in the Pacific; others read it as a cautionary note warning against taking on colonies. Those who favored expansion embraced the notion of the "white man's burden" as means to justify their position as a noble enterprise, that is, in "uplifting" those people of color who had not yet enjoyed the benefits of "civilization."

WHAT DID the readers of *McClure's* magazine understand as "the white man's burden"? How did this responsibility relate to the belief in a hierarchy of races and civilizations expressed in Kipling's poem?

The concept even made its way into advertising for soap. In 1789, London soapmaster Andrew Pears began producing a distinctive oval bar of transparent amber glycerin and marketing it as a luxury item under the name Pears Soap. He found a talented promoter in Thomas J. Barratt, considered a pioneer of modern advertising, who built an international market for the product. By the end of the nineteenth century, Pears Soap had achieved brand-name status among middle- and upper-class Americans.

Barratt's advertising presented Pears Soap as safe and beneficial but suitable only for discerning consumers. Among its many other advantages, Pears Soap promised a smooth, white complexion, underscoring this message by associating dark skins with "uncivilized" people. The man pictured in this ad is probably a colonial official. The advertisement appeared first in 1899 in *McClure's*—the same magazine in which Kipling's poetic exhortation was published.

Take up the White Man's burden—
Send forth the best ye breed—
Go bind your sons to exile
To serve your captives' need;
To wait in heavy harness,
On fluttered folk and wild—
Your new-caught, sullen peoples,
Half-devil and half-child.
Take up the White Man's burden—
In patience to abide,
To veil the threat of terror
And check the show of pride . . . ∎

The first step towards lightening

The White Man's Burden

is through teaching the virtues of cleanliness.

Pears' Soap

is a potent factor in brightening the dark corners of the earth as civilization advances, while amongst the cultured of all nations it holds the highest place—it is the ideal toilet soap.

Gypsies, as well as Eskimos, Syrians, Samoans, and Chinese. According to the guidebook, all these peoples had come "from the nightsome North and the splendid South, from the wasty West and the effete East, bringing their manners, customs, dress, religions, legends, amusements, that we might know them better."

By celebrating the brilliance of American industry and simultaneously presenting the "uncivilized" people of the world as a source of exotic entertainment, the planners of the fair delivered a powerful message. Former abolitionist Frederick Douglass, who attended the fair on "Colored People's Day," recognized it immediately. He noted that the physical layout of the fair, by carefully grouping exhibits, sharply divided the United States and Europe from the rest of the world, namely, from the nations of Africa, Asia, and the Middle East. Douglass objected to the stark contrast setting off Anglo-Saxons from people of color, an opposition between "civilization" and "savagery." He and Ida B. Wells also objected to the exclusion of African Americans from representation among the exhibits at the White City. Wells boycotted the special day set aside for African Americans, while Douglass attended, using the occasion to deliver a speech upbraiding white Americans for their racism.

Frederick Jackson Turner also spoke at the fair and read his famous essay about the disappearance of the frontier. Having passed "from the task of filling up the vacant spaces of the continent," the young historian warned, the nation is now "thrown back upon itself." His message was clear: if democracy were to survive, Americans required a new "frontier."

The Chicago World's Fair, which attracted 27 million visitors from all over the world, reassured Turner by marking the coming of age of the United States as a global power and by making a deliberate case for commercial expansion abroad. The exposition also gave material shape to prevalent ideas about the preeminence of American civilization as well as the superiority of the Anglo-Saxon race (see Seeing History).

Read the Document

Josiah Strong, from Our Country (1885) at **www.myhistorylab.com**

THE "IMPERIALISM OF RIGHTEOUSNESS"

Social gospeler Josiah Strong, a Congregational minister, provided a prescient commentary in 1885. Linking economic and spiritual expansion, he advocated an "imperialism of righteousness." He identified white Americans as the best agents for "Christianizing" and "civilizing" the people of Africa and the Pacific and beyond.

The push for overseas expansion coincided with a major wave of religious evangelism and foreign missions. Early in the nineteenth century, Protestant missionaries, hoping to fulfill what they believed to be a divine command to carry God's message to all peoples and to win converts for their church, had focused on North America. Many disciples, like Josiah Strong himself, headed west and stationed themselves on Indian reservations. Others worked among the immigrant populations of the nation's growing cities.

After the Civil War, the major evangelical Protestant denominations all sponsored missions directed at foreign lands. By the turn of the century, some 23 American Protestant churches had established missions in China, the

By the end of the nineteenth century, women represented 60 percent of the American missionary force in foreign lands. This photograph shows two Methodist women using "back chairs," a traditional form of transportation, at Mount Omei in Szechwan, China.

majority staffed by women. By 1900, the various Protestant denominations were supporting forty-one women's missionary boards; several years later more than 3 million women had enrolled in societies to support this work, together surpassing in size all other women's organizations in the United States.

Outside the churches, the YMCA and YWCA, which had set up nondenominational missions for the working poor in many American cities, also embarked on a worldwide crusade to reach non-Christians. As foreign branches multiplied, a close observer ironically suggested that the United States had three great occupying forces: the army, the navy, and the "Y."

The missionaries did more than spread the gospel. They taught school, provided rudimentary medical care, offered vocational training programs, and sometimes encouraged young men and women to pursue a college education in preparation for careers in their homelands. They also played an important role in preparing the way for American economic expansion.

THE QUEST FOR EMPIRE

Not only missionaries but also business and political leaders had set their sights on distant lands, which in turn meant new markets. Between 1870 and 1900, exports more than tripled, from about $400 million to over $1.5 billion, with textiles and agricultural products leading the way. But as European markets for American goods began to contract, business and political leaders, of necessity, looked more eagerly to Asia as well as to lands closer by.

Since the American Revolution, many Americans had regarded all nearby nations as falling naturally within their own territorial realm, destined to be acquired when opportunity allowed. With European nations launched on their own imperialist missions in Asia and Africa, the United States increasingly viewed the Caribbean as an "American lake" and all of Latin America as a vast potential market for U.S. goods. The crisis of the 1890s transformed this long-standing desire into a perceived economic necessity.

Americans focused their expansionist plans on the Western Hemisphere, determined to dislodge the dominant power, Great Britain. In 1867, when Canada became a self-governing dominion, American diplomats hoped to annex their northern neighbor. But Great Britain refused to give up Canada, and the United States backed away. Central and South America proved more accommodating to American designs (see Map 20.3).

Republican stalwart James G. Blaine, secretary of state under presidents Garfield and Harrison, determined to work out a Good Neighbor policy (a phrase coined by Henry Clay in 1820). Bilateral treaties with Mexico, Colombia, the British West Indies, El Salvador, and the Dominican Republic allowed American businesses to dominate local economies, importing their raw materials at low prices and flooding their local markets with goods manufactured in the United States. Often, American investors simply took over the principal industries of these small nations, undercutting national business classes.

The Good Neighbor policy depended, Blaine knew, on peace and order in the Latin American states. As early as 1875, when revolt shook Venezuela, the Department of State warned European powers not to meddle. If popular uprisings proved too much for local officials, the U.S. Navy would intervene and return American allies to power.

In 1883, wishing to enforce treaties and protect overseas investments, Congress appropriated funds to build up American sea power and in 1884 established the Naval War College in Newport, Rhode Island, to train the officer corps. Beginning with ninety small ships, over one-third of them wooden, the navy grew quickly to include modern steel fighting ships. The force behind this build-up of the U.S. Navy was Captain Alfred Thayer Mahan, one of the first presidents of the Naval War College.

Mahan achieved international fame for outlining an imperialist strategy based on command of the seas. His book, *The Influence of Sea Power upon History, 1660–1873*

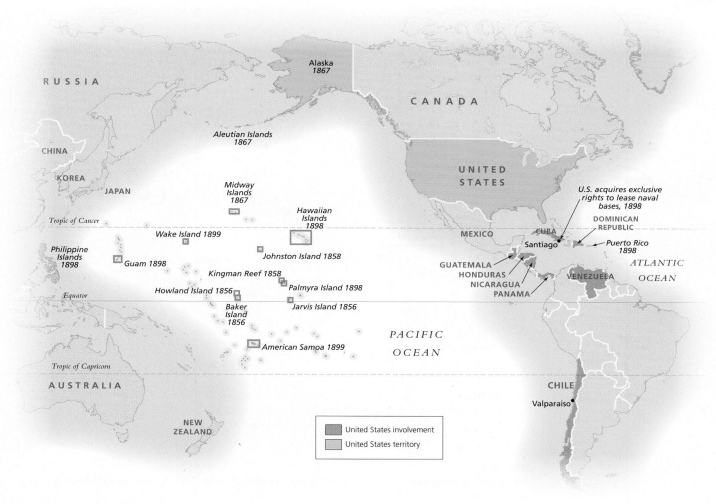

MAP 20.3

The American Domain, ca. 1900   The United States claimed numerous islands in the South Pacific and intervened repeatedly in Latin America to secure its own economic interests.

WHAT LIGHT does this map shed on American ambitions in Asia and Latin America?

(1890), helped to define foreign policy not only for the United States, but also for Great Britain, Japan, and Germany by identifying sea power as the key to world dominance. Viewing the U.S. Navy as the "handmaid of expansion," Mahan advocated the creation of bases in the Caribbean and the Pacific. In 1893, he came out for the annexation of Hawai'i. The Hawai'ian archipelago, he insisted, held key strategic value as stepping-stone to Asia and beyond.

ONTO A GLOBAL STAGE

Influenced by Alfred Thayer Mahan, McKinley became an advocate of expansion as a means to make the United States first in international commerce and as a means to implement its humanitarian and democratic goals. He also hoped to achieve these ends peacefully. Soon, however, McKinley found himself embroiled in a war with Spain that would establish the United States as a strong player in global imperialism (see

HOW DID the Spanish-American War change the place of the United States in world affairs?

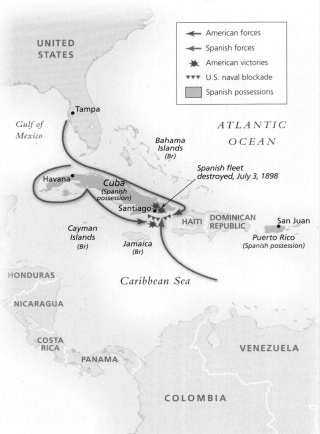

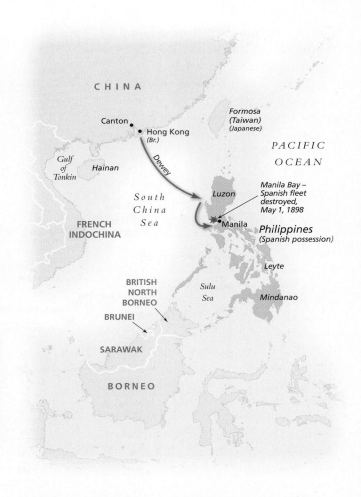

MAP 20.4

The Spanish-American War In two theaters of action, the United States used its naval power adeptly against a weak foe.

WHAT DID the United States gain from victories in each of these conflicts?

Map 20.4). By the end of the century, the United States had joined Europe and Japan in the quest for empire and claimed territories spread out from the Caribbean Sea across the Pacific.

A "SPLENDID LITTLE WAR" IN CUBA

In the mid-1860s, a movement for independence began in Cuba when Spain, its empire in ruins, began to impose stiff taxes on the island. After a series of defeats, insurgents rallied in the 1890s under the nationalist leadership of José Martí. In May 1895, Spanish troops ambushed and killed Martí, turning him into a martyr and fanning the flames of rebellion. In February 1896, Spain appointed General Valeriano Weyler as governor and gave him full authority to crush the rebellion. Weyler instituted a policy *of reconcentrado*, forcing civilians from the countryside into concentration camps so they could not aid the rebels. Thousands starved or died from the diseases that swept these crowded, dirty camps.

In the United States, the popular press whipped up support for the movement for *Cuba Libre*, circulating sensationalistic and even false stories of Spanish atrocities that Weyler. Newspapers ran stories on mass executions in the "death camps" and featured drawings of emaciated children. This so-called "yellow journalism," practiced brilliantly by publishers Joseph Pulitzer and William Randolph Hearst, boosted circulation and simultaneously aroused sympathy for the Cubans and abundant patriotic fervor.

Public sympathy, again whipped up by the press, turned into frenzy on February 15, 1898, when an explosion ripped through the battleship USS *Maine*, stationed in Havana harbor to protect American interests. The newspapers ran banner headlines charging a Spanish conspiracy, although there was no proof. The impatient public, meanwhile, demanded revenge for the death of 266 American sailors.

Finally, on April 11, President McKinley asked Congress for a declaration of war against Spain. Congress barely passed the war resolution on April 25, and only with the inclusion of an amendment by Senator Henry Teller (R-Colorado) that disclaimed "any disposition or intention to exercise sovereignty, jurisdiction or control over said island, except for the pacification thereof." McKinley called for volunteers, and by the end of April, the fighting had begun.

Ten weeks later, the war was all but over. On land, Lieutenant Colonel Theodore Roosevelt led his Rough Riders to victory. On July 3, the main Spanish fleet near Santiago Bay was destroyed; two weeks later Santiago itself surrendered, and the war drew to a close. Although poorly trained and lacking supplies, fewer than 400 Americans died in battle. Disease and the inept treatment of the wounded created a medical disaster, however, spreading sickness and disease to more than 20,000 in the regiments. Roosevelt, nevertheless, agreed with McKinley's Secretary of State John Hay that it had been a "splendid little war."

On August 12, at a small ceremony in McKinley's office marking Spain's surrender, the United States secured Cuba's independence from Spain, but not its own sovereignty. American businesses proceeded to tighten their hold on Cuban sugar plantations, while U.S. military forces oversaw the formation of a constitutional convention that made Cuba a protectorate of the United States. Under the Platt Amendment, sponsored by Republican senator Orville H. Platt of Connecticut in 1901, Cuba was required to provide land for American bases, including a navy base at Guantanomo Bay; to devote national revenues to pay back debts to the United States; to sign no treaty that would be detrimental to American interests; and to acknowledge the right of the United States to intervene at any time to protect its interests in Cuba.

WAR IN THE PHILIPPINES

The Philippines, another of Spain's colonies, seemed an especially attractive prospect, its 7,000 islands a natural way station to the markets of mainland Asia. At the first opportunity, McKinley acted to bring these islands into the U.S. strategic orbit. On May 4, shortly after Congress declared war on Spain, the president dispatched 5,000 troops to occupy the Philippines. George Dewey, a Civil War veteran who commanded the American Asiatic Squadron, was ordered to "start offensive action." During the first week of the conflict, he demolished the Spanish fleet in Manila Bay. Once the war ended, McKinley refused to sign the armistice unless Spain relinquished all claims to its Pacific islands. When Spain conceded, McKinley quickly drew up plans for colonial administration. After centuries of Spanish rule, however, the majority of islanders were eager to create their own nation.

The Filipino rebels, like the Cubans, at first welcomed American troops and fought with them against Spain. But when the Spanish-American War ended and they perceived

Brought to power with the assistance of American businessmen, Queen Lili'uokalani sought to limit outsider influence. American Marines, Christian missionaries, and sugar planters joined in 1893 to drive her from her throne. A century later, the U.S. government apologized to native Hawaiians for this illegal act.

View the Image
African American Troops in the Spanish-American War at **www.myhistorylab.com**

QUICK REVIEW

The Platt Amendment

- Cuba was required to provide land for American bases.
- Cuban national resources to be used to pay back debts to the United States.
- Cuba promised to sign no treaty detrimental to American interests.
- Cuba acknowledged the right of the United States to intervene to protect its interests in Cuba.

View the Image
Filipino Guerillas at **www.myhistorylab.com**

that American troops were not preparing to leave, the rebels, led by Emilio Aguinaldo, turned against their former allies and attacked the American base of operations in Manila in February 1899. Predicting a brief skirmish, American commanders seriously underestimated the population's capacity to endure great suffering for the sake of independence.

By the time the fighting slowed down in 1902, 4,300 American lives had been lost, and one of every five Filipinos had died in battle or from starvation or disease. On some of the Philippine islands, intermittent fighting lasted until 1935. In 1901, William Howard Taft headed a commission that established a special apparatus to rule in the Philippines; after 1905, the president appointed a Filipino governor general to maintain the provincial government. Meanwhile, Americans bought up the best land and invested heavily in the island's sugar economy.

The conquest of the Philippines, which remained a U.S. colony until 1946, evoked for its proponents the vision of empire. The Philippines joined Hawai'i as yet another stepping-stone for U.S. merchants en route to China. At the end of the Spanish-American War, the United States advanced its interests in the Caribbean to include Puerto Rico, ceded by Spain, and eventually the Virgin Islands of St. Thomas, St. John, and St. Croix, purchased from Denmark in 1917. The acquisition of Pacific territories, including Guam, marked the emergence of the United States as a global colonial power.

Once again, Josiah Strong proclaimed judgment over an era. His famous treatise *Expansion* (1900) roundly defended American overseas involvements as the best way to spread freedom around the world. Many began to wonder, however, whether the United States could become an empire without sacrificing its democratic spirit and to ask whether the subjugated people were really so fortunate under the rule of the United States.

CRITICS OF EMPIRE

No mass movement formed to forestall U.S. expansion, but distinguished figures like Mark Twain, Andrew Carnegie, William Jennings Bryan, and Harvard philosopher William James voiced their opposition strongly. To protest military action in the Philippines, a small group of prominent Bostonians organized the Anti-Imperialist League. Most members supported American economic expansion, but advocated free trade rather than political domination as the means to reach this goal.

The *National Labor Standard* expressed its common hope that all those "who believe in the Republic against Empire should join." By 1899, the league claimed a half-million members. A few outspoken anti-imperialists, such as former Illinois governor John Peter Altgeld, openly toasted Filipino rebels as heroes. Others, such as Samuel Gompers, a league vice president, felt no sympathy for conquered peoples and simply wanted to prevent colonized nonwhites from immigrating into the United States and "inundating" American labor.

Military leaders and staunch imperialists did not distinguish between racist and nonracist anti-imperialists. They called all dissenters "unhung traitors" and demanded their arrest. Newspaper editors accused universities of harboring antiwar professors, although college students as a group were enthusiastic supporters of the war.

Within the press, which overwhelmingly supported the Spanish-American War, the voices of opposition appeared primarily in African American and labor papers. The *Indianapolis Recorder* asked rhetorically in 1899, "Are the tender-hearted expansionists in the United States

"Uncle Sam Teaches the Art of Self-Government," editorial cartoon, 1898. Expressing a popular sentiment of the time, a newspaper cartoonist shows the rebels as raucous children who constantly fight among themselves and need to be brought into line by Uncle Sam. The Filipino leader, Emilio Aguinaldo, appears as a dunce for failing to learn properly from the teacher. The two major islands where no uprising took place, Puerto Rico and Hawai'i, appear as passive but exotically dressed women, ready to learn their lessons.

CHRONOLOGY

1867	Grange founded
	Secretary of State Seward negotiates the purchase of Alaska
1874	Granger laws begin to regulate railroad shipping rates
1877	Rutherford B. Hayes elected president
	Great Uprising of 1877
1879	Henry George publishes *Progress and Poverty*
1881	President James A. Garfield assassinated; Chester A. Arthur becomes president
1882	Chinese Exclusion Act
1883	Pendleton Act passed
1884	Grover Cleveland elected president
1887	Interstate Commerce Act creates the Interstate Commerce Commission
1888	Colored Farmers' Alliance formed
	Benjamin Harrison elected president
1889	National Farmers' Alliance formed
1890	Sherman Silver Purchase Act
	McKinley Tariff enacted
	National American Woman Suffrage Association formed
1892	Populist (People's) Party formed
	Coeur d'Alene miners' strike
	Homestead strike
	Ida B. Wells begins crusade against lynching
1893	Western Federation of Miners formed
	Financial panic and depression
	World's Columbian Exhibition opens in Chicago
1894	"Coxey's Army" marches on Washington, DC
	Pullman strike and boycott
1896	*Plessy* v. *Ferguson* upholds segregation
	William McKinley defeats William Jennings Bryan for president
1897	Dingley Tariff again raises import duties to an all-time high
1898	Eugene V. Debs helps found Social Democratic Party
	Hawai'i is annexed
	Spanish-American War begins
	Anti-Imperialist League formed
	Wilmington, North Carolina, massacre
1899	*Cumming* v. *Richmond County Board of Education* sanctions segregated education
	Guerrilla war begins in the Philippines
1900	Gold Standard Act
	Josiah Strong publishes *Expansion*

Congress really actuated by the desire to save the Filipinos from self-destruction or is it the worldly greed for gain?" The *Railroad Telegrapher* similarly commented, "The wonder of it all is that the working people are willing to lose blood and treasure in fighting another man's battle."

Most Americans put aside their doubts and welcomed the new era of imperialism. Untouched by the private tragedies of dead or wounded American soldiers and the mass destruction of civilian society in the Philippines, the vast majority could approve Theodore Roosevelt's defense of armed conflict: "No triumph of peace is quite so great as the supreme triumphs of war."

CONCLUSION

The conflicts marking the last quarter of the nineteenth century that pitted farmers, workers, and the proprietors of small businesses against powerful national interests had offered Americans an important moment of democratic promise. By the end of the century, however, the rural and working-class campaigns to retain a large degree of self-government in their communities had been defeated, their organizations destroyed, their autonomy eroded. The rise of a national governing class and its counterpart, the large bureaucratic state, established new rules of behavior, new sources of prestige, and new rewards for the most successful citizens.

The nation would eventually pay a steep price for the failure of democratic reform. Regional antagonisms, nativist movements against the foreign-born, and, above all, deepening racial tensions blighted American society. As the new century opened, progressive reformers moved to correct flaws in government while accepting the framework of a corporate society and its overseas empire. So, too, did the majority of citizens who shared their president's pride in expansion.

William Jennings Bryan made another bid for the presidency in 1900 on a strong anti-imperialist platform and was roundly defeated at the polls. The dream of Queen Lili'iokalani for an independent Hawai'i was likewise crushed, although in 1993, a century after her overthrow, President William Clinton signed a joint congressional resolution apologizing for the "alleged role the United States had played" in her deposing. But in 1900, Americans would find the widening divisions in their own society difficult—if not impossible—to overcome.

REVIEW QUESTIONS

1. Discuss some of the problems accompanying the expansion of government during the late nineteenth century. What role did political parties play in this process? Explain how a prominent reformer such as James Garfield might become a leading "machine" politician.

2. What were the major causes and consequences of the Populist movement of the 1880s and 1890s? Why did the election of 1896 prove so important to the future of American politics?

3. Discuss the role of women in both the Grange and the People's Party. What were their specific goals?

4. Discuss the causes and consequences of the financial crisis of the 1890s. How did various reformers and politicians respond to the event? What kinds of programs did they offer to restore the economy or reduce poverty?

5. How did the exclusion of African Americans affect the outcome of populism? Explain the rise of Jim Crow legislation in the South and discuss its impact on the status of African Americans.

6. Describe American foreign policy during the 1890s. Why did the United States intervene in Cuba and the Philippines? What were some of the leading arguments for and against overseas expansion?

KEY TERMS

Coxey's Army (p. 513)
Free silver (p. 516)
Grandfather clauses (p. 518)
Grange (p. 508)
Granger laws (p. 509)
Great Uprising of 1877 (p. 510)
Interstate Commerce Commission (ICC) (p. 505)
Jim Crow laws (p. 517)
Nativism (p. 517)

Pendleton Civil Service Reform Act (p. 507)
Plessy v. *Ferguson* (p. 518)
Populism (p. 508)
Protective association (p. 513)
Segregation (p. 517)
Sherman Silver Purchase Act (p. 516)
Southern Farmers' Alliance (p. 509)
Woman's Christian Temperance Union (WCTU) (p. 511)

PEARSON myhistorylab Connections

Reinforce what you learned in this chapter by studying the many documents, images, maps, review tools, and videos available at www.myhistorylab.com.

Read and Review

✓● Study and Review Chapter 20

●●● Read the Document

Frances E. Willard on the Reorganization of Government (1891)

The People's Party Platform (1892)

Jacob Coxey, Address of Protest (1894)

Eugene V. Debs, The Outlook for Socialism in America (1900)

William Jennings Bryan, "Cross of Gold" Speech (1896)

Josiah Strong, from Our Country (1885)

●● View the Image

Nast Cartoon: Boss Tweed

Homestead Strikers Surrendering

African American Troops in the Spanish-American War

Filipino Guerillas

Research and Explore

●●● Read the Document

Exploring America: White Man's Burden

Exploring America: Homestead Strike of 1892

Profiles
  Queen Liliuokalani
  Williams Jennings Bryan

((●● Hear the Audio

Hear the audio files for Chapter 20 at
www.myhistorylab.com.

Currency Reform

During the Civil War, farmers in the Midwest had gone deeply into debt to expand their crop production and meet the profitable demand for grain and other crops created by war. During the wild financial swings of booms and busts between 1865 and 1900, farmers again borrowed heavily to meet the demand for grains created by various world events. Farmers frequently had to borrow yearly to obtain the seeds and materials to plant their crops. If crop prices were low at harvest or a crop failure occurred, farmers were in deep financial trouble. Radical variations in international crop prices impacted the farmer's bottom line. Panics or depressions would also drive indebted farmers to the wall resulting in mortgage foreclosures and loss of their farms. Looking for simplistic explanations to complicated problems, farmers decided that the railroads and eastern financial interests were in a conspiracy to reduce them to economic slavery to the industrial East.

EXPLAIN AND describe the powerful political lure of currency reform in American presidential campaigns between 1874 and 1900. Where did various political groups and candidates stand on this issue and to whom did they attempt to appeal?

Simplistic explanations led to simplistic answers and currency reform became the central focus of many farmer political movements. After silver was dropped from the list of authorized coins for the U.S., farmers decided that was the focus of their problems and began demanding the free coinage of silver to create an artificial inflation that would raise crop prices and free them from debt, or so they believed. Currency reform became an emotional issue in politics between 1874 and 1900. ■

▲ McKinley stands upon the platform of a gold dollar coin supported by cheering workers, clerks, bankers and industrialists. Shipping and industry thrives behind the President under the banner: "Prosperity at Home, Prestige Abroad."

COINAGE ACT, FEBRUARY 12, 1873

AN ACT revising and amending the Laws relative to the Mints, Assay-offices, and Coinage of the United States.

Called the "Crime of '73" by farmers and Populists, the Coinage Act of 1873 demonetized silver by removing it from the list of dollar coins and relegating it to the minor coinage of the United States. Silver had become too expensive to coin, so the Treasury had ceased minting silver dollars. Demonetizing silver was really simply a housekeeping action by Congress, but farmers considered it a conspiracy mounted by eastern bankers to keep them in peonage to the industrial East. It is this law that launches the issue of free coinage of silver.

SEC. 14. That the gold coins of the United States shall be a One-dollar piece... a quartereagle, or two-and-a-half dollar piece; a three dollar piece; a half-eagle, or five-dollar piece; an eagle, or ten-dollar piece; and a double eagle, or twenty dollar piece... which coins shall be a legal tender in all payments at their nominal value....

SEC. I5. That the silver coins of the United States shall be... a half dollar, or fifty-cent piece, a quarter-dollar, or twenty five-cent piece, a dime, or ten-cent piece;... and said coins shall be a legal tender at their nominal value for any amount not exceeding five dollars in any one payment....

SEC. I7. That no coins, either of gold, silver, or minor coinage, shall hereafter be issued from the mint other than those of the denominations, standards, and weights herein set forth. ■

POPULIST PLATFORM, 1892

AUTHORED BY *Ignatius Donnelly, leader in the Grange movement and later with the Populists, this statement of demands along with others was adopted by the Populists at their 1892 convention in Omaha, Nebraska. Populists hoped to democratize the nation's economic system, but they never succeeded in their goal.*

Silver, which has been accepted as coin since the dawn of history, has been demonetized to add to the purchasing power of gold by decreasing the value of all forms of property as well as human labor, and the supply of currency is purposely abridged to fatten usurers, bankrupt enterprise, and enslave industry. A vast conspiracy against mankind has been organized on two continents, and it is rapidly taking possession of the world. If not met and overthrown at once it forebodes terrible social convulsions, the destruction of civilization, or the establishment of an absolute despotism. We demand a national currency, safe, sound, and flexible issued by the general government only, a full legal tender for all debts, public and private.... We demand free and unlimited coinage of silver and gold at the present legal ratio of 16 to 1. ■

WILLIAM H. HARVEY, *COIN'S FINANCIAL SCHOOL*, 1893

HARVEY WROTE Coin's Financial School *to explain to farmers the complicated economic issue of bimetallism and the demand for free coinage of silver.*

Hard times are with us; the country is distracted; very few things are marketable at a price above the cost of production; tens of thousands are out of employment; the jails, penitentiaries, workhouses and insane asylums are full... the cry of distress is heard on every hand...

Up to 1873 we were on what was known as a bimetallic basis, but what was in fact a silver basis, with gold as a companion metal enjoying the same privileges as silver, except that silver fixed the unit, and the value of gold was regulated by it. This was bimetallism....

Gold was considered the money of the rich. It was owned, principally by that class of people, and the poor people seldom handled it, and... seldom ever saw any of it....

It is proposed by the bimetallists to remonetize silver, and add it to the quantity of money that is to be used for measuring the value of all other property....

You increase the value of all property by adding to the number of money units in the land. You make it possible for the debtor to pay his debts; business to start anew, and revivify all the industries of the country, which must remain paralyzed so long as silver as well as all other property is measured by a gold standard....

The money lenders in the United States, who own substantially all our money, have a selfish interest in maintaining the gold standard. They, too, will not yield....

With silver remonetized, and gold at a premium, not one-tenth the hardships could result that now afflict us.... The bimetallic standard will make the United States the most prosperous nation on the globe. ■

WILLIAM JENNINGS BRYAN, "CROSS OF GOLD SPEECH," OFFICIAL PROCEEDINGS OF THE DEMOCRATIC NATIONAL CONVENTION, CHICAGO, ILLINOIS, JULY 9, 1896.

BRYAN BECAME *the champion of farmers and a candidate for president with this "Cross of Gold" speech, which advocated the free silver position of the earlier Populist movement.*

You come to us and tell us that the great cities are in favor of the gold standard. I tell you that the great cities rest upon these broad and fertile prairies. Burn down your cities and leave our farms, and your cities will spring up again as if by magic. But destroy our farms and the grass will grow in the streets of every city in the country....

If they dare to come out in the open field and defend the gold standard as a good thing, we shall fight them to the uttermost, having behind us the producing masses of the nation and the world. Having behind us the commercial interests and the laboring interests and all the toiling masses, we shall answer their demands for a gold standard by saying to them, you shall not press down upon the brow of labor this crown of thorns. You shall not crucify mankind upon a cross of gold. ■

Grant Hamilton, *Judge Magazine*, October 13, 1900 ▶
The cartoonist emphasizes the free silver issue in this cartoon that criticizes Bryan as "worth 53 cents only in free silver."

The women, trudging stoutly along under great difficulties, were able to complete their march only when troops of cavalry from Fort Meyers were rushed into Washington . . . No inauguration has ever produced such scenes . . .

—Washington Post, *March 4, 1913*

THE JUNGLE

UPTON SINCLAIR

VOTES FOR US WHEN ARE WOMEN

VOTES FOR WOMEN

Suffragettes display signs and American flags, while piled into a festooned car.

21

URBAN AMERICA AND THE PROGRESSIVE ERA

1900–1917

((•—[Hear the Audio

Hear the audio files for Chapter 21 at **www.myhistorylab.com**.

WHAT WERE the social and intellectual roots of progressive reform?

HOW DID progressives try to redefine the role of the government in American life?

HOW DID tensions between social justice and social control divide progressives?

WHAT GROUPS challenged the progressive vision of politics?

WHAT NEW forms of activism emerged among the working class, women, and African Americans?

WHAT ROLE did Theodore Roosevelt envision the federal government playing in national life?

AMERICAN COMMUNITIES

The Henry Street Settlement House: Women Settlement House Workers Create a Community of Reform

A FRIGHTENED YOUNG GIRL APPEARED AT THE WEEKLY HOME-NURSING CLASS for women on Manhattan's Lower East Side. Tugging on the teacher's skirt, the girl pleaded in broken English for the teacher to come home with her. "Mother," "baby," "blood," she kept repeating. The teacher gathered up the sheets that were part of the interrupted lesson in bed making. The two hurried through narrow, garbage-strewn streets, then groped their way up a pitch-dark staircase. They reached a two-room apartment, home to an immigrant family of seven and several boarders. There, in a vermin-infested bed, encrusted with dried blood, lay a mother and her newborn baby. The mother had been abandoned by a doctor because she could not afford his fee.

The teacher, Lillian Wald recalled this scene as her baptism by fire and the turning point in her life. Born in 1867, Wald had enjoyed a comfortable upbringing in a middle-class German Jewish family in Rochester. Despite her parents' objections, she moved to New York City to become a professional nurse. Horrified by the inhumane conditions at a juvenile asylum where she worked, Wald determined to find a way of caring for the sick in their neighborhoods and homes. With nursing school classmate Mary Brewster, Wald rented an apartment on the Lower East Side and established a visiting nurse service. The two provided professional care in the home to hundreds of families for a nominal fee. They also offered each family they visited information on basic health care, sanitation, and disease prevention. In 1895, philanthropist Jacob Schiff donated a red brick Georgian house on Henry Street as a new base of operation.

The Henry Street Settlement stood in the center of perhaps the most overcrowded neighborhood in the world, New York's Lower East Side. Population density was about 500 per acre, roughly four times the figure for the rest of New York City, and far more concentrated than even the worst slums of London or Calcutta. Home for most Lower East Siders was a small tenement apartment that might include paying boarders squeezed in alongside the immediate family. Residents were mostly recent immigrants from southern and eastern Europe. Men, women, and children toiled in the garment shops, small factories, retail stores, breweries, and warehouses that were found on nearly every street.

The Henry Street Settlement became a model for a new kind of reform community composed essentially of college-educated women who encouraged and supported one another in a wide variety of humanitarian, civic, and political activities. Settlement house living arrangements closely resembled those in the dormitories of such new women's colleges as Smith, Wellesley, and Vassar. Like these colleges, the settlement house was an "experiment," but one

designed, in settlement house pioneer Jane Addams's words, "to aid in the solution of the social and industrial problems which are engendered by the modern conditions of urban life." Unlike earlier moral reformers, who tried to impose their ideas from outside, settlement house residents lived in poor communities and worked for immediate improvements in the health and welfare of those communities. The college-educated women were beneficiaries as well. The settlement house allowed them to preserve a collegial spirit, satisfy the desire for service, and apply their academic training.

With its combined moral and social appeal, the settlement house movement attracted many educated young women and grew rapidly. Few women made settlement work a career, but those who did typically chose not to marry, and most lived together with female companions. As the movement flourished, settlement house residents called attention to the plight of the poor and fostered respect for different cultural heritages in countless articles and lectures. Leaders of the movement, including Jane Addams, Lillian Wald, and Florence Kelley, emerged as influential political figures during the progressive era.

The settlement house movement embodied the impulses toward social justice and civic engagement that were hallmarks of the progressive movement. But in a broader sense, the progressive era was defined by struggles over the true meaning of American democracy. If there was growing agreement that Americans needed to address the excesses of industrial growth and rapid urbanization, there was less consensus over precisely how. How might the power of government be used to restrain corporate excess and improve the lives of children, industrial laborers, and others in need of protection? Could the machinery of democracy be reformed to make politics less corrupt and more responsive to the needs of ordinary citizens? Did the calls to social action mean that full citizenship rights would be extended to African Americans, women, and new immigrants? What were the most effective ways to expose social problems and appeal to the public conscience?

During the first two decades of the twentieth century, millions of Americans identified themselves as "progressives" and most, like Lillian Wald, were first drawn to causes and campaigns rooted in their local communities. But many soon saw that confronting the grim realities of an urban and industrial society required national and even global strategies for pursuing reform. By the time America entered World War I in 1917, despite its contradictions, the progressive movement had reshaped the political and social landscape of the entire nation.

New York City

THE ORIGINS OF PROGRESSIVISM

Between the 1890s and World War I, a large and diverse number of Americans claimed the political label "progressive." Progressives could be found in all classes, regions, and races. They shared a fundamental belief that America needed a new social consciousness to cope with the problems brought on by the enormous rush of economic and social change in the post–Civil War decades. Yet **progressivism** was no unified movement with a single set of principles. It is best understood as a varied collection of reform communities, often fleeting, uniting citizens in a host of political, professional, and religious organizations, some of which were national in scope.

WHAT WERE the social and intellectual roots of progressive reform?

UNIFYING THEMES

Three basic attitudes underlay the various progressive crusades and movements. The first was anger over the excesses of industrial capitalism and urban growth. Unlike Populist-era reformers, who were largely rural and small-town oriented, progressives focused their energies on the social and political ills experienced by Americans in factories, mines, and cities. At the same time, progressives shared an essential optimism about the ability of citizens to improve social and economic conditions. They were reformers, not revolutionaries, who believed in using the democratic institutions available to them—the vote, the courts, the legislature—to address social problems. If those political processes were found to be corrupt or undemocratic, they would have to be reformed as well. Second, progressives emphasized social cohesion and common bonds as a way to understand how modern society and economics actually worked. They largely rejected the ideal of individualism that had informed nineteenth-century economic and political theory. For progressives, society's problems were structural rather than just the result of individual failures. Third, progressives believed in the need for citizens to intervene actively, both politically and morally, to improve social conditions. They looked to convert personal outrage into civic activism and to mobilize public opinion in new ways. Progressives thus called for expansion of the legislative and regulatory powers of the state. They moved away from the nineteenth-century celebration of minimal government as the surest way to allow all Americans to thrive.

Progressive rhetoric and methods drew on two distinct sources of inspiration. One was evangelical Protestantism, particularly the late nineteenth-century social gospel movement. Social gospelers emphasized both the capacity and the duty of Christians to purge the world of poverty, inequality, and economic greed. A second strain of progressive thought looked to natural and social scientists to develop rational measures for improving the human condition. They believed that experts trained in statistical analysis, engineering, and the sciences could make government and industry more efficient and set new standards for personal behavior. Progressivism thus offered an uneasy combination of social justice and social control, a tension that would characterize American reform for the rest of the twentieth century.

NEW JOURNALISM: MUCKRAKING

Changes in journalism helped fuel a new reform consciousness by drawing the attention of millions to urban poverty, political corruption, the plight of industrial workers, and immoral business practices. As early as 1890, journalist Jacob Riis had shocked the nation with his landmark book *How the Other Half Lives*, a portrait of New York City's poor (see Seeing History).

Within a few years, magazine journalists turned to uncovering the seamier side of American life. The key innovator was S. S. McClure, a young midwestern editor who in 1893 started America's first large-circulation magazine, *McClure's*. In 1902, McClure began hiring talented reporters to write detailed accounts of the nation's social problems. Lincoln Steffens's series *The Shame of the Cities* (1903) revealed the widespread graft at the center of American urban politics. Ida Tarbell, in her *History of the Standard Oil Company* (1904), thoroughly documented how John D. Rockefeller ruthlessly squeezed

progressivism A national movement focused on a variety of reform initiatives, including ending corruption, a more business like approach to government, and legislative responses to industrial excess.

Photographing Poverty in the Slums of New York

Jacob A. Riis was a twenty-year-old Danish immigrant when he arrived in New York City in 1870. After several years wandering the country as a casual laborer, he returned to New York and began a career as a reporter covering the police beat. By the early 1880s, Riis found himself drawn to report on perhaps the most overwhelming and rapidly worsening problem in the city: the deteriorating conditions of tenement house life. As he accompanied city police and Board of Health employees in their inspections of sanitary conditions, Riis's reports on the tenement districts reflected a keen outrage and new sense

HERE ARE two Riis photographs, "Five Cents a Spot" and "Home of an Italian Ragpicker." What visual information does each communicate about tenement life? How do they differ in their depiction of New York City's immigrant poor? How do you imagine Riis set up the scene for each of these photographs?

of purpose. Part of the story could be reduced to staggering statistics. By 1880, more than 600,000 New Yorkers lived in 24,000 tenements, each of which housed anywhere from four to several score families. Overcrowding kept getting worse, as in one Mulberry Street tenement that housed nearly two hundred people in small apartments meant for twenty families. Thousands of buildings had terrible sanitary conditions, with seriously defective plumbing, and often no ventilation or sewer connections. "It was upon my midnight trips with the sanitary police," he recalled, "that the wish kept cropping up in me that there were some way of putting before the people what I saw there."

In 1888, Riis taught himself the rudiments of photography, using the new "flash powder" technology to take pictures where there was no natural light. He shot many of these photographs in the dead of the night, taking his subjects by surprise. Other photographs were carefully staged to ensure maximum emotional impact on the middle- and upper-class audience Riis was trying to reach. Riis converted his photographs into "lantern slides," which could be projected as large images before audiences. He spent two years touring the country, presenting an illustrated lecture called "The Other Half: How It Lives and Dies in New York" to churches and reform groups, appealing to the conscience and Christian sympathy of his listeners. Newspapers reviewed Riis's slide lecture as both an "entertainment" and a new philanthropic campaign. In 1890, he published his landmark book, *How the Other Half Lives: Studies Among the Tenements*, illustrated with his photographs. The use of photography would become a key element for reform crusades in the progressive era and beyond. ■

out competitors with unfair business practices. Ray Stannard Baker wrote detailed portraits of life and labor in Pennsylvania coal towns.

McClure's and other magazines discovered that "exposure journalism" paid off handsomely in terms of increased circulation. The middle-class public responded to this new combination of factual reporting and moral exhortation. A series such as Steffens's fueled reform campaigns that swept individual communities. Between 1902 and 1908, magazines were full of articles exposing insurance scandals, patent medicine frauds, and stock market swindles. Upton Sinclair's 1906 novel *The Jungle* exposed the filthy sanitation and abysmal working conditions in the stockyards and the meatpacking industry. In an effort to boost sales, Sinclair's publisher devoted an entire issue of a monthly magazine it owned, *World's Work*, to articles and photographs that substantiated Sinclair's devastating portrait.

Muckraking crusades could take many forms. In the 1890s, the young African American newspaper editor Ida B. Wells set out to investigate an upsurge in lynchings around the city of Memphis. She paid special attention to the common white defense of lynching—that it was a necessary response to attempts by black men to rape white women. Her 1895 pamphlet *The Red Record* showed that the vast majority of black lynching victims had not even been accused of sexual transgression. Instead, Wells found that lynching was primarily a brutal device to eliminate African Americans who competed with white businesses or who had become too prosperous or powerful.

In 1906, David Graham Phillips, in a series for *Cosmopolitan* called "The Treason of the Senate," argued that many conservative U.S. senators were no more than mouthpieces for big business. President Theodore Roosevelt, upset by Phillips's attack on several of his friends and supporters, coined a new term when he angrily denounced Phillips and his colleagues as "muckrakers."

Lewis Hine, one of the pioneers of social documentary photography, made this evocative 1908 portrait of "Mamie," a typical young spinner working at a cotton mill in Lancaster, South Carolina. The National Child Labor Committee hired Hine to help document, publicize, and curb the widespread employment of children in industrial occupations. "These pictures," Hine wrote, "speak for themselves and prove that the law is being violated."

Lewis Hine (American, 1874–1940), "A Carolina Spinner," 1908. Gelatin silver print, 4 ¾ × 7 in. Milwaukee Art Museum, Gift of the Sheldon M. Barnett Family. M1973.83.

Read the Document

History Bookshelf: Upton Sinclair, The Jungle *(1906)* at **www.myhistorylab.com**

Read the Document

History Bookshelf: Ida B. Wells-Barnett, The Red Record *(1895)* at **www.myhistorylab.com**

INTELLECTUAL TRENDS PROMOTING REFORM

On a deeper level than muckraking, early twentieth-century thinkers challenged several core ideas in American intellectual life. Their new theories of education, law, economics, and society provided effective tools for reformers. The emergent fields of the social sciences—sociology, psychology, anthropology, and economics—emphasized observation of how people actually lived and behaved in their communities. Progressive reformers linked the systematic analysis of society and the individual characteristics of these new fields of inquiry to the project of improving the material conditions of Americans.

Sociologist Lester Frank Ward, in his pioneering work *Dynamic Sociology* (1883), offered an important critique of **social Darwinism**, the orthodox theory that attributed social inequality to natural selection and the "survival of the fittest." Ward argued that the conservative social theorists responsible for social Darwinism, such as Herbert Spencer and William Graham Sumner, had wrongly applied evolutionary theory to human affairs. They had confused organic evolution with social evolution. Nature's method was genetic: unplanned, involuntary, automatic, and mechanical. By contrast, civilization had been built on successful human intervention in the natural processes of organic evolution.

Philosopher John Dewey criticized the excessively rigid and formal approach to education found in most American schools. Dewey advocated developing what he called "creative intelligence" in students, which could then be put to use in improving society. Dewey's belief that education was the "fundamental method of social progress and reform" inspired generations of progressive educators.

muckraking Journalism exposing economic, social, and political evils, so named by Theodore Roosevelt for its "raking the muck" of American society.

social Darwinism The application of Charles Darwin's theory of biological evolution to society, holding that the fittest and wealthiest survive, the weak and the poor perish, and government action is unable to alter this "natural" process.

At the University of Wisconsin, John R. Commons founded the new field of industrial relations and organized a state industrial commission that became a model for other states. Working closely with Governor Robert M. La Follette, Commons and his students helped draft pioneering laws in worker compensation and public utility regulation. Another Wisconsin faculty member, economist Richard Ely, argued that the state was "an educational and ethical agency whose positive aim is an indispensable condition of human progress." Ely believed the state must intervene directly to help solve public problems. Like Commons, Ely worked with Wisconsin lawmakers to apply his expertise in economics to reforming the state's labor laws.

Progressive legal theorists began challenging the conservative view of constitutional law that had dominated American courts. Since the 1870s, the Supreme Court had interpreted the Fourteenth Amendment (1868) as a guarantee of broad rights for corporations. That amendment, which prevented states from depriving "any person of life, liberty, or property, without due process of law," had been designed to protect the civil rights of African Americans against violations by the states. But the Court, led by Justice Stephen J. Field, used the due process clause to strike down state laws regulating business and labor conditions.

The most important dissenter from this view was Oliver Wendell Holmes Jr. A scholar and Massachusetts judge, Holmes believed the law had to take into account changing social conditions. And courts should take care not to invalidate social legislation enacted democratically. After his appointment to the Supreme Court in 1902, Holmes wrote a number of notable dissents to conservative court decisions overturning progressive legislation. Criticizing the majority opinion in *Lochner* v. *New York* (1905), in which the Court struck down a state law setting a ten-hour day for bakers, Holmes insisted that the Constitution "is not intended to embody a particular theory."

Read the **Document**

History Bookshelf: *Jane Addams, The Spirit of Youth and City Streets (1909); Twenty Years at Hull House (1910)* at **www.myhistorylab.com**

THE FEMALE DOMINION

In the 1890s, the settlement house movement had begun to provide an alternative to traditional concepts of private charity and humanitarian reform. Settlement workers found they could not transform their neighborhoods without confronting a host of broad social questions: chronic poverty, overcrowded tenement houses, child labor, industrial accidents, public health. They soon discovered the need to engage the political and cultural life of the larger community. As on Henry Street, college-educated, middle-class women were a key vanguard in the crusade for social justice.

Jane Addams founded one of the first settlement houses, Hull House, in Chicago in 1889, after years of struggling to find work and a social identity equal to her talents. A member of one of the first generations of American women to attend college, Addams was a graduate of Rockford College. Many educated women were dissatisfied with the life choices conventionally available to them: early marriage or the traditional female professions of teaching, nursing, and library work. Settlement work provided an attractive alternative. Addams often spoke of the "subjective necessity" of settlement houses. By this she meant that they gave young, educated women a way to satisfy their powerful desire to connect with the real world. "There is nothing after disease, indigence and guilt," she wrote, "so fatal to life itself as the want of a proper outlet for active faculties."

Lillian Wald and her allies convinced the New York Board of Health to assign a nurse to every public school in the city. They lobbied the board of education to create the first school lunch programs. They persuaded the city to set up municipal milk stations to ensure the purity of milk. Henry Street also pioneered tuberculosis

A portrait of the young Jane Addams, probably taken around the time she founded Hull House in Chicago, in 1889.

OVERVIEW | Currents of Progressivism

	Key Figures	Issues
Local Communities	Jane Addams, Lillian Wald, Florence Kelley, Frederic C. Howe, Samuel Jones	• Improving health, education, welfare in urban immigrant neighborhoods • Child labor, eight-hour day • Celebrating immigrant cultures • Reforming urban politics • Municipal ownership/regulation of utilities
State	Robert M. La Follette, Hiram Johnson, Al Smith	• Limiting power of railroads, other corporations • Improving civil service • Direct democracy • Applying academic scholarship to human needs
National	James K. Vardaman, Hoke Smith, Theodore Roosevelt, Woodrow Wilson	• Disfranchisement of African Americans • Trust-busting • Conservation and western development • National regulation of corporate and financial excesses • Reform of national banking
Intellectual/Cultural	Jacob Riis, Lincoln Steffens, Ida Tarbell, Upton Sinclair, S. S. McClure John Dewey, Louis Brandeis, Edwin A. Ross	• Muckraking • Education reform • Sociological jurisprudence • Empowering "ethical elite"

treatment and prevention. Its leaders became powerful advocates for playground construction, improved street cleaning, and tougher housing inspection. Lillian Wald became a national figure—an outspoken advocate of child labor legislation and woman suffrage and a vigorous opponent of American involvement in World War I. She offered Henry Street as a meeting place to the National Negro Conference in 1909, out of which emerged the National Association for the Advancement of Colored People (NAACP).

Social reformer Florence Kelley helped direct the support of the settlement house movement behind groundbreaking state and federal labor legislation. Arriving at Hull House in 1891, Kelley found what she described as a "colony of efficient and intelligent women." In 1893, she wrote a report detailing the dismal conditions in sweatshops and the effects of long hours on the women and children who worked in them. This report became the basis for landmark legislation in Illinois that limited women to an eight-hour workday, barred children under fourteen from working, and abolished tenement labor. Moving to the Henry Street Settlement in 1898, Kelley served as general secretary of the new National Consumers' League. With Lillian Wald, she established the New York Child Labor Committee and pushed for the creation of the U.S. Children's Bureau, established in 1912. Its director, the first woman to head a federal bureau, was Julia Lathrop, another alumna of Hull House.

Kelley, Addams, Wald, Lathrop, and their circle consciously used their power as women to reshape politics in the progressive era. Electoral politics and the state were historically male preserves, but female social progressives turned their gender into an

advantage. Activists like Kelley used their influence in civil society to create new state powers in the service of social justice. "Women's place is Home," wrote reformer Rheta Childe Dorr, "but Home is not contained within the four walls of an individual home. Home is the community."

PROGRESSIVE POLITICS IN CITIES AND STATES

HOW DID progressives try to redefine the role of the government in American life?

Progressive reformers poured much of their zeal and energy into local political battles. In cities and states across the nation, progressive politicians became a powerful force, often balancing the practical need for partisan support with nonpartisan appeals to the larger citizenry. Although their motives and achievements were mixed, progressives were united in their attacks on corruption in government, the need to reign in corporate power, and calls for more activist city and state governments.

THE URBAN MACHINE

By the turn of the century, Democratic Party machines, usually dominated by first- and second-generation Irish, controlled the political life of most large American cities. The keys to machine strength were disciplined organization and the delivery of essential services to both immigrant communities and business elites. The successful machine politician viewed his work as a business, and he accumulated his capital by serving people who needed assistance. Recent immigrants in particular faced frequent unemployment, sickness, and discrimination. In exchange for votes, machine politicians offered their constituents a variety of services. These included municipal jobs, intervention with legal problems, and food and coal during hard times.

Read the **Document**

George W. Plunkitt, "Honest Graft" (1905) at **www.myhistorylab.com**

For those who did business with the city, staying on the machine's good side was simply another business expense. In exchange for valuable franchises and city contracts, businessmen routinely bribed machine politicians and contributed to their campaign funds. George Washington Plunkitt, a stalwart of New York's Tammany Hall machine, good-naturedly defended what he called "honest graft": making money from inside information on public improvements. "It's just like lookin' ahead in Wall Street or in the coffee or cotton market. . . . I seen my opportunities and I took 'em."

In the early twentieth century, to expand their base of support, political machines in the Northeast began concentrating more on passing welfare legislation beneficial to working-class and immigrant constituencies. In this way, machine politicians often allied themselves with progressive reformers in state legislatures. In New York, for example, Tammany Hall figures such as Robert Wagner, Al Smith, and Big Tim Sullivan worked with middle-class progressive groups to pass child labor laws, factory safety regulations, worker compensation plans, and other efforts to make government more responsive to social needs. As Jewish and Catholic immigrants expanded in number and proportion in the city population, urban machines also began to champion cultural pluralism, opposing prohibition and immigration restrictions and defending the contributions made by new ethnic groups in the cities.

Timothy D. **"Big** Tim" Sullivan, the popular and influential Democratic Party machine boss of the Bowery and Lower East Side districts of New York City, ca. 1901.

PROGRESSIVES AND URBAN REFORM

Political progressivism originated in the cities. It was both a challenge to the power of machine politics and a response to deteriorating urban conditions. City governments, especially in the Northeast and industrial Midwest, seemed hardly capable of providing the basic services needed to sustain large populations. For example, an impure water supply left Pittsburgh with one of the world's highest rates of death from typhoid, dysentery, and cholera.

Reformers placed much of the blame for urban ills on the machines and looked for ways to restructure city government. The "good government" movement, led by the National Municipal League, fought to make city management a nonpartisan, even nonpolitical, process by bringing the administrative techniques of large corporations to cities. Reformers revised city charters in favor of stronger mayoral power and expanded use of appointed administrators and career civil servants. They drew up blueprints for model charters, ordinances, and zoning plans designed by experts trained in public administration.

Business and professional elites became the biggest boosters of structural reforms in urban government. Leading businessmen convinced the state legislature to replace the mayor-council government with a small board of commissioners. Each commissioner was elected at large, and each was responsible for a different city department. Under this plan, voters could more easily identify and hold accountable those responsible for city services. By 1917, nearly 500 cities had adopted the commission form of government.

Progressive politicians who focused on the human problems of the industrial city championed a different kind of reform, one based on changing policies rather than the political structure. In Cleveland, for example, wealthy businessman Thomas L. Johnson served as mayor from 1901 to 1909. He emphasized both efficiency and social welfare. His popular program included lower streetcar fares, public baths, milk and meat inspection, and an expanded park and playground system.

STATEHOUSE PROGRESSIVES

On the state level, progressives focused on two major reform themes that sometimes coexisted uneasily. On the one hand, they looked to make politics more open and accessible by pushing through procedural reforms. The *direct primary*, for example, promised to take the selection of electoral candidates out of the smoke-filled backrooms of party bosses and into the hands of party voters. In 1902, Oregon was the first state to adopt two other reforms: the *initiative*, the popular power to initiate legislation, and the **referendum**, the right to a popular vote on proposed legislation. Several states also adopted a related reform, the "Australian," or secret ballot, which took the mechanics of ballot printing and distribution from the parties and made it the responsibility of the government. California and other states also established the *recall*: the power to remove elected officials from office. And in 1913, the states and Congress ratified the Seventeenth Amendment, shifting the selection of U.S. senators from the state legislatures to direct election by voters. On the other hand, progressive activists sought to remove some decisions from the electoral process entirely. They believed that judgments about railroad regulations, improving a city's sewer system, or establishing tax rates might best be made by informed, unbiased experts appointed to boards and commissions charged with setting policy.

In Wisconsin, Republican Robert M. La Follette forged a coalition of angry farmers, small businessmen, and workers with his attacks on railroads and other large corporations. Leader of the progressive faction of the state Republicans, "Fighting Bob" won three terms as governor (1900–06), and then served as a U.S. senator until his death in 1925. As governor, he pushed through tougher corporate tax rates, a direct primary, an improved civil service code, and a railroad commission designed to regulate freight charges. La Follette used faculty experts at the University of Wisconsin to help research and write his bills. Other states began copying the "Wisconsin Idea," the application of academic scholarship and theory to the needs of the people.

In New York, Theodore Roosevelt won the governor's race in 1898, propelled by his fame as a Spanish-American War hero. Although supported by the Republican Party

QUICK REVIEW

Municipal Reform

- Urban reformers sought to break alliances between city bosses and business leaders.
- Urban reformers developed the concept of the city commission and the city manager.
- Business groups often promoted these reforms.

referendum   Submission of a law, proposed or already in effect, to a direct popular vote for approval or rejection.

machine, Roosevelt embraced the progressive view that the people's interest ought to be above partisan politics, and he used his personal popularity with voters to assert independence from party leaders. As governor, he held frequent press conferences to communicate more directly with voters and gain support for progressive legislation. Roosevelt's administration strengthened the state's civil service system, set wage and hour standards for state employees, raised teachers' salaries, and placed a franchise tax on corporations controlling public utilities. Roosevelt also championed progressive conservation measures by expanding New York's forest preserves and reforming the fish and game service.

Western progressives targeted railroads, mining and timber companies, and public utilities for reform. An alliance between middle-class progressives and working-class voters reflected growing disillusionment with the ideology of individualism that had helped pave the way for the rise of the big corporation. In 1910, California elected progressive attorney Hiram Johnson governor, and he then pushed through laws regulating utilities and child labor, mandating an eight-hour day for working-women, and providing a state-worker compensation plan.

In the South, progressives organized to control both greedy corporations and "unruly" citizens. Citizen groups, city boards of trade, and newspapers pressed reluctant legislators to use state power to regulate big business. Between 1905 and 1909, nearly every southern state moved to regulate railroads by mandating lower passenger and freight rates. Southern progressives also directed their energies at the related problems of child labor and educational reform. Led by reform-minded ministers Edgar Gardner Murphy and Alexander McKelway and drawing on the activism of white club women, reformers attacked child labor by focusing on the welfare of children and their mothers and emphasizing the degradation of "Anglo Saxons." In 1903, Alabama and North Carolina enacted the first state child labor laws, setting twelve as a minimum age for employment.

But southern progressivism was for white people only. Indeed, southern progressives believed that the disenfranchisement of black voters and the creation of a legally segregated public sphere were necessary preconditions for political and social reform. With African Americans removed from political life, white southern progressives argued, the direct primary system of nominating candidates would give white voters more influence. Between 1890 and 1910, southern states passed a welter of statutes specifying poll taxes, literacy tests, and property qualifications with the explicit goal of preventing voting by blacks. This systematic disenfranchisement of African American voters stripped black communities of any political power.

Southern progressives also supported the push toward a fully segregated public sphere. Between 1900 and 1910, southern states strengthened Jim Crow laws requiring separation of races in restaurants, streetcars, beaches, and theaters. Schools were separate but hardly equal. A 1916 Bureau of Education study found that per capita expenditures for education in southern states averaged $10.32 a year for white children and $2.89 for black children. And African American teachers received far lower salaries than their white counterparts. The legacy of southern progressivism was thus closely linked to the strengthening of the legal and institutional guarantees of white supremacy.

Contradictions in the progressive approach to political reform were not limited to the South. Undermining party control of voting and elections may have also weakened politicians' incentives to get out the vote. Greater reliance on city commissions and other experts meant less in the way of promised favors for voters, which may have also made voters less interested in elections. Tightening up on residency requirements and voter registration rules in the cities cut into turnout in immigrant and ethnic neighborhoods. The effort to make politics more open, nonpartisan, and voter friendly also led, ironically, to a decline in voter participation and interest around the country.

SOCIAL CONTROL AND ITS LIMITS

Many middle- and upper-class Protestant progressives feared that immigrants and large cities threatened the stability of American democracy. They worried that alien cultural practices were disrupting what they viewed as traditional American morality. Edward A. Ross's landmark work *Social Control* (1901), a book whose title became a key phrase in progressive thought, argued that society needed an "ethical elite" of citizens "who have at heart the general welfare and know what kinds of conduct will promote this welfare." Progressive efforts at social control usually required some form of coercion. This was the moralistic and frequently xenophobic side of progressivism, and it provided a powerful source of support for the regulation of drinking, prostitution, leisure activities, and schooling.

THE PROHIBITION MOVEMENT

During the last two decades of the nineteenth century, the Woman's Christian Temperance Union (WCTU) had grown into a powerful mass organization. The WCTU appealed especially to women angered by men who used alcohol and then abused their wives and children. It directed most of its work toward ending the production, sale, and consumption of alcohol. Local WCTU chapters put their energy into nontemperance activities as well, including homeless shelters, Sunday schools, prison reform, child nurseries, and woman suffrage. The WCTU thus provided women with a political forum in which they could fuse their traditional moral posture as guardians of the home with broader public concerns. By 1911, the WCTU, with a quarter million members, was the largest women's organization in American history.

Other **temperance groups** had a narrower focus. The Anti-Saloon League, founded in 1893, began by organizing local-option campaigns in which rural counties and small towns banned liquor within their geographical limits. It drew much of its financial support from local businessmen, who saw a link between closing a community's saloons and increasing the productivity of workers. The league was a one-issue pressure group that played effectively on antiurban and anti-immigrant prejudice.

The battle to ban alcohol revealed deep ethnic and cultural divides within America's urban communities. Opponents of alcohol were generally "pietists," who viewed the world from a position of moral absolutism. These included native-born, middle-class Protestants associated with evangelical churches, along with some old-stock Protestant immigrant denominations. Opponents of **prohibition** were generally "ritualists" with less arbitrary notions of personal morality. These were largely new-stock, working-class Catholic and Jewish immigrants, along with some Protestants, such as German Lutherans.

THE SOCIAL EVIL

Many of the same reformers who battled the saloon and drinking also engaged in efforts to eradicate prostitution. Crusades against "the social evil" had appeared at intervals throughout the nineteenth century, but they reached a new level of intensity between 1895 and 1920. Antiprostitution campaigns epitomized the diverse makeup and mixed motives of so much progressive reform. Male business and civic leaders joined forces with feminists, social workers, and clergy to eradicate "commercialized vice."

Between 1908 and 1914, exposés of the "white slave traffic" became a national sensation. Dozens of books, articles, and motion pictures alleged an international conspiracy to seduce and sell girls into prostitution. Most of these materials exaggerated the practices they attacked. They also made foreigners, especially Jews and southern Europeans, scapegoats for the sexual anxieties of native-born whites. In 1910, Congress passed legislation that permitted the deportation of foreign-born prostitutes or any

HOW DID tensions between social justice and social control divide progressives?

QUICK REVIEW

Women's Christian Temperance Union

♦ The Women's Christian Temperance Union (WCTU) grew into a powerful mass organization in the late nineteenth century.

♦ Local chapters included non-temperance activities in their reform efforts.

♦ By 1911, the WCTU had a quarter million members.

●◄●―Read the **Document**

Report of the Vice Commission, Louisville, Kentucky (1915) at **www.myhistorylab.com**

temperance groups   Groups dedicated to reducing the sale and consumption of alcohol.

prohibition   A ban on the production, sale, and consumption of liquor, achieved temporarily through state laws and the Eighteenth Amendment.

foreigner convicted of procuring or employing them. That same year, the Mann Act made it a federal offense to transport women across state lines for "immoral purposes."

Reformers had trouble believing that any woman would freely choose to be a prostitute; such a choice was antithetical to conventional notions of female purity and sexuality. But for wage-earning women, prostitution was a rational choice in a world of limited opportunities. The anti-vice crusades succeeded in closing down many urban red-light districts and larger brothels, but the streetwalker and call girl, who were more vulnerable to harassment and control by policemen and pimps, replaced them. Rather than eliminating prostitution, reform efforts transformed the organization of the sex trade.

THE REDEMPTION OF LEISURE

Progressives faced a thorny issue in the growing popularity of commercial entertainment. For large numbers of working-class adults and children, leisure meant time and money spent at vaudeville and burlesque theaters, amusement parks, dance halls, and motion picture houses. For many cultural traditionalists, the flood of new urban commercial amusements posed a grave threat. One distinctively progressive response was the Playgrounds Movement. Los Angeles created the nation's first urban Department of Playgrounds in 1904, and proponents nationwide saw municipal playgrounds as a way to offer free, healthy, outdoor recreation for city children.

By 1908, movies had become the most popular form of cheap entertainment in America. One survey estimated that 11,500 movie theaters attracted 5 million patrons each day. Early movies were most popular in the tenement and immigrant districts of big cities and with children. As the films themselves became more sophisticated and as "movie palaces" began to replace cheap storefront theaters, the new medium attracted a large middle-class clientele as well.

Progressive reformers seized the chance to help regulate the new medium as a way of improving the commercial recreation of the urban poor. In 1909, New York City movie producers and exhibitors joined with the reform-minded People's Institute to establish the voluntary National Board of Censorship (NBC). A revolving group of civic activists reviewed new movies, passed them, suggested changes, or condemned them. Local censoring committees all over the nation subscribed to the board's weekly bulletin. They aimed at achieving what John Collier of the NBC called "the redemption of leisure."

STANDARDIZING EDUCATION

Along with reading, writing, and mathematics, schools inculcated patriotism, piety, and respect for authority. Progressive educators looked to the public school primarily as an agent of "Americanization." Elwood Cubberley, a leading educational reformer, expressed the view that schools could be the vehicle by which immigrant children could break free of the parochial ethnic neighborhood. "Our task," he argued in *Changing Conceptions of Education* (1909), "is to break up these groups or settlements, to assimilate and amalgamate these people as a part of our American race, and to implant in their children, so far as can be done, the Anglo-Saxon conception of righteousness, law and order, and popular government."

The most important educational trends in these years were the expansion and bureaucratization of the nation's public school systems. Children began school earlier and stayed there longer. Kindergartens spread rapidly in large cities. By 1918, every state had some form of compulsory school attendance. High schools also multiplied, extending the school's influence beyond the traditional grammar school curriculum. In 1890, only 4 percent of the nation's youth between fourteen and seventeen were enrolled in school; by 1930, the figure was 47 percent.

Watch the Video

What Was the Progressive Education Movement? at **www.myhistorylab.com**

High schools multiplied, reflecting a growing belief that schools should be comprehensive, multifunctional institutions. To support vocational training in high schools, the Smith-Hughes Act of 1917 provided federal grants and set up a Federal Board for Vocational Education.

CHALLENGES TO PROGRESSIVISM

While most progressive reformers had roots in Protestantism and the middle-class professions, other Americans vigorously challenged their political vision. Organized workers often invoked progressive rhetoric and ideals but for quite different, sometimes radical, ends. The Industrial Revolution, which had begun transforming American life and labor in the nineteenth century, reached maturity in the early twentieth century. The world of the industrial worker included large manufacturing towns in New England; barren mining settlements in the West; primitive lumber and turpentine camps in the South; steelmaking and coal-mining cities in Pennsylvania and Ohio; and densely packed immigrant ghettos from New York to San Francisco, where workers toiled in garment-trade sweatshops.

All these industrial workers shared the need to sell their labor for wages in order to survive. At the same time, differences in skill, ethnicity, and race proved powerful barriers to efforts at organizing trade unions that could bargain for improved wages and working conditions. So, too, did the economic and political power of the large corporations that dominated much of American industry. Yet these years saw many labor struggles that created effective trade unions or laid the groundwork for others. Industrial workers also became a force in local and national politics, adding a chorus of insistent voices to the calls for social justice.

WHAT GROUPS challenged the progressive vision of politics?

Newly landed European immigrant families on the dock at Ellis Island in New York Harbor, 1900. Originally a black-and-white photograph, this image was later color tinted for reproduction as a postcard or book illustration.

THE NEW GLOBAL IMMIGRATION

The first two decades of the twentieth century saw a profound transformation in both the size and scope of immigration, as over 14.5 million people from all over the world made their way to the United States. In the nineteenth century, much of the overseas migration had come from the industrial districts of northern and western Europe. By contrast, roughly 60 percent of early twentieth century immigrants came from southern and eastern Europe. Unlike their predecessors, nearly all the new immigrants lacked industrial skills. They thus entered the bottom ranks of factories, mines, mills, and sweatshops; by the eve of World War I, close to 60 percent of the industrial labor force was foreign-born (see Map 21.1).

These new immigrants had been driven from their European farms and towns by several forces, including the undermining of subsistence farming by commercial agriculture; a falling death rate that brought a shortage of land; and religious and political persecution. American corporations also sent agents to recruit cheap labor. Except for Jewish immigrants, a majority of whom fled virulent anti-Semitism in Russia and Poland, most newcomers planned on earning a stake and then returning home.

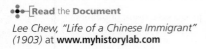

Read the Document

Lee Chew, "Life of a Chinese Immigrant"
(1903) at **www.myhistorylab.com**

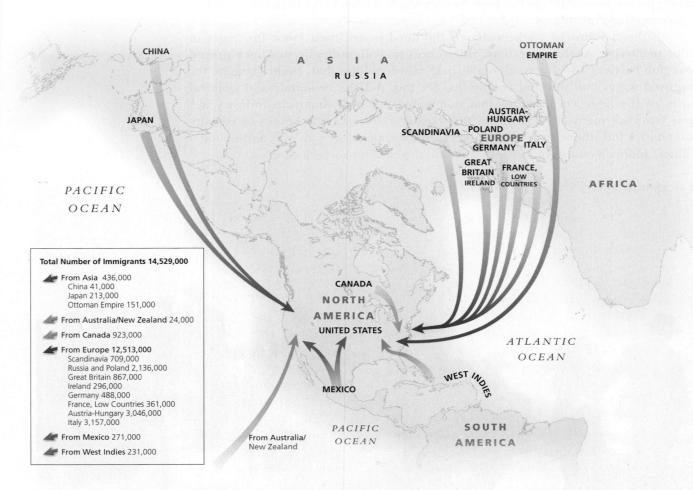

Total Number of Immigrants 14,529,000

From Asia 436,000
    China 41,000
    Japan 213,000
    Ottoman Empire 151,000

From Australia/New Zealand 24,000

From Canada 923,000

From Europe 12,513,000
    Scandinavia 709,000
    Russia and Poland 2,136,000
    Great Britain 867,000
    Ireland 296,000
    Germany 488,000
    France, Low Countries 361,000
    Austria-Hungary 3,046,000
    Italy 3,157,000

From Mexico 271,000

From West Indies 231,000

MAP 21.1
Immigration to the United States, 1901–1920

Adapted from Historical Statistics of the United States, Volume 1, Part A Population, Chapter Ad, International Migration (NY, 2006, Millennial Edition).

WHAT FORCES propelled so many people to emigrate from European countries to the United States?

The decision to emigrate usually occurred through social networks—people linked by kinship, personal acquaintance, and work experience. These "chains," extending from places of origin to specific destinations in the United States, helped immigrants cope with the considerable risks entailed by the long and difficult journey.

The low-paid, backbreaking work in basic industry became nearly the exclusive preserve of the new immigrants. In 1907, of the 14,359 common laborers employed at Pittsburgh's U.S. Steel mills, 11,694 were eastern Europeans. One-third of the immigrant steelworkers were single, and among married men who had been in the country less than five years, about two-thirds reported that their wives were still in Europe. Workers with families generally supplemented their incomes by taking in single men as boarders.

Not all of the recent immigrants came from Europe, as hemispheric migration increased sharply as well. Over 900,000 came from Canada between 1900 and 1920, including some 300,000 French Canadians, settling mostly in New England. The pull of jobs in New England's textile industry, along with its physical proximity, attracted male farmers and laborers unable to make a living in the rural districts of Quebec. Roughly one-third of female immigrants were domestic servants looking for the higher pay and greater independence associated with factory labor.

Mexican immigration also grew in these years, providing a critical source of labor for the West's farms, railroads, and mines. Between 1900 and 1920, the number of people of Mexican descent living and working in the United States nearly quadrupled from about 100,000 to 400,000. Economic and political crises spurred tens of thousands of Mexico's rural and urban poor to emigrate north. Large numbers of seasonal agricultural workers regularly came up from Mexico to work in the expanding sugar beet industry and then returned. But a number of substantial resident Mexican communities also emerged in the early twentieth century.

Throughout Texas, California, New Mexico, Arizona, and Colorado, western cities developed *barrios*, distinct communities of Mexicans. Mexican immigrants attracted by jobs in the smelting industry made El Paso the most thoroughly Mexican city in the United States. In southern California, labor agents for railroads recruited Mexicans to work on building new interurban lines around Los Angeles.

The Caribbean-born population of the United States grew significantly as well; approximately 230,000 immigrants from that region arrived between 1900 and 1920. New York City was the most popular destination for Caribbean immigrants, attracting tens of thousands who passed through Ellis Island in search of better paying jobs and career opportunities. By 1930, almost one-quarter of black Harlem was of Caribbean origin, and as many as one-third of all of New York's black professionals and business owners came from the ranks of Caribbean immigrants. These early Caribbean immigrants brought with them notably higher levels of literacy, formal education, and occupational skills, compared to European immigrants. Professionals and entrepreneurs from Barbados, Jamaica, Trinidad, and other islands flocked to New York. Yet, like native-born African Americans, Caribbean immigrants and their children often endured racial discrimination in their efforts to join craft unions, establish credit with banks, or integrate neighborhoods. Caribbean migration to the United States would not reach mass levels until after World War II, but the first wave of early twentieth-century immigrants laid the foundation for Afro-Caribbean communities in New York and elsewhere.

Over 200,000 Japanese also entered the United States during these decades. The vast majority were young men working as contract laborers in the West, mainly in California. American law prevented Japanese immigrants from obtaining American citizenship because they were not white. This legal discrimination, along with informal exclusion from many occupations, forced the Japanese to create niches for themselves within local economies. Most Japanese settled near Los Angeles, where they established small communities centered on fishing, truck farming, and the flower and nursery business.

URBAN GHETTOS

In large cities, new immigrant communities took the form of densely packed ghettos. By 1920, immigrants and their children constituted almost 60 percent of the population of cities over 100,000. They were an even larger percentage in major industrial centers such as Chicago, Pittsburgh, Philadelphia, and New York. The sheer size and dynamism of these cities made the immigrant experience more complex than in smaller cities and more isolated communities.

New York City had become the center of both Jewish immigration and America's huge ready-to-wear clothing industry. The city's Jewish population was 1.4 million in 1915, almost 30 percent of its inhabitants. In small factories, lofts, and tenement apartments, some 200,000 people, most of them Jews, some of them Italians, worked in the clothing trades. Most of the industry operated on the grueling piece-rate, or task, system, in which manufacturers and subcontractors paid individuals or teams of workers to complete a certain quota of labor within a specific time.

The garment industry was highly seasonal. A typical workweek was sixty hours, with seventy common during the busy season. But there were long stretches of unemployment in slack times. Often forced to work in cramped, dirty, and badly lit rooms, garment workers strained under a system in which time equaled money. In November 1909, two New York garment manufacturers responded to strikes by unskilled women workers by hiring thugs and prostitutes to beat up pickets. The strikers won the support of the Women's Trade Union League, a group of sympathetic female reformers that included Lillian Wald, Mary Dreier, and prominent society figures. The Uprising of the 20,000, as it became known, swept through the city's garment district. The strikers demanded union recognition, better wages, and safer and more sanitary conditions. They drew support from thousands of suffragists, trade unionists, and sympathetic middle-class women as well. After three cold months on the picket line, the strikers returned to work without union recognition. But the International Ladies Garment Workers Union (ILGWU), founded in 1900, did gain strength and negotiated contracts with some of the city's shirtwaist makers. The strike was an important breakthrough in the drive to organize unskilled workers into industrial unions.

On March 25, 1911, the issues raised by the strike took on new urgency when a fire raced through three floors of the Triangle Shirtwaist Company. As the flames spread, workers found themselves trapped by exit doors that had been locked from the outside. Within half an hour, 146 people, mostly young Jewish women, had been killed by smoke or had leaped to their deaths. In the bitter aftermath, women progressives led by Florence Kelley and Frances Perkins of the National Consumers' League joined with Tammany Hall leaders to create a New York State Factory Investigation Commission. Under Perkins's vigorous leadership, the commission conducted an unprecedented round of public hearings and on-site inspections, leading to a series of state laws that dramatically improved safety conditions and limited the hours for working women and children.

COMPANY TOWNS

Immigrant industrial workers and their families often established their communities in a company town, where a single large corporation was dominant. Workers had little or no influence over the economic and political institutions of these cities. In the more isolated company towns, residents often had no alternative but to buy their food, clothing, and supplies at company stores, usually for exorbitantly high

◀▶─Read the Document

Letters to the Jewish Daily Forward (1906–1907) at **www.myhistorylab.com**

QUICK REVIEW

Triangle Shirtwaist Fire

♦ 1911: fire kills 146 workers.

♦ Managers had locked the exits.

♦ Tragedy led to the enactment of new industrial safety laws.

New York City police set up this makeshift morgue to help identify victims of the disastrous Triangle Shirtwaist Company fire, March 25, 1911. Unable to open the locked doors of the sweatshop and desperate to escape from smoke and flames, many of the 146 who died had leaped eight stories to their death.

prices. They did maintain some community control in other ways. Family and kin networks, ethnic lodges, saloons, benefit societies, churches and synagogues, and musical groups affirmed traditional forms of community in a setting governed by individualism and private capital.

On the job, modern machinery and industrial discipline meant high rates of injury and death. A 1910 study of work accidents revealed that nearly a fourth of all new steelworkers were killed or injured each year. Mutual aid associations, organized around ethnic groups, offered some protection through cheap insurance and death benefits.

In steel and coal towns, women not only maintained the household and raised the children, but they also boosted the family income by taking in boarders, sewing, and laundry. Many women also tended gardens and raised chickens, rabbits, and goats. Their produce and income helped reduce dependence on the company store. Working-class women felt the burdens of housework more heavily than their middle-class sisters. The daily drudgery endured by working-class women far outlasted the "man-killing" shifts worked by their husbands. Many women struggled with the effects of their husbands' excessive drinking and faced early widowhood.

The power of large corporations in the life of company towns was most evident among the mining communities of the West, as was violent labor conflict. The Colorado Fuel and Iron Company (CFI) employed roughly half of the 8,000 coal miners who labored in that state's mines. In mining towns such as Ludlow and Trinidad, the CFI thoroughly dominated the lives of miners and their families. By the early twentieth century, new immigrants, such as Italians, Greeks, Slavs, and Mexicans, composed a majority of the population in these western mining communities.

In September 1913, the United Mine Workers led a strike in the Colorado coalfields, calling for improved safety, higher wages, and recognition of the union. Thousands of miners' families moved out of company housing and into makeshift tent colonies provided by the union. In October, Governor Elias Ammons ordered the Colorado National Guard into the tense strike region to keep order. By spring, the strike had bankrupted the state, forcing the governor to remove most of the troops. The coal companies then brought in large numbers of private mine guards who were extremely hostile toward the strikers. On April 20, 1914, a combination of guardsmen and private guards surrounded the largest of the tent colonies at Ludlow, where more than a thousand mine families lived. A shot rang out (each side accused the other of firing), and a pitched battle ensued that lasted until the poorly armed miners ran out of ammunition. At dusk, the troops burned the tent village to the ground, routing the families and killing fourteen, eleven of them children. Enraged strikers attacked mines throughout southern Colorado in an armed rebellion that lasted ten days, until President Woodrow Wilson ordered the U.S. Army into the region. News of the Ludlow Massacre shocked millions and aroused widespread protests and demonstrations against the policies of Colorado Fuel and Iron and its owner, John D. Rockefeller Jr.

COMPETING VISIONS OF UNIONISM: THE AFL AND THE IWW

Following the depression of the 1890s, the American Federation of Labor (AFL) emerged as the strongest and most stable organization of workers. Union membership climbed from under 500,000 in 1897 to 1.7 million by 1904. Most of this growth took place in AFL affiliates in coal mining, the building trades, transportation, and machine shops. The national unions—the United Mine Workers of America, the Brotherhood of Carpenters and Joiners, the International Association of Machinists—represented workers of specific occupations in collective bargaining. Trade autonomy and exclusive jurisdiction were the ruling principles within the AFL. But the strength of craft organization also gave rise to weakness. Each trade looked mainly to the welfare of its own, and many explicitly barred women and African Americans from membership.

Read the **Document**

Samuel Gompers, The American Labor Movement (1914) at
www.myhistorylab.com

open shop The name for a workplace where unions were not allowed.

Wobblies Popular name for the members of the Industrial Workers of the World (IWW).

AFL unions had a difficult time holding on to their gains. Economic slumps, technological changes, and aggressive counterattacks by employer organizations could be devastating. Trade associations using management-controlled efficiency drives fought union efforts to regulate output and shop practices. The National Association of Manufacturers (NAM), a group of smaller industrialists founded in 1903, launched an "**open shop**" campaign to eradicate unions altogether. Unfriendly judicial decisions also hurt organizing efforts.

Some workers developed more radical visions of labor organizing. In Idaho, Montana, and Colorado, miners suffered from low wages, poor food, and primitive sanitation, as well as injuries and death from frequent cave-ins and explosions. The Western Federation of Miners (WFM) had gained strength in the metal mining regions of the West by leading several strikes marred by violence. In 1899, during a strike in the silver mining district of Coeur d'Alene, Idaho, the Bunker Hill and Sullivan Mining Company had enraged the miners by hiring armed detectives and firing all union members. Desperate miners retaliated by destroying a company mill with dynamite. Idaho's governor declared martial law and obtained federal troops to enforce it. In a pattern that would become familiar in western labor relations, the soldiers served as strikebreakers, rounding up hundreds of miners and imprisoning them for months in makeshift bullpens.

In response to the brutal realities of labor organizing in the West, most WFM leaders embraced socialism and industrial unionism. In 1905, leaders of the WFM, the Socialist Party, and various radical groups gathered in Chicago to found the Industrial Workers of the World (IWW).

William D. "Big Bill" Haywood, an imposing, one-eyed, hardrock miner, emerged as the most influential and flamboyant spokesman for the IWW, or **Wobblies**, as they were called. Haywood, a charismatic speaker and effective organizer, regularly denounced the AFL for its conservative emphasis on organizing skilled workers by trade. He insisted that the IWW would exclude no one from its ranks. The Wobblies concentrated their efforts on miners, lumberjacks, sailors, "harvest stiffs," and other casual laborers.

The IWW briefly became a force among eastern industrial workers, tapping the rage and growing militance of immigrants and the unskilled. In 1909, an IWW-led steel strike at McKees Rocks, Pennsylvania, challenged the power of U.S. Steel. In the 1912 "Bread and Roses" strike in Lawrence, Massachusetts, IWW organizers turned a spontaneous walkout of textile workers into a successful struggle for union recognition. Wobbly leaders such as Haywood, Elizabeth Gurley Flynn, and Joseph Ettor used class-conscious rhetoric and multilingual appeals to forge unity among the ethnically diverse Lawrence workforce of 25,000.

The IWW failed to establish permanent organizations in the eastern cities, but it remained a force in the lumber camps, mines, and wheat fields of the West. But when the United States entered World War I, the Justice Department used the IWW's anticapitalist rhetoric and antiwar stance to crush it.

REBELS IN BOHEMIA

During the 1910s, a small but influential community of painters, journalists, poets, social workers, lawyers, and political activists coalesced in the New York City neighborhood of Greenwich Village. These cultural radicals, nearly all of middle-class backgrounds and hailing from provincial American towns, shared a deep sympathy toward the struggles of

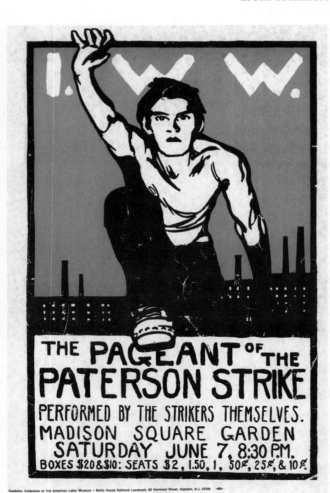

Publicity poster for the 1913 pageant, organized by John Reed and other Greenwich Village radicals, supporting the cause of striking silk workers in Paterson, New Jersey. This poster drew on aesthetic styles associated with the Industrial Workers of the World, typically including a heroic, larger-than-life image of a factory laborer.

labor, a passion for modern art, and an affinity for socialism and anarchism. Unlike most progressives, however, especially those from small towns and the nation's hinterlands, the "Village bohemians," particularly the women among them, challenged accepted middle-class morality and assumptions.

The Village scene was unique, if fleeting. The neighborhood offered cheap rents, studio space, and good ethnic restaurants, and it was close to the exciting political and labor activism of Manhattan's Lower East Side. The worldview of the Village's **bohemian** community found expression in *The Masses*, a monthly magazine founded in 1911. "The broad purpose of *The Masses*," wrote John Reed, one of its leading writers, "is a social one—to everlastingly attack old systems, old morals, old prejudices—the whole weight of outworn thought that dead men have saddled upon us." For some, Greenwich Village offered a chance to experiment with sexual relationships or work arrangements. For others, it was an escape from small-town conformity, or a haven for like-minded artists and activists. Yet the Village bohemians were united in their search for a new sense of community. Intellectuals and artists, as well as workers, feeling alienated from the rest of society, sought shelter in the collective life and close-knit social relations of the Village community.

WOMEN'S MOVEMENTS AND BLACK ACTIVISM

Like working-class radicals, politically engaged women and African American activists often found themselves at odds with more moderate and mainstream progressive reformers. They contested both gender and racial assumptions inherited from the nineteenth century. Women were at the forefront of several campaigns, such as the settlement house movement, prohibition, suffrage, and birth control. Millions of others took an active role in new women's associations that combined self-help and social mission.

In fighting racial discrimination, African Americans had a more difficult task. As racism gained ground in the political and cultural spheres, black progressives fought defensively to prevent the rights they had secured during Reconstruction from being further undermined.

THE NEW WOMAN

A steady proliferation of women's organizations attracted growing numbers of educated, middle-class women. With more men working in offices, more children attending school, and family size declining, the middle-class home was emptier. At the same time, more middle-class women were graduating from high school and college. In 1870, only 1 percent of college-age Americans had attended college, about 20 percent of them women; by 1910, about 5 percent of college-age Americans attended college, but the proportion of women among them had doubled to 40 percent.

Single-sex clubs brought middle-class women into the public sphere by celebrating the distinctive strengths associated with women's culture: cooperation, uplift, service. The women's club movement combined an earlier focus on self-improvement and intellectual pursuits with newer benevolent efforts on behalf of working women and children. The Buffalo Union, for example, sponsored art lectures for housewives and classes in typing, stenography, and bookkeeping for young working women. It also maintained a library, set up a "noon rest" downtown where women could eat lunch, and ran a school for training domestics.

For many middle-class women, the club movement provided a new kind of female-centered community. Club activity often led members to participate in other civic ventures, particularly "child-saving" reforms, such as child labor laws and mothers' pensions. Some took up the cause of working-class women, fighting for protective legislation and offering aid to trade unions. As wives and daughters of influential and well-off men in their communities, club women had access to funds and could generate support for projects they undertook.

WHAT NEW forms of activism emerged among the working class, women, and African Americans?

•◦•⌐**Read** the **Document**
Helen M. Todd, "Getting Out the Vote" (1911) at **www.myhistorylab.com**

bohemian   Artistic individual who lives with disregard for the conventional rules of behavior.

Other women's associations made even more explicit efforts to bridge class lines between middle-class homemakers and working-class women. The National Consumers' League (NCL), started in 1898 by Maud Nathan and Josephine Lowell, sponsored a "white label" campaign in which manufacturers who met safety and sanitary standards could put NCL labels on their food and clothing. Under the dynamic leadership of Florence Kelley, the NCL publicized labor abuses in department stores and lobbied for maximum-hour and minimum-wage laws in state legislatures.

BIRTH CONTROL

The phrase "birth control," coined by Margaret Sanger around 1913, described her campaign to provide contraceptive information and devices for women. In 1910, Sanger was a thirty-year-old nurse and housewife living with her husband and three children in a New York City suburb. Excited by a socialist lecture she had attended, she convinced her husband to move to the city. She became an organizer for the IWW, and in 1912, she wrote a series of articles on female sexuality for a socialist newspaper.

When postal officials confiscated the paper for violating obscenity laws, Sanger left for Europe to learn more about contraception. She returned to New York determined to challenge the obscenity statutes with her own magazine, the *Woman Rebel*. When she distributed her pamphlet *Family Limitation*, postal inspectors confiscated copies and she found herself facing forty-five years in prison. In October 1914, she fled to Europe again.

An older generation of feminists had advocated "voluntary motherhood," or the right to say no to a husband's sexual demands. The new birth control advocates embraced contraception as a way of advancing sexual freedom for middle-class women, as well as responding to the misery of those working-class women who bore numerous children while living in poverty. Sanger returned to the United States in October 1915. After the government

A supportive crowd surrounds birth control pioneer Margaret Sanger and her sister, Ethel Byrne, as they leave the Court of Special Services in New York City in 1917. Police had recently closed Sanger's first birth control clinic in the immigrant neighborhood of Brownsville, New York, and Sanger herself had spent a month in jail.

dropped the obscenity charges, she embarked on a national speaking tour. In 1916, she again defied the law by opening a birth control clinic in a working-class neighborhood in Brooklyn and offering birth control information without a physician present. Arrested and jailed, she gained more publicity for her crusade. Within a few years, birth control leagues and clinics could be found in every major city and most large towns in the country.

RACISM AND ACCOMMODATION

At the turn of the century, four-fifths of the nation's 10 million African Americans still lived in the South, where most eked out a living working in agriculture. In the cities, most blacks were relegated to menial jobs, but a small African American middle class of entrepreneurs and professionals gained a foothold by selling services and products to the black community. They all confronted a racism that was growing in both intensity and influence in American politics and culture. White racism came in many variants and had evolved significantly since slavery days. The more virulent strains, influenced by Darwin's evolutionary theory, held that blacks were genetically predisposed to vice, crime, and disease and destined to lose the struggle for existence with whites.

African Americans also endured a deeply racist popular culture that made hateful stereotypes of black people a normal feature of political debate and everyday life. In northern cities "coon songs," based on gross caricatures of black life, were extremely popular in theaters and as sheet music. These songs reduced African Americans to creatures of pure appetite—for food, sex, alcohol, and violence. Southern progressives articulated a more moderate racial philosophy. They also assumed the innate inferiority of blacks, but they believed that black progress was necessary to achieve the economic and political progress associated with a vision of the New South.

Amid this political and cultural climate, Booker T. Washington won recognition as the most influential black leader of the day. Born a slave in 1856, Washington was educated at Hampton Institute in Virginia, one of the first freedmen's schools devoted to industrial education. In 1881, he founded Tuskegee Institute, a black school in Alabama devoted to industrial and moral education. He became the leading spokesman for racial accommodation, urging blacks to focus on economic improvement and self-reliance, as opposed to political and civil rights. In an 1895 speech delivered at the Cotton States Exposition in Atlanta, Washington outlined the key themes of accommodationist philosophy. Washington told black people, they should focus on improving their vocational skills as industrial workers and farmers. "In all things that are purely social," he told attentive whites, "we can be as separate as the fingers, yet one as the hand in all things essential to mutual progress."

Washington's message won him the financial backing of leading white philanthropists and the respect of progressive whites. But Washington also gained a large following among African Americans, especially those who aspired to business success. With the help of Andrew Carnegie, he founded the National Negro Business League to preach the virtue of black business development in black communities.

Washington also had a decisive influence on the flow of private funds to black schools in the South. Publicly, he insisted that "agitation of questions of social equality is the extremest folly." Privately, Washington also spent money and worked behind the scenes trying to halt disfranchisement and segregation.

RACIAL JUSTICE, THE NAACP, AND BLACK WOMEN'S ACTIVISM

In the early 1900s, scholar and activist W. E. B. Du Bois created a significant alternative to Washington's leadership. A product of the black middle class, Du Bois had been educated at Fisk University and Harvard, where in 1895, he became the first African American to receive a PhD. In *The Souls of Black Folk* (1903), Du Bois declared prophetically that "the problem of the twentieth century is the problem of the color line." Through essays on black history, culture, education, and politics, Du Bois explored the concept of "double consciousness." Black people, he argued, would always feel the

•◦•—Read the Document

History Bookshelf: Booker T. Washington, Up From Slavery *(1901)* at **www.myhistorylab.com**

•◦•—Read the Document

History Bookshelf: W.E.B. DuBois, The Souls of Black Folk *(1903)* at **www.myhistorylab.com**

((•◦•—Hear the Audio

The Crisis *Magazine by W. E.B. DuBois* at **www.myhistorylab.com**

In July 1905, a group of African American leaders met in Niagara Falls, Ontario, to protest legal segregation and the denial of civil rights to the nation's black population. This portrait was taken against a studio backdrop of the falls. In 1909, the leader of the Niagara movement, W. E. B. Du Bois (second from right, middle row), founded and edited *The Crisis*, the influential monthly journal of the National Association for the Advancement of Colored People.
Photographs and Prints Division, Schomburg Center for Research in Black Culture, The New York Public Library, Astor, Lenox and Tilden Foundations.

((•─ **Hear** the **Audio**

The Progress of Colored Women by Mary Church Terrell at **www.myhistorylab.com**

WHAT ROLE did Theodore Roosevelt envision the federal government playing in national life?

Niagara movement African American group organized in 1905 to promote racial integration, civil and political rights, and equal access to economic opportunity.

National Association for the Advancement of Colored People Organization co-founded by W. E. B. Du Bois in 1910 dedicated to restoring African American political and social rights.

tension between an African heritage and their desire to assimilate as Americans. *Souls* represented the first effort to embrace African American culture as a source of collective black strength and something worth preserving.

The black community, he argued, must fight for the right to vote, for civic equality, and for higher education for the "talented tenth" of their youth. In 1905, Du Bois and editor William Monroe Trotter brought together a group of educated black men in Niagara Falls, Ontario, to oppose Washington's conciliatory views. The **Niagara movement** protested legal segregation, the exclusion of blacks from labor unions, and the curtailment of voting and other civil rights.

The Niagara movement failed to generate much change. But in 1909, many of its members, led by Du Bois, attended a National Negro Conference held at the Henry Street Settlement in New York. The group included a number of white progressives sympathetic to the idea of challenging Washington's philosophy. A new interracial organization emerged from this conference, the **National Association for the Advancement of Colored People**. Du Bois, the only black officer of the original NAACP, founded and edited *The Crisis*, the influential NAACP monthly journal. For the next several decades, the NAACP would lead struggles to overturn legal and economic barriers to equal opportunity.

The disenfranchisement of black voters in the South severely curtailed African American political influence. In response, African American women created new strategies to challenge white supremacy and improve life in their communities. Founded in 1900, the Women's Convention of the National Baptist Convention, the largest black denomination in the United States, offered African American women a new public space to pursue reform work and "racial uplift." They organized settlement houses and built playgrounds; they created daycare facilities and kindergartens; they campaigned for women's suffrage, temperance, and advances in public health.

NATIONAL PROGRESSIVISM

The progressive impulse had begun at local levels and percolated up. On the presidential level, both Republican Theodore Roosevelt and Democrat Woodrow Wilson laid claim to the progressive mantle—a good example of how on the national level, progressivism animated many perspectives. In their pursuit of reform agendas, both significantly reshaped the office of the president. As progressivism moved to Washington, nationally organized interest groups and public opinion began to rival the influence of the old political parties in shaping the political landscape.

THEODORE ROOSEVELT AND PRESIDENTIAL ACTIVISM

The assassination of William McKinley in 1901 made forty-two-year-old Theodore Roosevelt the youngest man to ever hold the office of president. Roosevelt viewed the presidency as a "bully pulpit," a platform from which he could exhort Americans to reform their society. Roosevelt preached the virtues of "the strenuous life," and he believed that educated and wealthy Americans had a special responsibility to serve, guide, and inspire those less fortunate. He also believed the nation was at a crossroads that required the national state to play a more active role in curbing the power of wealthy industrialists.

Roosevelt made key contributions to national progressivism and to changing the office of the president. He knew how to inspire and guide public opinion. In 1902, Roosevelt demonstrated his unique style of activism when he personally intervened in a bitter dispute in the anthracite coal industry. Using public calls for conciliation, a series of White House meetings, and private pressure on the mine owners, Roosevelt secured an arbitrated settlement that won better pay and working conditions for the miners but without recognition of their union. Roosevelt also pushed for efficient government as the solution to social problems. Unlike most nineteenth-century Republicans, who had largely ignored economic and social inequalities, Roosevelt frankly acknowledged them. Administrative agencies run by experts, he believed, could find rational solutions that would satisfy everyone.

TRUST-BUSTING AND REGULATION

One of the first issues Roosevelt faced was growing public concern with the rapid business consolidations taking place in the American economy. In 1902, he directed the Justice Department to begin a series of prosecutions under the **Sherman Antitrust Act**. The first target was the Northern Securities Company, a huge merger of transcontinental railroads. The deal would have created a giant holding company controlling nearly all the long-distance rail lines from Chicago to California. In *Northern Securities* v. *United States* (1904), the Supreme Court held that the stock transactions constituted an illegal combination in restraint of interstate commerce.

This case established Roosevelt's reputation as a "trustbuster." During his two terms, the Justice Department filed forty-three cases under the Sherman Antitrust Act to restrain or dissolve business monopolies. These included actions against the so-called tobacco and beef trusts and the Standard Oil Company. Roosevelt viewed these suits as necessary to publicize the issue and assert the federal government's ultimate authority over big business. But he did not really believe in the need to break up large corporations. Indeed, many of the legal cases against trusts were dropped after business executives met privately with Roosevelt in the White House. What was most important, in T. R.'s view, was to insist on the right and power of the federal government to reign in excessive corporate behavior.

After easily defeating Democrat Alton B. Parker in the 1904 election, Roosevelt felt more secure in pushing for regulatory legislation. In 1906, Roosevelt responded to public pressure for greater government intervention and, overcoming objections from a conservative Congress, signed three important measures into law. The **Hepburn Act** strengthened the Interstate Commerce Commission (ICC), established in 1887 as the first independent regulatory agency, by authorizing it to set maximum railroad rates and inspect financial records.

Two other laws passed in 1906 also expanded the regulatory power of the federal government. The battles surrounding these reforms demonstrate how progressive measures often attracted supporters with competing motives. The **Pure Food and Drug Act** established the Food and Drug Administration (FDA), which tested and approved drugs before they went on the market. The Meat Inspection Act empowered the Department of Agriculture to inspect and label meat products. In both cases, supporters hailed the new laws as providing consumer protection against adulterated or fraudulently labeled food and drugs.

Regulatory legislation found advocates among American big business as well. Large meatpackers such as Swift and Armour

Read the Document

Theodore Roosevelt, "The Strenuous Life" (1900) at **www.myhistorylab.com**

Sherman Antitrust Act   The first federal antitrust measure, passed in 1890; sought to promote economic competition by prohibiting business combinations in restraint of trade or commerce.

Hepburn Act   Act that strengthened the Interstate Commerce Commission (ICC) by authorizing it to set maximum railroad rates and inspect financial records.

Pure Food and Drug Act   Act that established the Food and Drug Administration (FDA), which tested and approved drugs before they went on the market.

This 1909 cartoon by Clifton Berryman depicts President Theodore Roosevelt slaying those trusts he considered "bad" for the public interest, while restraining those whose business practices he considered "good" for the economy. The image also plays on T. R.'s well-publicized fondness for big-game hunting.

strongly supported stricter federal regulation as a way to drive out smaller companies that could not meet tougher standards. The new laws also helped American packers compete more profitably in the European export market by giving their meat the official seal of federal inspectors. Large pharmaceutical manufacturers similarly supported new regulations that would eliminate competitors and patent medicine suppliers. Thus, these reforms won support from large corporate interests that viewed stronger federal regulation as a strategy for consolidating their economic power.

THE BIRTH OF ENVIRONMENTALISM

As a naturalist and outdoorsman, Theodore Roosevelt also believed in the need for government regulation of the natural environment. The conservation of forest and water resources, he argued, was a national problem of vital import. In 1905, he created the U.S. Forest Service and named conservationist Gifford Pinchot to head it. Pinchot recruited a force of forest rangers to manage the reserves. By 1909, total timber and forest reserves had increased from 45 to 195 million acres, and more than 80 million acres of mineral lands had been withdrawn from public sale.

On the broad issue of managing America's natural resources, the Roosevelt administration took the middle ground between preservation and unrestricted commercial development. But other voices championed a more radical vision of conservation, emphasizing the preservation of wilderness lands against the encroachment of commercial exploitation. The most influential and committed of these was John Muir, an essayist and founder of the modern environmentalist movement. Muir made a passionate and spiritual defense of the inherent value of the American wilderness. "Climb the mountains and get their good tidings," he advised. "Nature's peace will flow into you as the sunshine into the trees." Muir served as first president of the Sierra Club, founded in 1892 to preserve and protect the mountain regions of the West Coast as well as Yellowstone National Park in Wyoming, Montana, and Idaho.

A bitter, drawn-out struggle over new water sources for San Francisco revealed the deep conflicts between conservationists, represented by Pinchot, and preservationists, represented by Muir. After a devastating earthquake in 1906, San Francisco sought federal approval to dam and flood the spectacular Hetch Hetchy Valley, located 150 miles from the city in Yosemite National Park. The project promised to ease the city's chronic freshwater shortage and to generate hydroelectric power. Conservationists and their urban progressive allies argued that developing Hetch Hetchy would be a victory for the public good over greedy private developers, since the plan called for municipal control of the water supply. To John Muir and the Sierra Club, Hetch Hetchy was a "temple" threatened with destruction by the "devotees of ravaging commercialism." Congress finally approved the reservoir plan in 1913; utility and public development triumphed over the preservation of nature.

The Newlands Reclamation Act of 1902 represented another important victory for the conservation strategy of Roosevelt and Pinchot. With the goal of turning arid land into productive family farms through irrigation, the act established the Reclamation Bureau within the Department of the Interior and provided federal funding for dam and canal projects. But in practice, the bureau did more to encourage the growth of large-scale agribusiness and western cities than small farming. The Newlands Act established a growing federal presence in managing water resources, the critical issue in twentieth-century western development.

THE ELECTION OF 1912: A FOUR-WAY RACE

In 1908, Roosevelt kept his promise to retire after a second term. He chose Secretary of War William Howard Taft as his successor. Taft easily defeated Democrat William Jennings Bryan in the 1908 election. During Taft's presidency, the gulf between

●●●[**Read** the **Document**

History Bookshelf: *Gifford Pinchot, The Fight for Conservation (1910)* at **www.myhistorylab.com**

●●●[**Read** the **Document**

Profile: *John Muir* at **www.myhistorylab.com**

●●●[**Read** the **Document**

Exploring America: Hetchy Hetchy at **www.myhistorylab.com**

"insurgent" progressives and the "stand pat" wing split the Republican Party wide open. Compared with Roosevelt, the reflective and judicious Taft brought a much more restrained concept of the presidency to the White House. He supported some progressive measures, including the constitutional amendment legalizing a graduated income tax (ratified in 1913), safety codes for mines and railroads, and the creation of a federal Children's Bureau (1912). But in a series of bitter political fights involving tariff, antitrust, and conservation policies, Taft alienated Roosevelt and many other progressives.

After returning from an African safari and a triumphant European tour in 1910, Roosevelt threw himself back into national politics. He directly challenged Taft for the Republican Party leadership. In a dozen bitter state presidential primaries (the first ever held), Taft and Roosevelt fought for the nomination. Although Roosevelt won most of these contests, the old guard still controlled the national convention and renominated Taft in June 1912. Roosevelt's supporters stormed out, and in August, the new Progressive Party nominated Roosevelt and Hiram Johnson of California as its presidential ticket. Roosevelt's "New Nationalism" presented a vision of a strong federal government, led by an activist president, regulating and protecting the various interests in American society. The platform called for woman suffrage, the eight-hour day, prohibition of child labor, minimum-wage standards for working women, and stricter regulation of large corporations.

The Democrats chose Governor Woodrow Wilson of New Jersey as their candidate. Although not nearly as well known nationally as Taft and Roosevelt, Wilson had built a strong reputation as a reformer. Wilson declared himself and the Democratic Party to be the true progressives. Viewing Roosevelt rather than Taft as his main rival, Wilson contrasted his **New Freedom** campaign with Roosevelt's New Nationalism. Crafted largely by progressive lawyer Louis Brandeis, Wilson's platform was far more ambiguous than Roosevelt's. The New Freedom emphasized restoring conditions of free competition and equality of economic opportunity. Wilson did favor a variety of progressive reforms for workers, farmers, and consumers. But Wilson argued against allowing the federal government to become as large and paternalistic as Roosevelt advocated.

Socialist Party nominee Eugene V. Debs offered the fourth and most radical choice to voters. The socialists had more than doubled their membership since 1908, to exceed 100,000. By 1912, more than a thousand socialists held elective office in thirty-three states and 160 cities, including fifty-six mayors and one congressman. The party's 1912 platform called for collective ownership of all large-scale industry and all means of transportation and communication. It demanded shorter working hours, an end to child labor, and the vote for women. Debs and the socialists also took credit for pushing both Roosevelt and Wilson further toward the left. Both the Democratic and Progressive Party platforms contained proposals that had been considered extremely radical only ten years earlier.

In the end, the divisions in the Republican Party gave the election to Wilson (see Map 21.2). Even though he won with only 42 percent of the popular vote, Wilson swept the Electoral College with 435 votes to Roosevelt's 88 and Taft's 8, giving him the largest electoral majority up to that time. In several respects, the election of 1912 was the first "modern" presidential race. It featured the first direct primaries, challenges to traditional party loyalties, an issue-oriented campaign, and a high degree of interest-group activity.

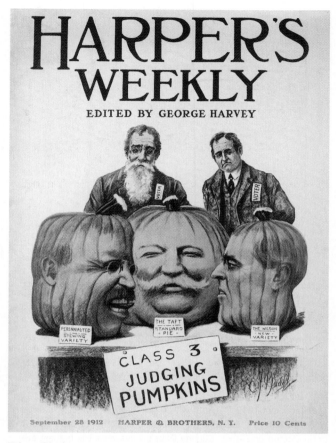

This political cartoon, drawn by Charles Jay Budd, appeared on the cover of *Harper's Weekly*, September 28, 1912. It employed the imagery of autumn county fairs to depict voters as unhappy with their three choices for president. Note that the artist did not include the fourth candidate, socialist Eugene V. Debs, who was often ignored by more conservative publications such as *Harper's*.

Read the **Document**
Theodore Roosevelt, "The New Nationalism" (1910) at **www.myhistorylab.com**

Read the **Document**
Woodrow Wilson, "The New Freedom" (1913) at **www.myhistorylab.com**

Hear the **Audio**
The Speech That Sent Debs to Jail at **www.myhistorylab.com**

New Freedom Woodrow Wilson's 1912 program for limited government intervention in the economy to restore competition by curtailing the restrictive influences of trusts and protective tariffs, thereby providing opportunities for individual achievement.

	Electoral Vote (%)	Popular Vote (%)
WOODROW WILSON (Democrat)	435 (82)	6,296,547 (42)
Theodore Roosevelt (Progressive)	88 (17)	4,118,571 (27)
William Taft (Republican)	8 (1)	3,486,720 (23)
Eugene Debs (Socialist)	—	900,672 (6)

MAP 21.2

The Election of 1912 The split within the Republican Party allowed Woodrow Wilson to become only the second Democrat since the Civil War to be elected president. Eugene Debs's votes were the highest ever polled by a socialist candidate.

WHERE WAS Theodore Roosevelt strongest? Why?

QUICK REVIEW

Democratic Victory in 1912

♦ Republicans split between Taft and Roosevelt.

♦ Democrats put themselves forward as the "true progressives."

♦ Wilson won with only 42 percent of the popular vote.

Underwood-Simmons Act of 1913
Reform law that lowered tariff rates and levied the first regular federal income tax.

Sixteenth Amendment Authorized a federal income tax.

Federal Reserve Act The 1913 law that revised banking and currency by extending limited government regulation through the creation of the Federal Reserve System.

WOODROW WILSON'S FIRST TERM

As president, Wilson followed Roosevelt's lead in expanding the activist dimensions of the office. He became more responsive to pressure for a greater federal role in regulating business and the economy. This increase in direct lobbying—from hundreds of local and national reform groups, Washington-based organizations, and the new Progressive Party—was itself a new and defining feature of the era's political life. With the help of a Democratic- controlled Congress, Wilson pushed through a significant battery of reform proposals.

The **Underwood-Simmons Act of 1913** substantially reduced tariff duties on a variety of raw materials and manufactured goods. Taking advantage of the newly ratified **Sixteenth Amendment**, which gave Congress the power to levy taxes on income, it also imposed the first graduated tax on personal incomes. The **Federal Reserve Act** that same year restructured the nation's banking and currency system. It created twelve Federal Reserve Banks, regulated by a central board in Washington. By giving central direction to banking and monetary policy, the Federal Reserve Board diminished the power of large private banks.

Wilson also supported the **Clayton Antitrust Act** of 1914, which replaced the old Sherman Act of 1890 as the nation's basic antitrust law. The Clayton Act reflected the growing political clout of the American Federation of Labor. It exempted unions from being construed as illegal combinations in restraint of trade, and it forbade federal courts from issuing injunctions against strikers. But Wilson adopted the view that permanent federal regulation was necessary for checking the abuses of big business. The **Federal Trade Commission (FTC)**, established in 1914, sought to give the federal government the same sort of regulatory control over corporations that the ICC had over railroads.

On social issues, Wilson proved more cautious in his first two years. His initial failure to support federal child labor legislation and rural credits to farmers angered many progressives. A Southerner, Wilson also issued an executive order that instituted legal segregation in federal employment, requiring African Americans to work separately from white employees in government offices around Washington, DC. As the reelection campaign of 1916 approached, Wilson worried about defections from the labor and social justice wings of his party. He proceeded to support a rural credits act providing government capital to federal farm banks, as well as federal aid to agricultural extension programs in schools. He also came out in favor of a worker compensation bill for federal employees, and he signed the landmark Keating-Owen Act, which banned children under fourteen from working in enterprises engaged in interstate commerce. But by 1916, the dark cloud of war in Europe had already begun to cast its long shadow over progressive reform.

CONCLUSION

In her memoirs, Lillian Wald summarized the growth of the Henry Street Settlement she founded in 1895 as a home health and visiting nurse service on New York's Lower East Side. "Our experience in one small East Side section," she recalled in 1934, "a block perhaps, has led to a next contact, and a next, in widening

CHRONOLOGY

1889	Jane Addams founds Hull House in Chicago
1890	Jacob Riis publishes *How the Other Half Lives*
1895	Booker T. Washington addresses Cotton States Exposition in Atlanta, emphasizing an accommodationist philosophy
	Lillian Wald establishes Henry Street Settlement in New York
1898	Florence Kelley becomes general secretary of the new National Consumers' League
1900	Robert M. La Follette is elected governor of Wisconsin
1901	Theodore Roosevelt succeeds the assassinated William McKinley as president
1903	Lincoln Steffens publishes *The Shame of the Cities*
1905	President Roosevelt creates U.S. Forest Service and names Gifford Pinchot head
	Industrial Workers of the World is founded in Chicago
1906	Upton Sinclair's *The Jungle* exposes conditions in the meatpacking industry
	Congress passes Pure Food and Drug Act and Meat Inspection Act and establishes Food and Drug Administration
1908	In *Muller* v. *Oregon*, the Supreme Court upholds a state law limiting maximum hours for working women
1909	Uprising of 20,000 garment workers in New York City's garment industries helps organize unskilled workers into unions
	National Association for the Advancement of Colored People (NAACP) is founded
1911	Triangle Shirtwaist Company fire kills 146 garment workers in New York City
	Socialist critic Max Eastman begins publishing *The Masses*
1912	Democrat Woodrow Wilson wins presidency, defeating Republican William H. Taft, Progressive Theodore Roosevelt, and socialist Eugene V. Debs
	"Bread and Roses" strike involves 25,000 textile workers in Lawrence, Massachusetts
	Margaret Sanger begins writing and speaking in support of birth control for women
1913	Sixteenth Amendment, legalizing a graduated income tax, is ratified
	Seventeenth Amendment, shifting the selection of U.S. senators to direct election by voters
1914	Clayton Antitrust Act exempts unions from being construed as illegal combinations in restraint of trade
	Federal Trade Commission is established
	Ludlow Massacre occurs
1916	National Park Service is established

circles, until our community relationships have come to include the city, the state, the national government, and the world at large." Much the same could be said of the progressive movement. What had begun as a series of interlocking, sometimes contradictory, reform initiatives had come to redefine Americans' relationship to government itself. Cities and state legislatures routinely made active interventions to improve the lives of their citizens. Real advances had been made through a range of social legislation covering working conditions, child labor, minimum wages, and worker compensation. Social progressives, too, had discovered the power of organizing into extraparty lobbying groups, such as the National Consumers' League and the National American Woman Suffrage Association. The national government had become the focus of political power and reform energy. The president was expected to provide leadership in policymaking, and new federal bureaucracies exerted more influence over the day-to-day lives of Americans.

Yet many progressive reforms had uneven or unintended consequences. The tensions between fighting for social justice and the urge toward social control remained unresolved. The emphasis on efficiency, uplift, and rational administration often collided with humane impulses to aid the poor, the immigrant, the slum dweller. The large majority of African Americans, blue-collar workers, and urban poor remained untouched by federal assistance programs. The drive for a more open and democratic

Clayton Antitrust Act Replaced the old Sherman Act of 1890 as the nation's basic antitrust law. It exempted unions from being construed as illegal combinations in restraint of trade, and it forbade federal courts from issuing injunctions against strikers.

Federal Trade Commission (FTC) Government agency established in 1914 to provide regulatory oversight of business activity.

political process, in particular, had the effect of excluding some people from voting while including others. For African Americans, progressivism largely meant disenfranchisement from voting altogether. Stricter election laws made it more difficult for third parties to get on the ballot. Voting itself steadily declined after 1916. Overall, party voting became a less important form of political participation. Interest-group activity, congressional and statehouse lobbying, and direct appeals to public opinion gained currency as ways of influencing government. Business groups and individual trade associations were among the most active groups pressing their demands on government. Political action often shifted from legislatures to the new administrative agencies and commissions created to deal with social and economic problems. Popular magazines and journals grew significantly in both number and circulation, becoming more influential in shaping and appealing to national public opinion. America's entry into World War I effectively drained the energy out of progressive reform. The progressive movement, however, with all its contradictions and internal tensions, had profoundly changed the landscape of American political and social life.

REVIEW QUESTIONS

1. Discuss the tensions within progressivism between the ideals of social justice and the urge for social control. What concrete achievements are associated with each wing of the movement? What were the driving forces behind them?

2. Describe the different manifestations of progressivism at the local, state, and national levels. To what extent did progressives redefine the role of the state in American politics?

3. How did workers use their own values and communities to restrain the power of large corporations during the progressive era?

4. How did the era's new immigration reshape America's cities and workplaces? What connections can you draw between the new immigrant experience and progressive era politics?

5. Analyze the progressive era from the perspective of African Americans. What political and social developments were most crucial, and what legacies did they leave?

6. How do the goals, methods, and language of progressives still find voice in contemporary America?

KEY TERMS

Bohemian (p. 551)

Clayton Antitrust Act (p. 558)

Federal Reserve Act (p. 558)

Federal Trade Commission (FTC) (p. 558)

Hepburn Act (p. 555)

Muckraking (p. 537)

National Association for the Advancement of Colored People (p. 554)

New Freedom (p. 557)

Niagara movement (p. 554)

Open shop (p. 550)

Progressivism (p. 535)

Prohibition (p. 543)

Pure Food and Drug Act (p. 555)

Referendum (p. 541)

Sherman Antitrust Act (p. 555)

Sixteenth Amendment (p. 560)

Social Darwinism (p. 537)

Temperance groups (p. 543)

Underwood-Simmons Act of 1913 (p. 558)

Wobblies (p. 550)

PEARSON myhistorylab Connections

Reinforce what you learned in this chapter by studying the many documents, images, maps, review tools, and videos available at www.myhistorylab.com.

Read and Review

✓●─ Study and Review **Chapter 21**

●ᐳ●─ Read the Document

George W. Plunkitt, "Honest Graft" (1905)

Report of the Vice Commission, Louisville, Kentucky (1915)

Lee Chew, "Life of a Chinese Immigrant" (1903)

Letters to the Jewish Daily Forward (1906-1907)

Samuel Gompers, The American Labor Movement (1914)

Helen M. Todd, "Getting Out the Vote" (1911)

Theodore Roosevelt, "The Strenuous Life" (1900)

Theodore Roosevelt, "The New Nationalism" (1910)

Woodrow Wilson, "The New Freedom" (1913)

Research and Explore

●ᐳ●─ Read the Document

Exploring America: Hetch Hetchy

The Struggle for Women Suffrage

History Bookshelf
Ida B. Wells-Barnett, The Red Record (1895)
Booker T. Washington, Up From Slavery (1901)
W.E.B. DuBois, The Souls of Black Folk (1903)
Upton Sinclair, The Jungle (1906)
Jane Addams, The Spirit of Youth and City Streets (1909)
Jane Addams, Twenty Years at Hull House (1910)
Margaret Sanger, Woman and the New Race (1920)
Gifford Pinchot, The Fight for Conservation (1910)

Profiles
John Muir
Margaret Sanger

((●─ Hear the Audio

The Crisis Magazine by W.E.B. Du Bois

The Progress of Colored Women by Mary Church Terrell

The Speech That Sent Debs to Jail

●●─ Watch the Video *What Was the Progressive Education Movement?*

((●─ **Hear** the **Audio**

Hear the audio files for Chapter 21 at
www.myhistorylab.com.

On the other hand, if there is little enthusiasm, the people everywhere are taking the war as a grim necessity, feeling that they have been forced into it by events beyond their control . . .
—Ray Stannard Baker, June 17, 1917

Female workers build a vehicle in an engineering shop in 1917.

The New York Times.

EXTRA
8:30 A.M.

LUSITANIA SUNK BY A SUBMARINE, PROBABLY 1,260 DEAD;
TWICE TORPEDOED OFF IRISH COAST; SINKS IN 15 MINUTES;
CAPT. TURNER SAVED, FROHMAN AND VANDERBILT MISSING;
WASHINGTON BELIEVES THAT A GRAVE CRISIS IS AT HAND

22

A GLOBAL POWER
THE UNITED STATES IN
THE ERA OF THE GREAT WAR
1901–1920

((•—[**Hear** the **Audio**

Hear the audio files for Chapter 22 at **www.myhistorylab.com**.

HOW DID the United States use military power as a component of U.S. foreign policy under Roosevelt, Taft, and Wilson?

WHY DID most Americans oppose U.S. involvement in World War I in 1914?

HOW DID the federal government try to change public opinion about U.S. involvement in World War I?

HOW DID the war affect American economic and political life?

WHAT STEPS did the federal government take to suppress the antiwar movement?

HOW CAN we explain Woodrow Wilson's failure to win the peace?

1901 | 1920

AMERICAN COMMUNITIES
The American Expeditionary Force in France

AT 5:30 A.M. ON SEPTEMBER 26, 1918, SOME 600,000 SOLDIERS OF THE American Expeditionary Force (AEF) headed into the dense gray fog on a twenty-mile front between the Meuse River and the Argonne Forest in northern France. The biggest and costliest American operation of World War I had begun. American commander General John J. Pershing aimed to overwhelm the undermanned and dispirited German lines with massive numbers and swift movement and thereby force a German surrender.

The American thrust quickly stalled as the Germans put up fierce resistance with well-placed machine gun nests and artillery batteries, spread out amidst a ghostly landscape littered with abandoned trenches, tangled barbed-wire fences, water-filled craters, and dead and mangled bodies everywhere. The scene was nothing like the storybooks of war, recalled Lieutenant Maury Maverick. "There were no bugles, no flags, no drums, and as far as we knew, no heroes. . . . I have never read in any military history a description of the high explosives that break overhead. There is a great swishing scream, a smash-bang, and it seems to tear everything loose from you. The intensity of it simply enters your heart and brain and tears every nerve to pieces."

After America's entry into the European conflict in April 1917, millions of Americans traded their civilian clothes for a uniform, creating a new kind of community of soldiers in a modern mechanized army. The Wilson administration had acted swiftly to mobilize the nation's economy and civilian population. The Selective Service Act required the registration and classification for military service of all men between ages twenty-one and thirty-five, and by war's end in November 1918, some 24 million men had registered for the draft, and another 2 million had volunteered. The numbers were there, but the looming question remained: could the nation create a cohesive, efficient, and mass fighting force where none had existed before? In 1917, one out of five soldiers was born in another country and overall illiteracy rates ran as high as 25 percent. Nearly 400,000 African Americans would enter the armed forces, but they faced rigid segregation and deep prejudice against their fitness to fight.

Despite the extraordinary differences of region, class, education, and ethnicity, the "**doughboys**," as AEF members were affectionately called, shared a great deal of common experiences. For many, the journey to training camp represented their first substantial trip away from home. Many progressives saw the army as a field for continuing social reform and education. In training camps, the War Department mounted a vigorous campaign against venereal disease, and the scientific discussions of sex to which recruits were subjected in lectures, pamphlets, and films were surely a first for the

vast majority. Accepting military discipline was new to most as well, and it often rubbed against traditional American notions of freedom and independence. As members of the AEF shipped off for the front, they also carried with them vague and often romantic notions of what to expect on the battlefield. Many doughboys carried to France images of war shaped by their grandfathers' stories about the Civil War or romantic accounts of medieval knights.

Their experiences in the Meuse-Argonne offensive brought those doughboys face-to-face with the very different reality of mass mechanized killing. Rather than the swift victory General Pershing had hoped for, the campaign turned into a slow, sometimes chaotic slog. Between September 25 and the Armistice ending the fighting on November 11, each day claimed an average of over 550 Americans dead, with a total of 26,000 Americans killed in the campaign. Behind the front, American inexperience with such a large-scale operation created enormous logistical problems. Huge traffic jams made it difficult to evacuate the wounded to hospitals and led to severe shortages of rations, water, and ammunition. Discipline frequently broke down with as many as 100,000 stragglers wandering in the rear areas, unable or unwilling to rejoin their units. Meanwhile, a lethal influenza outbreak, part of the worldwide pandemic that would claim over 20 million lives, swept through the AEF in France, afflicting 100,000 doughboys and killing about 10,000 of them.

Many AEF men would long remember their brief time in France as a life-changing high point of their lives, and for some it achieved a mythic significance. Revulsion at the horrors of warfare often coexisted with strong feelings of camaraderie. America's emergence as a global power required mass mobilization of the armed forces and created a new community of veterans. In early 1919, encouraged by some senior officers, a group of AEF veterans founded the American Legion, "to preserve the memories and incidents of our association in the great war . . . to consecrate and sanctify our comradeship." American Legion halls soon became a familiar sight in communities across America. The Legion had a political mission as well, however, one that would play out during the postwar "Red Scare." Legion leaders saw their group as a way to counter radical ideas that might "infect" returning veterans, especially those who suffered from unemployment or had trouble readjusting to civilian life. The American Legion would commemorate the war, celebrate sacrifice, and honor the dead, all in the name of promoting "100 Per Cent Americanism" and fighting against "dangerous" socialists and other radical groups. As much a political lobby as a veterans' organization, the American Legion would extend the memory and life of the AEF community well into the twentieth century.

Verdun

BECOMING A WORLD POWER

In the first years of the new century, the United States pursued a more vigorous and aggressive foreign policy than it had in the past. In addition to its newfound imperial presence in Asia, the United States marked out the Western Hemisphere as a site for establishing American hegemony. Presidents Theodore Roosevelt, William Howard Taft, and Woodrow Wilson all contributed to "progressive diplomacy," in which commercial expansion was backed by a growing military presence in the hemisphere. By 1917, when the United States entered the Great War, the nation was just as complicit in building empire as were the European states and Japan.

ROOSEVELT: THE BIG STICK

Theodore Roosevelt left a strong imprint on the nation's foreign policy. "T.R." took for granted the superiority of Protestant Anglo-American culture and the goal of spreading its values and influence. He believed that to maintain and increase its economic and political stature, America must be militarily strong. In 1900, Roosevelt summarized his activist views, declaring, "I have always been fond of the West African proverb, 'Speak softly and carry a big stick, you will go far.'"

Roosevelt brought the "big stick" approach to disputes in the Caribbean region. Since the 1880s, several British, French, and American companies had pursued plans for building a canal across the Isthmus of Panama, thereby connecting the Atlantic and Pacific Oceans. The canal was a top priority for Roosevelt, and he tried to negotiate a leasing agreement with Colombia, of which Panama was a province. When the Colombian Senate rejected a final American offer in the fall of 1903, Roosevelt invented a new strategy. A combination of native forces and foreign promoters associated with the canal project plotted a revolt against Colombia. Roosevelt kept in touch with at least one leader of the revolt, Philippe Bunau-Varilla, and the president let him know that U.S. warships were steaming toward Panama.

On November 3, 1903, just as the USS *Nashville* arrived in Colón harbor, the province of Panama declared itself independent of Colombia. The United States immediately recognized the new Republic of Panama. Less than two weeks later, Bunau-Varilla, serving as a minister from Panama, signed a treaty granting the United States full sovereignty in perpetuity over a ten-mile-wide canal zone. America guaranteed Panama's independence and agreed to pay it $10 million initially and an additional $250,000 a year for the Canal Zone.

The Panama Canal was a triumph of modern engineering and gave the United States a tremendous strategic and commercial advantage in the Western Hemisphere. It took eight years to build and cost hundreds of workers their lives. Several earlier attempts to build a canal in the region had failed. In 1914 the first merchant ships sailed through the canal.

"The inevitable effect of our building the Canal," wrote Secretary of State Elihu Root in 1905, "must be to require us to police the surrounding premises." Roosevelt agreed. He was especially concerned that European powers might step in if America did not. To prevent armed intervention by the Europeans, in 1904 Roosevelt proclaimed what became known as the **Roosevelt Corollary** to the Monroe Doctrine. "Chronic wrongdoing, or an impotence which results in a general loosening of the ties of civilized society," the statement read, justified "the exercise of an international police power" anywhere in the hemisphere. Roosevelt and later presidents cited the corollary to justify armed intervention in the internal affairs of the Dominican Republic, Cuba, Haiti, Nicaragua, and Mexico.

With the outbreak of the Russo-Japanese War in 1904, Roosevelt worried about the future of the **Open Door** policy in Asia. A total victory by Russia or

HOW DID the United States use military power as a component of U.S. foreign policy under Roosevelt, Taft, and Wilson?

doughboys Nickname for soldiers during the Civil War era who joined the army for money.

Roosevelt Corollary President Theodore Roosevelt's policy asserting U.S. authority to intervene in the affairs of Latin American nations; an expansion of the Monroe Doctrine.

Open Door American policy of seeking equal trade and investment opportunities in foreign nations or regions.

THE WORLD'S CONSTABLE.

This 1905 cartoon portraying President Theodore Roosevelt, "The World's Constable," appeared in *Judge* magazine. In depicting the president as a strong but benevolent policeman bringing order in a contentious world, the artist Louis Dalrymple drew on familiar imagery from Roosevelt's earlier days as a New York City police commissioner.

Japan could upset the balance of power in East Asia and threaten American business enterprises there. With this in mind, Roosevelt mediated a settlement of the Russo-Japanese War at Portsmouth, New Hampshire, in 1905. In this settlement, Japan won recognition of its dominant position in Korea and consolidated its economic control over Manchuria. Yet repeated incidents of anti-Japanese racism in California kept American–Japanese relations strained. In 1907, in the so-called Gentlemen's Agreement, Japan agreed not to issue passports to Japanese male laborers looking to emigrate to the United States, and Roosevelt promised to fight anti-Japanese discrimination.

Roosevelt did not want these conciliatory moves to be interpreted as weakness. He thus built up American naval strength in the Pacific, and in 1908, he sent battleships to visit Japan in a muscle-flexing display of sea power. In that same year, the two burgeoning Pacific powers reached a reconciliation. The Root-Takahira Agreement affirmed the "existing status quo" in Asia, mutual respect for territorial possessions in the Pacific, and the Open Door trade policy in China. From the Japanese perspective, the agreement recognized Japan's colonial dominance in Korea and southern Manchuria.

TAFT: DOLLAR DIPLOMACY

Roosevelt's successor, William Howard Taft, believed he could replace the militarism of the big stick with the more subtle and effective weapon of business investment. Taft and his secretary of state, corporate lawyer Philander C. Knox, followed a strategy (called

Read the **Document**

William H. Taft, "Dollar Diplomacy" (1912) at **www.myhistorylab.com**

"dollar diplomacy" by critics) in which they assumed that political influence would follow increased U.S. trade and investment.

Overall American investment in Central America grew rapidly, from $41 million in 1908 to $93 million by 1914. Most of this money went into railroad construction, mining, and plantations. But dollar diplomacy ended up requiring military support. The Taft administration sent the navy and the marines to intervene in political disputes in Honduras and Nicaragua, propping up factions pledged to protect American business interests. A contingent of U.S. Marines remained in Nicaragua until 1933 (see Map 22.1).

In China, Taft and Knox pressed for a greater share of the pie for U.S. investors. They gained a place for U.S. bankers in the European consortium, building the massive new Hukuang Railway in southern and central China. But Knox blundered by attempting

MAP 22.1

The United States in the Caribbean, 1865–1933   An overview of U.S. economic and military involvement in the Caribbean during the late nineteenth and early twentieth centuries. Victory in the Spanish-American War, the Panama Canal project, and rapid economic investment in Mexico and Cuba all contributed to a permanent and growing U.S. military presence in the region.

WHERE IN the Caribbean did the United States intervene militarily between 1865 and 1933? What role did economic considerations play in use of military force?

to "neutralize" the existing railroads in China. He tried to secure a huge international loan for the Chinese government that would allow it to buy up all the foreign railways and develop new ones. Both Russia and Japan, which had fought wars over their railroad interests in Manchuria, resisted this plan. Knox's "neutralization" scheme, combined with U.S. support for the Chinese Nationalists in their 1911 revolt against the ruling Manchu dynasty, prompted Japan to sign a new friendship treaty with Russia. The Open Door to China was now effectively closed, and American relations with Japan began a slow deterioration that ended in war thirty years later.

WILSON: MORALISM AND INTERVENTION IN MEXICO

President Woodrow Wilson brought to foreign affairs a set of fundamental principles that combined a moralist's faith in American democracy with a realist's understanding of the power of international commerce. He believed that American economic expansion, accompanied by democratic principles and Christianity, was a civilizing force in the world.

Wilson, like most corporate and political leaders of the day, emphasized foreign investments and industrial exports as the keys to the nation's prosperity. He believed that the United States, with its superior industrial efficiency, could achieve supremacy in world commerce if artificial barriers to free trade were removed. He championed and extended the Open Door principles of John Hay, advocating strong diplomatic and military measures "for making ourselves supreme in the world from an economic point of view." Wilson often couched his vision of a dynamic, expansive American capitalism in terms of a moral crusade. Yet he quickly found that the complex realities of power politics could interfere with moral vision.

This 1914 political cartoon comments approvingly on the interventionist role adopted by the United States in Latin American countries. By depicting President Woodrow Wilson as a schoolteacher giving lessons to children, the image captures the paternalistic views that American policymakers held toward nations like Mexico, Venezuela, and Nicaragua.

Wilson's policies toward Mexico, which foreshadowed the problems he would encounter in World War I, best illustrate his difficulties. The 1911 Mexican Revolution had overthrown the brutally corrupt dictatorship of Porfirio Díaz, and popular leader Francisco Madero had won wide support by promising democracy and economic reform for millions of landless peasants. But the U.S. business community was nervous about the future of its investments which, in the previous generation, had come to dominate the Mexican economy.

Wilson at first gave his blessing to the revolutionary movement, expressed regret over the Mexican-American War of 1846–48, and disavowed any interest in another war. But right before he took office, Wilson was stunned when Madero was ousted and murdered by his chief lieutenant, General Victoriano Huerta. Other nations, including Great Britain and Japan, recognized the Huerta regime, but Wilson refused. An armed faction opposed to Huerta, known as the Constitutionalists and led by Venustiano Carranza, emerged in northern Mexico. Both sides rejected an effort by Wilson to broker a compromise between them. Carranza, an ardent nationalist, pressed for the right to buy U.S. arms, which he won in 1914. Wilson also isolated Huerta diplomatically by persuading the British to withdraw their support in exchange for American guarantees of English property interests in Mexico.

Huerta stubbornly remained in power. In April 1914, Wilson used a minor insult to U.S. sailors in Tampico as an excuse to invade Mexico. American naval forces bombarded and then occupied Veracruz, the main port through which Huerta received arms shipments. The occupation brought the United States and Mexico close to war, and provoked anti-American demonstrations in Mexico and throughout Latin America. Wilson accepted the offer of the ABC Powers—Argentina, Brazil, and Chile—to mediate the dispute. Huerta rejected a plan for him to step aside in favor of a provisional government. In August, however, Carranza managed to overthrow Huerta. Playing to nationalist sentiment, Carranza also denounced Wilson for his intervention.

As war loomed in Europe, Mexico's revolutionary politics continued to frustrate Wilson. For a brief period, Wilson threw his support behind Francisco "Pancho" Villa, Carranza's former ally, who led a rebel army of his own in northern Mexico. But Carranza's forces dealt Villa a major setback in April 1915. In October, when its attention was focused on the war in Europe, the Wilson administration recognized Carranza as Mexico's de facto president. Meanwhile, Pancho Villa, feeling betrayed, turned on the United States and tried to provoke a crisis that might draw the United States into war with Mexico. In 1916, Villa led several raids in Mexico and across the border into the United States that killed a few dozen Americans.

In March 1916, enraged by Villa's defiance, Wilson dispatched General John J. Pershing to capture him. For a year, Pershing's troops chased Villa in vain, penetrating 300 miles into Mexico. The invasion made Villa a symbol of national resistance in Mexico, and his army grew from 500 men to 10,000 by the end of 1916. Villa's effective hit-and-run guerrilla tactics kept the U.S. forces at bay.

Skirmishes between American forces and Carranza's army brought the two nations to the brink of war again in June 1916. Although Wilson prepared a message to Congress asking permission for American troops to occupy all of northern Mexico, he never delivered it. There was fierce opposition to war with Mexico throughout the United States. Perhaps more important, mounting tensions with Germany caused Wilson to hesitate. Wilson thus accepted negotiations by a face-saving international commission.

Wilson's attempt to guide the course of Mexico's revolution suggested the limits of a foreign policy tied to a moral vision rooted in the idea of American exceptionalism. **Militarism** and **imperialism**, Wilson had believed, were hallmarks of the old European way. American liberal values—rooted in capitalist development, democracy, and free trade—were the wave of the future. Wilson believed the United States could lead the world in establishing a new international system based on peaceful commerce and political stability. In both the 1914 invasion and the 1916 punitive expedition, Wilson declared that he had no desire to interfere with Mexican sovereignty. But in both cases, that is exactly what he did. The United States, he argued, must actively use its enormous moral and material power to create the new order. That principle would soon engage America in Europe's bloodiest war and its most momentous revolution.

THE GREAT WAR

World War I, or the Great War as it was originally called, took an enormous human toll on an entire generation of Europeans. At the war's start in August 1914, both sides had confidently predicted a quick victory. Instead, the killing dragged on for more than four years, and in the end, transformed the old power relations and political map of Europe. The United States entered the war reluctantly, and American forces played a supportive, rather than a central, role in the military outcome.

THE GUNS OF AUGUST

Only a complex and fragile system of alliances had kept the European powers at peace with each other since 1871. Two great competing camps had evolved by 1907: the Triple Alliance (also known as the **Central Powers**), which included Germany, Austria-Hungary,

---

militarism   The tendency to see military might as the most important and best tool for the expansion of a nation's power and prestige.

imperialism   The policy and practice of exploiting nations and peoples for the benefit of an imperial power either directly through military occupation and colonial rule or indirectly through economic domination of resources and markets.

Central Powers   Germany and its World War I allies in Austria, Italy, Turkey, and Bulgaria.

•••—[Read the **Document**

Profile: *John J. Pershing* at **www.myhistorylab.com**

QUICK REVIEW

Wilson and Mexico

◆ Wilson refused to recognize the regime of General Victoriano Huerta.

◆ 1914: Wilson used the excuse of a minor event to attack Veracruz.

◆ Wilson's efforts to control events in Mexico led to the brink of war.

◆ Wilson's policies resulted in enduring distrust of the United States in Mexico.

WHY DID most Americans oppose U.S. involvement in World War I in 1914?

and Italy; and the Triple Entente (also known as the **Allies**), which included Great Britain, France, and Russia. The alliance system managed to keep small conflicts from escalating into larger ones for most of the late nineteenth and early twentieth centuries. But its inclusiveness was also its weakness: the alliance system threatened to entangle many nations in any war that did erupt. On June 28, 1914, Archduke Franz Ferdinand, heir to the throne of the unstable Austro-Hungarian Empire, was assassinated in Sarajevo, Bosnia. The archduke's killer was a Serbian nationalist who believed the Austro-Hungarian province of Bosnia ought to be annexed to neighboring Serbia. Germany gave Austria-Hungary a blank check to stamp out the Serbian threat, and the Serbians in turn asked Russia for help.

That summer both sides began mobilizing their armies, and by early August they had exchanged declarations of war. Germany invaded Belgium and prepared to move across the French border. At the beginning, most Europeans supported the war effort, believing there would be quick and glorious victories. After the German armies were stopped at the River Marne in September, however, the war settled into a long, bloody stalemate. New and grimly efficient weapons, such as the machine gun and the tank, and the horrors of trench warfare, meant unprecedented casualties for all involved. In northern France, Poland, and on the Italian front, the fighting killed 5 million people over the next two and a half years. Allied campaigns waged against German colonies in Africa and against the Ottoman Empire in the Middle East reflected the global nature of the war, as did the British and French dependence on colonial troops from India and Africa.

AMERICAN NEUTRALITY

The outbreak of war in Europe shocked Americans. President Wilson issued a formal proclamation of neutrality. In practice, powerful cultural, political, and economic factors made the impartiality advocated by Wilson impossible. Strong support for the Central Powers could be found among the 8 million German-Americans, as well as the 4 million Irish-Americans, who shared their ancestral homeland's historical hatred of English rule. On the other side, many Americans were at least mildly pro-Allies due to cultural and language bonds with Great Britain and the tradition of Franco-American friendship.

Both sides bombarded the United States with vigorous propaganda campaigns. The British effectively exploited their bonds of language and heritage with Americans. Reports of looting, raping, and the killing of innocent civilians by German troops circulated widely in the press. Wartime propaganda highlighted the terrible human costs of the war and, thus, strengthened the conviction that America should stay out of it.

Economic ties between the United States and the Allies were perhaps the greatest barrier to true neutrality. Early in the war, Britain imposed a blockade on all shipping to Germany. The United States, as a neutral country, might have insisted on the right of nonbelligerents to trade with both sides, as required by international law. In practice, although Wilson protested the blockade, he wanted to avoid antagonizing Britain and disrupting trade between the United States and the Allies. Trade with Germany all but ended while trade with the Allies increased dramatically. As America's annual export trade jumped from $2 billion in 1913 to nearly $6 billion in 1916 as a result of trade with the Allies, the nation enjoyed a great economic boom and the United States became neutral in name only.

PREPAREDNESS AND PEACE

In February 1915, Germany declared the waters around the British Isles to be a war zone, a policy that it would enforce with unrestricted submarine warfare. All enemy shipping would be subject to surprise submarine attack. Neutral powers were warned that the problems of identification at sea put their ships at risk. The United States issued

---

QUICK REVIEW

The Outbreak of War

- June 28, 1914: Archduke Franz Ferdinand assassinated.
- July 28, 1914: Austria declares war on Serbia with German support.
- Chain reaction draws all European powers into the war.

QUICK REVIEW

Anglo-American Ties

- 1915: United States gave tacit support to British naval blockade of Germany.
- Economic factors bound Britain and America together.
- Many Americans felt a cultural connection with Britain.

Allies　In World War I, Britain, France, Russia, and other belligerent nations fighting against the Central Powers but not including the United States.

a sharp protest to this policy, calling it "an indefensible violation of neutral rights," and threatened to hold Germany accountable.

On May 7, 1915, a German U-boat sank the British liner *Lusitania* off the coast of Ireland. Among the 1,198 people who died were 128 American citizens. The *Lusitania* was, in fact, secretly carrying war materials, and passengers had been warned about a possible attack. Wilson nevertheless denounced the sinking as illegal and inhuman. An angry exchange of diplomatic notes led Secretary of State William Jennings Bryan to resign in protest against a policy he thought too warlike.

Tensions heated up again in March 1916 when a German U-boat torpedoed the *Sussex*, an unarmed French passenger ship, injuring four Americans. President Wilson threatened to break off diplomatic relations with Germany unless it abandoned its submarine warfare. He won a temporary diplomatic victory when Germany promised that all vessels would be visited prior to attack. But the crisis also prompted Wilson to begin preparing for war. In June 1916, Congress passed the National Defense Act, which more than doubled the size of the regular army to

Patriotic marchers carry an over-sized American flag past spectators, as part of a "preparedness parade" in downtown Mobile Alabama, before American entry into World War I.
University of South Alabama Archives.

220,000 and integrated the state National Guards under federal control. In August, Congress passed a bill that dramatically increased spending for new battleships, cruisers, and destroyers.

Not all Americans supported these preparations for battle, and opposition to military buildup found expression in scores of American communities. As early as August 29, 1914, 1,500 women clad in black had marched down New York's Fifth Avenue in the Woman's Peace Parade. Out of this gathering evolved the American Union against Militarism, which lobbied against the **preparedness** campaign and against intervention in Mexico. Antiwar feeling was especially strong in the South and Midwest. A group of thirty to fifty House Democrats, led by majority leader Claude Kitchin of North Carolina, stubbornly opposed Wilson's military buildup. Jane Addams, Lillian D. Wald, and many other prominent progressive reformers spoke out for peace.

Wilson acknowledged the active opposition to involvement in the war by adopting the winning slogan "He Kept Us Out of War" in the 1916 presidential campaign. He made a point of appealing to progressives of all kinds, stressing his support for the eight-hour day and his administration's efforts on behalf of farmers. The war-induced prosperity no doubt helped him to defeat conservative Republican Charles Evans Hughes.

SAFE FOR DEMOCRACY

By the end of January 1917, Germany's leaders had decided against a negotiated peace settlement, placing their hopes instead in a final decisive offensive against the Allies. On February 1, 1917, with the aim of breaking the British blockade, Germany declared unlimited submarine warfare, with no warnings, against all neutral and belligerent shipping. This strategy went far beyond the earlier, more limited use of the U-boat.

Wilson was indignant and disappointed. He still hoped for peace, but Germany had made it impossible for him to preserve his twin goals of U.S. neutrality and freedom of the seas. Reluctantly, Wilson broke off diplomatic relations with Germany and called on Congress to approve the arming of U.S. merchant ships. On March 1, the White House

Read the **Document**

Eugene V. Debs, Critique of World War (1918) at **www.myhistorylab.com**

preparedness   Military buildup in preparation for possible U.S. participation in World War I.

THE NAVY NEEDS YOU! DON'T READ AMERICAN HISTORY— MAKE IT!

U·S·NAVY RECRUITING STATION
34 EAST 23rd ST., NEW YORK

James Montgomery Flagg's Navy recruiting poster from 1918 combined appeals to patriotism, the opportunity to "make history," and traditional images depicting liberty as a woman.

shocked the country when it made public a recently intercepted coded message, sent by German foreign secretary Arthur Zimmermann to the German ambassador in Mexico. The Zimmermann note proposed that an alliance be made between Germany and Mexico if the United States entered the war. The note caused a sensation and became a very effective propaganda tool for those who favored U.S. entry into the war.

Revelation of the Zimmermann note stiffened Wilson's resolve. He issued an executive order in mid-March, authorizing the arming of all merchant ships and allowing them to shoot at submarines. In that month, German U-boats sank seven U.S. merchant ships, with a heavy death toll. Anti-German feeling increased, and thousands took part in prowar demonstrations in New York, Boston, Philadelphia, and other cities. Wilson finally called a special session of Congress to ask for a declaration of war.

On April 2, before a packed and very quiet assembly, Wilson made his case. He reviewed the escalation of submarine warfare, which he called "warfare against mankind," and said that neutrality was no longer feasible or desirable. The conflict was not merely about U.S. shipping rights, Wilson argued. He employed highly idealistic language to make the case for war, reflecting his deeply held belief that America had a special mission as the world's most enlightened and advanced nation:

> It is a fearful thing to lead this great peaceful people into war, into the most terrible and disastrous of all wars, civilization itself seeming to be in the balance. But the right is more precious than peace, and we shall fight for the things which we have always carried nearest to our hearts— for democracy, for the right of those who submit to authority to have a voice in their own governments, for the rights and liberties of small nations, for a universal dominion of right by such a concert of free peoples as shall bring peace and safety to all nations and make the world itself at last free.

The Senate adopted the war resolution 82 to 6, the House 373 to 50. Wilson's eloquent speech won over not only the Congress, but also most of the press, and even his bitterest political critics, such as Theodore Roosevelt. On April 6, President Wilson signed the declaration of war. All that remained was to win over the American public.

AMERICAN MOBILIZATION

HOW DID the federal government try to change public opinion about U.S. involvement in World War I?

The overall public response to Wilson's war message was enthusiastic. Most newspapers, religious leaders, state legislatures, and prominent public figures endorsed the call to arms. The Wilson administration was less certain about the feelings of ordinary Americans and their willingness to fight in Europe. It therefore took immediate steps to strengthen public support for the war effort, to place a legal muzzle on antiwar dissenters, and to establish a universal military draft. War mobilization was, above all, a campaign to unify the country.

Committee on Public Information (CPI) Government agency during World War I that sought to shape public opinion in support of the war effort through newspapers, pamphlets, speeches, films, and other media.

SELLING THE WAR

Just a week after signing the war declaration, Wilson created the **Committee on Public Information (CPI)** to organize public opinion. Its civilian chairman, the journalist and reformer George Creel, quickly transformed the CPI into a sophisticated and aggressive agency for promoting the war. To sell the war, Creel adapted techniques from the emerging field of public relations. He enlisted more than 150,000 people to work on a score of CPI committees. They produced more than 100 million pieces of literature—pamphlets, articles, books—that explained the causes and meaning of the war. Across the nation, a volunteer army of 75,000 "Four Minute Men" gave brief patriotic speeches before stage and movie shows. The CPI also created posters, slides, newspaper advertising, and films to promote the war. It called upon movie stars to help sell war bonds at huge rallies. Many popular entertainers injected patriotic themes into their work as well, such as when Broadway composer George M. Cohan wrote the rousing prowar anthem "Over There" (see Seeing History).

The CPI led an aggressively negative campaign against all things German. Posters and advertisements depicted the Germans as Huns, bestial monsters outside the civilized world. German music and literature, indeed the German language itself, were deemed suspect. Many restaurants offered "liberty cabbage" and "liberty steaks" instead of sauerkraut and hamburgers. The CPI also urged ethnic Americans to abandon their Old World ties, to become "unhyphenated Americans." The CPI's push for conformity soon encouraged thousands of local, sometimes violent, campaigns of harassment against German-Americans, radicals, and peace activists.

FADING OPPOSITION TO WAR

By defining the call to war as a great moral crusade, President Wilson won over many Americans who had been reluctant to go to war. In particular, many liberals and progressives were attracted to the possibilities of war as a positive force for social change. Many identified with President Wilson's definition of the war as an idealistic crusade to defend democracy, spread liberal principles, and redeem European decadence and militarism.

The writer and cultural critic Randolph Bourne was an important voice of dissent among intellectuals. Bourne wrote a series of antiwar essays warning of the disastrous consequences for reform movements of all kinds. He was particularly critical of "war intellectuals" who were eager to shift their energies to serving the war effort. "War is essentially the health of the State," Bourne wrote, and he accurately predicted sharp infringements on political and intellectual freedoms.

The Woman's Peace Party, founded in 1915 by feminists opposed to preparations for war, dissolved. Most of its leading lights—Florence Kelley, Lillian D. Wald, and Carrie Chapman Catt—threw themselves into volunteer war work. A few lonely feminist voices, such as Jane Addams, continued steadfastly to oppose the war effort. But war work proved very popular among activist middle-class women. It gave them a leading role in their communities—selling bonds, coordinating food conservation drives, and working for hospitals and the Red Cross.

"YOU'RE IN THE ARMY NOW"

When war was declared, there were only about 200,000 men in the army. Traditionally, the United States had relied on volunteer forces organized at the state level. But volunteer rates after April 6 were less than they had been for the Civil War or the Spanish-American War, reflecting the softness of prowar sentiment. The administration thus introduced the **Selective Service Act**, which provided for the registration and classification for military service of all men between ages twenty-one and thirty-five. On June 5, 1917, nearly 10 million men registered for the draft. By the end of the war, some 24 million men had registered.

The vast, polyglot army posed unprecedented challenges of organization and control. But progressive elements within the administration also saw opportunities for pressing reform measures, especially for the one-fifth of U.S. soldiers born in another country. Army psychologists gave the new Stanford-Binet intelligence test to all recruits and were shocked to find illiteracy rates as high as 25 percent. The low test scores among recent immigrants and rural African Americans undoubtedly reflected the cultural biases embedded in the

Selective Service Act   The law establishing the military draft for World War I.

Selling War

The Committee on Public Information (CPI), chaired by the progressive Denver journalist George Creel, oversaw the crucial task of mobilizing public opinion for war. Creel employed the most sophisticated sales and public relations techniques of the day to get Americans behind the war effort. The CPI created a flood of pamphlets, billboards, and news articles; sent volunteer "Four Minute Men" to make hundreds of thousands of patriotic speeches in movie theaters between reels; sponsored government-funded feature films depicting life on the front lines; and staged celebrity-studded rallies to promote the sale of war bonds. CPI writers and artists worked closely with government agencies such as the Food Administration and the Selective Service, as well as private organizations like the YMCA and the Red Cross, in creating patriotic campaigns in support of the war.

HOW WOULD you contrast the different kind of patriotic appeals made by *Pershing's Crusaders, Americans All,* and *And They Thought We Couldn't Fight?* Which of these posters do you think makes the most compelling case for supporting the war? How do the artists portray gender differences as part of a visual strategy for winning the war?

The Division of Pictorial Publicity, headed by the popular artist Charles Dana Gibson, churned out posters and illustrations designed to encourage military enlistment, food conservation, war bond buying, and contributions for overseas victims of war.

The posters generally defined the war as a clear struggle between good and evil, in which American democracy and freedom opposed German militarism and despotism. Artists used a wide range of visual themes to illustrate these stark contrasts. World War I posters drew upon traditional ideas about gender differences (men as soldiers, women as nurturers), but they also illustrated the new wartime expectations of women working outside the home in support of the war effort. Appeals to American patriotism cutting across lines of ethnic and religious difference were common, as was the demonizing of the German enemy. And just as the wartime economy blurred the boundaries between public and private enterprises, businesses adapted patriotic appeals to their own advertising.

Creel aptly titled the memoir of his war experience *How We Advertised America.* These three images illustrate the range of World War I propaganda posters. ∎

tests and a lack of proficiency in English for many test takers. After the war, intelligence testing became a standard feature of America's educational system.

RACISM IN THE MILITARY

African Americans who served found severe limitations in the U.S. military. They were organized into totally segregated units, barred entirely from the marines and the Coast Guard, and largely relegated to working as cooks, laundrymen, stevedores, and the like in the army and navy. Thousands of black soldiers endured humiliating, sometimes violent, treatment, particularly from southern white officers. African American servicemen faced hostility from white civilians as well, North and South, and often were denied service in restaurants and admission to theaters near training camps. The ugliest incident occurred in Houston, Texas, in August 1917. Black infantrymen, incensed over continual insults and harassment by local whites, seized weapons from an armory and killed seventeen civilians. The army executed thirty black soldiers and imprisoned forty-one others for life, denying any of them a chance for appeal.

More than 200,000 African Americans eventually served in France, but only about one in five saw combat, as opposed to two out of three white soldiers. Black combat units served with distinction in various divisions of the French army. The French government awarded the Croix de Guerre to the all-black 369th U.S. Infantry regiment, and 171 officers and enlisted men were cited individually for exceptional bravery in action. African American soldiers by and large enjoyed a friendly reception from French civilians as well. The contrast with their treatment at home would remain a sore point with these troops upon their return to the United States.

AMERICANS IN BATTLE

President Wilson appointed General John J. Pershing as commander of the American Expeditionary Force (AEF). Pershing insisted that the AEF maintain its own identity, distinct from that of the French and British armies. He was also reluctant to send American troops into battle before they had received at least six months' training. Not until early

◆●●[Read the Document

Statement to French Concerning Black American Troops (1918) at
www.myhistorylab.com

QUICK REVIEW

African American Soldiers

◆ 200,000 African Americans served in France.

◆ One in five saw combat.

◆ African American combat units served with distinction.

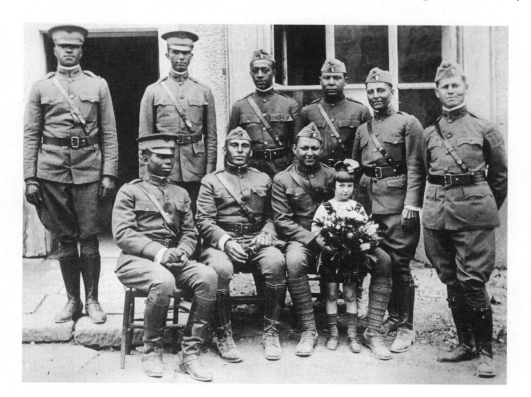

African American officers of the 367th Infantry Regiment, 77th Division, pose with a girl in France, 1918. Nicknamed the "Buffalos," a reference to the black "buffalo soldiers" who had served in the U.S. Army during the late nineteenth century campaigns against Indians, this was one of only two army units that commissioned African American officers.

See the Map
World War I at **www.myhistorylab.com**

Read the Document
Eugene Kennedy, "A 'Doughboy' Describes the Fighting Front" (1918) at **www.myhistorylab.com**

1918 did AEF units reach the front in large numbers; eight months later, the war was over (see Map 22.2).

Some 2 million men served in the AEF. Overall 60,000 Americans had died in battle with 206,000 wounded. Another 60,000 died from diseases, mainly influenza. These figures paled in comparison to the millions lost by the European nations. Yet the American contribution to winning the war was substantial. The prospect of facing seemingly unlimited quantities of American men and supplies convinced the exhausted German army to surrender.

THE RUSSIAN REVOLUTION, THE FOURTEEN POINTS, AND ALLIED VICTORY

Since early 1917, the turmoil of the Russian Revolution had changed the climate of both foreign affairs and domestic politics. The repressive and corrupt regime of Czar Nicholas II was overthrown in March 1917 by a coalition of forces demanding change. The new provisional government vowed to keep Russia in the fight against Germany. But the war had taken a terrible toll on Russian soldiers and civilians and had become

MAP 22.2
The Western Front, 1918 American units saw their first substantial action in late May, helping to stop the German offensive at the Battle of Cantigny. By September, more than 1 million American troops were fighting in a counteroffensive campaign at St. Mihiel, the largest single American engagement of the war.

HOW DID the entrance of the United States help turn the tide of World War I?

very unpopular. The radical **Bolsheviks**, led by V. I. Lenin, gained a large following by promising "peace, land, and bread," and they began plotting to seize power. The Bolsheviks followed the teachings of German revolutionary Karl Marx, emphasizing the inevitability of class struggle and the replacement of capitalism by communism. In November 1917, the Bolsheviks took control of the Russian government.

President Wilson refused to recognize the authority of the Bolshevik regime. Bolshevism represented a threat to the liberal-capitalist values that Wilson believed to be the foundation of America's moral and material power. Thus, in January 1918, Wilson outlined American war aims, known as the **Fourteen Points**, in a speech before Congress. He wanted to counter a fierce Bolshevik campaign to discredit the war as a purely imperialist venture, their sensational publication of secret treaties that the czar had signed with the Allies, and their revelations about annexationist plans across Europe.

As a blueprint for peace, the Fourteen Points contained three main elements. First, Wilson offered a series of specific proposals for setting postwar boundaries in Europe and creating new countries out of the collapsed Austro-Hungarian and Ottoman empires. The key idea here was the right of all peoples to "national self-determination." Second, Wilson listed general principles for governing international conduct, including freedom of the seas, free trade, open covenants instead of secret treaties, reduced armaments, and mediation for competing colonial claims. Third, and most important, Wilson called for a **League of Nations** to help implement these principles and resolve future disputes.

In March 1918, to the dismay of the Allies, the new Bolshevik government followed through on its promise and negotiated a separate peace with Germany, the Treaty of Brest-Litovsk. Russia's defection made possible a massive shift of German troops to the western front. In the early spring of 1918, the Germans launched a major offensive that brought them within fifty miles of Paris. In early June, about 70,000 AEF soldiers helped the French stop the Germans in the battles of Château-Thierry and Belleau Wood. In July, Allied forces led by Marshal Ferdinand Foch of France began a counteroffensive designed to defeat Germany once and for all.

In late September 1918, the AEF took over the southern part of a twenty-mile front in the Meuse-Argonne offensive. In seven weeks of fighting, U.S. soldiers used more ammunition than the entire Union army had in the four years of the Civil War. The Germans, exhausted and badly outnumbered, began to fall back and look for a cease-fire. On November 11, 1918, the war ended with the signing of an armistice.

OVER HERE

In one sense, World War I can be understood as the ultimate progressive crusade: an opportunity to expand the powers of the federal government in order to win the war. Nearly all the reform energy of the previous two decades turned toward that central goal. The federal government played a larger role than ever in managing and regulating the wartime economy. Planning, efficiency, scientific analysis, and cooperation were key principles for government agencies and large volunteer organizations. Although much of the regulatory spirit was temporary, the war experience started some important and lasting organizational trends in American life.

ORGANIZING THE ECONOMY

In the summer of 1917, President Wilson established the **War Industries Board (WIB)** as a clearinghouse for industrial mobilization to support the war effort. The WIB proved a major innovation in expanding the regulatory power of the federal government. Given broad authority over the conversion of industrial plants to wartime needs and the manufacture of war materials, the WIB had to balance price controls against war profits. Only by ensuring a fair rate of return on investment could it encourage stepped-up production.

Read the Document

Woodrow Wilson, "Fourteen Points" (1917) at **www.myhistorylab.com**

QUICK REVIEW

Wilson's Fourteen Points

- Wilson articulated U.S. war aims in his Fourteen Points.
- Self-determination was a key component of Wilson's plan.
- Wilson saw the League of Nations as the most important part of his postwar vision.

HOW DID the war affect American economic and political life?

Bolsheviks   Members of the Communist movement in Russia that established the Soviet government after the 1917 Russian Revolution.

Fourteen Points   Goals outlined by Woodrow Wilson for war.

League of Nations   International organization created by the Versailles Treaty after World War I to ensure world stability.

War Industries Board (WIB)   The federal agency that reorganized industry for maximum efficiency and productivity during World War I.

FOOD WILL WIN THE WAR
You came here seeking Freedom
You must now help to preserve it
WHEAT is needed for the allies
Waste nothing

A Food Administration poster blended a call for conservation of wheat with an imaginative patriotic appeal for recent immigrants to support the war effort.

Liberty Bonds Interest-bearing certificates sold by the U.S. government to finance the American World War I effort.

In August 1917, Congress passed the Food and Fuel Act, authorizing the president to regulate the production and distribution of the food and fuel necessary for the war effort. Wilson appointed Herbert Hoover to lead the Food Administration (FA). Hoover imposed price controls on certain agricultural commodities, such as sugar, pork, and wheat. The FA also raised the purchase price of grain, so that farmers would increase production. Hoover stopped short of imposing mandatory food rationing, preferring to rely on persuasion, high prices, and voluntary controls.

Hoover's success, like George Creel's at the CPI, depended on motivating hundreds of thousands of volunteers in thousands of American communities. The FA directed patriotic appeals for "Wheatless Mondays, Meatless Tuesdays, and Porkless Thursdays." These efforts resulted in a sharp cutback in the consumption of sugar and wheat as well as a boost in the supply of livestock. The resultant increase in food exports helped sustain the Allied war effort.

The enormous cost of fighting the war, about $33 billion. The tax structure shifted dramatically as a result. Taxes on incomes and profits replaced excise and customs levies as the major source of revenue. The bulk of war financing came from government borrowing, especially in the form of the popular **Liberty Bonds** sold to the American public. Bond drives became highly organized patriotic campaigns that ultimately raised a total of $23 billion for the war effort. The administration also used the new Federal Reserve Banks to expand the money supply, making borrowing easier. The federal debt jumped from $1 billion in 1915 to $20 billion in 1920.

THE GOVERNMENT–BUSINESS PARTNERSHIP

Overall, the war meant expansion and high profits for American business. Total capital expenditure in U.S. manufacturing jumped from $600 million in 1915 to $2.5 billion in 1918. Corporate profits as a whole nearly tripled between 1914 and 1919, and many large businesses did much better than that. The total value of farm produce rose from $9.8 billion in 1914 to $21.3 billion by 1918.

The most important and long-lasting economic legacy of the war was the organizational shift toward corporatism in American business. The wartime need for efficient management, manufacturing, and distribution could be met only by a greater reliance on the productive and marketing power of large corporations. Never before had business and the federal government cooperated so closely. Entire industries (such as radio manufacturing) and economic sectors (such as agriculture and energy) were organized, regulated, and subsidized. War agencies used both public and private power—legal authority and voluntarism—to hammer out and enforce agreements. Here was the genesis of the modern bureaucratic state.

Although many aspects of the government–business partnership proved temporary, some institutions and practices grew stronger in the postwar years. Among these were the Federal Reserve Board, the income tax system, the Chamber of Commerce, the Farm Bureau, and the growing horde of lobbying groups that pressed Washington for special interest legislation.

LABOR AND THE WAR

Organized labor's power and prestige, though by no means equal to those of business or government, clearly grew during the war. The expansion of the economy, combined with army mobilization and a decline in immigration from Europe, caused a growing wartime labor shortage. As the demand for workers intensified, the federal government was forced to recognize that labor would have to be more carefully tended to than in peacetime. For the war's duration, working people generally enjoyed higher wages and a better standard of living. In effect, the government took in labor as a junior partner in the mobilization of the economy.

Samuel Gompers, president of the AFL, emerged as the leading spokesman for the nation's trade union movement. Gompers pledged the AFL's patriotic support for the war effort, and in April 1918, President Wilson appointed him to the National War Labor Board (NWLB). During 1917, the nation had seen thousands of strikes involving more than a million workers. Wages were usually at issue, reflecting workers' concerns with spiraling inflation and higher prices. The NWLB acted as a kind of supreme court for labor, arbitrating disputes and working to prevent disruptions in production. The great majority of these interventions resulted in improved wages and reduced hours of work. Most important, the NWLB supported the right of workers to organize unions and furthered the acceptance of the eight-hour day for war workers—central aims of the labor movement. AFL unions gained more than a million new members during the war, and overall union membership rose from 2.7 million in 1914 to more than 5 million by 1920.

The war also brought widespread use of federal troops under the War Department's new "public utilities" doctrine, under which any private business remotely connected to war production was defined as a public utility. An influx of federal troops poured into lumber camps, coal districts, mining towns, and rail junctions across the nation, as employers requested help in guarding against threatened strikes or alleged "sabotage" by militant workers. Wartime conditions often meant severe disruptions and discomfort for America's workers as well. Overcrowding, rapid workforce turnover, and high inflation rates were typical in war-boom communities.

In the Southwest, the demand for wartime labor temporarily eased restrictions against the movement of Mexicans into the United States. The Immigration Act of 1917, requiring a literacy test and an $8 head tax, had cut Mexican immigration nearly in half, down to about 25,000 per year. But employers complained of severe shortages of workers.

Responding to these protests, in June 1917, the Department of Labor suspended the immigration law for the duration of the war and negotiated an agreement with the Mexican government permitting some 35,000 Mexican contract laborers to enter the United States. Pressure from southwestern employers kept the exemptions in force until 1921, well after the end of the war, demonstrating the growing importance of cheap Mexican labor to the region's economy.

If the war boosted the fortunes of the AFL, it also spelled the end for more radical elements of the U.S. labor movement. The Industrial Workers of the World (IWW), unlike the AFL, had concentrated on organizing unskilled workers into all-inclusive industrial unions. The Wobblies denounced capitalism as an unreformable system based on exploitation, and they opposed U.S. entry into the war. The IWW had grown in 1916 and 1917, gaining strength among workers in several areas crucial to the war effort: copper mining, lumbering, and wheat harvesting. In September 1917, the Wilson administration responded to appeals from western business leaders for a crackdown on the Wobblies. Justice Department agents, acting under the broad authority of the recently passed **Espionage Act**, swooped down on IWW offices in more than sixty towns and cities, arresting over 300 people and confiscating files. The mass trials and convictions that followed broke the back of America's radical labor movement and marked the beginning of a powerful wave of political repression.

WOMEN AT WORK

For many of the 8 million women already in the labor force, the war meant a chance to switch from low-paying jobs, such as domestic service, to higher-paying industrial employment. About a million women workers joined the labor force for the first time. Of the

---

QUICK REVIEW

National War Labor Board

- Federal and state governments created agencies to oversee the wartime economy.
- The National War Labor Board guaranteed the rights of unions to organize and bargain collectively.
- Labor unions sharply increased their membership under this protection.

Espionage Act   Law whose vague prohibition against obstructing the nation's war effort was used to crush dissent and criticism during World War I.

Women workers at the Midvale Steel and Ordnance Company in Pennsylvania, 1918. Wartime labor shortages created new opportunities for over 1 million women to take high-wage manufacturing jobs like the women shown here. The opportunities proved temporary, however, and with the war's end, nearly all of these women lost their jobs. By 1920, the number of women employed in manufacturing was lower than it had been in 1910.

estimated 9.4 million workers directly engaged in war work, some 2.25 million were women. World War I also marked the first time that women were mobilized directly into the armed forces. Over 16,000 women served overseas with the AEF in France, where most worked as nurses, clerical workers, telephone operators, and canteen operators. Another 12,000 women served stateside in the navy and U.S. Marine Corps. But the war's impact on women was greatest in the broader civilian economy.

In response to the widened range of female employment, the Labor Department created the Women in Industry Service (WIS). The service advised employers on using female labor and formulated general standards for the treatment of women workers. The WIS represented the first attempt by the federal government to take a practical stand on improving working conditions for women.

At war's end, women lost nearly all their defense-related jobs. But the war accelerated female employment in fields already dominated by women. By 1920, more women who worked outside the home did so in white-collar occupations—as telephone operators, secretaries, and clerks, for example—than in manufacturing or domestic service. The new awareness of women's work led Congress to create the Women's Bureau in the Labor Department, which continued the WIS wartime program of education and investigation through the postwar years.

WOMAN SUFFRAGE

The presence of so many new women wageworkers, combined with the highly visible volunteer work of millions of middle-class women, helped finally to secure the vote for women. Until World War I, the fight for woman suffrage had been waged largely within individual states. Western states and territories had led the way. Various forms of woman suffrage became law in Wyoming in 1869, followed by Utah (1870), Colorado (1893), and Idaho (1896).

The U.S. entry into the war provided a unique opportunity for suffrage groups to shift their strategy to a national campaign for a constitutional amendment granting the

The Mystery of 1920

The confident bearing and direct gaze of this woman voter, depicted on a 1920 cover of *Leslie's Illustrated Weekly*, suggests how the historic achievement of woman suffrage reinforced images of the "New Woman."

vote to women. At the same time, more militant suffragists, led by the young Quaker activist Alice Paul, injected new energy and more radical tactics into the movement. She joined forces with western women voters to form the National Woman's Party. Paul and her supporters picketed the White House, publicly burned President Wilson's speeches, and condemned the president and the Democrats for failing to produce an amendment. In one demonstration, they chained themselves to the White House fence, and after their arrest, went on a hunger strike in jail. The militants generated a great deal of publicity and sympathy.

Although some in the NAWSA objected to these tactics, Paul's radical approach helped make the NAWSA position more acceptable to Wilson. In 1917, the president urged Congress to pass a woman suffrage amendment as "vital to the winning of the war." The House did so in January 1918 and a more reluctant Senate approved it in June 1919. Another year of hard work was spent convincing the state legislatures. In August 1920,

•••⟨Read the Document
Profile: Alice Paul at
www.myhistorylab.com

QUICK REVIEW

Votes for Women

◆ Woman suffrage movement began in the mid-nineteenth century.

◆ Early twentieth-century leaders adopted activist tactics.

◆ Nineteenth Amendment ratified in 1920.

See the **Map**

Woman Suffrage before the Nineteenth Amendment at **www.myhistorylab.com**

Read the **Document**

Eighteenth Amendment, Prohibition of Intoxicating Liquor (1919) at **www.myhistorylab.com**

Tennessee gave the final vote needed to ratify the Nineteenth Amendment to the Constitution, finally making woman suffrage legal nationwide.

PROHIBITION

Another reform effort closely associated with women's groups triumphed at the same time. The movement to eliminate alcohol from American life had attracted many Americans, especially women, since before the Civil War. Temperance advocates saw drinking as the source of many of the worst problems faced by the working class, including family violence, unemployment, and poverty. By the early twentieth century, the Woman's Christian Temperance Union, with a quarter-million members, had become the single largest women's organization in American history.

In 1917, a coalition of progressives and rural fundamentalists in Congress pushed through a constitutional amendment providing for a national ban on alcoholic drinks. The Eighteenth Amendment was ratified by the states in January 1919 and became the law of the land one year later. Although Prohibition would create a host of problems in the postwar years, especially as a stimulus for the growth of organized crime, many Americans, particularly native-born Protestants, considered it a worthy moral reform.

PUBLIC HEALTH AND THE INFLUENZA PANDEMIC

Wartime mobilization brought deeper government involvement with public health issues, especially in the realm of sex hygiene, child welfare, and disease prevention. The rate of venereal disease among draftees was as high as 6 percent in some states, presenting a potential manpower problem for the army. In April 1917, the War Department mounted a vigorous campaign against venereal disease, which contributed to a 300 percent decline in venereal disease rates for soldiers during the war.

The wartime boost to government health work continued into the postwar years. The Children's Bureau, created in 1912 as a part of the Labor Department, undertook a series of reports on special problems growing out of the war: the increase in employment of married women, the finding of day care for children of working mothers, and the growth of both child labor and delinquency. In 1917, Julia C. Lathrop, chief of the bureau and a veteran of the settlement house movement, proposed a plan to institutionalize federal aid to the states for protection of mothers and children. Congress finally passed the Maternity and Infancy Act in 1921, appropriating over $1 million a year to be administered to the states by the Children's Bureau. In the postwar years, clinics for prenatal and obstetrical care grew out of these efforts and greatly reduced the rate of infant and maternal mortality and disease.

The disastrous influenza pandemic of 1918–19 offered the most serious challenge to national public health during the war years. Wartime conditions—large concentrations of people in military camps, on transport ships, and at the front—made its impact especially devastating. With no cure for the lethal combination of the "flu" and respiratory complications (mainly pneumonia), the pandemic killed over 21 million people worldwide. Few Americans paid attention to the disease until it swept through military camps and eastern cities in September 1918 and killed roughly 550,000 Americans in ten months. Most victims were young adults between the ages of twenty and forty.

REPRESSION AND REACTION

World War I exposed and intensified many of the deepest social tensions in American life. On the local level, vigilantes increasingly took the law into their own hands to punish those suspected of disloyalty. The push for national unity led the federal government to crack down on a wide spectrum of dissenters. The war inflamed racial hatred, and the worst race riots in the nation's history exploded in several

WHAT STEPS did the federal government take to suppress the antiwar movement?

cities. At war's end, a newly militant labor movement briefly asserted itself in mass strikes around the nation. Over each of these developments loomed the 1917 Bolshevik Revolution in Russia. Radicals around the world had drawn inspiration from what looked like the first successful revolution against a capitalist state. Many conservatives worried that similar revolutions were imminent. From 1918 through 1920, the federal government directed a repressive antiradical campaign that had crucial implications for the nation's future.

MUZZLING DISSENT: THE ESPIONAGE AND SEDITION ACTS

The Espionage Act of June 1917 became the government's key tool for the suppression of antiwar sentiment. It set severe penalties (up to twenty years' imprisonment and a $10,000 fine) for anyone found guilty of aiding the enemy, obstructing recruitment, or causing insubordination in the armed forces. The act also empowered the postmaster general to exclude from the mails any newspapers or magazines he thought treasonous.

To enforce the Espionage Act, the government had to increase its overall police and surveillance machinery. Civilian intelligence was coordinated by the newly created Bureau of Investigation in the Justice Department. This agency was reorganized after the war as the Federal Bureau of Investigation (FBI). In May 1918, the **Sedition Act**, an amendment to the Espionage Act, outlawed "any disloyal, profane, scurrilous, or abusive language intended to cause contempt, scorn, contumely, or disrepute" to the government, Constitution, or flag.

These acts became a convenient vehicle for striking out at socialists, pacifists, radical labor activists, and others who resisted the patriotic tide. The most celebrated prosecution came in June 1918, when federal agents arrested Eugene V. Debs in Canton, Ohio, after he gave a speech defending antiwar protesters. Debs served thirty-two months in federal prison before being pardoned by President Warren G. Harding on Christmas Day, 1921.

The Supreme Court upheld the constitutionality of the acts in several 1919 decisions. In *Schenck* v. *United States*, the Court unanimously ruled that Congress could restrict speech if the words "are used in such circumstances and are of such a nature as to create a clear and present danger." The decision upheld the conviction of Charles Schenck for having mailed pamphlets urging potential army inductees to resist conscription. In *Debs* v. *United States*, the Court affirmed the guilt of Eugene V. Debs for his antiwar speech in Canton. Finally, in *Abrams* v. *United States*, the Court upheld Sedition Act convictions of four Russian immigrants who had printed pamphlets denouncing American military intervention in the Russian Revolution.

In many western communities, local vigilantes used the superpatriotic mood to settle scores with labor organizers and radicals. In July 1917, for example, 2,000 armed vigilantes swept through the mining town of Bisbee, Arizona, acting on behalf of the Phelps-Dodge mining company and local businessmen. They wanted to break an IWW-led strike that had crippled Bisbee's booming copper industry. The vigilantes seized miners in their homes, on the street, and in restaurants and stores, delivering an ultimatum that any miner who refused to return to work would be deported. Some 1,400 miners were forced at gunpoint onto a freight train, which took them to Columbus, New Mexico, where they were dumped in the desert.

In thousands of other instances, government repression and local vigilantes reinforced each other. The American Protective League, founded with the blessing of the Justice Department, mobilized 250,000 self-appointed "operatives" in more than 600 towns and cities. Members of the league, mostly businessmen, bankers, and former policemen, spied on their neighbors and staged a series of well-publicized "slacker" raids on antiwar protesters and draft evaders.

•• Read the Document

Abrams v. *U.S.; Schenk* v. *U.S. (1919)* at **www.myhistorylab.com**

Sedition Act   Broad law restricting criticism of America's involvement in World War I or its government, flag, military, taxes, or officials.

Great Migration The mass movement of African Americans from the rural South to the urban North, spurred especially by new job opportunities during World War I and the 1920s.

•••┤Read the **Document**

Letters from the Great Migration (1917) at **www.myhistorylab.com**

•••┤Read the **Document**

The Chicago Riot (1919) at **www.myhistorylab.com**

THE GREAT MIGRATION AND RACIAL TENSIONS

Economic opportunity brought on by war prosperity triggered a massive migration of rural black Southerners to northern cities. From 1914 to 1920, between 300,000 and 500,000 African Americans left the rural South for the North. Acute labor shortages led northern factory managers to recruit black migrants to the expanding industrial centers. Black workers eagerly left low-paying jobs as field hands and domestic servants for the chance at relatively high-paying work in meatpacking plants, shipyards, and steel mills (see Table 22.1).

Kinship and community networks were crucial in shaping what came to be called the **Great Migration**. The networks spread news about job openings, urban residential districts, and boardinghouses in northern cities. Black clubs, churches, and fraternal lodges in southern communities frequently sponsored the migration of their members, as well as return trips to the South. Single African American women often made the trip first, because they could more easily obtain steady work as maids, cooks, and laundresses. Relatively few African American men actually secured high-paying skilled jobs in industry or manufacturing. Most had to settle for such low-paying occupations as construction laborers, teamsters, janitors, or porters.

Shut out of white neighborhoods by a combination of custom and law (such as restrictive covenants forbidding homeowners to sell to nonwhites), African American migrants found themselves forced to squeeze into less desirable and all-black neighborhoods. In 1920, for example, approximately 85 percent of Chicago's 110,000 black citizens lived within a narrow strip roughly three miles long and a quarter mile wide. The city's South Side ghetto had been born.

The persistence of lynching and other racial violence in the South no doubt contributed to the Great Migration, but racial violence was not limited to the South. On July 2, 1917, in East St. Louis, Illinois, a mob of whites attacked African Americans, killing at least 200. Before this riot, some of the city's manufacturers had steadily recruited black labor as a way to keep local union demands down. Unions had refused to allow black workers as members, and politicians had cynically exploited white racism in appealing for votes. In Chicago, on July 27, 1919, antiblack rioting broke out on a

TABLE 22.1

The Great Migration: Black Population Growth in Selected Northern Cities, 1910–20

| Northern Cities | 1910 | | 1920 | | |
	No.	Percent	No.	Percent	Percent Increase
New York	91,709	1.9%	152,467	2.7%	66.3%
Chicago	44,103	2.0	109,458	4.1	148.2
Philadelphia	84,459	5.5	134,229	7.4	58.9
Detroit	5,741	1.2	40,838	4.1	611.3
St. Louis	43,960	6.4	69,854	9.0	58.9
Cleveland	8,448	1.5	34,451	4.3	307.8
Pittsburgh	25,623	4.8	37,725	6.4	47.2
Cincinnati	19,739	5.4	30,079	7.5	53.2

U.S. Department of Commerce.

This southern African American family is shown arriving in Chicago around 1910. Black migrants to northern cities often faced overcrowding, inferior housing, and a high death rate from disease. But the chance to earn daily wages of $6 to $8 (the equivalent of a week's wages in much of the South), as well as the desire to escape persistent racial violence, kept the migrants coming.

Lake Michigan beach. For two weeks, white gangs hunted African Americans in the streets and burned hundreds out of their homes. Twenty-three African Americans and fifteen whites died, and more than 500 were injured. In 1921, the bloodiest race riot of all took place in Greenwood, a thriving African American neighborhood in Tulsa, Oklahoma. A group of armed blacks, many of them army veterans, confronted a white mob intent on lynching a young African American accused of rape. The next day, whites invaded the Greenwood district, burned it to the ground, and murdered some 300 African Americans.

African Americans had supported the war effort as faithfully as any group. In 1917, most African Americans thought the war might improve their lot. Black disillusionment with the war grew quickly, however, as did a newly militant spirit. A heightened sense of race consciousness and activism was evident among black veterans and the growing black communities of northern cities. By 1919, membership in the NAACP had reached 60,000 and the circulation of its journal exceeded half a million.

LABOR STRIFE

The relative labor peace of 1917 and 1918 dissolved after the armistice. In 1919 alone, more than 4 million American workers were involved in some 3,600 strikes. This unprecedented strike wave had several causes. Most of the modest wartime wage gains were wiped out by spiraling inflation and high prices for food, fuel, and housing. With the end of government controls on industry, many employers withdrew their recognition of unions. Difficult working conditions, such as the twelve-hour day in steel mills, were still routine in some industries.

Several of the postwar strikes received widespread national attention. In February 1919, a strike in the shipyards of Seattle, Washington, over wages escalated into a general citywide strike involving 60,000 workers. The local press and Mayor Ole Hanson denounced the strikers as revolutionaries. Hanson effectively ended the

strike by requesting federal troops to occupy the city. In September, Boston police-men went out on strike when the police commissioner rejected a citizens' commis-sion study that recommended a pay raise. Massachusetts Governor Calvin Coolidge called in the National Guard to restore order and won a national reputation by crush-ing the strike. The entire police force was fired.

The biggest strike took place in the steel industry and involved some 350,000 steel-workers. Centered in several midwestern cities, the strike lasted from September 1919 to January 1920. The major demands were union recognition, the eight-hour day, and wage increases. The steel companies used black strikebreakers and armed guards to keep the mills running. Elbert Gary, president of U.S. Steel, directed a sophisticated propaganda campaign that branded the strikers as revolutionaries. Public opinion turned against the strike and condoned the use of state and federal troops to break it. The failed steel strike proved to be the era's most bitter and devastating defeat for organized labor.

An Uneasy Peace

The armistice of November 1918 ended the fighting on the battlefield, but the war continued at the peace conference. In the old royal Palace of Versailles near Paris, delegates from twenty-seven countries spent five months hammering out a settlement. Yet neither Germany nor Russia were represented. The proceedings were dominated by leaders of the "Big Four": David Lloyd George (Great Britain), Georges Clemenceau (France), Vittorio Orlando (Italy), and Woodrow Wilson (United States).

PEACEMAKING AND THE SPECTER OF BOLSHEVISM

Even before November 1918, the Allies struggled with how to respond to the revolution-ary developments in Russia. President Wilson refused to recognize the authority of the Bolsheviks, seeing them as a threat to American values. At the same time, however, Wilson at first resisted British and French pressure to intervene in Russia, citing his com-mitment to national **self-determination** and noninterference in other countries' inter-nal affairs.

By August 1918, as the Russian political and military situation became increasingly chaotic, Wilson agreed to British and French plans for sending troops to Siberia and northern Russia. Meanwhile, Japan poured troops into Siberia and northern Manchuria in a bid to control the commercially important Chinese Eastern and Trans-Siberian rail-ways. After the Wilson administration negotiated an agreement that placed these strate-gic railways under international control, the restoration and protection of the railways became the primary concern of American military forces in Russia. Eventually, some 15,000 American troops served in northern and eastern Russia, with some remaining until 1920.

The Allied armed intervention widened the gulf between Russia and the West. In March 1919, Russian Communists established the Third International, or Comintern. Their call for a worldwide revolution deepened Allied mistrust, and the Paris Peace Conference essentially ignored the new political reality posed by the Russian Revolution.

WILSON IN PARIS

Wilson believed the Great War revealed the bankruptcy of diplomacy based on alliances and the "balance of power." He believed that peacemaking, based on the framework put forward in his Fourteen Points, meant an opportunity for America to lead the rest of the world toward a new vision of international relations. The most controversial element, both at home and abroad, would prove to be the League of Nations. The heart of the League Covenant, Article X, called for collective security as the ultimate method of

---

HOW CAN we explain Woodrow Wilson's failure to win the peace?

self-determination The right of a people or a nation to decide on its own political allegiance or form of government without external influence.

keeping the peace: "The members of the League undertake to respect and preserve as against external aggression the territorial integrity and existing political independence of all Members."

Much of the negotiating in Paris was done in secret among the Big Four. The ideal of self-determination found limited expression. The independent states of Austria, Hungary, Poland, Yugoslavia, and Czechoslovakia were carved out of the homelands of the defeated Central Powers. The Allies resisted Wilson's call for independence for the colonies of the defeated nations. A compromise mandate system of protectorates gave the French and British control of parts of the old German and Turkish empires in Africa and western Asia. Japan won control of former German colonies in China.

Another disappointment for Wilson came with the issue of war guilt. He had strongly opposed the extraction of harsh economic reparations from the Central Powers. But the French and British insisted on making Germany pay. The final treaty contained a clause attributing the war to "the aggression of Germany," and a commission later set German war reparations at $33 billion. Bitter resentment in Germany over the punitive treaty helped sow the seeds for the Nazi rise to power in the 1930s.

The final treaty was signed on June 28, 1919, in the Hall of Mirrors at the Palace of Versailles. The Germans had no choice but to accept its harsh terms. President Wilson had been disappointed by the endless compromising of his ideals, no doubt underestimating the stubborn reality of power politics in the wake of Europe's most devastating war. He had nonetheless won a commitment to the League of Nations, the centerpiece of his plan, and he was confident that the American people would accept the treaty.

Woodrow Wilson, Georges Clemenceau, and David Lloyd George are among the central figures depicted in John Christen Johansen's *Signing of the Treaty of Versailles*. The gathered statesmen appear dwarfed by their surroundings.

John Christen Johansen (1876–1964), *Signing of the Treaty of Versailles*, 1919, oil on canvas, 249 cm × 224.5 cm (98-1/16 × 88-3/8"). Gift of an anonymous donor through Mrs. Elizabeth Rogerson, 1926. National Portrait Gallery, Smithsonian Institution, Washington, DC/Art Resource, New York.

THE TREATY FIGHT

Preoccupied with peace conference politics in Paris, Wilson had neglected politics at home. His troubles had started earlier when Republicans captured both the House and the Senate in the 1918 elections. Wilson then made a tactical error by including no prominent Republicans in the U.S. peace delegation.

Wilson's most extreme enemies in the Senate were a group of about sixteen **"irreconcilables"** who were opposed to a treaty in any form. The less dogmatic, but more influential, opponents were led by Republican Henry Cabot Lodge of Massachusetts, powerful majority leader of the Senate. They had strong reservations about the League of Nations, especially the provisions for collective security should a member nation be attacked. Lodge proposed a series of amendments that would have weakened the League. Wilson refused to compromise, motivated in part by the long-standing hatred he and Lodge felt toward each other.

In September, Wilson set out on a speaking tour across the country to drum up support for the League and the treaty. The strain took its toll. On September 25, after speaking in Pueblo, Colorado, Wilson collapsed from exhaustion. A week later, back in Washington, the president suffered a stroke that left him partially paralyzed. In November, Lodge brought the treaty out of committee for a vote, having appended to it fourteen reservations—that is, recommended changes. A bedridden Wilson stubbornly refused to compromise and instructed Democrats to vote against the Lodge version of the treaty.

In the final vote, on March 19, 1920, twenty-one Democrats broke with the president and voted for the Lodge version, giving it a majority of 49 to 35. But this was seven votes short of the two-thirds needed for ratification. As a result, the United States never

•••••Read the Document

Henry Cabot Lodge, Objections to Treaty of Versailles (1919) at **www.myhistorylab.com**

irreconcilables Group of U.S. senators adamantly opposed to ratification of the Treaty of Versailles after World War I.

◉⟶ Read the Document

A. Mitchell Palmer, On the Menace of Communism (1920) at **www.myhistorylab.com**

signed the **Versailles Treaty**, nor did it join the League of Nations. The absence of the United States weakened the League and made it more difficult for the organization to realize Wilson's dream of a peaceful community of nations.

THE RED SCARE

Revolutionary changes taking place in Russia became an important backdrop for domestic politics. The accusation of Bolshevism became a powerful weapon for turning public opinion against strikers and political dissenters of all kinds. In truth, by 1919, the American radicals were already weakened and badly split. In the spring of 1919, a few extremists mailed bombs to prominent business and political leaders. That June, simultaneous bombings in eight cities killed two people and damaged the residence of Attorney General A. Mitchell Palmer. With public alarm growing, state and federal officials began a coordinated campaign to root out subversives and their alleged Russian connections.

Palmer used the broad authority of the 1918 Alien Act, which enabled the government to deport any immigrant found to be a member of a revolutionary organization prior to or after coming to the United States. In a series of raids in late 1919, Justice Department agents in eleven cities arrested and roughed up several hundred members of the IWW and the Union of Russian Workers. Little evidence of revolutionary intent was found, but 249 people were deported, including prominent anarchists Emma Goldman and Alexander Berkman. In early 1920, some 6,000 people in thirty-three cities, including many U.S. citizens and non-Communists, were arrested and herded into prisons and bullpens. The Palmer raids had a ripple effect around the nation, encouraging other repressive measures against radicals. In New York, the state assembly refused to seat five duly elected Socialist Party members.

Palmer's popularity had waned by the spring of 1920, when it became clear that his predictions of revolutionary uprisings were wildly exaggerated. A report prepared by a group of distinguished lawyers questioned the legality of the attorney general's tactics. As part of the resistance to Palmer's policies, a group of progressive activists formed the American Civil Liberties Union (ACLU) in 1920.

The **Red Scare** left an ugly legacy: wholesale violations of constitutional rights, deportations of hundreds of innocent people, fuel for the fires of nativism and intolerance. Business groups, such as the National Association of Manufacturers, found "Red-baiting" to be an effective tool in postwar efforts to keep unions out of their factories. In many communities, local vigilantes invoked the threat of Bolshevism and used the superpatriotic mood to settle scores with labor organizers and radicals.

The Red Scare took its toll on the women's movement as well. Before the war, many suffragists and feminists had maintained ties and shared platforms with socialist and labor groups. But the calls for "100 percent Americanism" during and after the war destroyed the fragile alliances that had made a group such as the National American Woman Suffrage Association so powerful. Hostility to radicalism marked the political climate of the 1920s, and this atmosphere narrowed the political spectrum for women activists.

THE ELECTION OF 1920

Ill and exhausted, Wilson did not run for reelection in 1920. A badly divided Democratic Party compromised on Governor James M. Cox of Ohio as its candidate. A proven vote-getter, Cox distanced himself from Wilson's policies, which had come under withering attack from many quarters.

The Republicans nominated Senator Warren G. Harding of Ohio. Harding's campaign was vague and elusive about the Versailles Treaty and almost everything else. He struck a chord with the electorate in calling for a retreat from Wilsonian idealism. "America's present need," he said, "is not heroics but healing; not nostrums but normalcy; not revolution but restoration."

Versailles Treaty The treaty ending World War I and creating the League of Nations.

Red Scare Post–World War I public hysteria over Bolshevik influence in the United States directed against labor activism, radical dissenters, and some ethnic groups.

CHRONOLOGY

1903	United States obtains Panama Canal rights
1905	President Theodore Roosevelt mediates peace treaty between Japan and Russia at Portsmouth Conference
1908	Root-Takahira Agreement with Japan affirms status quo in Asia and Open Door policy in China
1911	Mexican Revolution begins
1914	U.S. forces invade Mexico
	Panama Canal opens
	World War I begins in Europe
	President Woodrow Wilson issues proclamation of neutrality
1915	Germany declares war zone around Great Britain
	German U-boat sinks *Lusitania*
1916	Pancho Villa raids New Mexico and is pursued by General Pershing
	Wilson is reelected
	National Defense Act establishes preparedness program
1917	February: Germany resumes unrestricted submarine warfare
	March: Zimmermann note, suggesting a German-Mexican alliance, shocks Americans
	April: United States declares war on the Central Powers

	May: Selective Service Act is passed
	June: Espionage Act is passed
	November: Bolshevik Revolution begins in Russia
1918	January: Wilson unveils Fourteen Points
	May: Sedition Act is passed
	June: U.S. troops begin to see action in France
	September: Influenza outbreaks among AEF troops in France
	November: Armistice ends war
1919	January: Eighteenth Amendment (Prohibition) is ratified
	Wilson serves as chief U.S. negotiator at Paris Peace Conference
	June: Versailles Treaty is signed in Paris
	July: Race riot breaks out in Chicago
	Steel strike begins in several midwestern cities
	November: Palmer raids begin
1920	March: Senate finally votes down Versailles Treaty and League of Nations
	August: Nineteenth Amendment (woman suffrage) is ratified
	November: Warren G. Harding is elected president

The notion of a "return to normalcy" proved very attractive to voters exhausted by the war, inflation, big government, and social dislocation. Harding won the greatest landslide in history to that date, carrying every state outside the South and taking the popular vote by 16 million to 9 million. Republicans retained their majorities in the House and Senate as well. The overall vote repudiated Wilson and the progressive movement. Americans seemed eager to pull back from moralism in public and international controversies. Yet many of the economic, social, and cultural changes wrought by the war would accelerate during the 1920s. In truth, there could never be a "return to normalcy."

Read the Document

History Bookshelf: *Walter Lippmann,*
Public Opinion *(1922)* at
www.myhistorylab.com

CONCLUSION

The global impact of the Great War, including the United States' place in relation to the rest of the world, was profound. Although the casualties and social upheavals endured by the European powers might seem to dwarf the price paid by the United States, the war created economic, social, and political dislocations that helped reshape American life long after Armistice Day. The ability to raise and deploy the massive American Expeditionary Force overseas so quickly had proved decisive to ending the fighting. The government's direct intervention in every aspect of the wartime economy was unprecedented, and wartime production needs contributed to a "second industrial revolution" that transformed the economy in the decade following the war.

Republican administrations invoked the wartime partnership between government and industry to justify an aggressive peacetime policy fostering cooperation between the state and business. Although the United States would not join the League of Nations, the war turned the United States into a major global force: the world's new leading creditor nation would now also take its place as a powerful commercial and industrial engine in the global economy.

Patriotic fervor and the exaggerated threat of Bolshevism were used to repress radicalism, organized labor, feminism, and the entire legacy of progressive reform. The wartime measure of national prohibition evolved into perhaps the most contentious social issue of peacetime. Sophisticated use of sales techniques, psychology, and propaganda during the war helped define the newly powerful advertising and public relations industries of the 1920s. The growing visibility of immigrants and African Americans, especially in the nation's cities, provoked a xenophobic and racist backlash in the politics of the 1920s. More than anything else, the desire for "normalcy" reflected the deep anxieties evoked by America's wartime experience.

REVIEW QUESTIONS

1. What central issues drew the United States deeper into international politics in the early years of the century? How did American presidents justify a more expansive role? What diplomatic and military policies did they exploit for these ends?

2. Compare the arguments for and against American participation in the Great War. Which Americans were most likely to support entry? Which were more likely to oppose it?

3. How did mobilizing for war change the economy and its relationship to government? Which of these changes, if any, spilled over to the postwar years?

4. How did the war affect political life in the United States? What techniques were used to stifle dissent? What was the war's political legacy?

5. Analyze the impact of the war on American workers. How did the conflict affect the lives of African Americans and women?

6. What principles guided Woodrow Wilson's Fourteen Points? How would you explain the United States' failure to ratify the Treaty of Versailles?

KEY TERMS

Allies (p. 570)
Bolsheviks (p. 577)
Central Powers (p. 569)
Committee on Public Information (CPI) (p. 572)
Doughboys (p. 564)
Espionage Act (p. 579)
Fourteen Points (p. 577)
Great Migration (p. 584)
Imperialism (p. 569)
Irreconcilables (p. 587)
League of Nations (p. 577)

Liberty Bonds (p. 578)
Militarism (p. 569)
Open Door (p. 565)
Preparedness (p. 571)
Red Scare (p. 588)
Roosevelt Corollary (p. 565)
Sedition Act (p. 583)
Selective Service Act (p. 573)
Self-determination (p. 586)
Versailles Treaty (p. 588)
War Industries Board (WIB) (p. 577)

PEARSON
myhistorylab Connections

Reinforce what you learned in this chapter by studying the many documents, images, maps, review tools, and videos available at www.myhistorylab.com.

Read and Review

✓●─ Study and Review Chapter 22

●●●●─ Read the Document

William H. Taft, "Dollar Diplomacy" (1912)

Eugene V. Debs, Critique of World War (1918)

Joseph Buffington, "Friendly Words to the Foreign Born" (1917)

Statement to French Concerning Black American Troops (1918)

Eugene Kennedy, "A 'Doughboy' Describes the Fighting Front" (1918)

Woodrow Wilson, "Fourteen Points" (1917)

Eighteenth Amendment, Prohibition of Intoxicating Liquor (1919)

Abrams v. U.S.; Schenk v. U.S. (1919)

Letters from the Great Migration (1917)

The Chicago Riot (1919)

Henry Cabot Lodge, Objections to Treaty of Versailles (1919)

A. Mitchell Palmer, On the Menace of Communism (1920)

●●─ See the Map

World War I

Woman Suffrage before the Nineteenth Amendment

Research and Explore

●●●●─ Read the Document

Exploring America: Becoming American

Profiles
  Alice Paul
  General John J. Pershing

History Bookshelf: Walter Lippmann, Public Opinion *(1922)*

((●●─ Hear the Audio *Over There*

((●●─ Watch the Video

The Panama Canal

American Entry into WWI

The Outbreak of World War I

((●●─ **Hear** the **Audio**

Hear the audio files for Chapter 22 at
www.myhistorylab.com.

Happy times were here again.

—Upton Sinclair, *from* The Flivver King

Toward a Modern America: The 1920s. "More than a car. FORD: A National Institution" poster, 1923.

23

THE TWENTIES
1920–1929

((•—Hear the Audio

Hear the audio files for Chapter 23 at **www.myhistorylab.com**.

WHAT FACTORS combined to produce postwar prosperity in the United States?

HOW AND why did the Republican Party dominate 1920s' politics?

HOW DID the new mass media reshape American culture?

WHAT EXPLAINS the backlash against social and cultural change in the 1920s?

WHICH AMERICANS were less likely to share in postwar prosperity and why?

1920 1929

AMERICAN COMMUNITIES
The Movie Audience and Hollywood:
Mass Culture Creates a New National Community

INSIDE MIDTOWN MANHATTAN'S MAGNIFICENT NEW ROXY THEATER, A sellout crowd eagerly settled in for opening night. Outside, thousands of fans cheered wildly at the arrival of movie stars such as Charlie Chaplin, Gloria Swanson, and Harold Lloyd. A squadron of smartly uniformed ushers guided patrons under a five-story-tall rotunda to some 6,200 velvet-covered seats. The audience marveled at the huge gold- and rose-colored murals, classical statuary, plush carpeting, and Gothic-style windows. Suddenly, light flooded the orchestra pit and 110 musicians began playing "The Star Spangled Banner." A troupe of 100 performers took the stage, dancing ballet numbers and singing old southern melodies such as "My Old Kentucky Home" and "Swanee River." Congratulatory telegrams from President Calvin Coolidge and other dignitaries flashed on the screen. Finally, the evening's feature presentation, *The Love of Sunya*, starring Gloria Swanson, began. Samuel L. "Roxy" Rothapfel, the theater's designer, had realized his grand dream—to build "the cathedral of the motion picture."

When Roxy's opened in March 1927, nearly 60 million Americans "worshiped" each week at movie theaters across the nation. The remarkable popularity of motion pictures, and later radio, forged a new kind of community. People who may have had little in common in terms of ethnicity, background, or geographic location found themselves part of a virtual community of movie fans. Hollywood films also achieved a global popularity that represented the cultural side of America's newfound influence in the world. The Webb-Pomerene Act of 1918 proved a boon for the global expansion of Hollywood film, as it exempted export associations from antitrust laws, allowing them to form cartels, fix prices, and engage in other trade practices that would have been barred at home. Hollywood movies soon emerged as among the most widely circulated American commodities in the world. Producers found strong allies in the federal government, which touted the connections between the export of Hollywood movies and the growth of American trade around the world. "Trade follows the film," as one Commerce Department report put it, with movies supplying "an animated catalogue for ideas of dress, living, and comfort."

Hollywood's emergence might be thought of as part of a broader "second industrial revolution" that modernized industrial production and greatly expanded the availability of consumer goods

Hollywood

in the postwar years. The studios concentrated on producing big-budget feature films designed for mass audiences, with the "star system" providing the industry's version of product branding. The economies of large-scale production allowed studios to sign popular actors to long-term contracts and invest heavily in their salaries and promotion. The stars themselves had to be willing to sacrifice their privacy in order to promote their "celebrity" status. Movie stars like Charlie Chaplin, Mary Pickford, Rudolph Valentino, Gloria Swanson, and Douglas Fairbanks became popular idols as much for their highly publicized private lives as for their roles on-screen. Americans embraced the culture of celebrity, voraciously consuming fan magazines, gossip columns, and news of the stars. Indeed, during the 1920s, there was a tight connection between celebrity and the rapid growth of new networks of mass culture—movies, radio, advertising, musical recordings, and big-time sports.

Ordinary Americans found it easy to identify with movie stars despite their wealth and status. Unlike industrialists or politicians, stars had no social authority over large groups of employees or voters. They, too, had to answer to a boss, and most had risen from humble beginnings. But above all, Hollywood, like the movies it churned out, represented for millions of Americans new possibilities: freedom, material success, upward mobility, and the chance to remake one's very identity. By the end of the decade, the Hollywood "dream factory" had helped forge a national community whose collective aspirations and desires were increasingly defined by those possibilities, even if relatively few Americans realized them during the 1920s. And around the world, Hollywood movies became the preeminent version of the American way of life.

Of course, Hollywood films offered nothing near an accurate reflection of the complexities of American society. As American culture became increasingly defined by an urban-based mass media that claimed the entire nation for its audience, resentment toward and resistance against the new popular culture was widespread. Movies celebrated prosperity, new technologies, and expanded consumerism, but these were by no means shared equally among Americans in the decade following World War I. While Hollywood films touted the promise of the modern, and the potential for people to remake themselves, tenacious belief in the old-fashioned verities of prewar America fueled some of the strongest political and cultural currents of the decade.

POSTWAR PROSPERITY AND ITS PRICE

Republican Warren G. Harding won the presidency in 1920, largely thanks to his nostalgic call for a "return to normalcy." In the decade following the end of World War I, however, the American economy underwent profound structural changes that guaranteed life would never be "normal" again.

WHAT FACTORS combined to produce postwar prosperity in the United States?

THE SECOND INDUSTRIAL REVOLUTION

The prosperity of the 1920s rested on what historians have called the "second industrial revolution" in American manufacturing, in which technological innovations made it possible to increase industrial output without expanding the labor force. Electricity replaced steam as the main power source for industry in those years, making possible the replacement of older machinery with more efficient and flexible electric machinery.

Much of the newer, automatic machinery could be operated by unskilled and semi-skilled workers, and it boosted the overall efficiency of American industry. The machine industry itself, particularly the manufacture of electrical machinery, led in productivity gains, enjoying one of the fastest rates of expansion. It employed more workers than any other manufacturing sector—some 1.1 million in 1929—supplying not only a growing home market but 35 percent of the world market as well.

In the 1920s, modern mass-production techniques were increasingly applied to newer consumer-durable goods—automobiles, radios, washing machines, and telephones—permitting firms to make large profits while keeping prices affordable. Other consumer-based industries, such as canning, chemicals, synthetics, and plastics, began to change the everyday lives of millions of Americans. With more efficient management, greater mechanization, intensive product research, and ingenious sales and advertising methods, the consumer-based industries helped to nearly double industrial production in the 1920s.

The watchword for all this was efficiency, a virtue that progressives had emphasized in their prewar efforts to improve urban life and the mechanics of government itself. But efficiency became an obsession for American businessmen, who thought it defined modernity as well.

Read the Document
Frederick W. Taylor, "Scientific Management" (1911) at **www.myhistorylab.com**

THE MODERN CORPORATION

In the late nineteenth century, individual entrepreneurs such as John D. Rockefeller in oil and Andrew Carnegie in steel had provided a model for success. They maintained both corporate control (ownership) and business leadership (management) in their enterprises. In the 1920s, a managerial revolution increasingly divorced ownership of corporate stock from the everyday control of businesses (see Figure 23.1). A growing class of salaried executives, plant managers, and engineers formed a new elite, who made corporate policy without themselves having a controlling interest in the companies for which they worked. They stressed scientific management and the latest theories of behavioral psychology in their effort to make their workplaces more productive, stable, and profitable (see Figure 23.2). Modern managers also brought a more sophisticated understanding of global markets to their management. Exploiting overseas markets, especially in Europe, became a key element in corporate strategy, especially for car manufacturers, chemical companies, and businesses engaged in the new world of modern mass media.

During the 1920s, the most successful corporations were those that led in three key areas: the integration of production and distribution, product diversification, and the expansion of industrial research. Until the end of World War I, for example, the chemical manufacturer Du Pont

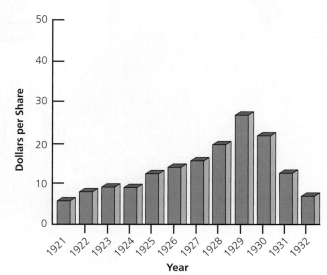

Figure 23.1 Stock Market Prices, 1921–32
Common stock prices rose steeply during the 1920s. Although only about 4 million Americans owned stocks during the period, "stock watching" became something of a national sport.

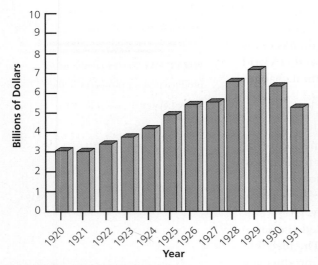

Figure 23.2 Consumer Debt, 1920–31
The expansion of consumer borrowing was a key component of the era's prosperity. These figures do not include mortgages or money borrowed to purchase stocks. They reveal the great increase in "installment buying" for such consumer durable goods as automobiles and household appliances.

had specialized in explosives such as gunpowder. After the war, Du Pont moved aggressively into the consumer market with a diverse array of products. The company created separate but integrated divisions that produced and distributed new fabrics (such as rayon), paints, dyes, and celluloid products (such as artificial sponges).

By 1929, the 200 largest corporations owned nearly half the nation's corporate wealth—that is, physical plant, stock, and property. Half the total industrial income—revenue from sales of goods—was concentrated in 100 corporations. Oligopoly—the control of a market by a few large producers—became the norm. National chain grocery stores, clothing shops, and pharmacies began squeezing out local neighborhood businesses. One grocery chain alone, the Great Atlantic and Pacific Tea Company (A&P), accounted for 10 percent of all retail food sales in America. A&P won out over thousands of older "mom and pop" grocery stores partly by selling its stores as "clean" and "modern," with no haggling over prices. These changes meant that Americans were increasingly members of national consumer communities, buying the same brands all over the country, as opposed to locally produced goods.

WELFARE CAPITALISM

The wartime gains made by organized labor, and the active sympathy shown to trade unions by government agencies such as the National War Labor Board (NWLB), troubled most corporate leaders. To challenge the power and appeal of trade unions and collective bargaining, large employers aggressively promoted a variety of new programs designed to improve worker well-being and morale while also fending off unionization. These schemes, collectively known as **welfare capitalism**, became a key part of corporate strategy in the 1920s.

Large corporations mounted an effective antiunion campaign in the early 1920s called "the American plan" as an alternative to trade unionism and the class antagonism associated with European labor relations. Backed by powerful business lobbies, campaign leaders called for the **open shop**, in which no employee would be compelled to join a union. In effect, an "open shop" meant that no known union member would be hired. If a union existed, nonmembers would still get whatever wages and rights the union had won—a policy that put organizers at a disadvantage in signing up new members.

The open shop undercut the gains won in a union shop, where new employees had to join an existing union, or a closed shop, where employers agreed to hire only union members. As alternatives, large employers such as U.S. Steel and International Harvester began setting up company unions. Their intent was to substitute largely symbolic employee representation in management conferences for the more confrontational process of collective bargaining. These management strategies contributed to a sharp decline in the ranks of organized labor. A conservative and timid union leadership was also responsible for the trend. William Green, who became president of the American Federation of Labor

The A&P grocery chain expanded from 400 stores in 1912 to more than 15,000 by the end of the 1920s, making it a familiar sight in communities across America. A&P advertisements, like this one from 1927, emphasized cleanliness, order, and the availability of name-brand goods at discount prices.

after the death of Samuel Gompers in 1924, showed no real interest in getting unorganized workers, such as those in the growing mass-production industries of automobiles, steel, and electrical goods, into unions.

Another approach encouraged workers to acquire property through stock-purchase plans or, less frequently, home-ownership plans. By 1927, 800,000 employees had more than $1 billion invested in more than 300 companies. Other programs offered workers insurance policies covering accidents, illness, old age, and death. By 1928, some 6 million workers had group insurance coverage valued at $7.5 billion. Many plant managers and personnel departments consciously worked to improve safety conditions, provide medical services, and establish sports and recreation programs for workers. Employers hoped such measures would encourage workers to identify personally with the company and discourage complaints on the job. To some extent they succeeded. But welfare capitalism could not solve the chronic problems faced by industrial workers: seasonal unemployment, low wages, long hours, and unhealthy factory conditions. Indeed, corporate policy reinforced economic insecurity for millions of workers and advanced growing income inequality.

welfare capitalism A paternalistic system of labor relations emphasizing management responsibility for employee well-being.

open shop Factory or business employing workers whether or not they are union members; in practice, such a business usually refuses to hire union members and follows antiunion policies.

THE AUTO AGE

No other single development matched the impact of the postwar automobile explosion on the way Americans worked, lived, and played. The auto industry offered the clearest example of the rise to prominence of consumer durables. During the 1920s, America made approximately 85 percent of all the world's passenger cars. By 1929, the motor vehicle industry was the most productive in the United States in terms of value. In that year, the industry added 4.8 million new cars to the more than 26 million—roughly one for every five people—already on American roads.

This extraordinary new industry had mushroomed in less than a generation. Its great pioneer, Henry Ford, had shown how the use of a continuous assembly line could drastically reduce the number of worker hours required to produce a single vehicle. Ford revolutionized the factory shop floor with new, custom-built machinery, such as the engine-boring drill press and the pneumatic wrench, and a more efficient layout. In 1913, it took thirteen hours to produce one automobile. In 1914, Ford's system finished one car every ninety minutes. By 1925, cars were rolling off his assembly line at the rate of one every ten seconds.

In 1914, Ford startled American industry by inaugurating a new wage scale: $5 for an eight-hour day. This was roughly double the going pay rate for industrial labor, along with a shorter workday as well. Ford acted less out of benevolence than out of shrewdness. He understood that workers were consumers as well as producers, and the new wage scale helped boost sales of Ford cars. It also reduced the high turnover rate in his labor force and increased worker efficiency. Ford's mass-production system and economies of scale permitted him to progressively reduce the price of his cars, bringing them within the reach of millions of Americans.

By 1927, Ford had produced 15 million Model Ts. But by then, the company faced stiff competition from General Motors (GM), which had developed an effective new marketing strategy. Under the guidance of Alfred P. Sloan, GM organized into separate divisions, each of which appealed to a different market segment. Cadillac, for example, produced GM's most expensive car, which was targeted at the wealthy buyer; Chevrolet produced its least expensive model, which was targeted at working-class and lower-middle-class buyers. The GM

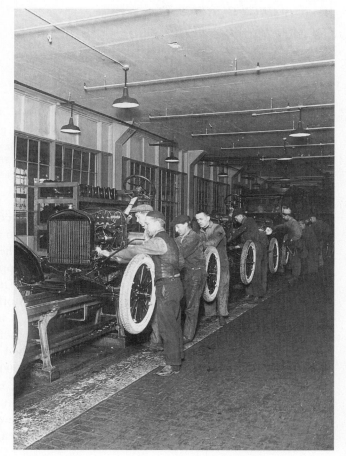

Finished automobiles roll off the moving assembly line at the Ford Motor Company, Highland Park, Michigan, ca. 1920. During the 1920s, Henry Ford achieved the status of folk hero, as his name became synonymous with the techniques of mass production. Ford cultivated a public image of himself as the heroic genius of the auto industry, greatly exaggerating his personal achievements.

Cancel distance &
conquer weather

Until 1924, Henry Ford had disdained national advertising for his cars. But as General Motors gained a competitive edge by making yearly changes in style and technology, Ford was forced to pay more attention to advertising. This ad was directed at "Mrs. Consumer," combining appeals to female independence and motherly duties.

Watch the Video

The Rise and Fall of the Automobile Economy at **www.myhistorylab.com**

QUICK REVIEW

The Automobile Industry

♦ 1920s: America made 85 percent of the world's passenger cars.

♦ By 1925, Ford's assembly line produced one new car every ten seconds.

♦ Auto industry provided a market for steel, rubber, glass, and petroleum products.

HOW AND why did the Republican Party dominate 1920s' politics?

---

business structure, along with its attempts to match production with demand through sophisticated market research and sales forecasting, became a widely copied model for other large American corporations. Both Ford and GM also pushed the idea of purchasing cars on credit, thus helping to make "installment buying" an underpinning of the new consumer culture.

The auto industry provided a large market for makers of steel, rubber, glass, and petroleum products. It stimulated public spending for good roads and extended the housing boom to new suburbs. Showrooms, repair shops, and gas stations appeared in thousands of communities. New small enterprises, from motels to billboard advertising to roadside diners, sprang up as motorists took to the highway. Automobiles widened the experience of millions of Americans. They made the exploration of the world outside the local community easier and more attractive. The automobile made leisure, in the sense of getting away from the routines of work and school, a more regular part of everyday life.

CITIES AND SUBURBS

Cars also promoted urban and suburban growth. The United States Census for 1920 was the first in American history in which the proportion of the population that lived in urban places (those with 2,500 or more people) exceeded the proportion of the population living in rural areas. More revealing of urban growth was the steady increase in the number of big cities. In 1910, there were sixty cities with more than 100,000 inhabitants; in 1920, there were sixty-eight; and by 1930, there were ninety-two.

Cities promised business opportunity, good jobs, cultural richness, and personal freedom. They attracted millions of Americans, white and black, from small towns and farms, as well as immigrants from abroad. Immigrants were drawn to cities by the presence there of family and people of like background in already-established ethnic communities. In a continuation of the Great Migration that began during World War I, roughly 1.5 million African Americans from the rural South migrated to cities in search of economic opportunities during the 1920s, doubling the black populations of New York, Chicago, Detroit, and Houston.

Houston offers a good example of how the automobile shaped an urban community. In 1910, it was a railroad town with a population of about 75,000 that served the Texas Gulf coast and interior. The enormous demand for gasoline and other petroleum products helped transform the city into a busy center for oil refining. Its population soared to 300,000 by the end of the 1920s. Abundant cheap land and the absence of zoning ordinances, combined with the availability of the automobile, pushed Houston to expand horizontally rather than vertically. It became the archetypal decentralized, low-density city, sprawling miles in each direction from downtown and thoroughly dependent on automobiles and roads for its sense of community.

THE STATE, THE ECONOMY, AND BUSINESS

Throughout the 1920s, a confident Republican Party dominated national politics, certain that it had ushered in a "new era" in American life. A new and closer relationship between the federal government and American business became the hallmark of Republican policy in both domestic and foreign affairs. Republicans never tired of claiming that the business–government partnership their policies promoted was responsible for the nation's economic prosperity.

HARDING AND COOLIDGE

Handsome, genial, and well-spoken, Warren Harding may have looked the part of a president—but acting like one was another matter. Harding was a product of small-town Marion, Ohio, and the machine politics in his native state. Republican Party officials had made a point of keeping Senator Harding, a compromise choice, as removed from the public eye as possible in the 1920 election. Harding understood his own limitations. He sadly told one visitor to the White House shortly after taking office, "I knew that this job would be too much for me."

Harding surrounded himself with a close circle of friends, the "Ohio gang," delegating to them a great deal of administrative power. In the summer of 1923, Harding began to get wind of the scandals for which his administration is best remembered. Soon after Harding's death from a heart attack later that year, a series of congressional investigations revealed a deep pattern of corruption. The worst affair was the Teapot Dome scandal involving Interior Secretary Albert Fall. Fall received hundreds of thousands of dollars in payoffs when he secretly leased navy oil reserves in Teapot Dome, Wyoming, and Elk Hills, California, to two private oil developers. He eventually became the first cabinet officer ever to go to jail.

The Harding administration's legacy was not all scandal. Andrew Mellon, an influential Pittsburgh banker, served as secretary of the treasury under all three Republican presidents of the 1920s. Mellon believed government ought to be run on the same conservative principles as a corporation. He was a leading voice for trimming the federal budget and cutting taxes on incomes, corporate profits, and inheritances. These cuts, he argued, would free up capital for new investment and, thus, promote general economic growth. Mellon's program sharply cut taxes both for higher-income brackets and for businesses.

When Calvin Coolidge succeeded to the presidency, he seemed to most people the temperamental opposite of Harding. Born and raised in rural Vermont, "Silent Cal" was the quintessential New England Yankee. Taciturn, genteel, and completely honest, Coolidge believed in the least amount of government possible. He spent only four hours a day at the office. His famous aphorism, "The business of America is business," perfectly captured the core philosophy of the Republican new era. He was in awe of wealthy men such as Andrew Mellon, and he thought them best suited to make society's key decisions.

Coolidge easily won election on his own in 1924. He benefited from the general prosperity and the contrast he provided with the disgraced Harding. Coolidge defeated little-known Democrat John W. Davis and Progressive Party candidate Robert M. La Follette of Wisconsin. In his full term, Coolidge showed most interest in reducing federal spending, lowering taxes, and blocking congressional initiatives. He saw his primary function as clearing the way for American businessmen.

HERBERT HOOVER AND THE "ASSOCIATIVE STATE"

The most influential figure of the Republican new era was Herbert Hoover, who as secretary of commerce dominated the cabinets of Harding and Coolidge before becoming president himself in 1929. A successful engineer, administrator, and politician, Hoover had earned an enviable reputation as wartime head of the U.S. Food Administration and director general of relief for Europe. He effectively embodied the belief that enlightened business, encouraged and informed by the government, would act in the public interest. In the modern industrial age, Hoover believed, the government needed only to advise private citizens' groups about what national or international polices to pursue.

Hoover thus fused a faith in old-fashioned individualism with a strong commitment to the progressive possibilities offered by efficiency and rationality. Unlike an earlier generation of Republicans, Hoover wanted not just to create a favorable climate for business but also to actively assist the business community. He spoke of creating an "associative state," in which the government would encourage voluntary cooperation among corporations, consumers, workers, farmers, and small businessmen. This became the central occupation of the Department of Commerce under Hoover's leadership.

Hoover actively encouraged the creation and expansion of national trade associations. By 1929, there were about 2,000 of them. At industrial conferences called by the Commerce Department, government officials explained the advantages of mutual cooperation in figuring prices and costs and then publishing the information. The idea was to improve efficiency by reducing competition. To some, this practice violated the spirit of antitrust laws, but in the 1920s, the Justice Department's Antitrust Division took a very lax view of its responsibility. In addition, the Supreme Court consistently upheld the legality of trade associations. The government thus provided an ideal climate for the concentration of corporate wealth and power. By 1929, the 200 largest American corporations owned almost half the total corporate wealth and about a fifth of the total national wealth. Concentration was particularly strong in manufacturing, retailing, mining, banking, and utilities.

WAR DEBTS, REPARATIONS, KEEPING THE PEACE

Rejection of the Treaty of Versailles and the League of Nations did not mean disengagement from the rest of the globe. The United States emerged from World War I as the strongest economic power in the world. The war transformed it from the world's leading debtor nation to its most important creditor. European governments owed the U.S. government about $10 billion in 1919. In the private sector, the war ushered in an era of expanding American investment abroad. By 1929, the U.S. trade surplus was $8 billion. New York replaced London as the center of international finance and capital markets. Yet America's postwar policies included a great contradiction: protectionism. The rest of the world owed the United States billions of dollars, but high tariffs on both farm products and manufactured goods made it much more difficult for debtor nations to repay by selling exports.

During the 1920s, war debts and reparations were the single most divisive issue in international economics. In France and Great Britain, which both owed the United States large amounts in war loans, many concluded that the Uncle Sam who had offered assistance during wartime was really a loan shark in disguise. In turn, many Americans viewed Europeans as ungrateful debtors. By the late 1920s, the European financial situation had become so desperate that the United States agreed to cancel a large part of these debts. Nonetheless, continued insistence by the United States that the Europeans pay at least a portion of the debt fed anti-American feeling in Europe and isolationism at home.

The Germans believed that war reparations, set at $33 billion by the Treaty of Versailles, not only unfairly punished the losers of the conflict but, by saddling their civilian economies with such massive debt, also deprived them of the very means to repay. In 1924, Herbert Hoover and Chicago banker Charles Dawes worked out a plan to aid the recovery of the German economy. The Dawes Plan reduced Germany's debt, stretched out the repayment period, and arranged for American bankers to lend funds to Germany. These measures helped stabilize Germany's currency and allowed it to make reparations payments to France and Great Britain. The Allies, in turn, were better able to pay their war debts to the United States.

In 1928, with great fanfare, the United States and sixty-two other nations signed the Pact of Paris (better known as the Kellogg-Briand Pact, for the U.S. Secretary of State Frank B. Kellogg and French Foreign Minister Aristide Briand who initiated it), which grandly and naively renounced war in principle. Peace groups, such as the Woman's

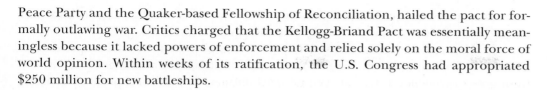

Peace Party and the Quaker-based Fellowship of Reconciliation, hailed the pact for formally outlawing war. Critics charged that the Kellogg-Briand Pact was essentially meaningless because it lacked powers of enforcement and relied solely on the moral force of world opinion. Within weeks of its ratification, the U.S. Congress had appropriated $250 million for new battleships.

GLOBAL COMMERCE AND U.S. FOREIGN POLICY

Throughout the 1920s, Secretary of State Charles Evans Hughes and other Republican leaders pursued policies designed to expand American economic activity abroad. They understood that capitalist economies must be dynamic; they must expand their markets if they were to thrive. The focus must be on friendly nations and investments that would help foreign citizens buy American goods. Toward this end, Republican leaders urged close cooperation between bankers and the government as a strategy for expanding American investment and economic influence abroad.

American oil, autos, farm machinery, and electrical equipment supplied a growing world market. Much of this expansion took place through the establishment of branch plants overseas by American companies. Leading the American domination of the world market were General Electric, Ford, and Monsanto Chemical. American oil companies, with the support of the State Department, also challenged Great Britain's dominance in the oil fields of the Middle East and Latin America, forming powerful cartels with English firms.

The strategy of maximum freedom for private enterprise, backed by limited government advice and assistance, significantly boosted the power and profits of American overseas investors. But in Central and Latin America, in particular, aggressive U.S. investment also fostered chronically underdeveloped economies, dependent on a few staple crops (sugar, coffee, cocoa, bananas) grown for export. American investments in Latin America more than doubled between 1924 and 1929, from $1.5 billion to over $3.5 billion. A large part of this money went to taking over vital mineral resources, such as Chile's copper and Venezuela's oil. The growing wealth and power of U.S. companies made it more difficult for these nations to grow their own food or diversify their economies. U.S. economic dominance in the hemisphere also hampered the growth of democratic politics by favoring autocratic, military regimes that could be counted on to protect U.S. investments.

WEAKENED AGRICULTURE, AILING INDUSTRIES

Amid prosperity and progress, there were large pockets of the country that lagged behind. Advances in real income and improvements in the standard of living for workers and farmers were uneven at best. The years 1914–19 had been a kind of golden age for the nation's farmers. Increased wartime demand, along with the devastation of much of European agriculture, had led to record-high prices for many crops. When the war ended, however, American farmers began to suffer from a chronic worldwide surplus of such farm staples as cotton, hogs, and corn.

In the South, farmers' dependency on "King Cotton" deepened, as the region lagged further behind the rest of the nation in both agricultural diversity and standard of living. Cotton acreage expanded, as large and heavily mechanized farms opened up new land in Oklahoma, west Texas, and the Mississippi-Yazoo delta. In most of the South, from North Carolina to east Texas, small one- and two-mule cotton farms, most under fifty acres, still dominated the countryside. With few large urban centers and inadequate transportation, even those southern farmers who had access to capital found it extremely difficult to find reliable markets for their products. Some 700,000 southern farmers, roughly half white and half black, still labored as sharecroppers. Modern conveniences such as electricity, indoor plumbing, automobiles, and phonographs remained far beyond the reach of the great majority of southern farmers. Widespread rural poverty, poor diet, and little access to capital meant the world of southern agriculture had changed very little since the days of the populist revolt in the 1890s.

To be sure, some farmers thrived. Improved transportation and chain supermarkets allowed for a wider and more regular distribution of such foods as oranges, lemons, and fresh green vegetables. Citrus, dairy, and truck farmers in particular profited from the growing importance of national markets. Wheat production jumped more than 300 percent during the 1920s. Across the Great Plains, wheat farmers brought the methods of industrial capitalism to the land. They hitched disc plows and combined harvester-threshers to gasoline-powered tractors, tearing up millions of acres of grassland to create a vast wheat factory. But when the disastrous dust storms of the 1930s rolled across the grassless plains, the long-range environmental impact of destroying so much native vegetation became evident.

Overall, per capita farm income remained well below what it had been in 1919, and the gap between farm and nonfarm income widened. By 1929, the average income per person on farms was $223, compared with $870 for nonfarm workers. By the end of the decade, hundreds of thousands had quit farming altogether for jobs in mills and factories. And fewer farmers owned their land. In 1930, 42 percent of all farmers were tenants, compared with 37 percent in 1919.

Large sectors of American industry also failed to share in the decade's general prosperity. As oil and natural gas gained in importance, America's coal mines became a less important source of energy. A combination of shrinking demand, new mining technology, and a series of losing strikes reduced the coal labor force by one-quarter. Economic hardship was widespread in many mining communities dependent on coal, particularly Appalachia and the southern Midwest. Those miners who did work earned lower hourly wages.

In textiles, shrinking demand and overcapacity (too many factories) were chronic problems. To improve profit margins, textile manufacturers in New England and other parts of the Northeast began a long-range shift of operations to the South, where nonunion shops and substandard wages became the rule. Older New England manufacturing centers such as Lawrence, Lowell, Nashua, Manchester, and Fall River were hard hit by this shift.

THE NEW MASS CULTURE

HOW DID the new mass media reshape American culture?

New communications media reshaped American culture in the 1920s, and much of the new mass culture was exported to the rest of the economically developed world. The phrase "Roaring Twenties" captures the explosion of image- and sound-making machinery that came to dominate so much of American life.

MOVIE-MADE AMERICA

The early movie industry, centered in New York and a few other big cities, had made moviegoing a regular habit for millions of Americans, especially immigrants and the working class. By 1914, there were about 18,000 "movie houses" showing motion pictures, with more than 7 million daily admissions and $300 million in annual receipts. With the shift of the industry westward to Hollywood, movies entered a new phase of business expansion.

Large studios such as Paramount, Fox, Metro-Goldwyn-Mayer (MGM), Universal, and Warner Brothers dominated the business with longer and more expensively produced movies—feature films. Each studio combined the three functions of production, distribution, and exhibition, and each controlled hundreds of movie theaters around the country. The era of silent films ended when Warner Brothers scored a huge hit in 1927 with *The Jazz Singer*, starring Al Jolson, which successfully introduced sound. New genres—musicals, gangster films, and screwball comedies—soon became popular. To maintain their hold on

European markets, the major studios established production facilities abroad that used foreign actors for the "dubbing" of American films into other languages. The higher costs associated with "talkies" also increased the studios' reliance on Wall Street investors and banks for working capital.

At the heart of Hollywood's success was the star system and the accompanying cult of celebrity, both of which help define American popular culture to this day (see Seeing History). For many in the audience, there was only a vague line separating the on-screen and off-screen adventures of the stars. Studio publicity, fan magazines, and gossip columns reinforced this ambiguity. Film idols, with their mansions, cars, parties, and private escapades, became the national experts on leisure and consumption. Their movies generally emphasized sexual themes and celebrated youth, athleticism, and the liberating power of consumer goods. Young Americans in particular looked to movies to learn how to dress, wear their hair, talk, or kiss.

Many Americans, however, particularly in rural areas and small towns, worried about Hollywood's impact on traditional sexual morality. They attacked the permissiveness associated with Hollywood life, and many states created censorship boards to screen movies before allowing them to be shown in theaters. To counter growing calls for government censorship, Hollywood's studios came up with a plan to censor themselves. In 1922, they hired Will Hays to head the Motion Picture Producers and Distributors of America. As the movie industry's czar, Hays lobbied against censorship laws, wrote pamphlets defending the movie business, and began setting guidelines for what could and could not be depicted on the screen.

RADIO BROADCASTING

In the fall of 1920, Westinghouse executive Harry P. Davis noticed that amateur broadcasts from the garage of an employee had attracted attention in the local Pittsburgh press. A department store advertised radio sets capable of picking up these "wireless concerts." Davis converted this amateur station to a stronger one at the Westinghouse main plant. Beginning with the presidential election returns that November, station KDKA offered regular nightly broadcasts. Radio broadcasting, begun as a service for selling cheap radio sets left over from World War I, would soon sweep the nation.

The "radio mania" of the early 1920s was a response to the new possibilities offered by broadcasting. By 1923, nearly 600 stations had been licensed by the Department of Commerce, and about 600,000 Americans had bought radios. Early programs included live popular music, the playing of phonograph records, talks by college professors, church services, and news and weather reports. For millions of Americans, especially in rural areas and small towns, radio provided a new and exciting link to the larger national community of consumption.

Who would pay for radio programs? The dominant corporations in the industry— General Electric, Westinghouse, Radio Corporation of America (RCA), and American Telephone and Telegraph (AT&T)—settled on the idea that advertisers would foot the bill for radio. Millions of listeners might be the consumers of radio shows, but sponsors were to be the customers. AT&T leased its nationwide system of telephone wires to allow the linking of many stations into powerful radio networks, such as the National Broadcasting Company (NBC) in 1926 and the Columbia Broadcasting System (CBS) in 1928. The rise of network radio squeezed out many of the stations and programs aimed at ethnic communities or broadcast in languages other than English, thus promoting a more homogenized culture.

NBC and CBS led the way in creating popular radio programs that relied heavily on older cultural forms. The variety show, hosted by vaudeville comedians, became network radio's first important format. Radio's first truly national hit, *The Amos 'n' Andy Show* (1928), was a direct descendant of nineteenth-century "blackface" minstrel entertainment. Radio

Creating Celebrity

A common definition for "celebrity" is one who is famous for being famous. Although politics, the arts, science, and the military have produced famous people for centuries, the celebrity is a twentieth-century phenomenon, one closely linked to the emergence of modern forms of mass media. In the 1920s, Hollywood's "star system," along with tabloid newspapers and the new profession of public relations, created the modern celebrity. Film producers were at first wary of identifying screen actors by name, but they soon discovered that promoting popular leading actors would boost the box office for their movies. The use of "close-ups" in movies and the fact that screen images were literally larger than life distinguished the images of film actors from, say, stage performers or opera singers.

WHAT VISUAL themes strike you as most powerful in the accompanying images? How do they compare—in contrasts and parallels—to celebrity images of today? Why do you think male stars such as Valentino and Fairbanks were so often portrayed as exotic foreigners? How did these posters convey a more open and accepting attitude toward sexuality?

Fans identified with their favorites in contradictory ways. Stars like Charlie Chaplin and Mary Pickford were like royalty, somehow beyond the realm of ordinary mortals. Yet audiences were also curious about the stars' private lives. Film studios took advantage of this curiosity by carefully controlling the public image of their stars through press releases, planted stories in newspapers, and carefully managed interviews and public appearances. Theda Bara, for example, one of the biggest female stars of the 1920s, was best known for her "vamp" roles depicting sexually aggressive and exotic women. According to the publicity from Fox Pictures, she was of Egyptian background, offspring of "a sheik and a princess, given in mystic marriage to the Sphinx, fought over by nomadic tribesmen, clairvoyant, and insatiably lustful." In truth, Theodosia Goodman was born and raised in Cincinnati, the daughter of middle-class Jewish parents, and became a stage actress after two years of college. By the 1920s, film stars were essentially studio–owned-and-operated commodities, requiring enormous capital investment. And the new media universe of newspapers, magazines, radio, movies, and advertising was held together by the public fascination with, and the commercial power of, celebrities. ■

did more than any previous medium to publicize and commercialize once-isolated forms of American music such as country-and-western, blues, and jazz. Broadcasts of baseball and college football games proved especially popular. By 1930, all the elements that characterize the present American system of broadcasting—regular daily programming paid for and produced by commercial advertisers, national networks carrying shows across the nation, and mass ownership of receiver sets in American homes—were in place.

Radio broadcasting created a national community of listeners, just as motion pictures created one of viewers. Like movies, it also transcended national boundaries. Broadcasting had a powerful hemispheric impact. In both Canada and Mexico, governments established national broadcasting systems to bolster cultural and political nationalism. Yet American shows—and advertising—continued to dominate Canadian airwaves. Large private Mexican radio stations were often started in partnership with American corporations such as RCA, as a way to create demand for receiving sets. Language barriers limited the direct impact of U.S. broadcasts, but American advertisers became the backbone of commercial radio in Mexico. Radio broadcasting thus significantly amplified the influence of American commercialism throughout the hemisphere.

NEW FORMS OF JOURNALISM

A new kind of newspaper, the tabloid, became popular in the postwar years. The *New York Daily News*, founded in 1919 by Joseph M. Patterson, was the first to develop the tabloid style. Its folded-in-half page size made it convenient to read on buses or subways. With a terse, lively reporting style that emphasized sex, scandal, and sports, *Daily News* circulation reached 400,000 in 1922 and 1.3 million by 1929. This success spawned a host of imitators in New York and elsewhere. The circulation of existing dailies was little affected. Tabloids had instead discovered an audience of millions who had never read newspapers before. Most of these new readers were poorly educated working-class city dwellers, many of whom were immigrants or children of immigrants.

The tabloid's most popular new feature was the gossip column, invented by Walter Winchell, who began writing his column "Your Broadway and Mine" for the *New York Daily Graphic* in 1924. Winchell described the secret lives of public figures with a distinctive, rapid-fire, slangy style that made the reader feel like an insider. By the end of the decade, scores of newspapers "syndicated" Winchell's column, making him the most widely read—and imitated—journalist in America.

Journalism followed the larger economic trend toward consolidation and merger. Newspaper chains flourished during the 1920s, producing a more standardized kind of journalism that could be found anywhere in the country. There was a sizable increase in the number of these chains and in the percentage of total daily circulation that was chain-owned.

ADVERTISING MODERNITY

A thriving advertising industry both reflected and encouraged the growing importance of consumer goods in American life. Previously, advertising had been confined mostly to staid newspapers and magazines and offered little more than basic product information. The successful efforts of the government's Committee on Public Information, set up to "sell" World War I to Americans, suggested that new techniques using modern communication media could convince people to buy a wide range of goods and services.

The larger ad agencies moved toward a more scientific approach by sponsoring market research and welcoming the language of psychology to their profession. Advertisers began focusing on the needs, desires, and anxieties of the consumer, rather than on the qualities of the product. "There are certain things that most people believe," noted one ad agency executive in 1927. "The moment your copy is linked to one of those beliefs, more than half your battle is won."

•◦•— Read the Document
Advertisements (1925, 1927) at **www.myhistorylab.com**

Ad agencies and their clients invested extraordinary amounts of time, energy, and money trying to discover and, to some extent, shape those beliefs. Above all, advertising celebrated consumption itself as a positive good. In this sense, the new advertising ethic was a therapeutic one, promising that products would contribute to the buyer's physical, psychic, or emotional well-being.

THE PHONOGRAPH AND THE RECORDING INDUSTRY

Like radio and movies, the phonograph came into its own in the 1920s as a popular entertainment medium. Originally marketed in the 1890s, early phonographs used wax cylinders that could both record and replay. But the sound quality was poor, and the cylinders were difficult to handle. The convenient permanently grooved disc recordings introduced around World War I were eagerly snapped up by the public, even though the discs could not be used to make recordings at home. The success of records transformed the popular music business, displacing both cylinders and sheet music as the major source of music in the home.

Record sales declined toward the end of the decade, due to competition from radio. But in a broader cultural sense, records continued to transform American popular culture. Record companies discovered lucrative regional and ethnic markets for country music, which appealed primarily to white Southerners, and blues and jazz, which appealed primarily to African Americans. Yet country and blues records were also played over the radio, and millions of Americans began to hear musical styles and performers who previously had been isolated from the general population. Jazz records by such African American artists as Louis Armstrong and Duke Ellington found a wide audience

This 1926 publicity photo shows Louis Armstrong and his Hot Five just after they made the historic recordings that established Armstrong as the most influential jazz soloist of the era. (L to R: Armstrong, Johnny St. Cyr, Johnny Dodds, Kid Ory, Lil Hardin Armstrong). Armstrong also had a huge impact as a singer, and his popularity extended to all racial groups.

overseas as well, and jazz emerged as a uniquely American cultural form with broad appeal around the globe. The combination of records and radio started an extraordinary cross-fertilization of American musical styles that continues to this day.

SPORTS AND CELEBRITY

During the 1920s, spectator sports enjoyed an unprecedented growth in popularity and profitability. As radio, newspapers, magazines, and newsreels exhaustively documented their exploits, athletes took their place alongside movie stars in defining a new culture of celebrity. Big-time sports, like the movies, entered a new corporate phase. The image of the modern athlete—rich, famous, glamorous, and often a rebel against social convention—came into its own during the decade.

Major league baseball had more fans than any other sport, and its greatest star, George Herman "Babe" Ruth, embodied the new celebrity athlete. Ruth's prodigious home-run hitting completely changed baseball strategy and attracted legions of new fans to the sport. Ruth was a larger-than-life character off the field as well. In New York, media capital of the nation, newspapers and magazines chronicled his enormous appetites—for food, whiskey, expensive cars, and big-city nightlife. Ruth became the first athlete avidly sought by manufacturers for celebrity endorsement of their products.

Baseball attendance exploded during the 1920s, reaching a one-year total of 10 million in 1929. The attendance boom prompted urban newspapers to increase their baseball coverage, and the larger dailies featured separate sports sections. William K. Wrigley, owner of the Chicago Cubs, discovered that by letting local radio stations broadcast his team's games, the club could win new fans, especially among housewives.

Among those excluded from major league baseball were African Americans, who had been banned from the game by an 1890s "gentleman's agreement" among owners. During the 1920s, black baseball players and entrepreneurs developed a world of their own, with several professional and semiprofessional leagues catering to expanding African American communities in cities. The largest of these was the Negro National League, organized in 1920 by Andrew "Rube" Foster. African Americans had their own baseball heroes, such as Josh Gibson and Satchel Paige, who no doubt would have been stars in the major leagues if not for racial exclusion.

The new media configuration of the 1920s created heroes in other sports as well. Radio broadcasts and increased journalistic coverage made college football a big-time sport. The center of college football shifted from the old elite schools of the Ivy League to the big universities of the Midwest and Pacific Coast, where most of the players were second-generation Irish, Italians, and Slavs. Athletes such as boxers Jack Dempsey and Gene Tunney, tennis players Bill Tilden and Helen Wills, golfer Bobby Jones, and swimmers Gertrude Ederle and Johnny Weissmuller became household names who brought legions of new fans to their sports.

A NEW MORALITY?

Movie stars, radio personalities, sports heroes, and popular musicians became the elite figures in a new culture of celebrity defined by the mass media. They were the model for achievement in the new age. The new media relentlessly created and disseminated images that are still familiar today: Babe Ruth trotting around the bases after hitting a home run; the wild celebrations that greeted Charles Lindbergh after he completed the first solo transatlantic airplane flight in 1927; the smiling gangster Al Capone, bantering with reporters who transformed his criminal exploits into important news events.

Images do not tell the whole story, however. Consider one of the most enduring images of the "Roaring Twenties," the flapper. She was usually portrayed on-screen, in novels, and in the press as a young, sexually aggressive woman with bobbed hair, rouged

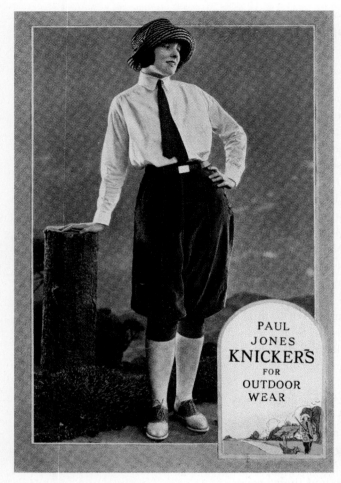

A woman in a man's shirt and necktie wears a pair of Paul Jones knickers in this 1922 advertisement. Her boyish, almost androgynous look reflects one way that notions of the "new woman" intersected with the worlds of fashion and advertising.

•••—Read the **Document**

History Bookshelf: *Margaret Sanger,* Woman and the New Race *(1920)* at **www.myhistorylab.com**

•••—Read the **Document**

Eleanor R. Wembridge, "Petting and the Campus" (1925) at **www.myhistorylab.com**

WHAT EXPLAINS the backlash against social and cultural change in the 1920s?

cheeks, and short skirt. She loved to dance to jazz music, enjoyed smoking cigarettes, and drank bootleg liquor in cabarets and dance halls. She could also be competitive, assertive, and a good pal.

Was the flapper a genuine representative of the 1920s? Did she embody the "new morality" that was so widely discussed and chronicled in the media of the day? The flapper certainly did exist, but she was neither as new nor as widespread a phenomenon as the image would suggest. The delight in sensuality, personal pleasure, and rhythmically complex dance and music had long been key elements of subcultures on the fringes of middle-class society. In the 1920s, these activities became normative for a growing number of white middle-class Americans, including women.

Several sources, most of them rooted in earlier years, can be found for the increased sexual openness of the 1920s. Troops in the armed forces during World War I had been exposed to government-sponsored sex education. New psychological and social theories stressed the central role of sexuality in human experience, maintaining that sex is a positive, healthy impulse that, if repressed, could damage mental and emotional health. The pioneering efforts of Margaret Sanger in educating women about birth control had begun before World War I (see Chapter 21). In the 1920s, Sanger campaigned vigorously—through her journal *Birth Control Review*, in books, and on speaking tours—to make contraception freely available to all women.

Sociological surveys also suggested that genuine changes in sexual behavior began in the prewar years among both married and single women. Katherine Bement Davis's pioneering study of 2,200 middle-class women, carried out in 1918 and published in 1929, revealed that most used contraceptives and described sexual relations in positive terms. Women born after the turn of the century were twice as likely to have had premarital sex as those born before 1900. The critical change took place in the generation that came of age in the late teens and early twenties. By the 1920s, male and female "morals" were becoming more alike.

The emergence of homosexual subcultures also reflected the newly permissive atmosphere of the postwar years. Although such subcultures had been a part of big city life since at least the 1890s, they had been largely confined to working-class saloons associated with the urban underworld. By the 1920s, middle-class enclaves of self-identified homosexuals took root in cities like New York, Chicago, and San Francisco. Even if these enclaves provided some sense of community and safety for homosexuals, the repressive shadow of the larger culture was never far away. Psychologists of the era condemned "perversion" as a mental illness and counseled the need for a "cure."

MODERNITY AND TRADITIONALISM

One measure of the profound cultural changes of the 1920s was the hostility and opposition expressed toward them by large sectors of the American public. Resentments over the growing power of urban culture, on full display in Hollywood movies, modern advertising, and over the airwaves, were very strong in rural and small-town America. Several trends and mass movements reflected this anger and the longing for a less complicated past.

PROHIBITION

The Eighteenth Amendment, banning the manufacture, sale, and transportation of alcoholic beverages, took effect in January 1920. Prohibition was the culmination of a long campaign that associated drinking with the degradation of working-class family life and the worst evils of urban politics. It became clear rather quickly that enforcing the new law would be extremely difficult. The **Volstead Act** of 1919 established a federal Prohibition Bureau to enforce the Eighteenth Amendment. Yet the bureau was severely understaffed with only about 1,500 agents to police the entire country.

The public demand for alcohol, especially in the big cities, led to widespread law-breaking. Drinking was such a routine part of life for so many Americans that "bootlegging" quickly became a big business. Nearly every town and city had at least one "speakeasy," where people could drink and enjoy music and other entertainment. Local law enforcement personnel, especially in the cities, were easily bribed to overlook these illegal establishments. By the early 1920s, many eastern states no longer made even a token effort at enforcing the law.

Liquor continued to be illegal, so Prohibition gave an enormous boost to violent organized crime. The profits to be made in the illegal liquor trade dwarfed the traditional sources of criminal income—gambling, prostitution, and robbery. The pattern of organized crime in the 1920s closely resembled the larger trends in American business: smaller operations gave way to larger and more complex combinations.

Organized crime, assisted by its huge profits from liquor, also made significant inroads into legitimate businesses, labor unions, and city government, especially in large cities. By the time Congress and the states ratified the Twenty-First Amendment in 1933, repealing Prohibition, organized crime was a permanent feature of American life.

IMMIGRATION RESTRICTION

Sentiment for restricting immigration, growing since the late nineteenth century, reached its peak immediately after World War I. Barriers against Asian immigrants were already in place with the Chinese Exclusion Act of 1882 and the so-called Gentleman's Agreement with Japan in 1907. The movement to curb European immigration reflected the growing preponderance after 1890 of "new immigrants"—those from southern and eastern Europe—over the immigrants from northern and western Europe, who had predominated before 1890 (see Figure 23.3).

The "new immigrants" were mostly Catholic and Jewish, and they were darker-skinned than the "old immigrants." To many old-stock Americans, they seemed more exotic, more foreign, and less willing and able to assimilate the nation's political and cultural values. They were also relatively poorer, more physically isolated in the nation's cities, and less politically strong than earlier immigrants. In the 1890s, the anti-Catholic American Protective Association called for a curb on immigration, and by exploiting the economic depression of that decade, it reached a membership of 2.5 million. In 1894, a group of prominent Harvard graduates, including Senator Henry Cabot Lodge (R-Massachusetts) and John Fiske, founded the Immigration Restriction League, providing an influential forum for the fears of the nation's elite. The league used newer scientific arguments, based on a flawed application of Darwinian evolutionary theory and genetics, to support its call for immigration restriction.

Theories of scientific racism, which had become more popular in the early 1900s, reinforced anti-immigrant bias and distorted genetic theory to argue that America was committing "race suicide." Eugenicists, who enjoyed considerable vogue in those years, held that heredity determined almost all of a person's capacities and that genetic inferiority predisposed people to crime and poverty. Such pseudoscientific thinking sought to explain historical and social development solely as a function of "racial" differences.

Volstead Act The 1920 law defining the liquor forbidden under the Eighteenth Amendment and giving enforcement responsibilities to the Prohibition Bureau of the Department of the Treasury.

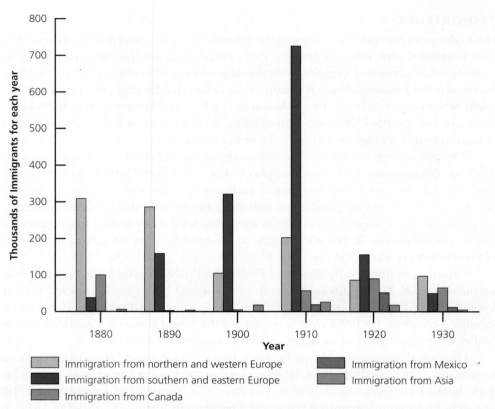

Figure 23.3 Immigration Trends to the United States by Continent/Region, 1880–1930

Reprinted with the permission of Cambridge University Press.

Immigration Act 1921 act setting a maximum of 357,000 new immigrants each year.

●•◦ Read the **Document**
Immigration Law (1924) at
www.myhistorylab.com

QUICK REVIEW

Restrictions on Immigration

◆ Immigration Act of 1921 reduced immigration and established quotas for nationalities.

◆ Immigration Act of 1924 restricted immigration on the basis of national origins.

◆ New laws became a permanent feature of national policy.

Against this background, the war and its aftermath provided the final push for the restriction of European immigration. The "100 percent American" fervor of the war years fueled nativist passions. So did the Red Scare of 1919–20, which linked foreigners with Bolshevism and radicalism of all kinds in the popular mindset. The postwar depression coincided with the resumption of massive immigration, bringing much hostile comment on the relationship between rising unemployment and the new influx of foreigners. Sensational press coverage of organized crime figures, many of them Italian or Jewish, also played a part.

In 1921, Congress passed the **Immigration Act**, setting a maximum of 357,000 new immigrants each year. Quotas limited annual immigration from any European country to 3 percent of the number of its natives counted in the 1910 U.S. Census. But restrictionists complained that the new law still allowed too many southern and eastern Europeans in, especially since the northern and western Europeans did not fill their quotas. The Reed-Johnson National Origins Act of 1924 revised the quotas to 2 percent of the number of foreign-born counted for each nationality in the census for 1890, when far fewer southern or eastern Europeans were present in the United States. The maximum total allowed each year was also cut to 164,000.

The 1924 National Origins Act in effect limited immigration to white Europeans eligible for immigration by country of origin (nationality), while it divided the rest of the world into "colored races" (black, mulatto, Chinese, and Indian) who were ineligible for immigration. These new restrictions dovetailed with two recent Supreme Court decisions, *Ozawa* v. *U.S.* (1922) and *U.S.* v. *Thind* (1923), in which the Court held that Japanese and Asian Indians were unassimilable aliens and racially ineligible for U.S. citizenship. By the 1920s, American law had thus created the peculiar new racial category of "Asian" and codified the principle of racial exclusion in immigration and naturalization law.

The Ku Klux Klan

If immigration restriction was resurgent nativism's most significant legislative expression, a revived Ku Klux Klan (KKK) was its most effective mass movement. The original Klan had been formed in the Reconstruction South as an instrument of white racial terror against newly freed slaves (see Chapter 17). It had died out in the 1870s. The new Klan, born in Stone Mountain, Georgia, in 1915, patterned itself on the secret rituals and antiblack hostility of its predecessor and, until 1920, it was limited to a few local chapters in Georgia and Alabama.

When Hiram W. Evans, a dentist from Dallas, became imperial wizard of the Klan in 1922, he transformed the organization. Evans hired professional fund-raisers and publicists and directed an effective recruiting scheme that paid a commission to sponsors of new members. The Klan advocated "100 percent Americanism" and "the faithful maintenance of White Supremacy." It staunchly supported the enforcement of Prohibition, and it attacked birth control and Darwinism. The new Klan made a special target of the Roman Catholic Church, labeling it a hostile and dangerous alien power and claiming that their allegiance to the Pope made Catholics unfit for citizenship.

By 1924, the new Klan counted more than 3 million members across the country. Its slogan, "Native, White, Protestant Supremacy," proved especially attractive in the Midwest and South, including many cities. Klansmen boycotted businesses, threatened families, and sometimes resorted to violence—public whippings, arson, and lynching—against their chosen enemies. The Klan's targets sometimes included white Protestants accused of sexual promiscuity, blasphemy, or drunkenness, but most victims were African Americans, Catholics, and Jews. Support for Prohibition enforcement probably united Klansmen more than any single issue.

On another level, the Klan was a popular social movement, a defensive bastion against forces of modernity. Many members were more attracted by the Klan's spectacular social events and its efforts to reinvigorate community life than by its attacks on those considered outsiders. Perhaps a half-million women joined the Women of the Ku Klux Klan, and women constituted nearly half of the Klan membership in some states. Klanswomen drew on family and community traditions, such as church suppers, kin reunions, and gossip campaigns, to defend themselves and their families against what they saw as corruption and immorality.

At its height, the Klan also became a powerful force in Democratic Party politics, and it had a strong presence among delegates to the 1924 Democratic National

•••—Read the Document

"Creed of Klanswomen" (1924) at
www.myhistorylab.com

Women members of the Ku Klux Klan in New Castle, Indiana, August 1, 1923. The revived Klan was a powerful presence in scores of American communities during the early 1920s, especially among native-born white Protestants, who feared cultural and political change. In addition to preaching "100 percent Americanism," local Klan chapters also served a social function for members and their families.

Convention. The Klan began to fade in 1925, when its Indiana leader, Grand Dragon David C. Stephenson, became involved in a sordid personal affair. With one of its most famous leaders disgraced and in jail, the new Klan began to lose members and influence.

FUNDAMENTALISM IN RELIGION

Paralleling political nativism in the 1920s was the growth of religious fundamentalism. In many eastern Protestant churches, congregations focused less on religious practice and worship than on progressive social and reform activities in the larger community. By the early 1920s, a fundamentalist revival had developed in reaction to these tendencies, particularly in the South and Midwest. The fundamentalists emphasized a literal reading of the Bible, and they rejected the tenets of modern science as inconsistent with the revealed word of God.

One special target of the fundamentalists was the theory of evolution, first set forth by Charles Darwin in his landmark work *The Origin of Species* (1859). Using fossil evidence, evolutionary theory suggested that, over time, many species had become extinct and that new ones had emerged through the process of natural selection. These ideas directly contradicted the account of one fixed creation in the Book of Genesis, and fundamentalists launched an attack on the teaching of Darwinism in schools and universities. By 1925, five southern state legislatures had passed laws restricting the teaching of evolution.

A young biology teacher, John T. Scopes, deliberately broke the Tennessee law prohibiting the teaching of Darwinism in 1925, in order to challenge it in court. The resulting trial drew international attention to the controversy. Scopes's defense team included attorneys from the American Civil Liberties Union and Clarence Darrow, the most famous trial lawyer in America. The prosecution was led by William Jennings Bryan, the old Democratic standard-bearer. The trial attracted thousands of reporters and partisans and was broadcast across the nation by the radio.

The Scopes "monkey trial"—so called because fundamentalists trivialized Darwin's theory into a claim that humans were descended from monkeys—became one of the most publicized and definitive moments of the decade. Scopes's guilt was never in question. The jury convicted him quickly, although the verdict was later thrown out on a technicality. The struggle over the teaching of evolution continued in an uneasy stalemate; state statutes were not repealed, but prosecutions for teaching evolution ceased. Fundamentalism, a religious creed and a cultural defense against the uncertainties of modern life, continued to have a strong appeal for millions of Americans.

Interpreting the Past: *The Scopes Monkey Trial as a Harbinger of Change, pp. 622–623*

PROMISES POSTPONED

The prosperity of the 1920s was unevenly distributed and enjoyed across America. Older progressive reform movements that had pointed out inequities faltered in the conservative political climate. But the new era did inspire a range of critics deeply troubled by unfulfilled promises in American life.

WHICH AMERICANS were less likely to share in postwar prosperity and why?

FEMINISM IN TRANSITION

The achievement of the suffrage removed the central issue that had given cohesion to the disparate forces of female reform activism. During the 1920s, the women's movement split into two main wings over a fundamental disagreement about female identity. Should activists stress women's differences from men—their vulnerability and the double burden of work and family—and continue to press for protective legislation, such as laws that limited the length of the workweek for women? Or should they emphasize the ways that women were like men—sharing similar aspirations—and push for full legal and civil equality?

In 1920, the National American Woman Suffrage Association reorganized itself as the **League of Women Voters**. The league represented the historical mainstream of the suffrage movement, those who believed that the vote for women would bring a nurturing sensibility and a reform vision to American politics. Most league members continued working in a variety of reform organizations, and the league itself concentrated on educating the new female electorate, encouraging women to run for office, and supporting laws for the protection of women and children.

A newer, smaller, and more militant group was the National Woman's Party (NWP), founded in 1916 by combative suffragist Alice Paul. The NWP downplayed the significance of suffrage and argued that women were still subordinate to men in every facet of life. The NWP opposed protective legislation for women, claiming that such laws reinforced sex stereotyping and prevented women from competing with men in many fields. Largely representing the interests of professional and business women, the NWP focused on passage of an Equal Rights Amendment (ERA) to the Constitution.

The most significant, if limited, victory for feminist reformers was the 1921 **Sheppard-Towner Act**, which established the first federally funded health care program, providing matching funds for states to set up prenatal and child health care centers. These centers also provided public health nurses for house calls. Although hailed as a genuine reform breakthrough, especially for women in rural and isolated communities, the act aroused much opposition. Many Republicans, including President Harding, had supported it as a way to curry favor with newly enfranchised women voters. Their support faded when it became clear that there was little "gender gap" in voting patterns. The NWP disliked Sheppard-Towner for its assumption that all women were mothers. Birth control advocates such as Margaret Sanger complained that contraception was not part of the program. The American Medical Association (AMA) objected to government-sponsored health care and to nurses who functioned outside the supervision of physicians. By 1929, largely as a result of intense AMA lobbying, Congress cut off funds for the program.

MEXICAN IMMIGRATION

While immigration restriction sharply cut the flow of new arrivals from Europe, the 1920s also brought a dramatic influx of Mexicans to the United States. Mexican immigration, which was not included in the immigration laws of 1921 and 1924, had picked up substantially after the outbreak of the Mexican Revolution in 1911, when politically inspired violence and economic hardships provided incentives to cross the border. According to the U.S. Immigration Service, an estimated 459,000 Mexicans entered the United States between 1921 and 1930, more than double the number for the previous decade (see Figure 23.4).

The primary pull was the tremendous agricultural expansion occurring in the American Southwest. Irrigation and large-scale agribusiness had begun transforming California's Imperial and San Joaquin Valleys into lucrative fruit and vegetable fields. Cotton pickers were needed in the vast plantations of Lower Rio Grande Valley in Texas and the Salt River Valley in Arizona. The sugar beet fields of Michigan, Minnesota, and Colorado attracted many Mexican farmworkers. American industry had also begun recruiting Mexican workers, first to fill wartime needs and later to fill the gap left by the decline in European immigration.

The new Mexican immigration appeared more permanent than previous waves—that is, more and more newcomers stayed—and, like other immigrants, more were attracted to cities. This was partly the unintended consequence of new policies designed to

League of Women Voters League formed in 1920 advocating for women's rights, among them the right for women to serve on juries and equal pay laws.

Sheppard-Towner Act The first federal social welfare law, passed in 1921, providing federal funds for infant and maternity care.

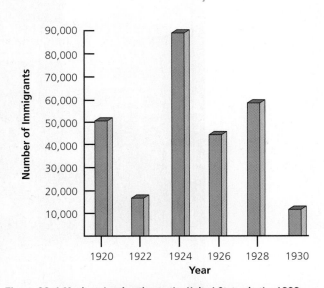

Figure 23.4 Mexican Immigration to the United States in the 1920s
Many Mexican migrants avoided official border-crossing stations so they would not have to pay visa fees. Thus, these official figures probably underestimated the true size of the decade's Mexican migration. As the economy contracted with the onset of the Great Depression, immigration from Mexico dropped off sharply.

make immigration more difficult. As the Border Patrol (established in 1924) made border crossing more difficult, what had once been a two-way process for many Mexicans became a one-way migration. Permanent communities of Mexicans in the United States grew rapidly.

Racism and local patterns of residential segregation confined most Mexicans to barrios. Housing conditions were generally poor, particularly for recent arrivals. Disease and infant mortality rates were much higher than average, and most Mexicans worked at low-paying, unskilled jobs and received inadequate health care. Legal restrictions passed by states and cities made it difficult for Mexicans to enter teaching, legal, and other professions. Mexicans were routinely banned from local public works projects as well. Many felt a deep ambivalence about applying for American citizenship. Loyalty to the Old Country was strong, and many cherished dreams of returning to live out their days in Mexico.

Mutual aid societies—*mutualistas*—became key social and political institutions in the Mexican communities of the Southwest and Midwest. They provided death benefits and widows' pensions for members and also served as centers of resistance to civil rights violations and discrimination. In 1928, the Federation of Mexican Workers Unions formed in response to a large farm labor strike in the Imperial Valley of California. A group of middle-class Mexican professionals in Texas organized the League of United Latin American Citizens (LULAC) in 1929.

THE "NEW NEGRO"

► Watch the Video

The Great Migration at
www.myhistorylab.com

The Great Migration spurred by World War I showed no signs of letting up during the 1920s, and African American communities in northern cities grew rapidly. By far the largest and most influential of these communities was New York City's Harlem. Previously a residential suburb, Harlem began attracting middle-class African Americans

Mexican workers gathered outside a San Antonio labor bureau in 1924. These employment agencies contracted Mexicans to work for Texas farmers, railroads, and construction companies. Note the three Anglo men in front (wearing suits and ties), who probably owned and operated this agency. During the 1920s, San Antonio's Mexican population doubled from roughly 40,000 to over 80,000, making it the second largest *colonia* in *El Norte* after Los Angeles.

in the prewar years. After the war, heavy black migration from the South and the Caribbean encouraged real estate speculators and landlords to remake Harlem as an exclusively black neighborhood (see Map 23.1).

Harlem emerged as the demographic and cultural capital of black America, but its appeal transcended national borders, as mass migration from the Caribbean helped reshape the community. By the late 1920s, about one-quarter of Harlem's population had been born in Jamaica, Barbados, Trinidad, the Bahamas, and other parts of the Caribbean. Some of the leading cultural, business, and political figures of the era—poet Claude McKay, newspaper publisher P. M. H. Savory, labor organizer Hubert Harrison, black nationalist Marcus Garvey—had roots in the West Indies. Most black Caribbean migrants came from societies where class differences mattered more than racial ones, and many refused to accept racial bigotry without protest. A large number also carried with them entrepreneurial experience that contributed to their success in running small businesses. Intraracial tensions and resentment between American-born blacks and an increasingly visible West Indian population were reflections of Harlem's transformation into a hemispheric center for black people.

Harlem was also headquarters to Marcus Garvey's Universal Negro Improvement Association. An ambitious Jamaican immigrant who had moved to Harlem in 1916, Garvey created a mass movement that stressed black economic self-determination and unity among the black communities of the United States, the Caribbean, and Africa. With a central message affirming pride in black identity, Garvey attracted as many as a million members worldwide. Garvey's best-publicized project was the Black Star Line, a black-owned

MAP 23.1

Black Population, 1920 Although the Great Migration had drawn hundreds of thousands of African Americans to the urban North, the southern states of the former Confederacy still remained the center of the African American population in 1920.

WHICH CITIES were the most popular destinations for African American migrants in the early twentieth century? Why?

and -operated fleet of ships that would link people of African descent around the world. But insufficient capital and serious financial mismanagement resulted in the spectacular failure of the enterprise. In 1923, Garvey was found guilty of mail fraud in his fund-raising efforts; he later went to jail and was subsequently deported to England. Despite the disgrace, Harlem's largest newspaper, the *Amsterdam News*, explained Garvey's continuing appeal to African Americans: "In a world where black is despised, he taught them that black is beautiful. He taught them to admire and praise black things and black people."

The demand for housing in this restricted geographical area led to skyrocketing rents, but most Harlemites held low-wage jobs. This combination produced extremely overcrowded apartments, unsanitary conditions, and the rapid deterioration of housing stock. Disease and death rates were abnormally high. Yet Harlem also boasted a large middle-class population and supported a wide array of churches, theaters, newspapers and journals, and black-owned businesses. It became a mecca, as poet and essayist James Weldon Johnson wrote, for "the curious, the adventurous, the enterprising, the ambitious, and the talented of the entire Negro world."

Harlem became the political and intellectual center for what writer Alain Locke called the "New Negro." Locke was referring to a new spirit in the work of black writers and intellectuals, an optimistic faith that encouraged African Americans to develop and celebrate their distinctive culture. This faith was the common denominator uniting the disparate figures associated with the **Harlem Renaissance**. The assertion of cultural independence resonated in the poetry of Langston Hughes and Claude McKay, the novels of Zora Neale Hurston and Jessie Fauset, the essays of Countee Cullen and James Weldon Johnson, the acting of Paul Robeson, and the blues singing of Bessie Smith.

There was a political side to the "New Negro" as well. The newly militant spirit that black veterans had brought home from World War I matured and found a variety of expressions in the Harlem of the 1920s. New leaders and movements began to appear alongside established organizations like the National Association for the Advancement of Colored People. A. Philip Randolph began a long career as a labor leader, socialist, and civil rights activist in these years, editing the *Messenger* and organizing the Brotherhood of Sleeping Car Porters.

Through the new mass media of radio and phonograph records, millions of Americans now listened and danced to a distinctively African American music, as jazz began to enter the cultural mainstream. Jazz found wildly enthusiastic fans in European capitals like Berlin and Paris, and noted classical composers such as Maurice Ravel and Igor Stravinsky treated it as a serious art form. The best jazz bands of the day, led by artists such as Duke Ellington, Fletcher Henderson, Cab Calloway, and Louis Armstrong, often had their performances broadcast live from such Harlem venues as the Cotton Club and Small's Paradise. These clubs themselves were rigidly segregated, however. Black dancers, singers, and musicians provided the entertainment, but no African Americans were allowed in the audience.

ALIENATED INTELLECTUALS

War, Prohibition, growing corporate power, and the deep currents of cultural intolerance troubled many intellectuals in the 1920s. Some felt so alienated from the United States that they left to live abroad. In the early 1920s, Gertrude Stein, an American expatriate writer living in Paris, told the young novelist Ernest Hemingway: "All of you young people who served in the war, you are a lost generation." The phrase "a lost generation" was widely adopted as a label for American writers, artists, and intellectuals of the postwar era. Yet it is difficult to generalize about so diverse a community. For one thing, living abroad attracted only a handful of American writers. Alienation and disillusion with American life were prominent subjects in the literature and thought of the 1920s, but artists and thinkers developed these themes in very different ways.

Read the **Document**

Exploring America: Harlem Renaissance
at **www.myhistorylab.com**

Watch the **Video**

The Harlem Renaissance at
www.myhistorylab.com

QUICK REVIEW

Harlem

- Harlem attracted middle-class African Americans in the prewar years.
- After the war, black people from the South and the Caribbean arrived in large numbers.
- Harlem became the political and intellectual center of African American culture.

Harlem Renaissance A new African American cultural awareness that flourished in literature, art, and music in the 1920s.

The mass slaughter of World War I provoked revulsion and a deep cynicism about the heroic and moralistic portrayal of war so popular in the nineteenth century. Novelists Ernest Hemingway and John Dos Passos, who both served at the front as ambulance drivers, depicted the war and its aftermath in world-weary and unsentimental tones.

Hemingway and F. Scott Fitzgerald were the most influential novelists of the era. Fitzgerald joined the army during World War I but did not serve overseas. His work celebrated the youthful vitality of the "Jazz Age" (a phrase he coined) but was also deeply distrustful of the promises of American prosperity and politics. His first novel, *This Side of Paradise* (1920), won a wide readership around the country with its exuberant portrait of a "new generation," "dedicated more than the last to the fear of poverty and the worship of success; grown up to find all Gods dead, all wars fought, all faiths in man shaken."

At home, many American writers engaged in sharp attacks on small-town America and what they viewed as its provincial values. Essayist H. L. Mencken, caustic editor of the *American Mercury*, heaped scorn on fundamentalists, Prohibition, and nativists, while ridiculing what he called the "American booboisie." Fiction writers also skewered small-town America, achieving commercial and critical success in the process. Sherwood Anderson's *Winesburg, Ohio* (1919) offered a spare, laconic, pessimistic, yet compassionate, view of Middle America. He had a lasting influence on younger novelists of the 1920s.

The most popular and acclaimed writer of the time was novelist Sinclair Lewis. In a series of novels satirizing small-town life, such as *Main Street* (1920) and especially *Babbitt* (1922), Lewis affectionately mocked his characters. His treatment of the central character in *Babbitt*—George Babbitt of Zenith—also had a strong element of self-mockery, because Lewis could offer no alternative set of values to Babbitt's crass self-promotion, hunger for success, and craving for social acceptance. In 1930, Lewis became the first American author to win the Nobel Prize for literature.

In the aftermath of the postwar Red Scare, American radicalism found itself on the defensive throughout the 1920s. But one *cause célèbre* did attract a great deal of support from intellectuals. In 1921, two Italian American immigrants, Nicola Sacco and Bartolomeo Vanzetti, were tried and convicted for murder in the course of robbing a shoe factory in South Braintree, Massachusetts. Neither Sacco, a shoemaker, nor Vanzetti, a fish peddler, had criminal records, but both had long been active in militant anarchist circles, labor organizing, and antiwar agitation. Their trial took place amidst an intense atmosphere of nativist and antiradical feeling, and both the judge and prosecuting attorney engaged in clearly prejudicial conduct toward the defendants. A six-year struggle to save Sacco and Vanzetti following the trial failed. The two men were finally executed in 1927, and for many years, their case would remain a powerful symbol of how the criminal justice system could be tainted by political bias and anti-immigrant fervor.

Another side of intellectual alienation was expressed by writers critical of industrial progress and the new mass culture. The most important of these were a group of poets and scholars centered in Vanderbilt University in Nashville, Tennessee, collectively known as the Fugitives. They included Allen Tate, John Crowe Ransom, Donald Davidson, and Robert Penn Warren, all of whom invoked traditional authority, respect for the past, and older agrarian ways as ideals to live by. The Fugitives attacked industrialism and materialism as modern-day ills. Self-conscious Southerners, they looked to the antebellum plantation-based society as a model for a community based on benevolence toward dependents (such as black people and women) and respect for the land. Their book of essays, *I'll Take My Stand* (1930), was a collective manifesto of their ideas.

THE ELECTION OF 1928

The presidential election of 1928 served as a kind of national referendum on the Republican new era. It also revealed just how important ethnic and cultural differences had become in defining American politics. The contest reflected many of the deepest

Read the **Document**

History Bookshelf: F. Scott Fitzgerald, This Side of Paradise *(1920)* at **www.myhistorylab.com**

Read the **Document**

History Bookshelf: Sinclair Lewis, Babbitt *(1922)* at **www.myhistorylab.com**

Read the **Document**

Nicola Sacco and Bartolomeo Vanzetti, *"Court Statements" (1927)* at **www.myhistorylab.com**

See the **Map**

African American Population, 1910 and 1950 at **www.myhistorylab.com**

tensions and conflicts in American society in the 1920s: native-born versus immigrant; Protestant versus Catholic; Prohibition versus legal drinking; small-town life versus the cosmopolitan city; fundamentalism versus modernism; traditional sources of culture versus the new mass media (see Map 23.2).

The 1928 campaign featured two politicians who represented profoundly different sides of American life. Al Smith, the Democratic nominee for president, was a pure product of New York City's Lower East Side. Smith came from a background that included Irish, German, and Italian ancestry, and he was raised as a Roman Catholic. He rose through the political ranks of New York's Tammany Hall machine. A personable man with a deep sympathy for poor and working-class people, Smith served four terms as governor of New York, pushing through an array of laws reforming factory conditions, housing, and welfare programs. Two of his closest advisers were the progressives Frances Perkins and Belle Moskowitz. Smith thus fused older-style machine politics with the newer reform emphasis on state intervention to solve social problems.

Herbert Hoover easily won the Republican nomination after Calvin Coolidge announced he would not run for reelection. Hoover epitomized the successful and forward-looking American. An engineer and self-made millionaire, he offered a unique combination of experience in humanitarian war relief, administrative efficiency, and probusiness policies. Above all, Hoover stood for a commitment to voluntarism and individualism as the best method for advancing the public welfare. He was one of the best-known men in America and promised to continue the Republican control of national politics.

Smith himself quickly became the central issue of the campaign. His sharp New York accent, jarring to many Americans who heard it over the radio, marked him clearly as a man of the city. So did his brown derby and fashionable suits, as well as his promise to work for the repeal of Prohibition. As the first Roman Catholic nominee of a major party, Smith also drew a torrent of anti-Catholic bigotry, especially in the South and Midwest. Bishop James Cannon, head of the Southern Methodist Episcopal Church, insisted that "no subject of the Pope" should be permitted to occupy the White House. For his part, Smith ran a largely conservative race. He appointed John Raskob, a Republican vice president of General Motors, to manage his campaign and tried to outdo Hoover in his praise for business. He avoided economic issues such as the unevenness of the prosperity, the plight of farmers, or the growing unemployment. Democrats remained regionally divided over Prohibition, Smith's religion, and the widening split between rural and urban values. Hoover did not have to do much, other than take credit for the continued prosperity.

Hoover polled 21 million votes to Smith's 15 million, and swept the Electoral College 444 to 87, including New York State. Even the solid South, reliably Democratic since the Civil War, gave five states to Hoover—a clear reflection of the ethnocultural split in the party. Yet the election offered important clues to the future of the Democrats. Smith was more successful in the big cities of the North and East than any Democrat in modern times. He outpolled Hoover in the aggregate vote of the nation's twelve largest cities and carried six of them, thus pointing the way to the Democrats' future dominance with urban, northeastern, and ethnic voters.

	Electoral Vote (%)	Popular Vote (%)
HERBERT HOOVER (Republican)	444 (82)	21,391,993 (58.2)
Alfred E. Smith (Democrat)	87 (17)	15,016,169 (40.9)
Norman Thomas (Socialist)	—	267,835 (0.7)
Other parties (Socialist Labor, Prohibition)	—	62,890 (0.2)

MAP 23.2
The Election of 1928 Although Al Smith managed to carry the nation's twelve largest cities, Herbert Hoover's victory in 1928 was one of the largest popular and electoral landslides in the nation's history.

WHAT EXPLAINS Al Smith's strength in the South? Why did Hoover win practically everywhere else?

Clifford K. Berryman's 1928 political cartoon interpreted that year's presidential contest along sectional lines. It depicted the two major presidential contenders as each setting off to campaign in the regions where their support was weakest. For Democrat Al Smith, that meant the West, and for Republican Herbert Hoover, the East.

CONCLUSION

America's big cities, if not dominant politically, now defined the nation's cultural and economic life as never before. With Hollywood movies leading the way, the new mass media brought cosmopolitan entertainment and values to the remotest small communities. The culture of celebrity knew no geographic boundaries. New consumer durable goods associated with mass-production techniques—automobiles, radios, telephones, household appliances—were manufactured largely in cities. The advertising and public relations companies that sang their praises were also distinctly urban enterprises. Even with the curtailing of European immigration, big cities attracted a kaleidoscopic variety of migrants: white people from small towns and farms, African Americans from the rural South, Mexicans from across the border, and intellectuals and professionals looking to make their mark.

Many Americans, of course, remained deeply suspicious of postwar cultural and economic trends. Yet the partisans of Prohibition, members of the Ku Klux Klan, and religious fundamentalists usually found themselves on the defensive against what they viewed as alien cultural and economic forces centered in the cities. Large sectors of the population did not share in the era's prosperity. But the large numbers who did—or at least had a taste of good times—ensured Republican political dominance throughout the decade. Thus, America in the 1920s balanced dizzying change in the cultural and economic realms with conservative politics. The reform crusades that attracted millions during the progressive era were a distant memory. Political activism was no match for the new pleasures promised by technology and prosperity.

CHRONOLOGY

1920	Prohibition takes effect
	Warren G. Harding is elected president
	Station KDKA in Pittsburgh goes on the air
	Census reports that urban population is greater than rural population for the first time
1921	First immigration quotas are established by Congress
	Sheppard-Towner Act establishes first federally funded health care program
1923	Equal Rights Amendment is first introduced in Congress
	Harding dies in office; Calvin Coolidge becomes president
1924	Ku Klux Klan is at height of its influence
	Dawes Plan for war reparations stabilizes European economies
	Reed-Johnson Immigration Act tightens quotas established in 1921
1925	Scopes trial pits religious fundamentalism against modernity
	F. Scott Fitzgerald publishes *The Great Gatsby*
1926	National Broadcasting Company establishes first national radio network
1927	McNary-Haugen Farm Relief bill finally passed by Congress but is vetoed by President Coolidge as unwarranted federal interference in the economy
	Warner Brothers produces *The Jazz Singer*, the first feature-length motion picture with sound
	Charles Lindbergh makes first solo flight across the Atlantic Ocean
1928	Kellogg-Briand Pact renounces war
	Herbert Hoover defeats Al Smith for the presidency
1929	Robert and Helen Lynd publish their classic community study, *Middletown*

REVIEW QUESTIONS

1. Describe the impact of the "second industrial revolution" on American business, workers, and consumers. Which technological and economic changes had the biggest impact on American society?

2. Analyze the uneven distribution of the 1920s' economic prosperity. Which Americans gained the most, and which were largely left out?

3. How did an expanding mass culture change the contours of everyday life in the decade following World War I? What role did new technologies of mass communication play in shaping these changes? What connections can you draw between the "culture of consumption" then and today?

4. What were the key policies and goals articulated by Republican political leaders of the 1920s? How did they apply these to both domestic and foreign affairs?

5. How did some Americans resist the rapid changes taking place in the post–World War I world? What cultural and political strategies did they employ?

6. Discuss the 1928 election as a mirror of the divisions in American society.

KEY TERMS

Harlem Renaissance (p. 616)

Immigration Act (p. 610)

League of Women Voters (p. 613)

Open shop (p. 596)

Sheppard-Towner Act (p. 613)

Volstead Act (p. 609)

Welfare capitalism (p. 596)

myhistorylab Connections

Reinforce what you learned in this chapter by studying the many documents, images, maps, review tools, and videos available at www.myhistorylab.com.

Read and Review

✓•—[Study and Review **Chapter 23**

•●•—[Read the Document

Frederick W. Taylor, "Scientific Management" (1911)

Edward E. Purinton, "Big Ideas from Big Business" (1921)

Advertisements (1925, 1927)

Eleanor R. Wembridge, "Petting and the Campus" (1925)

Immigration Law (1924)

"Creed of Klanswomen" (1924)

Nicola Sacco and Bartolomeo Vanzetti, "Court Statements" (1927)

◉—[See the Map *African American Population, 1910 and 1950*

Research and Explore

•●•—[Read the Document

Exploring America: Harlem Renaissance

Profiles
  Mary Pickford
  John B. Watson

History Bookshelf
  W.E.B. DuBois, The Negro *(1915)*
  Margaret Sanger, Woman and the New Race *(1920)*
  F. Scott Fitzgerald, This Side of Paradise *(1920)*
  Sinclair Lewis, Babbitt *(1922)*

((•—[Hear the Audio *Prohibition is a Failure*

⟨◉⟩—[Watch the Video

The Great Migration

The Rise and Fall of the Automobile Economy

The Harlem Renaissance

((•—[**Hear** the **Audio**

Hear the audio files for Chapter 23 at
www.myhistorylab.com.

The Scopes Monkey Trial as a Harbinger of Change

The Roaring '20's was a decade of turmoil and change in the United States on many levels. All this insecurity unsettled American traditionalists, especially religious fundamentalists. In rural states fundamentalists possessed a majority and control of the state legislature. John Washington Butler, a part time preacher and full time farmer served in the Tennessee legislature, had never read anything about evolution, but heard it denied the teachings of the Bible. He formulated a bill to forbid the teaching of evolution in the schools of Tennessee titled "AN ACT prohibiting the teaching of the Evolution Theory in all the Universities, Normals and all other public schools of Tennessee…"

The Butler Act immediately provoked a reaction from the American Civil Liberties Union. To challenge the law, John T. Scopes, part time biology teacher from Dayton, Tennessee, agreed to be arrested and placed on trial. The Scopes Monkey Trial, as it soon came to be known, became the first trial ever broadcast live on national radio. William Jennings Bryan, a prominent fundamentalist Christian, was seeking the Democratic presidential nomination again for the 1928 election and saw this trial as a vehicle to promote his candidacy. Clarence Darrow, nationally famous criminal lawyer, liberal, and agnostic, took the role of the defense. A circus of a trial followed.

EXAMINE THE history and impact of Tennessee's Butler Act (1925) and the trial of John T. Scopes that followed. Would contemporary observers have considered the jury decision to be the final decision on the issue of teaching evolution in the public schools of America or did they have an inkling of the future of this issue?

John T. Scopes was found guilty and fined. The sentence was appealed to the Tennessee Supreme Court, which upheld the Dayton sentence, but set the sentence aside on a legal technicality that the jury had not set the fine levied against Scopes. The Butler Act would not be repealed by the Tennessee state legislature until 1967. The U.S. Supreme Court would declare similar laws to be unconstitutional in an Arkansas case in 1968. ■

Scopes trial in Tennessee in 1925.
Clarence Darrow (standing) and
John T. Scopes (seated behind Darrow,
in a white shirt staring straight ahead).

BUTLER ACT, 1925

THAT IS shall be unlawful for any teacher in any of the Universities, Normals and all other public schools of the State which are supported in whole or in part by the public school funds of the State, to teach any theory that denies the story of the Divine Creation of man as taught in the Bible, and to teach instead that man has descended from a lower order of animals.

In the national media Clarence Darrow and William Jennings Bryan were the chief protagonists of the trial.

Darrow, the famous criminal lawyer, agnostic, and liberal stood for the defense. William Jennings Bryan volunteered for the prosecution and was given the honorary title of "colonel." During the trial a famous confrontation between Darrow and Bryan occurred when Bryan offered to testify as a biblical expert. Darrow demolished Bryan's arguments and even forced him to contradict the fundamentalist literal interpretation of Genesis as a seven-day creation event. ■

H. L. MENCKEN, AFTERMATH (OF THE SCOPES TRIAL), *BALTIMORE EVENING SUN*, SEPTEMBER 14, 1925

TRUE ENOUGH, even a superstitious man has certain inalienable rights. He has a right to harbor and indulge his imbecilities as long as he pleases, provided only he does not try to inflict them upon other men by force. He has a right to argue for them as eloquently as he can, in season and out of season. He has a right to teach them to his children. But certainly he has no right to be protected against the free criticism of those who do not hold them. He has no right to demand that they be treated as sacred. He has no right to preach them without challenge....

The meaning of religious freedom, I fear, is sometimes greatly misapprehended. It is taken to be a sort of immunity, not merely from governmental control but also from public opinion. A dunderhead gets himself a long-tailed coat, rises behind the sacred desk, and emits such bilge as would gag a Hottentot. Is it to pass unchallenged? If so, then what we have is not religious freedom at all, but the most intolerable and outrageous variety of religious despotism. Any fool, once he is admitted to holy orders, becomes infallible. Any half-wit, by the simple device of ascribing his delusions to revelation, takes on an authority that is denied to all the rest of us. ■

▲ What Would Their Verdict Be? *The Daily Star* (Montreal), reprinted in the *Literary Digest*, July 25, 1925

EPPERSON V. ARKANSAS, 393 U.S. 97 (1968)

IN THE present case, there can be no doubt that Arkansas has sought to prevent its teachers from discussing the theory of evolution because it is contrary to the belief of some that the Book of Genesis must be the exclusive source of doctrine as to the origin of man. No suggestion has been made that Arkansas' law may be justified by considerations of state policy other than the religious views of some of its citizens. It is clear that fundamentalist sectarian conviction was and is the law's reason for existence. Its antecedent, Tennessee's "monkey law," candidly stated its purpose: to make it unlawful "to teach any theory that denies the story of the Divine Creation of man as taught in the Bible, and to teach instead that man has descended from a lower order of animals." Perhaps the sensational publicity attendant upon the Scopes trial induced Arkansas to adopt less explicit language. It

eliminated Tennessee's reference to "the story of the Divine Creation of man" as taught in the Bible, but there is no doubt that the motivation for the law was the same: to suppress the teaching of a theory which, it was thought, "denied" the divine creation of man.

Arkansas' law cannot be defended as an act of religious neutrality. Arkansas did not seek to excise from the curricula of its schools and universities all discussion of the origin of man. The law's effort was confined to an attempt to blot out a particular theory because of its supposed conflict with the Biblical account, literally read. Plainly, the law is contrary to the mandate of the First, and in violation of the Fourteenth, Amendment to the Constitution.

The judgment of the Supreme Court of Arkansas is Reversed. ■

I remembered seeing the people passing on their way to California . . . It hurt me to see the people in their rickety old cars, their clothes in tatters, escaping from the drought and the dust bowls.

—*Carlotta Silvas Martin, January 1936*

NRA MEMBER U.S.

WE DO OUR PART

CONSERVATION US CIVILIAN CORPS Co. 272

Work Pays America!

PROSPERITY

WORKS PROGRESS ADMINISTRATION

Hands in their pockets, hungry men stand numbly in one of New York City's breadlines. Said one observer: "The wretched men, many without overcoats or decent shoes, usually began to line up soon after six o'clock— in good weather or bad, rain or snow."

24

THE GREAT DEPRESSION AND THE NEW DEAL

1929–1940

((●─[Hear the **Audio**

Hear the audio files for Chapter 24 at **www.myhistorylab.com**.

WHAT WERE the causes of the Great Depression, and what were its immediate consequences?

WHAT DID FDR hope to accomplish in his first hundred days in office?

HOW DID the Second New Deal differ from the First New Deal?

HOW DID the New Deal expand the scope of the federal government in the South and West?

WHAT WERE the limits of the New Deal's reforms, and what legacy did those reforms leave?

HOW DID the Great Depression affect American cultural life during the 1930s?

AMERICAN COMMUNITIES

Sit-Down Strike at Flint:
Automobile Workers Organize a New Union

ON FEBRUARY 11, 1937, 400 TIRED, BUT VERY HAPPY STRIKERS MARCHED out of a sprawling automobile factory in Flint, Michigan. A makeshift banner on top of the plant announced "Victory Is Ours." A wildly cheering parade line of a thousand supporters greeted the strikers at the gates. The celebrants marched to two other factories to greet other emerging strikers. After forty-four days, the great Flint sit-down strike was over.

Flint was the heart of production for General Motors, the largest corporation in the world. In 1936, GM's net profits had reached $285 million, and its total assets were $1.5 billion. Flint had boomed with the auto industry during the 1920s. Thousands of migrants streamed into the city, attracted by assembly-line jobs averaging about $30 a week. By 1930, Flint's population had grown to about 150,000 people, 80 percent of whom depended on work at General Motors.

The Great Depression hit Flint very hard. Employment at GM fell from a 1929 high of 56,000 to fewer than 17,000 in 1932. As late as 1938, close to half the city's families were receiving some kind of emergency relief. By that time, as in thousands of other American communities, Flint's private and county relief agencies had been overwhelmed by the needs of the unemployed and their families. Two new national agencies based in Washington, DC, the Federal Emergency Relief Administration and the Works Progress Administration, had replaced local sources of aid during the economic crisis.

The United Automobile Workers (UAW) came to Flint in 1936, seeking to organize GM workers into one industrial union. The previous year, Congress had passed the National Labor Relations Act (also known as the Wagner Act), which made union organizing easier by guaranteeing the right of workers to join unions and bargain collectively. The act established the National Labor Relations Board to oversee union elections and prohibit illegal antiunion activities by employers. But the obstacles to labor organizing were still enormous.

Unemployment was high, and GM had maintained a vigorous antiunion policy for years. By the fall of 1936, the UAW had signed up only a thousand members. The key moment came with the seizure of two Flint GM plants by a few hundred auto workers on December 30, 1936. The idea was to stay in the factories until strikers could achieve a collective bargaining agreement with General Motors.

The Flint strikers carefully organized themselves into what one historian called "the sit-down community." Each plant elected a strike committee and appointed its own police chief and sanitary engineer. Committees were organized for food preparation, recreation,

sanitation, education, and contact with the outside. A Women's Emergency Brigade—the strikers' wives, mothers, and daughters—provided crucial support preparing food and maintaining militant picket lines.

As the strike continued through January, support in Flint and around the nation grew. Overall production in the GM empire dropped from 53,000 vehicles per week to 1,500. Reporters and union supporters flocked to the plants. On January 11, strikers and their supporters clashed violently with Flint police and private GM guards. Michigan governor Frank Murphy, sympathetic to the strikers, brought in the National Guard to protect them. He refused to enforce an injunction obtained by GM to evict the strikers. In the face of determined unity by the sit-downers, GM gave in and recognized the UAW as the exclusive bargaining agent in all sixty of its factories.

The strike was perhaps the most important in American labor history, sparking a huge growth in union membership in the automobile and other mass-production industries. Out of the tight-knit, temporary community of the sit-down strike emerged a looser yet more permanent kind of community: a powerful, nationwide trade union of automobile workers. The national UAW, like other new unions in the mass-production industries, was composed of locals around the country. The permanent community of unionized auto workers won significant improvements in wages, working conditions, and benefits. Locals also became influential in the political and social lives of their larger communities—industrial cities such as Flint, Detroit, and Toledo.

Flint

More broadly, the Flint sit-down embodied the new political and economic dynamics of Depression-era America. Workers, farmers, and consumers hard hit by the worst economic catastrophe in U.S. history called for a more activist federal government to relieve suffering and offer greater economic security for Americans. In response, a rejuvenated Democratic Party, led by President Franklin D. Roosevelt and in solid control of Congress, created the New Deal, an ambitious collection of measures designed to promote relief, recovery, and reform. Organized labor provided crucial support for many of the social welfare initiatives associated with the New Deal throughout the 1930s and beyond. By the late 1930s, conservative resistance would limit the scope of New Deal reforms. But in communities around the nation, labor unions inspired by the Flint sit-down reached unprecedented levels of popularity and influence in economic and political life. Nationally, they would remain a crucial component of the New Deal political coalition, and a key power broker in the Democratic Party, for decades to come.

HARD TIMES

No twentieth-century event more profoundly affected American life than the **Great Depression**—the worst economic crisis in American history. Even today, the emotional and psychological toll of those years has left what one writer called an "invisible scar" on the lives and memories of millions of American families.

UNDERLYING WEAKNESSES OF THE 1920S' ECONOMY

Signs of deep economic weakness had already begun to surface amid the general prosperity of the 1920s. First, workers and consumers received too small a share of the enormous increases in labor productivity. Between 1923 and 1929, manufacturing output per worker-hour increased by 32 percent, while wages rose only 8 percent. Gains in wages and salaries were extremely uneven. While workers in newer industries such as automobiles and electrical manufacturing enjoyed pay increases, those in textiles and coal mining watched their wages fall. Moreover, the rise in productivity itself had encouraged overproduction in many industries, and the farm sector had never been able to regain the prosperity of the World War I years (see Chapter 23).

To be sure, Americans overall in the 1920s had more money to spend. But economic insecurity was still a brutal fact of life for millions of families, especially in rural communities. Most industrial workers endured regular bouts of unemployment and seasonal layoffs. Eighty percent of the nation's families had no savings at all, and an old age spent in poverty was far more likely for the average worker than "retirement." The most important weakness in the economy was the extremely unequal distribution of income, yielding the greatest concentration of wealth in the nation's history (see Table 24.1).

THE BULL MARKET AND THE CRASH

Stock trading in the late 1920s captured the imagination of the broad American public. The stock market resembled a sporting arena; millions followed stock prices as avidly as the exploits of Babe Ruth or Jack Dempsey. During the bull market of the 1920s, stock prices increased at roughly twice the rate of industrial production. By the end of the decade, stocks that once had been bought mainly on the basis of their earning power, which was passed on to stockholders in the form of dividends, came to be purchased only for the resale value after their prices rose.

Yet only about 3 million Americans—out of a total population of 120 million—owned any stocks at all. Many of these stock buyers had been lured into the market through easy-credit margin accounts, which allowed investors to purchase stocks with a small down payment (as low as 10 percent), borrowing the rest from a broker and using the shares as collateral on the loan. Investment trusts, similar to today's mutual funds,

WHAT WERE he causes of the Great Depression, and what were its immediate consequences?

◆◉◆─Read the Document
Dealing with Hard Times: The Great Depression at **www.myhistorylab.com**

Great Depression The nation's worst economic crisis, extending through the 1930s, producing unprecedented bank failures, unemployment, and industrial and agricultural collapse.

TABLE 24.1

Distribution of Total Family Income Among Various Segments of the Population, 1929–44 (in Percentages)

Year	Poorest Fifth	Second-Poorest Fifth	Middle Fifth	Second-Wealthiest Fifth	Wealthiest Fifth	Wealthiest 5 Percent
1929	12.5		13.8	19.3	54.4	30.0
1935–36	4.1	9.2	14.1	20.9	51.7	26.5
1941	4.1	9.5	15.3	22.3	48.8	24.0
1944	4.9	10.9	16.2	22.2	45.8	20.7

Adapted from U.S. Bureau of the Census, *Historical Statistics of the United States, Colonial Times to 1970*, Bicentennial Edition (Washington, DC: U.S. Government Printing Office, 1975), 301.

Rollin Kirby's 1929 cartoon depicts an individual investor losing his money as he clings to a bear running down Wall Street. The bear symbolizes an atmosphere of panic selling and heavy losses, the opposite of a "bull" market in which investor confidence spurs buying and faith in the future.

attracted many new investors with promises of high returns. Corporations found that lending excess capital to stockbrokers was more profitable than investing in new technologies. All these factors fed an expansive and optimistic atmosphere on Wall Street.

The bull market peaked in early September, and prices drifted downward. As expectations of an endless boom began to melt, the market had to decline. On Monday, October 28, the Dow lost 13 percent of its value. The next day—"Black Tuesday," October 29—the bottom fell out. Over 16 million shares, more than double the previous record, were traded as panic selling took hold. For many stocks, no buyers were available at any price.

The situation worsened. The market's fragile foundation of credit, based on the margin debt, quickly crumbled. Many investors with margin accounts had to sell when stock values fell. Since the shares themselves represented the security for their loans, more money had to be put up to cover the loans when prices declined. Half the value of the stocks listed in the *New York Times* index was lost in ten weeks.

The stock market crash undermined the confidence, investment, and spending of businesses and the well-to-do. Manufacturers cut production and began laying off workers, which brought further declines in consumer spending, and so another round of production cutbacks ensued. A large proportion of the nation's banking funds had been tied to the speculative bubble. Many banks began to fail as anxious depositors withdrew their funds, which were uninsured, costing thousands of families all their savings. And an 86 percent plunge in agricultural prices between 1929 and 1933 brought terrible suffering to America's farmers.

MASS UNEMPLOYMENT

At a time when unemployment insurance did not exist and public relief was completely inadequate, the loss of a job could mean economic catastrophe for workers and their families. Massive unemployment across America became the most powerful sign of a deepening depression. By 1933, 12.6 million workers—over one-quarter of the labor force—were without jobs. (Other sources put the figure that year above 16 million, or nearly one out of every three workers.)

Many Americans, raised believing that they were responsible for their own fate, blamed themselves for their failure to find work. Journalists and social workers noted the common feelings of shame and guilt expressed by the unemployed. One despondent Pennsylvania man asked a state relief agency, "Can you be so kind as to advise me as to which would be the most human way to dispose of my self and family, as this is about the only thing that I see left to do."

Unemployment upset the psychological balance in many families by undermining the traditional authority of the male breadwinner. Women, because their labor was cheaper than men's, found it easier to keep jobs. Female clerks, secretaries, maids, and waitresses earned much less than male factory workers, but their jobs were more likely to survive hard times. Men responded in a variety of ways to unemployment. Some withdrew emotionally; others became angry or took to drinking. A few committed suicide. Fear of unemployment and a deep desire for security marked the Depression generation.

HOOVER'S FAILURE

The enormity of the Great Depression overwhelmed traditional—and meager—sources of relief. In most communities across America, these sources were a patchwork of private agencies and local government units, such as towns, cities, or counties. They simply lacked the money, resources, and staff to deal with the worsening situation.

There was great irony, even tragedy, in President Hoover's failure to respond to human suffering. During World War I, he had effectively administered Belgian war relief abroad and won wide praise for his leadership of the Food Administration at home. As a leader of the progressive wing of the Republican Party, Hoover had long championed a kind of cooperative individualism that relied upon public-spirited citizens. Although he felt real personal anguish over the hardships people suffered, he lacked the political skill to demonstrate his compassion in public. Failing to face the facts of the depression, Hoover worried more about undermining individual initiative than providing actual relief for victims.

Dorothea Lange captured the lonely despair of unemployment in *White Angel Breadline, San Francisco, 1933.* During the 1920s, Lange had specialized in taking portraits of wealthy families, but by 1932, she could no longer stand the contradiction between her portrait business and "what was going on in the street." She said of this photograph: "There are moments such as these when time stands still and all you can do is hold your breath and hope it will wait for you."

Dorothea Lange, *White Angel Breadline, San Francisco, 1933.* Copyright the Dorothea Lange Collection, The Oakland Museum of California, City of Oakland. Gift of Paul S. Taylor.

Hoover's plan for recovery centered on restoring business confidence. His administration's most important institutional response to the depression was the Reconstruction Finance Corporation (RFC), established in early 1932. The RFC was designed to make government credit available to ailing banks, railroads, insurance companies, and other businesses, thereby stimulating economic activity. Given the public's low purchasing power, most businesses were not interested in obtaining loans for expansion. The RFC managed to save numerous banks and other businesses from going under, but its approach did not hasten recovery. Hoover was loath to use the RFC to make direct grants to states, cities, or individuals. In July 1932, congressional Democrats pushed through the Emergency Relief Act, which authorized the RFC to lend $300 million to states that had exhausted their own relief funds. Hoover grudgingly signed the bill, but less than $30 million was actually given out by the end of 1933.

Two other federal actions—in each case, the opposite of what should have been done—worsened the situation. First, the Federal Reserve tightened credit sharply. That caused interest rates to spike, putting heavy pressure on the nation's banking system, especially the smaller banks on which farmers, merchants, and local businessmen relied. Without any state or federal insurance, more than 5,000 rural banks and ethnic-group-oriented savings and loans institutions failed between 1929 and 1932, and more than 9 million depositors lost their savings. Second, in 1930 Congress passed (and Hoover signed) the Smoot-Hawley Tariff, raising import duties to their highest levels in American history. Supporters claimed that this would protect American farmers from global competition and raise farm prices. Other nations responded by raising their own tariffs, which caused world trade to decline steeply, thus exacerbating the economic collapse.

Bonus Army Unemployed veterans of World War I gathering in Washington in 1932 demanding payment of service bonuses not due until 1945.

Read the Document

Herbert Hoover, New York Campaign Speech (1932) at **www.myhistorylab.com**

QUICK REVIEW

The 1932 Election

- Republicans renominated Hoover
- The Democratic platform differed little from the Republican platform.
- Franklin D. Roosevelt's victory was a repudiation of Hoover.

	Electoral Vote (%)	Popular Vote (%)
FRANKLIN D. ROOSEVELT (Democrat)	472 (89)	22,809,638 (57)
Herbert Hoover (Republican)	59 (11)	15,758,901 (40)
Minor parties	—	1,153,306 (3)

MAP 24.1

The Election of 1932 Democrats owed their overwhelming victory in 1932 to the popular identification of the depression with the Hoover administration. Roosevelt's popular vote was about the same as Hoover's in 1928, and FDR's Electoral College margin was even greater.

DID THE election of 1932 represent a repudiation of Hoover or an affirmation of Roosevelt?

A GLOBAL CRISIS AND THE ELECTION OF 1932

By 1931, the depression had spread not only across the United States but also throughout the world, a sign of how interdependent the global economy had become. The immediate problem was the highly unstable system of international finance. The 1919 peace settlement had saddled Germany with $33 billion in war reparations, owed largely to Great Britain and France. The United States loaned money to the British and French during the war, and American banks loaned large sums to Germany in the 1920s. Germany used these loans to pay reparations to the British and French, who in turn used these reparations to repay their American debts. The 1929 stock market crash put an end to American loans for Germany, thus removing a critical link in the international cash flow. When Germany then defaulted on its reparations, Great Britain and France in turn stopped paying what they owed to this country. As German banks collapsed and unemployment swelled, nervous European investors sold their American stocks, depressing the stock market even further. Great Britain and several other European nations also abandoned the gold standard and devalued (lowered) their currency relative to the dollar. This made American goods more difficult to sell abroad, further dampening production at home. With many nations also raising their tariffs to protect national industries, international trade slowed to a crawl. American banks, badly hurt by both domestic depositors clamoring for their money and the foreign withdrawal of capital, began failing in record numbers.

By 1932, the desperate mood of many Americans was finding expression in direct, sometimes violent, protests that were widely covered in the press. On March 7, communist organizers led a march of several thousand Detroit auto workers and unemployed in Dearborn. Ford-controlled police fired tear gas and bullets, killing four demonstrators and seriously wounding fifty others. Desperate farmers in Iowa organized the Farmers' Holiday Association, aimed at raising prices by refusing to sell produce. In August, some 1,500 farmers dumped milk and other perishables into ditches.

The spring of 1932 also saw the "**Bonus Army**" begin descending on Washington, DC. This protest took its name from Congress's promise in 1924 to pay every veteran of World War I a $1,000 bonus—in the form of a bond that would not mature until 1945. The veterans who were gathering in Washington demanded immediate payment of the bonus in cash. By summer, they and their families numbered around 20,000 strong and were camping out all over the capital city. The House passed a bill for immediate payment, but when the Senate refused to agree, most of the downcast veterans left. At the end of July, U.S. Army troops forcibly evicted the remaining 2,000 veterans. The spectacle of these unarmed and unemployed men being driven off by bayonets and bullets, provided the most disturbing evidence yet of the failure of Hoover's administration.

In 1932, Democrats nominated Franklin D. Roosevelt, governor of New York, for the presidency. Roosevelt's acceptance speech stressed the need for reconstructing the nation's economy. "I pledge you, I pledge myself," he said, "to a new deal for the American people." Hoover bitterly condemned Roosevelt's ideas as a "radical departure" from the American way of life. The Democratic victory was overwhelming. Roosevelt carried forty-two states, taking the Electoral College 472 to 59 and the popular vote by about 23 million to 16 million. Democrats won big majorities in both the House and the Senate. The stage was set for FDR's "new deal" (see Map 24.1).

FDR AND THE FIRST NEW DEAL

No twentieth-century president had a greater impact on American life and politics than Franklin Delano Roosevelt (FDR). To a large degree, the New Deal was a product of his astute political skills and the sheer force of his personality. The only president ever elected to four terms, FDR would loom as the dominant personality in American political life through twelve years of depression and global war.

FDR THE MAN

Franklin Delano Roosevelt was born in 1882 in Dutchess County, New York, on his family's vast estate. In 1905, he married his distant cousin, Anna Eleanor Roosevelt, a niece of President Theodore Roosevelt. He was elected as a Democrat to the New York State Senate in 1910, served as assistant secretary of the navy from 1913 to 1920, and was nominated for vice president by the Democrats in the losing 1920 campaign.

In the summer of 1921, Roosevelt was stricken with polio; he was never to walk again without support. His illness proved the turning point in his life. The wealthy aristocrat, for whom everything had come relatively easily, now personally understood the meaning of struggle and hardship. Elected governor of New York in 1928, Roosevelt served two terms and won a national reputation for reform.

WHAT DID FDR hope to accomplish in his first hundred days in office?

This *New Yorker* magazine cover depicted an ebullient Franklin D. Roosevelt riding to his 1933 inauguration in the company of a glum Herbert Hoover. This drawing typified many mass media images of the day, contrasting the different moods and temperaments of the new president and the defeated incumbent.

●●●[Read the Document
*Franklin D. Roosevelt, Fireside Chat
(1933)* at **www.myhistorylab.com**

fireside chat   Speeches broadcast
nationally over the radio in which
President Franklin D. Roosevelt
explained complex issues and
programs in plain language, as
though his listeners were gathered
around the fireside with him.

Emergency Banking Act   1933 act
which gave the president broad
discretionary powers over all
banking transactions and foreign
exchange.

New Deal   The economic and
political policies of the Roosevelt
administration in the 1930s.

A recruitment poster represents the Civilian Conservation Corps
(CCC) as much more than simply an emergency relief measure,
stressing character building and the opportunity for self-
improvement. By the time the CCC expired in 1942, it had
become one of the most popular of all the New Deal programs.

"THE ONLY THING WE HAVE TO FEAR": RESTORING CONFIDENCE

In the first days of his administration, Roosevelt conveyed a sense of optimism and activism that helped restore the badly shaken confidence of the nation. "First of all," he told Americans in his Inaugural Address on March 4, 1933, "let me assert my firm belief that the only thing we have to fear is fear itself." The very next day he issued an executive order calling for a four-day "bank holiday" to stop the collapse of the country's financial system.

The new Congress was not scheduled to convene until the end of 1933, but Roosevelt convened a special session to deal with the banking crisis, unemployment aid, and farm relief. On March 12, he broadcast his first "**fireside chat**" to explain the steps he had taken to meet the financial emergency. These radio broadcasts gave courage to ordinary Americans and communicated a genuine sense of compassion from the White House.

Congress immediately passed the **Emergency Banking Act**, which gave the president broad discretionary powers over all banking transactions and foreign exchange. It authorized healthy banks to reopen only under licenses from the Treasury Department and provided for greater federal authority in managing the affairs of failed banks. By the middle of March, about half the country's banks, holding about 90 percent of the nation's deposits, were open for business again. The bank crisis had passed.

Roosevelt assembled a group of key advisers, the "brains trust," to counsel him in the White House. While they sometimes gave conflicting advice. Some advocated fiscal conservatism to restore confidence in the dollar; others pushed for central planning to manage the economy. But the "brain trusters" shared a basic belief in expert-directed government–business cooperation. Structural economic reform, they argued, must accept the modern reality of large corporate enterprise based on mass production and distribution.

THE HUNDRED DAYS

From March to June 1933—"the Hundred Days"—FDR pushed through Congress an extraordinary amount of depression-fighting legislation. What came to be called the **New Deal** was no unified program to end the depression but rather an improvised series of reform and relief measures, some of which completely contradicted each other. Still, all the New Deal programs were united by the fundamental goals of relief, reform, and recovery.

Five measures were particularly important and innovative. The Civilian Conservation Corps (CCC), established in March as an unemployment relief effort, provided work for jobless young men in protecting and conserving the nation's natural resources. Road construction, reforestation, flood control, and national park improvements were some of the major projects performed in work camps across the country. By the time the program was phased out in 1942, more than 2.5 million youths had worked in some 1,500 CCC camps.

In May, Congress authorized $500 million for the Federal Emergency Relief Administration (FERA). Half the money went as direct relief to the states; the rest was distributed on the basis of a dollar of federal aid for every three dollars of state and local funds spent for relief. To direct this massive undertaking, FDR tapped Harry Hopkins, a former New York City social worker driven by a deep moral passion to help the less fortunate and an impatience with bureaucracy. Hopkins would emerge as the key figure administering New Deal relief programs.

The Agricultural Adjustment Administration (AAA) was set up to provide immediate relief to the nation's farmers. The AAA established a new federal role in agricultural planning and price setting. It established prices for basic farm commodities, including corn, wheat, hogs, cotton, rice, and dairy products. The AAA also incorporated the principle of subsidy, whereby farmers received benefit payments in return for reducing acreage or otherwise cutting production where surpluses existed. New taxes on food processing would pay for these programs.

The AAA raised total farm income and was especially successful in pushing up the prices of wheat, cotton, and corn. It had some troubling side effects, however. Landlords often failed to share their AAA payments with tenant farmers, and they frequently used benefits to buy tractors and other equipment that displaced sharecroppers. Many Americans were disturbed, too, by the sight of surplus crops, livestock, and milk being destroyed while millions went hungry.

The **Tennessee Valley Authority (TVA)** proved to be one of the most unique and controversial projects of the New Deal era. The TVA, an independent public corporation, built dams and power plants, produced cheap fertilizer for farmers, and, most significantly, for the first time brought low-cost electricity to thousands of people in six southern states. Denounced by some as a dangerous step toward socialism, the TVA stood for decades as a model of how careful government planning could dramatically improve the social and economic welfare of an underdeveloped region.

On the very last of the Hundred Days, Congress passed the National Industrial Recovery Act, the closest attempt yet at a systematic plan for economic recovery. In theory, each industry would be self-governed by a code hammered out by representatives of business, labor, and consumers. Once approved by the National Recovery Administration (NRA) in Washington, the codes would have the force of law. In practice, almost all the National Recovery Administration codes were written by the largest firms in any given industry. The sheer administrative complexities involved with code writing and compliance made a great many people unhappy with the NRA's operation.

Finally, the Public Works Administration (PWA) authorized $3.3 billion for the construction of roads, public buildings, and other projects. The idea was to provide jobs and, through increased consumer spending, stimulate the economy. Eventually the PWA spent over $4.2 billion building roads, schools, post offices, bridges, courthouses, and other public buildings, which in thousands of communities today remain tangible reminders of the New Deal era.

During the Hundred Days and the months immediately following, Congress passed other legislation that would have important long-range effects. The Glass-Steagall Act created the Federal Deposit Insurance Corporation (FDIC), which provided protection to individual depositors in case of bank failure. Congress also established the Securities and Exchange Commission (SEC) to regulate stock exchanges and brokers, require full financial disclosures, and curb the speculative practices that had contributed to the 1929 crash. The 1934 National Housing Act, aimed at stimulating residential construction and making home financing more affordable, set up the Federal Housing Administration (FHA). The FHA insured loans made by banks and other private lenders for home building and home buying.

ROOSEVELT'S CRITICS, RIGHT AND LEFT

From the beginning, the New Deal had loud and powerful critics on the right who complained bitterly that FDR had overstepped the traditional boundaries of government action. Pro-Republican newspapers and the American Liberty League, a group of conservative businessmen organized in 1934, vehemently attacked the administration for what they considered its attack on property rights, the growing welfare state, and the alleged decline of personal liberty. In the 1934 election Democrats crushed their right-wing critics and increased their majorities in both houses of Congress.

In 1934, Father Charles E. Coughlin, a Catholic priest in suburban Detroit with a huge national radio audience of 40 million listeners, began attacking FDR in passionate broadcasts that also denounced Wall Street, international bankers, Jews, and "plutocratic capitalism." Roosevelt, he charged, wanted dictatorial powers, and New Deal policies were part of a communist conspiracy.

⊙ See the Map

The Tennessee Valley Authority at **www.myhistorylab.com**

QUICK REVIEW

The National Recovery Administration (NRA)

◆ Sought to halt the slide in prices, wages, and employment.

◆ Tended to help business, often at the expense of labor.

◆ Declared unconstitutional in 1935.

 Read the Document

Father Charles E. Coughlin, "A Third Party" (1936) at **www.myhistorylab.com**

Tennessee Valley Authority (TVA)
Federal regional planning agency established to promote conservation, produce electric power, and encourage economic development in seven Southern states.

OVERVIEW | Key Legislation of the First New Deal ("Hundred Days," March 9–June 16, 1933)

Legislation	Purpose
Emergency Banking Relief Act	Enlarged federal authority over private banks
	Government loans to private banks
Civilian Conservation Corps	Unemployment relief
	Conservation of natural resources
Federal Emergency Relief Administration	Direct federal money for relief, funneled through state and local governments
Agricultural Adjustment Administration	Federal farm aid based on parity pricing and subsidy
Tennessee Valley Authority	Economic development and cheap electricity for Tennessee Valley
National Industrial Recovery Act	Self-regulating industrial codes to revive economic activity
Public Works Administration	Federal public works projects to increase employment and consumer spending

 Read the Document

Huey Long, "Share Our Wealth" (1935) at
www.myhistorylab.com

More troublesome for Roosevelt were the vocal and popular movements on the left. These found the New Deal too timid. In California, the well-known novelist and socialist Upton Sinclair entered the 1934 Democratic primary for governor by running on a program he called EPIC ("End Poverty in California"). Sinclair shocked local and national Democrats by winning the primary easily. He lost a close general election only because the Republican candidate received heavy financial and tactical support from wealthy Hollywood studio executives and frightened regular Democrats. Another Californian, Francis E. Townsend won a large following among senior citizens with his Old Age Revolving Pension plan. He called for payments of $200 per month to all people over sixty, provided all the money was spent within thirty days. The pensions would be financed by a national 2 percent tax on commercial transactions.

Huey Long posed the greatest potential threat to Roosevelt's leadership. Long had captured Louisiana's governorship in 1928 by attacking the state's entrenched oil industry and calling for a radical redistribution of wealth. In office, he significantly improved public education, roads, medical care, and other public services, winning the loyalty of the state's poor farmers and industrial workers. Elected to the U.S. Senate in 1930, Long came to Washington with national ambitions. He at first supported Roosevelt, but in 1934, his own presidential ambitions and his impatience with the pace of New Deal measures led to a break with FDR.

Long organized the Share Our Wealth Society. Its purpose, he thundered, "was to break up the swollen fortunes of America and to spread the wealth among all our people." Although Long's economics were fuzzy, his "Every Man a King" slogan touched a deep popular nerve. Only his assassination that September by a political enemy of his corrupt political machine prevented Long's third-party candidacy, which might have proved disastrous for FDR.

A newly militant labor movement also loomed as a force to be reckoned with. Unemployed Councils, organized largely by the Communist Party in industrial cities, held marches and rallies demanding public works projects and relief payments. Section 7a of the National Industrial Recovery Act required that workers be allowed to bargain collectively with employers through representatives of their own choosing. Although this provision of the NIRA was not enforced, it did help raise expectations and sparked union organizing. Almost 1.5 million workers took part in some 1,800 strikes in 1934.

LEFT TURN AND THE SECOND NEW DEAL

The popularity of Coughlin, Sinclair, Townsend, and Long suggested Roosevelt might be losing electoral support among workers, farmers, the aged, and the unemployed. In addition, FDR had to contend with a conservative Supreme Court that did not share the public's enthusiasm for the New Deal. In May 1935, in *Schecter* v. *United States*, the Court found the NRA unconstitutional in its entirety. In early 1936, ruling in *Butler* v. *United States*, the Court invalidated the AAA, declaring it an unconstitutional attempt at regulating agriculture. Looking toward the 1936 election and eager for a popular mandate, Roosevelt and his closest advisers responded by turning left and offering new social-reform programs. What came to be called "the Second Hundred Days," marked the high point of progressive lawmaking in the New Deal.

THE SECOND HUNDRED DAYS

In April 1935, the administration pushed through Congress the Emergency Relief Appropriation Act, which allocated $5 billion for large-scale public works programs for the jobless. Over the next seven years, the WPA, under Harry Hopkins's leadership, oversaw the employment of more than 8 million Americans on a vast array of construction projects. Among the most innovative WPA programs were community service projects that employed thousands of jobless artists, musicians, actors, and writers.

The landmark Social Security Act of 1935 provided for old-age pensions and unemployment insurance. A payroll tax on workers and their employers created a fund from which retirees received monthly pensions after age sixty-five. The act's unemployment compensation plan established a minimum weekly payment and a minimum number of weeks during which those who lost jobs could collect.

In July 1935, Congress passed the **National Labor Relations Act**, often called the Wagner Act for its chief sponsor, Democratic senator Robert F. Wagner of New York. For the first time, the federal government guaranteed the right of American workers to join, or form, independent labor unions and to bargain collectively for improved wages, benefits, and working conditions. The The law also defined and prohibited unfair labor practices by employers, including firing workers for union activity.

Finally, the Resettlement Administration (RA) produced one of the most utopian New Deal programs, designed to create new kinds of model communities. Established by executive order, the RA helped destitute farm families relocate to more productive areas. It granted loans for purchasing land and equipment, and it directed reforestation and soil erosion projects, particularly in the hard-hit Southwest. Due to lack of funds and poor administration, however, only about 1 percent of the projected 500,000 families were actually moved.

LABOR'S UPSURGE: RISE OF THE CIO

The Wagner Act greatly facilitated union organizing and galvanized the moribund labor movement. In 1932, only 2.8 million workers were union members. By 1942, unions claimed more than 10.5 million members, nearly a third of the total nonagricultural work force. The growth in the size and power of the labor movement permanently changed the work lives and economic status of millions, as well as the national and local political landscapes.

HOW DID the Second New Deal differ from the First New Deal?

Watch the **Video**
Responding to the Great Depression: Whose New Deal? at
www.myhistorylab.com

QUICK REVIEW

The Social Security Act

◆ Provided unemployment compensation, old-age pensions, and aid for dependent mothers and children and the blind.

◆ The law excluded more than a fourth of all workers.

◆ Funded by a payroll tax.

Read the **Document**
Frances Perkins, The Social Security Act, (1935; 1960) at **www.myhistorylab.com**

Read the **Document**
Profile: *Frances Perkins* at
www.myhistorylab.com

National Labor Relations Act Act establishing Federal guarantee of right to organize trade unions and collective bargaining.

OVERVIEW | Key Legislation of the Second New Deal (1935–38)

Legislation	Purpose
Emergency Relief Appropriations Act (1935)	Large-scale public works program for the jobless (includes Works Progress Administration)
Social Security Act (1935)	Federal old-age pensions and unemployment insurance
National Labor Relations Act (1935)	Federal guarantee of right to organize trade unions and collective bargaining
Resettlement Administration (1935)	Relocation of poor rural families
	Reforestation and soil erosion projects
National Housing Act (1937)	Federal funding for public housing and slum clearance
Fair Labor Standards Act (1938)	Federal minimum wage and maximum hours

Committee for Industrial Organizations (CIO) An alliance of industrial unions that spurred the 1930s organizational drive among the mass-production industries.

Read the Document

Profile: *John Lewis* at www.myhistorylab.com

At the core of this growth was a series of dramatic successes in the organization of workers in large-scale, mass-production industries such as automobiles, steel, rubber, electrical goods, and textiles. The American Federation of Labor (AFL) had largely ignored workers in these industries. At the 1935 AFL convention, a group of more militant union officials led by John L. Lewis (of the United Mine Workers) and Sidney Hillman (of the Amalgamated Clothing Workers) formed the **Committee for Industrial Organization (CIO)** and set about organizing mass-production workers. They differed from nearly all old-line AFL unions by calling for the inclusion of black and women workers.

Lewis knew that establishing permanent unions in the mass-production industries would be a bruising battle. He committed the substantial resources of the United Mine Workers to a series of organizing drives, focusing first on the steel and auto industries. After the dramatic breakthrough in a 1937 sit-down strike against General Motors at Flint, Michigan, membership in CIO unions grew rapidly. CIO victories in the steel, rubber, and electrical industries followed, but often at a very high cost. One bloody example of the perils of union organizing was the 1937 Memorial Day Massacre in Chicago. In a field near the struck Republic Steel Mill in South Chicago, police fired into a crowd of union supporters, killing ten workers and wounding scores more.

In 1938, CIO unions withdrew from the AFL and reorganized themselves as the Congress of Industrial Organizations. For the first time ever, the labor movement had gained a permanent place in the nation's mass-production industries. Organized labor took its place as a key power broker in Roosevelt's New Deal and the national Democratic Party.

Photographer Milton Brooks won the first Pulitzer Prize for photography with this 1941 image for the *Detroit News*. He captured a violent labor confrontation in front of the Ford Motor Company's River Rouge plant, as private armed guards, employed by Ford, assault and beat organizers for the United Automobile Workers.

THE NEW DEAL COALITION AT HIGH TIDE

Both major political parties looked forward to the 1936 elections as a national referendum, and the campaign itself was exciting and hard fought. The Republicans nominated Governor Alfred M. Landon of Kansas. His campaign served as a lightning rod for all those, including many conservative Democrats, who were dissatisfied with Roosevelt and the direction he had taken.

Roosevelt attacked the "economic royalists" who denied that government "could do anything to protect the citizen in his right to work and his right to live." At the same time, FDR was careful to distance himself from radicalism. Huge and enthusiastic crowds greeted Roosevelt, especially in large cities. Still, the vast majority of the nation's newspapers endorsed Landon.

Election day erased all doubts: Roosevelt carried every state but Maine and Vermont, polling 61 percent of the popular vote. Democrats increased their substantial majorities in the House and Senate as well. In 1936, the Democrats forged a new coalition of voters that would dominate national politics for two generations. This "**New Deal coalition**," as it came to be known, included white Southern Democrats, ethnics who supported big-city political machines, unionized workers (including those being organized by the CIO), and many depression-hit farmers. Black voters in the North and West, long affiliated with the Republicans as "the party of Lincoln," went Democratic in record numbers.

THE NEW DEAL IN THE SOUTH AND WEST

The New Deal had its profoundest impact in the South and the West. Federal farm programs moved southern agriculture away from its longtime dependence upon sharecropping and tenant farming and helped reorganize it around new patterns of wage labor and agribusiness. New Deal dam building and power projects introduced electricity to millions of rural Southerners, transforming their lives. New Deal programs reshaped western agriculture, created new sources of water and energy, and changed Indian policy. In the process, the New Deal helped propel both the South and the West into the modern era and laid the groundwork for the postwar "Sunbelt."

MODERNIZING SOUTHERN FARMING AND LANDHOLDING

In 1930 over three-quarters of the South's African American farmers and nearly half its white farmers were sharecroppers or tenants. The continued dominance of a few crops—mainly cotton and tobacco—had only intensified the depression by glutting the market and keeping crop prices at rock bottom. The Agricultural Adjustment Administration succeeded in boosting prices by paying farmers to "plow under"—take their land out of production. Particularly in the South, however, these federal subsidies went overwhelmingly to large landowners. Most planters did not share these payments with sharecroppers and tenants.

New Deal policies helped destroy the old sharecropping and tenant system largely by helping landowners prosper. Those farmers who had access to government funds were able to diversify their crops, consolidate holdings, and work their land more efficiently with laborsaving machinery, such as tractors and mechanical harvesters. Mechanized farming and government-subsidized reductions of cultivated land cut the demand for labor and increased evictions. Uprooted tenants, sharecroppers, and day laborers found themselves on the road in search of work; many thousands migrated to cities and towns.

No New Deal initiative had more impact on southern communities than electrification. In the early 1930s, only about 3 percent of rural Southerners had access to electric power. The Tennessee Valley Authority and the Rural Electrification Administration (REA) helped millions of southern households move into the modern era by making electricity

New Deal coalition   Coalition that included traditional-minded white Southern Democrats, big-city political machines, industrial workers of all races, trade unionists, and many depression-hit farmers.

•••—**Read** the **Document**

Franklin D. Roosevelt, Second Inaugural Address (1937) at **www.myhistorylab.com**

HOW DID the New Deal expand the scope of the federal government in the South and West?

available for the first time. The TVA built sixteen dams across some 800 miles of the Tennessee River basin, bringing flood control and electric power to hundreds of thousands of families in seven southern states. It also significantly reduced consumer electric rates in many cities and towns by providing a cheaper alternative to private utilities.

AN ENVIRONMENTAL DISASTER: THE DUST BOWL

An ecological and economic catastrophe of unprecedented proportions struck the southern Great Plains in the mid-1930s. The region had suffered several drought years in the early 1930s. Such dry spells occurred regularly, in roughly twenty-year cycles. But this time, the parched earth became swept up in violent dust storms. The dust storms were largely the consequence of years of stripping the landscape of its natural vegetation. During World War I, wheat brought record-high prices on the world market, and for the next twenty years Great Plains farmers turned the region into a vast wheat factory.

As wheat prices fell in the 1920s, farmers broke still more land to make up the difference with increased production. Great Plains farmers had created an ecological time bomb that exploded when drought returned in the early 1930s. With native grasses destroyed to grow wheat, there was nothing left to prevent soil erosion. Dust storms blew away tens of millions of acres of rich topsoil, and thousands of farm families left the region. The hardest-hit regions were western Kansas, eastern Colorado, western Oklahoma, the Texas Panhandle, and eastern New Mexico—areas that a Denver journalist named the "Dust Bowl" (see Map 24.2).

Read the Document

Exploring America: The Dust Bowl at
www.myhistorylab.com

Watch the Video

The Plough that Broke the Plains at
www.myhistorylab.com

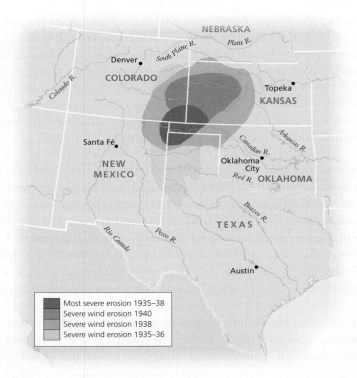

MAP 24.2

The Dust Bowl, 1935–40 This map shows the extent of the Dust Bowl in the southern Great Plains. Federal programs designed to improve soil conservation, water management, and farming practices could not prevent a mass exodus of hundreds of thousands out of the Great Plains.

WHAT WERE the reasons for this ecological disaster and why was it particularly damaging to people in the region?

Many thousands of Great Plains farm families were given direct emergency relief by the Resettlement Administration. Other federal assistance included crop and seed loans, moratoriums on loan payments, and temporary WPA jobs. The AAA paid wheat farmers millions of dollars not to grow what they could not sell and encouraged the diversion of acreage from soil-depleting crops like wheat to soil-enriching crops such as sorghum.

The federal government also pursued longer-range policies designed to alter land-use patterns, reverse soil erosion, and restore grasslands. By 1940, the acreage subject to dust storms in the Dust Bowl area of the southern plains had been reduced from roughly 50 million acres to fewer than 4 million acres.

While large landowners and ranchers were reaping sizable benefits from New Deal programs, thousands of tenant farmers and sharecropper families were being forced off the land in cotton-growing regions of Texas, Oklahoma, Missouri, and Arkansas. They became part of a stream of roughly 300,000 people, disparagingly called "Okies," who migrated to California in the 1930s. Once in California, most Okies could find work only as poorly paid agricultural laborers in the fertile San Joaquin and Imperial Valley districts. Only the outbreak of World War II and the pressing demand for labor allowed migrants to improve their situation significantly.

Mexican farm laborers faced stiff competition from Dust Bowl refugees. By the mid-1930s, they no longer dominated California's agricultural workforce. In 1936, an estimated 85 to 90 percent of the state's migratory workers were white Americans, as compared to less than 20 percent before the depression. Mexican farm worker families who managed to stay employed in California, Texas, and Colorado saw their wages plummet.

Southwestern communities campaigned to deport Mexicans and Mexican Americans. Employers, private charities, and the Immigration and Naturalization Service joined in this effort. Authorities made little effort to distinguish citizens from aliens; most of the children they deported had been born in the United States and, hence, were citizens. Los Angeles County had the most aggressive campaign, using boxcars to ship out more than 13,000 Mexicans between 1931 and 1934. The hostile climate convinced thousands more to leave voluntarily.

WATER POLICY

The New Deal ushered in the era of large-scale water projects, designed to provide irrigation and cheap power and to prevent floods. The long-range impact of these undertakings on western life was enormous. The key government agency in this realm was the Bureau of Reclamation of the Department of the Interior, which was given the responsibility of building huge multipurpose dams designed to control entire river systems (see Map 24.3).

The first of these projects, Boulder Dam (later renamed Hoover Dam), was designed to harness the Colorado River. The dam was completed in 1935 with the help of funds from the Public Works Administration. Los Angeles and neighboring cities built a 259-mile aqueduct to channel water to their growing populations. Lake Mead, created by construction of the dam, became the world's largest artificial lake, extending 115 miles up the canyon and providing a popular new recreation area. The dam's irrigation water helped make the Imperial Valley one of the most productive agricultural districts in the world.

Years of Dust. This 1936 poster by the artist and photographer Ben Shahn, served to publicize the work of the Resettlement Administration, which offered aid to destitute farm families hit hard by the Dust Bowl. Shahn's stark imagery here was typical of the documentary aesthetic associated with Depression-era art and photography.

QUICK REVIEW

The Federal Response to the Dust Bowl

- Many Great Plains families given direct emergency relief.
- Federal assistance included loans, debt relief, and temporary jobs.
- New federal policies designed to reverse soil erosion and restore grasslands.

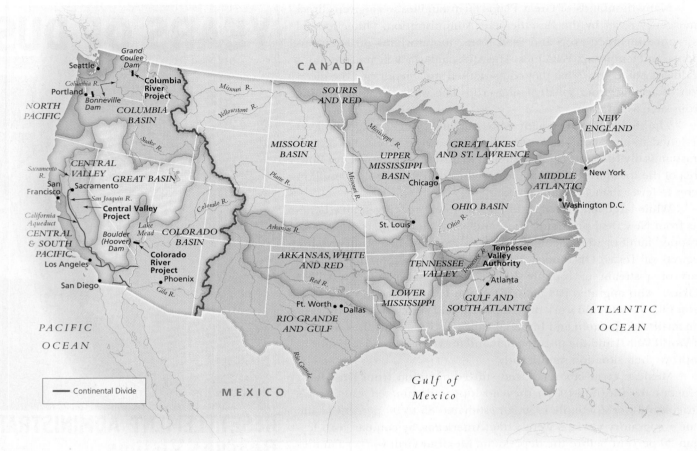

MAP 24.3

The New Deal and Water This map illustrates U.S. drainage areas and the major large-scale water projects begun or completed by federal agencies in them during the New Deal. By providing irrigation, cheap power, flood control, and recreation areas, these public works had a historically unprecedented impact on America's western communities.

WHAT WAS the impact of irrigation, cheap power, flood control, and recreation areas on America's western communities?

The success of Boulder Dam transformed the Bureau of Reclamation into a major federal agency commanding huge resources. In 1938, it completed the All-American Canal—an 80-mile channel connecting the Colorado River to the Imperial Valley and with a 130-mile branch to the Coachella Valley. This opened up more than a million acres of desert land to the cultivation of citrus fruits, melons, vegetables, and cotton.

The largest power and irrigation project of all was Grand Coulee Dam, northwest of Spokane, Washington. Completed in 1941, it was designed to convert the power of the Columbia River into cheap electricity and to irrigate previously uncultivated land, thereby stimulating economic development in the Pacific Northwest. Tens of thousands of workers built Grand Coulee, and the project pumped millions of dollars into the region's badly depressed economy. In the longer run, Grand Coulee provided the cheapest electricity in the United States and helped attract new manufacturing to a region previously dependent on the export of lumber and ore.

These projects were not without an environmental and human cost. Grand Coulee and smaller dams nearby reduced the Columbia River to a string of lakes. Spawning salmon could no longer run the river above the dam. In California, the federal guarantee of river water made a relative handful of large farmers fabulously wealthy. But tens of thousands of farm workers, mostly of Mexican descent, labored in the newly fertile fields for very low wages, and pesticides undermined their health. The Colorado River, its flow into the sea drastically diminished, began to build up salt deposits, making its water increasingly unfit for drinking or irrigation.

A NEW DEAL FOR INDIANS

The New Deal brought important changes and some limited improvements to the lives of Indians. In 1933, some 320,000 Indian people, belonging to about 200 tribes, lived on reservations, mostly in Oklahoma, Arizona, New Mexico, and South Dakota. Indians were the nation's poorest people with an infant mortality rate twice that of whites. The Bureau of Indian Affairs (BIA) had a long history of corruption and mismanagement. For years, it had tried to assimilate Indians through education, in the process routinely interfering with Indian religious and tribal customs.

In 1933, Roosevelt appointed John Collier to bring change to the BIA. As the new BIA head, Collier pledged to "stop wronging the Indians and to rewrite the cruel and stupid laws that rob them and crush their family lives." Collier became the driving force behind the Indian Reorganization Act (IRA) of 1934. The IRA reversed the allotment provisions of the Dawes Severalty Act of 1887, which had weakened tribal sovereignty by shifting the distribution of land from tribes to individuals (see Chapter 18). The new legislation permitted the restoration of surplus reservation lands to tribal ownership, and it allocated funds to purchase additional lands and for economic development. At its heart, the IRA sought to restore tribal structures by making the tribes instruments of the federal government. Any tribe that ratified the IRA could then elect a tribal council that would enjoy federal recognition as the legal tribal government.

Under Collier, the BIA became much more sensitive to Indian cultural and religious freedom. The number of Indian people employed by the BIA itself increased from a few hundred in 1933 to more than 4,600 in 1940. Collier trumpeted the principle of Indian political autonomy, a radical idea for the day. In practice, however, both the BIA and Congress regularly interfered with reservation governments, especially in money matters. For the long run, Collier's most important legacy was the reassertion of the status of Indian tribes as semisovereign nations.

THE LIMITS OF REFORM

In his second Inaugural Address, Roosevelt emphasized that much remained to be done to remedy the effects of the depression. With his stunning electoral victory, the future for further social reform seemed bright. Yet by 1937, the New Deal was in retreat. A rapid political turnaround over the next two years put continuing social reform efforts on the defensive.

WHAT WERE the limits of the New Deal's reforms, and what legacy did those reforms leave?

COURT PACKING

After his landslide reelection, and still smarting from the Supreme Court having struck down the NRA and the AAA, Roosevelt wanted more friendly justices. In February 1937, he asked Congress to allow him to make new Supreme Court appointments whenever a justice failed to retire upon reaching age seventy. This would expand the Court from nine to a maximum of fifteen justices, the majority presumably sympathetic to the New Deal. Newspapers almost unanimously denounced FDR's "court-packing bill."

The president fought on, disingenuously insisting that his purpose was simply to reduce the workload of elderly Supreme Court justices. As the battle dragged on through the spring and summer, FDR's claims weakened. Then a conservative justice retired, permitting Roosevelt to make his first Court appointment. More important, several justices began voting for rather than against Roosevelt's laws, so that the Court upheld the constitutionality of key measures from the second New Deal, including the Social Security Act and the National Labor Relations Act. At the end of August 1937, FDR backed off his court-packing scheme and accepted a compromise bill that reformed lower court procedures but left the Supreme Court untouched. The Court fight badly weakened Roosevelt's relations with Congress. Many more conservative Democrats felt free to oppose further New Deal measures.

THE WOMEN'S NETWORK

The New Deal brought a measurable, if temporary, increase in women's political influence. For those women associated with social reform, the New Deal opened up possibilities to effect change. A "women's network," linked by personal friendships and professional connections, made its presence felt in national politics and government. Most of the women in this network had deep roots in progressive-era movements promoting suffrage, labor law reform, and welfare programs (see Chapter 21).

The center of the women's network, First Lady Eleanor Roosevelt, became a powerful political figure, using her prominence to fight for liberal causes. Privately, she enjoyed great influence with her husband, and behind the scenes she supported a wide network of women professionals and reformers whom she had come to know in the 1920s. As a strong supporter of protective labor legislation for women, she owed much to the social reform tradition of the women's movement. One of her first public acts as First Lady was to convene a White House Conference on the Emergency Needs of Women in November 1933.

Eleanor Roosevelt worked vigorously for antilynching legislation, compulsory health insurance, and child-labor reform, and she fought racial discrimination in New Deal relief programs. She frequently testified before legislative committees, lobbied her husband privately and the Congress publicly, and wrote a widely syndicated newspaper column.

Mrs. Roosevelt's closest political ally was Molly Dewson. A longtime social worker and suffragist, Dewson wielded great political clout as director of the Women's Division of the national Democratic Party. Dewson proved a tireless organizer, traveling to cities

First Lady Eleanor Roosevelt rides with miners in a flag-decorated car during a visit to the mining town of Bellaire, Ohio, in 1935. Mrs. Roosevelt was more outspoken than the president in championing the rights of labor and African Americans, and she actively used her prestige as First Lady in support of social justice causes.

and towns around the country and educating women about Democratic policies and candidates. Her success impressed the president, and he relied on her judgment in recommending political appointments.

Perhaps Dewson's most important success came in persuading FDR to appoint Frances Perkins secretary of labor—the first woman cabinet member in U.S. history. As labor secretary, Perkins's department was responsible for creating the Social Security Act and the Fair Labor Standards Act of 1938, both of which incorporated protective measures long advocated by women reformers. New Deal agencies opened up spaces for scores of women in the federal bureaucracy. In addition, the social work profession, which remained roughly two-thirds female in the 1930s, grew enormously in response to the massive relief and welfare programs. By 1940, 25 percent of the workforce was female, as hard times increased the ranks of married working women. But sexual stereotyping still routinely forced most women into low-paying, low-status jobs. In sum, although the 1930s saw no radical challenges to existing male and female roles, working-class women and professional women held their own and managed to make some gains.

A NEW DEAL FOR MINORITIES?

Long near the bottom of the American economic ladder, African Americans suffered disproportionately in the Great Depression. The old saying among black workers that they were "last hired, first fired" was never truer than during times of high unemployment.

Overall, the Roosevelt administration made little overt effort to combat the racism and segregation entrenched in American life. FDR was especially worried about offending the powerful Southern Democratic congressmen. Local administration of many federal programs meant that most early New Deal programs routinely accepted discrimination. Racism was also embedded in the provisions of the Social Security Act and National Labor Relations Act, both of which explicitly excluded domestics and farm laborers—whose ranks were disproportionately African American and Hispanic—from coverage.

Yet some limited gains were made. Roosevelt issued an executive order in 1935 banning discrimination in WPA projects. Between 15 and 20 percent of all WPA employees were black people, although African Americans made up less than 10 percent of the nation's population. The Public Works Administration, under Harold Ickes, constructed a number of integrated housing complexes and employed more than its fair share of black workers in construction.

FDR appointed several African Americans to second-level positions in his administration. This group became known as "the Black Cabinet." Mary McLeod Bethune proved a superb leader of the Office of Minority Affairs in the National Youth Administration. Her most successful programs substantially reduced black illiteracy. Harvard-trained Robert Weaver advised the president on economic affairs, and in 1966, became the first black cabinet member when he was appointed secretary of housing and urban development.

Hard times were equally trying for Mexican Americans. As the Great Depression drastically reduced the demand for their labor, they faced massive layoffs, deepening poverty, and deportation. During the 1930s, more than 400,000 Mexican nationals and their children returned to Mexico. For those who stayed, the New Deal programs did little to help. The AAA benefited large growers, not laborers. Neither the National Labor Relations Act nor the Social Security Act made any provisions for farm laborers. After 1937, the WPA eliminated aliens from eligibility, causing great hardship for thousands of Mexican families.

While the New Deal made no explicit attempt to attack the deeply rooted patterns of racism and discrimination in American life, there were occasional symbolic victories for racial equality. In 1939, the conservative Daughters of the American Revolution

QUICK REVIEW

Impact of the New Deal on Women

♦ Women received a smaller percentage of jobs created by New Deal programs than men.

♦ Increase in the minimum wage brought greater improvements to women than to men.

♦ Women gained political influence under the New Deal.

QUICK REVIEW

Blacks and the New Deal

♦ Black unemployment rate was twice the rate for white people.

♦ Black people had less access to state and private aid and relief.

♦ New federal policies produced some limited gains for black people.

(DAR) refused to permit the world-renowned African American classical singer Marian Anderson to perform in the DAR's Washington hall. Eleanor Roosevelt and Interior Secretary Harold Ickes intervened to arrange for Anderson to perform at the Lincoln Memorial before an integrated audience of 75,000. More broadly, African Americans, especially in the cities, benefited from New Deal relief and work programs, even though this assistance was not color-blind. Black industrial workers made inroads into labor unions affiliated with the CIO. By 1936, an important political shift had begun: for the first time, a majority of black voters voted Democratic. Black voters and hardened white segregationists would coexist uneasily as partners in the New Deal coalition, a tension that would strain the Democratic Party for decades to come.

THE ROOSEVELT RECESSION AND THE EBBING OF THE NEW DEAL

The nation's economy had improved significantly by 1937. Unemployment had declined to *only* 14 percent, farm prices had improved to 1930 levels, and industrial production was slightly higher than the 1929 mark. Economic traditionalists, led by FDR's treasury secretary, called for reducing the federal deficit, which had grown to more than $4 billion in fiscal year 1936. Roosevelt, always uneasy about the growing national debt, called for large reductions in federal spending, and the Fed, worried about inflation, tightened credit policies.

This retrenchment caused a steep recession. The stock market plunged in August 1937, and industrial output and farm prices plummeted. Unemployment shot up alarmingly; by March 1938, it hovered around 20 percent.

The blunt reality was that even after five years, the New Deal had not brought about economic recovery. Throughout 1937 and 1938, the administration drifted. Emergency spending bills in the spring of 1938 put new life into the WPA and the PWA. But Republican gains in the 1938 congressional elections made it harder than ever to get new reform measures through. Conservative Southern Democrats increasingly allied themselves with Republicans in a coalition that would dominate Congress until the mid-1960s.

There were a couple of important exceptions. The 1938 Fair Labor Standards Act established the first federal minimum wage and set a maximum workweek of forty-four hours for all employees engaged in interstate commerce. The National Housing Act of 1937, also known as the Wagner-Steagall Act, funded public housing construction and slum clearance and provided rent subsidies for low-income families. But by and large, by 1938, the reform whirlwind of the New Deal was over.

DEPRESSION-ERA CULTURE

HOW DID the Great Depression affect American cultural life during the 1930s?

The Great Depression profoundly affected American culture, as it did all other aspects of national life. Yet contradictory messages coexisted, sometimes within the same novel or movie. With American capitalism facing its worst crisis in history, radical expressions of protest and revolution became more frequent. But there were also strong celebrations of individualism, nostalgia for a simpler, rural past, and many attempts to define American core virtues.

A NEW DEAL FOR THE ARTS

The depression hit America's writers, artists, and teachers just as hard as it did blue-collar workers. In 1935, the WPA allocated $300 million for the unemployed in these fields. Over the next four years, Federal Project No. 1, an umbrella agency covering writing, theater, music, and the visual arts offered work to desperate unemployed artists and intellectuals, enriched the cultural lives of millions, and left a substantial artistic and cultural legacy.

At its height, the Federal Writers Project employed 5,000 writers on a variety of programs. Work on the Writers Project helped many American writers to survive, to hone

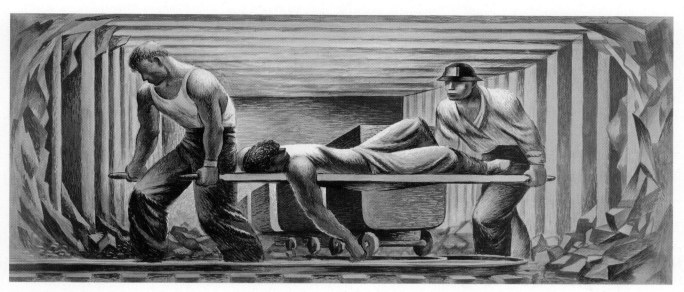

Fletcher Martin painted *Mine Rescue* (1939) in the Kellogg, Idaho, post office. The work was part of a Treasury Department program that employed unemployed artists to beautify government buildings. The mural was eventually removed under pressure from local citizens who worried that it might upset those who had lost loved ones in mine accidents.

Fletcher Martin (1904–1979), *Mine Rescue*, 1939, mural study for Kellog, Idaho Post Office; tempera on panel, 15-¾ × 36-½ in (40.0 × 92.7 cm). Copyright Smithsonian American Art Museum, Washington, DC/Art Resource, NY.

their craft, and later to achieve prominence—among them Ralph Ellison, Richard Wright, Margaret Walker, John Cheever, Saul Bellow, and Zora Neale Hurston. The Federal Theater Project (FTP) reached as many as 30 million Americans with its productions, expanding the audience for theater beyond the regular patrons of the commercial stage. The parallel Federal Music Project, under Nikolai Sokoloff of the Cleveland Symphony Orchestra, employed 15,000 musicians and financed hundreds of thousands of low-priced public concerts by touring orchestras. The Composers' Forum Laboratory commissioned new works by important young American classical composers.

Among the struggling painters, later world famous, who received government assistance through the Federal Art Project (FAP) were Willem de Kooning, Jackson Pollock, and Louise Nevelson. The FAP employed painters and sculptors to teach studio skills and art history in schools, churches, and settlement houses. It also commissioned artists to paint hundreds of murals on the walls of post offices, meeting halls, courthouses, and other government buildings.

THE DOCUMENTARY IMPULSE

During the 1930s, an enormous number of artists, novelists, journalists, photographers, and filmmakers tried to document the devastation wrought by the depression in American communities. They also depicted people's struggles to cope with, and reverse, hard times. Mainstream mass media, such as *Life* magazine with its photo essays or "March of Time" newsreels, also adapted this stance.

The "documentary impulse" became a prominent style in 1930s' cultural expression. The most direct and influential expression of the documentary style was the photograph. In 1935, Roy Stryker, chief of the Historical Section of the Resettlement Administration, gathered a remarkable group of photographers to help document the work of the agency. These photographers, including Dorothea Lange and Walker Evans, left the single most significant visual record of the Great Depression. They traveled through rural areas, small towns, and migrant labor camps, and they produced powerful images of despair and resignation, of hope and resilience (see Seeing History).

Watch the Video

Dorothea Lange and Migrant Mother at **www.myhistorylab.com**

Documenting Hard Times in Black and White and Color

Between 1935 and 1942, photographers working for the Farm Security Administration (FSA) created a remarkable pictorial record of depression life. The photography project had a political goal as well: to prod New Deal agricultural policy into providing greater support for the poorest agricultural workers. The photographers thus took aim at social, economic, and racial inequalities within American agriculture. They worked under difficult conditions. On the road for months, they worked in harsh weather, often eating bad food and staying in primitive accommodations, trying to capture the lives of subjects suspicious of their motives.

Many FSA photographs were published in newspapers and popular magazines as part of the agency's campaign to win public support for a greater federal role in building more migrant worker camps. Some of these photographs, such as those by Dorothea Lange and Walker Evans, have become among the most widely circulated images in the history of the medium. Even though Lange's *Migrant Mother* became a kind of universal symbol of suffering, its context and social-science origins have been lost. ■

HOW DOES Lee's portrait of the homesteader couple compare to Lange's portrait of the *Migrant Mother* as a document of rural life in the Great Depression? Are there differences beyond black and white and color?

That double vision, combining a frank portrayal of pain and suffering with a faith in the possibility of overcoming disaster, could be found in many other cultural works of the period. John Steinbeck's *Grapes of Wrath* (1939), soon made into an acclaimed film, sympathetically portrayed the hardships of Oklahoma Dust Bowl migrants on their way to California. Many writers interrupted their work to travel around the country and discover the thoughts and feelings of ordinary people.

WAITING FOR LEFTY

For some, capitalism itself was responsible for the Great Depression. Relatively few Americans became communists or socialists in the 1930s and many of these remained active for only a brief time. Yet Marxist analysis, with its emphasis on class conflict and the failures of capitalism, had a wide influence on thought and writing.

Some writers joined the Communist Party, seeing in the Soviet Union an alternative to an American system mired in exploitation, racial inequality, and human misery. Communist writers sought to radicalize art and literature and celebrated collective struggle rather than individual achievement.

A more common pattern for intellectuals, especially young ones, was brief flirtation with communism. Many African American writers, attracted by the Communist Party's militant opposition to lynching, job discrimination, and segregation, briefly joined the party or found their first supportive audiences there. These included Richard Wright, Ralph Ellison, and Langston Hughes. Playwrights and actors associated with New York's influential Group Theater were often part of the Communist Party orbit in those years. One production of the group, Clifford Odets's *Waiting for Lefty* (1935), depicted a union-organizing drive among taxi drivers. At the climax, someone yells that the organizer Lefty (for whom everyone has been waiting) has been killed by the police, and the audience joins the actors in shouting "Strike!" A commercial and political success, it offered perhaps the most celebrated example of radical, politically engaged art.

Left-wing influence reached its height after 1935 during the "Popular Front" period. Alarmed by the rise of fascism in Europe (see Chapter 25), communists around the world followed the Soviet line of aligning with liberals and other antifascists. Some 3,000 American men and women volunteered for the Communist Party–organized by the Abraham Lincoln Brigade, which fought in the Spanish Civil War on the republican side against the fascists led by Francisco Franco. The Lincolns' sense of commitment and sacrifice appealed to millions of Americans sympathetic to the republican cause. At home, the American Communist Party adopted the slogan "Communism is Twentieth-Century Americanism," and Communists proclaimed strong support of Roosevelt's New Deal (which before they had denounced). Their influence became especially strong within the labor movement as Communists and other radicals, known for their dedication and effectiveness, played a leading role in the difficult CIO unionizing drives in the auto, steel, and electrical industries. The radical presence was also strong within certain WPA arts projects. A decade later, many young idealists who came into the Communist Party orbit, no matter how briefly, would pay a heavy price.

RAISING SPIRITS: FILM, RADIO, AND THE SWING ERA

Despite the depression, the mass-culture industry expanded enormously during the 1930s. If mass culture offered little in the way of direct responses to the economic and social problems of the day, it nonetheless played a more integral role than ever in shaping the rhythms and desires of the nation's everyday life.

Toward the end of the 1920s, the coming of "talking pictures" helped make movies the most popular entertainment form of the day. More than 60 percent of Americans attended one of the nation's 20,000 movie houses each week, and millions followed the lives and careers of movie stars more avidly than ever. At the same time, the movie studios

QUICK REVIEW

Intellectuals and Communism

- Writers saw the Communist Party as a hope for political revolution.
- Black writers attracted to its stance against lynching, segregation, and discrimination.
- Communists supported Roosevelt's New Deal and WPA arts projects and fought in the Spanish Civil War against Francisco Franco.

themselves instituted a more stringent Production Code in 1933. For the next three decades, American filmmakers had to work within very narrow parameters of what was acceptable to depict on-screen. The code required unambiguous depictions of good triumphing over evil and a straight-laced treatment of sex.

By and large, Hollywood avoided social or political controversy. Some 1930s' filmmakers expressed highly personal visions of core American values. Two who succeeded in capturing both popular and critical acclaim were Walt Disney and Frank Capra. By the mid-1930s, Disney's animated cartoons (including Mickey Mouse) had become moral tales that preached following the rules. Capra's comedies idealized a small-town America, with close families and comfortable homes. Although Capra's films dealt with contemporary problems more than most, he seemed to suggest that most of the country's ills could be solved if only its leaders learned the old-fashioned values of "common people"—kindness, loyalty, and charity.

Radio broadcasting emerged as the most powerful medium of communication in the home, profoundly changing the rhythms and routines of everyday life. In 1930, roughly 12 million American homes (40 percent of the total) had radio sets; by the end of the decade, 90 percent had them. Advertisers dominated the structure and content of American radio, forming a powerful alliance with the two large networks, the National Broadcasting Company (NBC) and the Columbia Broadcasting System (CBS). The Federal Communications Commission, established in 1934, continued long-standing policies that favored commercial broadcasting over other arrangements, such as municipal or university programming.

The depression actually helped radio expand. An influx of talent arrived from the weakened worlds of vaudeville, ethnic theater, and the recording industry. The well-financed networks offered an attractive outlet to advertisers seeking a national audience. Radio programming achieved a regularity and professionalism absent in the 1920s, making it much easier for a listener to identify a show with its sponsor. Much of network radio was based on older cultural forms. The variety show, hosted by comedians and singers, and based on the old vaudeville format, was the first important style. Its stars constantly plugged the sponsor's product. The use of an audible studio audience re-created the human interaction so necessary in vaudeville. The popular comedy show *Amos 'n' Andy* adapted the minstrel "blackface" tradition to the new medium. Its two white comedians used only their voices to invent a world of stereotyped African Americans for millions of listeners.

Daytime serials, dubbed "soap operas," dominated radio drama. Aimed at women working in the home, these serials alone constituted 60 percent of all daytime shows by 1940. Soaps revolved around strong, warm female characters who provided advice and strength to weak, indecisive friends and relatives. Action counted very little; the development of character and relationships was all-important. Thrillers such as *The Shadow* aired in the evening when whole families could listen; they emphasized crime and suspense and made clever use of music and sound effects.

Radio news arrived in the 1930s, showing the medium's potential for direct and immediate coverage of political events. Network news and commentary shows multiplied rapidly. Complex political and economic issues and the impending European crisis (see Chapter 25) fueled a news hunger among Americans. A 1939 survey found that 70 percent of Americans relied on the radio as their prime source of news. Yet commercial broadcasting, dominated by big sponsors and large radio manufacturers, failed to cover politically controversial events such as labor struggles.

One measure of radio's cultural impact was its role in popularizing jazz. Before the 1930s, jazz was heard largely among African Americans and a small coterie of white fans. Regular broadcasts of live performances exposed a broader public to the music. Bands led by black artists such as Duke Ellington and Count Basie began to enjoy reputations outside of traditional jazz centers like Chicago, Kansas City, and New York.

CHRONOLOGY

1929	Stock market crash
1930	Democrats regain control of the House of Representatives
1932	Reconstruction Finance Corporation established to make government credit available
	"Bonus Army" marches on Washington
	Franklin D. Roosevelt elected president
1933	Roughly 13 million workers unemployed
	The "Hundred Days" legislation of the First New Deal
	Twenty-First Amendment repeals Prohibition (Eighteenth Amendment)
1934	Indian Reorganization Act repeals Dawes Severalty Act and reasserts the status of Indian tribes as semisovereign nations
	Growing popularity of Father Charles E. Coughlin and Huey Long, critics of Roosevelt
1935	Second New Deal
	Committee for Industrial Organization (CIO) established
	Dust storms turn the southern Great Plains into the Dust Bowl
	Boulder Dam completed
1936	Roosevelt defeats Alfred M. Landon in reelection landslide
	Sit-down strike begins at General Motors plants in Flint, Michigan
1937	General Motors recognizes United Automobile Workers
	Roosevelt's "Court-packing" plan causes controversy
	Memorial Day Massacre in Chicago demonstrates the perils of union organizing
	"Roosevelt recession" begins
1938	CIO unions withdraw from the American Federation of Labor to form the Congress of Industrial Organizations
	Fair Labor Standards Act establishes the first federal minimum wage

Benny Goodman became the key figure in the "swing era," largely through radio exposure. Goodman, a white, classically trained clarinetist, had been inspired by African American bandleaders who created big-band arrangements that combined harmonic call-and-response patterns with breaks for improvised solos. Goodman purchased a series of these arrangements, smoothing out the sound but keeping the strong dance beat. His band's late Saturday night broadcasts began to attract attention, and in 1935, at the Palomar Ballroom in Los Angeles, made the breakthrough that established his enormous popularity. When his band started playing, the young crowd, primed by radio broadcasts, roared its approval and began to dance wildly. Goodman's music was perfect for doing the jitterbug or lindy hop, dances borrowed from African American culture. As the "King of Swing," Goodman helped make big-band jazz a hit with millions of teenagers and young adults from all backgrounds. In the late 1930s, big-band music by artists like Goodman, Ellington, and Basie accounted for the majority of million-selling records.

CONCLUSION

Far from being the radical program its conservative critics charged, the New Deal did little to alter fundamental property relations or the distribution of wealth. Indeed, most of its programs largely failed to help the most powerless groups in America—migrant workers, tenant farmers and sharecroppers, African Americans, and other minorities. But the New Deal profoundly changed many areas of American life. Overall, it radically increased the role of the federal government in American lives and communities, creating a new kind of liberalism defined by an activist state. Social Security, unemployment insurance, and federal relief programs established at least the framework for a welfare state. The FDIC and the SEC established important new federal rules protecting individuals from financial ruin and unregulated stock markets. For the first time in American history, the national government took responsibility for assisting its needy citizens. And also for the first time, the federal government guaranteed the rights of workers to join trade unions, and it set standards for minimum wages and maximum hours. Western and southern communities in particular were transformed through federal intervention in water, power, and agricultural policies. In politics, the New Deal established the Democrats as the majority party. Some version of the Roosevelt New Deal coalition would dominate the nation's political life for another three decades.

The New Deal's efforts to end racial and gender discrimination were modest at best. Some of the more ambitious programs, such as subsidizing the arts or building model communities, enjoyed only brief success. Other reform proposals, such as national health insurance, never got off the ground. Conservative counterpressures, especially after 1937, limited what could be changed. Still, the New Deal did more than strengthen the presence of the national government in people's lives. It also fed expectations that the federal presence would intensify. Washington became a much greater center of economic regulation and political power, and the federal bureaucracy grew in size and influence. With the coming of World War II, the direct role of national government in shaping American communities would expand beyond the dreams of even the most ardent New Dealer.

REVIEW QUESTIONS

1. What were the underlying causes of the Great Depression? What consequences did it have for ordinary Americans, and how did the Hoover administration attempt to deal with the crisis?

2. Analyze the key elements of Franklin D. Roosevelt's first New Deal program. To what degree did these succeed in getting the economy back on track and in providing relief to suffering Americans?

3. How did the so-called Second New Deal differ from the first? What political pressures did Roosevelt face that contributed to the new policies?

4. How did the New Deal reshape western communities and politics? What specific programs had the greatest impact in the region? How are these changes still visible today?

5. Evaluate the impact of the labor movement and radicalism on the 1930s. How did they influence American political and cultural life?

6. To what extent were the grim realities of the depression reflected in popular culture? To what degree were they absent?

7. Discuss the long- and short-range effects of the New Deal on American political and economic life. What were its key successes and failures? What legacies of New Deal–era policies and political struggles can you find in contemporary America?

KEY TERMS

Bonus Army (p. 630)
Committee for Industrial Organizations (CIO) (p. 636)
Emergency Banking Act (p. 632)
Fireside chat (p. 632)

Great Depression (p. 627)
New Deal (p. 632)
New Deal coalition (p. 637)
Tennessee Valley Authority (TVA) (p. 633)

myhistórylab Connections

PEARSON

Reinforce what you learned in this chapter by studying the many documents,
images, maps, review tools, and videos available at www.myhistorylab.com.

Read and Review

✓● Study and Review Chapter 24

●●● Read the Document

*Herbert Hoover, New York Campaign
  Speech (1932)*

Franklin D. Roosevelt, Fireside Chat (1933)

Father Charles E. Coughlin, "A Third Party" (1936)

Huey Long, "Share Our Wealth" (1935)

*Frances Perkins, The Social Security Act,
  (1935; 1960)*

*Franklin D. Roosevelt, Second Inaugural
  Address (1937)*

👁 See the Map

The Great Depression

The Tennessee Valley Authority

Research and Explore

●●● Read the Document

Dealing with Hard Times: The Great Depression

Exploring America: The Dust Bowl

Profiles
  John Lewis
  Frances Perkins

📹 Watch the Video

*Responding to the Great Depression: Whose
  New Deal?*

Dorothea Lange and Migrant Mother

The Plough that Broke the Plains

((●● Hear the Audio

Hear the audio files for Chapter 24 at
www.myhistorylab.com.

> *The event was not spectacular, no fuses burned, no lights flashed. But to us it meant that release of atomic energy on a large scale would be only a matter of time.*
>
> —*Enrico Fermi, from* The First Reactor

On June 6, 1944, American, British, and Canadian forces seized a beachhead in German-occupied France. The landings began the final phase of World War II in Europe, which ended eleven months later with German surrender to the U.S., Britain, the Soviet Union, and their allies.

25

WORLD WAR II
1941–1945

((•─[Hear the **Audio**

Hear the audio files for Chapter 25 at **www.myhistorylab.com**.

WHAT STEPS did Roosevelt take in the late 1930s to prepare the United States for war?

WHAT WERE the economic consequences of the war for the United States?

WHAT MAJOR changes occurred in American society as a consequence of wartime mobilization?

HOW DID military service during World War II change the lives of American men and women?

WHAT WERE the main elements of the Allied war strategy?

HOW DID the relationship between the Allies change once victory was in sight?

1941 | 1945

AMERICAN COMMUNITIES
Los Alamos, New Mexico

ON MONDAY, JULY 16, 1945, THE FIRST ATOMIC BOMB EXPLODED IN A brilliant flash visible in three states. The heat generated by the blast was four times the temperature at the center of the sun, and the light produced rivaled that of nearly twenty suns. The giant fireball ripped a crater a half-mile wide in the ground, fusing the desert sand into glass. The shock wave blew out windows in houses more than 200 miles away. The blast killed every living creature—squirrels, rabbits, snakes, plants, and insects—within a mile, and the smells of death lingered for nearly a month.

Very early that morning, Ruby Wilkening had driven to a nearby mountain ridge, where she joined several other women waiting for the blast. Wilkening worried about her husband, a physicist, who was already at the test site. The Wilkenings were part of a unique community of scientists who had been marshaled for war. President Franklin D. Roosevelt had inaugurated a small nuclear research program in 1939. Then, after the United States entered World War II in 1941, the president released resources to create the Manhattan Project. By December 1942, a team headed by Italian-born Nobel Prize winner Enrico Fermi had produced the first chain reaction in uranium. Now the mission was to build the atomic bomb.

In March 1943, the government moved the key researchers and their families to Los Alamos, New Mexico. The scientists and their families formed an exceptionally close-knit community, united by the need for secrecy and their shared antagonism toward their army guardians. The military atmosphere was oppressive. Homes and laboratories were cordoned off by barbed wire and guarded by military police.

Los Alamos

Security personnel followed the scientists whenever they left Los Alamos. All outgoing mail was censored. Only a group thoroughly committed to the war effort could accept such restrictions on personal liberty.

A profound urgency motivated the research team, which included refugees from Nazi Germany and Fascist Italy and a large proportion of Jews. The director of the project, California physicist J. Robert Oppenheimer, promoted a scientific élan that offset the military style of commanding general Leslie Groves. Just thirty-eight, "Oppie" personified the idealism that helped the community of scientists overcome whatever moral reservations they held about placing such a potentially terrible weapon in the hands of the government.

The unprecedented scientific mobilization at Los Alamos mirrored changes occurring throughout American society as the nation rallied behind the war effort. Sixteen million men and women left home for military service and nearly as many moved to take advantage of wartime jobs. In becoming what President Franklin Roosevelt called "a great arsenal of democracy," the American economy quickly and fully recovered from the Great Depression. Several states in the South and Southwest experienced huge surges in population. Many broad social changes with roots in earlier times—the economic expansion of the West, the erosion of farm tenancy among black people in the South and white people in Appalachia, and the increasing employment of married women—accelerated during the war. The events of the war eroded old communities, created new ones like Los Alamos, and transformed nearly all aspects of American society.

THE COMING OF WORLD WAR II

The worldwide depression helped to undermine a political order that had been shaky since World War I. Political unrest spread across Europe and Asia as international trade dropped by as much as two-thirds and unemployment rose. Demagogues played on national and racial hatreds, fueled by old resentments and current despair, and offered solutions in the form of territorial expansion by military conquest.

THE SHADOWS OF WAR ACROSS THE GLOBE

Two major threats to peace gathered force in the 1930s in East Asia and in Central Europe. In Japan, devastated by the depression, military leaders decided that imperialism would make their nation the richest in the world, and in 1931 the Japanese army seized Manchuria from China. When the League of Nations objected, Japan simply quit the league. A full-scale Japanese invasion of China proper followed in 1937, and the world watched in horror the Rape of Nanking (today, Nanjing)—the destruction of what was then China's capital and the slaughter of as many as 300,000 Chinese men, women, and children. Within a year, Japan controlled most of coastal China.

In Europe, fanatical and tyrannical fascist leaders were taking power—first in Italy and later in Germany. "We have buried the putrid corpse of liberty," boasted Italy's fascist dictator Benito Mussolini in the 1920s. In Germany, nationalist resentment over the Treaty of Versailles fueled Adolf Hitler's National Socialist (Nazi) movement with its racist doctrine of "Aryan" supremacy that condemned nonwhites and Jews as "degenerate races." Renouncing the disarmament provisions imposed by the Versailles peace treaty, Hitler began to rebuild Germany's armed forces. No European powers opposed him.

Soon enough, Mussolini and Hitler began to act on their imperial visions. In 1935, Italy conquered Ethiopia and turned the African nation into a colony. In 1936, Hitler sent 35,000 troops to occupy the formerly demilitarized Rhineland region. In the Spanish Civil War that broke out later that year, Italy and Germany both supported General Francisco Franco's fascist rebels against the democratic republican regime. In November, Germany and Italy forged an alliance, the Rome–Berlin Axis.

In 1938, Hitler annexed Austria and then turned his attention to Czechoslovakia, the one remaining democracy in Central Europe, which Britain and France had pledged to assist. War seemed imminent. But Britain and France surprised the world by agreeing, at Munich on September 30, 1938, to allow Germany to annex the Sudetenland—the German-speaking parts of Czechoslovakia. "Appeasement," this was called: Hitler pledged that he would make no more territorial demands. Within six months, however, in March 1939, Germany seized the rest of the country.

By then, much of the world was aware of the horror of Hitler's racist regime. On the night of November 9, 1938, Nazi storm troopers rounded up Jews, beating them mercilessly and murdering an untold number. Reflecting the smashed windows of Jewish shops and burned synagogues, this attack came to be known as *Kristallnacht,* the "Night of Broken Glass." The Nazi government expropriated Jewish property and excluded Jews from all but the most menial jobs. Pressured by Hitler, his allies Hungary and Italy also enacted laws curtailing the civil rights of Jews.

On September 27, 1940, Germany, Italy, and Japan signed the anti-Communist Tripartite Pact and pledged to "stand by and co-operate with one another" for the next ten years.

ROOSEVELT READIES FOR WAR

FDR's instincts were to stand with other threatened democracies, but he knew that the American public and many members of Congress were strongly isolationist. In 1935, Congress passed the first of five Neutrality Acts to deter entanglements in future foreign wars. It required the president to embargo the sale and shipment of munitions to

WHAT STEPS did Roosevelt take in the late 1930s to prepare the United States for war?

Watch the **Video**
American Entry into WWI at
www.myhistorylab.com

View the **Image**
Nazi Book Bonfire at
www.myhistorylab.com

blitzkrieg German war tactic in World War II ("lightning war") involving the concentration of air and armored firepower to punch and exploit holes in opposing defensive lines.

Neutrality Act of 1939 Permitted the sale of arms to Britain, France, and China.

Lend-Lease Act An arrangement for the transfer of war supplies, including food, machinery, and services to nations whose defense was considered vital to the defense of the United States in Word War II.

Atlantic Charter Statement of common principles and war aims developed by President Franklin Roosevelt and British Prime Minister Winston Churchill at a meeting in August 1941.

QUICK REVIEW

Undeclared War

- March 1941: Lend-lease program approved by Congress.
- FDR ordered navy to offer support to Britain.
- August 1941: Atlantic Charter lays out British and American common ground.

all belligerents. As late as 1937, nearly 70 percent of Americans responding to a Gallup poll agreed that U.S. involvement in World War I had been a mistake.

Despite opposition, in October 1937, Roosevelt decided to call for international cooperation to "quarantine the aggressors." Although two-thirds of Congress opposed economic sanctions. Roosevelt nevertheless managed to secure $1 billion in appropriations to enlarge the navy. Another less stringent Neutrality Act passed in 1939 permitted wartime arms sales to Great Britain, France, and China.

War broke out in Europe in the fall of 1939. In August, Germany and the Soviet Union, hitherto mortal enemies, stunned the world by signing a nonaggression pact. A week later, on September 1, Hitler invaded Poland. Within days, Poland's allies, Great Britain and France, declared war on Germany. On September 17, Soviet troops invaded Poland too. Hitler and Stalin divided Poland between them.

Hitler began a crushing offensive against Western Europe in April 1940. In a *blitzkrieg* (lightning war), fast-moving columns of German tanks supported by air power struck first at Denmark and Norway and soon thereafter conquered Holland, Belgium, and Luxembourg. Hitler's army, joined at the last minute by the Italians, then easily overran France in June 1940. When Britain refused to surrender, Hitler launched the Battle of Britain. Nazi bombers pounded cities while U-boats tried to cut off incoming supplies.

The American public desperately hoped to stay out of the war, but they also agreed with Roosevelt that the nation's security depended on both a strong defense and Hitler's defeat. Invoking the **Neutrality Act of 1939**, which permitted the sale of arms to Britain, France, and China, the president affirmed his position: "All aid to the Allies short of war." In May 1940, when France collapsed, he began to transfer surplus U.S. warships and equipment to Britain. In September, while the Battle of Britain raged, Roosevelt and Congress enacted the nation's first peacetime military draft, which sent 1.4 million young men to army training camps by July 1941.

FDR could not yet admit the inevitability of U.S. involvement—especially in 1940, an election year. However, once reelected (defeating Republican Wendell Willkie), Roosevelt moved more aggressively to aid hard-pressed Great Britain. In his annual message to Congress in early 1941, he proposed a bill allowing the president to sell, exchange, or lease arms to any country whose defense he judged vital to U.S. security. Passed in March 1941, the **Lend-Lease Act** made Great Britain the first beneficiary of massive aid.

In August 1941, Roosevelt met on a warship off Newfoundland with Winston Churchill, the British prime minister. Roosevelt evaded Churchill's pleas to enter the war—he knew that Congress and the American public still hoped to stay out—but the two leaders declared common goals for the postwar world in what was called the **Atlantic Charter**, a lofty proclamation calling for all peoples to live in freedom from fear, want, and tyranny.

The European war widened. Having conquered the Balkans, Hitler broke the Nazi–Soviet Pact and in June 1941 invaded the Soviet Union. Roosevelt sent Lend-Lease supplies to the Soviets and ordered U.S. warships to "sink on sight" any lurking German submarines. The result was an undeclared and unpublicized naval war between the United States and Nazi Germany in the North Atlantic.

PEARL HARBOR

Throughout 1940 and 1941, the European struggle widened; war also escalated in East Asia. Anticipating trouble in the Pacific, in May 1940 Roosevelt transferred the Pacific fleet from its California bases to a forward position at Pearl Harbor in Hawai'i. Less than five

On December 7, 1941, Japanese attack planes devastated the U.S. fleet stationed at Pearl Harbor, on the Hawaiian island of Oahu. This photograph shows the explosion of the USS *Shaw*, a drydocked destroyer, during the second wave of Japanese attack. The "sneak" attack on Pearl Harbor became a symbol of Japanese treachery and the necessity for U.S. revenge.

months later, Japan formally joined Germany and Italy as a full Axis ally.

Both the United States and Japan were playing for time. Roosevelt wanted to bank resources to fight Germany (the greater danger, he thought); Japan's leaders gambled that America's preoccupation with Europe might allow them to conquer all Southeast Asia, including the oil-rich Dutch East Indies (today, Indonesia). Lacking petroleum, Japan was desperate to obtain a reliable source for oil. When Japan occupied French Indochina in July 1941, Roosevelt moved from economic sanctions, which had been in place for several months, to freezing Japanese assets in the United States and cutting off its oil supplies.

War with Japan looked more likely. The Japanese military decided to hit the Americans with a knock-out blow that would give them time to seize Southeast Asia and the western Pacific. But American intelligence had broken the Japanese secret diplomatic code, and the president knew that Japan was preparing to strike somewhere, most likely the Philippines. By the end of November, all American Pacific forces were put on high alert.

On December 7, 1941, carrier-borne Japanese bombers struck the Pacific fleet at Pearl Harbor. Within two hours, Japanese pilots destroyed nearly 200 American planes and badly damaged the fleet; more than 2,400 Americans were killed and nearly 1,200 wounded. (Fortunately, the U.S. carriers were spared, being out to sea on the morning of the attack.) That same day, Japan bombed U.S. bases on the Philippines, Guam, and Wake Island and attacked the British fleet and colonies in East Asia.

On December 8, declaring the attack on Pearl Harbor "a date which will live in infamy," Roosevelt asked Congress for a declaration of war against Japan. Congress agreed. On December 11, Germany and Italy declared war on the United States. World War II had begun for Americans.

On the day after the attack on Pearl Harbor, President Franklin D. Roosevelt addressed a joint session of Congress and asked for an immediate declaration of war against Japan. The resolution passed with one dissenting vote, and the United States entered World War II.

⬦⬦⬦⎯Read the **Document**

Franklin Roosevelt, Date Which Will Live in Infamy (1941) at **www.myhistorylab.com**

The Great Arsenal of Democracy

As early as 1938, the American economy had begun to benefit from sales to the British and French when those countries started rearming. In 1940, Roosevelt told Americans in a radio "fireside chat" that the nation must become the "great arsenal of democracy," and by the time the United States entered the war, the U.S. economy had already geared up for military purposes. After Pearl Harbor, the federal government poured unprecedented energy and money into wartime production and assigned a huge army of experts to manage it. During the next three years, the economic machinery that had failed during the 1930s was running at full speed. Defense spending would spark the greatest economic boom in the history of any nation. Suddenly, it seemed, the Great Depression ended.

WHAT WERE the economic consequences of the war for the United States?

Mobilizing for War

A few days after the United States declared war, Congress passed the **War Powers Act**, establishing a precedent for executive authority that would endure long after the war's end. Under the new law, the president could reorganize the federal government and create new

War Powers Act Gave the U.S. president the power to reorganize the federal government and create new agencies; to establish programs censoring news, information, and abridging civil liberties; to seize foreign-owned property; and award government contracts without bidding.

•◦•─ Read the Document

Exploring America: Propaganda at
www.myhistorylab.com

agencies, censor all news and information and abridge civil liberties, seize foreign-owned property, and even award government contracts without competitive bidding.

Roosevelt promptly used his authority to create special wartime agencies. At the top of his agenda was a massive reorientation and management of the economy, and to do that an alphabet soup of new agencies appeared. For example, the Supply Priorities and Allocation Board (SPAB) oversaw the use of scarce materials and resources vital to the war. The Office of Price Administration (OPA) used price controls to check inflation. The National War Labor Board (NWLB) mediated labor–management disputes.

Several new agencies took on the responsibility of creating propaganda to promote the war effort. Although Pearl Harbor brought an outpouring of rage against Japan, the government nevertheless tried to shape public opinion. In June 1942, the president created the Office of War Information (OWI) to engage the press, radio, and film industry in selling the war to the American people, as well as to publish leaflets for the armed services and to flood enemy ranks with subversive propaganda. Domestic propaganda also fueled the selling of war bonds.

The federal government sponsored various measures to prevent subversion. The attorney general authorized wiretapping in cases of espionage or sabotage, but the Federal Bureau of Investigation (FBI) also used it extensively—and illegally—for domestic surveillance. The Joint Chiefs of Staff created the Office of Strategic Services (OSS) to assess enemy military strength, gather intelligence, and conduct foreign espionage and engaged leading social scientists to plot psychological warfare.

In mid-1942, Roosevelt established an agency that would prove vital to the Allied victory and change the way science was conducted in the United States. The Office of Scientific Research and Development (OSRD) brought together government, business, and scientific leaders to coordinate military research. It developed better radar and early-warning systems, more effective medicines and pesticides, and improved weapons.

With the creation of these new agencies, the size of the federal government increased many times over its New Deal level. The number of federal employees nearly quadrupled, from a little over 1 million in 1940 to nearly 4 million by the war's end.

The New Deal itself, however, withered away. With the depression over and chronic unemployment giving way to acute labor shortages, FDR's administration directed all its resources toward securing the planes, ships, guns, and food—and the war workers—required for victory. Moreover, the 1942 elections weakened the New Deal coalition by unseating many liberal Democrats while sending fifty-five new and mostly conservative Republicans to Congress. Republicans quashed proposals to extend the social programs instituted during the 1930s. One by one, New Deal agencies vanished.

ORGANIZING THE WAR ECONOMY

Victory would ultimately depend less on military prowess and superior strategy than on the ability of the United States to outproduce its enemies. The nation enjoyed incomparable advantages: freedom from bombing and invasions, a huge industrial base, abundant natural resources, and a civilian population large enough to swell both its labor force and its armed forces. First, however, the entire civilian economy had to be both expanded and transformed for the production of arms and other military supplies.

Even before Pearl Harbor, by the summer of 1941, the federal government was pouring vast sums into defense production. Six months after the attack, allocations topped $100 billion for equipment and supplies, which exceeded what American firms had produced in all previous wars. Facing war orders too large to fill, American industries were primed for all-out production. Once-idled factories operated around-the-clock, seven days a week.

Defense production transformed entire regions. The impact was strongest in the West—the major staging area for the war in the Pacific—where the federal government spent nearly $40 billion for military and industrial expansion. California got 10 percent of all federal funds, and by 1944 Los Angeles was the nation's second largest manufacturing center. The South benefited from having 60 of the army's 100 new military camps, and its textile factories hummed: the army alone required nearly 520 million pairs of socks and 230 million pairs of pants. Much of the South's sharecropping and tenant-farming population migrated into well-paid urban industrial jobs, and unprecedented profits poured into southern businesses.

Across the nation, the rural population decreased by almost 20 percent, and American farmers could not keep up with rising demand. The war speeded the development of large-scale and mechanized crop production, including the first widespread use of chemical fertilizers and pesticides. By 1945, farm income had doubled, but thousands of small farms had disappeared.

Much like large-scale commercial agriculture, many big businesses did well during the war. Military contracts allowed huge profits. The government provided low-interest loans and even direct subsidies for the expansion of facilities, with generous tax write-offs for retooling. The 100 largest corporations, which manufactured 30 percent of all goods in 1940, garnered 70 percent of all war and civilian contracts and the bulk of war profits. On the other hand, many small businesses closed.

NEW WORKERS

The wartime economy required an unprecedented number of new workers. The *bracero* program, negotiated by the United States and Mexico in 1942, brought more than 200,000 Mexicans into the United States for short-term employment, mainly as farm and railroad workers. Sioux and Navajos were hired in large numbers to build ordnance depots and military training centers. African Americans joined white workers in defense industries—in iron and steel plants, shipyards and aircraft factories, and numerous government agencies. The number of black workers rose from 2.9 million to 3.8 million.

The war most dramatically altered the wage-earning patterns of women. The female labor force grew by more than 50 percent, reaching 19.5 million in 1945. The employment rate changed comparatively little for African American women; fully 90 percent had been in the labor force in 1940. However, many black women left domestic service for higher-paying industrial jobs.

Neither government nor industry rushed to recruit women. Well into the summer of 1942, the Department of War advised businesses to hold back from hiring women "until all available male labor in the area had first been employed." Likewise, neither government nor industry expected women to stay in their jobs when the war ended. "Rosie the Riveter" appeared in posters and advertisements as the model female citizen, but only "for the duration" (see Seeing History).

View the Image
Women Riveters in Navy Shipyard at
www.myhistorylab.com

Facing a shortage of workers and increased production demands, the War Manpower Commission and the Office of War Information conducted a campaign to recruit women into the labor force. Women were encouraged to "take a job for your husband/son/brother" and to "keep the world safe for your children." Higher wages also enticed many women to take jobs in factories. In this photograph, a woman is shown riveting the wing of an airplane.

Norman Rockwell's "Rosie, the Riveter"

During his long career as an artist-illustrator, Norman Rockwell published forty-seven covers of the popular family magazine *The Saturday Evening Post*, all venerating various aspects of American life. "Rosie, the Riveter" appeared on the magazine's cover May 29, 1943, and virtually enshrined women's contributions to the war effort. The *Post* donated the original painting to the U.S. Treasury Department, which took "Rosie" on a national tour to get Americans to buy war bonds.

IN WHAT ways does Rockwell's painting convey ideals related to gender roles during the war?

Now an iconic image, Rosie was modeled on a real-life woman, a telephone operator in Vermont. Rockwell took advantage of his artistic license by making Rosie older and more muscular than his slight nineteen-year-old model—who was quite surprised when she finally saw the portrait! There is no doubt, though, that Rockwell captured the spirit of wartime patriotism. The self-confident Rosie takes obvious pride in her work, keeping her riveter on her ample lap even during lunchtime. A halo encircles her head, the American flag waves in the background. To seal the message, Rockwell shows Rosie crushing Hitler's autobiography, *Mein Kampf,* under her penny loafer.

In calling attention to Rosie's impressive biceps, Rockwell nevertheless attended to the small details that assure viewers that his defense worker has lost none of her femininity. Like most other women in the 1940s, she wears lipstick and rouge and polishes her nails. She also keeps a lace hanky and compact in the pocket of her overalls and wears a necklace—albeit of merit buttons—around her neck. Moreover, Rockwell does not show Rosie riveting but instead eating a ham sandwich that she undoubtedly made at home.

Rockwell's painting, beloved during World War II, became even more popular with the rise of the women's liberation movement in the late 1960s and remains to this day an emblem of women's strength and determination. In May 2002, Sotheby's auctioned the original canvas for more than $4.9 million. ∎

TABLE 25.1

Strikes and Lockouts in the United States, 1940–45

	Number of Strikes	Number of Workers Involved	Number of Man-Days Idle	Percent of Total Employed
1940	2,508	576,988	6,700,872	2.3
1941	4,288	2,362,620	23,047,556	8.4
1942	2,968	839,961	4,182,557	2.8
1943	3,752	1,981,279	13,500,529	6.9
1944	4,956	2,115,637	8,721,079	7.0
1945	4,750	3,467,000	38,025,000	12.2

"Work Stoppages Caused by Labor–Management Disputes in 1945," *Monthly Labor Review*, May 1946, p. 720; and Martin Glaberman, *War Time Strikes* (Detroit: Bewick, 1980), p. 36.

Compared to the Great Depression, when married women were barred from many jobs, World War II opened up new fields. The number of women automobile workers jumped from 29,000 to 200,000, that of women electrical workers from 100,000 to 374,000. Polled near the end of the war, 75 percent of women workers said they wanted to keep working, preferably at the same jobs.

Although the war generated 17 million new jobs, the economic gains were not evenly distributed. Wages increased by as much as 50 percent, but never as fast as profits or prices. This widely reported disparity produced one of the most turbulent periods in American labor history (see Table 25.1). More workers went on strike in 1941, before the United States entered the war, than in any previous year except 1919. Total union membership increased from 10.5 million to 14.7 million, with the women's share alone rising from 11 to 23 percent. Unions also enrolled 1,250,000 African Americans, twice the prewar number.

Once the United States entered the war, the major unions patriotically agreed to no-strike pledges for the duration. Nevertheless, rank-and-file union members sporadically staged illegal "wildcat" strikes. The Democratic-majority Congress passed the first federal antistrike bill, giving the president power to penalize or even draft strikers. And yet the strikes reached a level greater than in any other four-year period in American history.

Despite "no-strike" pledges, workers staged wildcat strikes in the war years. Union leaders negotiated shorter hours, higher wages, and seniority rules and helped to build union membership to a new height. When the war ended, nearly 30 percent of all nonagricultural workers were union members.

THE HOME FRONT

Alone among the major combatants, the homelands of the United States and Canada were neither invaded nor bombed, except for remote Pearl Harbor. Nevertheless, Americans were not immune to the social upheavals that accompany war. Families were disrupted, and racial and ethnic hostilities flared repeatedly and sometimes violently.

FAMILIES IN WARTIME

Men and women rushed into marriage, despite (or maybe because of) wartime uncertainties. The wartime boom sent personal incomes surging, allowing many young couples to set up separate households for the first time since the depression struck. The prospect of wartime separation pushed other couples into marriage. The marriage rate peaked in 1946—but by then divorces were also setting records.

QUICK REVIEW

Rosie the Riveter

- Demand for labor drew women into the workplace.
- Companies opened positions for women in nontraditional jobs.
- Most women were forced to leave industrial jobs after the war.

WHAT MAJOR changes occurred in American society as a consequence of wartime mobilization?

Students at Officers' Training School at Northwestern University, who were not allowed to marry until they were commissioned as ensigns, apply for marriage licenses in Chicago, August 20, 1943, shortly before graduation. These young couples helped the marriage rate skyrocket during World War II.

Wartime wages made many Americans eager to stock up on consumer goods, including a few luxuries, but they soon discovered that even supplying a household was difficult. Shopping had to be squeezed in between long work hours. Rationing required extra planning for purchasing meat, cheese, sugar, milk, coffee, gasoline, and shoes. Illegal black markets flourished despite the high prices charged for scarce or rationed goods.

Many women found it nearly impossible to manage both a demanding job and a household. This dual responsibility contributed to high turnover and absentee rates in factories. Caring for small children became a major problem. Although the War Manpower Commission estimated that as many as 2 million children needed some form of child care, federally funded day-care centers served less than 10 percent of defense workers' children. In most communities, the limited facilities sponsored by industry or municipal governments could not keep up with the growing number of "latchkey" children.

Juvenile delinquency rose. With employers relaxing minimum age requirements, many teenagers quit school for high-wage factory jobs. Runaways drifted from city to city, finding temporary work at wartime plants or military installations. Urban gangs spawned brawling, prostitution, and automobile thefts for joy rides. To curb this trend, the U.S. Office of Education and the Children's Bureau sponsored a back-to-school campaign and appealed to employers to hire only older workers.

Public health improved greatly. Forced to forgo medical care during the Great Depression, many Americans spent large portions of their wartime paychecks on doctors, dentists, and prescription drugs. Even more important were the medical benefits provided to the more than 16 million men inducted into the armed forces and their dependents. Nationally, incidences of such communicable diseases dropped considerably, the infant death rate fell by more than a third, and life expectancy increased by three years. In the South and Southwest, however, racism and poverty combined to halt or even reverse these trends. These regions continued to have the nation's highest infant and maternal mortality rates.

THE INTERNMENT OF JAPANESE AMERICANS

No families suffered more from wartime dislocations than Japanese Americans who were interned for the duration. After Pearl Harbor, military officials feared an invasion of the mainland and suspected Japanese Americans of secret disloyalty. On December 8, 1941, the federal government froze the financial assets of those born in Japan, called Issei, who had been barred from U.S. citizenship. Meanwhile, in the name of national defense, a coalition of politicians, patriotic organizations, business groups, and military officials called for the removal of all Americans of Japanese descent from Pacific coastal areas.

On February 19, 1942, Roosevelt signed Executive Order 9066, which banned more than 120,000 Japanese American men, women, and children from designated military areas, mainly in California, but also in Oregon, Washington, and southern Arizona. The army prepared for forced evacuation, rounding up and removing Japanese Americans from communities where they had lived and worked, sometimes for generations.

During the spring of 1942, Japanese American families received one week's notice to close up their businesses and homes. Told to bring only what they could carry, they were then transported to one of the ten internment camps managed by the War Relocation Authority. The guarded camps were located as far away as Arkansas, although the majority had been set up in the remote desert areas of Utah, Colorado, Idaho, Arizona, Wyoming, and California. By August, virtually every West Coast resident with at least one Japanese grandparent had been interned.

The Japanese American Citizens League charged that "racial animosity," not military necessity, motivated the internment policy. Despite the protest of the American Civil Liberties Union and several church groups, the Supreme Court in *Korematsu* v. *United States* (1944) upheld the constitutionality of relocation on grounds of national security. As a result of internment, Japanese Americans had lost homes and businesses valued at $500 million in what many historians judge as being the worst violation of American civil liberties during the war. Not until 1988 did Congress vote to award each of the 60,000 surviving victims reparations of $20,000 and a public apology.

More than 110,000 Japanese Americans were interned during World War II, some for up to four years. This photograph, taken in May 1942 by Dorothea Lange (1895–1965), the famed photographer of depression-era migrant families, shows young boys waiting in the baggage-inspection line at the Assembly Center in Turlock, California.

•••─┤Read the **Document**
Executive Order 9066 (1942) at
www.myhistorylab.com

"DOUBLE V": VICTORY AT HOME AND ABROAD

Throughout the war, African American activists conducted a "Double V" campaign, mobilizing not only for Allied victory but also for their own rights as citizens. Black militants demanded, at a minimum, fair housing and equal employment opportunities, laying the foundation for the postwar civil rights movement.

Even before the United States entered the war, the foremost black labor leader—A. Philip Randolph, president of both the Brotherhood of Sleeping Car Porters and the National Negro Congress—began to mobilize against discrimination. At a planning meeting in Chicago, a black woman proposed sending African Americans to Washington, DC, in order to get some action from the White House. African Americans across the country began to prepare for a "great rally" of no less than 100,000 people at the Lincoln Memorial on the Fourth of July.

Eager to stop the March on Washington movement, Roosevelt met with Randolph, who proposed an executive order "making it mandatory that Negroes be permitted to work in [defense] plants." On June 25, 1941, Roosevelt issued Executive Order 8802, banning discrimination in defense industries and government. The president later appointed a Fair Employment Practices Committee to hear complaints and redress grievances. Randolph called off the march but remained determined to "shake up white America."

Other civil rights organizations formed during wartime to fight discrimination and Jim Crow, including segregation in the armed forces. The interracial Congress of

•••─┤Read the **Document**
Profile: A. Philip Randolph at
www.myhistorylab.com

•••─┤Read the **Document**
A. Philip Randolph, Why Should We March (1942) at **www.myhistorylab.com**

This painting is by Horace Pippin, a self-taught African American artist who began painting as therapy for an injury suffered while serving with the U.S. Army's 369th Colored Infantry Regiment during World War I. It is one of a series drawn during World War II illustrating the contradiction between the principles of liberty and justice, for which Americans were fighting abroad, and the reality of racial prejudice at home.

Horace Pippin (1888–1946), *Mr. Prejudice*, 1943. Oil on canvas, 18 × 14 inches. Philadelphia Museum of Art, Gift of Dr. and Mrs. Matthew T. Moore. Photo by Graydon Wood. 1984–108–1.

Racial Equality (CORE), formed by pacifists in 1942, staged sit-ins at Chicago, Detroit, and Denver restaurants that refused to serve African Americans. Membership in the NAACP, which fought discrimination in defense plants and the military, grew from 50,000 in 1940 to 450,000 in 1946. The Supreme Court ruling in *Smith* v. *Albright* (1944) overturning the legality of "white primaries" used in southern states to exclude black voters was a major victory paving the way for future civil rights struggles.

Despite these advances, racial conflict intensified during the war. Approximately 1.2 million African Americans left the rural South to take wartime jobs, and they faced not only serious housing shortages but also whites intent on keeping them out of their own jobs and neighborhoods. Racial violence reached its wartime peak during the summer of 1943, when 274 conflicts broke out in nearly fifty cities. In Detroit, where the black population had grown by more than a third since the beginning of the war, twenty-five blacks and nine whites were killed and more than 700 were injured.

ZOOT SUIT RIOTS

On the night of June 4, 1943, sailors poured into nearly 200 cars and taxis to drive through the streets of East Los Angeles in search of Mexican Americans dressed in "zoot suits." The sailors assaulted their victims at random, even chasing one youth into a movie theater and stripping him of his clothes while the audience cheered. Riots broke out and continued for five days.

Two communities had collided with tragic results. The sailors had only recently been uprooted from their hometowns and regrouped under the strict discipline of boot camp. Stationed in southern California while awaiting deployment overseas, they came face-to-face with Mexican American teenagers wearing long-draped coats, pegged pants, pocket watches with oversized chains, and big floppy hats. To the sailors, the zoot suit signaled defiance and a lack of patriotism.

The zoot-suiters, however, represented less than 10 percent of the Hispanic community's youth. More than 300,000 Mexican Americans were serving in the armed forces, often in the most hazardous branches, as paratroops and marines. Many others were employed in war industries in Los Angeles, which had become home to the nation's largest Mexican American community. For the first time, Mexican Americans were finding well-paying jobs, and like African Americans, they expected their government to protect them from discrimination.

Military and civilian authorities eventually contained the zoot suit riots by ruling several sections of Los Angeles off-limits to military personnel, and the city council passed legislation making the wearing of a zoot suit in public a criminal offense. Many Mexican Americans expressed concern about their personal safety; some feared that after the government rounded up the Japanese they would be the next group sent to internment camps.

POPULAR CULTURE AND "THE GOOD WAR"

Despite the sharpening racial divisions of the neighborhood and the workplace, popular music crossed racial lines. Transplanted southern musicians, black and white, brought their regional styles to northern cities. "Country" and "rhythm & blues" not only won new audiences but also inspired musicians to crisscross old boundaries. Musicians of the war years paved the way musically for the emergence of rock and roll a decade later.

Hollywood mobilized, as one screenwriters group explained, "to build morale" and to "stimulate . . . initiative and responsibility." With military cooperation, wartime movies encouraged Americans to think well of all the Allies—including the Soviet Union. Several films, such as *Tender Comrade*, plugged pro-Soviet views that would be abruptly reversed in the postwar years. Other films such as the Oscar-winning *Since You Went Away* portrayed the loyalty and resilience of American families with servicemen stationed overseas.

The fashion industry also did its part. Production of nylon stockings was halted because the material was needed for parachutes; to save cotton and woolen fabric for the production of uniforms, women's skirts were shortened, while the War Production Board encouraged cuffless "Victory Suits" for men. Executive Order M-217 restricted the colors of shoes manufactured during the war to "black, white, navy blue, and three shades of brown." For many civilians, including civil defense volunteers and Red Cross workers, wearing a uniform demonstrated patriotism, and padded shoulders and straight lines became popular among fashion-conscious men and women.

Much of this war fervor was spontaneous, but the government did all it could to encourage self-sacrificing patriotism. The Office of War Information screened all popular music, movies, radio programs, and advertisements to ensure that everyone got the message: only the collective effort of all Americans could preserve democracy at home and save the world from fascism.

By the mid-1940s, popular culture had helped to shape a collective memory of World War II as "the good war," the standard by which the nation's subsequent wars would be judged. It also played an important part in bringing diverse and sometimes antagonistic communities together, not only in support of the war but also as steadfast consumers of mass entertainment.

MEN AND WOMEN IN UNIFORM

World War II mobilized 16.4 million Americans into the armed forces. Although only 34 percent of men who served in the army saw combat—the majority during the final year of the war—the experience had a powerful impact on nearly everyone. Many men and women saw their lives reshaped in unpredictable ways. For those who survived, the war often proved to be the defining experience of their lives.

HOW DID military service during World War II change the lives of American men and women?

Hear the **Audio**
Soldier Boy Blues, 1943 at
www.myhistorylab.com

CREATING THE ARMED FORCES

Neither the army nor the navy was prepared for the scale of combat World War II entailed. Before 1939, when the European war broke out, most of the 200,000 men in the armed forces patrolled the Mexican border or occupied colonial possessions. Only the U.S. Marine Corps, which had been planning since the 1920s to seize the western Pacific from Japan in the event of war, were ready to fight.

On October 16, 1940, National Registration Day, all men between twenty-one and thirty-six had to register for military service. After the United States entered the war, the draft age was lowered to eighteen, and local boards were instructed to choose the youngest first. The draft law exempted those "who by religious training or belief" opposed war. About 25,000 conscientious objectors served in noncombatant roles in the military services; another 12,000 performed "alternative service." Approximately 6,000 men were jailed for refusing to register for the draft.

One-third of the men examined by the Selective Service were rejected. Surprising numbers were refused induction as physically unfit. For the first time, men were screened for "neuropsychiatric disorders or emotional problems," and approximately 1.6 million were rejected for that reason. At a time when only one American in four graduated from high school, many conscripts were turned away as functionally illiterate.

WOMEN ENTER THE MILITARY

In May 1942, the Women's Army Auxiliary Corps (WAAC), later changed to Women's Army Corps (WAC). In 1942–43, other bills established a women's division of the navy (WAVES), the Women's Air Force Service Pilots, and the Marine Corps Women's Reserve.

Overall, more than 350,000 women served in World War II, two-thirds of them in the WACS and WAVES. As a group, they were better educated and more skilled—although paid less—than the average enlisted man. However, military policy prohibited women from supervising male workers, even in desk jobs.

Barred from combat, women were not necessarily protected from danger. Nurses accompanied troops into combat, treated men under fire, and dug their own foxholes. More than 1,000 women flew planes, although not in combat missions. The vast majority remained far from battlefronts, however. Stationed mainly within the United States, most women served in administration, communications, clerical, or health care facilities.

The WACS and WAVES were subject to both hostile commentary and bad publicity. The overwhelming majority of soldiers believed that most WACS were prostitutes; the War Department itself, fearing "immorality" among women in the armed forces, closely monitored their conduct and established much stricter rules for women than for men.

OLD PRACTICES AND NEW HORIZONS

The draft brought hundreds of thousands of young black men into the army, and African Americans enlisted at a rate 60 percent above their proportion of the general population. By 1944, black soldiers represented 10 percent of the army's troops, and overall approximately 1 million African Americans served in the armed forces during World War II. The army, however, channeled black recruits into segregated, poorly equipped units, commanded by white officers. The majority of African Americans served mainly in construction or stevedore work.

Only toward the end of the war, when the shortage of infantry neared a crisis, were African Americans permitted to rise to combat status. The all-black 761st Tank Battalion, the first African American armored unit, served 183 days in action without relief. The 99th Pursuit Squadron, trained at the new base in Tuskegee, Alabama, earned high

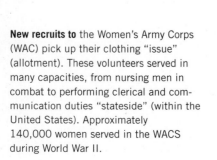

New recruits to the Women's Army Corps (WAC) pick up their clothing "issue" (allotment). These volunteers served in many capacities, from nursing men in combat to performing clerical and communication duties "stateside" (within the United States). Approximately 140,000 women served in the WACS during World War II.

marks in action against the feared German Luftwaffe. Even the Marine Corps and the Coast Guard agreed to end their historic exclusion of African Americans, although they recruited and promoted only a small number.

The ordinary black soldier, sailor, or marine encountered discrimination everywhere. Even the blood banks kept blood segregated by race. The year 1943 marked the peak of unrest, with violent confrontations between blacks and whites breaking out at military installations, especially in the South, where the majority of African American soldiers were stationed. Toward the end of the war, to improve morale among black servicemen, the army relaxed its policy of segregation, mainly in recreational facilities.

The army also grouped Japanese Americans into segregated units, sending most to fight far from the Pacific Theater. Better educated than the average soldier, many **Nisei** (second-generation Japanese American) soldiers who knew Japanese served stateside as interpreters and translators. When the army decided to create a Nisei regiment, more than 10,000 volunteers stepped forward, although only one in five was accepted. The Nisei 442nd fought heroically in Italy and France and became the most decorated regiment in the war.

Despite segregation, the armed forces ultimately pulled Americans of all varieties out of their separate communities. Many Jews and other second-generation European immigrants, for example, described their military stint as an "Americanizing" experience. For the first time in their lives, many Indian peoples left reservations as approximately 25,000 served in the armed forces. For many African Americans, military service provided a bridge to postwar civil rights agitation.

Many homosexuals also discovered a wider world in the service. Despite rules barring them from the military, most slipped through at the induction centers. Moreover, the emotional pressures of wartime, especially the fear of death, encouraged close friendships, and homosexuals in the military often found more room than in civilian life to express their sexual orientation openly.

Most veterans looked back on World War II, with all its dangers and discomforts, as the greatest experience they ever knew. As *The New Republic* predicted in 1943, they met other Americans from every part of the country and recognized for the first time in their lives "the bigness and wholeness of the United States." The army itself promoted these expectations of new experience. *Twenty-Seven Soldiers* (1944), a government-produced film for the troops, showed Allied soldiers of several nationalities all working together in harmony.

THE MEDICAL CORPS

By the time the war ended, nearly 500,000 Americans died in military actions. Although the European Theater produced the most casualties, the Pacific held grave dangers beyond enemy fire. For soldiers in humid jungles, malaria, typhus, diarrhea, or dengue fever posed the most common threat to their lives.

The prolonged stress of combat also took a toll in "battle fatigue"—the official army term for combat stress and what would today be called posttraumatic stress. More than 1 million soldiers suffered at one time or another from debilitating psychiatric symptoms. The cause, psychiatrists concluded, was not individual weakness but long stints in the front lines. In 1944, the army concluded that eight months in combat was the maximum. When replacements were available, a rotation system relieved exhausted soldiers.

The U.S. Marines recruited more than 400 Navajos to serve as code talkers by communicating in their own language. Deployed mainly to the Pacific Theater, they used radio and telegraph to transmit quickly vital information about battlefield activities, including troop movements. This photograph, taken in December 1943, shows Corporal Henry Bake, Jr., and Private First Class George H. Kirk operating a portable radio unit in a jungle clearing near the front lines.

Watch the Video
The Desegregation of the Military and Blacks in Combat at **www.myhistorylab.com**

Nisei U.S. citizens born of immigrant Japanese parents.

Army Medical Corps doctors worked on the front lines. There, in makeshift tent hospitals, these physicians pioneered advanced surgical techniques and used new "wonder drugs" such as penicillin to save many wounded soldiers who in earlier wars would have died. Much of the success in treatment came from the use of blood plasma, which reduced the often lethal effect of shock from severe bleeding.

Grateful for the care of skilled surgeons, many soldiers nevertheless named medics the true heroes of the battlefront. Thirty to forty medics were attached to each infantry battalion, and under fire they gave emergency first aid and transported the wounded to the aid station and, if necessary, the field hospital.

In the military hospitals, American nurses gave the bulk of care to recovering soldiers. Like medics, army nurses went first to training centers in the United States, learning how to dig foxholes and dodge bullets before being sent overseas. By 1945, approximately 56,000 women, including 500 African American women, were on active duty in the Army Nurse Corps, staffing medical facilities in every theater of the war.

The World at War

WHAT WERE the main elements of the Allied war strategy?

See the **Map**
World War II, European Theater at
www.myhistorylab.com

Read the **Document**
Profile: *Douglas MacArthur* at
www.myhistorylab.com

The Allies remained on the defensive almost until the end of 1942. During this time, from the Atlantic to deep in Russia, Hitler and his allies controlled most of continental Europe and continued to pound Great Britain from the air. A German army also swept across North Africa and almost took the Suez Canal from the British.

In the Pacific and East Asia, the situation was just as dire. Just two hours after the attack on Pearl Harbor, Japanese planes struck the main U.S. airbase in the Philippines and demolished half the warplanes commanded by General Douglas MacArthur. Japanese troops soon conquered the entire Philippines. The Japanese easily overran Britain's Southeast Asian colonies, the Dutch East Indies, and the entire western Pacific. Although China officially joined the Allies, Japanese forces on the Chinese mainland remained on the offensive (see Map 25.1).

The Allies did enjoy several important advantages: America's vast natural resources and a skilled workforce with sufficient reserves to accelerate the production of weapons and ammunitions; the determination of millions of antifascists throughout Europe and Asia; and the capacity of the Soviet people to endure immense losses. Slowly at first, but then with quickening speed, these advantages came into play.

SOVIETS HALT NAZI DRIVE

Unlike World War I, which was fought with poison gas and machine-gun fire by armies largely immobilized in trenches, World War II was a war of offensive maneuvers punctuated by surprise attacks. Its chief weapons—tanks and planes on land and aircraft carriers and submarines at sea—combined mobility and concentrated firepower. Also of major importance were artillery and explosives, which according to some estimates accounted for more than 30 percent of casualties. Major improvements in communication systems, mainly two-way radio transmission and radio-telephony that permitted commanders to stay in contact with division leaders, played a decisive role throughout the war.

From the beginning of the European war in 1939, Hitler had used these methods to seize the advantage, routing opposing armies in Western Europe. The Royal Air Force, however, fought the Luftwaffe to a standstill in the Battle of Britain, frustrating Hitler's hopes of invading England. By the spring of 1941, Hitler had turned his attention eastward, planning to conquer the Soviet Union. But he had to delay the invasion to rescue Mussolini, whose weak army faced defeat in North Africa and Greece. Not until June 22, 1941, six weeks behind schedule, did Hitler invade the Soviet Union.

MAP 25.1

The War in Europe   The Allies remained on the defensive during the first years of the war, but by 1943 the British and Americans, with an almost endless supply of resources, had turned the tide.

WHAT WERE the key turning points of the war in Europe?

Hitler's forces initially devastated the Red Army, killing or capturing nearly 3 million soldiers and leaving thousands to die from exposure or starvation. But the brutality of the Nazis kindled a desperate civilian resistance. The German army in Russia found its supply lines overextended and the brutal Russian winter just beginning, while Stalin was able to send every available resource to his troops concentrated just outside Moscow. The Red Army launched a massive counterattack, catching the frostbitten German troops off guard and driving them to retreat.

Hitler, however, remained stubbornly fixed on conquering Russia. In 1942, German troops had a new objective: occupying the rich oil fields of the Caucasus. But at Stalingrad, Hitler met his nemesis. In the battle for that city alone, the Soviets suffered more casualties than Americans did during the entire war. House-to-house fighting and a massive Red Army counterattack inflicted an even greater toll on the Nazis. Hitler ordered to his troops to die rather than surrender. In February 1943, the German Sixth Army, reduced to 100,000 starving men and overpowered by Soviet weaponry, at last gave up.

Already in retreat but plotting one last desperate attempt to halt the Red Army, the Germans threw most of their remaining armored vehicles into action at Kursk in July 1943. After another stunning defeat, the Germans had decisively lost the initiative. Their only option was to delay the advance of the Red Army toward their own homeland.

Meanwhile, the Soviet Union had begun to recover from its early losses, even as tens of millions of its people remained homeless and near starvation. Assisted by Lend-Lease, by 1942 the Soviets were outproducing Germany in many types of weapons and other supplies. Nazi officers and German civilians alike began to doubt that Hitler could win.

Soviet victories had turned the tide; the Soviet Union, not the Western Allies, bore by far the heaviest burden in stopping what had once seemed an unstoppable Nazi advance. The American and British people were grateful for this immense Soviet contribution and the British and American governments found themselves under enormous pressure from Stalin to open a second front in the west.

PLANNING AND INITIATING THE ALLIED OFFENSIVE

Despite the huge territories that Nazi Germany and Japan controlled in 1942, the Axis momentum was flagging. After Stalingrad, Hitler lost ground. In the Pacific that summer, Japan's plans to invade Hawai'i and Australia were stopped by the U.S. Navy. In the course of 1942 as well, American shipbuilding began to outpace the punishment Nazi U-boats could inflict on Allied shipping. The United States far outstripped Germany in building landing craft and amphibious vehicles, two of the most important innovations of the war. Now outnumbered by the Allies, the German Luftwaffe was increasingly limited to defensive action.

Against this backdrop, Roosevelt, Churchill, and their generals hammered out a strategy to defeat the Axis. They saw Japan as the lesser threat—one that for the moment should be contained rather than attacked. Germany, Roosevelt and Churchill agreed, must be beaten first, which meant eventually invading Europe and fighting Hitler's Reich from the west, while the Red Army advanced from the east.

But the Allies disagreed about where to attack Germany. Churchill and his generals wanted to strike through what he called "Europe's soft underbelly," the Mediterranean. The American generals retorted that only a direct, though meticulously prepared, assault through France would bring down Nazi Germany.

In the end, Roosevelt and Churchill compromised: they would first send smaller armies into the Mediterranean, while gathering a huge Anglo-American invasion army in Britain. This strategy was set in motion in late 1942. On October 23–24, near El Alamein in the desert of western Egypt, the British Eighth Army halted a major offensive by the German Afrika Korps, headed by General Erwin Rommel. Although suffering heavy losses, British forces destroyed the Italian North African Army and much of the Afrika Korps. Then, in November, American troops for the first time went into action in the

European Theater by joining the British in **Operation Torch**, an invasion of Morocco and Algeria. While at the eastern end, the British drove Rommel back from El Alamein, from the west, a mostly American army forced the Germans out of Tunisia. In six months, North Africa was cleared of Axis troops.

Operation Torch The Allied invasion of Axis-held North Africa in 1942.

In January 1943, while the fighting raged in North Africa, Roosevelt and Churchill met at Casablanca in Morocco and announced that they would accept nothing less than the unconditional surrender of their enemies. There would be no negotiations with Hitler and Mussolini. Roosevelt's supporters hailed the policy as a clear statement of goals, a promise to the world that the scourge of fascism would be completely banished. Stalin, who did not attend, criticized the policy, predicting that it would only increase enemy determination to fight to the end. Western critics charged that the demand for total capitulation would pro-long the war and swell the casualty list.

Allied aerial bombing was increasing the pressure on Germany. Some U.S. leaders believed that the B-17 Flying Fortress, "the mightiest bomber ever built," could win the war from the air without any western troops having to fight their way into Europe. The U.S. Army Air Corps (predecessor of the Air Force) described the B-17 as a "humane" weapon, capable of hitting specific military targets while sparing civilians. That claim was nonsense. Especially when weather or darkness required bombardiers to sight with radar, they could not distinguish between industrial, military, and civilian targets, and even with the best available targeting, bombs might land anywhere within a nearly two-mile radius. Bombing missions over the Rhineland and the Ruhr did take out many German factories, while also costing tens of thousands of civilian lives, but the Germans successfully relocated many industrial plants to the countryside.

Determined to break German resistance, the Royal Air Force redirected its main attack away from military targets to cities, fuel dumps, and transportation lines. Indiscriminate bombing practically leveled the great city of Hamburg, killing between 60,000 and 100,000 people and destroying 300,000 buildings. Sixty other cities were hit hard, leaving 20 percent of Germany's total residential area in ruins. Americans joined in the very worst air raid of the war—650,000 incen-diary bombs dropped on Dresden in 1945 destroying 8 square miles and killing perhaps 135,000 civilians. Dresden, famous for its archi-tecture and art galleries, had no military value. This was terror bombing. Hitler had started it, but the Allies more than repaid in kind.

Though the air war disappointed those who saw in it the means of a bloodless—to the attackers—victory, the Allied strategic air offensive did weaken the German economy and did terror-ize (but also enrage) German civilians. Moreover, in trying to defend German cities and factories, the Luftwaffe sacrificed most of its remaining fighter planes and aircraft fuel. When the Allies finally invaded Western Europe in the summer of 1944, they would enjoy total air superiority.

THE ALLIED INVASION OF EUROPE

In the summer of 1943, the Allies continued their Mediterranean offensive by attacking southern Italy. On July 10, British and American troops stormed Sicily, and by mid-August con-quered the island. After Allied troops landed

As part of the air war on Germany, Allied bombers launched a devastating attack on Dresden, a major economic center, in February 1945. Of the civilians who died, most from burns or smoke inhalation during the firestorm, a large number were women and children, refugees from the eastern front. The city was left in ruins.

D-Day landing, June 6, 1944, marked the greatest amphibious maneuver in military history. Troop ships ferried Allied soldiers from England to Normandy beaches. Within a month, nearly 1 million men had assembled in France, ready to retake western and central Europe from German forces.

near Naples, Italy surrendered to the Western Allies on September 8. Hitler, however, sent new divisions into northern and central Italy, stalling the Allied campaign. Almost until the end of the European war, a large Allied army was still bogged down on Italy's rugged terrain, battling a much smaller German force.

All across occupied Europe, resistance to the Nazis spread. Jews walled off in the Nazi-built Warsaw ghetto, realizing that they were marked for extermination, revolted in the summer of 1943 and fought to the death. Scattered revolts followed in the Nazi labor camps, where military prisoners of war and civilians were being worked on starvation rations. Underground fighters, known as partisans, resisted the Nazis from Norway to Greece and from Poland to France.

By early 1944, Anglo-American plans were being readied for **Operation Overlord**, a campaign to retake the Continent with a decisive counterattack through France. General Dwight D. Eisenhower, who was put in command, displayed great skill not only in strategizing but also in dealing with contentious British, Americans, and the prickly Free French leader, General Charles de Gaulle.

D-Day—the start of the Allied invasion—finally came on June 6, 1944. Under heavy German machine-gun and mortar fire, wave after wave of American, British, Canadian, and Free French troops hit the Normandy beaches, the tides swelling with the dead and the wounded. Some 2,500 men died in the initial assault, many before they could fire a shot. Although the Germans responded slowly—they expected the invasion near Calais and at first thought Normandy a feint—at Omaha Beach they had prepared their defense almost perfectly, and the Americans who landed there had a particularly difficult time gaining a toehold. Within days, though, more than 175,000 Allied troops and 20,000 vehicles were battling the Germans—the largest landing operation in history. Over the next six weeks, nearly 1 million more Allied soldiers came ashore. Not until mid-July did this invasion army finally break out of Normandy and drive into the French interior.

All eyes now turned to Paris. Allied bombers pounded roads, bridges, rail lines, and factories that were producing German munitions all around the French capital. With Free French and Allied troops, de Gaulle entered Paris on August 25 and announced a reconstituted French Republic. Belgium also fell swiftly to the liberators. But Allied troops had only reached a resting place between bloody battles, their supply lines stretched thin and German resistance stiffening.

THE HIGH COST OF EUROPEAN VICTORY

By September 1944, Allied commanders were searching for a way to end the war quickly. Missing a spectacular chance to move through largely undefended territory and on to Berlin, they turned north instead, intending to strike through the Netherlands into Germany's industrial heartland. Faulty intelligence reports overlooked a well-armed German division at the Dutch town of Arnhem, waiting to cut Allied paratroops to pieces. The Germans captured 6,000 Americans.

That winter, making a final, desperate effort to break the Allied momentum, Hitler sent his last reserves, a quarter-million men, against American lines in Belgium's dense

Operation Overlord United States and British invasion of France in June 1944 during World War II.

D-Day June 6, 1944, the day of the first paratroop drops and amphibious landings on the coast of Normandy, France, in the first stage of Operation Overlord during World War II.

Ardennes forest. In this so-called **Battle of the Bulge**, the Germans surprised the Americans, driving them fifty miles back before literally running out of gas. This last effort exhausted the German capacity for counterattack. After Christmas Day 1944, the Germans had to retreat into their own territory.

The end approached. In March 1945, discovery of a single intact bridge across the Rhine allowed the Allies to roll into the heart of Germany, taking the heavily industrialized Ruhr Valley.

By that time, Soviet offenses were crushing the German army in the east. The Red Army had reached Warsaw in the midsummer of 1944, but then stood by while the anti-Russian Polish resistance rose up—only to be destroyed (along with most of the city) by the Nazis. While that tragedy unfolded, the Soviets occupied the Balkans and battled the Germans in Hungary. Only in January 1945 did the Red Army sweep across Poland and by April besiege Berlin, where Hitler had holed up.

The defense of Germany, now hopeless, had fallen into the hands of teenagers, terrified elderly men, and a few desperate Nazis.

THE WAR IN ASIA AND THE PACIFIC

Six months after Pearl Harbor, the United States began regaining naval superiority in the central Pacific. The Americans had been supremely lucky that their aircraft carriers were out at sea during the Pearl Harbor attack; that luck was spectacularly demonstrated in the great naval battle of the Coral Sea on May 7–8, 1942, in which carrier-based American aircraft blocked a Japanese thrust at Australia. A month later, on June 4, the Japanese fleet converged on Midway Island, an outpost vital to American communications and to the defense of Hawai'i. There, the Americans had another lucky break; intelligence officers had broken the Japanese codes and thus knew when and where the attack would fall. Still separated by hundreds of miles of open sea, the Japanese and American carrier fleets clashed at long distance. Descending from the clouds, American warplanes sank four Japanese carriers and destroyed hundreds of planes, ending Japan's offensive threat to Hawai'i and the West Coast.

Even so, Japan controlled a vast arc of the western Pacific. That perimeter stretched from the outermost Aleutians (off Alaska) to northern New Guinea and the Solomon Islands (off Australia). Japan also dominated all of coastal China and the European colonies of Southeast Asia: Indochina, Malaya, present-day Indonesia, and Burma (see Map 25.2). In much of East Asia (except China), nationalistic and anticolonial sentiment played into Japanese hands at first. With only 200,000 troops, Japan easily overran Southeast Asia because so few people in the British, French, and Dutch colonies would fight for their imperial masters. Japan installed puppet governments in Burma and the Philippines, and independent Thailand became a Japanese ally. But the new Japanese empire proved terrifyingly cruel. Local nationalists from Indochina to the Philippines turned against the Japanese, forming guerrilla bands that harassed the invaders. In China, Japan's huge land army bogged down fighting both the Nationalist forces of Chiang Kai-shek and the Communist People's Liberation Army led by Mao Zedong.

Thus, in mid-1942, the war for the Pacific was still only beginning. Pulling back their offensive operations, the Japanese concentrated their remaining forces. Their commanders calculated that bitter fighting, with high casualties on both sides, would wear down the American military and public. The U.S. command, divided between MacArthur in the southwest Pacific and Admiral Chester Nimitz in the central Pacific, developed a strategy to strangle the Japanese import-dependent economy and to "**island-hop**" from one strategic outpost to another, closing in on the home islands.

In the Solomons and New Guinea, American and Australian ground troops began the counterattack. On Guadalcanal in the Solomons, American Marines struck at one Japanese stronghold, and during a six-month struggle endured tropical diseases, dangerous

See the Map
World War II, Pacific Theater at
www.myhistorylab.com

Battle of the Bulge   German offensive in December 1944 that penetrated deep into Belgium (creating a "bulge"). Allied forces, while outnumbered, attacked from the north and south. By January 1945, the German forces were destroyed or routed, but not without some 77,000 Allied casualties.

island-hop   The Pacific campaigns of 1944 that were the American naval versions of the *blitzkrieg*.

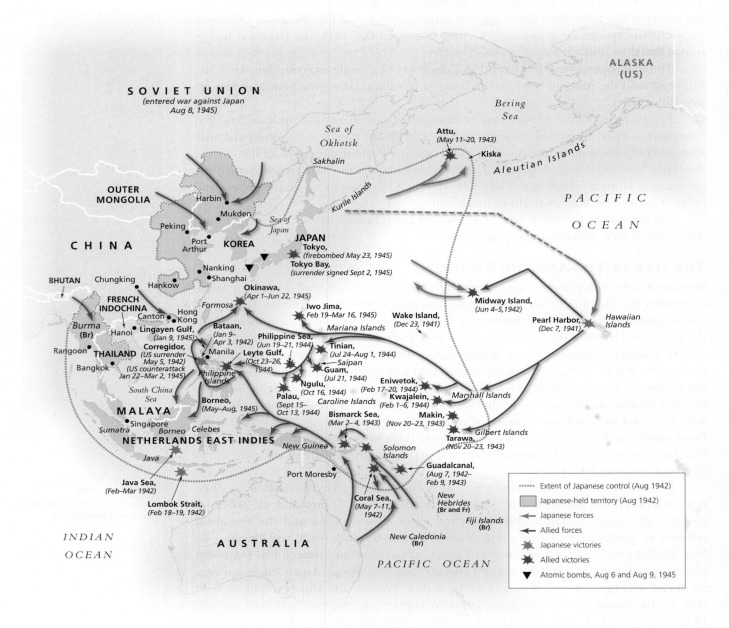

MAP 25.2

War in the Pacific Across an ocean battlefield utterly unlike the European Theater, Allies battled Japanese troops near their homeland.

HOW DID strategies in the Pacific differ from those in Europe?

parasites, food and ammunition shortages, and very high casualty rates against Japanese defenders who fought to the death. The marines were reduced to eating roots and berries to stay alive. Finally, with strong supply lines secured by a string of costly naval battles, in February 1943 the Americans finally prevailed, proving that they could defeat Japanese forces in brutal jungle combat.

For the next two years, the U.S. Navy and Marine Corps opened a path to Japan, capturing a series of important Pacific atolls but bypassing others, helplessly stranding well-armed Japanese defenders. Tarawa in the Gilbert Islands was first of these assaults in November 1943; it cost more than 1,000 U.S. Marine lives. In June 1944, simultaneously with the Normandy landings, the U.S. Navy inflicted crippling losses on the Japanese fleet in the Battle of the Philippine Sea. Then in August 1944, the Americans took Guam, Saipan, and Tinian in the Mariana Islands, for the first time bringing the Japanese home islands within bomber range. And in October of that year, MacArthur led an American force of 250,000 to retake the Philippines. Trying to hold the islands, practically all that remained of the Japanese navy threw itself at the Americans in the Battle of Leyte Gulf, the largest naval battle in history. The Japanese lost eighteen capital ships, leaving the United States in control of the Pacific. While MacArthur mopped up operations in the Philippines—at a cost of 100,000 Filipino lives and leaving Manila devastated—the small but strategically important island of Iwo Jima, south of Japan, fell. Here too, the American death toll was high; casualties were estimated at nearly 27,000.

Even bloodier was the struggle for Okinawa, an island 350 miles southwest of the Japanese home islands and the site of vital airbases. The invasion—the largest American amphibious operation in the Pacific war—began on Easter Sunday, April 1, 1945. Waves of Japanese *kamikaze* ("divine wind") pilots, flying suicide missions with a 500-pound bomb and only enough fuel for a one-way flight, met the marines on the beaches. The U.S. troops who survived this onslaught used flame-throwers, each with 300 gallons of napalm, to incinerate dug-in Japanese defenders. On Okinawa, more Americans died or were wounded than at Normandy. At the end of June, when the ghastly struggle ended, 140,000 Japanese were dead, including 42,000 civilians.

The war was over in Europe, and the Allies could concentrate on Japan alone. Tokyo and other Japanese cities were targeted by B-17s and new B-29s flying from Guam with devastating results. Massive fire bombings burned thousands of civilians alive in their mostly wooden or bamboo houses, and hundreds of thousands were left homeless. Meanwhile, U.S. submarines cut off the home islands from supplies on the East Asian mainland.

Japan could not hold out forever. Without a navy or air force, critically important oil, tin, rubber, and grain could not be transported to maintain its soldiers or feed its people. Great Britain and particularly the United States, however, pressed for a quick and unconditional surrender. They had special reasons to hurry. Earlier they had sought a commitment from the Soviet Union to invade Japan, but now they looked beyond the war, determined to prevent the Red Army from taking any Japanese-held territories. These calculations, as well as chilling forecasts of the bloody cost of invading and subjugating the home islands, set the stage for unleashing the top-secret weapon that American scientists had been building: the atomic bomb.

THE LAST STAGES OF WAR

From the attack on Pearl Harbor until mid-1943, Roosevelt and his advisers had focused on military strategy rather than on postwar plans. Once the defeat of Nazi Germany appeared in sight, high government officials began to consider long-range objectives. Roosevelt wanted both to crush the **Axis powers** and to establish a system of collective security to prevent another world war. He knew he could not succeed without the cooperation of the other key leaders, Stalin and Churchill.

In 1944 and early 1945, these "Big Three" met several times to hammer out the shape of the postwar world. Although none of these nations expected to reach a final agreement, neither did they anticipate how quickly they would confront momentous global events, including the obvious fact that the only thing holding the "Grand Alliance" together was the mission of destroying the Axis.

HOW DID he relationship between the Allies change once victory was in sight?

Axis powers   The opponents of the United States and its allies in World War II.

Holocaust The systematic murder of millions of European Jews and others deemed undesirable by Nazi Germany.

THE HOLOCAUST

Another fact also became clear, at least to the American public, as the European war entered its final stages: the full horror of Nazi atrocities. As part of a comprehensive plan for achieving Aryan superiority and the "final solution of the Jewish question," Hitler had ordered the extermination of "racial enemies" and others deemed undesirable, including mentally retarded and crippled German children and adults. The toll included some 6 million Jews, 250,000 Romany (Gypsies), 60,000 homosexuals, members of other "inferior races" (such as Slavs), and indeed anyone else deemed an enemy of the German Reich and its "master race." Beginning in 1933, but accelerating from 1941 onward, the Nazis murdered millions of people in Germany and in all the European nations they conquered. Gruesome "medical experiments" were also performed on Jews and Soviet prisoners of war (POWs).

These policies had begun at the outset of the Hitler regime in 1933, and at the beginning of 1942 the Nazis initiated mass murder in death camps like Auschwitz in Poland. Very soon, word of what the Nazis were doing was leaking out of occupied Europe. Throughout almost the entire war, however, the U.S. government released little information about what came to be known as the **Holocaust**. Although liberal magazines such as *The Nation* and small committees of intellectuals tried to call attention to what was happening in the Nazi camps, major news media like the *New York Times* and *Time* magazine treated reports of genocide as minor news items.

Leaders of the American Jewish community, however, were better informed than the general population, and since the mid-1930s they had been petitioning the government to suspend immigration quotas that barred significant numbers of German Jews from taking refuge in the United States. Backed by public opinion (fixated on foreigners threatening American jobs), Roosevelt and Congress refused. Even after the United States entered the war, the president maintained that the liberation of European Jews and other oppressed peoples depended on a speedy and total Allied victory. Not until January 1944 did Roosevelt agree to change government policy. At that time, Secretary of the Treasury Henry Morgenthau, himself Jewish, reported to the president on "one of the greatest crimes in history, the slaughter of the Jewish people in Europe," and suggested that anti-Semitism in the State Department had stalled the development of an aggressive plan of action. Within a week, in part to avoid scandal, Roosevelt issued an executive order creating the War Refugee Board. However, when American Jews pleaded for bombing rail lines leading to the notorious death camp at Auschwitz, in occupied Poland, both Roosevelt and the War Department refused. Attempts to rescue civilians—such was the government's unshaken position—would divert resources from military operations.

The extent of Nazi depravity was finally revealed to Americans when Allied troops invaded Germany and began liberating the Nazi camps. Touring Ohrdruf concentration camp in April 1945, Eisenhower found barracks crowded with corpses and crematories still reeking of burned flesh. "I want every American unit not actually in the front lines to see this place," Eisenhower ordered. "We are told that the American soldier does not know what he is fighting for. Now, at least, he will know what he is fighting against."

Belsen Camp: The *Compound for Women*, painted by American artist Leslie Cole, depicts Belsen as the Allied troops found it when they invaded Germany in 1945.

Leslie Cole, *Belsen Camp: The Compound for Women*. Imperial War Museum, London.

THE YALTA CONFERENCE

Roosevelt was elected to a fourth term in November 1944, defeating the moderately liberal Republican governor of New York, Thomas E. Dewey. Many loyal Democrats looked forward to a revival of the New Deal after the war was won. Elected with FDR was a new vice president, a middle-of-the-road Missouri senator named Harry S. Truman. Unknown to the public, however, Roosevelt was now exhausted and gravely ill—though, as was his habit, he kept his vice president totally uninformed of his plans and of the most important wartime secrets.

In early 1945, with the end of the war in sight, Allied leaders began to reassess their goals. The Atlantic Charter of 1941 had stated noble objectives for the world after the defeat of fascism: national self-determination, no territorial aggrandizement, equal access of all peoples to raw materials and collaboration for the improvement of economic opportunities, freedom of the seas, disarmament, and "freedom from fear and want." Now, four years later, Roosevelt realized that neither Great Britain nor the Soviet Union intended to abide by any code of conduct that compromised their national security or conflicted with their economic interests. Stalin and Churchill soon reached a new agreement, one projecting their respective spheres of influence in Eastern Europe.

In early February 1945, Roosevelt held still another wartime meeting with Churchill and Stalin, this time at Yalta, a Crimean resort on the Black Sea. Seeking his partners' cooperation, the president recognized that prospects for postwar peace also depended on compromise. Although diplomats avoided the touchy phrase "spheres of influence," it was clear that this opportunistic principle guided all negotiations. Neither the United States nor Great Britain raised serious objections to Stalin's demand to retain the Baltic states and eastern Poland—booty from the time of the Nazi–Soviet pact—and to create an East European "buffer zone" protecting Russia against future German aggression. In return, Churchill insisted on restoring the British Empire in Asia, and the United States hoped to retain captured Pacific islands from which Japanese military resurgence could be checked. Roosevelt hoped to ease the harshness of these imperialistic goals by creating a global peacekeeping organization, the United Nations, and by using promises of postwar American economic aid to persuade Stalin to behave with restraint in countries, like Poland, that the Red Army was liberating and occupying.

The biggest and most controversial item on the agenda at Yalta was the Soviet entry into the Pacific war, which Roosevelt believed necessary for a timely Allied victory. After driving a hard bargain involving Soviet rights to territory in China, Stalin agreed to declare war against Japan within three months of Germany's surrender. Roosevelt told Congress that the Yalta meeting had been a "great success," proof that the wartime alliance remained intact. Privately, however, the president concluded that the outcome of the conference revealed that the Atlantic Charter had been nothing more than "a beautiful idea."

The death of Franklin Roosevelt of a massive stroke on April 12, 1945, cast a dark shadow over all hopes for long-term, peaceful solutions to global problems. The president did not live to learn of Hitler's suicide in his Berlin bunker on April 30, 1945, or the unconditional surrender of Germany one week later, on May 8. Millions of Americans and people in other democratic nations deeply mourned the passing of the great pragmatic idealist, just as new and still greater challenges were looming.

THE ATOMIC BOMB

Roosevelt's death made Allied cooperation even more difficult. Harry Truman, an honest and plainspoken product of Kansas City machine politics, made a national reputation as a U.S. senator investigating wartime corruption, but he lacked foreign-policy experience and had none of FDR's finesse and prestige.

The wartime Big Three—now Stalin, Truman, and Churchill—held their final conference at Potsdam, just outside Berlin, from July 17 to August 2, 1945. A huge

● View the Image
Big Three at Yalta at
www.myhistorylab.com

Yalta Conference   Meeting of U.S. President Franklin Roosevelt, British Prime Minister Winston Churchill, and Soviet Premier Joseph Stalin held in February 1945 to plan the final stages of World War II and postwar arrangements.

agenda of thorny issues confronted the victorious leaders: the future of defeated and occupied Germany and other former Axis powers, the Soviet occupation of Eastern Europe, reparations and economic aid to rebuild a shattered Europe, and crucial details about organizing the new United Nations, on which the Americans set great store. The Big Three clashed sharply over most of these issues, but they held fast in demanding the unconditional surrender of reeling but still-defiant Japan.

It was while wrangling with Stalin at Potsdam that Truman learned a closely guarded secret: that on July 16 the United States had successfully tested an atomic bomb in New Mexico. As a senator and as vice president, Truman had not been informed of the existence of the Manhattan Project; he first heard about it upon Roosevelt's death. Until the moment of the test, Truman had been pressing Stalin to make good his Yalta promise to enter the Pacific war three months after Germany's surrender—a deadline that would fall on August 8. The president was eager to get Soviet participation in what everyone said would be a horrendously bloody U.S. invasion of Japan, and indeed he did extract Stalin's promise to attack Japan on schedule. But then Secretary of War Stimson received a cable: "Babies satisfactorily born." Truman and his advisers concluded that Soviet assistance was no longer needed to end the war.

On August 3, 1945, Japan announced its refusal to surrender. Its military leaders still demanded a fight to the death, and Japanese civilian politicians wanted Allied guarantees that the emperor, considered sacred, would keep his throne. This response the Americans deemed unsatisfactory: they still demanded unconditional surrender, preferably before the Red Army moved against Japan. Three days later, the B-29 bomber nicknamed *Enola Gay* dropped the five-ton uranium bomb that destroyed the Japanese city of Hiroshima. Instantly, some 40,000 people died; in the following weeks, 100,000 more perished from radiation poisoning or burns. By 1950, the death toll reached 200,000.

"This is not war, this is not even murder; this is pure nihilism . . . a crime against God which strikes at the very basis of moral existence." So wrote the Japanese *Nippon Times*. In the United States, several leading religious publications echoed this view. The *Christian Century* judged the use of the bomb as a "moral earthquake" that by comparison made the long-denounced use of poison gas by Germany in World War I utterly insignificant. Albert Einstein, whose physics provided the foundation for the Manhattan Project (but in which he had taken no part), said that the atomic bomb had changed everything—except the nature of man.

Americans first heard of the atomic bomb on August 7, when the news reported the destruction and death it had brought to Hiroshima. But fears about the implications of the appalling new weapon were overwhelmed by an outpouring of relief: Japan surrendered— still not unconditionally—on August 14, several days after a second nuclear bomb destroyed Nagasaki, killing another 73,000.

Allied insistence on unconditional surrender and the decision to atom-bomb Japan remain two of the most controversial political and moral questions about the conduct of World War II. Although Truman insisted in his memoirs (written years later) that he gave the order so as to save "a half a million American lives" in ground combat, no such official estimate exists. An intelligence document of April 30, 1946, stated that "the dropping of the bomb was the pretext seized upon by all [American] leaders as the reason for ending the war, but [even if the bomb had not been used] the Japanese would have capitulated upon the entry of Russia into the war." There is no question, however, that the use of nuclear weapons did strengthen U.S. policymakers' hand. It certainly did force caution upon Stalin, soon to emerge as America's primary adversary. Truman and his advisers knew that their nation's atomic monopoly would not last, but they hoped that in the meantime the United States could play the leading role in building the postwar world.

CHRONOLOGY

1931	September: Japan occupies Manchuria
1933	March: Adolf Hitler seizes power
	May: Japan quits League of Nations
1935	October: Italy invades Ethiopia
1935–1937	Neutrality Acts authorize the president to block the sale of munitions to belligerent nations
1936	July: Spanish Civil War begins
1937	August: Japan invades China
	October: Franklin D. Roosevelt calls for international cooperation against aggression
1938	March: Germany annexes Austria
	September: Munich Agreement lets Germany annex Sudetenland of Czechoslovakia
	November: *Kristallnacht*, Nazis attack Jews and destroy Jewish property
1939	March: Germany annexes remainder of Czechoslovakia
	August: Germany and the Soviet Union sign nonaggression pact
	September: Germany invades Poland; World War II begins
	November: Soviet Union invades Finland
1940	April–June: Germany's *bliztkrieg* sweeps over Western Europe
	September: Germany, Italy, and Japan—the Axis powers—conclude a military alliance
	First peacetime military draft in American history
	November: Roosevelt defeats Wendall Willkie and is elected to an unprecedented third term
1941	March: Lend-Lease Act extends aid to Great Britain
	May: German troops secure the Balkans
	A. Philip Randolph plans March on Washington movement for July
	June: Germany invades Soviet Union
	Fair Employment Practices Committee formed

	August: The United States and Great Britain agree to the Atlantic Charter
	December: Japanese attack Pearl Harbor; United States enters the war
1942	January: War mobilization begins
	February: Executive order mandates internment of Japanese Americans
	May–June: Battles of Coral Sea and Midway give the United States naval superiority in the Pacific
	August: Manhattan Project begins
	November: United States stages amphibious landing in North Africa; Operation Torch begins
1943	January: Casablanca Conference announces unconditional surrender policy
	February: Soviet victory over Germans at Stalingrad
	April–May: Coal miners strike
	May: German Afrika Korps troops surrender in Tunis
	July: Allied invasion of Italy
	Summer: Race riots break out in nearly fifty cities
1944	June–August: Operation Overlord and liberation of Paris
	November: Roosevelt elected to fourth term, defeating Thomas E. Dewey
1945	February: Yalta Conference renews American-Soviet alliance
	February–June: United States captures Iwo Jima and Okinawa in Pacific
	April: Roosevelt dies in office; Harry Truman becomes president
	May: Germany surrenders
	July–August: Potsdam Conference
	August: United States drops atomic bombs on Hiroshima and Nagasaki; Japan surrenders

CONCLUSION

The new tactics and weapons of World War II, such as massive air raids and the atomic bomb produced by the Los Alamos scientists, made warfare incomparably more deadly than before to both military and civilian populations. Between 40 and 50 million people died in World War II—four times the number in World War I—and half the casualties were women and children. More than 405,000 Americans died, and more than 670,000 were wounded. Although slight compared to the casualties suffered by other Allied nations—more than 20 million Soviets died during the war—the human cost of World War II for Americans was second only to that of the Civil War.

Coming at the end of two decades of resolutions to avoid military entanglements, the war pushed the nation's leaders to the center of global politics and into risky military and political alliances that would not outlive the war. The United States emerged the strongest nation in the world, but in a world where the prospects for lasting peace appeared increasingly remote. If World War II raised the nation's international commitments to a new height, its impact on ordinary Americans was not so easy to gauge. Many new communities formed as Americans migrated in mass numbers to new regions that were booming as a result of the wartime economy. Enjoying a rare moment of full employment, many workers new to well-paying industrial jobs anticipated further advances against discrimination. Exuberant at the Allies' victory over fascism and the return of the troops, the majority were optimistic as they looked ahead.

REVIEW QUESTIONS

1. How did President Franklin D. Roosevelt ready the nation for war?

2. What role did the federal government, business, and labor play in gearing up the economy for wartime production?

3. How did the war affect the lives of American women?

4. Discuss the causes and consequences of the Japanese American internment program.

5. Describe the role of popular culture in promoting the war effort at home.

6. How did military service affect the lives of those who served in World War II?

7. What were the main points of Allied military strategy in both Europe and Asia?

8. How successful were diplomatic efforts in ending the war and in establishing the terms of peace?

KEY TERMS

Atlantic Charter (p. 656)
Axis powers (p. 675)
Battle of the Bulge (p. 673)
Blitzkrieg (p. 656)
D-Day (p. 672)
Holocaust (p. 676)
Island-hop (p. 673)

Lend-Lease Act (p. 656)
Neutrality Act of 1939 (p. 656)
Nisei (p. 667)
Operation Overlord (p. 672)
Operation Torch (p. 671)
War Powers Act (p. 657)
Yalta Conference (p. 677)

PEARSON
myhistorylab Connections

Reinforce what you learned in this chapter by studying the many documents, images, maps, review tools, and videos available at www.myhistorylab.com.

Read and Review

✓● Study and Review Chapter 25

●●● Read the Document

Franklin Roosevelt, Date Which Will Live in Infamy (1941)

Executive Order 9066 (1942)

A. Philip Randolph, Why Should We March (1942)

👁 See the Map

World War II, European Theater

World War II, Pacific Theater

✺ View the Image

Nazi Book Bonfire

Women Riveters in Navy Shipyard

Big Three at Yalta

✺ Watch the Video *American Entry into WWI*

Research and Explore

●●● Read the Document

Exploring America: Propaganda

Profiles
  Douglas MacArthur
  A. Philip Randolph

Whose History Is It?: Exhibiting the Enola Gay

((●● Hear the Audio

Soldier Boy Blues, 1943

Obey the Ration Laws

✺ Watch the Video

Normandy Beach, June 6, 1944

The Desegregation of the Military and Blacks in Combat

((●● Hear the Audio

Hear the audio files for Chapter 25 at
www.myhistorylab.com.

To my mind we are in a situation no less dangerous than the one we were facing in 1939, and it is of the greatest importance that we realize it. We must realize . . . that democracy will not be saved by ideals alone.

—*Edward Teller*

As international tensions rose with the onset of the Cold War, Americans wondered how to prepare for a possible nuclear war. Many families stocked extra food and water and bought a battery-powered radio, but few actually installed backyard bomb shelters like the one being tested by this family in a Long Island suburb not far from Levittown.

26

THE COLD WAR BEGINS
1945–1952

((•—[**Hear** the **Audio**

Hear the audio files for Chapter 26 at **www.myhistorylab.com**.

WHAT STEPS did the United States take in the years following World War II to shape the economic and political future of Europe?

HOW DID the Truman Doctrine shape U.S. postwar foreign policy?

HOW DID the "Fair Deal" differ from the "New Deal"?

HOW DID concerns about national security lead to the abridgement of civil liberties?

WHAT ROLE did population growth and prosperity play in shaping Cold War culture?

HOW DID the Republicans win the presidency and control of Congress in 1952?

AMERICAN COMMUNITIES
University of Washington, Seattle: Students and Faculty Face the Cold War

IN MAY 1948, A PHILOSOPHY PROFESSOR AT THE UNIVERSITY OF WASHINGTON in Seattle answered a knock on his office door. Two state legislators, members of the state's Committee on Un-American Activities, entered. "Our information," they charged, "puts you in the center of a Communist conspiracy."

The accused professor, Melvin Rader, had never been a Communist. During the 1930s, alarmed by the rise of fascism, Rader had become a prominent political activist in his community. At one point, he served as president of the University of Washington Teacher's Union, which had formed during the upsurge of labor organizing during the New Deal. When invited to join the Communist Party, Rader bluntly refused.

Nonetheless, Rader was caught up in a second Red Scare—the first had been that of 1919–20 (see Chapter 22)—that curtailed free speech and political activity on campuses throughout the United States. At some universities, such as Yale, the FBI set up camp with the consent of the college administration, spying on students and faculty, screening the credentials of job or scholarship applicants, and enticing students to report on friends or roommates. The University of Washington administration turned down the Physics Department's recommendation to hire J. Robert Oppenheimer, the famed atomic scientist and former director of Los Alamos Scientific Laboratory who had become a vocal opponent of the arms race.

Although one state legislator claimed that "not less than 150 members" of the University of Washington faculty were subversives, the state's Committee on Un-American Activities turned up just six Communist Party members. These six were hauled before the university's Faculty Committee on Tenure and Academic Freedom. Three were ultimately dismissed, while the other three were placed on probation.

What had provoked this paranoia? Instead of peace in the wake of World War II, "Cold War"—tense, icy relations but no outright fighting—prevailed between the United States and the Soviet Union. Uneasy wartime allies, the two superpowers now viewed each other as archenemies. Within the United States, the Cold War demanded pledges of absolute loyalty from citizens in every institution, from universities to unions and from the media to government itself.

Without the Cold War, this era might have marked one of the most fruitful in the history of higher education. The Servicemen's Readjustment Act, popularly known as the G.I. Bill of Rights, passed by Congress in 1944, offered stipends covering tuition and living expenses to veterans attending vocational schools or college. By the 1947–48 academic year, the federal government was subsidizing nearly half of all male college students. At the University of Washington, the student population in 1946 had grown by 50 percent over its prewar peak of 10,000, and veterans represented two-thirds of the student body.

The Cold War squelched much of that. FBI director J. Edgar Hoover testified that the college campuses were centers of "red propaganda." Due to "Communistic" teachers and "Communist-line textbooks," a senator wailed, thousands of parents sent "their sons and daughters to college as good Americans," only to see them return home "four years later as wild-eyed radicals."

These extravagant charges were far from true. The overwhelming majority of college graduates in the late 1940s and 1950s were conservative and conformist. Nevertheless, several states, including Washington, enacted or revived loyalty-security programs, obligating all state employees to swear in writing their loyalty to the United States and to disclaim membership in any subversive organization. Nationwide, approximately 200 "radical" faculty members were dismissed outright and many others were denied tenure. Thousands of students simply left school, dropped out of organizations, or changed friends after "visits" from FBI agents or interviews with administrators.

This tense, gloomy mood reversed the wave of optimism that had swept through America only a few years earlier. V-J Day had escalated into two days of wild celebrations, ticker-tape parades, spontaneous dancing, and kisses for returning G.I.s. Americans, living in the richest and most powerful nation in the world, finally seemed to have gained the peace they had fought for and sacrificed to win. But peace proved fragile and elusive.

Seattle

GLOBAL INSECURITIES AT WAR'S END

The war that had engulfed the world from 1939 to 1945 created an international interdependence that no country could ignore. Never before, not even at the end of World War I, had hopes been so strong for a genuine "community of nations." But, as a 1945 opinion poll indicated, most Americans believed that prospects for a durable peace rested to a large degree on one factor: Soviet–American harmony.

FINANCING THE FUTURE

In 1941, Henry Luce, the publisher of *Time, Life,* and *Fortune* magazines, forecast the dawn of "the American Century." During the darkest days of World War II, he wrote that Americans must "accept wholeheartedly our duty and our opportunity as the most powerful and vital nation in the world and in consequence to assert upon the world the full impact of our influence, for such means as we see fit."

Americans had good reason to be confident about their prospects for setting the terms of reconstruction. Unlike Great Britain, France, and the Soviet Union, the United States had not only escaped the ravages of the war, but had actually prospered.

Yet many Americans recognized that massive wartime government spending, not the New Deal, had ended the nightmare of the Great Depression. A stark question loomed: What would happen when wartime production slowed and millions of troops returned home to claim jobs?

"We need markets—big markets—in which to buy and sell," answered Assistant Secretary of State for Economic Affairs Will Clayton. During the war, many business leaders had looked to the Soviet Union as a future customer. With that prospect vanishing, with potential Eastern European markets threatened, and with the enormous European colonies closed to American enterprise, U.S. business and government leaders decided to integrate Western Europe, Latin America, and Asia into an international economy open to American trade and investment.

During the final stages of the war, President Roosevelt's advisers laid plans to establish U.S. primacy in the postwar global economy. In July 1944, representatives from forty-four Allied nations met at Bretton Woods, New Hampshire, and established the International Bank for Reconstruction and Development (the World Bank) and the **International Monetary Fund (IMF)**. These institutions were expected to help rebuild war-torn Europe and Asia. The United States was the principal supplier of funds for the IMF and the World Bank (more than $7 billion to each) and thus, by determining the allocation of loans, could unilaterally reshape the global economy.

The Soviet Union participated at Bretton Woods, but refused to ratify the agreements. Accepting World Bank and IMF aid would, Stalin believed, make the Soviet Union an economic colony of the capitalist West. By spurning this aid, the Soviet Union economically isolated itself and its East European satellites.

THE DIVISION OF EUROPE

In the Atlantic Charter of 1941, the United States and Great Britain proclaimed the right of all nations to self-determination and renounced claims to new territories as spoils of war. Before the war ended, though,

WHAT STEPS did the United States take in the years following World War II to shape the economic and political future of Europe?

QUICK REVIEW

The IMF and the World Bank

- July 1944: Allies met at Bretton Woods, New Hampshire.
- International Monetary Fund and World Bank created to help rebuild and stabilize postwar economy.
- United States gained effective control of the new institutions.

International Monetary Fund (IMF) International organization established in 1945 to assist nations in maintaining stable currencies.

Representatives of the "Big Three" nations—the Soviet Union, the United Kingdom, and the United States—gathered at Potsdam, Germany, near Berlin, July 17–August 2, 1945. This photograph shows Stalin, Truman, and Churchill as they begin to discuss the terms of peace and postwar arrangements. They concluded by issuing the "Potsdam Declaration," which demanded Japan's unconditional surrender.

Churchill and Roosevelt violated the charter by dividing Europe into spheres of influence (see Chapter 25 and Map 26.1).

For Roosevelt, that strategy had seemed compatible with ensuring world peace. FDR balanced his internationalist idealism with a belief that the United States was entitled to extraordinary influence in Latin America and the Philippines and that other great powers might have similar privileges or responsibilities elsewhere. Roosevelt also recognized the diplomatic consequences of the brutal ground war that had been fought largely on Soviet territory: the Soviet Union's nonnegotiable demand for security along its western border.

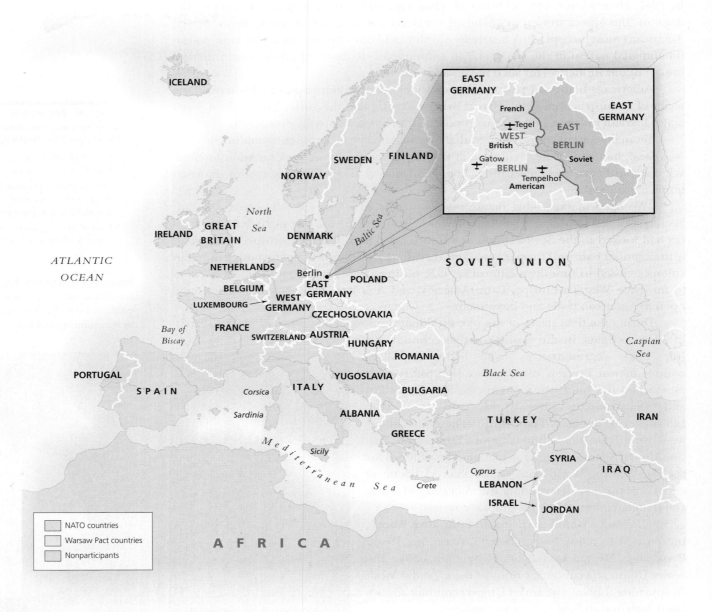

MAP 26.1

Divided Europe During the Cold War, Europe was divided into opposing military alliances, the North American Treaty Organization (NATO) and the Warsaw Pact (Communist bloc).

WHICH COUNTRIES were aligned with the United States, and which with the Soviet Union? How did the two superpowers exert influence and control over alliance members?

From the earliest days of fighting Hitler, the Soviet Union was intent on reestablishing its 1941 borders. At the Potsdam Conference, held in the bombed-out Berlin suburb in July 1945, Stalin not only regained but also extended his territory, annexing eastern Poland with Western approval and the little Baltic nations without it. Soviet influence quickly became paramount in all East European countries that the Red Army had occupied. The question remained: Did Stalin aim to bring all of Europe into the Communist domain?

At the Potsdam Conference, when the wartime allies began to plan Germany's future, that question loomed over all deliberations. They decided to divide the conquered nation into four occupation zones, each temporarily ruled by one of the Allied nations. They could not agree on long-term plans, however.

After the war, continuing disagreements about the future of Germany darkened hopes for Soviet-American cooperation. By July 1946, Americans had begun to withhold reparations due to the Soviets from their occupation zone and began to grant amnesty to some former Nazis. Then, in December, the Americans and British merged their zones and invited France and the Soviet Union to join. France agreed; Stalin, fearing a resurgence of a united Germany, refused.

The United States and the Soviet Union were now at loggerheads. Twice in the twentieth century, Germany had invaded Russia, and the Soviet Union interpreted any moves toward German reunification as menacing. For their part, American policymakers, assuming Stalin to be aggressively expansionist, envisioned a united Germany as a bulwark against further Soviet encroachments.

THE UNITED NATIONS AND HOPES FOR COLLECTIVE SECURITY

In 1944 at the Dumbarton Oaks Conference in Washington, and again in April 1945 at San Francisco, the Allies worked to shape the United Nations (UN) as a world organization that would arbitrate disputes among member nations and stop aggressors, by force if necessary.

The terms of membership, however, limited the UN's ability to mediate disputes. Although all fifty nations that signed the UN charter voted in the General Assembly, only five (the United States, Great Britain, the Soviet Union, France, and China) served permanently on the Security Council, and each had absolute veto power over the Council's decisions.

The UN achieved its greatest success with its humanitarian programs. Its relief agency gave war-torn European and Asian countries billions of dollars for medical supplies, food, and clothing. The UN also dedicated itself to the high principles enunciated in its 1948 Universal Declaration of Human Rights.

On other issues, however, the UN operated strictly along lines dictated by the emerging **Cold War**. The Western nations allied with the United States held the balance of power and controlled the admission of new members. For example, in 1949 when the Communists won the Chinese civil war (discussed later), the Western powers would block the new People's Republic from claiming China's UN seat, held by the defeated Nationalists on Taiwan. East–West polarization made negotiated settlements virtually impossible.

THE POLICY OF CONTAINMENT

In March 1946, in a speech delivered in Fulton, Missouri, Winston Churchill spoke to the end of wartime cooperation. With President Truman at his side, the former British prime minister solemnly intoned: "An iron curtain has descended across the [European] continent." He called directly upon the United States to recognize its "awe-inspiring accountability to the future" and, in alliance with Great Britain, act vigorously to stop Soviet expansion.

Although Truman at first responded cautiously to Churchill's warning, his administration ultimately rose to the challenge. As a policy uniting military, economic, and

Cold War The political and economic confrontation between the Soviet Union and the United States that dominated world affairs from 1946 to 1989.

HOW DID the Truman Doctrine shape U.S. postwar foreign policy?

Churchill's "Iron Curtain" Speech (1946) at **www.myhistorylab.com**

diplomatic strategies, the "containment" of communism had a powerful ideological dimension—an "us versus them" division of the world into "freedom" and "slavery."

THE TRUMAN DOCTRINE

• • Read the Document

George F. Kennan, The Long Telegram (1946) at **www.myhistorylab.com**

• • Read the Document

Exploring America: The Truman Doctrine at **www.myhistorylab.com**

Truman's attitude toward the Soviet Union was not always consistent; during the first years after the war, at times he attempted to be conciliatory. Among U.S. policymakers, however, an anti-Soviet consensus was growing, fed by perceptions that Stalin was taking a hard line. In February 1946, diplomat George F. Kennan sent an 8,000-word "long telegram" from Moscow to the State Department, insisting that Soviet fanaticism made cooperation impossible. The Soviet Union intended to extend its realm not by military means alone, he explained, but by "subversion" within "free" nations. In the long run, Kennan predicted, the Soviet system would collapse from within, but until that happened the West should pursue a policy of containment.

A perceived crisis in the Mediterranean marked the turning point. On February 21, 1947, amid a civil war in Greece, Great Britain informed the U.S. State Department that it could no longer afford to prop up the anti-Communist government there and announced its intention to withdraw all aid. Without U.S. intervention, Truman concluded, Greece, Turkey, and perhaps the entire oil-rich Middle East would fall under Soviet control. But, warned an influential Republican senator, Congress would not act unless the president "scare[d] hell out of the American people."

On March 12, 1947, the president made his case in a speech to Congress. Never naming the Soviet Union, he appealed for all-out resistance to a "certain ideology" wherever it appeared in the world. The preservation of peace and the freedom of all Americans depended, the president insisted, on containing communism.

Congress approved $400 million to aid Greece and Turkey, which helped conservative forces in those countries crush left-wing rebels. By dramatically opposing communism, Truman somewhat buoyed his sagging popularity and helped generate popular support for an anticommunist crusade at home and abroad.

The significance of what became known as the **Truman Doctrine** far outlasted events in the Mediterranean: the United States had declared its right to intervene to save other nations from communism. It was now the responsibility of the United States, the White House insisted, to safeguard what was coming to be called the Free World by any means necessary. They had fused anticommunism and internationalism into a strong foreign policy.

THE MARSHALL PLAN

The Truman Doctrine complemented the European Recovery Program, commonly known as the Marshall Plan. Introduced in a commencement speech at Harvard University on June 5, 1947, by Secretary of State George C. Marshall, the plan sought to reduce "hunger, poverty, desperation, and chaos" and to restore "the confidence of the European people in the economic future of their own countries and of Europe as a whole." Indirectly, the Marshall Plan aimed to turn back left-wing Socialist and Communist bids for votes in Western Europe. Not least, the plan was also designed to boost the U.S. economy by securing a European market for American goods.

Considered by many historians the most successful postwar U.S. diplomatic venture, the **Marshall Plan** improved the climate for a viable capitalist economy in Western Europe and, in effect, brought aid recipients into bilateral agreements with the United States. In addition, the United States and seventeen Western European nations ratified the tariff-cutting General Agreement on Tariffs and Trade pact, thus opening all to U.S. trade and investment.

As Truman later acknowledged, the Marshall Plan and the Truman Doctrine were "two halves of the same walnut." The Marshall Plan drove a deeper wedge between the

QUICK REVIEW

Postwar Foreign Policy

♦ Truman launched the nation into a global battle against communism.

♦ The United States pledged to help countries that faced external pressure or internal revolution.

♦ The United States played a decisive role in the rebuilding of Europe.

Truman Doctrine President Harry Truman's statement in 1947 that the United States should assist other nations that were facing external pressure or internal revolution.

Marshall Plan Secretary of State George C. Marshall's European Recovery Plan of June 5, 1947, committing the United States to help in the rebuilding of post–World War II Europe.

OVERVIEW | Major Cold War Policies

Date	Policy	Provisions
1947	Truman Doctrine	Pledged the United States to the containment of communism in Europe and elsewhere. The doctrine was the foundation of Truman's foreign policy. It impelled the United States to support any nation whose stability was threatened by communism or the Soviet Union.
1947	Federal Employees Loyalty and Security Program	Established by Executive Order 9835, this barred Communists and fascists from federal employment and outlined procedures for investigating current and prospective federal employees.
1947	Marshall Plan	U.S. program to aid war-torn Europe, also known as the European Recovery Program. The Marshall Plan was a cornerstone in the U.S. use of economic policy to contain communism.
1947	National Security Act	Established Department of Defense (to coordinate the three armed services), the National Security Council (to advise the president on security issues), and the Central Intelligence Agency (to gather and evaluate intelligence data).
1948	Smith-Mundt Act	Launched an overseas campaign of anti-Communist propaganda.
1949	North Atlantic Treaty Organization (NATO)	A military alliance of twelve nations formed to deter possible aggression of the Soviet Union against Western Europe.
1950	NSC-68	National Security Council Paper calling for an expanded and aggressive U.S. defense policy, including greater military spending and higher taxes.
1950	Internal Security Act (also known as the McCarran Act and the Subversive Activities Control Act)	Legislation providing for the registration of all Communist and totalitarian groups and authorizing the arrest of suspect persons during a national emergency.
1951	Psychological Strategy Board	Created to coordinate anti–Communist propaganda campaigns.
1952	Immigration and Nationality Act (also known as McCarran Walter Immigration Act)	Reaffirmed the national origins quota system but tightened immigration controls, barring homosexuals and people considered subversive from entering the United States.

United States and the Soviet Union. Although invited to participate, Stalin denounced the plan for what it was—an American scheme to rebuild Germany and incorporate it into an anti-Soviet bloc. Soon after the announcement of the Marshall Plan, the Soviet Union tightened its grip in Eastern Europe.

THE BERLIN CRISIS AND THE FORMATION OF NATO

Within a year of the start of the Marshall Plan, the United States and Britain moved closer to the goal of economically integrating their occupation zones in Germany into the western sphere of influence. A common currency was established for these zones. Stalin reacted on June 24, 1948, by halting all traffic to the western occupation zones of Berlin, deep within Soviet-occupied eastern Germany (see Map 26.1).

The **Berlin blockade** created both a crisis and an opportunity for the Truman administration. With help from the Royal Air Force, the United States began an unprecedented around-the-clock airlift delivering nearly 2 million tons of supplies to West Berliners. Stalin finally lifted the blockade in May 1949, clearing the way for the western powers to merge their occupation zones into a single nation, the Federal Republic of Germany. The

Berlin blockade Three-hundred-day Soviet blockade of land access to United States, British, and French occupation zones in Berlin, 1948–1949.

The Nazi occupation left Greece in economic ruins. Hunger and malnutrition were widespread. However, postwar foreign aid at first went mainly to fortify the military struggle against Communism. By 1949, after the civil war ended, government officials directed foreign aid to civilian needs. This photograph shows children lining up in Athens to receive bread made from wheat supplied by Marshall Plan.

Soviet Union countered by turning its zone into the communist-dominated German Democratic Republic.

In April 1949, ten European nations, Canada, and the United States formed the **North Atlantic Treaty Organization (NATO)**, a mutual-defense pact. NATO complemented the Marshall Plan, strengthening economic ties among the member nations. It also deepened divisions between Eastern and Western Europe, making a permanent military mobilization on both sides almost inevitable.

Global implications flowed from the forging of the North Atlantic alliance. Several Western European allies ruled valuable but restive colonial empires. During the war, FDR had urged British and French leaders to start dismantling their empires. In 1947, a financially strapped Britain granted independence to India and Pakistan, and under U.S. pressure, the Dutch gave up Indonesia in 1949. The French, however, were determined to regain Indochina, lost to Japan before Pearl Harbor (see Chapter 25). Cold War anticommunism now trumped traditional American anticolonialism. Because the most important fighter against France's attempt to reconquer Indochina was Vietnamese communist Ho Chi Minh, Truman decided that France deserved American support. The first seeds had been planted of what would eventually become an American commitment to fight communism in Vietnam.

The Truman administration took Latin America for granted and was satisfied when the right-wing dictators ruling much of that region proclaimed themselves staunchly anticommunist. The most positive gesture that the United States made toward Latin opinion was designating Puerto Rico a self-governing "commonwealth" in 1952. Beneath the surface, though, trouble was brewing for the United States throughout the hemisphere.

Between 1947 and 1949, the Truman administration had defined the policies that would shape the Cold War for decades to come. The Truman Doctrine explained the ideological basis of containment; the Marshall Plan put into place its economic underpinnings in Western Europe; and NATO created the mechanisms for military defense. When NATO extended membership to a rearmed West Germany in May 1955, the Soviet Union responded by creating a counterpart, the Warsaw Pact, including East Germany.

ATOMIC DIPLOMACY

The containment policy depended on the ability of the United States to back its commitments through military force, and Truman invested his faith in the U.S. monopoly of atomic weapons. After 1945, the United States began to build an atomic stockpile and to conduct tests on remote Pacific islands.

In August 1949, the Soviet Union tested its own atomic bomb and the arms race that scientists had feared since 1945 was now under way. By the early 1950s, both the United States and the Soviet Union were testing hydrogen bombs a thousand times more powerful than the weapons dropped on Hiroshima and Nagasaki in 1945. By the late 1950s, stockpiles of nuclear bombs were being supplemented by nuclear-armed missiles.

The United States and the Soviet Union were firmly locked into the Cold War. The nuclear arms race risked global catastrophe, diverted economic resources, and fed public fears of impending doom. Despite the Allied victory in World War II, the world had again divided into hostile camps.

North Atlantic Treaty Organization (NATO) Organization of ten European countries, Canada, and the United States whom together formed a mutual defense pact in April 1949.

COLD WAR LIBERALISM

Truman wanted to enlarge the New Deal, but settled on a modest domestic agenda to promote social welfare and an anti-isolationist, anti-Communist foreign policy. Fatefully, during his administration, domestic and foreign policy became increasingly entangled. Out of that entanglement emerged a distinctive brand of liberalism—Cold War liberalism.

HOW DID the "Fair Deal" differ from the "New Deal"?

"TO ERR IS TRUMAN"

Within a year of assuming office, Harry Truman's poll ratings were among the lowest of any twentieth-century president. The responsibilities of reestablishing peacetime conditions seemed to overwhelm the new president. "To err is Truman," critics sneered.

The task of converting from a wartime to a peacetime economy was enormous. Truman faced millions of restless would-be consumers tired of rationing and eager to spend their wartime savings. The demand for consumer items rapidly outran supply, fueling inflation and a huge black market.

In 1945 and 1946, the country appeared ready to explode. While homemakers protested rising prices by boycotting neighborhood stores, industrial workers struck in unprecedented numbers. In May 1946, Truman proposed to draft striking railroad workers. The usually conservative Senate killed this plan.

Congress defeated most of Truman's proposals to revive the New Deal. One week after Japan's surrender, the president introduced a twenty-one-point program that included greater unemployment compensation, higher minimum wages, and housing assistance. Later he added national health insurance and atomic-energy legislation. Congress rejected most of these bills and passed the Employment Act of 1946, but only with substantial modification. The act created the **Council of Economic Advisers**, experts who would counsel the president. In the midterm elections, voters gave Republicans majorities in both houses of Congress and many state capitols. Symbolically repudiating FDR, Republican-dominated state legislatures ratified the Twenty-Second Amendment, limiting future presidents to two terms.

The Republicans, dominant in Congress for the first time since 1931, mounted a counterattack on the New Deal, beginning with organized labor. Claiming that "Big Labor" had gone too far, the Eightieth Congress aimed at abolishing many practices legalized by the Wagner Act of 1935 (see Chapter 24). The resultant **Taft-Hartley Act of 1947**, passed over Truman's veto: outlawed the closed shop, the secondary boycott, and the use of union dues for political activities; mandated an eighty-day cooling-off period in the case of strikes affecting "national safety or health"; and required all union officials to swear that they were not Communists. Truman himself would later invoke the act against strikers.

Council of Economic Advisers   Board of three professional economists established in 1946 to advise the president on economic policy.

Taft-Hartley Act   Federal legislation of 1947 that substantially limited the tools available to labor unions in labor-management disputes.

Police and strikers confront each other in Los Angeles during one of many postwar strikes in 1946. Employers wanted to cut wages, and workers refused to give up the higher living standard achieved during the war.

THE 1948 ELECTION

Harry Truman had considered some of Roosevelt's advisers "crackpots and the lunatic fringe." By 1946, he forced out many of the remaining social planners who had

	Electoral Vote (%)	Popular Vote (%)
HARRY S. TRUMAN (Democrat)	303 (57)	24,105,812 (49.5)
Thomas E. Dewey (Republican)	189 (36)	21,970,065 (45.1)
Strom Thurmond (States' Rights)	39 (7)	1,169,063 (2.4)
Henry A. Wallace (Progressive)	—	1,157,172 (2.4)
Other candidates (Socialist, Prohibition, Socialist Labor, Socialist Workers)	—	272,713 (0.6)

MAP 26.2

The Election of 1948 Harry Truman holds up a copy of the *Chicago Daily Tribune* with headlines confidently and mistakenly predicting the victory of his opponent, Thomas E. Dewey. Initially an unpopular candidate, Truman made a whistle-stop tour of the country by train to win 49.5 percent of the popular vote to Dewey's 45.1 percent.

IN WHICH regions was Truman most popular? Why?

QUICK REVIEW

Truman's 1948 Presidential Campaign

- Truman conducted a vigorous campaign in all parts of the country.
- Truman tied Dewey to inflation, housing shortages, and fears about Social Security.
- Dewey's failure to campaign aggressively may have cost him the election.

Dixiecrat   States' Rights Democrats.

staffed the Washington bureaus for more than a decade. Truman also fired Roosevelt's secretary of commerce and former vice president, Henry Wallace, for advocating a more conciliatory policy toward the Soviet Union.

Wallace, refusing to fade away, vowed to run against Truman for president. He pledged to expand New Deal programs by moving boldly to establish full employment, racial equality, and stronger unions. He also promised peace with the Soviet Union. As the 1948 election neared, Wallace appeared a viable candidate on the new Progressive Party ticket.

Truman shrewdly repositioned himself. He deflated Wallace by branding him a tool of the Communists. Truman also attacked the conservative congressional Republicans, proposing federal funds for education, housing, and medical insurance. Summoning Congress back for a special session after the summertime political conventions of 1948, he dared it to enact the Republican platform—and when it predictably failed—lambasted the "do-nothing Congress."

Wallace and the Republican nominee, New York governor Thomas E. Dewey, had taken strong leads on civil rights, but Truman outflanked them. In July 1948, he issued executive decrees desegregating the armed forces and banning discrimination in the federal civil service. In response, some 300 southern delegates bolted from the Democratic National Convention and named a States' Rights ("**Dixiecrat**") ticket, headed by the segregationist governor of South Carolina, J. Strom Thurmond. With the South looking as good as lost, with Wallace threatening to siphon off left-leaning Democrats, and with soothing Dewey heading the Republicans, Truman appeared doomed.

But "Give 'em Hell Harry's" vigorous campaign slowly revived the New Deal coalition. Fear of Republicans who had passed Taft-Hartley won back the bulk of organized labor, and Truman's decision in May 1948 immediately to recognize the new State of Israel kept many liberal Jews loyally Democratic. The success of the Berlin airlift buoyed the president's popularity, and by Election Day growing anti-Communist sentiment among liberals was limiting the Wallace vote to the extreme left. Meanwhile, Dewey tried to coast to victory by appearing bland and "presidential."

Polls predicted a Dewey victory—but the pollsters stopped taking samples several weeks before Election Day and so missed a late Democratic surge. Truman won the popular vote by a 5 percent margin, trouncing Dewey 303 to 189 in electoral votes. Democrats regained majorities in both houses of Congress (see Map 26.2).

THE FAIR DEAL

"Every segment of our population and every individual has a right," Truman announced in January 1949, "to expect from our Government a fair deal." Democratic congressional majorities would, he hoped, translate campaign promises into laws and expand the New Deal. But a powerful bloc of conservative southern Democrats and midwestern Republicans turned back his domestic agenda.

The National Housing Act of 1949 provided federally funded low-income housing. Congress also raised the minimum wage (from 40 to 75 cents per hour) and brought an additional 10 million people under Social Security coverage. Otherwise Truman made no headway. He and congressional liberals introduced a variety of bills to weaken southern racism, including a federal antilynching law, outlawing poll taxes, and banning discrimination in interstate transportation. Southern-led filibusters killed them all, while conservative-dominated congressional committees bottled up his initiatives for national health insurance, federal aid to education, and a repeal or modification of Taft-Hartley.

Truman's greatest domestic achievement was to articulate the basic principles of Cold War liberalism, which would remain the northern Democratic agenda for decades to come. Truman's Fair Deal promoted bread-and-butter issues and economic growth. His administration insisted, therefore, on an ambitious program of expanded foreign trade, while relying on the federal government to encourage higher productivity. Equally important, Truman reshaped liberalism by making anticommunism a key element in both foreign policy and domestic affairs.

THE COLD WAR AT HOME

By the late 1940s, the Communist Party, U.S.A., formed in 1919 and at the peak of its influence in the 1930s, was steadily losing ground. Nevertheless, anticommunism now held center stage in domestic politics. The federal government, with help from the media, led the crusade, using the threat of communism to reorder its operation and to quell dissent. Seeking absolute security, Americans permitted a greater concentration of power in government and, while promising to lead the Free World, allowed many of their own rights to be circumscribed.

THE NATIONAL SECURITY ACT OF 1947

The imperative of national security destroyed old-fashioned isolation, forcing the United States into unprecedented alliances such as NATO and global leadership. Such responsibility required massive resources. Truman, therefore, demanded a substantial increase in the size of the federal government in both military forces and surveillance agencies. Security measures designed to keep the nation in a steady state of preparedness, readily justified during wartime, were now extended indefinitely.

The sweeping National Security Act, passed by Congress in July 1947, established the Department of Defense and the **National Security Council (NSC)** to administer and coordinate defense policies and advise the president. Ties between the armed forces and the State Department grew closer as retired military officers routinely filled positions in the State Department and diplomatic corps. The act also created the National Security Resources Board (NSRB) to coordinate plans throughout the government "in the event of war" and, for the first time in American history, to maintain military preparedness in peacetime.

The Department of Defense and the NSRB became the principal sponsor of scientific research during the first ten years of the Cold War. Federal agencies tied to military projects supplied well over 90 percent of the funding for research in the physical sciences, much of it in major universities.

The **Central Intelligence Agency (CIA)** was another product of the National Security Act. With roots in the wartime Office of Strategic Services (OSS), the new CIA became a permanent operation devoted to collecting political, military, and economic information for security purposes throughout the world. (It was barred from domestic intelligence gathering: that was the domain of its rival, the FBI.)

The national-security state required a huge workforce. Before World War II, approximately 900,000 civilians worked for the federal government, about 10 percent of them in security work; by the beginning of the Cold War, nearly 4 million people were on the government's payroll, 75 percent of them in national-security agencies.

National security absorbed increasingly large portions of the nation's resources. By the end of Truman's second term, defense allocations accounted for 10 percent of GNP, directly or indirectly employed hundreds of thousands of well-paid workers, and subsidized

HOW DID concerns about national security lead to the abridgement of civil liberties?

How Communism Works (1938) at **www.myhistorylab.com**

QUICK REVIEW

National Security Act of 1947

- Established Department of Defense, the National Security Council, and the National Security Resources Board (NSRB).

- Department of Defense and the NSRB became principal sponsors of scientific research.

- National security spending required a substantial increase in the size of the defense budget.

National Security Council (NSC)
The formal policy-making body for national defense and foreign relations, created in 1947 and consisting of the president, the secretary of defense, the secretary of state, and others appointed by the president.

Central Intelligence Agency (CIA)
Agency established in 1947 that coordinates the gathering and evaluation of military and economic information on other nations.

Published in 1947, this full-color comic book appeared as one of many sensationalistic illustrations of the threat of the "commie menace" to Americans at home. Approximately 4 million copies of *Is This Tomorrow?* were printed, the majority distributed to church groups or sold for ten cents a copy.

some of the nation's most profitable corporations. This vast financial outlay created the rationale for permanent, large-scale military spending and powerfully stimulated economic growth.

THE LOYALTY-SECURITY PROGRAM

National security required increased surveillance at home. Within two weeks of proclaiming the Truman Doctrine, the president signed **Executive Order 9835** on March 21, 1947, establishing a civilian loyalty program for all federal employees. The new Federal Employees Loyalty and Security Program in effect established a political test for federal employment. It also outlined procedures for investigating current and prospective federal employees. The loyalty review boards often asked employees about their opinions of the Soviet Union, the Marshall Plan, or NATO and whether they would report fellow workers if they found out they were Communists. Any employee could be dismissed merely on "reasonable grounds," including guilt by association (that is, knowing or being related to a "subversive" person), rather than on proof of disloyalty.

Many state and municipal governments enacted loyalty programs and required public employees, including teachers at all levels, to sign loyalty oaths. In all, some 6.6 million people underwent loyalty and security checks. An estimated 500 government workers were fired, and perhaps as many as 6,000 more chose to resign. Numerous private employers and labor unions also instituted loyalty programs.

Attorney General Tom C. Clark aided this effort by publishing a list of hundreds of potentially subversive organizations. There was no right of appeal for organizations so listed. The famous "Attorney General's List" effectively outlawed many political and social organizations, stigmatizing hundreds of thousands of individuals who had done nothing illegal. Church associations, civil rights organizations, musical groups, and even summer camps appeared on the list. Fraternal and social institutions, especially popular among aging Eastern European immigrants, were among the largest organizations destroyed. New York State, for example, legally dismantled the International Workers' Order, which had provided insurance to nearly 200,000 immigrants and their families.

In 1950, Congress overrode the president's veto to pass a bill that Truman called "the greatest danger to freedom of press, speech, and assembly since the Sedition Act of 1798." The Internal Security (or McCarran) Act required Communist organizations to register with the Subversive Activities Control Board—if they did not register, they were prosecuted—and authorized the arrest of suspect persons during a national emergency. The Immigration and Nationality Act, also sponsored by Republican senator Pat McCarran of Nevada and adopted in 1952, again over Truman's veto, barred people deemed "subversive" or "homosexual" from becoming citizens or even visiting the United States. It also empowered the attorney general to deport immigrants who were members of Communist organizations, even if they had become citizens.

THE SECOND RED SCARE

The supposed link between Hollywood and Communism was the particular focus of the **House Un-American Activities Committee (HUAC)**. HUAC had the power to subpoena witnesses and to compel them to answer all questions or face contempt of Congress charges. In well-publicized hearings held in Hollywood in October 1947, the mother of actress Ginger Rogers defended her daughter by saying that she had been duped into appearing in the 1943 pro-Soviet wartime film *Tender Comrade* and "had been forced" to

read the subversive line "Share and share alike, that's democracy." HUAC encouraged such testimony by other "friendly witnesses," including actors Ronald Reagan and Gary Cooper. The committee intimidated many others, who feared loss of their careers, into naming former friends and coworkers in order to be cleared for future work in Hollywood.

A small but prominent minority refused to cooperate with HUAC. By claiming the freedoms of speech and association guaranteed by the First and Sixth Amendments, they became known as "unfriendly witnesses," and a handful served prison sentences for refusing to "name names."

Hollywood studios would not employ any writer, director, or actor who refused to cooperate with HUAC. The resulting blacklist remained in effect until the 1960s and limited the production of films dealing with "controversial" social or political issues.

The labor movement also became a victim of this second Red Scare. Like the Hollywood film industry, a sizable portion of its leaders and members had affiliated with the Communist Party or supported liberal causes in the 1930s, and they emerged from their wartime experiences even more deeply committed to social justice. The Food, Tobacco, Agricultural, and Allied Workers-Congress of Industrial Organizations (FTA-CIO) organized a postwar campaign against discriminatory practices within southern industry and allied with local civil rights activists to spearhead a major organizing drive. In 1947, the R.J. Reynolds Tobacco Company struck back by characterizing union organizers and supporters as Moscow's pawns. A year later, CIO president Philip Murray decided to rid his organization of all Communists. Soon, eleven unions representing more than a million workers were expelled.

SPY CASES

In August 1948, *Time* magazine editor Whittaker Chambers appeared before HUAC to name Alger Hiss as a fellow Communist in the Washington underground during the 1930s. Hiss denied the charges and sued his accuser for slander. Chambers then

McCarthyism Anti-Communist attitudes and actions associated with Senator Joe McCarthy in the early 1950s, including smear tactics and innuendo.

revealed his trump card, a cache of films of secret documents that had been hidden in a hollowed-out pumpkin on his Maryland farm. The statute of limitations for espionage having run out, a federal grand jury in January 1950 convicted Hiss of perjury for denying he knew Chambers. He received a five-year prison term. Hiss was released two years later proclaiming his innocence, a position he held throughout his life. Historians remain divided on the question of his spying.

The most dramatic spy case of the era involved Julius Rosenberg, a former government engineer, and his wife Ethel, who were accused of conveying atomic secrets to Soviet agents during World War II. The Rosenberg case depended on testimony of alleged accomplices, some of them secretly coached by the FBI. Although the Rosenbergs maintained their innocence to the end, in March 1951 a jury found them both guilty. They died in the electric chair on June 19, 1953. Documents declassified in the 1990s provided evidence of Julius (but not Ethel) Rosenberg's guilt.

McCarthyism

((•●—|Hear the Audio

Joseph P. McCarthy Speech at
www.myhistorylab.com

On February 9, 1950, in a speech in Wheeling, West Virginia, Republican senator Joseph R. McCarthy of Wisconsin announced that the United States had been sold out by the "traitorous actions" of men holding important positions in the federal government. These acted as part of a conspiracy, he charged, of 205 card-carrying Communists in the State Department.

McCarthy refused to reveal names because, in reality, he had none. Nevertheless, a few days later, he told persistent reporters: "I'm not going to tell you anything. I just want you to know I've got a pailful [of dirt] . . . and I'm going to use it where it does the most good." Although investigations uncovered not a single Communist in the State Department, McCarthy launched a flamboyant offensive against New Deal Democrats and the Truman administration for failing to defend the nation's security. He gave his name to the era: **McCarthyism**.

Behind the blitz of publicity, the previously obscure junior senator from Wisconsin had struck a chord. Communism seemed to many Americans to be much more than a military threat; it was nothing less than a demonic force undermining all basic values. It compelled patriots to prepare Americans even for atomic warfare: "Better Dead Than Red."

Civil rights organizations faced the worst persecution since the 1920s. But attacks on women's organizations and homosexuals, which cloaked deep fears about changing sexual mores, also took a huge toll. Aided by FBI reports, the federal government fired up to sixty homosexuals per month in the early 1950s. Dishonorable discharges from the U.S. armed forces for homosexuality, an administrative procedure without appeal, also increased dramatically.

Joseph McCarthy and his fellow Redhunters eventually burned themselves out. During nationally televised congressional hearings in 1954, not only did McCarthy fail to prove his wild charges of Communist infiltration of the Army, but also in the glare of television appeared deranged. Cowed for four years, the Senate finally censured him for "conduct unbecoming a member."

The tables turned on Senator Joseph McCarthy (1908–57) after he instigated an investigation of the U.S. Army for harboring Communists. A special congressional committee then investigated McCarthy for attempting to make the Army grant special privileges to his staff aide, Private David Schine. During the televised hearings, Senator McCarthy discredited himself. In December 1954, the Senate voted to censure him, thus robbing him of his power. He died three years later.

COLD WAR CULTURE

As the Truman Doctrine revealed, the Cold War did not necessarily mean military confrontation. Nor was it defined exclusively by a quest for economic supremacy. The Cold War embodied the struggle of one "way of life" against another. It was, in short, a contest of values. If Americans were to rebuild the world based on their own values, they must rededicate themselves to defending their birthright: freedom and democracy.

AN ANXIOUS MOOD

Post-war anxieties surfaced as major themes in popular culture. *The Best Years of Our Lives* (1946), one of the most acclaimed Hollywood films of the era, showed three fictional veterans trying to readjust to civilian life. The former soldiers found that dreams of reunion with family and loved ones, which had sustained them through years of fighting, now seemed hollow. The feeling of community shared with wartime buddies dissipated, leaving only profound loneliness in a crass, selfish society.

The genre of *film noir* (French for "black film") deepened this postwar moodiness into a pessimistic aesthetic. American movies like *Out of the Past, Detour,* and *They Live by Night* told stories of relentless fate and ruthless betrayal. The high-contrast lighting of these black-and-white films accentuated the difficulty of distinguishing friend from foe.

Serious literature vividly captured a sense of anxious alienation. Playwright Arthur Miller in *Death of a Salesman* (1949) sketched an exacting portrait of self-destructive individualism. Willy Loman, the play's hero, is obsessively devoted to his career in sales, but is nevertheless a miserable failure. J.D. Salinger's novel *Catcher in the Rye* (1951) explored the mental anguish of a teenage boy estranged by his parents' psychological distance and materialism.

Cold War anxiety manifested itself in a flurry of unidentified flying object (UFO) sightings. Thousands of Americans imagined that a Communist-like invasion from outer space was already underway or hoped that superior creatures might arrive to show the way to world peace. Hollywood fed these beliefs. In *The Invasion of the Body Snatchers* (1956), for example, a small town is captured by aliens who take over the minds of its inhabitants when they fall asleep, a subtle warning against apathy toward the threat of communist "subversion" (see Seeing History).

THE FAMILY AS BULWARK

Postwar prosperity helped to strengthen the ideal of domesticity, although many Americans interpreted their rush toward marriage and parenthood, as one writer put it, as a "defense—an impregnable bulwark" against the era's anxieties.

Young couples were marrying younger and producing more children than at any time in the past century. The Census Bureau predicted that the "baby boom" would be temporary. To everyone's surprise, the birthrate continued to grow at a record pace (see Figure 26.1).

The new families who enjoyed postwar prosperity inaugurated a spending spree of trailblazing proportions. By the time Truman left office, two-thirds of all American households claimed at least one television set.

These two trends—the baby boom and high rates of consumer spending—encouraged a major change in the middle-class family. Having worked during World War II, often in occupations traditionally closed to them, many women wished to continue in full-time employment. Reconversion to peacetime production forced the majority from their factory positions, but most women quickly returned to the work force. By 1952, 2 million more wives worked than during the war. Gone, however,

WHAT ROLE did population growth and prosperity play in shaping Cold War culture?

Interpreting the Past: *Cold War Fears and Nuclear Holocaust, pp. 708–709*

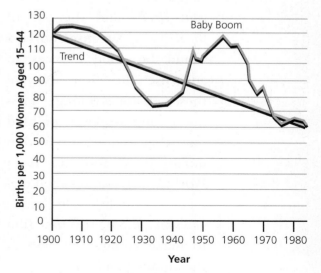

Figure 26.1 U.S. Birthrate, 1930–80
The bulge of the "baby boom," a leading demographic factor in the postwar economy, stands out for this fifty-year period.

National Archives and Records Administration.

The Hollywood Film
Invasion, U.S.A

Invasion, U.S.A. was the first of the genre of Red-scare films to do well at the box office. Shot in just seven days and released by Columbia Pictures in 1952, the film opens by depicting a group of well-off Americans, drinking casually in a New York bar and showing no particular concern about the imminent threat to their nation. Suddenly, they hear the news of horrific attacks by The Enemy. After atomic bombs fall and The Enemy approaches the nation's capital, they have all learned a potent lesson about complacency and begin to renounce their selfish ways. The group disperses, each character now understanding that freedom carries with it the price of vigilance.

HOW DID Hollywood and other forms of mass media help to shape Cold War culture in the late 1940s and early 1950s?

The Enemy is never named, but Slavic accents and references to the "People's Government" that takes over Manhattan strongly suggest that the evildoers are Russian Communists.

The film's poster builds on the foundation of fear. Studio publicists also advised local movie theaters to promote the movie along the same line: "Dress a young man in full paratroop regalia and have him walk through the principal streets of town in advance of playdate with a sign on his back reading HERE'S HOW IT WOULD HAPPEN IF IT HAPPENED NOW! SEE COLUMBIA PICTURES' *INVASION, U.S.A.* AT THE STATE THEATER FRIDAY!" The studio also suggested that blasts by air raid sirens and the use of local Civil Defense workers would be good choices to advertise the film. Despite these fear-provoking messages, one reviewer pointed out that poor production quality–stock footages from World War II–and stilted dialogue unintentionally made *Invasion, U.S.A,* the first film to make audiences laugh at the atomic bomb. ■

THEY PUSH A BUTTON AND VAST CITIES VANISH BEFORE YOUR VERY EYES!

INVASION U.S.A.

GERALD MOHR · PEGGIE CASTLE · DAN O'HERLIHY

were the high-paying unionized jobs in manufacturing. Instead, most women found low-wage jobs in the expanding service sector: clerical work, health care and education, and restaurant, hotel, and retail services. Women often worked out of "economic necessity" that is, to maintain a middle-class standard of living that now required more than one income (see Table 26.1).

Even though most women sought employment primarily to support their families, they ran up against popular opinion and expert advice urging them to go home. Polls registered resounding disapproval—by 86 percent of those surveyed—of a married woman working if jobs were scarce and her husband could support her. Noting that most Soviet women worked outside the home, many commentators appealed for a return to an imaginary "traditional" American family where men alone were breadwinners and women were exclusively homemakers.

Patterns of women's higher education reflected this conservative trend. Having made slight gains during World War II, when college-age men were serving in the armed forces or working in war industries, women lost ground after the **G.I. Bill** created a huge upsurge in male enrollment. Women represented 40 percent of all college graduates in 1940, but only 25 percent a decade later.

MILITARY-INDUSTRIAL COMMUNITIES IN THE AMERICAN WEST

All regions of the United States felt the impact of the Cold War, but none so directly as the West. World War II defense spending had stimulated the western economy and encouraged a mass westward migration of people eager to find wartime jobs. Following the war, many cities successfully converted to peacetime production. It was the Cold War, however, that by reviving defense funding gave the western economy its most important boost.

So much defense money—nearly 10 percent of the entire military budget—was poured by the federal government into California that the state's rate of economic growth between 1949 and 1952 outpaced that of the nation as a whole; nearly 40 percent came from aircraft manufacturing alone. Ten years later, an estimated one-third of all Los Angeles workers were employed by defense industries, particularly aerospace, and the absolute number of defense workers far exceeded those of the peak production

This photograph, taken in 1955, presents an ideal image of domestic life for American women during the Cold War. This young mother sits with her three small children in a well-equipped kitchen that depicts the high standard of living that symbolized the "American way of life."

 Read the Document

Ladies Home Journal, "Young Mother" (1956) at **www.myhistorylab.com**

QUICK REVIEW

Working Wives

♦ 1952: More wives worked than during the war but held lower-paying jobs.

♦ Many women worked to maintain a middle-class standard of living.

♦ Working women faced criticism by advocates of return to "traditional" family.

TABLE 26.1

Distribution of Total Personal Income among Various Segments of the Population, 1947–70 (in Percentages)*

Year	Poorest Fifth	Second Poorest Fifth	Middle Fifth	Second Wealthiest Fifth	Wealthiest Fifth	Wealthiest 5 Percent
1947	3.5	10.6	16.7	23.6	45.6	18.7
1950	3.1	10.5	17.3	24.1	45.0	18.2
1960	3.2	10.6	17.6	24.7	44.0	17.0
1970	3.6	10.3	17.2	24.7	44.1	16.9

Despite the general prosperity of the postwar era, the distribution of income remained essentially unchanged.

*Monetary income only.

Adapted from U.S. Bureau of the Census, *Historical Statistics of the United States, Colonial Times to 1970*, Bicentennial ed. (Washington, DC: U.S. Government Printing Office, 1975), p. 292.

G.I. Bill Legislation in June 1944 that eased the return of veterans into American society by providing educational and employment benefits.

years in World War II. The Bay Area also benefited economically from defense spending, and cities such as San Jose began their rise as home to the nation's budding high-technology industry.

The Cold War pumped new life into communities that had grown up during World War II. Hanford, Washington, and Los Alamos, New Mexico, both centers of the **Manhattan Project**, employed more people in the construction of the Cold War nuclear arsenal than in the development of the atom bomb. New communities accompanied the growth of the U.S. military bases and training camps in the West. Many of these installations, as well as hospitals and supply depots, not only survived but also expanded during the transition from the actual warfare of World War II to the threatened warfare of the Cold War. The availability of public lands with areas of sparse population made western states especially attractive to military planners designing such dangerous and secretive installations as the White Sands Missile Range in the New Mexico desert.

Local politicians, real estate agents, and merchants usually welcomed these developments as sources of revenue and employment. There were, however, heavy costs for speedy and unplanned federally induced growth. To accommodate the new populations, the government poured money into new highway systems but did little for public transportation. Uncontrolled sprawl, traffic congestion, air pollution, and strains on limited water and energy resources all grew with the military-industrial communities in the West. For those populations living near nuclear testing grounds, environmental degradation complemented the ultimate threat to their own physical well-being: over the next forty years, cancer rates soared.

"THE AMERICAN WAY"

Following the massive and spontaneous V-J Day celebrations, Americans began to retreat from public displays of patriotism, but soon new organizations, like the Freedoms Foundation of Valley Forge and the American Heritage Foundation, were joining the American Legion and the Chamber of Commerce in defining the "American way" in opposition to Soviet communism. These organizations sponsored events such as "freedom rallies" and "freedom fashion shows" to remind Americans of their nation's democratic values and commitment to free enterprise. In Mosinee, Wisconsin, for example, the American Legion used political theater to inculcate the American way, orchestrating an imaginary Communist coup in the small community.

Meanwhile, Attorney General Tom C. Clark, supported by Truman, by private donors, and by the American Heritage Foundation, was putting on the nation's rails the "Freedom Train." Carrying copies of the Bill of Rights, the Constitution, and the Emancipation Proclamation, the Freedom Train traveled to cities across the land.

Patriotic messages also permeated public education. Following guidelines set down by the Truman administration, teachers were to "strengthen national security through education" by designing their lesson plans to illustrate the superiority of the American democratic system over Soviet communism. In 1947, the federal Office of Education launched a "Zeal for Democracy" program for implementation by school boards nationwide. Meanwhile, in a national civil defense program, schoolchildren learned to "duck" under their desks and "cover" their heads in the event of a surprise Soviet nuclear attack.

Voices of protest were raised. The black poet Langston Hughes expressed his skepticism in verse, writing that he hoped the Freedom Train would carry no Jim Crow car. A brave minority of scholars protested infringements on academic freedom by refusing to sign loyalty oaths and by writing books pointing out the potential dangers of aggressively nationalistic foreign and domestic policies. But the chilling atmosphere made many individuals reluctant to express contrary opinions or ideas.

Manhattan Project   Scientific research project during World War II specifically devoted to developing the atomic bomb.

STALEMATE FOR THE DEMOCRATS

With Cold War tensions festering in Europe, neither the United States nor the Soviet Union would have predicted that events in Asia would bring them to the brink of a new world war. Yet in China, the most populous land on earth, Communists completed their seizure of power in late 1949. A few months later, in June 1950, Communist armies threatened to conquer all of Korea.

Truman sent American forces to conduct a "police action" in Korea, which within a few years absorbed more than 1.8 million U.S. troops with no victory in sight. For Truman, the "loss" of China and the Korean stalemate proved political suicide, ending the twenty-year Democratic lock on the presidency and the greatest era of reform in U.S. history.

HOW DID the Republicans win the presidency and control of Congress in 1952?

DEMOCRATIZING JAPAN AND "LOSING" CHINA

At the close of World War II, the United States acted deliberately to secure Japan firmly within its sphere of influence. General Douglas MacArthur directed an interim Japanese government in a modest reconstruction program that included land reform, creation of independent trade unions, abolition of contract marriages, granting of woman suffrage, sweeping demilitarization, and eventually a constitutional democracy that renounced war and barred Communists from all posts. American leaders worked to rebuild the nation's economy along capitalist lines and integrate Japan into an anti-Soviet bloc. Japan also housed huge U.S. military bases, placing U.S. troops and weapons on the doorstep of the Soviet Union's Asian rim.

China could not be handled so easily. After years of civil war, the pro–Western Nationalist government of Jiang Jeishi (Chiang Kai-shek) collapsed. Since World War II, the United States had been aiding Jiang's unpopular and corrupt regime, while warning him that without major reforms and a coalition with his political opponents, the Nationalists were heading for defeat. Jiang refused any concessions, and in the late 1940s the Truman administration cut off virtually all aid and then watched as Nationalist troops surrendered to the Communists, led by Mao Zedong. Abandoning the entire mainland, the defeated Nationalists fled to the island of Taiwan. On October 1, 1949, Mao proclaimed the People's Republic of China, and in February 1950, the Soviet Union and the People's Republic of China signed an alliance.

China's "fall" to communism set off an uproar in the United States. The Asia First wing of the Republican Party, which saw the Far East rather than Europe as the primary target of U.S. trade and investment, blamed Truman for the "loss" of China. The president's adversaries, pointing to the growing menace of "international communism," called the Democrats the "party of treason."

THE KOREAN WAR

At the end of World War II, the Allies had divided the Korean peninsula at the 38th Parallel. Although all Koreans hoped to reunite their nation under an independent government, the line between North and South hardened. While the United States backed the unpopular southern government of Syngman Rhee (the Republic of Korea), the Soviet Union sponsored a rival government in North Korea under Communist Kim Il-Sung (see Map 26.3).

Estimates runs as high as 6 million for the number of civilian refugees during the Korean War. This American news photograph, published in 1950, shows American soldiers heading toward battles sites while Korean refugees move in the opposite direction.

See the Map

The Korean War, 1950–1953 at
www.myhistorylab.com

On June 25, 1950, the U.S. State Department received a cablegram reporting an invasion of South Korea by the Communist North. Truman sought the Security Council's approval to send troops to defend South Korea under the UN's collective-security provisions. With the Soviet delegate withdrawn as an act to protest the exclusion of China, the Security Council backed the U.S. request for intervention.

Military events seemed at first to justify the president's decision. Seoul, the capital of South Korea, fell to North Korean troops within weeks, and Communist forces pushed south, occupying most of the peninsula. The situation appeared grim until Truman

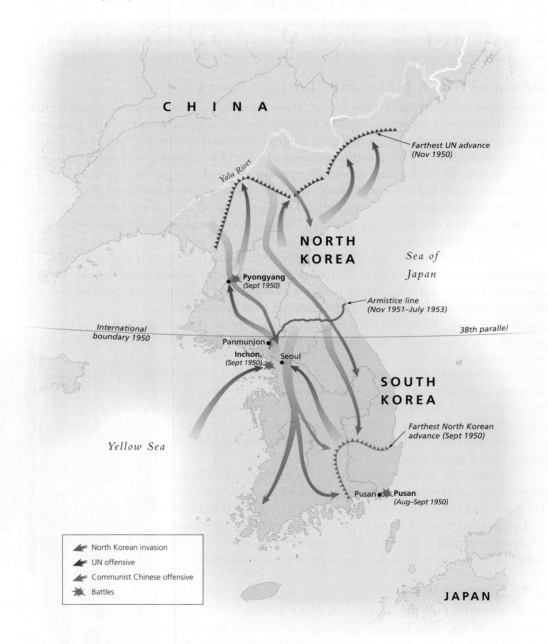

MAP 26.3

The Korean War The intensity of battles underscored the strategic importance of Korea in the Cold War.

HOW DID the United States' military campaign in Korea reflect Truman's doctrine of containment?

authorized General Douglas MacArthur to carry out an amphibious landing at Inchon, near Seoul, on September 15, 1950. The campaign not only halted the Communist drive, but also sent the North Koreans fleeing. By October, UN troops had retaken South Korea.

Basking in victory, the Truman administration could not resist the temptation to expand its war aims. The president decided to roll back the Communists beyond the 38th Parallel, uniting Korea as a showcase for democracy. China, not yet directly involved in the war, warned that crossing that dividing line would threaten its national security. Truman flew to Wake Island in the Pacific on October 15 to confer with MacArthur, who assured him of a speedy victory.

MacArthur had sorely miscalculated. Chinese troops massed along the Yalu River, the border between Korea and China. As the UN forces approached the Yalu, the Chinese attacked. MacArthur, who had foolishly divided his forces, suffered a crushing defeat. The Chinese drove the UN troops back into South Korea, where they regrouped south of the 38th Parallel. Finally, by the summer of 1951 a stalemate had been reached very near the old dividing line. Then, for the next eighteen months, negotiations for an armistice dragged out amid heavy fighting.

MacArthur tried to convince Truman to prepare for a new invasion of Communist territory. Encouraged by strong support at home, and defying the American tradition of civilian control over the military, MacArthur publicly criticized the president's policy, calling for bombing supply lines in China and blockading the Chinese coast. Such actions would certainly have led to a Chinese-American war. Finally, on April 10, 1951, Truman fired MacArthur for insubordination.

THE PRICE OF NATIONAL SECURITY

The Korean conflict had profound implications for the use of executive power. By unilaterally instituting a peacetime draft in 1948 and in 1950 ordering American troops into Korea without a declaration of war, Truman had bypassed congressional authority. Republican Senator Robert Taft called the president's actions "evidence of an 'imperial presidency'" that was guilty of "a complete usurpation" of checks and balances.

The president was acting at the prompting of **National Security Council Paper 68 (NSC-68)**, a sweeping declaration of Cold War policy. The document defined the struggle between the United States and the Soviet Union as "permanent" and the era one of "total war." American citizens, it declared, must be willing to sacrifice—"to give up some of the benefits which they have come to associate with their freedom"—to defend their way of life.

Initially hesitant, after the outbreak of the Korean war, Truman accepted the policies outlined in NSC-68 and agreed to a rapid and permanent military buildup. By the time the Korean conflict subsided, the defense budget had quadrupled, from $13.5 billion to more than $52 billion in 1953. At the same time, the federal government accelerated development of both conventional and nonconventional weapons. Its nuclear stockpile now included the thermonuclear hydrogen (or "H") bomb, first tested at full scale in November 1952. NCS-68 also proposed expensive "large-scale covert operations" for the "liberation" of Communist-dominated countries, particularly in Eastern Europe.

In Korea, peace negotiations and fighting proceeded in tandem until the summer of 1953, when a settlement was reached returning North and South Korea to almost the same territory each had held at the start of the war. Approximately 54,000 Americans died in Korea; North Korea and China lost well over 2 million. True to patterns of modern warfare that emerged during World War II, the majority of civilians killed were women and children. Nearly a million Koreans were left homeless.

The Korean conflict enlarged the geographical range of the Cold War to include East Asia. "Red China" and the United States would be implacable enemies for the next twenty years. Moreover, Korea did much to establish an ominous tradition of "unwinnable" conflicts that left many Americans skeptical of official policy.

Read the Document

National Security Council Memorandum Number 68 (1950) at **www.myhistorylab.com**

National Security Council Paper 68 (NSC-68) Policy statement that committed the United States to a military approach to the Cold War.

On September 23, 1952, Republican vice-presidential candidate Richard M. Nixon appeared on national television to defend himself against charges that he had taken illegal campaign contributions. This photograph shows him with one of those gifts, a black-and-white spotted cocker spaniel. He said: "And our little girl Tricia, the six year old, named it 'Checkers.' And you know, the kids, like all kids, love the dog, and I just want to say this, right now, that regardless of what they say about it, we're gonna keep it." This speech, which was simulcast on radio, won the hearts of many voters.

QUICK REVIEW

The Election of 1952

- Korean War the most important issue of the campaign.
- Truman's approval rating sank to 23%, leading to his decision not to run for a second term.
- Eisenhower positioned himself as a "modern Republican."

"I LIKE IKE": THE ELECTION OF 1952

Korea dominated the election campaign of 1952. Truman's popularity had wavered continually since he took office in 1945, but it sank to an all-time low in the early 1950s shortly after he fired MacArthur. Thousands of letters and telegrams poured into Congress demanding Truman's impeachment, while MacArthur returned home to a hero's welcome.

The case against Truman widened. The Asia First lobby argued that if in the late 1940s the president had aggressively turned back communism in China, there would have been no "limited war" in Korea. Large-scale corruption came to light in Truman's administration, with several agencies allegedly dealing in 5 percent kickbacks on government contracts. Business and organized labor complained about price and wage freezes during the Korean war. A late 1951 Gallup poll showed the president's approval rating at 23 percent. In March 1952, Truman announced he would not run for reelection.

Accepting political defeat and disgrace, Truman endorsed the uncharismatic governor of Illinois, Adlai E. Stevenson Jr. Admired for his eloquence, wit, honesty, and intelligence, Stevenson offered no solutions to the conflict in Korea, the accelerating arms race, or the Cold War generally. Accepting the Democratic nomination, he candidly admitted that "the ordeal of the twentieth century is far from over."

The Republicans made the most of the Democrats' dilemma. Without proposing any sweeping answers of their own, they zeroed in on "K_1C_2"—Korea, Communism, and Corruption. When opinion polls showed retired General Dwight D. Eisenhower with an "unprecedented" 64 percent approval rating, they found in "Ike" the perfect candidate.

Eisenhower styled himself the voice of "modern Republicanism." He wisely avoided the negative impressions made in 1948 by Dewey, who had seemed as aggressive as Truman abroad and bent on repealing the New Deal at home. Eisenhower knew better: voters wanted peace and a limited welfare state. He called New Deal reforms "a solid floor that keeps all of us from falling into the pit of disaster," and without going into specifics promised "an early and honorable" peace in Korea.

Richard Nixon, Eisenhower's vice presidential candidate, meanwhile waged a relentless and defamatory attack on "Adlai the Appeaser." Joe McCarthy chortled that with club in hand he might be able to make "a good American" of Stevenson. A month before the election, McCarthy went on network television with his requisite "exhibits" and "documents," purportedly showing that the Democratic presidential candidate had promoted communism at home and abroad. These outrageous charges kept the Stevenson campaign off balance.

The Republican campaign was itself not scandal-free: Nixon was caught accepting personal gifts from wealthy benefactors. On national television, he pathetically described his wife Pat's "good Republican cloth coat" and their struggling life, but then contritely admitted to indeed accepting one gift: a puppy named Checkers that his little daughters loved and that he refused to give back. The masterfully maudlin "Checkers Speech," defused the scandal without answering the most important charges. The speech also underscored how important television was becoming in molding voters' perceptions.

Soaring above the scandal, Eisenhower inspired voters as the peace candidate. Ten days before the election, he dramatically announced: "I shall go to Korea." Eisenhower carried 55 percent of the vote and thirty-nine states. Riding his coattails, the Republicans regained narrow control of Congress. The New Deal coalition—ethnic minorities, northern blacks, unionized workers, liberals, Catholics, Jews, and white southern conservatives—no longer commanded a majority.

CHRONOLOGY

1941 Henry Luce forecasts the dawn of "the American Century"

1944 G.I. Bill of Rights benefits World War II veterans

International Monetary Fund and World Bank founded

1945 Franklin D. Roosevelt dies in office; Harry S. Truman becomes president

United Nations charter signed

World War II ends

Strike wave begins

Truman proposes program of economic reforms

1946 Employment Act creates Council of Economic Advisers

Churchill's Iron Curtain speech

Atomic Energy Act establishes Atomic Energy Commission

Republicans win control of Congress

Benjamin Spock publishes *Baby and Child Care*

1947 Truman Doctrine announced; Congress appropriates $400 million in aid for Greece and Turkey

Federal Employees Loyalty and Security Program established and attorney general's list of subversive organizations authorized

Marshall Plan announced

Taft-Hartley Act restricts union activities

National Security Act establishes Department of Defense, the National Security Council, and the Central Intelligence Agency

House Un-American Activities Committee hearings in Hollywood

1948 Smith-Mundt Act passed by Congress

Ferdinand Lundberg and Marynia Farnham publish *Modern Woman: The Lost Sex*

State of Israel founded; immediately recognized by the United States

Berlin blockade begins

Henry Wallace nominated for president on Progressive Party ticket

Truman announces peacetime draft and desegregates U.S. armed forces and civil service

Truman elected president, defeating Dewey, Wallace, and Thurmond; Democrats sweep both houses of Congress

1949 Truman announces Fair Deal

North Atlantic Treaty Organization (NATO) created

Communists, led by Mao Zedong, take power in China

Berlin blockade ends

Soviet Union detonates atomic bomb

1950 Alger Hiss convicted of perjury

Senator Joseph McCarthy begins anti-Communist crusade

Soviet Union and the People's Republic of China sign an alliance

Adoption of NSC-68 consolidates presidential war powers

Korean war begins

Internal Security (McCarran) Act requires registration of Communist organizations and arrest of Communists during national emergencies

1951 Truman dismisses General Douglas MacArthur

Psychological Strategy Board created

Armistice talks begin in Korea

1952 Immigration and Nationality Act retains quota system, lifts ban on immigration of Asian and Pacific peoples, but bans "subversives" and homosexuals

United States detonates first hydrogen bomb

Dwight D. Eisenhower wins presidency, defeating Adlai Stevenson; Richard Nixon becomes vice president

1953 Julius and Ethel Rosenberg executed for atomic espionage

Armistice ends fighting in Korea

1954 Army–McCarthy hearings end, discrediting McCarthy

1955 Warsaw Pact created

CONCLUSION

In his farewell address, in January 1953, Harry Truman reflected: "I suppose that history will remember my term in office as the years when the 'cold war' began to overshadow our lives. I have hardly had a day in office that has not been dominated by this all-embracing struggle."

The election of Dwight Eisenhower helped to diminish the intensity of the country's dour mood without actually bringing a halt to the conflict. The new president pledged himself to liberate the world from communism by peaceful means rather than force. "Our aim is more subtle," he announced during his campaign, "more pervasive, more complete. We are trying to get the world, by peaceful means, to believe the truth. . . ." Increasing the budget of the CIA, Eisenhower took the Cold War out of the public eye by relying to a far greater extent than Truman on psychological warfare and covert operations.

"The Eisenhower Movement," wrote journalist Walter Lippmann, was a "mission in American politics" to restore a sense of community among the American people. In a larger sense, many of the issues of the immediate post–World War II years seemed to have been settled or put off for a distant future. The international boundaries of communism were frozen with the Chinese Revolution, the Berlin Crisis, and now the Korean war. Meanwhile, at home, Cold War defense spending had become a permanent part of the national budget, an undeniable drain on tax revenues but an important element in the government contribution to economic prosperity. If the nuclear arms race remained a cause for anxiety, joined by more personal worries about the changing patterns of family life, a sense of relative security nevertheless spread. Prospects for world peace had dimmed, but the worst nightmares of the 1940s had eased as well.

REVIEW QUESTIONS

1. Discuss the origins of the Cold War and the sources of growing tensions between the United States and the Soviet Union at the close of World War II.

2. Describe the basic elements of President Harry Truman's policy of containment. How did the threat of atomic warfare affect this policy?

3. Compare the presidencies of Franklin D. Roosevelt and Harry S. Truman, both Democrats.

4. Describe the impact of McCarthyism on American political life. How did the anti-Communist campaigns affect the media? What were the sources of Senator Joseph McCarthy's popularity? What brought about his downfall?

5. How did the Cold War shape mid-twentieth-century American culture?

6. Discuss the role of the United States in Korea in the decade after World War II. How did the Korean war affect the 1952 presidential election?

7. Why did Dwight D. Eisenhower win the 1952 presidential election?

KEY TERMS

Berlin blockade (p. 689)
Central Intelligence Agency (CIA) (p. 693)
Cold War (p. 687)
Council of Economic Advisers (p. 691)
Dixiecrat (p. 692)
Executive Order 9835 (p. 694)
G.I. Bill (p. 699)
House Un-American Activities Committee (HUAC) (p. 694)
International Monetary Fund (IMF) (p. 685)

Manhattan Project (p. 700)
Marshall Plan (p. 688)
McCarthyism (p. 696)
National Security Council (NSC) (p. 693)
National Security Council Paper 68 (NSC-68) (p. 703)
North Atlantic Treaty Organization (NATO) (p. 690)
Taft-Hartley Act (p. 691)
Truman Doctrine (p. 688)

PEARSON myhistorylab™ Connections

Reinforce what you learned in this chapter by studying the many documents, images, maps, review tools, and videos available at www.myhistorylab.com.

Read and Review

✓●─ **Study** and **Review** Chapter 26

●●●─ **Read** the **Document**

Churchill's "Iron Curtain" Speech (1946)

George F. Kennan, The Long Telegram (1946)

Ronald Reagan, Testimony before HUAC (1947)

Ladies Home Journal, "Young Mother" (1956)

National Security Council Memorandum Number 68 (1950)

●●─ **View** the **Image**

How Communism Works (1938)

Cover Illustration for "The Desi-Lucy Love Story" (1956)

👁─ **See** the **Map** The Korean War, 1950–1953

Research and Explore

●●●─ **Read** the **Document**

Exploring America: The Truman Doctrine

Profiles
Julius and Ethel Rosenberg
Strom Thurmond

((●─ **Hear** the **Audio** *Joseph P. McCarthy Speech*

((●─ **Hear** the **Audio**

Hear the audio files for Chapter 26 at
www.myhistorylab.com.

Cold War Fears and Nuclear Holocaust

In the 1950s and 1960s a multitude of grade B motion pictures appeared with a single theme, the total destruction of the United States by a nuclear holocaust. Some films focused on life after the holocaust in a radioactive nightmare of starvation, crazed mobs, and ruined cities. Others had radioactive spawned monsters of human, reptilian, or aquatic origin ravaging the survivors in a burned out world. The origin of these movies was the Cold War fear of total war or what the Eisenhower administration referred to as MAD (mutual assured destruction). By the middle 1950s the Soviet Union and the

TO WHAT extent did Cold War confrontations stimulate fear of world war and nuclear holocaust among the American people?

United States could deliver a complete knockout blow to each other by nuclear bombs carried by aircraft. By the late 1960s scientists were warning of a phenomenon called "nuclear winter" or a world-wide holocaust following any significant nuclear exchange among the world powers.

This was the great fear that motivated so much concern during the Cold War. ■

Test Mike—First Hydrogen Bomb Test—Eniwetok Atoll, October 31. 1952

Leo Szilard, a Petition to the President of the United States, July 3, 1945

Discoveries of which the people of the United States are not aware may affect the welfare of this nation in the near future. The liberation of atomic power which has been achieved places atomic bombs in the hands of the Army. It places in your hands, as Commander-in-Chief, the fateful decision whether or not to sanction the use of such bombs in the present phase of the war against Japan.

We, the undersigned scientists, have been working in the field of atomic power for a number of years. Until recently we have had to reckon with the possibility that the United States might be attacked by atomic bombs during this war and that her only defense might lie in a counterattack by the same means. Today with this danger averted we feel impelled to say what follows:

The war has to be brought speedily to a successful conclusion and the destruction of Japanese cities by means of atomic bombs may very well be an effective method of warfare. We feel, however, that such an attack on Japan could not be justified in the present circumstances. We believe that the United States ought not to resort to the use of atomic bombs in the present phase of the war, at least not unless the terms which will be imposed upon Japan after

the war are publicly announced and subsequently Japan is given an opportunity to surrender.

If such public announcement gave assurance to the Japanese that they could look forward to a life devoted to peaceful pursuits in their homeland and if Japan still refused to surrender, our nation would then be faced with a situation which might require a re-examination of her position with respect to the use of atomic bombs in the war.

Atomic bombs are primarily a means for the ruthless annihilation of cities. Once they were introduced as an instrument of war it would be difficult to resist for long the temptation of putting them to such use. . . .

Our use of atomic bombs in this war would carry the world a long way further on this path of ruthlessness.

In view of the foregoing, we, the undersigned, respectfully petition that you exercise your power as Commander-in-Chief to rule that the United States shall not, in the present phase of the war, resort to the use of atomic bombs. ■

Letter signed by Leo Szilard and 58 co-signers.

Dwight D. Eisenhower, Atoms for Peace Speech, December 8, 1953

ON JULY 16, 1945, the United States set off the world's first atomic explosion. Since that date in 1945, the United States of America has conducted 42 test explosions.

Atomic bombs today are more than 25 times as powerful as the weapons with which the atomic age dawned, while hydrogen weapons are in the ranges of millions of tons of TNT equivalent.

Today, the United States' stockpile of atomic weapons, which, of course, increases daily, exceeds by many times the explosive equivalent of the total of all bombs and all shells that came from every plane and every gun in every theatre of war in all of the years of World War II. . . .

But the dread secret, and the fearful engines of atomic might, are not ours alone. . . .

The secret is also known by the Soviet Union. . . .

Should such an atomic attack be launched against the United States, our reactions would be swift and resolute. But for me to say that the defense capabilities of the United States are such that they could inflict terrible losses upon an aggressor–for me to say that the retaliation capabilities of the United States are so great that such an aggressor's land would be laid waste–all this, while fact, is not the true expression of the purpose and the hope of the United States. . . .

Surely no sane member of the human race could discover victory in such desolation. . . . ■

Eisenhower's Farewell Address, January 17, 1961

. . . A VITAL element in keeping the peace is our military establishment. Our arms must be mighty, ready for instant action, so that no potential aggressor may be tempted to risk his own destruction.

Our military organization today bears little relation to that known by any of my predecessors in peace time, or indeed by the fighting men of World War II or Korea.

Until the latest of our world conflicts, the United States had no armaments industry. American makers of plowshares could, with time and as required, make swords as well. But now we can no longer risk emergency improvisation of national defense; we have been compelled to create a permanent armaments industry of vast proportions. Added to this, three and a half million men and women are directly engaged in the defense establishment. We annually spend on military security more than the net income of all United States corporations. . . .

In the councils of government, we must guard against the acquisition of unwarranted influence, whether sought or unsought, by the military-industrial complex.

▲ Hiroshima in ruins following the atomic bomb, dropped at end of WWII

The potential for the disastrous rise of misplaced power exists and will persist.

We must never let the weight of this combination endanger our liberties or democratic processes. . . . ■

John F. Kennedy, Cuban Missile Address, October 22, 1962

. . . THIS GOVERNMENT, as promised, has maintained the closest surveillance of the Soviet military build-up on the island of Cuba. Within the past week unmistakable evidence has established the fact that a series of offensive missile sites is now in preparation on that imprisoned island. . . .

The characteristics of these new missile sites indicate two distinct types of installations. Several of them include medium-range ballistic missiles capable of carrying a nuclear warhead for a distance of more than 1,000 nautical miles. Each of these missiles, in short, is capable of striking Washington, D.C., the Panama Canal, Cape Canaveral, Mexico City, or any other city in the southeastern part of the United States, in Central America, or in the Caribbean area.

Additional sites not yet completed appear to be designed for intermediate-range ballistic missiles capable of traveling more than twice as far—and thus capable of striking most of the major cities in the Western Hemisphere,

ranging as far north as Hudson Bay, Canada, and as far south as Lima, Peru. In addition, jet bombers, capable of carrying nuclear weapons, are now being uncrated and assembled in Cuba, while the necessary air bases are being prepared.

This urgent transformation of Cuba into an important strategic base—by the presence of these large, long-range, and clearly offensive weapons of sudden mass destruction—constitutes an explicit threat to the peace and security of all the Americas . . . This action also contradicts the repeated assurances of Soviet spokesmen . . . that the arms build-up in Cuba would retain its original defensive character . . .

In that sense missiles in Cuba add to an already clear and present danger . . . But this secret, swift, and extraordinary build-up of Communist missiles is a deliberately provocative and unjustifiable change in the status quo which cannot be accepted by this country if our courage and our commitments are ever to be trusted again by either friend or foe. ■

We were trapped. And I thought, Okay,
so I'm going to die here, in school . . .
Even the adults, the school officials, were panicked,
feeling like there was no protection . . .
[A] gentleman, who I believed to be the police chief,
said . . . "I'll get them out." And we were taken
to the basement of this place.
—*Melba Patillo Beals, from*

Voices of Freedom

MISSILE EQUIPMENT
MARIEL PORT FACILITY
4 NOVEMBER 1962

4 MISSILE TRANSPORTERS

OXIDIZER TRAILERS

OXIDIZER TRAILERS

Identical houses line the streets of Levittown, Long Island.

WE INSIST!
MAX ROACH'S – FREEDOM NOW SUITE

8002

FEATURING ABBEY LINCOLN
COLEMAN HAWKINS, OLATUNJI CANDID

27

AMERICA AT MIDCENTURY
1952–1963

((•—[Hear the Audio

Hear the audio files for Chapter 27 at **www.myhistorylab.com**.

HOW DID the Eisenhower administration's foreign policy differ from that of the Truman administration?

HOW DID postwar prosperity reshape American social and cultural life?

WHAT LARGER trends where reflected in the youth culture of the 1950s?

HOW DID television transform American culture?

HOW DID the Cold War shape the Kennedy presidency?

1952 1963

AMERICAN COMMUNITIES
Popular Music in Memphis

THE NINETEEN-YEAR-OLD MISSISSIPPIAN PEERED NERVOUSLY OUT OVER THE large crowd at Overton Park, Memphis's outdoor amphitheater. He knew that people had come that hot, sticky July day in 1954 to hear the headliner, country music star Slim Whitman. Sun Records, a local Memphis label, had just released the unknown young man's first record, and it had begun to receive some airplay on local radio. He and his two bandmates had never played in a setting even remotely as large as this one. And their music defied categories: it wasn't black and it wasn't white; it wasn't pop and it wasn't country. But when he launched into his version of a black blues song called "That's All Right," the crowd went wild. Elvis Presley had arrived.

Elvis, as anyone, defined the new music known as rock 'n' roll. An unprecedented cultural phenomenon, rock 'n' roll was made largely for and by teenagers. In communities all over America, rock 'n' roll brought teens together. It also demonstrated the enormous consumer power of an emerging youth culture. Postwar teenagers would constitute the most affluent generation of young people in American history. Their buying power helped define the affluent society of the postwar era.

Elvis Presley's life and career also personified many of the themes and tensions of postwar American life. Elvis was born in Tupelo, Mississippi, in 1935, but like many thousands of other poor rural whites, the Presley family moved to Memphis in 1949. Located halfway between St. Louis and New Orleans on the Mississippi River, Memphis enjoyed healthy growth during World War II, with lumber mills, furniture factories, and chemical manufacturing supplementing the cotton market as sources of jobs and prosperity. Memphis also boasted a remarkable diversity of popular theater and music, including a large opera house, vaudeville and burlesque, minstrel shows, and blues clubs. Like the rest of the South, Memphis was a legally segregated city. But music—in live clubs and on the radio—was an important means of breaking through the barriers of racial segregation.

As a boy, Elvis turned to music for emotional release and spiritual expression. He soaked up the wide range of musical styles available in Memphis. The all-white Assembly of God Church his family attended featured a renowned hundred-voice choir. Elvis also drew from the sounds he heard on Beale Street, the main black thoroughfare of Memphis. In the postwar years, local black rhythm and blues artists like B. B. King, Junior Parker, and Muddy Waters attracted legions of black and white fans with their emotional power and exciting showmanship. Elvis himself understood his debt to black music and black performers. "The colored folks," he told an interviewer in 1956, "been singing and playing it just like I'm doing now, man, for more years than I know. They played it like that in the shanties and in their juke joints and nobody paid it no mind until I goosed it up. I got it from them."

Dissatisfied with the cloying pop music of the day, white teenagers across the nation were increasingly turning to the rhythmic drive and emotional intensity of black rhythm and blues. They quickly adopted rock 'n' roll (the term had long been African American slang for dancing and sexual intercourse) as their music. But it was more than just music. For millions of young people, rock 'n' roll was an expression of revolt against the conformity and blandness found in so many new postwar suburbs. When Sun Records sold Presley's contract to RCA Records in 1956, Elvis became an international star. His appearances on network television shows contributed to his enormous popularity and demonstrated the extraordinary power of this new medium of communication. Television helped Elvis attract legions of new fans despite—and partly because of—the uproar over his overtly sexual performance style.

By helping to accustom white teenagers to the style and sound of black artists, Elvis helped establish rock 'n' roll as an interracial phenomenon. The considerable adult opposition to rock 'n' roll revolved largely around fears of race mixing. To a remarkable degree, the new music anticipated and contributed to the collapse of segregation, at least in the realm of popular culture. In a broader sense, rock 'n' roll heralded a generational shift in American society. Just as Elvis's extraordinary popularity led the way for a new kind of music, in 1960 the nation elected John F. Kennedy, the youngest president in its history and a leader who came to symbolize youthful idealism. His assassination cut short the promise of the new frontier, but not before young people had established a crucial new presence in the nation's economy, culture, and political life.

Memphis

UNDER THE COLD WAR'S SHADOW

By the time Dwight D. Eisenhower—universally called "Ike"—entered the White House in 1953, the confrontation with communism was already providing the framework for America's relations with the world. Eisenhower developed new strategies for the containment of what he called "international communism," including a greater reliance on nuclear deterrence and aggressively using the CIA for covert action. Yet Eisenhower also resolved to do everything possible to forestall an all-out nuclear conflict.

HOW DID the Eisenhower administration's foreign policy differ from that of the Truman administration?

THE EISENHOWER PRESIDENCY

Eisenhower's experience in foreign affairs had been one of his most attractive assets as a presidential candidate. As he had promised during his campaign, in December 1952 Eisenhower traveled to Korea just after his election and spent three days at the front. He returned home determined to end the fighting. The death of Soviet leader Joseph Stalin in March 1953, along with the exhaustion of Chinese and North Korean forces, created conditions favorable for a truce. In July 1953, a cease-fire agreement—not a peace settlement—brought the fighting to an uneasy end, freezing the division of North and South Korea near the 38th Parallel.

Eisenhower's success in ending the Korean fighting set the tone for his administration and increased his popularity. As president, Eisenhower kept up anti-Communist Cold War rhetoric while persuading Americans to accept the East–West stalemate as a more or less permanent fact. At home, Ike became the reassuring symbol of moderation and stability in a nation worried by threats ranging from communism and nuclear war to a new depression.

A conservative vision of community lay at the core of Eisenhower's political philosophy. He saw America as a corporate commonwealth, similar to Herbert Hoover's "associative state" of a generation earlier (see Chapter 23). As president, Eisenhower sought to limit New Deal trends that had expanded federal power, and he encouraged a voluntary, as opposed to a regulatory, government–business partnership. To him, social harmony and "the good life" at home were closely linked to maintaining a stable, American-led international order abroad. He was fond of the phrase "middle of the road." The majority of the American public agreed with Eisenhower's seemingly easygoing approach.

Eisenhower's "hidden hand presidency" relied on letting the states and corporate interests guide domestic policy and the economy. He appointed nine businessmen to his first cabinet. He appointed men congenial to the corporate interests they were supposed to regulate to the Federal Trade Commission, the Federal Communications Commission, and the Federal Power Commission.

At the same time, Eisenhower accepted the New Deal legacy of greater federal responsibility for social welfare. His administration agreed to a modest expansion of Social Security and unemployment insurance and small increases in the minimum wage. Ike also created the Department of Health, Education and Welfare, appointing as its head the second woman in history to hold a cabinet position, Oveta Culp Hobby. In agriculture, Eisenhower continued to sustain farm prices—and the interests of agribusiness—by means of New Deal–style parity payments.

Presidential contender Dwight D. Eisenhower hosts a group of Republican National Committee women at his campaign headquarters in 1952. Ike's status as America's biggest war hero, along with his genial public persona, made him an extremely popular candidate with voters across party lines.

Eisenhower, a fiscal conservative in Hoover's mold, hesitated to use fiscal policy (government spending) to pump up the economy when it twice went into recession: after the Korean war and again in 1958. Eisenhower feared inflation more than unemployment or poverty—and indeed, by the time he left office, he could boast that on his watch the average family's real wages (that is, factoring in inflation) had risen by 20 percent. With low inflation and steady, if modest, growth, the Eisenhower years were prosperous for most Americans.

THE "NEW LOOK" IN FOREIGN AFFAIRS

The death of Joseph Stalin in 1953, just two months after Eisenhower's inauguration, brought an internal power struggle in the Soviet Union. It also opened up the prospects for a thaw in the Cold War, giving Eisenhower hope for peaceful coexistence between the two superpowers. Although Eisenhower recognized that the United States was engaged in a long-term struggle with the Soviet Union, he feared that permanent Cold War mobilization might overburden the American economy and create a "garrison state." He therefore pursued a high-tech, capital-intensive defense policy that emphasized America's qualitative advantage in strategic weaponry and sought cuts in the military budget. As a percentage of the federal budget, military spending fell from 66 percent to 49 percent during Eisenhower's two terms.

Secretary of State John Foster Dulles gave shape to the "new look" in American foreign policy in the 1950s. A devout Presbyterian lawyer, Dulles brought to the job a strong sense of righteousness, an almost missionary belief in America's responsibility to preserve the Free World from godless, immoral communism. Dulles called not simply for "containing" communism, but for a "rollback." The key would be greater reliance on America's nuclear superiority. As part of a new strategic doctrine, Dulles emphasized the capacity of the Strategic Air Command to inflict devastating destruction with thermonuclear H-bombs.

The limits of a policy based on nuclear strategy became painfully clear when American leaders faced tense situations that offered no clear way to intervene without provoking full-scale war. When East Berliners rebelled against Communist rule in June 1953, Cold War hard-liners thought they saw the long-awaited moment for rollback. American agents had encouraged rebellion in East Berlin with implied promises of American support. It never came, and Soviet tanks crushed the uprising. But precisely how could the United States have responded? In the end, the United States did nothing except protest angrily. U.S. leaders faced the same dilemma in 1956 when Hungary revolted against Communist rule. The United States opened its gates to thousands of Hungarian refugees, but refused to intervene against Soviet tanks and troops. Eisenhower recognized that the Soviets would defend not just their own borders, but also their domination of Eastern Europe, by all-out war if necessary.

Nikita Khrushchev, who had emerged as Stalin's successor, in 1955 withdrew Soviet troops from eastern Austria in a conciliatory gesture. This first real rollback had been achieved by negotiation and a spirit of common hope, not by threats or force. In 1958, Khrushchev, probing American intentions and hoping to redirect the Soviet economy toward the production of more consumer goods, unilaterally suspended nuclear testing. Khrushchev made a twelve-day trip to America in 1959. If nothing else, such "summit" diplomacy offered a psychological thaw in the Cold War. In early 1960, Khrushchev called for another summit in Paris, to discuss German reunification and nuclear disarmament. Eisenhower prepared for a friendship tour of the Soviet Union.

Soviet Premier Nikita Khrushchev enjoys a bite to eat during his tour of an Iowa farm in 1959. A colorful, earthy, and erratic man, Khrushchev loomed as the most visible human symbol of the Soviet Union for Americans. On this trip he called for Soviet–American friendship, yet he also boasted "We will bury you."

All that collapsed in May 1960. The Soviets shot down an American U-2 spy plane gathering intelligence on nuclear facilities. Secret American surveillance and probes of Soviet air defenses had been going on for years. A deeply embarrassed Eisenhower at first denied the existence of U-2 flights, but then the Soviets produced the American pilot, who readily confessed. The summit collapsed when Eisenhower refused Khrushchev's demands for an apology and an end to spy flights.

Eisenhower often provided a moderating voice on issues of defense spending and missile development. The Soviet Union's dramatic launch of *Sputnik,* the first Earth-orbiting satellite, in October 1957 upset Americans' precarious sense of security. Critics attacked the Eisenhower administration for failure to keep up with the enemy. In addition to huge increases in defense spending, some panic-stricken pundits urged a massive program to build fallout shelters for the entire population in case of nuclear attack.

Eisenhower rejected these radical responses. He knew from U-2 evidence that the Soviet Union in fact trailed far behind the United States in ICBM development, but he kept this knowledge secret so as not to reveal to the Soviets the sources of American intelligence. Two measures did emerge from Congress with Eisenhower's support: creation of the National Aeronautics and Space Agency (NASA) to coordinate space exploration and missile development, and the National Defense Education Act, which funneled more federal aid into science and foreign-language education. A bipartisan majority in Congress also voted to increase the military budget by another $8 billion, accelerating the arms race and bloating the defense sector of the economy.

COVERT ACTION

A heavy reliance on covert CIA operations was the other side of Eisenhower's "New Look" defense policy of threatening massive retaliation on America's foreign enemies. He had been an enthusiastic supporter of covert operations during World War II, and during his presidency secret CIA-sponsored paramilitary operations became a key element of American foreign policy.

Eisenhower's new CIA chief was Allen Dulles, John Foster's brother. Under Dulles's command, the CIA far exceeded its mandate to collect and analyze information. All over the world, thousands of covert agents carried out operations that included making large, secret payments to friendly political parties (such as conservative Christian Democrats in Italy and Latin America) or to foreign trade unions that opposed the Communist Party.

Independence movements by now were shaking the European colonial empires throughout Asia and Africa, at the same time that dislike of U.S. hegemony was surging in Latin American. To the Eisenhower administration's alarm, the Soviet Union began winning influence in the "Third World," appealing to allegedly common anti-imperialist solidarity and by offering modest foreign aid. Widespread anti-Western feelings in these lands were fanned by publicity about America's racial problems and by resentment against foreign investors' control of natural resources, including oil and mineral wealth. If emerging nations questioned U.S. regional security arrangements by opting for neutrality—or, worse, expropriated American property—the Eisenhower administration was apt to try covert countermeasures and military intervention.

GLOBAL INTERVENTIONS

In Iran in 1953, the CIA produced a swift, major victory. The popular Iranian prime minister, Mohammed Mossadegh, had nationalized Britain's Anglo-Iranian Oil Company, and the State Department worried that this might set a precedent throughout the oil-rich Middle East. A CIA-sponsored opposition movement drove Mossadegh from office and put in power an autocratic monarch (shah), Riza Pahlavi. The shah proved his loyalty to his American sponsors by renegotiating oil contracts, assuring American companies 40 percent of Iran's oil concessions. But U.S. identification with the shah's repressive regime in the long run created a groundswell of anti-Americanism among Iranians.

U.S. policy throughout the Middle East was complicated by the conflict between Israel and its Arab neighbors. Immediately after the United States and the Soviet Union recognized the newborn Jewish state in 1948, the Arab countries launched an all-out attack. Israel repulsed the attack, drove thousands of Palestinians from their homes, and seized territory considerably beyond the lines of the projected UN partition of Palestine into a Jewish and an Arab state. While the Arab world boycotted Israel economically and refused to recognize its right to exist. Israel became a reliable U.S. ally in an unstable region.

Arab nationalism continued to vex American policymakers, culminating in the 1956 Suez Crisis. Egyptian president Gamal Abdel Nasser, a leading voice of Arab nationalism, dreamed of building the Aswan High Dam on the Nile to create more arable land and provide cheap electric power. To build the dam, he sought American and British economic aid. When negotiations broke down, Nasser turned to the Soviet Union for aid and announced he would nationalize the strategically vital—and British-controlled—Suez Canal. Eisenhower refused European appeals for help in forcibly returning the canal to the British. British, French, and Israeli forces then invaded Egypt in October 1956. The United States sponsored a UN cease-fire resolution demanding withdrawal of foreign forces. Yielding to this pressure and to Soviet threats, the British, French, and eventually Israeli forces withdrew. The end of crisis, however, brought no lasting peace to the troubled region. Arab nationalists continued to look primarily to the Soviet Union for support against Israel.

Guatemala saw the most publicized CIA intervention of the Eisenhower years (see Map 27.1). In that impoverished Central American country—where 2 percent of the population held 72 percent of all farmland and the American-based United Fruit Company owned vast banana plantations—a fragile democracy took root in 1944. President Jácobo Arbenz Guzmán, elected in 1950, aggressively pursued land reform, encouraged the formation of trade unions, and tried to buy (at assessed value) enormous acreage that United Fruit owned but did not cultivate. The company demanded far more compensation for this land than Guatemala offered and, having powerful friends in the administration (CIA director Dulles had sat on United Fruit's board of directors), it began lobbying intensively for U.S. intervention, linking land-reform programs to international communism.

U.S. intervention began when the Navy stopped Guatemala-bound ships and seized their cargoes, and on June 14, 1954, the U.S.-trained antigovernment force invaded from Honduras. Guatemalans resisted by seizing United Fruit buildings, but U.S. Air Force bombing gave the invaders cover. Guatemala appealed in vain to the United Nations for help, while Eisenhower publicly denied any knowledge of CIA involvement. A newly appointed Guatemalan leader, Carlos Castillo Armas, flew to the Guatemalan capital in a U.S. embassy plane. In the widespread terror that followed, unions were outlawed and thousands were arrested. In 1957, Castillo Armas was assassinated, initiating a decades-long civil war between military factions and peasant guerrillas.

The global anti-Communist strategy that the Truman and Eisenhower administrations embraced led to American backing of France's desperate attempt to maintain its colonial empire in Indochina (see Chapter 26). From 1950 to 1954, the United States poured $2.6 billion in military aid and CIA assistance into the fight against the nationalist Vietminh movement, led by Communist Ho Chi Minh. When in March 1954, Vietminh forces surrounded 25,000 French troops at Dien Bien Phu, France pleaded for direct American intervention. Secretary of State Dulles and Vice President Nixon, among others, called for using tactical nuclear weapons and U.S. ground troops to rescue the French. But Eisenhower, remembering Korea, refused. "I can conceive of no greater tragedy," he said, "than for the United States to become engaged in all-out war in Indochina."

•••─ Read the Document

Dwight D. Eisenhower, "Dien Bien Phu" (1954) at **www.myhistorylab.com**

MAP 27.1
The United States in the Caribbean, 1948–66 U.S. military intervention and economic presence grew steadily in the Caribbean following World War II. After 1960, opposition to the Cuban Revolution dominated U.S. Caribbean policies.

WHAT NATIONAL interests did U.S. policy makers feel were at stake in the Caribbean? How did they justify military intervention in Cuba and Guatemala?

Still, Eisenhower feared that the loss of one country to communism would inevitably lead to the loss of others. After the French surrender at Dien Bin Phu, an international conference in Geneva established a cease-fire and a "temporary" division into a Communist northern state and a non-Communist southern state. National elections and reunification were promised in 1956. But the United States refused to sign the accord. Instead, the Eisenhower administration created the Southeast Asia Treaty Organization (SEATO), a NATO-like and U.S.-dominated security pact including the United States, Great Britain, France, Australia, New Zealand, Thailand, the Philippines, and Pakistan.

Ngo Dinh Diem quickly emerged as South Vietnam's president. Supported by Eisenhower, Diem refused to permit the promised 1956 elections, knowing that the popular hero Ho Chi Minh would easily win. American economic and military aid, along with covert CIA activity, kept the increasingly isolated Diem in power. His corrupt and repressive policies alienated many peasants. By 1959, his Saigon regime faced a civil war against the thousands of peasants who were joining guerrilla bands to drive him out. Eisenhower's commitment of military advisers and economic aid to South Vietnam, based on Cold War assumptions, had laid the foundation for the Vietnam war of the 1960s.

QUICK REVIEW

U.S. Intervention Abroad

• U.S. policy shaped by Secretary of State John Foster Dulles.

• Eisenhower used the CIA to subvert democratically elected governments in Iran and Guatemala.

• The United States replaced France as the supporter of pro–Western Vietnamese in the south.

THE AFFLUENT SOCIETY

With the title of his influential book *The Affluent Society* (1958), economist John Kenneth Galbraith labeled postwar America. Galbraith observed that American capitalism had worked "quite brilliantly" in the years since World War II. But Americans, he argued, needed to spend less on personal consumption and devote more public funds to schools, medical care, culture, and social services. For most Americans, however, strong economic growth was the defining fact of the postwar period, and a fierce desire for consumer goods and the "good life" permeated American culture.

SUBSIDIZING PROSPERITY

During the Eisenhower years, the federal government played a crucial role in subsidizing programs that helped millions of Americans achieve middle-class status. Federal aid helped people to buy homes, attend colleges and technical schools, and live in new suburbs. Much of this assistance expanded on programs begun during the New Deal and World War II. The Federal Housing Administration (FHA), established in 1934, extended the government's role in subsidizing the housing industry by insuring long-term mortgage loans to private lenders for home building. By putting "the full faith and credit" of the federal government behind residential mortgages, the FHA attracted new private capital into home building and revolutionized the industry. In addition, homeowners benefited from the provision in the Internal Revenue Code (dating back to 1913) that allowed the deduction of all forms of interest payments from taxes.

Yet FHA policies had long-range drawbacks. FHA insurance went overwhelmingly to new residential developments. FHA policy favored the construction of single-family projects while discouraging multiunit housing, refused loans to repair older structures and rental units, and required for any loan guarantee an "unbiased professional estimate" rating of the property, the prospective borrower, and the neighborhood. In practice, these estimates resulted in blatant discrimination against racially mixed communities. Thus, the FHA reinforced racial and income segregation.

Most suburbs were built as planned communities. One of the first, Levittown, opened in 1947 in Hempstead, Long Island, on 1,500 acres of former potato fields. Developer William Levitt was the first entrepreneur to bring mass-production techniques to home building, allowing his company to put up hundreds of identical houses each week. Eventually, Levittown encompassed more than 17,000 houses and 82,000 people. Yet in 1960 not one of Levittown's residents was African American, and owners who rented out their homes were told to specify that their houses would not be "used or occupied by any person other than members of the Caucasian race."

The 1944 Servicemen's Readjustment Act—the G.I. Bill of Rights—made an unprecedented impact on American life. In addition to educational grants, the act gave returning veterans low-interest mortgages and business loans, thus subsidizing suburban growth as much as the postwar expansion of higher education. By 1956, of the roughly 15.4 million military veterans of World War II, 12.4 million, or 78 percent, received some form of benefits from the law. Over 2 million enrolled in colleges and universities, and nearly 6 million received vocational training. Another 3 million got loans to run businesses and farms.

Another key boost to postwar growth, especially in suburbs, came from the National Interstate and Defense Highways Act of

An aerial view of 1950s tract houses in the suburban development of Levittown, New York. Mass production techniques were key to providing affordable housing in the new postwar suburbs—but they required a "cookie cutter" approach to architecture, with little or no variation among the houses.

1956. It is significant that the program was sold to the country partly as a civil defense measure (supposedly to facilitate evacuating American cities in case of nuclear attack). By 1972, the program had become the single largest public works program in American history, laying out 41,000 miles of highway at a cost of $76 billion. Federal subsidies for interstate highway construction stimulated both the automobile industry and suburb building and helped transform the American landscape with motels, fast-food outlets, and other businesses servicing road-tripping Americans. The interstate also accelerated the decline of American mass transit and of older cities.

Cold War jitters also prompted the federal government to launch new initiatives to aid education. In the wake of the Soviet launch of the *Sputnik* satellite in the fall of 1957, the Eisenhower administration pledged to strengthen support for educating American students in mathematics, science, and technology. The National Defense Education Act (NDEA) of 1958 allocated $280 million in grants for state universities to upgrade their science facilities. The NDEA also created low-interest loans for college students and fellowship support for graduate students planning to go into college and university teaching.

In a broader sense, the postwar economy floated on a sea of Cold War–justified military spending. That spending provided an enormous boost to defense-industry employers like Boeing and Douglas Aircraft and created hundreds of thousands of new jobs. New military bases, along with the growing aviation industry, spurred enormous economic and population growth across communities in southern California, around Seattle and Charleston, and on New York's Long Island. Military spending, which many associated with high-paying jobs and prosperous communities, thus acquired enormous local political support and powerful patrons in Congress, all devoted to keeping federal contracts flowing into their districts.

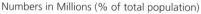

Read the Document

National Defense Education Act (1958) at **www.myhistorylab.com**

SUBURBAN LIFE

For millions of Americans, the Great Depression and World War II had meant squeezing into cramped apartments or run-down houses, often sharing space with relatives and boarders. Suburban home owning was irresistibly alluring for them. Unquestionably, suburban living meant a huge improvement in material conditions for many postwar American families, and the suburban boom strengthened the domestic ideal of the nuclear family as the model for American life. The image of the perfect suburban wife—efficient, patient, always charming—permeated television, movies, and magazines.

That glowing image often masked a stifling existence defined by housework, child care, and boredom. In the late 1950s, Betty Friedan, a wife, mother, and journalist, began a systematic survey of her Smith College classmates. She found "a strange discrepancy between the reality of our lives as women and the image to which we were trying to conform." Extending her research, in 1963 Friedan published her landmark book *The Feminine Mystique*, which gave voice to the silent frustrations of suburban women and helped to launch a new feminist movement.

For millions of suburban families, only two incomes could yield the middle-class life. The expansion of the female labor force was a central economic fact of the post–World War II years. By 1960, 40 percent of women were employed full-time or part-time, and 30 percent of married women looked to supplement the family income and ensure a solidly middle-class standard of living (see Figure 27.1).

The powerful postwar rebirth of American religion was strongly associated with suburban living. In 1940, less than half the American population

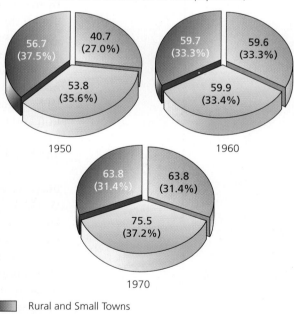

Numbers in Millions (% of total population)

1950 — 56.7 (37.5%), 40.7 (27.0%), 53.8 (35.6%)

1960 — 59.7 (33.3%), 59.6 (33.3%), 59.9 (33.4%)

1970 — 63.8 (31.4%), 63.8 (31.4%), 75.5 (37.2%)

■ Rural and Small Towns
□ Suburbs
▨ Central Cities

Figure 27.1 The Growth of the Suburbs, 1950–70
Suburban growth, at the expense of older inner cities, was one of the key social trends in the twenty-five years following World War II. By 1970, more Americans lived in suburbs than in either inner cities or rural areas.

Adapted from U.S. Bureau of the Census, Current Censuses, 1930–1970 (Washington, DC: U.S. Government Printing Office, 1975).

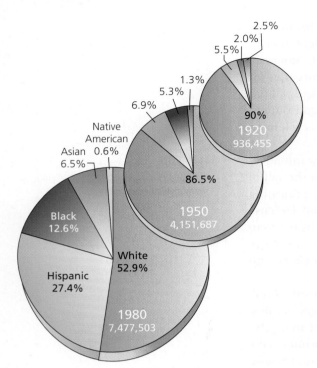

2.5%
2.0%
5.5%
1.3%
5.3%
6.9%
Native
American
Asian   0.6%
6.5%
90%
1920
936,455
86.5%
1950
4,151,687
Black
12.6%
White
52.9%
Hispanic
27.4%
1980
7,477,503

Figure 27.2 L.A. County Population 1920–80

👁 See the **Map**
Population Shifts, 1940–1950 at
www.myhistorylab.com

Landrum-Griffin Act   1959 Act that
widened government control over
union affairs and further restricted
union use of picketing and
secondary boycotts during strikes.

belonged to institutional churches; by the mid-1950s, nearly three-quarters
called themselves church members, and a church-building boom was part of
the nation's suburban expansion. Most popular religious writers emphasized
the importance of belonging, of fitting in—an appeal that meshed perfectly
with the conventional aspirations of suburban social life and with the ideal of
family-centered domesticity.

California came to embody postwar suburban life, centered on the
automobile. Cars were a necessity for commuting to work. California led
the nation in creating automobile-oriented facilities: motels ("motor
hotels"), drive-in movies, drive-through fast-food eateries and banks, and
parking-lot-encircled shopping malls. In Orange County, southeast of Los
Angeles, the "centerless city" emerged as the dominant form of community
(see Figure 27.2).

Contemporary journalists, novelists, and social scientists fed the popular image of suburban life as essentially dull, conformist, and peopled exclusively by the educated middle class. Yet these writers tended to obscure the
real class and ethnic differences among and between different suburban
communities. Many new suburbs had a distinctively blue-collar cast. Milpitas,
California, for example, grew up around a Ford auto plant about fifty miles
outside San Jose. Its residents were blue-collar assembly-line workers and
their families. Self-segregation and zoning ordinances gave some new suburbs distinctively Italian, Jewish, or Irish ethnic identities, similar to older
urban neighborhoods.

ORGANIZED LABOR AND THE AFL-CIO

By the mid-1950s, American trade unions reached a historic high point in their penetration of the labor market, reflecting enormous gains made during the organizing drives in
core mass-production industries during the New Deal era and World War II. Union influence in political life, especially within the Democratic Party, had also increased. Yet the
Republican sweep to power in 1952 meant that for the first time in a generation organized labor was without an ally in the White House. New leaders in the nation's two major
labor organizations, the American Federation of Labor (dominated by old-line construction and craft unions) and the Congress of Industrial Organizations (new unions in mass-
production industry), pushed for a merger of the two rival groups as the way to protect
and build on the movement's recent gains.

George Meany, the head of the AFL, had worked his way through the AFL
bureaucracy and had played a leading role on the National War Labor Board during
World War II. An outspoken anti-Communist, Meany pushed the AFL closer to the
Democratic Party but took pride in never having been on a strike or a picket line.
Unions, he believed, must focus on improving the economic well-being of their members. Meany's counterpart in the CIO was Walter Reuther. Reuther believed strongly
that American unions ought to stand for something beyond the bread-and-butter needs
of their members. His support of a broader social vision, including racial equality,
aggressive union organizing, and expansion of the welfare state, reflected the more
militant tradition of the CIO unions. Despite their differences, both Meany and
Reuther believed a merger of their two organizations offered the best strategy for the
labor movement. In 1955, the newly combined AFL-CIO brought some 12.5 million
union members under one banner.

The merger marked the apex of trade union membership, and after 1955 its share
of the labor market began a slow but steady decline. Scandals involving union corruption
and racketeering hurt the labor movement's public image. In 1959, after highly publicized hearings into union corruption, Congress passed the **Landrum-Griffin Act**, which

widened government control over union affairs and further restricted union use of picketing and secondary boycotts during strikes.

While union membership as a percentage of the total workforce declined, important growth did take place in new areas, reflecting a broader shift in the American workplace from manufacturing to service jobs. During the 1950s and 1960s, union membership among public sector employees increased dramatically as millions of civil servants, postal employees, teachers, police, and firefighters joined unions for the first time.

LONELY CROWDS AND ORGANIZATION MEN

Perhaps the most ambitious and controversial critique of postwar suburban America was sociologist David Riesman's *The Lonely Crowd* (1950). Riesman argued that modern America had given birth to a new kind of character type, the "other-directed" man. The "other-directed" person typical of the modern era was peer-oriented. Morality and ideals came from the overarching desire to conform. Americans, Riesman thought, were now less likely to take risks or act independently. Their thinking and habits had come to be determined by cues they received from the mass media.

Similarly, William H. Whyte's *Organization Man* (1956), a study of the Chicago suburb of Park Forest, offered a picture of people obsessed with fitting into their communities and jobs. In place of the old Protestant ethic of hard work, thrift, and competitive struggle, Whyte believed, middle-class suburbanites now strove mainly for a comfortable, secure niche in the system.

The most radical critic of postwar society, and the one with the most enduring influence, was Texas-reared sociologist C. Wright Mills. In *White Collar* (1951), Mills analyzed the job culture that typified life for middle-class salaried employees, office workers, and bureaucrats. "When white collar people get jobs," he wrote, "they sell not only their time and energy, but their personalities as well. They sell by the week or month their smiles

A crowded commuter train in Philadelphia, ca. 1955. The rapid growth of suburbs in the postwar era made commuting to work, either by mass transit or auto, a routine part of life for millions of Americans.

and their kindly gestures, and they must practice the prompt repression of resentment and aggression." In *The Power Elite* (1956), Mills argued that a small, interconnected group of corporate executives, military men, and political leaders had come to dominate American society.

THE EXPANSION OF HIGHER EDUCATION

American higher education grew explosively after the war, creating the system of postsecondary training that still exists. This expansion both reflected and reinforced other postwar social trends. The number of students enrolled in colleges and universities climbed from 2.6 million in 1950 to 3.2 million in 1960, and then more than doubled—to 7.5 million— by 1970, as the baby boomers reached college age.

A college degree opened a gateway to the middle class. It became a requirement for a whole range of expanding white-collar occupations in banking, insurance, real estate, advertising and marketing, and corporate management in general. Most administrators accommodated large business interests, which were well represented on university boards of trustees. Universities themselves were increasingly run like businesses, with administrators adopting the language of input-output, cost effectiveness, and quality control.

HEALTH AND MEDICINE

Dramatic improvements in medical care allowed many Americans to enjoy longer and healthier lives. Perhaps the most celebrated achievement of postwar medicine was the victory over poliomyelitis. Between 1947 and 1951, this disease, which usually crippled those it did not kill, struck an average of 39,000 Americans every year. In 1955, Jonas Salk pioneered the first effective vaccine against the disease, using a preparation of killed virus. A nationwide program of polio vaccination, later supplemented by the oral Sabin vaccine, virtually eliminated polio by the 1960s.

Yet access to new drugs and advanced medical techniques was not shared equally. More sophisticated treatments and expensive new hospital facilities sharply increased the costs of health care. Poor and many elderly Americans found themselves unable to afford modern medicine. Thousands of communities, especially in rural areas and small towns, lacked doctors or decent hospital facilities.

The American Medical Association (AMA), which certified medical schools, did nothing to increase the flow of new doctors. The number of physicians per 100,000 people actually declined between 1950 and 1960; doctors trained in other countries made up the shortfall. The AMA also lobbied hard against efforts to expand government responsibility for the public's health. Until 1965, with the advent of Medicare (for the elderly) and Medicaid (for the poor)—both of which it also opposed—the AMA successfully fought any form of direct federal involvement in health care.

YOUTH CULTURE

During the fifteen years after World War II, unprecedented attention was paid to America's adolescents. Adults expressed deep fears about everything from teenage sexuality and juvenile delinquency to young people's driving habits, hairstyles, and choice of clothing. At the same time, advertisers and businesses pursued the disposable income of America's affluent youth with a vengeance.

THE YOUTH MARKET

Birthrates had accelerated gradually during the late 1930s and more rapidly during the war years. The children born in those years came of age in a society that, compared with that of their parents and the rest of the world, was uniquely affluent. Converging, the demographic growth of teens and the postwar economic expansion created an explosive and profitable youth market. Manufacturers and advertisers rushed to cash in on the special needs and desires of young consumers: cosmetics, clothing, radios and phonographs, and cars. In addition, advertisers and market researchers found that teenagers often played a critical, if hard to measure, role as "secret persuaders" in a family's large purchase decisions. Specialized market research organizations sprang up to serve business clients eager to attract teen consumers and instill brand loyalty.

The special status of teenagers was also made apparent to the public by the increasing uniformity of public school education. In 1900, about one of every eight teenagers was in school; six out of eight were by the 1950s. Psychologists wrote guidebooks for parents, with titles like Dorothy Baruch's *How to Live with Your Teenager* (1953) and Paul Landis's *Understanding Teenagers* (1955). Traditional sources of adult authority and socialization—the marketplace, schools, child-rearing manuals, the mass media—all reinforced the notion of teenagers as a special community, united by age, rank, and status.

"HAIL! HAIL! ROCK 'N' ROLL!"

The demands of the new teen market, combined with structural changes in the postwar American mass media, reshaped the nation's popular music. In the recording industry, change was in the air. Small independent record labels led the way in aggressively recording African American rhythm-and-blues artists. Atlantic Records, in New York, developed the most. On radio, over jukeboxes, and in record stores, African American artists including Ray Charles, Chuck Berry, and Little Richard "crossed over," adding millions of white teenagers to their solid base of black fans.

The older, more established record companies had largely ignored black music. They responded to the new trend with slick, toned-down "cover" versions of rhythm-and-blues originals by white pop singers. The major labels' superior promotional power, as well as institutional racism in the music business, ensured that white cover versions almost always outsold the black originals. At live shows, however, white and black teenagers often listened and danced together to the music of African American performers. Alan Freed, a white Cleveland DJ, popularized the term *rock 'n' roll* to describe the black rhythm and blues that he played on the air and promoted in live concerts before enthusiastic, racially mixed teen audiences.

The stage was thus set for the arrival of white rock 'n' roll artists who could exploit the new sounds and styles. As a rock 'n' roll performer and recording artist, Elvis Presley reinvented American popular music. His success challenged the old lines separating black music from white and pop from rhythm and blues or country. As a symbol of rebellious youth and as the embodiment of youthful sexuality, Elvis revitalized American popular culture. But the greatest songwriter and most influential guitarist to emerge from this first "golden age of rock 'n' roll" was Chuck Berry, an African American from St. Louis. With humor, irony, and passion, Berry proved especially adept at capturing the teen spirit. Composing hits around the trials and tribulations of school, young love, and cars, Berry created music that defined what it meant to be young in postwar America.

QUICK REVIEW

Teenagers

- Teenagers became consumers in the 1950s.
- Advertisers directed their message at the youth market.
- Teenagers developed a shared culture.

Read the **Document**

Whose History Is It?: Any Old Way You Choose It: Rock and Roll as History, Myth, and Commerce at **www.myhistorylab.com**

The marquee at the Paramount Theater, New York City, advertises Alan Freed's "Holiday of Stars" rock 'n' roll show, 1957. Freed promoted live shows featuring both white and African American performers, attracting enthusiastic mixed race audiences.

ALMOST GROWN

Teenage consumers remade into their own turf the landscape of popular music. The dollar value of annual record sales nearly tripled between 1954 and 1959, from $213 million to $603 million. New magazines aimed exclusively at teens flourished in the postwar years, focusing on the rituals, pleasures, and sorrows surrounding teenage courtship. Paradoxically, behavior patterns among white middle-class teenagers in the 1950s and early 1960s exhibited a new kind of youth orientation and at the same time a more pronounced identification with adults.

While parents were worrying about the separate world inhabited by their teenage children, many teens seemed determined to become adults as quickly as possible. Postwar affluence multiplied the number of two-car families, making it easier for sixteen-year-olds to win driving privileges formerly reserved for eighteen-year-olds. Girls began dating, wearing brassieres and nylon stockings, and using cosmetics at an earlier age than before—twelve or thirteen rather than fifteen or sixteen. Several factors contributed to this trend, including a continuing decline in the age of menarche (first menstruation), the sharp drop in the age of marriage after World War II, and the precocious social climate of junior high schools (institutions that became widespread only after 1945). By the late 1950s, eighteen had become the most common age at which American females married. Teenagers often felt torn between their identification with youth culture and pressures to assume adult responsibilities—a dilemma for which teen-oriented magazines, music, and movies routinely dispensed advice and sympathy.

DEVIANCE AND DELINQUENCY

Many adults blamed rock 'n' roll for the apparent decline of parental control over teens. Much of the opposition to rock 'n' roll, particularly in the South, played on long-standing racist fears of white females being attracted to black music and black performers. The undercurrent beneath all this opposition was a deep anxiety over the more open expression of sexual feelings by both performers and audiences.

Paralleling the rise of rock 'n' roll was a growing concern with an alleged increase in juvenile delinquency. An endless stream of magazine articles, books, and newspaper stories asserted that criminal behavior among the nation's young was chronic. Although crime statistics do suggest an increase in juvenile crime during the 1950s, particularly in the suburbs, the public perception of the severity of the problem was surely exaggerated.

In retrospect, the juvenile delinquency controversy tells us more about anxieties over family life and the erosion of adult authority than about crime patterns. Teenagers seemed more defined by and loyal to their peer culture than to their parents. A great deal of their music, speech, dress, and style seemed alien and threatening. The growing importance of the mass media in defining youth culture brought efforts to regulate or censor media forms believed to cause juvenile delinquency.

As reactions to two of the most influential "problem youth" movies of the postwar era indicate, teens and their parents frequently interpreted depictions of youthful deviance in the mass media in very different ways. In *The Wild One* (1954), Marlon Brando played the crude, moody leader of a vicious motorcycle gang. Most adults thought of the film as a critique of mindless gang violence, but many teenagers identified with the Brando character, who, when asked, "What are you rebelling against?" coolly replied, "Whattaya got?" In *Rebel Without a Cause* (1955), James Dean, Natalie Wood, and Sal Mineo played emotionally troubled youths in an affluent California suburb. The movie suggests that parents can cause delinquency when they fail to conform to conventional roles—Dean's father does housework wearing an apron, and his mother is domineering.

Elvis, Brando, and Dean (who died in a car crash at the height of his popularity) were probably the most popular and widely imitated teen idols of the era. For most parents, they were vaguely threatening figures whose sexual energy and lack of discipline placed them outside the bounds of middle-class respectability. For teens, however, they offered an irresistible combination of rough exterior and sensitive core. They embodied, as well, the contradiction of individual rebellion versus the attractions of a community defined by youth.

MASS CULTURE AND ITS DISCONTENTS

No mass medium ever achieved such power and popularity as rapidly as television. By 1960, nearly nine in ten American families owned at least one set, which was turned on an average of more than five hours a day. Television reshaped leisure time and political life. It also helped create a new kind of national community defined by the buying and selling of consumer goods.

HOW DID television transform American culture?

Dissident voices challenged the economic trends and cultural conformity of the postwar years. Academics, journalists, novelists, and poets offered a variety of works criticizing the overall direction of American life. These critics of what was dubbed "mass society" were troubled by the premium American culture put on conformity, status, and material consumption.

TELEVISION: TUBE OF PLENTY

Television was a radical change from radio, and its development as a mass medium was quicker and less chaotic. The three main television networks—NBC, CBS, and ABC—grew directly from radio corporations. Nearly all TV stations were affiliated with one or more of the networks; only a handful of independent stations struggled for survival.

Television not only depended on advertising, but it also transformed the advertising industry. The television business, like radio, was based on the selling of time to advertisers who wanted to reach the mass audiences tuning into specific shows. Radio had offered entire shows produced by and for single sponsors. But the higher costs of television production forced key changes. Sponsors left the production of programs to the networks, independent producers, and Hollywood studios.

A 1950s' family watching *I Love Lucy*, one of the most popular situation comedies in the early days of television. Manufacturers designed and marketed TV sets as living room furniture and emphasized their role in fostering family togetherness.

Fess Parker, the actor who starred as Davy Crockett in Walt Disney's popular television series, greets young fans at New York's Idlewild Airport in 1955. The series generated enormous sales of coonskin caps and other Crockett-inspired merchandise, demonstrating the extraordinary selling power of the new medium of television.

Sponsors bought scattered time slots for spot advertisements instead of bankrolling an entire show. Ad agencies switched their creative energy to producing slick thirty-second commercials rather than entertainment programs. A shift from broadcasting live shows to filming them opened up lucrative opportunities for reruns and exports.

The staple of network radio, the comedy-variety show, was now produced visually. The first great national TV hit, *The Milton Berle Show,* followed this format when it premiered in 1948. Boxing, wrestling, the roller derby, and other sporting events were also quite popular. For a brief time, original live drama. In addition, early television featured an array of situation comedies with deep roots in radio and vaudeville.

Set largely among urban ethnic families, early shows often featured working-class families struggling with the dilemmas posed by a consumer society. Most plots turned around comic tensions created and resolved by consumption: contemplating home ownership, going out on the town, moving to the suburbs, buying on credit, purchasing a new car. Generational discord and the loss of ethnic identity were also common themes. To some degree, these early shows mirrored and spoke to the real dilemmas facing families in the early 1950s.

By the late 1950s, all the urban ethnic comedy shows were off the air. A new breed of situation comedies presented nonethnic white, affluent, and insular suburban middle-class families. Their plots focused on genial crises, usually brought on by children's mischief or wives' inability to cope with money matters, but patiently resolved by kindly fathers. In retrospect, what is most striking about these shows is what is absent: virtually unrepresented were politics, social issues, cities, white ethnic groups, African Americans, and Latinos.

Television also demonstrated a unique ability to create overnight fads and crazes across the nation. A memorable example of TV's influence came in 1955 when Walt Disney produced a series of three one-hour shows on the life of frontier legend Davy Crockett. The tremendous success of the series instantly created a $300 million industry of Davy Crockett shirts, dolls, toys, and "coonskin" caps.

TELEVISION AND POLITICS

Prime-time entertainment shows carefully avoided any references to the political issues of the day. Network executives bowed to the conformist climate created by the Cold War. Any hint of political controversy could scare off sponsors, ever wary of public protest.

As in Hollywood, the Cold War chill severely restricted the range of political discussion on television. Any honest treatment of the conflicts in American society threatened the consensus mentality at the heart of the television business. Even public affairs and documentary programs were largely devoid of substantial political debate. Television news did not come into its own until 1963, with the beginning of half-hour nightly network newscasts. Only then did television's extraordinary power to rivet the nation's attention during a crisis become clear.

Some of the ways that TV would alter the nation's political life were already emerging in the 1950s. Television made Democratic senator Estes Kefauver of Tennessee a national political figure through live coverage of his 1951 Senate investigation into organized crime. In 1952, Republican vice presidential candidate Nixon's rambling, emotionally manipulative television appeal to voters—the famous "Checkers" speech (see Chapter 26)—saved his career.

The 1952 election brought the first use of TV political advertising for presidential candidates. The Republican Party hired a high-powered ad agency to create a series of short, sophisticated advertisements touting Ike. Ever since, television image-making has been the single most important element in American electoral politics.

CULTURE CRITICS

Critics argued that the audiences for the mass media were atomized, anonymous, and detached. The media themselves had become omnipotent, capable of manipulating the attitudes and behavior of the isolated individuals in the mass. Many of these critics achieved great popularity themselves, suggesting that the public was deeply ambivalent about mass culture. These critics undoubtedly overestimated the media's power. They ignored the preponderance of research suggesting that most people watched and responded to mass media in family, peer group, and other social settings. The critics also missed the genuine vitality and creative brilliance to be found within mass culture: African American music; the films of Nicholas Ray, Elia Kazan, and Howard Hawks; the experimental television of Ernie Kovacs; even the madcap satire of teen-oriented *Mad* magazine.

Some of the sharpest dissents from the cultural conformity of the day came from a group of writers known collectively as the **Beats**. Led by the novelist Jack Kerouac and the poet Allen Ginsberg, the Beats shared a distrust of the American virtues of progress, power, and material gain. The Beats' sensibility celebrated spontaneity, friendship, jazz, open sexuality, drug use, and the outcasts of American society. Kerouac's 1957 novel *On the Road,* chronicling the tumultuous adventures of Kerouac's circle of friends as they traveled by car back and forth across America, became the Beat manifesto.

Beat writers received a largely antagonistic, even virulent reception from the literary establishment, and the mass media soon trivialized them. A San Francisco journalist coined the word *beatnik,* which by the late 1950s had become popularly associated with scruffy, bearded men and promiscuous women, all dressed in black, sporting sunglasses and berets, and acting rebellious and alienated. By challenging America's official culture, however, Beat writers foreshadowed the mass youth rebellion and counterculture of the 1960s.

Jack Kerouac, founding voice of the Beat literary movement, ca. 1957, the year he published *On the Road.* Kerouac's public readings, often accompanied by live jazz music, underlined the connections between his writing style and the rhythms and sensibilities of contemporary jazz musicians.

THE COMING OF THE NEW FRONTIER

The handsome son of a prominent, wealthy Irish American diplomat, husband of a fashionable, trendsetting heiress, forty-two-year-old John Fitzgerald Kennedy embodied youth, excitement, and sophistication. As only the second Catholic candidate for president—the first was Al Smith in 1928—Kennedy ran under the banner of his self-proclaimed "**New Frontier**." His liberalism inspired idealism and hope in millions of young people at home and abroad, and his presidency seemed to embody the call for a new sense of national purpose beyond simply enjoying affluence.

THE ELECTION OF 1960

John F. Kennedy's political career began in Massachusetts, which elected him to the House in 1946 and then the Senate in 1952. Kennedy won the Democratic nomination after a bruising series of primaries in which he defeated Hubert Humphrey of Minnesota and Lyndon B. Johnson of Texas. Vice President Richard M. Nixon, the Republican nominee, was far better known than his younger opponent. The Kennedy campaign stressed its

HOW DID the Cold War shape the Kennedy presidency?

Beats   A group of writers from the 50s whose writings challenged American culture.

beatnik   Term used to designate members of the Beats.

New Frontier   John F. Kennedy's domestic and foreign policy initiatives, designed to reinvigorate sense of national purpose and energy.

candidate's youth and his war-hero image. During his World War II tour of duty in the Pacific, Kennedy had bravely rescued one of his crew after their PT boat had been sunk. Kennedy's supporters made much of his intellectual ability. JFK had won the Pulitzer Prize in 1957 for his book *Profiles in Courage*, which in fact had been written largely by his aides.

The 1960 election featured the first televised presidential debates. Political analysts have long argued over the impact of these four encounters, but agree that they moved television to the center of presidential politics, making image and appearance more critical than ever. Nixon, just recovering from illness, looked nervous, and heat from studio lights made his makeup run and his jowls look unshaven. Kennedy benefited from a confident manner, telegenic good looks, and less propensity to sweat.

Kennedy squeaked to victory (see Map 27.2), winning by a little more than 100,000 votes out of nearly 69 million cast. By solemnly promising to keep church and state separate, he had countered residual anti-Catholic prejudice among conservative Protestants and suspicious liberals. Kennedy imbued the presidency with an aura of celebrity. The new administration promised to be exciting and stylish, a modern-day Camelot peopled by heroic young men and beautiful women. The new president's ringing inaugural address ("Ask not what your country can do for you—ask what you can do for your country") resonated through a whole generation of young Americans.

Just before Kennedy took office, President Eisenhower delivered a televised farewell address that included a stark and unexpected warning against what he called (coining a phrase) "the military-industrial complex." Throughout the 1950s, the small numbers of peace advocates in the United States had pointed to the ultimate illogic of Ike's "new look" in national-defense policy. Increasing reliance on nuclear weapons, they

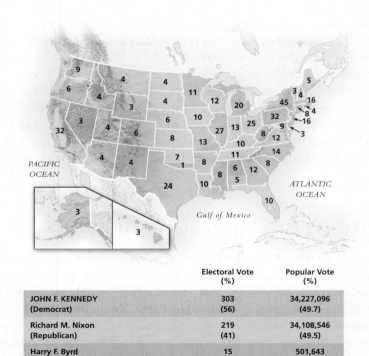

	Electoral Vote (%)	Popular Vote (%)
JOHN F. KENNEDY (Democrat)	303 (56)	34,227,096 (49.7)
Richard M. Nixon (Republican)	219 (41)	34,108,546 (49.5)
Harry F. Byrd (Independent)	15 (3)	501,643 (0.7)

MAP 27.2

The Election of 1960 Kennedy's popular vote margin over Nixon was only a little over 100,000 votes, making this one of the closest elections in American history.

IN WHICH regions was Kennedy strongest? What explains his strong showing in the South and Southwest?

Presidential candidates John F. Kennedy and Richard M. Nixon during the second of three televised debates held during the 1960 election campaign. Moderator Frank McGee sits at a desk upstage, facing a panel of newsmen. Eighty-five million viewers watched at least one of the first-ever televised debates, which both reflected and increased the power of television in the electoral process.

argued, did not strengthen national security—it threatened the entire planet with extinction. Peace advocates had demonstrated at military camps, nuclear-test sites, and missile-launching ranges. Reports of radioactive fallout around the globe rallied a larger group of scientists and prominent intellectuals against further nuclear testing.

Eisenhower came to share some of the protesters' anxiety and doubts about the arms race, because he had found it difficult to rein in the "New Look" system he helped create. Frustrated—and disturbed by the incoming Democrats' demands for increased military spending, he used his farewell address to express alarm at the growing influence of a large military and defense-industry establishment. "We annually spend on military security more than the net income of all United States corporations," Eisenhower warned the country. "This conjunction of an immense military establishment and a large arms industry is new in the American experience. The total influence—economic, political, even spiritual—is felt in every city, every State house, every office of the Federal government. . . . Our toil, resources and livelihood are all involved; so is the very structure of our society."

The old soldier understood better than most the dangers of raw military force, and in later years, critics of American foreign policy and budget priorities would adapt the sentiments behind this language. Eisenhower's public posture of restraint and caution in foreign affairs accompanied an enormous expansion of American economic, diplomatic, and military strength. Yet the Eisenhower years also demonstrated the limits of power and intervention in a world that did not always conform to the simple dualistic assumptions of Cold War ideology.

NEW FRONTIER LIBERALISM

As president, John F. Kennedy promised to revive the liberal domestic agenda, stalled since Truman's presidency. His New Frontier advocated such liberal programs as medical care for the elderly, greater federal aid for education and public housing, raising Social Security benefits and the minimum wage, and various antipoverty measures. Yet the thin

Read the Document

Dwight D. Eisenhower, "Farewell to the Nation" (1961) at **www.myhistorylab.com**

margin of his victory and stubborn opposition by conservative southern Democrats in Congress made it difficult to achieve these goals.

There were a few New Frontier achievements: modest increases in the minimum wage (to $1.25 per hour), Social Security benefits, and $5 billion appropriated for public housing. The Manpower Retraining Act provided $435 million to train the unemployed. The Area Redevelopment Act provided federal funds for rural, depressed Appalachia. The Higher Education Act of 1963 offered aid to colleges for constructing buildings and upgrading libraries.

The Peace Corps was the New Frontier's best-publicized initiative. It sent thousands of mostly young men and women overseas for two-year stints to provide technical and educational assistance to underdeveloped Third World countries. Volunteers set up health care programs, helped villagers modernize farm technology, and taught English. As a force for change, the Peace Corps produced modest results, but it epitomized Kennedy's promise to provide opportunities for service for a new generation of idealistic young people.

Kennedy's Presidential Commission on the Status of Women, led by Eleanor Roosevelt, helped revive attention to women's rights issues. The commission's 1963 report was the most comprehensive study of women's lives ever produced by the federal government. It documented the ongoing discrimination faced by American women in the workplace and in the legal system, as well as the inadequacy of social services such as day care. It called for federally supported day-care programs, continuing education programs for women, and an end to sex bias in Social Security and unemployment benefits. The **Equal Pay Act of 1963**, a direct result of the commission's work, mandated equal wages for men and women employed in industries engaged in interstate commerce. Kennedy also directed executive agencies to prohibit sex discrimination in hiring and promotion. The work of the commission contributed to a new generation of women's rights activism.

Kennedy took a more aggressive stance on stimulating economic growth and creating new jobs than had Eisenhower. The administration pushed lower business taxes through Congress, even at the cost of a higher federal deficit. Kennedy also gained approval for lower U.S. tariffs as a way to increase foreign trade. To help keep inflation down, he intervened in the steel industry in 1961 and 1962, pressuring labor to keep its wage demands low and management to curb price increases.

A wholly new realm of government spending also won Kennedy's enthusiastic backing: the space program. The **National Aeronautics and Space Administration (NASA)** had been established in reaction to *Sputnik*, and in 1961, Kennedy pushed through a greatly expanded space program. Dramatically, he announced the goal of landing an American on the moon by the end of the decade.

Kennedy's longest-lasting achievement as president may have been his strengthening of the executive branch itself. He insisted on direct presidential control of details that Eisenhower had left to advisers and appointees. Moreover, under Kennedy the White House staff assumed many of the decision-making and advisory functions previously held by cabinet members. This arrangement increased Kennedy's authority, since these appointees, unlike cabinet secretaries, escaped congressional oversight and confirmation proceedings. White House aides lacked independent constituencies; their power derived solely from their ties to the president. Kennedy's aides—"the best and the brightest," he called them—dominated policymaking. Kennedy intensified a pattern whereby American presidents increasingly operated through small groups of fiercely loyal aides, often in secret.

Equal Pay Act of 1963 Act that made it illegal for employers to pay men and women different wages for the same job.

National Aeronautics and Space Administration (NASA) Federal agency created in 1958 to manage American space flights and exploration.

KENNEDY AND THE COLD WAR

During Kennedy's three years as president, his approach to foreign policy shifted from aggressive containment to efforts at easing U.S.–Soviet tensions. Certainly when he first entered office, Kennedy and his chief aides saw their main task as confronting the

Communist threat. In his first State of the Union Address, Kennedy told Congress that America must seize the initiative in the Cold War. The nation must "move outside the home fortress, and . . . challenge the enemy in fields of our own choosing." Kennedy believed that Eisenhower had timidly accepted stalemate when the Cold War could have been won.

Between 1960 and 1962, defense appropriations increased by nearly a third, from $43 billion to $56 billion. JFK expanded Eisenhower's policy of covert operations, deploying the Army's elite Special Forces to supplement covert CIA operations against Third World guerrillas. These soldiers, fighting under the direct orders of the president, could provide "rapid response" to "brush-fire" conflicts where Soviet influence threatened American interests. The Special Forces, authorized by Kennedy to wear the green berets that gave them their unofficial name, reflected the president's desire to acquire greater flexibility, secrecy, and independence in the conduct of foreign policy.

But incidents in Southeast Asia showed there were limits to advancing American interests with covert actions and Green Berets. In Laos, the United States had ignored the 1954 Geneva agreement and installed a friendly, CIA-backed military regime, but it could not defeat Soviet-supported Pathet Lao guerrillas. The president had to arrange with the Soviets to neutralize Laos. In neighboring South Vietnam, a more difficult situation developed when Communist Vietcong guerrillas launched an insurgency against the U.S.-supported Diem regime. Kennedy began sending hundreds of Green Berets and other military advisers to bolster Diem. In May 1961, in response to North Vietnamese aid to the Vietcong, Kennedy ordered a covert action against Ho Chi Minh's northern regime that included sabotage and intelligence gathering.

Kennedy's approach to Vietnam reflected an analysis of the situation in that country by two aides, General Maxwell Taylor and Walt Rostow, who saw things solely through Cold War spectacles. "The Communists are pursuing a clear and systematic strategy in Southeast Asia," Taylor and Rostow concluded, ignoring the inefficiency, corruption, and unpopularity of the Diem government. By 1963, with Diem's army unable to contain the Vietcong rebellion, Kennedy had sent nearly 16,000 support and combat troops to South Vietnam. At that time, a wide spectrum of South Vietnamese society had joined the revolt against the hated Diem, including highly respected Buddhist monks and their students. Americans watched in horror as evening newscasts showed Buddhists burning themselves to death on the streets of Saigon—the ultimate protest against Diem's repressive rule. American press and television also reported the mounting casualty lists of U.S. forces in Vietnam. The South Vietnamese army, bloated by U.S. aid and weakened by corruption, continued to disintegrate. In the fall of 1963, American military officers and CIA operatives stood aside with approval as a group of Vietnamese generals toppled Diem, killing him and his top advisers. It was the first of many coups that racked the South Vietnamese government over the next few years.

In Latin America, where millions of impoverished peasants were forced to relocate to already-overcrowded cities, various revolutionary movements were also gaining ground—and Kennedy looked for ways to forestall them. In 1961, he unveiled the "**Alliance for Progress**," a ten-year, $100 billion plan to spur economic development in Latin America. The United States committed $20 billion to the project with the Latin nations responsible for the rest. The main goals included greater industrial growth and agricultural productivity, a more equitable distribution of income, and improved health and housing.

Kennedy saw the Alliance for Progress as a Marshall Plan that would benefit Latin America's poor and middle classes. It did help raise growth rates in Latin American economies. But the expansion in export crops and in consumption by the tiny upper class did little to aid the poor or encourage democracy. The United States hesitated to challenge the dictators and extreme conservatives who were its staunchly anti-Communist allies.

Alliance for Progress   Program of economic aid to Latin America during the Kennedy administration.

THE CUBAN REVOLUTION AND THE BAY OF PIGS

The direct impetus for the Alliance for Progress was the 1959 Cuban Revolution, which loomed over Latin America—inspiring the left and alarming the right. The U.S. economic domination of Cuba, beginning with the Spanish-American War (see Chapter 20), had continued through the 1950s. American-owned businesses controlled all of Cuba's oil production, 90 percent of its mines, and roughly half of its railroads and sugar and cattle industries. U.S. crime syndicates shared control—with dictator Fulgencio Batista—of the island's lucrative gambling, prostitution, and drug trade. As a response, in the early 1950s a peasant-based revolutionary movement, led by a middle-class student named Fidel Castro, began gaining strength in the rural districts and mountains outside Havana.

On New Year's Day 1959, after years of guerrilla war, the rebels entered Havana and, amid great public rejoicing, seized power. For a brief time, Castro seemed a hero in North America as well. The *New York Times* had conducted sympathetic interviews with Castro in 1958, while he was still fighting in Cuba's mountains. The CIA and President Eisenhower shared none of this exuberance. Castro's land-reform program, involving the seizure of acreage from the tiny minority that controlled much of the fertile land, threatened to set an example for other Latin American countries. Although Castro had not yet joined the Cuban Communist Party, he turned to the Soviet Union after the United States withdrew economic aid. He began to sell sugar to the Soviets and soon nationalized American-owned oil companies and other enterprises. Eisenhower established an economic boycott of Cuba in 1960 and then severed diplomatic relations.

Kennedy inherited from Eisenhower plans for a U.S. invasion of Cuba, including the secret arming and training of Cuban exiles. The CIA drafted the invasion plan, which was based on the assumption that a U.S.-led invasion would trigger a popular uprising and bring down Castro. Kennedy went along with the plan, but at the last moment decided not to supply Air Force cover for the invaders. On April 17, 1961, a ragtag army of 1,400 counterrevolutionaries led by CIA operatives landed at the **Bay of Pigs** on Cuba's southern coast. Castro's efficient and loyal army easily subdued them.

The debacle revealed that the CIA, blinded by Cold War assumptions, had failed to understand the Cuban Revolution. There was no popular uprising against Castro. An embarrassed Kennedy reluctantly took the blame for the disaster, and his administration was censured time and again by Third World delegates in the United Nations. American liberals criticized Kennedy for plotting Castro's overthrow, while conservatives blamed him for not supporting the invasion. Despite the failure, Kennedy remained committed to getting rid of Castro.

The botched invasion had strengthened "Fidel's" standing among the urban poor and peasants, already attracted by his programs of universal literacy and medical care. As Castro stifled internal opposition, many Cuban intellectuals and professionals fled to the United States. These middle-class émigrés would transform Miami from a retirement resort into a bustling entrepreneurial center, but the growing Cuban presence in electoral-vote-rich Florida also created a powerful lobby for rigid anti-Castro U.S. policies. Even before the end of Kennedy's administration, the CIA's support for anti-Castro operations included at least eight attempts to assassinate Fidel, and the U.S. economic embargo against Cuba continues to this day.

Bay of Pigs Site in Cuba of an unsuccessful landing by fourteen hundred anti-Castro Cuban refugees in April 1961.

Cuban missile crisis Crisis between the Soviet Union and the United States over the placement of Soviet nuclear missiles in Cuba.

THE 1962 MISSILE CRISIS

The aftermath of the Bay of Pigs led to the Cold War's most serious superpower confrontation: the **Cuban missile crisis** of October 1962. Frightened by U.S. belligerency, Castro asked Soviet Premier Khrushchev for military help. Khrushchev responded in the summer of 1962 by shipping to Cuba a large amount of sophisticated weaponry, including intermediate-range nuclear missiles capable of hitting Washington, the Northeast, and the Midwest. In early October, American U-2 reconnaissance planes found camouflaged missile silos dotting the island. Several Kennedy aides and the Joint Chiefs of Staff demanded an immediate bombing of these missile sites, arguing that the Soviet move had decisively eroded the United States' strategic global advantage. The president and his advisers pondered their options in a series of tense meetings.

Kennedy went on national television on October 22 to announce discovery of the missile sites. He publicly demanded the removal of all missiles and proclaimed a naval "quarantine" of offensive military equipment shipped to Cuba. (This was actually a blockade; Kennedy avoided the word because a blockade is an act of war.) Requesting an emergency meeting of the UN Security Council, he promised that any missiles launched from Cuba would bring "a full retaliatory response upon the Soviet Union." For a grim week, Americans wondered whether the long-dreaded nuclear Armageddon was imminent. Eyeball to eyeball, each superpower waited for the other to blink. On October 26 and 27, Khrushchev blinked, ordering twenty-five Soviet ships off their course to Cuba, thus avoiding a challenge to the U.S. Navy.

Khrushchev offered to remove the missiles in return for a pledge from the United States not to invade Cuba and later added a demand for removal of American weapons from Turkey, which is as close to the Soviet Union as Cuba is to the United States. Secretly, Kennedy assured Khrushchev that the United States would dismantle its obsolete missiles in Turkey. On November 20, after weeks of delicate negotiations, Kennedy announced the withdrawal of Soviet missiles and bombers from Cuba. He also pledged to respect Cuban sovereignty and promised not to invade the island.

The crisis had passed. The Soviets, determined not to be intimidated again, began the largest weapons buildup in their history. For his part, Kennedy, perhaps chastened by this brush with nuclear disaster, made important gestures toward peaceful coexistence with the Soviets. In a June 1963 address at American University, Kennedy called for a rethinking of Cold War diplomacy.

Shortly after, Washington and Moscow set up a "hot line"—a direct phone connection to permit instant communication during times of crisis. More substantial was the **Limited Nuclear Test-Ban Treaty**, signed in August 1963 by the United States, the Soviet Union, and Great Britain. The treaty prohibited above-ground, outer-space, and underwater nuclear weapons tests, easing global anxieties about radioactive fallout. But underground testing continued to accelerate for years. The limited test ban was perhaps more symbolic than substantive, a psychological breakthrough in East–West relations after three particularly tense years.

By November 1963, the situation in South Vietnam was deteriorating; Diem's overthrow and murder in a U.S.-backed coup was symptomatic of U.S. failure to secure an anti-Communist alternative to Ho Chi Minh's revolutionary movement. Kennedy understood this. There are some indications that he was thinking of cutting losses, perhaps after winning reelection in 1964; there are other signs that he was preparing to escalate the U.S. commitment. Most likely, he meant to keep all options open. But we will never know what he would have done about Vietnam.

Shoppers in an appliance store watch President John F. Kennedy deliver an address to the nation during the Cuban missile crisis in October 1962. Kennedy's presidency coincided with the emergence of television as the nation's dominant mass medium.

Read the Document

John F. Kennedy, Cuban Missile Crisis Address (1962) at **www.myhistorylab.com**

QUICK REVIEW

The Cuban Missile Crisis

◆ October 15, 1962: United States acquired evidence of construction of missile launching sites in Cuba.

◆ In response, Kennedy imposed a blockade.

◆ The Soviets removed the launchers in exchange for removal of U.S. missiles from Turkey and a U.S. promise not to invade Cuba.

Limited Nuclear Test-Ban Treaty Treaty, signed by the United States, Britain, and the Soviet Union, outlawing nuclear testing in the atmosphere, in outer space, and under water.

Televising a National Tragedy

The assassination of President John F. Kennedy on Friday, November 22, 1963, marked the emerging power of television as a medium capable of focusing the entire nation's attention on an extraordinary news event.

Kennedy had traveled to Texas on November 21 to shore up popularity in a state crucial to his reelection hopes for 1964.

Only local stations covered the presidential arrival and motorcade. But once the president had been shot and declared dead, the networks cut into regular program-

WHAT STRIKES you as most powerful about these images from more than four decades ago? Can you think of any recent national events that have brought the nation together via television coverage? How has that coverage changed—or remained similar—in terms of both techniques and subjects covered?

ming, combining live coverage with videotape from local stations. The hasty inauguration of Vice President Lyndon B. Johnson aboard *Air Force One* was not televised, but widespread dissemination of still photos showed Americans how the constitutional process of succession proceeded side by side with the personal grief of the president's widow, Jacqueline Kennedy.

The next day, Saturday, audiences watched television coverage of world leaders arriving in Washington for the presidential funeral. On Sunday, NBC offered live coverage of the accused assassin, Lee Harvey Oswald, being transferred from police custody to the county jail. Millions were stunned to suddenly see Jack Ruby, a shadowy Dallas underworld figure, emerge from the crowd and shoot Oswald himself to death—the first nationally televised murder.

On Monday, November 25, virtually the entire nation watched Kennedy's televised funeral: the ceremony at the National Cathedral and the procession to Arlington Cemetery. The images of the Kennedy family, especially five-year-old Caroline and three-year-old John Jr. saluting, lent a quiet dignity amid deep mourning. Critic Marya Mannes wrote of the four days of television coverage: "This was not viewing. This was total involvement. . . . I stayed before the set, knowing—as millions knew—that I must give myself over entirely to an appalling tragedy, and that to evade it was a treason of the spirit." ∎

CHRONOLOGY

1950	David Riesman publishes *The Lonely Crowd*
1952	Dwight D. Eisenhower is elected president, defeating Adlai Stevenson
1953	CIA installs Riza Shah Pahlavi as monarch of Iran
1954	Vietminh force French surrender at Dien Bien Phu
	CIA overthrows government of Jácobo Arbenz Guzmán in Guatemala
	United States explodes first hydrogen bomb
1955	Jonas Salk pioneers vaccine for polio
	James Dean stars in the movie *Rebel Without a Cause*
1956	Congress passes the National Interstate and Defense Highways Act
	Elvis Presley signs with RCA
	Eisenhower is reelected, defeating Stevenson a second time
	Allen Ginsberg publishes *Howl*
1957	Soviet Union launches *Sputnik*, first space-orbiting satellite
	Jack Kerouac publishes *On the Road*
1958	National Defense Education Act authorizes grants and loans to college students
1959	Nikita Khrushchev visits the United States
1960	Soviets shoot down U-2 spy plane and cancel planned summit meeting with Eisenhower
	John F. Kennedy is elected president, defeating Richard Nixon
	Almost 90 percent of American homes have television
1961	President Kennedy creates "Green Berets"
	Bay of Pigs invasion of Cuba fails
1962	Cuban missile crisis brings the world to the brink of a superpower confrontation
1963	Report by the Presidential Commission on the Status of Women documents ongoing discrimination
	Betty Friedan publishes *The Feminine Mystique*
	Limited Nuclear Test-Ban Treaty is signed
	President Kennedy is assassinated; Lyndon B. Johnson becomes president

THE ASSASSINATION OF PRESIDENT KENNEDY

The assassination of John F. Kennedy in Dallas on November 22, 1963, sent the entire nation into shock and mourning. Just forty-six years old and president for only three years, Kennedy quickly ascended to martyrdom in the nation's consciousness. Millions had identified his strengths—intelligence, optimism, wit, charm, coolness under fire—as those of American society. In life, Kennedy had helped put television at the center of American politics. In the aftermath of his death, television riveted a badly shocked nation. One day after the assassination, the president's accused killer, an obscure misfit named Lee Harvey Oswald, was himself gunned down before television cameras covering his arraignment in Dallas. Two days later, tens of millions watched the televised spectacle of Kennedy's funeral, trying to make sense of the brutal murder (see Seeing History). Although a special commission headed by Chief Justice Earl Warren found the killing to be the work of Oswald acting alone, many Americans doubted this conclusion. Kennedy's death gave rise to a host of conspiracy theories, none of which seems provable.

We will never know, of course, what Kennedy might have achieved in a second term. In his 1,000 days as president, he demonstrated a capacity to change and grow in office. Having gone to the brink during the missile crisis, he managed to launch new initiatives toward peaceful coexistence. At the time of his death, relations between the United States and the Soviet Union were more amicable than at any time since the end of World War II. Much of the domestic liberal agenda of the New Frontier would be finally implemented by Kennedy's successor, Lyndon B. Johnson, who dreamed of creating a **Great Society**.

Great Society Theme of Lyndon Johnson's administration, focusing on poverty, education, and civil rights.

CONCLUSION

America in 1963 still enjoyed its postwar economic boom. To be sure, millions of Americans, particularly African Americans and Latinos, did not share in the good times. But millions had managed to reach the middle class since the early 1950s. An expanding economy, cheap energy, government subsidies, and dominance in the global marketplace had made the "the good life" available to more Americans than ever. The postwar "American dream" promised home ownership, college education, secure employment at decent wages, affordable appliances, and the ability to travel—for one's children if not for one's self. The nation's public culture—its schools, mass media, politics, advertising—presented a powerful consensus based on the idea that the American dream was available to all who would work for it.

The presidential transition of 1961—from grandfatherly war hero Dwight Eisenhower to charismatic young war hero Jack Kennedy—symbolized for many a generational shift as well. By 1963, young people had more influence than ever before in shaping the nation's political life, its media images, and its burgeoning consumer culture. Kennedy himself inspired millions of young Americans to pursue public service and to express their idealism. But even by the time of Kennedy's death, the postwar consensus and the conditions that nurtured it were beginning to unravel.

REVIEW QUESTIONS

1. How did Cold War politics and assumptions shape American foreign policy in these years? What were the key interventions the United States made in Europe and the Third World?

2. How did postwar economic prosperity change the lives of ordinary Americans? Which groups benefited most and which were largely excluded from "the affluent society"?

3. What role did federal programs play in expanding economic opportunities?

4. Analyze the origins of postwar youth culture. How was teenage life different in these years from previous eras? How did popular culture both reflect and distort the lives of American youth?

5. How did mass culture become even more central to American everyday life in the two decades following World War II? What problems did various cultural critics identify with this trend?

6. Evaluate the domestic and international policies associated with John F. Kennedy and the New Frontier. What continuities with Eisenhower-era politics do you find in the Kennedy administration? How did JFK break with past practices?

KEY TERMS

Alliance for Progress (p. 731)
Bay of Pigs (p. 732)
Beatnik (p. 727)
Beats (p. 727)
Cuban missile crisis (p. 732)
Equal Pay Act of 1963 (p. 730)

Great Society (p. 735)
Landrum-Griffin Act (p. 720)
Limited Nuclear Test-Ban Treaty (p. 733)
New Frontier (p. 727)
National Aeronautics and Space Administration (NASA) (p. 730)

PEARSON myhistorylab Connections

Reinforce what you learned in this chapter by studying the many documents, images, maps, review tools, and videos available at www.myhistorylab.com.

Read and Review

✓• Study and Review Chapter 27

•••• Read the Document

Dwight D. Eisenhower, "Dien Bien Phu" (1954)

National Defense Education Act (1958)

John F. Kennedy, "Inaugural Address" (1961)

Dwight D. Eisenhower, "Farewell to the Nation" (1961)

John F. Kennedy, Cuban Missile Crisis Address (1962)

👁 See the Map *Population Shifts, 1940–1950*

Research and Explore

•••• Read the Document

Exploring America: How to Lie with Statistics

Profiles
John Foster Dulles
Jack Kerouac

Whose History Is It?: Any Old Way You Choose It: Rock and Roll as History, Myth, and Commerce

◉ Watch the Video

Newsreel: JFK 1917–1963

The Polio Epidemic and Polio Vaccine

((•• Hear the Audio

Hear the audio files for Chapter 27 at
www.myhistorylab.com.

"We have discovered a new and powerful weapon—nonviolent resistance."
—*Martin Luther King, Jr., December 1956 address on Montgomery bus boycott*

The Black Panthers march in New York City.

28

THE CIVIL RIGHTS MOVEMENT
1945–1966

((•—⌈Hear the Audio

Hear the audio files for Chapter 28 at **www.myhistorylab.com**.

WHAT WERE the legal and political origins of the African American civil rights struggle?

HOW DID student protesters and direct action shape the civil rights struggle in the South?

HOW DID the civil rights movement intersect with national politics in the 1960s?

HOW DID the African American struggle for civil rights inspire other American minority groups?

AMERICAN COMMUNITIES

The Montgomery Bus Boycott: An African American Community Challenges Segregation

ON DECEMBER 1, 1955, ROSA PARKS, A SEAMSTRESS AND WELL-KNOWN activist in the African American community of Montgomery, Alabama, was taken from a bus, arrested, and jailed for refusing to give up her seat to a white passenger. Composing roughly half the city's 100,000 people, Montgomery's black community had long endured the humiliation of a strictly segregated bus system.

Protesting Mrs. Parks's arrest, more than 30,000 African Americans answered a hastily organized call to boycott the city's buses. On the day of the boycott, a steady stream of cars and pedestrians jammed the streets around Holt Street Baptist Church. By early evening, a patient, orderly, and determined crowd of more than 5,000 African Americans packed the church and spilled over onto the sidewalks. Reverend Martin Luther King Jr. addressed the gathering. "We are here this evening," he began slowly, "for serious business. We are here in a general sense because first and foremost we are American citizens, and we are determined to apply our citizenship to the fullness of its means."

Dr. King laid out the key principles that would guide the boycott—nonviolence, Christian love, unity. His brief but stirring address created a powerful sense of communion. "If we are wrong, justice is a lie," he told the clapping and shouting throng. "And we are determined here in Montgomery to work and fight until justice runs down like water and righteousness like a mighty stream."

Dr. King's prophetic speech catapulted him into leadership of the Montgomery bus boycott—but he had not started what would become known simply as the Movement. When Rosa Parks was arrested, local activists with deep roots in the black protest tradition galvanized the community with the idea of a boycott. Mrs. Parks herself had served for twelve years as secretary of the local NAACP chapter. E. D. Nixon, president of the Alabama NAACP and head of the local Brotherhood of Sleeping Car Porters union, saw Mrs. Parks's arrest as the right case on which to make a stand. It was Nixon who brought Montgomery's black ministers together on December 5 to coordinate an extended boycott of city buses. They formed the Montgomery Improvement Association (MIA) and chose Dr. King as their leader. Significantly, Mrs. Parks's lawyer was Clifford Durr, a white liberal with a history of representing black clients. And two white ministers, Rev. Robert Graetz and Rev. Glenn Smiley, would offer important support to the MIA.

While Nixon organized black ministers, Jo Ann Robinson, an English teacher at Alabama State College, spread the word to the larger black community. Robinson led the Women's Political Council (WPC), an organization of black professional women founded in 1949. WPC members wrote, mimeographed, and distributed 50,000 copies of a leaflet telling the story of Mrs. Parks's arrest and urging all African Americans to stay off city buses on December 5. They did. Now the MIA faced the more difficult task of keeping the boycott going.

The MIA coordinated an elaborate system of car pools, using hundreds of private cars and volunteer drivers to provide as many as 20,000 rides each day. Many people walked. Local authorities, although shocked by the discipline and sense of purpose shown by Montgomery's African American community, refused to engage in serious negotiations. With the aid of the NAACP, the MIA brought suit in federal court against bus segregation in Montgomery. Police harassed boycotters with traffic tickets and arrests. White racists exploded bombs in the homes of Dr. King and E. D. Nixon. The days turned into weeks, then months, but still the boycott continued. All along, mass meetings in Montgomery's African American churches helped boost morale with singing, praying, and stories of individual sacrifice.

On June 4, 1956, a panel of three federal judges struck down Montgomery's bus segregation ordinances as unconstitutional. On November 13, the Supreme Court affirmed the district court ruling. After eleven hard months and against all odds, the boycotters had won.

The boycotters' victory inspired a new mass movement for African American civil rights. A series of local struggles to dismantle segregation would coalesce into a broad-based national movement at the center of American politics. By 1963, the massive March on Washington would win the endorsement of President John F. Kennedy, and his successor, Lyndon B. Johnson, would push through the landmark Civil Rights Act and Voting Rights Act.

The struggle to end legal segregation took root in scores of southern cities and towns. African American communities led these fights, developing a variety of tactics, leaders, and ideologies. With white allies, they engaged in direct-action protests such as boycotts, sit-ins, and mass civil disobedience, as well as strategic legal battles in state and federal courts. In the process, the civil rights movement created new social identities for African Americans, inspired a new "rights consciousness" among other minority groups, and profoundly changed American society.

Montgomery

ORIGINS OF THE MOVEMENT

The civil rights movement arose out of the aspirations and community strength of African Americans. Its deepest roots lay in the historic injustices of slavery, racism, and segregation. African Americans' experiences during and immediately after World War II laid the foundation for the civil rights struggle of the 1950s and 1960s.

CIVIL RIGHTS AFTER WORLD WAR II

Between 1939 and 1945, almost 1 million black men and women served in the armed forces. The discrepancy between fighting totalitarianism abroad while enduring segregation and racism in the military embittered many combat veterans and their families. African American newspapers like the *Pittsburgh Courier* fought for the "Double V" campaign—victory over fascism abroad and over segregation at home. But wartime stress on national unity largely muted political protests. With the war's end, African Americans and their white allies determined to push ahead for full political and social equality.

The wartime boom spurred a mass northward migration of nearly a million black Southerners. Although racial discrimination in housing and employment was by no means absent in northern cities, greater economic opportunities and political freedom continued to attract rural African Americans after the war. With the growth of African American communities in cities like New York, Chicago, and Detroit, black people gained significant influence in urban political machines. Within industrial unions white and black workers learned the power of biracial unity in fighting for better wages and working conditions.

After the war, civil rights issues returned to the national political stage for the first time since Reconstruction. The shift of black voters from the Republicans to the Democrats that had begun during the New Deal continued under Truman. In 1946, Truman created a President's Committee on Civil Rights. Its 1947 report, *To Secure These Rights*, set out an ambitious program to end racial inequality: creating a permanent civil rights division in the Justice Department, protecting voting rights, passing antilynching legislation, and challenging laws that permitted segregated housing. Although he publicly endorsed nearly all these proposals, Truman introduced no legislation to make them law.

Truman and his advisers understood that black voters in several key northern states would be pivotal in the 1948 election. At the same time, they worried about the loyalty of white southern Democrats adamantly opposed to changing the racial status quo. In July 1948, the president made his boldest move on behalf of civil rights, issuing an executive order ending segregation in the armed forces. Later that summer, when liberals forced the Democratic National Convention to adopt a strong civil rights plank, outraged southern delegates walked out and nominated Governor Strom Thurmond. The deep split over race issues would continue to wrack the national Democratic Party for a generation.

Electoral politics was not the only arena for civil rights work. During the war, membership in the National Association for the Advancement of Colored People had mushroomed from 50,000 to 500,000. The NAACP conducted voter registration drives and lobbied against discrimination in housing and employment. Its Legal Defense and

WHAT WERE the legal and political origins of the African American civil rights struggle?

▶ Watch the Video
The Civil Rights Movement at
www.myhistorylab.com

Charlie Parker (alto sax) and Miles Davis (trumpet) with their group in 1947, at the Three Deuces Club in New York City. Parker and Davis were two creative leaders of the "bebop" movement of the 1940s. Working in northern cities, boppers reshaped jazz music and created a distinct language and style that were widely imitated by young people. They challenged older stereotypes of African American musicians by insisting that they be treated as serious artists.

Education Fund mounted several significant legal challenges to segregation laws. In *Morgan* v. *Virginia* (1946), the Supreme Court used the interstate-commerce clause to declare segregation on interstate buses unconstitutional. Other Supreme Court decisions struck down all-white election primaries, racially restrictive housing covenants, and the exclusion of blacks from law and graduate schools. The NAACP's legal work demonstrated the potential for using federal courts in attacking segregation. Federal enforcement of court decisions was often lacking, however.

Two symbolic "firsts" raised black expectations and inspired pride. In 1947, Jackie Robinson broke the color barrier in major league baseball, winning rookie-of-the-year honors with the Brooklyn Dodgers. In 1950, United Nations diplomat Ralph Bunche won the Nobel Peace Prize for arranging the 1948 Arab-Israeli truce. Bunche, however, later declined an appointment as undersecretary of state because he did not want to subject his family to Washington, DC's humiliating segregation laws.

Cultural change could have political implications as well. In the 1940s, African American musicians created a new form of jazz that revolutionized American music and asserted a militant black consciousness. Black artists such as Charlie Parker, Dizzy Gillespie, Thelonius Monk, Bud Powell, and Miles Davis revolted against the standard big-band format of swing, preferring small groups and competitive jam sessions to express their musical visions. The new music, dubbed "bebop," demanded a much more sophisticated knowledge of harmony and melody and featured more complex rhythms and extended improvisation than did previous jazz styles. Serious about both their music and the way it was presented, the "boppers" refused to cater to white stereotypes of grinning, easygoing black performers.

THE SEGREGATED SOUTH

In the postwar South, still home to over half the nation's 15 million African Americans, the racial situation had changed little since the Supreme Court sanctioned "separate but equal" segregation in *Plessy* v. *Ferguson* (see Chapter 20). In practice, segregation meant separate but unequal.

In the late 1940s, only about 10 percent of eligible southern black people voted, most of these in urban areas. A combination of legal and extralegal measures kept all but the most determined blacks disenfranchised. African Americans who insisted on exercising their right to vote, especially in remote rural areas, faced physical violence—beatings, shootings, and lynchings. A former president of the Alabama Bar Association expressed a commonly held view when he declared, "No Negro is good enough and no Negro will ever be good enough to participate in making the law under which the white people of Alabama have to live."

The South's racial code forced African Americans to accept, at least outwardly, social conventions that reinforced their low standing with whites. A black person did not shake hands with a white person, or enter a white home through the front door, or address a white person except formally. In these circumstances, survival and self-respect depended to a great degree on patience and stoicism. Black people learned to endure humiliation by keeping their thoughts and feelings hidden from white people.

The consequences of violating the code could be fatal. In the summer of 1955, Emmett Till, a fourteen-year-old African American boy from Chicago was visiting relatives near Money, Mississippi. Leaving a store with some friends, Till spoke in an informal tone to the white wife of the store owner. Several days later, Till was kidnapped from his uncle's house in the middle of the night, and shortly thereafter his body was dragged out of the Tallahatchie River. Till's murderers were acquitted in a trial that attracted national attention and underlined the stark realities of southern segregation.

Broad demographic and economic changes were also remaking the postwar South. On the eve of World War II, more than 40 percent of Southerners lived on

⊙ **Watch** the **Video**

Jackie Robinson and the Integration of Baseball at **www.myhistorylab.com**

QUICK REVIEW

The Postwar NAACP

◆ During the war, membership increased from 50,000 to 500,000.

◆ The NAACP used law suits to attack segregation.

◆ Lack of federal enforcement of court decisions undermined effectiveness.

◦▪◦ **Read** the **Document**

Sterling A. Brown, "Out of Their Mouths" (1942) at **www.myhistorylab.com**

Signs designating "White" and "Colored" rest rooms, waiting rooms, entrances, benches, and even water fountains were a common sight in the segregated South. They were a constant reminder that legal separation of the races in public spaces was the law of the land.

farms; two-thirds of the South's 35 million people resided in places with fewer than 2,500 inhabitants. During the 1950s, tens of thousands of nonagricultural jobs were created in factories, mills, and office buildings across the region. More and more national corporations, attracted by the region's cheaper labor costs, began establishing a southern presence, and the region's towns and cities competed to lure them. A more highly mechanized agriculture and rapid industrialization pushed more Southerners, black and white, into cities and suburbs. By 1960, roughly half of all Southerners inhabited metropolitan districts and only 15 percent lived on farms.

Brown v. *Board* of Education

Since the late 1930s, the NAACP had chipped away at the legal foundations of segregation. Rather than making a frontal assault on the *Plessy* separate-but-equal rule, civil rights attorneys launched a series of suits seeking complete equality in segregated facilities. Their strategy was to make segregation so prohibitively expensive that the South would be forced to dismantle it. In the 1939 case *Missouri* v. *ex rel. Gaines*, the Supreme Court ruled that the University of Missouri law school must either admit African Americans or build another, fully equal law school for them. NAACP lawyers pushed their arguments further, asserting that equality could not be measured simply by money or physical plant. In *McLaurin* v. *Oklahoma State Regents* (1950), the Court agreed with NAACP special counsel Thurgood Marshall's argument that regulations forcing a black law student to sit, eat, and study in areas apart from white students inevitably created a "badge of inferiority."

Brown v. Board of Education
Supreme Court decision in 1954 that declared that "separate but equal" schools for children of different races violated the Constitution.

•◦•─Read the Document

Brown v. Board of Education of Topeka (1954) at **www.myhistorylab.com**

◦◦•─Watch the Video

How Did the Civil Rights Movement Change American Schools? at **www.myhistorylab.com**

•◦•─Read the Document

The Southern Manifesto (1956) at **www.myhistorylab.com**

By 1951, Marshall had begun coordinating the NAACP's legal resources for a direct attack on the separate-but-equal doctrine, aiming to overturn *Plessy* and the constitutionality of segregation itself. For a test case, Marshall combined five lawsuits challenging segregation in public schools. One of these suits argued the case of Oliver Brown of Topeka, Kansas, who sought to overturn a state law permitting cities to maintain segregated schools. By law, Brown's eight-year-old daughter Linda was forced to travel by bus to a black school even though she lived only three blocks from an all-white elementary school. The Supreme Court heard initial arguments on the cases, grouped together as *Brown v. Board of Education*, in December 1952.

In his argument before the Court, Thurgood Marshall argued that separate facilities, by definition, denied black people their full rights as American citizens. Marshall used sociological and psychological evidence that went beyond standard legal arguments. For example, he cited the research of African American psychologist Kenneth B. Clark, who had studied the self-esteem of black children whose work illustrated how black children educated in segregated schools developed a negative self-image. After hearing further arguments, the Court remained divided on the issue of overturning *Plessy*. Chief Justice Earl Warren, eager for a unanimous decision, patiently worked at convincing two holdouts. Using his political skills to persuade and achieve compromise, Warren urged his colleagues to affirm a simple principle as the basis for the decision.

On May 17, 1954, Warren read aloud the Court's unanimous decision overturning *Plessy*. Warren made a point of citing several of the psychological studies of segregation's effects. He ended by directly addressing the constitutional issue. Segregation deprived the plaintiffs of the equal protection of the laws guaranteed by the Fourteenth Amendment. "We conclude that in the field of public education the doctrine of 'separate but equal' has no place. Separate educational facilities are inherently unequal . . . Any language in *Plessy* v. *Ferguson* contrary to this finding is rejected."

African Americans and their liberal allies around the country hailed the decision. But the issue of enforcement soon dampened this enthusiasm. To gain a unanimous decision, Warren had to agree to let the Court delay for one year its ruling on how to implement desegregation. This second *Brown* ruling, handed down in May 1955, assigned responsibility for desegregation plans to local school boards. The Court left it to federal district judges to monitor compliance, requiring only that desegregation proceed "with all deliberate speed." Thus, although the Court had made a momentous and clear constitutional ruling, the need for compromise dictated gradual enforcement by unspecified means.

CRISIS IN LITTLE ROCK

Resistance to *Brown* took many forms. Most affected states passed laws transferring authority for pupil assignment to local school boards. This prevented the NAACP from bringing statewide suits against segregated school systems. Counties and towns created layers of administrative delays designed to stop implementation of *Brown*. Some school boards transferred public school property to new, all-white private "academies." In 1956, 101 members of Congress from the former

Four African American students walk swiftly past barricaded sidewalks as they integrate Central High School in Little Rock, Arkansas, in September 1957. Soldiers from the 101st Airborne Division, sent to Little Rock by President Eisenhower, protect the students during the tense racial confrontation.

Visualizing Civil Rights

Images from the front lines of the civil rights struggle were crucial to the evolution of "The Movement," and they could be used for very different purposes. They attracted local activists to the cause and helped to turn a regional battle into a national crusade. Photos of the racist violence that marked confrontations in Little Rock, the Freedom Rides, and in Birmingham circulated widely in foreign newspapers, complicating the freedom vs. tyranny narrative of Cold War era policymakers.

HOW DID compelling visual images help turn the civil rights movement from a regional struggle to a national one? Was the strategy of inciting violent reactions from its opponents hypocritical or cynical for a Movement devoted to non-violence?

The growth of The Movement also converged with the emergence of television as the dominant mass medium in American life. By 1957, some eighty-five percent of American homes watched TV five hours each day. To the nascent world of television news, The Movement offered dramatic confrontations, compelling visuals, and a sharp distinction between good and evil that resembled familiar forms like Hollywood westerns or coverage of the Cold War. But images could also provide a more intimate and human sense of what was at stake.

Watch the Video
Photographing the Civil Rights Movement: Birmingham, 1963 at **www.myhistorylab.com**

When SCLC leaders planned the Birmingham campaign in the spring of 1963, they counted on a violent response from local authorities—and they got it. Images of demonstrators being attacked by police dogs or getting blasted by high pressure water hoses circulated all over the globe.

Two years later, SCLC looked to exploit the short temper and violent reputation of Sheriff Jim Clark when it brought its voting rights campaign to Selma, Alabama. As Andrew Young noted, "We're only saying to [Sheriff Clark] that if he still wants to beat heads he'll have to do it on Main Street, at noon, in front of CBS, NBC, and ABC television cameras." On March 7, 1965, when local police and Alabama state troopers attacked civil rights marchers on the Edmund Pettus Bridge, news cameras captured the searing moment. That night, ABC interrupted its premiere broadcast of the movie *Judgement at Nuremberg* with footage from Selma. The national outcry provided the final push for passage of the Voting Rights Act. As Selma's Mayor Joseph Smitherman later recalled, "I did not understand how big it was until I saw it on television." ■

Confederate states signed the **Southern Manifesto**, urging their states to refuse compliance with desegregation. President Eisenhower declined to publicly endorse *Brown*, contributing to the southern resistance.

In Little Rock, Arkansas, the tense controversy over school integration became a test case of state versus federal power. A federal court ordered public schools to begin desegregation in September 1957, and the local school board made plans to comply. But Governor Orval Faubus, facing a tough reelection fight, decided to make a campaign issue out of defying the court order. He dispatched Arkansas National Guard troops to Central High School to prevent nine black students from entering. For three weeks, armed troops stood guard at the school. Screaming crowds, encouraged by Faubus, menaced the black students, beat up two black reporters, and chanted "Two, four, six, eight, we ain't going to integrate."

At first, Eisenhower tried to intervene quietly, gaining Faubus's assurance that he would protect the nine black children. But when Faubus suddenly withdrew his troops, leaving the black students at the mercy of the white mob, Eisenhower had to move. On September 24, he placed the Arkansas National Guard under federal command and ordered a thousand paratroopers of the 101st Airborne Division to Little Rock. With fixed bayonets, the soldiers protected the students as they finally integrated Central High School in Little Rock. Eisenhower, the veteran military commander, justified his actions on the basis of upholding federal authority and enforcing the law. He also defended his intervention as crucial to national prestige abroad, noting the propaganda victory Faubus was handing the Communist world.

No Easy Road to Freedom, 1957–62

Widespread opposition to *Brown* showed the limits of a strictly legal strategy in the fight for civil rights. Although they welcomed Eisenhower's intervention in Little Rock, civil rights activists noted his reluctance to endorse desegregation, suggesting that they could not rely on federal help. As the Montgomery bus boycott had proved, black communities would have to help themselves first.

HOW DID student protesters and direct action shape the civil rights struggle in the South?

Martin Luther King Jr. and the SCLC

Martin Luther King Jr. was an extraordinary and complex man. Born in 1929 in Atlanta, he enjoyed a middle-class upbringing as the son of a prominent Baptist minister. After graduating from prestigious Morehouse College, an all-black school, King earned a divinity degree at Crozer Theological Seminary in Pennsylvania and a Ph.D. in theology from Boston University. In graduate school he was drawn to the Social Christianity of American theologian Walter Rauschenbusch, who insisted on connecting religious faith with struggles for social justice. Above all, King admired Mohandas Gandhi, the leader of a successful nonviolent resistance movement against British colonial rule in India. Gandhi taught his followers to confront authorities with a readiness to suffer in order to expose injustice and force those in power to end it. This tactic of nonviolent civil disobedience required discipline and sacrifice from its followers, who were sometimes called upon to lay their lives on the line against armed police and military forces. Crucially, King believed Gandhian nonviolence to be not merely a moral imperative but a potent political strategy. Two northern pacifists, Bayard Rustin of the War Resisters' League and Glenn Smiley of the Fellowship of Reconciliation, helped deepen King's commitment to the Gandhian philosophy.

In a December 1956 address celebrating the Montgomery bus boycott victory, King laid out six key lessons from the yearlong struggle: "(1) We have discovered that we can stick together for a common cause; (2) our leaders do not have to sell out; (3) threats and violence do not necessarily intimidate those who are sufficiently aroused and nonviolent;

Southern Manifesto   A document signed by 101 members of Congress from Southern states in 1956 that argued that the Supreme Court's decision in *Brown* v. *Board of Education of Topeka* itself contradicted the Constitution.

(4) our church is becoming militant, stressing a social gospel as well as a gospel of personal salvation; (5) we have gained a new sense of dignity and destiny; (6) we have discovered a new and powerful weapon—nonviolent resistance."

King recognized the need to exploit the momentum of the Montgomery movement. In early 1957, with the help of Rustin and others, he brought together nearly 100 black ministers to found the **Southern Christian Leadership Conference (SCLC)**. The clergymen elected King president and his close friend, the Reverend Ralph Abernathy, treasurer. The SCLC called upon black people "to understand that nonviolence is not a symbol of weakness or cowardice, but as Jesus demonstrated, nonviolent resistance transforms weakness into strength and breeds courage in the face of danger."

King and other black leaders believed white Southerners could be divided roughly into three groups: first, a tiny minority—often with legal training, social connections, and money—that might be counted on to help overthrow segregation; second, extreme segregationists who were willing and able to use violence and terror in defense of white supremacy; and third, a broad middle group who favored and benefited from segregation but were unwilling to take personal risks to prevent its destruction. In the battles to come, civil rights leaders made this nuanced view of the white South central to their larger political strategy. Extreme segregationists could be counted on to overreact, often violently, to civil rights campaigns, and thereby help to win sympathy and support for the cause. White moderates, especially in the business community, might be reluctant to initiate change, but they would try to distance themselves from the desperate violence of extremists and present themselves as pragmatic supporters of order and peace.

The SCLC gained support among black ministers, but the organization failed to generate the kind of mass, direct-action movement that had made history in Montgomery. Instead, the next great spark to light the fire of protest came from what seemed at the time a most unlikely source: black college students.

Sit-Ins: Greensboro, Nashville, Atlanta

On Monday, February 1, 1960, four black freshmen from North Carolina Agricultural and Technical College in Greensboro sat down at the whites-only lunch counter in Woolworth's and politely ordered coffee and doughnuts. As the students had anticipated, they were refused service. Nonetheless, the four students stayed at the counter until closing time. Word of their actions spread quickly, and the next day they returned with more than two dozen supporters. On the third day, students occupied sixty-three of the sixty-six lunch counter seats. By Thursday, they had been joined by three white students from the Women's College of the University of North Carolina in Greensboro. On Friday, hundreds of black students and a few white sympathizers jammed the lunch counters.

The week's events put Greensboro on the national news. City officials, looking to end the protest, offered to negotiate in exchange for an end to demonstrations. White business leaders and politicians proved unwilling to change the racial status quo, however, and the sit-ins resumed on April 1. In response to the April 21 arrest of forty-five students for trespassing, an outraged African American community organized a boycott of targeted stores that cut deeply into merchants' profits. Greensboro's leaders reluctantly gave in. On July 25, 1960, the first African American ate a meal at Woolworth's.

The Greensboro sit-in sent a shock wave throughout the South. During the next eighteen months, 70,000 people—most of them black students, a few of them white allies—participated in sit-ins against segregation in dozens of communities. More than 3,000 were arrested. African Americans had discovered a new form of direct-action protest, dignified and powerful, that white people could not ignore.

In Nashville, Reverend James Lawson, a northern-born black minister, had led workshops in nonviolent resistance since 1958. Lawson gathered around him a group of

Southern Christian Leadership Conference (SCLC) Black civil rights organization founded in 1957 by Martin Luther King Jr., and other clergy.

The second day of the sit-in at the Greensboro, North Carolina, Woolworth lunch counter, February 2, 1960. From left: Ronald Martin, Robert Patterson, and Mark Martin. The Greensboro protest sparked a wave of sit-ins across the South, mostly by college students, demanding an end to segregation in restaurants and other public places.

deeply committed black students from Fisk and Vanderbilt universities and other Nashville colleges. Young activists there talked not only of ending segregation but also of creating a "Beloved Community" based on Christian idealism and Gandhian principles.

In the spring of 1960, more than 150 Nashville students were arrested in disciplined sit-ins aimed at desegregating downtown lunch counters. Lawson, who preached the need for sacrifice in the cause of justice, found himself expelled from the divinity school at Vanderbilt. Lawson and other veterans of the Nashville sit-ins, such as John Lewis, Diane Nash, and Marion Barry, would go on to play influential roles in the national civil rights movement. The Nashville group developed rules of conduct that became a model for protesters elsewhere: "Don't strike back or curse if abused. . . . Show yourself courteous and friendly at all times. . . . Report all serious incidents to your leader in a polite manner. Remember love and nonviolence."

The most ambitious sit-in campaign unfolded in Atlanta, the South's largest and wealthiest city, and home to the region's most powerful and prestigious black community. Students from Morehouse, Spelman, and the other all-black schools that made up Atlanta University took the lead. On March 15, 1960, 200 young black people staged a well-coordinated sit-in at restaurants in City Hall, the State Capitol, and other government offices. Police arrested and jailed seventy-six demonstrators that day, but the experience only strengthened the activists' resolve. Led by Julian Bond and Lonnie King, two Morehouse undergraduates, the students formed the Committee on an Appeal for Human Rights. Over the summer they planned a fall campaign of large-scale sit-ins at major Atlanta department stores and a boycott of downtown merchants. In October 1960, Martin Luther King Jr. and thirty-six students were arrested when they sat down in the all-white Magnolia Room restaurant in Rich's Department Store. The campaign stretched on for months, and hundreds of protesters went to jail. The city's business leaders finally relented in September 1961, and desegregation came to Atlanta.

SNCC and the "Beloved Community"

The sit-in movement pumped fresh energy into the civil rights cause, creating a new generation of activists and leaders. Mass arrests, beatings, and vilification in the southern white press only strengthened the resolve of those in the Movement. Students also had to deal with the fears of their families, many of whom had made great sacrifices to send them to college.

The new student militancy also caused discord within black communities. The authority of local African American elites had traditionally depended on their influence and cooperation with the white establishment. Black lawyers, school principals, and businessmen had to maintain regular and cordial relations with white judges, school boards, and politicians. Student calls for freedom disturbed many community leaders worried about upsetting traditional patronage networks. Some black college presidents, pressured by trustees and state legislators, sought to moderate or stop the Movement altogether.

An April 1960 conference of 120 black student activists in Raleigh, North Carolina, underlined the generational and radical aspects of the new movement. The meeting had been called by Ella Baker, executive director of the SCLC, to help the students assess their experiences and plan future actions. Fifty-five at the time, Baker had for years played an important behind-the-scenes role in the civil rights cause, serving as a community organizer and field secretary for the NAACP before heading the staff of the SCLC. She counseled the student activists to resist affiliating with any of the national civil rights organizations, and she also encouraged the trend toward group-centered leadership among the students.

With Baker's encouragement, the conference voted to establish a new group, the Student Nonviolent Coordinating Committee (SNCC, pronounced "Snick"). In the fall of 1960, SNCC established an organizational structure, a set of principles, and a new style of civil rights protest. The emphasis was on fighting segregation through direct confrontation, mass action, and civil disobedience. SNCC field-workers initiated and supported local, community-based activity. Three-quarters of the first field-workers were less than twenty-two years old. Leadership was vested in a nonhierarchical Coordinating Committee, but local groups were free to determine their own direction. SNCC people distrusted bureaucracy and structure; they stressed spontaneity and improvisation. A small but dedicated group of young white Southerners, inspired by SNCC's idealism and activism, joined the cause. Over the next few years SNCC was at the forefront of nearly every major civil rights battle.

The Election of 1960 and Civil Rights

The race issue was kept from center stage during the very close presidential campaign of 1960. As vice president, Richard Nixon had been a leading Republican voice for stronger civil rights legislation, whereas Democratic nominee Senator John F. Kennedy had played virtually no role in the 1950s' congressional battles over civil rights. During the campaign, however, their roles reversed. Kennedy praised the sit-in movement as part of a revival of national reform spirit. While the Republican platform contained a strong civil rights plank, Nixon, eager to court southern white voters, minimized his own identification with the Movement.

In October, Martin Luther King Jr. was jailed after leading a demonstration in Atlanta and faced the strong possibility of being sent to a notorious state prison. Kennedy

●●●─┤Read the Document

Profile: Ella Baker (1960) at **www.myhistorylab.com**

●●●─┤Read the Document

Student Non-Violent Coordinating Committee, "Statement of Purpose" (1960) at **www.myhistorylab.com**

telephoned King's wife, Coretta Scott King, to reassure her and express his personal support. Senator Kennedy's brother and campaign manager Robert telephoned the judge in the case and angrily warned him that he had violated King's civil rights and endangered the national Democratic ticket. The judge released King soon afterward. The Kennedy campaign effectively played up the story among black voters all over the country, using black churches as a grapevine. Kennedy won 70 percent of the black vote, which helped put him over the top in such critical states as Illinois, Texas, Michigan, and Pennsylvania and secure his narrow victory over Nixon. Many civil rights activists optimistically looked forward to a new president who would have to acknowledge his political debt to the black vote.

The very closeness of his victory constrained Kennedy on race. Kennedy had to worry about alienating conservative Southern Democrats who chaired key congressional committees. Passage of major civil rights legislation would be virtually impossible. The president did appoint some forty African Americans to high federal positions, including Thurgood Marshall to a federal appellate court. He also established a Committee on Equal Employment Opportunity, chaired by Vice President Lyndon B. Johnson, to fight discrimination in the federal civil service and in corporations that received government contracts.

Most significantly, the Kennedy administration sought to invigorate the Civil Rights Division of the Justice Department. The division had been created by the Civil Rights Act of 1957, which authorized the attorney general to seek court injunctions to protect people denied their right to vote. But the Eisenhower administration had made little use of this new power. Robert Kennedy, the new attorney general, encouraged his staff to get out of Washington and into the field wherever racial troubles arose. In early 1961, when Louisiana school officials balked at a school desegregation order, Robert Kennedy warned them that he would ask the federal court to hold them in contempt. When Marshall started court proceedings, the state officials gave in. The new, more aggressive mood at Justice could not solve the central political dilemma: how to move forward on civil rights without alienating southern Democrats. Pressure from the newly energized southern civil rights movement soon revealed the true difficulty of that problem. The movement would also provoke murderous outrage from white extremists determined to maintain the racial status quo (see Map 28.1).

FREEDOM RIDES

In the spring of 1961, James Farmer, national director of the **Congress of Racial Equality (CORE)**, announced plans for an interracial Freedom Ride through the South. The goal was to test compliance with court orders banning segregation in interstate travel and terminal accommodations. Farmer designed the Freedom Ride to induce a crisis, in the spirit of the sit-ins. "Our intention," Farmer declared, "was to provoke the southern authorities into arresting us and thereby prod the Justice Department into enforcing the law of the land."

On May 4, seven blacks and six whites split into two interracial groups and left Washington on public buses bound for Alabama and Mississippi. At first the two buses encountered only isolated harassment and violence as they headed south. But when one bus entered Anniston, Alabama, on May 14, an angry mob surrounded it, smashing windows and slashing tires. Six miles out of town, the tires went flat. A firebomb tossed through a window forced the passengers out. The mob then beat the Freedom Riders with blackjacks, iron bars, and clubs, and the bus burst into flames. A caravan of cars organized by the Birmingham office of the SCLC rescued the wounded. Another mob attacked the second bus in Anniston, leaving one Freedom Rider near death and permanently brain damaged.

The violence escalated. In Birmingham, a mob of forty whites attacked the bus that managed to get out of Anniston. Although police had been warned to expect trouble, they did nothing to stop the mob from beating the Freedom Riders with pipes and fists, nor did they make any arrests. FBI agents observed and took notes but did nothing.

Congress of Racial Equality (CORE)
Civil rights group formed in 1942 and committed to nonviolent civil disobedience.

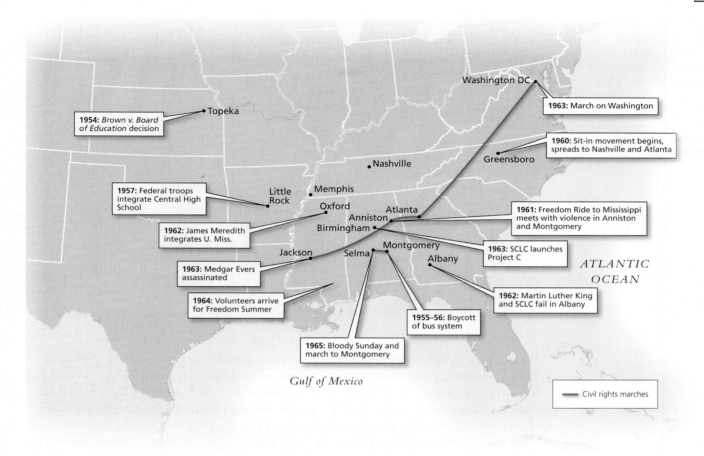

MAP 28.1
The Civil Rights Movement Key battlegrounds in the struggle for racial justice in communities across the South.

HOW DID Movement leaders choose their targets for protest activities?

Stranded and frightened, the remaining Freedom Riders reluctantly boarded a special flight to New Orleans arranged by the Justice Department. On May 17, the CORE-sponsored Freedom Ride disbanded.

That was not the end of the Freedom Rides. SNCC leaders in Atlanta and Nashville assembled a fresh group of volunteers to continue the trip. On May 20, twenty-one Freedom Riders left Birmingham for Montgomery. The bus station in the Alabama capital was eerily quiet and deserted as they pulled in. But when the passengers left the bus, a mob of several hundred whites rushed them, yelling "Get those niggers!" and clubbing people to the ground. It took police more than an hour to halt the rioting. Montgomery's police commissioner later said, "We have no intention of standing guard for a bunch of troublemakers coming into our city."

The mob violence and the indifference of Alabama officials made the Freedom Ride first-page news around the country and throughout the world. The Kennedy administration, preparing for the president's first summit meeting with Soviet premier Nikita Khrushchev, saw the situation as a threat to the nation's global prestige. The attorney general called for a cooling-off period, but King, Farmer, and the SNCC leaders announced that the Freedom Ride would continue. A bandaged but spirited group of twenty-seven Freedom Riders prepared to leave Montgomery for Jackson, Mississippi, on May 24. To avoid further violence, Robert Kennedy arranged a compromise through

A Freedom Riders' bus burns after being firebombed in Anniston, Alabama, May 14, 1961. After setting the bus afire, whites attacked the passengers fleeing the smoke and flames. Violent scenes like this one received extensive publicity in the mass media and helped compel the Justice Department to enforce court rulings banning segregation on interstate bus lines.

Mississippi's Senator James Eastland. In exchange for a guarantee of safe passage through Mississippi, the federal government promised not to interfere with the arrest of the Freedom Riders in Jackson. This Freedom Ride and several that followed thus escaped violence. But more than 300 people were arrested that summer in Jackson on charges of traveling "for the avowed purpose of inflaming public opinion."

The Freedom Rides exposed the ugly face of southern racism to the world and inspired grassroots activists around the South. But they also reinforced white resistance to desegregation and showed the limits of federal action against Jim Crow. Eventually the Justice Department did petition the Interstate Commerce Commission to issue clear rules prohibiting segregation on interstate carriers. By creating a crisis, the Freedom Rides had forced the Kennedy administration to act. But they also revealed the unwillingness of the federal government to fully enforce the law of the land. The jailings and brutality experienced by Freedom Riders made clear to the civil rights community the limits of moral persuasion alone for effecting change.

THE ALBANY MOVEMENT: THE LIMITS OF PROTEST

Charles Sherrod, SNCC Memorandum (1961) at **www.myhistorylab.com**

In Albany, a small city in southwest Georgia, activists from SNCC, the NAACP, and other local groups formed a coalition known as the **Albany Movement**. For more than a year, beginning in October 1961, thousands of Albany's black citizens marched, sat in, and boycotted as part of a citywide campaign to integrate public facilities and win voting rights. More than a thousand people spent time in jail. In December, the arrival of Martin Luther King Jr. and the SCLC transformed Albany into a national symbol of the struggle.

The gains at Albany proved minimal. Albany police chief Laurie Pritchett shrewdly deprived the movement of the kind of national sympathy won by the Freedom Riders. Pritchett filled the jails with black demonstrators, kept their mistreatment to a minimum, and prevented white mobs from running wild. King himself was twice arrested in the summer of 1962, but Albany officials quickly freed him to avoid negative publicity. By late 1962, the Albany movement had collapsed, and Pritchett proudly declared the city "as segregated as ever." Albany showed that mass protest without violent white reaction and direct federal intervention could not end Jim Crow.

Albany Movement Coalition formed in 1961 in Albany, a small city in southwest Georgia, of activists from SNCC, the NAACP, and other local groups.

In contrast to the failure at Albany, a successful battle to integrate the University of Mississippi reinforced the importance of federal intervention for guaranteeing African

American civil rights. In the fall of 1962, James Meredith tried to register as the first black student at "Ole Miss." Defying a federal court order, Governor Ross Barnett personally blocked Meredith at the admissions office. When Barnett refused to assure Robert Kennedy that Meredith would be protected, the attorney general dispatched 500 federal marshals to the campus. An enraged mob of several thousand whites, many of them armed, laid siege to the campus on September 30. A night of violence left two people dead and 160 marshals wounded, 28 from gunfire. President Kennedy ordered 5,000 Army troops onto the campus to stop the riot. A federal guard remained to protect Meredith, who graduated the following summer.

THE MOVEMENT AT HIGH TIDE, 1963–65

The tumultuous events of 1960–62 convinced civil rights strategists that segregation could not be dismantled merely through orderly protest and moral persuasion. Only comprehensive civil rights legislation, backed by federal power, could guarantee full citizenship rights for African Americans. To build the national consensus needed for new laws, civil rights activists looked for ways to gain broader support for their cause. By 1963, their sense of urgency had led them to plan dramatic confrontations that would expose the violence and terror routinely faced by southern blacks.

HOW DID the civil rights movement intersect with national politics in the 1960s?

BIRMINGHAM

At the end of 1962, Martin Luther King and his SCLC allies decided to launch a new campaign against segregation in Birmingham, Alabama. Birmingham, the most segregated big city in America, had a deep history of racial violence. African Americans endured total segregation in schools, restaurants, city parks, and department store dressing rooms. Although black people constituted more than 40 percent of the city's population, fewer than 10,000 of Birmingham's 80,000 registered voters were black.

Working closely with local civil rights groups led by the longtime Birmingham activist Reverend Fred Shuttlesworth, the SCLC carefully planned its campaign. The strategy was to fill the city jails with protesters, boycott downtown department stores, and enrage Public Safety Commissioner Eugene "Bull" Connor, a die-hard segregationist. In April, King arrived with a manifesto demanding an end to racist hiring practices and segregated public accommodations and the creation of a biracial committee to oversee desegregation. Connor's police began jailing hundreds of demonstrators, including King himself. Held in solitary confinement for several days, King managed to write a response to a group of Birmingham clergy who had deplored the protests. King's "Letter from a Birmingham Jail" set out the key moral issues at stake, and scoffed at those who claimed the campaign was illegal and ill timed.

After King's release on bail, the campaign intensified. The SCLC kept up the pressure by recruiting thousands of Birmingham's young students for a "children's crusade." In early May, Connor unleashed high-powered water cannons, billy clubs, and snarling police dogs to break up demonstrations. Millions of Americans reacted with horror to the violent scenes from Birmingham shown on national television. On May 10, mediators from the Justice Department negotiated an uneasy truce. The SCLC agreed to an immediate end to the protests. In exchange, businesses would desegregate and begin hiring African Americans over the next three months, and a biracial city committee would oversee desegregation of public facilities.

A few days after the announcement, more than a thousand robed Ku Klux Klansmen burned a cross in a park on the outskirts of Birmingham. When bombs rocked SCLC headquarters and the home of King's brother, a Birmingham minister, enraged blacks took to the streets and pelted police and firefighters with stones and bottles. President Kennedy ordered 3,000 Army troops into the city and prepared to nationalize the Alabama National Guard. The violence receded, and white businesspeople and politicians began to carry out the agreed-upon pact. But in September, a bomb killed four black girls in a Birmingham Baptist church, reminding the city and the world that racial harmony was still a long way off.

The Birmingham campaign and the other protests it sparked over the next seven months engaged more than 100,000 people and led to nearly 15,000 arrests. The civil rights community now drew support from millions of Americans, black and white. At the same time, Birmingham changed the nature of black protest. The black unemployed and working poor who joined in the struggle brought a different perspective from that of the students, professionals, and members of the religious middle class who had dominated the Movement before Birmingham. They cared less about the philosophy of nonviolence and more about immediate gains in employment and housing and an end to police brutality.

JFK AND THE MARCH ON WASHINGTON

The growth of black activism and of white support convinced President Kennedy the moment had come to press for sweeping civil rights legislation. On June 11, the president went on national television and offered his personal endorsement of the Movement. The next week, Kennedy asked Congress for a broad law that would ensure voting rights, outlaw segregation in public facilities, and bolster federal authority to deny funds for discriminatory programs. Knowing they would face a stiff fight from congressional conservatives,

Part of the huge throng of marchers at the historic March on Washington for "jobs and freedom," August 28, 1963. The size of the crowd, the stirring oratory and song, and the live network television coverage produced one of the most memorable political demonstrations in the nation's history.

administration officials began an intense lobbying effort in support of the law. After three years of fence sitting, Kennedy finally committed his office and his political future to the civil rights cause.

Movement leaders lauded the president's initiative. Yet they understood that racial hatred still haunted the nation. Only hours after Kennedy's television speech, a gunman murdered Medgar Evers, leader of the Mississippi NAACP, outside his home in Jackson, Mississippi. To pressure Congress and demonstrate the urgency of their cause, a broad coalition of civil rights groups planned a massive, nonviolent **March on Washington**. The idea had deep roots in black protest. A. Philip Randolph, head of the Brotherhood of Sleeping Car Porters, had originally proposed such a march in 1941 to protest discrimination against blacks in defense industries (see Chapter 25). More than twenty years later, Randolph, along with his aide Bayard Rustin, revived the concept and convinced leaders of the major civil rights groups to support it.

Leaders from the SCLC, the NAACP, SNCC, the Urban League, and CORE—the leading organizations in the civil rights community—put aside their tactical differences to forge a broad consensus for the event. John Lewis, the young head of SNCC, planned a speech that denounced the Kennedys as hypocrites. Lewis's speech enraged Walter Reuther, the white liberal leader of the United Auto Workers union, which had helped finance the march. Randolph, the Movement's acknowledged elder statesman, convinced Lewis to tone down his remarks. "We've come this far," he implored. "For the sake of unity, change it."

On August 28, 1963, more than a quarter of a million people, including 50,000 whites, gathered at the Lincoln Memorial to rally for "jobs and freedom." At the end of a long, exhilarating day of speeches and freedom songs, Martin Luther King Jr. provided the emotional climax. Combining the democratic promise of the Declaration of Independence with the religious fervor of his Baptist heritage, King stirred the crowd and the nation with his dream for America.

The following year, at age 35, King received the Nobel Peace Prize, which both solidified his reputation as the premier voice of the Movement and added greatly to his stature within mainstream American culture. The award also demonstrated the truly global impact of the Movement he led.

LBJ AND THE CIVIL RIGHTS ACT OF 1964

An extraordinary demonstration of interracial unity, the March on Washington stood as the high-water mark in the struggle for civil rights. It buoyed the spirits of Movement leaders, as well as of liberals pushing the new civil rights bill through Congress. But the assassination of John F. Kennedy on November 22, 1963, in Dallas threw an ominous cloud over the whole nation and the civil rights movement in particular.

Lyndon Baines Johnson (LBJ), Kennedy's successor, had never been much of a friend to civil rights. Throughout the 1950s, as a senator from Texas, he had worked to obstruct the passage and enforcement of civil rights laws. But as vice president he had ably chaired Kennedy's working group on equal employment. Even so, civil rights activists looked upon Johnson warily as he took over the Oval Office.

As president, Johnson realized that he faced a new political reality, created by the civil rights movement. Eager to unite the Democratic Party and prove himself as a national leader, he seized on civil rights as a golden political opportunity. Throughout the early months of 1964, the new president let it be known that he would brook no compromise on civil rights. Johnson exploited all his skills as a political insider to persuade key members of the House and Senate. Working with the president, the fifteen-year-old Leadership Conference on Civil Rights coordinated a sophisticated lobbying effort in Congress. Groups such as the NAACP, the AFL-CIO, the National Council of Churches, and the American Jewish Congress made the case for a strong civil rights bill. The House

Read the **Document**

John Lewis, Address at the March on Washington (1963) at **www.myhistorylab.com**

Watch the **Video**

Civil Rights March on Washington (1963) at **www.myhistorylab.com**

March on Washington Historic gathering of over 250,000 people in Washington D.C. in 1963 marching for jobs and freedom.

OVERVIEW | Court Decisions, and Executive Orders

Year	Decision, Law, or Executive Order	Significance
1939	*Missouri* v. *ex. rel. Gaines*	Required University of Missouri Law School either to admit African Americans or build another fully equal law school
1941	Executive Order 8802 (by President Roosevelt)	Banned racial discrimination in defense industry and government offices; established Fair Employment Practices Committee to investigate violations
1946	*Morgan* v. *Virginia*	Ruled that segregation on interstate buses violated federal law and created an "undue burden" on interstate commerce
1948	Executive Order 9981 (by President Truman)	Desegregated the U.S. armed forces
1950	*McLaurin* v. *Oklahoma State Regents*	Ruled that forcing an African American student to sit, eat, and study in segregated facilities was unconstitutional because it inevitably created a "badge of inferiority"
1950	*Sweatt* v. *Painter*	Ruled that an inferior law school created by the University of Texas to serve African Americans violated their right to equal protection and ordered Herman Sweatt to be admitted to University of Texas Law School
1954	*Brown* v. *Board of Education of Topeka I*	Declared "separate educational facilities are inherently unequal," thus overturning *Plessy* v. *Ferguson* (1896) and the "separate but equal" doctrine as it applied to public schools
1955	*Brown* v. *Board of Education of Topeka II*	Ordered school desegregation to begin with "all deliberate speed," but offered no timetable
1957	Civil Rights Act	Created Civil Rights Division within the Justice Department
1964	Civil Rights Act	Prohibited discrimination in employment and most places of public accommodation on basis of race, color, religion, sex, or national origin; outlawed bias in federally assisted programs; created Equal Employment Opportunity Commission
1965	Voting Rights Act	Authorized federal supervision of voter registration in states and counties where fewer than half of voting age residents were registered; outlawed literacy and other discriminatory tests in voter registration

•••─Read the Document

The Civil Rights Act of 1964 at **www.myhistorylab.com**

Civil Rights Act of 1964 Federal legislation that outlawed discrimination in public accommodations and employment on the basis of race, skin color, sex, religion, or national origin.

passed the bill in February by a 290–130 vote. The more difficult fight would be in the Senate, where a southern filibuster promised to block or weaken the bill. By June, however, Johnson's persistence paid off. The southern filibuster collapsed.

On July 2, 1964, Johnson signed the **Civil Rights Act of 1964.** This landmark law represented the most significant civil rights legislation since Reconstruction. It prohibited discrimination in most places of public accommodation; it banned discrimination in employment on the basis of race, color, religion, sex, or national origin; it outlawed bias in federally assisted programs; it authorized the Justice Department to institute suits to desegregate public schools and other facilities; and it provided technical and financial aid to communities desegregating their schools. The act also created the Equal Employment Opportunity Commission (EEOC) to investigate and litigate cases of job discrimination.

There were important unintended consequences of this landmark legislation as well. It gave legal foundation to affirmative action policies and to the assertion of equal rights for women and nonblack minorities. And on a political level, LBJ was perhaps more prescient than he realized when he commented after signing the bill that the Civil Rights Act "delivered the South to the Republican Party."

MISSISSIPPI FREEDOM SUMMER

While Johnson and his liberal allies won the congressional battle for the new civil rights bill, a coalition of workers led by SNCC launched the Freedom Summer project, an ambitious effort to register black voters and directly challenge the iron rule of segregation. Mississippi stood as the toughest test for the civil rights movement. It was the nation's poorest state and by most statistical measures the most backward, and it had remained largely untouched by the freedom struggle.

Planned by Bob Moses of SNCC and Dave Dennis of CORE, the project recruited over 900 volunteers, mostly white college students, to aid in voter registration, teach in "freedom schools," and help build a "Freedom Party" as an alternative to Mississippi's all-white Democratic Party. Organizers expected violence, which was precisely why they wanted white volunteers. Dave Dennis later explained their reasoning: "The death of a white college student would bring on more attention to what was going on than for a black college student getting it. That's cold, but that was also in another sense speaking the language of this country."

On June 21, while most project volunteers were still training in Ohio, three activists disappeared in Neshoba County, Mississippi, when they went to investigate the burning of a black church that was supposed to serve as a freedom school. Six weeks later, FBI agents discovered the bodies of the three—northern white students Michael Schwerner and

QUICK REVIEW

Johnson and Civil Rights

- Johnson had worked to obstruct civil rights legislation in the 1950s.
- Saw civil rights for African Americans as a way of uniting the Democratic Party.
- Applied personal political skills to passage of Civil Rights Act of 1964.

An interracial group of volunteers singing in front of a bus during the Freedom Summer Project in Mississippi, 1964. Images portraying black and white unity in the civil rights struggle reflected the powerful idealism that attracted many young people to "the Movement."

Andrew Goodman, and a local black activist, James Chaney—buried in an earthen dam. Over the summer, at least three other civil rights workers died violently. Project workers suffered 1,000 arrests, 80 beatings, 35 shooting incidents, and 30 bombings in homes, churches, and schools.

Within the project, simmering problems tested the ideal of the Beloved Community. Black veterans of SNCC resented the affluent white volunteers, many of whom had not come to terms with their own racial prejudices. White volunteers often found it difficult to communicate in the southern communities with local African Americans, wary of breaking old codes of deference. Sexual tensions between black male and white female volunteers also strained relations. A number of both black and white women, led by Ruby Doris Robinson, Mary King, and Casey Hayden, began to raise the issue of women's equality as a companion goal to racial equality. The day-to-day reality of violent reprisals, police harassment, and constant fear took a hard toll on everyone.

The project did manage to rivet national attention on Mississippi racism, and it won enormous sympathy from northern liberals. Among their concrete accomplishments, the volunteers could point with pride to more than forty freedom schools that brought classes in reading, arithmetic, politics, and African American history to thousands of black children. Some 60,000 black voters signed up to join the Mississippi Freedom Democratic Party (MFDP). In August 1964, the MFDP sent a slate of delegates to the Democratic National Convention looking to challenge the credentials of the all-white regular state delegation.

At the Democrats' Atlantic City convention, the idealism of **Freedom Summer** collided with the more cynical needs of the national Democratic Party. Concerned that Republicans might carry a number of southern states in November, President Johnson opposed seating the MFDP because he wanted to avoid a divisive floor fight. Led by Senator Hubert Humphrey, whom LBJ had already picked as his running mate, Johnson's forces offered a compromise that would have given the MFDP two token seats on the floor. Bitter over what they saw as a betrayal, the MFDP delegates turned the offer down. Within SNCC, the defeat of the MFDP intensified African American disillusionment with the Democratic Party and the liberal establishment.

MALCOLM X AND BLACK CONSCIOUSNESS

Frustrated with the limits of nonviolent protest and electoral politics, younger activists within SNCC found themselves increasingly drawn to the militant rhetoric and vision of Malcolm X, who since 1950 had been the preeminent spokesman for the black nationalist religious sect, the **Nation of Islam (NOI)**. Founded in depression-era Detroit by Elijah Muhammad, the NOI, like the followers of black-nationalist leader Marcus Garvey in the 1920s (see Chapter 23), aspired to create a self-reliant, highly disciplined, and proud community—a separate "nation" for black people. During the 1950s, the NOI (also called Black Muslims) successfully organized in northern black communities. It operated restaurants, retail stores, and schools as models for black economic self-sufficiency.

The man known as Malcolm X had been born Malcolm Little in 1925 and raised in Lansing, Michigan. His father, a preacher and a follower of Marcus Garvey, was killed in a racist attack by local whites. In his youth, Malcolm led a life of petty crime, eventually ending up in prison. While in jail he educated himself and converted to the Nation of Islam. He took the surname "X" to symbolize his original African family name, lost through slavery. Emerging from jail in 1952, he became a dynamic organizer, editor, and speaker for the Nation of Islam. He encouraged his audiences to take pride in their African heritage and to consider armed self-defense rather than relying solely on nonviolence—in short, to break free of white domination "by any means necessary."

In 1964, troubled by Elijah Muhammad's personal scandals (he faced paternity suits brought by two young female employees) and eager to find a more politically effective

---

Read the Document

Fannie Lou Hammer, Voting Rights in Mississippi (1962–1964) at **www.myhistorylab.com**

Watch the Video

Malcolm X at **www.myhistorylab.com**

Freedom Summer   Voter registration effort in rural Mississippi organized by black and white civil rights workers in 1964.

Nation of Islam (NOI)   Religious movement among black Americans that emphasizes self-sufficiency, self-help, and separation from white society.

Born Malcolm Little, Malcolm X (1925–65) took the name "X" as a symbol of the stolen identity of African slaves. He emerged in the early 1960s as the foremost advocate of racial unity and black nationalism. The Black Power movement, initiated in 1966 by SNCC members, was strongly influenced by Malcolm X.

approach to improving conditions for blacks, Malcolm X broke with the Nation of Islam. He made the pilgrimage to Mecca, the Muslim holy city, where he met Islamic peoples of all colors and underwent a "radical alteration in my whole outlook about 'white' men." He returned to the United States as El-Hajj Malik El-Shabazz, abandoned his black separatist views, and founded the Organization of Afro-American Unity. Malcolm now looked for common ground with the civil rights movement. He stressed the international links between the civil rights struggle in America and the problems facing emerging African nations. On February 21, 1965, Malcolm X was assassinated. His assailants were members of a New Jersey branch of the NOI, possibly infiltrated by the FBI.

In his death, Malcolm X became a martyr for the idea that soon became known as Black Power. As much as anyone, he pointed the way to a new black consciousness that celebrated black history, black culture, African heritage, and black self-sufficiency.

SELMA AND THE VOTING RIGHTS ACT OF 1965

Lyndon Johnson won reelection in 1964 by a landslide, capturing 61 percent of the popular vote. Of the 6 million black people who voted in the election—2 million more than in 1960—an overwhelming 94 percent cast their ballots for Johnson. Republican candidate Barry Goldwater managed to carry only his home state of Arizona and five Deep South states. With Democrats in firm control of both the Senate and the House, civil rights leaders believed the time was ripe for further legislative gains. The 1964 ratification of the Twenty-Fourth Amendment to the Constitution outlawed the poll tax or any other tax as a condition of voting. Johnson and his staff began drafting a tough voting rights bill (see Map 28.2).

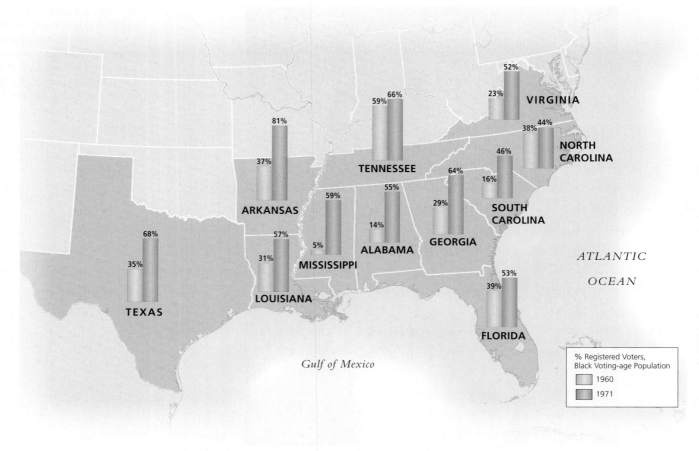

MAP 28.2

Impact of the Voting Rights Act of 1965 Voter registration among African Americans in the South increased significantly between 1960 and 1971.

IN WHICH states was the increase in registered African American voters particularly dramatic? Why?

Once again, Movement leaders decided to create a crisis that would arouse national indignation, pressure Congress, and force federal action. King and his aides chose Selma, Alabama, as their target. In 1963, local activists had invited SNCC workers to aid voter registration efforts in the community. But they had met a violent reception from county sheriff Jim Clark. Sensing that Clark might be another Bull Connor, King arrived in Selma in January 1965, just after accepting the Nobel Peace Prize in Oslo. King, the SCLC staff, and SNCC workers led daily marches on the Dallas County Courthouse, where hundreds of black citizens tried to get their names added to voter lists. By early February, Clark had imprisoned more than 3,000 protesters.

In early March SCLC staffers called on black activists to march from Selma to Montgomery, where they planned to deliver a list of grievances to Governor Wallace. On Sunday, March 7, while King preached to his church in Atlanta, a group of 600 marchers crossed the Pettus Bridge on the Alabama River, on their way to Montgomery. A group of mounted, heavily armed county and state lawmen blocked their path and ordered them to turn back. When the marchers did not move, the lawmen attacked with billy clubs and tear gas, driving the protesters back over the bridge.

The dramatic "Bloody Sunday" attack received extensive coverage on network television, prompting a national uproar. King issued a public call for civil rights supporters to come to Selma for a second march on Montgomery. But a federal court temporarily enjoined the SCLC from proceeding with the march. He reluctantly accepted a face-saving compromise: in return for a promise from Alabama authorities not to harm marchers, King would lead his followers across the Pettus Bridge, stop, pray briefly, and then turn back. This plan outraged the more militant SNCC activists and sharpened their distrust of King and the SCLC.

Just when it seemed the Selma movement might die, white racist violence revived it. A gang of white toughs attacked four white Unitarian ministers who had come to Selma to participate in the march. One of them, Reverend James J. Reeb of Boston, died of multiple skull fractures. His death brought new calls for federal action. On March 15, President Johnson delivered a televised address to a joint session of Congress to request passage of a voting rights bill. Johnson prevailed upon federal judge Frank Johnson to issue a ruling allowing the march to proceed and warned Governor Wallace not to interfere.

On March 21, Martin Luther King Jr. led more than 3,000 black and white marchers out of Selma on the road to Montgomery, where the bus boycott that marked the beginning of his involvement had occurred nine years before. Four days later, they arrived at the Alabama statehouse. Their ranks had been swelled by more than 30,000 supporters, including hundreds of prominent politicians, entertainers, and black leaders.

In August 1965, President Johnson signed the **Voting Rights Act** into law. It authorized federal supervision of registration in states and counties where fewer than half of voting-age residents were registered. It also outlawed literacy and other discriminatory tests that had been used to prevent blacks from registering to vote. Between 1964 and 1968, the number of southern black voters grew from 1 million to 3.1 million. For the first time in their lives, black Southerners in hundreds of small towns and rural communities could enjoy full participation in American politics. Ten years after the Montgomery bus boycott, the civil rights movement had reached a peak of national influence and interracial unity.

Yet even amid this triumph, the growing mood of desperation among African Americans in northern ghettoes suggested the limits of the Movement and interracial unity. There had been a violent uprising in New York's Harlem in the summer of 1964 and a far more widespread and destructive rebellion in the Watts section of Los Angeles in August 1965 (see Chapter 29). These marked the first of the "long, hot summer" uprisings that would alienate many white citizens who had been sympathetic to

Voting rights demonstrators on the historic four-day, fifty-four mile trek from Selma to Montgomery Alabama, March 1965. Intensive media coverage helped swell the original 3,000 marchers to over 30,000 supporters at a climactic rally in front of the Alabama state capitol in Montgomery.

Voting Rights Act Legislation in 1965 that overturned a variety of practices by which states systematically denied voter registration to minorities.

the nonviolent civil rights struggle. They served notice as well that the growing frustration and alienation of northern blacks could not be addressed with the same principles, tactics, and solutions that had made the southern civil rights movement successful.

CIVIL RIGHTS BEYOND BLACK AND WHITE

HOW DID the African American struggle for civil rights inspire other American minority groups?

Minorities other than African Americans also had long been denied their civil rights. After World War II, Latinos, Indian peoples, and Asian Americans began making their own halting efforts to improve their political, legal, and economic status.

MEXICAN AMERICANS AND MEXICAN IMMIGRANTS

The Mexican American community in the West and Southwest included both longtime U.S. citizens and noncitizen immigrants from Mexico. After World War II, several Mexican American political organizations sought to secure equal rights and equal opportunity for their community by stressing its American identity. The most important of these groups were the League of United Latin American Citizens (LULAC), launched in Texas in 1928, and the GI Forum, founded in Texas in 1948 by Mexican American veterans of World War II. Both emphasized learning English, assimilating into American society, improving education, and voting to gain political power. LULAC successfully pursued two important legal cases that anticipated *Brown* v. *Board of Education*. In *Mendez* v. *Westminster*, a 1947 California case, and in the 1948 *Delgado* case in Texas, the Supreme Court upheld lower-court rulings that declared segregation of Mexican Americans unconstitutional. LULAC won another significant legal battle in the 1954 *Hernandez* decision, in which the Supreme Court ended the exclusion of Mexican Americans from Texas jury lists.

Mexican migration to the United States increased dramatically during and after World War II. The *bracero* program, a cooperative effort between the U.S. and Mexican governments, brought some 300,000 Mexicans to the United States during the war as temporary agricultural and railroad workers. American agribusiness came to depend on

Delegates to the 1948 National Convention of the League of United Latin American Citizens met in Kingsville, Texas. After World War II, LULAC grew to about 15,000 members active in 200 local councils, mostly in Texas and California.

Mexicans as a key source of cheap farm labor, and the program continued after the war. Most *braceros* endured harsh work, poor food, and substandard housing in migratory labor camps. Some migrated into the newly emerging *barrios*—Hispanic neighborhoods—in cities such as San Antonio, Los Angeles, El Paso, and Denver. Many *braceros* and their children became American citizens, but most returned to Mexico. Another group of postwar Mexican immigrants were the *mojados*, or "wetbacks," so called because many swam the Rio Grande to enter the United States illegally.

This continued flow of immigrant workers into the Southwest heightened tensions within the Mexican American community. LULAC and the GI Forum contended that Mexican American civil rights activists needed to focus their efforts on American citizens of Mexican descent. Yet within Mexican American communities, where citizens and noncitizens shared language and work experience and made families together, this distinction had always been blurry.

In 1954, trying to curb the flow of undocumented immigrants from Mexico, the Eisenhower administration launched the massive "Operation Wetback." For three years, Immigration and Naturalization Service (INS) agents rounded up some 3.7 million allegedly undocumented migrants and sent them back over the border. INS agents made little effort to distinguish so-called illegals from *braceros* and Mexican American citizens. Many families were broken up, and thousands who had lived in the United States for a decade or more found themselves deported. Many deportees were denied basic civil liberties, such as due process, and suffered physical abuse and intimidation.

The government campaign against aliens pushed LULAC, the GI Forum, and other activist groups to change their strategy in a critical way. The campaign to win full civil rights for American citizens of Mexican descent would increasingly be linked to improving the lives—and asserting the rights—of all Mexican immigrants, both documented and undocumented. If the government and the broader American public refused to distinguish between a Mexican national, a resident alien of the United States, a naturalized American citizen, or a native-born Spanish-speaking American, why should Mexican Americans cling to these distinctions? By the 1960s, a new civil rights movement emerged, *la raza*, based on the shared ethnicity and historical experiences of the broader Mexican American community.

PUERTO RICANS

The United States seized Puerto Rico in 1898, during the final stages of the Spanish-American War. The Jones Act of 1917 made the island an unincorporated territory of the United States and granted U.S. citizenship to all Puerto Ricans. Over the next several decades, Puerto Rico's economic base shifted from a diversified, subsistence-oriented agriculture to a single export crop—sugar. U.S. absentee owners dominated the sugar industry, claiming most of the island's arable land, previously tilled by small farmers growing crops for local consumption. Puerto Rico's sugar industry grew enormously profitable, but few island residents benefited from this expansion. By the 1930s, unemployment and poverty were widespread and the island was forced to import its foodstuffs.

Small communities of Puerto Rican migrants had begun to form in New York City during the 1920s. The largest was on the Upper East Side of Manhattan—*el barrio* in East Harlem. During World War II, labor shortages led the federal government to sponsor the recruitment of Puerto Rican workers for industrial jobs in New Jersey, Philadelphia, and Chicago. But the "great migration" took place from 1945 to 1964. During these two decades, the number of Puerto Ricans living on the mainland jumped from fewer than 100,000 to roughly 1 million. Economic opportunity was the chief impetus for this migration, because the island suffered from high unemployment and low wages.

The Puerto Rican community in East (or Spanish) Harlem mushroomed, and new communities in the South Bronx and Brooklyn began to emerge. By 1970, there were about 800,000 Puerto Ricans in New York—more than 10 percent of the city's population. New Puerto Rican communities also took root in Connecticut, Massachusetts, New Jersey, and the Midwest. Puerto Ricans frequently circulated between the island and the mainland, often returning home when economic conditions on the mainland were less favorable.

The experience of Puerto Rican migrants both resembled and differed from that of other immigrant groups in significant ways. Like Mexican immigrants, Puerto Ricans were foreign in language, culture, and experience; unlike Mexicans, they entered the continental United States as citizens. Many Puerto Ricans were also black. Racial and ethnic discrimination came as a double shock, since Puerto Ricans, as citizens, came to America with a sense of entitlement. In New York, Puerto Ricans found themselves barred from most craft unions, excluded from certain neighborhoods, and forced to take jobs largely in the low-paying garment industry and service trades. Puerto Rican children were not well served by a public school system insensitive to language differences and too willing to track Spanish-speaking students into obsolete vocational programs.

By the early 1970s, Puerto Rican families were substantially poorer on average than the total U.S. population, and they had the lowest median income of any Latino group. The steep decline in manufacturing jobs and in the garment industry in New York during the 1960s and 1970s hit the Puerto Rican community especially hard. The structural shift in the U.S. economy away from manufacturing and toward service and high-technology jobs reinforced the Puerto Rican community's goal of improving educational opportunities for its members. The struggle to establish and improve bilingual education in schools became an important part of this effort. Most Puerto Ricans, especially those who had succeeded in school and achieved middle-class status, continued to identify strongly with their Puerto Rican heritage and Spanish language.

JAPANESE AMERICANS

The harsh relocation program of World War II devastated the Japanese American community on the West Coast (see Chapter 25). But the war against Nazism also helped weaken older notions of white superiority and racism. During the war, the state of California had aggressively enforced an alien land law by confiscating property declared illegally held by Japanese. In November 1946, a proposition supporting the law appeared on the state ballot. Thanks in part to a campaign by the Japanese American Citizens League (JACL) reminding voters of the wartime contributions of Nisei (second-generation Japanese American) soldiers, voters overwhelmingly rejected the referendum. Two years later, the Supreme Court declared the law unconstitutional, calling it "nothing more than outright racial discrimination."

The 1952 Immigration and Nationality Act (see Chapter 26) removed the old ban against Japanese immigration and also made Issei (first-generation Japanese Americans) eligible for naturalized citizenship. Japanese Americans, who lobbied hard for the new law, greeted it with elation. "It gave the Japanese equality with all other immigrants," said JACL leader Harry Takagi, "and that was the principle we had been struggling for from the very beginning." By 1965, some 46,000 immigrant Japanese, most of them elderly Issei, had taken their citizenship oaths.

INDIAN PEOPLES

The postwar years also brought significant changes in the status and lives of Indian peoples. Congress reversed New Deal policies that had stressed Indian sovereignty and cultural independence. Responding to a variety of pressure groups, including mining and other economic interests wishing to exploit natural resources on reservations, Congress

•••—Read the Document

Exploring America: The American Indian Movement at **www.myhistorylab.com**

adopted a policy known as "termination," designed to cancel Indian treaties and termi-nate sovereignty rights. In 1953, Congress passed **House Concurrent Resolution 108**, which allowed Congress to terminate a tribe as a political entity by passing legislation spe-cific to that tribe. Supporters of termination had varied motives, but the policy added up to the return of enforced assimilation for solving the "Indian problem."

Between 1954 and 1962, Congress passed twelve termination bills covering more than sixty tribes, nearly all in the West. Even when tribes consented to their own termina-tion, they discovered that dissolution brought unforeseen problems. For example, mem-bers of the Klamaths of Oregon and the Paiutes of Utah received large cash payments from the division of tribal assets. But after these one-time payments were spent, members had to take poorly paid, unskilled jobs to survive. Many Indian peoples became depen-dent on state social services and slipped into poverty and alcoholism.

Along with termination, the federal government gave greater emphasis to a reloca-tion program aimed at speeding up assimilation. The Bureau of Indian Affairs encour-aged reservation Indians to relocate to cities, where they were provided with housing and jobs. For some, relocation meant assimilation, intermarriage with whites, and loss of tribal identity. Others, homesick and unable to adjust to an alien culture and place, either returned to reservations or wound up on the margins of city life. Still others regu-larly traveled back and forth. In some respects, this urban migration paralleled the larger postwar shift of rural peoples to cities and suburbs.

Indians increasingly came to see termination as a policy geared mainly to exploiting resources on Indian lands. By the early 1960s, a new movement was emerging to defend Indian sovereignty. The National Congress of American Indians (NCAI) condemned ter-mination, calling for a review of federal policies and a return to self-determination. The NCAI led a political and educational campaign that challenged the goal of assimilation and created a new awareness among white people that Indians had the right to remain Indians. When the termination policy ended in the early 1960s, it had affected only about 3 percent of federally recognized Indian peoples.

Taking their cue from the civil rights movement, Indian activists used the court sys-tem to reassert sovereign rights. Indian and white liberal lawyers, many with experience in civil rights cases, worked through the Native American Rights Fund. A series of Supreme Court decisions, culminating in *United States* v. *Wheeler* (1978), reasserted the principle of "unique and limited" sovereignty. The Court recognized tribal indepen-dence except where limited by treaty or Congress.

The Indian population had been growing since the early years of the century, but most reservations had trouble making room for a new generation. Indians suffered increased rates of poverty, chronic unemployment, alcoholism, and poor health. The average Indian family in the early 1960s earned only one-third of the average family income in the United States. Those who remained in the cities usually became "ethnic Indians," identifying themselves more as simply "Indians" than as members of specific tribes. By the late 1960s, ethnic Indians had begun emphasizing civil rights over tribal rights, making common cause with African Americans and other minorities. The National Indian Youth Council (NIYC), founded in 1960, tried to unite the two causes of equality for individual Indians and special status for tribes. But the organization faced dif-ficult contradictions between a common Indian identity, emphasizing Indians as a single ethnic group, and tribal identity, stressing the citizenship of Indians in separate nations.

REMAKING THE GOLDEN DOOR: THE IMMIGRATION AND NATIONALITY ACT OF 1965

The egalitarian political climate created by the civil rights movement nurtured efforts to modernize and reform the country's immigration policies. In 1965, Congress passed a new **Immigration and Nationality Act**, abolishing the national origins quotas that had

QUICK REVIEW

Termination

♦ Cancellation of treaties and sov-ereignty rights under pressure from mining and other economic interests.

♦ 1954–1962: Termination bills passed covering sixty tribes.

♦ Termination contributed to poverty and social problems among Indian peoples.

House Concurrent Resolution 108 Resolution passed in 1953 that allowed Congress to pass legislation to terminate a specific tribe as a political entity.

Immigration and Nationality Act Act passed in 1965 that abolished national origin quotas and established overall hemisphere quotas.

been in place since the 1920s and substituting overall hemispheric limits: 120,000 visas annually for immigrants from the Western Hemisphere and 170,000 for those from the Eastern Hemisphere (with a 20,000 limit from any single country). The act was intended to redress the grievances of Eastern and Southern European ethnic groups who had been largely shut out since 1924.

Exempted from numerical quotas were immigrants seeking family reunification with American citizens or resident aliens. In addition, preferences to those with specialized job skills and training, in fields like medicine and engineering, were extended to people from the nations of the Eastern Hemisphere. The high priority given family reunification created an unprecedented cycle of "chain immigration and sponsorship" of people seeking to join relatives already in the United States. As initial immigrants attained permanent resident or citizenship status, they would sponsor family members and relatives to come over. Once these family members and relatives arrived in the United States and became resident aliens or citizens, they in turn could sponsor their family members, and so on.

The consequences for Asian American communities in particular were profound. The number of Asian Americans soared from about 1 million in 1965 to 11 million by the end of the century. Immigrants from India and the Philippines included a high percentage of health care professionals, whereas many Chinese and Korean immigrants found work in professional and managerial occupations as well as their own small businesses. At the same time, low-skilled and impoverished Asians poured into the "Chinatowns" and "Koreatowns" of cities like New York and Los Angeles, taking jobs in restaurants, hotels, and garment manufacturing. Four times as many Asians settled in the United States in this period as in the entire previous history of the nation.

The 1965 act also created conditions that increased undocumented immigration from Latin America. The new limits on Western Hemisphere migration, along with the simultaneous ending of the *bracero* program, tempted many thousands to enter the United States illegally. The Immigration and Naturalization Service arrested and deported 500,000 undocumented aliens each year in the decade following the act, most of them from Mexico, Central America, and the Caribbean. By the 1980s, more than 80 percent of all legal immigrants to the United States came from either Asia or Latin America; if one included illegal immigrants, the figure would surpass 90 percent.

CONCLUSION

The mass movement for civil rights was arguably the most important domestic event in twentieth-century American history. The struggle that began in Montgomery, Alabama, in December 1955 ultimately transformed race relations in thousands of American communities. By the early 1960s, this community-based movement had placed civil rights at the very center of national political life. It achieved its greatest successes by invoking the Constitution—the supreme law of the land—to destroy legal segregation and win individual freedom for African Americans. The Civil Rights Act of 1964 and the Voting Rights Act of 1965 testified to the power of an African American and white liberal coalition. Yet the persistence of racism, poverty, and ghetto slums challenged a central assumption of liberalism: that equal protection of constitutional rights would give all Americans equal opportunities in life. By the mid-1960s, many black people had begun to question the core values of liberalism, the benefits of alliance with whites, and the philosophy of nonviolence. At the same time, a

CHRONOLOGY

1941   Executive Order 8802 forbids racial discrimination in defense industries and government

1946   In *Morgan* v. *Virginia*, U.S. Supreme Court rules that segregation on interstate buses is unconstitutional

President Harry Truman creates the President's Committee on Civil Rights

1947   Jackie Robinson becomes the first African American on a major league baseball team

1948   President Truman issues executive order desegregating the armed forces

1954   In *Brown* v. *Board of Education*, Supreme Court rules segregated schools inherently unequal

1955   Supreme Court rules that school desegregation must proceed "with all deliberate speed"

Montgomery bus boycott begins

1956   Montgomery bus boycott ends in victory as the Supreme Court affirms a district court ruling that segregation on buses is unconstitutional

1957   Southern Christian Leadership Conference (SCLC) is founded

President Dwight Eisenhower sends in federal troops to protect African American students integrating Little Rock, Arkansas, high school

1960   Sit-in movement begins as four college students sit at a lunch counter in Greensboro, North Carolina, and ask to be served

Student Nonviolent Coordinating Committee (SNCC) founded

Board of Indian Commissioners is created

1961   Freedom Rides begin

1962   James Meredith integrates the University of Mississippi

The Albany movement fails to end segregation in Albany, Georgia

1963   SCLC initiates campaign to desegregate Birmingham, Alabama

Medgar Evers, leader of the Mississippi NAACP, is assassinated

March on Washington; Martin Luther King Jr. delivers his historic "I Have a Dream" speech

1964   Mississippi Freedom Summer project brings students to Mississippi to teach and register voters

President Johnson signs the Civil Rights Act of 1964

Civil rights workers Michael Schwerner, James Chaney, and Andrew Goodman are found buried in Philadelphia, Mississippi

Mississippi Freedom Democratic Party (MFDP) is denied seats at the 1964 Democratic Presidential Convention

1965   SCLC and SNCC begin voter registration campaign in Selma, Alabama

Malcolm X is assassinated

Civil rights marchers walk from Selma to Montgomery

Voting Rights Act of 1965 is signed into law

Immigration and Nationality Act

---

conservative white backlash against the gains made by African Americans further weakened the liberal political consensus.

In challenging the persistence of widespread poverty and institutional racism, the civil rights movement called for deep structural changes in American life. By 1967, Martin Luther King Jr. was articulating a broad and radical vision linking the struggle against racial injustice to other defects in American society. "The black revolution," he argued, "is much more than a struggle for the rights of Negroes. It is forcing America to face all its interrelated flaws—racism, poverty, militarism, and materialism. It is exposing evils that are deeply rooted in the whole structure of our society." Curing these ills would prove far more difficult than ending legal segregation.

REVIEW QUESTIONS

1. What were the key legal and political antecedents to the civil rights struggle in the 1940s and early 1950s? What organizations played the most central role? Which tactics continued to be used, and which were abandoned?

2. How did African American communities challenge legal segregation in the South? Compare the strategies of key organizations, such as the NAACP, SNCC, SCLC, and CORE.

3. Discuss the varieties of white resistance to the civil rights movement. Which were most effective in slowing the drive for equality?

4. Analyze the civil rights movement's complex relationship with the national Democratic Party between 1948 and 1964. How was the party transformed by its association with the movement? What political gains and losses did that association entail?

5. What legal and institutional impact did the movement have on American life? How did it change American culture and politics? Where did it fail?

6. What relationship did the African Americans who struggled for civil rights have with other American minorities? How—if at all—did these minorities benefit? Did they build their own versions of the movement?

KEY TERMS

Albany Movement (p. 752)

Brown v. *Board of Education* (p. 744)

Civil Rights Act of 1964 (p. 756)

Congress of Racial Equality (CORE) (p. 750)

Freedom Summer (p. 758)

House Concurrent Resolution 108 (p. 765)

Immigration and Nationality Act (p. 765)

March on Washington (p. 755)

Nation of Islam (NOI) (p. 758)

Southern Manifesto (p. 746)

Southern Christian Leadership Conference (SCLC) (p. 747)

Voting Rights Act (p. 761)

PEARSON
myhistorylab Connections

Reinforce what you learned in this chapter by studying the many documents,
images, maps, review tools, and videos available at www.myhistorylab.com.

Read and Review

✓●—[Study and Review Chapter 28

●●●—[Read the Document

Sterling A. Brown, "Out of Their Mouths" (1942)

Brown v. Board of Education of Topeka (1954)

The Southern Manifesto (1956)

*Student Non-Violent Coordinating Committee,
"Statement of Purpose" (1960)*

Charles Sherrod, SNCC Memorandum (1961)

*John Lewis, Address at the March on
Washington (1963)*

The Civil Rights Act of 1964

*Fannie Lou Hammer, Voting Rights in Mississippi
(1962–1964)*

👁—[See the Map *Impact of the Voting Rights Act
of 1965*

Research and Explore

●●●—[Read the Document

*Exploring America: The American Indian
Movement*

The Civil Rights Movement

Profiles
Ella Baker
César Chávez

((●—[Watch the Video

Malcolm X

The Civil Rights Movement

Civil Rights March on Washington, 1963

Jackie Robinson and the Integration of Baseball

*Photographing the Civil Rights Movement:
Birmingham, 1963*

*How Did the Civil Rights Movement Change
American Schools?*

((●—[Hear the Audio

Hear the audio files for Chapter 28 at
www.myhistorylab.com.

The Quest for African American Equality

Booker T. Washington was a leading African American educator in the late 19th century. Born into slavery, he would rise to the position of principal of the Tuskegee Normal Institute (teacher's college) in Alabama, later Tuskegee University. Washington's proposed that African Americans accept the racial separation of Jim Crow laws and the refusal of southern states to grant them voting rights for the time being in exchange for immediate guarantees of economic security and the right to work in industry and agriculture. Against critics angered by his temporary acceptance of Jim Crow, Washington explained that any attempt to challenge segregation would be disastrous for blacks who could later use their enhanced economic status to effect permanent change.

IN THE late 19th and early 20th centuries, Booker T. Washington and W.E.B. Du Bois both held strong positions of leadership in a segregationist society. How and in what manner were the goals of either man like those of Dr. Martin Luther King, Jr. during the civil rights movement of the 1950s and 1960s? How do the style and techniques of both men compare to those used by Dr. King?

W. E. B. Du Bois was among Washington's strongest critics and a founder of the Niagara Movement. Du Bois was the first black graduate of Harvard University. He was a principal in establishing the National Association for the Advancement of Colored People (NAACP) in 1909 and became its director of publications in 1910. Du Bois argued that segregation should be confronted directly and aggressively and was in complete opposition to a position of accommodation.

The Reverend Dr. Martin Luther King Jr., was the foremost civil rights leader of the 20th century. Beginning with the Montgomery Bus Boycott (Alabama) in 1955 that ended with a U.S. Supreme Court decision banning segregation in all forms of public transportation, King conducted an activist civil rights movement that challenged Jim Crow on both the social and political fronts in the South. King was instrumental in the establishment of a civil rights program that was founded on the philosophy of nonviolent civil disobedience based on the teachings of both Mahatma Gandhi and Henry David Thoreau. ■

JUSTICE JOHN MARSHALL HARLAN, DISSENTING OPINION, *PLESSY v. FERGUSON* (1896)

IF EVILS will result from the commingling of the two races upon public highways established for the benefit of all, they will be infinitely less than those that will surely come from state legislation regulating the enjoyment of civil rights upon the basis of race. We boast of the freedom enjoyed by our people above all other peoples. But it is difficult to reconcile that boast with a state of the law which, practically, puts the brand of servitude and degradation upon a large class of our fellow citizens,-our equals before the law. The thin disguise of 'equal' accommodations for passengers in railroad coaches will not mislead any one, nor atone for the wrong this day done....

'People of the United States,' for whom, and by whom through representatives, our government is administered. Such a system is inconsistent with the guaranty given by the constitution to each state of a republican form of government, and may be stricken down by congressional action, or by the courts in the discharge of their solemn duty to maintain the supreme law of the land, anything in the constitution or laws of any state to the contrary notwithstanding.

For the reason stated, I am constrained to withhold my assent from the opinion and judgment of the majority. ■

Booker T. Washington, Atlanta Compromise Speech (1895)

THE WISEST among my race understand that the agitation of questions of social equality is the extremist folly, and that progress in the enjoyment of all the privileges that will come to us must be the result of severe and constant struggle rather than of artificial forcing. No race that has anything to contribute to the markets of the world is long in any degree ostracized. It is important and right that all privileges of the law be ours, but it is vastly more important that we be prepared for the exercise of these privileges. The opportunity to earn a dollar in a factory just now is worth infinitely more than the opportunity to spend a dollar in an opera-house. ■

W.E.B. Du Bois, Of Mr. Booker T. Washington and Others (1903)

THE BLACK men of America have a duty to perform, a duty stern and delicate, - a forward movement to oppose a part of the work of their greatest leader. So far as Mr. Washington preaches Thrift, Patience, and Industrial Training for the masses, we must hold up his hands and strive with him, rejoicing in his honors and glorying in the strength of this Joshua called of God and of man to lead the headless host. But so far as Mr. Washington apologizes for injustice, North or South, does not rightly value the privilege and duty of voting, belittles the emasculating effects of caste distinctions, and opposes the higher training and ambition of our brighter minds, – so far as he, the South, or the Nation, does this, - we must unceasingly and firmly oppose them. By every civilized and peaceful method we must strive for the rights which the world accords to men, clinging unwaveringly to those great words which the sons of the Fathers would fain forget: "We hold these truths to be self-evident: That all men are created equal; that they are endowed by their Creator with certain unalienable rights; that among these are life, liberty, and the pursuit of happiness." ■

▲ Booker T. Washington

▲ W.E.B. Du Bois

▲ Martin Luther King Jr.

Interpreting the Past

*We opened the hatch and Neil, with me as navigator,
begin backing out the tiny opening. It seemed like
a small eternity before I heard Neil say,
"That's one small step for man . . .
one giant leap for mankind."*
—Edwin E. "Buzz" Aldrin, Jr

On Monday, May 4, 1970, Ohio National Guardsmen fired
into a crowd of students, killing four and wounding nine others
on the campus of Kent State University.

29

WAR ABROAD, WAR AT HOME
1965–1974

((•—[**Hear** the **Audio**

Hear the audio files for Chapter 29 at **www.myhistorylab.com**.

WHY DID Johnson escalate the war in Vietnam?

HOW DID campus protests shape national political debate?

WHAT WERE the goals of Johnson's Great Society?

WHY DID divisions within American society deepen in 1968?

HOW DID race, gender, and sexual orientation gain new political importance in the 1960s?

WHAT WERE the most important successes and failures of the Nixon administration?

1965 | 1974

AMERICAN COMMUNITIES
Uptown, Chicago, Illinois

DURING THE FREEDOM SUMMER OF 1964, WHILE TEAMS OF NORTHERN college students traveled south to join voter registration campaigns among African Americans, a small group moved to Chicago to help the city's poor people take control of their communities. They targeted a neighborhood known as Uptown. The student organizers hoped to mobilize the community "so as to demand an end to poverty and the construction of a decent social order."

With the assistance of the Packinghouse Workers union, the students formed Jobs or Income Now (JOIN), opened a storefront office, and invited local residents to work with them to demand jobs and better living conditions. They spent hours listening to people, drawing out their ideas, and helping them develop scores of programs. They helped establish new social clubs, a food-buying cooperative, a community theater, and a health clinic. Within a few years, Uptown street kids had formed the Young Patriots organization, put out a community newspaper, and staffed free breakfast programs.

Chicago JOIN was one of ten similar projects sponsored by Students for a Democratic Society (SDS). Impatient with the nation's chronic poverty and Cold War politics, twenty-nine students from nine universities had met in June 1960 to form a new kind of campus-based political organization. By its peak in 1968, SDS had 350 chapters and between 60,000 and 100,000 members. Its principle of participatory democracy—with its promise to give people control over the decisions affecting their lives—appealed to a wider following of more than a million students.

In June 1962, in Port Huron, Michigan, SDS issued a declaration of principles, drafted mainly by graduate student Tom Hayden. According to the statement, poverty and social injustice were not the only problems facing America. A deeper ailment plagued American society. Everyone, including middle-class students with few material wants, suffered from a sense of "loneliness, estrangement, and alienation." *The Port Huron Statement* defined SDS as a new kind of political movement that would bring people "out of isolation and into community" so that not just the poor but all Americans could overcome their feelings of "powerlessness [and hence] resignation before the enormity of events."

SDS began with a campaign to reform the university, especially to disentangle the financial ties between campus-based research programs and the military-industrial complex. SDS also sent small groups of students to live and organize in the poor communities. Ultimately, none of these projects recruited large numbers of people. Nevertheless, organizers did succeed, to some degree, in realizing the goal specified in its slogan: "Let the People Decide." By late 1967, SDS prepared to leave JOIN in the hands of the people it had organized, which was its intention from the beginning.

Initially, even Lyndon Baines Johnson promoted civic participation. The Great Society, as the president called his domestic program, promised more than the abolition of poverty and racial inequality. In May 1964, at the University of Michigan, the president described his goal as a society "where every child can find knowledge to enrich his mind and to enlarge his talents," where "the city of man serves not only the needs of the body and the demands of commerce but the desire for beauty and the hunger for community."

By 1967, the Vietnam War had pushed aside such ambitions. SDS threw its energies into building a movement against the war in Vietnam. President Johnson, meanwhile, pursued a foreign policy that would swallow up the funding for his own plans for a war on poverty and would precipitate a very different war at home, Americans against Americans. As hawks and doves lined up on opposite sides, the Vietnam War created a huge and enduring rift.

The dream of community did not vanish, but consensus became increasingly remote by the late 1960s. By that time, parents and children were at odds over values and aspirations, urban uprisings were rocking the nation, and political leaders were struck down by assassins' bullets. New protest groups—Black Power, Women's Liberation, Gay Liberation, as well as Chicano, Native American, and Asian—were staking out a highly charged "politics of identity." Political conservatives managed to triumph in the election of Richard Nixon, who went on to disgrace the office. Meanwhile, the United States continued to fight—and eventually lost—the longest war in its history.

The Vietnam War

The Vietnam War had its roots in the Truman Doctrine and its goal of containing communism (see Chapter 26). In 1954, after the Communist forces of Ho Chi Minh defeated the French colonialists and created a new government in the north, Vietnam emerged as a major zone of Cold War contention. President John Kennedy called it "the cornerstone of the Free World in Southeast Asia. President Lyndon Johnson's Secretary of Defense Robert McNamara warned that failure in Vietnam would result in "a complete shift of world power," with the "prestige and integrity" of the United States severely damaged. With the stakes so high, Johnson concluded that Americans had little choice but to fight.

JOHNSON'S WAR

Although President Kennedy had greatly increased the number of military advisers and Special Forces in South Vietnam (see Chapter 27), it was his successor, Lyndon B. Johnson, who made the decision to engage the United States in a major war there.

Throughout the winter and spring of 1964, as conditions worsened in South Vietnam, Johnson's advisers quietly laid the groundwork for a sustained bombing campaign against North Vietnam. In early August, they found a pretext to set this plan in motion. The National Security Agency reported two attacks against U.S. destroyers by North Vietnamese patrol boats in the Gulf of Tonkin, off the coast of North Vietnam. Although the second alleged attack never took place, the report prompted Johnson to order retaliatory air strikes against bases in North Vietnam.

Johnson appealed to Congress to give him the authority "to take all necessary measures" and "all necessary steps" to defend U.S. armed forces and "to prevent further aggression." The **Gulf of Tonkin resolution** moved unanimously through the House and passed the Senate on August 7 with only two dissenting votes.

Ironically, Johnson continued his presidential campaign in 1964 with a call for restraint in Vietnam. This strategy helped him win a landslide victory over conservative Republican Barry Goldwater of Arizona, who had advocated systematic bombing of North Vietnam as a prelude to invasion.

With the election behind him, Johnson faced a hard decision. U.S. forces failed to slow the Communist insurgency into South Vietnam. Meanwhile, the U.S.-backed government in Saigon, the capital city of South Vietnam, appeared near collapse. His advisors pressed him hard to chart a new course if he hoped to avoid, as National Security Advisor McGeorge Bundy put it, a "disastrous defeat."

DEEPER INTO THE QUAGMIRE

In early February 1965, the Johnson Administration found a rationale to escalate the war. The Vietcong had dispatched a suicide bomb squad to the U.S. military base at Pleiku in the central highlands of Vietnam, killing seven and wounding more than 100 Americans. Johnson ordered immediate reprisal bombing and one week later, on February 13, authorized Operation Rolling Thunder, a campaign of gradually intensifying air attacks against North Vietnam.

Once Rolling Thunder began, President Johnson hesitated to speak frankly with the American public about his plan to widen the war by sending in more ground troops. Initially, he announced that only two battalions of Marines were being assigned to Danang to defend the airfields where bombing runs began. But six weeks later, 50,000 U.S. combat troops were in Vietnam. By November 1965, the total topped 165,000, and more troops were on the way.

The strategy pursued by the Johnson administration and implemented by General William Westmoreland—a war of attrition—was based on the premise that continuous use of heavy artillery and air power would eventually exhaust North Vietnam's resources. Meanwhile, U.S. ground forces would defeat the Vietcong in South Vietnam and thereby

WHY DID Johnson escalate the war in Vietnam?

Watch the Video
Vietnam War at **www.myhistorylab.com**

Read the Document
Johnson's Defense of the U.S. Presence in Vietnam (1965) at **www.myhistorylab.com**

Gulf of Tonkin resolution Request to Congress from President Lyndon Johnson in response to North Vietnamese torpedo boat attacks in which he sought authorization for "all necessary measures" to protect American forces and stop further aggression.

The massive bombing and ground combat created huge numbers of civilian casualties in Vietnam. The majority killed were women and children.

See the **Map**

The Vietnam War at
www.myhistorylab.com

HOW DID campus protests shape national political debate?

restore political stability to South Vietnam's pro-Western government. As Johnson once boasted, the strongest military power in the world surely could crush a Communist rebellion in a "pissant" country of peasants.

In practice, the United States wreaked havoc in South Vietnam, tearing apart its society and bringing ecological devastation to its land. Intending to eradicate the support network of the Vietcong, U.S. ground troops conducted search-and-destroy missions throughout the countryside. They attacked villagers and their homes. Seeking to ferret out Vietcong sympathizers, U.S. troops turned at any one time as many as 4 million people—approximately one-quarter of the population of South Vietnam—into refugees. By late 1968, the United States had dropped more than 3 million tons of bombs on Vietnam. Using herbicides such as Agent Orange to defoliate forests, the United States also conducted the most destructive chemical warfare in history.

Several advisers urged the president to keep the American people informed about his decisions in Vietnam, even to declare a state of national emergency. But Johnson feared he would lose momentum on domestic reform if he drew attention to foreign policy. Thus, he held to a course of intentional deceit.

THE CREDIBILITY GAP

Johnson's popularity had surged at the time of the Gulf of Tonkin resolution, but it waned rapidly. To stem the tide, Johnson worked hard to control the news media. Despite his efforts, he found himself accused of lying to the American public.

During the early 1960s, network news had either ignored Vietnam or unquestioningly supported U.S. policy. Beginning with a CBS News report by Morley Safer in August 1965, however, the tenor changed. Although government officials described the U.S. operation in the South Vietnamese village Cam Ne as an attack on "fortified Vietcong bunkers," the *CBS Evening News* showed Marines setting fire to the thatched homes of civilians. By 1967, according to a noted media observer, "every subject tended to become Vietnam." Scenes of human suffering and devastation, now broadcast daily, ultimately weakened the administration's moral justification of U.S. involvement as a defense of freedom and democracy in South Vietnam.

Skeptics stepped forward in the U.S. Congress. Democratic Senator J. William Fulbright of Arkansas, who had personally speeded the passage of the Gulf of Tonkin resolution, became the most vocal critic of Johnson's war policy. A strong supporter of the Cold War, Fulbright had nevertheless concluded that the war in Vietnam was both unwinnable and destructive to domestic reform. Meanwhile, some of the nation's most trusted European allies called for restraint in Vietnam.

The impact of the war, which cost Americans $21 billion per year, was also felt by Americans at home. Johnson convinced Congress to levy a 10 percent surcharge on individual and corporate taxes. Later adjustments tapped the Social Security fund, heretofore safe from interference. Inflation raced upward, fed by spending on the war. Johnson promised that the end of the war was in sight. As casualties multiplied, however, more and more Americans began to question his credibility and to mistrust his handling of the war.

A GENERATION IN CONFLICT

As the Vietnam war escalated, Americans from all walks of life began to doubt the wisdom of the administration's leadership. Between 1965 and 1971, much of this skepticism took on a distinctly generational character. At the forefront were the baby boomers just coming of age who broadened the definition of politics to encompass not only U.S. foreign policy but also everyday life.

"THE TIMES THEY ARE A-CHANGIN'"

The free speech movement at the University of California at Berkeley marked the beginning of a new kind of protest movement. In the fall of 1964, civil rights activists returned from Freedom Summer in Mississippi to the 27,000-student campus and decided to picket Bay Area stores that practiced discrimination in hiring. When the university administration tried to stop them from setting up information booths on campus, eighteen student groups objected, including the archconservative Students for Goldwater, claiming that their right to free speech had been abridged. The administration sent police to break up the protest rally and arrest participants. After university president Clark Kerr announced his intention to press charges against the free speech movement's leaders, a huge crowd gathered. Joining folk singer Joan Baez in singing "We Shall Overcome," nearly 1,000 people marched toward the university's administration building, where they planned to stage a sit-in until Kerr rescinded his order. The police moved in, detaining nearly 800 protestors in the largest mass arrest in California history.

Mario Savio, a Freedom Summer volunteer and philosophy student, explained that the **free speech movement** aspired to more than just the right to conduct political activity on campus. They wanted, in the phrase coined by SDS, participatory democracy. Across the country—and in many nations around the world—college students began to demand a say in their education. Students also spoke out against campus rules that treated students as children instead of as adults. After a string of campus protests, most large universities relinquished *in loco parents* (in the place of parents) policies and allowed students to live off-campus and to set their own hours.

Across the bay in San Francisco, other young adults staked out a new form of community—a **counterculture**. In 1967, the "Summer of Love," the population of the Haight-Ashbury district swelled by 75,000 as youthful adventurers from around the world gathered for a huge "be-in." Although the *San Francisco Chronicle* featured a headline reading "Mayor Warns Hippies to Stay Out of Town," masses of long-haired young men and women dressed in bell-bottoms and tie-dyed T-shirts congregated in "the Haight" to listen to music, take drugs, and "be" with each other.

The generational rebellion took many forms, including a revolution in sexual behavior. During the 1960s, more teenagers experienced premarital sex and far more talked about it openly than in previous eras. With birth control widely available, including the newly developed "pill," many young women were no longer deterred from sex by fear of pregnancy. Many heterosexual couples chose to live together outside marriage, a practice few parents condoned. A much smaller but significant number formed communes—approximately 4,000 by 1970—where members could share housekeeping and child care as well as sexual partners.

Mood-altering drugs played a large part in this counterculture. Soon-to-be-former Harvard professor Timothy Leary urged young people to "turn on, tune in, drop out" and also advocated the mass production and distribution of LSD (lysergic

free speech movement Student movement at the University of California, Berkeley, formed in 1964 to protest limitations on political activities on campus.

counterculture Various alternatives to mainstream values and behaviors that became popular in the 1960s, including experimentation with psychedelic drugs, communal living, a return to the land, Asian religions, and experimental art.

Folk and rock musician Henry Diltz was something of a hippie himself in the 1960s and took many photographs of the "alternative culture," including the famed event at Woodstock, New York. In this photograph, taken in Los Angeles in 1967, he captures a young hippie girl making a flower out of tissue paper.

acid diethylamide), which was not criminalized until 1968. Marijuana, illegal yet readily available, was often paired with rock music in a collective ritual of love and laughter.

Music played a large part in defining the counterculture. With the emergence of rock 'n' roll in the 1950s, popular music had begun to express a deliberate generational identity (see Chapter 27). Folk music, popular on campuses since the early 1960s, served as a voice of protest.

Many considered the Woodstock Music Festival the apotheosis of the counter-culture. At a farm near Woodstock, New York, more than 400,000 people gathered in August 1969 for a three-day rock concert. Thousands took drugs while security officials and local police stood by, some stripped off their clothes to dance or swim, and a few even made love in the grass.

The Woodstock Nation, as the counterculture was mythologized, did not actually represent the sentiments of most young people. Nor would its good vibes persist. The attitudes and styles of the counterculture, especially the efforts to create a new community, did speak for the large minority seeking a peaceful alternative to the intensifying climate of war. The slogan "Make Love, Not War" linked generational rebellion and opposition to the U.S. war in Vietnam.

FROM CAMPUS PROTEST TO MASS MOBILIZATION

Three weeks after the announcement of Operation Rolling Thunder in 1965, peace activists called for a daylong boycott of classes so that students and faculty might meet to discuss the war. "Teach-ins" soon spread across the United States and to Europe and Japan. Meanwhile, SDS mobilized 20,000 people in an antiwar march on the nation's capital.

Students also protested against war-related research on their campuses. The expansion of higher education in the 1960s had depended largely on federally funded programs, including military research on counterinsurgency tactics and chemical weapons. Student protesters demanded an end to these programs and, receiving no response from university administrators, turned to civil disobedience. Between 1967 and 1970, demonstrations took place on campuses in every region of the country.

The peace movement spread well beyond the campus. In April 1967, a daylong antiwar rally in Manhattan's Central Park drew more than 300,000 people. Meanwhile, 60,000 protesters turned out in San Francisco. By summer, Vietnam Veterans Against the War had

Read the Document

The Report of the President's Commission on Campus Unrest (1970) at **www.myhistorylab.com**

Watch the Video

Protests against the Vietnam War at **www.myhistorylab.com**

Watch the Video

Newsreel: Peace March, Thousands Oppose Vietnam War at **www.myhistorylab.com**

On May 8, 1970, New York construction workers surged into Wall Street in Lower Manhattan, violently disrupting an anti-war rally and attacking the protesters with lead pipes and crowbars. Known as the "hard hat riots," the well-publicized event was followed later in the month by a march, 100,000 strong, of hard-hat workers unfurling American flags and chanting "All the way U.S.A."

begun to organize returning soldiers and sailors, encouraging them to cast off the medals and ribbons they had won in battle.

The steadily increasing size of antiwar demonstrations provoked conservatives and prowar Democrats to take a stronger stand. Secretary of State Dean Rusk, appearing on NBC's *Meet the Press*, declared that "authorities in Hanoi" might conclude, incorrectly, that the majority of Americans did not back their president. He predicted that "the net effect of these demonstrations will be to prolong the war, not to shorten it."

Many demonstrators themselves, concluding that peaceful protest alone had little impact on U.S. policy, decided to change tactics—"from protest to resistance"—and serve as moral witnesses. Despite a 1965 congressional act providing for a five-year jail term and a $10,000 fine for destroying a draft card, thousands of young men burned their draft cards. Approximately a half-million more refused induction. Other activists determined to "bring the war home" went beyond civil disobedience. An estimated 40,000 bombing incidents or bomb threats took place from January 1969 to April 1970; more than $21 million of property was damaged, and forty-three people were killed.

Parallel wars were now being fought, one between two systems of government in Vietnam, another between the American government and masses of its citizens. Those Americans sent to Vietnam were caught in between.

TEENAGE SOLDIERS

The average age of soldiers who fought in Vietnam hovered around nineteen. Until late 1969, the Selective Service System—the draft—gave deferments to college students and to workers in selected occupations, while focusing intense recruiting in poor communities by advertising the armed forces as a provider of vocational training and social mobility. Working-class young men, disproportionately African American and Latino, signed up in large numbers under these inducements. They also bore the brunt of combat. High school dropouts were the most likely to serve in Vietnam and by far the most likely to die there. The casualty rate for African Americans during the early years of the war was disproportionately higher than the overall death rate for U.S. forces in Southeast Asia. These disparities created a rupture that would last well past the end of the war.

The soldiers were not entirely isolated from the changes affecting their generation, but most condemned antiwar protest as the self-indulgent behavior of their privileged peers who did not have to fight. As the war dragged on, however, some soldiers showed their frustration. By 1971, many G.I.s were putting peace symbols on their combat helmets and joining antiwar demonstrations. Sometimes entire companies refused to carry out duty assignments or even to enter battle. A smaller number took revenge by intentionally wounding or killing—"fragging"—reckless commanding officers with grenades meant for the enemy. Some African American soldiers complained about fighting "a white man's war" and emblazoned their helmets with slogans like "No Gook Ever Called Me Nigger."

The war's course fed these feelings of disaffection. U.S. troops entering South Vietnam expected a warm welcome from the people whose homeland they had been sent to defend. Instead, they encountered anti-American demonstrations. Moreover, despite their superior arms and air power, soldiers found themselves stumbling into booby traps as they chased an elusive guerrilla enemy. They could never be sure who was friend and who was foe.

Vietnam veterans returned to civilian life quietly and without fanfare. They reentered a society divided over the cause for which they had risked their lives. Tens of thousands suffered debilitating physical injuries. As many as 40 percent of the 8.6 million who served came back with drug dependencies or symptoms of posttraumatic stress disorder, haunted and depressed by troubling memories of atrocities. Moreover, finding and keeping a job proved to be particularly hard in the shrinking economy of the 1970s.

QUICK REVIEW

Opposition to the War

- Antiwar activists and students challenged the "Cold Warriors."
- In 1966 and 1967 antiwar activity intensified.
- Antiwar activists directed their anger against the draft system.

WHAT WERE the goals of
Johnson's Great Society?

QUICK REVIEW

The Great Society

◆ Most ambitious reform program
since the New Deal.

◆ Office of Economic Opportunity
launched a War on Poverty.

◆ Programs had mixed results.

---

war on poverty   Set of programs
introduced by Lyndon Johnson
between 1963 and 1966 designed to
break the cycle of poverty by
providing funds for job training,
community development, nutrition,
and supplementary education.

Office of Economic Opportunity (OEO)
Federal agency that coordinated
many programs of the War on
Poverty between 1964 and 1975.

WARS ON POVERTY

Hoping to build on Kennedy's legacy, President Johnson pledged to expand the antipoverty program that he had inherited. Over the next several years, he used the political momentum of the civil rights movement and the overwhelming Democratic majorities in the House and Senate to push through the most ambitious reform program since the New Deal. Ironically, violence at home as well as abroad ultimately undercut his aspiration to wage "an unconditional **war on poverty**" (see Figures 29.1 and 29.2).

THE GREAT SOCIETY

The cornerstone of Johnson's plan for a Great Society was the Economic Opportunity Act, enacted in August 1964. The legislation established the **Office of Economic Opportunity (OEO)**, which coordinated a network of community-based programs designed to help the poor help themselves by providing opportunities for education and employment. The results were mixed. The Job Corps provided vocational training mostly for urban black youth considered unemployable. Trainees often found themselves learning factory skills that were already obsolete. The Neighborhood Youth Corps provided work for about 2 million young people, but nearly all the jobs were low paying and dead-end. Educational programs proved more successful. VISTA (Volunteers in Service to America), a kind of domestic Peace Corps, brought several thousand idealistic volunteers into poor communities for social service work.

The most innovative and controversial element of the OEO was the Community Action Program (CAP), which mandated "maximum feasible participation" of local residents. In theory, community action would empower the poor by giving them a direct say in mobilizing resources. What often resulted was a tug-of-war between local government officials and the poor over who should control funding and decision making.

More successful and popular were the so-called national-emphasis programs, designed in Washington and administered according to federal guidelines. The Legal Services Program, staffed by attorneys, helped millions of poor people in legal battles with housing authorities, welfare departments, police, and slumlords. Head Start and Follow Through reached more than 2 million poor children and significantly improved

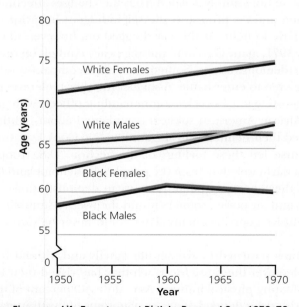

Figure 29.1 Comparative Figures on Life Expectancy at Birth by Race and Sex, 1950–70
Shifting mortality statistics suggested that the increased longevity of females increasingly cut across race lines, but did not diminish the difference between white people and black people as a whole.

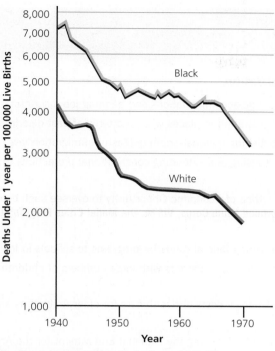

Figure 29.2 Comparative Figures on Infant Mortality by Race, 1940–70

Figure 29.2 Comparative Figures on Infant Mortality by Race, 1940–70
The causes of infant mortality, such as inadequate maternal diets, prenatal care, and medical services, were all rooted in poverty, both rural and urban. Despite generally falling rates of infant mortality, nonwhite people continued to suffer the effects more than white people.

Medicare Basic medical insurance for the elderly, financed through the federal government; program created in 1965.

the long-range educational achievement of participants. Comprehensive Community Health Centers provided basic medical services to patients who could not afford to see doctors. Upward Bound helped low-income teenagers develop the skills and confidence needed for college. Birth control programs dispensed contraceptive supplies and information to hundreds of thousands of poor women (see Figure 29.3).

But the root cause of poverty lay in the unequal distribution of power as well as of income. The Johnson administration never committed itself to reallocating income or wealth. Spending on social welfare jumped from 7.7 percent of the GNP in 1960 to 16 percent in 1974. But roughly three-quarters of social welfare payments went to the nonpoor. The largest sums went to **Medicare**, established by Congress in 1965 to provide basic health care for the aged, and to expanded Social Security payments and unemployment compensation.

Having made the largest commitment to federal spending on social welfare since the New Deal, Johnson could take pride in the number of programs passed by Congress. At the same time, he had raised expectations higher than could be reached without a more drastic redistribution of economic and political power. Even in the short run, the president could not sustain the welfare programs and simultaneously fight a lengthy and expensive war abroad.

CRISIS IN THE CITIES

With funds for new construction limited during the Great Depression and World War II, and the postwar building boom taking place in the suburbs, the housing stock in the nation's cities declined. City officials meanwhile spearheaded civic revitalization programs that more often than not sliced up poor neighborhoods with new super highways, demolished them to build new office complexes, or, as in Chicago's Uptown, favored residential developments for the

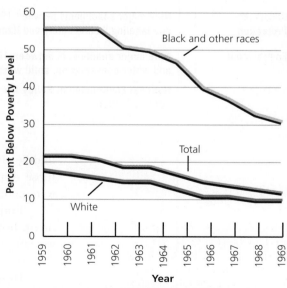

Figure 29.3 Percent of Population Below Poverty Level, by Race, 1959–69

NOTE: The poverty threshold for a nonfarm family of four was $3,743 in 1969 and $2,973 in 1959.

From *Congressional Quarterly, Civil Rights: A Progress Report*, 1971. Copyright 1971 by CQ-ROLL CALL GROUP. Reproduced with permission of CQ-ROLL CALL GROUP in the format Other book via Copyright Clearance Center.

OVERVIEW | The Great Society

Major Legislation

Civil Rights	**Civil Rights Act of 1964**, forbidding segregation in public accommodations and banning job discrimination
	Voting Rights Act of 1965, ensuring minority voter registration in places where patterns of past discrimination existed
	Immigration and Nationality Services Act of 1965, abolishing national-origin quotas in immigration law
	Civil Rights Act of 1968, banning discrimination in housing and extending constitutional protections to Native Americans on reservations
The War on Poverty	**Economic Opportunity Act of 1964**, establishing the Office of Economic Opportunity to oversee such community-based antipoverty programs as the **Job Corps**, the **Neighborhood Youth Corps, VISTA**, the **Model Cities Program, Upward Bound**, the **Community Action Program**, and **Project Head Start**
Education	**Elementary and Secondary Education Act of 1965**, providing federal funds for programs to schools in low-income areas
	Bilingual Education Act of 1968, providing federal aid to school districts with large numbers of children needing to learn English as a second language
Health	**Social Security Act of 1965**, funding Medicare to help cover costs of health care for older Americans and Medicaid to provide funds for medical care of welfare recipients
Culture	**National Foundation on the Arts and Humanities Act of 1965**, creating the National Endowment for the Arts and the National Endowment for the Humanities
	Public Broadcasting Act of 1967, chartering the Corporation for Public Broadcasting, which later established the Public Broadcasting Services (PBS) and National Public Radio (NPR)
Transportation	**Urban Mass Transportation Act of 1964**, funding large-scale urban public and private rail projects
	National Traffic and Motor Vehicle Safety Act of 1966, laying the foundation for the National Highway Traffic Safety Administration to effect policy to reduce traffic injuries and fatalities
	Highway Safety Act of 1966, permitting the federal government to set standards for motor vehicles and highways
	Department of Transportation, established in 1966
Consumer Protection	**Nine major enactments between 1965 and 1968, covering such areas as cigarette warning labels, motor safety, "fair packaging and labeling," child safety and flammable fabrics, meat and poultry packaging, "truth in lending," and radiation safety**
Environment	**Nine major enactments between 1964 and 1968, covering such areas as wilderness and endangered species protection, land and water conservation, solid waste disposal, air pollution, aircraft noise abatement, and historic preservation**
	National Environmental Policy Act of 1969, consolidating many of these gains, was passed in the first year of the Nixon administration

middle class rather than for the poor. In 1968, a federal survey showed that 80 percent of those displaced under these programs—dubbed "Negro removal" by former residents—were people of color.

Employment opportunities declined along with the housing stock. Black unemployment, however, was nearly twice that of white unemployment. Moreover, the proportion working in the low-paying service sector continued to rise. In short, African Americans were steadily falling further behind whites.

Despite deteriorating conditions, millions of Americans continued to move to the cities, mainly African Americans from the Deep South, white people from the Appalachian Mountains, and Latinos from Puerto Rico. By the mid-1960s, African Americans had become near majorities in the nation's decaying inner cities. Many had fled rural poverty only to find themselves earning minimum wages at best and living in miserable, racially segregated neighborhoods. These conditions brought urban pressures to the boiling point.

URBAN UPRISINGS

Just as the Vietnam War was heating up, more than 100 urban uprisings rocked the nation during the "long, hot summers" of 1964 to 1968 (see Map 29.1). The first major uprising erupted in August 1965 in the Watts section of Los Angeles. There, one in three men was unemployed, and the nearest hospital was twelve miles away. It took only a minor arrest to set off the uprising, which quickly spread outward for fifty miles. After six days, 34 people lay dead, 900 were injured, and 4,000 more had been arrested. The Los Angeles police chief blamed civil rights agitators, the mayor accused Communists, and both feigned ignorance when the media reported that white police assigned to "charcoal alley," their name for the Watts district, had customarily called their nightsticks "nigger knockers."

The following summer, large-scale uprisings occurred in San Francisco, Milwaukee, Dayton, and Cleveland. On July 12, 1967, in Newark, New Jersey, a city with severe housing shortages and the nation's highest black unemployment rate, the beating and arrest of a black taxi driver by a white police officer sparked a protest. Five days of looting and burning of buildings ended with 25 people dead. One week later, Detroit police raided a bar and arrested the after-hours patrons. Army tanks and paratroopers were brought in to quell the disturbance, which lasted a week and left 34 people dead and 7,000 under arrest.

MAP 29.1
Urban Uprisings, 1965–1968 After World War II, urban uprisings precipitated by racial conflict increased in African American communities. In Watts in 1965 and in Detroit and Newark in 1967, rioters struck out at symbols of white control of their communities, such as white-owned businesses and residential properties.

WHY WERE cities the focal points of racial unrest in the 1960s?

In July 1967, President Johnson created the National Advisory Commission on Civil Disorders to investigate the riots. Headed by Illinois Governor Otto Kerner, the eleven-member commission indicted "white racism" for creating an "explosive mixture" of poverty and police brutality. But the Johnson administration and Congress disregarded the commission's advice to direct funds into housing and jobs and to reduce segregation. By this time, the escalating costs of the Vietnam War left little federal money for antipoverty programs.

1968: YEAR OF TURMOIL

WHY DID divisions within

American society deepen in 1968?

The urban uprisings of the summer of 1967 marked the most drawn-out violence in the United States since the Civil War. Rather than offering a respite, however, 1968 proved to be even more turbulent.

THE TET OFFENSIVE

On January 30, 1968, the North Vietnamese and their Vietcong allies launched the Tet Offensive (named for the Vietnamese lunar New Year holiday), stunning the U.S. military command in South Vietnam. The Vietcong pushed into the major cities and provincial capitals of the South. U.S. troops ultimately halted the offensive, with comparatively modest casualties of 1,100 dead and 8,000 wounded. The North Vietnamese and Vietcong suffered more than 40,000 deaths, about one-fifth of their total forces. Civilian casualties ran to the tens of thousands. As many as 1 million South Vietnamese became refugees, their villages totally ruined (see Map 29.2).

The Tet Offensive, despite the U.S. success in stopping it, weakened the resolve of many Americans. The United States chalked up a major military victory, but lost the war at home. For the first time, polls showed strong opposition to the war, 49 percent concluding that the entire operation in Vietnam was a mistake. Meanwhile, in Rome, Berlin, Paris, and London, huge crowds protested U.S. involvement in Vietnam. President Johnson, facing the 1968 election campaign, watched his popularity plummet to an all-time low.

On March 31, the president appeared on television to declare a pullback in bombing over North Vietnam and the readiness of the United States to enter into comprehensive peace talks with Hanoi. He then shocked the nation: "I shall not seek, and I will not accept, the nomination of my party for another term as president." Like Truman almost thirty years earlier, Johnson had lost his presidency in Asia.

KING, THE WAR, AND THE ASSASSINATION

By 1968, the civil rights leadership stood firmly against the war, and Martin Luther King Jr. had reached a turning point in his life. The FBI had been harassing King, tapping his telephones and spreading malicious rumors about him. Despite these threats, King abandoned his customary caution in criticizing U.S. policy in Vietnam. As early as 1965, he had connected domestic unrest with the war abroad. He became yet more outspoken in his opposition to the war, even if it meant losing the support of those liberal Democrats loyal to Johnson.

In the spring of 1968, King chose Memphis, Tennessee, home of striking sanitation workers, to launch a Poor People's Campaign for peace and justice. There he delivered, in what was to be his final speech, a message of hope. "I have a dream this afternoon that the brotherhood of man will become a reality," King told the crowd. "With this faith, I will go out and carve a tunnel of hope from a mountain of despair." The next evening, April 4, 1968, as he stood on the balcony of his motel, King was shot and killed.

Throughout the world, crowds turned out to mourn King's death. Riots broke out in more than a hundred cities, on college campuses, and on military bases in Vietnam.

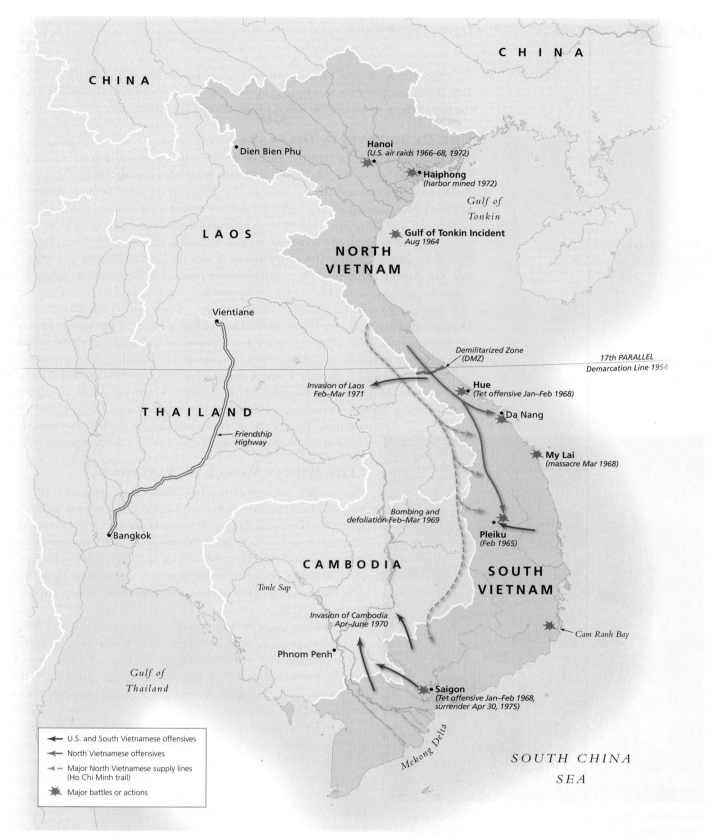

MAP 29.2
The Southeast Asian War The Indo-Chinese subcontinent, home to long-standing regional conflict, became the center of a prolonged war with the United States.

WHAT LIGHT does this map shed on the difficulties the United States had in precipitating and winning decisive battles in the Vietnam War?

Chicago Mayor Richard Daley ordered his police to shoot to kill. In Washington, DC, U.S. Army units set up machine guns outside the Capitol and the White House. King's dream of the nation as a "Beloved Community" died with him.

THE DEMOCRATS IN DISARRAY

The dramatic events of the first part of the year had a direct impact on the presidential campaign. For those liberals dissatisfied with Johnson's conduct of the war, and especially for African Americans suffering the loss of their greatest leader, Senator Robert F. Kennedy of New York emerged as the candidate of choice. Kennedy enjoyed a strong record on civil rights, and, like King, he had begun to interpret the war as a mirror of injustice at home.

Ironically, Kennedy faced an opponent who agreed with him, Senator Eugene McCarthy of Minnesota. McCarthy did well with liberal Democrats and white suburbanites. On college campuses, his popularity with antiwar students was so great that his campaign became known as the "children's crusade."

Kennedy captured the votes of African Americans and Latinos and emerged as the Democratic Party's strongest candidate. Having won all but the Oregon primary, he moved on to California. But on June 4, as the final tabulation of his victory came in just past midnight, Robert Kennedy was struck down by an assassin's bullet.

Vice President Hubert H. Humphrey, who had announced his candidacy in April, was now the sole Democrat with the credentials to succeed Johnson. Without entering a single state primary, he lined up delegates loyal to city bosses, labor leaders, and conservative southern Democrats. As the candidate least likely to rock the boat, he secured his party's nomination well before delegates met in convention.

"THE WHOLE WORLD IS WATCHING!"

The events surrounding the Democratic convention in Chicago, August 21–26, demonstrated how deep the divisions within the United States had become. Mayor Richard Daley refused to issue parade permits to the antiwar activists, who had called for a massive demonstration at the convention center. According to later accounts, he sent hundreds of undercover police into the crowds to encourage rock throwing and generally to incite violence so that retaliation would appear necessary and reasonable.

Daley's strategy boomeranged when his officers staged what a presidential commission later termed a "police riot," randomly assaulting demonstrators, casual passersby, and the television crews broadcasting the events. Angered by the embarrassing publicity, Daley sent his agents to raid McCarthy's campaign headquarters where antiwar Democrats had gathered.

Inside the convention hall, a raging debate over a peace resolution underscored the depth of the division within the party. When the resolution failed, McCarthy delegates put on black armbands and sang "We Shall Overcome." Later, as tear gas used against the demonstrators outside turned the amphitheater air acrid, the beaming Humphrey praised Mayor Daley and Johnson's conduct of the Vietnam War. The crowd outside chanted, "The whole world is watching! The whole world is watching!" Indeed, through satellite transmission, it was.

Protest had spread worldwide. Across the United States the antiwar movement picked up steam. In Paris, students and workers scrawled on building walls such humorous and half-serious slogans as "Be Realistic, Demand the Impossible!" Meanwhile, demonstrations in Japan, Italy, Ireland, Germany, and England all brought young people

●●●─┤Read the Document

Profile: *Eugene McCarthy* at
www.myhistorylab.com

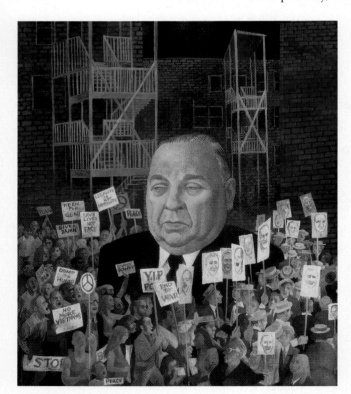

Bernard Perlin, *Mayor* Daley, 1968, Oil on canvas. In 1968, Richard J. Daley had been elected mayor of Chicago four times and held power as a traditional city boss. In December of that year, the National Commission on Violence released a report that concluded that Chicago police, acting under Mayor Daley's orders, had been "unrestrained and indiscriminate" in their attacks on demonstrators at the National Democratic Convention held the previous August. In response, Mayor Daley brazenly announced a 22 percent salary increase for members of the city's police and fire personnel.

into the streets to demand democratic reforms in their own countries and an end to the U.S. war in Vietnam.

THE REPUBLICAN VICTORY

The Republicans stepped into the breach. Presidential contender Richard Nixon deftly built on voter hostility toward youthful protesters and the counterculture. He wooed a growing constituency that he later termed the "silent majority"—those Americans who worked, paid taxes, and did not demonstrate or picket. Recovering from election defeats for president in 1960 and California governor in 1962, Nixon claimed to be the one candidate who could restore law and order. He chose as his running mate the governor of Maryland, Spiro T. Agnew, known for treating dissent as near treason (see Map 29.3).

After signing the landmark Civil Rights Act of 1964, President Johnson said privately, "I think we just delivered the South to the Republicans for a long time to come." Republican strategists moved quickly to make this prediction come true. They also recognized the growing electoral importance of the Sunbelt, where populations grew with the rise of high-tech industries and retirement communities. A powerful conservatism dominated this region, home to many military bases, defense plants, and an increasingly influential religious right.

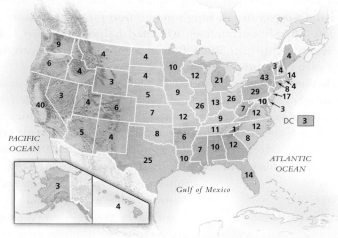

	Electoral Vote (%)	Popular Vote (%)
RICHARD M. NIXON (Republican)	301 (56)	31,785,480 (43.4)
Hubert H. Humphrey (Democrat)	191 (36)	31,275,165 (42.7)
George C. Wallace (American Independent)	46 (8)	9,906,473 (13.5)
Other candidates (Dick Gregory, Socialist Labor; Fred Halstead and Paul Boutelle, Socialist Workers; Eugene McCarthy, Peace and Freedom; E. Harold Munn and Rolland E. Fisher, Prohibition)	—	221,134 (0.3)

MAP 29.3

The Election of 1968 Although the Republican Nixon-Agnew team won the popular vote by only a small margin, the Democrats lost in most of the northern states that had voted Democratic since the days of FDR. Segregationist Governor George Wallace of Alabama polled more than 9 million votes.

HOW DID the civil rights struggle of the 1950s and 1960s shape the results of the 1968 election?

HOW DID race, gender, and sexual orientation gain new political importance in the 1960s?

Black Power Philosophy emerging after 1965 that real economic and political gains for African Americans could come only through self-help, self-determination, and organizing for direct political influence.

Black Panther Party Political and social movement among black Americans, founded in Oakland, California, in 1966 and emphasizing black economic and political power.

The Nixon-Agnew team ushered in the greatest political realignment since Franklin Roosevelt's victory in 1932. They captured the popular vote by the slim margin of 43.4 percent to Democrat Hubert Humphrey and Maine senator Edmund Muskie's 42.7 percent, but they took nearly all the West's electoral votes. Bitterly divided by the campaign, the Democrats would remain out of presidential contention for more than two decades, except when the Republicans suffered scandal and disgrace. The Republicans in 1968 had paved the way for the conservative ascendancy.

THE POLITICS OF IDENTITY

The tragic events of 1968 brought whole sectors of the counterculture to political activism. With great media fanfare, gay liberation and women's liberation movements took shape while young Latinos, Asian Americans, and Indian peoples pressed their own claims. In different ways, these groups drew their own lessons from Black Power, the nationalist movement that formed in the wake of Malcolm X's death. Soon, "Brown Power," "Yellow Power," and "Red Power" became the slogans of movements constituted distinctly as new communities of protest.

BLACK POWER

Impatient with tactics based on voting rights and integration, many young activists spurned the civil disobedience of King's generation for direct action and militant self-defense. In 1966, Stokely Carmichael, who had helped turn SNCC into an all-black organization, began to advocate **Black Power** as a means for African Americans to take control of their own communities.

The **Black Panther Party**, founded in Oakland, California, in 1966 by Huey P. Newton and Bobby Seale, demanded "land, bread, housing, education, clothing, and justice." They adopted a paramilitary style that infuriated the authorities. Monitoring local police was their major activity. In several communities, volunteers also ran free breakfast programs for schoolchildren, established medical clinics, and conducted educational classes. Persecuted by police and the FBI, their leaders were arrested, prosecuted, and sentenced to long terms in jail that effectively destroyed the organization.

Black Power nevertheless continued to grow into a multifaceted movement. The Reverend Jesse Jackson, for example, rallied African Americans in Chicago to boycott the A&P supermarket chain until the firm hired 700 black workers. A dynamic speaker and skillful organizer, Jackson encouraged African Americans to support their own businesses and services.

Cultural nationalism became the most enduring component of Black Power. In their popular book *Black Power* (1967), Stokely Carmichael and Charles V. Hamilton urged African Americans "to assert their own definitions, to reclaim their history, their culture; to create their own sense of community and togetherness." Thousands of college students responded by calling for more classes on African American history and culture.

Meanwhile, trendsetters put aside Western dress for African-style dashikis and hairdos, and

The war in Vietnam contributed to the growing racial militancy in the United States. African Americans served on the front lines in Vietnam in disproportionate numbers, and many came to view the conflict as a "white man's war."

OVERVIEW | Protest Movements of the 1960s

Year	Organization/Movement	Description
1962	**Students for a Democratic Society (SDS)**	Organization of college students that became the largest national organization of left-wing white students. Calling for "participatory democracy," SDS involved students in community-based campaigns against poverty and for citizens' control of neighborhoods. SDS played a prominent role in the campaign to end the war in Vietnam.
1964	**Free Speech Movement**	Formed at the University of California at Berkeley to protest the banning of on-campus political fundraising. Decried the bureaucratic character of the "multiuniversity" and advocated an expansion of student rights.
1965	**Anti–Vietnam War Movement**	Advocated grassroots opposition to U.S. involvement in Southeast Asia. By 1970, a national mobilization committee organized a demonstration of a half-million protesters in Washington, DC.
1965	La raza	A movement of Chicano youth to advance the cultural and political self-determination of Mexican Americans. *La raza* included the Brown Berets, which addressed community issues, and regional civil rights groups such as the Crusade for Social Justice, formed in 1965.
1966	**Black Power**	Militant movement that emerged from the civil rights campaigns to advocate independent institutions for African Americans and pride in black culture and African heritage. The idea of Black Power, a term coined by Stokely Carmichael, inspired the formation of the paramilitary Black Panthers.
1968	**American Indian Movement (AIM)**	Organization formed to advance the self-determination of Indian peoples and challenge the authority of the Bureau of Indian Affairs. Its most effective tactic was occupation. In February 1973, AIM insurgents protesting land and treaty violations occupied Wounded Knee, South Dakota, the location of an 1890 massacre, until the FBI and BIA agents drove them out.
1968	**Women's Liberation**	Movement of mainly young women that took shape following a protest at the Miss America Beauty Pageant. Impatient with the legislative reforms promoted by the National Organization for Women, founded in 1966, activists developed their own agenda shaped by the slogan "The Personal Is Political." Activities included the formation of "consciousness-raising" groups and the establishment of women's studies programs.
1968	Asian American **Political Alliance (AAPA)**	Formed at the University of California at Berkeley, the AAPA was one of the first pan-Asian political organizations to struggle against racial oppression. The AAPA encouraged Asian Americans to claim their own cultural identity and to protest the war against Asian peoples in Vietnam.
1969	**Gay Liberation**	Movement to protest discrimination against homosexuals and lesbians that emerged after the Stonewall Riots in New York City. Unlike earlier organizations such as the Mattachine Society, which focused on civil rights, gay liberationists sought to radically change American society and government, which they believed were corrupt.

black parents gave their children African names. Many well-known activists and artists such as Imamu Amiri Baraka (formerly LeRoi Jones), Muhammad Ali (formerly Cassius Clay), and Kwame Touré (formerly Stokely Carmichael) rejected their "slave names." The new holiday Kwanzaa followed Christmas as a weeklong celebration of African heritage and culture. This deepening sense of racial pride was summed up in the popular slogan "Black Is Beautiful."

SISTERHOOD IS POWERFUL

In 1966, Betty Friedan's best-selling *Feminine Mystique* (see Chapter 27) sparked the formation of the **National Organization for Women (NOW)**. Members campaigned for the enforcement of laws banning sex discrimination in work and in education, for maternity leaves, and for government funding of day-care centers. NOW also backed the Equal Rights Amendment, first introduced in Congress in 1923, and demanded the repeal of legislation that prohibited abortion or restricted birth control.

In 1971, Congress passed a joint resolution, introduced by Rep. Bella Abzug (D-NY), that designates August 26 each year as "Women's Equality Day" to commemorate the passage of the 19th Amendment to the Constitution granting women full voting rights. This photo shows a parade of women marking the first celebration of this day in 1971.

Read the **Document**

Shirley Chisholm, Equal Rights for Women (1969) at **www.myhistorylab.com**

By the time Nixon took office, a different kind of movement had emerged: women's liberation. The women's liberation movement attracted young women who had been active in civil rights, SDS, and campus antiwar movements. Impatient with NOW's legislative agenda and angered by the sexism of male activists, these women organized separately under the slogan "Sisterhood Is Powerful."

The women's liberation movement issued a scathing critique of patriarchy—that is, the power of men to dominate all institutions, from the family to business and government to the protest movements themselves. One New York group created a lot of publicity for the movement by storming the 1968 Miss America Beauty Pageant in Atlantic City. They crowned a live sheep as queen and threw "implements of female torture" (bras, girdles, curlers, and copies of the *Ladies' Home Journal*) into a "freedom trash can."

The media focused on such audacious acts and brazen pronouncements, but the majority of activists were less flamboyant women simply trying to rise above the limitations imposed on them because of their gender. They met more often outside the limelight in consciousness-raising groups, where they examined the relationship between public events and private lives. Here women established the constituency for the movement's most important principle, expressed in the aphorism "The personal is political." Believing that no aspect of life lacked a political dimension, consciousness-raising groups explored the power dynamics of the family and marriage as well as the workforce and government.

Women's liberation activism ranged widely. Some feminists staged sit-ins at *Newsweek* to protest demeaning media depictions of women. Others established health clinics, day-care centers, rape crisis centers, and shelters for women fleeing abusive husbands or lovers. The movement also had a significant educational impact. Feminist bookstores and publishing companies, such as the Feminist Press, reached out to eager readers. In January 1972, *Ms. Magazine* hit the newsstands. Meanwhile, campus activists demanded women's studies programs and women's centers (see Figure 29.4).

The women's liberation movement remained, however, a bastion of white middle-class women. The appeal to sisterhood did not unite women across race or class or even sexual orientation. Lesbians, who charged the early NOW leaders with homophobia, found large pockets of "heterosexism" in the women's liberation movement and broke off

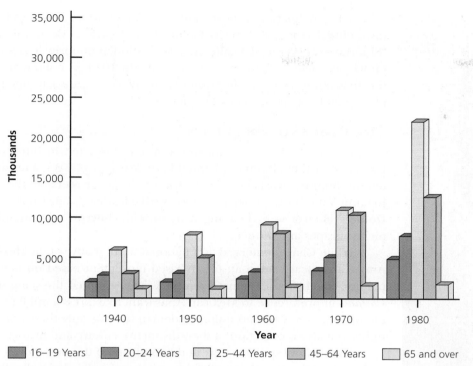

Figure 29.4 Women in the Workforce, 1940–80

U.S. Bureau of the Census.

to form their own organizations. The majority of African American women remained wary of white women's appeals to sisterhood. African American women formed their own "womanist" movement to address their distinct cultural and political concerns. Similarly, by 1970, a Latina feminist movement addressed issues uniquely relevant to women of color in an Anglo-dominated society.

GAY LIBERATION

The gay community had been generations in the making, but gained visibility only during World War II (see Chapter 25). In the mid-1950s, two pioneering homophile organizations, the Mattachine Society and the Daughters of Bilitis, campaigned against discrimination in employment, the armed forces, and all areas of social and cultural life. But it was during the tumultuous late 1960s that a sizeable movement formed to encourage gays and lesbians to "come out": "Say It Loud, Gay Is Proud."

The major event prompting gays to organize followed repeated police raids of gay bars. On Friday, June 27, 1969, New York police raided the Stonewall Inn, a well-known gay bar in Greenwich Village, and provoked an uprising that lasted the entire night. The next day, "Gay Power" graffiti appeared throughout the neighborhood.

In New York City, the Gay Liberation Front (GLF) announced itself as "a revolutionary homosexual group of men and women . . . who reject society's attempt to impose sexual roles and definitions of our nature." Taking a stand against the war in Vietnam, the GLF quickly adopted the forms of public protest, such as street demonstrations and sitins, developed by civil rights activists and given new direction by antiwar protesters.

Changes in public opinion and policies followed. Several churches opened their doors to gay activists. In 1973, the American Psychiatric Association, which since World War II had viewed homosexuality as a treatable mental illness, reclassified it as a normal sexual orientation. Meanwhile, a slow process of decriminalization of homosexual acts between consenting adults began. In 1975, the U.S. Civil Service Commission ended its ban on the employment of homosexuals.

•●•⌐Read the Document

Gay Liberation Front (1970) at **www.myhistorylab.com**

The gay liberation movement encouraged more than legal and institutional changes. "Gay Is Good" (like "Black Is Beautiful" and "Sisterhood Is Powerful") called to a large hidden minority to demand public acceptance of their sexual identity. In 1970, to commemorate the first anniversary of the Stonewall raid, Gay Pride parades took place in at least eight American cities.

THE CHICANO REBELLION

To many Americans, the Chicano movement seemed to burst onto the scene in 1965, when the United Farm Workers (UFW), a union of mainly migrant workers, struck against grape growers of the San Joaquin Valley in California. By 1968, strike leaders César Chávez and Dolores Huerta were heading a nationwide boycott of non-union-picked grapes and lettuce.

Labor activist César Chávez spearheaded the organization of Chicano agricultural workers into the United Farm Workers (UFW), the first successful union of migrant workers. In 1965, a strike of grape pickers in the fields around Delano, California, and a nationwide boycott of table grapes brought Chávez and the UFW into the media spotlight. Like Martin Luther King Jr., he advocated nonviolent methods for achieving justice and equality.

⬢ Read the Document

Chávez, He Showed Us the Way (1978) at **www.myhistorylab.com**

While Chávez emerged as a national hero, many young Mexican Americans spearheaded an urban-based movement based on identity politics, which Chávez himself rejected. They adopted the slang term *Chicano*, in preference to Mexican American, to express a militant ethnic nationalism. Chicano militants demanded not only their full civil rights, but also recognition of their distinctive culture and history.

High school students were at the forefront of this new movement. In March 1968, the Brown Berets, a group modeled on the Black Panthers, helped to plan the "blow out" (walkout) that sent nearly 15,000 Chicano teenagers into the streets of East Los Angeles. The high school students demanded educational reform, including courses on the history, literature, art, and language of Mexican Americans. After the police arrested the protesters, students in San Antonio and Denver expressed their solidarity by conducting their own blow outs. Meanwhile, college students demanded Chicano studies programs.

The larger Chicano movement found vivid expression in the performing and visual arts and in literature. *Teatro*, comprising film and drama, flourished as an exploration of the political dimensions of Mexican American society. One of the most popular and visible media was the mural, often inspired by art of Mexican masters such as Diego Rivera. Artistic expression found its way into music and dance. The rock group Los Lobos, for example, dedicated its first recorded album to the UFW. One of the most important writers to capture the excitement of the Chicano movement was Oscar Zeta Acosta, whose *The Revolt of the Cockroach People*, published in 1973, renders into fiction some of the major events of the era.

RED POWER

The phrase "**Red Power**," attributed to Vine Deloria Jr., commonly expressed a pan-Indian identity. At the forefront of this movement was the **American Indian Movement (AIM)**. Founded in 1968, AIM represented mainly urban Indian communities. Like Black Panthers and Brown Berets, its young, militant leaders organized initially to monitor law enforcement practices. They soon built a network of urban centers, churches, and philanthropic organizations as well as the "powwow circuit" that publicized news of protest and educational activities across the country (see Map 29.4).

The movement's major catalyst was the occupation of the deserted federal prison on Alcatraz Island in San Francisco Bay. On November 20, 1969, a group of eighty-nine "Indians of All Tribes" claimed the island according to the terms of an 1868 Sioux treaty that gave Indians rights to unused federal property on Indian land. Although the protes-

Red Power Term for pan-Indian identity.

American Indian Movement (AIM) Group of Native-American political activists who used confrontations with the federal government to publicize their case for Indian rights.

MAP 29.4
Major Indian Reservations, 1976   Although sizable areas, designated Indian reservations represented only a small portion of territory occupied in earlier times.

HOW DID Indian activists attempt to reclaim lost territory in the 1960s?

tors ultimately failed to achieve their specific goals, which included a deed to the land and federal funding for a cultural center, they rallied the larger Indian community.

Another series of dramatic events began in 1972, when AIM sponsored the "**Trail of Broken Treaties**" caravan. First they went to Washington, DC, where they staged a week-long occupation of the Bureau of Indian Affairs. AIM insurgents then headed west, to the Pine Ridge Reservation, the site of the 1890 massacre at Wounded Knee, South Dakota. There, in the spring of 1973, they demanded a restoration of treaty rights and began a siege that lasted ten weeks. Dozens of FBI agents with shoot-to-kill orders poured in, leaving two Indians dead and an unknown number of casualties on both sides.

The Red Power movement culminated in the "Longest Walk," a five-month march in 1978 from San Francisco to Washington, DC. Again, activists emphasized the history of the forced removal of Indians from their homelands and the U.S. government's repeated violations of treaty rights. By this time, several tribes had won in court small parts of what had been taken from them. Despite these victories, many tribal lands continued to suffer from industrial and government waste-dumping and other commercial uses. On reservations and in urban areas with heavy Indian concentrations, alcohol abuse and ill health remained serious problems.

Read the **Document**

Exploring America: The American Indian Movement at **www.myhistorylab.com**

Trail of Broken Treaties   1972 event staged by the American Indian Movement (AIM) that culminated in a week-long occupation of the Bureau of Indian Affairs in Washington, D.C.

THE ASIAN AMERICAN MOVEMENT

In 1968, groups of Chinese, Japanese, and Filipino students began to identify for the first time as Asian Americans. Students at San Francisco State University formed the Asian American Political Alliance (AAPA), while UC-Berkeley students mobilized to "express Asian American solidarity in a predominantly white society." These groups stood firmly against the Vietnam War, condemning it as a violation of the national sovereignty of the small Asian country. They also protested the racism directed against Southeast Asian peoples and proclaimed their solidarity with their "Asian brothers and sisters" in Vietnam.

Throughout 1968 and 1969, Asian American college students boycotted classes and demanded the establishment of ethnic studies programs. Meanwhile, artists, writers, documentary filmmakers, oral historians, and anthropologists worked to recover the Asian American past.

Looking to the example of the Black Panthers, Yellow Power activists also took their struggle into the community. In 1968, a group presented the San Francisco municipal government with a list of grievances about conditions in Chinatown and organized a protest march down the neighborhood's main street. The Redress and Reparations Movement, begun by Sansei (third-generation Japanese Americans) encouraged children to ask their parents about their wartime internment experiences and prompted older civil rights organizations, such as the Japanese American Citizens League, to raise the issue of reparations. Trade unionists organized new Asian workers, mainly in service industries and garment trades. Other campaigns reflected the growing diversity of the Asian population. Filipinos, the fastest-growing group, demonstrated against the U.S.-backed Philippine dictator Ferdinand Marcos. Students from South Korea similarly denounced the repressive government in their homeland. Samoans publicized the damage caused by nuclear testing in the Pacific Islands. Ultimately, however, in blurring intergroup differences, the Asian American movement failed to reach the growing immigrant populations, especially the numerous Southeast Asians fleeing their devastated homeland.

THE NIXON PRESIDENCY

WHAT WERE the most important successes and failures of the Nixon administration?

Richard M. Nixon inherited not only an increasingly unpopular war but also a nation riven by internal discord. Without specifying his plans, he promised a "just and honorable peace" in Southeast Asia and the restoration of law and order at home. Yet, once in office, Nixon puzzled both friends and foes. He ordered unprecedented illegal government action against private citizens while agreeing with Congress to enhance several welfare programs and improve environmental protection. He widened and intensified the war in Vietnam, yet made stunning moves toward détente with the People's Republic of China. An architect of the Cold War in the 1950s, Nixon became the first president to foresee its end. Nixon worked hard in the White House, centralizing authority and reigning defiantly as an "Imperial President"—until he brought himself down.

DOMESTIC POLICY

Although Nixon showed comparatively little interest in domestic policy, he nevertheless promised to restore order in American society. Despite his efforts to dismantle many of Johnson's poverty programs, however, Nixon had some surprises for conservatives. Determined to win reelection in 1972, he supported new Social Security benefits and subsidized housing for the poor and oversaw the creation of the Environmental Protection Agency and the Occupational Safety and Health Administration.

Nixon also embraced a policy of fiscal liberalism, even accepting the idea of deficit spending. In August 1971, he ordered the dollar's value to float against other currencies on the world market rather than being tied to a fixed value of gold, thereby ending the international monetary policy established at Bretton Woods. His ninety-day freeze on wages, rents, and prices, designed to halt the inflation caused by the massive spending on the Vietnam War, also closely resembled Democratic policies. Finally, Nixon's support adjustments or quotas favoring minority contractors in construction projects created an explosive precedent for "set-aside" programs later blamed on liberals.

Yet, for the most part, Nixon remained committed to the "Southern Strategy" that brought him into office. He lined up with conservatives on most civil rights issues and thus enlarged his southern Republican base. He slowed school desegregation and rejected the busing programs required to achieve racial balance. His nominees to the Supreme Court were far more conservative than those appointed by Eisenhower.

NIXON'S WAR

Nixon promised to bring "peace with honor." Yet, despite this pledge, the Vietnam War raged for four more years before a peace settlement was reached (see Figure 29.5).

Much of the responsibility for prolonging the war rested with Henry A. Kissinger, Nixon's national security adviser. Kissinger insisted that the United States could not retain its global leadership by appearing weak to either allies or enemies. After centralizing foreign policymaking in the White House, Kissinger and Nixon together overpowered those State Department members who had concluded that the majority of Americans no longer supported the war (see Figure 29.6).

In public, Nixon followed a policy of "Vietnamization." On May 14, 1969, he announced that the time was approaching "when the South Vietnamese . . . will be able to take over some of the fighting." During the next several months, he ordered the withdrawal of 60,000 U.S. troops. In private, Nixon mulled over the option of a "knockout blow" to the North Vietnamese.

On April 30, 1970, Nixon made one of the most controversial decisions of his presidency. Without seeking congressional approval, he ordered U.S. troops to invade the tiny nation of Cambodia. Nixon hoped in this way to end North Vietnamese infiltration into the South, but he also decided to live up to what he privately called his "wild man" or "mad bomber" reputation. The enemy would be unable to anticipate the location or severity of the next U.S. strike, Nixon reasoned, and would thus feel compelled to negotiate.

The invasion of Cambodia triggered the largest series of demonstrations and police–student confrontations in the nation's history. At Kent State University in Ohio, the National Guard shot into an unarmed crowd of students, killing four and wounding nine. Ten days later, on May 14, at Jackson State University, a black school in Mississippi, state troopers entered a campus dormitory and began shooting wildly, killing two students and wounding twelve others. Huge demonstrations took place on fifty campuses, and thirty-seven college and university presidents signed a letter calling on the president to end the war. A few weeks later the Senate adopted a bipartisan resolution outlawing the use of funds for U.S. military operations in Cambodia, starting July 1, 1970.

The president did not accept defeat easily. In February 1971, Nixon directed the South Vietnamese army to invade Laos and cut supply lines, but the demoralized invading force suffered a quick and humiliating defeat. In April 1972, Nixon ordered the

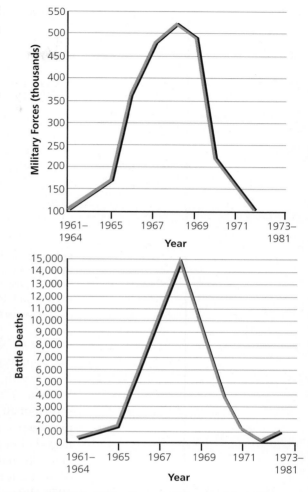

Figure 29.5 U.S. Military Forces in Vietnam and Casualties, 1961–81

The U.S. government estimated battle deaths between 1969 and 1973 for South Vietnamese troops at 107,504 and North Vietnamese and Vietcong at more than a half million. Although the United States suffered fewer deaths, the cost was enormous.

U.S. Department of Defense, *Selected Manpower Statistics*, annual and unpublished data; beginning 1981, National Archives and Records Service, "Combat Area Casualty File" (3-330-80-3).

●●●—Read the Document

Richard Nixon, Peace with Honor at **www.myhistorylab.com**

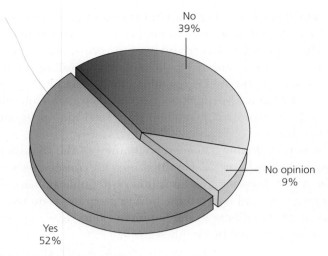

No
39%

No opinion
9%

Yes
52%

Figure 29.6 Public Opinion on the War in Vietnam
By 1969, Americans were sharply divided in their assessments of the progress of the war and peace negotiations. The American Institute of Public Opinion, founded in 1935 by George Gallup, charted a growing dissatisfaction with the war in Vietnam.

mining of North Vietnamese harbors and directed B-52s to conduct massively destructive bombing missions in Cambodia and North Vietnam (see Seeing History).

Nixon also sent Kissinger to Paris for secret negotiations with delegates from North Vietnam. They agreed to a cease-fire specifying the withdrawal of all U.S. troops and the return of all U.S. prisoners of war. Knowing these terms ensured defeat, South Vietnam's president refused to sign the agreement. On Christmas Day 1972, hoping for a better negotiating position, Nixon ordered one final wave of bomb attacks on North Vietnam's cities. To halt the bombing, the North Vietnamese resumed negotiations. But the terms of the Paris Peace Agreement, signed by North Vietnam and the United States in January 1973, differed little from the settlement Nixon could have procured in 1969.

The last U.S. troops withdrew from Vietnam in March 1973. Two years later, in April 1975, the North Vietnamese took over Saigon, and the Communist-led Democratic Republic of Vietnam soon united the small nation.

The war was finally over. It had cost the United States 58,000 lives and $150 billion. The nation had not only failed to achieve its stated war goal, but also had lost an important post in Southeast Asia. Equally important, the United States proved it could not sustain the policy of containment introduced by President Truman.

While Nixon was maneuvering to bring about "peace with honor," the chilling crimes of war had already begun to haunt Americans. In 1971, the army court-martialed a lieutenant, William L. Calley Jr., for the murder of "at least" twenty-two Vietnamese civilians during a 1968 search-and-destroy mission subsequently known as the **My Lai Massacre**. Calley's platoon had destroyed a village and slaughtered more than 350 unarmed South Vietnamese, raping and beating many of the women before killing them. The platoon commander at My Lai, Calley was first sentenced to life imprisonment before receiving a reduced term of ten years. The secretary of the army paroled Calley after three years of house arrest.

NIXON'S FOREIGN POLICY

Apart from Vietnam, Nixon's foreign policy defied the expectations of liberals and conservatives alike. Nixon pursued a policy of détente that replaced U.S.–Soviet bipolarity with multilateral relations that included the People's Republic of China, a rising world power more rigidly Communist than the Soviet Union. Despite criticism from

QUICK REVIEW

The Nixon Doctrine

♦ Nixon responded to antiwar protesters by reducing the role of U.S. ground forces in Vietnam.

♦ "Vietnamization": The withdrawal of U.S. troops as fast as possible without undermining the South Vietnamese government.

♦ The Nixon Doctrine substituted weapons and money for troops.

My Lai Massacre   Killing of twenty-two Vietnamese civilians by U.S. forces during a 1968 search-and-destroy mission.

Kim Phuc, Fleeing a Napalm Attack near Trang Bang

In 1972, during the phase of the war termed "Vietnamization," South Vietnamese aircraft bombed the village of Trang Bang, about twenty-five miles from Saigon. They were attacking North Vietnamese and Vietcong fighters, but mistakenly targeted a Buddhist pagoda. The incendiary bombs contained black, oily napalm that burned the villagers gathered there.

WHAT DOES this photograph suggest about the role of the news media during the Vietnam war? In focusing on civilians, what does Nick Ut's photograph suggest about the course of the war?

News photographer Nick Ut had been assigned to meet up with the South Vietnamese army at Trang Bang. "When we [the reporters] moved closer to the village we saw the first people running," he recalled in 1999. "I thought 'Oh my God' when I suddenly saw a woman with her left leg badly burned by napalm. Then came a woman carrying a baby, who died, then another woman carrying a small child with its skin coming off. When I took a picture of them I heard a child screaming and saw that young girl who had pulled off all her burning clothes. She yelled to her brother on her left. Just before the napalm was dropped soldiers [of the South Vietnamese Army] had yelled to the children to run but there wasn't enough time."

The Associated Press, which syndicates photographs to the media worldwide, at first refused to transmit the picture because of the nine-year-old girl's nudity but eventually concluded that the news value of the photograph was such that it could run, provided no-close up of the girl be transmitted. Ut, who took the severely burned girl to the hospital before delivering his film, won a Pulitzer Prize for the photograph.

In 1996, Phan Thi Kim Phuc, by then thirty-three, came to the United States, visited the Vietnam Veterans Memorial in Washington, DC, and resolved to form a foundation to help children victimized by war. She still wants the photograph to be seen: "Let the world see how horrible wars can be." ■

Students at hundreds of colleges and universities turned out in mass demonstrations to protest widening the war in Southeast Asia and the increasing violence on campus. Following the Kent State "massacre," approximately 5 million students joined the national student strike, boycotting classes for the remainder of the week. This photograph, taken at George Washington University, shows a confrontation between Washington Metropolitan Police and an unidentified student.

both the right and the left, Nixon persisted in his plan to restore the prestige of the United States and secure global stability by improving U.S. relations with China and the Soviet Union.

Nixon and Kissinger understood that the People's Republic of China was too important to be isolated by the West and too obviously hostile to the Soviet Union to be discounted as a potential ally. "Ping-Pong diplomacy" began in April 1971, when the Chinese hosted a table tennis team from the United States. Henry Kissinger embarked on a secret mission a few months later. Finally, in February 1972, Nixon flew to Beijing. It was a momentous and surprising event, one that marked a new era in East-West diplomacy. Nixon claimed that he succeeded in bridging "16,000 miles and twenty-two years of hostility."

Next, the president went to Moscow to negotiate with Soviet leader Leonid Brezhnev, who was anxious about U.S. involvement with China and eager for economic assistance. Nixon agreed to cooperate on science and technology, including a joint space mission. Nixon also completed negotiations of the **Strategic Arms Limitation Treaty** (SALT, known later as SALT I). A limited measure, SALT I represented the first success at strategic arms control since the start of the Cold War and a major public relations victory for the leaders of the two superpowers.

Nixon's last major diplomatic foray was far less effective. The president sent Kissinger on a two-year mission of "shuttle diplomacy" to mediate Israeli-Arab disputes, to ensure the continued flow of oil, and to increase lucrative U.S. arms sales to Arab countries. The Egyptians and Israelis agreed to a cease-fire in their October 1973 Yom Kippur War, but little progress toward peace in the area was achieved.

Apart from the highly publicized tour to China, Nixon revealed little to the American people about his policy for other parts of the globe. Unknown to most Americans, he accelerated the delivery of arms supplies to foreign dictators, including the shah of Iran, Ferdinand Marcos of the Philippines, and the white supremacist apartheid government in South Africa. In Latin America, Nixon gave financial assistance and military aid to repressive regimes such as that of Anastasio Somoza of Nicaragua, notorious for its blatant corruption and repeated violations of human rights.

Strategic Arms Limitation Treaty
Treaty signed in 1972 by the United States and the Soviet Union to slow the nuclear arms race.

Still more controversial was Nixon's plan to overthrow the democratically elected socialist government of Salvador Allende in Chile. The CIA destabilized the regime by funding right-wing parties, launching demonstrations, and preparing the Chilean army for a coup. In September 1973, a military junta killed President Allende and captured, tortured, or murdered thousands of his supporters. Nixon and Kissinger welcomed the new ruler, General Augusto Pinochet, granting him financial assistance to restabilize the country.

Toward the end of Nixon's term, members of Congress who had been briefed on these policies began to break silence, and reports of clandestine operations flooded the media. Several former CIA agents issued anguished confessions of their activities in other countries. More troubling to Nixon, in spite of all his efforts, the United States continued to lose ground as a superpower.

DIRTY TRICKS AND THE 1972 ELECTION

As Nixon approached the 1972 reelection campaign, he tightened his inner circle of White House staff who assisted him in withholding information from the public, discrediting critics, and engaging in assorted "dirty tricks." They also formed a secret squad, "the plumbers," to halt the troublesome information leaks. This team, headed by former CIA agent E. Howard Hunt and former FBI agent G. Gordon Liddy, assisted in conspiracy at the highest levels of government.

The first person on the squad's "hit list" was Daniel Ellsberg, a former researcher with the Department of Defense, who in 1971 had turned over to the press secret documents outlining the history of U.S. involvement in Vietnam. The so-called **Pentagon Papers** exposed the role of presidents and military leaders in deceiving the public and Congress about the conduct of the United States in Southeast Asia. When his attempts to suppress the Pentagon Papers failed, Nixon directed the Department of Justice to prosecute Ellsberg on charges of conspiracy, espionage, and theft. Meanwhile, Hunt and Liddy, seeking to discredit Ellsberg, broke into the office of his former psychiatrist. By 1973, the charges against Ellsberg were dropped after the Nixon administration itself stood guilty of misconduct.

During the 1972 presidential campaign, the Committee to Re-Elect the President (CREEP) enjoyed a huge war chest and spent a good portion on dirty tricks designed to divide the Democrats and discredit them in the eyes of the voting public. They charged George McGovern, Nixon's Democratic opponent, with advocating "abortion, acid [LSD], and amnesty" for draft resisters and deserters. They also informed the news media that McGovern's running mate, Senator Thomas Eagleton, had earlier undergone electric shock therapy for depression, thus forcing his resignation from the Democratic team.

In the short run, the Republicans tallied a monumental success. Nixon presented himself as the candidate of "middle Americans," the Great Silent Majority, and won reelection by a landslide, winning every state but Massachusetts. More important in the long run, the Republicans captured the once solidly Democratic South and the majority of blue-collar, Catholic, and urban voters.

Nixon had achieved the grandest moment of his long and complex political career. Nevertheless, even with this huge mandate from voters, the most audacious plan of his reelection committee—wiretapping the Democratic National Committee headquarters—ultimately backfired.

WATERGATE: NIXON'S DOWNFALL

On June 17, 1972, a security team had tripped up a group of intruders hired by CREEP to install listening devices in the Washington, DC, Watergate apartment and office complex where the Democrats were headquartered. The police arrested five men, who were later found guilty of conspiracy and burglary. Although Nixon disclaimed any knowledge of

Pentagon Papers   Classified Defense Department documents on the history of the United States' involvement in Vietnam, prepared in 1968 and leaked to the press in 1971.

QUICK REVIEW

Dirty Tricks

- Inner circle aided Nixon in attacks on political enemies.
- Secret group known as the "plumbers" worked to halt leaks to the public.
- Installed listening devices in Democratic headquarters in Watergate building.

Richard Nixon bid a final farewell to his White House staff as he left Washington, DC, on August 9, 1974. The first president to resign from office, Nixon had become so entangled in the Watergate scandal that his impeachment appeared certain. He was succeeded by Vice President Gerald Ford. After taking the oath of office later that day, President Ford remarked that the wounds of Watergate were "more painful and more poisonous than those of foreign wars."

◆◆◆ Read the Document

House Judiciary Committee's Assessment of Nixon's Activities (1974) at **www.myhistorylab.com**

Watergate A complex scandal involving attempts to cover up illegal actions taken by administration officials and leading to the resignation of President Richard Nixon in 1974.

the plan, two *Washington Post* reporters, Bob Woodward and Carl Bernstein, followed a trail of evidence back to the nation's highest office.

Televised Senate hearings opened to public view more than a pattern of presidential wrongdoing: they showed an attempt to impede investigations of the **Watergate** case. Testifying before the committee, a former Nixon aide revealed evidence of secret tape recordings of conversations held in the Oval Office. After special prosecutor Archibald Cox refused to allow Nixon to claim executive privilege and withhold the tapes, the president ordered Cox fired. This "Saturday Night Massacre," as it came to be called, further tarnished Nixon's reputation and swelled curiosity about the tapes. On June 24, 1974, the Supreme Court voted unanimously that Nixon had to release the tapes to a new special prosecutor, Leon Jaworski.

Although incomplete, the Watergate tapes proved damning. The tapes proved that Nixon had not only known about plans to cover up the Watergate break-in, but had in fact ordered it. In July 1974, the House Judiciary Committee adopted three articles of impeachment, charging Nixon with obstructing justice, abusing the power of his office, and acting in contempt of Congress.

Charges of executive criminality had clouded the Nixon administration since his vice president left in disgrace. In 1972, Spiro Agnew admitted to accepting large kickbacks while serving as governor of Maryland. Pleading no contest to this and to charges of federal income tax evasion, Agnew resigned in October 1973. Gerald Ford, a moderate Republican representative from Michigan, replaced him and now stood in the wings while the president's drama unfolded.

A delegation from Congress, led by Senator Barry Goldwater, approached Nixon with the news that impeachment and conviction were certain. On August 8, 1974, Nixon announced his intention to step down, becoming the first U.S. president to resign from office.

CONCLUSION

The resignations of Richard Nixon and Spiro Agnew did little to relieve the feeling of national exhaustion that followed the Vietnam War. U.S. troops pulled out of Vietnam in 1973 and the war officially ended in 1975, but bitterness lingered over

CHRONOLOGY

1964   President Lyndon Johnson calls for "an unconditional war on poverty" in his state of the union address

Gulf of Tonkin resolution

The Economic Opportunity Act establishes the Office of Economic Opportunity

Free speech movement gets under way at University of California at Berkeley

Johnson defeats conservative Barry Goldwater for president

1965   President Johnson authorizes Operation Rolling Thunder, the bombing of North Vietnam

Teach-ins begin on college campuses

First major march on Washington for peace is organized

Watts uprising begins a wave of rebellions in black communities

1966   J. William Fulbright publishes *The Arrogance of Power*

Black Panther Party is formed

National Organization for Women (NOW) is formed

1967   Antiwar rally in New York City draws 300,000

Vietnam Veterans Against the War is formed

Uprisings in Newark, Detroit, and other cities

Hippie "Summer of Love"

1968   U.S. ground troop levels in Vietnam number 500,000

Tet Offensive in Vietnam, followed by international protests against U.S. policies

Martin Luther King Jr. is assassinated; riots break out in more than 100 cities

Vietnam peace talks begin in Paris

Robert Kennedy is assassinated

Democratic National Convention, held in Chicago, nominates Hubert Humphrey; "police riot" against protesters

Richard Nixon elected president

American Indian Movement (AIM) founded

1969   Woodstock music festival marks the high tide of the counterculture

Stonewall Riot in Greenwich Village sparks the gay liberation movement

Apollo 11 lands on the moon

1970   U.S. incursion into Cambodia sparks campus demonstrations; students killed at Kent State and Jackson State universities

1971   Lieutenant William Calley Jr. court-martialed for My Lai Massacre

The New York Times starts publishing the Pentagon Papers

1972   *Ms. Magazine* publishes first issue

Nixon visits China and Soviet Union

SALT I limits offensive intercontinental ballistic missiles

Intruders attempting to "bug" Democratic headquarters in the Watergate complex are arrested

Nixon is reelected in a landslide

Nixon orders Christmas Day bombing of North Vietnam

1973   Paris Peace Agreement ends war in Vietnam

FBI seizes Indian occupants of Wounded Knee, South Dakota

Watergate burglars tried; congressional hearings on Watergate

CIA destabilizes elected Chilean government, which is overthrown

Vice President Spiro T. Agnew resigns

1974   House Judiciary Committee adopts articles of impeachment against Nixon

Nixon resigns the presidency

the unprecedented—and, for many, humiliating—defeat. Moreover, confidence in the government's highest office was severely shaken. The passage of the War Powers Act in 1973, written to compel any future president to seek congressional approval for armed intervention abroad and passed over Nixon's veto, dramatized both the widespread suspicion of an "Imperial Presidency" and a yearning for peace. But the positive dream of community that had inspired Johnson, King, and a generation of student activists could not be revived. No other vision took its place.

In 1968, seven prominent antiwar protesters had been brought to trial for allegedly conspiring to disrupt the Democratic National Convention in Chicago. Just a few years later, the majority of Americans had concluded that presidents Johnson and Nixon had conspired to do far worse. They had intentionally deceived the public about the nature and fortunes of the war. This moral failure signaled a collapse at the center of the American political system. Since Dwight Eisenhower left office warning of the potential danger embedded in the "military-industrial complex," no president had survived the presidency with his honor intact. Watergate, then, appeared to cap the politics of the Cold War, its revelations only reinforcing futility and cynicism. The United States was left psychologically at war with itself.

REVIEW QUESTIONS

1. Discuss the events that led up to and contributed to U.S. involvement in Vietnam. How did U.S. involvement in the war affect domestic programs?

2. Discuss the reasons the protest movement against the Vietnam War started on college campuses. Describe how these movements were organized and how the opponents of the war differed from the supporters.

3. Discuss the programs sponsored by Johnson's plan for a Great Society. What was their impact on urban poverty in the late 1960s?

4. What was the impact of the assassinations of Martin Luther King Jr. and Robert Kennedy on the election of 1968? How were various communities affected?

5. How were the "politics of identity" movements different from earlier civil rights organizations? In what ways did the various movements resemble one another?

6. Why did Richard Nixon enjoy such a huge electoral victory in 1972? Discuss his foreign and domestic policies. What led to his sudden downfall?

KEY TERMS

American Indian Movement (AIM) (p. 792)
Black Panther Party (p. 788)
Black Power (p. 788)
Counterculture (p. 777)
Gulf of Tonkin resolution (p. 775)
Free speech movement (p. 777)
Medicare (p. 781)
My Lai Massacre (p. 796)
National Organization of Women (NOW) (p. 789)

Office of Economic Opportunity (OEO) (p. 780)
Pentagon Papers (p. 799)
Red Power (p. 792)
Strategic Arms Limitation Treaty (p. 798)
Trail of Broken Treaties (p. 793)
War on poverty (p. 780)
Watergate (p. 800)

PEARSON myhistorylab Connections

Reinforce what you learned in this chapter by studying the many documents,
images, maps, review tools, and videos available at www.myhistorylab.com.

Read and Review

✓• Study and Review Chapter 29

•••• Read the Document

Johnson's Defense of the U.S. Presence in Vietnam (1965)

The Report of the President's Commission on Campus Unrest (1970)

Stokely Carmichael and Charles V. Hamilton, from Black Power: The Politics of Liberation in America (1966)

Shirley Chisholm, Equal Rights for Women (1969)

Gay Liberation Front (1970)

Chávez, He Showed Us the Way (1978)

Richard Nixon, Peace with Honor (1973)

House Judiciary Committee's Assessment of Nixon's Activities (1974)

👁 See the Map *The Vietnam War*

Research and Explore

•••• Read the Document

Exploring America: Rachel Carson

Profiles
Janis Joplin
Eugene McCarthy

Whose History Is It? The Vietnam Memorial

Watch the Video

Richard Nixon Presidential Campaign Ad: A Wavering Hubert Humphrey

Richard Nixon, "I am not a crook"

LBJ Signing the Civil Rights Bill

Protests against the Vietnam War

The Vietnam War

Newsreel: Peace March, Thousands Oppose Vietnam War

((•• Hear the Audio

Hear the audio files for Chapter 29 at
www.myhistorylab.com.

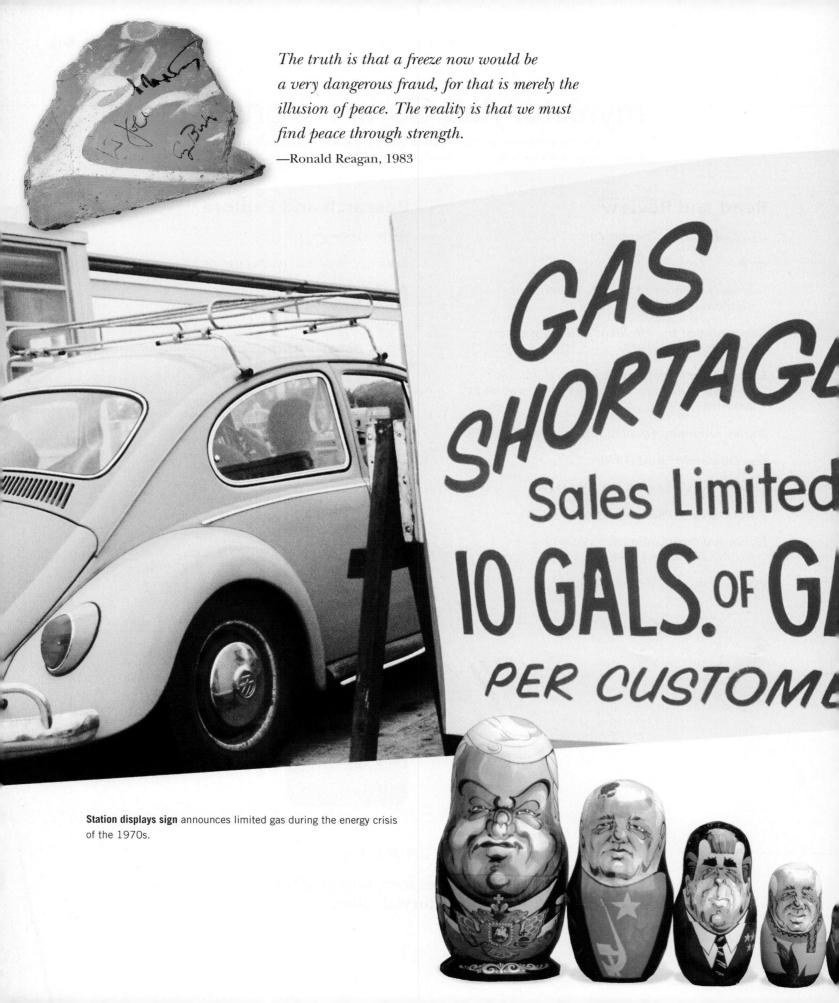

The truth is that a freeze now would be a very dangerous fraud, for that is merely the illusion of peace. The reality is that we must find peace through strength.

—Ronald Reagan, 1983

Station displays sign announces limited gas during the energy crisis of the 1970s.

30

THE CONSERVATIVE ASCENDANCY
1974–1991

((•─|Hear the Audio

Hear the audio files for Chapter 30 at **www.myhistorylab.com**.

WHAT EXPLAINS the weakness of the U.S. economy in the 1970s?

WHAT EXPLAINS the rise of the New Right in the 1980s?

WHAT ECONOMIC assumptions underlay "Reaganomics"?

WHY DID the gap between rich and poor grow in the 1980s?

HOW DID the Cold War end?

WHAT FACTORS led to U.S. involvement in the Persian Gulf War?

AMERICAN COMMUNITIES

Grassroots Conservatism in Orange County, California

IN 1962, BEE GATHRIGHT INVITED HER NEIGHBORS TO HER SUBURBAN Garden Grove home to hear a political talk by a man from the nearby Knott's Berry Farm Freedom Center. "This is when I discovered that I was a conservative," she later recalled. She convinced her skeptical husband Neil to share her new conviction. They soon joined the California Republican Assembly, a volunteer organization committed to electing conservatives to office. In 1964, the Gathrights' home served as a local headquarters for the presidential campaign of conservative Arizona Senator Barry Goldwater.

In Orange County in the 1960s and 1970s, thousands of "kitchen table" activists like the Gathrights began a transformation of American conservatism and American politics that culminated in the presidential election of Ronald Reagan in 1980. Most of them were middle-class men and women, including large numbers of professionals and small business owners. Orange County's 800 square miles lie at the center of the southern California basin, and citrus groves dominated the economy until the 1940s. World War II and Cold War defense-related spending accelerated the county's growth, creating thousands of new manufacturing jobs. By 1960, more than 700,000 people lived in Orange County, an increase of nearly 400 percent since 1940, and the population doubled again to top 2 million in the 1980s.

While Barry Goldwater's 1964 campaign ignited great enthusiasm in Orange County, his national defeat forced conservatives to consider ways to shed the "extremism" label. In 1966, they successfully backed the gubernatorial campaign of Ronald Reagan, a former Hollywood actor and New Deal liberal who had evolved in the 1950s into a prominent conservative. As governor, Reagan sought to limit state support for welfare and other social services, while expanding state power to enforce law and order.

Reagan's success in California, as well as Richard Nixon's election as president in 1968, signaled an important new turn for American conservatives. They still championed anticommunism but no longer engaged in the loose talk about using nuclear weapons that had hurt Goldwater. They attacked "big government," but no longer spoke openly about repealing popular New Deal programs like Social Security. Instead, they emphasized so-called family issues, in which

Orange County

opposition to sex education, obscenity, abortion rights, gay liberation, and the Equal Rights Amendment were all linked. On the economic side, conservatives began to tap a deep well of resentment over rising property taxes and high inflation.

Two central themes of this new conservatism resonated with millions of Americans well beyond Orange County. One was the 1978 "revolt" of homeowners that led to a sharp reduction in the property tax rate and soon spread to other states.

Orange County also helped form the second new force reshaping conservatism, "born-again" evangelical Christianity. Orange County's religious revival featured educated professionals and middle-class suburbanites who turned to Christianity for spirituality and as a way to assert order amid rapid cultural and social change. "Born-again" Christians found community not only in Sunday services, but also in a wide range of tightly organized activities: Bible study groups, summer retreats, "singles' fellowships," prayer breakfasts, and "Christian" consumer culture, which allowed people to simultaneously embrace faith, modern business techniques, and worldly goods. The political implications of the new evangelicalism soon became clear.

President Jimmy Carter, who took office in 1976, was a "born-again" Christian, and his successor, Ronald Reagan, raced to victory in 1980 with the strong backing of newly politicized Christian voters. Unlike Carter, who advised Americans to accept limits, Reagan promised to not only restore but also enhance American global supremacy. As president, Reagan introduced a new economic program—"Reaganomics"—that reduced income taxes for wealthy Americans and at the same time increased federal spending for the largest military buildup in American history. Abolishing the Great Society antipoverty programs, he fostered the growth of a two-tiered society characterized by a disproportionate number of women and children filling the ranks of the nation's poor. Meanwhile, the increases in military spending complemented Reagan's foreign policy, which included a revival of Cold War patriotism, interventions in the Caribbean and Central America, and labeling the Soviet Union an "Evil Empire." However, it was Reagan's successor, George H. W. Bush, who presided during one of the most dramatic events of the era: the dissolution of the Soviet Union.

THE OVEREXTENDED SOCIETY

I n the 1970s, the economic growth that had followed World War II ground to a halt, and Americans saw their standard of living decline. In addition, the decade presented Americans with an unfamiliar combination of skyrocketing prices and rising unemployment. Economists termed this novel condition "stagflation."

The United States had come to an unhappy turning point in its economic history. Emerging from World War II as the world's richest nation and retaining this status through the 1960s, the country suddenly found itself falling behind Western Europe and Japan. Moreover, the proportion of families living in poverty, which had shrunk during the 1960s, grew at an alarming rate. Nixon's successors, presidents Gerald Ford and Jimmy Carter, hoped to restore integrity to the office that Nixon had tarnished, but when it came to the economy, they promised little and, as many voters concluded, delivered even less.

A TROUBLED ECONOMY

The most vivid sign of the troubled economy, the energy crisis, seemed to appear suddenly in the fall of 1973, although it had been decades in the making. The United States, which used about 70 percent of all oil produced in the world, had a sufficient domestic supply until the mid-1950s. By 1973 the nation was importing one-third of its crude oil, mainly from the Middle Eastern countries around the Persian Gulf. On October 17, the Arab members of the government-controlled **Organization of Petroleum Exporting Countries (OPEC)**, in retaliation for U.S. support of Israel during the Yom Kippur War, announced an embargo on oil shipments to the United States and its Western European allies (see Map 30.1). As a result, Americans faced a severe oil shortage. OPEC ended the embargo five months later, but limited production to keep prices high.

President Nixon responded to the crisis by appointing an "energy czar" and paving the way for the creation of the Department of Energy in 1977. He also initiated a number of energy-saving measures. But the impact of these measures was slight, and the effects of the oil embargo rippled throughout the economy. While the cost of gasoline, oil, and electricity jumped to new heights, many other prices also rose, from apartment rents and telephone bills to restaurant checks (see Figure 30.1).

WHAT EXPLAINS the weakness of the U.S. economy in the 1970s?

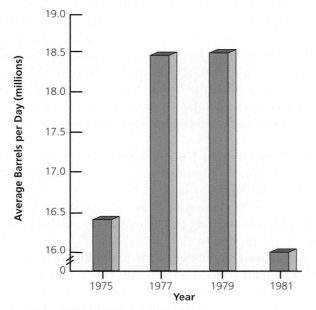

Figure 30.1 Decline of U.S. Oil Consumption, 1975–81
Boycotts causing shortages and high prices spurred the reduction in oil consumption. However, in the 1980s consumption once again began to rise to reach record highs.
Department of Energy, *Monthly Energy Review,* June 1982.

Organization of Petroleum Exporting Countries (OPEC)   Cartel of oil producing nations in Asia, Africa, and Latin America that gained substantial power over the world economy in the mid- to late-1970s by controlling the production and price of oil.

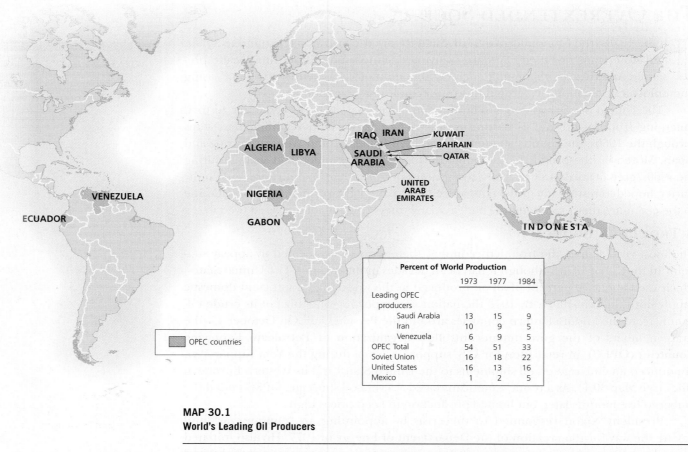

Percent of World Production			
	1973	1977	1984
Leading OPEC producers			
Saudi Arabia	13	15	9
Iran	10	9	5
Venezuela	6	9	5
OPEC Total	54	51	33
Soviet Union	16	18	22
United States	16	13	16
Mexico	1	2	5

MAP 30.1
World's Leading Oil Producers

WHY DID OPEC's share of world oil production drop between 1973 and 1984?

The economic downturn had deeper roots in the failure of the United States to keep up with the rising industrial efficiency of other nations. Manufacturers from Asia, Latin America, and Europe now produced cheaper and better products, including automobiles, long considered the monopoly of Detroit. U.S. automakers, determined to reduce costs, turned to "outsourcing"—that is, making cars and trucks from parts cheaply produced abroad and imported into the United States. In high-tech electronics, the United States could scarcely compete with Japanese companies. For the first time in the twentieth century, the balance of trade had tipped: Americans were importing more goods than exporting.

An AFL-CIO leader complained that the United States was becoming "a nation of hamburger stands . . . a country stripped of industrial capacity and meaningful work." Between 1970 and 1982 the AFL-CIO, since the early 1930s a leading source of support to the Democratic Party, lost nearly 30 percent of its membership (see Figure 30.2). The only real union growth took place among public employees, including teachers, civil service workers, and health professionals.

Typical of hard times, an increasing number of women sought jobs to support their families. By 1980, more than half of all married women with children in their care were working outside the home. Yet despite their numerical gains, women lost ground relative to men. In 1955, women earned 64 percent of the average wages paid to men; in 1980, they earned only 59 percent.

African American women made some gains. Through Title VII of the Civil Rights Act, which outlawed workplace discrimination by sex or race, and the establishment of the Equal Employment Opportunity Commission to enforce it, they managed to climb the lower levels of the job ladder. By 1980, northern black women's median earnings were about 95 percent of white women's earnings. In contrast, Hispanic women, whose labor force participation leaped by 80 percent during the decade, were restricted to only a few occupations, mostly at or only slightly above the minimum wage.

THE ENDANGERED ENVIRONMENT

The roots of the modern environmentalist movement trace back to marine biologist Rachel Carson's 1962 best-seller, *Silent Spring,* which detailed the devastating effects of DDT and other pesticides. By the end of the decade, concerned citizens were advocating conservation practices such as recycling glass bottles and newspapers and providing popular support for the proclamation of Earth Day, first celebrated on April 22, 1970.

The oil embargo of 1973 and the high prices of energy that followed helped to underscore even more boldly the environmental downside of the post–World War II economic boom. Air and water pollution, climate change, and depletion of the ozone layer became major political issues. Sometimes environmental campaigns succeeded in blocking massive construction projects, such as nuclear energy plants; more often they halted small-scale destruction of a natural habitat or historic urban district.

Congress responded to growing pressure by passing during the1970s more than twenty new bills and amending earlier legislation to protect endangered species, reduce pollution caused by automobile emissions, limit and ban the use of some pesticides and fluorocarbon gases, and control strip-mining practices. The **Environmental Protection Agency (EPA)**, established in 1970, grew to become the federal government's largest regulatory agency.

Business-based groups fought back and sometimes found unexpected allies. City officials, both Democratic and Republican, generally avoided congressional mandates for reduction in air pollution by requesting lengthy extensions of deadlines for compliance. Top labor officials such as George Meany, president of the AFL-CIO, denounced environmentalists as enemies of economic growth, and United Auto Workers lobbyists joined auto makers in resisting compulsory gas mileage and tighter emissions controls in new models. Again and again, efforts at more environmentally attuned policies on energy met defeat. Despite the introduction of lead-free gasoline, the air in major metropolitan areas grew worse because automobile traffic increased.

"LEAN YEARS PRESIDENTS": FORD AND CARTER

Gerald R. Ford and Jimmy Carter presided over not only a depressed economy but also a nation of disillusioned citizens. The revelations of the Watergate break-in and Nixon's subsequent resignation as president had cast a pall over politics. Replacing Nixon in August 1974, Gerald Ford reassured the public that "our long national nightmare is over," but then quickly pardoned Nixon for all the federal crimes he may have committed while in office. At the time, the pardon reinforced public cynicism toward government and Ford in particular.

To many Americans, Ford seemed a pleasant person but an inept leader. Ford only narrowly won nomination in 1976 after holding off a challenge from Ronald Reagan. Democrats chose Jimmy Carter, a former navy officer and governor of Georgia, who presented himself as a political outsider.

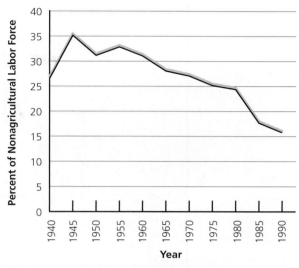

Figure 30.2 Union Membership, 1940–90
After reaching a peak during World War II, union membership steadily declined. In the 1980s, overseas production took an especially big toll on industrial unions.

Bureau of Labor Statistics, in Mary Kupiec et al., eds., *Encyclopedia of American Social History,* Vol. II. New York: Scribner's, 1993, p. 4188. Copyright © 1993 Scribner's. Reprinted by permission of Cengage Learning.

Read the **Document**

Exploring America: Rachel Carson at **www.myhistorylab.com**

Read the **Document**

Profile: Jimmy Carter at **www.myhistorylab.com**

Environmental Protection Agency (EPA)   Federal agency created in 1970 to oversee environmental monitoring and cleanup programs.

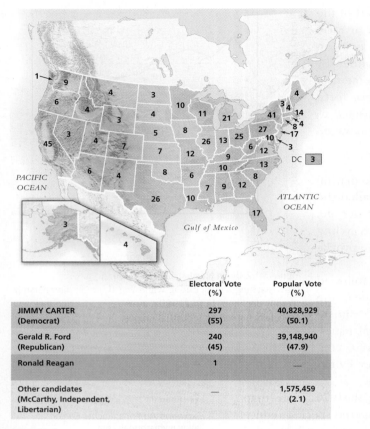

	Electoral Vote (%)	Popular Vote (%)
JIMMY CARTER (Democrat)	297 (55)	40,828,929 (50.1)
Gerald R. Ford (Republican)	240 (45)	39,148,940 (47.9)
Ronald Reagan	1	—
Other candidates (McCarthy, Independent, Libertarian)	—	1,575,459 (2.1)

MAP 30.2

The Election of 1976   Incumbent Gerald Ford could not prevail over the disgrace brought to the Republican Party by Richard Nixon. The lingering pall of the Watergate scandal, especially Ford's pardon of Nixon, worked to the advantage of Jimmy Carter, who campaigned as an outsider to national politics. Although Carter and his running mate Walter Mondale won by only a narrow margin, the Democrats gained control of both the White House and Congress.

WHY DID Ford pardon Nixon? Did it cost him the election?

QUICK REVIEW

The Election of 1976

♦ Pardon of Nixon reinforced cynicism about Ford.

♦ Jimmy Carter, governor of Georgia, positioned himself as a political outsider.

♦ Carter's campaign focus on domestic issues won him 50 percent of the popular vote.

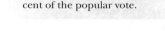

Jimmy Carter, The "Crisis of Confidence" Speech (1979) at **www.myhistorylab.com**

A born-again Christian and successful southern politician, Carter was the first Democratic presidential candidate since the 1930s who declined to call himself a liberal, offering instead personal integrity as his chief qualification for the nation's highest office. On domestic issues, Carter campaigned as a moderate. Counting on support from both conservative and southern voters who would ordinarily vote Republican, he defended existing entitlement programs while opposing Senator Edward Kennedy's call for comprehensive health coverage. He capitalized on Ford's unpopular Nixon pardon and, with his running mate Senator Walter Mondale of Minnesota, won with just over 50 percent of the popular vote and a 297-to-240 margin in the Electoral College (see Map 30.2).

If his outsider status helped win the election, Carter's lack of experience in national politics did little to prepare him to govern. Congress continued to pull tight on the reins of power, while the new president seemed to many observers enigmatic, even uninterested in the major issues. His most successful initiative, deregulation of the airlines, brought lower fares for millions of passengers. He also gained reforms in civil service, Social Security, and Medicare and created the Department of Education. Inflation proved to be his worst enemy. Half of all the inflation since 1940 had occurred in just ten years. Interest rates rose, driving mortgages out of reach for many would-be home buyers. Rents in many locations doubled, sales of automobiles and other consumer products slumped, and many small businesses went under. Tuition costs skyrocketed along with unemployment, and many young men and women who could neither afford to go to college nor find a job moved back home.

An outspoken fiscal conservative, Carter could not deliver on his promise to turn the economy around or even to lower the federal deficit. He had managed to discredit the liberal tradition of the Democratic Party even while distancing himself from it, making his presidency the symbol of a larger political collapse.

THE LIMITS OF GLOBAL POWER

President Carter pledged to inaugurate a new era in U. S. foreign policy, and, noting a shameful "loss of morality" in recent times, he placed international human rights at the top of his agenda. Carter condemned policies that allowed the United States to support "right-wing monarchs and military dictators" in the name of anticommunism. His secretary of state, Cyrus R. Vance, and the assistant secretary for human rights and humanitarian affairs, Pat Derrian, worked to punish or at least to censure repressive military regimes in Brazil, Argentina, and Chile. For the first time, leading U.S. diplomats spoke out against the South African apartheid regime. In line with this policy, Carter tried to reform operations at the CIA, particularly to halt covert interventions in the affairs of foreign governments.

Early in his administration, Carter met privately with Israeli prime minister Menachem Begin to encourage conciliation with Egypt. When negotiations between the two countries stalled in 1978, Carter brought Begin together with Egyptian president Anwar el-Sadat for a thirteen-day retreat at Camp David, Maryland.

President Carter signs the Middle East Peace Treaty with Egyptian President Anwar Sadat and Israeli Prime Minister Menachem Begin, in Washington, DC, March 1979. President Carter had invited both leaders to Camp David, the presidential retreat in Maryland, where for two weeks he mediated between them on territorial rights to the West Bank and Gaza Strip. Considered Carter's greatest achievement in foreign policy, the negotiations, known as the Camp David Peace Accords, resulted in not only the historic peace treaty but also the Nobel Peace Prize for Begin and Sadat.

The **Camp David Accords**, signed in September 1978, set the formal terms for peace in the region. Egypt became the first Arab country to recognize Israel's right to exist, as the two nations established mutual diplomatic relations for the first time since the founding of Israel in 1948. In return, Egypt regained control of the Sinai Peninsula, including important oil fields and airfields.

But disappointment lay ahead. Carter staked his hopes for regional peace on the final achievement of statehood, or at least political autonomy, for Palestinians in a portion of their former lands now occupied by the Israelis. The accords specified that Israel would eventually return to its approximate borders of 1967. However, although Begin agreed to dismantle some Israeli settlements in the Sinai, the Israeli government continued to sponsor more and more Jewish settlements, expropriating Palestinian holdings. The final status of the Palestinians remained in limbo.

Carter scored his biggest moral victory in foreign affairs by paving the way for Panama to assume the ownership, operation, and defense of the Panama Canal Zone. Carter pressured the Senate to ratify new treaties in 1978 that would turn the Panama Canal over to Panama by the year 2000.

Carter also succeeded in achieving full diplomatic relations with the Peoples Republic of China in January, 1979 and in paving the way for cultural and trade exchanges between the two nations. The agreement angered conservatives because it stipulated that the United States sever ties with its ally, the national regime on Taiwan.

Mired in problems inherited from his predecessors, however, Carter often found himself disoriented, and, despite his commitment to human rights, putting aside his principles. He chose to stabilize repressive regimes in nations considered vital to U.S. interests, such as South Korea and the Philippines. In Nicaragua, the overthrow in 1979 of the brutal dictator Anastasio Somoza Debayle, longtime U.S. ally, left Carter without a successor to support. When the new Sandinista revolutionary government pleaded for help, Congress turned down Carter's request for $75 million in aid to Nicaragua. Meanwhile, in El Salvador, the Carter administration continued to back a repressive government.

Carter's campaign for international human rights worsened the prospect for **détente** with the Soviet Union. Only after softening his criticism of the Soviet policy

Camp David Accords Agreement signed by Israel in Egypt in 1978 that set the formal terms for peace in the Middle East.

Détente French for "easing of tension," the term used to describe the new U.S. relations with China and the Soviet Union in 1972.

Iranians demonstrate outside the U.S. Embassy in Tehran, raising a poster with a caricature of President Carter. The Iran hostage crisis, which began November 8, 1979, when a mob of Iranians seized the U.S. embassy in Tehran, contributed to Carter's defeat at the polls the following year. Fifty-two embassy employees were held hostage for 444 days.

QUICK REVIEW

Iranian Hostages

- November 4, 1979: Iranian fundamentalists seized U.S. embassy in Tehran.
- Fifty-two Americans held hostage for 444 days.
- Crisis doomed the Carter presidency.

WHAT EXPLAINS the rise of the New Right in the 1980s?

---

toward political dissidents did Carter achieve in June 1979 the SALT II agreement on arms control. But the thaw proved only temporary.

Carter's reaction to the Soviet occupation of Afghanistan produced a major setback. In December 1979, 30,000 Soviet troops invaded their neighbor to put down a revolt by Islamic insurgents against the weakening Soviet-backed government. Noting that the Soviet occupation of Afghanistan posed "a grave threat to the free movement of Middle East oil," President Carter issued his own corollary to the Monroe Doctrine by affirming the right of the United States to use military force if necessary to protect its interests in the Persian Gulf. He backed up his increasingly hard-line policies by halting exports of grain and high technology to the Soviet Union, by supporting Afghan resistance against the Russians, and by canceling American participation in the 1980 Moscow Olympics. Carter also called for ever-larger increases in the military budget. The prospect of détente dried up.

THE IRAN HOSTAGE CRISIS

On November 4, 1979, Iranian militants seized the U.S. embassy in Tehran and took nearly seventy American employees hostage. For decades, U.S. foreign policy in the Middle East had depended on a friendly government in Iran. After the CIA had helped to overthrow the reformist, constitutional government and installed the Pahlavi royal family and the shah of Iran in 1953, millions of U.S. dollars had poured into the Iranian economy and the shah's armed forces. By early 1979, however, a revolution led by the Islamic leader Ayatollah Ruhollah Khomeini overthrew the shah. After Carter had allowed the deposed Reza Shah Pahlavi to enter the United States for medical treatment, a group of Khomeini's followers retaliated, storming the U.S. embassy and demanding the return of the Shah to Iran to face trial.

Carter refused the militants' demands, and months passed without a resolution. Finally, after 444 days, the President ordered U.S. military forces to stage a nighttime helicopter rescue mission. But a sandstorm caused some of the aircrafts to crash and burn, leaving eight Americans dead, their charred corpses displayed by the enraged Iranians. Short of an all-out attack, which surely would have resulted in the hostages' deaths, Carter had used up his options.

The political and economic fallout was heavy. Cyrus Vance resigned, the first secretary of state in sixty-five years to leave office over a political difference with the president. The price of oil rose by 60 percent. Carter had failed in the one area he had proclaimed central to the future of the United States: energy. He had also violated his own human rights policy, which he had intended to be his distinctive mark on American foreign affairs.

THE NEW RIGHT

The failures in U.S. foreign policy, accompanied by the faltering economy, played a large part in mobilizing what one writer termed "the politics of resentment." Sizable numbers of white taxpayers begrudged the tax hikes required to fund the welfare programs that benefited minorities and expanded social services for the poor and, at the same time, slowed economic development. In economically hard-pressed urban areas, conservative white voters who resented the gains made by African Americans, Latinos, and women formed a powerful backlash movement against liberalism.

What distinguished the New Right from the old was an emphasis on "moral values" and its populist character. One element in this coalition comprised conservative ideologues, some of them former Democrats who had become disenchanted with liberalism. By far, the largest component comprised evangelical or born-again Protestants like the Gathrights who organized to become a powerful political force.

NEOCONSERVATISM

By the mid-1970s, a new variation of conservatism appeared on the political landscape: neoconservatism. The most prestigious leaders of this new movement had been liberal Democrats, some even socialists, in the preceding decades. The unsettling social movements of the 1960s had prompted them to turn against New Deal–style liberalism and the welfare state. They continued to believe in equal opportunity, but forcefully rejected the goal of equality of outcome. They sought to repeal affirmative action programs and dismantle the antipoverty programs enacted during the Johnson administration.

The heart of the neoconservatism was, however, foreign policy. Angered over the failure to pursue victory in Vietnam, neoconservatives called for a stronger national defense against communism. They opposed Carter's move toward détente and accused the president of allowing Communists to advance in Third World countries.

Neoconservatives played an important role in building the institutional foundation for the rightward turn in American politics. Richly funded by corporate donors, they established think tanks to engage scholars and intellectuals in policy-shaping discussions. The growing intellectual prominence of neoconservatives smoothed the way for broader public support.

THE RELIGIOUS RIGHT

Evangelical Protestants, more than 50 million Americans by the late 1970s, became the backbone of the new conservatism. The Religious Right typically endorsed neoconservative positions on foreign and domestic policy. They supported a balanced budget amendment to the Constitution, sought unsuccessfully to return prayer to the public schools, and endorsed the Supreme Court's reinstatement of the death penalty in 1976. As grassroots activists, they moved conservatism from the margins to the center of the Republican Party.

Finding huge audiences among the growing evangelical and Pentecostal congregations, Protestant ministers took to the airwaves. Televangelists such as Pat Robertson, Jimmy Swaggart, and Jim and Tammy Bakker frequently mixed conservative politics with appeals for both prayer and money. By the late 1970s, more than 1,400 radio stations and 30 TV stations specialized in religious broadcasts that reached perhaps 20 million listeners weekly and became a major source of fundraising for conservative organizations and campaigns.

In 1979, the Reverend Jerry Falwell, a Bible Baptist, formed the Moral Majority. As a major political lobbying group, the Moral Majority advocated tough laws against homosexuality and pornography and promoted a reduction of government services (especially welfare payments to single mothers) and increased spending for a stronger national defense. The Moral Majority also waged well-publicized campaigns against public school integration and especially the busing of schoolchildren.

THE PRO-FAMILY MOVEMENT

Most of all, the New Right embraced what they termed "traditional family values": defeating the Equal Rights Amendment (ERA) stood at the top of their political agenda. Approved by Congress in March 1972, nearly fifty years after its introduction (see Chapter 22), the ERA stated: "Equality of rights under the law shall not be denied or abridged by the United States or by any State on account of sex." Endorsed by both the Democratic and Republican parties, the amendment appeared likely to be ratified by the individual states.

◉ Watch the **Video**

Evangelical Religion and Politics, Then and Now at **www.myhistorylab.com**

•◦• Read the **Document**

Profile: *Jerry Falwell* at **www.myhistorylab.com**

Phyllis Schlafly rallied her supporters in Springfield, Illinois, to demonstrate against the Equal Rights Amendment in March 1975. She also renamed her Stop ERA group the Eagle Forum, which would continue to serve, as she put it, as "the alternative to women's lib."

◆◆◆ Read the Document

Roe v. Wade (1973) at
www.myhistorylab.com

Watch the Video

Ronald Reagan Presidential Campaign
Ad: A Bear in the Woods at
www.myhistorylab.com

Roe v. Wade U.S. Supreme Court decision (1973) that disallowed state laws prohibiting abortion during the first three months (trimester) of pregnancy and established guidelines for abortion in the second and third trimesters.

Phyllis Schlafly, a self-described suburban housewife and popular lecturer, headed the STOP-ERA campaign. Under Schlafly's leadership, the New Right mounted large, expensive campaigns in each swing state and overwhelmed pro-ERA resources. Her supporters also built a strong, religious-based coalition, with southern Protestants, western Mormons, northeastern Catholics, and Orthodox Jews temporarily putting aside differences to join forces to defeat the amendment that they believed was "against God's plan."

Although thirty-five states had ratified the ERA by 1979, the amendment remained three votes short of passage. Despite a three-year extension, the ERA died in Congress in 1982.

Meanwhile, the anti-ERA campaign had grown into a comprehensive "pro-family" movement that placed eliminating abortion rights at the top of its political agenda. In 1973, the Supreme Court had ruled in *Roe v. Wade* that state laws decreeing abortion a crime during the first two trimesters of pregnancy constituted a violation of a woman's right to privacy. Opponents of *Roe* rallied for a constitutional amendment defining conception as the beginning of life and then argued that the "rights of the unborn" supersede a woman's right to control her own body.

Antiabortion groups, such as the Orange County Pro-Life Political Action Committee, founded in 1973, also rallied against sex education programs in public schools. They picketed Planned Parenthood counseling centers, intimidating potential clients. A small minority turned to more extreme actions and bombed dozens of abortion clinics.

THE 1980 ELECTION

Despite the upsurge of the new right, Carter went into the 1980 presidential campaign determined to win a second term. His prospects, he knew, depended to a large extent on an uptick in the economy and a resolution to the hostage crisis in Iran.

On the Republican side, former California governor Ronald Reagan had been building his campaign since his near nomination in 1976. Former CIA director and Texas oil executive George H. W. Bush, more moderate than Reagan, became the Republican candidate for vice president.

Reagan rode the crest of the swelling conservative wave, repeatedly asking voters, "Are you better off now than you were four years ago?" While Carter implored Americans to tighten their belts, Reagan promised to cut their taxes. He assured them that "America's best days lay ahead." He also embraced the conservative heart of the GOP platform.

The Republicans cruised to victory. Carter won only 41.2 percent of the popular vote to Reagan's 50.9 percent, 49 votes in the Electoral College to Reagan's 489. The Republicans won control of the Senate for the first time since 1952 and with the largest majority since 1928. White working people, the traditional supporters of the Democratic Party, had defected to the Republicans in large numbers, although women and African Americans voted for Reagan in far fewer numbers. Reagan's first term began on a high note: the Iranians released the American hostages on January 20, 1981, the day he took the oath of office (see Seeing History).

The Inaugurations of Carter and Reagan

Presidents-elect commonly plan their inauguration ceremonies to reflect symbolically their values and campaign pledges. In 1977, Jimmy Carter staged a "people's inaugural," and hoped to emphasize the unassuming style and frugality that would mark his presidency. He took the oath of office wearing a plain business suit and then broke tradition to walk hand-in-hand with his wife Rosalynn along the parade route. There were no flowers on display on the cold January day, and the White House reviewing stand was heated by solar energy.

Ronald Reagan hoped to convey a different message, not one of thrift but of wealth and security. On January 21, 1981, he became the nation's fortieth president wearing a formal black coat, striped pants, and black shoes and accompanied First Lady Nancy Reagan down the parade route in a limousine.

WHY DID the newly elected President Carter choose to celebrate thrift and humility? Why did his successor Ronald Reagan choose to celebrate wealth? What had happened in the United States between the mid-1970s and the beginning of the 1980s to make such a display of wealth and power acceptable to the public?

Everything about Reagan's inauguration, including eight formal balls spread across four days of festivities, reflected what Nancy Reagan described as her aspiration to put the White House "symbolically back up on a hill in people's minds, to have stature and loftiness." The Reagans hired a public relations expert to ensure that every event was telecast. All the inaugural balls, concerts, and receptions, including the opening evening event (an $800,000 light show and concert on the steps of the Lincoln Memorial), were planned to entertain and astound at-home audiences. Festivities at the Washington, DC, balls were also beamed through a $2 million satellite hookup to "mini-balls" held simultaneously across the nation. The Reagan inauguration cost nearly five times that of Carter.

Newspapers and magazines published many photographs of Nancy Reagan, noting that she had restored high style to the image of the First Lady. Whereas Rosalynn Carter had worn an old blue chiffon evening dress to the inaugural ball in 1977, Nancy Reagan had chosen a hand-beaded, crystal-studded gown designed by a leader in the fashion industry. Overall, her inaugural wardrobe was estimated to cost around $25,000. Unlike Rosalynn Carter, who appeared at the swearing-in ceremony in a modest cloth coat, Nancy Reagan chose a full-length mink.

Reagan's inauguration, touted by the press as the most expensive in U.S. history, showcased the theme the president-elect had chosen for his administration: "America—A New Beginning." Not the belt-tightening, "homespun ways" of the Carter presidency, noted one reporter, but an unabashed celebration of wealth would prevail. ■

THE REAGAN REVOLUTION

No other twentieth-century president except Franklin D. Roosevelt left as deep a personal imprint on American politics as Ronald Reagan. Ironically, Reagan himself began his political life as an ardent New Deal Democrat. But by the time he entered the White House in 1981, Reagan had rejected the activist welfare state legacy of the New Deal era. "In the present crisis. . .," he declared, "government is not the solution to our problem, government is the problem." Reagan and his allies proceeded to reshape the political and social landscape of the nation along conservative lines (see Map 30.3).

WHAT ECONOMIC assumptions underlay "Reagonomics"?

THE GREAT COMMUNICATOR

Even as he took office, most Americans knew Ronald Reagan mainly from his Hollywood movies and television appearances. Although never a big star, on-screen he appeared tall, handsome, and affable.

By midcentury, Reagan had emerged as one of the most prominent conservative politicians in the nation. While serving as president of the Screen Actors Guild from 1947 to 1952, he distanced himself from other New Deal Democrats by leading the anti-Communist forces in Hollywood.

Reagan switched his party affiliation and became a successful fundraiser and popular speaker for the California Republican Party. With the financial backing of some wealthy conservatives, he won the 1966 race for California governor. He won reelection in 1970. As governor, Reagan cut the state welfare rolls, reduced the number of state employees, and funneled a large share of state tax revenues back to local governments. He vigorously attacked student protesters and black militants, thereby tapping into the conservative backlash against the 1960s' activism.

When Reagan entered the White House in January 1981, his supporters interpreted his election as a popular mandate for the conservatism that had been growing since Nixon took office. The "Reagan Revolution," they confidently predicted, would usher in a new age in American political life.

•••[Read the Document

Ronald Reagan, First Inaugural Address (1981) at **www.myhistorylab.com**

•••[Read the Document

Paul Craig Robert, The Supply-Side Revolution (1984) at **www.myhistorylab.com**

	Electoral Vote (%)	Popular Vote (%)
RONALD REAGAN (Republican)	489 (91)	43,201,220 (50.9)
Jimmy Carter (Democrat)	49 (9)	34,913,332 (41.2)
John B. Anderson (Independent)	—	5,581,379 (6.6)
Other candidates (Libertarian)	—	921,299 (1.1)

MAP 30.3
The Election of 1980 Ronald Reagan won a landslide victory over incumbent Jimmy Carter, who managed to carry only six states and the District of Columbia. Reagan attracted millions of traditionally Democratic voters to the Republican camp.

WHAT ATTRACTED many Democratic voters to Ronald Reagan?

REAGANOMICS

Supply-side theory, dubbed "Reaganomics" by the media, dominated the Reagan administration's economic planning and helped redirect the American economy. Supply-side theorists urged a sharp break with the Keynesian policies that had prevailed since the New Deal era (see Chapter 24). During recessions, Keynesians traditionally favored moderate tax cuts and increases in government spending to stimulate the economy and reduce unemployment. By putting more money in people's pockets, they argued, greater consumer demand would lead to economic expansion.

By contrast, supply-siders called for simultaneous tax cuts and reductions in public spending. This combination would give private entrepreneurs and investors greater incentives to start businesses, take risks, invest capital, and thereby create new wealth and jobs. Whatever revenues were lost in lower tax rates would be offset by revenue from new economic growth. At the same time, spending cuts would keep the federal deficit under control and thereby keep interest rates down.

Reagan quickly won bipartisan approval for two key bills that culminated in the largest tax cut in the nation's history. The

Economic Recovery Tax Act of 1981 brought across-the-board cuts for corporations and individuals. The new legislation also reduced the maximum tax on all income from 70 percent to 50 percent, lowered the maximum capital gains tax—the tax paid on profitable investments—from 28 percent to 20 percent, and eliminated the distinction between earned and unearned income. This last measure proved a boon to the smallest although richest fraction of the population that derives most of its income from rent, dividends, and interest instead of from wages.

With the help of conservative southern and western Democrats in the House, the administration also pushed through a comprehensive program of spending cuts, known as the Omnibus Reconciliation Act of 1981. This bill mandated huge cuts affecting more than 200 social and cultural programs. The hardest-hit areas included education, the environment, health, housing, urban aid, food stamps, research on synthetic fuels, and the arts.

While reducing spending on domestic programs, the Reagan administration greatly increased the defense budget, a trend already under way during Carter's final two years as president. Overall, the military buildup indicated a significant shift in federal budget priorities.

Ronald Reagan, the fortieth president of the United States, was known for his ability to articulate broad principles of government in a clear fashion. The most popular president since Dwight Eisenhower, he built a strong coalition of supporters from long-term Republicans, disillusioned Democrats, and evangelical Protestants.

Meanwhile, the Reagan administration created a chilly atmosphere for organized labor. In the summer of 1981, some 13,000 federal employees, all members of the Professional Air Traffic Controllers Organization (PATCO), went on strike. The president retaliated by firing all the strikers, and a crash course started by the Federal Aviation Administration permanently replaced them. Conservative appointees to the National Labor Relations Board and the federal courts toughened their antiunion position. By 1990, fewer than 15 percent of American workers belonged to a labor union, the lowest proportion since before World War II.

Deregulation also served as a key element in Reaganomics. The president's appointments to head the Environmental Protection Agency, the Occupational Safety and Health Administration, and the Consumer Product Safety Commission abolished or weakened hundreds of rules governing environmental protection, workplace safety, and consumer protection, all to increase the efficiency and productivity of business. Secretary of the Interior James Watt opened up formerly protected wilderness areas and wetlands to private developers. Secretary of Transportation Andrew L. "Drew" Lewis Jr. eliminated regulations passed in the 1970s aimed at reducing air pollution and improving fuel efficiency in cars and trucks.

Following supply-side theory, the Reagan administration weakened the Justice Department's Antitrust Division, the Securities and Exchange Commission, and the Federal Home Loan Bank Board. The appointment of Alan Greenspan in 1983, to succeed Carter appointee Paul Volker, greatly encouraged trends toward speculation in market trading. By the late 1980s, the unfortunate consequences of deregulation would become apparent in a series of unprecedented scandals in the nation's financial and banking industries.

THE ELECTION OF 1984

Hoping to win back disgruntled voters, Democrats chose Carter's vice president, Walter F. Mondale, as their nominee. A former senator from Minnesota, Mondale had close ties with the party's liberal establishment, but also the support of its more military-minded wing. At the Democratic National Convention, Mondale named New York Representative Geraldine Ferraro as his running mate, a first for women in American politics.

While Mondale emphasized the growing deficit, called attention to Americans who were left out of prosperity, and promised to raise taxes, Reagan cruised above it all. He

QUICK REVIEW

Key Components of Reagonomics

♦ Lower personal income tax rates.

♦ Increase defense spending.

♦ Deregulate industry.

Economic Recovery Tax Act of 1981
A major revision of the federal income tax system.

Deregulation   Reduction or removal of government regulations and encouragement of direct competition in many important industries and economic sectors.

offered the voters a choice between a Democratic "government of pessimism, fear, and limits" or his own, based on "hope, confidence, and growth."

"It's morning again in America," Reagan's campaign ads promised, and in one of the biggest landslides in American history, Reagan won 59 percent of the popular vote and carried every state but Minnesota and the District of Columbia. A majority of blue-collar voters cast their ballots for the president. Even a quarter of all Democrats voted for Reagan.

RECESSION, RECOVERY, AND FISCAL CRISIS

Reagan's supply-side policies produced a mixed record but a highly favorable outcome for the wealthiest Americans. In 1982, a severe recession, the worst since the 1930s, gripped the nation. The official unemployment rate reached nearly 11 percent. But by 1983, the economy recovered and headed into one of the longest periods of growth and expansion in American history. The stock market boomed, pushing the Dow Jones industrial average from 776 in August 1982 to an all-time high of 2,722 in August 1987. The administration took credit for the turnaround, hailing the supply-side policies that had drastically cut taxes and domestic spending. But critics pointed to other factors: the Federal Reserve Board's tight-money policies, an energy resource glut and a consequent sharp drop in energy prices, and the billions of dollars pumped into the economy for defense spending.

Most financial experts, however, believed that the supply-side formula intensified a significant fiscal crisis. Although Reagan had promised to balance the federal budget, his policies had the opposite effect. The national debt tripled, growing from $914 billion in 1980 to over $2.7 trillion in 1989.

During the Reagan presidency, the fiscal crisis became a structural problem with profound and long-lasting implications for the American economy. Big deficits kept interest rates high. Foreign investors, attracted by high interest rates on government securities, pushed up the value of the dollar in relation to foreign currencies. The overvalued dollar made it difficult for foreigners to buy American products, while making overseas goods cheaper to American consumers. Basic American industries found it difficult to compete abroad and at home. Since World War I, the United States had been the world's leading creditor; in the mid-1980s, it became its biggest debtor (see Figure 30.3).

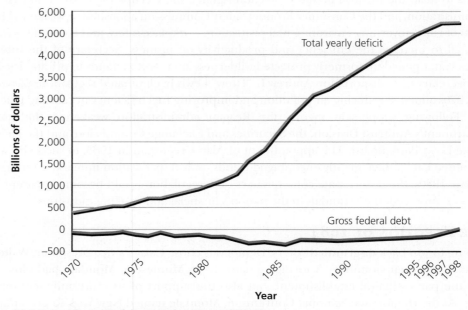

Figure 30.3 Federal Budget Deficit and National Debt, 1970–98
Tax cuts combined with huge increases in defense spending created a sharp increase in the budget deficit during the Republican administrations.

Statistical abstract of the United States, in Nash et al., *The American People,* 5th ed., p. 988.

On Wall Street, the bull market ended abruptly in the fall of 1987. After reaching its new high, the Dow Jones average of thirty leading industrial stocks began to slide downward and then crashed. On October 19, "Black Monday," the Dow lost almost one-quarter of its value. Although the causes for the panic remain uncertain, at the time many commentators pointed to anxiety spurred by the raging federal deficit.

BEST OF TIMES, WORST OF TIMES

The celebration of wealth, moneymaking, and entrepreneurship dominated much of popular culture, politics, and intellectual life in the 1980s, establishing a pattern that would persist into the twenty-first century. The dapper stock speculator Ivan Boesky, who was later indicted for criminal insider trading, boasted of making more than $100 million on just two deals. "I think greed is healthy," he told cheering business students in 1986: "You can be greedy and still feel good about yourself." However, few Americans in the 1980s could actually live by these principles.

Various data indicated that the nation was moving toward greater inequality, that while income soared for the wealthiest Americans, poverty was also on the rise. Many Americans feared that the future looked uncertain at best. Two of their most cherished beliefs—that life would improve for most people and their children, and that membership in the comfortable middle class was possible for all who worked for it—looked shaky by the end of the decade (see Tables 30.1, 30.2, and 30.3).

A TWO-TIERED SOCIETY

Until the mid-1970s, the rise in income had been fairly evenly distributed among Americans. During the Reagan presidency, in contrast, affluent Americans gained the most, with the top 1 percent way out in front. Before Reagan took office, a CEO of a major corporation earned about forty times that of a typical blue-collar worker; at the end of his second term, the typical CEO made ninety-three times as much. Poverty grew at an alarming rate. The number of fully employed workers earning below poverty-level incomes increased by 50 percent. Nearly one-quarter of all children lived in poverty.

The gains for African Americans achieved by the civil rights movement were steadily eroded. In 1954, black families earned about 53 percent of the income of white families. This figure rose to 60 percent in 1969, peaked at 62 percent in 1975, and steadily dropped during the next decade. By 1992, 33 percent of all African Americans lived in poverty, as did 29 percent of Hispanics.

The majority of African Americans lived in central cities with high unemployment rates, and the bleak prospects took a toll especially on the young. Among black teenagers, the unemployment rate topped 40 percent. Meanwhile, the high school dropout rate skyrocketed, and the number of serious crimes, such as burglary, car theft, and murder, perpetrated by black teenagers increased at an alarming rate.

Moreover, opportunities for advancement into the middle class were dwindling. By 1980, fewer black students attended integrated schools than in 1954, except in the South, where about half the black students did. The turnabout resulted in part from increasing opposition by white parents to court-ordered school busing, which had served as the principal means of achieving racial balance in urban school systems. During the 1980s, the busing controversy nearly disappeared because federal judges hesitated to mandate such programs. But more important

WHY DID the gap between rich and poor grow in the 1980s?

TABLE 30.1

Percentage Share of Aggregate Family Income, 1980–92

	1980	**1992**
Top 5 Percent	15.3%	17.6%
Highest Fifth	41.6	44.6
Fourth Fifth	24.3	24.0
Third Fifth	17.5	16.5
Second Fifth	11.6	10.5
Lowest Fifth	5.1	4.4

U.S. Bureau of the Census, *Current Population Reports: Consumer Incomes,* Series P-60, Nos. 167 and 184, 1990, 1993. U.S. federal data compiled by Ed Royce, Rollins College.

TABLE 30.2

Share of Total Net Worth of American Families

	1983	**1989**
Richest 1 percent of families	31%	37%
Next richest 9 percent	35	31
Remaining 90 percent	33	32

The New York Times, April 21, 1992, from Federal Reserve Survey of Consumer Finances. Copyright © 1992 The New York Times. Reprinted by permission.

TABLE 30.3

Measures of Average Earnings, 1980–92 (In 1990 Dollars)

Year	Average Weekly Earnings	Average Hourly Earnings
1980	$373.81	$10.59
1985	363.30	10.41
1992	339.37	9.87

U.S. House of Representatives, Committee on Ways and Means, *Overview of Entitlement Programs* (Washington, DC: GPO, 1993), table 35, p. 557. U.S. federal data compiled by Ed Royce, Rollins College.

TABLE 30.4

Number of Poor, Rate of Poverty, and Poverty Line, 1979–92

	1979	1992
Millions of poor	26.1	36.9
Rate of poverty	11.7%	14.5%
Poverty line (family of four)	$7,412	$14,335

U.S. Bureau of the Census, *Current Population Reports: Consumer Income,* Series P-60, Nos. 161 and 185, 1988, 1993. U.S. federal data compiled by Ed Royce, Rollins College.

Affirmative action A set of policies to open opportunities in business and education for members of minority groups and women by allowing race and sex to be factors included in decisions to hire, award contracts, or admit students to higher education programs.

Sunbelt The states of the American South and Southwest.

TABLE 30.5

Net New Job Creation by Wage Level, 1979–87

	Number of Net New Jobs Created	Percentage of Net New Jobs Created
Low-wage jobs (less than $11,611)	5,955,000	50.4%
Middle-wage jobs ($11,612 to $46,444)	4,448,000	31.7%
High-wage jobs ($46,445 and above)	1,405,000	11.9%

U.S. Senate, Committee on the Budget, *Wages of American Workers in the 1980s* (Washington, DC: U.S. Government Printing Office, 1988). U.S. federal data compiled by Ed Royce, Rollins College.

TABLE 30.6

Median Family Income and Ratio to White, by Race, and Hispanic Origin, 1980–92 (in 1992 Dollars)

Year	All Races	White	Black	Hispanic
1980	$35,839	$37,341	$21,606 (58%)	$25,087 (67%)
1985	36,164	38,011	21,887 (58%)	25,596 (67%)
1992	36,812	38,909	21,161 (54%)	23,901 (61%)

U.S. Bureau of the Census, *Current Population Reports,* Series P-60, No. 184, 1993. U.S. federal data compiled by Ed Royce, Rollins College.

was the change in the racial composition of American cities. As a consequence of "white flight" to the suburbs, big-city school systems were serving mainly African American and Latino children, making the issue of integration moot (see Tables 30.4, 30.5, and 30.6).

New legal rulings closed off important routes to employment in the professions. A 1978 U.S. Supreme Court decision dealt a sharp blow to **affirmative action**. To ensure acceptance of a minimum number of minority students, the University of California at Davis Medical School had established a quota system under affirmative action guidelines. In 1973 and 1974, the school denied admission to Allan Bakke, a white student. Bakke sued the university for "reverse discrimination," claiming his academic record was better than that of the sixteen minority students who were admitted. The U.S. Supreme Court handed down a five-to-four decision on June 18, 1978, stating that the use of an "explicit racial classification" in situations where no earlier discrimination had been demonstrated violated the equal protection clause of the Fourteenth Amendment. During the 1980s, therefore, affirmative action programs could operate only when "a legacy of unequal treatment" could be proved.

THE FEMINIZATION OF POVERTY

While the gap between the rich and poor was growing to its widest point since 1945, the experience of poverty became the lot of primarily women and children. Throughout the era, women with young children continued to enter the labor force at a fast pace, but the majority of jobs available to them paid too little to support their children.

The rising rate of divorce and desertion paralleled the increasing number of women and children in poverty. Most women usually lost ground following a divorce, which now affected nearly half of all new marriages. Moreover, the majority of men defaulted on child-support payments within one year after separation. Whereas divorced men enjoyed a sizable increase in their standard of living, divorced women and their children suffered a formidable decline.

A sharp rise in teenage pregnancy reinforced this trend. Nearly one in four babies was born to unmarried mothers. Many of these mothers were too young to have gained either the education or skills to secure jobs that paid enough to support themselves and their children. By 1992, female-headed households, comprising 13.7 million people, accounted for 37 percent of the nation's poor. Among black women, the number of female-headed families increased in just one decade from 30 percent in 1970 to 47 percent in 1980.

SUNBELT/RUSTBELT COMMUNITIES

A distinctive pattern of poverty and prosperity mirrored changes in the nation's political tenor. The bastion of prosperity as well as the bulwark of political conservatism was the **Sunbelt**, which extended from Florida to Orange County, California. This region boasted a gross product greater than many nations along with a growing number of Republicans.

Much of the Sunbelt's growth depended on a huge outlay of federal funds, including defense spending and the allocation of Social Security benefits. The number of residents over age sixty-five increased by 30 percent during the 1970s, reaching 26 million by the time President Reagan took office. Immigrants from Latin America, the Caribbean, and Asia joined Americans fleeing the depressed Northeast to boost the region's population (see Map 30.4).

The Sunbelt witnessed a dramatic turnaround in demographic and economic trends. Southern cities reversed the century-long trend of out-migration among African Americans. The Southwest and West changed yet more dramatically. Aided by air conditioning, water diversions, public improvements, and large-scale development and subsidies to agribusiness, California became the nation's most populous state; Texas moved to third, behind New York. Former farms and deserts were turned almost overnight into huge metropolitan areas ringed by new automobile-dependent suburbs (see Figure 30.4).

Much Sunbelt wealth tended to be temporary or sharply cyclical, producing a boom-and-bust economy. Income was also distributed unevenly. Older Hispanic populations made only modest gains, while recent Mexican immigrants and Indian peoples suffered from a combination of low wages and poor public services. The Sunbelt states directed their tax and federal dollars to strengthening police forces, building roads or sanitation systems for the expanding suburbs, and creating budget surpluses.

The "Rustbelt" states, longtime centers of voting strength for the Democratic Party, meanwhile suffered severe population losses accompanying the sharp decline of manufacturing. The production of steel, automobiles, and heavy machinery suffered from foreign competition and from new, more efficient factories that opened in the South. Of the nineteen metropolitan areas that lost population, all were old manufacturing centers. The rural areas of the Midwest and Plains States also

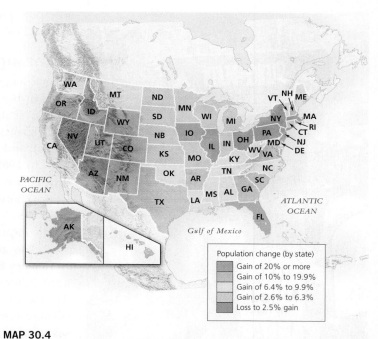

MAP 30.4
Population Shifts, 1970–80   Industrial decline in the Northeast coincided with an economic boom in the Sunbelt, encouraging millions of Americans to head for warmer climates and better jobs.

HOW WERE the changes in population between 1970 and 1980 reflected in the American economy?

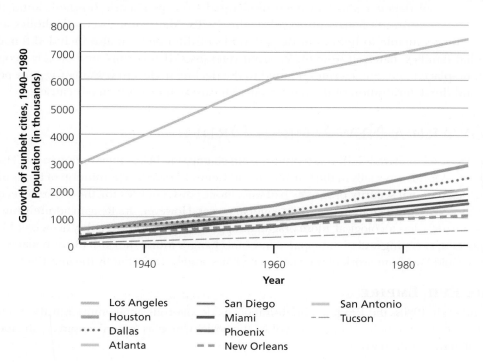

Figure 30.4 Growth of Sunbelt Cities, 1940–80
The old industrial cities in the Northeast and Midwest steadily lost population to the southern and western decentralized cities and their surrounding suburbs.

From Statistical abstract of the United States, in Nash et al., *The American People*, 5th ed., p. 988. Reprinted by permission of Longman Publishing Group, a division of Pearson Education.

lost population, as farmers abandoned land that no longer produced a decent livelihood.

EPIDEMICS: DRUGS, AIDS, HOMELESSNESS

Illegal drug addiction and drug trafficking took on frightening new dimensions in the early 1980s. Even the urban poor could afford the new arrival, "crack," a cheap, smokable, and highly addictive form of cocaine. The crack trade spawned a new generation of young drug dealers who were willing to risk jail and death for enormous profits.

In 1982, the Reagan administration declared a highly publicized "**war on drugs**," a multibillion-dollar paramilitary operation to halt drug trafficking. Critics charged that the war on drugs focused on supply from abroad when it needed to look at demand here at home. They urged more federal money for drug education, treatment, and rehabilitation.

Also new to the 1980s was the outbreak of the **Acquired Immune Deficiency Syndrome (AIDS)** epidemic. Because the majority of early victims were homosexual men who acquired AIDS through sexual contact, many Americans perceived AIDS as a disease of homosexuals. But other victims became infected through intravenous drug use, blood transfusions, heterosexual transmission, or birth from AIDS-carrying mothers.

AIDS provoked fear, anguish, and anger. It also brought an upsurge of organization and political involvement. In city after city, the gay community responded to the AIDS crisis with energy and determination. Most gay men changed their sexual habits, practicing "safe sex" to lessen the chances of infection. President Reagan, playing to antigay prejudices, had largely ignored the epidemic.

Homelessness emerged as a chronic social problem during the 1980s. In the early 1980s, the Department of Housing and Urban Development placed the number of the nation's homeless at between 250,000 and 350,000. Advocates for the homeless estimated that the number was as high as 3 million.

Who were the homeless? Analysts agreed that at least a third were mental patients who had been discharged from psychiatric hospitals amid the deinstitutionalization trend of the 1970s. Many more were alcoholics and drug addicts unable to hold jobs. But the ranks of the homeless also included female-headed families, battered women, Vietnam veterans, AIDS victims, and elderly people with no place to go. Some critics pointed to the decline in decent housing for poor people and the deterioration of the nation's health care system as the major causes.

In May 1987, members of the Lesbian and Gay Community Services in downtown Manhattan organized ACT-UP. Protesting what they perceived to be the Reagan administration's mismanagement of the AIDS crisis, they used nonviolent direct action, which often took the form of dramatic acts of civil disobedience. ACT-UP grew to more than seventy chapters in the United States and around the world.

HOW DID the Cold War end?

War on drugs A paramilitary operation to halt drug trafficking in the United States.

Acquired Immune Deficiency Syndrome (AIDS) A complex of deadly pathologies resulting from infection with the human immunodeficiency virus (HIV).

TOWARD A NEW WORLD ORDER

Reagan revived Cold War patriotism and championed U.S. intervention in the Third World, especially in the Caribbean and Central America. His infusion of funds into national security programs had enormous consequences for the domestic economy as well as for the nation's status as a global power. However, the Reagan administration also pursued a less ideological, more pragmatic approach in key foreign policy decisions. Most important, sweeping and unanticipated internal changes within the Soviet Union made the entire Cold War framework of international affairs largely irrelevant by the late 1980s.

THE EVIL EMPIRE

In the early 1980s, the Reagan administration made vigorous anticommunism the centerpiece of its foreign policy. Reagan described the Soviet Union as "an evil empire. . . the focus of evil in the modern world."

Administration officials argued that during the 1970s the nation's military strength had fallen dangerously behind that of the Soviet Union. Critics disputed this assertion, pointing out that the Soviet advantage in intercontinental ballistic missiles (ICBMs) was offset by U.S. superiority in submarine-based forces and strategic aircraft. Nonetheless, the administration proceeded with plans to secure global military supremacy, including enlarging America's nuclear strike force. U.S. defense spending jumped by 50 percent, reaching $1.5 trillion.

In 1983, President Reagan introduced an unsettling new element into superpower relations when he presented his **Strategic Defense Initiative (SDI)**, a plan for a space-based ballistic-missile defense system. This proposal for a five-year, $26 billion program promised to give the United States the capacity to shoot down incoming missiles with laser beams and homing rockets. As critics pointed out, this plan was unworkable, impossibly expensive, and likely to destabilize existing arms treaties. The Reagan administration pressed ahead, but without achieving any convincing results. The prospect of meaningful arms control dimmed in this atmosphere, and U.S.-Soviet relations deteriorated.

THE REAGAN DOCTRINE

Reagan moved beyond President Truman's "containment" policy and confidently promised to "roll back" communism. He reasserted America's right to intervene anywhere in the world and pledged to supply overt and covert aid to anti-Communist resistance movements, including those led by right-wing dictators. The so-called Reagan Doctrine assumed that all political instability in the Third World resulted not from indigenous factors such as poverty or corruption but from the pernicious influence of the Soviet Union.

One of Reagan's most successful interventions took place in Afghanistan, which the Soviet Union had invaded in 1979. Reagan greatly expanded the U.S. aid initiated by President Carter to include supplies of weapons and antiaircraft missiles. During the course of his administration, the CIA also sent billions of U.S. dollars to the mujahedeen. These fundamentalist Islamic "holy warriors" managed to drive out the Soviet Union but also eventually gave rise to the Taliban and Osama bin Laden's al-Qaeda, which would emerge in the 1990s as major agent of global terrorism.

The Reagan doctrine found its most important expression in Central America, where the United States hoped to reestablish its historical control over the Caribbean basin (see Map 30.5). Claiming that all problems throughout the Western Hemisphere stemmed from a "Moscow-Havana" alliance, the administration worked to support anti-Communist groups in Cuba and elsewhere in Latin America.

In October 1983, the administration directed U.S. Marines to invade Grenada, claiming that the tiny island governed by Marxists since 1979 had become a Cuban military base and, therefore, would soon serve as "an outpost of communism" and terrorism. Condemned by the United Nations General Assembly as "a flagrant violation of International law," the invasion proved popular with most Grenadans and Americans.

In other nations such as El Salvador, this sort of unilateral military action proved politically and strategically more difficult to carry out. But the Reagan administration directed nearly $5 billion to shore up El Salvador's pro-American yet highly repressive regime. By 1983, right-wing death squads had tortured and assassinated thousands of opposition leaders.

In Nicaragua, the Reagan administration claimed that the revolutionary Sandinista government posed "an unusual and extraordinary threat to the national security." U.S. officials accused the Sandinistas of shipping arms to antigovernment rebels in El Salvador. In December 1981, Reagan approved a CIA plan to arm and organize Nicaraguan exiles, known as **Contras**, to fight against the Sandinista government. In 1984, the CIA secretly mined Nicaraguan harbors. When Nicaragua won a judgment against the United States in the World Court over this violation of its sovereignty, the Reagan administration refused to

Strategic Defense Initiative (SDI) President Reagan's program, announced in 1983, to defend the United States against nuclear missile attack with untested weapons systems and sophisticated technologies.

Contras Nicaraguan exiles armed and organized by the CIA to fight the Sandinista government of Nicaragua.

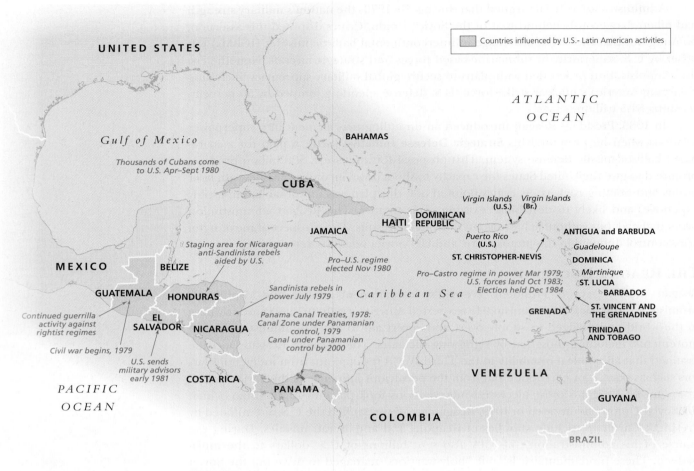

Countries influenced by U.S.- Latin American activities

UNITED STATES

ATLANTIC OCEAN

Gulf of Mexico

BAHAMAS

Thousands of Cubans come to U.S. Apr–Sept 1980

CUBA

Virgin Islands (U.S.)   Virgin Islands (Br.)

HAITI   DOMINICAN REPUBLIC

JAMAICA

Puerto Rico (U.S.)

ANTIGUA and BARBUDA

Guadeloupe

ST. CHRISTOPHER-NEVIS

DOMINICA

Pro–U.S. regime elected Nov 1980

Pro–Castro regime in power Mar 1979; U.S. forces land Oct 1983; Election held Dec 1984

Martinique

ST. LUCIA

MEXICO   BELIZE

Staging area for Nicaraguan anti-Sandinista rebels aided by U.S.

BARBADOS

GUATEMALA   HONDURAS

Sandinista rebels in power July 1979

Caribbean Sea

GRENADA

ST. VINCENT AND THE GRENADINES

Continued guerrilla activity against rightist regimes

EL SALVADOR   NICARAGUA

Panama Canal Treaties, 1978: Canal Zone under Panamanian control, 1979 Canal under Panamanian control by 2000

TRINIDAD AND TOBAGO

Civil war begins, 1979

VENEZUELA

U.S. sends military advisors early 1981

COSTA RICA

PACIFIC OCEAN

PANAMA

GUYANA

COLOMBIA

BRAZIL

MAP 30.5
The United States in Central America, 1978–90   U.S. intervention in Central America reached a new level of intensity with the so-called Reagan Doctrine. The bulk of U.S. aid came in the form of military support for the government of El Salvador and the Contra rebels in Nicaragua.

HOW DID Reagan explain and justify U.S. policy in Central America?

recognize the court's jurisdiction in the case and ignored the verdict. Predictably, the U.S. covert war pushed the Sandinistas closer to Cuba and the Soviet bloc.

In 1984, Congress sought to rein in the covert war by passing legislation that forbade government agencies from supporting "directly or indirectly military or paramilitary operations" in Nicaragua. Denied funding by Congress, President Reagan turned to the National Security Council (NSC) to find a way to keep the Contra war going. Between 1984 and 1986, the NSC staff secretly assisted the Contras, raising enough money privately to support the largest mercenary army in hemispheric history. In 1987, the revelation of this unconstitutional scheme exploded before the public as part of the Iran-Contra affair.

THE MIDDLE EAST AND THE IRAN-CONTRA SCANDAL

In 1987, the revelations of what became known as the Iran-Contra scandal laid bare the contradictions in Reagan's foreign policy. The scandal also revealed how overzealous and secretive government officials subverted the Constitution and compromised presidential authority under the guise of patriotism.

Terrorist acts, including the seizing of Western hostages and the bombing of commercial airplanes and cruise ships, continued to redefine the politics of the Middle East. Many of these attacks were desperate acts of retaliation by small pro-Palestinian sects or Islamic extremists opposed to U.S. support of Israel. However, the Reagan administration insisted that behind international terrorism lay the sinister influence of the Soviet bloc, the Ayatollah Khomeini of Iran, and Libyan leader Muammar el-Qaddafi. In the spring of 1986, the president, eager to demonstrate his antiterrorist resolve, ordered the bombing of Tripoli in a failed effort to kill Qaddafi.

As a fierce war between Iran and Iraq escalated, the administration tilted publicly toward Iraq, Iraq's dictator, Saddam Hussein, was treated as an ally and provided much sophisticated weaponry. But in 1986, Reagan's advisers changed course and began secret negotiations with the revolutionary Iranian government. They eventually offered to supply Iran with weapons for use against Iraq in exchange for help in securing the release of Americans who were being held hostage by radical Islamic groups in Lebanon (see Map 30.6).

Subsequent disclosures elevated the arms-for-hostages deal into a major scandal in the summer of 1987. The American public learned that the NSC had sold weapons and missiles to the Iranians, using Israel as a go-between. The public also found out that millions of dollars from the weapons sale had been secretly diverted into covert aid of the Nicaraguan Contras.

In the televised congressional hearings, NSC staffer and Marine Lieutenant Colonel Oliver North defended his grossly illegal actions in the name of patriotism. Some Americans saw North as a hero; most were appalled by his and Admiral John Poindexter's admissions that they had lied to Congress, shredded evidence, and refused to keep the president fully informed in order to guarantee his "plausible deniability." Both North and Poindexter were convicted of felonies, but higher courts overturned their convictions on technical grounds. Reagan held fast to a plea of ignorance.

Lt. Col. Oliver North, who once described the scheme to sell arms to Iran to help the Contras as a "neat idea," is shown testifying in July 1987 before a joint Congressional committee formed to investigate the Iran-Contra affair.

THE COLLAPSE OF COMMUNISM

Meanwhile, momentous political changes within the Soviet Union ultimately led to the end of the Cold War. In 1985, a reform-minded leader, Mikhail Gorbachev, took over as Soviet leader. Gorbachev encouraged open political discussion and released longtime dissidents from prison. His government also took the first halting steps toward a profit-based market economy.

In Gorbachev's view, improving the economic performance of the Soviet system depended first on halting the arms race. Over 10 percent of the Soviet GNP went to

In August 1961, the border between East and West Berlin was closed, and the Berlin Wall was built to divide the city into two sections. After twenty-eight years, on November 9, 1989, the government in East Germany lifted travel restrictions. This photograph shows demonstrators defiantly tearing down the Berlin Wall, which for three decades had embodied the political divisions of the Cold War.

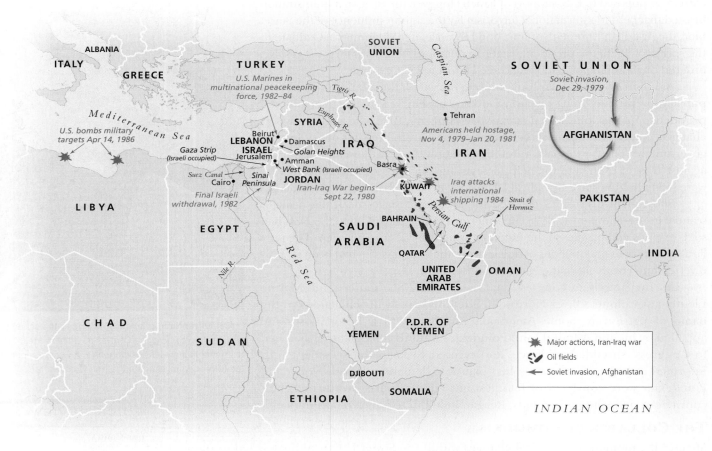

MAP 30.6
The United States in the Middle East in the 1980s The volatile combination of ancient religious and ethnic rivalries, oil, and emerging Islamic fundamentalism made peace and stability elusive in the Middle East.

IN WHAT ways was the U.S. involved in the Middle East in the 1980s?

Watch the Video
The Berlin Wall at **www.myhistorylab.com**

QUICK REVIEW

The Fall of Gorbachev and the Soviet Union

- August 1991: Old-line communists attempted a coup against Gorbachev.
- Coup failed and all fifteen Soviet republics declared their independence.
- Gorbachev lost control of the government and resigned.

defense spending. Fully aware that the Soviet Union could not compete with Reagan's Star Wars program, Gorbachev took the lead to end the arms race with the United States. Between 1985 and 1988 Reagan and Gorbachev had four separate summit meetings with the new Soviet leader. Culminating in a modest treaty allowing comprehensive, mutual, on-site inspections, the meetings also provided an important psychological breakthrough. At one of the summits, a Soviet leader humorously announced, "We are going to do something terrible to you Americans—we are going to deprive you of an enemy."

Indeed, the reforms initiated by Gorbachev—and, more immediately, the failed Soviet war in Afghanistan—led to the dissolution of the Soviet Union and to the end of Communist rule throughout Eastern Europe. In March 1989, the Soviet Union held its first open elections since 1917, and Gorbachev announced that he would not use force to keep the satellite nations in line. In June 1989, when Poland held its first free elections since 1945, prodemocracy demonstrations forced out longtime Communist leaders in Hungary, Czechoslovakia, Bulgaria, and Romania. Most dramatic of all were the events in East Germany. The Berlin Wall came down on November 9, 1989. Hundreds of thousands of East Germans immediately rushed into West Berlin, paving the way for German reunification the following year. On Christmas Day 1991, Gorbachev signed a decree officially dissolving the Soviet Union and then resigned as president.

The Soviet Union's dissolution marked the end of the great superpower rivalry that had shaped American foreign policy and domestic politics for nearly a half century. Reagan's successor, President George H. W. Bush, proclaimed the end of the Cold War as an event of "biblical proportions."

"A KINDER, GENTLER NATION"

During the 1988 presidential campaign, moderate Republican George Herbert Walker Bush, hoped to ride on Reagan's conservative coattails. He made a clear-cut pledge to voters: "Read my lips: no new taxes." He also promised to energize the war against drugs and back initiatives to allow prayer in public schools. Bush won the general election handily over Massachusetts governor George Dukakis in forty states and with 56 percent of the popular vote. After winning such widespread support, he concluded that he could set his own agenda. President Bush began to distance himself from Reagan and infuriate conservatives, promising in his inaugural address to deliver a "kinder and gentler nation."

REAGAN'S SUCCESSOR: GEORGE H. W. BUSH

President Bush carried over several policies from the Reagan administration, such as the war on illegal drugs. In December 1989, President Bush sent U.S. troops to Panama on a mission to capture General Manuel Noriega, an international drug dealer who at one time had been on the CIA payroll. Thousands of Panamanians died before Noriega was taken into custody and brought to the United States to stand trial on drug trafficking and racketeering charges. During the Bush presidency, the federal budget for drug control tripled.

As a self-proclaimed "compassionate" Republican, President Bush endorsed the **Americans with Disabilities Act**, which had been introduced during the Reagan administration and now passed through Congress. The act penalized employers who discriminated against qualified workers with disabilities and required employers and local governments to provide access to their facilities. President Bush signed the bill in July 1990. Showing less compassion, he vetoed a family-leave bill that would have provided up to six months of unpaid leave to workers with new children or with family emergencies.

Bush also endorsed several bills to enhance environmental legislation, including revisions to the Clean Water and the Clean Air Act passed during the 1970s. He also approved federal initiatives to raise local educational standards. But Bush angered conservative Republicans when he broke his "no new taxes" promise and allowed Congress to impose a small hike on wealthy taxpayers.

THE PERSIAN GULF WAR

President Bush soon saw that the end of the Cold War did not bring world peace but instead let loose renewed nationalism, ethnic and religious conflict, and widening divisions between the world's rich and poor. Just as dramatically, as the old geopolitical order disappeared, ideological rivalry shifted to the Middle East and other areas in the world where Islamic militants had forcefully turned against the West.

On August 2, 1990, Iraqi troops swept into neighboring Kuwait and quickly seized control of its rich oil fields. The motives of Saddam Hussein, Iraq's military dictator, were mixed. Like most Iraqis, Hussein believed that oil-rich Kuwait was actually an ancient province of Iraq. Control of Kuwait would give Saddam Hussein control of its huge oil reserves, as well as major Persian Gulf ports for his almost landlocked country. Iraqis also resented Kuwait's production of oil beyond OPEC quotas, which had helped send the world price of oil plummeting from the highs of the 1970s and early 1980s.

The United States responded swiftly to news of the invasion. On August 15, President Bush ordered U.S. forces to Saudi Arabia and the Persian Gulf, calling the action Operation Desert Shield. The United States also led a broad coalition in the

WHAT FACTORS led to U.S. involvement in the Persian Gulf War?

Watch the **Video**
President George Bush's Early Response in the Persian Gulf War at **www.myhistorylab.com**

Americans with Disabilities Act An act that required employers to provide access to their facilities for qualified employees with disabilities.

Read the **Document**

*George H. W. Bush, Gulf War Address
(1990)* at **www.myhistorylab.com**

United Nations, including the Soviet Union, that condemned the Iraqi invasion of Kuwait and declared strict economic sanctions against Iraq if it did not withdraw.

In early November, President Bush announced a change in policy to what he called "an offensive military option." The UN sanctions failed to budge Hussein from Kuwait, and the drift to war looked inevitable. In January 1991, Congress narrowly passed a joint resolution authorizing the president to use military force.

After a last-minute UN peace mission failed to break the deadlock, President Bush announced, on January 16, 1991, the start of **Operation Desert Storm**. U.S.-led air strikes began forty-two days of massive bombing of Iraqi positions in Kuwait, as well as Baghdad and other Iraqi cities. The ground war, which began on February 24, took only 100 hours to force Saddam Hussein's troops out of Kuwait.

Victory in the Gulf War rekindled national pride, and many Americans declared the end of the "Vietnam syndrome." But for the 18 million people of Iraq, it produced the worst possible outcome. The ecological damage in the Gulf region was extensive and long-lasting. Human rights groups reported an appalling death toll among civilians.

The limits of military power to solve complex political and economic disputes became clear in the aftermath of victory. The **Persian Gulf War** failed to dislodge Saddam Hussein, who remained in power despite CIA attempts to overthrow him and repeated bombings of Iraqi military positions. Iraqi Kurds, who had supported the U.S. invasion in hopes it would topple Saddam, faced violent reprisals, including gassing and chemical weapons, from the Iraqi army. Trade sanctions did little to weaken Hussein's rule.

The repercussions of the Gulf War were long-lasting. The leading U.S. ally in the region, Saudi Arabia, had served as the launching pad for the invasion of Iraq, and following the war the Saudis had allowed the continuing presence of U.S. troops and weapons. This occupation of Saudi territory, which included Islamic holy sites, intensified the hatred of Americans among many Muslims and prompted appeals for revenge.

See the **Map**

The Middle East in the 1980s and 1990s
at **www.myhistorylab.com**

Among those actively opposed to the U.S. role in the region was Saudi millionaire Osama bin Laden, just a few years earlier a close ally of the United States during the Soviet invasion of Afghanistan. Using his own funds and a vast tribal network, bin Laden built his shadowy Al Qaeda organization, training small groups in terror tactics to be used against Western interests, particularly to force U.S. troops out of the Middle East.

THE ECONOMY AND THE ELECTION OF 1992

Politically, the Persian Gulf War marked the high point of Bush's popularity, with his approval rating rising to nearly 90 percent. Basking in his success, the president proclaimed the United States the leader in the creation of a "new world order" that would be "freer from the threat of terror, stronger in the pursuit of justice, and more secure in the quest for peace, an era in which the nations of the world, East and West, North and South, can prosper and live in harmony."

However, it was the economy rather than foreign affairs that fueled the 1992 presidential election campaign. Just as Bush was about to take office in 1989, many of the nation's savings and loan institutions, which had been deregulated by Reagan, collapsed. Then, on Friday, October 13, 1989, the stock market took its worst nosedive since 1987, signaling a major recession. With the national debt reaching $4 trillion, the paradoxes of the Reagan-Bush years became readily apparent.

American consumers had been spending extravagantly, many falling deep into debt, and now, with the prospect of a recession, they pulled back. Real estate prices plummeted, unemployment hovered at 7 percent, and many businesses filed for bankruptcy. Eventually, Bush reneged on his campaign promise and worked with Democrats in Congress to raise taxes.

As the 1992 campaign heated up, President Bush found himself facing a formidable opponent, William Jefferson Clinton. In the Democrats' campaign headquarters a sign humorously reminded the staff: "It's the economy, stupid." Candidate Clinton promised

Operation Desert Storm U.S. military campaign to force Iraqi forces out of Kuwait.

Persian Gulf War War initiated by President Bush in reponse to Iraq's invasion of Kuwait.

CHRONOLOGY

1973	*Roe* v. *Wade* legalizes abortion
	Arab embargo sparks oil crisis in the United States
1974	Richard Nixon resigns presidency; Gerald Ford takes office
	President Ford pardons Nixon and introduces anti-inflation program
1975	Unemployment rate reaches nearly 9 percent
	South Vietnamese government falls to communists
	Antibusing protests break out in Boston
1976	Percentage of African Americans attending college peaks at 9.3 percent and begins a decline
	Democrat Jimmy Carter defeats incumbent Gerald Ford in presidential election
1977	President Carter announces human rights as major tenet in foreign policy
1978	*Bakke* v. *University of California* decision places new limits on affirmative action programs
	Camp David meeting sets terms for Middle East peace
	California passes Proposition 13, cutting taxes and government social programs
1979	Three Mile Island nuclear accident threatens a meltdown
	Nicaraguan Revolution overthrows Anastasio Somoza
	Iranian fundamentalists seize the U.S. embassy in Tehran and hold U.S. citizens hostage for 444 days
	Soviets invade Afghanistan
1980	Inflation reaches 13.5 percent
	Republican Ronald Reagan defeats incumbent Jimmy Carter in presidential election
1981	Reagan administration initiates major cuts in taxes and domestic spending
	Military buildup accelerates
	AIDS is recognized and named
1982	Economic recession grips the nation
1983	Reagan announces the Strategic Defense Initiative, labeled "Star Wars" by the media
	241 U.S. Marines killed in Beirut terrorist bombing
1985	Mikhail Gorbachev initiates reforms in the Soviet Union
1986	Iran-Contra hearings before Congress reveal arms-for-hostages deal and funds secretly and illegally diverted to Nicaraguan rebels
1988	Republican George H. W. Bush defeats Michael Dukakis in presidential election
	Communist authority collapses in Eastern Europe
1990	Iraqi invasion of Kuwait leads to massive U.S. military presence in the Persian Gulf
1991	Operation Desert Storm forces Iraq out of Kuwait
	Soviet Union dissolves into Commonwealth of Independent States
1992	Democrat Bill Clinton defeats incumbent George H. W. Bush and independent candidate Ross Perot in the presidential election

economic leadership. While promising deficit reduction and a tax cut for the middle class, he also took advantage of Bush's betrayal of his own campaign promise not to raise taxes.

Clinton effectively adopted many of the conservative themes that proved so advantageous to Republicans over the past twelve years. He called for "responsibility" on the part of recipients of social programs and spoke of the importance of stable families, promised to be tough on crime and to reduce the bureaucracy, and stressed the need for encouraging private investment to create new jobs. Economic issues also fueled the independent campaign of Texas billionaire H. Ross Perot, who argued that someone as successful in business as himself was better qualified to solve the nation's economic woes than Washington insiders.

Clinton received 43 percent of the popular vote. He also carried thirty-two states. Although failing to carry a single state, Perot scored 19 percent of the popular vote. The newly elected Clinton interpreted Perot's relative success at the polls as a mandate to focus, as he put it, "like a laser beam on the economy."

CONCLUSION

The success of conservatives to halt and in some cases actually reverse key trends in American politics, from Franklin Roosevelt's New Deal to Lyndon Johnson's Great Society, was made possible by the legacy of the Cold War and the trauma of defeat in Vietnam. But that success also owed a great deal to a deepening anxiety about cultural changes and a growing pessimism about the ability of politicians to offer solutions, especially at the national level. Those community activists struggling to broaden the 1960s' protest movements into an updated, comprehensive reformism encompassing such issues as feminism, ecology, and affirmative action readily recognized that the liberal era had ended.

President Ronald Reagan, a charismatic figure who sometimes invented his own past and seemed to believe in it, offered remedies for a weary and nostalgic nation. By insisting that the rebellious 1960s had been a terrible mistake, lowering national self-confidence along with public morals and faith in the power of economic individualism, he successfully wedded the conservatism of Christian fundamentalists, many suburbanites, and Sunbelt voters with the more traditional conservatism of corporate leaders. In many respects, the Reagan administration actually continued and added ideological fervor to the downscaling of government services and upscaling of military spending already evident under President Jimmy Carter, while offering supporters the hope of a sweeping conservative revolution.

In the end, critics suggested, supporters of Ronald Reagan and Reaganism could not go back to the 1950s—just as the erstwhile rebels of the 1960s could not go back to their favorite era. Economically, conservatives achieved many of their goals, including widespread acceptance of sharper economic divisions within society and fewer restraints on corporations and investments. But socially and culturally, their grasp was much less secure.

REVIEW QUESTIONS

1. Evaluate the significance of the major population shifts in the United States from the 1940s through the 1970s. What was their impact on local and national politics?

2. Discuss the connections between the energy crisis and the rise of the environmental movement.

3. Interpret the decline of liberalism and the rise of conservative political groups. How did these changes affect the outcome of presidential elections?

4. Was the Iran hostage crisis a turning point in American politics or only a thorn in Carter's reelection campaign? How did the Iran-Contra scandal affect the Republicans?

5. Describe the central philosophical assumptions behind Reaganomics. What were the key policies by which it was implemented? To what extent were these policies a break with previous economic approaches?

6. Evaluate Reagan's foreign policy. How did it differ from Carter's approach to foreign affairs?

7. Analyze the key structural factors underlying recent changes in American economic and cultural life. Do you see any political solutions for the growth of poverty and inequality?

KEY TERMS

Acquired Immune Deficiency Syndrome (AIDS) (p. 822)
Affirmative action (p. 820)
Americans with Disabilities Act (p. 827)
Camp David Accords (p. 811)
Contras (p. 823)

Deregulation (p. 817)
Détente (p. 811)
Economic Recovery Tax Act of 1981 (p. 817)
Environmental Protection Agency (EPA) (p. 809)

PEARSON
myhistorylab Connections

Reinforce what you learned in this chapter by studying the many documents, images, maps, review tools, and videos available at www.myhistorylab.com.

READ AND REVIEW

✓• Study and Review Chapter 30

•••• Read the Document

Jimmy Carter, The "Crisis of Confidence" Speech (1979)

Roe v. Wade (1973)

Ronald Reagan, First Inaugural Address (1981)

Paul Craig Robert, The Supply-Side Revolution (1984)

Ronald Reagan, Address to the National Association of Evangelicals (1983)

George H. W. Bush, Gulf War Address (1990)

👁 See the Map *The Middle East in the 1980s and 1990s*

RESEARCH AND EXPLORE

•••• Read the Document

Exploring America: Growing Inequality

Profiles
  Jimmy Carter
  Jerry Falwell

🎞 Watch the Video

Evangelical Religion and Politics, Then and Now

Ronald Reagan Presidential Campaign Ad: A Bear in the Woods

Ronald Reagan on the Wisdom of Tax Cuts

The Berlin Wall

President George Bush's Early Response in the Persian Gulf War

President Bush on the Gulf War

((•• Hear the Audio

Hear the audio files for Chapter 30 at
www.myhistorylab.com.

. . . the looks on the faces of the people
coming out of the city that day will haunt me forever . . .
everyone was the same color . . . dust white . . .
women crying . . . men crying . . . we must never forget
the men and women that died that day . . .
—*John McNamara,* The September 11 Digital Archive, *April 13, 2002*

The twisted ruins of the World Trade Center in the aftermath of the terrorist attacks of September 11, 2001.

31

THE UNITED STATES IN A GLOBAL AGE

1992–2010

((●—[Hear the **Audio**

Hear the audio files for Chapter 31 at **www.myhistorylab.com**.

WHAT WERE Bill Clinton's priorities as president?

WHAT TRENDS shaped American society and culture in the 1990s?

HOW DID the threat of international terrorism transform the American political landscape in the first decade of the twenty-first century?

WHAT CHALLENGES did Barack Obama face in early years of his presidency?

1992 2010

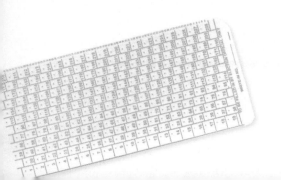

AMERICAN COMMUNITIES
Transnational Communities in San Diego and Tijuana

As THE NEW MILLENNIUM BEGAN, NORMA OJEIDA CROSSED THE U.S.-MEXICO border on a daily basis, leaving for work in the morning and returning home at night. She held a position at a high-powered research institute in Rosarito, a suburb of the booming city of Tijuana in Baja, California, Mexico, and made her home in suburban San Diego. Ojeida therefore had plenty of company in making the daily journey across the busiest border crossing in North America. Thousands of other affluent, educated professionals made the same trip southward, while a steady stream of 40,000 Mexicans left Tijuana to work on the U.S. side of the border.

Tijuana, hardly more than a small, poor town of 60,000 in 1950, had depended on a lucrative tourist trade since at least 1919, when a transnational railroad connected it with San Diego. Since midcentury, Tijuana served as a mecca not only for a growing number of American tourists, but also for Mexicans looking for better jobs. Poor people from distant regions of Mexico were migrating to the rich agricultural valleys and hills surrounding Tijuana, often to prepare for *El Norte*, the trip north to the United States.

Meanwhile, San Diego, which grew from a Spanish mission and fishing village to a Navy boomtown during World War II, developed into a major center of defense-industry manufacturing and research. Tourism, upscale retirement communities, and a major research branch of the University of California helped to make San Diego the second-largest city in California and the seventh in the United States, with mainly Hispanics and Asians accounting for the major share of population growth since 1985.

In 1961, the Border Industrialization Program paved the way for a closer economic relationship between Tijuana and San Diego. The program fostered the creation of *maquiladoras*, assembly plants for such American-owned firms as Ford Motors and General Electric; in the 1990s, the adoption of the North American Free Trade Agreement (NAFTA) helped to secure these economic structures. By the end of the twentieth century, Tijuana, the fourth-largest city in Mexico and home to 1.5 million people, had become the only Mexican border city where the size of the middle class most nearly approached that of the impoverished population. Shoppers from Tijuana were able to pour about $2.8 billion a year into the San Diego economy.

San Diego and Tijuana, one of eight transnational metropolitan regions on the 2,000-mile U.S.-Mexico border, had come to share not only people but also problems that flout political boundaries. For example, unregulated growth on both sides of the border threatened ecological disaster, created bumper-to-bumper traffic on highways, and encouraged the kind of suburban sprawl that surrounded most large American cities. The Tijuana River, which flows into the San Diego Bay, by the 1990s was carrying 1.5 million gallons of untreated sewage per day. The virtually unregulated airborne pollution of the *maquiladoras* posed additional threats to the region. The continuous cross-border traffic in goods and people also caused substantial amounts of native vegetation to succumb to exotic weedy grasses.

By the end of the century, the Californian and Mexican governments began to catch up with problems festering for decades. A joint feasibility study was funded by the California legislature for the construction of an aqueduct to the Colorado River to bring more water into the region. Other plans included mass transit on the San Diego side and airport expansion on the Tijuana side to relieve congestion at San Diego's overtaxed international airport. The bright promise of the transnational San Diego/Tijuana community was held in check, however, by the dark shadows of world recession and environmental exhaustion that gathered in the first decade of the twenty-first century.

The governments of Mexico and the United States continued to explore scores of binational projects, while San Diego and Tijuana invested in a major border initiative to promote sustainable development and effective public health programs on both sides of the border. In 2006, the governors from the border states of the United States and Mexico met to affirm once again their "common values and . . . vision for the prosperity of the border region." It seemed clear to everyone that the accelerating diffusion of information technologies, such as television, film, and the Internet, continued to create sources of community where none had previously existed. The key word of the new era, "globalization," however, held together many contradictory tendencies. For one, international terrorism offered dramatic and unwelcome proof that no part of the world was far removed—or safe—from the conflicts of any other part.

THE PRESIDENCY OF BILL CLINTON

During his campaign, Bill Clinton promised to bring a new kind of Democratic leadership to the presidency. Since 1985, he had been active in the Democratic Leadership Council (DLC). Responding to the conservative challenge, members of the DLC sought to distance the Democratic Party even further from the liberal tradition established by Franklin D. Roosevelt and revived by Lyndon Johnson in the 1960s. They sought to recapture the blue-collar and white southern defectors "by redefining and reclaiming the political center."

Clinton carried this mission to the White House. He presented a bold agenda that included balancing the federal budget, reforming welfare, reducing crime, promoting economic growth, and ensuring a strong national defense. Trimming the federal government and promoting free markets worldwide became hallmarks of his administration.

A "NEW DEMOCRAT" IN THE WHITE HOUSE

Despite his remarkable powers of persuasion, President Clinton got off to a rocky start. His biggest stumbling block during his first term was health care reform. Nearly 40 million Americans had no health insurance. Many simply could not afford it; others were denied coverage by private insurers because of preexisting conditions. For millions of others, health insurance was tied to the workplace and a loss or change of jobs threatened their coverage. Private spending on health care had skyrocketed from $246 billion in 1980 to more than $880 billion during the year Clinton took office.

In a controversial move, President Clinton appointed First Lady Hillary Rodham Clinton, an accomplished attorney, to head a task force charged with preparing a sweeping legislative overhaul of health care. The task force, in trying to find a political middle ground, ultimately produced an impossibly complicated compromise. Opposed by powerful lobbying groups and most Republicans, the plan died in Congress in August, 1994, just as the midterm election campaign moved into its final phase.

In the 1994 midterm elections, Clinton's defeat on health care reform helped the Republicans gain control of both the House and Senate for the first time in forty years. Congress was now dominated by conservative Republicans led by the new House Speaker, Newt Gingrich of Georgia. Gingrich challenged Clinton's leadership by presenting his own set of proposals labeled the "**Contract with America**." The House did indeed pass much of the "Contract," including a large tax cut, an increase in military spending, cutbacks in federal regulatory power in the environment and at the workplace, a tough anti-crime bill, and a sharp reduction in federal welfare programs.

Meanwhile, Clinton undercut the Republicans by adapting many of their proposals to his own. He endorsed the goal of a balanced federal budget. Clinton opposed his own party's efforts to block a Republican plan to dismantle the federal welfare system and instead backed new legislation—the **Welfare Reform Act**—that abolished the sixty-year-old Aid to Families with Dependent Children program (AFDC). Poor mothers with dependent children would now have access to aid for only a limited period and only if they were preparing for or seeking work. After Congress passed the act in August 1996, Clinton held a public signing ceremony and declared "an end to welfare as we know it."

With such deft maneuvers, Clinton set the theme for his 1996 reelection campaign against Robert Dole of Kansas, the Republican majority leader of the Senate. Clinton won a resounding reelection victory in November, confounding the predictions of the media pundits who had pronounced his political death. It was a victory without coattails, however: the Republicans retained control of both houses of Congress.

The Republican majority worked with Clinton to achieve a sweeping deregulation of the banking industry. The Republicans managed to get sufficient bipartisan support for this initiative, and Congress passed the controversial Financial Services Modernization Act

---

WHAT WERE Bill Clinton's priorities as president?

Read the **Document**

Statements of the Clinton Health Care Plan (1993) at **www.myhistorylab.com**

Contract with America　Platform proposing a sweeping reduction in the role and activities of the federal government on which many Republican candidates ran for Congress in 1994.

Welfare Reform Act　Act passed by Congress in 1996 that abolished the Aids to Families with Dependent Children (AFDC) welfare program.

Chief Justice William Rehnquist administers the oath of office to President William Jefferson Clinton on January 20, 1993. Daughter Chelsea and wife Hillary Rodham Clinton stand by his side. In his Inaugural Address as the nation's 42nd president, Clinton invited his fellow citizens to "celebrate the mystery of the American renewal" and to help him "revitalize our democracy."

of 1999. The bill, signed by President Clinton in November, repealed sections of the Glass-Steagall Act of 1933 and allowed banking, securities, and insurance companies to consolidate services and to combine (see Chapter 24).

THE "GLOBALIZATION" PRESIDENT

Following in the footsteps of his Democratic predecessor, Jimmy Carter, Clinton insisted that U.S. foreign policy reflect "the moral principles most Americans share" and promote humanitarian goals. But even more central to his vision was the goal of enlarging "the world's free community of market democracies" under the leadership of the United States. The editors of *Foreign Affairs* dubbed Clinton the "globalization" president.

These principles drove Clinton's policy toward the People's Republic of China (PRC). During the spring of 1989, Chinese government forces had brutally attacked prodemocracy demonstrators in Beijing's Tiananmen Square. During the 1992 election campaign, Clinton criticized Bush for continuing "to coddle" China in light of such gross human rights violations. Then, after taking office, he modified his position and recommended restoring Most Favored Nation (MFN) status with the PRC. Clinton acknowledged that serious human rights abuses continued, but he pointed out that China, the world's most populous nation, had the world's fastest-growing economy—as well as a nuclear arsenal and veto in the Security Council of the UN. He promoted free enterprise as a principal means to advance democracy in not only the PRC but also in other nations, such as Turkey, Saudi Arabia, and Indonesia.

During his first term, President Clinton pushed through Congress two major trade agreements to expand markets and encourage "free trade." Approved in November 1993, the **North American Free Trade Agreement (NAFTA)** eased the international flow of goods, services, and investments among the United States, Mexico, and Canada by eliminating tariffs and other trade barriers. The second trade agreement, which led to the establishment of the **World Trade Organization (WTO)** in 1995, continued the GATT policy of keeping tariffs low on thousands of goods throughout the world and phased out many import quotas imposed by the United States and other industrialized nations. Critics and supporters argued over whether these trade agreements would encourage global competition, thereby boosting American export industries and creating new high-wage jobs for American workers, or simply erode the U.S. industrial base and accelerate environmental degradation.

On humanitarian grounds, Clinton's accomplishments fell short of his lofty goals. During his first year in office, in October 1993, the United States took part in a UN mission to restore civil order in Somalia in East Africa. Eighteen ill-equipped American soldiers were killed in battle, while several thousand Somalian fighters and civilians died in the ill-fated attack. The president aborted the military mission and adopted a more cautious policy of intervention for humanitarian reasons.

In 1995, acting reluctantly, Clinton committed U.S. troops to a multinational effort in **Bosnia** where, following the collapse of communism and the dissolution of Yugoslavia, ethnic and religious rivalry among Serbs, Croats, and Muslims had erupted into a civil war. As reports of "ethnic cleansing"—forced removal and murder of Croats and Muslims by Bosnian Serbs—increased, and as the numbers of refugees grew, Clinton joined NATO in bombing Serbian strongholds in Bosnia. After negotiating with Yugoslav president Slobodan Milosevic, on November 27, Clinton announced a peace accord that called for a federated, multiethnic state of Bosnia.

North American Free Trade Agreement (NAFTA) Agreement reached in 1993 by Canada, Mexico, and the United States to substantially reduce barriers to trade.

World Trade Organization (WTO) International organization that sets standards and practices for global trade, and the focus of international protests over world economic policy in the late 1990s.

Bosnia A nation in southeast Europe that split off from Yugoslavia and became the site of bitter civil and religious war, requiring NATO and U.S. intervention in the 1990s.

Clinton's worst foreign crisis erupted in **Kosovo**, Yugoslavia, where intensifying clashes between Serbs and Albanians spread to neighboring Macedonia and to Albania itself. He once again tried to negotiate, but failed to resolve the problems through diplomacy. In March 1999, following NATO authorized air strikes, U.S. armed forces joined the attack on Serbian forces in Kosovo.

The so-called Clinton Doctrine, articulated in 1999 to justify the dispatch of U.S. troops to Yugoslavia, departed sharply from Cold War policies that sanctioned intervention primarily on the grounds of strategic interest and national security. In a later statement, Clinton insisted that "genocide is in and of itself a national interest where we should act." In 1998, he acknowledged that the United States, as part of the global community, must share the blame for failing to intervene in Rwanda in 1994, where a struggle for power led to genocide in the killing of up to 1 million Tutsis and moderate Hutu by Hutu extremists. At the time the Clinton administration had known about the genocide and had chosen not to act.

Nor did Clinton's understanding of the global community extend to include the most important international environmental issue of the 1990s: climate change. During the late 1970s, scientists had presented data indicating that the earth was warming. They pointed to the emission of "greenhouse gases," the by-products of the fossil fuels burned to run factories and automobiles, as the main cause. Delegates from various nations began to work on ways to limit greenhouse gas emissions, but the United States refused to make a commitment. The controversy came to a head at the world summit held in 1997 in Kyoto, Japan, where delegates outlined a protocol that included targets and timetables for the reduction of greenhouse gases. Although the fifteen-member nations of the European Union endorsed the terms of the treaty, both Japan and the United States held out.

After the 1994 midterm election gave Republicans control of the House of Representatives for the first time in forty years, the new Speaker, Newt Gingrich of Georgia, presented a list of legislative initiatives to be completed within the first one hundred days of the new session. On April 7, 1995, he appeared at a rally on Capitol Hill to celebrate the success of the Republicans' "Contract with America."

PRESIDING OVER THE BOOM

Between 1992 and 2000, the economy produced more than 20 million new jobs, and by 2000 the unemployment rate fell below 4 percent, the lowest in more than thirty years. With government spending down and economic growth increasing tax revenues, the largest federal budget deficit in American history became a surplus nearly as large by the time Clinton left office.

A soaring stock market provided a great boost to Clinton's second term as president. The record highs of the Bush years, when the Dow Jones index of thirty industrials approached 4,000, paled by comparison to the leap in 1999 when the Dow hit 10,000 in March and then peaked above 11,000 in May.

By the end of the century, Americans had 60 percent of their investments and savings in stocks, more than double the proportion in 1982. An estimated 78.7 million people held stocks, often through mutual funds or in retirement fund portfolios managed by their employers or unions.

The downside of the economic boom was nearly invisible. Productivity had risen sharply since the 1970s while labor costs had actually declined, hoisting profits to new levels. But while a corporate official had earned around twenty or thirty times the pay of a blue-collar worker at the same company a few decades earlier, corporate executive income was now more than two hundred times greater than that of a blue-collar employee. In the blue-collar sector, industrial jobs continued to disappear as factories closed or companies moved production across borders or overseas.

Kosovo Province of Yugoslavia where the United States and NATO intervened militarily in 1999 to protect ethnic Albanians from expulsion.

U.S. Army Military Police stop and search vehicles for weapons and explosives at this checkpoint near Vitina, Kosovo in Yugoslavia, 1999. They were part of the NATO led international force sent to attack Serbian forces in Kosovo.

HIGH CRIMES AND MISDEMEANORS

During his second term as president, Clinton had to answer many questions about his moral conduct. Real estate deals involving both him and Hillary Rodham Clinton blew up into a scandal known as Whitewater. A former Arkansas state employee, Paula Jones, charged Clinton with sexual assault during his gubernatorial term. Attorney General Janet Reno appointed an independent counsel, former judge Kenneth Starr, to investigate these allegations. In the summer of 1998, Starr instead delivered to the House Judiciary Committee a report focusing on an extramarital affair with a young White House intern, Monica Lewinsky. Starr's report outlined several potential impeachable offenses allegedly committed by the president to keep secret his relationship with Lewinsky. For only the third time in history, in October 1998, the House of Representatives voted to open an inquiry into possible grounds for impeachment.

Republicans hoping to reap a wholesale victory from the scandal in the midterm elections were bitterly disappointed. Contrary to predictions, the president's party added seats, trimming the Republican majority in the 105th Congress. The election also brought a shakeup in the Republican leadership. Newt Gingrich, under pressure from Republican colleagues angry about a campaign strategy that had narrowly focused on Clinton's impeachment problem, announced his resignation as Speaker of the House and from his seat in Congress.

After the 1998 midterm election, the House Judiciary Committee voted to bring four articles of impeachment—charging President Clinton with perjury, obstruction of justice, witness tampering, and abuse of power—to the full House. Unlike the bipartisan case the Judiciary Committee brought against Richard Nixon in 1974 (see Chapter 29), this time the votes were strictly along party lines. On February 12, 1999, the Senate trial concluded with the president's acquittal. When Clinton left office, he enjoyed the highest approval rating of any president since Dwight Eisenhower.

CHANGING AMERICAN COMMUNITIES

WHAT TRENDS shaped American society and culture in the 1990s?

During the Clinton administration, economists coined the phrase "the new economy" to underscore the increasing importance of globalization and corporate restructuring as well as the growing service sector. This included all those workers not directly involved in producing or processing a physical product. In 1965, an estimated 50 percent of all jobs were in the service sector; by 2000, the figure had grown to about 70 percent.

The new economy helped to change American society in significant ways. It depended on a global workforce and attracted millions of immigrants who were forming new communities throughout the United States. It created new forms of social relationships and communication based on electronic media. It also helped to widen the fissures in American society by reshaping manners and morals.

SILICON VALLEY

Silicon Valley The region of California including San Jose and San Francisco that holds the nation's greatest concentration of electronics firms.

The real and symbolic capital of the new economy was a thirty-by-ten-mile strip of Santa Clara County, California. Dubbed "**Silicon Valley**" in 1971 after the material used in semiconductor chips, the region flourished thanks to its unique combination of research facilities, investment capital, attractive environment, and a large pool of highly educated people. Silicon Valley firms gave birth to pocket calculators, video games, home computers, cordless telephones, digital watches, and almost every other new development in electronics. It became home to thousands of high-tech firms that specialized in gathering, processing, or distributing information or in manufacturing information technology.

By the end of the twentieth century, Silicon Valley had become the home and workplace of a diverse population. The managers and engineers, nearly all of whom were white males, had settled in affluent communities such as Palo Alto, Mountain View, and Sunnyvale. Manual workers on assembly lines and in low-paying service jobs clustered in San Jose and Gilroy. Most of these were immigrants or temporary workers who constituted a cheap, nonunionized labor pool with an extremely high turnover rate.

Silicon Valley was part of a global enterprise. Its firms were closely linked to the microelectronics industry of the greater Pacific Rim. American companies competed on the world market against similar companies in Japan, Korea, China, and Malaysia or protected themselves against such competition by owning a large share of the plants in those countries.

By the end of Clinton's administration, the rate of growth slowed, dramatized by a sharp plunge of technology stocks in March 2000. By this time, high prices in housing, traffic jams, inflated cost of living, and unemployment were already highlighting the downside to the new economy.

Yi Li, a graduate student from Taiwan, uses a computer terminal at the New York Public Library to gain access to the Internet. By the 1990s banks of personal computers had become a familiar sight in American offices, businesses, schools, and libraries. Millions of Americans made connecting with the new world of cyberspace a part of their daily routines.

New Media and Virtual Communities

The technological developments produced in Silicon Valley helped reconfigure cultural life in the United States and the world. Revolutions in computers and telecommunications merged telephones, televisions, computers, cable, and satellites into a global system of information exchange.

The new technologies changed the way people worked, played, and conducted business and politics. The twin arrivals of pay cable services and videocassette recorders (VCR) expanded and redefined the power of television and by the early 1990s had penetrated roughly two-thirds of American homes.

New digital technologies continued to reshape American culture. Compact discs (CDs) and digital video discs (DVDs) emerged as the dominant media for popular music and movies. Millions of Americans now used digital cameras to document their vacations and everyday lives. Digital telephones—"cell phones"—became ubiquitous in the streets, malls, campuses, cars, and workplaces of American communities.

Perhaps no aspect of the electronic culture was more revolutionary than the creation of cyberspace, the conceptual region occupied by people linked through computers and communications networks. It began with ARPANET, the first computer network, which the Department of Defense developed in the early 1970s. In the mid-1980s, alongside the launch of Microsoft Word and Windows operating programs, the boom in cheap personal computers capable of linking individuals to the worldwide telecommunications network began a population explosion in cyberspace. By then, tens of thousands of researchers and scholars at universities and in private industry were linked to the **Internet**, the U.S. government–sponsored successor to ARPANET. The establishment of the World Wide Web and easy-to-use browser software such as Netscape, introduced in 1994, made the "information highway" accessible to millions of Americans with few computer skills and created a popular communications medium with global dimensions.

By the beginning of the new century, more than half of all households had at least one computer and more than 40 percent were connected to the Internet. By 2010, surveys indicated that children and teenagers spent 7.5 hours per day using an electronic device.

Internet The system of interconnected computers and servers that allows the exchange of email, posting of Web sites, and other means of instant communication.

Americans used their computers to play games, access information and entertainment, and purchase a huge array of goods and services. These electronic media, Americans created "virtual" communities, widening their base of friends and acquaintances through social networking sites accessed through their computers and smart phones.

These new information technologies gave birth to "virtual" communities that transcended national boundaries. During the 1980s, exports from Hollywood to the rest of the world doubled in value. The number of hours of television watched throughout the world nearly tripled: MTV was broadcast to an estimated 250 million households. By the mid-1990s, there were more television sets in China than in the United States. Americans, however, owned a disproportionate share of the largest media corporations in the world. More than 40 percent of television programs in the world originated in the United States.

THE NEW IMMIGRANTS

During the 1990s, the nation's population grew by 32.7 million, a number greater than that of any other decade in U.S. history. In October 2006, the U.S. population hit 300 million.

More than a third of the nation's population growth came from the influx of new immigrants (see Figure 31.1). Nationally, at the turn of the century the percentage of Americans born outside the United States was 11.2 percent, its highest point since 1930; in California, the percentage of foreign-born approached 26 percent.

The Immigration Act of 1965 had revolutionary, if largely unintended, consequences (see Chapter 28). The act abolished the discriminatory national origins quotas that had been in place since the 1920s. It also for the first time limited immigration from the Western Hemisphere, while giving preference to people from the nations of the Eastern Hemisphere who had specialized job skills and training. This provision created the conditions for Asian immigrants to become the fastest-growing ethnic group in the United States.

Hispanics also benefited from the changes in immigration law. By 1990, Hispanics had already formed over a third of the population of New Mexico, a quarter of the population of Texas, and over 10 percent of the populations of California, Arizona, and Colorado. Demographers predicted that Hispanics, who had grown from 22.4 million in 1990 to 35.3 million in 2000, according to U.S. Census data, would replace African Americans as the nation's largest minority group by the middle of the twenty-first century.

Mexicans were the largest Hispanic group in the United States at 20.6 million, representing nearly 60 percent of the total Hispanic population. The boom of the U.S. economy in the 1990s provided a significant "pull" for these newcomers. But other factors encouraged Mexican immigration. First, a drop in worldwide oil prices followed by the deflation of the Mexican national currency dramatically lowered living standards in Mexico in the mid-1990s. NAFTA and the greater integration of the U.S. and Mexican economies brought new jobs but often with increasingly expensive living conditions. Tens and perhaps hundreds of thousands of Mexicans worked in the United States temporarily while planning a permanent move north—with or without legal documentation.

The cultural implications of immigration were far-reaching. In the 2000 U.S. Census, 6.8 million Americans nationwide listed themselves as multiracial. Identities blurred as popular entertainment created new mixes of traditions and styles.

At the same time, many native-born Americans became increasingly concerned about the impact of "illegal aliens" on their communities, particularly in California and throughout the Southwest. The Immigration Reform and Control Act of 1986 marked a break with the previous attempts to address this problem. Instead of mass deportation programs, the law strengthened the

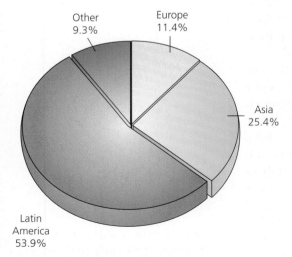

Figure 31.1 Continent of Birth for Immigrants, 1990–2000
By 2000, the number of foreign-born residents and their children—56 million according to the U.S. Census Bureau—had reached the highest level in U.S. history.

Other 9.3%
Europe 11.4%
Asia 25.4%
Latin America 53.9%

The sign at this 1996 vigil in Echo Park, Los Angeles, reads, "This fruit is the product of immigrants' labor." Members of the city's Latino community bless fruit baskets as they protest a state crackdown on illegal immigration and the increase of border patrol guards.

patrols along the border with Mexico and simultaneously offered amnesty to all undocumented workers who had entered the country since 1982. Four years later, additional revisions of this act enlarged the quota of immigrants, once again giving priority to skilled and professional workers. In many communities, however, opposition to immigration mounted. For example, in 1994, a California ballot initiative, **Proposition 187**, called for denying social services, public schooling, and health care to undocumented immigrants. In 1997, a federal judge ruled the law unconstitutional.

GROWING SOCIAL DISPARITIES

The prosperity of the 1990s, which encouraged immigration, did little to alleviate inequality. By 2000, the United States outstripped sixteen other developed countries in terms of income inequality. Roughly one in every eight Americans lived below the poverty line; the figure for children was one in five. And the new economy had done little to close the gap between the highest and lowest income earners. To the contrary, while the poorest fifth of households saw their income decrease since 1990, the wealthiest fifth saw their income grow nearly 30 percent. Women as a group made few gains, earning 73 cents to each dollar earned by men. With African Americans and Latinos continuing to earn, on average, far less than non-Hispanic whites, race relations benefited little from the economic boom of the 1990s.

In the spring of 1992, an upheaval in Los Angeles offered the starkest evidence that racial tensions had not eased. Outrage over police brutality ignited the worst riot of the century. A year earlier, Rodney King, a black motorist, had been pulled from his vehicle and severely beaten by four white police officers. When, despite the graphic evidence of an amateur videotape of the incident, a jury acquitted the officers of all but one of eleven counts of assault, South Central Los Angeles erupted. More than fifty people were killed, and 500 buildings were destroyed before L.A. police and National Guard troops restored order.

More than a quarter century after the uprising in Watts, the situation in South Central Los Angeles in 1992 seemed more desperate than ever to most African Americans. The poverty rate was 30.3 percent, more than twice the national average. The unemployment rate for adult black males hovered around 40 percent, and a quarter of the population was on welfare. Drug dealing and gang warfare had escalated, reflecting the sense of despair among young people.

•••• Read the Document

Illegal Immigration Reform and Immigrant Responsibility Act at **www.myhistorylab.com**

QUICK REVIEW

Los Angeles Riots

♦ Spring 1992: Riots sparked by acquittal of officers in Rodney King case.

♦ Fifty-one people were killed and $850 million in damage was reported.

♦ Riots exposed ethnic and economic divisions in the city.

Proposition 187 California legislation adopted by popular vote in California in 1994, which cuts off state-funded health and education benefits to undocumented or illegal immigrants.

The California ballot initiative Proposition 187 was designed to deny basic social services, including health and education, to undocumented immigrants. To express their opposition to the legislation, as many as 250,000 people took the streets in downtown Los Angeles. This photograph shows Grace Lee and a group of fellow students demonstrating in the Westwood section of the city shortly after voters approved the bill known as "the last gasp of White America in California" on November 8, 1994.

The events in Los Angeles exposed deep animosity among various groups. Almost 2,000 Korean businesses were destroyed, and Koreans angrily accused the police of making no effort to defend their stores. The division was sharpest, though, between whites and the minority populations. "We are all quite isolated in our own communities," a resident of Westwood, a mostly white upper-middle-class neighborhood, explained. "We don't know and don't care about the problems in the inner cities."

The situation in Los Angeles was not unique. Segregation was on the rise, not only in many large cities, but also in their surrounding suburbs. Similarly, in the nation's schools, the gains from the civil rights era diminished and, in some communities, disappeared altogether. Despite the increasing racial and ethnic diversity of the nation's youth, segregation was more pronounced in grades K–12.

The U.S. criminal justice system reflected these disparities. Despite a drop in violent crime in the past twenty years, the prison population in the United States grew to be the largest in the world. By 2009, one in 100 American adults were imprisoned, with ethnic and racial minorities accounting for the majority. The Bureau of Justice estimated that nearly one-third of African American men would enter a state or federal prison during their lifetimes.

THE CULTURE WARS

At the 1992 Republican National Convention, the conservative Patrick Buchanan gave the opening speech. "There is a religious war going on in our country for the soul of America," he declared. "It is a cultural war, as critical to the kind of nation we will one day be as was the Cold War itself." Into the twenty-first century, politics focused on issues like reproductive rights and reproductive technology, homosexuality and gay rights, the curriculum in public schools, codes of speech and standards in the arts, gun control, and scientific developments such as cloning, genetic alteration, and fetal tissue research, and even the validity of Darwin's theory of evolution.

The growing racial and ethnic diversity of American society, as well as the expansion of rights for groups such as women and gays, had sparked a broad and controversial movement known as "**multiculturalism**." Unlike earlier descriptions of America as a "melting pot," new metaphors such as "salad bowl" or "mosaic" became popular expressions to call attention to the unique attributes and achievements of formerly marginal groups and recent immigrants. On college campuses, multiculturalism marked the high point of the curricular reform that had been ongoing since the late 1960s and early 1970s (see Chapter 29).

Similar controversies surrounded gay rights, particularly around a push for the legal recognition of civil unions and marriage for same-sex couples. In 2000, Vermont became the first state to recognize civil unions, allowing same-sex couples to receive many, although not all, of the legal benefits of marriage. Several other states passed versions of civil union or domestic partner laws. By 2010, five states, either by legislation or court ruling, had recognized the right of same sex couples to marry and receive state benefits. Meanwhile, thirty states passed constitutional amendments prohibiting same sex marriage. Gay marriage would continue to be a powerful symbolic issue.

multiculturalism   Movement that emphasized the unique attributes and achievements of formerly marginal groups and recent immigrants.

Women's reproductive rights also remained a prime "hot button" issue, with extreme opponents targeting providers of abortion services. Operation Rescue launched a well-publicized and illegal blockade of three abortion clinics in Wichita, Kansas, in September 1991. Antiabortion protests became increasingly violent in the wake of the "war in Wichita." Several medical providers were murdered outside their clinics. In 1994, with the support of President Clinton, Congress enacted the Freedom of Access to Clinic Entrance Act, which provides protection to any abortion clinic requesting it. The number of violent incidents declined from the peak of thirty-two bombings, arsons, or attempted attacks in 1992 and twelve murders or attempted murders in 1994. After the turn of the century, the attacks continued to diminish but did not stop.

Nearly as volatile was the controversy sparked by government financing of human embryonic stem cell research. These microscopic clusters of cells have the potential to grow into any tissue in the body, so embryonic stem cells hold promise, scientists believe, for refurbishing or replacing damaged tissues or organs and, therefore, might prove useful in treating or perhaps even curing diseases such as diabetes, Parkinson's, and Alzheimer's. Religious conservatives opposed this research because it may involve the destruction of human embryos, usually derived from the excess products of *in vitro* fertilization processes.

PRESIDENT GEORGE W. BUSH AND THE WAR ON TERROR

HOW DID the threat of international terrorism transform the American political landscape in the first decade of the twenty-first century?

The end of the Cold War had reconfigured global politics, ending the bilateralism that had dominated international affairs since the end of World War II. The United States alone held fast to its superpower status, but this achievement did not necessarily make Americans more secure or safe. The old enemy, Soviet communism, was succeeded by more-fanatic, less-predictable foes: terrorist organizations.

THE ELECTION OF 2000

Voters went to the polls as usual on election day 2000, watched as late-night television newscasters projected a victory for the Democratic candidate, Clinton's vice president Al Gore, and then woke up the next morning to learn that perhaps the winner was not the vice president but his Republican opponent, Governor George W. Bush of Texas, son of former president George H. W. Bush. It was clear that Gore and his running mate, Connecticut Senator Joseph Lieberman, had won the popular vote. In doubt was the number of votes in the Electoral College. The cliffhanger ended early the next morning when Florida earmarked the state's decisive twenty-five electoral votes for the Republicans. Bush's margin of victory in Florida was only a few hundred votes, however, so narrow that Florida law mandated a machine recount in all sixty-seven counties (see Map 31.1).

After Florida completed its machine recount of votes, the Democrats requested a hand tally in selected counties where the ballots were in dispute. The Republicans responded by suing in the Miami district court to prohibit the manual recounting. Meanwhile, Florida election officials, mainly Republicans, set November 14 as the date to certify the election results, thereby disallowing the

	Electoral Vote (%)	Popular Vote (%)
GEORGE W. BUSH (Republican)	271 (50.5)	50,456,169 (48.0)
Al Gore (Democrat)	266 (49.5)	50,996,116 (48.0)

MAP 31.1

The Election of 2000 The 2000 presidential election was the closest one in U.S. history and the first one to be decided by a decision of the Supreme Court.

WHAT REGIONAL divisions were reflected in the results of the 2000 presidential election?

More than 5,000 activists gathered in Seattle in November 1999 to demonstrate against the meeting of the World Trade Organization. The event, which was marked by a violent clash with police and the arrest of dozens of protestors, marked the beginning of a movement for global economic justice.

QUICK REVIEW

Election Controversy

- Al Gore secured a majority of the popular vote.
- Both sides needed Florida's contested electoral votes to secure election.
- The U.S. Supreme Court voted 5–4 to end the recount in Florida, making George W. Bush the new president.

Read the Document

George W. Bush, Address to Congress (2001) at **www.myhistorylab.com**

returns on overseas ballots that might favor Al Gore. In turn, Democrats sued to extend the deadline. Eventually, appeals by both parties reached the Florida Supreme Court and finally the U.S. Supreme Court, which voted five to four along partisan lines to halt the counting. On December 12, Gore conceded defeat, despite having received over 500,000 more votes than Bush.

TERRORIST ATTACK ON AMERICA

On September 11, 2001, hijackers crashed two jetliners into New York's World Trade Center towers, while a third jetliner slammed into the Pentagon in Virginia. A fourth plane, diverted from its terrorist mission by courageous passengers, hurtled to the ground near Pittsburgh. At the Pentagon, the death toll soon reached 184, including 59 people who had been on board the hijacked airliner. In New York City, the collapse of the twin towers killed 2,752 people, including hundreds of police and rescue workers who had run into the buildings to help. The stark images of the attack and its aftermath were replayed over and over again on televisions throughout the world (see Seeing History).

The September 11, 2001 attacks sparked a massive response. While the media recalled Pearl Harbor, President Bush declared the deadly attacks an act of war and vowed to hunt down those responsible for the "evil, despicable acts of terror." Congress, with only one dissenting vote, granted him power to take whatever steps necessary. For the first time ever, NATO invoked the mutual defense clause in its founding treaty, which in effect supported any U.S. military action.

The day following the highly coordinated terrorist attack, President Bush identified the Saudi Arabian Osama bin Laden as the prime suspect and linked the airline hijackers, all presumed to be Islamic fundamentalists, to his Al Qaeda network. In 1998, bin Laden had issued a decree that granted religious legitimacy to all efforts to expel the United States from the lands of Islam in the Middle East. He had based Al Qaeda's operations in Afghanistan, where he enjoyed the protection of a government run by the Taliban, a radical Islamist group.

RESHAPING U.S. FOREIGN POLICY

At a memorial service for victims, President Bush outlined a new approach to U.S. foreign policy. "From this day forward," he announced, "any nation that continues to harbor or support terrorists will be regarded by the United States as a hostile regime." The first theater of the campaign against terrorism would be Afghanistan. With the support of a United Nations Security Council resolution, the United States delivered an ultimatum to the Taliban-dominated government of Afghanistan: hand over Osama bin Laden and other Al Qaeda leaders presumed to be responsible, and close all terrorist training camps immediately and unconditionally.

On October 7, after the Taliban had refused to comply, President Bush announced the beginning of Operation Enduring Freedom, a joint American-British military campaign aimed at capturing bin Laden and overthrowing the Taliban regime that had sheltered him. Fierce fighting continued through December as U.S.-led coalition troops grew to a force of over 10,000. The Taliban government toppled, but bin Laden and much of the Al Qaeda leadership escaped, presumably into a mountainous region of Pakistan.

The 9/11 Attacks

The first plane hit at 8:48 A.M.; the second, at 9:03 A.M. Then, as millions of disbelieving television viewers watched, the 110-story Twin Towers collapsed. Already, many Americans were saying that they would forever remember where they were and what they were doing when they heard the news.

WHAT ROLE did the media play in shaping our understanding of the events of September 11, 2001? How does the ability of modern media to dramatize the horror and immediacy of such events enhance their "value" to terrorists launching attacks? In what ways did the 9/11 attacks facilitate the Bush administration's decision to go to war in Iraq?

Journalists and ordinary Americans alike repeatedly invoked two twentieth-century catastrophes as parallels to 9/11: the Japanese attack at Pearl Harbor on December 7, 1941, and the assassination of John F. Kennedy on November 22, 1963. Neither of the earlier disasters played out in real time over modern media, however.

The World Trade Center attack occurred virtually before the eyes of millions. Video cameras caught the image of the second plane hitting the South Tower, panic on the faces of those fleeing, smoke billowing from the towers, and their collapse. Reporters were soon pulling comments from traumatized survivors. The networks immediately preempted regular programming and allowed millions of horrified Americans to watch endless replays. Newscasters drew out the Pearl Harbor analogy as another "Day of Infamy." Within days, pro-

grammers edited the videotapes to enhance the drama—adding images of cell phones (to remind viewers of the final calls many of the victims made), overlaying images of the collapsing towers with an unfurling American flag, and piping in patriotic music. To enhance the emotional impact, they borrowed such cinematic techniques as slowing the pace and using jump cuts that fast-timed images of the burning towers with close-ups of anguished observers' faces.

Some seventy history-oriented institutions created an Internet site, 911history.net, to collect oral histories and artifacts. Said Diane Kresh of the Library of Congress, "The Internet has become for many the public commons, a place where they can come together and talk." Importance of the Internet aside, the searing pictures of the burning towers will likely remain the preeminent image for 9/11. ∎

•••⌐Read the Document

*George W. Bush, From National Security
Strategy of the U.S. (2002)* at
www.myhistorylab.com

In his January 2002 State of the Union address, President Bush expanded on his vision of a global war on terrorism. He argued that America now faced a grave and unprecedented danger not merely from Al Qaeda terrorists but also from nation-states seeking chemical, biological, or nuclear weapons of mass destruction. He denounced the regimes of North Korea, Iran, and Iraq as an "axis of evil, arming to threaten the peace of the world."

The new focus on the threat of weapons of mass destruction formed a central part of a sweeping reformulation of American foreign policy. In the fall of 2002, the Bush administration released a new National Security Strategy Report that offered the most radical revision of American foreign policy since the Truman administration in the early days of the Cold War (see Chapter 26). It argued that "the struggle against global terrorism is different from any other war in our history," requiring the United States to "deter and defend against the threat before it is unleashed," acting preemptively and alone if necessary.

The war on terrorism had a domestic front as well. The partisan bitterness of the 2000 election largely dissolved amid post–9/11 calls for national unity, making it easier for the Bush administration to push new legislation through Congress. Signed into law in the fall of 2001, the **USA Patriot Act** gave federal officials greater authority to track and intercept communications for law-enforcement and intelligence-gathering purposes, new powers to curb foreign money laundering, and broader discretion in tightening borders against suspected foreign terrorists. It created new crimes and penalties against suspected domestic and international terrorists. In the months after the 9/11 attacks, more than a thousand Muslims, some of them U.S. citizens, were arrested and detained. Only a few of these suspects were actually charged with crimes related to terrorism. Congress passed the USA Patriot Act II in 2003, further expanding the ability of law-enforcement and intelligence-gathering authorities to perform surveillance and authorize secret arrests.

The Bush administration also created a new cabinet-level **Department of Homeland Security (DHS)**, consolidating twenty-two different domestic agencies. Its components included the Immigration and Naturalization Service, the U.S. Customs Service, the Secret Service, the Coast Guard, and the Federal Emergency Management Agency.

Many questions remained unanswered about the events and circumstances surrounding the 9/11 attacks, particularly the multiple failures within the U.S. intelligence community. The Bush administration at first resisted efforts to mount a full-scale inquiry. Pressure from the families of 9/11 victims, as well as widespread calls for a bipartisan investigation, forced the administration to reverse its opposition. In July 2004, a panel of five Democrats and five Republicans issued its final report concluding that the government "failed to protect the American people" because it did not understand the "gravity of the threat."

INVASION OF IRAQ

The president's pledge to confront threats to security before they reached American shores—a policy of "preemptive defense"—became known as the Bush Doctrine, and its first major test was Iraq. Planning for a U.S.-led invasion and the overthrow of Saddam Hussein had actually begun in the first weeks after the September 11 attacks. President Bush himself had come to believe that "regime change" was necessary, a position supported by several major figures in his administration including Vice President Dick Cheney, Secretary of Defense Donald Rumsfeld, and his deputy secretary, Paul Wolfowitz.

Proponents of war made three central arguments. First, Saddam Hussein must be removed by force because he possessed biological and chemical weapons—weapons of mass destruction—and was planning to develop nuclear weapons. Second, they argued that Saddam's intelligence services had direct connections to the September 11 hijackers and to Al Qaeda operatives around the world. Third, toppling Saddam would make possible a democratic Iraq that could then serve as a herald of political change throughout the Middle East and Muslim world. The majority of the Iraqi people, they asserted, would welcome and support a U.S.-led campaign, ensuring a swift and fairly painless victory.

USA Patriot Act   Federal legislation adopted in 2001 in response to the terrorist attacks on September 11 to facilitate anti-terror actions by federal law enforcement and intelligence agencies.

Department of Homeland Security (DHS)   Cabinet-level department created by George Bush to manage U.S. security.

Throughout late 2002 and early 2003, while U.S. military planners prepared for battle, opponents of war refuted the arguments of the Bush administration. Many political analysts and veteran diplomats doubted that Saddam had the weapon capability credited to him. They charged that Vice President Cheney and Secretary Rumsfeld had manipulated Pentagon intelligence estimates to make their case. Others doubted Saddam's links to Al Qaeda and argued that war with Iraq would sideline the hunt for bin Laden. A growing number of Americans questioned the assumption that removing Saddam would make America safer, envisioning an invasion instead as a boost to the recruitment efforts of Al Qaeda and other terrorist organizations. Millions of citizens began organizing against the push for war via Internet organizations such as MoveOn.org and in vigils and gatherings in their local communities.

The antiwar movement went global. On February 15, 2003, millions of demonstrators turned out in more than 300 cities, including 500,000 in New York, 2 million in London, and 1 million in Rome. This was the single largest expression of antiwar sentiment in history.

Meanwhile, Secretary of State Powell tried but failed to gain support for war from the UN Security Council. Nonetheless, the Bush administration decided to invade Iraq with what it called a "coalition of the willing," with Great Britain as its major partner. On March 19, President Bush announced the beginning of war (see Map 31.2).

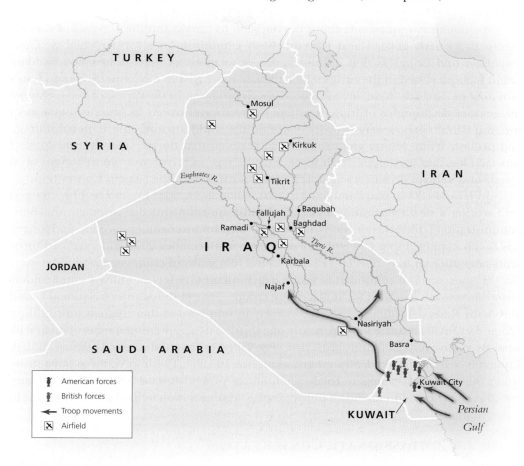

MAP 31.2

Invasion in Iraq   On March 20, 2003, American and British troops poured into Iraq from bases in Kuwait, crossing the Iraqi border to the east near Safwan. The American Third Infantry Division used armored bulldozers to create wide gaps in the Iraqi defensive line.

WHY DID the quick defeat of the Iraqi army fail to bring peace to the country?

The American and British forces overwhelmed the regular Iraqi army fairly easily and secured Baghdad and several other major cities. On May 1, 2003, on the flight deck of the USS *Abraham Lincoln*, anchored off the San Diego coast, President Bush announced the official end of combat operations. "In the battle of Iraq," the president declared, "the United States and our allies have prevailed."

The purely military act of removing Saddam's regime from power proved far simpler than bringing peace and stability to Iraq. The invasion turned into an occupation, and the plight of ordinary Iraqis and American soldiers worsened quickly. Amid widespread civil disorder and massive looting, millions of Iraqis had their electricity, water, and basic food supplies disrupted. Well-organized resistance movements fought back and also fought among themselves. The American invasion created about 4.5 million refugees in Iraq, roughly half of whom fled the country. Rather than weaken terrorists, the U.S. occupation instead strengthened a new generation of terror networks now drawn to do battle with U.S. forces in Iraq.

In early 2004, the well-coordinated, heavily armed, and well-financed resistance to the American occupation gained strength. Badly stretched U.S. forces, which included a high percentage of National Guard and Army Reserve units, were forced back into combat. A year after President Bush had confidently declared the fighting over, American troops engaged in the toughest fighting since the Vietnam War.

Troubling new questions about the decision to invade and the conduct of the war emerged. In early 2004, David Kay, the Bush administration's former chief weapons inspector, told Congress that any stockpiles of weapons of mass destruction Saddam might have possessed in the early 1990s had been destroyed by UN inspections and Iraq's own actions. Nor was there any nuclear weapons program. In the spring of 2004, graphic images and descriptions of Iraqi detainees abused and tortured by American guards in the Abu Ghraib prison were broadcast around the world, inciting international outrage and protest. White House memos, however, revealed that the president's legal counsel Alberto Gonzales had urged Bush to declare the war on terror and the treatment of Al Qaeda and Taliban prisoners exempt from the provisions of the Geneva Convention.

In January 2005, Iraq conducted its first national elections for an assembly charged with writing a new constitution by 2006. Amidst enormous media coverage, the Bush administration hailed the elections as a historic step toward democracy. Saddam Hussein was finally captured in a U.S. military operation in December 2003 and executed three years later after an Iraqi Special Tribunal found him guilty of crimes against humanity.

The occupation continued to take a heavy toll on U.S. forces. Military commanders found themselves strapped for replacement troops. Tens of thousands of National Guard and Army Reserve soldiers were forced to stay in Iraq beyond their regular tour of duty. When they finally returned home, nearly one-third of troops presented signs of mental illness. By 2005, over 1,500 Americans had been killed in Iraq and nearly 12,000 wounded. Estimates of Iraqi civilian deaths ranged as high as 100,000. The Iraq War also put a heavy strain on the federal budget. Total expenditures pushed toward $800 billion. Military spending on the war on terrorism during Bush's administration helped push the deficit to a record high.

BUSH'S "COMPASSIONATE CONSERVATISM"

National security and the war on terrorism became the keynotes in Bush's 2004 reelection campaign. With Iraq dominating the news, he described himself as a "wartime president" and appealed to patriotism and national unity.

Democrats, nominated the Vietnam War hero Senator John Kerry of Massachusetts as their presidential candidate. However, the Democrat's campaign quickly faltered and President Bush won reelection with 51 percent of the popular vote to Kerry's 48 percent, a 3-million-vote margin. Though not as close as the 2000 election, few would dispute that the 2004 election revealed a nation that was as politically divided as any time since the Civil War. President Bush interpreted the 2004 election results as support for the Iraq war and as a mandate for the "compassionate conservatism" that marked his first administration. On the domestic front, he promised to spend his "political capital" by advancing the Republican agenda that President Reagan had shaped: tax cuts, strong military defense, and the overhaul of Social Security and Medicare.

Lowering federal income taxes became an important signature of the Bush presidency. During his first term, Bush promoted the Economic Growth and Tax Relief Reconciliation Act, which had squeaked through Congress with bipartisan support in 2001. The act lowered tax rates, disproportionately for the wealthy, and gave most Americans a small rebate from the IRS as "reconciliation" for paying too much in taxes. While many Americans did see a decline in their income tax payments, many found that increases in local property taxes, college tuitions, and other fees more than made up for the savings.

Domestically, Bush's earliest Congressional victory came in education with the No Child Left Behind Act. Passed by Congress in 2001, the act provided for the implementation of standards and assessments for math and reading skills for children in grades three to eight and allowed parents to transfer their children out of schools that did not reach these goals.

A U.S. Coast Guard helicopter rescues flood-stranded victims of Hurricane Katrina from their homes in New Orleans, September 2005. Images like this one received wide circulation in the news media, prompting criticism of the government's failures to offer more and swifter help to Katrina's victims.

Bush won a decisive victory in gaining approval for the addition of a prescription drug benefit to Medicare. This 2003 bill, which included a $400 billion price tag, helped older Americans cover the skyrocketing costs of prescription medicine while providing huge subsidies to drug manufacturers and private insurers. However, Bush failed in his persistent efforts to "reinvent Social Security." Congress refused to heed Bush's call for a major overhaul of the popular New Deal–era social insurance program by substituting private investment accounts. Moreover, national statistics indicated that the typical American family made no economic gains since he took office. During his second term, President Bush saw the post–9/11 political consensus largely dissolve as victory in Iraq, as well as the larger "war on terror," proved elusive and increasingly difficult to define.

The Bush administration endured a heated and prolonged controversy sparked by its response to one of the most cataclysmic events of the new century—Hurricane Katrina. On August 25, Hurricane Katrina made its way through Florida, killing six people, destroying homes, and uprooting trees before heading into the Gulf of Mexico. Local officials called for the evacuation of New Orleans, a city below sea level, and opened the Superdome "as a refuge of last resort." President Bush directed the **Federal Emergency Management Agency (FEMA)** to coordinate federal assistance to state and local governments in the case of disaster.

Hurricane Katrina struck New Orleans on August 31 and destroyed several parishes, including the Lower Ninth Ward, the home to an African American population already steeped in poverty. Canal levees failed, submerging 80 percent of the city. President Bush, who had been vacationing at his ranch in Crawford, Texas, did not rush to the area but instead four days later flew over in *Air Force One* on his early return to the White House. Meanwhile, the rescue operations stalled amid bureaucratic mishaps. Conditions at the Superdome deteriorated to a point that newscasters described a reign of anarchy. Shortages of food, water, blankets, sanitary facilities, and medical supplies put the lives of the 5,000 refugees at risk. Only slowly did FEMA relocate staff to the area and, worse, actually hampered private relief efforts.

Federal Emergency Management Agency (FEMA)   Agency charged with providing assistance to communities hit by natural disasters.

The press largely vilified President Bush, labeling his response to this disaster as "a national disgrace." Much of the shame resulted from the way unfolding events underscored the race and class dimensions of the tragedy. The population of New Orleans, with a poverty rate 76 percent higher than the national average, was two-thirds African American, and more than a quarter of those black citizens of New Orleans lacked access to an automobile. When the mandatory evacuation order came, the majority of white residents drove away from the city, while many black residents had no choice but to board the special buses headed for the ill-equipped Superdome.

More than 1,600 people had died in New Orleans alone, and nearly a million had fled the greater region. Only very slowly did business activity—especially tourism in the French Quarter—revive. President Bush was left with the legacy of having one of the nation's most important cities nearly destroyed during his administration.

DIVIDED GOVERNMENT, DIVIDED NATION

The 2006 midterm elections, occurring in the aftermath of Hurricane Katrina, brought a return of the divided government that had characterized the Clinton years. Democrats took control of both the House (233–202) and the Senate (51–49) for the first time since 1992. A record-breaking number of women were elected to Congress, and Nancy Pelosi (D-CA) became the first woman to serve as Speaker of the House.

Although a large number of Democrats had originally supported the invasion, many had since changed their minds and now believed that a military "victory" was both impossible and an illusion. Democrats tried to attach deadlines for withdrawal to the president's funding bills, but enjoying only a narrow majority, they could not override President Bush's vetoes.

Rather than scaling back, President Bush asked for yet greater funding. In January 2007, he unveiled his new and costly plan, a "surge" of some 30,000 additional American troops to Iraq. The goal was to clamp down on sectarian violence and thereby create space for the Iraqi political system to govern more effectively. The Bush administration touted the success of its new strategy, pointing to a substantial decline in both political violence and attacks on U.S. forces throughout 2007–8.

Even though the "surge" represented a tactical success, the larger picture in Iraq remained grim. The Iraqi government proved unable to provide basic security and services in many parts of the country. Some 2 million Iraqis, including much of the nation's educated middle class and professionals, fled the country to nearby nations such as Syria, Jordan, and Egypt. Another 2 million Iraqis, forced to leave their neighborhoods and towns, found themselves refugees within their own country. Moreover, violence continued. Although the number of American casualties dropped from their peak in 2007, by the time President Bush left office in 2009, nearly 4,400 American troops had been killed in Iraq and more than 31,600 wounded, many of them gravely.

By the end of his second term, President Bush faced growing disillusionment with the Iraq War, the single issue that most clearly defined his presidency. He continued to defend the war as part of a broader, long-term struggle against global terrorism carried out by well-armed Islamic extremists. By this time, the argument had lost credibility. The Senate Intelligence Committee concluded in 2008 that the Bush administration had knowingly "misrepresented the intelligence and the threat from Iraq."

To fund the wars in Afghanistan and Iraq and the open-ended war on terror, Bush pushed the deficit to record levels. When he left office, the federal debt had reached an estimated $1.3 trillion. Moreover, whereas in the previous decades, the federal debt was held by Americans in the form of government securities, about 45 percent was now held mainly by foreign governments, with Japan and China the largest creditors. President Bush left office with nearly three-quarters of Americans disapproving of the way he had governed during his two terms. Approximately two-thirds of those polled had also come to oppose the Iraq war.

BARACK OBAMA AND THE AUDACITY OF HOPE

The 2008 election brought the first African American to the presidency of the United States. Running on a platform promising change, Barack Obama inspired many Americans, especially young people and first-time voters, to get involved in his quest for the White House. The nation's worst economic downturn since the Great Depression of the 1930s also loomed over the political landscape, raising fundamental questions about the strength and the future of the nation's economy.

THE ELECTION OF 2008

On January 20, 2009, 143 years after the end of slavery, Barack Hussein Obama took the oath as the nation's first African American president. Only a year earlier, such a prospect seemed highly unlikely, even impossible in the eyes of most Americans. When Senator Obama announced his candidacy for president in January 2007, he was relatively unknown outside Illinois. Born in 1961, child of a Kenyan father and a white Kansan mother who had met in Hawaii, Obama had grown up in an extended multiracial family. After graduating from New York's Columbia University in 1983, Obama moved to Chicago where he worked for five years as a community organizer among low-income residents whose neighborhoods had been devastated by the loss of manufacturing jobs. He then moved on to Harvard Law School, graduating in 1991 as the first African American editor of the prestigious law review. He returned to Chicago, working as a civil rights attorney and lecturer at the University of Chicago Law School.

Obama made the leap into electoral politics in 1996, and won election to the Illinois State Senate. After an unsuccessful campaign for Congress, he set his sights on the U.S. Senate. In 2002, while still a state senator, he began to attract national attention for his vocal opposition to the American invasion of Iraq. After winning the Democratic Senate nomination, Obama was invited to give the keynote address at the 2004 National Democratic convention, where he impressed the national audience with his passionate oratory and his emphasis on what united, rather than what divided, Americans. That fall, Obama became only the third African American elected to the U.S. Senate since Reconstruction.

Obama launched his campaign for the presidency barely two years later. Obama had a carefully thought-out electoral strategy that relied heavily on his experiences as a community organizer. He focused on registering new voters, especially among the young and people of color. He defined himself as an outsider, looking to shake up Washington's "politics as usual." Although his policy positions largely reflected those of mainstream liberal Democrats, he carefully framed his appeals to attract independent voters and even Republicans disgruntled with the Bush presidency. His surprise victory in the January 2008 Iowa caucuses vindicated his strategy, proved his appeal to white voters, and revealed his campaign's fund-raising prowess.

Senator Hillary Clinton (D-NY) emerged as Obama's main rival, and their battle for the Democratic nomination continued into the spring and across a string of primary states. An accomplished attorney, former First Lady, a savvy campaigner and fund-raiser, and influential U.S. Senator, her status as a pioneer for women in politics added a special dimension to her appeal. Throughout their primary battles, the fundamental issue of race simmered in media coverage and soured the increasingly tense relations between the campaigns. The issue boiled over in March 2008 when highly controversial videos of Rev. Jeremiah Wright, the longtime pastor of Obama's church in Chicago, surfaced. Wright's militant oratory, fusing Black Nationalist rhetoric and anti-American epithets, received endless replay on television and the Internet. The uproar raised questions about why Obama had not left the church, jeopardized his carefully crafted message of racial unity, and threatened to sink the campaign.

WHAT CHALLENGES did Barack Obama face in the first years of his presidency?

Watch the **Video**
The Historical Significance of the 2008 Presidential Election at **www.myhistorylab.com**

Hear the **Audio**
Barack Obama, Excerpt from The Audacity of Hope at **www.myhistorylab.com**

In response, Obama took on Rev. Wright and the broader issue of race in American history in a speech delivered at the National Constitution Center in Philadelphia. He offered a condensed review of the nation's racial history, acknowledging the racial resentments of both African Americans and working-class whites. He invoked his own multiracial background and family experiences. Obama stressed the progress the nation had made against racism. "What we have already achieved,' he declared, "gives us hope—the audacity to hope—for what we can and must achieve tomorrow." Most commentators judged Obama's presentation as the most thoughtful, nuanced, and historically grounded speech on race relations ever delivered by a political candidate.

Obama clinched the Democratic nomination in June, and then he and his running mate, Sen. Joseph Biden (D-DE) took to the campaign trail. Obama's network of organizers helped register hundreds of thousands of new voters, especially among minorities, and turned out huge crowds wherever Obama appeared. Avoiding public financing, organizers raised record-breaking sums, mainly from individual donors. They also made use of the Internet to direct their message to prospective voters among the population under age thirty. The campaign slogans "Change we can believe in" and "Yes we can" reaffirmed Obama's basic message of hope and created what many observers believed was a genuine political movement that would persist past election day.

The Republican campaign generated no less excitement. The Republicans nominated Sen. John McCain (R-AZ), who had lost his 2000 bid for the presidency to George W. Bush. McCain supporters stressed his national security and military credentials, and compared his long experience to Obama's thin resume. Yet McCain's judgment came under fire when he announced his surprise pick for vice-president, Governor Sarah Palin (R-AL). Palin, a mother of five and a social conservative with working-class roots, excited the Republican base, and she instantly became a national celebrity. A series of national media interviews exposed her uninformed, at times embarrassing, views on foreign policy and raised serious doubts among many, including some high-level Republicans.

In November, Obama won the election with the biggest margin by any candidate in twenty years. He took the Electoral College by 365–173 and the popular vote by nearly 10 million. Observers noted Obama's reversal of some long-standing trends. He was the first Democratic candidate since Lyndon B. Johnson in 1964 to receive more than 50% of the popular vote. This reflected large gains made for his party among young voters, Latinos, and suburbanites. He attracted a higher percentage of white voters than either John Kerry in 2004 or Al Gore in 2000, helping him to carry several states, such as Virginia and North Carolina, that had not gone Democratic in decades. Although the broken economy no doubt contributed to Obama's victory, his election also reflected the changing demography of the twenty-first century: the electorate was younger, more non-white, and less divided by racial polarization. To drive home the symbolism, Obama chose to celebrate on election night in Chicago's Grant Park, site of the police attack on peace demonstrators at the 1968 Democratic convention (see Chapter 29).

THE GREAT RECESSION

Much of the final phase of Obama's election campaign had focused on the economic crisis facing the nation—and much of the world—and helped to give him an edge over his Republican opponent. While McCain remained aloof from the tense, high-stakes negotiations going on in Washington, Obama dived into the public debates over how to rescue the economy. By the time he took office in January 2009, however, there was no time for basking in his victory. Wall Street's woes had quickly spread to Main Street, and the recession was deepening to become the worst economic crisis since the Great Depression.

The immediate cause of the recession was the abrupt burst of the "real estate bubble" that had artificially inflated the value of houses for years. Approximately 80 percent of mortgages recently contracted had been in the hands of risky borrowers, homeowners who had been encouraged by the banks to buy with little or no money down and take sub-prime or adjustable-rate mortgages. When housing prices slid downward and interest rates moved up, many of these new homeowners could not make their payments or realized that the money they still owed on their mortgages far exceeded the market value of their homes, putting them "underwater." Hundreds of thousands defaulted on their loans and let the lending agencies take over their property. Hundreds of billions of dollars in mortgage-backed stocks and bonds that were owned and traded by large financial institutions became worthless when the real estate market collapsed. As a result, leading banks, investment houses, and insurance companies suddenly faced imminent failure. In the fall of 2008, the bankruptcy of Bear Stearns and Lehman Brothers, two of Wall Street's wealthiest investment banks that had securitized many subprime mortgages, shocked the international financial markets. So did the near-collapse of American International Group, one of the world's biggest insurers.

In its final months, the Bush Administration worked frantically to stabilize the financial system, eventually pushing through Congress an unprecedented bailout package. The Troubled Asset Relief Program (TARP) allowed the Department of Treasury to buy or insure up to $700 billion in bad loans and other "toxic" assets held by financial institutions. A recalcitrant Congress agreed to pass TARP only after the Dow Jones industrial average dropped nearly 800 points, wiping out $1.2 trillion from the stock market in the biggest one-day decline since the crash of 1987. Despite the infusion of funds, banks continued to collapse. By early 2010, the Federal Deposit Insurance Corporation had taken over nearly 200 banks and many more were assigned to the federal government's secret list of "troubled" banks.

OBAMA IN OFFICE

President Obama pushed through Congress in February 2009 the largest stimulus package in U.S. history. While Bush's TARP program made capital available to big financial institutions, the $787 billion American Recovery and Reinvestment Act targeted ordinary Americans. It combined tax breaks with spending on infrastructure projects, extensions of welfare and unemployment benefits, and education. While the Obama administration hoped to jump-start recovery, as well as create or save 3.5 million jobs by 2011, many economists warned that the funds allocated were too small.

Recovery proved hard to measure. By early 2010, nearly one in four American homeowners owed more on their mortgages than their property was worth. Millions could not make payments and faced foreclosure on their houses. The stock market crash, the most severe since 1974, had wiped out large portions of retirement savings that were invested in equities rather than tied to employer-sponsored pensions, and many older Americans put off retirement. Many colleges and universities, their endowments cut by one-third or more, raised tuition, putting higher education out of reach for many Americans. Whole industries, such as automaking, continued to teeter on the brink of bankruptcy. The unemployment rate topped 10 percent, and the sense that most lost jobs might never return reinforced a deep sense insecurity and frustration. The future remained uncertain and the consensus continued to hold that America was in the grip of the worst economic crisis since the Great Depression.

Beyond the economy, Obama faced many hurdles during his first year in office. His two biggest issues were foreign policy and health care reform, both key elements in his election campaign. He swiftly set to work on these two issues. Opposition would be strong and steady. Obama's stimulus bill had passed without a single Republican vote in the House and only three in the Senate and previewed the difficulty of realizing his oft-stated goal of bringing a more bipartisan, even "post-partisan" tone to Washington. Such opposition also forecast the resistance the ambitious president would face in passing legislation that would fulfill his campaign promises.

President Obama signing the Health Care and Education Reconciliation Act in March 2010. It represented the most ambitious overhaul of America's health-care system since the enactment of Medicare in 1965.

In foreign policy, Obama had campaigned promising to end the unilateral actions that had made President Bush unpopular with many other heads of state. To help reach this goal, as well as demonstrate his political savvy, he named his toughest rival, Hillary Clinton, as secretary of state. Clinton agreed with Obama that there was "a lot of damage to repair" from the Bush administration. She also supported Obama's boldest moves in foreign policy that, surprisingly to some observers, made less of a break with Bush-era policies than anticipated.

Within days of taking office, Obama ordered the closing of the notorious Guantanamo Bay Naval Camp prison, relocation of its 250 terror suspects to the United States, and trials by American courts. This policy provoked enormous opposition and proved slow to implement; in early 2010, plans for the removal of the prisoners had stalled.

Obama also began the difficult process of repairing America's standing and prestige on the global stage. In June 2009, he traveled to Cairo, Egypt where he called for "a new beginning between the United States and Muslims around the world; one based upon mutual interest and mutual respect; and one based upon the truth that America and Islam are not exclusive, and need not be in competition." It would take more than a speech to undo the damage wrought by the Iraq War and the legacy of Islamist terrorism. The speech, however, and the largely positive reaction to it, at least temporarily, placed the United States in a new diplomatic light.

Renewing his campaign promise, President Obama announced a process for a gradual troop drawdown from Iraq. By summer 2010 Obama had removed all combat troops, leaving roughly 50,000 military personnel as training forces scheduled to leave by the end of 2011. At the same time, he pledged to expand the war in Afghanistan. The failure to capture Osama bin Laden and the revival of the Taliban had once again made that country a haven for al Qaeda and other terrorist groups. In December 2009, the president announced a plan to deploy 30,000 additional troops to Afghanistan. This announcement came as he prepared to accept the Nobel Peace Prize. "Let us reach for the world that ought to be," he said to the Oslo audience in justifying his leadership in the conduct of two wars: "Clear-eyed, we can understand that there will be war and still strive for peace."

CHRONOLOGY

1981	MTV and CNN start broadcasting as cable channels
1986	Immigration Reform and Control Act addresses concerns about undocumented aliens
1988	George H. W. Bush is elected president
1989	Tiananmen Square demonstration in China
1990	Iraqi invasion of Kuwait leads to massive U.S. military presence in the Persian Gulf
1991	Operation Desert Storm forces Iraq out of Kuwait
	Operation Rescue launched in Wichita, Kansas
1992	Rodney King verdict sparks rioting in Los Angeles
	Bill Clinton is elected president
1993	Terrorist bombing of World Trade Center kills six people
	Clinton administration introduces comprehensive health care reform, but it fails to win passage in Congress
	Congress approves the North American Free Trade Agreement (NAFTA)
1994	Republicans win control of Senate and House for first time in forty years
	Congress approves the General Agreement on Tariffs and Trade (GATT)
	Congress passes the Comprehensive AIDS Revenue Emergency Act
	Congress passes Defense of Marriage Act
	California voters approve Proposition 187
1995	Bombing of Alfred P. Murrah Federal Building in Oklahoma City kills 168 people

1996	Congress passes Welfare Reform Act
	Congress enacts the Antiterrorism and Effective Death Penalty Act
	President Bill Clinton is reelected
1997	Kyoto Protocol endorsed by European Union but not United States
1998	U.S. embassies in Kenya and Tanzania bombed by terrorists
	House of Representatives votes to impeach President Clinton, but vote fails in Senate
1999	U.S. joins NATO forces in Kosovo
	Protesters disrupt meetings of the World Trade Organization in Seattle
2000	USS *Cole* bombed by terrorists
2001	George W. Bush becomes president after contested election
	Terrorists attack World Trade Center and Pentagon
	U.S. begins military campaign in Afghanistan
	Homeland Security Department established
	USA Patriot Act passed
2003	Invasion of Iraq and occupation
	USA Patriot Act II passed
2004	Release of *The 9/11 Commission Report*
	Reelection of George W. Bush
2005	Elections in Iraq
	Hurricane Katrina devastates New Orleans and the Gulf Coast

On several domestic issues, Obama signaled new directions. The first bill he signed into law, the Lilly Ledbetter Fair Pay Act, allowed workers more time to sue employers over unequal pay. He issued an executive order lifting Bush-era restrictions on funding for international aid groups that provided abortions. He overturned a ban on federal funding for stem cell research, and ramped up public spending for research into curing Parkinson's and other diseases. He supported some $30 billion in bridge loans to help automakers General Motors and Chrysler emerge from bankruptcy. For his first Supreme Court nomination, Obama chose Sandra Sotomayor, a federal court judge with Puerto Rican roots who became the first-ever Latino Supreme Court justice in 2009. His second appointment, former Harvard law School dean Elena Kagan, was sworn in the next year.

On the domestic front, Obama's biggest challenge was health care reform. Throughout the first year of his term, deep partisan divisions in Congress stalled Obama's effort to create a comprehensive universal system of health insurance. The bill that finally emerged from the House and Senate, and that Obama signed into law in

March 2010, included a series of reforms to be fully implemented by 2014. Some 32 million uninsured Americans would gain coverage. With no government run "public option" to compete with private insurers, the legislation itself was more focused on reforming insurance industry practices than on overhauling how patient care was delivered and paid for.

President Obama and Democrats in Congress hailed the new law as an historic achievement in social legislation. Yet not a single Republican in either the House or Senate had supported it. In their eyes, it represented an unwarranted expansion of federal power. The political fallout remained unclear, but the debate over health care reform epitomized how sharply the two parties, and Americans, were divided.

REVIEW QUESTIONS

1. How is the "new economy" different from the old economy? How has it reshaped American business and financial practices? Explain the relationship between the new economy and electronic media, such as the Internet and cable television.

2. Evaluate the presidency of Bill Clinton. Compare his domestic and foreign policies to those of the Republican presidents who preceded and followed him in office. What was the impact of the scandals that plagued his presidency?

3. Describe the major demographic trends revealed by the 2000 U. S. Census. Identify the racial and ethnic groups with the greatest gains in population. How have various legislative acts since 1965 affected immigration to the United States? How have communities changed as a result of the influx of new immigrants?

4. The concept of globalization is highly controversial. Are borders between nations "melting away" as some scholars contend? How does this concept square with the description of the United States as the single superpower in the world? Does this concept apply primarily to economics, or is it useful for discussing issues related to culture, media, the environment, and population trends?

5. How has the "war on terror" differed from other wars in this century? How and why did the 9/11 attacks lead to fundamental changes in the conduct of U.S. foreign policy? What arguments for the American invasion of Iraq in 2003 do you find most and least persuasive?

KEY TERMS

Bosnia (p. 836)

Contract with America (p. 835)

Department of Homeland Security (DHS) (p. 846)

Federal Emergency Management Agency (FEMA) (p. 849)

Internet (p. 839)

Kosovo (p. 837)

Multiculturalism (p. 842)

North American Free Trade Agreement (NAFTA) (p. 836)

Proposition 187 (p. 841)

Silicon Valley (p. 838)

USA Patriot Act (p. 846)

Welform Reform Act (p. 835)

World Trade Organization (WTO) (p. 836)

myhistorylab Connections

Reinforce what you learned in this chapter by studying the many documents,
images, maps, review tools, and videos available at www.myhistorylab.com.

Read and Review

✓● Study and Review **Chapter 31**

●●● Read the Document

Statements of the Clinton Health Care Plan (1993)

Illegal Immigration Reform and Immigrant Responsibility Act

George W. Bush, Address to Congress (2001)

George W. Bush, From National Security Strategy of the U.S. (2002)

👁 See the Map *Immigration to the United States, 1945–1990*

Research and Explore

●●● Read the Document

Exploring America: Globalization

Profiles
  Bill Gates
  Jesse Jackson

((●● Hear the Audio *Barack Obama, Excerpt from The Audacity of Hope*

◉ Watch the Video

Bill Clinton Sells Himself to America: Presidential Campaign Ad, 1992

Bill Clinton First Inauguration

The Historical Significance of the 2008 Presidential Election

The Connection between Obama and Lincoln

((●● **Hear** the **Audio**

Hear the audio files for Chapter 31 at
www.myhistorylab.com.

The Threat of War to Democratic Institutions

As early as 1798 and the Alien and Sedition Act of the Adams administration, American governments have been willing to suppress civil liberties in the name of national defense. Adams was fearful of French immigrants who added to the voting power of Democratic Republicans and the poisoned pens of Democratic Republicans whose newspaper torn at his public reputation. In the Civil War Lincoln suspended the right of habeas corpus in Maryland and arrested members of Congress who were known secessionists.

HOW HAS the use of the Patriot Act and its later revisions in line with wartime actions of earlier American governments during wartime or times of perceived threat to the United States?

In the twentieth century, the events of the 18th and 19th century during war were paralleled during World War One, World War Two, the Cold War, and during the current War on Terror which began on September 11, 2001. In World War II hysteria over the Japanese attack on Pearl Harbor combined with a long standing racism against Asians in West Coast states resulted in the imprisonment of approximately 120,000 Japanese Americans, many native born citizens, under Roosevelt's Executive Order 9066. During the Cold War and the era of Joseph McCarthy Americans lost their jobs, faced government investigation of the most intrusive nature, and public disgrace. Civil libertarians have criticized the Patriot Act of 2001 also called The Uniting and Strengthening America by Providing Appropriate Tools Required to Intercept and Obstruct Terrorism Act of 2001 (Public Law 107–56), as an inappropriate curtailment of constitutional rights and a dangerous expansion of executive police powers. ∎

GEORGE W. BUSH, PRESIDENT'S STATEMENT ON H.R. 3199, THE "USA PATRIOT IMPROVEMENT AND REAUTHORIZATION ACT OF 2005," MARCH 9, 2006

TODAY, I have signed into law H.R. 3199, the "USA PATRIOT Improvement and Reauthorization Act of 2005," and then S. 2271, the "USA PATRIOT Act Additional Reauthorizing Amendments Act of 2006." The bills will help us continue to fight terrorism effectively and to combat the use of the illegal drug methamphetamine that is ruining too many lives.

The executive branch shall construe the provisions of H.R. 3199 that call for furnishing information to entities outside the executive branch, such as sections 106A and 119, in a manner consistent with the President's constitutional authority to supervise the unitary executive branch and to withhold information the disclosure of which could impair foreign relations, national security, the deliberative processes of the Executive, or the performance of the Executive's constitutional duties.

The executive branch shall construe section 756(e)(2) of H.R. 3199, which calls for an executive branch official to submit to the Congress recommendations for legislative action, in a manner consistent with the President's constitutional authority to supervise the unitary executive branch and to recommend for the consideration of the Congress such measures as he judges necessary and expedient. ∎

SEDITION ACT OF 1918, MAY 16, 1918 (REPEALED 1921)

SECTION 3. Whoever, when the United States is at war, shall willfully make or convey false reports or false statements with intent to interfere with the operation or success of the military or naval forces of the United States, or to promote the success of its enemies, or shall willfully make or convey false reports, or false statements, . . . or incite insubordination, disloyalty, mutiny, or refusal of duty, in the military or naval forces of the United States, or shall willfully obstruct . . . the recruiting or enlistment service of the United States, or . . . shall willfully utter, print, write, or publish any disloyal, profane, scurrilous, or abusive language about the form of government of the United States, or the Constitution of the United States, or the military or naval forces of the United States . . . or shall willfully display the flag of any foreign enemy, or shall willfully . . . urge, incite, or advocate any curtailment of production . . . or advocate, teach, defend, or suggest the doing of any of the acts or things in this section enumerated and whoever shall by word or act support or favor the cause of any country with which the United States is at war or by word or act oppose the cause of the United States therein, shall be punished by a fine of not more than $10,000 or imprisonment for not more than twenty years, or both. . . . ■

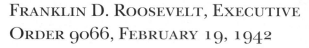 Esther C. Brunauer, an employee of the State Department, testified before the Senate Subcommittee on Foreign Relations to defend herself against allegations made against her by Senator Joseph McCarthy.

FRANKLIN D. ROOSEVELT, EXECUTIVE ORDER 9066, FEBRUARY 19, 1942

I HEREBY authorize and direct the Secretary of War, and the Military Commanders whom he may from time to time designate, whenever he or any designated Commander deems such action necessary or desirable, to prescribe military areas in such places and of such extent as he or the appropriate Military Commander may determine, from which any or all persons may be excluded, and with respect to which, the right of any person to enter, remain in, or leave shall be subject to whatever restrictions the Secretary of War or the appropriate Military Commander may impose in his discretion. ■

The hysteria and fear following the Pearl Harbor attack resulted in the internment of 110,000 Japanese Americans in "War Relocation Centers" located in isolated areas of the West for the duration of the war. In 1944 the U.S. Supreme Court upheld this action by the government with the comment that it was a "pressing public necessity."

Camp X-ray Detainees – Guantanamo Bay Detention Camp
In his War on Terrorism President Bush deemed it necessary to intern approximately 775 enemy prisoners captured in Afghanistan and elsewhere in a military facility. Bush claimed these prisoners did not possess rights under the terms of the Geneva Conventions. The U.S. Supreme Court ruled against his position in 2006 and ordered the U.S. military to extend international rights granted under the Geneva Conventions to enemy combatants to these individuals.

THE DECLARATION OF INDEPENDENCE

When in the course of human events it becomes necessary for one people to dissolve the political bands which have connected them with another and to assume, among the powers of the earth, the separate and equal station to which the laws of nature and of nature's God entitle them, a decent respect to the opinions of mankind requires that they should declare the causes which impel them to the separation.

We hold these truths to be self-evident, that all men are created equal; that they are endowed by their Creator with certain unalienable rights; that among these are life, liberty, and the pursuit of happiness. That, to secure these rights, governments are instituted among men, deriving their just powers from the consent of the governed; that, whenever any form of government becomes destructive of these ends, it is the right of the people to alter or to abolish it, and to institute a new government, laying its foundation on such principles, and organizing its powers in such form, as to them shall seem most likely to effect their safety and happiness. Prudence, indeed, will dictate that governments long established should not be changed for light and transient causes; and, accordingly, all experience hath shown that mankind are more disposed to suffer, while evils are sufferable, than to right themselves by abolishing the forms to which they are accustomed. But when a long train of abuses and usurpations, pursuing invariably the same object, evinces a design to reduce them under absolute despotism, it is their right, it is their duty, to throw off such government and to provide new guards for their future security. Such has been the patient sufferance of these colonies, and such is now the necessity which constrains them to alter their former systems of government. The history of the present King of Great Britain is a history of repeated injuries and usurpations, all having, in direct object, the establishment of an absolute tyranny over these States. To prove this, let facts be submitted to a candid world:

He has refused his assent to laws the most wholesome and necessary for the public good.

He has forbidden his governors to pass laws of immediate and pressing importance, unless suspended in their operation till his assent should be obtained; and, when so suspended, he has utterly neglected to attend to them.

He has refused to pass other laws for the accommodation of large districts of people, unless those people would relinquish the right of representation in the legislature, a right inestimable to them and formidable to tyrants only.

He has called together legislative bodies at places unusual, uncomfortable, and distant from the depository of their public records, for the sole purpose of fatiguing them into compliance with his measures.

He has dissolved representative houses, repeatedly for opposing, with manly firmness, his invasions on the rights of the people.

He has refused, for a long time after such dissolutions, to cause others to be elected; whereby the legislative powers, incapable of annihilation, have returned to the people at large for their exercise; the state remaining, in the meantime, exposed to all the danger of invasion from without and convulsions within.

He has endeavored to prevent the population of these States; for that purpose, obstructing the laws for naturalization of foreigners, refusing to pass others to encourage their migration hither, and raising the conditions of new appropriations of lands.

He has obstructed the administration of justice by refusing his assent to laws for establishing judiciary powers.

He has made judges dependent on his will alone for the tenure of their offices and the amount and payment of their salaries.

He has erected a multitude of new offices and sent hither swarms of officers to harass our people and eat out their substance.

He has kept among us, in time of peace, standing armies, without the consent of our legislatures.

He has affected to render the military independent of, and superior to, the civil power.

He has combined with others to subject us to a jurisdiction foreign to our Constitution and unacknowledged by our laws, giving his assent to their acts of pretended legislation—

For quartering large bodies of armed troops among us;

For protecting them by mock trial, from punishment for any murders which they should commit on the inhabitants of these States;

For cutting off our trade with all parts of the world;

For imposing taxes on us without our consent;

For depriving us, in many cases, of the benefit of trial by jury;

For transporting us beyond seas to be tried for pretended offences;

For abolishing the free system of English laws in a neighboring province, establishing therein an arbitrary government, and enlarging its boundaries, so as to render it at once an example and fit instrument for introducing the same absolute rule into these colonies;

For taking away our charters, abolishing our most valuable laws, and altering, fundamentally, the powers of our governments.

For suspending our own legislatures and declaring themselves invested with power to legislate for us in all cases whatsoever.

He has abdicated government here by declaring us out of his protection and waging war against us.

He has plundered our seas, ravaged our coasts, burnt our towns, and destroyed the lives of our people.

He is, at this time, transporting large armies of foreign mercenaries to complete the works of death, desolation, and tyranny already begun with circumstances of cruelty and perfidy scarcely paralleled in the most barbarous ages, and totally unworthy the head of a civilized nation.

He has constrained our fellow citizens, taken captive on the high seas, to bear arms against their country, to become the executioners of their friends and brethren, or to fall themselves by their hands.

He has excited domestic insurrections amongst us and has endeavored to bring on the inhabitants of our frontiers, the merciless Indian savages, whose known rule of warfare is an undistinguished destruction of all ages, sexes, and conditions.

In every stage of these oppressions, we have petitioned for redress in the most humble terms; our repeated petitions have been answered only by repeated injury. A prince whose character is thus marked by every act which may define a tyrant is unfit to be the ruler of a free people.

Nor have we been wanting in attention to our British brethren. We have warned them, from time to time, of attempts made by their legislature to extend an unwarrantable jurisdiction over us. We have reminded them of the circumstances of our emigration and settlement here. We have appealed to their native justice and magnanimity, and we have conjured them, by the ties of our common kindred, to disavow these usurpations, which would inevitably interrupt our connections and correspondence. They, too, have been deaf to the voice of justice and consanguinity. We must, therefore, acquiesce in the necessity which denounces our separation, and hold them, as we hold the rest of mankind, enemies in war, in peace, friends.

We, therefore, the representatives of the United States of America, in general Congress assembled, appealing to the Supreme Judge of the world for the rectitude of our intentions, do, in the name and by the authority of the good people of these colonies, solemnly publish and declare, that these united colonies are, and of right ought to be, free and independent states: that they are absolved from all allegiance to the British Crown, and that all political connection between them and the state of Great Britain is, and ought to be, totally dissolved; and that, as free and independent states, they have full power to levy war, conclude peace, contract alliances, establish commerce, and to do all other acts and things which independent states may of right do. And, for the support of this declaration, with a firm reliance on the protection of Divine Providence, we mutually pledge to each other our lives, our fortunes, and our sacred honor.

THE ARTICLES OF CONFEDERATION AND PERPETUAL UNION*

Between the states of New Hampshire, Massachusetts-bay Rhode Island and Providence Plantations, Connecticut, New York, New Jersey, Pennsylvania, Delaware, Maryland, Virginia, North Carolina, South Carolina, and Georgia.

ARTICLE 1

The Stile of this Confederacy shall be "The United States of America."

ARTICLE 2

Each state retains its sovereignty, freedom, and independence, and every power, jurisdiction, and right, which is not by this Confederation expressly delegated to the United States, in Congress assembled.

ARTICLE 3

The said States hereby severally enter into a firm league of friendship with each other, for their common defense, the security of their liberties, and their mutual and general welfare, binding themselves to assist each other, against all force offered to, or attacks made upon them, or any of them, on account of religion, sovereignty, trade, or any other pretense whatever.

ARTICLE 4

The better to secure and perpetuate mutual friendship and intercourse among the people of the different States in this Union, the free inhabitants of each of these States, paupers, vagabonds, and fugitives from justice excepted, shall be entitled to all privileges and immunities of free citizens in the several States; and the people of each State shall have free ingress and regress to and from any other State, and shall enjoy therein all the privileges of trade and commerce, subject to the same duties, impositions, and restrictions as the inhabitants thereof respectively, provided that such restrictions shall not extend so far as to prevent the removal of property imported into any State, to any other State of which the owner is an inhabitant; provided also that no imposition, duties or restriction shall be laid by any State, on the property of the United States, or either of them.

If any person guilty of, or charged with, treason, felony, or other high misdemeanor in any State, shall flee from justice, and be found in any of the United States, he shall, upon demand of the Governor or executive power of the State from which he fled, be delivered up and removed to the State having jurisdiction of his offense.

Full faith and credit shall be given in each of these States to the records, acts, and judicial proceedings of the courts and magistrates of every other State.

ARTICLE 5

For the most convenient management of the general interests of the United States, delegates shall be annually appointed in such manner as the legislatures of each State shall direct, to meet in Congress on the first Monday in November, in every year, with a power reserved to each State to recall its delegates, or any of them, at any time within the year, and to send others in their stead for the remainder of the year.

No State shall be represented in Congress by less than two, nor by more than seven members; and no person shall be capable of being a delegate for more than three years in any term of six years; nor shall any person, being a delegate, be capable of holding any office under the United States, for which he, or another for his benefit, receives any salary, fees or emolument of any kind.

Each State shall maintain its own delegates in a meeting of the States, and while they act as members of the committee of the States.

In determining questions in the United States in Congress assembled, each State shall have one vote.

Freedom of speech and debate in Congress shall not be impeached or questioned in any court or place out of Congress, and the members of Congress shall be protected in

---

*Agreed to in Congress November 15, 1777; ratified March 1781.

their persons from arrests or imprisonments, during the time of their going to and from, and attendence on Congress, except for treason, felony, or breach of the peace.

ARTICLE 6

No State, without the consent of the United States in Congress assembled, shall send any embassy to, or receive any embassy from, or enter into any conference, agreement, alliance or treaty with any King, Prince or State; nor shall any person holding any office of profit or trust under the United States, or any of them, accept any present, emolument, office or title of any kind whatever from any King, Prince or foreign State; nor shall the United States in Congress assembled, or any of them, grant any title of nobility.

No two or more States shall enter into any treaty, confederation or alliance whatever between them, without the consent of the United States in Congress assembled, specifying accurately the purposes for which the same is to be entered into, and how long it shall continue.

No State shall lay any imposts or duties, which may interfere with any stipulations in treaties, entered into by the United States in Congress assembled, with any King, Prince or State, in pursuance of any treaties already proposed by Congress, to the courts of France and Spain.

No vessel of war shall be kept up in time of peace by any State, except such number only, as shall be deemed necessary by the United States in Congress assembled, for the defense of such State, or its trade; nor shall any body of forces be kept up by any State in time of peace, except such number only, as in the judgement of the United States in Congress assembled, shall be deemed requisite to garrison the forts necessary for the defense of such State; but every State shall always keep up a well-regulated and disciplined militia, sufficiently armed and accoutered, and shall provide and constantly have ready for use, in public stores, a due number of filed pieces and tents, and a proper quantity of arms, ammunition and camp equipage.

No State shall engage in any war without the consent of the United States in Congress assembled, unless such State be actually invaded by enemies, or shall have received certain advice of a resolution being formed by some nation of Indians to invade such State, and the danger is so imminent as not to admit of a delay, till the United States in Congress assembled can be consulted; nor shall any State grant commissions to any ships or vessels of war, nor letters of marque or reprisal, except it be after a declaration of war by the United States in Congress assembled, and then only against the Kingdom or State and the subjects thereof, against which war has been so declared, and under such regulations as shall be established by the United States in Congress assembled, unless such State be infested by pirates, in which case vessels of war may be fitted out for that occasion, and kept so long as the danger shall continue, or until the United States in Congress assembled shall determine otherwise.

ARTICLE 7

When land forces are raised by any State for the common defense, all officers of or under the rank of colonel, shall be appointed by the legislature of each State respectively, by whom such forces shall be raised, or in such manner as such State shall direct, and all vacancies shall be filled up by the State which first made the appointment.

ARTICLE 8

All charges of war, and all other expenses that shall be incurred for the common defense or general welfare, and allowed by the United States in Congress assembled, shall be defrayed out of a common treasury, which shall be supplied by the several States in proportion to the value of all land within each State, granted to or surveyed for any person, as such land and the buildings and improvements thereon shall be estimated according to such mode as the United States in Congress assembled, shall from time to time direct and appoint.

The taxes for paying that proportion shall be laid and levied by the authority and direction of the legislatures of the several States within the time agreed upon by the United States in Congress assembled.

ARTICLE 9

The United States in Congress assembled, shall have the sole and exclusive right and power of determining on peace and war, except in the cases mentioned in the sixth article; of sending and receiving ambassadors; entering into treaties and alliances, provided that no treaty of commerce shall be made whereby the legislative power of the respective States shall be restrained from imposing such imposts and duties on foreigners, as their own people are subjected to, or from prohibiting the exportation or importation of any species of goods or commodities whatsoever; of establishing rules for deciding in all cases, what captures on land or water shall be legal, and in what manner prizes taken by land or naval forces in the service of the United States shall be divided or appropriated; of granting letters of marque and reprisal in times of peace; appointing courts for the trial of piracies and felonies committed on the high seas and establishing courts for receiving and determining finally appeals in all cases of captures, provided that no member of Congress shall be appointed a judge of any of the said courts.

The United States in Congress assembled shall also be the last resort on appeal in all disputes and differences now subsisting or that hereafter may arise between two or more States concerning boundary, jurisdiction or any other causes whatever; which authority shall always be exercised in the manner following. Whenever the legislative or executive authority or lawful agent of any State in controversy with another shall present a petition to Congress stating the matter in question and praying for a hearing, notice thereof shall be given by order of Congress to the legislative or executive authority of the other State in controversy, and a day assigned for the appearance of the parties by their lawful agents, who shall then be directed to appoint by joint consent, commissioners or judges to constitute a court for hearing and determining the matter in question: but if they cannot agree, Congress shall name three persons out of each of the United States, and from the list of such persons each party shall alternately strike out one, the petitioners beginning, until the number shall be reduced to thirteen; and from that number not less than seven, nor more than nine names as Congress shall direct, shall in the presence of Congress be drawn out by lot, and the persons whose names shall be so drawn or any five of them, shall be commissioners or judges, to hear and finally determine the controversy, so always as a major part of the judges who shall hear the cause shall agree in the determination: and if either party shall neglect to attend at the day appointed, without showing reasons, which Congress shall judge sufficient, or being present shall refuse to strike, the Congress shall proceed to nominate three persons out of each State, and the secretary of Congress shall strike in behalf of such party absent or refusing; and the judgement and sentence of the court to be appointed, in the manner before prescribed, shall be final and conclusive; and if any of the parties shall refuse to submit to the authority of such court, or to appear or defend their claim or cause, the court shall nevertheless proceed to pronounce sentence, or judgement, which shall in like manner be final and decisive, the judgement or sentence and other proceedings being in either case transmitted to Congress, and lodged among the acts of Congress for the security of the parties concerned: provided that every commissioner, before he sits in judgement, shall take an oath to be administered by one of the judges of the supreme or superior court of the State, where the cause shall be tried, "well and truly to hear and determine the matter in question, according to the best of his judgement, without favor, affection or hope of reward:" provided also, that no State shall be deprived of territory for the benefit of the United States.

All controversies concerning the private right of soil claimed under different grants of two or more States, whose jurisdictions as they may respect such lands, and the States which passed such grants are adjusted, the said grants or either of them being at the same time claimed to have originated antecedent to such settlement of jurisdiction, shall on the petition of either party to the Congress of the United States, be finally determined as near as may be in the same manner as is before prescribed for deciding disputes respecting territorial jurisdiction between different States.

The United States in Congress assembled shall also have the sole and exclusive right and power of regulating the alloy and value of coin struck by their own authority, or by that of the respective States; fixing the standards of weights and measures throughout the United States; regulating the trade and managing all affairs with the Indians not members of any of the States; provided that the legislative right of any State within its own limits be not infringed or violated; establishing or regulating post offices from one State to another, throughout all the United States, and exacting such postage on the papers passing through the same as may be requisite to defray the expenses of the said office; appointing all officers of the land forces in the service of the United States, excepting regimental officers; appointing all the officers of the naval forces, and commissioning all officers whatever in the service of the United States; making rules for the government and regulation of the said land and naval forces, and directing their operations.

The United States in Congress assembled shall have authority to appoint a committee, to sit in the recess of Congress, to be denominated "A Committee of the States," and to consist of one delegate from each State; and to appoint such other committees and civil officers as may be necessary for managing the general affairs of the United States under their direction; to appoint one of their members to preside, provided that no person be allowed to serve in the office of president more than one year in any term of three years; to ascertain the necessary sums of money to be raised for the service of the United States, and to appropriate and apply the same for defraying the public expenses; to borrow money, or emit bills on the credit of the United States, transmitting every half year to the respective States an account of the sums of money so borrowed or emitted; to build and equip a navy; to agree upon the number of land forces, and to make requisitions from each State for its quota, in proportion to the number of white inhabitants in such State; which requisition shall be binding, and thereupon the legislature of each State shall appoint the regimental officers, raise the men and cloath, arm and equip them in a soldierlike manner, at the expense of the United States; and the officers and men so cloathed, armed and equipped shall march to the place appointed, and within the time agreed on by the United States in Congress assembled; but if the United States in Congress assembled shall, on consideration of circumstances judge proper that any State should not raise men, or should raise a smaller number of men than the quota thereof, such extra number shall be raised, officered, cloathed, armed and equipped in the same manner as the quota of each State, unless the legislature of such State shall judge that such extra number cannot be safely spared out in the same, in which case they shall raise, officer, cloath, arm and equip as many of such extra number as they judge can be safely spared. And the officers and men so cloathed, armed, and equipped, shall march to the place appointed, and within the time agreed on by the United States in Congress assembled.

The United States in Congress assembled shall never engage in a war, nor grant letters of marque or reprisal in time of peace, nor enter into any treaties or alliances, nor coin money, nor regulate the value thereof, nor ascertain the sums and expenses necessary for the defense and welfare of the United States, or any of them, nor emit bills, nor borrow money on the credit of the United States, nor appropriate money, nor agree upon the number of vessels of war, to be built or purchased, or the number of land or sea forces to be raised, nor appoint a commander in chief of the army or navy, unless nine States assent to the same: nor shall a question on any other point, except for adjourning from day to day be determined, unless by the votes of the majority of the United States in Congress assembled.

The Congress of the United States shall have power to adjourn to any time within the year, and to any place within the United States, so that no period of adjournment be for a longer duration than the space of six months, and shall publish the journal of their proceedings monthly, except such parts thereof relating to treaties, alliances or military operations, as in their judge-ment require secrecy; and the yeas and nays of the delegates of each State on any question shall be entered on the journal, when it is desired by any delegates of a State, or any of them, at his or their request shall be furnished with a transcript of the said journal, except such parts as are above excepted, to lay before the legislatures of the several States.

ARTICLE 10

The Committee of the States, or any nine of them, shall be authorized to execute, in the recess of Congress, such of the powers of Congress as the United States in Congress assembled, by the consent of the nine States, shall from time to time think expedient to vest them with; provided that no power be delegated to the said Committee, for the exercise of which, by the Articles of Confederation, the voice of nine States in the Congress of the United States assembled is requisite.

ARTICLE 11

Canada acceding to this confederation, and adjoining in the measures of the United States, shall be admitted into, and entitled to all the advantages of this Union; but no other colony shall be admitted into the same, unless such admission be agreed to by nine States.

ARTICLE 12

All bills of credit emitted, monies borrowed, and debts contracted by, or under the authority of Congress, before the assembling of the United States, in pursuance of the present confederation, shall be deemed and considered as a charge against the United States, for payment and satisfaction whereof the said United States, and the public faith are hereby solemnly pledged.

ARTICLE 13

Every State shall abide by the determination of the United States in Congress assembled, on all questions which by this confederation are submitted to them. And the Articles of this Confederation shall be inviolably observed by every State, and the Union shall be perpetual; nor shall any alteration at any time hereafter be made in any of them; unless such alteration be agreed to in a Congress of the United States, and be afterwards confirmed by the legislatures of every State.

These articles shall be proposed to the legislatures of all the United States, to be considered, and if approved of by them, they are advised to authorize their delegates to ratify the same in the Congress of the United States; which being done, the same shall become conclusive.

THE CONSTITUTION OF THE UNITED STATES OF AMERICA

We the people of the United States, in order to form a more perfect union, establish justice, insure domestic tranquillity, provide for the common defense, promote the general welfare, and secure the blessings of liberty to ourselves and our posterity, do ordain and establish this Constitution for the United States of America.

ARTICLE I

SECTION 1. All legislative powers herein granted shall be vested in a Congress of the United States, which shall consist of a Senate and House of Representatives.

SECTION 2. 1. The House of Representatives shall be composed of members chosen every second year by the people of the several States, and the electors in each State shall have the qualifications requisite for electors of the most numerous branch of the State legislature.

2. No person shall be a representative who shall not have attained to the age of twenty-five years, and been seven years a citizen of the United States, and who shall not, when elected, be an inhabitant of that State in which he shall be chosen.

3. Representatives and direct taxes[1] shall be apportioned among the several States which may be included within this Union, according to their respective numbers, which shall be determined by adding to the whole number of free persons, including those bound to service for a term of years, and excluding Indians not taxed, three fifths of all other persons.[2] The actual enumeration shall be made within three years after the first meeting of the Congress of the United States, and within every subsequent term of ten years, in such manner as they shall by law direct. The number of representatives shall not exceed one for every thirty thousand, but each State shall have at least one representative; and until such enumeration shall be made,

the State of New Hampshire shall be entitled to choose three, Massachusetts eight, Rhode Island and Providence Plantations one, Connecticut five, New York six, New Jersey four, Pennsylvania eight, Delaware one, Maryland six, Virginia ten, North Carolina five, South Carolina five, and Georgia three.

4. When vacancies happen in the representation from any State, the executive authority thereof shall issue writs of election to fill such vacancies.

5. The House of Representatives shall choose their speaker and other officers; and shall have the sole power of impeachment.

SECTION 3. 1. The Senate of the United States shall be composed of two senators from each State, chosen by the legislature thereof,[3] for six years; and each senator shall have one vote.

2. Immediately after they shall be assembled in consequence of the first election, they shall be divided as equally as may be into three classes. The seats of the senators of the first class shall be vacated at the expiration of the second year, of the second class at the expiration of the fourth year, and of the third class at the expiration of the sixth year, so that one third may be chosen every second year; and if vacancies happen by resignation, or otherwise, during the recess of the legislature of any State, the executive thereof may make temporary appointments until the next meeting of the legislature, which shall then fill such vacancies.[4]

3. No person shall be a senator who shall not have attained to the age of thirty years, and been nine years a citizen of the United States, and who shall not, when elected, be an inhabitant of that State for which he shall be chosen.

4. The Vice President of the United States shall be President of the Senate, but shall have no vote, unless they be equally divided.

5. The Senate shall choose their other officers, and also a president pro tempore, in the absence of the Vice President,

---

[1]See the Sixteenth Amendment.
[2]See the Fourteenth Amendment.

[3]See the Seventeenth Amendment.
[4]See the Seventeenth Amendment.

or when he shall exercise the office of the President of the United States.

6. The Senate shall have the sole power to try all impeachments. When sitting for that purpose, they shall be on oath or affirmation. When the President of the United States is tried, the chief justice shall preside: and no person shall be convicted without the concurrence of two thirds of the members present.

7. Judgment in cases of impeachment shall not extend further than to removal from office, and disqualification to hold and enjoy any office of honor, trust or profit under the United States: but the party convicted shall nevertheless be liable and subject to indictment, trial, judgment and punishment, according to law.

SECTION 4. 1. The times, places, and manner of holding elections for senators and representatives, shall be prescribed in each State by the legislature thereof; but the Congress may at any time by law make or alter such regulations, except as to the places of choosing senators.

2. The Congress shall assemble at least once in every year, and such meeting shall be on the first Monday in December, unless they shall by law appoint a different day.

SECTION 5. 1. Each House shall be the judge of the elections, returns and qualifications of its own members, and a majority of each shall constitute a quorum to do business; but a smaller number may adjourn from day to day, and may be authorized to compel the attendance of absent members, in such manner, and under such penalties as each House may provide.

2. Each House may determine the rules of its proceedings, punish its members for disorderly behavior, and, with the concurrence of two thirds, expel a member.

3. Each House shall keep a journal of its proceedings, and from time to time publish the same, excepting such parts as may in their judgment require secrecy; and the yeas and nays of the members of either House on any question shall, at the desire of one fifth of those present, be entered on the journal.

4. Neither House, during the session of Congress, shall, without the consent of the other, adjourn for more than three days, nor to any other place than that in which the two Houses shall be sitting.

SECTION 6. 1. The senators and representatives shall receive a compensation for their services, to be ascertained by law, and paid out of the Treasury of the United States. They shall in all cases, except treason, felony, and breach of the peace, be privileged from arrest during their attendance at the session of their respective Houses, and in going to and returning from the same; and for any speech or debate in either House, they shall not be questioned in any other place.

2. No senator or representative shall, during the time for which he was elected, be appointed to any civil office under the authority of the United States, which shall have been created, or the emoluments whereof shall have been increased, during such time; and no person holding any office under the United States shall be a member of either House during his continuance in office.

SECTION 7. 1. All bills for raising revenue shall originate in the House of Representatives; but the Senate may propose or concur with amendments as on other bills.

2. Every bill which shall have passed the House of Representatives and the Senate, shall, before it become a law, be presented to the President of the United States; If he approves he shall sign it, but if not he shall return it, with his objections, to that House in which it shall have originated, who shall enter the objections at large on their journal, and proceed to reconsider it. If after such reconsideration two thirds of that House shall agree to pass the bill, it shall be sent, together with the objections, to the other House, by which it shall likewise be reconsidered, and if approved by two thirds of that House, it shall become a law. But in all such cases the votes of both Houses shall be determined by yeas and nays, and the names of the persons voting for and against the bill shall be entered on the journal of each House respectively. If any bill shall not be returned by the President within ten days (Sundays excepted) after it shall have been presented to him, the same shall be a law, in like manner as if he had signed it, unless the Congress by their adjournment prevent its return, in which case it shall not be a law.

3. Every order, resolution, or vote to which the concurrence of the Senate and the House of Representatives may be necessary (except on a question of adjournment) shall be presented to the President of the United States; and before the same shall take effect, shall be approved by him, or being disapproved by him, shall be repassed by two thirds of the Senate and House of Representatives, according to the rules and limitations prescribed in the case of a bill.

SECTION 8. The Congress shall have the power

1. To lay and collect taxes, duties, imposts, and excises, to pay the debts and provide for the common defense and general welfare of the United States; but all duties, imposts, and excises shall be uniform throughout the United States.

2. To borrow money on the credit of the United States;

3. To regulate commerce with foreign nations, and among the several States, and with the Indian tribes;

4. To establish a uniform rule of naturalization, and uniform laws on the subject of bankruptcies throughout the United States;

5. To coin money, regulate the value thereof, and of foreign coin, and fix the standard of weights and measures;

6. To provide for the punishment of counterfeiting the securities and current coin of the United States;

7. To establish post offices and post roads;

8. To promote the progress of science and useful arts, by securing for limited times to authors and inventors the exclusive right to their respective writings and discoveries;

9. To constitute tribunals inferior to the Supreme Court;

10. To define and punish piracies and felonies committed on the high seas, and offenses against the law of nations;

11. To declare war, grant letters of marque and reprisal, and make rules concerning captures on land and water;

12. To raise and support armies, but no appropriation of money to that use shall be for a longer term than two years;

13. To provide and maintain a navy;

14. To make rules for the government and regulation of the land and naval forces;

15. To provide for calling forth the militia to execute the laws of the Union, suppress insurrections and repel invasions;

16. To provide for organizing, arming, and disciplining the militia, and for governing such part of them as may be employed in the service of the United States, reserving to the States respectively, the appointment of the officers, and the authority of training the militia according to the discipline prescribed by Congress;

17. To exercise exclusive legislation in all cases whatsoever, over such district (not exceeding ten miles square) as may, by cession of particular States, and the acceptance of Congress, become the seat of the government of the United States, and to exercise like authority over all places purchased by the consent of the legislature of the State in which the same shall be, for the erection of forts, magazines, arsenals, dockyards, and other needful buildings; and

18. To make all laws which shall be necessary and proper for carrying into execution the foregoing powers, and all other powers vested by this Constitution in the government of the United States, or any department or officer thereof.

SECTION 9. 1. The migration or importation of such persons as any of the States now existing shall think proper to admit, shall not be prohibited by the Congress prior to the year one thousand eight hundred and eight, but a tax or duty may be imposed on such importation, not exceeding ten dollars for each person.

2. The privilege of the writ of habeas corpus shall not be suspended, unless when in cases of rebellion or invasion the public safety may require it.

3. No bill of attainder or ex post facto law shall be passed.

4. No capitation, or other direct, tax shall be laid, unless in proportion to the census or enumeration herein-before directed to be taken.[5]

5. No tax or duty shall be laid on articles exported from any State.

6. No preference shall be given by any regulation of commerce or revenue to the ports of one State over those of another: nor shall vessels bound to, or from, one State be obliged to enter, clear, or pay duties in another.

7. No money shall be drawn from the treasury, but in consequence of appropriations made by law; and a regular statement and account of the receipts and expenditures of all public money shall be published from time to time.

8. No title of nobility shall be granted by the United States: and no person holding any office of profit or trust under them, shall, without the consent of the Congress, accept of any present, emolument, office, or title, of any kind whatever, from any king, prince, or foreign State.

SECTION 10. 1. No State shall enter into any treaty, alliance, or confederation; grant letters of marque and reprisal; coin money; emit bills of credit; make any thing but gold and silver coin a tender in payment of debts; pass any bill of attainder, ex post facto law, or law impairing the obligation of contracts, or grant, any title of nobility.

2. No State shall, without the consent of the Congress, lay any imposts or duties on imports or exports, except what may be absolutely necessary for executing its inspection laws: and the net produce of all duties and imposts laid by any State on imports or exports, shall be for the use of the treasury of the United States; and all such laws shall be subject to the revision and control of the Congress.

3. No State shall, without the consent of the Congress, lay any duty of tonnage, keep troops, or ships of war in time of peace, enter into any agreement or compact with another State, or with a foreign power, or engage in war, unless actually invaded, or in such imminent danger as will not admit of delay.

ARTICLE II

SECTION 1. 1. The executive power shall be vested in a President of the United States of America. He shall hold his office during the term of four years, and, together with the Vice President, chosen for the same term, be elected, as follows:

2. Each State shall appoint, in such manner as the legislature thereof may direct, a number of electors, equal to the whole number of senators and representatives to which the State may be entitled in the Congress: but no senator or representative, or person holding any office of trust or profit under the United States, shall be appointed an elector.

The electors shall meet in their respective States, and vote by ballot for two persons, of whom one at least shall not be an inhabitant of the same State with themselves. And they shall make a list of all the persons voted for, and of the number of votes for each; which list they shall sign and certify, and transmit sealed to the seat of the government of the United States, directed to the president of the Senate. The president of the Senate shall, in the presence of the Senate and House of Representatives, open all the certificates, and the votes shall then be counted. The person having the greatest number of votes shall be the President, if such number be a majority of the whole number of electors appointed; and if there be more than one who have such majority, and have an equal number of votes, then the House of Representatives shall immediately choose by ballot one of them for President; and if no person have a majority, then from the five highest on the list the said House shall in like manner choose the President. But in choosing the President, the votes shall be taken by States, the representation from each State having one vote; a quorum for this purpose shall consist of a member or members from two thirds of the States, and a majority of all the States shall be necessary to a choice. In every case after the choice of the President, the person having the greatest number of votes of the electors shall be the Vice President. But if there should remain two or more who have equal votes, the Senate shall choose from them by ballot the Vice President.[6]

3. The Congress may determine the time of choosing the electors, and the day on which they shall give their votes; which day shall be the same throughout the United States.

4. No person except a natural born citizen, or a citizen of the United States, at the time of the adoption of this Constitution, shall be eligible to the office of President; neither shall any person be eligible to the office who shall not have attained to the age of thirty-five years, and been fourteen years a resident within the United States.

5. In case of the removal of the President from office, or of his death, resignation, or inability to discharge the powers and duties of the said office, the same shall devolve on the Vice President, and the congress may by law provide for the case of removal, death, resignation or inability, both of the President and Vice President, declaring what officer shall then act as President, and such officer shall act accordingly until the disability be removed, or a President shall be elected.

6. The President shall, at stated times, receive for his services a compensation which shall neither be increased nor diminished during the period for which he shall have been elected, and he shall not receive within that period any other emolument from the United States, or any of them.

---

[5]See the Sixteenth Amendment.

[6]Superseded by the Twelfth Amendment.

7. Before he enter on the execution of his office, he shall take the following oath or affirmation:—"I do solemnly swear (or affirm) that I will faithfully execute the office of President of the United States, and will to the best of my ability, preserve, protect and defend the Constitution of the United States."

SECTION 2. 1. The President shall be commander in chief of the army and navy of the United States, and of the militia of the several States, when called into the actual service of the United States; he may require the opinion in writing, of the principal officer in each of the executive departments, upon any subject relating to the duties of their respective offices, and he shall have power to grant reprieves and pardons for offenses against the United States, except in cases of impeachment.

2. He shall have power, by and with the advice and consent of the Senate, to make treaties, provided two thirds of the senators present concur; and he shall nominate, and by and with the advice and consent of the Senate, shall appoint ambassadors, other public ministers and consuls, judges of the Supreme Court, and all other officers of the United States, whose appointments are not herein otherwise provided for, and which shall be established by law; but the Congress may by law vest the appointment of such inferior officers, as they think proper, in the President alone, in the courts of laws, or in the heads of departments.

3. The President shall have power to fill up all vacancies that may happen during the recess of the Senate, by granting commissions which shall expire at the end of their next session.

SECTION 3. He shall from time to time give to the Congress information of the state of the Union, and recommend to their consideration such measures as he shall judge necessary and expedient; he may, on extraordinary occasions, convene both Houses, or either of them, and in case of disagreement between them with respect to the time of adjournment, he may adjourn them to such time as he shall think proper; he shall receive ambassadors and other public ministers; he shall take care that the laws be faithfully executed, and shall commission all the officers of the United States.

SECTION 4. The President, Vice President, and all civil officers of the United States, shall be removed from office on impeachment for, and conviction of, treason, bribery, or other high crimes and misdemeanors.

ARTICLE III

SECTION 1. The judicial power of the United States shall be vested in one Supreme Court, and in such inferior courts as the Congress may from time to time ordain and establish. The judges, both of the Supreme and inferior courts, shall hold their offices during good behavior, and shall, at stated times, receive for their services, a compensation, which shall not be diminished during their continuance in office.

SECTION 2. 1. The judicial power shall extend to all cases, in law and equity, arising under this Constitution, the laws of the United States, and treaties made, or which shall be made, under their authority;—to all cases of admiralty and maritime jurisdiction;—to controversies to which the United States shall be a party;[7]—to

controversies between two or more States;—between a State and citizens of another State;—between citizens of different States;—between citizens of the same State claiming lands under grants of different States, and between a State, or the citizens thereof, and foreign States, citizens or subjects.

2. In all cases affecting ambassadors, other public ministers and consuls, and those in which a State shall be party, the Supreme Court shall have original jurisdiction. In all the other cases before mentioned, the Supreme Court shall have appellate jurisdiction, both as to law and fact, with such exceptions, and under such regulations as the Congress shall make.

3. The trial of all crimes, except in cases of impeachment, shall be by jury; and such trial shall be held in the State where the said crimes shall have been committed; but when not committed within any State, the trial shall be such place or places as the congress may by law have directed.

SECTION 3. 1. Treason against the United States shall consist only in levying war against them, or in adhering to their enemies, giving them aid and comfort. No person shall be convicted of treason unless on the testimony of two witnesses to the same overt act, or on confession in open court.

2. The Congress shall have power to declare the punishment of treason, but no attainder of treason shall work corruption of blood, or forfeiture except during the life of the person attained.

ARTICLE IV

SECTION 1. Full faith and credit shall be given in each State to the public acts, records, and judicial proceedings of every other State. And the Congress may by general laws prescribe the manner in which such acts, records and proceedings shall be proved, and the effect thereof.

SECTION 2. 1. The citizens of each State shall be entitled to all privileges and immunities of citizens in the several States.[8]

2. A person charged in any State with treason, felony, or other crime, who shall flee from justice, and be found in another State, shall on demand of the executive authority of the State from which he fled, be delivered up to be removed to the State having jurisdiction of the crime.

3. No person held to service or labor in one State under the laws thereof, escaping into another, shall, in consequence of any law or regulation therein, be discharged from such service or labor, but shall be delivered up on claim of the party to whom such service or labor may be due.[9]

SECTION 3. 1. New States may be admitted by the Congress into this Union; but no new State shall be formed or erected within the jurisdiction of any other State, nor any State be formed by the junction of two or more States, or parts of States, without the consent of the legislatures of the States concerned as well as of the Congress.

2. The Congress shall have power to dispose of and make all needful rules and regulations respecting the territory or other property belonging to the United States; and nothing in this Constitution shall be so construed as to prejudice any claims of the United States, or of any particular State.

---

[7]See the Eleventh Amendment.

[8]See the Fourteenth Amendment, Sec. 1.
[9]See the Thirteenth Amendment.

SECTION 4. The United States shall guarantee to every State in this Union a republican form of government, and shall protect each of them against invasion; and on application of the legislature, or of the executive (when the legislature cannot be convened) against domestic violence.

ARTICLE V

The Congress, whenever two thirds of both Houses shall deem it necessary, shall propose amendments to this Constitution, or, on the application of the legislatures of two thirds of the several States, shall call a convention for proposing amendments, which in either case shall be valid to all intents and purposes, as part of this Constitution, when ratified by the legislatures of three fourths of the several States, or by conventions in three fourths thereof, as the one or the other mode of ratification may be proposed by the Congress; Provided that no amendment which may be made prior to the year one thousand eight hundred and eight shall in any manner affect the first and fourth clauses in the ninth section of the first article; and that no State, without its consent, shall be deprived of its equal suffrage in the Senate.

ARTICLE VI

1. All debts contracted and engagements entered into, before the adoption of this Constitution, shall be as valid against the United States under this Constitution, as under the Confederation.[10]

2. This Constitution, and the laws of the United States which shall be made in pursuance thereof; and all treaties made, or which shall be made, under the authority of the United States, shall be the supreme law of the land; and the judges in every State shall be bound thereby, any thing in the Constitution or laws of any State to the contrary notwithstanding.

3. The senators and representatives before mentioned, and the members of the several State legislatures, and all executive and judicial officers, both of the United States and of the several States, shall be bound by oath or affirmation to support this Constitution; but no religious test shall ever be required as a qualification to any office or public trust under the United States.

ARTICLE VII

The ratification of the conventions of nine States shall be sufficient for the establishment of this Constitution between the States so ratifying the same.

Done in Convention by the unanimous consent of the States present the seventeenth day of September in the year of our Lord one thousand seven hundred and eighty-seven, and of the independence of the United States of America the twelfth. In witness whereof we have hereunto subscribed our names.

[Signatories' names omitted]

* * *

Articles in addition to, and amendment of, the Constitution of the United States of America, proposed by Congress, and ratified by the legislatures of the several States, pursuant to the fifth article of the original Constitution.

---

[10]See the Fourteenth Amendment, Sec. 4.

Amendment I
[First ten amendments ratified December 15, 1791]

Congress shall make no law respecting an establishment of religion, or prohibiting the free exercise thereof; or abridging the freedom of speech, or of the press; or the right of the people peaceably to assemble, and to petition the government for a redress of grievances.

Amendment II

A well regulated militia, being necessary to the security of a free State, the right of the people to keep and bear arms, shall not be infringed.

Amendment III

No soldier shall, in time of peace be quartered in any house, without the consent of the owner, nor in time of war, but in a manner to be prescribed by law.

Amendment IV

The right of the people to be secure in their persons, houses, papers, and effects, against unreasonable searches and seizures, shall not be violated, and no warrants shall issue, but upon probable cause, supported by oath or affirmation, and particularly describing the place to be searched, and the persons or things to be seized.

Amendment V

No person shall be held to answer for a capital or otherwise infamous crime, unless on a presentment or indictment of a grand jury, except in cases arising in the land or naval forces, or in the militia, when in actual service in time of war or public danger; nor shall any person be subject for the same offense to be twice put in jeopardy of life or limb; nor shall be compelled in any criminal case to be a witness against himself, nor be deprived of life, liberty, or property, without due process of law; nor shall private property be taken for public use, without just compensation.

Amendment VI

In all criminal prosecutions, the accused shall enjoy the right to a speedy and public trial, by an impartial jury of the State and district wherein the crime shall have been committed, which district shall have been previously ascertained by law, and to be informed of the nature and cause of the accusation; to be confronted with the witnesses against him; to have compulsory process for obtaining witnesses in his favor, and to have the assistance of counsel for his defense.

Amendment VII

In suits at common law, where the value in controversy shall exceed twenty dollars, the right of trial by jury shall be preserved, and no fact tried by a jury shall be otherwise reexamined in any court of the United States, than according to the rules of the common law.

Amendment VIII

Excessive bail shall not be required, nor excessive fines imposed, nor cruel and unusual punishments inflicted.

Amendment IX

The enumeration in the Constitution of certain rights shall not be construed to deny or disparage others retained by the people.

Amendment X

The powers not delegated to the United States by the Constitution, nor prohibited by it to the States, are reserved to the States respectively, or to the people.

Amendment XI [January 8, 1798]

The judicial power of the United States shall not be construed to extend to any suit in law or equity, commended or prosecuted against one of the United States by citizens of another State, or by citizens or subjects of any foreign State.

Amendment XII [September 25, 1804]

The electors shall meet in their respective States, and vote by ballot for President and Vice President, one of whom, at least, shall not be an inhabitant of the same State with themselves; they shall name in their ballots the person voted for as President, and in distinct ballots, the person voted for as Vice President, and they shall make distinct lists of all persons voted for as President and of all persons voted for as Vice President, and of the number of votes for each, which lists they shall sign and certify, and transmit sealed to the seat of the government of the United States, directed to the President of the Senate;—The President of the Senate shall, in the presence of the Senate and House of Representatives, open all the certificates and the votes shall then be counted;—The person having the greatest number of votes for President, shall be the President, if such number be a majority of the whole number of electors appointed; and if no person have such majority, then from the persons having the highest numbers not exceeding three on the list of those voted for as President, the House of Representatives shall choose immediately, by ballot, the President. But in choosing the President, the votes shall be taken by States, the representation from each State having one vote; a quorum for this purpose shall consist of a member or members from two thirds of the States, and a majority of all the States shall be necessary to a choice. And if the House of Representatives shall not choose a President whenever the right of choice shall devolve upon them, before the fourth day of March next following, then the Vice President shall act as President, as in the case of the death or other constitutional disability of the President. The person having the greatest number of votes as Vice President shall be the Vice President, if such number be a majority of the whole number of electors appointed, and if no person have a majority, then from the two highest numbers on the list, the Senate shall choose the Vice President; a quorum for the purpose shall consist of two thirds of the whole number of Senators, and a majority of the whole number shall be necessary to a choice. But no person constitutionally ineligible to the office of President shall be eligible to that of Vice President of the United States.

Amendment XIII [December 18, 1865]

SECTION 1. Neither slavery nor involuntary servitude, except as a punishment for crime whereof the party shall have been duly convicted, shall exist within the United States, or any place subject to their jurisdiction.

SECTION 2. Congress shall have power to enforce this article by appropriate legislation.

Amendment XIV [July 28, 1868]

SECTION 1. All persons born or naturalized in the United States, and subject to the jurisdiction thereof, are citizens of the United States and of the State wherein they reside. No State shall make or enforce any law which shall abridge the privileges or immunities of citizens of the United States; nor shall any State deprive any person of life, liberty, or property, without due process of law; nor deny to any person within its jurisdiction the equal protection of the laws.

SECTION 2. Representatives shall be apportioned among the several States according to their respective numbers, counting the whole number of persons in each State, excluding Indians not taxed. But when the right to vote at any election for the choice of electors for President and Vice President of the United States, representatives in Congress, the executive and judicial officers of a State, or the members of the legislature thereof, is denied to any of the male inhabitants of such State, being twenty-one years of age, and citizens of the United States, or in any way abridged, except for participating in rebellion, or other crime, the basis of representation there shall be reduced in the proportion which the number of such male citizens shall bear to the whole number of male citizens twenty-one years of age in such State.

SECTION 3. No person shall be a senator or representative in Congress, or elector of President and Vice President, or hold any office, civil or military, under the United States, or under any State, who having previously taken an oath, as a member of Congress, or as an officer of the United States, or as a member of any State legislature, or as an executive or judicial officer of any State, to support the Constitution of the United States, shall have engaged in insurrection or rebellion against the same, or given aid or comfort to the enemies thereof. But Congress may by a vote of two thirds of each House, remove such disability.

SECTION 4. The validity of the public debt of the United States, authorized by law, including debts incurred for payment of pensions and bounties for services in suppressing insurrection or rebellion; shall not be questioned. But neither the United States nor any State shall assume or pay any debt or obligation incurred in aid of insurrection or rebellion against the United States, or any claim for the loss or emancipation of any slave; but all such debts, obligations, and claims shall be held illegal and void.

SECTION 5. The Congress shall have the power to enforce, by appropriate legislation, the provisions of this article.

Amendment XV [March 30, 1870]

SECTION 1. The right of citizens of the United States to vote shall not be denied or abridged by the United States or by any State on account of race, color, or previous condition of servitude.

SECTION 2. The Congress shall have power to enforce this article by appropriate legislation.

Amendment XVI [February 25, 1913]

The Congress shall have power to lay and collect taxes on incomes, from whatever source derived, without apportionment among the several States, and without regard to any census or enumeration.

Amendment XVII [May 31, 1913]

The Senate of the United States shall be composed of two senators from each State, elected by the people thereof, for six years; and each senator shall have one vote. The electors in each State shall have the qualifications requisite for electors of the most numerous branch of the State legislature.

When vacancies happen in the representation of any State in the Senate, the executive authority of such State shall issue writs of election to fill such vacancies: Provided, That the legislature of any State may empower the executive thereof to make temporary appointments until the people fill the vacancies by election as the legislature may direct.

This amendment shall not be so construed as to affect the election or term of any senator chosen before it becomes valid as part of the Constitution.

Amendment XVIII[11] [January 29, 1919]

After one year from the ratification of this article, the manufacture, sale, or transportation of intoxicating liquors within, the importation thereof into, or the exportation thereof from the United States and all territory subject to the jurisdiction thereof for beverage purposes is thereby prohibited.

The Congress and the several States shall have concurrent power to enforce this article by appropriate legislation.

This article shall be inoperative unless it shall have been ratified as an amendment to the Constitution by the legislatures of the several States, as provided in the constitution, within seven years from the date of the submission hereof to the States by Congress.

Amendment XIX [August 26, 1920]

The right of citizens of the United States to vote shall not be denied or abridged by the United States or by any State on account of sex.

Congress shall have the power to enforce this article by appropriate legislation.

Amendment XX [January 23, 1933]

Section 1. The terms of the President and Vice President shall end at noon on the 20th day of January and the terms of Senators and Representatives at noon on the 3d day of January, of the years in which such terms would have ended if this article had not been ratified; and the terms of their successors shall then begin.

Section 2. The Congress shall assemble at least once in every year, and such meeting shall begin at noon on the 3d day of January, unless they shall by law appoint a different day.

Section 3. If, at the time fixed for the beginning of the term of President, the President-elect shall have died, the Vice President-elect shall become President. If a President shall not have been chosen before the time fixed for the beginning of his term, or if the President-elect shall have failed to qualify, then the Vice President-elect shall act as President until a President shall have qualified; and the Congress may by law provide for the case wherein neither a President-elect nor a Vice President-elect shall have qualified, declaring who shall then act as President, or the manner in which one who is to act shall be selected, and such person shall act accordingly until a President or Vice President shall have qualified.

Section 4. The Congress may by law provide for the case of the death of any of the persons from whom, the House of Representatives may choose a President whenever the right of choice shall have devolved upon them, and for the case of the death of any of the persons from whom the Senate may choose a Vice President whenever the right of choice shall have devolved upon them.

Section 5. Sections 1 and 2 shall take effect on the 15th day of October following the ratification of this article.

Section 6. This article shall be inoperative unless it shall have been ratified as an amendment to the Constitution by the legislatures of three-fourths of the several States within seven years from the date of its submission.

Amendment XXI [December 5, 1933]

Section 1. The Eighteenth Article of amendment to the Constitution of the United States is hereby repealed.

Section 2. The transportation or importation into any State, Territory, or possession of the United States for delivery or use therein of intoxicating liquors in violation of the laws thereof, is hereby prohibited.

Section 3. This article shall be inoperative unless it shall have been ratified as an amendment to the Constitution by conventions in the several States, as provided in the Constitution, within seven years from the date of the submission thereof to the States by the Congress.

Amendment XXII [March 1, 1951]

No person shall be elected to the office of the President more than twice, and no person who has held the office of President, or acted as President, for more than two years of a term to which some other person was elected President shall be elected to the office of the President more than once.

But this article shall not apply to any person holding the office of President when this article was proposed by the Congress, and shall not prevent any person who may be holding the office of President, or acting as President, during the term within which this article becomes operative from holding the office of President or acting as President during the remainder of such term.

This article shall be inoperative unless it shall have been ratified as an amendment to the Constitution by the legislatures of three-fourths of the several States within seven years from the date of its submission to the States by the Congress.

Amendment XXIII [March 29, 1961]

Section 1. The District constituting the seat of Government of the United States shall appoint in such manner as the Congress may direct.

A number of electors of President and Vice President equal to the whole number of Senators and Representatives in Congress to which the District would be entitled if it were a State, but in no event more than the least populous State; they shall be in addition to those appointed by the States, but they shall be considered, for the purposes of the election of President and Vice President, to be electors appointed by a State; and they shall meet in the District and perform such duties as provided by the twelfth article of amendment.

Section 2. The Congress shall have power to enforce this article by appropriate legislation.

Amendment XXIV [January 23, 1964]

Section 1. The right of citizens of the United States to vote in any primary or other election for President or Vice President, for electors for President or Vice President, or for Senator or Representative in Congress, shall not be denied or abridged by

---

[11]Repealed by the Twenty-first Amendment

the United States or any State by reason of failure to pay any poll tax or other tax.

SECTION 2. The Congress shall have power to enforce this article by appropriate legislation.

Amendment XXV [February 10, 1967]

SECTION 1. In case of the removal of the President from office or of his death or resignation, the Vice President shall become President.

SECTION 2. Whenever there is a vacancy in the office of the Vice President, the President shall nominate a Vice President who shall take office upon confirmation by a majority of both Houses of Congress.

SECTION 3. Whenever the President transmits to the President pro tempore of the Senate and the Speaker of the House of Representatives his written declaration that he is unable to discharge the powers and duties of his office, and until he transmits to them a written declaration to the contrary, such powers and duties shall be discharged by the Vice President as Acting President.

SECTION 4. Whenever the Vice President and a majority of either the principal officers of the executive departments or of such other body as Congress may by law provide, transmit to the President pro tempore of the Senate and the Speaker of the House of Representatives their written declaration that the President is unable to discharge the powers and duties of his office, the Vice President shall immediately assume the powers and duties of the office as Acting President.

Thereafter, when the President transmits to the President pro tempore of the Senate and the Speaker of the House of Representatives his written declaration that no inability exists, he shall resume the powers and duties of his office unless the Vice President and a majority of either the principal officers of the executive departments or of such other body as Congress may by law provide, transmit within four days to the President pro tempore of the Senate and the Speaker of the House of Representatives their written declaration that the President is unable to discharge the powers and duties of his office. Thereupon Congress shall decide the issue, assembling within forty-eight hours for that purpose if not in session. If the Congress, within twenty-one days after receipt of the latter written declaration, or, if Congress is not in session, within twenty-one days after Congress is required to assemble, determines by two-thirds vote of both Houses that the President is unable to discharge the powers and duties of his office, the Vice President shall continue to discharge the same as Acting President; otherwise, the President shall resume the powers and duties of his office.

Amendment XXVI [June 30, 1971]

SECTION 1. The right of citizens of the United States who are eighteen years of age or older to vote shall not be denied or abridged by the United States or by any State on account of age.

SECTION 2. The Congress shall have power to enforce this article by appropriate legislation.

Amendment XXVII[12] [May 7, 1992]

No law, varying the compensation for services of the Senators and Representatives, shall take effect until an election of Representatives shall have intervened.

---

[12]James Madison proposed this amendment in 1789 together with the ten amendments that were adopted as the Bill of Rights, but it failed to win ratification at the time. Congress, however, had set no deadline for its ratification, and over the years—particularly in the 1980s and 1990s—many states voted to add it to the Constitution. With the ratification of Michigan in 1992 it passed the threshold of 3/4ths of the states required for adoption, but because the process took more than 200 years, its validity remains in doubt.

•◦•─[Read the Document

Admission of States to the Union
Demographics of the United States

PRESIDENTS AND VICE PRESIDENTS

1. George Washington (1789)
   John Adams (1789)

2. John Adams (1797)
   Thomas Jefferson (1797)

3. Thomas Jefferson (1801)
   Aaron Burr (1801)
   George Clinton (1805)

4. James Madison (1809)
   George Clinton (1809)
   Elbridge Gerry (1813)

5. James Monroe (1817)
   Daniel D. Thompkins (1817)

6. John Quincy Adams (1825)
   John C. Calhoun (1825)

7. Andrew Jackson (1829)
   John C. Calhoun (1829)
   Martin Van Buren (1833)

8. Martin Van Buren (1837)
   Richard M. Johnson (1837)

9. William H. Harrison (1841)
   John Tyler (1841)

10. John Tyler (1841)

11. James K. Polk (1845)
    George M. Dallas (1845)

12. Zachary Taylor (1849)
    Millard Fillmore (1849)

13. Millard Fillmore (1850)

14. Franklin Pierce (1853)
    William R. King (1853)

15. James Buchanan (1857)
    John C. Breckinridge (1857)

16. Abraham Lincoln (1861)
    Hannibal Hamlin (1861)
    Andrew Johnson (1865)

17. Andrew Johnson (1865)

18. Ulysses S. Grant (1869)
    Schuyler Colfax (1869)
    Henry Wilson (1873)

19. Rutherford B. Hayes (1877)
    William A. Wheeler (1877)

20. James A. Garfield (1881)
    Chester A. Arthur (1881)

21. Chester A. Arthur (1881)

22. Grover Cleveland (1885)
    T. A. Hendricks (1885)

23. Benjamin Harrison (1889)
    Levi P. Morgan (1889)

24. Grover Cleveland (1893)
    Adlai E. Stevenson (1893)

25. William McKinley (1897)
    Garret A. Hobart (1897)
    Theodore Roosevelt (1901)

26. Theodore Roosevelt (1901)
    Charles Fairbanks (1905)

27. William H. Taft (1909)
    James S. Sherman (1909)

28. Woodrow Wilson (1913)
    Thomas R. Marshall (1913)

29. Warren G. Harding (1921)
    Calvin Coolidge (1921)

30. Calvin Coolidge (1923)
    Charles G. Dawes (1925)

31. Herbert C. Hoover (1929)
    Charles Curtis (1929)

32. Franklin D. Roosevelt (1933)
    John Nance Garner (1933)
    Henry A. Wallace (1941)
    Harry S. Truman (1945)

33. Harry S. Truman (1945)
    Alben W. Barkley (1949)

34. Dwight D. Eisenhower (1953)
    Richard M. Nixon (1953)

35. John F. Kennedy (1961)
    Lyndon B. Johnson (1961)

36. Lyndon B. Johnson (1963)
    Hubert H. Humphrey (1965)

37. Richard M. Nixon (1969)
    Spiro T. Agnew (1969)
    Gerald R. Ford (1973)

38. Gerald R. Ford (1974)
    Nelson A. Rockefeller (1974)

39. James E. Carter Jr. (1977)
    Walter F. Mondale (1977)

40. Ronald W. Reagan (1981)
    George H. Bush (1981)

41. George H. Bush (1989)
    James D. Quayle III (1989)

42. William J. Clinton (1993)
    Albert Gore (1993)

43. George W. Bush (2001)
    Richard Cheney (2001)

44. Barack H. Obama (2009)
    Joseph Biden (2009)

PRESIDENTIAL ELECTIONS

Year	Number of States	Candidates	Party	Popular Vote*	Electoral Vote[†]	Percentage of Popular Vote*
1789	11	GEORGE WASHINGTON	No party designations		69	
		John Adams			34	
		Other Candidates			35	
1792	15	GEORGE WASHINGTON	No party designations		132	
		John Adams			77	
		George Clinton			50	
		Other Candidates			5	
1796	16	JOHN ADAMS	Federalist		71	
		Thomas Jefferson	Democratic-Republican		68	
		Thomas Pinckney	Federalist		59	
		Aaron Burr	Democratic-Republican		30	
		Other Candidates			48	
1800	16	THOMAS JEFFERSON	Democratic-Republican		73	
		Aaron Burr	Democratic-Republican		73	
		John Adams	Federalist		65	
		Charles C. Pinckney	Federalist		64	
		John Jay	Federalist		1	
1804	17	THOMAS JEFFERSON	Democratic-Republican		162	
		Charles C. Pinckney	Federalist		14	
1808	17	JAMES MADISON	Democratic-Republican		122	
		Charles C. Pinckney	Federalist		47	
		George Clinton	Democratic-Republican		6	
1812	18	JAMES MADISON	Democratic-Republican		128	
		DeWitt Clinton	Federalist		89	
1816	19	JAMES MONROE	Democratic-Republican		183	
		Rufus King	Federalist		34	
1820	24	JAMES MONROE	Democratic-Republican		231	
		John Quincy Adams	Independent-Republican		1	
1824	24	JOHN QUINCY ADAMS	Democratic-Republican	108,740	84	30.5
		Andrew Jackson	Democratic-Republican	153,544	99	43.1
		William H. Crawford	Democratic-Republican	46,618	41	13.1
		Henry Clay	Democratic-Republican	47,136	37	13.2
1828	24	ANDREW JACKSON	Democrat	647,286	178	56.0
		John Quincy Adams	National-Republican	508,064	83	44.0
1832	24	ANDREW JACKSON	Democrat	687,502	219	55.0
		Henry Clay	National-Republican	530,189	49	42.4
		William Wirt	Anti-Masonic	33,108	7	
		John Floyd	National-Republican		11	2.6
1836	26	MARTIN VAN BUREN	Democrat	765,483	170	50.9
		William H. Harrison	Whig		73	
		Hugh L. White	Whig	739,795	26	49.1
		Daniel Webster	Whig		14	
		W. P. Mangum	Whig		11	

*Percentage of popular vote given for any election year may not total 100 percent because candidates receiving less than 1 percent of the popular vote have been omitted.
[†]Prior to the passage of the Twelfth Amendment in 1904, the electoral college voted for two presidential candidates; the runner-up became Vice-President. Data from Historical Statistics of the United States, Colonial Times to 1957 (1961), pp. 682–683, and The World Almanac.

PRESIDENTIAL ELECTIONS   (CONTINUED)

Year	Number of States	Candidates	Party	Popular Vote	Electoral Vote	Percentage of Popular Vote
1840	26	WILLIAM H. HARRISON	Whig	1,274,624	234	53.1
		Martin Van Buren	Democrat	1,127,781	60	46.9
1844	26	JAMES K. POLK	Democrat	1,338,464	170	49.6
		Henry Clay	Whig	1,300,097	105	48.1
		James G. Birney	Liberty	62,300		2.3
1848	30	ZACHARY TAYLOR	Whig	1,360,967	163	47.4
		Lewis Cass	Democrat	1,222,342	127	42.5
		Martin Van Buren	Free-Soil	291,263		10.1
1852	31	FRANKLIN PIERCE	Democrat	1,601,117	254	50.9
		Winfield Scott	Whig	1,385,453	42	44.1
		John P. Hale	Free-Soil	155,825		5.0
1856	31	JAMES BUCHANAN	Democrat	1,832,955	174	45.3
		John C. Frémont	Republican	1,339,932	114	33.1
		Millard Fillmore	American ("Know Nothing")	871,731	8	21.6
1860	33	ABRAHAM LINCOLN	Republican	1,865,593	180	39.8
		Stephen A. Douglas	Democrat	1,382,713	12	29.5
		John C. Breckinridge	Democrat	848,356	72	18.1
		John Bell	Constitutional Union	592,906	39	12.6
1864	36	ABRAHAM LINCOLN	Republican	2,206,938	212	55.0
		George B. McClellan	Democrat	1,803,787	21	45.0
1868	37	ULYSSES S. GRANT	Republican	3,013,421	214	52.7
		Horatio Seymour	Democrat	2,706,829	80	47.3
1872	37	ULYSSES S. GRANT	Republican	3,596,745	286	55.6
		Horace Greeley	Democrat	2,843,446		*43.9
1876	38	RUTHERFORD B. HAYES	Republican	4,036,572	185	48.0
		Samuel J. Tilden	Democrat	4,284,020	184	51.0
1880	38	JAMES A. GARFIELD	Republican	4,453,295	214	48.5
		Winfield S. Hancock	Democrat	4,414,082	155	48.1
		James B. Weaver	Greenback-Labor	308,578		3.4
1884	38	GROVER CLEVELAND	Democrat	4,879,507	219	48.5
		James G. Blaine	Republican	4,850,293	182	48.2
		Benjamin F. Butler	Greenback-Labor	175,370		1.8
		John P. St. John	Prohibition	150,369		1.5
1888	38	BENJAMIN HARRISON	Republican	5,447,129	233	47.9
		Grover Cleveland	Democrat	5,537,857	168	48.6
		Clinton B. Fisk	Prohibition	249,506		2.2
		Anson J. Streeter	Union Labor	146,935		1.3
1892	44	GROVER CLEVELAND	Democrat	5,555,426	277	46.1
		Benjamin Harrison	Republican	5,182,690	145	43.0
		James B. Weaver	People's	1,029,846	22	8.5
		John Bidwell	Prohibition	264,133		2.2

*Because of the death of Greeley, Democratic electors scattered their votes.

PRESIDENTIAL ELECTIONS (CONTINUED)

Year	Number of States	Candidates	Party	Popular Vote	Electoral Vote	Percentage of Popular Vote
1896	45	WILLIAM MCKINLEY	Republican	7,102,246	271	51.1
		William J. Bryan	Democrat	6,492,559	176	47.7
1900	45	WILLIAM MCKINLEY	Republican	7,218,491	292	51.7
		William J. Bryan	Democrat; Populist	6,356,734	155	45.5
		John C. Woolley	Prohibition	208,914		1.5
1904	45	THEODORE ROOSEVELT	Republican	7,628,461	336	57.4
		Alton B. Parker	Democrat	5,084,223	140	37.6
		Eugene V. Debs	Socialist	402,283		3.0
		Silas C. Swallow	Prohibition	258,536		1.9
1908	46	WILLIAM H. TAFT	Republican	7,675,320	321	51.6
		William J. Bryan	Democrat	6,412,294	162	43.1
		Eugene V. Debs	Socialist	420,793		2.8
		Eugene W. Chafin	Prohibition	253,840		1.7
1912	48	WOODROW WILSON	Democrat	6,296,547	435	41.9
		Theodore Roosevelt	Progressive	4,118,571	88	27.4
		William H. Taft	Republican	3,486,720	8	23.2
		Eugene V. Debs	Socialist	900,672		6.0
		Eugene W. Chafin	Prohibition	206,275		1.4
1916	48	WOODROW WILSON	Democrat	9,127,695	277	49.4
		Charles E. Hughes	Republican	8,533,507	254	46.2
		A. L. Benson	Socialist	585,113		3.2
		J. Frank Hanly	Prohibition	220,506		1.2
1920	48	WARREN G. HARDING	Republican	16,143,407	404	60.4
		James M. Cox	Democrat	9,130,328	127	34.2
		Eugene V. Debs	Socialist	919,799		3.4
		P. P. Christensen	Farmer-Labor	265,411		1.0
1924	48	CALVIN COOLIDGE	Republican	15,718,211	382	54.0
		John W. Davis	Democrat	8,385,283	136	28.8
		Robert M. La Follette	Progressive	4,831,289	13	16.6
1928	48	HERBERT C. HOOVER	Republican	21,391,993	444	58.2
		Alfred E. Smith	Democrat	15,016,169	87	40.9
1932	48	FRANKLIN D. ROOSEVELT	Democrat	22,809,638	472	57.4
		Herbert C. Hoover	Republican	15,758,901	59	39.7
		Norman Thomas	Socialist	881,951		2.2
1936	48	FRANKLIN D. ROOSEVELT	Democrat	27,752,869	523	60.8
		Alfred M. Landon	Republican	16,674,665	8	36.5
		William Lemke	Union	882,479		1.9
1940	48	FRANKLIN D. ROOSEVELT	Democrat	27,307,819	449	54.8
		Wendell L. Willkie	Republican	22,321,018	82	44.8
1944	48	FRANKLIN D. ROOSEVELT	Democrat	25,606,585	432	53.5
		Thomas E. Dewey	Republican	22,014,745	99	46.0
1948	48	HARRY S TRUMAN	Democrat	24,105,812	303	49.5
		Thomas E. Dewey	Republican	21,970,065	189	45.1
		J. Strom Thurmond	States' Rights	1,169,063	39	2.4
		Henry A. Wallace	Progressive	1,157,172		2.4

PRESIDENTIAL ELECTIONS   (CONTINUED)

Year	Number of States	Candidates	Party	Popular Vote	Electoral Vote		Percentage of Popular Vote
1952	48	DWIGHT D. EISENHOWER	Republican	33,936,234	442		55.1
		Adlai E. Stevenson	Democrat	27,314,992	89		44.4
1956	48	DWIGHT D. EISENHOWER	Republican	35,590,472	457	*	57.6
		Adlai E. Stevenson	Democrat	26,022,752	73		42.1
1960	50	JOHN F. KENNEDY	Democrat	34,227,096	303	†	49.9
		Richard M. Nixon	Republican	34,108,546	219		49.6
1964	50	LYNDON B. JOHNSON	Democrat	42,676,220	486		61.3
		Barry M. Goldwater	Republican	26,860,314	52		38.5
1968	50	RICHARD M. NIXON	Republican	31,785,480	301		43.4
		Hubert H. Humphrey	Democrat	31,275,165	191		42.7
		George C. Wallace	American Independent	9,906,473	46		13.5
1972	50	RICHARD M. NIXON‡	Republican	47,165,234	520		60.6
		George S. McGovern	Democrat	29,168,110	17		37.5
1976	50	JAMES E. CARTER JR.	Democrat	40,828,929	297		50.1
		Gerald R. Ford	Republican	39,148,940	240		47.9
		Eugene McCarthy	Independent	739,256			
1980	50	RONALD W. REAGAN	Republican	43,201,220	489		50.9
		James E. Carter Jr.	Democrat	34,913,332	49		41.2
		John B. Anderson	Independent	5,581,379			
1984	50	RONALD W. REAGAN	Republican	53,428,357	525		59.0
		Walter F. Mondale	Democrat	36,930,923	13		41.0
1988	50	GEORGE H. W. BUSH	Republican	48,901,046	426		53.4
		Michael Dukakis	Democrat	41,809,030	111		45.6
1992	50	WILLIAM J. CLINTON	Democrat	43,728,275	370		43.2
		George H. W. Bush	Republican	38,167,416	168		37.7
		H. Ross Perot	United We Stand, America	19,237,247			19.0
1996	50	WILLIAM J. CLINTON	Democrat	45,590,703	379		49.0
		Robert Dole	Republican	37,816,307	159		41.0
		H. Ross Perot	Reform	7,874,283			8.0
2000	50	GEORGE W. BUSH	Republican	50,459,624	271		47.9
		Albert Gore	Democrat	51,003,328	266		49.4
		Ralph Nader	Green	2,882,985	0		2.7
2004	50	GEORGE W. BUSH	Republican	59,117,523	286		51.1
		John Kerry	Democrat	55,557,584	252		48.0
		Ralph Nader	Green	405,623	0		0.3
2008	50	BARACK H. OBAMA	Democrat	69,456,897	365		52.9
		John McCain	Republican	59,934,814	173		45.7

*Walter B. Jones received 1 electoral vote.

†Harry F. Byrd received 15 electoral votes.

‡Resigned August 9, 1974: Vice President Gerald R. Ford became President.

Acquired Immune Deficiency Syndrome (AIDS)   A complex of deadly pathologies resulting from infection with the human immunodeficiency virus (HIV).

Act of Toleration   Act passed in 1661 by King Charles II ordering a stop to religious persecution in Massachusetts.

Affirmative action   A set of policies to open opportunities in business and education for members of minority groups and women by allowing race and sex to be factors included in decisions to hire, award contracts, or admit students to higher education programs.

Alamo   Franciscan mission at San Antonio, Texas that was the site in 1836 of a siege and massacre of Texans by Mexican troops.

Albany Conference   A 1754 meeting, held in Albany, NY, between the British and leaders of the Iroquois Confederacy.

Albany Movement   Coalition formed in 1961 in Albany, a small city in southwest Georgia, of activists from SNCC, the NAACP, and other local groups.

Alien Act   Act passed by Congress in 1798 that authorized the president to imprison or deport suspected aliens during wartime.

Alliance for Progress   Program of economic aid to Latin America during the Kennedy administration.

Allies   In World War I, Britain, France, Russia, and other belligerent nations fighting against the Central Powers but not including the United States.

American Colonization Society   Organization founded in 1817 by antislavery reformers, that called for gradual emancipation and the removal of freed blacks to Africa.

American Federation of Labor (AFL)   Union formed in 1886 that organized skilled workers along craft lines and emphasized a few workplace issues rather than a broad social program.

American Indian Movement (AIM)   Group of Native-American political activists who used confrontations with the federal government to publicize their case for Indian rights.

American Society for the Promotion of Temperance   Largest reform organization of its time dedicated to ending the sale and consumption of alcoholic beverages.

American System   A technique of production pioneered in the United States in the first half of the nineteenth century that relied on precision manufacturing with the use of interchangeable parts.

American System   The program of government subsidies favored by Henry Clay and his followers to promote American economic growth and protect domestic manufacturers from foreign competition.

Americans with Disabilities Act   An act that required employers to provide access to their facilities for qualified employees with disabilities.

Annapolis Convention   Conference of state delegates at Annapolis, Maryland, that issued a call in September 1786 for a convention to meet at Philadelphia to consider fundamental changes.

Anti-Federalists   Opponents of the Constitution in the debate over its ratification.

Archaic period   The period roughly 10,000 to 2,500 years ago marked by the retreat of glaciers.

Articles of Confederation   Written document setting up the loose confederation of states that comprised the first national government of the United States.

Athapascan   A people that began to settle the forests in the northwestern area of North America around 5000 BCE.

Atlantic Charter   Statement of common principles and war aims developed by President Franklin Roosevelt and British Prime Minister Winston Churchill at a meeting in August 1941.

Axis powers   The opponents of the United States and its allies in World War II.

Aztecs   A warrior people who dominated the Valley of Mexico from 1100–1521.

Bank War   The political struggle between President Andrew Jackson and the supporters of the Second Bank of the United States.

Battle of the Bulge   German offensive in December 1944 that penetrated deep into Belgium (creating a "bulge"). Allied forces, while outnumbered, attacked from the north and south. By January 1945, the German forces were destroyed or routed, but not without some 77,000 Allied casualties.

Bay of Pigs   Site in Cuba of an unsuccessful landing by fourteen hundred anti-Castro Cuban refugees in April 1961.

Beatnik   Term used to designate members of the Beats.

Beats   A group of writers from the 50s whose writings challenged American culture.

Beaver Wars   Series of bloody conflicts, occurring between 1640s and 1680s, during which the Iroquois fought the French for control of the fur trade in the east and the Great Lakes region.

Beringia   A subcontinent bridging Asia and North America, named after the Bering Straits.

Berlin blockade   Three-hundred-day Soviet blockade of land access to United States, British, and French occupation zones in Berlin, 1948–1949.

Bill for Establishing Religious Freedom   A bill authored by Thomas Jefferson establishing religious freedom in Virginia.

Bill of Rights   A written summary of inalienable rights and liberties. The first ten amendments to the Constitution.

Black codes   Laws passed by states and municipalities denying many rights of citizenship to free black people.

Black Panther Party   Political and social movement among black Americans, founded in Oakland, California, in 1966 and emphasizing black economic and political power.

Black Power   Philosophy emerging after 1965 that real economic and political gains for African Americans could come only through self-help, self-determination, and organizing for direct political influence.

Bleeding Kansas   Violence between pro- and antislavery forces in Kansas Territory after the passage of the Kansas-Nebraska Act in 1854.

Blitzkrieg   German war tactic in World War II ("lightning war") involving the concentration of air and armored firepower to punch and exploit holes in opposing defensive lines.

Bohemian   Artistic individual who lives with disregard for the conventional rules of behavior.

Bolsheviks   Members of the Communist movement in Russia that established the Soviet government after the 1917 Russian Revolution.

Bonus Army   Unemployed veterans of World War I gathering in Washington in 1932 demanding payment of service bonuses not due until 1945.

Bosnia   A nation in southeast Europe that split off from Yugoslavia and became the site of bitter civil and religious war, requiring NATO and U.S. intervention in the 1990s.

Boston Massacre   After months of increasing friction between townspeople and the British troops stationed in the city, on March 5, 1770, British troops fired on American civilians in Boston.

Boston Tea Party   Incident that occurred on December 16, 1773, in which Bostonians, disguised as Indians, destroyed £18,000 worth of tea belonging to the British East India Company in order to prevent payment of the duty on it.

Brown v. Board of Education   Supreme Court decision in 1954 that declared that "separate but equal" schools for children of different races violated the Constitution.

Cahokia   One of the largest urban centers created by Mississippian peoples, containing 30,000 residents in 1250.

Californios   Californians of Spanish descent.

Calvinist Theology of Election   Belief that salvation was the result of God's sovereign decree and that few people would receive God's grace.

Camp David Accords   Agreement signed by Israel in Egypt in 1978 that set the formal terms for peace in the Middle East.

Carpetbaggers   Northern transplants to the South, many of whom were Union soldiers who stayed in the South after the war.

Central Intelligence Agency (CIA)   Agency established in 1947 that coordinates the gathering and evaluation of military and economic information on other nations.

Central Powers   Germany and its World War I allies in Austria, Italy, Turkey, and Bulgaria.

Chinese Exclusion Act   Act which suspended Chinese immigration, limited the civil rights of resident Chinese, and forbade their naturalization.

Civil Rights Act of 1964   Federal legislation that outlawed discrimination in public accommodations and employment on the basis of race, skin color, sex, religion, or national origin.

Civil Rights Bill   The 1866 act that gave full citizenship to African Americans.

Clayton Antitrust Act   Replaced the old Sherman Act of 1890 as the nation's basic antitrust law. It exempted unions from being construed as illegal combinations in restraint of trade, and it forbade federal courts from issuing injunctions against strikers.

Coercive Acts   Legislation passed by Parliament in 1774; included the Boston Port Act, the Massachusetts Government Act, the Administration of Justice Act, and the Quartering Act of 1774.

Cold War   The political and economic confrontation between the Soviet Union and the United States that dominated world affairs from 1946 to 1989.

Committee for Industrial Organizations (CIO)   An alliance of industrial unions that spurred the 1930s organizational drive among the mass-production industries.

Committee on Public Information (CPI)   Government agency during World War I that sought to shape public opinion in support of the war effort through newspapers, pamphlets, speeches, films, and other media.

Compromise of 1850   The four-step compromise which admitted California as a free state, allowed the residents of the New Mexico and Utah territories to decide the slavery issue for themselves, ended the slave trade in the District of Columbia, and passed a new fugitive slave law to enforce the constitutional provision stating that a slave escaping into a free state shall be delivered back to the owner.

Compromise of 1877   The Congressional settling of the 1876 election which installed Republican Rutherford B. Hayes in the White House and gave Democrats control of all state governments in the South.

Confederate States of America   Nation proclaimed in Montgomery, Alabama, in February 1861, after the seven states of the Lower South seceded from the United States.

Congress of Racial Equality (CORE)   Civil rights group formed in 1942 and committed to nonviolent civil disobedience.

Congressional Reconstruction   Name given to the period 1867–1870 when the Republican-dominated Congress controlled Reconstruction-era policy.

Conspicuous consumption   Highly visible displays of wealth and consumption.

Constitution   The written document providing for a new central government of the United States.

Constitutional Convention   Convention of delegates from the colonies that first met to organize resistance to the Intolerable Acts.

Constitutional Union Party   National party formed in 1860, mainly by former Whigs, that emphasized allegiance to the Union and strict enforcement of all national legislation.

Continental Army   The regular or professional army authorized by the Second Continental Congress and commanded by General George Washington during the Revolutionary War.

Contract with America   Platform proposing a sweeping reduction in the role and activities of the federal government on which many Republican candidates ran for Congress in 1994.

Contras   Nicaraguan exiles armed and organized by the CIA to fight the Sandinista government of Nicaragua.

Copperheads   A term Republicans applied to Northern war dissenters and those suspected of aiding the Confederate cause during the Civil War.

Council of Economic Advisers   Board of three professional economists established in 1946 to advise the president on economic policy.

Counterculture   Various alternatives to mainstream values and behaviors that became popular in the 1960s, including experimentation with psychedelic drugs, communal living, a return to the land, Asian religions, and experimental art.

Coureurs de bois   French for "woods runner," an independent fur trader in New France.

Covenant Chain   An alliance between the Iroquois Confederacy and the colony of New York which sought to establish Iroquois dominance over all other tribes.

Coxey's Army   A protest march of unemployed workers, led by Populist businessman Jacob Coxey, demanding inflation and a public works program during the depression of the 1890s.

Cuban missile crisis   Crisis between the Soviet Union and the United States over the placement of Soviet nuclear missiles in Cuba.

Culpeper's Rebellion   The overthrow of the established government in the Albermarle region of North Carolina by backcountry men in 1677.

D-Day   June 6, 1944, the day of the first paratroop drops and amphibious landings on the coast of Normandy, France, in the first stage of Operation Overlord during World War II.

Dawes Severalty Act   An 1887 law terminating tribal ownership of land and allotting some parcels of land to individual Indians with the remainder opened for white settlement.

Declaration of Sentiments   The resolutions passed at the Seneca Falls Convention in 1848 calling for full female equality, including the right to vote.

Declaratory Act   Law passed in 1776 to accompany repeal of the Stamp Act that stated that Parliament had the authority to legislate for the colonies "in all cases whatsoever."

Democrats   Political party formed in the 1820s under the leadership of Andrew Jackson; favored states' rights and a limited role for the federal government.

Denmark Vesey's Conspiracy   The most carefully devised slave revolt in which rebels planned to seize control of Charleston in 1822 and escape to freedom in Haiti, a free black republic, but they were betrayed by other slaves, and seventy-five conspirators were executed.

Department of Homeland Security (DHS)   Cabinet-level department created by George Bush to manage U.S. security.

Deregulation   Reduction or removal of government regulations and encouragement of direct competition in many important industries and economic sectors.

Desert culture   A way of life based on hunting small game and the foraging of plant foods.

Détente   French for "easing of tension," the term used to describe the new U.S. relations with China and the Soviet Union in 1972.

Dixiecrat   States' Rights Democrats.

Doughboys   Nickname for soldiers during the Civil War era who joined the army for money.

***Dred Scott* Decision**   Supreme Court ruling, in a lawsuit brought by Dred Scott, a slave demanding his freedom based on his residence in a free state, that slaves could not be U.S. citizens and that Congress had no jurisdiction over slavery in the territories.

Economic Recovery Tax Act of 1981   A major revision of the federal income tax system.

Edmunds Act   1882 act that effectively disenfranchised those who believed in or practiced polygamy and threatened them.

Edmunds-Tucker Act   1887 act which destroyed the temporal power of the Mormon Church by confiscating all assets over $50,000 and establishing a federal commission to oversee all elections in the Utah territory.

Emancipation Proclamation   Decree announced by President Abraham Lincoln in September 1862 and formally issued on January 1, 1863, freeing slaves in all Confederate states still in rebellion.

Embargo Act   Act passed by Congress in 1807 prohibiting American ships from leaving for any foreign port.

Emergency Banking Act   1933 act which gave the president broad discretionary powers over all banking transactions and foreign exchange.

Empresarios   Agents who received a land grant from the Spanish or Mexican government in return for organizing settlements.

Enclave   Self-contained community.

Enlightenment   Intellectual movement stressing the importance of reason and the existence of discoverable natural laws.

Enumerated goods   Items produced in the colonies and enumerated in acts of Parliament that could be legally shipped from the colony of origin only to specified locations.

Environmental Protection Agency (EPA)   Federal agency created in 1970 to oversee environmental monitoring and cleanup programs.

Equal Pay Act of 1963   Act that made it illegal for employers to pay men and women different wages for the same job.

Era of Good Feelings   The period from 1817 to 1823 in which the disappearance of the Federalists enabled the Republicans to govern in a spirit of seemingly nonpartisan harmony.

Espionage Act   Law whose vague prohibition against obstructing the nation's war effort was used to crush dissent and criticism during World War I.

Executive Order 9835   Signed by Harry Truman in 1947 to establish a loyalty program requiring federal employees to sign loyalty oaths and undergo security checks.

Federal Emergency Management Agency (FEMA)   Agency charged with providing assistance to communities hit by natural disasters.

Federal Reserve Act   The 1913 law that revised banking and currency by extending limited government regulation through the creation of the Federal Reserve System.

Federal Trade Commission (FTC)   Government agency established in 1914 to provide regulatory oversight of business activity.

Federalists   Supporters of the Constitution who favored its ratification.

Female Moral Reform Society   Antiprostitution group founded by evangelical women in New York in 1834.

Fifteenth Amendment   Passed by Congress in 1869, guaranteed the right of American men to vote, regardless of race.

Fireside chat   Speeches broadcast nationally over the radio in which President Franklin D. Roosevelt explained complex issues and programs in plain language, as though his listeners were gathered around the fireside with him.

First Continental Congress   Meeting of delegates from most of the colonies held in 1774 in response to the Coercive Acts.

First Reconstruction Act   1877 act that divided the South into five military districts subject to martial law.

Forest Efficiency   Creation of a comfortable life through the development of a sophisticated knowledge of available resources.

Forest Management Act   1897 act which, along with the National Reclamation Act, set the federal government on the path of large-scale regulatory activities.

Fourteen Points   Goals outlined by Woodrow Wilson for war.

Frame of Government   William Penn's constitution for Pennsylvania which included a provision allowing for religious freedom.

Free silver   Philosophy that the government should expand the money supply by purchasing and coining all the silver offered to it.

Free speech movement   Student movement at the University of California, Berkeley, formed in 1964 to protest limitations on political activities on campus.

Freedmen's Bureau   Agency established by Congress in March 1865 to provide social, educational, and economic services, advice, and protection to former slaves and destitute whites; lasted seven years.

Freedom Summer   Voter registration effort in rural Mississippi organized by black and white civil rights workers in 1964.

French and Indian War   The last of the Anglo-French colonial wars (1754–1763) and the first in which fighting began in North America. The war ended with France's defeat. Also known as the Seven Years' War.

Fugitive Slave Law   Part of the Compromise of 1850 that required the authorities in the North to assist Southern slave catchers and return runaway slaves to their owners.

G.I. Bill   Legislation in June 1944 that eased the return of veterans into American society by providing educational and employment benefits.

Gang System   The organization and supervision of slave field hands into working teams on Southern plantations.

General Land Revision Act of 1891   Act which gave the president the power to establish forest reserves to protect watersheds against the threats posed by lumbering, overgrazing, and forest fires.

Gilded Age   Term applied to late nineteenth-century America that refers to the shallow display and worship of wealth characteristic of that period.

Gospel of wealth   Thesis that hard work and perseverance lead to wealth, implying that poverty is a character flaw.

Grandfather clauses   Rules that required potential voters to demonstrate that their grandfathers had been eligible to vote; used in some Southern states after 1890 to limit the black electorate.

Grange   The National Grange of the Patrons of Husbandry, a national organization of farm owners formed after the Civil War.

Granger Laws   State laws enacted in the Midwest in the 1870s that regulated rates charged by railroads, grain elevator operators, and other middlemen.

Great Awakening   North American religious revival in the middle of the eighteenth century. Tremendous religious revival in colonial America striking first in the Middle Colonies and New England in the 1740s and then spreading to the southern colonies.

Great Compromise   Plan proposed at the 1787 Constitutional Convention for creating a national bicameral legislature in which all states would be equally represented in the Senate and proportionally represented in the House.

Great Depression   The nation's worst economic crisis, extending through the 1930s, producing unprecedented bank failures, unemployment, and industrial and agricultural collapse.

Great Migration   The mass movement of African Americans from the rural South to the urban North, spurred especially by new job opportunities during World War I and the 1920s.

Great Sioux War   From 1865 to 1867 the Oglala Sioux warrior Red Cloud waged war against the U.S. Army, forcing the U.S. to abandon its forts built on land relinquished to the government by the Sioux.

Great Society   Theme of Lyndon Johnson's administration, focusing on poverty, education, and civil rights.

Great Uprising of 1877   Unsuccessful railroad strike to protest wage cuts and the use of federal troops against strikers; the first nationwide work stoppage in American history.

Gulf of Tonkin Resolution   Request to Congress from President Lyndon Johnson in response to North Vietnamese torpedo boat attacks in which he sought authorization for "all necessary measures" to protect American forces and stop further aggression.

Harlem Renaissance   A new African American cultural awareness that flourished in literature, art, and music in the 1920s.

Hepburn Act   Act that strengthened the Interstate Commerce Commission (ICC) by authorizing it to set maximum railroad rates and inspect financial records.

Hispanic-American Alliance   Organization formed to protect and fight for the rights of Spanish Americans.

Holocaust   The systematic murder of millions of European Jews and others deemed undesirable by Nazi Germany.

Homestead Act   Law passed by Congress in May 1862 providing homesteads with 160 acres of free land in exchange for improving the land within five years of the grant.

Homestead Act of 1862   1862 act which granted a quarter section (160 acres) of the public domain free to any settler who lived on the land for at least five years and improved it.

Horizontal Combination   The merger of competitors in the same industry.

House Concurrent Resolution 108   Resolution passed in 1953 that allowed Congress to pass legislation to terminate a specific tribe as a political entity.

House of Burgesses   The legislature of colonial Virginia. First organized in 1619, it was the first institution of representative government in the English colonies.

House Un-American Activities Committee (HUAC)   Originally intended to ferret out pro-Fascists, it later investigated "un-American propaganda" that attacked constitutional government.

Huguenots   French Protestant religious dissenters who planted the first French colonies in North America.

Immigration Act   1921 act setting a maximum of 357,000 new immigrants each year.

Immigration and Nationality Act   Act passed in 1965 that abolished national origin quotas and established overall hemisphere quotas.

Imperialism   The policy and practice of exploiting nations and peoples for the benefit of an imperial power either directly through military occupation and colonial rule or indirectly through economic domination of resources and markets.

Indentured Servants   Individuals who contracted to serve a master for a period of four to seven years in return for payment of the servant's passage to America.

Indian Removal Act   President Andrew Jackson's measure that allowed state officials to override federal protection of Native Americans.

Indios   Name first used by Christopher Columbus for the Taino people of the Caribbean.

Industrial Revolution   Revolution in the means and organization of production.

Intercourse Act   Passed in 1790, this law regulated trade and intercourse with the Indian tribes and declared public treaties between the United States and Indian nations the only means of obtaining Indian lands.

International Monetary Fund (IMF)   International organization established in 1945 to assist nations in maintaining stable currencies.

Internet   The system of interconnected computers and servers that allows the exchange of email, posting of Web sites, and other means of instant communication.

Interstate Commerce Commission (ICC)   The 1887 law that expanded federal power over business by prohibiting pooling and discriminatory rates by railroads and establishing the first federal regulatory agency, the Interstate Commerce Commission.

Intolerable Acts   American term for the Coercive Acts and the Quebec Act.

Irreconcilables   Group of U.S. senators adamantly opposed to ratification of the Treaty of Versailles after World War I.

Island-hop   The Pacific campaigns of 1944 that were the American naval versions of the *blitzkrieg.*

Jay's Treaty   Treaty with Britain negotiated in 1794 in which the United States made major concessions to avert a war over the British seizure of American ships.

Jim Crow Laws   Segregation laws that became widespread in the South during the 1890s.

Judicial review   A power implied in the Constitution that gives federal courts the right to review and determine the constitutionality of acts passed by Congress and state legislatures.

Judiciary Act of 1789　Act of Congress that implemented the judiciary clause of the Constitution by establishing the Supreme Court and a system of lower federal courts.

Kansas-Nebraska Act　Law passed in 1854 creating the Kansas and Nebraska Territories but leaving the question of slavery open to residents, thereby repealing the Missouri Compromise.

King George's War　The third Anglo-French war in North America (1744–1748), part of the European conflict known as the War of the Austrian Succession.

King William's War　The first of a series of colonial struggles between England and France, these conflicts occur principally on the frontiers of northern New England and New York between 1689 and 1697.

Knights of Labor　Labor union founded in 1869 that included skilled and unskilled workers irrespective of race or gender.

Know-Nothings　Name given to the anti-immigrant party formed from the wreckage of the Whig Party and some disaffected Northern democrats in 1854.

Kosovo　Province of Yugoslavia where the United States and NATO intervened militarily in 1999 to protect ethnic Albanians from expulsion.

Ku Klux Klan　Perhaps the most prominent of the vigilante groups that terrorized black people in the South during Reconstruction era, founded by the Confederate veterans in 1866.

Land Ordinance of 1785　Act passed by Congress under the Articles of Confederation that created the grid system of surveys by which all subsequent public land was made available for sale.

Landrum-Griffin Act　1959 Act that widened government control over union affairs and further restricted union use of picketing and secondary boycotts during strikes.

League of Nations　International organization created by the Versailles Treaty after World War I to ensure world stability.

League of Women Voters　League formed in 1920 advocating for women's rights, among them the right for women to serve on juries and equal pay laws.

Lecompton constitution　Proslavery draft written in 1857 by Kansas territorial delegates elected under questionable circumstances; it was rejected by two governors, supported by President Buchanan, and decisively defeated by Congress.

Legal Tender Act　Act creating a national currency in February 1862.

Lend-Lease Act　An arrangement for the transfer of war supplies, including food, machinery, and services to nations whose defense was considered vital to the defense of the United States in World War II.

Liberal Republicans　Disaffected Republicans that emphasized the doctrines of classical economics.

Liberty Bonds　Interest-bearing certificates sold by the U.S. government to finance the American World War I effort.

Liberty Party　The first antislavery political party, formed in 1840.

Limited Nuclear Test-Ban Treaty　Treaty, signed by the United States, Britain, and the Soviet Union, outlawing nuclear testing in the atmosphere, in outer space, and under water.

Loyalists　British colonists who opposed independence from Britain.

Manhattan Project　Scientific research project during World War II specifically devoted to developing the atomic bomb.

Manifest Destiny　Doctrine, first expressed in 1845, that the expansion of white Americans across the continent was inevitable and ordained by God.

Manumission　The freeing of a slave.

Marbury v. *Madison*　Supreme Court decision of 1803 that created the precedent of judicial review by ruling as unconstitutional part of the Judiciary Act of 1789.

March on Washington　Historic gathering of over 250,000 people in Washington D.C. in 1963 marching for jobs and freedom.

Market revolution　The outcome of three interrelated developments: rapid improvements in transportation, commercialization, and industrialization.

Marshall Plan　Secretary of State George C. Marshall's European Recovery Plan of June 5, 1947, committing the United States to help in the rebuilding of post–World War II Europe.

Massachusetts Bay Company　A group of wealthy Puritans who were granted a royal charter in 1629 to settle in Massachusetts Bay.

McCarthyism　Anti-Communist attitudes and actions associated with Senator Joe McCarthy in the early 1950s, including smear tactics and innuendo.

Medicare　Basic medical insurance for the elderly, financed through the federal government; program created in 1965.

Mercantilism　Economic system whereby the government intervenes in the economy for the purpose of increasing national wealth.

Mesoamerica　The region stretching from central Mexico to Central America.

Mexican-American War　War fought between Mexico and the United States between 1846 and 1848 over control of territory in southwest North America.

Middle Passage　The voyage between West Africa and the New World slave colonies.

Militarism　The tendency to see military might as the most important and best tool for the expansion of a nation's power and prestige.

Missouri Compromise　Sectional compromise in Congress in 1820 that admitted Missouri to the Union as a slave state and Maine as a free state and prohibited slavery in the northern Louisiana Purchase territory.

Monroe Doctrine　Declaration by President James Monroe in 1823 that the Western Hemisphere was to be closed off to further European colonization and that the United States would not interfere in the internal affairs of European nations.

Mormonism　The doctrines based on the Book of Mormon, taught by Joseph Smith and the succeeding prophets and leaders of the Church.

Morrill Act of 1862　Act by which "land-grant" colleges acquired space for campuses in return for promising to institute agricultural programs.

Morrill Land Grant Act　Law passed by Congress in July 1862 awarding proceeds from the sale of public lands to the states for the establishment of agricultural and mechanical colleges.

Morrill Tariff Act　Act that raised tariffs to more than double their prewar rate.

Muckraking　Journalism exposing economic, social, and political evils, so named by Theodore Roosevelt for its "raking the muck" of American society.

Multiculturalism　Movement that emphasized the unique attributes and achievements of formerly marginal groups and recent immigrants.

My Lai Massacre　Killing of twenty-two Vietnamese civilians by U.S. forces during a 1968 search-and-destroy mission.

Nat Turner's Revolt   Uprising of slaves in Southampton County, Virginia, in the summer of 1831 led by Nat Turner that resulted in the death of fifty-five white people.

Nation of Islam (NOI)   Religious movement among black Americans that emphasizes self-sufficiency, self-help, and separation from white society.

National Aeronautics and Space Administration (NASA)   Federal agency created in 1958 to manage American space flights and exploration.

National Association for the Advancement of Colored People   Organization co-founded by W. E. B. Du Bois in 1910 dedicated to restoring African American political and social rights.

National Bank Act   Act prohibiting state banks from issuing their own notes and forcing them to apply for federal charters.

National Labor Relations Act   Act establishing Federal guarantee of right to organize trade unions and collective bargaining.

National Organization for Women (NOW)   Organization founded to campaign for the enforcement of laws related to women's issues.

National Reclamation Act   1902 act which added 1 million acres of irrigated land to the United States.

National Security Council (NSC)   The formal policy-making body for national defense and foreign relations, created in 1947 and consisting of the president, the secretary of defense, the secretary of state, and others appointed by the president.

National Security Council Paper 68 (NSC-68)   Policy statement that committed the United States to a military approach to the Cold War.

Nativism   Favoring the interests and culture of native-born inhabitants over those of immigrants.

Neutrality Act of 1939   Permitted the sale of arms to Britain, France, and China.

New Deal   The economic and political policies of the Roosevelt administration in the 1930s.

New Deal coalition   Coalition that included traditional-minded white Southern Democrats, big-city political machines, industrial workers of all races, trade unionists, and many depression-hit farmers.

New Freedom   Woodrow Wilson's 1912 program for limited government intervention in the economy to restore competition by curtailing the restrictive influences of trusts and protective tariffs, thereby providing opportunities for individual achievement.

New Frontier   John F. Kennedy's domestic and foreign policy initiatives, designed to reinvigorate sense of national purpose and energy.

New Jersey Plan   Proposal of the New Jersey delegation for a strengthened national government in which all states would have an equal representation in a unicameral legislature.

New Lights   People who experienced conversion during the revivals of the Great Awakening.

Niagara movement   African American group organized in 1905 to promote racial integration, civil and political rights, and equal access to economic opportunity.

Nisei   U.S. citizens born of immigrant Japanese parents.

Nonimportation movement   A tactical means of putting economic pressure on Britain by refusing to buy its exports to the colonies.

North American Free Trade Agreement (NAFTA)   Agreement reached in 1993 by Canada, Mexico, and the United States to substantially reduce barriers to trade.

North Atlantic Treaty Organization (NATO)   Organization of ten European countries, Canada, and the United States whom together formed a mutual defense pact in April 1949.

Northwest Ordinance of 1787   Legislation that prohibited slavery in the Northwest Territories and provided the model for the incorporation of future territories into the union as co-equal states.

Nullification   A constitutional doctrine holding that a state has a legal right to declare a national law null and void within its borders.

Nullification Crisis   Sectional crisis in the early 1830s in which a states' rights party in South Carolina attempted to nullify federal law.

Office of Economic Opportunity (OEO)   Federal agency that coordinated many programs of the War on Poverty between 1964 and 1975.

Old Lights   Religious faction that condemned emotional enthusiasm as part of the heresy of believing in a personal and direct relationship with God outside the order of the church.

Omaha Act of 1882   Act which allowed the establishment of individual title to tribal lands.

Open Door   American policy of seeking equal trade and investment opportunities in foreign nations or regions.

Open shop   Factory or business employing workers whether or not they are union members; in practice, such a business usually refuses to hire union members and follows antiunion policies. The name for a workplace where unions were not allowed.

Operation Desert Storm   U.S. military campaign to force Iraqi forces out of Kuwait.

Operation Overlord   United States and British invasion of France in June 1944 during World War II.

Operation Torch   The Allied invasion of Axis-held North Africa in 1942.

Oregon Trail   Overland trail of more than two thousand miles that carried American settlers from the Midwest to new settlements in Oregon, California, and Utah.

Organization of Petroleum Exporting Countries (OPEC)   Cartel of oil producing nations in Asia, Africa, and Latin America that gained substantial power over the world economy in the mid- to late-1970s by controlling the production and price of oil.

Pan-Indian Military Resistance Movement   Movement calling for the political and cultural unification of Indian tribes in the late eighteenth and early nineteenth centuries.

Panic of 1857   Banking crisis that caused a credit crunch in the North; it was less severe in the South, where high cotton prices spurred a quick recovery.

Patriots   British colonists who favored independence from Britain.

Pendleton Civil Service Reform Act   A law of 1883 that reformed the spoils system by prohibiting government workers from making political contributions and creating the Civil Service Commission to oversee their appointment on the basis of merit rather than politics.

Peninsular Campaign   Union offensive led by McClellan with the objective of capturing Richmond.

Pentagon Papers   Classified Defense Department documents on the history of the United States' involvement in Vietnam, prepared in 1968 and leaked to the press in 1971.

Pequot War   Conflict between English settlers and Pequot Indians over control of land and trade in eastern Connecticut.

Persian Gulf War   War initiated by President Bush in reponse to Iraq's invasion of Kuwait.

Plan of Union   Plan put forward by Benjamin Franklin in 1754 calling for an intercolonial union to manage defense and Indian affairs. The plan was rejected by participants at the Albany Congress.

Plessy v. *Ferguson* Supreme Court decision holding that Louisiana's railroad segregation law did not violate the Constitution as long as the railroads or the state provided equal accommodations.

Popular sovereignty A solution to the slavery crisis suggested by Michigan senator Lewis Cass by which territorial residents, not Congress, would decide slavery's fate.

Populism A mass movement of the 1890s formed on the basis of the Southern Farmers' Alliance and other reform organizations.

Powhatan Confederacy A village of communities of the Chesapeake united under Chief Wahunsonacook, who was called King Powhatan by the colonists.

Preparedness Military buildup in preparation for possible U.S. participation in World War I.

Progressivism A national movement focused on a variety of reform initiatives, including ending corruption, a more business like approach to government, and legislative responses to industrial excess.

Prohibition A ban on the production, sale, and consumption of liquor, achieved temporarily through state laws and the Eighteenth Amendment.

Proposition 187 California legislation adopted by popular vote in California in 1994, which cuts off state-funded health and education benefits to undocumented or illegal immigrants.

Proprietary Colony A colony created when the English monarch granted a huge tract of land to an individual or group of individuals, who became "lords proprietor."

Protective association Organizations formed by mine owners in response to the formation of labor unions.

Protestant Reformation Martin Luther's challenge to the Catholic Church, initiated in 1517, calling for a return to what he understood to be the purer practices and beliefs of the early church.

Protestants All European supporters of religious reform under Charles V's Holy Roman Empire.

Pueblo Revolt Rebellion in 1680 of Pueblo Indians in New Mexico against their Spanish overlords.

Pure Food and Drug Act Act that established the Food and Drug Administration (FDA), which tested and approved drugs before they went on the market.

Puritans Individuals who believed that Queen Elizabeth's reforms of the Church of England had not gone far enough in improving the church. Puritans led the settlement of Massachusetts Bay Colony.

Putting-out system Production of goods in private homes under the supervision of a merchant who "put out" the raw materials, paid a certain sum per finished piece, and sold the completed item to a distant market.

Quakers Members of the Society of Friends, a radical religious group that arose in the mid-seventeenth century. Quakers rejected formal theology, focusing instead on the Holy Spirit that dwelt within them.

Quartering Act Acts of Parliament requiring colonial legislatures to provide supplies and quarters for the troops stationed in America.

Quasi-War Undeclared naval war of 1797 to 1800 between the United States and France.

Québec Act Law passed by Parliament in 1774 that provided an appointed government for Canada, enlarged the boundaries of Quebec, and confirmed the privileges of the Catholic Church.

Queen Anne's War American phase (1702–1713) of Europe's War of the Spanish Succession.

Radical Republicans A shifting group of Republican congressmen, usually a substantial minority, who favored the abolition of slavery from the beginning of the Civil War and later advocated harsh treatment of the defeated South.

Rancherias Dispersed settlements of Indian farmers in the Southwest.

Reconquista The long struggle (ending in 1492) during which Spanish Christians reconquered the Iberian peninsula from Muslim occupiers.

Red Power Term for pan-Indian identity.

Red Scare Post–World War I public hysteria over Bolshevik influence in the United States directed against labor activism, radical dissenters, and some ethnic groups.

Referendum Submission of a law, proposed or already in effect, to a direct popular vote for approval or rejection.

Renaissance The intellectual and artistic flowering in Europe during the fourteenth, fifteenth, and sixteenth centuries sparked by a revival of interest in classical antiquity.

Republican Party Party that emerged in the 1850s in the aftermath of the bitter controversy over the Kansas-Nebraska Act, consisting of former Whigs, some Northern Democrats, and many Know-Nothings.

Republicanism A complex, changing body of ideas, values, and assumptions that influenced American political behavior during the eighteenth and nineteenth centuries.

Roe v. *Wade* U.S. Supreme Court decision (1973) that disallowed state laws prohibiting abortion during the first three months (trimester) of pregnancy and established guidelines for abortion in the second and third trimesters.

Roosevelt Corollary President Theodore Roosevelt's policy asserting U.S. authority to intervene in the affairs of Latin American nations; an expansion of the Monroe Doctrine.

Royal Proclamation of 1763 Royal proclamation declaring the trans-Appalachian region to be "Indian Country."

Rush-Bagot Treaty of 1817 Treaty between the United States and Britain that effectively demilitarized the Great Lakes by sharply limiting the number of ships each power could station on them.

Sabbatarianism Reform movement that aimed to prevent business on Sundays.

Sand Creek Massacre The near annihilation in 1864 of Black Kettle's Cheyenne band by Colorado troops under Colonel John Chivington's orders to "kill and scalp all, big and little."

Santa Fé Trail The 900-mile trail opened by American merchants for trading purposes following Mexico's liberalization of the formerly restrictive trading policies of Spain.

Scalawags Southern whites, mainly small landowning farmers and well-off merchants and planters, who supported the Southern Republican party during Reconstruction.

Second American Party System The basic pattern of American politics of two parties, each with appeal among voters of all social voters and in all sections of the country.

Second Great Awakening Religious revival among black and white Southerners in the 1790s.

Sedition Act An act passed by Congress in 1798 that provided fines for anyone convicted of writing, publishing, or speaking out against the government or its officers. Broad law restricting criticism of America's involvement in World War I or its government, flag, military, taxes, or officials.

Segregation A system of racial control that separated the races, initially by custom but increasingly by law during and after Reconstruction.

Selective Service Act The law establishing the military draft for World War I.

Self-determination The right of a people or a nation to decide on its own political allegiance or form of government without external influence.

Seneca Falls Convention The first convention for women's equality in legal rights, held in upstate New York in 1848.

Shakers The followers of Mother Ann Lee, who preached a religion of strict celibacy and communal living.

Sharecropping Labor system that evolved during and after Reconstruction whereby landowners furnished laborers with a house, farm animals, and tools and advanced credit in exchange for a share of the laborers' crop.

Sheppard-Towner Act The first federal social welfare law, passed in 1921, providing federal funds for infant and maternity care.

Sherman Antitrust Act The first federal antitrust measure, passed in 1890; sought to promote economic competition by prohibiting business combinations in restraint of trade or commerce.

Sherman Silver Purchase Act 1890 act which directed the Treasury to increase the amount of currency coined from silver mined in the West and also permitted the U.S. government to print paper currency backed by the silver.

Silicon Valley The region of California including San Jose and San Francisco that holds the nation's greatest concentration of electronics firms.

Sixteenth Amendment Authorized a federal income tax.

Slaughterhouse cases Group of cases resulting in one sweeping decision by the U.S. Supreme Court in 1873 that contradicted the intent of the Fourteenth Amendment by decreeing that most citizenship rights remained under state, not federal, control.

Slave codes A series of laws passed mainly in the Southern colonies in the late seventeenth and early eighteenth centuries to defend the status of slaves and codify the denial of basic civil rights to them.

Social Darwinism The application of Charles Darwin's theory of biological evolution to society, holding that the fittest and wealthiest survive, the weak and the poor perish, and government action is unable to alter this "natural" process.

Sons of Liberty Secret organizations in the colonies formed to oppose the Stamp Act.

Southern Christian Leadership Conference (SCLC) Black civil rights organization founded in 1957 by Martin Luther King Jr., and other clergy.

Southern Farmers' Alliance The largest of several organizations that formed in the post-Reconstruction South to advance the interests of beleaguered small farmers.

Southern Manifesto A document signed by 101 members of Congress from Southern states in 1956 that argued that the Supreme Court's decision in *Brown* v. *Board of Education of Topeka* itself contradicted the Constitution.

Special Field Order 15 Order by General William T. Sherman in January 1865 to set aside abandoned land along the southern Atlantic coast for forty-acre grants to freedmen; rescinded by President Andrew Johnson later that year.

Specie Circular Proclamation issued by President Andrew Jackson in 1836 stipulating that only gold or silver could be used as payment for public land.

Stamp Act Law passed by Parliament in 1765 to raise revenue in America by requiring taxed, stamped paper for legal documents, publications, and playing cards.

States' Rights Favoring the rights of individual states over rights claimed by the national government.

Stono Rebellion One of the largest and most violent slave uprisings during the Colonial Period that occurred in Stono, South Carolina.

Strategic Arms Limitation Treaty Treaty signed in 1972 by the United States and the Soviet Union to slow the nuclear arms race.

Strategic Defense Initiative (SDI) President Reagan's program, announced in 1983, to defend the United States against nuclear missile attack with untested weapons systems and sophisticated technologies.

Suffrage The right to vote in a political election.

Sugar Act Law passed in 1764 to raise revenue in the American colonies. It lowered the duty from 6 pence to 3 pence per gallon on foreign molasses imported into the colonies and increased the restrictions on colonial commerce.

Sunbelt The states of the American South and Southwest.

Taft-Hartley Act Federal legislation of 1947 that substantially limited the tools available to labor unions in labor-management disputes.

Tammany Society A fraternal organization of artisans begun in the 1780s that evolved into a key organization of the new mass politics in New York City.

Tariff of 1816 A tax imposed by Congress on imported goods.

Tea Act Act of Parliament that permitted the East India Company to sell through agents in America without paying the duty customarily collected in Britain, thus reducing the retail price.

Tejanos Persons of Spanish or Mexican descent born in Texas.

Temperance Reform movement originating in the 1820s that sought to eliminate the consumption of alcohol.

Temperance groups Groups dedicated to reducing the sale and consumption of alcohol.

Tenements Four- to six-story residential dwellings, once common in New York, built on tiny lots without regard to providing ventilation or light.

Tennessee Valley Authority (TVA) Federal regional planning agency established to promote conservation, produce electric power, and encourage economic development in seven Southern states.

Tenure of Office Act Act stipulating that any officeholder appointed by the president with the Senate's advice and consent could not be removed until the Senate had approved a successor.

Thirteenth Amendment Constitutional amendment ratified in 1865 that freed all slaves throughout the United States.

Tories A derisive term applied to Loyalists in America who supported the king and Parliament just before and during the American Revolution.

Townshend Revenue Acts Act of Parliament, passed in 1767, imposing duties on colonial tea, lead, paint, paper, and glass.

Trail of Broken Treaties 1972 event staged by the American Indian Movement (AIM) that culminated in a week-long occupation of the Bureau of Indian Affairs in Washington, D.C.

Trail of Tears The forced march in 1838 of the Cherokee Indians from their homelands in Georgia to the Indian Territory in the West.

Treaty of Fort Laramie The treaty acknowledging U.S. defeat in the Great Sioux War in 1868 and supposedly guaranteeing the Sioux perpetual land and hunting rights in South Dakota, Wyoming, and Montana.

Treaty of Ghent Treaty signed in December 1814 between the United States and Britain that ended the War of 1812.

Treaty of Greenville Treaty of 1795 in which Native Americans in the Old Northwest were forced to cede most of the present state of Ohio to the United States.

Treaty of Paris The formal end to British hostilities against France and Spain in February 1763.

Truman Doctrine President Harry Truman's statement in 1947 that the United States should assist other nations that were facing external pressure or internal revolution.

Underwood-Simmons Act of 1913 Reform law that lowered tariff rates and levied the first regular federal income tax.

Union League Republican party organizations in Northern cities that became an important organizing device among freedmen in Southern cities after 1865.

USA Patriot Act Federal legislation adopted in 2001 in response to the terrorist attacks on September 11 to facilitate anti-terror actions by federal law enforcement and intelligence agencies.

Versailles Treaty The treaty ending World War I and creating the League of Nations.

Vertical Integration The consolidation of numerous production functions, from the extraction of the raw materials to the distribution and marketing of the finished products, under the direction of one firm.

Virginia Company A group of London investors who sent ships to Chesapeake Bay in 1607.

Virginia Plan Proposal calling for a national legislature in which the states would be represented according to population.

Virtual Representation The notion that parliamentary members represented the interests of the nation as a whole, not those of the particular district that elected them.

Volstead Act The 1920 law defining the liquor forbidden under the Eighteenth Amendment and giving enforcement responsibilities to the Prohibition Bureau of the Department of the Treasury.

Voting Rights Act Legislation in 1965 that overturned a variety of practices by which states systematically denied voter registration to minorities.

War Democrats Those from the North and the border states who broke with the Democratic Party and supported Abraham Lincoln's military policies during the Civil War.

War Hawks Members of Congress, predominantly from the South and West, who aggressively pushed for a war against Britain after their election in 1810.

War Industries Board (WIB) The federal agency that reorganized industry for maximum efficiency and productivity during World War I.

War of 1812 War fought between the United States and Britain from June 1812 to January 1815 largely over British restrictions on American shipping.

War on Drugs A paramilitary operation to halt drug trafficking in the United States.

War on Poverty Set of programs introduced by Lyndon Johnson between 1963 and 1966 designed to break the cycle of poverty by providing funds for job training, community development, nutrition, and supplementary education.

War Powers Act Gave the U.S. president the power to reorganize the federal government and create new agencies; to establish programs censoring news, information, and abridging civil liberties; to seize foreign-owned property; and award government contracts without bidding.

Watergate A complex scandal involving attempts to cover up illegal actions taken by administration officials and leading to the resignation of President Richard Nixon in 1974.

Welfare capitalism A paternalistic system of labor relations emphasizing management responsibility for employee well-being.

Welfare Reform Act Act passed by Congress in 1996 that abolished the Aids to Families with Dependent Children (AFDC) welfare program.

Whigs The name used by advocates of colonial resistance to British measures during the 1760s and 1770s.

Whiskey Rebellion Armed uprising in 1794 by farmers in western Pennsylvania who attempted to prevent the collection of the excise tax on whiskey.

Wilmot Proviso The amendment offered by Pennsylvania Democrat David Wilmot in 1846 which stipulated that "as an express and fundamental condition to the acquisition of any territory from the Republic of Mexico . . . neither slavery nor involuntary servitude shall ever exist in any part of said territory."

Wobblies Popular name for the members of the Industrial Workers of the World (IWW).

Woman's Christian Temperance Union (WCTU) Women's organization whose members visited schools to educate children about the evils of alcohol, addressed prisoners, and blanketed men's meetings with literature.

Women's Educational and Industrial Union Boston organization offering classes to wage-earning women.

World Trade Organization (WTO) International organization that sets standards and practices for global trade, and the focus of international protests over world economic policy in the late 1990s.

XYZ Affair Diplomatic incident in 1798 in which Americans were outraged by the demand of the French for a bribe as a condition for negotiating with American diplomats.

Yalta Conference Meeting of U.S. President Franklin Roosevelt, British Prime Minister Winston Churchill, and Soviet Premier Joseph Stalin held in February 1945 to plan the final stages of World War II and postwar arrangements.

Yeoman Independent farmers of the South, most of whom lived on family-sized farms.

Text, Tables, Maps and Figures

Chapter 1   Page 10: "Corn Mother" from AMERICAN INDIAN MYTHS AND LEGENDS by Richard Erdoes and Alfonso Ortiz, copyright © 1984 by Richard Erdoes and Alfonso Ortiz. Used by permission of Pantheon Books, a division of Random House, Inc.

Chapter 4   Figure 4.1: From *Voyages: The Trans-Atlantic Slave Trade Database.* http://www.slavevoyages.org (accessed 2010). **Figure 4.2:** From *Time on the Cross: The Economics of American Negro Slavery*, by Robert William Fogel and Stanley L. Engerman. Copyright © 1974 by Robert William Fogel and Stanley L. Engerman. Used by permission of W. W. Norton & Company, Inc. **Figure 4.3:** From *Shipping, Maritime Trade and the Economic Development of Colonial America*, James J. Shepherd, and Gary M. Walton, Eds. Copyright © 1972 Cambridge University Press. Reprinted with the permission of Cambridge University Press.

Chapter 5   Figure 5.1: *Historical Statistics of the United States* (Washington, DC: Government Printing Office, 1976), 1168. **Figure 5.2:** From "The European Ancestry of the United States Population," by Thomas L. Purvis. *William and Mary Quarterly* 61 (1984): 85–101. Reprinted by permission of the *William and Mary Quarterly*.

Chapter 8   Figure 8.1: From "How Much Is That in Real Money?" *Proceedings of the American Antiquarian Society*, N.S. 102 (1992): 297–359. Copyright © 1992 American Antiquarian Society. Courtesy of American Antiquarian Society. Used by permission.

Chapter 10   Figure 10.1: From *Atlas of Antebellum Southern Agriculture*, by Sam B. Hilliard. (Baton Rouge: Louisiana State University Press, 1984), pp. 67–71. Copyright © 1984 Louisiana State University Press. Reprinted by permission. **Map 10.2:** From *Atlas of Antebellum Southern Agriculture*, by Sam B. Hilliard. (Baton Rouge: Louisiana State University Press, 1984), pp. 67–71. Copyright © 1984 Louisiana State University Press. Reprinted by permission. **Map 10.3:** From *Historical Atlas of the United States* (Washington, DC: National Geographic Society, 1988). Copyright © 1988 National Geographic Society. Reprinted by permission.

Chapter 11   Figure 11.1: From *The Right to Vote*, by Alexander Keyssar. Copyright © 2009 Alexander Keyssar. Reprinted by permission of Basic Books, a member of the Perseus Books Group.

Chapter 13   Figure 13.1: From *Immigrant Life in New York City, 1825–1863* by Robert Ernst. Copyright 1994 by Syracuse University Press. Reprinted by permission. **Map 13.2:** Reprinted from *Whitney R. Cross, The Burned-Over District: The Social and Intellectual History of Enthusiastic Religion in Western New York, 1800–1850.* Copyright © 1950 by Cornell University. Used with permission of the publisher, Cornell University Press.

Chapter 14   Figure 14.1: From *The Plains Across: The Overland Emigrants and the Trans-Mississippi West, 1840–60.* Copyright 1979 by Board of Trustees of the University of Illinois. Used with permission of the University of Illinois Press.

Chapter 16   Figure 16.1: From *The Times Atlas of World History.* Copyright © 1978, Hammond. Reprinted by permission of the publisher.

Chapter 18   Map 18.1: From *The Historical Atlas of Oklahoma* by Morris, Goins, McReynolds. Copyright 1965 University of Oklahoma Press. Reprinted by permission. **Map 18.4:** "THE MORMON CULTURE REGION: STRATEGIES AND PATTERNS IN THE GEOGRAPHY OF THE AMERICAN WEST, 1847-1964" by Donald W. Meinig, from *The Annals of the Association of American Geographers* 55, no. 2, June 1965., reprinted by permission of the publisher (Taylor & Francis Group, http://www.informaworld.com).

Chapter 19   Table 19.1: From THE GILDED AGE edited by Charles W. Calhoun. © 1996. Reprinted by permission of Rowman & Littlefield. **Map 19.2:** From LORD. *Historical Atlas of the United States*, 1E. © 1962 Wadsworth, a part of Cengage Learning, Inc. Reproduced by permission. www.cengage.com/permissions.

Chapter 20   Map 20.1: From *Geographical Inquiry and American Historical Problems*, edited by Earl Carville. (Stanford, CA: Stanford University Press, 1992). Originally published in the *Third Annual Report of the Commissioner of Labor*, 1887.

Chapter 23   Figure 23.3: Reprinted with the permission of Cambridge University Press.

Chapter 29   Figure 29.3: From Congressional Quarterly, *Civil Rights: A Progress Report*, 1971. Copyright 1971 by CQ-ROLL CALL GROUP. Reproduced with permission of CQ-ROLL CALL GROUP in the format Other book via Copyright Clearance Center. **Figure 29.6:** From THE GALLUP POLL 1835–1971 by George Gallup. Copyright © 1972 The Gallup Organization. All rights reserved. Reprinted by permission.

Chapter 30   Figure 30.2: From Bureau of Labor Statistics, in Mary Kupiec et al., eds., *Encyclopedia of American Social History*, Vol. II. New York: Scribner's, 1993, p. 4188. Copyright © 1993 Scribner's. Reprinted by permission of Cengage Learning. **Table 30.2:** From *The New York Times*, April 21, 1992, from Federal Reserve Survey of Consumer Finances. Copyright © 1992 The New York Times. Reprinted by permission. **Figure 30.4:** From Statistical abstract of the United States, in Nash et al., *The American People*, 5th ed., p. 988. Reprinted by permission of Longman Publishing Group, a division of Pearson Education.

Photos

Chapter 1   Chapter Opener   Center: Cahokia Mounds State Historic Site, painting by Michael Hampshire. **Bottom:** © Warren Morgan/CORBIS All Rights Reserved **Page 5:** James Chatters/Agence France Presse/Getty Images **Page 7:** © Warren Morgan/CORBIS All Rights Reserved **Page 9:** Courtesy of the Denver Museum of Nature and Science **Page 10:** Image #1739-3, courtesy the Library, American Museum of Natural History. **Page 11:** Mimbres black on white bowl, with painted representations of man and woman under a blanket. Grant County, New Mexico. Diam. 26.7 cm. Courtesy National Museum of the American Indian, Smithsonian Institution, 24/3198 **Page 12:** David Muench/CORBIS- NY **Page 13:** © Tony Linck/SuperStock **Page 14:** "Nursing Mother Effigy Bottle." From the Whelpley Collection at the St. Louis Science Center. Photograph © 1985 the Detroit Institute of Arts/The Bridgeman Art Library, NY **Page 17:** Bayerische Staatsbibliothek Munchen...Rar. 5k. **Page 19:** Neg. No. 324281, Photographed by Rota, Engraving by DeBry. American Museum of Natural History Library. **Page 20:** Courtesy of the Library of Congress.

Chapter 2   Chapter Opener   Center: The French, under the command of Jean Ribault, discover the River of May (St. Johns River) in Florida on 1 May 1562: colored engraving, 1591, by Theodor de Bry after a now lost drawing by Jacques Le Moyne de Morgues. The Granger Collection. **Top left:** © Hulton-Deutsch Collection/CORBIS **Bottom right:** © Stapleton Collection/CORBIS **Page 28:** October, from Tres Riches Heures du Duc de Berry. Musee Conde, Chantilly/Bridgeman-Giraudon, Art Resource, NY **Page 30:** © National Maritime Museum Picture Library, London, England. Neg. #E5555-3 **Page 31:** Beinecke Rare Book and Manuscript Library, Yale University **Page 33:** Beinecke Rare Book and Manuscript Library, Yale University **Page 34:** De Bry engraving of Spanish attack on native village **Page 38:** Olive and Arthur Kelsall/Nova Scotia Museum **Page 39:** Jacques Le Moyne, *Rene de Loudonniere and Chief Athore*, 1564. Gouache and metallic pigments on vellum. Print Collection, The New York Public Library, New York. The New York Public Library/Art Resource, NY **Page 40:** *Elizabeth I*, Armada portrait, c. 1588 (oil on panel) by English School (C16th) Private Collection/The Bridgeman Art Library, London/New York.

Chapter 3   Chapter Opener   Center: Beinecke Rare Book and Manuscript Library, Yale University **Top left:** © Dorling Kindersley **Bottom left:** Photodisc/Getty Images **Top:** © Bettmann/CORBIS **Top right:** Courtesy of Pilgrim Hall Museum, Plymouth, Massachusetts. **Page 49:** Lowell Georgia/CORBIS- NY **Page 53:** Courtesy of the Library of Congress **Page 54:** From Samuel de Champlain, Les Voyages, Paris, 1613. Illustration opp. pg. 232. Rare Books Division, The New York Public Library, Astor Lenox and Tilden Foundations. The New York Public Library/Art Resource, NY **Page 55:** The Granger Collection **Page 58:** Courtesy, American Antiquarian Society **Page 59:** Courtesy of The John Carter Brown Library, at Brown University. **Page 60:** The Freake-Gibbs Painter (American, Active 1670), "David, Joanna, and Abigail Mason," 1670. Oil on canvas, 39 ½ × 42 ½ in.; Frame: 42 ¾ × 45 ½ × 1 ½ in. Fine Arts Museums of San Francisco, Gift of Mr. and Mrs. John D. Rockefeller 3rd to The Fine Arts Museums of San Francisco, 1979.7.3 **Page 62:** Fort New Amsterdam, New York, 1651. Engraving. Collection of The New-York Historical Society, 77354d **Page 64:** "Courtesy of the Osher Map Library, University of Southern Maine." **Page 68:** Courtesy of the Pilgrim Hall Museum, Plymouth, Massachusetts **Page 69:** Eliot Elisofon/Getty Images/Time Life Pictures.

Chapter 4 Chapter Opener Center: Courtesy of the Library of Congress **Top right:** Courtesy, American Antiquarian Society **Page 73:** The Granger Collection **Page 74:** Beinecke Rare Book and Manuscript Library, Yale University **Page 78:** Royal Albert Memorial Museum, Exeter, Devon, UK/Bridgeman Art Library **Page 79 (top):** The Granger Collection, New York **Page 79 (bottom):** The Granger Collection, New York **Page: 82:** Thomas Coram, "View of Mulberry Street, House and Street." Oil on paper, 10 × 17.6 cm. Gibbes Museum of Art/Carolina Art Association. 68.18.01 **Page 86:** Abby Aldrich Rockefeller Folk Art Museum, The Colonial Williamsburg Foundation, Williamsburg, VA. **Page 87:** Thomas Moran (American, 1837–1926), "Slave Hunt, Dismal Swamp, Virginia," 1862. Gift of Laura A. Clubb, 1947.8.44. ©2008 The Philbrook Museum of Art, Inc.,Tulsa, Oklahoma. **Page 89:** Samuel Scott, "Old Custom House Quay" Collection. V&A IMAGES, THE VICTORIA AND ALBERT MUSEUM, LONDON **Page 93:** Virginia Historical Society, Richmond, Virginia/Bridgeman Art Library, NY.

Chapter 5 Chapter Opener Center: North Wind Picture Archives **Top left:** © Judith Miller/Dorling Kindersley/Sara Covelli **Bottom left:** David Murray © Dorling Kindersley **Top right:** © National Maritime Museum, London **Bottom:** Liz McAulay © Dorling Kindersley, Courtesy of the Worthing Museum and Art Gallery **Page 100:** Gustavus Hesselius, *Tishcohan*, Native American Portrait, 1735. Courtesy of The Historical Society of Pennsylvania Collection, Atwater Kent Museum of Philadelphia. **Page 102:** The Granger Collection, New York **Page 103:** Jack W. Dykinga/Dykinga Photography **Page 105:** EROS Data Center, U.S. Geological Survey **Page 106:** Peter Cooper, *The South East Prospect of the City of Philadelphia*, ca. 1720. The Library Company of Philadelphia. **Page 110 (left):** The Granger Collection **Page 110 (right):** The Granger Collection **Page 114:** *Human Races (Las Castas)*, 18th century, oil on canvas, 1.04 × 1.48 m. Museo Nacional del Virreinato, Tepotzotlan, Mexico. Schalkwijk/Art Resource, NY **Page 117:** Henry Dawkins, *Baptismal Ceremony Beside the Schuykill.* Engraving, 1770. John Carter Brown Library at Brown University.

Chapter 6 Chapter Opener Center: The Granger Collection, New York **Top:** Steve Gorton © Dorling Kindersley **Top left, Bottom:** Getty Images, Inc. **Top right:** Dave King © Dorling Kindersley **Page 123:** The Library Company of Philadelphia **Page 126:** Benjamin West (1738–1820), "The Death of General Wolfe," 1770. Oil on canvas, 152.6 × 214.5 cm. Transfer from the Canadian War Memorials, 1921 (Gift of the 2nd Duke of Westminster, England, 1918). Photo ©National Gallery of Canada, Ottawa, Ontario. **Page 128:** National Museum of the American Indian/Smithsonian Institution **Page 130:** Art Resource/The New York Public Library **Page 132:** John Singleton Copley (1738–1815), "Samuel Adams," ca. 1772. Oil on canvas, 49 ½ × 39 ½ in. (125.7 cm × 100.3 cm). Deposited by the City of Boston, 30.76c. Courtesy, Museum of Fine Arts, Boston. Reproduced with permission. ©2000 Museum of Fine Arts, Boston. All Rights Reserved. **Page 136:** Library of Congress **Page 138:** American Antiquarian Society, Worcester, Massachusetts/ Bridgeman Art Library. **Page 141:** The New York Public Library, Prints Division, Stokes Collection **Page 144:** The Granger Collection.

Chapter 7 Chapter Opener Center: John Trumbull (American 1756–1843), *The Surrender of Lord Cornwallis at Yorktown, 19 October 1781*, 1787–c. 1828. Oil on canvas, 53.3 × 77.8 × 1.9 cm (21 × 30 5/8 × 3/4 in.), 1832.4. Yale University Art Gallery/Art Resource., NY **Top:** Getty Images Inc. - Hulton Archive Photos **Top left:** Courtesy of the Library of Congress **Top right:** Photograph courtesy of the Concord Museum, Concord, MA and the archives of the Lexington Historical Society, Lexington, MA Photograph by David Bohl. **Bottom:** © CORBIS **Page 151:** Anne S.K. Brown Military Collection, John Hay Library, Brown University **Page 152:** The Granger Collection **Page 153:** John Singleton Copley (American, 1738–1815), "Mrs. James Warren (Mercy Otis)," ca.1763. Oil on canvas. 49 ⅝ × 39 ½ in. (126 × 100.3 cm). Bequest of Winslow Warren. Courtesy, Museum of Fine Arts, Boston (31.212). Reproduced with permission. © [2000] Museum of Fine Arts, Boston. All Rights Reserved. **Page 156:** Gilbert Stuart, "The Mohawk Chief Joseph Brant," 1786. Oil on canvas, 30 × 25 in. Fenimore Art Museum, Cooperstown, New York **Page 159:** William Ranney, *The Battle of Cowpens.* Oil on canvas. Photo by Sam Holland. Courtesy South Carolina State House. **Page 163:** Library of Congress **Page 165:** Beinecke Rare Book and Manuscript Library, Yale University **Page 169:** © Bettmann/CORBIS All Rights Reserved **Page 170:** ©Bettmann/CORBIS.

Chapter 8 Chapter Opener Center: Courtesy of The Historical Society of Pennsylvania Collection, Atwater Kent Museum of Philadelphia. **Top left:** Library of Congress **Bottom:** The Library Company of Philadelphia **Top right:** Gallery of the Republic **Page 179:** Print and Picture Collection, The Free Library of Philadelphia. **Page 181:** The Federal Edifice "On the Erection of the Eleventh Pillar," caricature from the "Massachusetts Centinal, August 2, 1788. Neg. #33959. Collection of The New-York Historical Society **Page 182 (left):** Smithsonian Institution, NNC, Douglas Mudd. **Page 182 (right):** Smithsonian Institution, NNC, Douglas Mudd. **Page 183:** John Trumbull (1756–1843), "Portrait of Alexander Hamilton" (1755/57-1804), statesman, 1806, oil on canvas, 76.2 × 61 cm (20 × 24 in). Gift of Henry Cabot Lodge. National Portrait Gallery, Smithsonian Institution, Washington, DC/Art Resource, NY **Page 185:** Little Turtle, or Mich-i-kin-i-qua, Miami War Chief, Conqueror of Harmar and St. Clair. Lithograph made from a portrait painted in 1797 by Gilbert Stuart. Indiana Historical Society Library (negative no. C2584). **Page 187:** Beinecke Rare Book and Manuscript Library, Yale University **Page 189:** Francis Kemmelmeyer, "General George Washington Reviewing the Western Army at Fort Cumberland the 18th of October 1794," after 1794. Oil on paper backed with linen, 18 ⅛ × 23 1/8. Courtesy of Winterthur Museum **Page 192:** Collection of The New-York Historical Society, Neg. #33995. **Page 193:** The Granger Collection **Page 195:** John Singleton Copley (1738–1815), "Portrait of Mrs. John Stevens (Judith Sargent, later Mrs. John Murray)," 1770–72. Commissioned on the occasion of her first marriage, at age eighteen. Oil on canvas, 50 × 40 in. Daniel J. Terra Art Acquisition Endowment Fund, 2000.6. © Terra Foundation for American Art, Chicago/Art Resource, New York.

Chapter 9 Chapter Opener Center: Mac G. Morris Collection **Top left:** Collection of The New-York Historical Society **Bottom left:** Getty Images Inc. - Hulton Archive Photos **Top right:** National Museum of American History/Smithsonian Institution, Photographic Collection **Page 202:** Illustration by Kittlitz, F. H. v. (Friedrich Heinrich von) in Litke, F. P. (Fedor Petrovich), Voyage autour du monde, exécuté par ordre de Sa Majesté l'empereur Nicolas 1er, sur la corvette le Séniavine, dans les années 1826, 1827, 1828. [Rare Book C0024] Alaska and Polar Regions Collections, Elmer E. Rasmuson Library, University of Alaska Fairbanks. **Page 204:** Peabody Essex Museum, Salem, Massachusetts, USA/The Bridgeman Art Library **Page 206:** Courtesy of the Library of Congress **Page 207:** Courtesy of the Library of Congress **Page 213 (left):** The Granger Collection, New York **Page 213 (right):** 1830. Oil on canvas. 29 × 24 in. (73.7 × 60.9 cm) Location: Smithsonian American Art Museum, Washington, DC, U.S.A. **Page 215:** Courtesy of the Library of Congress **Page 217:** Courtesy of the Bostonian Society/Old State House **Page 220 (top):** Courtesy of the Bostonian Society/Old State House **Page 220 (bottom):** Courtesy of the Bostonian Society/Old State House.

Chapter 10 Chapter Opener Center: The Granger Collection **Top left:** Library of Congress **Bottom:** Library of Congress **Top right:** © Dorling Kindersley **Page 232:** National Museum of American History/Smithsonian Institution **Page 233:** Culver Pictures, Inc. **Page 237:** Monticello/Thomas Jefferson Foundation, Inc. **Page 238:** Collection of The New-York Historical Society. Photograph by G.N. Barnard, Bagoe Collection, ca. 1865, negative number 48169. **Page 239:** John Antrobus, *Negro Burial.* Oil painting. The Historic New Orleans Collection. #1960.46 **Page 240:** The Granger Collection **Page 241 (top right):** Library of Congress **Page 241 (bottom left):** American Numismatic Society of New York **Page 241 (bottom right):** American Numismatic Society of New York **Page 243:** © Andre Jenny/Alamy **Page 245:** © Bettmann/CORBIS All Rights Reserved.

Chapter 11 Chapter Opener Center: © Bettmann/CORBIS **Top left:** National Numismatic Collection/Smithsonian Institution **Bottom:** Courtesy, American Antiquarian Society **Top right:** Getty Images, Inc.- Photodisc./Royalty Free **Page 259:** George Caleb Bingham (American, 1811–1879), *Stump Speaking*, 1853–54. Oil on canvas, 42 ½ × 58 in. Saint Louis Art Museum, Gift of Bank of America. **Page 261:** Richard Caton Woodville, *Politics in an Oyster House*, 1848. Oil on canvas. The Walters Art Museum, Baltimore. **Page 263:** Courtesy of the Library of Congress **Page 264:** Courtesy of the Library of Congress **Page 265 (top left):** The Granger Collection, New York **Page 265 (center):** Matthew H. Joulett (1788–1827), *Henry Clay*, c. 1824. Oil on panel. (attr. to Jouett) © Chicago Historical Society, Chicago, USA **Page 265 (top right):** The Granger Collection **Page 270:** CORBIS- NY **Page 271:** CORBIS- NY **Page 274:** Asher Brown Durand, *Kindred Spirits*, 1849. Oil on canvas, 44 × 36 in. Collection of the New York Public Library, Astor, Lenox and Tilden Foundations. **Page 278:** Courtesy of the Library of Congress **Page 279:** The Granger Collection, New York.

Astor, Lenox and Tilden Foundations **Page 555:** The Granger Collection, New York. **Page 557:** Theodore Roosevelt Collection, Harvard College Library.

Chapter 22 Chapter Opener Center: Getty Images Inc. - Hulton Archive Photos/3306891 **Top left:** © Bettmann/CORBIS **Bottom:** © Bettmann/CORBIS **Top right:** Richard Ward © Dorling Kindersley **Page 566:** The Granger Collection **Page 568:** The Granger Collection, New York **Page 571:** University of South Alabama Archives. **Page 572:** Courtesy of the Library of Congress **Page 574 (left):** Courtesy of the Library of Congress **Page 574 (middle):** © CORBIS All Rights Reserved **Page 574 (right):** Courtesy of the Library of Congress **Page 575:** Getty Images Inc. - Hulton Archive Photos **Page 578:** Russ Lappa/Prentice Hall School Division **Page 580:** National Archives and Records Administration **Page 581:** New York Public Library/Art Resource, NY : Leslie's Illustrated Newspaper, Sept. 11, 1920 **Page 585:** © Stock Montage **Page 587:** John Christen Johansen (1876–1964), *Signing of the Treaty of Versailles*, 1919, oil on canvas, 249 cm × 224.5 cm (98-⅟₁₆ × 88-⅜"). Gift of an anonymous donor through Mrs. Elizabeth Rogerson, 1926. National Portrait Gallery, Smithsonian Institution, Washington D.C./Art Resource, New York

Chapter 23 Chapter Opener Center: © Swim Ink/CORBIS **Top:** Getty Images - Photodisc-Royalty Free/msi_017 **Top left:** Getty Images Inc. - Hulton Archive Photos/82874980 **Top right:** Getty Images Inc. RF/OS25011 **Page 596:** A&P Food Stores LTD **Page: 597** Brown Brothers **Page 598:** Ford Motor Company **Page 604 (left):** Picture Desk, Inc./Kobal Collection **Page 604 (middle):** Everett Collection **Page 604 (right):** Everett Collection **Page 606:** JAN PERSSON/Lebrecht Music & Arts Photo Library **Page 608:** CORBIS- NY **Page 611:** Ball State University Libraries, Archives & Special Collections, W.A. Swift Photo Collection **Page 614:** Goldbeck Collection, Harry Ransom Humanities Research Center, University of Texas at Austin. Photo by Summerville. **Page 619:** Courtesy of the Library of Congress. **Page 622:** Courtesy of the Library of Congress **Page 623:** Courtesy of the Library of Congress.

Chapter 24 Chapter Opener Center: Culver Pictures, Inc./SuperStock. D. © CORBIS **Top:** © CORBIS; © David J. & Janice L. Frent Collection/CORBIS **Bottom left:** © CORBIS **Top right:** Courtesy of the Library of Congress **Page 628:** The Granger Collection **Page 629:** Dorothea Lange, *White Angel Breadline, San Francisco, 1933*. Copyright the Dorothea Lange Collection, The Oakland Museum of California, City of Oakland. Gift of Paul S. Taylor. **Page 631:** Franklin D. Roosevelt Library **Page 632:** ALBERT EINSTEIN and related rights TM/© of The Hebrew University of Jerusalem, used under license. Represented exclusively by Corbis Corporation **Page 636:** Milton Brooks/AP Wide World Photos **Page 639:** © CORBIS All Rights Reserved **Page 642:** AP Wide World Photos **Page 645:** Fletcher Martin (1904–1979), *Mine Rescue*, 1939, mural study for Kellog, Idaho Post Office; tempera on panel, 15-¾ × 36-½ in (40.0 × 92.7 cm). Copyright Smithsonian American Art Museum, Washington, DC/Art Resource, NY **Page 646 (bottom left):** Courtesy of the Library of Congress **Page 646 (bottom right):** Courtesy of the Library of Congress.

Chapter 25 Chapter Opener Center: The Granger Collection, New York **Top left:** Andy Crawford/Dorling Kindersley © Imperial War Museum, London; Andy Crawford/Dorling Kindersley © Imperial War Museum, London **Top:** © Minnesota Historical Society/CORBIS **Top right:** © CORBIS **Bottom:** Getty Images Inc. - Hulton Archive Photos/3346808 **Page 656:** U.S. Navy News Photo **Page 657:** AP Wide World Photos **Page 659:** CORBIS- NY **Page 660:** Printed by permission of the Norman Rockwell Family Agency. Copyright © 1943 the Norman Rockwell Family Entities. © 1943 SEPS: Licensed by Curtis Publishing, Indianapolis, IN. All rghts reserved. www.curtispublishing.com **Page 662:** © Bettmann/CORBIS **Page 663:** National Archives and Records Administration **Page 664:** Horace Pippin (1888–1946), *Mr. Prejudice*, 1943. Oil on canvas, 18 × 14 inches. Philadelphia Museum of Art, Gift of Dr. and Mrs. Matthew T. Moore. Photo by Graydon Wood. 1984-108-1 **Page 666:** National Archives and Records Administration. **Page 667:** Stilpx/NARA National/National Archives and Records Administration **Page 671:** Fred Ramage/Getty Images Inc. - Hulton Archive Photos **Page 672:** courtesy of the Library of Congress **Page 676:** Leslie Cole, *Belsen Camp. The Compound for Women*. Imperial War Museum, London.

Chapter 26 Chapter Opener Center: Getty Images/Time Life Pictures/50605483 **Top left:** CORBIS- NY/BE064604 **Bottom:** © CORBIS **Top right:** Getty Images Inc. - Hulton Archive Photos/HGE:3070762 **Page 685:** Courtesy of the Library of Congress **Page 690:** © Bettmann/CORBIS All Rights Reserved **Page 691:** AP Wide World Photos **Page 694:** "The Michael Barson Collection" **Page 695:** Southern California Library for Social Studies & Research **Page 696:** Hank Walker/Getty Images/Time Life Pictures **Page 698:** Conelrad Collection **Page 699:** Harold M. Lambert/Getty Images - Bambu Productions **Page 701:** Courtesy of the Library of Congress **Page 704:** AP Wide World Photos. **Page 708:** U.S. Air Force/AP Wide World Photos **Page 709:** Bernard Hoffman/Stringer/© Time & Life Pictures/Getty Images.

Chapter 27 Chapter Opener Center: Getty Images Inc. - Hulton Archive Photos/3207617 **Top:** © CORBIS **Bottom left:** Dorling Kindersley/© Dorling Kindersley **Top right:** © CORBIS **Page 713:** © Bettmann/CORBIS **Page 714:** © Bettmann/CORBIS **Page 718:** Bernard Hoffman/Life Magazine/©1950 TimePix **Page 721:** [Photographer]/Hulton Archive/Getty Images **Page 723:** Hulton Archive/Getty Images Inc. - Hulton Archive Photos **Page 725:** PPP/Popperfoto/Getty Images/Retrofile **Page 726:** Bettmann/CORBIS-NY **Page 727:** © Alan Ginsberg/CORBIS All Rights Reserved **Page 729:** Bettmann/CORBIS- NY **Page 733:** Ralph Crane/Getty Images/Time Life Pictures **Page 734 (top right):** AP Wide World Photos **Page 734 (center):** Robert Jackson/Bob Jackson **Page 734 (bottom left):** [Photographer]/Hulton Archive/Getty Images.

Chapter 28 Chapter Opener Center: CORBIS- NY/BE004329 **Top left:** Courtesy of the Library of Congress **Bottom:** John F. Kennedy Library, National Archives, document MS 2003-036 **Top right:** Courtesy of the Library of Congress **Page 741:** Frank Driggs Collection **Page 743:** Dan McCoy/Black Star **Page 744:** Ed Clark/Getty Images/Time Life Pictures **Page 748:** CORBIS- NY **Page 752:** UPI/CORBIS- NY **Page 754:** Francis Miller/Time Life Pictures/Getty Images/Time Life Pictures **Page 757:** Steve Schapiro/Black Star **Page 759:** Library of Congress **Page 761:** Bill Hudson/AP Wide World Photos **Page 762:** Benson Latin American Collection **Page 771 (left):** Library of Congress **Page 771 (middle):** Library of Congress **Page 771 (right):** Courtesy of the Library of Congress.

Chapter 29 Chapter Opener Center: © John Paul Filo/Hulton/Archive **Top left, Bottom:** © Royalty-Free/CORBIS **Top:** © Royalty-Free/CORBIS **Bottom left:** Wayne State University Archives of Labor and Urban Affairs **Top right:** © Henry Diltz/CORBIS **Page 776:** Jim Pickerell/Black Star **Page 777:** © Henry Diltz/CORBIS All Rights Reserved **Page 778:** AP Wide World Photos **Page 786:** Library of Congress **Page 788:** Naval Historical Foundation **Page 790:** © Bettmann/CORBIS All Rights Reserved **Page 792:** Paul Fusco/Magnum Photos, Inc. **Page 797:** Nick Ut/AP Wide World Photos **Page 798:** Wally McNamee/CORBIS- NY **Page 800:** CORBIS- NY.

Chapter 30 Chapter Opener Center: CORBIS- NY/OF012892 **Top left:** CORBIS- NY/0000359851-005 **Bottom:** © Neil Beer/CORBIS **Top right:** © Dorling Kindersley **Page 811:** CORBIS- NY **Page 812:** AP Wide World Photos **Page 814:** AP Wide World Photos **Page 815 (left):** The White House Photo Office **Page 815 (right):** Ron Edmonds/CORBIS- NY **Page 817:** Wally McNamee/CORBIS- NY **Page 822:** AP Wide World Photos **Page 825 (top right):** AP Wide World Photos **Page 825 (bottom):** Robert Maass/CORBIS- NY.

Chapter 31 Chapter Opener Center: CORBIS- NY/UT0089971 **Bottom left:** Steve Gorton © Dorling Kindersley **Top right:** © Dorling Kindersley; Geoff Dann © Dorling Kindersley, Courtesy of the Imperial War Museum, London **Bottom:** Agence France Presse/Getty Images **Page 836:** Susan Walsh/AP Wide World Photos **Page 837:** AP Wide World Photos **Page 838:** [Photographer]/Getty Images, Inc. **Page 839:** AP Wide World Photos **Page 841:** AP Wide World Photos **Page 842:** Chris Pizzello/AP Wide World Photos **Page 844:** Agence France Presse/Getty Images **Page 845:** Getty Images, Inc. **Page 849:** David J. Phillip/AP Wide World Photos **Page 854:** Jewel SAMAD/Getty Images Inc. RF **Page 859 (top):** Harris and Ewing Photos/Harris and Ewing Photos Courtesy Harry S. Truman Library **Page 859 (center):** National Archives and Records Administration **Page 859 (bottom):** AP Wide World Photos.

A

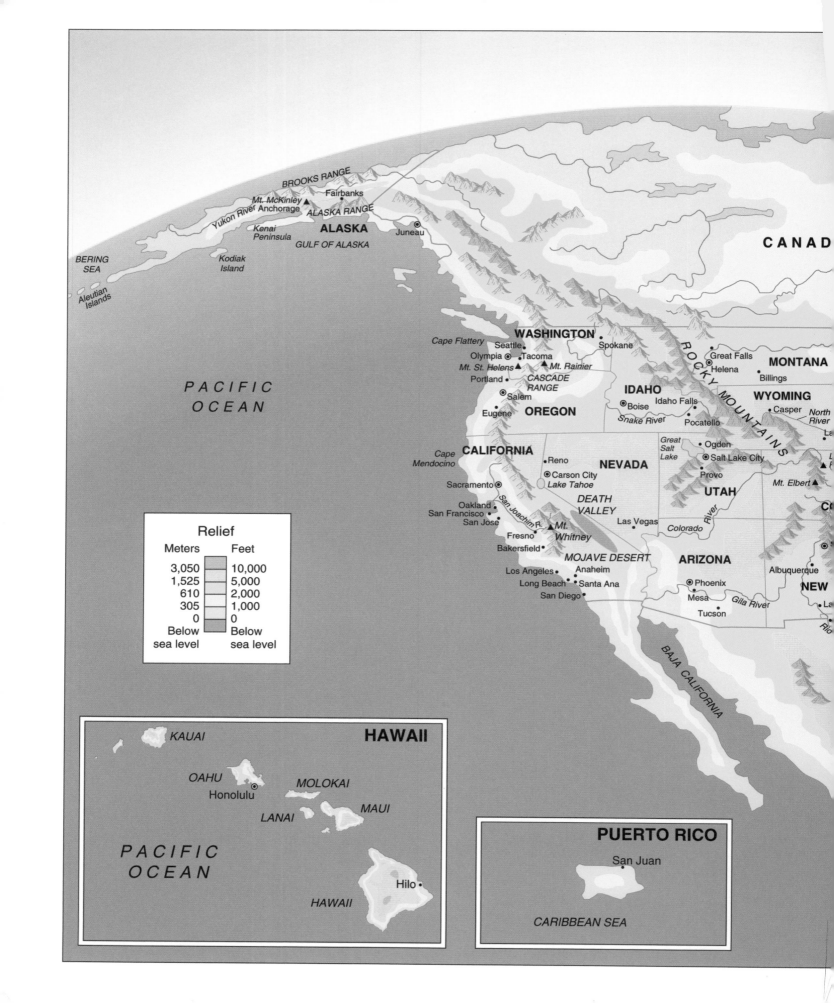

BROOKS RANGE

Mt. McKinley ▲ Fairbanks •
Yukon River Anchorage • **ALASKA RANGE**
Kenai
Peninsula
ALASKA
Juneau ⊙

GULF OF ALASKA

**BERING
SEA**

Kodiak
Island

Aleutian
Islands

**PACIFIC
OCEAN**

CANAD

Cape Flattery • **WASHINGTON** •
Seattle • Spokane •
Olympia ⊙ • Tacoma
Mt. St. Helens ▲ • Mt. Rainier **Great Falls** ⊙
Portland • **CASCADE
RANGE** Helena •
Salem ⊙ **MONTANA**
Eugene • **OREGON** Billings •
IDAHO **WYOMING**
Boise ⊙ Idaho Falls •
Snake River Pocatello • Casper •
**North
River**

Cape
Mendocino • **CALIFORNIA**
Reno •
Carson City ⊙ **NEVADA**
Sacramento ⊙ Lake Tahoe Great
Salt
Lake Ogden •
Salt Lake City ⊙
Provo • Mt. Elbert ▲
Oakland • San Joachim R. **DEATH
VALLEY** **UTAH**
San Francisco • San Jose • Mt. Whitney ▲ Las Vegas • Colorado **CO**
Fresno •
Bakersfield • River
MOJAVE DESERT **ARIZONA**
Los Angeles • Anaheim • Albuquerque •
Long Beach • • Santa Ana Phoenix • **NEW**
San Diego • Mesa • Gila River • La
Tucson • Rio

BAJA CALIFORNIA

Relief

Meters	Feet
3,050	10,000
1,525	5,000
610	2,000
305	1,000
0	0
Below sea level	Below sea level

HAWAII

KAUAI

OAHU ⊙ MOLOKAI
Honolulu
LANAI MAUI

**PACIFIC
OCEAN**

Hilo •

HAWAII

PUERTO RICO

San Juan •

CARIBBEAN SEA